Understanding
LINUX
NETWORK
INTERNALS

Other Linux resources from O'Reilly

Related titles

Linux in a Nutshell

Linux Network
  Administrator's Guide

Running Linux

Linux Device Drivers

Understanding the Linux
  Kernel

Building Secure Servers with
  Linux

LPI Linux Certification in a
  Nutshell

Learning Red Hat Linux

Linux Server Hacks™

Linux Security Cookbook

Managing RAID on Linux

Linux Web Server CD
  Bookshelf

Building Embedded Linux
  Systems

Linux Books Resource Center

linux.oreilly.com is a complete catalog of O'Reilly's books on Linux and Unix and related technologies, including sample chapters and code examples.

ONLamp.com is the premier site for the open source web platform: Linux, Apache, MySQL, and either Perl, Python, or PHP.

Conferences

O'Reilly brings diverse innovators together to nurture the ideas that spark revolutionary industries. We specialize in documenting the latest tools and systems, translating the innovator's knowledge into useful skills for those in the trenches. Visit *conferences.oreilly.com* for our upcoming events.

Safari Bookshelf (*safari.oreilly.com*) is the premier online reference library for programmers and IT professionals. Conduct searches across more than 1,000 books. Subscribers can zero in on answers to time-critical questions in a matter of seconds. Read the books on your Bookshelf from cover to cover or simply flip to the page you need. Try it today with a free trial.

Understanding
LINUX
NETWORK
INTERNALS

Christian Benvenuti

O'REILLY®

Beijing · Cambridge · Farnham · Köln · Paris · Sebastopol · Taipei · Tokyo

Understanding Linux Network Internals
by Christian Benvenuti

Published by O'Reilly Media, Inc., 1005 Gravenstein Highway North, Sebastopol, CA 95472.

O'Reilly books may be purchased for educational, business, or sales promotional use. Online editions are also available for most titles (*safari.oreilly.com*). For more information, contact our corporate/institutional sales department: (800) 998-9938 or *corporate@oreilly.com*.

Editor:	Andy Oram
Production Editor:	Philip Dangler
Cover Designer:	Karen Montgomery
Interior Designer:	David Futato

Printing History:

December 2005:   First Edition.

[M]
ISBN: 0-596-00255-6   [7/06]

Table of Contents

Part I.   General Background

Part II. System Initialization

Part III. Transmission and Reception

Part VII. Routing

Preface

Today more than ever before, networking is a hot topic. Any electronic gadget in its latest generation embeds some kind of networking capability. The Internet continues to broaden in its population and opportunities. It should not come as a surprise that a robust, freely available, and feature-rich operating system like Linux is well accepted by many producers of embedded devices. Its networking capabilities make it an optimal operating system for networking devices of any kind. The features it already has are well implemented, and new ones can be added easily. If you are a developer for embedded devices or a student who would like to experiment with Linux, this book will provide you with good fodder.

The performance of a pure software-based product that uses Linux cannot compete with commercial products that can count on the help of specialized hardware. This of course is not a criticism of software; it is a simple recognition of the consequence of the speed difference between dedicated hardware and general-purpose CPUs. However, Linux can definitely compete with low-end commercial products that are entirely software-based. Of course, simple extensions to the Linux kernel allow vendors to use Linux on hybrid systems as well (software and hardware); it is only a matter of writing the necessary device drivers.

Linux is also often used as the operating system of choice for the implementation of university projects and theses. Not all of them make it to the official kernel (not right away, at least). A few do, and others are simply made available online as patches to the official kernel. Isn't it a great satisfaction and reward to see your contribution to the Linux kernel being used by potentially millions of users? There is only one drawback: if your contribution is really appreciated, you may not be able to cope with the numerous emails of thanks or requests for help.

The momentum for Linux has been growing continually over the past years, and apparently it can only keep growing.

I first encountered Linux at the University of Bologna, where I was a grad student in computer science around 10 years ago. What a wonderful piece of software! I could work on my image processing projects at home on an i286/486 computer without having to compete with other students for access to the few Sun stations available at the university labs.

Since then, my marriage to Linux has never seen a gray day. It has even started to displace my fond memories of the glorious C64 generation, when I was first introduced to programming with Assembly language and the various dialects of BASIC. Yes, I belong to the C64 generation, and to some extent I can compare the joy of my first programming experiences with the C64 to my first journeys into the Linux kernel.

When I was first introduced to the beautiful world of networking, I started playing with the tools available on Linux. I also had the fortune to work for a UNESCO center in Italy where I helped develop their networking courses, based entirely on Linux boxes. That gave me access to a good lab equipped with all sorts of network devices and documentation, plus plenty of Linux enthusiasts to learn from and to collaborate with.

Unfortunately for my own peace of mind (but fortunately, I hope, for the reader of this book who benefits from the results), I am the kind of person that likes to understand everything and takes very little for granted. So at UNESCO, I started looking into the kernel code. This not only proved to be a good way to burn in my knowledge, but it also gave me more confidence in making use of user-space configuration tools: whenever a configuration tool did not provide a specific option, I usually knew whether it would be possible to add it or whether it would have required significant changes to the kernel. This kind of study turns into a path without an end: you always want more.

After developing a few tools as extensions to the Linux kernel (some revision of versions 2.0 and 2.2), my love for operating systems and networking led me to the Silicon Valley (Cisco Systems). When you learn a language, be it a human language or a computer programming language, a rule emerges: the more languages you know, the easier it becomes to learn new ones. You can identify each one's strengths and weaknesses, see the reasons behind design compromises, etc. The same applies to operating systems.

When I noticed the lack of good documentation about the networking code of the Linux kernel and the availability of good books for other parts of the kernel, I decided to try filling in the gap—or at least part of it. I hope this book will give you the starting documentation that I would have loved to have had years ago.

I believe that this book, together with O'Reilly's other two kernel books (*Understanding the Linux Kernel* and *Linux Device Drivers*), represents a good starting point for anyone willing to learn more about the Linux kernel internals. They complement each other and, when they do not address a given feature, point the reader to external documentation sources (when available).

However, I still suggest you make some coffee, turn on the music, and spend some time on the source code trying to understand how a given feature is implemented. I believe the knowledge you build in this way lasts longer than that built in any other way. Shortcuts are good, but sometimes the long way has its advantages, too.

The Audience for This Book

This book can help those who already have some knowledge of networking and would like to see how the engine of the Internet—that is, the Internet Protocol (IP) and its friends—is implemented on a first-class operating system. However, there is a theoretical introduction for each topic, so newcomers will be able to get up to speed quickly, too. Complex topics are accompanied by enough examples to make them easier to follow.

Linux doesn't just support basic IP; it also has quite a few advanced features. More important, its implementation must be sophisticated enough to play nicely with other kernel features such as symmetric multiprocessing (SMP) and kernel preemption. This makes the networking code of the Linux kernel a very good gym in which to train and keep your networking knowledge in shape.

Moreover, if you are like me and want to learn everything, you will find enough details in this book to keep you satisfied for quite a while.

Background Information

Some knowledge of operating systems would help. The networking code, like any other component of the operating system, must follow both common sense and implicit rules for coexistence with the rest of the kernel, including proper use of locking; fair use of memory and CPU; and an eye toward modularity, code cleanliness, and good performance. Even though I occasionally spend time on those aspects, I refer you to the other two O'Reilly kernel books mentioned earlier for a deeper and detailed discussion on generic operating system services and design.

Some knowledge of networking, and especially IP, would also help. However, I think the theory overview that precedes each implementation description in this book is sufficient to make the book self-contained for both newcomers and experienced readers.

The theoretical description of the topics covered in the book does not require any programming experience. However, the descriptions of the associated implementations require an intermediate knowledge of the C language. Chapter 1 will go through a series of coding conventions and tricks that are often used in the code, which should help especially those with less experience with C and kernel programming.

Organization of the Material

Some aspects of networking code require as many as seven chapters, while for other aspects one chapter is sufficient. When the topic is complex or big enough to span different chapters, the part of the book devoted to that topic always starts with a concept chapter that covers the theory necessary to understand the implementation, which is described in another chapter. All of the reference and secondary material is usually located in one miscellaneous chapter at the end of the part. No matter how big the topic is, the same scheme is used to organize its presentation.

For each topic, the implementation description includes:

- The big picture, which shows where the described kernel component falls in the network stack.
- A brief description of the main data structures and a figure that shows how they relate to each other.
- A description of which other kernel features the component interfaces with—for example, by means of notification chains or data structure cross-references. The firewall is an example of such a kernel feature, given the numerous hooks it has all over the networking code.
- Extensive use of flow charts and figures to make it easier to go through the code and extract the logic from big and seemingly complex functions.

The reference material always includes:

- A detailed description of the most important data structures, field by field
- A table with a brief description of all functions, macros, and data structures, which you can use as a quick reference
- A list of the files mentioned in the chapter, with their location in the kernel source tree
- A description of the interface between the most common user-space tools used to configure the topic of the chapter and the kernel
- A description of any file in /proc that is exported

The Linux kernel's networking code is not just a moving target, but a fast runner. The book does not cover all of the networking features. New ones are probably being added right now while you are reading. Many new features are driven by the needs of single users or organizations, or as university projects, but they find their way into the official kernel when they're considered useful for a large audience. Besides detailing the implementation of a subset of those features, I try to give you an idea of what the generic implementation of a feature might look like. This will help you greatly in understanding changes to the code and learning how new features are implemented. For example, given any feature, you need to take the following points into consideration:

- How do you design the data structures and the locking semantics?
- Is there a need for a user-space configuration tool? If so, is it going to interact with the kernel via an existing system call, an ioctl command, a */proc* file, or the Netlink socket?
- Is there any need for a new notification chain, and is there a need to register to an already existing chain?
- What is the relationship with the firewall?
- Is there any need for a cache, a garbage collection mechanism, statistics, etc.?

Here is the list of topics covered in the book:

Interface between user space and kernel
> In Chapter 3, you will get a brief overview of the mechanisms that networking configuration tools use to interact with their counterparts inside the kernel. It will not be a detailed discussion, but it will help you to understand certain parts of the kernel code.

System initialization
> Part II describes the initialization of key components of the networking code, and how network devices are registered and initialized.

Interface between device drivers and protocol handlers
> Part III offers a detailed description of how *ingress* (incoming or received) packets are handed by the device drivers to the upper-layer protocols, and vice versa.

Bridging
> Part IV describes transparent bridging and the Spanning Tree Protocol, the L2 (Layer two) counterpart of routing at L3 (Layer three).

Internet Protocol Version 4 (IPv4)
> Part V describes how packets are received, transmitted, forwarded, and delivered locally at the IPv4 layer.

Interface between IPv4 and the transport layer (L4) protocols
> Chapter 20 shows how IPv4 packets addressed to the local host are delivered to the transport layer (L4) protocols (TCP, UDP, etc.).

Internet Control Message Protocol (ICMP)
> Chapter 25 describes the implementation of ICMP, the only transport layer (L4) protocol covered in the book.

Neighboring protocols
> These find local network addresses, given their IP addresses. Part VI describes both the common infrastructure of the various protocols and the details of the ARP neighboring protocol used by IPv4.

Routing
> Part VII, the biggest one of the book, describes the routing cache and tables. Advanced features such as Policy Routing and Multipath are also covered.

What Is Not Covered

For lack of space, I had to select a subset of the Linux networking features to cover. No selection would make everyone happy, but I think I covered the core of the networking code, and with the knowledge you can gain with this book, you will find it easier to study on your own any other networking feature of the kernel.

In this book, I decided to focus on the networking code, from the interface between device drivers and the protocol handlers, up to the interface between the IPv4 and L4 protocols. Instead of covering all of the features with a compromise on quality, I preferred to keep quality as the first goal, and to select the subset of features that would represent the best start for a journey into the kernel networking implementation.

Here is a partial list of the features I could not cover for lack of space:

Internet Protocol Version 6 (IPv6)
> Even though I do not cover IPv6 in the book, the description of IPv4 can help you a lot in understanding the IPv6 implementation. The two protocols share naming conventions for functions and often for variables. Their interface to Netfilter is also similar.

IP Security protocol
> The kernel provides a generic infrastructure for cryptography along with a collection of both ciphers and digest algorithms. The first interface to the cryptographic layer was synchronous, but the latest improvements are adding an asynchronous interface to allow Linux to take advantage of hardware cards that can offload the work from the CPU.
>
> The protocols of the IPsec suite—Authentication Header (AH), Encapsulating-Security Payload (ESP), and IP Compression (IPcomp)—are implemented in the kernel and make use of the cryptographic layer.

IP multicast and IP multicast routing
> Multicast functionality was implemented to conform to versions 2 and 3 of the Internet Group Management Protocol (IGMP). Multicast routing support is also present, conforming to versions 1 and 2 of Protocol Independent Multicast (PIM).

Transport layer (L4) protocols
> Several L4 protocols are implemented in the Linux kernel. Besides the two well-known ones, UDP and TCP, Linux has the newer Stream Control Transmission Protocol (SCTP). A good description of the implementation of those protocols would require a new book of this size, all on its own.

Traffic Control
> This is the Quality of Service (QoS) layer of Linux, another interesting and powerful component of the kernel's networking code. Traffic control is implemented as a general infrastructure and as a collection of traffic classifiers and queuing disciplines. I briefly describe it and the interface it provides to the main transmission routine in Chapter 11. A great deal of documentation is available at *http://lartc.org*.

Netfilter

The firewall code infrastructure and its extensions (including the various NAT flavors) is not covered in the book, but I describe its interaction with most of the networking features I cover. At the Netfilter home page, *http://www.netfilter.org*, you can find some interesting documentation about its kernel internals.

Network filesystems

Several network filesystems are implemented in the kernel, among them NFS (versions 2, 3, and 4), SMB, Coda, and Andrew. You can read a detailed description of the Virtual File System layer in *Understanding the Linux Kernel*, and then delve into the source code to see how those network filesystems interface with it.

Virtual devices

The use of a dedicated virtual device underlies the implementation of networking features. Examples include 802.1Q, bonding, and the various tunneling protocols, such as IP-over-IP (IPIP) and Generalized Routing Encapsulation (GRE). Virtual devices need to follow the same guidelines as real devices and provide the same interface to other kernel components. In different chapters, where needed, I compare real and virtual device behaviors. The only virtual device that is described in detail is the bridge interface, which is covered in Part IV.

DECnet, IPX, AppleTalk, etc.

These have historical roots and are still in use, but are much less commonly used than IP. I left them out to give more space to topics that affect more users.

IP virtual server

This is another interesting piece of the networking code, described at *http://www.linuxvirtualserver.org/*. This feature can be used to build clusters of servers using different scheduling algorithms.

Simple Network Management Protocol (SNMP)

No chapter in this book is dedicated to SNMP, but for each feature, I give a description of all the counters and statistics kept by the kernel, the routines used to manipulate them, and the */proc* files used to export them, when available.

Frame Diverter

This feature allows the kernel to kidnap ingress frames not addressed to the local host. I will briefly mention it in Part III. Its home page is *http://diverter.sourceforge.net*.

Plenty of other network projects are available as separate patches to the kernel, and I can't list them all here. One that I find particularly fascinating and promising, especially in relation to the Linux routing code, is the highly configurable Click router, currently offered at *http://pdos.csail.mit.edu/click/*.

Because this is a book about the kernel, I do not cover user-space configuration tools. However, for each topic, I describe the interface between the most common user-space configuration tools and the kernel.

Conventions Used in This Book

The following is a list of the typographical conventions used in this book:

Italic

> Used for file and directory names, program and command names, command-line options, URLs, and new terms

`Constant Width`

> Used in examples to show the contents of files or the output from commands, and in the text to indicate words that appear in C code or other literal strings

`Constant Width Italic`

> Used to indicate text within commands that the user replaces with an actual value

`Constant Width Bold`

> Used in examples to show commands or other text that should be typed literally by the user

Pay special attention to notes set apart from the text with the following icons:

> This is a tip. It contains useful supplementary information about the topic at hand.

> This is a warning. It helps you solve and avoid annoying problems.

Using Code Examples

This book is here to help you get your job done. In general, you may use the code in this book in your programs and documentation. The code samples are covered by a dual BSD/GPL license.

We appreciate, but do not require, attribution. An attribution usually includes the title, author, publisher, and ISBN. For example: "*Understanding Linux Network Internals*, by Christian Benvenuti. Copyright 2006 O'Reilly Media, Inc., 0-596-00255-6."

We'd Like to Hear from You

Please address comments and questions concerning this book to the publisher:

O'Reilly Media, Inc.
1005 Gravenstein Highway North
Sebastopol, CA 95472
(800) 998-9938 (in the United States or Canada)
(707) 829-0515 (international or local)
(707) 829-0104 (fax)

We have a web page for this book, where we list errata, examples, and any additional information. You can access this page at:

http://www.oreilly.com/catalog/understandlni/

To comment or ask technical questions about this book, send email to:

bookquestions@oreilly.com

For more information about our books, conferences, Resource Centers, and the O'Reilly Network, see our web site at:

http://www.oreilly.com

Safari Enabled

 When you see a Safari® Enabled icon on the cover of your favorite technology book, that means the book is available online through the O'Reilly Network Safari Bookshelf.

Safari offers a solution that's better than e-books. It's a virtual library that lets you easily search thousands of top tech books, cut and paste code samples, download chapters, and find quick answers when you need the most accurate, current information. Try it for free at *http://safari.oreilly.com*.

Acknowledgments

This book would not have been possible without an interesting topic to talk about, and an audience. The interesting topic is Linux, this modern operating system that anyone has an opportunity to be part of, and the audience is the incredible number of users that often decide not only to take advantage of the good work of others, but also to contribute to its success by getting involved in its development. I have always loved sharing knowledge and passion for the things I like, and with this book, I have tried my best to add a lane or two to the highway that takes interested people into the wonderful world of the Linux kernel.

Of course, I did not do everything while lying in a hammock by the beach, with an ice cream in one hand and a mouse in the other. It took quite a lot of work to investigate the reasons behind some of the implementation choices. It is incredible how much information you can dig out of the development mailing lists, and how much people are willing to share their knowledge when you show genuine interest in their work.

For sure, this book would not be what it is without the great help and suggestions of my editor, Andy Oram. Due to the frequent changes that the networking code experiences, a few chapters had to undergo substantial updates during the writing of the book, but Andy understood this and helped me get to the finish line.

I also would like to thank all of those people that supported me in this effort, and Cisco Systems for giving me the flexibility I needed to work on this book.

A special thanks also goes to the technical reviewers for being able to review a book of this size in a short amount of time, still providing useful comments that allowed me to catch errors and improve the quality of the material. The book was reviewed by Jerry Cooperstein, Michael Boerner, and Paul Kinzelman (in alphabetical order, by first name). I also would like to thank Francois Tallet for reviewing Part IV and Andi Kleen for his feedback on Part V.

## PART I

General Background

The information in this part of the book represents the basic knowledge you need to understand the rest of the book comfortably. If you are already familiar with the Linux kernel, or you are an experienced software engineer, you will be able to go pretty quickly through these chapters. For other readers, I suggest getting familiar with this material before proceeding with the following parts of the book:

Chapter 1, *Introduction*
> The bulk of this chapter is devoted to introducing a few of the common programming patterns and tricks that you'll often meet in the networking code.

Chapter 2, *Critical Data Structures*
> In this chapter, you can find a detailed description of two of the most important data structures used by the networking code: the socket buffer sk_buff and the network device net_device.

Chapter 3, *User-Space-to-Kernel Interface*
> The discussion of each feature in this book ends with a set of sections that shows how user-space configuration tools and the kernel communicate. The information in this chapter can help you understand those sections better.

## CHAPTER 1

Introduction

To do research in the source code of a large project is to enter a strange, new land with its own customs and unspoken expectations. It is useful to learn some of the major conventions up front, and to try interacting with the inhabitants instead of merely standing back and observing.

The bulk of this chapter is devoted to introducing you to a few of the common programming patterns and tricks that you'll often meet in the networking code.

I encourage you, when possible, to try interacting with a given part of the kernel networking code by means of user-space tools. So in this chapter, I'll give you a few pointers as to where you can download those tools if they're not already installed on your preferred Linux distribution, or if you simply want to upgrade them to the latest versions.

I'll also describe some tools that let you find your way gracefully through the enormous kernel code. Finally, I'll explain briefly why a kernel feature may not be integrated into the official kernel releases, even if it is widely used in the Linux community.

Basic Terminology

In this section, I'll introduce terms and abbreviations that are going to be used extensively in this book.

Eight-bit quantities are normally called *octets* in the networking literature. In this book, however, I use the more familiar term *byte*. After all, the book describes the behavior of the kernel rather than some network abstraction, and kernel developers are used to thinking in terms of bytes.

The terms *vector* and *array* will be used interchangeably.

When referring to the layers of the TCP/IP network stack, I will use the abbreviations L2, L3, and L4 to refer to the link, network, and transport layers, respectively.

The numbers are based on the famous (if not exactly current) seven-layer OSI model. In most cases, L2 will be a synonym for Ethernet, L3 for IP Version 4 or 6, and L4 for UDP, TCP, or ICMP. When I need to refer to a specific protocol, I'll use its name (i.e., TCP) rather than the generic *Ln protocol* term.

In different chapters, we will see how data units are received and transmitted by the protocols that sit at a given layer in the network stack. In those contexts, the terms *ingress* and *input* will be used interchangeably. The same applies to *egress* and *output*. The action of receiving or transmitting a data unit may be referred to with the abbreviations RX and TX, respectively.

A data unit is given different names, such as *frame*, *packet*, *segment*, and *message*, depending on the layer where it is used (see Chapter 13 for more details). Table 1-1 summarizes the major abbreviations you'll see in the book.

Table 1-1. Abbreviations used frequently in this book

Abbreviation	Meaning
L2	Link layer (e.g., Ethernet)
L3	Network layer (e.g., IP)
L4	Transport layer (e.g., UDP/TCP/ICMP)
BH	Bottom half
IRQ	Interrupt
RX	Reception
TX	Transmission

Common Coding Patterns

Each networking feature, like any other kernel feature, is just one of the citizens inside the kernel. As such, it must make proper and fair use of memory, CPU, and all other shared resources. Most features are not written as standalone pieces of kernel code, but interact with other kernel components more or less heavily depending on the feature. They therefore try, as much as possible, to follow similar mechanisms to implement similar functionalities (there is no need to reinvent the wheel every time).

Some requirements are common to several kernel components, such as the need to allocate several instances of the same data structure type, the need to keep track of references to an instance of a data structure to avoid unsafe memory deallocations, etc. In the following subsections, we will view common ways in Linux to handle such requirements. I will also talk about common coding tricks that you may come across while browsing the kernel's code.

This book uses *subsystem* as a loose term to describe a collection of files that implement a major set of features—such as IP or routing—and that tend to be maintained by the same people and to change in lockstep. In the rest of the chapter, I'll also use the term *kernel component* to refer to these subsystems, because the conventions discussed here apply to most parts of the kernel, not just those involved in networking.

Memory Caches

The kernel uses the kmalloc and kfree functions to allocate and free a memory block, respectively. The syntax of those two functions is similar to that of the two sister calls, malloc and free, from the *libc* user-space library. For more details on kmalloc and kfree, please refer to *Linux Device Drivers* (O'Reilly).

It is common for a kernel component to allocate several instances of the same data structure type. When allocation and deallocation are expected to happen often, the associated kernel component initialization routine (for example, fib_hash_init for the routing table) usually allocates a special memory cache that will be used for the allocations. When a memory block is freed, it is actually returned to the same cache from which it was allocated.

Some examples of network data structures for which the kernel maintains dedicated memory caches include:

Socket buffer descriptors
> This cache, allocated by skb_init in *net/core/sk_buff.c*, is used for the allocation of sk_buff buffer descriptors. The sk_buff structure is probably the one that registers the highest number of allocations and deallocations in the networking subsystem.

Neighboring protocol mappings
> Each neighboring protocol uses a memory cache to allocate the data structures that store L3-to-L2 address mappings. See Chapter 27.

Routing tables
> The routing code uses two memory caches for two of the data structures that define routes. See Chapter 32.

Here are the key kernel functions used to deal with memory caches:

kmem_cache_create
kmem_cache_destroy
> Create and destroy a cache.

kmem_cache_alloc
kmem_cache_free
> Allocate and return a buffer to the cache. They are usually called via wrappers, which manage the requests for allocation and deallocation at a higher level. For example, the request to free an instance of an sk_buff buffer with kfree_skb ends up calling kmem_cache_free only when all the references to the buffer have been released and all the necessary cleanup has been done by the interested subsystems (for instance, the firewall).

The limit on the number of instances that can be allocated from a given cache (when present) is usually enforced by the wrappers around kmem_cache_alloc, and are sometimes configurable with a parameter in */proc*.

For more details on how memory caches are implemented and how they interface to the slab allocator, please refer to *Understanding the Linux Kernel* (O'Reilly).

Caching and Hash Tables

It is pretty common to use a cache to increase performance. In the networking code, there are caches for L3-to-L2 mappings (such as the ARP cache used by IPv4), for the routing table cache, etc.

Cache lookup routines often take an input parameter that says whether a cache miss should or should not create a new element and add it to the cache. Other lookup routines simply add missing elements all the time.

Caches are often implemented with hash tables. The kernel provides a set of data types, such as one-way and bidirectional lists, that can be used as building blocks for simple hash tables.

The standard way to handle inputs that hash to the same value is to put them in a list. Traversing this list takes substantially longer than using the hash key to do a lookup. Therefore, it is always important to minimize the number of inputs that hash to the same value.

When the lookup time on a hash table (whether it uses a cache or not) is a critical parameter for the owner subsystem, it may implement a mechanism to increase the size of the hash table so that the average length of the collision lists goes down and the average lookup time improves. See the section "Dynamic resizing of per-netmask hash tables" in Chapter 34 for an example.

You may also find subsystems, such as the neighboring layer, that add a random component (regularly changed) to the key used to distribute elements in the cache's buckets. This is used to reduce the damage of Denial of Service (DoS) attacks aimed at concentrating the elements of a hash table into a single bucket. See the section "Caching" in Chapter 27 for an example.

Reference Counts

When a piece of code tries to access a data structure that has already been freed, the kernel is not very happy, and the user is rarely happy with the kernel's reaction. To avoid those nasty problems, and to make garbage collection mechanisms easier and more effective (see the section "Garbage Collection" later in this chapter), most data structures keep a reference count. Good kernel citizens increment and decrement the reference count of every data structure every time they save and release a reference, respectively, to the structure. For any data structure type that requires a reference count, the kernel component that owns the structure usually exports two functions that can be used to increment and decrement the reference count. Such functions are usually called *xxx*_hold and *xxx*_release, respectively. Sometimes the release function is called *xxx*_put instead (e.g., dev_put for net_device structures).

While we like to assume there are no bad citizens in the kernel, developers are human, and as such they do not always write bug-free code. The use of the reference count is a simple but effective mechanism to avoid freeing still-referenced data structures. However, it does not always solve the problem completely. This is the consequence of forgetting to balance increments and decrements:

- If you release a reference to a data structure but forget to call the *xxx*_release function, the kernel will never allow the data structure to be freed (unless another buggy piece of code happens to call the release function an extra time by mistake!). This leads to gradual memory exhaustion.

- If you take a reference to a data structure but forget to call *xxx*_hold, and at some later point you happen to be the only reference holder, the structure will be prematurely freed because you are not accounted for. This case definitely can be more catastrophic than the previous one; your next attempt to access the structure can corrupt other data or cause a kernel panic that brings down the whole system instantly.

When a data structure is to be removed for some reason, the reference holders can be explicitly notified about its going away so that they can politely release their references. This is done through notification chains. See the section "Reference Counts" in Chapter 8 for an interesting example.

The reference count on a data structure typically can be incremented when:

- There is a close relationship between two data structure types. In this case, one of the two often maintains a pointer initialized to the address of the second one.

- A timer is started whose handler is going to access the data structure. When the timer is fired, the reference count on the structure is incremented, because the last thing you want is for the data structure to be freed before the timer expires.

- A successful lookup on a list or a hash table returns a pointer to the matching element. In most cases, the returned result is used by the caller to carry out some task. Because of that, it is common for a lookup routine to increase the reference count on the matching element, and let the caller release it when necessary.

When the last reference to a data structure is released, it may be freed because it is not needed anymore, but not necessarily.

The introduction of the new *sysfs* filesystem has helped to make a good portion of the kernel code more aware of reference counts and consistent in its use of them.

Garbage Collection

Memory is a shared and limited resource and should not be wasted, particularly in the kernel because it does not use virtual memory. Most kernel subsystems implement some sort of garbage collection to reclaim the memory held by unused or stale data structure instances. Depending on the needs of any given feature, you will find two main kinds of garbage collection:

Asynchronous

> This type of garbage collection is unrelated to particular events. A timer that expires regularly invokes a routine that scans a set of data structures and frees the ones considered eligible for deletion. The conditions that make a data structure eligible for deletion depend on the features and logic of the subsystem, but a common criterion is the presence of a null reference count.

Synchronous

> There are cases where a shortage of memory, which cannot wait for the asynchronous garbage collection timer to kick in, triggers immediate garbage collection. The criteria used to select the data structures eligible for deletion are not necessarily the same ones used by asynchronous cleanup (for instance, they could be more aggressive). See Chapter 33 for an example.

In Chapter 7, you will see how the kernel manages to reclaim the memory used by initialization routines and that is no longer needed after they have been executed.

Function Pointers and Virtual Function Tables (VFTs)

Function pointers are a convenient way to write clean C code while getting some of the benefits of the object-oriented languages. In the definition of a data structure type (the object), you include a set of function pointers (the methods). Some or all manipulations of the structure are then done through the embedded functions. C-language function pointers in data structures look like this:

```
struct sock {
    ...
    void    (*sk_state_change)(struct sock *sk);
    void    (*sk_data_ready)(struct sock *sk, int bytes);
    ...

};
```

A key advantage to using function pointers is that they can be initialized differently depending on various criteria and the role played by the object. Thus, invoking sk_ state_change may actually invoke different functions for different sock sockets.

Function pointers are used extensively in the networking code. The following are only a few examples:

- When an ingress or egress packet is processed by the routing subsystem, it initializes two routines in the buffer data structure. You will see this in Chapter 35. Refer to Chapter 2 for a complete list of function pointers included in the sk_buff data structure.

- When a packet is ready for transmission on the networking hardware, it is handed to the hard_start_xmit function pointer of the net_device data structure. That routine is initialized by the device driver associated with the device.

- When an L3 protocol wants to transmit a packet, it invokes one of a set of function pointers. These have been initialized to a set of routines by the address resolution protocol associated with the L3 protocol. Depending on the actual routine to which the function pointer is initialized, a transparent L3-to-L2 address resolution may take place (for example, IPv4 packets go through ARP). When the address resolution is unnecessary, a different routine is used. See Part VI for a detailed discussion on this interface.

We see in the preceding examples how function pointers can be employed as interfaces between kernel components or as generic mechanisms to invoke the right function handler at the right time based on the result of something done by a different subsystem. There are cases where function pointers are also used as a simple way to allow protocols, device drivers, or any other feature to personalize an action.

Let's look at an example. When a device driver registers a network device with the kernel, it goes through a series of steps that are needed regardless of the device type. At some point, it invokes a function pointer on the net_device data structure to let the device driver do something extra if needed. The device driver could either initialize that function pointer to a function of its own, or leave the pointer NULL because the default steps performed by the kernel are sufficient.

A check on the value of a function pointer is always necessary before executing it to avoid NULL pointer dereferences, as shown in this snapshot from register_netdevice:

```
if (dev->init && dev->init(dev) != 0) {
    ...
}
```

Function pointers have one main drawback: they make browsing the source code a little harder. While going through a given code path, you may end up focusing on a function pointer call. In such cases, before proceeding down the code path, you need to find out how the function pointer has been initialized. It could depend on different factors:

- When the selection of the routine to assign to a function pointer is based on a particular piece of data, such as the protocol handling the data or the device driver a given packet is received from, it is easier to derive the routine. For example, if a given device is managed by the *drivers/net/3c59x.c* device driver, you can derive the routine to which a given function pointer of the net_device data structure is initialized by reading the device initialization routine provided by the device driver.

- When the selection of the routine is based instead on more complex logic, such as the state of the resolution of an L3-to-L2 address mapping, the routine used at any time depends on external events that cannot be predicted.

A set of function pointers grouped into a data structure are often referred to as a *virtual function table* (VFT). When a VFT is used as the interface between two major subsystems, such as the L3 and L4 protocol layers, or when the VFT is simply exported as an interface to a generic kernel component (set of objects), the number of function pointers in it may swell to include many different pointers that accommodate a wide range of protocols or other features. Each feature may end up using only a few of the many functions provided. You will see an example in Part VI. Of course, if this use of a VFT is taken too far, it becomes cumbersome and a major redesign is needed.

goto Statements

Few C programmers like the goto statement. Without getting into the history of the goto (one of the longest and most famous controversies in computer programming), I'll summarize some of the reasons the goto is usually deprecated, but why the Linux kernel uses it anyway.

Any piece of code that uses goto can be rewritten without it. The use of goto statements can reduce the readability of the code, and make debugging harder, because at any position following a goto you can no longer derive unequivocally the conditions that led the execution to that point.

Let me make this analogy: given any node in a tree, you know what the path from the root to the node is. But if you add vines that entwine around branches randomly, you do not always have a unique path between the root and the other nodes anymore.

However, because the C language does not provide explicit exceptions (and they are often avoided in other languages as well because of the performance hit and coding complexity), carefully placed goto statements can make it easier to jump to code that handles undesired or peculiar events. In kernel programming, and particularly in networking, such events are very common, so goto becomes a convenient tool.

I must defend the kernel's use of goto by pointing out that developers have by no means gone wild with it. Even though there are more than 30,000 instances, they are mainly used to handle different return codes within a function, or to jump out of more than one level of nesting.

Vector Definitions

In some cases, the definition of a data structure includes an optional block at the end. This is an example:

```
struct abc {
    int age;
    char *name[20];
    ...
    char    placeholder[0];
}
```

The optional block starts with `placeholder`. Note that `placeholder` is defined as a vector of size 0. This means that when `abc` is allocated with the optional block, `placeholder` points to the beginning of the block. When no optional block is required, `placeholder` is just a pointer to the end of the structure; it does not consume any space.

Thus, if `abc` is used by several pieces of code, each one can use the same basic definition (avoiding the confusion of doing the same thing in slightly different ways) while extending `abc` differently to personalize its definition according to its needs.

We will see this kind of data structure definition a few times in the book. One example is in Chapter 19.

Conditional Directives (#ifdef and family)

Conditional directives to the compiler are sometimes necessary. An excessive use of them can reduce the readability of the code, but I can state that Linux does not abuse them. They appear for different reasons, but the ones we are interested in are those used to check whether a given feature is supported by the kernel. Configuration tools such as *make xconfig* determine whether the feature is compiled in, not supported at all, or loadable as a module.

Examples of feature checks by `#ifdef` or `#if defined` C preprocessor directives are:

To include or exclude fields from a data structure definition

```
    struct sk_buff {
        ...
    #ifdef CONFIG_NETFILTER_DEBUG
        unsigned int nf_debug;
    #endif
        ...
    }
```

In this example, the Netfilter debugging feature requires an `nf_debug` field in the `sk_buff` structure. When the kernel does not have support for Netfilter debugging (a feature needed by only a handful of developers), there is no need to include the field, which would just take up more memory for every network packet.

To include or exclude pieces of code from a function

```
int ip_route_input(...)
{
        ...
        if (rth->fl.fl4_dst == daddr &&
            rth->fl.fl4_src == saddr &&
            rth->fl.iif == iif &&
            rth->fl.oif == 0 &&
#ifndef CONFIG_IP_ROUTE_FWMARK
            rth->fl.fl4_fwmark == skb->nfmark &&
#endif
            rth->fl.fl4_tos == tos) {
                ...
        }
}
```

The routing cache lookup routine ip_route_input, described in Chapter 33, checks the value of the tag set by the firewall only when the kernel has been compiled with support for the "IP: use netfilter MARK value as routing key" feature.

To select the right prototype for a function

```
#ifdef CONFIG_IP_MULTIPLE_TABLES
struct fib_table * fib_hash_init(int id)
#else
struct fib_table * __init fib_hash_init(int id)
{
    ...
}
```

In this example, the directives are used to add the __init tag* to the prototype when the kernel does not have support for Policy Routing.

To select the right definition for a function

```
#ifndef CONFIG_IP_MULTIPLE_TABLES
...
static inline struct fib_table *fib_get_table(int id)
{
    if (id != RT_TABLE_LOCAL)
        return ip_fib_main_table;
    return ip_fib_local_table
}
...
#else
...
static inline struct fib_table *fib_get_table(int id)
{
    if (id == 0)
        id = RT_TABLE_MAIN;
    return fib_tables[id];
}
```

---

* See Chapter 7 for a description of this macro.

```
...
#endif
```
Note that this case differs from the previous one. In the previous case, the function body lies outside the #ifdef/#endif blocks, whereas in this case, each block contains a complete definition of the function.

The definition or initialization of variables and macros can also use conditional compilation.

It is important to know about the existence of multiple definitions of certain functions or macros, whose selection at compile time is based on a preprocessor macro as in the preceding examples. Otherwise, when you look for a function, variable, or macro definition, you may be looking at the wrong one.

See Chapter 7 for a discussion of how the introduction of special macros has reduced, in some cases, the use of conditional compiler directives.

Compile-Time Optimization for Condition Checks

Most of the time, when the kernel compares a variable against some external value to see whether a given condition is met, the result is extremely likely to be predictable. This is pretty common, for example, with code that enforces sanity checks. The kernel uses the likely and unlikely macros, respectively, to wrap comparisons that are likely to return a true (1) or false (0) result. Those macros take advantage of a feature of the *gcc* compiler that can optimize the compilation of the code based on that information.

Here is an example. Let's suppose you need to call the do_something function, and that in case of failure, you must handle it with the handle_error function:

```
err = do_something(x,y,z);
if (err)
    handle_error(err);
```

Under the assumption that do_something rarely fails, you can rewrite the code as follows:

```
err = do_something(x,y,z);
if (unlikely(err))
    handle_error(err);
```

An example of the optimization made possible by the likely and unlikely macros is in handling options in the IP header. The use of IP options is limited to very specific cases, and the kernel can safely assume that most IP packets do not carry IP options. When the kernel forwards an IP packet, it needs to take care of options according to the rules described in Chapter 18. The last stage of forwarding an IP packet is taken care of by ip_forward_finish. This function uses the unlikely macro to wrap the condition that checks whether there is any IP option to take care of. See the section "ip_forward_finish Function" in Chapter 20.

Mutual Exclusion

Locking is used extensively in the networking code, and you are likely to see it come up as an issue under every topic in this book. Mutual exclusion, locking mechanisms, and synchronization are a general topic—and a highly interesting and complex one—for many types of programming, especially kernel programming. Linux has seen the introduction and optimization of several approaches to mutual exclusion over the years. Thus, this section merely summarizes the locking mechanisms seen in networking code; I refer you to the high-quality, detailed discussions available in O'Reilly's *Understanding the Linux Kernel* and *Linux Device Driver*.

Each mutual exclusion mechanism is the best choice for particular circumstances. Here is a brief summary of the alternative mutual exclusion approaches you will see often in the networking code:

Spin locks

> This is a lock that can be held by only one thread of execution at a time. An attempt to acquire the lock by another thread of execution makes the latter loop until the lock is released. Because of the waste cause by looping, spin locks are used only on multiprocessor systems, and generally are used only when the developer expects the lock to be held for short intervals. Also because of the waste caused to other threads, a thread of execution must not sleep while holding a spin lock.

Read-write spin locks

> When the uses of a given lock can be clearly classified as read-only and read-write, the use of read-write spin locks is preferred. The difference between spin locks and read-write spin locks is that in the latter, multiple readers can hold the lock at the same time. However, only one writer at a time can hold the lock, and no reader can acquire it when it is already held by a writer. Because readers are given higher priority over writers, this type of lock performs well when the number of readers (or the number of read-only lock acquisitions) is a good deal bigger than the number of writers (or the number or read-write lock acquisitions).
>
> When the lock is acquired in read-only mode, it cannot be promoted to read-write mode directly: the lock must be released and reacquired in read-write mode.

Read-Copy-Update (RCU)

> RCU is one of the latest mechanisms made available in Linux to provide mutual exclusion. It performs quite well under the following specific conditions:
>
> - Read-write lock requests are rare compared to read-only lock requests.
> - The code that holds the lock is executed atomically and does not sleep.
> - The data structures protected by the lock are accessed via pointers.
>
> The first condition concerns performance, and the other two are at the base of the RCU working principle.

Note that the first condition would suggest the use of read-write spin locks as an alternative to RCU. To understand why RCU, when its use is appropriate, performs better than read-write spin locks, you need to consider other aspects, such as the effect of the processor caches on SMP systems.

The working principle behind the design of RCU is simple yet powerful. For a clear description of the advantages of RCU and a brief description of its implementation, refer to an article published by its author, Paul McKenney, in the Linux Journal (*http://linuxjournal.com/article/6993*).* You can also refer to *Understanding the Linux Kernel* and *Linux Device Drivers*.

An example where RCU is used in the networking code is the routing subsystem. Lookups are more frequent than updates on the cache, and the routine that implements the routing cache lookup does not block in the middle of the search. See Chapter 33.

Semaphores are offered by the kernel but are rarely used in the networking code covered in this book. One example, however, is the code used to serialize configuration changes, which we will see in action in Chapter 8.

Conversions Between Host and Network Order

Data structures spanning more than one byte can be stored in memory with two different formats: Little Endian and Big Endian. The first format stores the least significant byte at the lowest memory address, and the second does the opposite. The format used by an operating system such as Linux depends on the processor in use. For example, Intel processors follow the Little Endian model, and Motorola processors use the Big Endian model.

Suppose our Linux box receives an IP packet from a remote host. Because it does not know which format, Little Endian or Big Endian, was used by the remote host to initialize the protocol headers, how will it read the header? For this reason, each protocol family must define what "endianness" it uses. The TCP/IP stack, for example, follows the Big Endian model.

But this still leaves the kernel developer with a problem: she must write code that can run on many different processors that support different endianness. Some processors might match the endianness of the incoming packet, but those that do not require conversion to the endianness used by the processor.

Therefore, every time the kernel needs to read, save, or compare a field of the IP header that spans more than one byte, it must first convert it from network byte order to host byte order or vice versa. The same applies to the other protocols of the

---

* For more documentation, you can refer to the following URL maintained by the author: *http://www.rdrop. com/users/paulmck/rclock*.

TCP/IP stack. When both the protocol and the local host are Big Endian, the conversion routines are simply no-ops because there is no need for any conversion. They always appear in the code to make the code portable; only the conversion routines themselves are platform dependent. Table 1-2 lists the main macros used for the conversion of two-byte and four-byte fields.

Table 1-2. Byte-ordering conversion routines

Macro	Meaning (short is 2 bytes, long is 4 bytes)
htons	Host-to-network byte order (short)
htonl	Host-to-network byte order (long)
ntohs	Network-to-host byte order (short)
ntohl	Network-to-host byte order (long)

The macros are defined in the generic header file *include/linux/byteorder/generic.h*. This is how each architecture tailors the definition of those macros based on their endianness:

- For each architecture there is a *byteorder.h* file in the per-architecture directory *include/asm-XXX/*.
- That file includes either *include/linux/byteorder/big_endian.h* or *include/linux/byteorder/little_endian.h*, depending on the processor's endianness.
- Both *little_endian.h* and *big_endian.h* include the generic file *include/linux/byteorder/generic.h*. The definitions of the macros in Table 1-2 are based on other macros that are defined differently by *little_endian.h* and *big_endian.h*, and this is how the endianness of the architecture influences the definition of the macros of Table 1-2.

For each macro *xxx* in Table 1-2 there is a sister macro, __constant_*xxx*, that is used when the input field is a constant value, such as an element of an enumeration list (see the section "ARP Protocol Initialization" in Chapter 28 for an example). Note that the macros in Table 1-2 are commonly used in the kernel code even when their input is a constant value (see the section "Setting the Ethernet Protocol and Length" in Chapter 13 for an example).

We said earlier in the section that endianness is important when a data field spans more than one byte. Endianness is actually important also when a field of one or more bytes is defined as a collection of bitfields. See, for example, what the IPv4 header looks like in Figure 18-2 in Chapter 18, and how the kernel defines the iphdr structure in *include/linux/ip.h*. The kernel defines __LITTLE_ENDIAN_BITFIELD and __BIG_ENDIAN_BITFIELD, respectively, in the *little_endian.h* and *big_endian.h* files mentioned earlier.

Catching Bugs

A few functions are supposed to be called under specific conditions, or are *not* supposed to be called under certain conditions. The kernel uses the BUG_ON and BUG_TRAP macros to catch cases where such conditions are not met. When the input condition to BUG_TRAP is false, the kernel prints a warning message. BUG_ON instead prints an error message and panics.

Statistics

It is a good habit for a feature to collect statistics about the occurrence of specific conditions, such as cache lookup successes and failures, memory allocation successes and failures, etc. For each networking feature that collects statistics, this book lists and describes each counter.

Measuring Time

The kernel often needs to measure how much time has passed since a given moment. For example, a routine that carries on a CPU-intensive task often releases the CPU after a given amount of time. It will continue its job when it is rescheduled for execution. This is especially important in kernel code, even though the kernel supports kernel preemption. A common example in the networking code is given by the routines that implement garbage collection. We will see plenty in this book.

The passing of time in kernel space is measured in ticks. A tick is the time between two consecutive expirations of the timer interrupt. The timer takes care of different tasks (we are not interested in them here) and regularly expires HZ times per second. HZ is a variable initialized by architecture-dependent code. For example, it is initialized to 1,000 on i386 machines. This means that the timer interrupt expires 1,000 times per second when Linux runs on an i386 system, and that there is one millisecond between two consecutive expirations.

Every time the timer expires it increments the global variable called jiffies. This means that at any time, jiffies represents the number of ticks since the system booted, and the generic value $n*HZ$ represents n seconds of time.

If all a function needs is to measure the passing of time, it can save the value of jiffies into a local variable and later compare the difference between jiffies and that timestamp against a time interval (expressed in number of ticks) to see how much time has passed since measurement started.

The following example shows a function that needs to do some kind of work but does not want to hold the CPU for more than one tick. When do_something says the work is completed by setting job_done to a nonzero value, the function can return:

```
unsigned long start_time = jiffies;
int job_done = 0;
```

```
do {
    do_something(&job_done);
    If (job_done)
        return;
while (jiffies - start_time < 1);
```

For a couple of examples involving real kernel code using jiffies, see the section "Backlog Processing: The process_backlog Poll Virtual Function" in Chapter 10, or the section "Asynchronous cleanup: the neigh_periodic_timer function" in Chapter 27.

User-Space Tools

Different tools can be used to configure the many networking features available on Linux. As mentioned at the beginning of the chapter, you can make thoughtful use of these tools to manipulate the kernel for learning purposes and to discover the effects of these changes.

The following tools are the ones I will refer often to in this book:

iputils
> Besides the perennial command ping, *iputils* includes arping (used to generate ARP requests), the Network Router Discovery daemon rdisc, and others.

net-tools
> This is a suite of networking tools, where you can find the well-known *ifconfig*, *route*, *netstat*, and *arp*, but also *ipmaddr*, *iptunnel*, *ether-wake*, *netplugd*, etc.

IPROUTE2
> This is the new-generation networking configuration suite (although it has been around for a few years already). Through an omnibus command named *ip*, the suite can be used to configure IP addresses and routing along with all of its advanced features, neighboring protocols, etc.

IPROUTE2's source code can be downloaded from *http://linux-net.osdl.org/index. php/Iproute2*, and the other packages can be downloaded from the download server of most Linux distributions.

These packages are included by default on most (if not all) Linux distributions. Whenever you do not understand how the kernel code processes a command from user space, I encourage you to look at the user-space tool source code and see how the command from the user is packaged and sent to the kernel.

At the following URLs, you can find good documentation on how to use the aforementioned tools, including active mailing lists:[*]

---

[*] I do not cover the firewall infrastructure design in this book, but I often show where the firewall hooks are located when analyzing various network protocols and layers.

- *http://lartc.org*
- *http://www.policyrouting.org*
- *http://www.netfilter.org*

If you want to follow the latest changes in the networking code, keep an eye on the following mailing list:

- The Linux Network Development List Archives (*http://oss.sgi.com/projects/netdev/archive*)

Other, more specific URLs will be given in the associated chapters.

Browsing the Source Code

The Linux kernel has gotten pretty big, and browsing the code with our old friend *grep* is definitely not a good idea anymore. Nowadays you can count on different pieces of software to make your journey into the kernel code a better experience.

One that I would like to suggest to those that do not know it already is *cscope*, which you can download from *http://cscope.sourceforge.net*. It is a simple yet powerful tool for searching, for example, where a function or variable is defined, where it is called, etc. Installing the tool is straightforward and you can find all the necessary instructions on the web site.

Each of us has his preferred editor, and probably the majority of us are fans of some form of either Emacs or *vi*. Both editors can use a special file called a "tags" file, to allow the user to move through source code. (*cscope* also uses a similar database file.) You can easily create such files with a synonymous target in the kernel root tree's *makefile*. The three databases: TAGS, tags, and cscope.out, are created, respectively, with *make TAGS*, *make tags*, and *make cscope*.[*]

Be aware that those files are pretty big, especially the one used by *cscope*. Therefore, make sure before building the file that you have a lot of free disk space.

If you are already using other source navigation tools, fine. But if you are not using any and have been lazy so far, it is time to say goodbye to *grep* and invest 15 minutes in learning how to use the aforementioned tools—they are well worth it.

Dead Code

The kernel, like any other large and dynamic piece of software, includes pieces of code that are no longer invoked. Unfortunately, you rarely see comments in the code that tell you this. You may sometimes find yourself having trouble trying to understand how a given function is used or a given variable is initialized simply because

---

[*] The *tags* and *TAGS* files are created with the help of the *ctags* utility.

you are looking at dead code. If you are lucky, that code does not compile and you can guess its out-of-date status. Other times you may not be that lucky.

Each kernel subsystem is supposed to be assigned one or more maintainers. However, some maintainers simply have too much code to look at, and insufficient free time to do it. Other times they may have lost interest in maintaining their subsystems but could not find any substitutes for their role. It is therefore good to keep this in mind when looking at code that seems to do something strange or that simply does not adhere to general, common-sense programming rules.

In this book, I tried, whenever meaningful, to alert you about functions, variables, and data structure fields that are not used, perhaps because they were left behind when removing a feature or because they were introduced for a new feature whose coding was never completed.

When a Feature Is Offered as a Patch

The kernel networking code is continuously evolving. Not only does it integrate new features, but existing components sometimes undergo design changes to achieve more modularity and higher performance. This obviously makes Linux very attractive as an embedded operating system for network appliance products (routers, switches, firewalls, load balancers, etc.).

Because anyone can develop a new feature for the Linux kernel, or extend or reimplement an existing one, the greatest thrill for any "open" developer is to see her work make it to the official kernel release. Sometimes, however, that is not possible or it may take a long time, even when a project has valuable features and is well implemented. Common reasons include:

- The code may not have been written following the guidelines in *Documentation/ CodingStyle*.

- Another major project that provides the same functionality has been around for some time and has already received the green light from the Linux community and from the key kernel developers that maintain the associated kernel area.

- There is too much overlap with another kernel component. In a case like this, the best approach is to remove the redundant functionality and use existing functionality where possible, or to extend the latter so that it can be used in new contexts. This situation underlines the importance of modularity.

- The size of the project and the amount of work required to maintain it in a quick-changing kernel may lead the new project's developers to keep it as a separate patch and release a new version only once in a while.

- The feature would be used only in very specific scenarios, considered not necessary in a general-purpose operating system. In this case, a separate patch is often the best solution.
- The overall design may not satisfy some key kernel developers. These experts usually have the big picture in mind, concerning both where the kernel is and where it is going. Often, they request design changes to make a feature fit into the kernel the right way.

Sometimes, overlap between features is hard to remove completely, perhaps, for example, because a feature is so flexible that its different uses become apparent only after some time. For example, the firewall has hooks in several places in the network stack. This makes it unnecessary for other features to implement any filtering or marking of data packets going in any direction: they can simply rely on the firewall. Of course, this creates dependencies (for example, if the routing subsystem wants to mark traffic matching specific criteria, the kernel must include support for the firewall). Also, the firewall maintainers must be ready to accept reasonable enhancement requests when they are deemed to be required by other kernel features. However, the compromise is often worth the gain: less redundant code means fewer bugs, easier code maintenance, simplified code paths, and other benefits.

An example of a recent cleanup of feature overlap is the removal of stateless Network Address Translation (NAT) support by the routing code in version 2.6 of the kernel. The developers realized that the stateful NAT support in the firewall is more flexible, and therefore that it was no longer worthwhile maintaining stateless NAT code (although it is faster and consumes less memory). Note that a new module could be written for Netfilter at any time to provide stateless NAT support if necessary.

CHAPTER 2
Critical Data Structures

A few key data structures are referenced throughout the Linux networking code. Both when reading this book and when studying the source code directly, you'll need to understand the fields in these data structures. To be sure, going over data structures field by field is less fun than unraveling functions, but it's an important foundation to have. "Show me your data," said the legendary software engineer, Frederick P. Brooks.

This chapter introduces the following data structures, and mentions some of the functions and macros that manipulate them:

struct sk_buff
> This is where a packet is stored. The structure is used by all the network layers to store their headers, information about the user data (the payload), and other information needed internally for coordinating their work.

struct net_device
> Each network device is represented in the Linux kernel by this data structure, which contains information about both its hardware and its software configuration. See Chapter 8 for details on when and how net_device data structures are allocated.

Another critical data structure for Linux networking is struct sock, which stores the networking information for sockets. Because this book does not cover sockets, I have not included sock in this chapter.

The Socket Buffer: sk_buff Structure

This is probably the most important data structure in the Linux networking code, representing the headers for data that has been received or is about to be transmitted. Defined in the *<include/linux/skbuff.h>* include file, it consists of a tremendous heap of variables that try to be all things to all people.

The structure has changed many times in the history of the kernel, both to add new options and to reorganize existing fields into a cleaner layout. Its fields can be classified roughly into the following categories:

- Layout
- General
- Feature-specific
- Management functions

This structure is used by several different network layers (MAC or another link protocol on the L2 layer, IP on L3, TCP or UDP on L4), and various fields of the structure change as it is passed from one layer to another. L4 appends a header before passing it to L3, which in turn puts on its own header before passing it to L2. Appending headers is more efficient than copying the data from one layer to another. Since adding space to the beginning of a buffer—which means changing the variable that points to it—is a complicated operation, the kernel provides the skb_reserve function (described later in this chapter) to carry it out. Thus, one of the first things done by each protocol, as the buffer passes down through layers, is to call skb_reserve to reserve space for the protocol's header.* In the later section "Data reservation and alignment: skb_reserve, skb_put, skb_push, and skb_pull," we will see an example of how the kernel makes sure enough space is reserved at the head of the buffer to allow each layer to add its own header while the buffer traverses the layers.

When the buffer passes up through the network layers, each header from the old layer is no longer of interest. The L2 header, for instance, is used only by the device drivers that handle the L2 protocol, so it is of no interest to L3. Instead of removing the L2 header from the buffer, the pointer to the beginning of the payload is moved ahead to the beginning of the L3 header, which requires fewer CPU cycles.

The rest of this section explains a basic principle about conditional (optional) fields, and then covers each of the categories just listed.

Networking Options and Kernel Structures

As you can see from glancing at TCP/IP specifications or configuring a kernel, network code provides an enormous number of options that are useful but not always required, such as a Firewall, Multicasting, and other features. Most of these options require additional fields in kernel data structures. Therefore, sk_buff is peppered with C preprocessor #ifdef directives. For example, near the bottom of the sk_buff definition you can find:

```
struct sk_buff {
    ... ... ...
```

---

* skb_reserve is also used by device drivers to align the IP header of ingress frames. See Chapter 10.

```
#ifdef CONFIG_NET_SCHED
    __u32     tc_index;
#ifdef CONFIG_NET_CLS_ACT
    __u32     tc_verd;
    __u32     tc_classid;
#endif
#endif
}
```

This shows that the field tc_index is part of the data structure only if the CONFIG_NET_ SCHED symbol is defined at compile time, which means that the right option (in this example, "Device Drivers → Networking support → Networking options → QoS and/ or fair queueing") has been enabled with some version of *make config* by an administrator or by an automated installation utility.

The previous example actually shows two nested options: the fields used by CONFIG_ NET_CLS_ACT (packet classifier) are considered for inclusion only if support for "QoS and/or fair queueing" is present.

Notice, by the way, that the QoS option cannot be compiled as a module. The reason is that most of the consequences of enabling the option will not be reversible after the kernel is compiled. In general, any option that causes a change in a kernel data structure (such as adding the tc_index field to the sk_buff structure) renders the option unfit to be compiled as a module.

You'll often want to find out which compile option from *make config* or its variants is associated with a given #ifdef symbol, to understand when a block of code is included in the kernel. The fastest way to make the association, in the 2.6 kernels, is to look for the symbol in the *kconfig* files that are spread all over the source tree (one per directory). In 2.4 kernels, you can consult the file *Documentation/Configure.help*.

Layout Fields

A few of the sk_buff's fields exist just to facilitate searching and to organize the data structure itself. The kernel maintains all sk_buff structures in a doubly linked list. But the organization of this list is somewhat more complicated than that of a traditional doubly linked list.

Like any doubly linked list, this one is tied together by next and prev fields in each sk_buff structure, the next field pointing forward and the prev field pointing backward. But this list has another requirement: each sk_buff structure must be able to find the head of the whole list quickly. To implement this requirement, an extra structure of type sk_buff_head is inserted at the beginning of the list, as a kind of dummy element. The sk_buff_head structure is:

```
struct sk_buff_head {
    /* These two members must be first. */
    struct sk_buff    * next;
    struct sk_buff    * prev;
```

```
    __u32        qlen;
    spinlock_t   lock;
};
```

qlen represents the number of elements in the list. lock is used to prevent simultaneous accesses to the list and is described in the section "List management functions," later in this chapter.

The first two elements of both sk_buff and sk_buff_head are the same: the next and
prev pointers. This allows the two structures to coexist in the same list, even though
sk_buff_head is positively skimpy in comparison to sk_buff. In addition, the same
functions can be used to manipulate both sk_buff and sk_buff_head.

To add to the complexity, every sk_buff structure contains a pointer to the single sk_
buff_head structure. This pointer has the field name list. See Figure 2-1 for help
finding your way around these data structures.

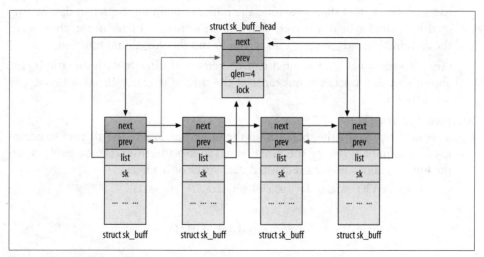

Figure 2-1. List of sk_buff elements

Other interesting fields of sk_buff follow:

struct sock *sk

> This is a pointer to a sock data structure of the socket that owns this buffer. This
> pointer is needed when data is either locally generated or being received by a
> local process, because the data and socket-related information is used by L4
> (TCP or UDP) and by the user application. When a buffer is merely being for-
> warded (that is, neither the source nor the destination is on the local machine),
> this pointer is NULL.

unsigned int len

> This is the size of the block of data in the buffer. This length includes both the
> data in the main buffer (i.e., the one pointed to by head) and the data in the

fragments.* Its value changes as the buffer moves from one network layer to the next, because headers are discarded while moving up in the stack and are added while moving down the stack. len accounts for protocol headers as well, as shown in Figure 2-8 in the section "Data reservation and alignment: skb_reserve, skb_put, skb_push, and skb_pull."

unsigned int data_len
Unlike len, data_len accounts only for the size of the data in the fragments.

unsigned int mac_len
This is the size of the MAC header.

atomic_t users
This is the reference count, or the number of entities using this sk_buff buffer. The main use of this parameter is to avoid freeing the sk_buff structure when someone is still using it. For this reason, each user of the buffer should increment and decrement this field when necessary. This counter covers only the users of the sk_buff data structure; the buffer containing the actual data is covered by a similar field (dataref) that will be introduced later in the chapter, in the section "The skb_shared_info structure and the skb_shinfo function."

users is sometimes incremented and decremented directly with the atomic_inc and atomic_dec functions, but most of the time it is manipulated with skb_get and kfree_skb.

unsigned int truesize
This field represents the total size of the buffer, including the sk_buff structure itself. It is initially set by the function alloc_skb to len+sizeof(sk_buff) when the buffer is allocated for a requested data space of len bytes.

```
struct sk_buff *alloc_skb(unsigned int size,int gfp_mask)
{
    ... ... ...
    skb->truesize = size + sizeof(struct sk_buff);
    ... ... ...
}
```

The field gets updated whenever skb->len is increased.

unsigned char *head
unsigned char *end
unsigned char *data
unsigned char *tail
These represent the boundaries of the buffer and the data within it. When each layer prepares the buffer for its activities, it may allocate more space for a header or for more data. head and end point to the beginning and end of the space allocated to the buffer, and data and tail point to the beginning and end of the actual data. See Figure 2-2. The layer can then fill in the gap between head and

---

* See Chapter 21 for a discussion of fragmented buffers.

data with a protocol header, or the gap between tail and end with new data. You will see in the later section "Allocating memory: alloc_skb and dev_alloc_skb" that the buffer on the right side of Figure 2-2 includes an additional header at the bottom.

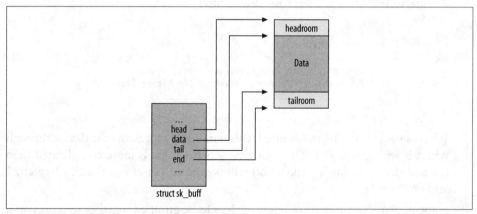

Figure 2-2. head/end versus data/tail pointers

void (*destructor)(...)
> This function pointer can be initialized to a routine that performs some activity when the buffer is removed. When the buffer does not belong to a socket, the destructor is usually not initialized. When the buffer belongs to a socket, it is usually set to sock_rfree or sock_wfree (by the skb_set_owner_r and skb_set_owner_w initialization functions, respectively). The two sock_*xxx* routines are used to update the amount of memory held by the socket in its queues.

General Fields

This section covers the majority of sk_buff fields, which are not associated with specific kernel features:

struct timeval stamp
> This is usually meaningful only for a received packet. It is a timestamp that represents when a packet was received or (occasionally) when one is scheduled for transmission. It is set by the function netif_rx with net_timestamp, which is called by the device driver after the reception of each packet and is described in Chapter 21.

struct net_device *dev
> This field, whose type (net_device) will be described in more detail later in the chapter, describes a network device. The role of the device represented by dev depends on whether the packet stored in the buffer is about to be transmitted or has just been received.

When a packet is received, the device driver updates this field with the pointer to the data structure representing the receiving interface, as illustrated by the following piece of code from vortex_rx, the function called by the driver of the 3c59x Ethernet card series when receiving a frame (in *drivers/net/3c59x.c*):

```
static int vortex_rx(struct net_device *dev)
{
        ... ... ...
        skb->dev = dev;
        ... ... ...
        skb->protocol = eth_type_trans(skb, dev);
        netif_rx(skb); /* Pass the packet to the higher layer */
        ... ... ...
}
```

When a packet is to be transmitted, this parameter represents the device through which it will be sent out. The code that sets the value is more complicated than the code for receiving a packet, so I will postpone a discussion until Chapter 21 and Chapter 35.

Some network features allow a few devices to be grouped together to represent a single virtual interface (that is, one that is not directly associated with a hardware device), served by a virtual device driver. When the device driver is invoked, the dev parameter points to the virtual device's net_device data structure. The driver chooses a specific device from its group and changes the dev parameter to point to the net_device data structure of that device. Under these circumstances, therefore, the pointer to the transmitting device may be changed during packet processing.

struct net_device *input_dev

This is the device the packet has been received from. It is a NULL pointer when the packet has been generated locally. For Ethernet devices, it is initialized in eth_type_trans (see Chapters 10 and 13). It is used mainly by Traffic Control.

struct net_device *real_dev

This field is meaningful only for virtual devices, and represents the real device the virtual one is associated with. The Bonding and VLAN interfaces use it, for example, to remember where the real device ingress traffic is received from.

union {...} h
union {...} nh
union {...} mac

These are pointers to the protocol headers of the TCP/IP stack: h for L4, nh for L3, and mac for L2. Each field points to a union of various structures, one structure for each protocol understood by the kernel at that layer. For instance, h is a union that includes a field for the header of each L4 protocol understood by the kernel. One member of each union is called raw and is used for initialization; all later accesses are through the protocol-specific members.

When receiving a data packet, the function responsible for processing the layer *n* header receives a buffer from layer *n-1* with skb->data pointing to the beginning of the layer *n* header. The function that handles layer *n* initializes the proper pointer for this layer (for instance, skb->nh for L3 handlers) to preserve the skb->data field, because the contents of this pointer will be lost during the processing at the next layer, when skb->data is initialized to a different offset within the buffer. The function then completes the layer *n* processing and, before passing the packet to the layer *n+1* handler, updates skb->data to make it point to the end of the layer *n* header, which is the beginning of the layer *n+1* header (see Figure 2-3).

Sending a packet reverses this process, with the added complexity of adding a new header at each layer.

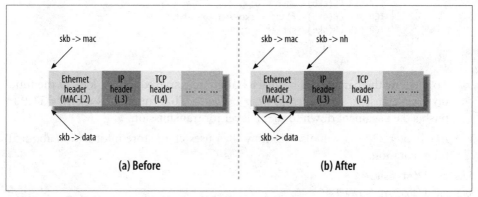

Figure 2-3. Header's pointer initializations while moving from layer two to layer three

struct dst_entry dst
    This is used by the routing subsystem. Because the data structure is quite complex and requires knowledge of how other subsystems work, I'll postpone a description of it until Part VII.

char cb[40]
    This is a "control buffer," or storage for private information, maintained by each layer for internal use. It is statically allocated within the sk_buff structure (currently with a size of 40 bytes) and is large enough to hold whatever private data is needed by each layer. In the code for each layer, access is done through macros to make the code more readable. TCP, for example, uses that space to store a tcp_skb_cb data structure, which is defined in *include/net/tcp.h*:

```
struct tcp_skb_cb {
    ... ... ...
    __u32       seq;        /* Starting sequence number */
    __u32       end_seq;    /* SEQ + FIN + SYN + datalen*/
    __u32       when;       /* used to compute rtt's    */
    __u8        flags;      /* TCP header flags.         */
    ... ... ...
};
```

And this is the macro used by the TCP code to access the structure. The macro consists simply of a pointer cast:

```
#define TCP_SKB_CB(__skb)    ((struct tcp_skb_cb *)&((__skb)->cb[0]))
```

Here is an example where the TCP subsystem fills in the structure upon receipt of a segment:

```
int tcp_v4_rcv(struct sk_buff *skb)
{
        ... ... ...
        th = skb->h.th;
        TCP_SKB_CB(skb)->seq = ntohl(th->seq);
        TCP_SKB_CB(skb)->end_seq = (TCP_SKB_CB(skb)->seq + th->syn + th->fin +
                                    skb->len - th->doff * 4);
        TCP_SKB_CB(skb)->ack_seq = ntohl(th->ack_seq);
        TCP_SKB_CB(skb)->when = 0;
        TCP_SKB_CB(skb)->flags = skb->nh.iph->tos;
        TCP_SKB_CB(skb)->sacked = 0;
        ... ... ...
}
```

To see how the parameters in the cb buffer are retrieved, take a look at the function tcp_transmit_skb in *net/ipv4/tcp_output.c*. That function is used by TCP to push a data segment down to the IP layer for transmission.

In Chapter 22, you will also see how IPv4 uses cb to store information about IP fragmentation.

unsigned int csum
unsigned char ip_summed

> These represent the checksum and associated status flag. Their use is described in Chapter 19.

unsigned char cloned

> A boolean flag that, when set, indicates that this structure is a clone of another sk_buff buffer. See the later section "Cloning and copying buffers."

unsigned char pkt_type

> This field classifies the type of frame based on its L2 destination address. The possible values are listed in *include/linux/if_packet.h*. For Ethernet devices, this parameter is initialized by the function eth_type_trans, which is described in Chapter 13.

> The main values it can be assigned are:

PACKET_HOST

> The destination address of the received frame is that of the receiving interface; in other words, the packet has reached its destination.

PACKET_MULTICAST

> The destination address of the received frame is one of the multicast addresses to which the interface is registered.

PACKET_BROADCAST

> The destination address of the received frame is the broadcast address of the receiving interface.

PACKET_OTHERHOST

> The destination address of the received frame does not belong to the ones associated with the interface (unicast, multicast, and broadcast); thus, the frame will have to be forwarded if forwarding is enabled, and dropped otherwise.

PACKET_OUTGOING

> The packet is being sent out; among the users of this flag are the Decnet protocol and the function that gives each network tap a copy of the outgoing packet (see dev_queue_xmit_nit in Chapter 11).

PACKET_LOOPBACK

> The packet is being sent out to the loopback device. Thanks to this flag, when dealing with the loopback device, the kernel can skip some operations needed for real devices.

PACKET_FASTROUTE

> The packet is being routed using the Fastroute feature. Fastroute support is not available anymore in 2.6 kernels.

Chapter 13 details how those values are set based on the L2 destination address value.

__u32 priority

> This indicates the Quality of Service (QoS) class of a packet being transmitted or forwarded. If the packet is generated locally, the socket layer defines the priority value. If instead the packet is being forwarded, the function rt_tos2priority (called from the ip_forward function) defines the value of the field according to the value of the Type of Service (ToS) field in the IP header itself. The value of this parameter has nothing to do with the DiffServ Code Point (DSCP) described in Chapter 18. I will discuss its role in the section "ip_forward Function" in Chapter 20.

unsigned short protocol

> This is the protocol used at the next-higher layer from the perspective of the device driver at L2. Typical protocols listed here are IP, IPv6, and ARP; a complete list is available in *include/linux/if_ether.h*. Since each protocol has its own function handler for the processing of incoming packets, this field is used by the driver to inform the layer above it what handler to use. Each driver calls netif_rx to invoke the handler for the upper network layer, so the protocol field must be initialized before that function is invoked. See Chapters 10 and 13 for more detail.

unsigned short security

> This is the security level of the packet. This field was originally introduced for use with IPsec but is no longer used.

Feature-Specific Fields

The Linux kernel is modular, allowing you to select what to include and what to leave out. Thus, some fields are included in the sk_buff data structure only if the kernel is compiled with support for particular features such as firewalling (Netfilter) or QoS:

```
unsigned long nfmark
__u32 nfcache
__u32 nfctinfo
struct nf_conntrack *nfct
unsigned int nfdebug
struct nf_bridge_info *nf_bridge
```
These parameters are used by Netfilter (the firewall code), and more specifically by the kernel option "Device Drivers → Networking support → Networking options → Network packet filtering" and its two suboptions, "Network packet filtering debugging" and "Bridged IP/ARP packets filtering."

union {...} private
This union is used by the High Performance Parallel Interface (HIPPI). The associated kernel option is "Device Drivers → Networking support → Network device support → HIPPI driver support."

```
__u32 tc_index
__u32 tc_verd
__u32 tc_classid
```
These parameters are used by the Traffic Control, and more specifically by the kernel option "Device Drivers → Networking support → Networking options → QoS and/or fair queueing" and its suboption, "Packet classifier API."

struct sec_path *sp
This is used by the IPsec protocol suite to keep track of transformations.

Management Functions

Lots of functions, usually very short and simple, are offered by the kernel to manipulate sk_buff elements or lists of elements. With the help of Figure 2-4, I'll describe the most important ones. First we will see the functions used to allocate and free buffers, and then the ones used to manipulate the pointers (i.e., skb->data) to reserve space at the head or at the tail of a frame.

If you take a look at the files *include/linux/skbuff.h* and *net/core/skbuff.c*, you will notice that almost all of the functions exist in two versions, with names like do_something and __do_something. Usually, the first one is a wrapper that adds extra sanity checks or locking mechanisms around a call to the second one. The internal __do_something form is generally not called directly (unless specific conditions are met—i.e., lock requirements, to name one). Exceptions to that rule are usually poorly coded functions that will be fixed eventually.

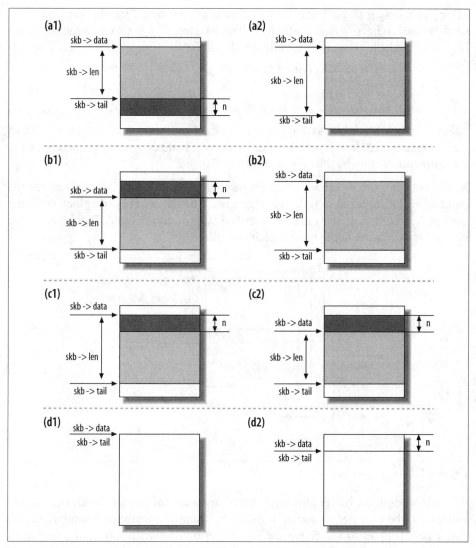

Figure 2-4. Before and after: (a)skb_put, (b)skb_push, (c)skb_pull, and (d)skb_reserve

Allocating memory: alloc_skb and dev_alloc_skb

alloc_skb is the main function for the allocation of buffers and is defined in *net/core/skbuff.c*. We have already seen that the data buffer and the header (the sk_buff data structure) are two different entities, which means that creating a single buffer involves two allocations of memory (one for the buffer and one for the sk_buff structure).

`alloc_skb` takes an `sk_buff` data structure from a cache by calling the function `kmem_cache_alloc`, and gets a data buffer by calling `kmalloc`, which also uses cached memory if it is available. The code (slightly simplified) is:

```
skb = kmem_cache_alloc(skbuff_head_cache, gfp_mask & ~__GFP_DMA);
... ... ...
size = SKB_DATA_ALIGN(size);
data = kmalloc(size + sizeof(struct skb_shared_info), gfp_mask);
```

Before calling `kmalloc`, the `size` parameter is tuned with the macro `SKB_DATA_ALIGN` to force alignment. Before returning, the function initializes a few parameters in the structure, producing the final result shown in Figure 2-5.

At the bottom of the memory block on the right side of Figure 2-5 you can see the padding area introduced to force the alignment. The `skb_shared_info` block is mainly used to handle IP fragments and is described later in this chapter. The fields shown on the left side of the figure were explained earlier.

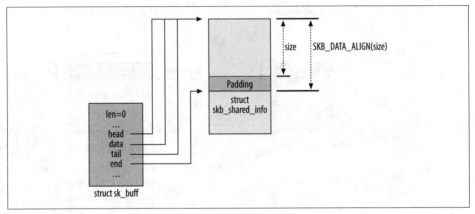

Figure 2-5. alloc_skb function

`dev_alloc_skb` is the buffer allocation function meant for use by device drivers and expected to be executed in interrupt mode. It is simply a wrapper around `alloc_skb` that adds 16 bytes to the requested size for optimization reasons and asks for an atomic operation (`GFP_ATOMIC`) since it will be called from within an interrupt handler routine:

```
static inline struct sk_buff *dev_alloc_skb(unsigned int length)
{
    return __dev_alloc_skb(length, GFP_ATOMIC);
}


static inline
struct sk_buff *__dev_alloc_skb(unsigned int length, int gfp_mask)
{
    struct sk_buff *skb = alloc_skb(length + 16, gfp_mask);
    if (likely(skb))
```

```
        skb_reserve(skb, 16);
    return skb;
}
```

This definition of __dev_alloc_skb is the default one used when there is no architecture-specific definition.

Freeing memory: kfree_skb and dev_kfree_skb

These two functions release a buffer, which results in its return to the buffer pool (cache). kfree_skb is both called directly and invoked through the dev_kfree_skb wrapper. The latter is defined for use by device drivers, to have a name that parallels dev_alloc_skb but consists of a simple macro that does nothing but call kfree_skb. This basic function releases a buffer only when the skb->users counter is 1 (when no users of the buffer are left). Otherwise, the function simply decrements that counter. So if a buffer had three users, only the third call to dev_kfree_skb or kfree_skb would free memory.

The flowchart in Figure 2-6 shows all the steps involved in freeing a buffer. As you will see in Chapter 33, an sk_buff structure can hold a reference on a dst_entry data structure. When the sk_buff structure is freed, therefore, dst_release also has to be called to decrement the reference count on the associated dst_entry data structure.

When the destructor function pointer has been initialized, it is called here (see the section "Layout Fields" earlier in this chapter).

We have seen in Figure 2-5 what a simple scenario looks like: an sk_buff data structure is associated to another memory block where the actual data is stored. However, the skb_shared_info data structure at the bottom of that data block, as shown in Figure 2-5, can hold pointers to other memory fragments. See Chapter 21 for some examples. kfree_skb releases the memory held by those fragments as well, when they are present. Finally, the sk_buff data structure is returned to the skbuff_head_cache cache.

Data reservation and alignment: skb_reserve, skb_put, skb_push, and skb_pull

skb_reserve reserves some space (headroom) at the head of the buffer and is commonly used to allow the insertion of a header or to force data to be aligned on some boundary. The function shifts the data and tail pointers (discussed earlier in the section "Layout Fields") that mark the beginning and the end of the payload, respectively. Figure 2-4(d) shows the result of calling skb_reserve(skb,n). This function is usually called soon after the allocation of the buffer, when data and tail are still the same.

If you look at the receive function of one of the Ethernet drivers (for instance, vortex_rx in *drivers/net/3c59x.c*) you will see that they all use the following command before storing any data in the buffer they have just allocated:

```
skb_reserve(skb, 2);    /* Align IP on 16 byte boundaries */
```

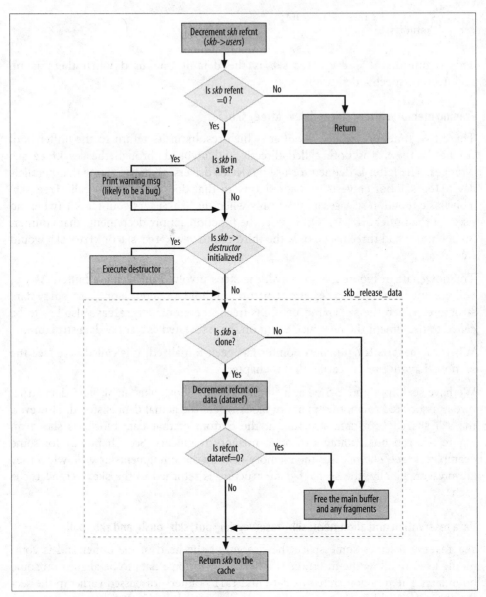

Figure 2-6. kfree_skb function

Because they know that they are about to copy an Ethernet frame that has a header 14 octets long into the buffer, the argument of 2 shifts the head of the buffer 2 bytes. This keeps the IP header, which follows immediately after the Ethernet header, aligned on a 16-byte boundary from the beginning of the buffer, as shown in Figure 2-7.

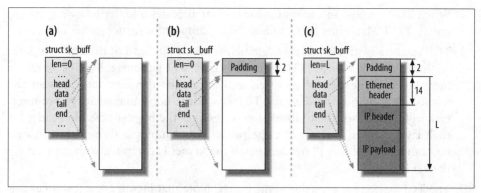

Figure 2-7. (a) before skb_reserve, (b) after skb_reserve, and (c) after copying the frame on the buffer

Figure 2-8 shows an example of using skb_reserve in the opposite direction, during data transmission.

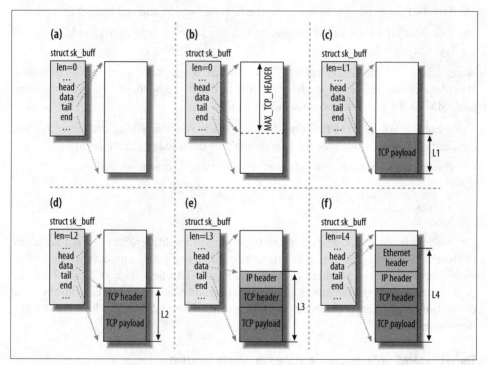

Figure 2-8. Buffer that is filled in while traversing the stack from the TCP layer down to the link layer

1. When TCP is asked to transmit some data, it allocates a buffer following certain criteria (TCP Maximum Segment Size (mss), support for scatter gather I/O, etc.).

2. TCP reserves (with skb_reserve) enough space at the head of the buffer to hold all the headers of all layers (TCP, IP, link layer). The parameter MAX_TCP_HEADER is the sum of all headers of all levels and is calculated taking into account the worst-case scenarios: because the TCP layer does not know what type of interface will be used for the transmission, it reserves the biggest possible header for each layer. It even accounts for the possibility of multiple IP headers (because you can have multiple IP headers when the kernel is compiled with support for IP over IP).

3. The TCP payload is copied into the buffer. Note that Figure 2-8 is just an example. The TCP payload could be organized differently; for example, it could be stored as fragments. In Chapter 21, we will see what a fragmented buffer (also commonly called a paged buffer) looks like.

4. The TCP layer adds its header.

5. The TCP layer hands the buffer to the IP layer, which adds its header as well.

6. The IP layer hands the IP packet to the neighboring layer, which adds the link layer header.

Note that while the buffer travels down the network stack, each protocol moves skb->data down, copies in its header, and updates skb->len. All of this is accomplished with the functions we saw in Figure 2-4.

Note that the skb_reserve function does not really move anything into or within the data buffer; it simply updates the two pointers as depicted in Figure 2-4(d).

```
static inline void skb_reserve(struct sk_buff *skb, unsigned int len)
{
    skb->data+=len;
    skb->tail+=len;
}
```

skb_push adds one block of data to the beginning of the buffer, and skb_put adds one to the end. Like skb_reserve, these functions don't really add any data to the buffer; they simply move the pointers to its head or tail. The new data is supposed to be copied explicitly by other functions. skb_pull removes a block of data from the head of the buffer by moving the head pointer forward. Figure 2-4 shows how these functions work.

The skb_shared_info structure and the skb_shinfo function

As shown in Figure 2-5, there is a structure called skb_shared_info at the end of the data buffer that keeps additional information about the data block. The data structure immediately follows the end pointer that marks the end of the data. This is the definition of the data structure:

```
struct skb_shared_info {
    atomic_t        dataref;
    unsigned int    nr_frags;
    unsigned short  tso_size;
    unsigned short  tso_seqs;
    struct sk_buff  *frag_list;
    skb_frag_t      frags[MAX_SKB_FRAGS];
};
```

dataref represents the number of "users" of the data block and is described in the next section, "Cloning and copying buffers." nr_frags, frag_list, and frags are used to handle IP fragments and are described in Chapter 21. The skb_is_nonlinear routine can be used to check whether the buffer is fragmented, and skb_linearize* can be used to collapse the fragments into a single flat buffer. Collapsing the fragments involves copying, which introduces a performance penalty.

Some network interface cards (NICs) can handle in hardware some of the tasks that have traditionally been done by the CPU. The most common example is the computation of the L3 and L4 checksums. Some NICs can even maintain the L4 protocol's state machines. For the sake of the code shown here, we are interested in TCP segmentation offload, where the NIC implements a subset of the TCP layer. tso_size and tso_seqs are used by this feature.

Note that there is no field inside the sk_buff structure pointing at the skb_shared_ info data structure. To access that structure, functions need to use the skb_shinfo macro, which simply returns the end pointer:

```
#define skb_shinfo(SKB)    ((struct skb_shared_info *)((SKB)->end))
```

The following statement, for instance, shows how the macro is used to increment a field of the private block:

```
skb_shinfo(skb)->nr_frags++;
```

Cloning and copying buffers

When the same buffer needs to be processed independently by different consumers, and they may need to change the content of the sk_buff descriptor (the h and nh pointers to the protocol headers), the kernel does not need to make a complete copy of both the sk_buff structure and the associated data buffers. Instead, to be more efficient, the kernel can *clone* the original, which consists of making a copy of the sk_ buff structure only and playing with the reference counts to avoid releasing the shared data block prematurely. Buffer cloning is done with the skb_clone function.

---

* See the section "dev_queue_xmit Function" in Chapter 11 for an example of its use.

An example of a situation using cloning is when an ingress packet needs to be delivered to multiple recipients, such as the protocol handler and one or more network taps (see Chapter 21).

The sk_buff clone is not linked to any list and has no reference to the socket owner. The field skb->cloned is set to 1 in both the clone and the original buffer. skb->users is set to 1 in the clone so that the first attempt to remove it succeeds, and the number of references (dataref) to the buffer containing the data is incremented (since now there is one more sk_buff data structure pointing to it). Figure 2-9 shows an example of a cloned buffer.

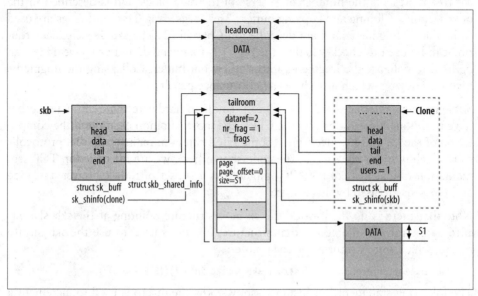

Figure 2-9. skb_clone function

The skb_clone routine can be used to check the cloned status of an skb buffer.

Figure 2-9 shows an example of a fragmented buffer—that is to say, a buffer that has some data stored in data fragments linked with the frags array. We will see how fragmented buffers are used in Chapter 21; for now, let's not bother with those details.

The skb_share_check routine can be used to check the reference count skb->users and clone the buffer skb when the users field says the buffer is shared.

When a buffer is cloned, the contents of the data block cannot be modified. This means that code can access the data without any need for locking. When, however, a function needs to modify not only the contents of the sk_buff structure but the data too, it needs to clone the data block as well. In this case, the programmer has two options. When he knows he needs to modify only the contents of the data in the area between skb->start and skb->end, he can use pskb_copy to clone just that area. When he thinks he may need to modify the content of the fragment data blocks too, he must use `skb_copy`. The result of both `pskb_copy` and `skb_copy` is shown in Figure 2-10. You will see in Chapter 21 that the `skb_shared_info` data structure can include a list of `sk_buff` structures too (linked to a field called `frag_list`). That list is handled by `pskb_copy` and `skb_copy` in the same way as the `frags` array (this detail has been omitted from Figure 2-10 to keep the latter more readable).

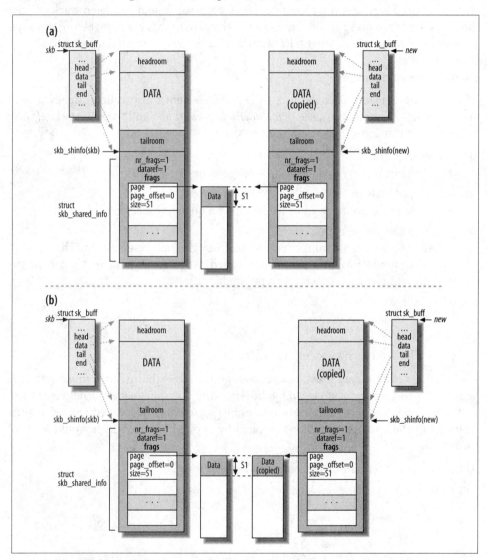

Figure 2-10. (a) pskb_copy function and (b) skb_copy function

You may not be able to appreciate all of the details in Figures 2-9 and 2-10 at this point. Later in the book, especially once you have gone through Part V, everything will make more sense.

While discussing the various topics of this book, I will sometimes emphasize that a given function needs to clone or copy a buffer. When deciding to make a clone or copy of a buffer, programmers of each subsystem cannot anticipate whether other kernel components (or other users of their subsystems) will need the original information in that buffer. The kernel is very modular and changes in a very dynamic and unpredictable way, so each subsystem is ignorant of what other subsystems may do with a buffer. Therefore, the programmers of each subsystem just keep track of any modifications they make to the buffer, and take care to make a copy before modifying anything in case some other part of the kernel needs the original information.

List management functions

These functions manipulate the lists of sk_buff elements, also called queues. For a complete list of functions, see *<include/linux/skbuff.h>* and *<net/core/skbuff.c>*. Some of the most commonly used functions are:

skb_queue_head_init
> Initializes an sk_buff_head with an empty queue of elements.

skb_queue_head, skb_queue_tail
> Adds one buffer to the head or to the tail of a queue, respectively.

skb_dequeue, skb_dequeue_tail
> Dequeues an element from the head or from the tail, respectively. The second function should probably have been called skb_dequeue_head to be consistent with the names of the other queueing functions.

skb_queue_purge
> Empties a queue.

skb_queue_walk
> Runs a loop on each element of a queue in turn.

All functions of this class must be executed atomically—that is, they must grab the spin lock provided by the sk_buff_head structure for the queue. Otherwise, they could be interrupted by asynchronous events that enqueue or dequeue elements from the queues, such as functions invoked by expired timers, which would lead to race conditions.

Thus, each function is implemented as follows:

```
static inline function_name ( parameter_list )
{
        unsigned long flags;

        spin_lock_irqsave(...);
        __function_name ( parameter_list )
        spin_unlock_irqrestore(...);
}
```

The function consists of a wrapper that grabs the lock, does its work by invoking a function whose name begins with two underscores, and releases the lock.

net_device Structure

The net_device data structure stores all information specifically regarding a network device. There is one such structure for each device, both real ones (such as Ethernet NICs) and virtual ones (such as bonding* or VLAN†). In this section, I will use the words *interface* and *device* interchangeably, even though the difference between them is important in other contexts.

The net_device structures for all devices are put into a global list to which the global variable dev_base points. The data structure is defined in *include/linux/netdevice.h*. The registration of network devices is described in Chapter 8. In that chapter, you can find details on how and when most of the net_device fields are initialized.

Like sk_buff, this structure is quite big and includes many feature-specific parameters, along with parameters from many different layers. For this reason, the overall organization of the structure will probably see some changes soon for optimization reasons.

Network devices can be classified into *types* such as Ethernet cards and Token Ring cards. While certain fields of the net_device structure are set to the same value for all devices of the same type, some fields must be set differently by each model of device. Thus, for almost every type, Linux provides a general function that initializes the parameters whose values stay the same across all models. Each device driver invokes this function in addition to setting those fields that have unique values for its model. Drivers can also overwrite fields that were already initialized by the kernel (for instance, to improve performance). You can find more details in Chapter 8.

The fields of the net_device structure can be classified into the following categories:

- Configuration
- Statistics
- Device status
- List management
- Traffic management
- Feature specific
- Generic
- Function pointers (or VFT)

---

* Bonding, also called EtherChannel (Cisco terminology) and trunking (Sun terminology), allows a set of interfaces to be grouped together and be treated as a single interface. This feature is useful when a system needs to support point-to-point connections at a high bandwidth. A nearly linear speedup can be achieved, with the virtual interface having a throughput nearly equal to the sum of the throughputs of the individual interfaces.

† VLAN stands for Virtual LAN. The use of VLANs is a convenient way to isolate traffic using the same L2 switch in different broadcast domains by means of an additional tag, called the VLAN tag, that is added to the Ethernet frames. You can find an introduction to VLANs and their use with Linux at *http://www.linuxjournal.com/article/7268*.

Identifiers

The net_device structure includes three identifiers, not to be confused:

int ifindex

> A unique ID, assigned to each device when it is registered with a call to dev_new_index.

int iflink

> This field is mainly used by (virtual) tunnel devices and identifies the real device that will be used to reach the other end of the tunnel.

unsigned short dev_id

> Currently used by IPv6 with the zSeries OSA NICs. The field is used to differentiate between virtual instances of the same device that can be shared between different OSes concurrently. See comments in *net/ipv6/addrconf.c.*

Configuration

Some of the configuration fields are given a default value by the kernel that depends on the class of network device, and some fields are left to the driver to fill. The driver can change defaults, as mentioned earlier, and some fields can even be changed at runtime by commands such as ifconfig and ip. In fact, several parameters—base_addr, if_port, dma, and irq—are commonly set by the user when the module for the device is loaded. On the other hand, these parameters are not used by virtual devices.

char name[IFNAMSIZ]

> Name of the device (e.g., *eth0*).

unsigned long mem_start
unsigned long mem_end

> These fields describe the shared memory used by the device to communicate with the kernel. They are initialized and accessed only within the device driver; higher layers do not need to care about them.

unsigned long base_addr

> The beginning of the I/O memory mapped to the device's own memory.

unsigned int irq

> The interrupt number used by the device to talk to the kernel. It can be shared among multiple devices. Drivers use the request_irq function to allocate this variable and free_irq to release it.

unsigned char if_port

> The type of port being used for this interface. See the next section, "Interface types and ports."

unsigned char dma

> The DMA channel used by the device (if any). To obtain and release a DMA channel from the kernel, the file *kernel/dma.c* defines the functions request_dma

and free_dma. To enable or disable a DMA channel after obtaining it, the functions enable_dma and disable_dma are provided in various *include/asm-architecture* files (e.g., *include/asm-i386*). The routines are used by ISA devices; Peripheral Component Interconnect (PCI) devices do not need them because they use others instead.

DMA is not available for all devices because some buses don't use it.

unsigned short flags
unsigned short gflags
unsigned short priv_flags

Some bits in the flags field represent capabilities of the network device (such as IFF_MULTICAST) and others represent changing status (such as IFF_UP or IFF_RUNNING). You can find the complete list of these flags in *include/linux/if.h*. The device driver usually sets the capabilities at initialization time, and the status flags are managed by the kernel in response to external events. The settings of the flags can be viewed through the familiar ifconfig command:

```
bash# ifconfig lo
lo          Link encap:Local Loopback
            inet addr:127.0.0.1  Mask:255.0.0.0
            UP LOOPBACK RUNNING  MTU:3924  Metric:1
            RX packets:198 errors:0 dropped:0 overruns:0 frame:0
            TX packets:198 errors:0 dropped:0 overruns:0 carrier:0
            collisions:0 txqueuelen:0
```

In this example, the words UP LOOPBACK RUNNING correspond to the flags IFF_UP, IFF_LOOPBACK, and IFF_RUNNING.

priv_flags stores flags that are not visible to the user space. Right now this field is used by the VLAN and Bridge virtual devices. gflags is almost never used and is there for compatibility reasons. Flags can be changed through the dev_change_flags function.

int features

Another bitmap of flags used to store some other device capabilities. It is not redundant for this data structure to contain multiple flag variables. The features field reports the card's capabilities for communicating with the CPU, such as whether the card can do DMA to high memory, or checksum all the packets in hardware. The list of the possible features is defined inside the structure net_device itself. This parameter is initialized by the device driver. You can find the list of NETIF_F_XXX features, along with good comments, inside the net_device data structure definition.

unsigned mtu

MTU stands for Maximum Transmission Unit and it represents the maximum size of the frames that the device can handle. Table 2-1 shows the values for the most common network technologies.

Table 2-1. MTU values for different device types

Device type	MTU
PPP	296
SLIP	296
Ethernet	1,500
ISDN	1,500
PLIP	1,500 (`ether_setup`)
Wavelan	1,500 (`ether_setup`)
EtherChannel	2,024
FDDI	4,352
Token Ring 4 MB/s (IEEE 802.5)	4,464
Token Bus (IEEE 802.4)	8,182
Token Ring 16 MB/s (IBM)	17,914
Hyperchannel	65,535

The Ethernet MTU deserves a little clarification. The Ethernet frame specification defines the maximum payload size as 1,500 bytes. Sometimes you find the Ethernet MTU defined as 1,518 or 1,514: the first is the maximum size of an Ethernet frame including the header, and the second includes the header but not the frame check sequence (4 bytes of checksum).

In 1998, Alteon Networks (acquired by Nortel Networks in 2000) promoted an initiative to increase the maximum payload of Ethernet frames to 9 KB. This proposal was later formalized with an IETF Internet draft, but the IEEE never accepted it. Frames exceeding the 1,500 bytes of payload in the IEEE specification are commonly called jumbo frames and are used with Gigabit Ethernet to increase throughput. This is because bigger frames mean fewer frames for large data transfers, fewer interrupts, and therefore less CPU usage, less header overhead, etc.). For a discussion of the benefits of increasing the Ethernet MTU and why IEEE does not agree on standardizing this extension, you can read the white paper "Use of Extended Frame Sizes in Ethernet Networks" that can be found with an Internet search, as well as at *http://www.ietf.org/proceedings/01aug/I-D/ draft-ietf-isis-ext-eth-01.txt*.

`unsigned short type`
> The category of devices to which it belongs (Ethernet, Frame Relay, etc.). *include/linux/if_arp.h* contains the complete list of possible types.

`unsigned short hard_header_len`
> The size of the device header in octets. The Ethernet header, for instance, is 14 octets long. The length of each device header is defined in the header file for that device. For Ethernet, for instance, ETH_HLEN is defined in *<include/linux/if_ether.h>*.

```
unsigned char broadcast[MAX_ADDR_LEN]
```
The link layer broadcast address.

```
unsigned char dev_addr[MAX_ADDR_LEN]
unsigned char addr_len
```
dev_addr is the device link layer address; do not confuse it with the L3 or IP address. The address's length in octets is given by addr_len. The value of addr_len depends on the type of device. Ethernet addresses are six octets long.

```
int promiscuity
```
See the later section "Promiscuous mode."

Interface types and ports

Some devices come with more than one connector (the most common combination is BNC + RJ45) and allow the user to select one of them depending on her needs. This parameter is used to set the port type for the device. When the device driver is not forced by configuration commands to select a specific port type, it simply chooses a default one. There are also cases where a single device driver can handle different interface models; in those situations, the interface can discover the port type to use by simply trying all of them in a specific order. This piece of code shows how one device driver sets the interface mode depending on how it has been configured:

```
switch (dev->if_port) {
case IF_PORT_10BASE2:
    writeb((readb(addr) & 0xf8) | 1, addr);
    break;
case IF_PORT_10BASET:
    writeb((readb(addr) & 0xf8), addr);
    break;
}
```

Promiscuous mode

Certain network administration tasks require a system to receive all the frames that travel across a shared cable, not just the ones directly addressed to it; a device that receives all packets is said to be in *promiscuous mode*. This mode is needed, for instance, by applications that check performance or security breaches on their local network segment. Promiscuous mode is also used by bridging code (see Part IV). Finally, it has obvious value to malicious snoopers, unfortunately; for this reason, no data is secure from other users on a local network unless it is encrypted.

The net_device structure contains a counter named promiscuity that indicates a device is in promiscuous mode. The reason it is a counter rather than a simple flag is that several clients may ask for promiscuous mode; therefore, each increments the counter when entering the mode and decrements the counter when leaving the mode. The device does not leave promiscuous mode until the counter reaches zero. Usually the field is manipulated by calling the function dev_set_promiscuity.

Whenever promiscuity is nonzero (such as through a call to dev_set_promiscuity), the IFF_PROMISC bit flag of flags is also set and is checked by the functions that configure the interface.

The following piece of code, taken from the *drivers/net/3c59x.c* driver, shows how the different receive modes are set based on the flags (bits) in the flags field:

```
static void set_rx_mode(struct net_device *dev)
{
        int ioaddr = dev->base_addr;
        int new_mode;

        if (dev->flags & IFF_PROMISC) {
            if (corqscreq_debug > 3)
                        printk("%s: Setting promiscuous mode.\n", dev->name);
            new_mode = SetRxFilter | RxStation | RxMulticast | RxBroadcast | RxProm;
        } else if ((dev->mc_list) || (dev->flags & IFF_ALLMULTI)) {
            new_mode = SetRxFilter | RxStation | RxMulticast | RxBroadcast;
        } else
            new_mode = SetRxFilter | RxStation | RxBroadcast;

        outw(new_mode, ioaddr + EL3_CMD);
}
```

When the IFF_PROMISC flag is set, the new_mode variable is initialized to accept the traffic addressed to the card (RxStation), multicast traffic (RxMulticast), broadcast traffic (RxBroadcast), and all the other traffic (RxProm). EL3_CMD is the offset to the ioaddr memory address that represents where commands are supposed to be copied when interacting with the device.

Statistics

Instead of providing a collection of fields to keep statistics, the net_device structure includes a pointer named priv that is set by the driver to point to a private data structure storing information about the interface. The private data consists of statistics such as the number of packets transmitted and received and the number of errors encountered.

The format of the structure pointed at by priv depends both on the device type and on the particular model: thus, different Ethernet cards may use different private structures. However, nearly all structures include a field of type net_device_stats (defined in *include/linux/netdevice.h*) that contains statistics common to all the network devices and that can be retrieved with the method get_stats, described later.

Wireless devices behave so differently from wired devices that wireless ones do not find the net_device_stats data structure appropriate. Instead, they provide a field of type iw_statistics that can be retrieved using a method called get_wireless_stats, described later.

The data structure to which priv points sometimes has a name reflecting the interface (e.g., vortex_private for the Vortex and Boomerang series, also called the 3c59x family), and other times is simply called net_local. Still, the fields in net_local are defined uniquely by each device driver.

The private data structure may be more or less complex depending on the card's capabilities and on how much the device driver writer is willing to employ sophisticated statistics and complex design to enhance performance. Compare, for instance, the generic net_local structure used by the 3c507 Ethernet card in *drivers/net/3c507.c* with the highly detailed vortex_private structure used by the 3c59x Ethernet card in *drivers/net/3c59x.c*. Both, however, include a field of type net_device_stats.

As you will see in Chapter 8, the private data structure is sometimes appended to the net_device structure itself (requiring only one malloc for both) and sometimes allocated as a separate block.

Device Status

To control interactions with the NIC, each device driver has to maintain information such as timestamps and flags indicating what kind of behavior the interface requires. In a symmetric multiprocessing (SMP) system, the kernel also has to make sure that concurrent accesses to the same device from different CPUs are handled correctly. Several fields of the net_device structure are dedicated to these types of information:

unsigned long state
    A set of flags used by the network queuing subsystem. They are indexed by the constants in the enum netdev_state_t, which is defined in *include/linux/netdevice.h* and defines constants such as __LINK_STATE_XOFF for each bit. Individual bits are set and cleared using the general functions set_bit and clear_bit, usually invoked through a wrapper that hides the details of the bit used. For example, to stop a device queue, the subsystem invokes netif_stop_queue, which looks like this:

```
static inline void netif_stop_queue(struct net_device *dev)
{
    ...
    set_bit(__LINK_STATE_XOFF, &dev->state);
}
```

    The Traffic Control subsystem is briefly introduced in Chapter 11.

enum {...} reg_state
    The registration state of the device. See Chapter 8.

unsigned long trans_start
    The time (measured in jiffies) when the last frame transmission started. The device driver sets it just before starting transmission. The field is used to detect problems with the card if it does not finish transmission after a given amount of time. An overly long transmission means there is something wrong; in that case, the driver usually resets the card.

unsigned long last_rx

The time (measured in jiffies) when the last packet was received. At the moment, it is not used for any specific purpose, but is available in case of need.

struct net_device *master

Some protocols exist that allow a set of devices to be grouped together and be treated as a single device. These protocols include EQL (Equalizer Load-balancer for serial network interfaces), Bonding (also called EtherChannel and trunking), and the TEQL (true equalizer) queuing discipline of Traffic Control. One of the devices in the group is elected to be the so-called master, which plays a special role. This field is a pointer to the net_device data structure of the master device of the group. If the interface is not a member of such a group, the pointer is simply NULL.

spinlock_t xmit_lock
int xmit_lock_owner

The xmit_lock lock is used to serialize accesses to the driver function hard_start_xmit. This means that each CPU can carry out only one transmission at a time on any given device. xmit_lock_owner is the ID of the CPU that holds the lock. It is always 0 on single-processor systems and −1 when the lock is not taken on SMP systems. It is possible to have lockless transmissions, too, when the device driver supports it. See Chapter 11 for both the lock and the lockless cases.

void *atalk_ptr
void *ip_ptr
void *dn_ptr
void *ip6_ptr
void *ec_ptr
void *ax25_ptr

These six fields are pointers to data structures specific to particular protocols, each data structure containing parameters that are used privately by that protocol. ip_ptr, for instance, points to a data structure of type in_device (even though it is declared as void *) that contains different IPv4-related parameters, among them the list of IP addresses configured on the interface (see Chapter 19). Other sections of this book describe the fields of the data structures used by protocols covered in the book. Most of the time only one of these fields is in use.

List Management

net_device data structures are inserted into a global list and into two hash tables, as described in Chapter 8. The following fields are used to accomplish these tasks:

struct net_device *next

Links each net_device data structure to the next in the global list.

struct hlist_node name_hlist
struct hlist_node index_hlist

Link the net_device structure to the bucket's list of two hash tables.

Link Layer Multicast

Multicast is a mechanism used to deliver data to multiple recipients. Multicasting can be available both at the L3 network layer (i.e., IP) and at the L2 link layer (i.e., Ethernet). In this section, we are concerned with the latter.

Link layer multicast delivery can be achieved by using special addresses or control information in the link layer header. (When it is not supported by the link layer protocol, it may be emulated.) Ethernet natively supports multicasting: we will see in Chapter 13 how an Ethernet address can be classified as unicast, multicast, or broadcast.

Multicast addresses are distinguished from the range of other addresses by a specific bit. This means that 50% of the possible addresses are multicast, and 50% of 2^{48} is a huge number! When an interface is asked to join a lot of multicast groups (each identified by a multicast address), it may be more efficient and faster for it to simply listen to all the multicast addresses instead of maintaining a long list and wasting time filtering ingress L2 multicast frames based on the list. One of the flags in the net_device data structure indicates whether the device should listen to all addresses. The decision about when to set or clear this flag is controlled by the all_multi field shown in this section.

Each device keeps an instance of the dev_mc_list structure for each link layer multicast address it listens to. Link layer multicast addresses can be added and removed with the functions dev_mc_add and dev_mc_delete, respectively. Relevant fields in the *net-device* structure include:

struct dev_mc_list *mc_list
> Pointer to the head of this device's list of dev_mc_list structures.

int mc_count
> The number of multicast addresses for this device, which is also the length of the list to which mc_list points.

int allmulti
> When nonzero, causes the device to listen to all multicast addresses. Like promiscuity, discussed earlier in this chapter, allmulti is a reference count rather than a simple Boolean. This is because multiple facilities (VLANs and bonding devices, for instance) may independently require listening to all addresses. When the variable goes from 0 to nonzero, the function dev_set_allmulti is called to instruct the interface to listen to all multicast addresses. The opposite happens when allmulti goes to 0.

Traffic Management

The Traffic Control subsystem of Linux has grown quite a lot and represents one of the strengths of the Linux kernel. The associated kernel option is "Device drivers → Networking support → Networking options → QoS and/or fair queueing." Relevant fields in the *net-device* structure include:

`struct net_device *next_sched`
>   Used by one of the software interrupts described in Chapter 11.

`struct Qdisc *qdisc`
`struct Qdisc *qdisc_sleeping`
`struct Qdisc *qdisc_ingress`
`struct list_head qdisc_list`
>   These fields are used to manage the ingress and egress packet queues and access to the device from different CPUs.

`spinlock_t queue_lock`
`spinlock_t ingress_lock`
>   The Traffic Control subsystem defines a private egress queue for each network device. queue_lock is used to avoid simultaneous accesses to it (see Chapter 11). ingress_lock does the same for ingress traffic.

`unsigned long tx_queue_len`
>   The length of the device's transmission queue. When Traffic Control support is present in the kernel, tx_queue_len may not be used (only a few queuing discipline use it). Table 2-2 shows the values used for the most common device types. Its value can be tuned with the *sysfs* filesystem (see the */sys/class/net/device_name/* directories).

Table 2-2. tx_queue_len values for different device types

Device type	tx_queue_len
Ethernet	1,000
Token Ring	100
EtherChannel	100
Fibre Channel	100
FDDI	100
TEQL (true link equalizer)[a]	100
ISDN	30
HIPPI	25
PLIP	10
SLIP	10
AX25	10
EQL (Equalizer load balancer for serial network interfaces)	5

Table 2-2. tx_queue_len values for different device types (continued)

Device type	tx_queue_len
Generic PPP	3
Bonding	0
Loopback	0
Bridge	0
VLAN	0

ᵃ TEQL is one of the queuing disciplines you can configure with Traffic Control (the QoS layer).

Depending on the queuing discipline—the strategy used to queue incoming and outgoing packets—in use, tx_queue_len may or may not be used. It is usually used when the queue type is FIFO (First In, First Out) or something else relatively simple.

Note that all devices with a queue length of 0 are virtual devices: they rely on the associated real devices to do any queuing (with the exception of the loopback device, which does not need it because it is internal to the kernel and delivers all traffic immediately).

Feature Specific

As we saw when describing sk_buff, a few parameters are included in the definition of net_device only if the features they belong to have been included in the kernel:[*]

struct divert_blk *divert
> Diverter is a feature that allows you to change the source and destination addresses of the incoming packet. This makes it possible to reroute traffic with specific characteristics specified by the configuration to a different interface or a different host. To work properly and to make sense, diverter needs other features such as bridging. The data structure pointed to by this field stores the parameters needed by the diverter feature. The associated kernel option is "Device drivers → Networking support → Networking options → Frame Diverter."

struct net_bridge_port *br_port
> Extra information needed when the device is configured as a bridged port. The bridging code and the Spanning Tree Protocol (STP) are covered in Part IV. The associated kernel option is "Device drivers → Networking support → Networking options → 802.1d Ethernet Bridging."

---

[*] The fields are actually included only when the associated feature is part of the kernel. See, for example, br_port.

```
void (*vlan_rx_register)(...)
void (*vlan_rx_add_vid)(...)
void (*vlan_rx_kill_vid)(...)
```
These three function pointers are used by the VLAN code to register a device as VLAN tagging capable (see *net/8021q/vlan.c*), add a VLAN to the device, and delete the VLAN from the device, respectively. The associated kernel option is "Device drivers → Networking support → Networking options → 802.1Q VLAN Support."

```
int netpoll_rx
void (*poll_controller)(...)
```
Used by the optional Netpoll feature that is briefly mentioned in Chapter 10.

Generic

In addition to the list management fields of the net_device structure discussed earlier, a few other fields are used to manage structures and make sure they are removed when they are not needed:

```
atomic_t refcnt
```
Reference count. The device cannot be unregistered until this counter has gone to zero (see Chapter 8).

```
int watchdog_timeo
struct timer_list watchdog_timer
```
Along with the tx_timeout variable discussed earlier, these fields implement the timer discussed in the section "Watchdog timer" in Chapter 11.

```
int (*poll)(...)
struct list_head poll_list
int quota
int weight
```
Used by the NAPI feature described in Chapter 10.

```
const struct iw_handler_def *wireless_handlers
struct iw_public_data *wireless_data
```
Additional parameters and function pointers used by wireless devices. See also get_wireless_stats.

```
struct list_head todo_list
```
The registration and unregistration of a network device is done in two steps. todo_list is used to handle the second one. See Chapter 8.

```
struct class_device class_dev
```
Used by the new generic kernel driver infrastructure.

Function Pointers

We saw in Chapter 1 that the networking code makes heavy use of function pointers. The net_device data structure includes quite a few of them. Such functions are used mainly to:

- Transmit and receive a frame
- Add or parse the link layer header on a buffer
- Change a part of the configuration
- Retrieve statistics
- Interact with a specific feature

A few function pointers were already introduced in the previous sections when describing the fields used to accomplish a specific task. Here are the generic ones:

struct ethtool_ops *ethtool_ops
> Pointer to a set of function pointers used to set or get the configuration of different device parameters. See the section "Ethtool" in Chapter 8.

int (*init)(...)
void (*uninit)(...)
void (*destructor)(...)
int (*open)(...)
int (*stop)(...)
> Used to initialize, clean up, destroy, enable, and disable a device. Not all of them are always used. See Chapter 8.

struct net_device_stats* (*get_stats)(...)
struct iw_statistics* (*get_wireless_stats)(...)
> Some statistics collected by the device driver can be displayed with user-space applications such as ifconfig and ip, and others are strictly used by the kernel and are discussed in the section "Device Status" earlier in this chapter. These two methods are used to collect statistics. get_stats operates on a normal device and get_wireless_stats on a wireless device. See also the earlier section "Statistics."

int (*hard_start_xmit)(...)
> Used to transmit a frame. See Chapter 11.

int (*hard_header)(...)
int (*rebuild_header)(...)
int (*hard_header_cache)(...)
void (*header_cache_update)(...)
int (*hard_header_parse)(...)
int (*neigh_setup)(...)
> Used by the neighboring layer. See the sections "Methods Provided by the Device Driver" and "Neighbor Initialization" in Chapter 27.

```
int (*do_ioctl)(...)
```
ioctl is the system call used to issue commands to devices (see Chapter 3). This method is called to process some of the ioctl commands (see Chapter 8).

```
void (*set_multicast_list)(...)
```
We have already seen in the section "Link Layer Multicast" that mc_list and mc_count are used to manage the list of L2 multicast addresses. This method is used to ask the device driver to configure the device to listen to those addresses. Usually it is not called directly, but through wrappers such as dev_mc_upload or its lockless version, __dev_mc_upload. When a device cannot install a list of multicast addresses, it simply enables all of them.

```
int (*set_mac_address)(...)
```
Changes the device MAC address. When the device does not provide this capability (as in the case of Bridge virtual devices), it is set to NULL.

```
int (*set_config)(...)
```
Configures driver parameters, such as the hardware parameters irq, io_addr, and if_port. Higher-layer parameters (such as protocol addresses) are handled by do_ioctl. Not many devices use this method, especially among the new devices that are better able to implement probe functions. A good example with some documentation can be found in sis900_set_config in *drivers/net/sis900.c*.

```
int (*change_mtu)(...)
```
Changes the device MTU (see the description of mtu in the earlier section, "Configuration"). Changing this field has no effect on the device driver but simply forces the kernel software to respect the new MTU and to handle fragmentation accordingly.

```
void (*tx_timeout)(...)
```
The method invoked at the expiration of the watchdog timer, which determines whether a transmission is taking a suspiciously long time to complete. The watchdog timer is not even started unless this method is defined. See the section "Watchdog timer" in Chapter 11 for more information.

```
int (*accept_fastpath)(...)
```
Fast switching (also called FASTROUTE) was a kernel feature that allowed device drivers to route incoming traffic during interrupt context using a small cache (bypassing all the software layers). Fast switching is no longer supported, starting with the 2.6.8 kernel. This method was used to test whether the fast-switching feature could be used on the device.

Files Mentioned in This Chapter

Figure 2-11 shows the main files referenced in this chapter. The missing ones will be introduced in upcoming chapters.

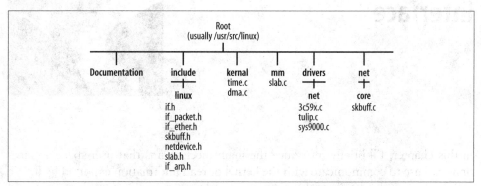

Figure 2-11. Files referenced in this chapter

CHAPTER 3

User-Space-to-Kernel Interface

In this chapter, I'll briefly introduce the main mechanisms that user-space applications can use to communicate with the kernel or read information exported by it. We will not look at the details of their implementations, because each mechanism would deserve a chapter of its own. The purpose of this chapter is to give you enough pointers to the code and to external documentation so that you can further investigate the topic if interested. For example, with this chapter, you have the information you need to find how and where a given directory is added to /proc, kernel handler which processes a given ioctl command, and what functions are provided by Netlink, currently the preferred interface for user-space network configuration.

This chapter focuses only on the mechanisms that I will often mention in the book when talking about the interface between the user-space configuration commands such as *ifconfig* and *route* and the kernel handlers that apply the requested configurations. For analysis of the generic messaging systems available for intrakernel communication as well as kernel-to-user-space communication, please refer to *Understanding the Linux Kernel* (O'Reilly).

The discussion of each feature in this book ends with a set of sections that show how user-space configuration tools and the kernel communicate. The information in this chapter can help you understand those sections better.

Overview

The kernel exports internal information to user space via different interfaces. Besides the classic set of system calls the application programmer can use to ask for specific information, there are three special interfaces, two of which are virtual filesystems:

procfs (/proc filesystem)
> This is a virtual filesystem, usually mounted in /proc, that allows the kernel to export internal information to user space in the form of files. The files don't actually exist on disk, but they can be read through *cat* or *more* and written to

with the > shell redirector; they even can be assigned permission like real files. The components of the kernel that create these files can therefore say who can read from or write to any file. Directories cannot be written (i.e., no user can add or remove a file or a directory to or from any directory in */proc*).

The default kernel that comes with most (if not all) Linux distributions includes support for *procfs*. It cannot be compiled as a module. The associated kernel option from the configuration menu is "Filesystems → Pseudo filesystems → /proc file system support."

sysctl (/proc/sys directory)

This interface allows user space to read and modify the value of kernel variables. You cannot use it for every kernel variable: the kernel has to explicitly say what variables are visible through this interface. From user space, you can access the variables exported by *sysctl* in two ways. One is the sysctl system call (see *man sysctl*) and the other one is *procfs*. When the kernel has support for *procfs*, it adds a special directory (*/proc/sys*) to */proc* that includes a file for each kernel variable exported by *sysctl*.

The *sysctl* command that comes with the *procps* package can be used to configure variables exported with the *sysctl* interface. The command talks to the kernel by writing to */proc/sys*.

The default kernel that comes with most (if not all) Linux distributions includes support for *sysctl*. It cannot be compiled as a module. The associated kernel option from the configuration menu is "General setup → Sysctl support."

sysfs (/sys filesystem)

procfs and *sysctl* have been abused over the years, and this has led to the introduction of a newer filesystem: *sysfs*. *sysfs* exports plenty of information in a very clean and organized way. You can expect part of the information currently exported with *sysctl* to migrate to *sysfs*.

sysfs is available only with kernels starting at 2.6. The default kernel that comes with most (if not all) Linux distributions includes support for *sysfs*. It cannot be compiled as a module. The associated kernel option from the configuration menu is "Filesystems → Pseudo filesystems → sysfs filesystem support (NEW)." The option is visible only if you first enable the following option: "General setup → Configure standard kernel features (for small systems)."

You can find a detailed analysis of *sysfs* in the latest edition of the O'Reilly book *Linux Device Drivers*. In Chapter 17, we will see how the bridging code uses it.

You also use the following interfaces to send commands to the kernel, either to configure something or to dump the configuration of something else:

ioctl *system call*

The ioctl (input/output control) system call operates on a file and is usually used to implement operations needed by special devices that are not provided by the standard filesystem calls. ioctl can be passed a socket descriptor too, as returned by the *socket* system call, and that is how it is used by the networking code. This interface is used by old-generation commands like *ifconfig* and *route*, among others.

Netlink socket

This is the newest and preferred mechanism for networking applications to communicate with the kernel. Most commands in the IPROUTE2 package use it. Netlink represents for Linux what the routing socket represents in the BSD world.

Most network kernel features can be configured using either Netlink or ioctl interfaces, because the kernel supports both the newer configuration tools (IPROUTE2) and the legacy ones (*ifconfig*, *route*, etc.).

procfs Versus sysctl

Both *procfs* and *sysctl* export kernel-internal information, but *procfs* mainly exports read-only data, while most *sysctl* information is writable too (but only by the superuser).

As far as exporting read-only data, the choice between *procfs* and *sysctl* depends on how much information is supposed to be exported. Files associated with a simple kernel variable or data structure are exported with *sysctl*. The others, which are associated with more complex data structures and may need special formatting, are exported with *procfs*. Examples of the latter category are caches and statistics.

procfs

Most networking features register one or more files in */proc* when they get initialized, either at boot time or at module load time. When a user reads the file, it causes the kernel to indirectly run a set of kernel functions that return some kind of output. The files registered by the networking code are located in */proc/net*.

Directories in */proc* can be created with proc_mkdir. Files in */proc/net* can be registered and unregistered with proc_net_fops_create and proc_net_remove, defined in *include/linux/proc_fs.h*. These two routines are wrappers around the generic APIs create_proc_entry and remove_proc_entry. In particular, proc_net_fops_create takes care of creating the file (with proc_net_create) and initializing its file operation handlers. Let's look at an example.

This is how the ARP protocol registers its *arp* file in */proc/net*:

```
static struct file_operations arp_seq_fops = {
    .owner      = THIS_MODULE,
    .open       = arp_seq_open,
    .read       = seq_read,
```

```
        .llseek      = seq_lseek,
        .release     = seq_release_private,
    };

    static int __init arp_proc_init(void)
    {
        if (!proc_net_fops_create("arp", S_IRUGO, &arp_seq_fops))
            return -ENOMEM;
        return 0;
    }
```

The three input parameters to proc_net_fops_create tell you that the filename is *arp*, it must be assigned read permission only, and the set of file operation handlers is arp_seq_ops. When a user reads the file, the use of the file_operations data structure allows *procfs* to return data to the user in chunks. This is useful when the data consists of a collection of objects of the same type. For example, the ARP cache is returned one entry at a time, the routing table is returned one route at a time, etc.

The routine to which open is initialized (arp_seq_open in the previous example) makes another important initialization: it registers an array of function pointers that includes all the routines *procfs* uses to walk through the data that is to be returned to the user: one routine to start the dump, another to advance one item, and another one to dump one item. Those routines internally take care of saving the necessary context information (in this example, how much of the ARP cache has been dumped already) needed to remember what point the dump is at and to resume it from the right position.

```
    static struct seq_operations arp_seq_ops = {
        .start   = clip_seq_start,
        .next    = neigh_seq_next,
        .stop    = neigh_seq_stop,
        .show    = clip_seq_show,
    };

    static int arp_seq_open(struct inode *inode, struct file *file)
    {
        ...
        rc = seq_open(file, &arp_seq_ops);
        ...
    }
```

sysctl: Directory /proc/sys

What the user sees as a file somewhere under */proc/sys* is actually a kernel variable. For each variable, the kernel can define:

- Where to place it in */proc/sys*. Variables associated with the same kernel component or feature are usually located within a common directory. For instance, in */proc/sys/net/ipv4* you can find IPv4-related files.

- What name to give it. Most of the time, the files are simply given the same name as the associated kernel variables, but sometimes their name is changed to be a little more user friendly.
- The permission. A file may, for instance, be readable by anyone but modified only by the superuser.

The content of the variables exported in */proc/sys* can be read or written by accessing the associated file (provided that you have the necessary permissions), or more directly with the *sysctl* system call.

Some directories and files are defined statically at boot time; others are added at runtime. Examples of events that lead to the runtime creation of directories or files are:

- When a kernel module implements a new feature or a protocol is loaded or unloaded.
- When a new network device is registered or unregistered. There are configuration parameters (and thus files in */proc/sys*) that have one instance per device. For example, the directories */proc/sys/net/ipv4/conf* (discussed in Chapter 36) and */proc/sys/net/ipv4/neigh* (discussed in Chapter 29) have one subdirectory for each registered network device.

Both files and directories in */proc/sys* are defined with ctl_table structures. ctl_table structures are registered and unregistered with the register_sysctl_table and unregister_sysctl_table functions, defined in *kernel/sysctl.c*.

Here are the key fields of ctl_data:

const char *procname
> Filename that will be used in */proc/sys*.

int maxlen
> Size of the kernel variable that is exported.

mode_t mode
> Permissions to be assigned to the associated file or directory in */proc/sys*.

ctl_table *child
> Used to build the parent-child relationships between directories and files. We will see examples later in this section.

proc_handler
> Function that performs the read or write operation when you read from or write to a file in */proc/sys*. All ctl_instances associated with files (i.e., the leaves of the tree) must have proc_handler initialized. Directories are assigned a default one by the kernel.

strategy

> Function that can optionally be initialized to a routine that performs additional formatting of data before displaying or storing it. It is invoked when the file in */proc/sys* is accessed with the sysctl system call.

extra1
extra2

> Two optional parameters commonly used to define the minimum and maximum values for the variable. I'll often refer to these two parameters as the min/max parameters.

Depending on what kind of variable is associated with a file, proc_handler and strategy are initialized differently. For example, proc_dointvec is the proc_handler routine to use when the kernel variable consists of one or more integer values. Tables 3-1 and 3-2 list some of the routines that can be used to initialize proc_handler and strategy, respectively. All routines are defined and well commented in *kernel/sysctl.c*.

Table 3-1. Routines for initializing proc_handler

Function	Description
proc_dostring	Reads/writes a string.
proc_dointvec	Reads/writes an array of one or more integers.
proc_dointvec_minmax	Similar to proc_dointvec, but makes sure the input falls within a min/max range. Values that do not respect the range are rejected.
proc_dointvec_jiffies	Reads/writes an array of integers. The kernel variable is expressed in jiffies but is converted into seconds before being returned to the user, and vice versa.
proc_dointvec_ms_jiffies	Reads/writes an array of integers. The kernel variable is expressed in jiffies but is converted into milliseconds before being returned to the user, and vice versa.
proc_doulongvec_minmax	Similar to proc_dointvec_minmax, but the values are longs rather than integers.
proc_doulongvec_ms_jiffies_minmax	Reads/writes an array of longs. The kernel variable is expressed in jiffies but is converted into milliseconds before being returned to the user, and vice versa. The kernel variable must be assigned values within a min/max range.

Table 3-2. Routines for initializing strategy

Function	Description
sysctl_string	Reads/writes a string
sysctl_intvec	Reads/writes an array of integers and makes sure that they respect the min/max range
sysctl_jiffies	Reads/writes a value expressed in jiffies and converts it into seconds
sysctl_ms_jiffies	Reads/writes a value expressed in jiffies and converts it into milliseconds

It is not uncommon for a strategy or proc_handler function to be initialized to a routine that is a wrapper around one of the routines in Tables 3-1 or 3-2. The wrapper may be necessary to add some kind of logic or sanity check that depends on the meaning of the associated kernel variable. An example is in the next section.

Anytime we look at the *procfs* interface for the configuration of any of the features covered in this book, I will always refer to the proc_handler function for simplicity.

Examples of ctl_table initialization

Let's first see what the initialization of a ctl_table structure for a file and a directory looks like, and then how they are actually used.

This is the initialization of the ctl_table instance used for the */proc/sys/net/ipv4/conf/ default/forwarding* file, defined in *net/ipv4/devinet.c*. Its use is described in Chapter 36.

```
{
    .ctl_name     = NET_IPV4_CONF_FORWARDING,
    .procname     = "forwarding",
    .data         = &ipv4_devconf.forwarding,
    .maxlen       = sizeof(int),
    .mode         = 0644,
    .proc_handler = &devinet_sysctl_forward,
}
```

From this snapshot, you can't really tell where in */proc/sys* the file will be placed. We will see in a moment how you can find that information. What you can tell from the code is that the file is called *forwarding*, the kernel variable whose value is exported with the *forwarding* file is ipv4_devconf.forwarding (a field within a more complex structure), the parameter is declared as an integer, the permissions on the file are 0644 (i.e., read permission for anyone, write permission for the superuser only), and the proc_handler routine is initialized to devinet_sysctl_forward.

Now let's see an example of a declaration of a directory from *kernel/sysctl.c*:

```
{
    .ctl_name  = CTL_NET,
    .procname  = "net",
    .mode      = 0555,
    .child     = net_table,
}
```

This is the ctl_table instance that defines the directory */proc/sys/net*. No proc_handler is needed this time (the kernel provides a default one that suits the needs of all directories), but there is a child field instead. child is a pointer to another ctl_table instance, which is nothing but the head element of a list of ctl_table instances (there will be one instance for each file or subdirectory created within the *net* directory).

Registering a file in /proc/sys

We saw that a file can be registered to and unregistered from */proc/sys* with register_sysctl_table and unregister_sysctl_table, respectively. The registration function, well documented in the source code, requires two input parameters:

- A pointer to a ctl_table instance
- A flag that tells where to put the new element in the list of ctl_table instances located in the same directory: at the head (1) or at the tail (0)

Note that the input to register_sysctl_table does not include a reference to the location in the */proc/sys* filesystem where the input ctl_table is added. The reason is that all insertions are made into the */proc/sys* directory. If you wanted to register a file into a subdirectory of */proc/sys*, you would need to provide the full path by building a tree (by means of multiple ctl_table instances linked with the child field) and pass to register_sysctl_table the ctl_table instance that represents the root of the tree you have built. When any of the nodes of the tree do not exist already, they are created.

Let's take two examples, starting with a simpler one. This piece of code from *drivers/scsi/scsi_sysctl.c* shows how the file *logging_level* is defined and placed in the */proc/sys/dev/scsi/* directory:

```
static ctl_table scsi_table[] = {
    { .ctl_name     = DEV_SCSI_LOGGING_LEVEL,
      .procname     = "logging_level",
      .data         = &scsi_logging_level,
      .maxlen       = sizeof(scsi_logging_level),
      .mode         = 0644,
      .proc_handler = &proc_dointvec },
    { }
};

static ctl_table scsi_dir_table[] = {
    { .ctl_name     = DEV_SCSI,
      .procname     = "scsi",
      .mode         = 0555,
      .child        = scsi_table },
    { }
};

static ctl_table scsi_root_table[] = {
    { .ctl_name     = CTL_DEV,
      .procname     = "dev",
      .mode         = 0555,
      .child        = scsi_dir_table },
    { }
};

int __init scsi_init_sysctl(void)
{
    scsi_table_header = register_sysctl_table(scsi_root_table, 1) :
}
```

Note that register_sysctl_table is passed scsi_root_table, which is the root of the ctl_table tree defined in the code. The result is shown in Figure 3-1.

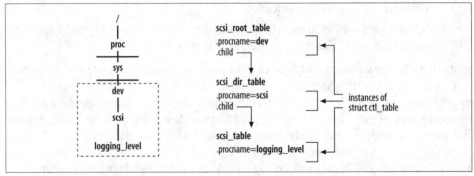

Figure 3-1. Registration of the /proc/sys/dev/scsi/logging_level file

Note also that if later you wanted to add another file to the same directory—say, *abc*—you would need to define a similar tree (i.e., the same two ctl_table instances for the *dev* and *scsi* directories, plus one new ctl_table instance for the new file *abc*).

What developers sometimes do to simplify the addition of new files to an already existing directory is to define a template and reuse it any time a new file is to be added to the same directory. The good part about using templates is that the ctl_table instances that are used to navigate the directories (e.g., scsi_root_table and scsi_dir_table in the previous example) need to be initialized only once: after that, every time you add a new file you will initialize only the leaf nodes (i.e., the real files). See, for example, how the neighboring subsystem defines neigh_sysctl_template and uses it with neigh_sysctl_register in *net/core/neighbour.c* (see also Chapter 29).

Core networking files and directories

Figure 3-2 shows the main directories used by the networking code in */proc/sys*. For each one, it tells you in what chapter its files are described.

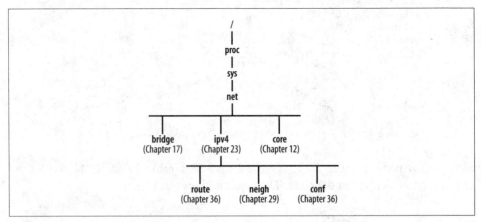

Figure 3-2. Core directories in /proc/sys/net

Let's see, based on what we saw in the previous section, how the tree rooted in *net* is defined and registered at boot time.

For each directory in Figure 3-2, and for each file in those directories, there is an instance of ctl_table. Figure 3-3 shows where the ctl_table instances of most of the directories in Figure 3-2 are defined, and what the child-parent relationships are. Not all directories have been included to make the figure more readable.

The three boxes in Figure 3-3 show three examples of ctl_table initializations. Note that:

- The *netdev_max_backlog* file is assigned a proc_handler routine but not a strategy routine. Because netdev_max_backlog is an integer, the input from the user is read with proc_dointvec.
- The *min_delay* file is assigned both the proc_handler and strategy routines. Because the kernel variable ip_rt_min_delay is expressed in jiffies but the user input and output are in seconds, the two routines take care of converting seconds to jiffies.
- The *ip_local_port_range* file is an interesting case. It is used to allow the user to configure a range, defined as two values. The range must respect a minimum and a maximum value. Therefore, the strategy and proc_handler routines selected are able to manage an array of integer values (two of them in this case). These values, extra1 and extra2, express the range and are used to make sure that the input from the user respects it.

ioctl

At the top of Figure 3-4, you can see how an ioctl call is issued. Let's see an example involving *ifconfig*.

We said earlier that the *ifconfig* command uses ioctl to communicate with the kernel. For example, when the system administrator types a command like *ifconfig eth0 mtu 1250* to change the MTU of the interface *eth0*, *ifconfig* opens a socket, initializes a local data structure with the information received from the system administrator (data in the example), and passes it to the kernel with an ioctl call. SIOCSIFMTU is the command identifier.

```
struct ifreq data;
fd = socket(PF_INET, SOCK_DGRAM, 0);
< ... initialize "data" ...>
err = ioctl(fd, SIOCSIFMTU, &data);
```

ioctl commands are processed by the kernel in different places. Figure 3-4 shows how the most common ioctl commands used by the networking code are dispatched by sock_ioctl and routed to the right function handler. We will not see how sock_ioctl is invoked or how transport protocols like UDP and TCP register their handlers. If you desire to dig into this part of the code, you can use the figure as a

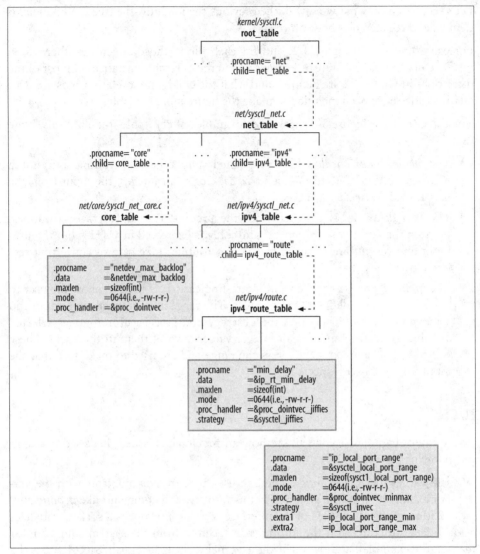

Figure 3-3. Creation of the core directories in /proc/sys/net

starting point. For the routines that we cover in this book, the figure provides a reference to the right chapter.

The name of the `ioctl` commands in the figure is parsed (split into components) for your convenience. For example, the command used to add a route to a routing table, SIOCADDRT, is shown as SIOC ADD RT to emphasize the two interesting components: ADD, which says you are adding something, and RT, which says a route is what you are adding. Most commands follow this syntax. Often, when a given object type can be both read and written, you have one more component in the command

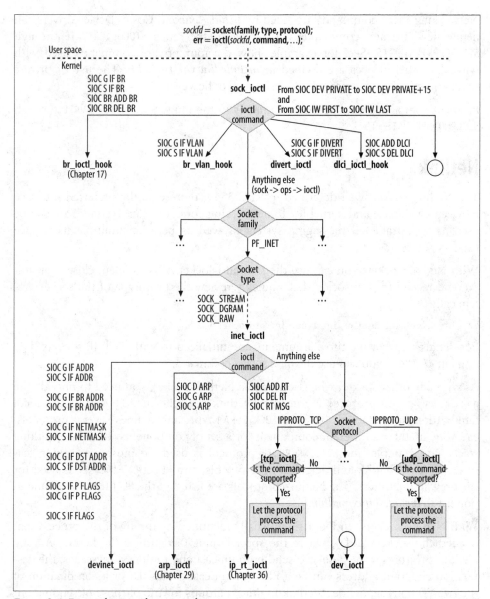

Figure 3-4. Dispatching ioctl commands

name: G for get or S for set. The two commands that add and remove an IP address from an interface, SIOCGIFADDR and SIOCSIFADDR, are an example. SIOCSIFMTU, which we saw in the earlier *ifconfig* example, sets (S) the interface's (IF) maximum transport unit (MTU). SIOCSIFMTU, which is taken care of by dev_ioctl, does not appear in Figure 3-4.

Networking ioctl commands are listed in *include/linux/sockios.h*. Device drivers can define new (private) commands with codes in the range SIOCDEVPRIVATE through SIOCDEVPRIVATE+15. See, for example, how the four private commands used with (virtual) tunnel devices are defined in *include/linux/if_tunnel.h*. The use of private ioctl commands is deprecated and discouraged, however.

Protocols can also define private commands in the range SIOCPROTOPRIVATE through SIOCPROTOPRIVATE+15.

Netlink

The Netlink socket, well described in RFC 3549, represents the preferred interface between user space and kernel for IP networking configuration. Netlink can also be used as an intrakernel messaging system as well as between multiple user-space processes.

With Netlink sockets you can use the standard socket APIs to open, close, transmit on, and receive from a socket. Let's quickly review the prototype of the socket system call:

```
int socket(int domain, int type, int protocol)
```

For details on what the three arguments are initialized to with TCP/IP sockets (i.e., domain PF_INET), you can use the *man socket* command.

As with any other socket, when you open a Netlink socket, you need to provide the domain, type, and protocol arguments. Netlink uses the new PF_NETLINK protocol family (domain), supports only the SOCK_DGRAM type, and defines several protocols, each one used for a different component (or a set of components) of the networking stack. For example, the NETLINK_ROUTE protocol is used for most networking features, such as routing and neighboring protocols, and NETLINK_FIREWALL is used for the firewall (Netfilter). The Netlink protocols are listed in the NETLINK_*XXX* enumeration list in *include/linux/netlink.h*.

With Netlink sockets, endpoints are usually identified by the ID of the process that opened the sockets (PID), where the special value 0 identifies the kernel. Among Netlink's features is the ability to send both unicast and multicast messages: the destination endpoint address can be a PID, a multicast group ID, or a combination of the two. The kernel defines Netlink multicast groups for the purpose of sending out notifications about particular kinds of events, and user programs can register to those groups if they are interested in them. The groups are listed in the enumeration list RTMGRP_*XXX* in *include/linux/rtnetlink.h*. Among them are the RTMGRP_IPV4_ROUTE and RTMGRP_NEIGH groups, used respectively for notifications regarding changes to the routing tables and to the L3-to-L2 address mappings. We will see how these two groups are used in Parts VI and VII.

Another interesting feature is the ability to send both positive and negative acknowledgments.

One of the advantages of Netlink over other user-kernel interfaces such as ioctl is that the kernel can initiate a transmission instead of just returning information in answer to user-space requests.

Serializing Configuration Changes

Any time you apply a configuration change, the handler that takes care of it inside the kernel acquires a semaphore (rtnl_sem) that ensures exclusive access to the data structures that store the networking configuration. This is true regardless of whether the configuration is applied via ioctl or Netlink.

## PART II

System Initialization

In this part of the book, we will see how and when network devices are initialized and registered with the kernel. I'll put special emphasis on Peripheral Component Interconnect (PCI) devices, both because they are increasingly common and because they have special requirements.

Many tasks related to the network interface card (NIC) have to be accomplished before getting a network up and running. First, key kernel components need to be initialized. Then device drivers must initialize and register all the devices they are responsible for and allocate the resources the kernel will use to communicate with them (IRQ, I/O ports, etc.).

It's important to distinguish between two kinds of registration. First, when a device is discovered, it is registered with the kernel as a generic device. Second, an NIC device is registered with the network stack as a network device. For example, a PCI Ethernet card is registered both as a generic PCI device with the PCI layer, and as an Ethernet card (where the device gets a name such as *eth0*) with the network stack. The first kind of registration is covered in Chapter 6 and the second in Chapter 8.

Here is what is covered in each chapter:

Chapter 4, *Notification Chains*
> The mechanism that kernel components use to notify each other about specific events.

Chapter 5, *Network Device Initialization*
> How network devices are initialized.

Chapter 6, *The PCI Layer and Network Interface Cards*
> How PCI device drivers register with the kernel, and how PCI devices are identified and associated with their drivers.

Chapter 7, *Kernel Infrastructure for Component Initialization*
> The kernel mechanism that ensures that the necessary initialization functions are invoked at boot time or module load time. We'll learn how initialization routines can be tagged with special macros to optimize memory usage and therefore

reduce the size of the kernel image. We will also see how the kernel can be passed boot options and how these can be used to configure NICs.

Chapter 8, *Device Registration and Initialization*

How devices are registered with the kernel and initialized.

## CHAPTER 4

Notification Chains

The kernel's many subsystems are heavily interdependent, so an event detected or generated by one of them could be of interest to others. To fulfill the need for interaction, Linux uses so-called *notification chains*.

In this chapter, we will see:

- How notification chains are declared and what chains are defined by the networking code
- How a kernel subsystem can register to a notification chain
- How a kernel subsystem generates a notification on a chain

Note that notification chains are used only between kernel subsystems. Notifications between kernel and user space rely on other mechanisms, such as those introduced in Chapter 3.

Reasons for Notification Chains

Suppose we had the Linux router in Figure 4-1 with four interfaces. The figure shows the relationship between the router and five networks, along with a simplified version of its routing table.

Let's look at some examples of the topology in Figure 4-1. Network A is directly connected to RT on interface *eth0*, and network F is not directly connected to RT, but RT's *eth3* is directly connected to another router that has an interface with address IP1, and that second router knows how to reach network F. The other cases are similar. In short, some networks are directly connected and others require the help of one or more additional routers to be reached.

For a detailed description of how the routing code handles this situation, refer to Part VII. In this chapter, we will concentrate on the role of notification chains. Suppose that interface *eth3* went down, due to a break in the network, an administrative command (such as `ifconfig eth3 down`) or a hardware failure. Networks D, E, and F

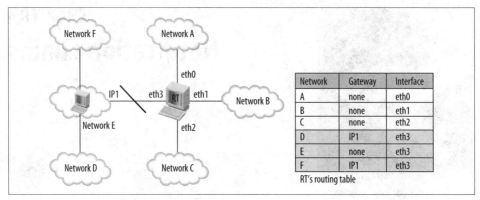

Figure 4-1. Example of Linux router

would become unreachable by RT (and by systems in A, B, and C relying on RT for their connections) and should be removed from the routing table. Who is going to tell the routing subsystem about that interface failure? A notification chain.

Figure 4-2 shows a slightly more complicated example where the routing subsystem interacts with dynamic routing protocols—protocols that can adjust the routing table or tables* to the network topology and therefore cope with interface failures when the topology allows it (i.e., when there are redundant paths).

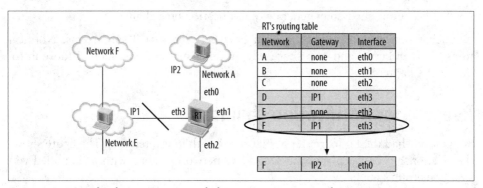

Figure 4-2. Example of a Linux router with dynamic routing protocols

In Figure 4-2, network F could be reached by RT by passing through both network A and network E. E was chosen initially because of its smaller cost,† but now that E is no longer reachable, the routing table should update the route for network F to go through network A. The basis for such a decision could include local host events, such as device registration and unregistration, as well as complex factors in router

---

* It is possible to have multiple routing tables at the same time. We will cover this feature in Chapter 31.

† The cost of a link is one of the metrics that routing protocols can use to compare links and choose among them. See Chapter 30.

configuration and the routing protocols used. In any case, the routing subsystem that manages the tables must be informed of the relevant information by some other subsystem, demonstrating the need for notification chains.

Overview

A notification chain is simply a list of functions to execute when a given event occurs. Each function lets one other subsystem know about an event that occurred within, or was detected by, the subsystem calling the function.

Thus, for each notification chain there is a passive side (the notified) and an active side (the notifier), as in the so-called publish-and-subscribe model:

- The *notified* are the subsystems that ask to be notified about the event and that provide a callback function to invoke.
- The *notifier* is the subsystem that experiences an event and calls the callback function.

The functions executed are chosen by the notified subsystems. It is never up to the owner of the chain (the subsystem that generates the notifications) to decide what functions to execute. The owner simply defines the list; any kernel subsystem can register a callback function with that chain to receive the notification.

The use of notification chains makes the source code easier to write and maintain. Imagine how a generic routine might notify external subsystems about an event without using notification chains:

```
If (subsystem_X_enabled) {
    do_something_1
}
if (subsystem_Y_enabled) {
    do_something_2
}
If (subsystem_Z_enabled) {
    do_something_3
}
... ... ...
```

In other words, a conditional clause would have to be included for every possible subsystem that might be interested in an event, and the maintainer of this subsystem would have to add a new clause every time somebody else added a subsystem to the kernel.

No subsystem maintainer is expected to keep track of every subsystem added to the kernel. However, each subsystem maintainer should know:

- The kinds of events from other subsystems he is interested in
- The kinds of events he knows about and that other subsystems may be interested in

Thus, notification chains allow each subsystem to share the occurrence of an event with others, without having to know what the others are and why they are interested.

Defining a Chain

The elements of the notification chain's list are of type `notifier_block`, whose definition is the following:

```
struct notifier_block
{
    int (*notifier_call)(struct notifier_block *self, unsigned long, void *);
    struct notifier_block *next;
    int priority;
};
```

`notifier_call` is the function to execute, `next` is used to link together the elements of the list, and `priority` represents the priority of the function. Functions with higher priority are executed first. But in practice, almost all registrations leave the `priority` out of the `notifier_block` definition, which means it gets the default value of 0 and execution order ends up depending only on the registration order (i.e., it is a semirandom order). The return values of `notifier_call` are listed in the upcoming section, "Notifying Events on a Chain."

Common names for `notifier_block` instances are *xxx*_chain, *xxx*_notifier_chain, and *xxx*_notifier_list.

Registering with a Chain

When a kernel component is interested in the events of a given notification chain, it can register it with the general function `notifier_chain_register`. The kernel also provides a set of wrappers around `notifier_chain_register`, some of which are shown in Table 4-1.

Table 4-1 lists the main APIs and the associated wrappers used to register and unregister to the three chains `inetaddr_chain`, `inet6addr_chain`, and `netdev_chain`.

Table 4-1. Main functions and wrappers for a few chains

Operation	Function prototype	
Registration	`int notifier_chain_register(struct notifier_block **list, struct notifier_block *n)`	
	Wrappers	
	`inetaddr_chain`	`register_inetaddr_notifier`
	`inet6addr_chain`	`register_inet6addr_notifier`
	`netdev_chain`	`register_netdevice_notifier`

Table 4-1. Main functions and wrappers for a few chains (continued)

Operation	Function prototype	
Unregistration	int notifier_chain_unregister(struct notifier_block **nl, struct notifier_block *n)	
	Wrappers	
	inetaddr_chain	unregister_inetaddr_notifier
	inet6addr_chain	unregister_inet6addr_notifier
	netdev_chain	unregister_netdevice_notifier
Notification	int notifier_call_chain(struct notifier_block **n, unsigned long val, void *v)	

For each chain, the notifier_block instances are inserted into a list, which is sorted by priority. Elements with the same priority are sorted based on insertion time: new ones go to the tail.

Accesses to the notification chains are protected by the notifier_lock lock. The use of a single lock for all the notification chains is not a big constraint and does not affect performance, because subsystems usually register their notifier_call functions only at boot time or at module load time, and from that moment on access the lists in a read-only manner (that is, shared).

Because the notifier_chain_register function is called to insert callbacks into all lists, it requires that the list be specified as an input parameter. However, this function is rarely called directly; generic wrappers are used instead.

```
int notifier_chain_register(struct notifier_block **list, struct notifier_block *n)
{
    write_lock(&notifier_lock);
    while(*list)
    {
        if(n->priority > (*list)->priority)
            break;
        list= &((*list)->next);
    }
    n->next = *list;
    *list=n;
    write_unlock(&notifier_lock);
    return 0;
}
```

Notifying Events on a Chain

Notifications are generated with notifier_call_chain, defined in *kernel/sys.c*. This function simply invokes, in order of priority, all the callback routines registered against the chain. Note that callback routines are executed in the context of the process that calls notifier_call_chain. A callback routine could, however, be implemented so that it queues the notification somewhere and wakes up a process that will look at it.

```
int notifier_call_chain(struct notifier_block **n, unsigned long val, void *v)
{
    int ret = NOTIFY_DONE;
    struct notifier_block *nb = *n;

    while (nb)
    {
        ret = nb->notifier_call(nb, val, v);
        if (ret & NOTIFY_STOP_MASK)
        {
            return ret;
        }
        nb = nb->next;
    }
    return ret;
}
```

This is the meaning of its three input parameters:

n

Notification chain.

val

Event type. The chain itself identifies a class of events; val unequivocally identifies an event type (i.e., NETDEV_REGISTER).

v

Input parameter that can be used by the handlers registered by the various clients. This can be used in different ways under different circumstances. For instance, when a new network device is registered with the kernel, the associated notification uses v to identify the net_device data structure.

The callback routines called by notifier_call_chain can return any of the NOTIFY_*XXX* values defined in *include/linux/notifier.h*:

NOTIFY_OK

Notification was processed correctly.

NOTIFY_DONE

Not interested in the notification.*

NOTIFY_BAD

Something went wrong. Stop calling the callback routines for this event.

NOTIFY_STOP

Routine invoked correctly. However, no further callbacks need to be called for this event.

---

* This return value is sometimes improperly used in place of NOTIFY_OK.

NOTIFY_STOP_MASK

This flag is checked by `notifier_call_chain` to see whether to stop invoking the callback routines, or keep going. Both `NOTIFY_BAD` and `NOTIFY_STOP` include this flag in their definitions.

`notifier_call_chain` captures and returns the return value received by the last callback routine invoked. This is true regardless of whether all the callbacks have been invoked, or one of them interrupted the loop due to a return value of `NOTIFY_BAD` or `NOTIFY_STOP`.

Note that it is possible for `notifier_call_chain` to be called for the same notification chain on different CPUs at the same time. It is the responsibility of the callback functions to take care of mutual exclusion and serialization where needed.

Notification Chains for the Networking Subsystems

The kernel defines at least 10 different notification chains. Here we are interested in the ones that are used to signal events of particular importance to the networking code. The main ones are:

`inetaddr_chain`

Sends notifications about the insertion, removal, and change of an Internet Protocol Version 4 (IPv4) address on a local interface. Chapter 23 describes when such notifications are generated. Internet Protocol Version 6 (IPv6) uses a similar chain (`inet6addr_chain`).

`netdev_chain`

Sends notifications about the registration status of network devices. Chapter 8 describes when such notifications are generated.

For these chains, and others used by the networking subsystems, their purposes and uses are described in the chapter about the relevant notifier subsystem.

The networking code can register to notifications generated by other kernel components, too. For example, some NIC device drivers register with the `reboot_notifier_list` chain, which is a chain that warns when the system is about to reboot.

Wrappers

Most notification chains come with a set of wrappers used to register to them and unregister from them. For example, this is the wrapper used to register to `netdev_chain`:

```
int register_netdevice_notifier(struct notifier_block *nb)
{
        return notifier_chain_register(&netdev_chain, nb);
}
```

Common names for wrappers include [un]register_*xxx*_notifier, *xxx*_[un]register_notifier, and *xxx*_[un]register.

Examples

Registrations to notification chains usually take place when the interested kernel component is initialized. For example, the following snapshot from *net/ipv4/fib_frontend.c* shows ip_fib_init, which is the initialization routine used by the routing code that is described in the section "Routing Subsystem Initialization" in Chapter 32:

```
static struct notifier_block fib_inetaddr_notifier = {
    .notifier_call = fib_inetaddr_event,
};

static struct notifier_block fib_netdev_notifier = {
    .notifier_call = fib_netdev_event,
};

void __init ip_fib_init(void)
{
    ... ... ...
    register_netdevice_notifier(&fib_netdev_notifier);
    register_inetaddr_notifier(&fib_inetaddr_notifier);
}
```

The routing code registers to both of the chains introduced in the earlier section, "Notification Chains for the Networking Subsystems." The routing tables are affected both by changes to locally configured IP addresses and by changes to the registration status of local devices.

Tuning via /proc Filesystem

There is no file of interest in */proc* as far as this chapter is concerned.

Functions and Variables Featured in This Chapter

Table 4-2 summarizes the functions and data structures introduced in this chapter.

Table 4-2. Functions, macros, and data structures used for notification chains

Name	Description
Functions and macros	
`notifier_chain_register` + wrappers `notifier_chain_unregister` + wrappers `notifier_call_chain`	The first two functions register and unregister a callback handler for a notification chain. The third sends out all the notifications about events in a specific class.
Data structure	
`struct notifier_block`	Defines the handler for a notification. It includes the callback function to invoke.

Files and Directories Featured in This Chapter

Figure 4-3 lists the files referred to in this chapter.

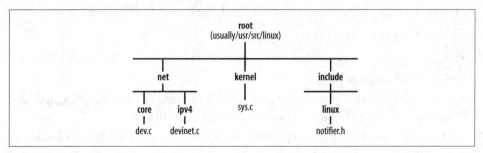

Figure 4-3. Files related to notification chains

CHAPTER 5
Network Device Initialization

The flexibility of modern operating systems introduces complexity into initialization. First, a device driver can be loaded as either a module or a static component of the kernel. Furthermore, devices can be present at boot time or inserted (and removed) at runtime: the latter type of device, called a *hot-pluggable* device, includes USB, PCI CardBus, IEEE 1394 (also called FireWire by Apple), and others. We'll see how hot-plugging affects what happens in both the kernel and the user space.

In this first chapter, we will cover:

- A piece of the core networking code initialization.
- The initialization of an NIC.
- How an NIC uses interrupts, and how IRQ handlers can be allocated and released. We will also look at how drivers can share IRQs.
- How the user can provide configuration parameters to device drivers loaded as modules.
- Interaction between user space and kernel during device initialization and configuration. We will look at how the kernel can run a user-space helper to either load the correct device driver for an NIC or apply a user-space configuration. In particular, we will look at the Hotplug feature.
- How virtual devices differ from real ones with regard to configuration and interaction with the kernel.

System Initialization Overview

It's important to know where and how the main network-related subsystems are initialized, including device drivers. However, because this book is concerned only with the networking aspect of such initializations, I will not cover device drivers in general, or generic kernel services (e.g., memory management). For an understanding of that background, I recommend that you read *Linux Device Drivers* and *Understanding the Linux Kernel*, both published by O'Reilly.

Figure 5-1 shows briefly where, and in what sequence, some of the kernel subsystems are initialized at boot time (see *init/main.c*).

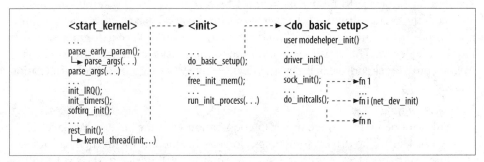

Figure 5-1. Kernel initialization

When the kernel boots up, it executes `start_kernel`, which initializes a bunch of subsystems, as partially shown in Figure 5-1. Before `start_kernel` terminates, it invokes the `init` kernel thread, which takes care of the rest of the initializations. Most of the initialization activities related to this chapter happen to be inside `do_basic_setup`.

Among the various initialization tasks, we are mainly interested in three:

Boot-time options
> Two calls to `parse_args`, one direct and one indirect via `parse_early_param`, handle configuration parameters that a boot loader such as LILO or GRUB has passed to the kernel at boot time. We will see how this task is handled in the section "Boot-Time Kernel Options."

Interrupts and timers
> Hardware and software interrupts are initialized with `init_IRQ` and `softirq_init`, respectively. Interrupts are covered in Chapter 9. In this chapter, we will see just how device drivers register a handler with an IRQ and how IRQ handlers are organized in memory. Timers are also initialized early in the boot process so that later tasks can use them.

Initialization routines
> Kernel subsystems and built-in device drivers are initialized by `do_initcalls`. `free_init_mem` frees a piece of memory that holds unneeded code. This optimization is possible thanks to smart routine tagging. See Chapter 7 for more details.

`run_init_process` determines the first process run on the system, the parent of all other processes; it has a PID of 1 and never halts until the system is done. Normally the program run is *init*, part of the SysVinit package. However, the administrator can specify a different program through the `init=` boot time option. When no such option is provided, the kernel tries to execute the *init* command from a set of well-known locations, and panics if it cannot find any. The user can also provide boot-time options that will be passed to *init* (see the section "Boot-Time Kernel Options").

Device Registration and Initialization

For a network device to be usable, it must be recognized by the kernel and associated with the correct driver. The driver stores, in private data structures, all the information needed to drive the device and interact with other kernel components that require the device. The registration and initialization tasks are taken care of partially by the core kernel and partially by the device driver. Let's go over the initialization phases:

Hardware initialization

> This is done by the device driver in cooperation with the generic bus layer (e.g., PCI or USB). The driver, sometimes alone and sometimes with the help of user-supplied parameters, configures such features of each device as the IRQ and I/O address so that they can interact with the kernel. Because this activity is closer to the device drivers than to the higher-layer protocols and features, we will not spend much time on it. We will see one example for the PCI layer.

Software initialization

> Before the device can be used, depending on what network protocols are enabled and configured, the user may need to provide some other configuration parameters, such as IP addresses. This task is addressed in other chapters.

Feature initialization

> The Linux kernel comes with lots of networking options. Because some of them need per-device configuration, the device initialization boot sequence must take care of them. One example is Traffic Control, the subsystem that implements Quality of Service (QoS) and that decides, therefore, how packets are queued on and dequeued from the device egress's queue (and with some limitations, also queued on and dequeued from the ingress's queue).

We already saw in Chapter 2 that the net_device data structure includes a set of function pointers that the kernel uses to interact with the device driver and special kernel features. The initialization of these functions depends in part on the type of device (e.g., Ethernet) and in part on the device's make and model. Given the popularity of Ethernet, this chapter focuses on the initialization of Ethernet devices (but other devices are handled very similarly).

Chapter 8 goes into more detail on how device drivers register their devices with the networking code.

Basic Goals of NIC Initialization

Each network device is represented in the Linux kernel by an instance of the net_device data structure. In Chapter 8, you will see how net_device data structures are allocated and how their fields are initialized, partly by the device driver and partly by core kernel routines. In this chapter, we focus on how device drivers allocate the resources needed to establish device/kernel communication, such as:

IRQ line

As you will see in the section "Interaction Between Devices and Kernel," NICs need to be assigned an IRQ and to use it to call for the kernel's attention when needed. Virtual devices, however, do not need to be assigned an IRQ: the loopback device is an example because its activity is totally internal (see the later section "Virtual Devices").

The two functions used to request and release IRQ lines are introduced in the later section "Hardware Interrupts." As you will see in the later section "Tuning via /proc Filesystem," the */proc/interrupts* file can be used to view the status of the current assignments.

I/O ports and memory registration

It is common for a driver to map an area of its device's memory (its configuration registers, for example) into the system memory so that read/write operations by the driver will be made on system memory addresses directly; this can simplify the code. I/O ports and memory are registered and released with request_region and release_region, respectively.

Interaction Between Devices and Kernel

Nearly all devices (including NICs) interact with the kernel in one of two ways:

Polling

Driven on the kernel side. The kernel checks the device status at regular intervals to see if it has anything to say.

Interrupt

Driven on the device side. The device sends a hardware signal (by generating an interrupt) to the kernel when it needs the kernel's attention.

In Chapter 9, you can find a detailed discussion of NIC driver design alternatives as well as software interrupts. You will also see how Linux can use a combination of polling and interrupts to increase performance. In this chapter, we will look only at the interrupt-based case.

I won't go into detail on how interrupts are reported by the hardware, the difference between hardware exceptions and device interrupts, how the driver and bus kernel infrastructures are designed, etc.; you can refer to *Linux Device Drivers* and *Understanding the Linux Kernel* for those topics. But I'll give a brief overview on interrupts to help you understand how device drivers initialize and register the devices they are responsible for, with special attention to the networking aspect.

Hardware Interrupts

You do not need to know the low-level background about how hardware interrupts are handled. However, there are details worth mentioning because they can make it easier to understand how NIC device drivers are written, and therefore how they interact with the upper networking layers.

Every interrupt runs a function called an *interrupt handler*, which must be tailored to the device and therefore is installed by the device driver. Typically, when a device driver registers an NIC, it requests and assigns an IRQ. It then registers and (if the driver is unloaded) unregisters a handler for a given IRQ with the following two architecture-dependent functions. They are defined in *kernel/irq/manage.c* and are overridden by architecture-specific functions in *arch/XXX/kernel/irq.c*, where *XXX* is the architecture-specific directory:

`int request_irq(unsigned int irq, void (*handler)(int, void*, struct pt_regs*), unsigned long irqflags, const char * devname, void *dev_id)`
> This function registers a handler, first making sure that the requested interrupt is a valid one, and that it is not already allocated to another device unless both devices understand shared IRQs (see the later section "Interrupt sharing").

`void free_irq(unsigned int irq, void *dev_id)`
> Given the device identified by dev_id, this function removes the handler and disables the IRQ line if no more devices are registered for that IRQ. Note that to identify the handler, the kernel needs both the IRQ number and the device identifier. This is especially important with shared IRQs, as explained in the later section "Interrupt sharing."

When the kernel receives an interrupt notification, it uses the IRQ number to find out the driver's handler and then executes this handler. To find handlers, the kernel stores the associations between IRQ numbers and function handlers in a global table. The association can be either one-to-one or one-to-many, because the Linux kernel allows multiple devices to use the same IRQ, a feature described in the later section "Interrupt sharing."

In the following sections, you will see common examples of the information exchanged between devices and drivers by means of interrupts, and how an IRQ can be shared by multiple devices under some conditions.

Interrupt types

With an interrupt, an NIC can tell its driver several different things. Among them are:

Reception of a frame
> This is the most common and standard situation.

Transmission failure

This kind of notification is generated on Ethernet devices only after a feature called exponential binary backoff has failed (this feature is implemented at the hardware level by the NIC). Note that the driver will not relay this notification to higher network layers; they will come to know about the failure by other means (timer timeouts, negative ACKs, etc.).

DMA transfer has completed successfully

Given a frame to send, the buffer that holds it is released by the driver once the frame has been uploaded into the NIC's memory for transmission on the medium. With synchronous transmissions (no DMA), the driver knows right away when the frame has been uploaded on the NIC. But with DMA, which uses asynchronous transmissions, the device driver needs to wait for an explicit interrupt from the NIC. You can find an example of each case at points where dev_kfree_skb* is called within the driver code *drivers/net/3c59x.c* (DMA) and *drivers/net/3c509.c* (non-DMA).

Device has enough memory to handle a new transmission

It is common for an NIC device driver to disable transmissions by stopping the egress queue when that queue does not have sufficient free space to hold a frame of maximum size (e.g., 1,536 bytes for an Ethernet NIC). The queue is then re-enabled when memory becomes available. The rest of this section goes into this case in more detail.

The final case in the previous list covers a sophisticated way of throttling transmissions in a manner that can improve efficiency if done properly. In this system, a device driver disables transmissions for lack of queuing space, asks the NIC to issue an interrupt when the available memory is bigger than a given amount (typically the device's Maximum Transmission Unit, or MTU), and then re-enables transmissions when the interrupt comes.

A device driver can also disable the egress queue before a transmission (to prevent the kernel from generating another transmission request on the device), and re-enable it only if there is enough free memory on the NIC; if not, the device asks for an interrupt that allows it to resume transmission at a later time. Here is an example of this logic, taken from the el3_start_xmit routine, which the *drivers/net/3c509.c* driver installs as its hard_start_xmit† function in its net_device structure:

```
static int
el3_start_xmit(struct sk_buff *skb, struct net_device *dev)
{
    ... ... ...
    netif_stop_queue (dev);
    ... ... ...
```

---

* Chapter 11 describes this function in detail.

† The hard_start_xmit virtual function is described in Chapter 11.

```
    if (inw(ioaddr + TX_FREE) > 1536)
        netif_start_queue(dev);
    else
        outw(SetTxThreshold + 1536, ioaddr + EL3_CMD);
    ... ... ...
}
```

The driver stops the device queue with netif_stop_queue, thus inhibiting the kernel from submitting further transmission requests. The driver then checks whether the device's memory has enough free space for a packet of 1,536 bytes. If so, the driver starts the queue to allow the kernel once again to submit transmission requests; otherwise, it instructs the device (by writing to a configuration register with an outw call) to generate an interrupt when that condition will be met. An interrupt handler will then re-enable the device queue with netif_start_queue so that the kernel can restart transmissions.

The netif_xxx_queue routines are described in the section "Enabling and Disabling Transmissions" in Chapter 11.

Interrupt sharing

IRQ lines are a limited resource. A simple way to increase the number of devices a system can host is to allow multiple devices to share a common IRQ. Normally, each driver registers its own handler to the kernel for that IRQ. Instead of having the kernel receive the interrupt notification, find the right device, and invoke its handler, the kernel simply invokes all the handlers of those devices that registered for the same shared IRQ. It is up to the handlers to filter spurious invocations, such as by reading a registry on their devices.

For a group of devices to share an IRQ line, all of them must have device drivers capable of handling shared IRQs. In other words, each time a device registers for an IRQ line, it needs to explicitly say whether it supports interrupt sharing. For example, the first device that registers for one IRQ, saying something like "assign me IRQ *n* and use this routine *fn* as the handler," must also specify whether it is willing to share the IRQ with other devices. When another device driver tries to register the same IRQ number, it is refused if either it, or the driver to which the IRQ is currently assigned, is incapable of sharing IRQs.

Organization of IRQs to handler mappings

The mapping of IRQs to handlers is stored in a vector of lists, one list of handlers for each IRQ (see Figure 5-2). A list includes more than one element only when multiple devices share the same IRQ. The size of the vector (i.e., the number of possible IRQ numbers) is architecture dependent and can vary from 15 (on an x86) to more than 200. With the introduction of interrupt sharing, even more devices can be supported on a system at once.

The section "Hardware Interrupts" already introduced the two functions provided by the kernel to register and unregister a handler, respectively. Let's now see the data structure used to store the mappings.

Mappings are defined with `irqaction` data structures. The `request_irq` function introduced in the earlier section "Hardware Interrupts" is a wrapper around `setup_irq`, which takes an `irqaction` structure as input and inserts it into the global `irq_desc` vector. `irq_desc` is defined in *kernel/irq/handler.c* and can be overridden in the per-architecture files *arch/XXX/kernel/irq.c*. `setup_irq` is defined in *kernel/irq/manage.c* and can be overridden in the per-architecture files *arch/XXX/kernel/irq.c*.

The kernel function that handles interrupts and passes them to drivers is architecture dependent. It is called `handle_IRQ_event` on most architectures.

Figure 5-2 shows how `irqaction` instances are stored: there is an instance of `irq_desc` for each possible IRQ and an instance of `irqaction` for each successfully registered IRQ handler. The vector of `irq_desc` instances is called `irq_desc` as well, and its size is given by the architecture-dependent symbol `NR_IRQS`.

Note that when you have more than one `irqaction` instance for a given IRQ number (that is, for a given element of the `irq_desc` vector), interrupt sharing is required (each structure must have the `SA_SHIRQ` flag set).

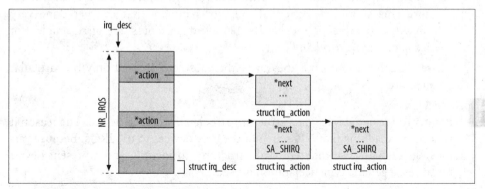

Figure 5-2. Organization of IRQ handlers

Let's see now what information is stored about IRQ handlers in the fields of an `irqaction` data structure:

`void (*handler)(int irq, void *dev_id, struct pt_regs *regs)`
> Function provided by the device driver to handle notifications of interrupts: whenever the kernel receives an interrupt on line `irq`, it invokes `handler`. Here are the function's input parameters:

> `int irq`
>> IRQ number that generated the notification. Most of the time it is not used by the NICs' device drivers to accomplish their job; the device ID is sufficient.

void *dev_id

Device identifier. The same driver can be responsible for different devices at the same time, so it needs the device ID to process the notification correctly.

struct pt_regs *regs

Structure used to save the content of the processor's registers at the moment the interrupt interrupted the current process. It is normally not used by the interrupt handler.

unsigned long flags

Set of flags. The possible values SA_XXX are defined in *include/asm-XXX/signal.h*. Here are the main ones from the x86 architecture file:

SA_SHIRQ

When set, the device driver can handle shared IRQs.

SA_SAMPLE_RANDOM

When set, the device is making itself available as a source of random events. This can be useful to help the kernel generate random numbers for internal use, and is called contributing to *system entropy*. This is further described in the later section "Initializing the Device Handling Layer: net_dev_init."

SA_INTERRUPT

When set, the handler runs with interrupts disabled on the local processor. This should be specified only for handlers that can get done very quickly. See one of the handle_IRQ_event instances for an example (for instance, */kernel/irq/handle.c*).

There are other values, but they are either obsolete or used only by particular architectures.

void *dev_id

Pointer to the net_device data structure associated with the device. The reason it is declared void * is that NICs are not the only devices to use IRQs. Because various device types use different data structures to identify and represent device instances, a generic type declaration is used.

struct irqaction *next

All the devices sharing the same IRQ number are linked together in a list with this pointer.

const char *name

Device name. You can read it by dumping the contents of */proc/interrupts*.

Initialization Options

Both components built into the kernel and components loaded as modules can be passed input parameters so that users can fine-tune the functionality implemented by the components, override defaults compiled into them, or change them from one system boot to the next. The kernel provides two kinds of macros to define options:

Module options (macros of the `module_param` *family)*
These define options you can provide when you load a module. When a component is built into the kernel, you cannot provide values for these options at kernel boot time. However, with the introduction of the */sys* filesystem, you can configure the options via those files at runtime. The */sys* interface is relatively new, compared to the */proc* interface. The later section "Module Options" goes into a little more detail on these options.

Boot-time kernel options (macros of the `__setup` *family)*
These define options you can provide at boot time with a boot loader. They are used mainly by modules that the user can build into the kernel, and kernel components that cannot be compiled as modules. You will see those macros in the section "Boot-Time Kernel Options" in Chapter 7.

It is interesting to note that a module can define an initialization option in both ways: one is effective when the module is built-in and the other is effective when the module is loaded separately. This can be a little confusing, especially because different modules can define passing parameters of the same name at module load time without any risk of name collision (i.e., the parameters are passed just to the module being loaded), but if you pass those parameters at kernel boot time, you must make sure there is no name collision between the various modules' options.

We will not go into detail on the pros and cons of the two approaches. You can look at the *drivers/block/loop.c* driver for a clear example using both `module_param` and `__setup`.

Module Options

Kernel modules define their parameters by means of macros such as `module_param`; see *include/linux/moduleparam.h* for a list. `module_param` requires three input parameters, as shown in the following example from *drivers/net/sis900.c*:

```
...
module_param(multicast_filter_limit, int 0444);
module_param(max_interrupt_work, int 0444);
module_param(debug, int, 0444);
...
```

The first input parameter is the name of the parameter to be offered to the user. The second is the type of the parameter (e.g., integer), and the third represents the permissions assigned to the file in /sys to which the parameter will be exported.

This is what you would get when listing the module's directory in /sys:

```
[root@localhost src]# ls -la /sys/module/sis900/parameters/
total 0
drwxr-xr-x  2 root root     0 Apr  9 18:31 .
drwxr-xr-x  4 root root     0 Apr  9 18:31 ..
-r--r--r--  1 root root     0 Apr  9 18:31 debug
-r--r--r--  1 root root  4096 Apr  9 18:31 max_interrupt_work
-r--r--r--  1 root root  4096 Apr  9 18:31 multicast_filter_limit
[root@localhost src]#
```

Each module is assigned a directory in /sys/modules. The subdirectory /sys/modules/module/parameters holds a file for each parameter exported by module. The previous snapshot from drivers/net/sis900.c shows three options that are readable by anyone, but not writable (they cannot be changed).

Permissions on /sys files (and on /proc files, incidentally) are defined using the same syntax as common files, so you can specify read, write, and execute permissions for the owner, the group, and everybody else. A value of 400 means, for example, read access for the owner (who is the root user) and no other access for anyone. When a value of 0 is assigned, no one has any permissions and you would not even see the file in /sys.

If the component programmer wants the user to be able to read the values of parameters, she must give at least read permission. She can also provide write permission to allow users to modify values. However, take into account that the module that exports the parameter is not notified about any change to the file, so the module must have a mechanism to detect the change or be able to cope with changes.

For a detailed description of the /sys interface, refer to Linux Device Drivers.

Initializing the Device Handling Layer: net_dev_init

An important part of initialization for the networking code, including Traffic Control and per-CPU ingress queues, is performed at boot time by net_dev_init, defined in net/core/dev.c:

```
static int __init net_dev_init(void)
{
    ...
}
subsys_initcall(net_dev_init);
```

See Chapter 7 for how the subsys_initcall macros ensure that net_dev_init runs before any NIC device drivers register themselves, and why this is important. You also will see why net_dev_init is tagged with the __init macro.

Let's walk through the main parts of net_dev_init:

- The per-CPU data structures used by the two networking software interrupts (softirqs) are initialized. In Chapter 9, we will see what a softirq is and go into detail on how the networking code uses softirqs.

- When the kernel is compiled with support for the */proc* filesystem (which is the default configuration), a few files are added to */proc* with dev_proc_init and dev_mcast_init. See the later section "Tuning via /proc Filesystem" for more details.

- netdev_sysfs_init registers the net class with *sysfs*. This creates the directory */sys/class/net*, under which you will find a subdirectory for each registered network device. These directories include lots of files, some of which used to be in */proc*.

- net_random_init initializes a per-CPU vector of seeds that will be used when generating random numbers with the net_random routine. net_random is used in different contexts, described later in this section.

- The protocol-independent destination cache (DST), described in Chapter 33, is initialized with dst_init.

- The protocol handler vector ptype_base, used to demultiplex ingress traffic, is initialized. See Chapter 13 for more details.

- When the OFFLINE_SAMPLE symbol is defined, the kernel sets up a function to run at regular intervals to collect statistics about the devices' queue lengths. In this case, net_dev_init needs to create the timer that runs the function regularly. See the section "Average Queue Length and Congestion-Level Computation" in Chapter 10.

- A callback handler is registered with the notification chain that issues notifications about CPU hotplug events. The callback used is dev_cpu_callback. Currently, the only event processed is the halting of a CPU. When this notification is received, the buffers in the CPU's ingress queue are dequeued and are passed to netif_rx. See Chapter 9 for more detail on per-CPU ingress queues.

Random number generation is a support function that the kernel performs to help randomize some of its own activity. You will see in this book that many networking subsystems use randomly generated values. For instance, they often add a random component to the delay of timers, making it less likely for timers to run simultaneously and load down the CPU with background processing. Randomization can also defend against a Denial of Service (DoS) attack by someone who tries to guess the organization of certain data structures.

The degree to which the kernel's numbers can be considered truly random is called *system entropy*. It is improved through contributions by kernel components whose activity has a nondeterministic aspect, and networking often falls in this category. Currently, only a few NIC device drivers contribute to system entropy (see earlier discussion on SA_SAMPLE_RANDOM). A patch for kernel 2.4 adds a compile time option that you can use to enable or disable the contribution to system entropy by NICs. Search the Web using the keyword "SA_SAMPLE_NET_RANDOM," and you will find the current version.

Legacy Code

I mentioned in the previous section that the subsys_initcall macros ensure that net_dev_init is executed before any device driver has a chance to register its devices. Before the introduction of this mechanism, the order of execution used to be enforced differently, using the old-fashioned mechanism of a one-time flag.

The global variable dev_boot_phase was used as a Boolean flag to remember whether net_dev_init had to be executed. It was initialized to 1 (i.e., net_dev_init had not been executed yet) and was cleared by net_dev_init. Each time register_netdevice was invoked by a device driver, it checked the value of dev_boot_phase and executed net_dev_init if the flag was set, indicating the function had not yet been executed.

This mechanism is not needed anymore, because register_netdevice cannot be called before net_dev_init if the correct tagging is applied to key device drivers' routines, as described in Chapter 7. However, to detect wrong tagging or buggy code, net_dev_init still clears the value of dev_boot_phase, and register_netdevice uses the macro BUG_ON to make sure it is never called when dev_boot_phase is set.[*]

User-Space Helpers

There are cases where it makes sense for the kernel to invoke a user-space application to handle events. Two such helpers are particularly important:

/sbin/modprobe
> Invoked when the kernel needs to load a module. This helper is part of the *module-init-tools* package.

/sbin/hotplug
> Invoked when the kernel detects that a new device has been plugged or unplugged from the system. Its main job is to load the correct device driver (module) based on the device identifier. Devices are identified by the bus they are plugged into (e.g., PCI) and the associated ID defined by the bus specification.[†] This helper is part of the *hotplug* package.

The kernel provides a function named call_usermodehelper to execute such user-space helpers. The function allows the caller to pass the application a variable number

---

[*] The use of the macros BUG_ON and BUG_TRAP is a common mechanism to make sure necessary conditions are met at specific code points, and is useful when transitioning from one design to another.

[†] See the section "Registering a PCI NIC Device Driver" in Chapter 6 for an example involving PCI.

of both arguments in arg[] and environment variables in env[]. For example, the first argument arg[0] tells call_usermodehelper what user-space helper to launch, and arg[1] can be used to tell the helper itself what configuration script to use (often called the user-space agent). We will see an example in the later section "/sbin/hotplug."

Figure 5-3 shows how two kernel routines, request_module and kobject_hotplug, invoke call_usermodehelper to invoke */sbin/modprobe* and */sbin/hotplug*, respectively. It also shows examples of how arg[] and envp[] are initialized in the two cases. The following subsections go into a little more detail on each of those two user-space helpers.

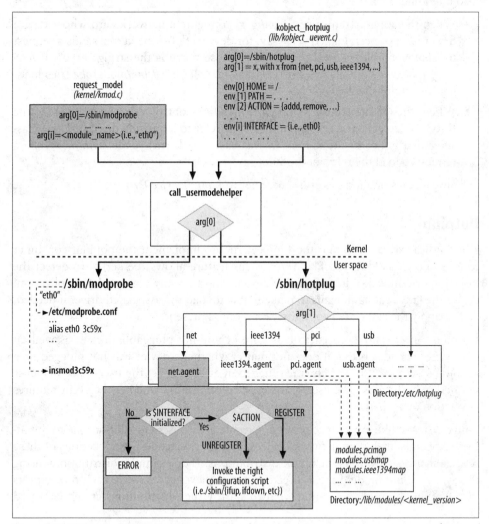

Figure 5-3. Event propagation from kernel to user space

kmod

kmod is the kernel module loader that allows kernel components to request the loading of a module. The kernel provides more than one routine, but here we'll look only at request_module. This function initializes arg[1] with the name of the module to load. */sbin/modprobe* uses the configuration file */etc/modprobe.conf* to do various things, one of which is to see whether the module name received from the kernel is actually an alias to something else (see Figure 5-3).

Here are two examples of events that would lead the kernel to ask */sbin/modprobe* to load a module:

- When the administrator uses *ifconfig* to configure a network card whose device driver has not been loaded yet—say, for device *eth0*[*]—the kernel sends a request to */sbin/modprobe* to load the module whose name is the string "eth0". If */etc/modprobe.conf* contains the entry "alias eth0 3c59x", */sbin/modprobe* tries loading the module *3c59x.ko*.

- When the administrator configures Traffic Control on a device with the IPROUTE2 package's *tc* command, it may refer to a queuing discipline or a classifier that is not in the kernel. In this case, the kernel sends */sbin/modprobe* a request to load the relevant module.

For more details on modules and kmod, refer to *Linux Device Drivers*.

Hotplug

Hotplug was introduced into the Linux kernel to implement the popular consumer feature known as Plug and Play (PnP). This feature allows the kernel to detect the insertion or removal of hot-pluggable devices and to notify a user-space application, giving the latter enough details to make it able to load the associated driver if needed, and to apply the associated configuration if one is present.

Hotplug can actually be used to take care of non-hot-pluggable devices as well, at boot time. The idea is that it does not matter whether a device was hot-plugged on a running system or if it was already plugged in at boot time; the user-space helper is notified in both cases. The user-space application decides whether the event requires any action on its part.

Linux systems, like most Unix systems, execute a set of scripts at boot time to initialize peripherals, including network devices. The syntax, names, and locations of these scripts change with different Linux distributions. (For example, distributions using the System V *init* model have a directory per run level in */etc/rc.d/*, each one with its own configuration file indicating what to start. Other distributions are either based

---

[*] Note that because the device driver has not been loaded yet, *eth0* does not exist yet either.

on the BSD model, or follow the BSD model in compatibility mode with System V.) Therefore, notifications for devices already present at boot time may be ignored because the scripts will eventually configure the associated devices.

When you compile the kernel modules, the object files are placed by default in the directory */lib/modules/kernel_version/*, where *kernel_version* is, for instance, 2.6.12. In the same directory you can find two interesting files: *modules.pcimap* and *modules.usbmap*. These files contain, respectively, the PCI IDs[*] and USB IDs of the devices supported by the kernel. The same files include, for each device ID, a reference to the associated kernel module. When the user-space helper receives a notification about a hot-pluggable device being plugged, it uses these files to find out the correct device driver.

The *modules.xxxmap* files are populated from ID vectors provided by device drivers. For example, you will see in the section "Example of PCI NIC Driver Registration" in Chapter 6 how the Vortex driver initializes its instance of pci_device_id. Because that driver is written for a PCI device, the contents of that table go into the *modules.pcimap* file.

If you are interested in the latest code, you can find more information at *http://linux-hotplug.sourceforge.net*.

/sbin/hotplug

The default user-space helper for Hotplug is the script[†] */sbin/hotplug*, part of the Hotplug package. This package can be configured with the files located in the default directories */etc/hotplug/* and */etc/hotplug.d/*.

The kobject_hotplug function is invoked by the kernel to respond to the insertion and removal of a device, among other events. kobject_hotplug initializes arg[0] to */sbin/hotplug* and arg[1] to the agent to be used: */sbin/hotplug* is a simple script that delegates the processing of the event to another script (the agent) based on arg[1].

The user-space helper agents can be more or less complex based on how fancy you want the auto-configuration to be. The scripts provided with the Hotplug package try to recognize the Linux distribution and adapt the actions to their configuration file's syntax and location.

Let's take networking, the subject of this book, as an example of hotplugging. When an NIC is added to or removed from the system, kobject_hotplug initializes arg[1] to *net*, leading */sbin/hotplug* to execute the *net.agent* agent.

---

[*] The section "Example of PCI NIC Driver Registration" in Chapter 6 gives a brief description of a PCI device identifier.

[†] The administrator can write his own scripts or use the ones provided by the most common Linux distributions.

Unlike the other agents shown in Figure 5-3, *net.agent* does not represent a medium or bus type. While the *net* agent is used to configure a device, other agents are used to load the correct modules (device drivers) based on the device identifiers.

net.agent is supposed to apply any configuration associated with the new device, so it needs the kernel to provide at least the device identifier. In the example shown in Figure 5-3, the device identifier is passed by the kernel through the INTERFACE environment variable.

To be able to configure a device, it must first be created and registered with the kernel. This task is normally driven by the associated device driver, which must therefore be loaded first. For instance, adding a PCMCIA Ethernet card causes several calls to */sbin/hotplug*; among them:

- One leading to the execution of */sbin/modprobe*,* which will take care of loading the right module device driver. In the case of PCMCIA, the driver is loaded by the *pci.agent* agent (using the action ADD).

- One configuring the new device. This is done by the *net.agent* agent (again using the action ADD).

Virtual Devices

A virtual device is an abstraction built on top of one or more real devices. The association between virtual devices and real devices can be many-to-many, as shown by the three models in Figure 5-4. It is also possible to build virtual devices on top of other virtual devices. However, not all combinations are meaningful or are supported by the kernel.

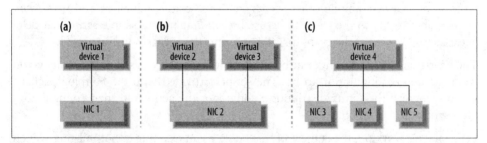

Figure 5-4. Possible relationship between virtual and real devices

Examples of Virtual Devices

Linux allows you to define different kinds of virtual devices. Here are a few examples:

---

* Unlike */sbin/hotplug*, which is a shell script, */sbin/modprobe* is a binary executable file. If you want to give it a look, download the source code of the *modutil* package.

Bonding

With this feature, a virtual device bundles a group of physical devices and makes them behave as one.

802.1Q

This is an IEEE standard that extends the 802.3/Ethernet header with the so-called VLAN header, allowing for the creation of Virtual LANs.

Bridging

A bridge interface is a virtual representation of a bridge. Details are in Part IV.

Aliasing interfaces

Originally, the main purpose for this feature was to allow a single real Ethernet interface to span several virtual interfaces (*eth0:0*, *eth0:1*, etc.), each with its own IP configuration. Now, thanks to improvements to the networking code, there is no need to define a new virtual interface to configure multiple IP addresses on the same NIC. However, there may be cases (notably routing) where having different virtual NICs on the same NIC would make life easier, perhaps allowing simpler configuration. Details are in Chapter 30.

True equalizer (TEQL)

This is a queuing discipline that can be used with Traffic Control. Its implementation requires the creation of a special device. The idea behind TEQL is a bit similar to Bonding.

Tunnel interfaces

The implementation of IP-over-IP tunneling (IPIP) and the Generalized Routing Encapsulation (GRE) protocol is based on the creation of a virtual device.

This list is not complete. Also, given the speed with which new features are included into the Linux kernel, you can expect to see new virtual devices being added to the kernel.

Bonding, bridging, and 802.1Q devices are examples of the model in Figure 5-4(c). Aliasing interfaces are examples of the model in Figure 5-4(b). The model in Figure 5-4(a) can be seen as a special case of the other two.

Interaction with the Kernel Network Stack

Virtual devices and real devices interact with the kernel in slightly different ways. For example, they differ with regard to the following points:

Initialization

Most virtual devices are assigned a net_device data structure, as real devices are. Often, most of the virtual device's net_device's function pointers are initialized to routines implemented as wrappers, more or less complex, around the function pointers used by the associated real devices.

However, not all virtual devices are assigned a net_device instance. Aliasing devices are an example; they are implemented as simple labels on the associated real device (see the section "Old-generation configuration: aliasing interfaces" in Chapter 30).

Configuration

It is common to provide ad hoc user-space tools to configure virtual devices, especially for the high-level fields that apply only to those devices and which could not be configured using standard tools such as *ifconfig*.

External interface

Each virtual device usually exports a file, or a directory with a few files, to the */proc* filesystem. How complex and detailed the information exported with those files is depends on the kind of virtual device and on the design. You will see the ones used by each virtual device listed in the section "Virtual Devices" in their associated chapters (for those devices covered in this book). Files associated with virtual devices are extra files; they do not replace the ones associated with the physical devices. Aliasing devices, which do not have their own net_device instances, are again an exception.

Transmission

When the relationship of virtual device to real device is not one-to-one, the routine used to transmit may need to include, among other tasks, the selection of the real device to use.* Because QoS is enforced on a per-device basis, the multiple relationships between virtual devices and associated real devices have implications for the Traffic Control configuration.

Reception

Because virtual devices are software objects, they do not need to engage in interactions with real resources on the system, such as registering an IRQ handler or allocating I/O ports and I/O memory. Their traffic comes secondhand from the physical devices that perform those tasks. Packet reception happens differently for different types of virtual devices. For instance, 802.1Q interfaces register an Ethertype and are passed only those packets received by the associated real devices that carry the right protocol ID.† In contrast, bridge interfaces receive any packet that arrives from the associated devices (see Chapter 16).

External notifications

Notifications from other kernel components about specific events taking place in the kernel‡ are of interest as much to virtual devices as to real ones. Because virtual devices' logic is implemented on top of real devices, the latter have no knowledge about that logic and therefore are not able to pass on those notifica-

---

* See Chapter 11 for more details on packet transmission in general, and dev_queue_xmit in particular.

† Chapter 13 discusses the demultiplexing of ingress traffic based on the protocol identifier.

‡ Chapter 4 defines notification chains and explains what kind of notifications they can be used for.

tions. For this reason, notifications need to go directly to the virtual devices. Let's use Bonding as an example: if one device in the bundle goes down, the algorithms used to distribute traffic among the bundle's members have to be made aware of that so that they do not select the devices that are no longer available.

Unlike these software-triggered notifications, hardware-triggered notifications (e.g., PCI power management) cannot reach virtual devices directly because there is no hardware associated with virtual devices.

Tuning via /proc Filesystem

Figure 5-5 shows the files that can be used either to tune or to view the status of configuration parameters related to the topics covered in this chapter.

In */proc/sys/kernel* are the files *modprobe* and *hotplug* that can change the pathnames of the two programs introduced earlier in the section "User-Space Helpers."

A few files in */proc* export the values within internal data structures and configuration parameters, which are useful to track what resources were allocated by device drivers, shown earlier in the section "Basic Goals of NIC Initialization." For some of these data structures, a user-space command is provided to print their contents in a more user-friendly format. For example, *lsmod* lists the modules currently loaded, using */proc/modules* as its source of information.

In */proc/net*, you can find the files created by net_dev_init, via dev_proc_init and dev_mcast_init (see the earlier section "Initializing the Device Handling Layer: net_dev_init"):

dev

> Displays, for each network device registered with the kernel, a few statistics about reception and transmission, such as bytes received or transmitted, number of packets, errors, etc.

dev_mcast

> Displays, for each network device registered with the kernel, the values of a few parameters used by IP multicast.

wireless

> Similarly to *dev*, for each wireless device, prints the values of a few parameters from the wireless block returned by the dev->get_wireless_stats virtual function. Note that dev->get_wireless_stats returns something only for wireless devices, because those allocate a data structure to keep those statistics (and so */proc/net/wireless* will include only wireless devices).

softnet_stat

> Exports statistics about the software interrupts used by the networking code. See Chapter 12.

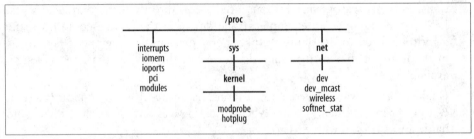

Figure 5-5. /proc files related to the routing subsystem

There are other interesting directories, including */proc/drivers*, */proc/bus*, and */proc/irq*, for which I refer you to *Linux Device Drivers*. In addition, kernel parameters are gradually being moved out of */proc* and into a directory called */sys*, but I won't describe the new system for lack of space.

Functions and Variables Featured in This Chapter

Table 5-1 summarizes the functions, macros, variables, and data structures introduced in this chapter.

Table 5-1. Functions, macros, variables, and data structures related to system initialization

Name	Description
Functions and macros	
request_irq free_irq	Registers and releases, respectively, a callback handler for an IRQ line. The registration can be exclusive or shared.
request_region release_region	Allocates and releases I/O ports and I/O memory.
call_usermodehelper	Invokes a user-space helper application.
module_param	Macro used to define configuration parameters for modules.
net_dev_init	Initializes a piece of the networking code at boot time.
Global variables	
dev_boot_phase	Boolean flag used by legacy code to enforce the execution of net_dev_init before NIC device drivers register themselves.
irq_desc	Pointer to the vector of IRQ descriptors.
Data structure	

Table 5-1. *Functions, macros, variables, and data structures related to system initialization*

Name	Description
struct irq_action	Each IRQ line is defined by an instance of this structure. Among other fields, it includes a callback function.
net_device	Describes a network device.

Files and Directories Featured in This Chapter

Figure 5-6 lists the files and directories referred to in this chapter.

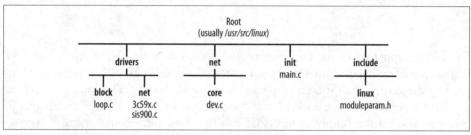

Figure 5-6. Files and directories featured in this chapter

CHAPTER 6

The PCI Layer and Network Interface Cards

Given the popularity of the PCI bus, on the x86 as well as other architectures, we will spend a few pages on it so that you can understand how PCI devices are managed by the kernel, with special emphasis on network devices. This chapter will help you find a context for the code about device registration we will see in Chapter 8. You will also learn a bit about how PCI handles some nifty kernel features such as probing and power management. For an in-depth discussion of PCI, such as device driver design, PCI bus features, and implementation details, refer to *Linux Device Drivers* and *Understanding the Linux Kernel*, as well as PCI specifications.

The PCI subsystem (also known as the PCI layer) in the kernel provides all the generic functions that are used in common by various PCI device drivers. This subsystem takes a lot of work off the shoulders of the programmer for each individual device, lets drivers be written in a clean manner, and makes it easier for the kernel to collect and maintain information about the devices, such as accounting information and statistics.

In this chapter, we will see the meaning of a few key data structures used by the PCI layer and how these structures are initialized by one common NIC device driver. I'll conclude with a few words on the PCI power management and Wake-on-LAN features.

Data Structures Featured in This Chapter

Here are a few key data structure types used by the PCI layer. There are many others, but the following ones are all we need to know for our overview in this book. The first one is defined in *include/linux/mod_devicetable.h*, and the other two are defined in *include/linux/pci.h*.

pci_device_id

> Device identifier. This is not a local ID used by Linux, but an ID defined accordingly to the PCI standard. The later section "Registering a PCI NIC Device Driver" shows the ID's definition, and the later section "Example of PCI NIC Driver Registration" presents an example.

pci_dev

Each PCI device is assigned a `pci_dev` instance, just as network devices are assigned `net_device` instances. This is the structure used by the kernel to refer to a PCI device.

pci_driver

Defines the interface between the PCI layer and the device drivers. This structure consists mostly of function pointers. All PCI devices use it. See the later section "Example of PCI NIC Driver Registration" for its definition and an example of its initialization.

PCI device drivers are defined by an instance of a `pci_driver` structure. Here is a description of its main fields, with special attention paid to the case of NIC devices. The function pointers are initialized by the device driver to point to appropriate functions within that driver.

char *name

Name of the driver.

const struct pci_device_id *id_table

Vector of IDs the kernel will use to associate devices to this driver. The section "Example of PCI NIC Driver Registration" shows an example.

int (*probe)(struct pci_dev *dev, const struct pci_device_id *id)

Function invoked by the PCI layer when it finds a match between a device ID for which it is seeking a driver and the id_table mentioned previously. This function should enable the hardware, allocate the `net_device` structure, and initialize and register the new device.* In this function, the driver also allocates any additional data structures (e.g., buffer rings used during transmission or reception) that it may need to work properly.

void (*remove)(struct pci_dev *dev)

Function invoked by the PCI layer when the driver is unregistered from the kernel or when a hot-pluggable device is removed. It is the counterpart of probe and is used to clean up any data structure and state.

Network devices use this function to release the allocated I/O ports and I/O memory, to unregister the device, and to free the `net_device` data structure and any other auxiliary data structure that could have been allocated by the device driver, usually in its probe function.

int (*suspend)(struct pci_dev *dev, pm_message_t state)
int (*resume)(struct pci_dev *dev)

Functions invoked by the PCI layer when the system goes into suspend mode and when it is resumed, respectively. See the later section "Power Management and Wake-on-LAN."

---

* NIC registration is covered in Chapter 8.

```
int (*enable_wake)(struct pci_dev *dev, u32 state, int enable)
```
With this function, a driver can enable or disable the capability of the device to wake the system up by generating specific Power Management Event signals. See the later section "Power Management and Wake-on-LAN."

```
struct pci_dynids dynids
```
Dynamic IDs. See the following section.

See the later section "Example of PCI NIC Driver Registration" for an example of initialization of a pci_driver instance.

Registering a PCI NIC Device Driver

PCI devices are uniquely identified by a combination of parameters, including vendor, model, etc. These parameters are stored by the kernel in a data structure of type pci_device_id, defined as follows:

```
struct pci_device_id {
    unsigned int vendor, device;
    unsigned int subvendor, subdevice;
    unsigned int class, class_mask;
    unsigned long driver_data;
};
```

Most of the fields are self-explanatory. vendor and device are usually sufficient to identify the device. subvendor and subdevice are rarely needed and are usually set to a wildcard value (PCI_ANY_ID). class and class_mask represent the class the device belongs to; NETWORK is the class that covers the devices we discuss in this chapter. driver_data is not part of the PCI ID; it is a private parameter used by the driver.

Each device driver registers with the kernel a vector of pci_device_id instances that lists the IDs of the devices it can handle.

PCI device drivers register and unregister with the kernel with pci_register_driver and pci_unregister_driver, respectively. These functions are defined in *drivers/pci/pci.c*. There is also pci_module_init, an alias for pci_register_driver. A few drivers still use pci_module_init, which is the name of the routine the kernel provided in older kernel versions before the introduction of pci_register_driver.

pci_register_driver requires a pci_driver data structure as an argument. Thanks to the pci_driver's id_table vector, the kernel knows what devices the driver can handle, and thanks to all the virtual functions that are part of pci_driver, the kernel has a mechanism to interact with any device that will be associated with the driver.

One of the great advantages of PCI is its elegant support for *probing* to find the IRQ and other resources each device needs. A module can be passed input parameters at load time to tell it how to configure all the devices for which it is responsible, but sometimes (especially with buses such as PCI) it is easier to let the driver itself check the devices on the system and configure the ones for which it is responsible. The user can still fall back on manual configuration if necessary.

The /sys filesystem exports information about system buses (PCI, USB, etc.), including the various devices and relationships between them. /sys also allows an administrator to define new IDs for a given device driver so that besides the static IDs registered by the drivers with their pci_driver structures' id_table vector, the kernel can use the user-configured parameters.

We will not cover the probing mechanism used by the kernel to look up a driver based on the device IDs. However, it is worth mentioning that there are two types of probing:

Static

Given a device PCI ID, the kernel can look up the right PCI driver (i.e., the pci_driver instance) based on the id_table vectors. This is called static probing.

Dynamic

This is a lookup based on IDs the user configures manually, a rare practice but one that is occasionally useful, as for debugging. Dynamic refers to the system administrator's ability to add an ID; it does not mean the ID can change on its own.

Since dynamic IDs are configured on a running system, they are useful only when the kernel is compiled with support for Hotplug.

Power Management and Wake-on-LAN

PCI power management events are processed by the suspend and resume functions of the pci_driver data structure. Besides taking care of the PCI state, by saving and restoring it, respectively, these functions need to take special steps in the case of NICs:

- suspend mainly stops the device egress queue so that no transmission will be allowed on the device.
- resume re-enables the egress queue so that the device is available again for transmissions.

Wake-on-LAN (WOL) is a feature that allows an NIC to wake up a system that's in standby mode when it receives a specific type of frame. WOL is normally disabled by default. The feature can be turned on and off with pci_enable_wake.

When the WOL feature was first introduced, only one kind of frame could wake up a system: "Magic Packets."* These special frames have two main characteristics:

- The destination MAC address belongs to the receiving NIC (whether the address is unicast, multicast, or broadcast).
- Somewhere (anywhere) in the frame a sequence of 48 bits is set (i.e., FF:FF:FF:FF:FF:FF) followed by the NIC MAC address repeated at least 16 times in a row.

---

* WOL was introduced by AMD with the name "Magic Packet Technology."

Now it is possible to allow other frame types to wake up the system, too. A handful of devices can enable or disable the WOL feature based on a parameter that can be set at module load time (see *drivers/net/3c59x.c* for an example).The *ethtool* tool allows an administrator to configure what kind of frames can wake up the system. One choice is ARP packets, as described in the section "Wake-on-LAN Events" in Chapter 28. The *net-utils* package includes a command, *ether-wake*, that can be used to generate WOL Ethernet frames.

Whenever a WOL-enabled device recognizes a frame whose type is allowed to wake up the system, it generates a power management notification that does the job.

For more details on power management, refer to the later section "Interactions with Power Management" in Chapter 8.

Example of PCI NIC Driver Registration

Let's use the Intel PRO/100 Ethernet driver in *drivers/net/e100.c* to illustrate a driver registration:

```
#define INTEL_8255X_ETHERNET_DEVICE(device_id, ich) {\
    PCI_VENDOR_ID_INTEL, device_id, PCI_ANY_ID, PCI_ANY_ID, \
    PCI_CLASS_NETWORK_ETHERNET << 8, 0xFFFF00, ich }
static struct pci_device_id e100_id_table[] = {
    INTEL_8255X_ETHERNET_DEVICE(0x1029, 0),
    INTEL_8255X_ETHERNET_DEVICE(0x1030, 0),
    ...
}
```

We saw in the section "Registering a PCI NIC Device Driver" that a PCI NIC device driver registers with the kernel a vector of pci_device_id structures that lists the devices it can handle. e100_id_table is, for instance, the structure used by the *e100.c* driver. Note that:

- The first field (which corresponds to vendor in the structure's definition) has the fixed value of PCI_VENDOR_ID_INTEL which is initialized to the vendor ID assigned to Intel.[*]

- The third and fourth fields (subvendor and subdevice) are often initialized to the wildcard value PCI_ANY_ID, because the first two fields (vendor and device) are sufficient to identify the devices.

- Many devices use the macro __devinitdata on the table of devices to mark it as initialization data, although e100_id_table does not. You will see in Chapter 7 exactly what that macro is used for.

---

[*] You can find an updated list at *http://pciids.sourceforge.net*.

The module is initialized by `e100_init_module`, as specified by the `module_init` macro.[*] When the function is executed by the kernel at boot time or at module loading time, it calls `pci_module_init`, the function introduced in the section "Registering a PCI NIC Device Driver." This function registers the driver, and, indirectly, all the associated NICs, as briefly described in the later section "The Big Picture."

The following snapshot shows the key parts of the e100 driver with regard to the PCI layer interface:

```
NAME "e100"

static int __devinit e100_probe(struct pci_dev *pdev,
    const struct pci_device_id *ent)
{
    ...
}
static void __devexit e100_remove(struct pci_dev *pdev)
{
    ...
}


#ifdef CONFIG_PM
static int e100_suspend(struct pci_dev *pdev, u32 state)
{
    ...
}
static int e100_resume(struct pci_dev *pdev)
{
    ...
}
#endif

static struct pci_driver e100_driver = {
    .name =         DRV_NAME,
    .id_table =     e100_id_table,
    .probe =        e100_probe,
    .remove =       __devexit_p(e100_remove),
#ifdef CONFIG_PM
    .suspend =      e100_suspend,
    .resume =       e100_resume,
#endif
};

static int __init e100_init_module(void)
{
    ...
    return pci_module_init(&e100_driver);
}

static void __exit e100_cleanup_module(void)
```

---

[*] See Chapter 7 for more details on module initialization code.

```
{
    pci_unregister_driver(&e100_driver);
}

module_init(e100_init_module);
module_exit(e100_cleanup_module);
```

Also note that:

- suspend and resume are initialized only when the kernel has support for power management, so the two routines e100_suspend and e100_resume are included in the image only when that condition is true.

- The remove field of pci_driver is tagged with the __devexit_p macro, and e100_remove is tagged with __devexit.

- e100_probe is tagged with __devinit.

You will see in Chapter 7 what the __dev*XXX* macros mentioned in the list are used for.

The Big Picture

Let's put together what we saw in the previous sections and see what happens at boot time in a system with a PCI bus and a few PCI devices.*

When the system boots, it creates a sort of database that associates each bus to a list of detected devices that use the bus. For example, the descriptor for the PCI bus includes, among other parameters, a list of detected PCI devices. As we saw in the section "Registering a PCI NIC Device Driver," each PCI device is uniquely identified by a large collection of fields in the structure pci_device_id, although only a few are usually necessary. We also saw how PCI device drivers define an instance of pci_driver and register with the PCI layer with pci_register_driver (or its alias, pci_module_init). By the time device drivers are loaded, the kernel has already built its database:† let's then take the example of Figure 6-1(a) with three PCI devices and see what happens when device drivers A and B are loaded.

When device driver A is loaded, it registers with the PCI layer by calling pci_register_driver and providing its instance of pci_driver. The pci_driver structure includes a vector with the IDs of those PCI devices it can drive. The PCI layer then uses that table to see what devices match in its list of detected PCI devices. It thus creates the driver's device list shown in Figure 6-1(b). In addition, for each matching device, the PCI layer invokes the probe function provided by the matching driver in its pci_driver structure. The probe function creates and registers the associated network device. In this case, device *Dev3* needs an additional device driver, called B. When driver B eventually registers with the kernel, *Dev3* will be assigned to it. Figure 6-1(c) shows the results of loading the driver.

---

* Other buses behave in a similar way. Please refer to *Linux Device Drivers* for details.

† This may not be possible for all bus types.

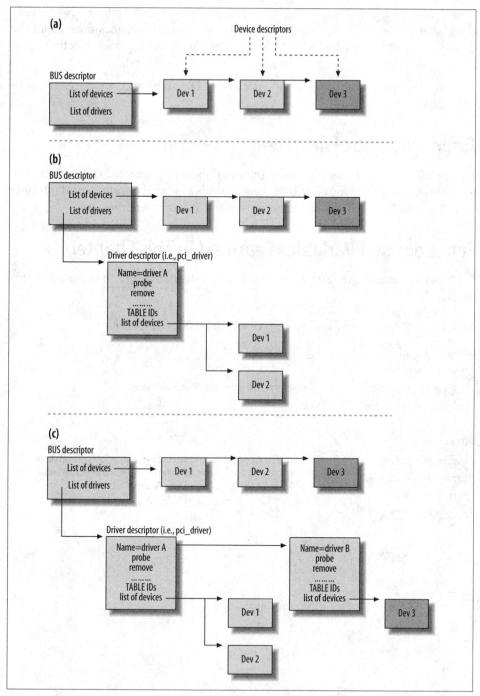

Figure 6-1. Binding between bus and drivers, and between driver and devices

When the driver is unloaded later, the module's `module_exit` routine invokes `pci_unregister_driver`. The PCI layer then, thanks to its database, goes through all the devices associated with the driver and invokes the driver's remove function. This function unregisters the network device.

You can find more details about the internals of the probe and remove functions in Chapter 8.

Tuning via /proc Filesystem

The */proc/pci* file can be used to dump information about registered PCI devices. The *lspci* command, part of the *pciutils* package, can also be used to print useful information about the local PCI devices, but it retrieves its information from */sys*.

Functions and Variables Featured in This Chapter

Table 6-1 summarizes the functions, macros, and data structures introduced in this chapter.

Table 6-1. Functions, macros, and data structures related to PCI device handling

Name	Description
Functions and macros	
`pci_register_driver`	Register, unregister, and initialize a PCI driver.
`pci_unregister_driver`	
`pci_module_init`	
Data structure	
`struct pci_driver`	The first data structure defines a PCI driver (and consists mostly of virtual function callbacks). The second stores the universal ID associated with a PCI device. The last one represents a PCI device in kernel space.
`struct pci_device_id`	
`struct pci_dev`	

Files and Directories Featured in This Chapter

Figure 6-2 lists the files and directories referred to in the chapter. The figure does not include all the files used by the topics covered in the chapter. For example, the *drivers/pci/* directory includes several other files.

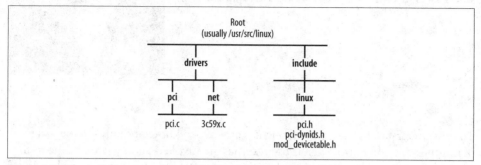

Figure 6-2. Files and directories featured in this chapter

CHAPTER 7

Kernel Infrastructure for Component Initialization

To fully understand a kernel component, you have to know not only what a given set of routines does, but also when those routines are invoked and by whom. The initialization of a subsystem is one of the basic tasks handled by the kernel according to its own model. This infrastructure is worth studying to help you understand how core components of the networking stack are initialized, including NIC device drivers.

The purpose of this chapter is to show how the kernel handles routines used to initialize kernel components, both for components statically included into the kernel and those loaded as kernel modules, with a special emphasis on network devices. We will therefore see:

- How initialization functions are named and identified by special macros
- How these macros are defined, based on the kernel configuration, to optimize memory usage and make sure that the various initializations are done in the correct order
- When and how the functions are executed

We will not cover all details of the initialization infrastructure, but you'll have a sufficient overview to navigate the source code comfortably.

Boot-Time Kernel Options

Linux allows users to pass kernel configuration options to their boot loaders, which then pass the options to the kernel; experienced users can use this mechanism to fine-tune the kernel at boot time.[*] During the boot phase, as shown in Figure 5-1 in Chapter 5, the two calls to parse_args take care of the boot-time configuration input.

---

[*] You can find some documentation and examples of the use of boot options in the *Linux BootPrompt* HOWTO.

We will see in the next section why parse_args is called twice, with details in the later section "Two-Pass Parsing."

parse_args is a routine that parses an input string with parameters in the form *name_variable=value*, looking for specific keywords and invoking the right handlers. parse_args is also used when loading a module, to parse the command-line parameters provided (if any).

We do not need to know the details of how parse_args implements the parsing, but it is interesting to see how a kernel component can register a handler for a keyword and how the handler is invoked. To have a clear picture we need to learn:

- How a kernel component can register a keyword, along with the associated handler that will be executed when that keyword is provided with the boot string.

- How the kernel resolves the association between keywords and handlers. I will offer a high-level overview of how the kernel parses the input string.

- How the networking device subsystem uses this feature.

All the parsing code is in *kernel/params.c*. We'll cover the points in the list one by one.

Registering a Keyword

Kernel components can register a keyword and the associated handler with the __setup macro, defined in *include/linux/init.h*. This is its syntax:

```
__setup(string, function_handler)
```

where string is the keyword and function_handler is the associated handler. The example just shown instructs the kernel to execute function_handler when the input boot-time string includes string. string has to end with the = character to make the parsing easier for parse_args. Any text following the = will be passed as input to function_handler.

The following is an example from *net/core/dev.c*, where netdev_boot_setup is registered as the handler for the netdev= keyword:

```
__setup("netdev=", netdev_boot_setup);
```

The same handler can be associated with different keywords. For instance *net/ethernet/eth.c* registers the same handler, netdev_boot_setup, for the ether= keyword.

When a piece of code is compiled as a module, the __setup macro is ignored (i.e., defined as a no-op). You can check how the definition of the __setup macro changes in *include/linux/init.h* depending on whether the code that includes the latter file is a module.

The reason why start_kernel calls parse_args twice to parse the boot configuration string is that boot-time options are actually divided into two classes, and each call takes care of one class:

Default options

Most options fall into this category. These options are defined with the __setup macro and are handled by the second call to parse_args.

Early options

Some options need to be handled earlier than others during the kernel boot. The kernel provides the early_param macro to declare these options instead of __setup. They are then taken care of by parse_early_params. The only difference between early_param and __setup is that the former sets a special flag so that the kernel will be able to distinguish between the two cases. The flag is part of the obs_kernel_param data structure that we will see in the section ".init.setup Memory Section."

The handling of boot-time options has changed with the 2.6 kernel, but not all the kernel code has been updated accordingly. Before the latest changes, there used to be only the __setup macro. Because of this, legacy code that is to be updated now uses the macro __obsolete_setup. When the user passes the kernel an option that is declared with the __obsolete_setup macro, the kernel prints a message warning about its obsolete status and provides a pointer to the file and source code line where the latter is declared.

Figure 7-1 summarizes the relationship between the various macros: all of them are wrappers around the generic routine __setup_param.

Note that the input routine passed to __setup is placed into the .init.setup memory section. The effect of this action will become clear in the section "Boot-Time Initialization Routines."

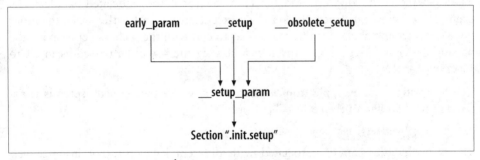

Figure 7-1. setup_param macro and its wrappers

Two-Pass Parsing

Because boot-time options used to be handled differently in previous kernel versions, and not all of them have been converted to the new model, the kernel handles both models. When the new infrastructure fails to recognize a keyword, it asks the obsolete infrastructure to handle it. If the obsolete infrastructure also fails, the keyword and value are passed on to the init process that will be invoked at the end of the init kernel thread via `run_init_process` (shown in Figure 5-1 in Chapter 5). The keyword and value are added either to the arg parameter list or to the `envp` environment variable list.

The previous section explained that, to allow early options to be handled in the necessary order, boot-string parsing and handler invocation are handled in two passes, shown in Figure 7-2 (the figure shows a snapshot from `start_kernel`, introduced in Chapter 5):

1. The first pass looks only for higher-priority options that must be handled early, which are identified by a special flag (`early`).

2. The second pass takes care of all other options. Most of the options fall into this category. All options following the obsolete model are handled in this pass.

The second pass first checks whether there is a match with the options implemented according to the new infrastructure. These options are stored in `kernel_param` data structures, filled in by the `module_param` macro introduced in the section "Module Options" in Chapter 5. The same macro makes sure that all of those data structures are placed into a specific memory section (`__param`), delimited by the pointers `__start___param` and `__stop___param`.

When one of these options is recognized, the associated parameter is initialized to the value provided with the boot string. When there is no match for an option, `unknown_bootoption` tries to see whether the option should be handled by the obsolete model handler (Figure 7-2).

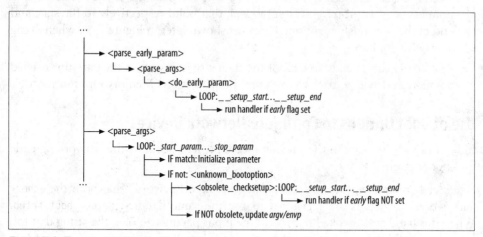

Figure 7-2. Two-pass option parsing

Obsolete and new model options are placed into two different memory areas:

`__setup_start ... __setup_end`

We will see in a later section that this area is freed at the end of the boot phase: once the kernel has booted, these options are not needed anymore. The user cannot view or change them at runtime.

`__start___param ... __stop___param`

This area is not freed. Its content is exported to *sys*, where the options are exposed to the user.

See Chapter 5 for more details on module parameters.

Also note that all obsolete model options, regardless of whether they have the early flag set, are placed into the `__setup_start ... __setup_end` memory area.

.init.setup Memory Section

The two inputs to the `__setup` macro we introduced in the previous section are placed into a data structure of type obs_kernel_param, defined in *include/linux/init.h*:

```
struct obs_kernel_param {
    const char *str;
    int (*setup_func)(char*);
    int early;
};
```

str is the keyword, setup_func is the handler, and early is the flag we introduced in the section "Two-Pass Parsing."

The `__setup_param` macro places all of the obs_kernel_params instances into a dedicated memory area. This is done mainly for two reasons:

- It is easier to walk through all of the instances—for instance, when doing a lookup based on the str keyword. We will see how the kernel uses the two pointers `__setup_start` and `__setup_end`, that point respectively to the start and end of the previously mentioned area (as shown later in Figure 7-3), when doing a keyword lookup.
- The kernel can quickly free all of the data structures when they are not needed anymore. We will go back to this point in the section "Memory Optimizations."

Use of Boot Options to Configure Network Devices

In light of what we saw in the previous sections, let's see how the networking code uses boot options.

We already mentioned in the section "Registering a Keyword" that both the ether= and netdev= keywords are registered to use the same handler, netdev_boot_setup. When this handler is invoked to process the input parameters (i.e., the string that follows the matching keyword), it stores the result into data structures of type netdev_boot_setup, defined in *include/linux/netdevice.h*. The handler and the data structure type happen to share the same name, so make sure you do not confuse the two.

```
struct netdev_boot_setup {
    char name[IFNAMSIZ];
    struct ifmap map;
};
```

name is the device's name, and ifmap, defined in *include/linux/if.h*, is the data structure that stores the input configuration:

```
struct ifmap
{
    unsigned long mem_start;
    unsigned long mem_end;
    unsigned short base_addr;
    unsigned char irq;
    unsigned char dma;
    unsigned char port;
    /* 3 bytes spare */
};
```

The same keyword can be provided multiple times (for different devices) in the boottime string, as in the following example:

LILO: linux ether=5,0x260,eth0 ether=15,0x300,eth1

However, the maximum number of devices that can be configured at boot time with this mechanism is NETDEV_BOOT_SETUP_MAX, which is also the size of the static array dev_boot_setup used to store the configurations:

```
static struct netdev_boot_setup dev_boot_setup[NETDEV_BOOT_SETUP_MAX];
```

netdev_boot_setup is pretty simple: it extracts the input parameters from the string, fills in an ifmap structure, and adds the latter to the dev_boot_setup array with netdev_boot_setup_add.

At the end of the booting phase, the networking code can use the netdev_boot_setup_ check function to check whether a given interface is associated with a boot-time configuration. The lookup on the array dev_boot_setup is based on the device name dev->name:

```
int netdev_boot_setup_check(struct net_device *dev)
{
    struct netdev_boot_setup *s = dev_boot_setup;
    int i;

    for (i = 0; i < NETDEV_BOOT_SETUP_MAX; i++) {
        if (s[i].name[0] != '\0' && s[i].name[0] != ' ' &&
            !strncmp(dev->name, s[i].name, strlen(s[i].name))) {
            dev->irq       = s[i].map.irq;
            dev->base_addr = s[i].map.base_addr;
            dev->mem_start = s[i].map.mem_start;
            dev->mem_end   = s[i].map.mem_end;
            return 1;
        }
    }
    return 0;
}
```

Devices with special capabilities, features, or limitations can define their own keywords and handlers if they need additional parameters on top of the basic ones provided by ether= and netdev= (one driver that does this is PLIP).

Module Initialization Code

Because the examples in the following sections often refer to modules, a couple of initial concepts have to be made clear.

Kernel code can be either statically linked to the main image or loaded dynamically as a module when needed. Not all kernel components are suitable to be compiled as modules. Device drivers and extensions to basic functionalities are good examples of kernel components often compiled as modules. You can refer to *Linux Device Drivers* for a detailed discussion of the advantages and disadvantages of modules, as well as the mechanisms that the kernel can use to dynamically load them when they are needed and unload them when they are no longer needed.

Every module must provide two special functions, called init_module and cleanup_module. The first one is called at module load time to initialize the module. The second one is invoked by the kernel when removing the module, to release any resources (memory included) that have been allocated for use by the module.

The kernel provides two macros, module_init and module_exit, that allow developers to use arbitrary names for the two routines. The following snapshot is an example from the *drivers/net/3c59x.c* Ethernet driver:

```
module_init(vortex_init);
module_exit(vortex_cleanup);
```

In the section "Memory Optimizations," we will see how those two macros are defined and how their definition can change based on the kernel configuration. Most of the kernel uses these two macros, but a few modules still use the old default names init_module and cleanup_module. In the rest of this chapter, I will use module_init and module_exit to refer to the initialization and cleanup functions.

Let's first see how module initialization code used to be written with older kernels, and then how the current kernel model, based on a set of new macros, works.

Old Model: Conditional Code

Regardless of whether a kernel component is compiled as a module or is built statically into the kernel, it needs to be initialized. Because of that, the initialization code of a kernel component may need to distinguish between the two cases by means of conditional directives to the compiler. In the old model, this forced developers to use conditional directives like #ifdef all over the place.

Here is a snapshot from the *drivers/net/3c59x.c* driver of kernel 2.2.14: note how many times #ifdef MODULE and #if defined (MODULE) are used.

```
...
#if defined(MODULE) && LINUX_VERSION_CODE > 0x20115
MODULE_AUTHOR("Donald Becker <becker@cesdis.gsfc.nasa.gov>");
MODULE_DESCRIPTION("3Com 3c590/3c900 series Vortex/Boomerang driver");
MODULE_PARM(debug, "i");
...
#endif
...
#ifdef MODULE
...
int init_module(void)
{
    ...
}
#else
int tc59x_probe(struct device *dev)
{
    ...
}
#endif  /* not MODULE */
...
static int vortex_scan(struct device *dev, struct pci_id_info pci_tbl[])
{
    ...
#if defined(CONFIG_PCI) || (defined(MODULE) && !defined(NO_PCI))
    ...
#ifdef MODULE
    if (compaq_ioaddr) {
        vortex_probe1(0, 0, dev, compaq_ioaddr, compaq_irq,
            compaq_device_id, cards_found++);
        dev = 0;
    }
#endif

    return cards_found ? 0 : -ENODEV;
}
...
#ifdef MODULE
void cleanup_module(void)
{
    ... ... ...
}
#endif
```

This snapshot shows how the old model let a programmer specify some of the things done differently, depending on whether the code is compiled as a module or statically into the kernel image:

The initialization code is executed differently

The snapshot shows that the cleanup_module routine is defined (and therefore used) only when the driver is compiled as a module.

Pieces of code could be included or excluded from the module

> For example, vortex_scan calls vortex_probe1 only when the driver is compiled as a module.

This model made source code harder to follow, and therefore to debug. Moreover, the same logic is repeated in every module.

New Model: Macro-Based Tagging

Now let's compare the snapshot from the previous section to its counterpart from the same file from a 2.6 kernel:

```
static char version[] __devinitdata = DRV_NAME " ... ";

static struct vortex_chip_info {
    ...
} vortex_info_tbl[] __devinitdata = {
    {"3c590 Vortex 10Mbps",
    ... ... ...
}

static int __init vortex_init (void)
{
    ...
}
static void __exit vortex_cleanup (void)
{
    ...
}

module_init(vortex_init);
module_exit(vortex_cleanup);
```

You can see that #ifdef directives are no longer necessary.

To remove the mess introduced by conditional code, and therefore make code more readable, kernel developers introduced a set of macros that module developers now can use to write cleaner initialization code (most drivers are good candidates for the use of those macros). The snapshot just shown uses a few of them: __init, __exit, and __devinitdata.

Later sections describe how some of the new macros are used and how they work.

These macros allow the kernel to determine behind the scenes, for each module, what code is to be included in the kernel image, what code is to be excluded because it is not needed, what code is to be executed only at initialization time, etc. This removes the burden from each programmer to replicate the same logic in each module.[*]

---

[*] Note that the use of these macros does not eliminate completely the use of conditional directives. The kernel still uses conditional directives to set off options that the user can configure when compiling the kernel.

It should be clear that for these macros to allow programmers to replace the old conditional directives, as shown in the example of the previous section, they must be able to provide at least the following two services:

- Define routines that need to be executed when a new kernel component is enabled, either because it is statically included in the kernel or because it is loaded at runtime as a module
- Define some kind of order between initialization functions so that dependencies between kernel components can be respected and enforced

Optimized Macro-Based Tagging

The Linux kernel uses a variety of different macros to mark functions and data structures with special properties: for instance, to mark an initialization routine. Most of those macros are defined in *include/linux/init.h*. Some of those macros tell the linker to place code or data structures with common properties into specific, dedicated memory areas (memory sections) as well. By doing so, it becomes easier for the kernel to take care of an entire class of objects (routines or data structures) with a common property in a simple manner. We will see an example in the section "Memory Optimizations."

Figure 7-3 shows some of the kernel memory sections: on the left side are the names of the pointers that delimit the beginning and the end of each area section (when meaningful).

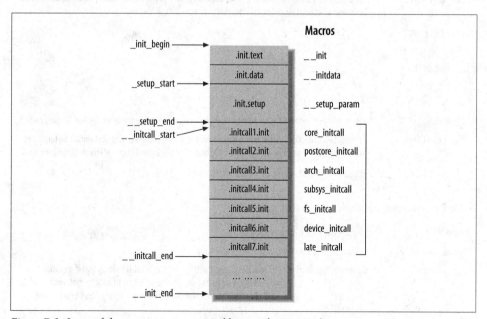

Figure 7-3. Some of the memory sections used by initialization code

On the right side are the names of the macros used to place data and code into the associated sections. The figure does not include all the memory sections and associated macros; there are too many to list conveniently.

Tables 7-1 and 7-2 list some of the macros used to tag routines and data structures, respectively, along with a brief description. We will not look at all of them for lack of space, but we will spend a few words on the *xxx*_initcall macros in the section "xxx_initcall Macros" and on __init and __exit in the section "__init and __exit Macros."

The purpose of this section is not to describe how the kernel image is built, how modules are handled, etc., but rather to give you just a few hints about why those macros exist, and how the ones most commonly used by device drivers work.

Table 7-1. Macros for routines

Macro	Kind of routines the macro is used for
__init	Boot-time initialization routine: for routines that are not needed anymore at the end of the boot phase.
	This information can be used to get rid of the routine under some conditions (see the later section "Memory Optimizations").
__exit	Counterpart to __init. Called when the associated kernel component is shut down. Often used to mark module_exit functions.
	This information can be used to get rid of the routine under some conditions (see the later section "Memory Optimizations").
core_initcall postcore_initcall arch_initcall subsys_initcall fs_initcall device_initcall late_initcall	Set of macros, listed in decreasing order of priority, used to tag initialization routines that need to be executed at boot time. See the later section "xxx_initcall Macros."
__initcall	Obsolete macro, defined as an alias to device_initcall. See the later section "Legacy code."
__exitcall[a]	One-shot exit function, called when the associated kernel component is shut down. So far, it has been used only to mark module_exit routines. See the later section "Memory Optimizations."

[a] __exitcall and __initcall are defined on top of __exit_call and __init_call.

Table 7-2. Macros for initialized data structures

Macro	Kind of data the macro is used for
__initdata	Initialized data structure used at boot time only.
__exitdata	Data structure used only by routines tagged with __exitcall. It follows that if a routine tagged with __exitcall is not going to be used, the same is true of data tagged with __exitdata. The same kind of optimization can therefore be applied to __exitdata and __exitcall.

Before we go into some more detail on a few of the macros listed in Tables 7-1 and 7-2, it is worth stressing the following points:

- Most macros come in couples: one (or a set of them) takes care of initialization, and a sister macro (or a sister set) takes care of removal. For example, __exit is __init's sister; __exitcalls is __initcall's sister, etc.

- Macros take care of two points (one or the other, not both): one is when a routine is to be executed (i.e., __initcall, __exitcall); the other is the memory section a routine or a data structure is to be placed in (i.e., __init, __exit).

- The same routine can be tagged with more than one macro. For example, the following snapshot says that pci_proc_init is to be run at boot time (__initcall), and can be freed once it is executed (__init):

```
static int __init pci_proc_init(void)
{
...
}

__initcall(pci_proc_init)
```

Initialization Macros for Device Initialization Routines

Table 7-3 lists a set of macros commonly used to tag routines used by device drivers to initialize their devices, and that can introduce memory optimizations when the kernel does not have support for Hotplug. In the section "Example of PCI NIC Driver Registration" in Chapter 6, you can find an example of their use. In the later section "Other Optimizations," you can see when the macros in Table 7-3 facilitate memory optimizations.

Table 7-3. Macros for device initialization routines

Name	Description
__devinit	Used to tag routines that initialize a device.
	For instance, for a PCI driver, the routine to which pci_driver->probe is initialized is tagged with this macro.
	Routines that are exclusively invoked by another routine tagged with __devinit are commonly tagged with __devinit as well.
__devexit	Used to tag routines to be invoked when a device is removed.
__devexit_p	Used to initialize pointers to routines tagged with __devexit.
	__devexit_p(fn) returns fn if the kernel supports both modules and Hotplug, and returns NULL otherwise. See the later section "Other Optimizations."
__devinitdata	Used to tag initialized data structures that are used by functions that take care of device initialization (i.e., are tagged with __devinit), and that therefore share their properties.
__devexitdata	Same as __devinitdata but associated with __devexit.

Boot-Time Initialization Routines

Most initialization routines have two interesting properties:

- They need to be executed at boot time, when all the kernel components get initialized.
- They are not needed once they are executed.

The next section, "xxx_initcall Macros," describes the mechanism used to run initialization routines at boot time, taking into consideration these properties as well as priorities among modules. The later section "Memory Optimizations" shows how routines and data structures that are no longer needed can be freed at link time or runtime by using smart tagging.

xxx_initcall Macros

The early phase of the kernel boot consists of two main blocks of initializations:

- The initialization of various critical and mandatory subsystems that need to be done in a specific order. For instance, the kernel cannot initialize a PCI device driver before the PCI layer has been initialized. See the later section "Example of dependency between initialization routines" for another example.
- The initialization of other kernel components that do not need a strict order: routines in the same priority level can be run in any order.

The first part is taken care of by the code that comes before do_initcalls in Figure 5-1 in Chapter 5. The second part is taken care of by the invocation of do_initcalls shown close to the end of do_basic_setup in the same figure. The initialization routines of this second part are classified based on their role and priority. The kernel executes those initialization routines one by one, starting from the ones placed in the highest-priority class (core_initcall). The addresses of those routines, which are needed to invoke them, are placed in the .initcallN.init memory sections of Figure 7-3 by tagging them with one of the xxx_initcall macros in Table 7-1.

The area used to store the addresses of the routines tagged with the xxx_initcall macros is delimited by a starting address (__initcall_start) and an ending address (__initcall_end). In the excerpt of the do_initcalls function that follows, you can see that it simply takes the function addresses one by one from that area and executes the functions they point to:

```
static void __init do_initcalls(void)
{
        initcall_t *call;
        int count = preempt_count();

        for (call = __initcall_start; call < __initcall_end; call++) {
           ... ... ...
           (*call)();
           ... ... ...
```

```
        }
        flush_scheduled_work( );
}
```

The routines invoked by do_initcalls are not supposed to change the preemption status or disable IRQs. Because of that, after each routine execution, do_initcalls checks whether the routine has made any changes, and adjusts the preemption and IRQ status if necessary (not shown in the previous snapshot).

It is possible for the *xxx*_initcall routines to schedule some work that takes place later. This means that the tasks handled by those routines may terminate asynchronously, at unknown times. The call to flush_scheduled_work is used to make do_initcalls wait for those asynchronous tasks to complete before returning.

Note that do_initcalls itself is marked with __init: because it is used only once within do_basic_setup during the booting phase, the kernel can discard it once the latter is done.

__exitcall is the counterpart of __initcall. It is not used much directly, but rather via other macros defined as aliases to it, such as module_exit, which we introduced in the section "Module Initialization Code."

Example of __initcall and __exitcall routines: modules

I said in the section "Module Initialization Code" that the module_init and module_exit macros, respectively, are used to tag routines to be executed when the module is initialized (either at boot time if built into the kernel or at runtime if loaded separately) and unloaded.

This makes a module the perfect candidate for our __initcall and __exitcall macros: in light of what I just said, the following definition from *include/linux/init.h* of the macros module_init and module_exit should not come as a surprise:

```
#ifndef MODULE
... ... ...
#define module_init(x)    __initcall(x);
#define module_exit(x)    __exitcall(x);

#else
... ... ...
#endif
```

module_init is defined as an alias to __initcall for code statically linked to the kernel: its input function is classified as a boot-time initialization routine.

module_exit follows the same scheme: when the code is built into the kernel, module_exit becomes a shutdown routine. At the moment, shutdown routines are not called when the system goes down, but the code is in place to allow it.*

---

* User-Mode Linux is the only architecture that actually makes use of shutdown routines. It does not use __exitcall macros, but defines its own macro, __uml_exitcall. The home page of the User-Mode Linux project is *http://user-mode-linux.sourceforge.net*.

Example of dependency between initialization routines

net_dev_init was introduced in Chapter 5. Device drivers register with the kernel with their module_init routine, which, as described in the section "The Big Picture" in Chapter 6, registers its devices with the networking code. Both net_dev_init and the various module_init functions for built-in drivers are invoked at boot time by do_initcalls. Because of that, the kernel needs to make sure no device registrations take place before net_dev_init has been executed. This is enforced transparently thanks to the marking of device driver initialization routines with the macro device_initcall (or its alias, __initcall), while net_dev_init is marked with subsys_initcall. In Figure 7-3, you can see that subsys_initcall routines are executed earlier than device_initcall routines (the memory sections are sorted in priority order).

Legacy code

Before the introduction of the set of *xxx*_initcall macros, there was only one macro to mark initialization functions: __initcall. The use of only a single macro created a heavy limitation: no execution order could be enforced by simply marking routines with the macro. In many cases, this limitation is not acceptable due to intermodule dependencies, and other considerations. Therefore, the use of __initcall could not be extended to all the initialization functions.

__initcall used to be employed mostly by device drivers. For backward compatibility with pieces of code not yet updated to the new model, it still exists and is simply defined as an alias to device_initcall.

Another limitation, which is still present in the current model, is that no parameters can be provided to the initialization routines. However, this does not seem to be an important limitation.

Memory Optimizations

Unlike user-space code and data, kernel code and data reside permanently in main memory, so it is important to reduce memory waste in every way possible. Initialization code is a good candidate for memory optimization. Given their nature, most initialization routines are executed either just once or not at all, depending on the kernel configuration. For example:

- The module_init routines are executed only once when the associated module is loaded. When the module is statically included in the kernel, the kernel can free the module_init routine right at boot time, after it runs.
- The module_exit routines are never executed when the associated modules are included statically in the kernel. In this case, therefore, there is no need to include module_exit routines into the kernel image (i.e., the routines can be discarded at link time).

The first case is a runtime optimization, and the second one is a link-time optimization.

Code and data that are used only during the boot and are not needed thereafter are placed in one of the memory sections shown in Figure 7-3. Once the kernel has completed the initialization phase, it can discard that entire memory area. This is accomplished by the call to free_init_mem,[*] as shown in Figure 5-1 in Chapter 5. Different macros are used to place code into the different memory sections of Figure 7-3.

If you look at the example in the earlier section "New Model: Macro-Based Tagging," you can see that the two input routines to module_init and module_exit are (usually) tagged with __init and __exit, respectively: this is done precisely to take advantage of the two properties mentioned at the start of this section.

__init and __exit Macros

The initialization routines executed in the early phase of the kernel are tagged with the macro __init.

As mentioned in the previous section, most module_init input routines are tagged with this macro. For example, most of the functions in Figure 5-1 in Chapter 5 (before the call to free_initmem) are marked with __init.

As shown by its definition here, the __init macro places the input routine into the .text.init memory section:

```
#define __init    __attribute__ ((__section__ (".text.init")))
```

This section is one of the memory areas freed at runtime by free_initmem.

__exit is the counterpart of __init. Routines used to shut down a module are placed into the .text.exit section. This section can be discarded at link time directly for modules build into the kernel. However, a few architectures discard it a runtime to deal with cross-references. Note that the same section, for modules loaded separately, can be removed at load time when the kernel does not support module unloading. (There is a kernel option that keeps the user from unloading modules.)

xxx_initcall and __exitcall Sections

The memory sections where the kernel places the addresses to the routines tagged with the xxx_initcall and __exitcall macros are also discarded:

- The xxx_initcall sections shown in Figure 7-3 are discarded at runtime by free_initmem.

- The .text.exit section used for __exitcall functions is discarded at link time because right now the kernel does not call the __exitcall routines on system shutdown (i.e., it does not use a mechanism similar to do_initcalls).

---

[*] This is the memory that boot-time messages of the following sort refer to: "Freeing unused kernel memory: 120k freed".

Other Optimizations

Other examples of optimizations include the macros in Table 7-3:

__devinit

When the kernel is not compiled with support for Hotplug, routines tagged with __devinit are not needed anymore at the end of the boot phase (after all the devices have been initialized). Because of this, when there is no support for Hotplug, __devinit becomes an alias to __init.

__devexit

When a PCI driver is built into a kernel without support for Hotplug, the routine to which pci_driver->remove is initialized, and which is tagged with __devexit, can be discarded because it is not needed. The routine can be discarded also when the module is loaded separately into a kernel that does not have support for module unloading.

__devinitdata

When there is no support for Hotplug, this data too is needed only at boot time. Normally, device drivers use this macro to tag the banner strings that the pci_driver-> probe functions print when initializing a device. PCI drivers, for instance, tag the pci_device_id tables with __devinitdata: once the system has finished booting and there is no support for Hotplug, the kernel does not need the tables anymore.

This section has given you only a few examples of removing code. You can learn more by browsing the source code, starting, for instance, from the architecture-dependent definitions of the /DISCARD/ section.

Dynamic Macros' Definition

In the previous sections, I introduced a few macros, such as __init and the various versions of *xxx*_initcall. We have also seen that the routines passed to the module_init macro are tagged with macros such as __initcall. Because most kernel components can be either compiled as modules or statically linked to the kernel, the choice made changes the definitions of these macros to apply the memory optimizations introduced in the previous section.

In particular, the definition of the macros in Table 7-1, as you can see in *include/linux/init.h*, change depending on whether the following symbols are defined within the scope of the file that includes *include/linux/init.h*:

CONFIG_MODULE

Defined when there is support for a loadable module in the kernel (the "Loadable module support" configuration option)

MODULE

Defined when the kernel component that the file belongs to is compiled as a module

CONFIG_HOTPLUG

   Defined when the kernel is compiled with "Support for hot-pluggable devices" (an option in the "General setup" menu)

While MODULE can have different values for different files, the other two symbols are kernel-wide properties and therefore are either set or not set consistently throughout a kernel.

Among the macros in Tables 7-1 and 7-2, we are mostly interested in the following ones from the perspective of NIC driver initialization: __init, __exit, __initcall, and __exitcall. Summarizing what was discussed so far, Figure 7-4 shows the effectiveness of the macros in the previous list in saving memory, based on whether the symbols MODULE and CONFIG_HOTPLUG are defined (let's suppose the kernel had support for loadable modules—i.e., that CONFIG_MODULE is defined). As you can see from the figure, there is a lot going on when the kernel does not have support for both loadable modules and Hotplug, compared to when both of those options are supported: the more restrictions you have, the more optimizations you get.

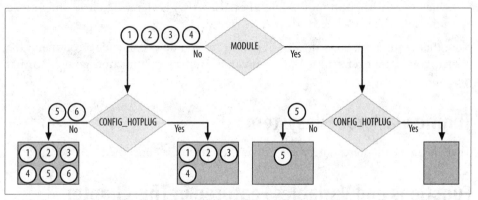

Figure 7-4. Effect of macros in Table 7-1, following numbered lists in text

Let's see one by one the meaning of the points 1 through 6 in Figure 7-4, keeping in mind the generic structure of a device driver as shown earlier in the section "New Model: Macro-Based Tagging" and the definitions of __initcall and __exitcall that we saw earlier in the section "Memory Optimizations."

Here are the optimizations that can be applied when compiling a module as part of the kernel:

1. module_exit routines will never be used; so by tagging them with __exit, the programmer makes sure they will not be included in the image at link time.

2. module_init routines will be executed only once at boot time, so by tagging them with __init, the programmer lets them be discarded once they are executed.

3. module_init(fn) becomes an alias to __initcall(fn), which makes sure fn will be executed by do_initcalls, as we saw in the section "xxx_initcall Macros."

4. module_exit(fn) becomes an alias to __exitcall(fn). This places the address to the input function in the .exitcall.exit memory section, which makes it easier for the kernel to run it at shutdown time, but the section is actually discarded at link time.

Let's use PCI devices as a reference, and see what other optimizations the lack of support for Hotplug introduces. These concern the pci_driver->remove function, which is called when a module is unloaded, once for each device registered by that module (see the section "The Big Picture" in Chapter 6).

5. Regardless of whether MODULE is defined, when there is no support for Hotplug in the kernel, devices cannot be removed from a running system. Therefore, the remove function will never be invoked by the PCI layer and can be initialized to a NULL pointer. This is indicated by the __devexit_p macro.

6. When there is no support for Hotplug or for modules in the kernel, the driver's routine that would be used to initialize pci_driver->remove is not needed by the module. This is indicated by the __devexit macro. Note that this is not true when there is support for modules. Because a user is allowed to load and unload a module, the kernel needs the remove routine.

Note that point 5 is a consequence of point 6: if you do not include a routine in the kernel, you cannot refer to it (i.e., you cannot initialize a function pointer to that routine).[*]

Tuning via /proc Filesystem

There is no file of interest in /proc as far as this chapter is concerned.

Functions and Variables Featured in This Chapter

Table 7-4 summarizes the functions, macros, structures, and variables introduced in the chapter.

Table 7-4. Functions, macros, variables, and data structures introduced in this chapter

Name	Description
Functions and macros	
__init, __exit, __initcall, __exitcall, __initdata, __exitdata, __devinit, __devexit, __devexit_p, __devinitdata, __devexitdata, xxx_initcall	Macros used to tag pieces of code with special characteristics. These tags can be used to optimize the kernel image size, leaving out unneeded code, for instance.
do_initcalls	Executes at boot time all the functions tagged with the xxx_initcall macros.

[*] See the snapshot in the section "Example of PCI NIC Driver Registration" in Chapter 6.

Table 7-4. Functions, macros, variables, and data structures introduced in this chapter (continued)

Name	Description
init_module, cleanup_module, module_init, module_exit	The first two are the names of the functions that each module should provide to respectively initialize and remove a module. The other two are macros that allow device driver writers to use an arbitrary name for the previous two routines.
netdev_boot, setup_check, netdev_boot_setup_add	Apply the boot-time configuration (if any) to a specific device.
module_param	Defines optional module parameters that can be provided when loading the module.
Data structures	
kernel_param	Stores the input to the module_param macro.
obs_kernel_param	Stores the input to the __setup macro.
netdev_boot_setup, ifmap	netdev_boot_setup stores boot-time parameters for the ether= and netdev= options.
	ifmap is one of the fields of netdev_boot_setup.
Variables	
dev_boot_setup	Array of netdev_boot_setup structures.
NETDEV_BOOT_SETUP_MAX	Size of dev_boot_setup.

Files and Directories Featured in This Chapter

Figure 7-5 lists the files and directories referred to in the chapter.

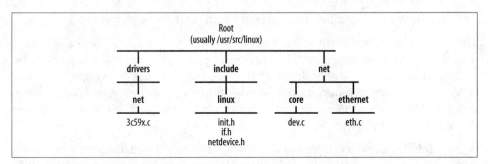

Figure 7-5. Files and directories featured in this chapter

CHAPTER 8
Device Registration and Initialization

In Chapters 5 and 6, we saw how NICs are recognized by the kernel, and the initialization that the kernel performs so that the NICs can talk to their device drivers. In this chapter, we will discuss additional stages of initialization:

- When and how network devices register with the kernel
- How a network device registers with the network device database and gets assigned an instance of a net_device structure
- How net_device structures are organized into hash tables and lists to allow different kinds of lookups
- How net_device instances are initialized, partly by kernel core routines and partly by their device drivers
- How virtual devices differ from real ones with regard to registration

This chapter does not strive to be a guide on how to write NIC device drivers. I sometimes go into detail on an NIC device driver's code, but I will not cover the entire design of an NIC device driver. We are interested here only in registration and in the interface between device drivers and features such as link state change detection and power management. Refer to *Linux Device Drivers* (O'Reilly) for a detailed discussion of device drivers.

Before an NIC can be used, its associated net_device data structure must be initialized, added to the kernel network device database, configured, and enabled. It is important not to confuse registration and unregistration with enabling and disabling. They are two different concepts:

- Registration and unregistration, if we exclude the act of loading a device driver module, are user independent; the kernel drives them. A device that has been only registered is not operative yet. We will see when a device is registered and unregistered in the sections "When a Device Is Registered" and "When a Device Is Unregistered."

- Enabling and disabling a device require user intervention. Once a device has been registered by the kernel, the user can see it by means of user commands, configure it, and enable it. See the later section "Enabling and Disabling a Network Device."

Let's start by seeing what events trigger the registration and unregistration of network devices.

When a Device Is Registered

The registration of a network device takes place in the following situations:

Loading an NIC's device driver
An NIC's device driver is initialized at boot time if it is built into the kernel, and at runtime if it is loaded as a module. Whenever initialization occurs, all the NICs controlled by that driver are registered.

Inserting a hot-pluggable network device
When a user inserts a hot-pluggable NIC, the kernel notifies its driver, which then registers the device. (For the sake of simplicity, we'll assume the device driver is already loaded.)

In the first situation, the registration model that applies is described in the later section "Skeleton of NIC Registration and Unregistration." It applies to all bus types, and is the same whether the registration routine ends up being called by the bus infrastructure or by the module initialization code. For example, we saw in Chapter 6 how loading a PCI device driver leads to the execution of the pci_driver-> probe routine, usually named something like *xxx*_probe, which is provided by the driver and which takes care of device registration. In this chapter, we will look at how those probe routines are implemented.

The registration of devices using other bus types (USB, PCMCIA, etc.) shares the same skeleton. We will not look at how the infrastructure of those buses ends up calling their probe counterpart, as we saw for PCI in Chapter 6. Older buses may not be able to automatically detect the presence of devices and may require the device drivers to do it by manually probing specific memory addresses, using default parameters or boot-time parameters provided by the user.* We will not look at this case either.

---

* See, for example, net_olddevs_init in *drivers/net/Space.c*. This function, which is tagged with the device_ initcall macro introduced in Chapter 7, is executed at boot time. The same function takes care of the registration of the loopback device.

When a Device Is Unregistered

Two main conditions trigger the unregistration of a device:

Unloading an NIC device driver
> This can be done only for drivers loaded as modules, of course, not for those built into the kernel. When the administrator unloads an NIC's device driver, all the associated NICs must be unregistered.
>
> For example, we saw in Chapter 6 how unloading a PCI device driver leads to the execution of the pci_driver->remove routine provided by the driver, often called something like *xxx*_remove_one, which will take care of device unregistration. This routine is invoked by the PCI layer once for each device registered against the driver being unloaded. In this chapter, we will look at how those routines are implemented.

Removing a hot-pluggable network device
> When a user removes a hot-pluggable NIC from a system whose running kernel has support for hot-pluggable devices, the network device is unregistered.

Allocating net_device Structures

Network devices are defined with net_device structures. Because they are usually named dev in the kernel code, I use that name frequently in this chapter for a net_device. These data structures are allocated with alloc_netdev, defined in *net/core/dev.c*, which requires three input parameters:

Size of private data structure
> We will see in the section "Organization of net_device Structures" that the net_device data structure can be extended by device drivers with a private data block to store the driver's parameters. This parameter specifies the size of the block.

Device name
> This may be a partial name that the kernel will complete through some scheme that ensures unique device names.

Setup routine
> This routine is used to initialize a portion of the net_device's fields. See the sections "Device Initialization" and "Device Type Initialization: xxx_setup Functions" for more details.

The return value is a pointer to the net_device structure allocated, or NULL in case of errors.

Every device is assigned a name that depends on the device type and that, to be unique, contains a number that is assigned sequentially as devices of the same type are registered. Ethernet devices, for instance, are called *eth0*, *eth1*, and so on. A single device may be called with different names depending on the order with which the devices are registered. For instance, if you had two cards handled by two different modules, the names of the devices would depend on the order in which the two modules were loaded. Hot-pluggable devices lend themselves particularly to unanticipated name changes.

Because user-space configuration tools refer to the kernel-assigned device name, the order with which devices register is important. As this is a user-space detail, I will not bother with it further, except to mention that there are tools, such as *nameif* from the *net-tools* package, that allow you to assign fixed names to interfaces based on the MAC address.

When the name of the device passed to alloc_netdev is in the form *name*%d (e.g., "eth%d"), the kernel completes the name using the function dev_alloc_name. The latter changes %d to the first unassigned number for that device type.

The kernel also provides a set of wrappers around alloc_netdev, a few of which are listed in Table 8-1, which can be used to feed alloc_netdev the correct parameters for a set of common device types.* For example, alloc_etherdev is used for Ethernet devices, and therefore creates a device name in the form of the string eth followed by a unique number. As its second argument, it specifies ether_setup as the setup routine, which initializes a portion of the net_device structure to values common to all Ethernet devices.

Table 8-1. Wrappers for the alloc_netdev function

Network device type	Wrapper name	Wrapper definition
Ethernet	alloc_etherdev	return alloc_netdev(sizeof_priv, "eth%d", ether_setup);
Fiber Distributed Data Interface	alloc_fddidev	return alloc_netdev(sizeof_priv, "fddi%d", fddi_setup);
High Performace Parallel Interface	alloc_hippi_dev	return alloc_netdev(sizeof_priv, "hip%d", hippi_setup);
Token Ring	alloc_trdev	return alloc_netdev(sizeof_priv, "tr%d", tr_setup);
Fibre Channel	alloc_fcdev	return alloc_netdev(sizeof_priv, "fc%d", fc_setup);
Infrared Data Association	alloc_irdadev	return alloc_netdev(sizeof_priv, "irda%d", irda_device_setup);

---

* There are other, similar wrappers that do not follow the alloc_*xxx*dev naming convention. Furthermore, some devices call alloc_netdev directly to register with the kernel instead of using a wrapper.

Skeleton of NIC Registration and Unregistration

Figure 8-1(a) shows the generic scheme for an NIC's device driver to register with the networking code. Figure 8-1(b) shows the complementary action that takes place for unregistration. Although the example shows a PCI Ethernet NIC, the scheme is the same for other device types; only the name of the routine that takes care of it, or the way that routine is invoked, may change depending on how the bus code is implemented.

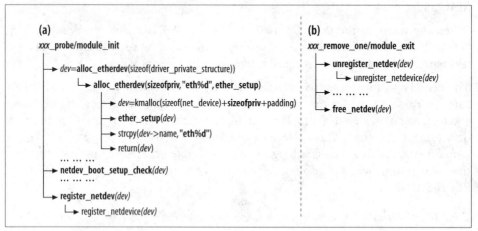

Figure 8-1. (a) Device registration model; (b) device unregistration model

The function starts by allocating the `net_device` structure with `alloc_etherdev`. `alloc_etherdev` also initializes all the parameters that are common to all Ethernet devices. The driver then initializes another portion of the `net_device` structure, and concludes the device registration with a call to the `register_netdev` routine.

Note that:

- The driver calls the appropriate wrapper around `alloc_netdev` (`alloc_etherdev` in the example), and provides only the size of its private data block. A few wrappers are listed in Table 8-1.

- The wrapper calls `alloc_netdev` using the parameter provided by the driver, and adds the other two (the device name and the initialization routine).

- The size of the memory block allocated by `alloc_netdev` includes the `net_device` structure, the driver's private block, and some padding to force an alignment. See Figure 8-2 later in the chapter.

- Some drivers call `netdev_boot_setup_check` to check whether the user provided any boot-time parameter when loading the kernel. See the section "Use of Boot Options to Configure Network Devices" in Chapter 7.

- The new net_device instance is inserted into the device database with register_ netdevice (see the later section "Device Registration"). Incidentally, I use the term *database* here, and in other parts of the book, to refer loosely to a combination of data structures that provides convenient access to information on the terms the kernel needs.

The unregistration of a device, shown in its simple form in Figure 8-1(b), always includes a call to unregister_netdevice and free_netdev. The call to free_netdev is sometimes made explicitly, and sometimes indirectly via the dev->destructor function,* as shown later in Figure 8-4. The device driver also needs to release any resources used by the device (IRQ, memory mappings, etc.), but we are not interested in those details in this chapter.

Device Initialization

In the section "When a Device Is Registered," we saw what needs to be initialized for the kernel to communicate to the NIC. In the rest of this chapter we will look at higher-level initialization tasks.

The net_device structure is pretty big. Its fields are initialized in chunks by different routines, each one responsible for a different subset of fields.[†] In particular:

Device drivers
    Parameters such as IRQ, I/O memory, and I/O port, whose values depend on the hardware configuration, are taken care of by the device driver. See Chapter 5.

Device type
    The initialization of fields common to all the devices of a device type family is taken care by the *xxx*_setup routines. For example, Ethernet devices use ether_ setup. See the section "Device Type Initialization: xxx_setup Functions."

Features
    Mandatory and optional features also need to be initialized. For example, the queuing discipline (i.e., QoS) is initialized in register_netdevice, as described in the section "register_netdevice Function." Other features can be initialized when the associated modules are notified about the registration of the new device (see the section "Device Registration Status Notification").

The device type initialization is done as part of the device driver initialization (that is, *xxx*_setup is called by *xxx*_probe) so that the driver has a chance to overwrite the default device type's initializations. See the section "Optional Initializations and Special Cases" for an example.

---

* The device drivers of only a few virtual devices use this approach (see, for example, *net/8021q/vlan.c*). The two calls in Figure 8-4 are mutually exclusive.

† An interesting exception is the loopback device, whose initialization is hardcoded in the loopback_dev definition in *drivers/net/loopback.c*.

Table 8-2 shows the function pointers that are initialized by the *xxx*_setup routines and what is left to the device driver[*] (*xxx*_probe): what is device-type specific and what is device-model specific. Note that not all device drivers respect the distinction in Table 8-2. For instance, there are cases where the *xxx*_setup function does not initialize any function pointer (an example is irda_device_setup in *net/irda/irda_device.c*) and others where it initializes all of them (an example is wifi_setup in *drivers/net/wireless/airo.c*).

Table 8-2. net_device function pointers initialized by xxx_setup and xxx_probe

Initializer	Function pointer name
*xxx*_setup	change_mtu set_mac_address rebuild_header hard_header hard_header_cache header_cache_update hard_header_parse
Device driver's probe routine	open stop hard_start_xmit tx_timeout watchdog_timeo get_stats get_wireless_stats set_multicast_list do_ioctl init uninit poll ethtool_ops *(this is actually an array of routines)*

Table 8-3 is similar to Table 8-2, but instead of function pointers it lists some of the other net_device fields.

Table 8-3. net_device fields initialized by xxx_setup and xxx_probe

Initializer	Variable name
*xxx*_setup	type hard_header_len mtu addr_len tx_queue_len broadcast flags
Device driver's probe routine	base_addr irq if_port priv features

[*] Chapter 2 contains a detailed description of all the parameters of the net_device data structure.

For more details on the meaning of the fields in Tables 8-2 and 8-3, refer to Chapter 2.

Device Driver Initializations

The net_device fields initialized by the device driver are usually taken care of by the *xxx*_probe function introduced in the section "The Big Picture" in Chapter 6, and depicted in Figure 8-1(a).

Some drivers can handle different device models; so the same parameters can be initialized differently based on the device model and capabilities. The following snapshot, from the *drivers/net/3c59x.c* driver, shows that the function hard_start_xmit, which we will introduce in Chapter 11, is initialized differently depending on the device's capabilities:*

```
if (vp->capabilities & CapBusMaster) {
    vp->full_bus_master_tx = 1;
        ... ... ...
}
... ... ...
if (vp->full_bus_master_tx) {
    dev->hard_start_xmit = boomerang_start_xmit;
        ... ... ...
} else {
    dev->hard_start_xmit = vortex_start_xmit;
}
```

Device Type Initialization: xxx_setup Functions

For the most common network device types there is an *xxx*_setup function to initialize the fields of the net_device structure (both parameters and function pointers) that are common to all the devices of the same type—for instance, all Ethernet cards.

In Table 8-1, you saw how the various alloc_ *xxx*dev functions pass the right *xxx*_setup routine to alloc_netdev (as the third input parameter). Here is the ether_setup routine, which is the *xxx*_setup routine used by Ethernet devices:

```
void ether_setup(struct net_device *dev)
{
    dev->change_mtu            = eth_change_mtu;
    dev->hard_header           = eth_header;
    dev->rebuild_header        = eth_rebuild_header;
    dev->set_mac_address       = eth_mac_addr;
    dev->hard_header_cache     = eth_header_cache;
    dev->header_cache_update   = eth_header_cache_update;
    dev->hard_header_parse     = eth_header_parse;
```

---

* Capabilities can be hardcoded into the driver or retrieved by reading a register on the NIC.

```
        dev->type               = ARPHRD_ETHER;
        dev->hard_header_len     = ETH_HLEN;
        dev->mtu                 = 1500;
        dev->addr_len            = ETH_ALEN;
        dev->tx_queue_len        = 1000;
        dev->flags               = IFF_BROADCAST|IFF_MULTICAST;

        memset(dev->broadcast,0xFF, ETH_ALEN);
    }
```

As you can see, this function initializes only the fields and function pointers that can be shared by any Ethernet card: an MTU of 1,500, a link-layer broadcast address of FF:FF:FF:FF:FF:FF, an egress queue length of 1,000 packets,[*] etc.

The use of a generic allocation wrapper and the *xxx*_setup routine, as shown in Table 8-1, is the most common approach. However:

- Some classes of devices define setup functions but do not provide a generic wrapper similar to the ones in Table 8-1. Among them are ARCNET[†] devices (see arcdev_setup in *drivers/net/arcnet/arcnet.c*) and IrDA[‡] devices (see irda_device_setup in *net/irda/irda_device.c*).

- A generic *xxx*_setup may be used by devices that do not belong to the indicated class. ether_setup is an example: it is used by non-Ethernet devices as well. When most of the initializations of a particular *xxx*_setup routine suit the needs of a device driver, the latter may use that *xxx*_setup routine and simply override those initializations that are not correct. But this approach is not common.

- An Ethernet driver can use the default initialization provided by ether_setup (which is invoked indirectly by alloc_etherdev) but override some of the initializations. For example, the *3c59x.c* driver does not use the net_device->mtu value set by ether_setup, but overrides it with a local variable. This variable is initialized to the same default that would be set by ether_setup, but the driver can set bigger values for NIC models that can handle them.

Optional Initializations and Special Cases

There are cases when some net_device parameters are not initialized simply because they are meaningless for that type of device; the associated function pointer or value is not initialized and therefore is left to NULL.

---

[*] This is Linux's implementation choice; it is not derived from any protocol specification. Depending on the egress queuing discipline configured, this value may not be used.

[†] ARCNET (Attached Resource Computer) is a LAN technology based on a token bus design (similar to 802.4) that has found its natural habit in the industrial automation industry thanks to its deterministic performance. Linux provides a general layer for ARCNET and a few device drivers.

[‡] IrDA (Infrared Data Association) is a standard for infrared wireless communication.

To avoid NULL pointer references, the kernel always makes sure that optional function pointers are initialized before invoking them,[*] as in the following example from register_netdevice:

```
if (dev->init && dev->init(dev) != 0) {
    ...
}
```

It is important to note that external factors could also change how and where the fields of Tables 8-2 and 8-3 are initialized. One example involves the net_device->mtu field. Virtual devices usually inherit configuration parameters from the real devices they are associated with, and then adjust them if needed. For example, virtual tunnel interfaces created by the IP-over-IP protocol inherit dev->mtu from the real devices they are associated with. (This is not automatic; the virtual device driver takes care of it.) However, due to the extra IP header needed by the IP-over-IP protocol, the MTU needs to be lowered accordingly (see ipip_tunnel_xmit in *net/ipv4/ipip.c,* which assumes an underlying Ethernet device).

Organization of net_device Structures

Some of the subtler aspects of the net_device structure include the following:

- We saw in the section "Allocating net_device Structures" that when alloc_netdev is called to allocate a net_device structure, it is passed the size of the driver's private data block (whose size depends on the driver—some do not even use private data at all). alloc_netdev appends the private data to the net_device structure. Figure 8-1 showed how that parameter is passed and Figure 8-2 shows the effect on the memory allocation.

- Figure 8-2 also shows the relationship between the net_device data structure and the optional driver's private data structure. Normally, the second part is allocated together with the first one so that a single kmalloc is sufficient, but there are also cases where the driver prefers to allocate its private block by itself (see driver C in Figure 8-2).

- As shown in the example in Figure 8-2, the size of the driver's private block and its content change not only from one device type to another (e.g., Token Ring versus Ethernet) but also among devices of the same type (e.g., two different Ethernet cards).

- dev_base (introduced later in this section) and the next pointer in net_device point to the beginning of the net_device structure, not to the beginning of the allocated block. However, the size of the initial padding is saved in dev->padded, which allows the kernel to release the whole memory block when it is time to do so.

---

[*] In Chapter 1, you can find some more details on the use of VFTs.

net_device data structures are inserted both in a global list, as shown in Figure 8-2, and in two hash tables, as shown in Figure 8-3. These different structures allow the kernel to easily browse or look up the net_device database as required. Here are the details:

dev_base

This global list of all net_device instances allows the kernel to easily browse devices in case, for instance, it has to get some statistics, change a configuration across all devices as a consequence of a user command, or find devices matching given search criteria.

Because each driver has its own definition for the private data structure, the global list of net_device structures may link together elements of different sizes (see Figure 8-2).

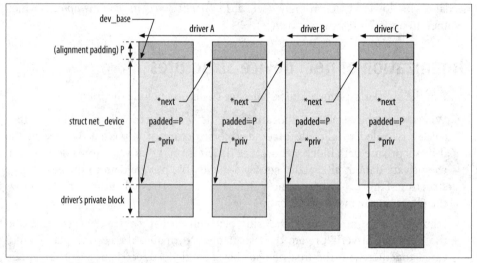

Figure 8-2. Global list of registered devices

dev_name_head

This is a hash table indexed on the device name. It is useful, for instance, when applying a configuration change via the ioctl interface. The old-generation configuration tools that talk to the kernel via the ioctl interface usually refer to devices by their names.

dev_index_head

This is a hash table indexed on the device ID dev->ifindex. Cross-references to net_device structures usually store either device IDs or pointers to net_device structures; dev_index_head is useful for the former. Also, the new-generation configuration tool *ip* (from the IPROUTE2 package), which talks to the kernel via the Netlink socket, usually refers to devices by their ID.

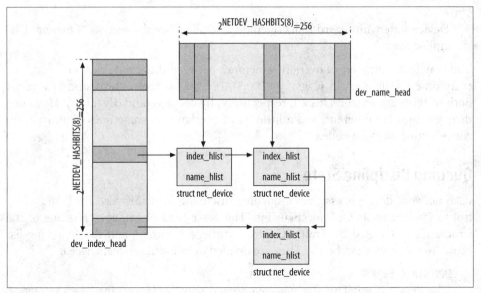

Figure 8-3. Hash tables used to search net_device instances based on device name and device index

Lookups

The most common lookups are based either on the device name or on the device ID. These two lookup types are implemented by dev_get_by_name and dev_get_by_index, which use the two hash tables discussed in the previous section. It is also possible to search net_device instances based on their device type, MAC address, etc. These kinds of lookups use the dev_base list.

All lookups, both on the dev_base list and on the two hash tables, are protected by the dev_base_lock lock.

All lookup routines are defined in *net/core/dev.c*.

Device State

The net_device structure includes different fields that define the current state of the device. These include:

flags

> Bitmap used to store different flags. Most of them represent a device's capabilities. However, one of them, IFF_UP, is used to say whether the device is enabled (up) or disabled (down). You can find the list of IFF_*XXX* flags in *include/linux/if. h*. See also the section "Enabling and Disabling a Network Device."

reg_state

> Device registration state. The section "Registration State" lists the values this field can be assigned and when its value changes.

state

> Device state with regard to its queuing discipline. See the section "Queuing Discipline State."

You may find a little bit of overlap sometimes between these variables. For example, every time IFF_UP is set in flags, __LINK_STATE_START is set in state, and vice versa. Both of them are set and cleared, respectively, by dev_open and dev_close. However, their domains are different, and a little bit of overlap may sometimes be introduced when writing modular code.

Queuing Discipline State

Each network device is assigned a queuing discipline, which is used by Traffic Control to implement its QoS mechanisms. The state field of net_device is one of the structure's fields used by Traffic Control. state is a bitmap, and the following list shows the flags that can be set. They are defined in *include/linux/netdevice.h.*

__LINK_STATE_START

> The device is up. This flag can be checked with netif_running. See the section "Enabling and Disabling a Network Device."

__LINK_STATE_PRESENT

> The device is present. This flag may look superfluous; but take into account that hot-pluggable devices can be temporally removed. The flag is also cleared and restored, respectively, when the system goes into suspend mode and then resumes. The flag can be checked with netif_device_present. See the section "register_netdevice Function."

__LINK_STATE_NOCARRIER

> There is no carrier. The flag can be checked with netif_carrier_ok. See the section "Link State Change Detection."

__LINK_STATE_LINKWATCH_EVENT

> The device's link state has changed. See the section "Scheduling and processing link state change events."

__LINK_STATE_XOFF
__LINK_STATE_SHED
__LINK_STATE_RX_SCHED

> These three flags are used by the code that manages ingress and egress traffic on the device. We will see how they are used in Part III.

Registration State

The state of a device with regard to its registration with the network stack is saved in the reg_state field of the net_device structure. The NETREG_*XXX* values it can take are defined in *include/linux/netdevice.h*, within the net_device structure definition. In the next section, we will see how they relate to each other. Here is a brief description:

NETREG_UNINITIALIZED

> Defined as 0. When the net_device data structure is allocated and its contents zeroed, this value represents the 0 in dev->reg_state.

NETREG_REGISTERING

> The net_device structure has been added to the structures listed in the later section "Organization of net_device Structures," but the kernel still needs to add an entry to the */sys* filesystem.

NETREG_REGISTERED

> The device has been fully registered.

NETREG_UNREGISTERING

> The net_device structure has been removed from the structures listed in the later section "Organization of net_device Structures."

NETREG_UNREGISTERED

> The device has been fully unregistered (which includes removing the entry from */sys*), but the net_device structure has not been freed yet.

NETREG_RELEASED

> All the references to the net_device structure have been released. The data structure can be freed, from the networking code's perspective. However, it will be up to *sysfs* to take care of it. See the section "Reference Counts."

Registering and Unregistering Devices

Network devices are registered and unregistered with the kernel with register_ netdev and unregister_netdev, respectively. These are simple wrappers that take care of locking and then invoke the routines register_netdevice and unregister_ netdevice, respectively. We already briefly introduced these functions in Figure 8-1. All of them are defined in *net/core/dev.c*.

Figure 8-4 shows the registration states a net_device can be set to, and shows where the aforementioned routines come into the picture. It also shows where other key routines are called. All of them will be described in later sections. In particular, note that:

- Changes of state may use intermediate states between NETREG_UNINITIALIZED and NETREG_REGISTERED. These progressions are handled by netdev_run_todo, described in the section "Split Operations: netdev_run_todo."

- The two net_device virtual functions init and uninit can be used by device drivers to initialize and clean up private data, respectively, when registering and unregistering a device. They are mainly used by virtual devices. See the section "Virtual Devices."

- The unregistration of a device cannot be completed until all references to the associated net_device data structure have been released: netdev_wait_allrefs does not return until that condition is met. See the section "Reference Counts."

- Both the registration and unregistration of a device are completed by netdev_run_todo. We will see in the section "Split Operations: netdev_run_todo" how register_netdevice and unregister_netdevice interact with netdev_run_todo.

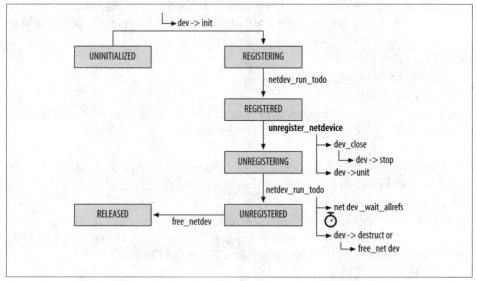

Figure 8-4. net_device's registration state machine

Split Operations: netdev_run_todo

register_netdevice takes care of a portion of the registration, and then lets netdev_run_todo complete it. At first, it may not be clear how this happens by looking at the code. Let's see how it works with the help of Figure 8-5(a).

Changes to net_device structures are protected with the Routing Netlink semaphore via rtnl_lock and rtnl_unlock, which is why register_netdev acquires the lock (semaphore) at the beginning and releases it before returning (more details in the section "Locking"). Once register_netdevice is done with its job, it adds the new net_device structure to net_todo_list with net_set_todo. That list contains the devices whose registration (or unregistration, as we will see in a moment) has to be completed. The list is not processed by a separate kernel thread or by means of a periodic timer; it will be up to register_netdev to indirectly process it when releasing the lock.

Thus, `rtnl_unlock` not only releases the lock, but also calls `netdev_run_todo`.[*] The latter function browses the `net_todo_list` array and completes the registration of all its `net_device` instances.

Only one CPU can be running `net_run_todo` at any one time. Serialization is enforced with the `net_todo_run_mutex` mutex.

The unregistration of a device is handled exactly the same way (as shown in Figure 8-5(b)).

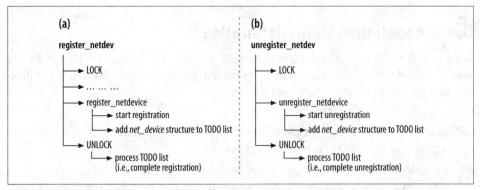

Figure 8-5. Structure of register_netdev and unregister_netdev

What `netdev_run_todo` does, exactly, to complete the registration or unregistration of a device is described at the end of the sections "register_netdevice Function" and "unregister_netdevice Function," respectively.

Note that since the registration and unregistration tasks handled by `netdev_run_todo` do not hold the lock, this function can safely sleep and leave the semaphore available. You will see one example why this is a good thing in the section "Reference Counts."

Given the model of Figure 8-5, it may seem that the kernel cannot have more than one `net_device` instance in `net_todo_list` by the time `netdev_run_todo` is called. How can there be more than one element if `register_netdev` and `unregister_netdev` add only one `net_device` instance to the list and then process the latter right away when releasing the lock? Well, for example, it is possible for a device driver to use a loop like the following to unregister all of its devices in one shot (see, for instance, tun_cleanup in *drivers/net/tun.c*):

```
rtnl_lock();
loop for each device driven by this driver {
    ... ... ...
    unregister_netdevice(dev);
    ... ... ...
```

---

[*] `rtnl_unlock` is a wrapper around the semaphore primitive up. When up is called directly, as in `rtnetlink_rcv`, `netdev_run_todo` is called explicitly. See also the section "Locking."

```
    }
    rtnl_unlock();
```

This is better than the following approach, which gets and releases the lock and processes net_todo_list at each iteration of the loop:

```
loop for each device driven by this driver {
    ... ... ...
    unregister_netdev(dev);
    ... ... ...
}
```

Device Registration Status Notification

Both kernel components and user-space applications may be interested in knowing when a network device is registered, unregistered, goes down, or comes up. Notifications about these events are sent via two channels:

netdev_chain
> Kernel components can register with this notification chain. See the following section, "netdev_chain notification chain."

Netlink's RTMGRP_LINK *multicast group*
> User-space applications, such as monitoring tools or routing protocols, can register with RTnetlink's RTMGRP_LINK multicast group. See the section "RTnetlink link notifications."

netdev_chain notification chain

We saw what notification chains are and how they are used in Chapter 4. The progress through the various stages of registering and unregistering a device is reported with the netdev_chain notification chain. This chain is defined in *net/core/dev.c*, and kernel components interested in these kinds of events register and unregister with the chain with register_netdevice_notifier and unregister_netdevice_notifier, respectively.

All the NETDEV_XXX events that are reported via netdev_chain are listed in *include/linux/notifier.h*. Here are the ones we have seen in this chapter, together with the conditions that trigger them:

NETDEV_UP
NETDEV_GOING_DOWN
NETDEV_DOWN
> NETDEV_UP is sent to report about a device that has been enabled, and is generated by dev_open.

> NETDEV_GOING_DOWN is sent when the device is about to be disabled. NETDEV_DOWN is sent when the device has been disabled. They are both generated by dev_close.

For more details on these three events, see the section "Enabling and Disabling a Network Device."

NETDEV_REGISTER

The device has been registered. This event is generated by register_netdevice. See the section "register_netdevice Function."

NETDEV_UNREGISTER

The device has been unregistered. This event is generated by unregister_netdevice. See the section "unregister_netdevice Function."

And here are the other ones:

NETDEV_REBOOT

The device has restarted due to a hardware failure. Currently not used.

NETDEV_CHANGEADDR

The hardware address (or the associated broadcast address) of the device has changed.

NETDEV_CHANGENAME

The device has changed its name.

NETDEV_CHANGE

The device status or configuration of the device has changed. This is used in all the cases not covered by NETDEV_CHANGEADDR and NETDEV_CHANGENAME. It is currently used when something changes in dev->flags.

The NETDEV_CHANGE*XXX* notifications are usually generated in response to a user configuration change.

Note that register_netdevice_notifier, when registering with the chain, also replays (to the new registrant only) all the past NETDEV_REGISTER and NETDEV_UP notifications for the devices currently registered in the system. This gives the new registrant a clear picture of the current status of the registered devices.

Quite a few kernel components register to netdev_chain. Among them are:

Routing

For instance, the routing subsystem uses this notification to add or remove all the routing entries associated with the device. See Chapter 32.

Firewall

For example, if the firewall had buffered any packet from a device that now is down, it has to either drop the packet or take another action according to its policies.

Protocol code (i.e., ARP, IP, etc.)

For example, when you change the MAC address of a local device, the ARP table must be updated accordingly. See the associated protocol chapters for more details.

Virtual devices
> See the section "Virtual Devices."

RTnetlink
> See the following section, "RTnetlink link notifications."

RTnetlink link notifications

Notifications are sent to the Link multicast group `RTMGRP_LINK` with `rtmsg_ifinfo` when something changed in the device's state or configuration. Among these notifications are:

- When a notification is received on the `netdev_chain` notification chain. RTnetlink registers to the `netdev_chain` chain introduced in the previous section and replays the notifications it receives.
- When a disabled device is enabled or vice versa (see `netdev_state_change`).
- When a flag in `net_device->flags` is changed, for example, via a user configuration command (see `dev_change_flags`).

netplugd is a daemon, part of the *net-utils* package, that listens to these notifications and reacts according to a user configuration file. See the *netplugs* manpage for details.

Device Registration

Device registration, whose basic model is shown in Figure 8-1(a), does not consist simply of inserting the `net_device` structure into the global list and hash tables introduced in the section "Organization of net_device Structures." It also involves the initialization of some parameters in the `net_device` structure, the generation of a broadcast notification that will inform other kernel components about the registration, and other tasks. Devices are registered with `register_netdev`, which is a simple wrapper around `register_netdevice`. The wrapper mainly takes care of locking and name completion as described earlier in the section "Allocating net_device Structures." The lock protects the `dev_base` list of registered devices.

register_netdevice Function

As described in Figure 8-5(a), `register_netdevice` starts device registration and calls `net_set_todo`, which ultimately asks `netdev_run_todo` to complete the registration.

Here are the main tasks carried out by `register_netdevice`:

- Initialize some of the `net_device`'s fields, including the ones used for locking, listed in the section "Locking."

- When the kernel has support for the Divert feature, allocate a configuration block needed by the feature and link it to dev->divert. This is taken care of by alloc_divert_blk.

- If the device driver had initialized dev->init, execute that function. See the section "Virtual Devices."

- Assign the device a unique identifier with dev_new_index. The identifier is generated using a counter that is incremented every time a new device is added to the system. This counter is a 32-bit variable, so dev_new_index includes an if clause to handle wraparound as well as another if clause to handle the possibility that the variable hits a value that was already assigned.

- Append net_device to the global list dev_base and insert it into the two hash tables described in the section "Organization of net_device Structures." Even though adding the structure at the head of dev_base would be faster, the kernel has a chance to check for duplicate device names by browsing the entire list. The device name is checked against invalid names with dev_valid_name.

- Check the feature flags for invalid combinations. For example:

  - Scather/Gather-DMA is useless without L4 hardware checksumming support and is therefore disabled in that situation.

  - TCP Segmentation Offload (TSO) requires Scather/Gather-DMA, and is therefore disabled when the latter is not supported.

  See Chapter 19 for more details on L4 checksums.

- Set the __LINK_STATE_PRESENT flag in dev->state to make the device available (visible and usable) to the system. The flag is cleared, for example, when a hot-pluggable device is unplugged, or when a system with support for power management goes into suspend mode. See the section "Queuing Discipline State."

  The initialization of this flag does not trigger any action; instead, its value is checked in well-defined cases to filter out illegal requests or to get the device state.

- Initialize the device's queuing discipline, used by Traffic Control to implement QoS, with dev_init_scheduler. The queuing discipline defines how egress packets are queued to and dequeued from the egress queue, defines how many packets can be queued before starting to drop them, etc. See the section "Queuing Discipline Interface" in Chapter 11.

- Notify all the subsystems interested in device registration via the netdev_chain notification chain. Notification chains are described in Chapter 4.

When netdev_run_todo is called to complete the registration, it just updates dev->reg_state and registers the device in the *sysfs* filesystem.

Aside from memory allocation problems, device registration can fail only if the device name is invalid or is a duplicate, or when dev->init fails for some reason.

Device Unregistration

To unregister a device, the kernel and the associated device driver need to undo all the operations that were executed during its registration, and more:

- Disable the device with dev_close, described in the section "Enabling and Disabling a Network Device."
- Release all the allocated resources (IRQ, I/O memory, I/O port, etc.)
- Remove the net_device structure from the global list dev_base and the two hash tables introduced in the section "Organization of net_device Structures."
- Once all the references to the structure have been released, free the net_device data structure, the driver's private data structure, and any other memory block linked to it (see Figure 8-2). The net_device structure is freed with free_netdev. When the kernel is compiled with support for *sysfs*, free_netdev lets it take care of freeing the structure.
- Remove any file that may have been added to the */proc* and */sys* filesystems.

Note that whenever there is a dependency between devices, unregistering one of them may force the unregistration of all (or part) of the others. See the section "Virtual Devices" for an example.

Three function pointers in net_device (represented by a variable named dev) come into the picture when unregistering a device:

dev->stop

> This function pointer is initialized by the device driver to one of its local routines. It is invoked by dev_stop when disabling a device (see the section "Enabling and Disabling a Network Device"). Common tasks handled here include stopping the egress queue with netif_stop_queue,[*] releasing hardware resources, stopping any timers used by the device driver, etc.
>
> Virtual devices do not need to release any hardware resources, but they may need to take care of other, high-level issues. See the section "Virtual Devices."

dev->uninit

> This function pointer is also initialized by the device driver to one of its local routines. Only a few, tunneling virtual devices currently initialize it; they point it to a routine that mainly takes care of reference counts.

dev->destructor

> When used, this is normally initialized to free_netdev or to a wrapper around it. However, destructor is not commonly initialized; only a few virtual devices use it. Most device drivers call free_netdev directly after unregister_netdevice.

---

[*] netif_*xxx*_queue routines are described in Chapter 11.

Figure 8-4 shows when and in what order these three routines are invoked.

unregister_netdevice Function

unregister_netdevice accepts one parameter, the pointer to the net_device structure it is to remove:

```
int unregister_netdevice(struct net_device *dev)
```

In Chapter 9, we will see in detail how the networking code uses software interrupts (softirqs) to handle packet transmission (net_tx_action) and reception (net_rx_action). You can look at those functions, for now, as the interface between device drivers and upper-layer protocols. Two calls to synchronize_net are used to synchronize unregister_netdevice with the receive engine (net_rx_action) so that it will not access old data after it has been updated by unregister_netdevice.

Other tasks taken care of by unregister_netdevice include:

- If the device was not disabled, it has to be disabled first with dev_close (see the section "Enabling and Disabling a Network Device").

- The net_device instance is then removed from the global list dev_base and the two hash tables introduced in the section "Organization of net_device Structures." Note that this is not sufficient to forbid kernel subsystems from using the device: they may still hold a pointer to the net_device data structure. This is why net_device uses a reference count to keep track of how many references are left to the structure (see the section "Reference Counts").

- All the instances of queuing discipline associated with the device are destroyed with dev_shutdown.

- A NETDEV_UNREGISTER notification is sent on the netdev_chain notification chain to let other kernel components know about it. See the section "Device Registration Status Notification."

- User space has to be notified about the unregistration. For instance, in a system with two NICs that could be used to access the Internet, this notification could be used to start the secondary device. See the section "Device Registration Status Notification."

- Any data block linked to the net_device structure is freed. For example, the multicast data dev->mc_list is removed with dev_mc_discard, the Divert block is removed with free_divert_blk, etc. The ones that are not explicitly removed in unregister_netdevice are supposed to be removed by the function handlers that process the notifications mentioned in the previous bullet.

- Whatever was done by dev->init in register_netdevice is undone here with dev->uninit.

- Features such as bonding allow you to group a set of devices together and treat them as a single virtual device with special characteristics. Among those devices, one is often elected master because it plays a special role within the group. For obvious reasons, the device being removed should release any reference to the master device: having dev->master non-NULL at this point would be a bug. If we stick to the bonding example, the dev->master reference is cleared thanks to the NETDEV_UNREGISTER notifications sent just a few lines of code earlier.

Finally, net_set_todo is called to let net_run_todo complete the unregistration, as described in the section "Split Operations: netdev_run_todo," and the reference count is decreased with dev_put. net_run_todo unregisters the device from *sysfs*, changes dev->reg_state to NETREG_UNREGISTERED, waits until all the references are gone, and completes the unregistration with a call to dev->destructor.

Reference Counts

net_device structures cannot be freed until all the references to it are released. The reference count for the structure is kept in dev->refcnt, which is updated every time a reference is added or removed, respectively, with dev_hold and dev_put.

When a device is registered with register_netdevice, dev->refcnt is initialized to 1. This first reference is therefore kept by the kernel code that is responsible for the network devices database. This reference will be released only with a call to unregister_netdevice. This means that dev->refcnt will never drop to zero until the device is to be unregistered. Therefore, unlike other kernel objects that are freed by the *xxx_put* routine when the reference count drops to zero, net_device data structures are not freed until you unregister the device from the kernel. We saw already the conditions that lead to the unregistration of a device in the section ""When a Device Is Unregistered."

In summary, the call to dev_put at the end of unregister_netdevice is not sufficient to make a net_device instance eligible for deletion: the kernel still needs to wait until all the references are released. But because the device is no longer usable after it is unregistered, the kernel needs to notify all the reference holders so that they can release their references. This is done by sending a NETDEV_UNREGISTER notification to the netdev_chain notification chain. This also means that reference holders should register to the notification chain; otherwise, they will not be able to receive such notifications and take action accordingly.

As we mentioned in the section "Split Operations: netdev_run_todo," unregister_netdevice starts the unregistration process and lets netdev_run_todo complete it. netdev_run_todo calls netdev_wait_allrefs to indefinitely wait until all references to the net_device structure have been released. The next section goes into detail on the internals of netdev_wait_allrefs.

Function netdev_wait_allrefs

netdev_wait_allrefs, depicted in Figure 8-6, consists of a loop that ends only when the value of dev->refcnt drops to zero. Every second it sends out a NETDEV_UNREGISTER notification, and every 10 seconds it prints a warning on the console. The rest of the time it sleeps. The function does not give up until all the references to the input net_device structure have been released.

Two common cases that would require more than one notification to be sent are:

A bug

> For example, a piece of code could hold references to net_device structures, but it may not release them because it has not registered to the netdev_chain notification chain, or because it does not process notifications correctly.

A pending timer

> For example, suppose the routine that is executed when some timer expires needs to access data that includes references to net_device structures. In this case, you would need to wait until the timer expires and its handler hopefully releases its references.

Note that since netdev_run_todo is started by unregister_netdevice when it releases the lock, as described in the section "Split Operations: netdev_run_todo," it means that whoever started the unregistration, most probably the driver, is going to sleep waiting for netdev_run_todo to complete its job.

When the function sends the notification, it also processes the pending link state change events. Link state change events are covered in the section "Link State Change Detection." Here, suffice it to say that when a device is being unregistered, the kernel does not need to do anything when informed about a link state change event on the device. When the current device state is that the device is about to be removed, events associated with devices being removed are associated with no-ops when the link state change event list is processed, so the result is that the event list is cleared and only events for other devices are actually processed. This is just an easy way to clean up the link state change queue from events associated with a device about to disappear.

Enabling and Disabling a Network Device

Once a device has been registered it is available for use, but it will not transmit and receive traffic until it is explicitly enabled by the user (or a user-space application). Requests to enable a device are taken care of by dev_open, defined in *net/core/dev.c*. Enabling a device consists of the following tasks:

* Call dev->open if it is defined. Not all device drivers initialize this function.
* Set the __LINK_STATE_START flag in dev->state to mark the device as up and running.

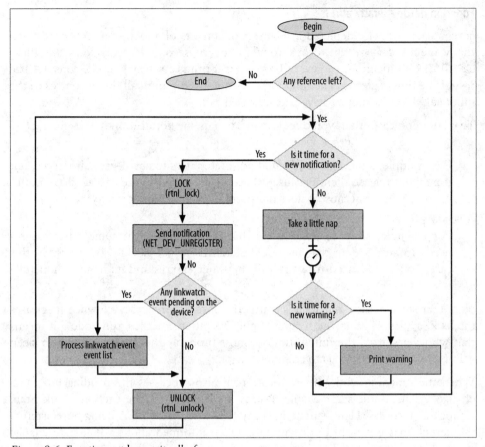

Figure 8-6. Function netdev_wait_allrefs

- Set the IFF_UP flag in dev->flags to mark the device as up.

- Call dev_activate to initialize the egress queuing discipline used by Traffic Control, and start the watchdog timer.* If there is no user configuration for Traffic Control, assign a default First In, First Out (FIFO) queue.

- Send a NETDEV_UP notification to the netdev_chain notification chain to notify interested kernel components that the device is now enabled.

While a device needs to be explicitly enabled, it can be disabled either explicitly by a user command or implicitly by other events. For example, before a device is unregistered, it is first disabled (see the section "Device Unregistration"). Network devices are disabled with dev_close. Disabling a device consists of the following tasks:

- Send a NETDEV_GOING_DOWN notification to the netdev_chain notification chain to notify interested kernel components that the device is about to be disabled.

---

* See Chapter 11 for more details on the watchdog timer.

- Call `dev_deactivate` to disable the egress queuing discipline, thus making sure the device cannot be used for transmission anymore, and stop the watchdog timer because it is not needed anymore.
- Clear the `__LINK_STATE_START` flag in `dev->state` to mark the device as down.
- If a polling action was scheduled to read ingress packets on the device, wait for that action to complete. Because the `__LINK_STATE_START` flag has been cleared, no more receive polling will be scheduled on the device, but one could have been pending before the flag was cleared. See Chapter 10 for more detail on receive polling.
- Call `dev->stop` if it is defined. Not all device drivers initialize this function.
- Clear the `IFF_UP` flag in `dev->flags` to mark the device as down.
- Send a `NETDEV_DOWN` notification to the `netdev_chain` notification chain to notify interested kernel components that the device is now disabled.

Updating the Device Queuing Discipline State

We saw in the section "Queuing Discipline State" which flags can be set in `dev->state` to define the device queuing discipline state. In this section, we will see how two of those flags are used to handle power management and link state changes.

Interactions with Power Management

When the kernel has support for power management, NIC device drivers can be notified when the system goes into suspend mode, when it is resumed, etc. We saw in the section "Example of PCI NIC Driver Registration" in Chapter 6 how the `suspend` and `resume` function pointers of the `pci_driver` structures are initialized depending on whether the kernel has support for power management. This is, for example, how the *drivers/net/3c59x.c* device driver initializes its `pci_driver` instance:

```
static struct pci_driver vortex_driver = {
    .name        "3c59x",
    .probe       vortex_init_one,
    .remove      __devexit_p(vortex_remove_one),
    .id_table    vortex_pci_tbl,
#ifdef CONFIG_PM
    .suspend     vortex_suspend,
    .resume      vortex_resume,
#endif
};
```

When the system goes into suspend mode, the `suspend` routines provided by device drivers are executed to let drivers take action accordingly. Power management state changes do not affect the registration status `dev->reg_state`, but the device state `dev->state` needs to be changed.

Suspending a device

When a device is suspended, its device driver handles the event, by calling, for example, the pci_driver's suspend routine for PCI devices. Besides the driver-specific actions, a few additional actions must be performed by every device driver:

- Clear the __LINK_STATE_PRESENT flag from dev->state because the device is temporarily not going to be operational.
- If the device was enabled, disable its egress queue with netif_stop_queue* to prevent the device from being used to transmit any other packet. Note that a device that is registered is not necessarily enabled: when a device is recognized, it gets assigned to its device driver by the kernel and is registered; however, the device will not be enabled (and therefore usable) until an explicit user configuration requests it.

These tasks are succinctly implemented by netif_device_detach:

```
static inline void netif_device_detach(struct net_device *dev)
{
    if (test_and_clear_bit(__LINK_STATE_PRESENT, &dev->state) &&
        netif_running(dev)) {
        netif_stop_queue(dev);
    }
}
```

Resuming a device

When a device is resumed, its device driver handles the event, by calling, for example, the pci_driver's resume routine for PCI devices. Again, a few tasks are shared by all device drivers:

- Set the __LINK_STATE_PRESENT flag in dev->state because the device is now available again.
- If the device was enabled before being suspended, re-enable its egress queue with netif_wake_queue, and restart a watchdog timer used by Traffic Control (see the section "Watchdog timer" in Chapter 11).

These tasks are implemented by netif_device_attach:

```
static inline void netif_device_attach(struct net_device *dev)
{
    if (!test_and_set_bit(__LINK_STATE_PRESENT, &dev->state) &&
        netif_running(dev)) {
        netif_wake_queue(dev);
        __netdev_watchdog_up(dev);
    }
}
```

---

* See Chapter 11 for more detail on the routines used to start, stop, and restart the egress queue.

Link State Change Detection

When an NIC device driver detects the presence or absence of a carrier or signal, either because it was notified by the NIC or via an explicit check by reading a configuration register on the NIC, it can notify the kernel with netif_carrier_on and netif_carrier_off, respectively. These routines are to be called when there is a change in the carrier status; therefore, they do nothing when they are invoked inappropriately.

Here are a few common cases that may lead to a link state change:

- A cable is plugged into or unplugged from an NIC.
- The device at the other end of the cable is powered down or disabled. Examples of devices include hubs, bridges, routers, and PC NICs.

When netif_carrier_on is called by a device driver that has detected the carrier on one of its devices, the function:

- Clears the __LINK_STATE_NOCARRIER flag from dev->state.
- Generates a link state change event and submits it for processing with linkwatch_fire_event. See the section "Scheduling and processing link state change events."
- If the device was enabled, starts a watchdog timer. The timer is used by Traffic Control to detect whether a transmission fails and gets stuck (in which case the timer times out). See the section "Watchdog timer" in Chapter 11.

```
static inline netif_carrier_on(struct net_device *dev)
{
    if (test_and_clear_bit(__LINK_STATE_NOCARRIER, &dev->state))
        linkwatch_fire_event(dev);
    if (netif_running(dev)
        __netdev_watchdog_up(dev);
}
```

When netif_carrier_off is called by a device driver that has detected the loss of a carrier from one of its devices, the function:

- Sets the __LINK_STATE_NOCARRIER flag in dev->state.
- Generates a link state change event and submits it for processing with linkwatch_fire_event. See the section "Scheduling and processing link state change events."

Note that both routines generate a link state change event and submit it for processing with linkwatch_fire_event, described in the next section.

```
static inline netif_carrier_off(struct net_device *dev)
{
    if (!test_and_set_bit(__LINK_STATE_NOCARRIER, &dev->state))
        linkwatch_fire_event(dev);
}
```

Scheduling and processing link state change events

Link state change events are defined with lw_event structures. It's a pretty simple structure: it includes just a pointer to the associated net_device structure and another field used to link the structure to the global list of pending link state change events, lweventlist. The list is protected by the lweventlist_lock lock.

Note that the lw_event structure does not include any parameter to distinguish between detection and loss of carrier. This is because no differentiation is needed. All the kernel needs to know is that there was a change in the link status, so a reference to the device is sufficient. There will never be more than one lw_event instance in lweventlist for any device, because there's no reason to record a history or track changes: either the link is operational or it isn't, so the link state is either on or off. Two state changes equal no change, three changes equal one, etc., so new events are not queued when the device already has a pending link state change event. The condition can be detected by checking the __LINK_STATE_LINKWATCH_PENDING flag in dev->state, as shown in the flowchart in Figure 8-7.

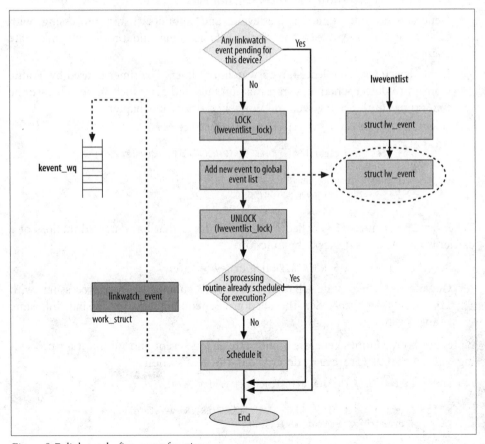

Figure 8-7. linkwatch_fire_event function

Once the lw_event data structure has been initialized with a reference to the right net_device instance and it has been added to the lweventlist list, and the __LINK_STATE_LINKWATCH_PENDING flag has been set in dev->state, linkwatch_fire_event needs to launch the routine that will actually process the elements on the lweventlist list. This routine, linkwatch_event, is not called directly. It is scheduled for execution by submitting a request to the keventd_wq kernel thread: a work_struct data structure is initialized with a reference to the linkwatch_event routine and is submitted to keventd_wq.

To avoid having the processing routine linkwatch_event run too often, its execution is rate limited to once per second.

linkwatch_event processes the elements of the lweventlist list with linkwatch_run_queue, under the protection of the rtnl lock described in the section "Locking." Processing lw_event instances consists simply of:

- Clearing the __LINK_STATE_LINKWATCH_PENDING flag on dev->state.
- Sending a NETDEV_CHANGE notification on the netdev_chain notification chain
- Sending an RTM_NEWLINK notification to the RTMGRP_LINK RTnetlink group. See the section "RTnetlink link notifications."

The two notifications are sent with netdev_state_change, but only when the device is enabled (dev->flags & IFF_UP): no one cares about link state changes on disabled devices.

Linkwatch flags

The code in *net/core/linkwatch.c* defines two flags that can be set in the global variable linkwatch_flags:

LW_RUNNING

> When this flag is set, linkwatch_event has been scheduled for execution. The flag is cleared by linkwatch_event itself.

LW_SE_USED

> Because lweventlist usually has at most one element, the code optimizes lw_event data structure allocations by statically allocating one and always using it as the first element of the list. Only when the kernel needs to keep track of more than one pending event (events on more than one device) does it allocate additional lw_event structures; otherwise, it simply recycles the same one.

Configuring Device-Related Information from User Space

Different tools can be used to configure or dump the current status of media and hardware parameters for network devices. Among them are:

- *ifconfig* and *mii-tool*, from the *net-tools* package
- *ethtool*, from the *ethtool* package
- *ip link*, from the *IPROUTE2* package

You can refer to the associated manpages for details on the syntax of those commands. The section "Ethtool" describes the interface between *ethtool* and the kernel, and the section "Media Independent Interface (MII)" describes the interface between *mii-tool* and the kernel. Later chapters return to the *ifconfig* and *ip* commands for the L3 configuration.

Figure 8-8 is a high-level overview of what we will cover in these sections. The figure does not show the locking details. Suffice it to say that both dev_ethtool and the call to dev->do_ioctl are protected with the routing Netlink lock (see the section "Locking").

Ethtool

This section gives an overview of *ethtool* along with its relationship to *mii-tool* and the do_ioctl function pointer in net_device.

The net_device data structure includes a pointer to a VFT of type ethtool_ops. The latter structure is a collection of function pointers that can be used to both read and initialize a bunch of parameters on the net_device structure, or to trigger an action (i.e., restart auto-negotiation).

Not all device drivers currently support this feature; and those that do support it don't always support all of its functions. The initialization of dev->ethtool_ops is normally done in the probe routine introduced at the beginning of the chapter.

The interface between user space and the functions is the old ioctl system call. Figure 8-8 shows how the user-space command *ethtool* ends up invoking dev_ethtool on the kernel side. The figure also shows the skeleton of dev_ethtool, and how this function interfaces to the generic Media Independent Interface Kernel library. We will address the last point in the section "Media Independent Interface (MII)."

Without going into too much detail on how the kernel dispatches ioctl commands to the right handlers, I'll just say that the request first arrives to inet_ioctl, which invokes dev_ioctl, which ends up calling dev_ethtool. (You can browse the code and see how it works step by step; the code is pretty clear.)

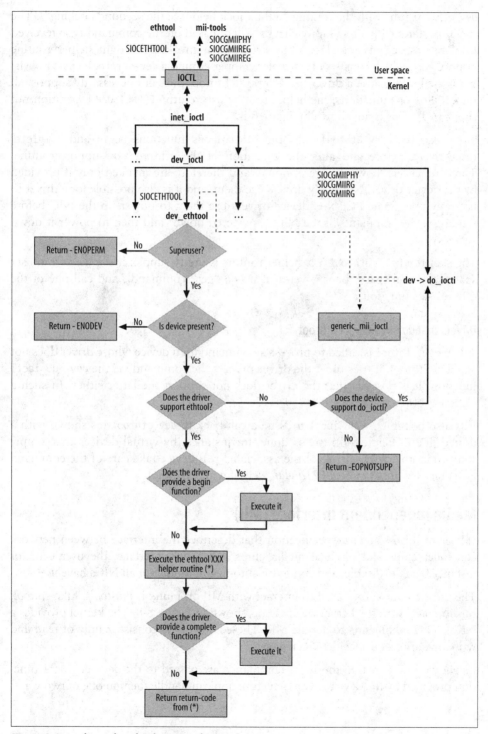

Figure 8-8. ioctl interface for device configuration

dev_ethtool runs with the routing Netlink lock held (see the section "Locking"). The function starts with a few sanity checks. Then, based on the command type received from user space via an ifreq data structure, it invokes the right helper routine ethtool_*xxx*, which consists of a simple wrapper around a dev->ethtool_ops->*xxx* virtual function. Because a driver that supports Ethtool does not necessarily support all the ethtool_ops functions, the helper routine can return −EOPNOTSUPP (operation not supported). This is not shown in Figure 8-8.

Note also that dev_ethtool calls the ethtool_ops functions begin and complete, respectively, before and after the execution of the ethtool_*xxx* support routine. Those functions, however, are optional, and therefore are invoked only if provided by the device driver. Not many drivers use them, and it is also possible for a driver to use only one. Some PCI NIC device drivers use them to power up the NIC before sending it the command (if the NIC is powered down) and then to power it down again.

The skeleton of an ethtool_*xxx* helper routine is pretty simple: move data from user space to kernel space (or vice versa, if it is a "get" command), and call one of the ethtool_ops functions.

Drivers that do not support ethtool

When dev_ethtool is called to process a command for a device whose driver does not support Ethtool, it tries to let the driver process the command via the dev->do_ioctl function. It is possible that the driver does not support the latter either. In such a case, dev_ethtool returns -EOPNOTSUPP.

It is also possible for do_ioctl to issue a call back to dev_ethtool (as shown with a dotted line in Figure 8-8): this is done, for instance, by virtual devices that simply want to let the device driver of the associated real device take care of the command (see vlan_dev_ioctl in *net/8021q/vlan_dev.c* for an example).

Media Independent Interface (MII)

MII is an IEEE standard specification that describes the interface between network controller chips and physical media chips. With this interface, the user can, for instance, enable, disable, and configure auto-negotiation. Not all NICs have it.

The most common tool used to interact with MII on Linux is *mii-tools*. Like *ethtool*, this interacts with the kernel via ioctl, as shown in Figure 8-8. The kernel provides a set of ioctl commands to handle MII. These commands consist mainly of read and write operations on specific NIC registers.

As shown in Figure 8-8, the ioctl commands are passed to the dev->do_ioctl function provided by the device driver. The function can handle them in one of two ways:

- Recognize only the three MII ioctl commands and process them with device driver code. This is the most common case.
- Rely on the kernel MII library *drivers/net/mii.c* by processing the input command with `generic_mii_ioctl`.

It is also possible, especially for virtual devices, to have `dev->do_ioctl` functions that recognize and process other commands besides the MII ones.

The following is a common model for the `dev->do_ioclt` function for those drivers that rely on the kernel MII library and do not implement special commands:

```
if (!netif_running(dev)) {
    return -EINVAL;
}
<lock private data structure>
err = generic_mii_ioctl(...);
<unlock private data structure>
return err;
```

Note in Figure 8-8 that an *ethtool* command may end up invoking a routine from the MII kernel library (for example, to restart auto-negotiation).

Virtual Devices

In the section "Virtual Devices" in Chapter 5, we saw how virtual devices differ from real ones with regard to initialization. As far as registration is concerned, virtual devices need to be registered and enabled just like real ones, to be used. However, there are differences:

- Virtual devices sometimes call `register_netdevice` and `unregister_netdevice` rather than their wrappers, and take care of locking by themselves. They may need to handle locking to keep the lock for a little longer than a real device does. With this approach, the lock could also be misused and hold longer than needed, by making it protect additional pieces of code (besides `register_netdev`) that could be protected in other ways.
- Real devices cannot be unregistered (i.e., destroyed) with user commands; they can only be disabled. Real devices are unregistered at the time their drivers are unloaded (when loaded as modules, of course). Virtual devices, in contrast, may be created and unregistered with user commands, too. Whether this is possible depends on the virtual device driver's design.

We also saw in the sections "register_netdevice Function" and "Device Unregistration" that virtual devices, unlike most real ones, use `dev->init`, `dev->uninit`, and `dev->destructor`. Because most virtual devices implement some kind of more or less complex logic on top of real devices, they use `dev->init` and `dev->uninit` to take care of extra initialization and cleanup. `dev->destructor` is often initialized to `free_netdev` (as shown in Figure 8-4) so that the driver does not need to explicitly call the latter function after unregistration.

We saw in the section "Device Initialization" how the initialization of net_device structures is split between the device driver's probe routine and generic setup routines. Because virtual devices do not have a probe routine, the classification in Tables 8-2 and 8-3 does not apply to them.

Virtual device drivers register to the netdev_chain notification chain described in the section "Device Registration Status Notification" because most virtual devices are defined on top of real devices, so changes to real devices affect virtual ones, too. Let's see two examples:

Bonding

Bonding is a virtual device that allows you to bundle a set of interfaces and make them look like a single one. Traffic can be distributed between the set of interfaces using different algorithms, one of which is a simple round robin. Let's take the example in Figure 8-9(a). When *eth0* goes down, the bonding interface *bond0* needs to know about it to take it into account when distributing traffic between the real devices. In case *eth1* went down too, *bond0* would have to be disabled because there would not be any working real device left.

VLAN interfaces

Linux supports the 802.1Q protocol and allows you to define Virtual LAN (VLAN) interfaces. Consider the example in Figure 8-9(b), where the user has defined two VLAN interfaces on *eth0*. When *eth0* goes down, all virtual (VLAN) interfaces must go down, too.

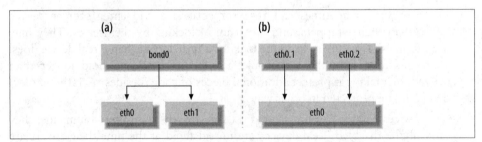

Figure 8-9. a) Bonding interface b) VLAN interfaces

Locking

We saw in the section "Organization of net_device Structures" that the dev_base list and the two hash tables dev_name_head and dev_name_index are protected by the dev_base_list lock. That lock, however, is used only to serialize accesses to the list and tables, not to serialize changes to the contents of net_device data structures. net_device content changes are taken care of by the Routing Netlink semaphore (rtnl_sem), which is acquired and released with rtnl_lock and rtnl_unlock, respectively.[*] This semaphore is used to serialize changes to net_device instances from:

Runtime events
> For example, when the link state changes (e.g., a network cable is plugged or unplugged), the kernel needs to change the device state by modifying dev->flags.

Configuration changes
> When the user applies a configuration change with commands such as *ifconfig* and *route* from the *net-tools* package, or *ip* from the *IPROUTE2* package, the kernel is notified via ioctl commands and the Netlink socket, respectively. The routines invoked via these interfaces must use locks.

The net_device data structure includes a few fields used for locking, among them:

ingress_lock
queue_lock
> Used by Traffic Control when dealing with ingress and egress traffic scheduling, respectively.

xmit_lock
xmit_lock_owner
> Used to synchronize accesses to the device driver hard_start_xmit function.

For more details on these locks, please refer to Chapter 11.

Tuning via /proc Filesystem

There are no files in */proc* that can be used to tune the device registration and unregistration tasks.

---

[*] Other routines can also be used to acquire and release the semaphore. See *include/linux/rtnetlink.h* for more details.

Functions and Variables Featured in This Chapter

Table 8-4 summarizes the functions, data structures, and variables introduced in this chapter.

Table 8-4. Functions, data structures, and variables introduced in this chapter

Name	Description
Functions	
alloc_netdev alloc_*xxx*dev wrappers	Allocate and partially initialize a net_device structure.
free_netdev	Frees a net_device structure.
dev_alloc_name	Completes a device name.
register_netdevice, register_netdev unregister_netdevice, unregister_netdev	Register and unregister a network device. The *xxx*_netdev APIs are wrappers for the *xxx*_netdevice APIs.
*xxx*_setup	Helper routines used to initialize part of the net_device structure. There is one for each of the most common interface types.
dev_hold dev_put	Increment and decrement the reference count on a net_device structure.
netif_carrier_on netif_carrier_off netif_carrier_ok	Called when the carrier on a device is detected, lost, or to be read, respectively.
netif_device_attach netif_device_detach	Called when a device is plugged into and unplugged from the system, respectively. Called also when the system goes into suspend mode and then resumes.
netif_start_queue netif_stop_queue netif_queue_stopped	Called to start, stop, and check the status of the device egress queue, respectively.
dev_ethtool	Processes ioctl commands from the ethtool user-space command.
Variables	
dev_base dev_name_head dev_index_head dev_base_lock	dev_base is a flat list of registered network devices. dev_*xxx*_head are two hash tables for net_device structures, indexed on the device's name and ID. The previous three structures are protected by the dev_base_lock lock.
lweventlist lweventlist_lock	lweventlist is a list of pending lw_event events. The list is protected by lweventlist_lock.
Data structure	
lw_event	Link state change event.

Files and Directories Featured in This Chapter

Figure 8-10 shows where the files and directories mentioned in this chapter are located in the kernel source tree.

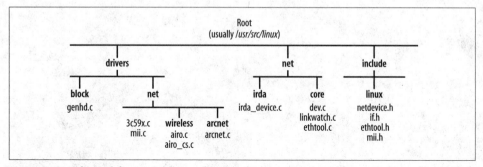

Figure 8-10. Files and directories featured in this chapter

## PART III

Transmission and Reception

The aim of these five chapters is to put into context all the features that can influence the path of a packet inside the kernel, and to give you an idea of the big picture. You will see what each subsystem is supposed to do and when it comes into the picture. This chapter will not touch upon routing, which has a large chapter of its own, or firewalling, which is beyond the scope of this book.

In general usage, the term *transmission* is often used to refer to communications in any direction. But in kernel discussions, transmission refers only to sending frames outward, whereas reception refers to frames coming in. In some places, I use the terms *ingress* for reception and *egress* for transmission.

Forwarded packets—which both originate and terminate in remote systems but use the local system for routing—constitute yet another category that combines elements of reception and transmission. Some aspects of forwarding are presented in Chapter 10; a more thorough discussion appears in Parts V and VII.

We saw in Chapter 1 the difference between the terms *frame, datagram,* and *packet.* Because the chapters in Part III discuss the interface between L2 and L3, both the terms *frame* and *packet* would be correct in most cases. Even though I'll mostly use the term *frame*, I may sometimes use *packet* when referring to a data unit with no reference to any particular layer. The word *packet* is the one most commonly seen in the code we are discussing.

Here is what we will see in each chapter of Part III:

Chapter 9, *Interrupts and Network Drivers*
  In this chapter, you will be given an overview on both bottom half handlers and kernel synchronization mechanisms.

Chapter 10, *Frame Reception*
  This chapter goes on to describe the path through the L2 layer of a received frame.

Chapter 11, *Frame Transmission*
   Chapter 11 does the same as Chapter 10, but for a transmitted (outgoing) frame.

Chapter 12, *General and Reference Material About Interrupts*
   This is a repository of reference material for the previous chapters.

Chapter 13, *Protocol Handlers*
   This chapter will conclude this part of the book with a discussion of how ingress frames are handed to the right L3 protocol receive routines.

## CHAPTER 9

Interrupts and Network Drivers

The previous chapters gave an overview of how the initialization of core components in the networking code is taken care of. The remainder of the book offers a feature-by-feature or subsystem-by-subsystem analysis of how networking is implemented, why features were introduced, and, when meaningful, how they interact with each other.

This chapter begins an explanation of how packets travel between the L2 or driver layer and the IP or network layer described in detail in Part V. I'll be referring a lot to the data structures introduced in Chapters 2 and 8, so you should be ready to turn back to those chapters as needed.

Even before the kernel is ready to handle the frame that is coming from or going to the L2 layer, it must deal with the subtle and complex system of interrupts set up to make the handling of thousands of frames per second possible. That is the subject of this chapter.

A couple of other general issues affect the discussion in this chapter:

- When the Linux kernel is compiled with support for symmetric multiprocessing (SMP) and runs on a multiprocessor system, the code for receiving and transmitting packets takes full advantage of that power. The data structures involved are designed with that goal in mind. In this chapter, we will look at one aspect of SMP support in particular: the differences between the new softirq queues and the old backlog queue.

- When talking about the ingress path, I will cover both the old interface, which is still used by most network drivers, and the new interface, called NAPI, which can significantly increase performance under medium to high loads.

In this chapter, you will be given an overview on both bottom half handlers and kernel synchronization mechanisms. However, for a more detailed discussion, you can refer to the other two O'Reilly books, *Understanding the Linux Kernel* and *Linux Device Drivers*.

Decisions and Traffic Direction

The paths taken by packets through the network stack differ for received, transmitted, and forwarded packets (see Figure 9-1). Differences in processing also depend on the features compiled into the kernel and how they are configured. Finally, the devices involved can make a difference because different devices support different features.

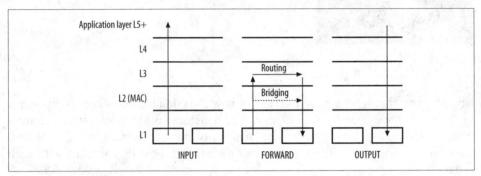

Figure 9-1. Traffic directions

Virtual devices, such as the familiar loopback interface (lo), tend to use shortcuts inside the network stack. These devices are software only. For instance, the loopback interface is not associated with any piece of hardware, but bonding interfaces are associated indirectly with one or more network cards. Some virtual interfaces can therefore dispense with some of the limitations found with hardware (such as the Maximum Transmission Unit, or MTU) and thus speed up performance.

Figure 9-2 gives an idea of the big picture. It is certainly very sketchy; for instance, it the does not show all of the conditions that can lead to dropping a frame.* The figure includes extra details about the ingress path; you can find more detailed graphs about the egress path in Parts V, VI, and VII. We will go through all the links that should be part of the graph in the rest of this chapter.

Notifying Drivers When Frames Are Received

In Chapter 5, I mentioned that devices and the kernel can use two main techniques for exchanging data: polling and interrupts. I also said that a combination of the two is also a valid option. This section offers a brief overview of the most common ways for a driver to notify the kernel about the reception of a frame, along with the main

---

* Frames can be dropped for a variety of reasons: no memory in the input queue, no memory in the output queue (only for forwarded or transmitted frames), no route to destination, firewall policy, a failed sanity check, etc.

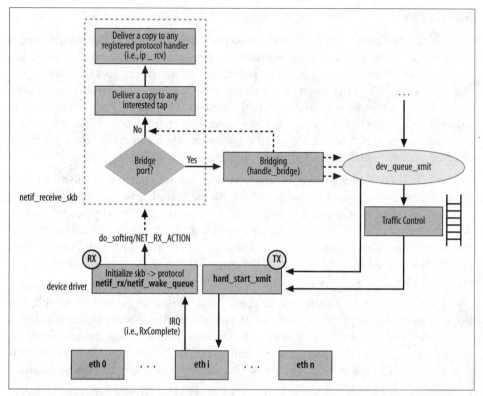

Figure 9-2. Ingress path (frame reception)

pros and cons for each one. Some approaches depend on the availability of specific features on the devices (such as ad hoc timers), and some need changes to the driver, the operating system, or both.

This discussion could theoretically apply to any device type, but it best describes those devices like network cards that can generate a high number of interactions (that is, the reception of frames).

Polling

With this technique, the kernel constantly keeps checking whether the device has anything to say. It can do that by continually reading a memory register on the device, for instance, or returning to check it when a timer expires. As you can imagine, this approach can easily waste quite a lot of system resources, and is rarely employed if the operating system and device can use other techniques such as interrupts. Still, there are cases where polling is the best approach. We will come back to this point later.

Interrupts

Here the device driver, on behalf of the kernel, instructs the device to generate a hardware interrupt when specific events occur. The kernel, interrupted from its other activities, will then invoke a handler registered by the driver to take care of the device's needs. When the event is the reception of a frame, the handler queues the frame somewhere and notifies the kernel about it. This technique, which is quite common, still represents the best option under low traffic loads. Unfortunately, it does not perform well under high traffic loads: forcing an interrupt for each frame received can easily make the CPU waste all of its time handling interrupts.

The code that takes care of an input frame is split into two parts: first the driver copies the frame into an input queue accessible by the kernel, and then the kernel processes it (usually passing it to a handler dedicated to the associated protocol such as IP). The first part is executed in interrupt context and can preempt the execution of the second part. This means that the code that accepts input frames and copies them into the queue has higher priority than the code that actually processes the frames.

Under a high traffic load, the interrupt code would keep preempting the processing code. The consequence is obvious: at some point the input queue will be full, but since the code that is supposed to dequeue and process those frames does not have a chance to run due to its lower priority, the system collapses. New frames cannot be queued since there is no space, and old frames cannot be processed because there is no CPU available for them. This condition is called *receive-livelock* in the literature.

In summary, this technique has the advantage of very low latency between the reception of the frame and its processing, but does not work well under high loads. Most network drivers use interrupts, and a large section later in this chapter will discuss how they work.

Processing Multiple Frames During an Interrupt

This approach is used by quite a few Linux device drivers. When an interrupt is notified and the driver handler is executed, the latter keeps downloading frames and queuing them to the kernel input queue, up to a maximum number of frames (or a window of time). Of course, it would be possible to keep doing that until the queue gets empty, but let's remember that device drivers should behave as good citizens. They have to share the CPU with other subsystems and IRQ lines with other devices. Polite behavior is especially important because interrupts are disabled while the driver handler is running.

Storage limitations also apply, as they did in the previous section. Each device has a limited amount of memory, and therefore the number of frames it can store is limited. If the driver does not process them in a timely manner, the buffers can get full and new frames (or old ones, depending on the driver policies) could be dropped. If a loaded device kept processing incoming frames until its queue emptied out, this form of starvation could happen to other devices.

This technique does not require any change to the operating system; it is implemented entirely within the device driver.

There could be other variations to this approach. Instead of keeping all interrupts disabled and having the driver queue frames for the kernel to handle, a driver could disable interrupts only for a device that has frames in its ingress queue and delegate the task of polling the driver's queue to a kernel handler. This is exactly what Linux does with its new interface, NAPI. However, unlike the approach described in this section, NAPI requires changes to the kernel.

Timer-Driven Interrupts

This technique is an enhancement to the previous ones. Instead of having the device asynchronously notify the driver about frame receptions, the driver instructs the device to generate an interrupt at regular intervals. The handler will then check if any frames have arrived since the previous interrupt, and handles all of them in one shot. Even better would be to have the driver generate interrupts at intervals, but only if it has something to say.

Based on the granularity of the timer (which is implemented in hardware by the device itself; it is not a kernel timer), the frames that are received by the device will experience different levels of latency. For instance, if the device generated an interrupt every 100 ms, the notification of the reception of a frame would have an average delay of 50 ms and a maximum one of 100 ms. This delay may or may not be acceptable depending on the applications running on top of the network connections using the device.*

The granularity available to a driver depends on what the device has to offer, since the timer is implemented in hardware. Only a few devices provide this capability currently, so this solution is not available for all the drivers in the Linux kernel. One could simulate that capability by disabling interrupts for the device and using a kernel timer instead. However, one would not have the support of the hardware, and the CPU cannot spend as much of its resources as the device can on handling timers, so one would not be able to schedule the timers nearly as often. This workaround would, in the end, become a polling approach.

---

* This discussion applies mainly to Ethernet devices, which already do not guarantee an upper bound on the transmission time (and therefore on the reception) because of the congestion algorithm they use.

Combinations

Each approach described in the previous sections has some advantages and disadvantages. Sometimes, it is possible to combine them and obtain something even better. We said that under low load, the pure interrupt model guarantees a low latency, but that under high load it performs terribly. On the other hand, the timer-driven interrupt may introduce too much latency and waste too much CPU time under low load, but it helps a lot in reducing the CPU usage and solving the receive-livelock problem under high load. A good combination would use the interrupt technique under low load and switch to the timer-driven interrupt under high load. The tulip driver included in the Linux kernel, for instance, can do this (see *drivers/net/tulip/interrupt.c*[*]).

Example

A balanced approach to processing multiple frames is shown in the following piece of code, taken from the *drivers/net/3c59x.c* Ethernet driver. It is a selection of key lines from vortex_interrupt, the function registered by the driver as the handler of interrupts from devices in 3Com's Vortex family:

```
static irqreturn_t vortex_interrupt(int irq, void *dev_id, struct pt_regs *regs)
{
    int work_done = max_interrupt_work;
    ioaddr = dev->base_addr;
    ... ... ...
    status = inw(ioaddr + EL3_STATUS);
    do {
        ... ... ...
        if (status & RxComplete)
            vortex_rx(dev);
        if (--work_done < 0) {
            /* Disable all pending interrupts. */
            ... ... ...
            /* The timer will re-enable interrupts. */
            mod_timer(&vp->timer, jiffies + 1*HZ);
            break;
        }
        ... ... ...
    } while ((status = inw(ioaddr + EL3_STATUS)) & (IntLatch | RxComplete));
    ... ... ...
}
```

Other drivers that follow the same model will have something very similar. They probably will call the EL3_STATUS and RxComplete symbols something different, and their implementation of an *xxx*_rx function may be different, but the skeleton will be very close to the one shown here.

---

[*] This is not a trivial driver. Going through the other three chapters of this part of the book first is advisable.

In vortex_interrupt, the driver reads from the device the reasons for the interrupt and stores it into status. Network devices can generate an interrupt for different reasons, and several reasons can be grouped together in a single interrupt. If RxComplete (a symbol specially defined by this driver to mean a new frame has been received) is among those reasons, the code invokes vortex_rx.* During its execution, interrupts are disabled for the device. However, the driver can read a hardware register on the card and find out if in the meantime, a new interrupt was posted. The IntLatch flag is true when a new interrupt has been posted (and it is cleared by the driver when it is done processing it).

vortex_interrupt keeps processing incoming frames until the register says there is an interrupt pending (IntLatch) and that it is due to the reception of a frame (RxComplete). This also means that only multiple occurrences of RxComplete interrupts can be handled in one shot. Other types of interrupts, which are much less frequent, can wait.

Finally—here is where good citizenship enters—the loop terminates if it reaches the maximum number of input frames that can be processed, stored in work_done. This driver uses a default value of 32 and allows that value to be tuned at module load time.

Interrupt Handlers

A good deal of the frame handling we discuss in this chapter takes place in response to interrupts from network hardware. The scheduling of functions triggered by interrupts is a complicated topic and deserves some study, even though it doesn't concern networking in particular. Therefore, in this section, we discuss the various ways that interrupts are handled by different network drivers and introduce the concepts of bottom halves and softirqs.

In Chapter 5, we saw how device drivers register their handlers with an IRQ number, but we did not see how hardware interrupts delegate frame processing to software interrupt handlers. This section will describe how an interrupt request associated with the reception of a frame is handled all the way to the point where protocol handlers discussed in Chapter 13 receive their packets. We will see the relationship between hardware IRQs and software IRQs and why the latter category is needed. We will briefly see how interrupts were handled with the old kernels and then compare the old approach to the new one introduced with kernel version 2.4. This discussion will show the advantages of the new model over the old one, especially in the area of performance.

---

* vortex_rx is passed the device as an input parameter because a device driver can handle more instances of the same device type or family. Therefore, when it is invoked it needs to know which device it is dealing with.

Before launching into softirqs, we need a small introduction to the concept of bottom half handlers. However, I will not go into much detail about them because they are documented in other resources, notably *Understanding the Linux Kernel* and *Linux Device Drivers*.

Reasons for Bottom Half Handlers

Whenever a CPU receives an interrupt notification, it invokes the handler associated with that interrupt, which is identified by a number. During the handler's execution—in which the kernel code is said to be in *interrupt context*—interrupts are disabled for the CPU serving the interrupt. This means that if a CPU is busy serving one interrupt, it cannot receive other interrupts, whether of the same type or of different types.* Nor can the CPU execute any other process: it belongs totally to the interrupt handler and cannot be preempted.

In the simplest situation, these are the main events touched off by an interrupt:

1. The device generates an interrupt and the hardware notifies the kernel.

2. If the kernel is not serving another interrupt (and if interrupts are not disabled for other reasons) it will see the notification.

3. The kernel disables interrupts for the local CPU and executes the handler associated with the interrupt type received.

4. The kernel exits the interrupt handler and re-enables interrupts for the local CPU.

In short, interrupt handlers are nonpreemptible and non-reentrant. (A function is defined as non-reentrant when it cannot be interrupted by another invocation of itself. In the case of interrupt handlers, it simply means that they are executed with interrupts disabled.) This design choice helps reduce the likelihood of race conditions. However, because the CPU is so limited in what it can do, the nonpreemptible design has potentially serious effects on performance by the kernel as well as the processes waiting to be served by the CPU.

Therefore, the work done by interrupt handlers should be as quick as possible. The amount of processing needed by the interrupt handlers during interrupt context depends on the type of event. A keyboard, for instance, may simply send an interrupt every time a key is pressed, which requires very little effort to be handled: the handler simply needs to store the code of the key somewhere, and run a few times per second at most. At other times, the actions required to handle an interrupt are not trivial and their executions could require much CPU time. Network devices, for instance, have a relatively complex job: they need to allocate a buffer (sk_buff), copy

---

* We saw in Chapter 5 that an interrupt handler that is declared as a slow handler is executed with the interrupts enabled on the local CPU.

the received data into it, initialize a few parameters within the buffer structure (protocol) to tell the higher-layer protocol handlers what kind of data is coming from the driver, and so on.

Here is where the concept of a *bottom half* handler comes into play. Even if the action triggered by an interrupt needs a lot of CPU time, most of this action can usually wait. Interrupts are allowed to preempt the CPU in the first place because if the operating system makes the hardware wait too long, it may lose data. This is obviously true of real-time streaming data, but also is true of any hardware that has to store incoming data in fixed-size buffers. And if the hardware loses data, there is usually no way to get it back.

On the other hand, if the kernel or a user-space process has to be delayed or preempted, no data will be lost (with the exception of real-time systems, which entail a completely different way of handling processes as well as interrupts). In light of these considerations, modern interrupt handlers are divided into a top half and a bottom half. The top half consists of everything that has to be executed before releasing the CPU, to preserve data. The bottom half contains everything that can be done at relative leisure.

One can define a bottom half as an asynchronous request to execute a particular function. Normally, when you want to execute a function, you do not have to request anything—you simply invoke it. When an interrupt arrives, you have a lot to do and don't want to do it right away. Thus, you package most of the work into a function that you submit as a bottom half.

The following model allows the kernel to keep interrupts disabled for much less time than the simple model shown previously:

1. The device signals the CPU to notify it of the interrupt.
2. The CPU executes the associated top half, disabling further interrupt notifications until this handler has finished its job.
3. Typically, a top half performs the following:
   a. It saves somewhere in RAM all the information that the kernel will need later to process the interrupt event.
   b. It marks a flag somewhere (or triggers something using another kernel mechanism) to make sure the kernel will know about the interrupt and will use the data saved by the handler to complete the event processing.
   c. Before terminating, it re-enables the interrupt notifications for the local CPU.
4. At some later point, when the kernel is free of more pressing matters, it checks the flag set by the interrupt handler (signaling the presence of data to be processed) and calls the associated bottom half handler. It also clears the flag so that it can later recognize when the interrupt handler sets the flag again.

Over time, Linux developers have tried different types of bottom halves, which obey different rules. Networking has played a large role in the development of new implementations, because of networking's need for low latency—that is, a minimal amount of time between the reception of a frame and its delivery. Low latency is more important for network device drivers than for other types of devices because of the high number of tasks involved in reception and transmission. As described earlier in the section "Interrupts," it can be disastrous to let a large number of frames build up while waiting to be handled. Sound cards are another example of devices requiring fast response.

Bottom Halves Solutions

The kernel provides different mechanism for implementing bottom halves and for deferring work in general. These mechanisms differ mainly with regard to the following points:

Running context
> Interrupts are seen by the kernel as having a different running context from user-space processes or other kernel code. When the function executed by a bottom half is capable of going to sleep, it is restricted to mechanisms allowed in process context, as opposed to interrupt context.

Concurrency and locking
> When a mechanism can take advantage of SMP, this has implications for how serialization is enforced (if necessary) and how locking influences scalability.

In this chapter, we will look only at those mechanisms that do not need a process context—namely, softirqs and tasklets. In the next section, we will briefly see their implications for concurrency and locking.

When you need to defer the execution of a function that may sleep, you need to use a dedicated kernel thread or work queues. A work queue is simply a queue where you can queue a request to execute a function, and a kernel thread will take care of it. In this case, the function would be executed in the context of a kernel thread, and therefore sleeping is allowed. Since the networking code mainly uses softirq and tasklets, we will not look at work queues.

Concurrency and Locking

Before launching into the code that network drivers use to handle bottom halves, we need some background on *concurrency*, which refers to functions that can interfere with each other either because they are scheduled on different CPUs or because one is suspended by the kernel to run another. Related topics are locks and the disabling of interrupts. (Concurrency is discussed in detail in both *Understanding the Linux Kernel* and *Linux Device Drivers*.)

Three different types of functions will be introduced in this chapter to handle interrupts, old-style bottom halves, softirqs, and tasklets. All of them can be used to schedule the execution of a function, but they come with some big differences. As far as concurrency is concerned, we can summarize the differences as follows:

- Only one old-style bottom half can run at any time, regardless of the number of CPUs (kernel 2.2).

- Only one instance of each tasklet can run at any time. Different tasklets can run concurrently on different CPUs. This means that given any tasklet, there is no need to enforce any serialization because already it is enforced by the kernel: you cannot have multiple instances of the same tasklet running concurrently.

- Only one instance of each softirq can run at the same time on a CPU. However, the same softirq can run on different CPUs concurrently. This means that given any softirq you need to make sure that accesses to shared data by different CPUs use proper locking. To increase parallelization, the softirqs should be designed to access only per-CPU data as much as possible, reducing the need for locking considerably.

Therefore, these three features require different kinds of locking mechanisms. The higher the concurrency allowed, the more carefully the programmer has to design the code executed, for the sake of both accuracy and performance. Whether a softirq or a tasklet represents the best choice for any given context depends on both locking and concurrency requirements. In most cases, tasklets are the way to go. But given the tight response requirements of the receive and transmit networking tasks, softirqs are preferred in those two specific cases. We will see later in this chapter how the networking code uses softirqs.

In some cases, the programmer has to disable hardware interrupts, software interrupts, or both. A detailed discussion of the contexts requires a background in SMP, preemption in the Linux kernel, and other matters outside the scope of this book. However, to understand the networking code you need to know the meaning of the main functions used to enable and disable interrupts. Table 9-1 summarizes the ones we need in this chapter (you can find many more in *kernel/softirq.c*, *include/asm-XXX/hardirq.h*, *include/asm-XXX/spinlock.h*, and *include/linux/spinlock.h*). Some of them may be defined globally and others per architecture.

Table 9-1. A few APIs related to software and hardware interrupts

Function/macro	Description
in_interrupt	in_interrupt returns TRUE if the CPU is currently serving a hardware or software interrupt, or preemption is disabled.
in_softirq	in_softirq returns TRUE if the CPU is currently serving a software interrupt.

Function/macro	Description
`in_irq`	`in_irq` returns TRUE if the CPU is currently serving a hardware interrupt.
	In the section "Preemption," and with the help of Figure 9-3, you can see how these three routines are implemented.
`softirq_pending`	Returns TRUE if there is at least one softirq pending (i.e., scheduled for execution) for the CPU whose ID was passed as the input argument.
`local_softirq_pending`	Returns TRUE if there is at least one softirq pending for the local CPU.
`__raise_softirq_irqoff`	Sets the flag associated with the input softirq type to mark it pending.
`raise_softirq_irqoff`	This is a wrapper around `__raise_softirq_irqoff` that also wakes up `ksoftirqd` when `in_interrupt()` returns FALSE.
`raise_softirq`	This is a wrapper around `raise_softirq_irqoff` that disables hardware interrupts before calling it and restores them to their original status.

`__local_bh_enable`
`local_bh_enable`
`local_bh_disable`
	`__local_bh_enable` enables bottom halves (and thus softirqs/tasklets) on the local CPU, and `local_bh_enable` also invokes `invoke_softirq` if any softirq is pending and `in_interrupt()` returns FALSE.
	`local_bh_disable` disables bottom halves on the local CPU.

`local_irq_disable` `local_irq_enable`	Disable and enable interrupts on the local CPU.
`local_irq_save` `local_irq_restore`	`local_irq_save` first saves the current state of interrupts on the local CPU and then disables them. `local_irq_restore` restores the state of interrupts on the local CPU thanks to the information previously saved with `local_irq_save`.
`spin_lock_bh` `spin_unlock_bh`	Acquire and release a spinlock, respectively. Both functions disable and then re-enable bottom halves and preemption during the operation.

Preemption

In time-sharing systems, the kernel has always been able to preempt user processes at will, but the kernel itself is often nonpreemptive, which means that once it starts running it will not be interrupted until it is ready to give up control. A nonpreemptive kernel sometimes holds up high-priority processes when they are ready to run because the kernel is executing a system call for a lower-priority process. To support real-time extensions and for other reasons, the Linux kernel was made fully preemptible during the 2.5 kernel development cycle. With this new kernel feature, system calls and other kernel tasks can be preempted by other kernel tasks with higher priorities.

Because much work had already been done to eliminate critical sections (nonpreemptible code) from the kernel to support SMP locking mechanisms, adding full preemption was not a major change to the kernel. Once preemption was added, developers just had to define explicitly where to disable it (in hardware and software interrupt code, in the scheduler itself, in the code protected by spin locks and read/write locks, etc.).

However, there are times when preemption, just like interrupts, must be disabled. In this section, I'll cover just a few functions related to preemption that you may bump into while browsing the code, and then briefly show how some of the locking macros have been updated to deal with preemption.

The following functions control preemption:

preempt_disable

> Disables preemption for the current task. Can be called repeatedly, incrementing a reference counter.

preempt_enable
preempt_enable_no_resched

> The reverse of preempt_disable, allowing preemption to be enabled again. preempt_enable_no_resched simply decrements a reference counter, which allows preemption to be re-enabled when it reaches zero. preempt_enable, in addition, checks whether the counter is zero and forces a call to schedule( ) to allow any higher-priority task to run.

preempt_check_resched

> This function is called by preempt_enable and differentiates it from preempt_enable_no_resched.

The networking code does not deal with these routines directly. However, preempt_enable and preempt_disable are indirectly called, for instance, by locking primitives, like rcu_read_lock and rcu_read_unlock, spin_lock and spin_unlock, etc. Routines used to access per-CPU data structures, like get_cpu and get_cpu_var, also disable preemption before reading the data.

A counter for each process, named preempt_count and embedded in the thread_info structure, indicates whether a given process allows preemption. The field can be read with preempt_count( ) and is manipulated indirectly through the inc_preempt_count and dec_preempt_count functions defined in *include/linux/preempt.h*. There are situations in which the kernel should not be preempted. These include when it is servicing hardware, as well as when it uses one of the calls just shown to disable preemption. Therefore, preempt_count is split into three components. Each byte is a counter for a different condition that requires nonpreemption: hardware interrupts, software interrupts, and general nonpreemption. The layout of preempt_count is shown in Figure 9-3.

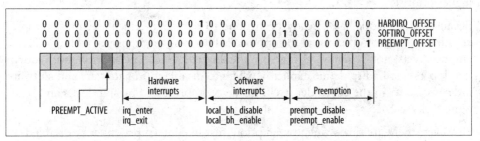

Figure 9-3. Structure of preempt_count

The figure shows, in addition to the purpose of each byte, the main functions that manipulate it. The high-order byte is not fully used at the moment, but its second least significant bit is set before calling the schedule function and tells that function that it has been called to preempt the current task.* In *include/asm-xxx/hardirq.h* you can find several macros that make it easier to read and write preempt_counter; some of these include the XXX_OFFSET variables shown in Figure 9-3 and used by the functions listed in the figure to increment or decrement the right byte.

Despite all this complexity, whenever a check has to be done on the current process to see if it can be preempted, all the kernel needs to know is whether preempt_count is NULL (it does not really matter why preemption is disabled).

Bottom-Half Handlers

The infrastructure for bottom halves must address the following needs:

- Classifying the bottom half as the proper type
- Registering the association between a bottom half type and its handler
- Scheduling a bottom half for execution
- Notifying the kernel about the presence of scheduled BHs

Let's first see how kernels up to version 2.2 handled bottom half handlers, and then how they are handled with the softirqs used by kernels 2.4 and 2.6.

Bottom-half handlers in kernel 2.2

The 2.2 model for bottom-half handlers divides them into a large number of types, which are differentiated by when and how often the kernel checks for them and runs

---

* The PREEMPT_ACTIVE flag is defined on a per-architecture basis. The figure shows the most common definition.

them. The 2.2 list is as follows, taken from *include/linux/interrupt.h*. In this book, we are most interested in NET_BH.

```
enum {
        TIMER_BH = 0,
        CONSOLE_BH,
        TQUEUE_BH,
        DIGI_BH,
        SERIAL_BH,
        RISCOM8_BH,
        SPECIALIX_BH,
        AURORA_BH,
        ESP_BH,
        NET_BH,
        SCSI_BH,
        IMMEDIATE_BH,
        KEYBOARD_BH,
        CYCLADES_BH,
        CM206_BH,
        JS_BH,
        MACSERIAL_BH,
        ISICOM_BH
};
```

Each bottom-half type is associated with a function handler by means of init_bh. The networking code, for instance, initializes the NET_BH bottom-half type to the net_bh handler in net_dev_init, which is covered in Chapter 5.

```
__initfunc(int net_dev_init(void))
{
        ... ... ...
        init_bh(NET_BH, net_bh);
        ... ... ...
}
```

The main function used to unregister a BH handler is remove_bh. (There are other related functions too, such as enable_bh/disable_bh, but we do not need to see all of them.)

Whenever an interrupt handler wants to trigger the execution of a bottom half handler, it has to set the corresponding flag with mark_bh. This function is very simple: it sets a bit into a global bitmap bh_active, which, as we will see in a moment, is tested in several places.

```
extern inline void mark_bh(int nr)
{
        set_bit(nr, &bh_active);
};
```

For instance, you will see later in the chapter that every time a network device driver has successfully received a frame, it signals the kernel about it with a call to netif_rx. The latter queues the newly received frame into the ingress queue backlog (shared by all the CPUs) and marks the NET_BH bottom-half handler flag.

```
skb_queue_tail(&backlog, skb);
mark_bh(NET_BH);
return
```

During several routine operations, the kernel checks whether any bottom halves are scheduled for execution. If any are waiting, the kernel runs the function do_bottom_half (currently in *kernel/softirq.c*), to execute them. The checks are performed during:

do_IRQ

> Whenever the kernel is notified by an IRQ about a hardware interrupt, it calls do_IRQ to execute the associated handler. Since a good number of bottom halves are scheduled for transmission by interrupt handlers, what could give them less latency than an invocation right at the end of do_IRQ? For this reason, the regular timer interrupt that expires with frequency HZ represents an upper bound between two consecutive executions of do_bottom_half.

Returns from interrupts and exceptions (which includes system calls)

> See *arch/XXX/kernel/entry.S* for the assembly language code that takes care of this case.

schedule

> This function, which decides what to execute next on the CPU, checks if any bottom-half handlers are pending and gives them higher priority over other tasks.
>
> ```
> asmlinkage void schedule(void)
> {
>
>         /* Do "administrative" work here while we don't hold any locks */
>         if (bh_mask & bh_active)
>                 goto handle_bh;
> handle_bh_back:
>         ... ... ...
> handle_bh:
>         do_bottom_half();
>         goto handle_bh_back;
>         ... ... ...
> }
> ```

run_bottom_half, the function used by do_bottom_half to execute the pending interrupt handlers, looks like this:

```
active = get_active_bhs();
clear_active_bhs(active);
bh = bh_base;
do {
        if (active & 1)
                (*bh)();
        bh++;
        active >>= 1;
} while (active);
```

The order in which the pending handlers are invoked depends on the positions of the associated flags inside the bitmap and the direction used to scan those flags (returned by get_active_bhs). In other words, bottom halves are not run on a first-come-first-served basis. And since networking bottom halves can take a long time, those that have the misfortune to be dequeued last can experience high latency.

Bottom halves in 2.2 and earlier kernels suffer from a ban on concurrency. Only one bottom half can run at any time, regardless of the number of CPUs.

Bottom-half handlers in kernel 2.4 and above: the introduction of the softirq

The biggest improvement between kernels 2.2 and 2.4, as far as interrupt handling is concerned, was the introduction of software interrupts (softirqs), which can be seen as the multithreaded version of bottom half handlers. Not only can many softirqs run concurrently, but also the same softirq can run on different CPUs concurrently. The only restriction on concurrency is that only one instance of each softirq can run at the same time on a CPU.

The new softirq model has only six types (from *include/linux/interrupt.h*):

```
enum
{
    HI_SOFTIRQ=0,
    TIMER_SOFTIRQ,
    NET_TX_SOFTIRQ,
    NET_RX_SOFTIRQ,
    SCSI_SOFTIRQ,
    TASKLET_SOFTIRQ
};
```

All the *XXX*_BH bottom-half types in the old model are still available to old drivers, but have been reimplemented to run as softirqs of the HI_SOFTIRQ type (which means they take priority over the other softirq types). The two types used by networking code, NET_TX_SOFTIRQ and NET_RX_SOFTIRQ, are introduced in the later section "How the Networking Code Uses softirqs." The next section will introduce tasklets.

Softirqs, like the old bottom halves, run with interrupts enabled and therefore can be suspended at any time to handle a new, incoming interrupt. However, the kernel does not allow a new request for a softirq to run on a CPU if another instance of that softirq has been suspended on that CPU; this drastically reduces the amount of locking needed. Each softirq type can maintain an array of data structures of type softnet_data, one per CPU, to hold state information about the current softirq; we'll see the contents of this structure in the section "softnet_data Structure." Since different instances of the same type of softirq can run simultaneously on different CPUs, the functions run by softirqs still need to lock other data structures that are shared, to avoid race conditions.

The functions used to register and schedule a softirq handler, and the logic behind them, are very similar to the ones used with 2.2 bottom halves.

softirq handlers are registered with the open_softirq function, which, unlike init_bh, accepts an extra parameter so that the function handler can be passed some input data if needed. None of the softirqs, however, currently uses that extra parameter, and a proposal has been floated to remove it. open_softirq simply copies the input parameters into the global array softirq_vec, declared in *kernel/softirq.c*, which holds the associations between types and handlers.

```
static struct softirq_action softirq_vec[32] __cacheline_aligned_in_smp;

void open_softirq(int nr, void (*action)(struct softirq_action*), void *data)
{
    softirq_vec[nr].data = data;
    softirq_vec[nr].action = action;
}
```

A softirq can be scheduled for execution on the local CPU by the following functions:

__raise_softirq_irqoff
> This function, the counterpart of mark_bh in 2.2, simply sets the bit flag associated to the softirq to run. Later on, when the flag is checked, the associated handler will be invoked.

raise_softirq_irqoff
> This is a wrapper around __cpu_raise_softirq that additionally schedules the ksoftirqd thread (discussed later in this chapter) if the function is not called from a hardware or software interrupt context and preemption has not been disabled. If the function is called from interrupt context, invoking the thread is not necessary because, as we will see, do_softirq will be called anyway.

raise_softirq
> This is a wrapper around raise_softirq_irqoff that executes the latter with hardware interrupts disabled.

The following code, taken from kernel 2.4.5,[*] shows the model used at an early stage of softirq development. It is very similar to the 2.2 model, and invokes the function do_softirq, which is a counterpart to the 2.2 function do_bottom_half discussed in the previous section. do_softirq is called if at least one softirq has been scheduled for execution:

```
asmlinkage void schedule(void)
{

        /* Do "administrative" work here while we don't hold any locks */
        if (softirq_active(this_cpu) & softirq_mask(this_cpu))
                goto handle_softirq;
handle_softirq_back:
        ... ... ...
```

[*] It has been removed in 2.4.6.

```
handle_softirq:
        do_softirq();
        goto handle_softirq_back;
        ... ... ...
}
```

The only difference between this early stage of softirqs and the 2.2 bottom-half model is that the softirq version has to check the flags on a per-CPU basis, since each CPU has its own bitmap of pending softirqs.

The implementation of do_softirq is also very similar to its counterpart do_bottom_half in 2.2. The kernel also calls the function at some of the same points, but not entirely the same. The main change is the introduction of a new per-CPU kernel thread, ksoftirqd.

Here are the main points where do_softirq may be invoked:[*]

do_IRQ

The skeleton for do_IRQ, which is defined in the per-architecture files *arch/arch-name/kernel/irq.c*, is:

```
fastcall unsigned int do_IRQ(struct pt_regs * regs)
{
    irq_enter();
    ... ... ...
    /* handle the IRQ number "irq" with the registered handler */
    ... ... ...
    irq_exit();
    return 1;
}
```

In kernel 2.4, the function also called do_softirq. For most architectures in 2.6, a call to do_softirq is made inside irq_exit instead. A minority still have it inside do_IRQ.

Since nested calls to irq_enter are allowed, irq_exit calls invoke_softirq only when all the usual conditions are met (there are softirqs pending, etc.) and the reference count associated with the interrupt context has reached zero, indicating that the kernel is leaving the interrupt context.

Here is the generic definition of irq_exit from *kernel/softirq.c*, but there are architectures that define their own versions:

```
void irq_exit(void)
{
    ...
    sub_preempt_count(IRQ_EXIT_OFFSET);
    if (!in_interrupt() && local_softirq_pending())
        invoke_softirq();
    preempt_enable_no_resched();
}
```

---

[*] It is also possible to call invoke_softirq instead of do_softirq directly. The former could be an alias to do_softirq or to its helper routine, __do_softirq, depending on whether the __ARCHIRQ_EXIT_IRQS_DISABLED symbol is defined.

`smp_apic_timer_interrupt`, which handles SMP timers in *arch/XXX/kernel/apic.c*, also uses `irq_enter/irq_exit`.

Returns from interrupts and exceptions (which include system calls)
>   This is the same as kernel 2.2.

`local_bh_enable`
>   When softirqs are re-enabled on a CPU, pending requests are processed (if any) with a call to `do_softirq`.

The kernel threads, `ksoftirqd_CPUn`
>   To keep softirqs from monopolizing all the CPUs (which could happen easily on a heavily loaded network because the `NET_TX_SOFTIRQ` and `NET_RX_SOFTIRQ` interrupts have a higher priority than user processes), developers introduced a new set of per-CPU threads. These have the names `ksoftirqd_CPU0`, `ksoftirqd_CPU1`, and so on, and can be seen by a *ps* command. More details on these threads appear in the section "ksoftirqd Kernel Threads."

I have described i386 behavior in general; other architectures may use different naming conventions or have additional timers that also invoke `do_softirq`.

Another interesting place where `do_softirq` is called is from within `netif_rx_ni`, which is briefly described in the section "Old Interface Between Device Drivers and Kernel: First Part of netif_rx" in Chapter 10. The traffic generator built into the kernel (*net/core/pktgen.c*) also calls `do_softirq`.

Tasklets

Most of the bottom halves of the 2.2 kernel variety have been converted to either softirqs or tasklets. A tasklet is a function that some interrupt or other task has deferred to execute later. Tasklets are built on top of softirqs and are usually kicked off by interrupt handlers. (But other parts of the kernel, such as the neighboring subsystem discussed in Part VI, also use tasklets).*

In the section "Bottom-half handlers in kernel 2.4 and above: the introduction of the softirq," we saw the list of softirqs. `HI_SOFTIRQ` is used to implement high-priority tasklets, and `TASKLET_SOFTIRQ` is used for lower-priority ones. Each time a request for a deferred execution is issued, an instance of a `tasklet_struct` structure is queued onto either a list processed by `HI_SOFTIRQ` or another one that is instead processed by `TASKLET_SOFTIRQ`.

Since softirqs are handled independently by each CPU, it should not be a surprise that there are two lists of pending `tasklet_structs` for each CPU, one associated

---

* The kernel provides work queues as well. We will not cover them because they are not used much by the networking code. Refer to *Understanding the Linux Kernel* for a discussion of work queues.

with HI_SOFTIRQ and one with TASKLET_SOFTIRQ. These are their definitions from *kernel/softirq.c*:

```
static DEFINE_PER_CPU(struct tasklet_head tasklet_vec) = { NULL };
static DEFINE_PER_CPU(struct tasklet_head tasklet_hi_vec) = { NULL };
```

At first sight, tasklets may seem to be just like the old bottom halves, but there actually are substantial differences:

- There is no limit on the number of different tasklets, whereas the old bottom halves were limited to one type for each bit flag of bh_base.
- Tasklets provide two levels of priority.
- Different tasklets can run concurrently on different CPUs.
- Tasklets, unlike old bottom halves and softirqs, are dynamic and do not need to be statically declared in an *XXX*_BH or *XXX*_SOFTIRQ enumeration list.

The tasklet_struct data structure is defined in *include/linux/interrupt.h* as follows:

```
struct tasklet_struct
{
    struct tasklet_struct *next;
    unsigned long state;
    atomic_t count;
    void (*func)(unsigned long);
    unsigned long data;
};
```

The following is the field-by-field description:

struct tasklet_struct *next

A pointer used to link together the pending structures associated with the same CPU. New elements are added at the head by the functions tasklet_hi_schedule and tasklet_schedule.

unsigned long state

A bitmap flag whose possible values are represented by the TASKLET_STATE_*XXX* enums listed in *include/linux/interrupt.h*:

TASKLET_STATE_SCHED

The tasklet has been scheduled for execution, and the data structure is already in the list associated with HI_SOFTIRQ or TASKLET_SOFTIRQ, based on the priority assigned. The same tasklet cannot be scheduled concurrently on different CPUs. If other requests to execute the tasklet arrive when the first one has not started its execution yet, they will be dropped. Since for any given tasklet, there can be only one instance in execution, there is no reason to schedule it for execution more than once.

TASKLET_STATE_RUN

The tasklet is being executed. This flag is used to prevent multiple instances of the same tasklet from being executed concurrently. It is meaningful only for SMP systems. The flag is manipulated with the three locking functions tasklet_trylock, tasklet_unlock, and tasklet_unlock_wait.

`atomic_t count`

> There are cases where you may need to temporarily disable and later re-enable a tasklet. This is accomplished by this counter: a value of zero means that the tasklet is disabled (and thus not executable) and nonzero means the tasklet is enabled. Its value is incremented and decremented by the `tasklet[_hi]_enable` and `tasklet[_hi]_disable` functions described later in this section.

`void (*func)(unsigned long)`
`unsigned long data`

> `func` is the function to execute and `data` is an optional input that can be passed to `func`.

The following are some important kernel functions that handle tasklets, from *kernel/softirq.c* and *include/linux/interrupt.h*:

`tasklet_init`

> Fills in the fields of a `tasklet_struct` structure with the `func` and `data` values provided as arguments.

`tasklet_action, tasklet_hi_action`

> Execute low-priority and high-priority tasklets, respectively.

`tasklet_schedule, tasklet_hi_schedule`

> Schedule a low-priority and a high-priority tasklet, respectively, for execution. They add the `tasklet_struct` structure to the list of pending tasklets associated with the local CPU and then schedule the associated softirq (`TASKLET_SOFTIRQ` or `HI_SOFTIRQ`). If the tasklet is already scheduled (but not running), these APIs do nothing (see the `TASKLET_STATE_SCHED` flag).

`tasklet_enable, tasklet_hi_enable`

> These two functions are identical and are used to enable a tasklet.

`tasklet_disable, tasklet_disable_nosync`

> Both of these functions disable a tasklet and can be used with low- and high-priority tasklets. Tasklet_disable is a wrapper to `tasklet_disable_nosync`. While the latter returns right away (it is asynchronous), the former returns only when the tasklet has terminated its execution in case it was running (it is synchronous).
>
> `tasklet_enable`, `tasklet_hi_enable`, and `tasklet_disable_nosync` manipulate the value of the count field to declare the tasklet enabled or disabled. Nested calls are allowed.

Softirq Initialization

During kernel initialization, `softirq_init` initializes the software IRQ layer with the two general-purpose softirqs: `tasklet_action` and `tasklet_hi_action`, which are associated with `TASKLET_SOFTIRQ` and `HI_SOFTIRQ`, respectively.

```
void __init softirq_init()
{
    open_softirq(TASKLET_SOFTIRQ, tasklet_action, NULL);
    open_softirq(HI_SOFTIRQ, tasklet_hi_action, NULL);
}
```

The two softirqs used by the networking code NET_RX_SOFTIRQ and NET_TX_SOFTIRQ are initialized in net_dev_init, one of the networking initialization functions (see the section "How the Networking Code Uses softirqs").

The other softirqs listed in the section "Bottom-half handlers in kernel 2.4 and above: the introduction of the softirq" are registered in the associated subsystems (SCSI_SOFTIRQ in *drivers/scsi/scsi.c*, TIMER_SOFTIRQ in *kernel/timer.c*, etc.).

HI_SOFTIRQ is mainly used by sound card device drivers.[*]

Users of TASKLET_SOFTIRQ include:

- Drivers for network interface cards (not only Ethernets)
- Numerous other device drivers
- Media layers (USB, IEEE 1394, etc.)
- Networking subsystems (Neighboring, ATM qdisc, etc.)

Pending softirq Handling

We explained in the section "Bottom-half handlers in kernel 2.4 and above: the introduction of the softirq" when do_softirq is invoked to take care of the pending softirqs. Here we will see the internals of the function. You will notice how much it resembles the one by kernel 2.2 described in the section "Bottom-half handlers in kernel 2.2."

do_softirq stops and does nothing if the CPU is currently serving a hardware or software interrupt. The function checks for this by calling in_interrupt, which is equivalent to if (in_irq() || in_softirq()).

If do_softirq decides to proceed, it saves pending softirqs in pending with local_softirq_pending.

```
#ifndef __ARCH_HAS_DO_SOFTIRQ

asmlinkage void do_softirq(void)
{
    if (in_interrupt())
        return;

    local_irq_save(flags);
```

---

[*] In 2.4 kernels, all the bottom-half handlers of kernel version 2.2 were converted to high-priority tasklets by defining the mark_bh function as a wrapper around tasklet_hi_schedule.

```
        pending = local_softirq_pending( );
        if (pending)
            _ _do_softirq( );
        local_irq_restore;
    }

    EXPORT_SYMBOL(do_softirq);
    #endif
```

From the preceding snapshot, it could seem that do_softirq runs with IRQs disabled, but that's not true. IRQs are kept disabled only when manipulating the bitmap of pending softirqs (i.e., accessing the softnet_data structure). You will see in a moment that _ _do_softirq internally re-enables IRQs when running the softirq handlers.

_ _do_softirq function

It is possible for the same softirq type to be scheduled multiple times while do_softirq is running. Since IRQs are enabled when running the softirq handlers, the bitmap of pending softirq can be manipulated while serving an interrupt, and therefore any of the softirq handlers that has been executed by _ _do_softirq could be re-scheduled during the execution of _ _do_softirq itself.

For this reason, before _ _do_softirq re-enables IRQs, it saves the current bitmap of the pending softirq on the local variable pending and clears it from the softnet_data instance associated with the local CPU using local_softirq_pending( )=0. Then based on pending, it calls all the necessary handlers.

Once all the handlers have been called, _ _do_softirq checks whether in the meantime any softirqs were scheduled again (this request disables IRQs). If there was at least one pending softirq, it will repeat the whole process. However, _ _do_softirq repeats it only up to MAX_SOFTIRQ_RESTART times (experimentation has found that 10 times works well).

The use of MAX_SOFTIRQ_RESTART is a design decision made to keep a single type of interrupt—particularly a stream of networking interrupts—from starving other interrupts out of one of the CPUs. Without the limit in _ _do_softirq, starvation could easily happen when a server is highly loaded by network traffic and the number of NET_RX_SOFTIRQ interrupts goes through the roof.

Let's see how starvation could take place. do_IRQ would raise a NET_RX_SOFTIRQ interrupt that would cause do_softirq to be executed. _ _do_softirq would clear the NET_RX_SOFTIRQ flag, but before it ended it would be interrupted by an interrupt that would set NET_RX_SOFTIRQ again, and so on, indefinitely.

Let's see now how the central part of _ _do_softirq manages to invoke the softirq handler. Every time one softirq type is served, its bit is cleared from the local copy of the active softirqs, pending. h is initialized to point to the global data structure softirq_vec that holds the associations between softirq types and their function handlers (for instance, NET_RX_SOFTIRQ is handled by net_rx_action). The loop ends when the bitmap is cleared.

Finally, if there are pending softirqs that cannot be handled because do_softirq must return, having repeated its job MAX_SOFTIRQ_RESTART times already, the ksoftirqd thread is awakened and given the responsibility of handling them later. Because do_softirq is invoked at so many points within the kernel, it is actually likely that a later invocation of do_softirq will handle these interrupts before the ksoftirqd thread is scheduled.

```
#define MAX_SOFTIRQ_RESTART 10

asmlinkage void __do_softirq(void)
{
    struct softirq_action *h;
    __u32 pending;
    int max_restart = MAX_SOFTIRQ_RESTART;
    int cpu;

    pending = local_softirq_pending();

    local_bh_disable();
    cpu = smp_processor_id();
restart:
    /* Reset the pending bitmask before enabling irqs */
    local_softirq_pending() = 0;

    local_irq_enable();

    h = softirq_vec;

    do {
        if (pending & 1) {
            h->action(h);
            rcu_bh_qsctr_inc(cpu);
        }
        h++;
        pending >>= 1;
    } while (pending);

    local_irq_disable();

    pending = local_softirq_pending();
    if (pending && --max_restart)
        goto restart;

    if (pending)
        wakeup_softirqd();

    __local_bh_enable();
}
```

Per-Architecture Processing of softirq

The do_softirq function provided in *kernel/softirq.c* can be overridden by another function provided by the architecture code (which ends up calling __do_softirq anyway). This explains why the definition of do_softirq in *kernel/softirq.c* is wrapped with the check on __ARCH_HAS_DO_SOFTIRQ (see the previous section).

A few architectures, including i386 (see *arch/i386/kernel/irq.c*), define their own version of do_softirq. Such architecture versions are used when the architectures use 4 KB stacks (instead of 8 KB) and use the remaining 4 K to implement stacked handling of both hard IRQs and softirqs. Please refer to *Understanding the Linux Kernel* for more detail.

ksoftirqd Kernel Threads

Background kernel threads are assigned the job of checking for softirqs that have been left unexecuted by the functions previously described, and executing as many of those softirqs as they can before needing to give that CPU back to other activities. There is one kernel thread for each CPU, named ksoftirqd_CPU0, ksoftirqd_CPU1, and so on. The section "Starting the threads" describes how these threads are started at CPU boot time.

The function ksoftirqd associated to these threads is pretty simple and is defined in the same file *softirq.c*:

```
static int ksoftirqd(void * __bind_cpu)
{
    set_user_nice(current, 19);
    ...
    while (!kthread_should_stop()) {
        if (!local_softirq_pending())
            schedule();

        __set_current_state(TASK_RUNNING);

        while (local_softirq_pending()) {
            /* Preempt disable stops cpu going offline.
               If already offline, we'll be on wrong CPU:
               don't process */
            preempt_disable();
            if (cpu_is_offline((long)__bind_cpu))
                goto wait_to_die;
            do_softirq();
            preempt_enable();
            cond_resched();
        }
        set_current_state(TASK_INTERRUPTIBLE);
    }
    __set_current_state(TASK_RUNNING);
    return 0;
    ...
}
```

There are a couple of small details I want to emphasize. The priority of a process, also called the nice priority, is a number ranging from −20 (maximum) to +19 (minimum). The ksoftirqd threads are given a low priority of 19. This is done so that frequently running softirqs such as NET_RX_SOFTIRQ cannot completely kidnap the CPU, which would leave almost no resources to other processes. We already saw that do_softirq can be invoked from different places in the code, so this low priority doesn't represent a handicap. Once started, the loop simply keeps calling do_softirq (always with preemption disabled) until one of the following conditions becomes true:

- There are no more pending softirqs to handle (local_softirq_pending( ) returns FALSE).

  In this case, the function sets the thread's state to TASK_INTERRUPTIBLE and calls schedule( ) to release the CPU. The thread can be awakened by means of wakeup_softirqd, which can be called from both _ _do_softirq itself and raise_softirq_irqoff.

- The thread has run for too long and is asked to release the CPU.

  The handler associated with the timer interrupt, among other things, sets the need_resched flag to signal that the current process/thread has used its time slot. In this case, ksoftirqd releases the CPU, keeping its state as TASK_RUNNING, and will soon be resumed.

Starting the threads

There is one ksoftirqd thread for each CPU. When the system's first CPU comes online, the first thread is started at kernel boot time inside do_pre_smp_initcalls.* The ksoftirqd threads for the other CPUs that come up at boot time, and for any other CPU that may be enabled later on a system that can handle hot-pluggable CPUs, are taken care of through the cpu_chain notification chain.

Notification chains were introduced in Chapter 4. The cpu_chain chain lets various subsystems know when a CPU is up and running or when one dies. The softirq subsystem registers to the cpu_chain with spawn_ksoftirqd, called from the function do_pre_smp_initcalls mentioned previously. The callback routine cpu_callback that processes notifications from cpu_chain is used to initialize the necessary per-CPU data structures and start the ksoftirqd thread on the CPU.

The complete list of CPU_XXX notifications is in *include/linux/notifier.h*, but we need only four of them in the context of this chapter:

CPU_UP_PREPARE
   Generated when the CPU starts coming up, but is not ready yet.

CPU_ONLINE
   Generated when the CPU is ready.

---

* See Chapter 7 for details about how the kernel takes care of basic initializations at boot time.

CPU_UP_CANCELLED
CPU_DEAD

These two messages are generated only when the kernel is compiled with support for hot-pluggable CPUs. The first is used when one of the tasks triggered by a previous CPU_UP_PREPARE notification failed and therefore does not allow the CPU to go online. The second one is used when a CPU dies.

CPU_PREPARE_UP creates the thread and binds it to the associated CPU, but does not wake up the thread. CPU_ONLINE wakes up the thread. When a CPU dies, its associated ksoftirqd instance is killed:

```
static int __devinit cpu_callback(struct notifier_block *nfb, unsigned long action,
void *hcpu)
{
    ...
    switch(action) {
        ...
    }
    return NOTIFY_OK;
}

static struct notifier_block __devinitdata cpu_nfb = {
    .notifier_call = cpu_callback
};

__init int spawn_ksoftirqd(void)
{
    void *cpu = (void *)(long)smp_processor_id();
    cpu_callback(&cpu_nfb, CPU_UP_PREPARE, cpu);
    cpu_callback(&cpu_nfb, CPU_ONLINE, cpu);
    register_cpu_notifier(&cpu_nfb);
    return 0;
}
```

Note that spawn_ksoftirqd places two direct calls to cpu_callback before registering with cpu_chain via register_cpu_notifier. This is necessary because CPU notifications are not generated for the first CPU that comes online.

Tasklet Processing

The two handlers for low-latency tasklets (TASKLET_SOFTIRQ) and high-latency tasklets (HI_SOFTIRQ) are identical; they simply work on two different lists. For this reason, we will describe only one of them: tasklet_action, the one associated with TASKLET_SOFTIRQ.

Only one instance of each tasklet can be waiting for execution at any time. When tasklet_schedule or tasklet_hi_schedule schedules a tasklet, the function sets the TASKLET_STATE_SCHED bit described earlier in the section "Tasklets." Attempts to reschedule the same tasklet will be ignored because TASKLET_STATE_SCHED is already set. The bit is cleared only when the tasklet starts its execution; thus, during or after its execution another instance can be scheduled.

The `tasklet_action` function starts by copying the list of tasklets waiting to be processed into a local variable first; it then clears the global list.* This is the only part of the function that is executed with interrupts disabled. Disabling them is necessary to avoid race conditions with interrupt handlers that could add new elements to the list while `tasklet_action` accesses it.

At this point, the function goes through the list tasklet by tasklet. For each element it invokes the handler if both of the following are true:

- The tasklet is not already running—in other words, `TASKLET_STATE_RUN` is clear. (The function runs `tasklet_trylock` to see whether `TASKLET_STATE_RUN` is already set; if not, `tasklet_trylock` sets the bit.)
- The tasklet is enabled (count is zero).

The part of the function implementing these activities follows:

```
struct tasklet_struct *list;

local_irq_disable( );
list = __get_cpu_var(tasklet_vec).list;
__get_cpu_var(tasklet_vec).list = NULL;
local_irq_enable( );

while (list) {
    struct tasklet_struct *t = list;

    list = list->next;

    if (tasklet_trylock(t)) {
        if (!atomic_read(&t->count)) {
```

At this stage, since the tasklet was not already being executed and it was extracted from the list of pending tasklets, it must have the `TASKLET_STATE_SCHED` flag set:

```
            if (!test_and_clear_bit(TASKLET_STATE_SCHED, &t->state))
                BUG( );
            t->func(t->data);
            tasklet_unlock(t);
            continue;
        }
        tasklet_unlock(t);
    }
```

If the handler cannot be executed, the tasklet is put back into the list and `TASKLET_SOFTIRQ` is rescheduled to take care of all of those tasklets that for one of the two reasons listed earlier cannot be handled now:

```
    local_irq_disable( );
    t->next = __get_cpu_var(tasklet_vec).list;
```

* We will see that one of the networking softirq handlers (net_tx_action) does something similar.

```
        __get_cpu_var(tasklet_vec).list = t;
        __raise_softirq_irqoff(TASKLET_SOFTIRQ);
        local_irq_enable();
    }
}
```

How the Networking Code Uses softirqs

The networking subsystem has been assigned two different softirqs. NET_RX_SOFTIRQ handles incoming traffic and NET_TX_SOFTIRQ handles outgoing traffic. Both are registered in net_dev_init (described in Chapter 5) through the following lines:

```
open_softirq(NET_TX_SOFTIRQ, net_tx_action, NULL);
open_softirq(NET_RX_SOFTIRQ, net_rx_action, NULL);
```

Because different instances of the same softirq handler can run concurrently on different CPUs (unlike tasklets), networking code is both low latency and scalable.

Both networking softirqs are higher in priority than normal tasklets (TASKLET_SOFTIRQ) but are lower in priority than high-priority tasklets (HI_SOFTIRQ). This prioritization guarantees that other high-priority tasks can proceed in a responsive and timely manner even when a system is under a high network load.

The internals of the two handlers are covered in the sections "Processing the NET_RX_SOFTIRQ: net_rx_action" in Chapter 10 and "Processing the NET_TX_SOFTIRQ: net_tx_action" in Chapter 11.

softnet_data Structure

We will see in Chapter 10 that each CPU has its own queue for incoming frames. Because each CPU has its own data structure to manage ingress and egress traffic, there is no need for any locking among different CPUs. The data structure for this queue, softnet_data, is defined in *include/linux/netdevice.h* as follows:

```
struct softnet_data
{
    int               throttle;
    int               cng_level;
    int               avg_blog;
    struct sk_buff_head    input_pkt_queue;
    struct list_head       poll_list;
    struct net_device      *output_queue;
    struct sk_buff         *completion_queue;
    struct net_device      backlog_dev;
}
```

The structure includes both fields used for reception and fields used for transmission. In other words, both the NET_RX_SOFTIRQ and NET_TX_SOFTIRQ softirqs refer to the structure. Ingress frames are queued to `input_pkt_queue`,[*] and egress frames are placed into the specialized queues handled by Traffic Control (the QoS layer) instead of being handled by softirqs and the `softnet_data` structure, but softirqs are still used to clean up transmitted buffers afterward, to keep that task from slowing transmission.

Fields of softnet_data

The following is a brief field-by-field description of this data structure; details will be given in later chapters. Some drivers use the NAPI interface, whereas others have not yet been updated to NAPI; both types of driver use this structure, but some fields are reserved for the non-NAPI drivers.

`throttle`
`avg_blog`
`cng_level`

> These three parameters are used by the congestion management algorithm and are further described following this list, as well as in the "Congestion Management" section in Chapter 10. All three, by default, are updated with the reception of every frame.

`input_pkt_queue`

> This queue, initialized in `net_dev_init`, is where incoming frames are stored before being processed by the driver. It is used by non-NAPI drivers; those that have been upgraded to NAPI use their own private queues.

`backlog_dev`

> This is an entire embedded data structure (not just a pointer to one) of type `net_device`, which represents a device that has scheduled `net_rx_action` for execution on the associated CPU. This field is used by non-NAPI drivers. The name stands for "backlog device." You will see how it is used in the section "Old Interface Between Device Drivers and Kernel: First Part of netif_rx" in Chapter 10.

`poll_list`

> This is a bidirectional list of devices with input frames waiting to be processed. More details can be found in the section "Processing the NET_RX_SOFTIRQ: net_rx_action" in Chapter 10.

`output_queue`
`completion_queue`

> `output_queue` is the list of devices that have something to transmit, and `completion_queue` is the list of buffers that have been successfully transmitted and therefore can be released. More details are given in the section "Processing the NET_TX_SOFTIRQ: net_tx_action" in Chapter 11.

---

[*] You will see in Chapter 10 that this is no longer true for drivers using NAPI.

throttle is treated as a Boolean variable whose value is true when the CPU is overloaded and false otherwise. Its value depends on the number of frames in input_pkt_ queue. When the throttle flag is set, all input frames received by this CPU are dropped, regardless of the number of frames in the queue.[*]

avg_blog represents the weighted average value of the input_pkt_queue queue length; it can range from 0 to the maximum length represented by netdev_max_backlog. avg_ blog is used to compute cng_level.

cng_level, which represents the congestion level, can take any of the values shown in Figure 9-4. As avg_blog hits one of the thresholds shown in the figure, cng_level changes value. The definitions of the NET_RX_*XXX* enum values are in *include/linux/ netdevice.h*, and the definitions of the congestion levels mod_cong, lo_cong, and no_ cong are in *net/core/dev.c*.[†] The strings within brackets (/DROP and /HIGH) are explained in the section "Congestion Management" in Chapter 10. avg_blog and cng_level are recalculated with each frame, by default, but recalculation can be postponed and tied to a timer to avoid adding too much overhead.

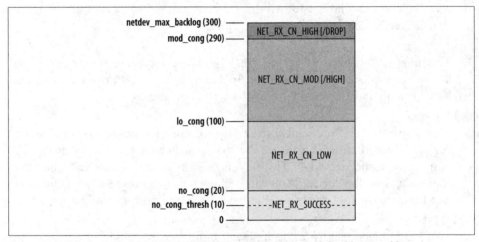

Figure 9-4. Congestion level (NET_RX_XXX) based on the average backlog avg_blog

avg_blog and cng_level are associated with the CPU and therefore apply to non-NAPI devices, which share the queue input_pkt_queue that is used by each CPU.

---

[*] Drivers using NAPI might not drop incoming traffic under these conditions.

[†] The NET_RX_*XXX* values are also used outside this context, and there are other NET_RX_*XXX* values not used here. The value no_cong_thresh is not used; it used to be used by process_backlog (described in Chapter 10) to remove a queue from the throttle state under some conditions when the kernel still had support for the feature (which has been dropped).

Initialization of softnet_data

Each CPU's softnet_data structure is initialized by net_dev_init, which runs at boot time and is described in Chapter 5. The initialization code is:

```
for (i = 0; i < NR_CPUS; i++) {
    struct softnet_data *queue;

    queue = &per_cpu(softnet_data,i);
    skb_queue_head_init(&queue->input_pkt_queue);
    queue->throttle = 0;
    queue->cng_level = 0;
    queue->avg_blog = 10; /* arbitrary non-zero */
    queue->completion_queue = NULL;
    INIT_LIST_HEAD(&queue->poll_list);
    set_bit(__LINK_STATE_START, &queue->backlog_dev.state);
    queue->backlog_dev.weight = weight_p;
    queue->backlog_dev.poll = process_backlog;
    atomic_set(&queue->backlog_dev.refcnt, 1);
}
```

NR_CPUS is the maximum number of CPUs the Linux kernel can handle and softnet_ data is a vector of struct softnet_data structures.

The code also initializes the fields of softnet_data->blog_dev, a structure of type net_ device, a special device representing non-NAPI devices. The section "Backlog Processing: The process_backlog Poll Virtual Function" in Chapter 10 describes how non-NAPI device drivers are handled transparently with the old netif_rx interface.

CHAPTER 10
Frame Reception

In the previous chapter, we saw that the functions that deal with frames at the L2 layer are driven by interrupts. In this chapter, we start our discussion about frame reception, where the hardware uses an interrupt to signal the CPU about the availability of the frame.

As shown in Figure 9-2 in Chapter 9, the CPU that receives an interrupt executes the do_IRQ function. The IRQ number causes the right handler to be invoked. The handler is typically a function within the device driver registered at device driver initialization time. IRQ function handlers are executed in interrupt mode, with further interrupts temporarily disabled.

As discussed in the section "Interrupt Handlers" in Chapter 9, the interrupt handler performs a few immediate tasks and schedules others in a bottom half to be executed later. Specifically, the interrupt handler:

1. Copies the frame into an sk_buff data structure.*

2. Initializes some of the sk_buff parameters for use later by upper network layers (notably skb->protocol, which identifies the higher-layer protocol handler and will play a major role in Chapter 13).

3. Updates some other parameters private to the device, which we do not consider in this chapter because they do not influence the frame's path inside the network stack.

4. Signals the kernel about the new frame by scheduling the NET_RX_SOFTIRQ softirq for execution.

Since a device can issue an interrupt for different reasons (new frame received, frame transmission successfully completed, etc.), the kernel is given a code along with the

---

* If DMA is used by the device, as is pretty common nowadays, the driver needs only to initialize a pointer (no copying is involved).

interrupt notification so that the device driver handler can process the interrupt based on the type.

Interactions with Other Features

While perusing the routines introduced in this chapter, you will often see pieces of code for interacting with optional kernel features. For features covered in this book, I will refer you to the chapter on that feature; for other features, I will not spend much time on the code. Most of the flowcharts in the chapter also show where those optional features are handled in the routines.

Here are the optional features we'll see, with the associated kernel symbols:

802.1d Ethernet Bridging (CONFIG_BRIDGE/CONFIG_BRIDGE_MODULE)
Bridging is described in Part IV.

Netpoll (CONFIG_NETPOLL)
Netpoll is a generic framework for sending and receiving frames by polling the network interface cards (NICs), eliminating the need for interrupts. Netpoll can be used by any kernel feature that benefits from its functionality; one prominent example is Netconsole, which logs kernel messages (i.e., strings printed with printk) to a remote host via UDP. Netconsole and its suboptions can be turned on from the *make xconfig* menu with the "Networking support → Network console logging support" option. To use Netpoll, devices must include support for it (which quite a few already do).

Packet Action (CONFIG_NET_CLS_ACT)
With this feature, Traffic Control can classify and apply actions to ingress traffic. Possible actions include dropping the packet and consuming the packet. To see this option and all its suboptions from the *make xconfig* menu, you need first to select the "Networking support → Networking options → QoS and/or fair queueing → Packet classifier API" option.

Enabling and Disabling a Device

A device can be considered enabled when the __LINK_STATE_START flag is set in net_device->state. The section "Enabling and Disabling a Device" in Chapter 8 covers the details of this flag. The flag is normally set when the device is open (dev_open) and cleared when the device is closed (dev_close). While there is a flag that is used to explicitly enable and disable transmission for a device (__LINK_STATE_XOFF), there is none to enable and disable reception. That capability is achieved by other means—i.e., by disabling the device, as described in Chapter 8. The status of the __LINK_STATE_START flag can be checked with the netif_running function.

Several functions shown later in this chapter provide simple wrappers that check the correct status of flags such as `__LINK_STATE_START` to make sure the device is ready to do what is about to be asked of it.

Queues

When discussing L2 behavior, I often talk about queues for frames being received (ingress queues) and transmitted (egress queues). Each queue has a pointer to the devices associated with it, and to the `skb_buff` data structures that store the ingress/egress buffers. Only a few specialized devices work without queues; an example is the loopback device. The loopback device can dispense with queues because when you transmit a packet out of the loopback device, the packet is immediately delivered (to the local system) with no need for intermediate queuing. Moreover, since transmissions on the loopback device cannot fail, there is no need to requeue the packet for another transmission attempt.

Egress queues are associated directly to devices; Traffic Control (the Quality of Service, or QoS, layer) defines one queue for each device. As we will see in Chapter 11, the kernel keeps track of devices waiting to transmit frames, not the frames themselves. We will also see that not all devices actually use Traffic Control. The situation with ingress queues is a bit more complicated, as we'll see later.

Notifying the Kernel of Frame Reception: NAPI and netif_rx

In version 2.5 (then backported to a late revision of 2.4 as well), a new API for handling ingress frames was introduced into the Linux kernel, known (for lack of a better name) as NAPI. Since few devices have been upgraded to NAPI, there are two ways a Linux driver can notify the kernel about a new frame:

By means of the old function `netif_rx`
> This is the approach used by those devices that follow the technique described in the section "Processing Multiple Frames During an Interrupt" in Chapter 9. Most Linux device drivers still use this approach.

By means of the NAPI mechanism
> This is the approach used by those devices that follow the technique described in the variation introduced at the end of the section "Processing Multiple Frames During an Interrupt" in Chapter 9. This is new in the Linux kernel, and only a few drivers use it. *drivers/net/tg3.c* was the first one to be converted to NAPI.

A few device drivers allow you to choose between the two types of interfaces when you configure the kernel options with tools such as *make xconfig*.

The following piece of code comes from vortex_rx, which still uses the old function netif_rx, and you can expect most of the network device drivers not yet using NAPI to do something similar:

```
skb = dev_alloc_skb(pkt_len + 5);
    ... ... ...
if (skb != NULL) {
    skb->dev = dev;
    skb_reserve(skb, 2);    /* Align IP on 16 byte boundaries */
        ... ... ...
        /* copy the DATA into the sk_buff structure */
        ... ... ...
    skb->protocol = eth_type_trans(skb, dev);
    netif_rx(skb);
    dev->last_rx = jiffies;
        ... ... ...
}
```

First, the sk_buff data structure is allocated with dev_alloc_skb (see Chapter 2), and the frame is copied into it. Note that before copying, the code reserves two bytes to align the IP header to a 16-byte boundary. Each network device driver is associated with a given interface type; for instance, the Vortex device driver *driver/net/3c59x.c* is associated with a specific family of Ethernet cards. Therefore, the driver knows the length of the link layer's header and how to interpret it. Given a header length of $16*k+n$, the driver can force an alignment to a 16-byte boundary by simply calling skb_reserve with an offset of $16-n$. An Ethernet header is 14 bytes, so $k=0$, $n=14$, and the offset requested by the code is 2 (see the definition of NET_IP_ALIGN and the associated comment in *include/linux/sk_buff.h*).

Note also that at this stage, the driver does not make any distinction between different L3 protocols. It aligns the L3 header to a 16-byte boundary regardless of the type. The L3 protocol is probably IP because of IP's widespread usage, but that is not guaranteed at this point; it could be Netware's IPX or something else. The alignment is useful regardless of the L3 protocol to be used.

eth_type_trans, which is used to extract the protocol identifier skb->protocol, is described in Chapter 13.[*]

Depending on the complexity of the driver's design, the block shown may be followed by other housekeeping tasks, but we are not interested in those details in this book. The most important part of the function is the notification to the kernel about the frame's reception.

---

[*] Different device types use different functions; for instance, eth_type_trans is used by Ethernet devices and tr_type_trans by Token Ring interfaces.

Introduction to the New API (NAPI)

Even though some of the NIC device drivers have not been converted to NAPI yet, the new infrastructure has been integrated into the kernel, and even the interface between netif_rx and the rest of the kernel has to take NAPI into account. Instead of introducing the old approach (pure netif_rx) first and then talking about NAPI, we will first see NAPI and then show how the old drivers keep their old interface (netif_rx) while sharing some of the new infrastructure mechanisms.

NAPI mixes interrupts with polling and gives higher performance under high traffic load than the old approach, by reducing significantly the load on the CPU. The kernel developers backported that infrastructure to the 2.4 kernels.

In the old model, a device driver generates an interrupt for each frame it receives. Under a high traffic load, the time spent handling interrupts can lead to a considerable waste of resources.

The main idea behind NAPI is simple: instead of using a pure interrupt-driven model, it uses a mix of interrupts and polling. If new frames are received when the kernel has not finished handling the previous ones yet, there is no need for the driver to generate other interrupts: it is just easier to have the kernel keep processing whatever is in the device input queue (with interrupts disabled for the device), and re-enable interrupts once the queue is empty. This way, the driver reaps the advantages of both interrupts and polling:

- Asynchronous events, such as the reception of one or more frames, are indicated by interrupts so that the kernel does not have to check continuously if the device's ingress queue is empty.

- If the kernel knows there is something left in the device's ingress queue, there is no need to waste time handling interrupt notifications. A simple polling is enough.

From the kernel processing point of view, here are some of the advantages of the NAPI approach:

Reduced load on the CPU (because there are fewer interrupts)
Given the same workload (i.e., number of frames per second), the load on the CPU is lower with NAPI. This is especially true at high workloads. At low workloads, you may actually have slightly higher CPU usage with NAPI, according to tests posted by the kernel developers on the kernel mailing list.

More fairness in the handling of devices
We will see later how devices that have something in their ingress queues are accessed fairly in a round-robin fashion. This ensures that devices with low traffic can experience acceptable latencies even when other devices are much more loaded.

net_device Fields Used by NAPI

Before looking at NAPI's implementation and use, I need to describe a few fields of the net_device data structure, mentioned in the section "softnet_data Structure" in Chapter 9.

Four new fields have been added to this structure for use by the NET_RX_SOFTIRQ soft-irq when dealing with devices whose drivers use the NAPI interface. The other devices will not use them, but they will share the fields of the net_device structure embedded in the softnet_data structure as its backlog_dev field.

poll

> A virtual function used to dequeue buffers from the device's ingress queue. The queue is a private one for devices using NAPI, and softnet_data->input_pkt_queue for others. See the section "Backlog Processing: The process_backlog Poll Virtual Function."

poll_list

> List of devices that have new frames in the ingress queue waiting to be processed. These devices are known as being in *polling state*. The head of the list is softnet_data->poll_list. Devices in this list have interrupts disabled and the kernel is currently polling them.

quota
weight

> quota is an integer that represents the maximum number of buffers that can be dequeued by the poll virtual function in one shot. Its value is incremented in units of weight and it is used to enforce some sort of fairness among different devices. Lower quotas mean lower potential latencies and therefore a lower risk of starving other devices. On the other hand, a low quota increases the amount of switching among devices, and therefore overall overhead.

> For devices associated with non-NAPI drivers, the default value of weight is 64, stored in weight_p at the top of *net/core/dev.c*. The value of weight_p can be changed via */proc*.

> For devices associated with NAPI drivers, the default value is chosen by the drivers. The most common value is 64, but 16 and 32 are used, too. Its value can be tuned via *sysfs*.

> For both the */proc* and *sysfs* interfaces, see the section "Tuning via /proc and sysfs Filesystems" in Chapter 12.

The section "Old Versus New Driver Interfaces" describes how and when elements are added to poll_list, and the section "Backlog Processing: The process_backlog Poll Virtual Function" describes when the poll method extracts elements from the list and how quota is updated based on the value of weight.

Devices using NAPI initialize these four fields and other net_device fields according to the initialization model described in Chapter 8. For the fake backlog_dev devices, introduced in the section "Initialization of softnet_data" in Chapter 9 and described later in this chapter, the initialization is taken care of by net_dev_init (described in Chapter 5).

net_rx_action and NAPI

Figure 10-1 shows what happens each time the kernel polls for incoming network traffic. In the figure, you can see the relationships among the poll_list list of devices in polling state, the poll virtual function, and the software interrupt handler net_rx_action. The following sections will go into detail on each aspect of that diagram, but it is important to understand how the parts interact before moving to the source code.

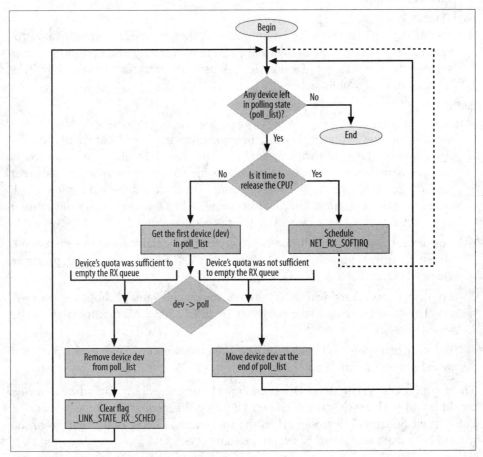

Figure 10-1. net_rx_action function and NAPI overview

We already know that net_rx_action is the function associated with the NET_RX_ SOFTIRQ flag. For the sake of simplicity, let's suppose that after a period of very low activity, a few devices start receiving frames and that these somehow trigger the execution of net_rx_action—how they do so is not important for now.

net_rx_action browses the list of devices in polling state and calls the associated poll virtual function for each device to process the frames in the ingress queue. I explained earlier that devices in that list are consulted in a round-robin fashion, and that there is a maximum number of frames they can process each time their poll method is invoked. If they cannot clear the queue during their slot, they have to wait for their next slot to continue. This means that net_rx_action keeps calling the poll method provided by the device driver for a device with something in its ingress queue until the latter empties out. At that point, there is no need anymore for polling, and the device driver can re-enable interrupt notifications for the device. It is important to underline that interrupts are disabled only for those devices in poll_ list, which applies only to devices that use NAPI and do not share backlog_dev.

net_rx_action limits its execution time and reschedules itself for execution when it passes a given limit of execution time or processed frames; this is enforced to make net_rx_action behave fairly in relation to other kernel tasks. At the same time, each device limits the number of frames processed by each invocation of its poll method to be fair in relation to other devices. When a device cannot clear out its ingress queue, it has to wait until the next call of its poll method.

Old Versus New Driver Interfaces

Now that the meaning of the NAPI-related fields of the net_device structure, and the high-level idea behind NAPI, should be clear, we can get closer to the source code.

Figure 10-2 shows the difference between a NAPI-aware driver and the others with regard to how the driver tells the kernel about the reception of new frames.

From the device driver perspective, there are only two differences between NAPI and non-NAPI. The first is that NAPI drivers must provide a poll method, described in the section "net_device fields used by NAPI." The second difference is the function called to schedule a frame: non-NAPI drivers call netif_rx, whereas NAPI drivers call __netif_rx_schedule, defined in *include/linux/netdevice.h*. (The kernel provides a wrapper function named netif_rx_schedule, which checks to make sure that the device is running and that the softirq is not already scheduled, and then it calls __netif_rx_schedule. These checks are done with netif_rx_schedule_prep. Some drivers call netif_rx_schedule, and others call netif_rx_schedule_prep explicitly and then __netif_rx_schedule if needed).

As shown in Figure 10-2, both types of drivers queue the input device to a polling list (poll_list), schedule the NET_RX_SOFTIRQ software interrupt for execution, and therefore end up being handled by net_rx_action. Even though both types of drivers

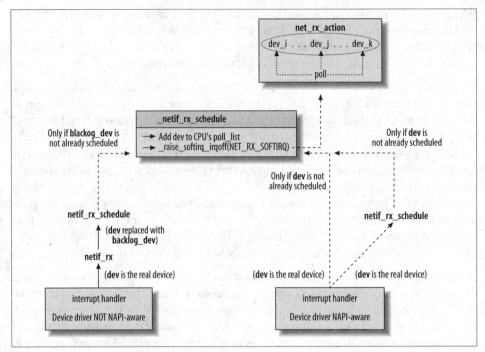

Figure 10-2. NAPI-aware drivers versus non-NAPI-aware devices

ultimately call __netif_rx_schedule (non-NAPI drivers do so within netif_rx), the NAPI devices offer potentially much better performance for the reasons we saw in the section "Notifying Drivers When Frames Are Received" in Chapter 9.

An important detail in Figure 10-2 is the net_device structure that is passed to __netif_rx_schedule in the two cases. Non-NAPI devices use the one that is built into the CPU's softnet_data structure, and NAPI devices use net_device structures that refer to themselves.

Manipulating poll_list

We saw in the previous section that any device (including the fake one, backlog_dev) is added to the poll_list list with a call to netif_rx_schedule or __netif_rx_schedule.

The reverse operation, removing a device from the list, is done with netif_rx_complete or __netif_rx_complete (the second one assumes interrupts are already disabled on the local CPU). We will see when these two routines are called in the section "Processing the NET_RX_SOFTIRQ: net_rx_action."

A device can also temporarily disable and re-enable polling with netif_poll_disable and netif_poll_enable, respectively. This does not mean that the device driver has decided to revert to an interrupt-based model. Polling might be disabled on a device, for instance, when the device needs to be reset by the device driver to apply some kind of hardware configuration changes.

I already said that netif_rx_schedule filters requests for devices that are already in the poll_list (i.e., that have the __LINK_STATE_RX_SCHED flag set). For this reason, if a driver sets that flag but does not add the device to poll_list, it basically disables polling for the device: the device will never be added to poll_list. This is how netif_poll_disable works: if __LINK_STATE_RX_SCHED was not set, it simply sets it and returns. Otherwise, it waits for it to be cleared and then sets it.

```
static inline void netif_poll_disable(struct net_device *dev)
{
    while (test_and_set_bit(__LINK_STATE_RX_SCHED, &dev->state)) {
        /* No hurry. */
        current->state = TASK_INTERRUPTIBLE:
        schedule_timeout(1);
    }
}
```

Old Interface Between Device Drivers and Kernel: First Part of netif_rx

The netif_rx function, defined in *net/core/dev.c*, is normally called by device drivers when new input frames are waiting to be processed;[*] its job is to schedule the softirq that runs shortly to dequeue and handle the frames. Figure 10-3 shows what it checks for and the flow of its events. The figure is practically longer than the code, but it is useful to help understand how netif_rx reacts to its context.

netif_rx is usually called by a driver while in interrupt context, but there are exceptions, notably when the function is called by the loopback device. For this reason, netif_rx disables interrupts on the local CPU when it starts, and re-enables them when it finishes.[†]

When looking at the code, one should keep in mind that different CPUs can run netif_rx concurrently. This is not a problem, since each CPU is associated with a private softnet_data structure that maintains state information. Among other things, the CPU's softnet_data structure includes a private input queue (see the section "softnet_data Structure" in Chapter 9).

---

[*] There is an interesting exception: when a CPU of an SMP system dies, the dev_cpu_callback routine drains the input_pkt_queue queue of the associated softnet_data instance. dev_cpu_callback is the callback routine registered by net_dev_init in the cpu_chain introduced in Chapter 9.

[†] netif_rx_ni is a sister to netif_rx and is used in noninterrupt contexts. Among the systems using it is the TUN (Universal TUN/TAP) device driver in *drivers/net/tun.c*.

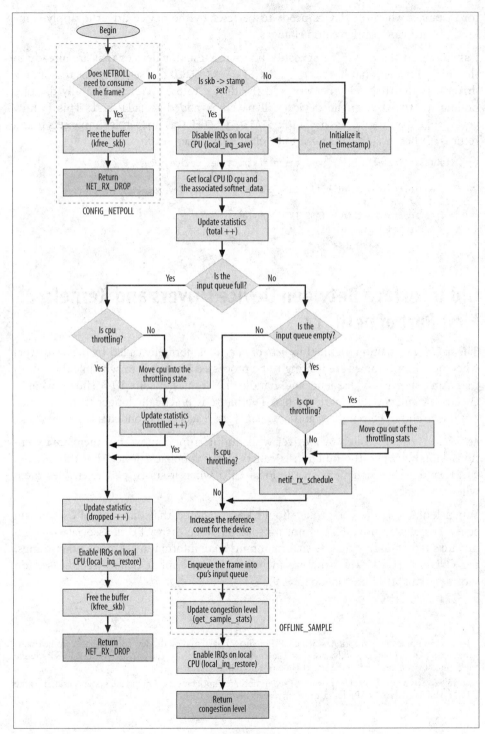

Figure 10-3. netif_rx function

This is the function's prototype:

```
int netif_rx(struct sk_buff *skb)
```

Its only input parameter is the buffer received by the device, and the output value is an indication of the congestion level (you can find details in the section "Congestion Management").

The main tasks of netif_rx, whose detailed flowchart is depicted in Figure 10-3, include:

- Initializing some of the sk_buff data structure fields (such as the time the frame was received).

- Storing the received frame onto the CPU's private input queue and notifying the kernel about the frame by triggering the associated softirq NET_RX_SOFTIRQ. This step takes place only if certain conditions are met, the most important of which is whether there is space in the queue.

- Updating the statistics about the congestion level.

Figure 10-4 shows an example of a system with a bunch of CPUs and devices. Each CPU has its own instance of softnet_data, which includes the private input queue where netif_rx will store ingress frames, and the completion_queue where buffers are sent when they are not needed anymore (see the section "Processing the NET_TX_ SOFTIRQ: net_tx_action" in Chapter 11). The figure shows an example where CPU 1 receives an RxComplete interrupt from *eth0*. The associated driver stores the ingress frame into CPU 1's queue. CPU m receives a DMADone interrupt from *ethn* saying that the transmitted buffer is not needed anymore and can therefore be moved to the completion_queue queue.[*]

Initial Tasks of netif_rx

netif_rx starts by saving the time the function was invoked (which also represents the time the frame was received) into the stamp field of the buffer structure:

```
if (skb->stamp.tv_sec == 0)
        net_timestamp(&skb->stamp);
```

Saving the timestamp has a CPU cost—therefore, net_timestamp initializes skb-> stamp only if there is at least one interested user for that field. Interest in the field can be advertised by calling net_enable_timestamp.

Do not confuse this assignment with the one done by the device driver right before or after it calls netif_rx:

```
netif_rx(skb);
dev->last_rx = jiffies;
```

---

[*] Both input_pkt_queue and completion_queue keep only the pointers to the buffers, even if the figure makes it look as if they actually store the complete buffers.

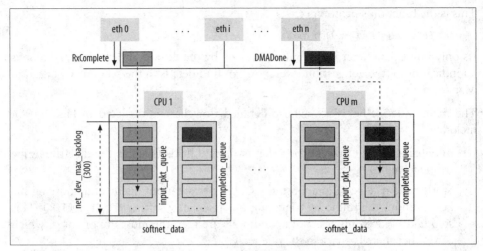

Figure 10-4. CPU's ingress queues

The device driver stores in the net_device structure the time its *most recent* frame was received, and netif_rx stores the time the frame was received in the buffer itself. Thus, one timestamp is associated with a device and the other one is associated with a frame. Note, moreover, that the two timestamps use two different precisions. The device driver stores the timestamp of the most recent frame in jiffies, which in kernel 2.6 comes with a precision of 10 or 1 ms, depending on the architecture (for instance, before 2.6, the i386 used the value 10, but starting with 2.6 the value is 1). netif_rx, however, gets its timestamp by calling get_fast_time, which returns a far more precise value.

The ID of the local CPU is retrieved with smp_processor_id( ) and is stored in the local variable this_cpu:

```
this_cpu = smp_processor_id( );
```

The local CPU ID is needed to retrieve the data structure associated with that CPU in a per-CPU vector, such as the following code in netif_rx:

```
queue = &__get_cpu_var(softnet_data);
```

The preceding line stores in queue a pointer to the softnet_data structure associated with the local CPU that is serving the interrupt triggered by the device driver that called netif_rx.

Now netif_rx updates the total number of frames received by the CPU, including both the ones accepted and the ones discarded (because there was no space in the queue, for instance):

```
netdev_rx_stat[this_cpu].total++
```

Each device driver also keeps statistics, storing them in the private data structure that dev->priv points to. These statistics, which include the number of received frames, the number of dropped frames, etc., are kept on a per-device basis (see Chapter 2), and the ones updated by `netif_rx` are on a per-CPU basis.

Managing Queues and Scheduling the Bottom Half

The input queue is managed by `softnet_data->input_pkt_queue`. Each input queue has a maximum length given by the global variable `netdev_max_backlog`, whose value is 300. This means that each CPU can have up to 300 frames in its input queue waiting to be processed, regardless of the number of devices in the system.[*]

Common sense would say that the value of `netdev_max_backlog` should depend on the number of devices and their speeds. However, this is hard to keep track of in an SMP system where the interrupts are distributed dynamically among the CPUs. It is not obvious which device will talk to which CPU. Thus, the value of `netdev_max_backlog` is chosen through trial and error. In the future, we could imagine it being set dynamically in a manner reflecting the types and number of interfaces. Its value is already configurable by the system administrator, as described in the section "Tuning via /proc and sysfs Filesystems" in Chapter 12. The performance issues are as follows: an unnecessarily large value is a waste of memory, and a slow system may simply never be able to catch up. A value that is too small, on the other hand, could reduce the performance of the device because a burst of traffic could lead to many dropped frames. The optimal value depends a lot on the system's role (host, server, router, etc.).

In the previous kernels, when the `softnet_data` per-CPU data structure was not present, a single input queue, called `backlog`, was shared by all devices with the same size of 300 frames. The main gain with `softnet_data` is not that n CPUs leave room on the queues for $n*300$ frames, but rather, that there is no need for locking among CPUs because each has its own queue.

The following code controls the conditions under which `netif_rx` inserts its new frame on a queue, and the conditions under which it schedules the queue to be run:

```
        if (queue->input_pkt_queue.qlen <= netdev_max_backlog) {
            if (queue->input_pkt_queue.qlen) {
                if (queue->throttle)
                    goto drop;

enqueue:
                dev_hold(skb->dev);
                __skb_queue_tail(&queue->input_pkt_queue,skb);
#ifndef OFFLINE_SAMPLE
                get_sample_stats(this_cpu);
#endif
```

---

[*] This applies to non-NAPI devices. Because NAPI devices use private queues, the devices can select the maximum length they prefer. Common values are 16, 32, and 64. The 10-Gigabit Ethernet driver *drivers/net/s2io. c* uses a larger value (90).

```
                    local_irq_restore(flags);
                return queue->cng_level;
            }

            if (queue->throttle)
                queue->throttle = 0;

            netif_rx_schedule(&queue->backlog_dev);
            goto enqueue;
        }

        ... ... ...

    drop:
        __get_cpu_var(netdev_rx_stat).dropped++;
        local_irq_restore(flags);

        kfree_skb(skb);
        return NET_RX_DROP;
    }
```

The first if statement determines whether there is space. If the queue is full and the statement returns a false result, the CPU is put into a throttle state, which means that it is overloaded by input traffic and therefore is dropping all further frames. The code instituting the throttle is not shown here, but appears in the following section on congestion management.

If there is space on the queue, however, that is not sufficient to ensure that the frame is accepted. The CPU could already be in the "throttle" state (as determined by the third if statement), in which case, the frame is dropped.

The throttle state can be lifted when the queue is empty. This is what the second if statement tests for. When there is data on the queue and the CPU is in the throttle state, the frame is dropped. But when the queue is empty and the CPU is in the throttle state (which an if statement tests for in the second half of the code shown here), the throttle state is lifted.[*]

The dev_hold(skb->dev) call increases the reference count for the device so that the device cannot be removed until this buffer has been completely processed. The corresponding decrement, done by dev_put, takes place inside net_rx_action, which we will analyze later in this chapter.

If all tests are satisfactory, the buffer is queued into the input queue with __skb_queue_tail(&queue->input_pkt_queue,skb), the IRQ's status is restored for the CPU, and the function returns.

---

[*] This case is actually rare because net_rx_action probably lifts the throttle state (indirectly via process_backlog) earlier. We will see this later in this chapter.

Queuing the frame is extremely fast because it does not involve any memory copying, just pointer manipulation. input_pkt_queue is a list of pointers. __skb_queue_tail adds the pointer to the new buffer to the list, without copying the buffer.

The NET_RX_SOFTIRQ software interrupt is scheduled for execution with netif_rx_schedule. Note that netif_rx_schedule is called only when the new buffer is added to an empty queue. The reason is that if the queue is not empty, NET_RX_SOFTIRQ has already been scheduled and there is no need to do it again.

In the section "Pending softirq Handling" in Chapter 9, we saw how the kernel takes care of scheduled software interrupts. In the upcoming section "Processing the NET_RX_SOFTIRQ: net_rx_action," we will see the internals of the NET_RX_SOFTIRQ softirq's handler.

Congestion Management

Congestion management is an important component of the input frame-processing task. An overloaded CPU can become unstable and introduce a big latency into the system. The section "Interrupts" in Chapter 9 explained why the interrupts generated by a high load can cripple the system. For this reason, congestion management mechanisms are needed to make sure the system's stability is not compromised under high network load. Common ways to reduce the CPU load under high traffic loads include:

Reducing the number of interrupts if possible
> This is accomplished by coding drivers either to process several frames with a single interrupt (see the section "Processing Multiple Frames During an Interrupt" in Chapter 9), or to use NAPI.

Discarding frames as early as possible in the ingress path
> If code knows that a frame is going to be dropped by higher layers, it can save CPU time by dropping the frame quickly. For instance, if a device driver knew that the ingress queue was full, it could drop a frame right away instead of relaying it to the kernel and having the latter drop it.

The second point is what we cover in this section.

A similar optimization applies to the egress path: if a device driver does not have resources to accept new frames for transmission (that is, if the device is out of memory), it would be a waste of CPU time to have the kernel pushing new frames down to the driver for transmission. This point is discussed in Chapter 11 in the section "Enabling and Disabling Transmissions."

In both cases, reception and transmission, the kernel provides a set of functions to set, clear, and retrieve the status of the receive and transmit queues, which allows device drivers (on reception) and the core kernel (on transmission) to perform the optimizations just mentioned.

A good indication of the congestion level is the number of frames that have been received and are waiting to be processed. When a device driver uses NAPI, it is up to the driver to implement any congestion control mechanism. This is because ingress frames are kept in the NIC's memory or in the receive ring managed by the driver, and the kernel cannot keep track of traffic congestion. In contrast, when a device driver does not use NAPI, frames are added to per-CPU queues (softnet_data-> input_pkt_queue) and the kernel keeps track of the congestion level of the queues. In this section, we cover this latter case.

Queue theory is a complex topic, and this book is not the place for the mathematical details. I will content myself with one simple point: the current number of frames in the queue does not necessarily represent the real congestion level. An average queue length is a better guide to the queue's status. Keeping track of the average keeps the system from wrongly classifying a burst of traffic as congestion. In the Linux network stack, average queue length is reported by two fields of the softnet_data structure, cng_level and avg_blog, that were introduced in "softnet_data Structure" in Chapter 9.

Being an average, avg_blog could be both bigger and smaller than the length of input_pkt_queue at any time. The former represents recent history and the latter represents the present situation. Because of that, they are used for two different purposes:

- By default, every time a frame is queued into input_pkt_queue, avg_blog is updated and an associated congestion level is computed and saved into cng_ level. The latter is used as the return value by netif_rx so that the device driver that called this function is given a feedback about the queue status and can change its behavior accordingly.

- The number of frames in input_pkt_queue cannot exceed a maximum size. When that size is reached, following frames are dropped because the CPU is clearly overwhelmed.

Let's go back to the computation and use of the congestion level. avg_blog and cng_ level are updated inside get_sample_stats, which is called by netif_rx.

At the moment, few device drivers use the feedback from netif_rx. The most common use of this feedback is to update statistics local to the device drivers. For a more interesting use of the feedback, see *drivers/net/tulip/de2104x.c*: when netif_rx returns NET_RX_DROP, a local variable drop is set to 1, which causes the main loop to start dropping the frames in the receive ring instead of processing them.

So long as the ingress queue input_pkt_queue is not full, it is the job of the device driver to use the feedback from netif_rx to handle congestion. When the situation gets worse and the input queue fills in, the kernel comes into play and uses the softnet_data->throttle flag to disable frame reception for the CPU. (Remember that there is a softnet_data structure for each CPU.)

Congestion Management in netif_rx

Let's go back to `netif_rx` and look at some of the code that was omitted from the previous section of this chapter. The following two excerpts include some of the code shown previously, along with new code that shows when a CPU is placed in the throttle state.

```
if (queue->input_pkt_queue.qlen <= netdev_max_backlog) {
    if (queue->input_pkt_queue.qlen) {
        if (queue->throttle)
            goto drop;
        ... ... ...
        return queue->cng_level;
    }
    ... ...    ...
}

if (!queue->throttle) {
    queue->throttle = 1;
    __get_cpu_var(netdev_rx_stat).throttled++;
}
```

`softnet_data->throttle` is cleared when the queue gets empty. To be exact, it is cleared by `netif_rx` when the first frame is queued into an empty queue. It could also happen in `process_backlog`, as we will see in the section "Backlog Processing: The process_backlog Poll Virtual Function."

Average Queue Length and Congestion-Level Computation

The value of `avg_blog` and `cng_level` is always updated within `get_sample_stats`. The latter can be invoked in two different ways:

- Every time a new frame is received (`netif_rx`). This is the default.
- With a periodic timer. To use this technique, one has to define the `OFFLINE_SAMPLE` symbol. That's the reason why in `netif_rx`, the execution of `get_sample_stats` depends on the definition of the `OFFLINE_SAMPLE` symbol. It is disabled by default.

The first approach ends up running `get_sample_stats` more often than the second approach under medium and high traffic load.

In both cases, the formula used to compute `avg_blog` should be simple and quick, because it could be invoked frequently. The formula used takes into account the recent history and the present:

```
new_value_for_avg_blog = (old_value_of_avg_blog + current_value_of_queue_len) / 2
```

How much to weight the present and the past is not a simple problem. The preceding formula can adapt quickly to changes in the congestion level, since the past (the old value) is given only 50% of the weight and the present the other 50%.

get_sample_stats also updates cng_level, basing it on avg_blog through the mapping shown earlier in Figure 9-4 in Chapter 9. If the RAND_LIE symbol is defined, the function performs an extra operation in which it can randomly decide to set cng_level one level higher. This random adjustment requires more time to calculate but, oddly enough, can cause the kernel to perform better under one specific scenario.

Let's spend a few more words on the benefits of random lies. Do not confuse this behavior with Random Early Detection (RED).

In a system with only one interface, it does not really make sense to drop random frames here and there if there is no congestion; it would simply lower the throughput. But let's suppose we have multiple interfaces sharing an input queue and one device with a traffic load much higher than the others. Since the greedy device fills the shared ingress queue faster than the other devices, the latter will often find no space in the ingress queue and therefore their frames will be dropped.* The greedy device will also see some of its frames dropped, but not proportionally to its load. When a system with multiple interfaces experiences congestion, it should drop ingress frames across all the devices proportionally to their loads. The RAND_LIE code adds some fairness when used in this context: dropping extra frames randomly should end up dropping them proportionally to the load.

Processing the NET_RX_SOFTIRQ: net_rx_action

net_rx_action is the bottom-half function used to process incoming frames. Its execution is triggered whenever a driver notifies the kernel about the presence of input frames. Figure 10-5 shows the flow of control through the function.

Frames can wait in two places for net_rx_action to process them:

A shared CPU-specific queue
> Non-NAPI devices' interrupt handlers, which call netif_rx, place frames into the softnet_data->input_pkt_queue of the CPU on which the interrupt handlers run.

Device memory
> The poll method used by NAPI drivers extracts frames directly from the device (or the device driver receive rings).

The section "Old Versus New Driver Interfaces" showed how the kernel is notified about the need to run net_rx_action in both cases.

---

* When sharing a queue, it is up to the users to behave fairly with others, but that's not always possible. NAPI does not encounter this problem because each device using NAPI has its own queue. However, non-NAPI drivers still using the shared input queue input_pkt_queue have to live with the possibility of overloading by other devices.

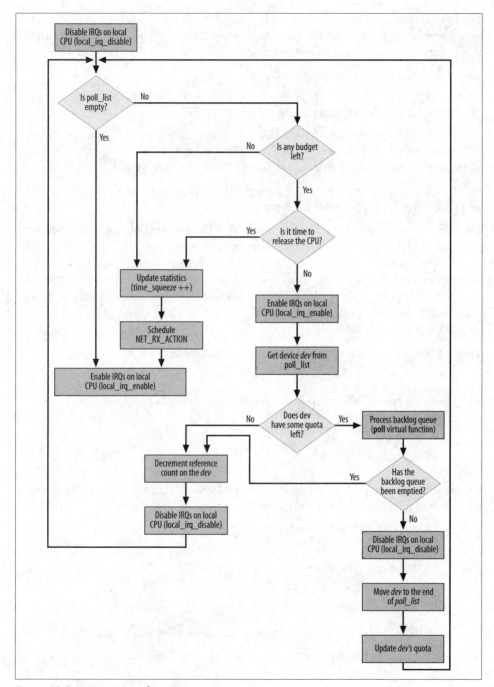

Figure 10-5. net_rx_action function

The job of net_rx_action is pretty simple: to browse the poll_list list of devices that have something in their ingress queue and invoke for each one the associated poll virtual function until one of the following conditions is met:

- There are no more devices in the list.
- net_rx_action has run for too long and therefore it is supposed to release the CPU so that it does not become a CPU hog.
- The number of frames already dequeued and processed has reached a given upper bound limit (budget). budget is initialized at the beginning of the function to netdev_max_backlog, which is defined in *net/core/dev.c* as 300.

As we will see in the next section, net_rx_action calls the driver's poll virtual function and depends partly on this function to obey these constraints.

The size of the queue, as we saw in the section "Managing Queues and Scheduling the Bottom Half," is restricted to the value of netdev_max_backlog. This value is considered the *budget* for net_rx_action. However, because net_rx_action runs with interrupts enabled, new frames could be added to a device's input queue while net_rx_action is running. Thus, the number of available frames could become greater than budget, and net_rx_action has to take action to make sure it does not run too long in such cases.

Now we will see in detail what net_rx_action does inside:

```
static void net_rx_action(struct softirq_action *h)
{
    struct softnet_data *queue = &__get_cpu_var(softnet_data);
    unsigned long start_time = jiffies;
    int budget = netdev_max_backlog;

    local_irq_disable();
```

If the current device has not yet used its entire quota, it is given a chance to dequeue buffers from its queue with the poll virtual function:

```
    while (!list_empty(&queue->poll_list)) {
        struct net_device *dev;

        if (budget <= 0 || jiffies - start_time > 1)
            goto softnet_break;

        local_irq_enable();

        dev = list_entry(queue->poll_list.next, struct net_device, poll_list);
```

If dev->poll returns because the device quota was not large enough to dequeue all the buffers in the ingress queue (in which case, the return value is nonzero), the device is moved to the end of poll_list:

```
        if (dev->quota <= 0 || dev->poll(dev, &budget)) {
            local_irq_disable();
```

```
            list_del(&dev->poll_list);
            list_add_tail(&dev->poll_list, &queue->poll_list);
            if (dev->quota < 0)
                dev->quota += dev->weight;
            else
                dev->quota = dev->weight;
        } else {
```

When instead poll manages to empty the device ingress queue, net_rx_action does not remove the device from poll_list: poll is supposed to take care of it with a call to netif_rx_complete (__netif_rx_complete can also be called if IRQs are disabled on the local CPU). This will be illustrated in the process_backlog function in the next section.

Furthermore, note that budget was passed by reference to the poll virtual function; this is because that function will return a new budget that reflects the frames it processed. The main loop in net_rx_action checks budget at each pass so that the overall limit is not exceeded. In other words, budget allows net_rx_action and the poll function to cooperate to stay within their limit.

```
            dev_put(dev);
            local_irq_disable( );
        }
    }
out:
    local_irq_enable( );
    return;
```

This last piece of code is executed when net_rx_action is forced to return while buffers are still left in the ingress queue. In this case, the NET_RX_SOFTIRQ softirq is scheduled again for execution so that net_rx_action will be invoked later and will take care of the remaining buffers:

```
softnet_break:
    __get_cpu_var(netdev_rx_stat).time_squeeze++;
    __raise_softirq_irqoff(NET_RX_SOFTIRQ);
    goto out;
}
```

Note that net_rx_action disables interrupts with local_irq_disable only while manipulating the poll_list list of devices to poll (i.e., when accessing its softnet_data structure instance). The netpoll_poll_lock and netpoll_poll_unlock calls, used by the NETPOLL feature, have been omitted. If you can access the kernel source code, see *net_rx_action* in *net/core/dev.c* for details.

Backlog Processing: The process_backlog Poll Virtual Function

The poll virtual function of the net_device data structure, which is executed by net_rx_action to process the backlog queue of a device, is initialized by default to process_backlog in net_dev_init for those devices not using NAPI.

As of kernel 2.6.12, only a few device drivers use NAPI, and initialize dev->poll with a pointer to a function of its own: the Broadcom Tigon3 Ethernet driver in *drivers/net/tg3.c* was the first one to adopt NAPI and is a good example to look at. In this section, we will analyze the default handler process_backlog defined in *net/core/dev.c*. Its implementation is very similar to that of a poll method of a device driver using NAPI (you can, for instance, compare process_backlog to tg3_poll).

However, since process_backlog can take care of a bunch of devices sharing the same ingress queue, there is one important difference to take into account. When process_backlog runs, hardware interrupts are enabled, so the function could be preempted. For this reason, accesses to the softnet_data structure are always protected by disabling interrupts on the local CPU with local_irq_disable, especially the calls to __skb_dequeue. This lock is not needed by a device driver using NAPI:[*] when its poll method is invoked, hardware interrupts are disabled for the device. Moreover, each device has its own queue.

Let's see the main parts of process_backlog. Figure 10-6 shows its flowchart.

The function starts with a few initializations:

```
static int process_backlog(struct net_device *backlog_dev, int *budget)
{
    int work = 0;
    int quota = min(backlog_dev->quota, *budget);
    struct softnet_data *queue = &__get_cpu_var(softnet_data);
    unsigned long start_time = jiffies;
```

Then begins the main loop, which tries to dequeue all the buffers in the input queue and is interrupted only if one of the following conditions is met:

- The queue becomes empty.
- The device's quota has been used up.
- The function has been running for too long.

The last two conditions are similar to the ones that constrain net_rx_action. Because process_backlog is called within a loop in net_rx_action, the latter can respect its constraints only if process_backlog cooperates. For this reason, net_rx_action passes its leftover budget to process_backlog, and the latter sets its quota to the minimum of that input parameter (budget) and its own quota.

budget is initialized by net_rx_action to 300 when it starts. The default value for dev->quota is 64 (and most devices stick with the default). Let's examine a case where several devices have full queues. The first four devices to run within this function receive a value of budget greater than their internal quota of 64, and can empty their queues.

---

[*] Because each CPU has its own instance of softnet_data, there is no need for extra locking to take care of SMP.

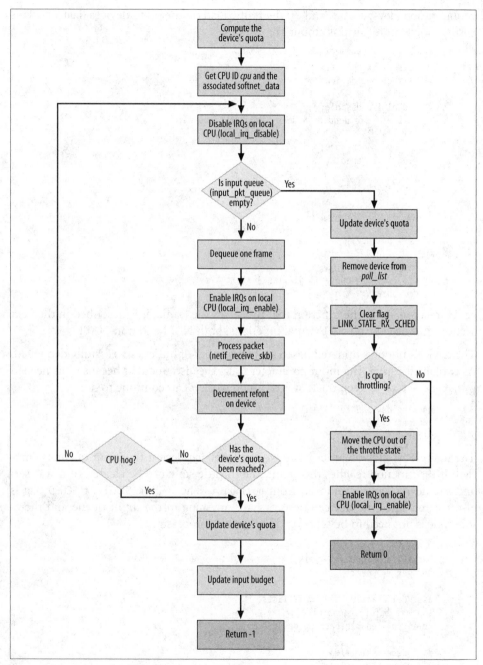

Figure 10-6. process_backlog function

The next device may have to stop after sending a part of its queue. That is, the number of buffers dequeued by process_backlog depends both on the device configuration (dev->quota), and on the traffic load on the other devices (budget). This ensures some more fairness among the devices.

```
for (;;) {
    struct sk_buff *skb;
    struct net_device *dev;

    local_irq_disable();
    skb = __skb_dequeue(&queue->input_pkt_queue);
    if (!skb)
        goto job_done;
    local_irq_enable();

    dev = skb->dev;

    netif_receive_skb(skb);

    dev_put(dev);

    work++;
    if (work >= quota || jiffies - start_time > 1)
        break;
```

netif_receive_skb is the function that processes the frame; it is described in the next section. It is used by all poll virtual functions, both NAPI and non-NAPI.

The device's quota is updated based on the number of buffers successfully dequeued. As explained earlier, the input parameter budget is also updated because it is needed by net_rx_action to keep track of how much work it can continue to do:

```
backlog_dev->quota -= work;
*budget -= work;
return -1;
```

The main loop shown earlier jumps to the label job_done if the input queue is emptied. If the function reaches this point, the throttle state can be cleared (if it was set) and the device can be removed from poll_list. The __LINK_STATE_RX_SCHED flag is also cleared since the device does not have anything in the input queue and therefore it does not need to be scheduled for backlog processing.

```
job_done:
    backlog_dev->quota -= work;
    *budget -= work;

    list_del(&backlog_dev->poll_list);
    smp_mb__before_clear_bit();
    netif_poll_enable(backlog_dev);

    if (queue->throttle)
        queue->throttle = 0;
    local_irq_enable();
    return 0;
}
```

Actually, there is another difference between process_backlog and a NAPI driver's poll method. Let's return to *drivers/net/tg3.c* as an example:

```
if (done) {
        spin_lock_irqsave(&tp->lock, flags);
        __netif_rx_complete(netdev);
        tg3_restart_ints(tp);
        spin_unlock_irqrestore(&tp->lock, flags);
}
```

done here is the counterpart of job_done in process_backlog, with the same meaning that the queue is empty. At this point, in the NAPI driver, the __netif_rx_complete function (defined in the same file) removes the device from the poll_list list, a task that process_backlog does directly. Finally, the NAPI driver re-enables interrupts for the device. As we anticipated at the beginning of the section, process_backlog runs with interrupts enabled.

Ingress Frame Processing

As mentioned in the previous section, netif_receive_skb is the helper function used by the poll virtual function to process ingress frames. It is illustrated in Figure 10-7.

Multiple protocols are allowed by both L2 and L3. Each device driver is associated with a specific hardware type (e.g., Ethernet), so it is easy for it to interpret the L2 header and extract the information that tells it which L3 protocol is being used, if any (see Chapter 13). When net_rx_action is invoked, the L3 protocol identifier has already been extracted from the L2 header and stored into skb->protocol by the device driver.

The three main tasks of netif_receive_skb are:

- Passing a copy of the frame to each protocol tap, if any are running
- Passing a copy of the frame to the L3 protocol handler associated with skb->protocol[*]
- Taking care of those features that need to be handled at this layer, notably bridging (which is described in Part IV)

If no protocol handler is associated with skb->protocol and none of the features handled in netif_receive_skb (such as bridging) consumes the frame, it is dropped because the kernel doesn't know how to process it.

Before delivering an input frame to these protocol handlers, netif_receive_skb must handle a few features that can change the destiny of the frame.

---

[*] See Chapter 13 for more details on protocol handlers.

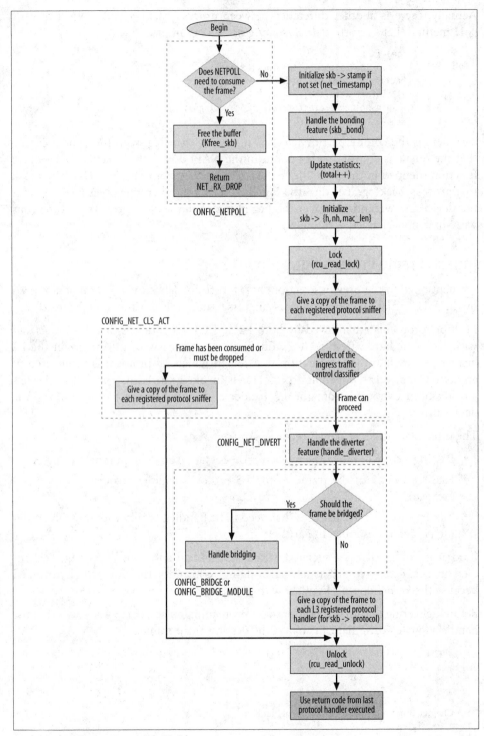

Figure 10-7. The netif_receive_skb function

Bonding allows a group of interfaces to be grouped together and be treated as a single interface. If the interface from which the frame was received belonged to one such group, the reference to the receiving interface in the sk_buff data structure must be changed to the device in the group with the role of master before netif_receive_skb delivers the packet to the L3 handler. This is the purpose of skb_bond.

```
skb_bond(skb);
```

The delivery of the frame to the sniffers and protocol handlers is covered in detail in Chapter 13.

Once all of the protocol sniffers have received their copy of the packet, and before the real protocol handler is given its copy, Diverter, ingress Traffic Control, and bridging features must be handled (see the next section).

When neither the bridging code nor the ingress Traffic Control code consumes the frame, the latter is passed to the L3 protocol handlers (usually there is only one handler per protocol, but multiple ones can be registered). In older kernel versions, this was the only processing needed. The more the kernel network stack was enhanced and the more features that were added (in this layer and in others), the more complex the path of a packet through the network stack became.

At this point, the reception part is complete and it will be up to the L3 protocol handlers to decide what to do with the packets:

- Deliver them to a recipient (application) running in the receiving workstation.
- Drop them (for instance, during a failed sanity check).
- Forward them.

The last choice is common for routers, but not for single-interface workstations. Parts V and VI cover L3 behavior in detail.

The kernel determines from the destination L3 address whether the packet is addressed to its local system. I will postpone a discussion of this process until Part VII; let's take it for granted for the moment that somehow the packet will be delivered to the above layers (i.e., TCP, UDP, ICMP, etc.) if it is addressed to the local system, and to ip_forward otherwise (see Figure 9-2 in Chapter 9).

This finishes our long discussion of how frame reception works. The next chapter describes how frames are transmitted. This second path includes both frames generated locally and received frames that need to be forwarded.

Handling special features

netif_receive_skb checks whether any Netpoll client would like to consume the frame.

Traffic Control has always been used to implement QoS on the egress path. However, with recent releases of the kernel, you can configure filters and actions on ingress traffic, too. Based on such a configuration, `ing_filter` may decide that the input buffer is to be dropped or that it will be processed further somewhere else (i.e., the frame is consumed).

Diverter allows the kernel to change the L2 destination address of frames originally addressed to other hosts so that the frames can be diverted to the local host. There are many possible uses for this feature, as discussed at *http://diverter.sourceforge.net*. The kernel can be configured to determine the criteria used by Diverter to decide whether to divert a frame. Common criteria used for Diverter include:

- All IP packets (regardless of L4 protocol)
- All TCP packets
- TCP packets with specific port numbers
- All UDP packets
- UDP packets with specific port numbers

The call to `handle_diverter` decides whether to change the destination MAC address. In addition to the change to the destination MAC address, `skb->pkt_type` must be changed to `PACKET_HOST`.

Yet another L2 feature could influence the destiny of the frame: Bridging. Bridging, the L2 counterpart of L3 routing, is addressed in Part IV. Each `net_device` data structure has a pointer to a data structure of type `net_bridge_port` that is used to store the extra information needed to represent a bridge port. Its value is NULL when the interface has not enabled bridging. When a port is configured as a bridge port, the kernel looks only at L2 headers. The only L3 information the kernel uses in this situation is information pertaining to firewalling.

Since `net_rx_action` represents the boundary between device drivers and the L3 protocol handlers, it is right in this function that the Bridging feature must be handled. When the kernel has support for bridging, `handle_bridge` is initialized to a function that checks whether the frame is to be handed to the bridging code. When the frame is handed to the bridging code and the latter consumes it, `handle_bridge` returns 1. In all other cases, `handle_bridge` returns 0 and `netif_receive_skb` will continue processing the frame skb.

```
if (handle_bridge(skb, &pt_prev, &ret));
    goto out;
```

## CHAPTER 11

Frame Transmission

Transmission is the term used for frames that leave the system, either because they were sent by the system or because they are being forwarded. In this chapter, we will cover the main tasks involved during the frame transmission data path:

- Enabling and disabling frame transmission for a device
- Scheduling a device for transmission
- Selecting the next frame to transmit among the ones waiting in the device's egress queue
- The transmission itself (we will examine the main function)

Much about transmission is symmetric to the reception process we discussed in Chapter 10: NET_TX_SOFTIRQ is the transmission counterpart of the NET_RX_SOFTIRQ softirq, net_tx_action is the counterpart of net_rx_action, and so on. Thus, if you have studied the earlier chapter, you should find it easy to follow this one. Figure 11-1 compares the logic behind scheduling a device for reception and scheduling a device for transmission. Here are some more similarities:

- poll_list is the list of devices that are polled because they have a nonempty receive queue. output_queue is the list of devices that have something to transmit. poll_list and output_queue are two fields of the softnet_data structure introduced in Chapter 9.
- Only open devices (ones with the __LINK_STATE_START flag set) can be scheduled for reception. Only devices with transmission enabled (ones with the __LINK_STATE_XOFF flag cleared) can be scheduled for transmission.
- When a device is scheduled for reception, its __LINK_STATE_RX_SCHED flag is set. When a device is scheduled for transmission, its __LINK_STATE_SCHED flag is set.

dev_queue_xmit plays the same role for the egress path that netif_rx plays for the ingress path: each transfers one frame between the driver's buffer and the kernel's queue. The net_tx_action function is called both when there are devices waiting to transmit something and to do housekeeping with the buffers that are not needed

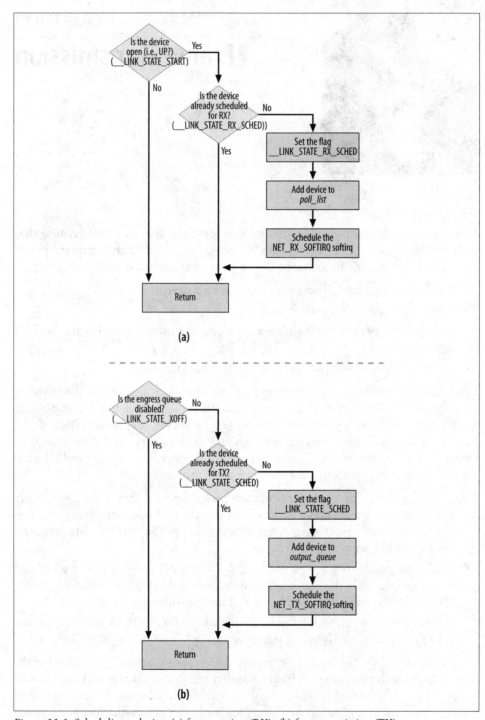

Figure 11-1. Scheduling a device: (a) for reception (RX); (b) for transmission (TX)

anymore. Just as there are queues for ingress traffic, there are queues for egress traffic. The egress queues, handled by Traffic Control (the QoS layer), are actually much more complex than the ingress ones: while the latter are just ordinary First In, First Outs (FIFOs), the former can be hierarchical, represented by trees of queues. Even though Traffic Control has support for ingress queueing too, it's used more for policing and management reasons rather than real queuing: Traffic Control does not use real queues for ingress traffic, but only classifies and applies actions.

Enabling and Disabling Transmissions

In the section "Congestion Management" in Chapter 10, we learned about some conditions under which frame reception must be disabled, either on a single device or globally. Something similar applies to frame transmission as well.

The status of the egress queue is represented by the flag `__LINK_STATE_XOFF` in `net_device->state`. Its value can be manipulated and checked with the following functions, defined in *include/linux/netdevice.h*:[*]

`netif_start_queue`

> Enables transmission for the device. It is usually called when the device is activated and can be called again later if needed to restart a stopped device.

`netif_stop_queue`

> Disables transmission for the device. Any attempt to transmit something on the device will be denied. Later in this section is an example of a common case where this function is used.

`netif_queue_stopped`

> Returns the status of the egress queue: enabled or disabled. This function is simply:
>
> ```
> static inline int netif_queue_stopped(const struct net_device *dev)
> {
>     return test_bit(__LINK_STATE_XOFF, &dev->state);
> }
> ```

Only device drivers enable and disable transmission of devices.

Why stop and start a queue once the device is running? One reason is that a device can temporarily use up its memory, thus causing a transmission attempt to fail. In the past, the transmitting function (which I introduce later in the section "dev_queue_xmit Function") would have to deal with this problem by putting the frame back into the queue (requeuing it). Now, thanks to the `__LINK_STATE_XOFF` flag, this extra processing can be avoided. When the device driver realizes that it does not have enough space to store a frame of maximum size (MTU), it stops the egress queue

---

[*] The other flags in the list are described in Chapters 8 and 10.

with `netif_stop_queue`. In this way, it is possible to avoid wasting resources with future transmissions that the kernel already knows will fail. The following example of this throttling at work is taken from `vortex_start_xmit` (the `hard_start_xmit` method used by the *drivers/net/3c59x.c* driver):

```
outsl(ioaddr + TX_FIFO, skb->data, (skb->len + 3) >> 2);
dev_kfree_skb (skb);
if (inw(ioaddr + TxFree) > 1536) {
    netif_start_queue (dev);     /* AKPM: redundant? */
} else {
    /* Interrupt us when the FIFO has room for max-sized packet. */
    netif_stop_queue(dev);
    outw(SetTxThreshold + (1536>>2), ioaddr + EL3_CMD);
}
```

Shortly after the transmission by `outsl`, the code checks whether there is space for a frame of maximum size (1536), and uses `netif_stop_queue` to stop the device's egress queue if there is not. This is a relatively crude technique used to avoid transmission failures due to a shortage of memory. Of course, the transmission of a frame of 300 bytes would succeed when just a little more than 300 bytes are left; therefore, checking for 1,536 bytes could disable transmission unnecessarily. The code could compromise by using a lower value, such as 500, but in the end, the gain would not be that big and there could be failures when bigger frames arrive while transmission is enabled.

To cover all eventualities, the code calls `netif_start_queue` when there is enough memory on the device. The redundant? comment in the code refers to the practice of restarting the queue on two types of interrupts. The driver requests a restart to the queue when the device indicates that it has finished transmitting, and when it indicates that there is enough space in its memory for another frame. Probably, the queue would be restarted promptly if the driver did so on only one of these interrupts, but that's not guaranteed. So the request to restart the queue is issued under both circumstances.

The code also sends a `SetTxThreshold` command to the device, which instructs the device to generate an interrupt when a given amount of memory (the size of the MTU, in this case) becomes available.

You may wonder when and how the queue will be re-enabled in the previous scenario. In the case of the Vortex driver, it asks the device to generate an interrupt when a given amount of memory (the size of the MTU, in this case) becomes available. This is the piece of code that handles such an interrupt:

```
static void vortex_interrupt(int irq, void *dev_id, struct pt_regs *regs)
{
        ... ... ...
        if (status & TxAvailable) {
            if (vortex_debug > 5)
                printk(KERN_DEBUG "    TX room bit was handled.\n");
            /* There's room in the FIFO for a full-sized packet. */
```

```
            outw(AckIntr | TxAvailable, ioaddr + EL3_CMD);
            netif_wake_queue (dev);
        }
        ... ... ...
    }
```

The bits of the status variable represent the reasons why the interrupt was generated by the card. The TxAvailable bit indicates that space is available and that it's
therefore safe to wake up the device (this is called waking the queue, and is carried
out by netif_wake_queue). Values such as EL3_CMD are simply offsets from ioaddr used
by the driver to read or write the network card registers at the right positions.

Note that the egress queue is re-enabled with netif_wake_queue instead of netif_
start_queue. That new function, which we will see later in more detail, not only
enables the egress queue but also asks the kernel to check whether anything in that
queue is waiting to be transmitted. The reason is that during the time the queue was
disabled, there could have been transmission attempts. In this case, they would have
failed, and those frames that could not be sent would have been put back into the
egress queue.

Scheduling a Device for Transmission

When describing the ingress path, we saw that when a device receives a frame, its
driver invokes a kernel function (the one invoked depends on whether the driver uses
NAPI) that adds the device to a polling list and schedules the NET_RX_SOFTIRQ for
execution.

Something very similar happens on the egress path. To transmit frames, the kernel
provides the dev_queue_xmit function, described later in its own section. This function dequeues a frame from the device's egress queue and feeds it to the device's
hard_start_xmit method. However, dev_queue_xmit might not be able to transmit for
various reasons—for instance, because the device's egress queue is disabled, as we
saw in the previous section, or because the lock on the device queue is already taken.
To handle the latter case, the kernel provides a function called __netif_schedule that
schedules a device for transmission (somewhat similar to what netif_rx_schedule
does on the reception path). This function is never called directly, but through two
wrappers shown later in this section.

Here is the function's definition from *include/linux/netdevice.h*:

```
    static inline void __netif_schedule(struct net_device *dev)
    {
        if (!test_and_set_bit(__LINK_STATE_SCHED, &dev->state)) {
            unsigned long flags;
            struct softnet_data *sd;

            local_irq_save(flags);
            sd = &__get_cpu_var(softnet_data);
            dev->next_sched = sd->output_queue;
```

```
        sd->output_queue = dev;
        raise_softirq_irqoff(cpu, NET_TX_SOFTIRQ);
        local_irq_restore(flags);
    }
}
```

__netif_schedule accomplishes two main tasks:

- It adds the device to the head of the output_queue list. This list is the counterpart to the poll_list list used by reception. There is one output_queue for each
  CPU, just as there is one poll_list for each CPU. However, output_queue is used
  by both NAPI and non-NAPI devices, and poll_list is used only to handle NAPI
  devices. The devices in the output_queue list are linked together with the net_
  device->next_sched pointer. You will see in the section "Processing the NET_
  TX_SOFTIRQ: net_tx_action" how that list is used.

  We already saw in the section "softnet_data Structure" in Chapter 9 that output_
  queue represents a list of devices that have something to send (because they failed
  on previous attempts, as described in the section "Queuing Discipline Interface") or whose egress queues have been re-enabled after having been disabled
  for a while. Because __netif_schedule may be called both inside and outside
  interrupt context, it disables interrupts while adding the input device to the
  output_queue list.

- It schedules the NET_TX_SOFTIRQ softirq for execution. __LINK_STATE_SCHED is used
  to mark devices that are in the output_queue list because they have something to
  send. (__LINK_STATE_SCHED is the counterpart of the reception path's __LINK_
  STATE_RX_SCHED.) Note that if the device was already scheduled for transmission,
  __netif_schedule would not do anything.

Since it does not make sense to schedule a device for transmission if transmission is
disabled on the device, the kernel provides two functions to be used instead, both
wrappers around __netif_schedule:

netif_schedule*

Simply makes sure transmission is enabled on the device before scheduling it for
transmission:

```
static inline void netif_schedule(struct net_device *dev)
{
    if (!test_bit(__LINK_STATE_XOFF, &dev->state))
        __netif_schedule(dev);
}
```

netif_wake_queue

Enables transmission for the device and, if transmission was previously disabled, schedules the device for transmission. This scheduling is needed because

---

* For consistency, netif_tx_schedule would probably have been a better name.

there could have been transmission attempts while the device queue was disabled. We saw an example of its use in the previous section.

```
static inline void netif_wake_queue(struct net_device *dev)
{
    ...
    if (test_and_clear_bit(__LINK_STATE_XOFF, &dev->state))
        __netif_schedule(dev);
}
```

`test_and_clear_bit` clears the `__LINK_STATE_XOFF` flag if it is set, and returns the old value.

Note that a call to netif_wake_queue is equivalent to a call to both netif_start_queue and netif_schedule. I said in the section "Enabling and Disabling Transmissions" that it is the responsibility of the driver, not higher-layer functions, to disable and enable transmission on devices. Usually, high-level functions schedule transmissions on devices, and device drivers disable and re-enable the queue when required, such as to handle a shortage of memory. Therefore, it should not come as a surprise that netif_wake_queue is the one used by device drivers, and netif_schedule is the one used elsewhere (for example, by net_tx_action* and Traffic Control).

A device driver uses netif_wake_queue in the following cases:

- We will see in the section "Watchdog timer" that device drivers use a watchdog timer to recover from a transmission that hangs. In such a situation, the virtual function net_device->tx_timeout usually resets the card. During that black hole in which the device is not usable, there could be other transmission attempts, so the driver needs to first enable the device's queue and then schedule the device for transmission. The same applies to interrupts that signal error conditions (look at *drivers/net/3c59x.c* for some examples).

- When (as previously requested by the driver itself) the device signals to the driver that it has enough memory to handle the transmission of a frame of a given size, the device can be awakened. We already saw an example of this practice in the previous section in relation to the TxAvailable interrupt. The reason for using this function, again, is that during the time the driver has disabled the queue, there could have been transmission attempts. A similar consideration applies to the interrupt type that tells the driver when a driver-to-card DMA transfer has completed.

Queuing Discipline Interface

Almost all devices use a queue to schedule egress traffic, and the kernel can use algorithms known as *queuing disciplines* to arrange the frames in the most efficient order

---

* net_tx_action schedules a device for transmission when it cannot grab the dev->queue_lock lock on the device's egress queue and therefore cannot transmit.

for transmission. Although a detailed discussion of Traffic Control and its queuing disciplines is outside the scope of this book, in this section I'll provide a brief overview of the interface between device drivers and the transmission layer discussed in this chapter.

Each Traffic Control queuing discipline can provide different function pointers to be called by higher layers to accomplish different tasks. Among the most important functions are:

enqueue
> Adds an element to the queue

dequeue
> Extracts an element from the queue

requeue
> Puts back on the queue an element that was previously extracted (e.g., because of a transmission failure)

Whenever a device is scheduled for transmission, the next frame to transmit is selected by the qdisc_run function, which indirectly calls the dequeue virtual function of the associated queuing discipline.

Once again, the real job is actually done by another function, qdisc_restart. The qdisc_run function, defined in *include/linux/pkt_sched.h*, is simply a wrapper that filters out requests for devices whose egress queues are disabled:

```
static inline void qdisc_run(struct net_device *dev)
{
    while (!netif_queue_stopped(dev) && qdisc_restart(dev) < 0)
        /* NOTHING */;
}
```

qdisc_restart function

We saw earlier the common cases where a device is scheduled for transmission. Sometimes it is because something in the egress queue is waiting to be transmitted. But at other times, the device is scheduled because the queue has been disabled for a while and therefore there could be something waiting in the queue from previous failed transmission attempts. The driver does not know whether anything has actually arrived; it must schedule the device in case data is waiting. If in fact no data is waiting, the subsequent call to the dequeue method fails. Even if data is waiting, the call can fail because complex queuing disciplines may decide not to transmit any of the data. Therefore, qdisc_restart, defined in *net/sched/sch_generic.c*, takes various actions based on the return value of the dequeue method.

```
int qdisc_restart(struct net_device *dev)
{
    struct Qdisc *q = dev->qdisc;
    struct sk_buff *skb;

    if ((skb = q->dequeue(q)) != NULL) {
```

The dequeue function is called at the very start. Let's suppose it succeeded. Transmitting a frame requires the acquisition of two locks:

- The lock that protects the queue (dev->queue_lock). This is acquired by the caller of qdisc_restart (dev_queue_xmit).
- The lock on the driver's transmit routine hard_start_xmit (dev->xmit_lock). The lock is managed by this function. When the device driver already implements its own locking, it indicates this by setting the NETIF_F_LLTX flag (lockless transmission feature) in dev->features to tell the upper layers that there is no need to acquire the dev->xmit_lock lock as well. The use of NETIF_F_LLTX allows the kernel to optimize the transmit data path by not acquiring dev->xmit_lock when it is not needed. Of course, there is no need to acquire the lock if the queue is empty.

Note that qdisc_restart does not release the queue_lock immediately after dequeuing a buffer, because the function might have to requeue the buffer right away if it fails to acquire the lock on the driver. The function releases queue_lock when it has the driver lock in hand, and reacquires queue_lock before returning. Ultimately, dev_queue_xmit will take care of releasing it.

When the driver does not support NETIF_F_LLTX and the driver lock is already taken (i.e., spin_trylock returns 0), transmission fails. If qdisc_restart fails to grab the lock on the driver, it means that another CPU is transmitting through the same device. All that qdisc_restart can do in this case is put the frame back into the queue and reschedule the device for transmission, since it does not want to wait. If the function is running on the same CPU that is holding the lock, a loop (i.e., a bug in the code) has been detected and the frame is dropped; otherwise, it is just a collision.

```
        if (!spin_trylock(&dev->xmit_lock)) {
        collision:
            ...
            goto requeue;
        }
        ...
requeue:
        q->ops->requeue(skb, q);
        netif_schedule(dev);
```

Once the driver lock is successfully acquired, the lock on the queue is released so that other CPUs can access the queue. Sometimes, there is no need to acquire the driver lock because NETIF_F_LLTX is set. In either case, qdisc_restart is ready to start its real job.

```
        if (!netif_queue_stopped(dev)) {
            int ret;
            if (netdev_nit)
                dev_queue_xmit_nit(skb, dev);

            ret = dev->hard_start_xmit(skb, dev);
            if (ret == NETDEV_TX_OK) {
                if (!nolock) {
```

```
                              dev->xmit_lock_owner = -1;
                              spin_unlock(&dev->xmit_lock);
                          }
                          spin_lock(&dev->queue_lock);
                          return -1;
                      }
                      if (ret == NETDEV_TX_LOCKED && nolock) {
                          spin_lock(&dev->queue_lock);
                          goto collision;
                      }
                  }
```

We saw in the previous section that qdisc_run has already checked the status of the egress queue with netif_queue_stopped, but here qdisc_restart checks it again. The second check is not superfluous. Consider this scenario: when qdisc_run called netif_queue_stopped, the lock on the driver was not taken yet. By the time the lock is taken, another CPU could have sent something and the card could have run out of buffer space. Therefore, netif_queue_stopped may have returned FALSE before but would now return TRUE.

netdev_nit represents the number of protocol sniffers registered. If any are registered, dev_queue_xmit_nit is used to deliver a copy of the frame to each. (We saw something similar for reception in netif_receive_skb in Chapter 10.)

Finally we get to the invocation of the device driver's virtual function for frame transmission. The function provided by the device driver is dev->hard_start_xmit, which is defined for each device at initialization time (see Chapter 8). The NETDEV_TX_XXX values returned by hard_start_xmit routines are listed in *include/linux/netdevice.h*. Here is how qdisc_restart handles them:

NETDEV_TX_OK*
> The transmission succeeded. The buffer is not released yet (kfree_skb is not issued). We will see in the section "Processing the NET_TX_SOFTIRQ: net_tx_action" that the driver does not release the buffer itself but asks the kernel to do so by means of the NET_TX_SOFTIRQ softirq. This provides more efficient memory handling than if each driver did its own freeing.

NETDEV_TX_BUSY
> The driver has discovered that the NIC lacks sufficient room in its transmit buffer pool. When this condition is detected, the driver often calls netif_stop_queue too (see the section "Enabling and Disabling Transmissions").

NETDEV_TX_LOCKED
> The driver is locked. This return value is used only by drivers that support NETIF_F_LLTX.

---

* The NETDEV_TX_XXX values were introduced relatively recently in kernel version 2.6.9. Before their introduction, hard_start_xmit functions used to just return 0 in case of success and 1 in case of error (e.g., if there was no room in the NIC's memory). So far, only a few drivers have been updated to use the NETDEV_TX_XXX values (mainly those that support NETIF_F_LLTX); all the others still use the values 0 and 1 directly.

In summary, transmission fails and a frame must be put back onto the queue when one of the following conditions is true:

- The queue is disabled (netif_queue_stopped(dev) is true).
- Another CPU is holding the lock on the driver.
- The driver failed (hard_start_xmit did not return NETDEV_TX_OK).

See Figure 11-2 for details of the disc_restart function.

dev_queue_xmit Function

This function is the interface to the device driver that performs a transmission. As shown in Figure 9-2 in Chapter 9, dev_queue_xmit can lead to the execution of the driver transmit function hard_start_xmit through two alternate paths:

Interfacing to Traffic Control (the QoS layer)
> This is done through the qdisc_run function that we already described in the previous section.

Invoking hard_start_xmit *directly*
> This is done only for devices that do not use the Traffic Control infrastructures (i.e., virtual devices).

We will look at these cases soon, but let's start with the checks and tasks common to both.

When dev_queue_xmit is called, all the information required to transmit the frame, such as the outgoing device, the next hop, and its link layer address, is ready. Parts VI and VII describe how those parameters are initialized.

Figures 11-3(a) and 11-3(b) describe dev_queue_xmit.

dev_queue_xmit receives only an sk_buff structure as input. This contains all the information the function needs. skb->dev, for instance, is the outgoing device, and skb->data points to the beginning of the payload, whose length is skb->len.

```
int dev_queue_xmit(struct sk_buff *skb)
```

The main tasks of dev_queue_xmit are:

- Checking whether the frame is composed of fragments and whether the device can handle them through scatter/gather DMA; combining the fragments if the device is incapable of doing so. See Chapter 21 for a discussion of fragmented buffers.
- Making sure the L4 checksum (that is, TCP/UDP) is computed, unless the device computes the checksum in hardware. See Chapter 18 for more details on checksumming.
- Selecting which frame to transmit (the one pointed to by the input sk_buff may not be the one to transmit because there is a queue to honor).

In the following code, the data payload is a list of fragments when skb_shinfo(skb)->
frag_list is non-NULL; otherwise, the payload is a single block. If there are fragments, the code checks whether scatter/gather DMA is a feature supported by the
device, and if not, combines the fragments into a single buffer itself. The function
must also combine the fragments if any of them are stored in a memory area whose
address is too big to be addressed by the device (that is, if illegal_highdma(dev, skb)
is true).[*]

```
if (skb_shinfo(skb)->frag_list &&
    !(dev->features&NETIF_F_FRAGLIST) &&
    __skb_linearize(skb, GFP_ATOMIC)) {
    goto out_kfree_skb;
}

if (skb_shinfo(skb)->nr_frags &&
    (!(dev->features&NETIF_F_SG) || illegal_highdma(dev, skb)) &&
    __skb_linearize(skb, GFP_ATOMIC)) {
    goto out_kfree_skb;
}
```

The defragmentation of fragments is done by __skb_linearize, which can fail for one
of the following reasons:

- The new buffer required to store the joined fragments failed to be allocated.
- The sk_buff buffer is shared with some other subsystems (that is, the reference
  count is bigger than one). In this case, the BUG() macro is invoked, leading to a
  kernel panic.

The L4 checksum can be calculated both in software and in hardware.[†] Not all network cards can compute the checksum in hardware; the ones that can will set the
associated bit flag in net_device->features during device initialization. This tells
higher network layers that they do not need to worry about checksumming. The
checksum must instead be calculated in software if:

- There is no support for hardware checksumming.
- The interface can use hardware checksumming only for TCP/UDP packets over
  IP, but the packet being transmitted does not use IP or uses another L4 protocol
  over IP.

The software checksum is calculated with skb_checksum_help:

```
if (skb->ip_summed == CHECKSUM_HW &&
    (!(dev->features & (NETIF_F_HW_CSUM | NETIF_F_NO_CSUM)) &&
    (!(dev->features & NETIF_F_IP_CSUM) ||
    skb->protocol != htons(ETH_P_IP))))
    if (skb_checksum_help(skb, 0))
        goto out_kfree_skb;
```

---

[*] Some devices can use only 16-bit addresses, which constrains the portion of addressable memory.

[†] The algorithm used by each protocol to compute the checksum is analyzed in the associated chapters.

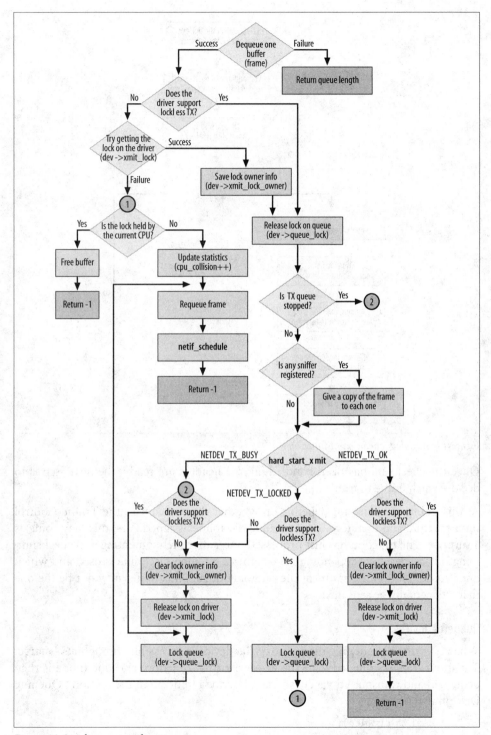

Figure 11-2. qdisc_restart function

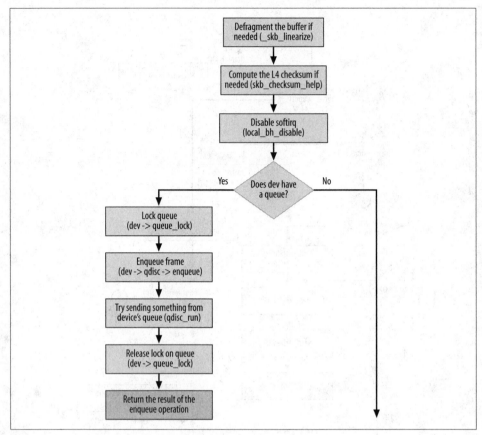

Figure 11-3(a). dev_queue_xmit function

Once the checksum has been handled, all the headers are ready; the next step is to decide which frame to transmit.

At this point, the behavior depends on whether the device uses the Traffic Control infrastructure and therefore has a queuing discipline assigned. Yes, this may come as a surprise. The function has just processed one buffer (defragmenting and checksumming it if needed) but depending on whether a queuing discipline is used and which one is used, and on the status of the outgoing queue, this buffer may not be the one that will actually be sent next.

Queueful devices

When it exists, the queuing discipline of the device is accessible through dev->qdisc. The input frame is queued with the enqueue virtual function, and one frame is then dequeued and transmitted via qdisc_run, described in detail in the section "Queuing Discipline Interface."

```
local_bh_disable( );
```

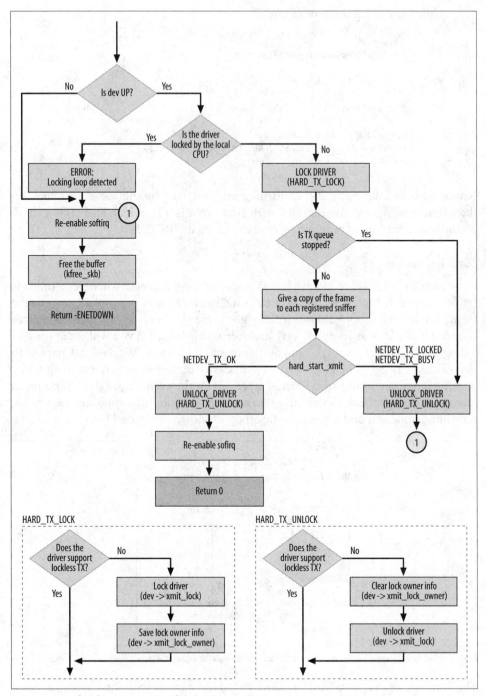

TFigure 11-3(b). dev_queue_xmit function

```
        q = rcu_dereference(dev->qdisc);
        ...
        if (q->enqueue) {
            spin_lock(&dev->queue_lock);

            rc = q->enqueue(skb, q);

            qdisc_run(dev);

            spin_unlock_bh(&dev->queue_lock);
            rc = rc == NET_XMIT_BYPASS ? NET_XMIT_SUCCESS : rc;
            goto out;
        }
```

Note that both enqueuing and dequeuing are protected by the queue_lock lock on the queue. Softirqs are also disabled with local_bh_disable, which also takes care of disabling preemption as required by read-copy-update (RCU).

Queueless devices

Some devices, such as the loopback device, do not have a queue: whenever a frame is transmitted, it is immediately delivered. (But because there is no place to requeue them, frames are dropped if something goes wrong; they are not given a second chance.) If you look at loopback_xmit in *drivers/net/loopback.c*, you will see at the end a direct call to netif_rx, bypassing all the queuing business. We saw in Chapter 10 that netif_rx is the API called by non-NAPI device drivers to put an incoming frame into the input queue and signal higher layers about the event. Since there is no input queue for the loopback device, the transmission function accomplishes two tasks: transmit on one side and receive on the other, as shown in Figure 11-4.

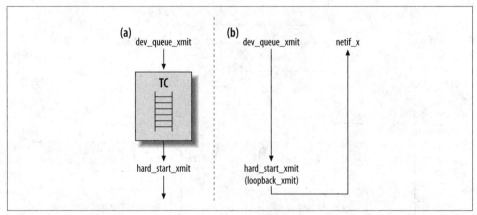

Figure 11-4. (a) Queueful device transmission; (b) loopback transmission

The last part of dev_queue_xmit is used to handle devices without a queuing discipline and therefore without an egress queue. It closely resembles the behavior of qdisc_run covered in the section "Queuing Discipline Interface." There are, however, two differences in the case where no queue is used:

- When a transmission fails, the driver cannot put the buffer back into any queue because there is no queue, so the buffer is dropped by dev_queue_xmit. If the higher layers are using a reliable protocol such as TCP, the data will eventually be retransmitted; otherwise, it will be lost.

- The NETIF_F_LLTX feature introduced in the section "qdisc_restart function" is taken care of by the two macros HARD_TX_LOCK and HARD_TX_UNLOCK. HARD_TX_LOCK uses spin_lock rather than spin_trylock: when the driver lock is already taken, dev_queue_xmit spins, waiting for it to be released.

Processing the NET_TX_SOFTIRQ: net_tx_action

We saw in Chapter 10 that the net_rx_action function is the handler associated with NET_RX_SOFTIRQ software interrupts. It is triggered by device drivers (and by itself under some specific conditions) and handles the part of the input frame processing that is postponed by device drivers to the "after interrupt handling phase." In this way, the code executed in interrupt context by the driver does only what is strictly necessary (copy the data in memory and signal the kernel about its existence by generating a software interrupt) and does not force the rest of the system to wait long; later on, the software interrupt takes care of that part of the frame processing that can wait.

net_tx_action works in a similar way. It can be triggered with raise_softirq_irqoff(NET_TX_SOFTIRQ) by devices in two different contexts, to accomplish two main tasks:

- By netif_wake_queue when transmission is enabled on a device. In this case, it makes sure that frames waiting to be sent are actually sent when all the needed conditions are met (for instance, when the device has enough memory).

- By dev_kfree_skb_irq when a transmission has completed and the device driver signals with the former routine that the associated buffer can be released. In this case, it deallocates the sk_buff structures associated with successfully transmitted buffers.

The reason for the second task is as follows. We know that when code from the device driver runs in interrupt context, it needs to be as quick as possible. Releasing a buffer can take time, so it is deferred by asking the net_tx_action softirq to take care of it. Instead of using dev_kfree_skb, device drivers use dev_kfree_skb_irq. While the former deallocates the sk_buff (which actually consists of the buffer going back into a per-CPU cache), the latter simply adds the pointer to the buffer being released to the completion_queue list of the softnet_data structure associated with the CPU and lets net_tx_action do the real job later.

Let's see how net_tx_action accomplishes its two tasks.

It starts by deallocating all the buffers that have been added to the completion_queue list by the device drivers' calls to dev_kfree_skb_irq. Because net_tx_action is running outside interrupt context, a device driver could add elements to the list at any time, so net_tx_action must disable interrupts while accessing the softnet_data structure. To keep interrupts disabled as little as possible, it clears the list by setting completion_queue to NULL and saves the pointer to the list in a local variable clist, which no one else can access (note also that each CPU has its own list). This way, it can walk through the list and free each element with __kfree_skb, while drivers can continue adding new elements to completion_queue.

```
if (sd->completion_queue) {
    struct sk_buff *clist;

    local_irq_disable();
    clist = sd->completion_queue;
    sd->completion_queue = NULL;
    local_irq_enable();

    while (clist != NULL) {
        struct sk_buff *skb = clist;
        clist = clist->next;

        BUG_TRAP(!atomic_read(&skb->users));
        __kfree_skb(skb);
    }
}
```

The second half of the function, which transmits frames, works similarly: it uses a local variable to remain safe from hardware interrupts. Note that for each device, before transmitting anything, the function needs to grab the lock on the output device's queue (dev->queue_lock). If the function fails to grab the lock (because another CPU holds it), it simply reschedules the device for transmission with netif_schedule.

```
if (sd->output_queue) {
    struct net_device *head;

    local_irq_disable();
    head = sd->output_queue;
    sd->output_queue = NULL;
    local_irq_enable();

    while (head) {
        struct net_device *dev = head;
        head = head->next_sched;

        smp_mb__before_clear_bit();
        clear_bit(__LINK_STATE_SCHED, &dev->state);

        if (spin_trylock(&dev->queue_lock)) {
            qdisc_run(dev);
```

```
                    spin_unlock(&dev->queue_lock);
            } else {
                netif_schedule(dev);
            }
        }
    }
```

We already saw in the section "Queuing Discipline Interface" how qdisc_run works. Devices are handled in a sequential order starting from the head of the list. Because the netif_schedule function (calling __netif_schedule internally) adds elements at the head of the list, devices are served in Last In, First Out (LIFO) order, which in some conditions may be unfair.

That completes the net_tx_action function; let's look at some contexts where it can be invoked to free buffers. Some functions that desire to release a buffer can be invoked in different contexts, inside or outside interrupt context. A wrapper is available to handle these cases elegantly:

```
static inline void dev_kfree_skb_any(struct sk_buff *skb)
{
    if (in_irq() || irqs_disabled())
        dev_kfree_skb_irq(skb);
    else
        dev_kfree_skb(skb);
}
```

The dev_kfree_skb_irq function runs when the calling function is in interrupt context, and looks like this:

```
static inline void dev_kfree_skb_irq(struct sk_buff *skb)
{
    if (atomic_dec_and_test(&skb->users)) {
        struct softnet_data *sd;
        unsigned long flags;

        local_irq_save(flags);
            sd = &__get_cpu_var(softnet_data);
        skb->next = sd->completion_queue;
        sd->completion_queue = skb;
        raise_softirq_irqoff(NET_TX_SOFTIRQ);
        local_irq_restore(flags);
    }
}
```

A buffer can be freed only if there are no other references to it (that is, if skb->users is 0).

Let's see an example of how the execution of net_tx_action is triggered by an indirect call to cpu_raise_softirq(cpu, NET_TX_SOFTIRQ) by a device driver. (Another example can be found in the section "Enabling and Disabling Transmissions.")

Among the interrupt types handled by the vortex_interrupt function in *drivers/net/3c59x.c* we introduced earlier is an interrupt invoked by the device to tell the driver that a DMA transfer from the CPU to the device is completed (DMADone). Since the buffer has been transferred to the device, the sk_buff structure can now be freed. Because the interrupt handler is running in interrupt context, the driver calls dev_kfree_skb_irq.

```
if (status & DMADone) {
    if (inw(ioaddr + Wn7_MasterStatus) & 0x1000) {
        outw(0x1000, ioaddr + Wn7_MasterStatus); /* Ack the event. */
        pci_unmap_single(VORTEX_PCI(vp), vp->tx_skb_dma,
                (vp->tx_skb->len + 3) & ~3, PCI_DMA_TODEVICE);
        dev_kfree_skb_irq(vp->tx_skb); /* Release the transferred buffer */
        if (inw(ioaddr + TxFree) > 1536) {
            netif_wake_queue(dev);
        } else { /* Interrupt when FIFO has room for max-sized packet. */
            outw(SetTxThreshold + (1536>>2), ioaddr + EL3_CMD);
            netif_stop_queue(dev);
        }
    }
}
```

Watchdog timer

We saw in the section "Enabling and Disabling Transmissions" that transmission can be disabled by a device driver when certain conditions are met. The disabling of transmission is supposed to be temporary, so when transmission is not re-enabled within a reasonable amount of time, the kernel assumes the device is experiencing some problems and should be restarted.

This is achieved by a per-device timer that is started with dev_watchdog_up when the device is activated with dev_activate. The timer regularly expires, makes sure everything is OK with the device, and restarts itself. When it detects a problem—because the device's egress queue is disabled (netif_queue_stopped returns TRUE) and too much time has passed since the last frame transmission took place—the timer's handler invokes a routine registered by the device driver, which resets the NIC.

Here are the net_device fields used to implement this mechanism:

trans_start
    This is the timestamp initialized by the device driver when the last frame transmission started.

watchdog_timer
    This is the timer started by Traffic Control. The handler executed when the timer expires is dev_watchdog, defined in *net/sched/sch_generic.c*.

watchdog_timeo
    This is the amount of time to wait. This is initialized by the device driver. When it is set to 0, watchdog_timer is not started.

tx_timeout

> This is the routine provided by the device driver that will be invoked by dev_watchdog to reset the device.

When the timer expires, the kernel handler dev_watchdog takes action by calling the function to which tx_timeout points. The latter normally resets the card and restarts the interface scheduler with netif_wake_queue.

The proper value for watchdog_timeo depends on the interface. If the driver does not set it, it defaults to 5 seconds. The parameters to take into account when defining the value are:

The likelihood of transmission collisions

> This is zero for point-to-point links, but can be high on shared and overloaded Ethernet links plugged into hubs.

The interface speed

> The slower the interface, the bigger the timeout should be.

The value of watchdog_timeo is usually defined as a multiple of the variable HZ, which represents 1 second. HZ is a global variable whose value depends on the platform (it is defined in the architecture-dependent file *include/asm-XXX/param.h*). As you can see in Table 11-1, even devices of the same type may take different values for the timeout. The table lists only a few examples; it is not a complete list.

Table 11-1. Transmission timeout used by the most common network cards

Device driver	watchdog_timeo (timeout used)
3c501	HZ
3c505	10*HZ
3c509	(400*HZ)/1000
3c515	(400*HZ)/1000
3c523	HZ
3c527	5*HZ
3c59x	5*HZ
dl2k	4*HZ
Natsemi	2*HZ
Aironet 4500	8*HZ
s2io (10Gbit)	5*HZ
8390	(20*HZ)/100
8139too	6*HZ
b44	5*HZ
tg3	5*HZ
e100	2*HZ
e1000	5*HZ

Table 11-1. Transmission timeout used by the most common network cards (continued)

Device driver	watchdog_timeo (timeout used)
SIS 900	4*HZ
Tulip family	4*HZ
Intel EtherExpress 16	2*HZ
SLIP	20*HZ

The watchdog timer mechanism is provided by the Traffic Control code. However, advanced device drivers may implement their own watchdog timers, too. See *drivers/net/e1000_main.c* for an example.

## CHAPTER 12

General and Reference Material About Interrupts

This chapter contains several general types of information that apply to the material presented in the previous three chapters on interrupts and frame handling.

Statistics

Statistics about frame reception are kept in the per-CPU array netdev_rx_stat, whose elements are of type netif_rx_stats (see *include/linux/netdevice.h*):

```
struct netif_rx_stats netdev_rx_stat[NR_CPUS];

struct netif_rx_stats
{
        unsigned total;
        unsigned dropped;
        unsigned time_squeeze;
        unsigned throttled;
        unsigned fastroute_hit;
        unsigned fastroute_success;
        unsigned fastroute_defer;
        unsigned fastroute_deferred_out;
        unsigned fastroute_latency_reduction;
        unsigned cpu_collision;
} ____cacheline_aligned;
```

The elements of netif_rx_stats are:

total

>Total number of ingress frames processed, including any that might be discarded. This value is updated both in netif_rx and in netif_receive_skb, which means that (by mistake) the same frame is accounted for twice when the driver does not use NAPI (i.e., it uses the netif_rx interface; see Figure 10-2 in Chapter 10).

dropped

> Number of frames that were dropped because they were received when the CPU was in the throttle state.

time_squeeze

> Number of times net_rx_action had to return while frames were still in the CPU ingress queue, so as not to become a CPU hog. See the section "Processing the NET_RX_SOFTIRQ: net_rx_action" in Chapter 10.

throttled

> Number of times the CPU went into the throttle state. This value is incremented by netif_rx.

fastroute_hit
fastroute_success
fastroute_defer
fastroute_latency_reduction
fastroute_deferred_out

> Fields that used to be used by the Fastroute feature. This feature has been dropped in kernel 2.6.8.

cpu_collision

> Number of times the CPU failed to grab the lock on a device driver (more precisely, on dev->xmit_lock) because the lock was already taken by another CPU. This counter is updated in qdisc_restart, which handles only frame transmission, not reception. cpu_collision is the only statistic about transmission that has been included in this structure.

The fact that some of the preceding counters are currently updated only by netif_rx (which is used only by non-NAPI drivers), means that their values are not correct when using NAPI drivers.

The contents of the netdev_rx_stat vector can be viewed via the /proc interface. See the next section.

Other statistics are kept by the driver in private data structures (see Chapter 2), by higher-layer protocols, and by the Traffic Control queuing disciplines. Some of those values can be read with user-space applications such as *ifconfig*, *tc*, *ip*, or *netstat*, and others are also exported via /proc.

Tuning via /proc and sysfs Filesystems

All of the files in */proc/sys/net/core* listed in Table 12-1 are defined in *net/core/sysctl_net_core.c*, where you can find the association between files and kernel variables.

Table 12-1. /proc/sys/net/core/ files usable for tuning frame reception

Filename	Kernel variable[a]	Default value
netdev_max_backlog	netdev_max_backlog	300
mod_cong	mod_cong	290
lo_cong	lo_cong	100
no_cong	no_cong	20
no_cong_thresh	no_cong_thresh	10
dev_weight	weight_p	64

[a] All of these variables are defined in *net/core/dev.c*.

I would like to stress that NAPI drivers do not need any of the fields in Table 12-1. NAPI drivers are expected to initialize net_device->weight using local (to the driver) values rather than weight_p. But they could use weight_p if they wanted, particularly because they usually use the same default value of 64. Starting with kernel 2.6.12, the value of net_device's weight field can be tuned at runtime with *sysfs* via the per-device files */sys/class/net/device_name/weight*. The *weight* file is created in *net/core/net-sysfs.c*.

The statistics collected with the netdev_rx_stats structures described in the section "Statistics" can be read via the file */proc/net/softnet_stat* (the output is in hexadecimal).

Functions and Variables Featured in This Part of the Book

Table 12-2 summarizes the main functions, variables, and data structures introduced or referenced in the previous three chapters. Additional ones can be found in Table 9-1 in Chapter 9.

Table 12-2. Functions, variables, and data structures related to interrupts and frame handling

Name	Description
Functions	
netif_rx	Queues an input frame into a CPU's queue. See the section "Old Versus New Driver Interfaces" in Chapter 10.
netif_rx_schedule __netif_rx_schedule	Schedules the NET_RX_SOFTIRQ software interrupt for execution. See the section "Old Versus New Driver Interfaces" in Chapter 10.
netif_rx_complete	Called by the net_device->poll virtual function when the latter has cleared the queue.
netif_start_queue netif_stop_queue	Enables and disables transmission on a device, respectively. See the section "Enabling and Disabling Transmissions" in Chapter 11.
netif_queue_stopped	Checks whether a device is enabled for transmission.

Name	Description
netif_schedule[a] netif_wake_queue	netif_schedule schedules a device for transmission. netif_wake_queue enables transmission on a device and schedules the device for transmission. See the section "Scheduling a Device for Transmission" in Chapter 11.
qdisc_run	Dequeues a frame from the egress queue of a device and pushes it down to the device driver for transmission. See the section "Queuing Discipline Interface" in Chapter 11.
process_backlog	poll virtual function used by non-NAPI device drivers. See the section "Backlog Processing: The process_backlog Poll Virtual Function" in Chapter 10.
netif_receive_skb	Processes input frames by passing them to higher-layer protocol handlers. See the section "Ingress Frame Processing" in Chapter 10.
dev_queue_xmit	Main function for frame transmission. See the section "dev_queue_xmit Function" in Chapter 11.
dev_kfree_skb dev_kfree_skb_irq dev_kfree_skb_any	Releases an sk_buff structure. See the section "Processing the NET_TX_SOFTIRQ: net_tx_action" in Chapter 11.
do_IRQ	Takes care of a hardware interrupt notification by invoking the associated handler.
open_softirq raise_softirq, raise_softirq_irqoff	Registers and schedules for execution a software interrupt, respectively. See the section "Bottom-half handlers in kernel 2.4 and above: the introduction of the softirq" in Chapter 9.
do_softirq invoke_softirq	Takes care of the pending software interrupts by invoking the associated handlers. See the section "Pending softirq Handling" in Chapter 9.
net_rx_action net_tx_action	The handlers for the NET_RX_SOFTIRQ and NET_TX_SOFTIRQ software interrupts, respectively. See the section "How the Networking Code Uses softirqs" in Chapter 9.
tasklet_init	Initializes a tasklet_struct structure.
tasklet_action tasklet_hi_action	Handlers for the TASKLET_SOFTIRQ and HI_SOFTIRQ software interrupts, respectively. See the section "Tasklets" in Chapter 9.
tasklet_enable, tasklet_hi_enable tasklet_disable, tasklet_disable_nosync	Enables and disables a tasklet, respectively. See the section "Tasklets" in Chapter 9.
tasklet_schedule tasklet_hi_schedule	Schedules a tasklet for execution. See the section "Tasklets" in Chapter 9.
Variables	
mod_cong lo_cong no_cong no_cong_thresh	Congestion levels for the input queue (used with non-NAPI devices). See the section "Fields of softnet_data" in Chapter 9.
netdev_max_backlog	Maximum size for the CPU's input queues. See Figure 9-4 in Chapter 9.
Data structures	
softnet_data	The two NET_*XXX*_SOFTIRQ software interrupts use one such structure for each CPU. See the section "softnet_data Structure" in Chapter 9.
tasklet_struct	Represents a tasklet. See the section "Tasklets" in Chapter 9.

[a] For consistency with the reception function names, it should probably have been called netif_tx_schedule.

Files and Directories Featured in This Part of the Book

Figure 12-1 shows the files and directories we have referenced in the first four chapters of Part III. The *xxx* keyword in the figure represents an architecture (e.g., i386).[*] Some architectures do not require particular architecture specific files, because a general-purpose file can sometimes be used by multiple architectures.

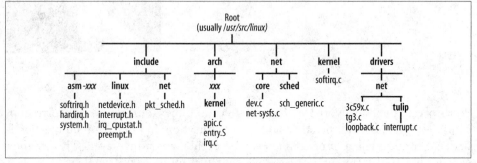

Figure 12-1. Files and directories featured in this part of the book

---

[*] The *irq.c* file may not always be inside a directory called *kernel*.

CHAPTER 13
Protocol Handlers

Protocols are the framework for all communication: they indicate to each correspondent how to understand the other side of a conversation. In Linux, communication is understood through a *protocol handler* at each networking layer. This chapter explains how these handlers are installed, chosen at runtime, and invoked.

To understand the relationship among communication layers and protocols, imagine a possible situation in real life where I have to talk to a stranger. What language should I use? If I'm in Italy I'll begin with Italian, and if I'm in the United States I'll try English. If these don't work, there may be ways to negotiate the use of a different language.

On top of that basic protocol, there are others. When writing a letter, for instance, my relationship with the correspondent determines whether I begin "Dear Madam" or "Hi, gal!" These sorts of choices take place at many layers of real-life communication. Networks have layers too, and the choice of protocols becomes formalized in network code.

Overview of Network Stack

Readers of this book are expected to be familiar with the basic TCP/IP protocols, but there are some other protocols in common use—such as Logical Link Control (LLC) and Subnetwork Access Protocol (SNAP)—that you may not know. This section introduces key protocols and shows their relationships.

The two best-known models for network protocols are the seven-layer OSI model and the five-layer TCP/IP model, shown in Figure 13-1. The OSI model remains an important reference point for networking discussions even though it never took off for a variety of reasons. The TCP/IP model covers most of the protocols used by computers today.[*]

---

[*] For more information on these two models, I suggest *Computer Networks, Second Edition* (Prentice Hall).

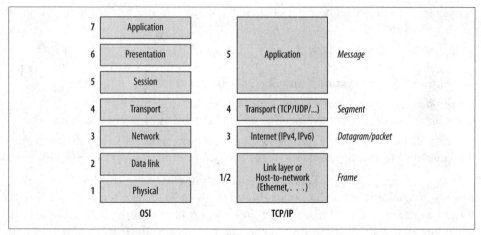

Figure 13-1. OSI and TCP/IP models

At each layer, numerous protocols are available. At the lowest level, where interfaces exchange data, the protocol in use is predetermined. A driver for that protocol is associated with the interface, and all data that comes in on the interface is assumed to follow the protocol (i.e., Ethernet); if it doesn't, errors are reported and no communication takes place.

But once the driver has to hand over data to a higher layer, a choice of protocols ensues. Should data at L3 be handled by IPv4, IPv6, IPX (the Novell NetWare protocol), DECnet, or some other network-layer protocol? And a similar choice must be made going from L3 to L4, where TCP, UDP, ICMP, and other protocols reside.

This chapter deals with the lower three layers and briefly touches on the fourth one.

An individual package of transmitted data is commonly called a *frame* on the link layer, L2; a *packet* on the network layer; a *segment* on the transport layer; and a *message* on the application layer.

The layers are often called the *network stack*, because communication travels down the layers until it is physically transmitted across the wire (or wireless bands) and then travels back up. Headers are also added and removed in a LIFO manner.

The Big Picture

Figure 13-2 builds on the TCP/IP model in Figure 13-1. Figure 13-2 shows which chapter covers each interface between adjacent layers. Some of these interfaces involve communication down the stack, whereas others involve communication upward:

Going up in the stack (for receiving a message)
> This chapter describes how ingress traffic is handed to the right protocol handler. (The meaning of ptype_base and ptype_all will become clear in the section "Protocol Handler Organization.")

Chapter 10 describes how device drivers notify the kernel about the reception of ingress frames.

Chapter 24 describes how the IPv4 protocol delivers ingress IPv4 packets to the right L4 protocol (IPv4 is the only network layer protocol we cover in the book). The IPv4 receive routine is described in Chapter 19.

Going down in the stack (for sending a message)
Chapter 21 describes the functions provided by the IPv4 layer for transmission.

Part VI describes how the neighboring layer interfaces the L3 protocols to the transmitting routine dev_queue_xmit. The latter is described in Chapter 11.

As shown in Figure 13-2, the socket interface is not covered in this book. However, there is one point worth mentioning about the AF_PACKET socket type. It's the Linux way to capture frames at the link layer and inject frames into the link layer, directly bypassing all the intermediate protocol layers. Network sniffers such as *tcpdump* and Ethereal are common users of AF_PACKET sockets. You can see from the figure that AF_PACKET sockets hand frames directly to dev_queue_xmit, and receive ingress frames directly from the network protocol dispatcher routine (this latter point is addressed in Chapter 10).

Figure 13-2 shows only two protocol families (PF_INET, PF_PACKET), but several others are implemented in the Linux kernel. Among them are:

PF_NETLINK
Used as the preferred interface for network configuration. See Chapter 3.

PF_KEY
Used as a key management interface for network security services. IPsec is one of these services.

PF_LLC
See the section "Logical Link Control (LLC)."

Link Layer Choices for Ethernet (LLC and SNAP)

Although the link layer protocol is fairly fixed by the hardware in use, the Ethernet standard allows some choice between protocols. The first attempt at standardizing this choice was called Logical Link Control (LLC). Since it offered very limited options, it never saw much use. The IEEE 802 committee then standardized the Sub-network Access Protocol (SNAP), which is found in use fairly often. The implementation of both of these subprotocols is described later in this chapter.

In LLC, the header contains a field specifying the protocol for the Source Service Access Point (SSAP) and the protocol for the Destination Service Access Point (DSAP). Each field, however, contains only 8 bits, one of which is dedicated to a flag that indicates whether multicast is in use and another dedicated to a flag that indicates whether the address is local to one network or is recognized worldwide.

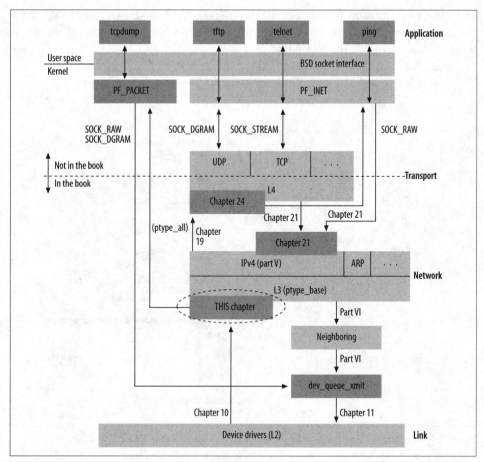

Figure 13-2. The big picture

Therefore, with 6 bits left to specify a protocol, LLC supports a maximum of 64 protocols, which is too few to make the technology popular.

Therefore, the IEEE 802 committee extended LLC by providing a special value in the SSAP and DSAP fields that indicates that the protocol in use by that source or destination is identified by another 5 bytes in the header. With this extension, called SNAP, there are 40 bits that can be assigned to various protocols.

How the Network Stack Operates

Let's briefly examine a sample communication to see how choices are made at communication points.

In Figure 13-3, assume that a user at Host X wants to download an HTML page using a web browser from the web server running on Server Y. Some of the questions to answer include the following:

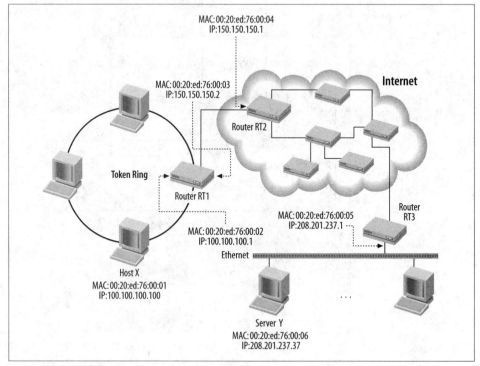

Figure 13-3. Example of communication between two remote stations (Host X and Server Y)

- Because Host X and Server Y are on different local area networks, how will they be able to talk to each other?
- Because Host X does not know where Server Y is physically located, how will it find out where to send its request?
- If Server Y is running more than one application (not just the web server), how can its operating system determine which application should handle the request from Host X?
- If Host X is running more than one application (not just the browser), how can its operating system determine which application receives the data that returns?

Let's follow the request for a web page through the network stack to see how these questions are answered. We'll use Figures 13-3* and 13-4 as references.

---

* The figure shows only the details needed for our discussion.

Application layer, Host X

The browser reads the URL requested by the user; suppose it is *http://www.oreilly.com*. The browser uses the Domain Name System (a topic beyond the scope of this book) to resolve the domain *www.oreilly.com* to an IP address, which we'll suppose is 208.201.239.37. It is up to the IP protocol (L3, the network layer) to find a path between Host X and Server Y using this address.

The browser now initiates an HTTP session on the application layer to 208.201.239.37. It then invokes TCP to carry the traffic to the remote web server. (TCP is used instead of UDP because HTTP requires a reliable channel that can deliver large amounts of data without corrupting it.) The request is now traveling down the network stack.

Transport layer, Host X

The TCP layer breaks the HTTP message request into segments, if needed, and adds a TCP header to each. Among other things, TCP adds the source and destination port. The port number lets the operating system direct the request to the proper application. The web server on Server Y listens on the default HTTP port 80 unless it is explicitly configured to use a different port number, and picks up all traffic there. Server Y directs responses back to Host X's port 5000, which is the source port number the server got from the request received from the host.

Port numbers are an L4 concept, so a separate set of ports exist for TCP and UDP.

The TCP layer on Host X knows the destination port is 80 because the browser uses the default port assigned to the HTTP protocol unless a different one is provided in the URL. The source port assigned to the browser (which will be used to identify the target application when processing ingress traffic) is assigned by the OS (unless a specific one is asked by the application). Let's assume that port was 5000. Different ports can be used for the two sides of the conversation. Network Address Translation (NAT) and proxying firewalls complicate the issue even further, but the outlines of how applications reach each other should be clear from this discussion.

The TCP layer does not know how to get the segments to the destination system. To accomplish that, the TCP layer invokes the IP layer, passing the destination IP address in each transmission request.

Network layer, Host X

The IP layer does not care about applications or ports. All it does is examine the IP addresses on the packets and the network options related to IP. Its big task is to consult routing tables (a complex process discussed in detail in Part VII) to discover that the packet should go through Router RT1. The IPv4 protocol is described in detail in Part V.

The packet is going to drop down another layer to be sent to the router, but the IP layer has to find the right address on this layer for the router. Since L2 involves communication between neighboring hosts (such as hosts sharing a LAN or a point-to-point link), the process used by the IP layer to find the L2 address associated with a given IP address is called a *neighbor protocol*. It is discussed in Part VI.

Link layer, Host X and Router RT1

This layer is implemented partly by a device driver. On LANs, Ethernet is the most common protocol, but ATM, Token Ring, FDDI, and others exist. Long-distance links use dedicated copper or fiber lines; the simplest of these is the dial-up connection that millions of home and small-office users still establish with their ISPs. LANs use their own (L2) addressing schemes that have nothing to do with TCP/IP; on Ethernet (and in IEEE 802 networks in general), addresses are 6 octets long and are commonly called MAC addresses. On a dedicated line (e.g., dial-up), no L2 addressing is needed at all because each side simply sends to the other side.

Different types of headers might be used on different links, because each is hardware-specific. These headers do not carry any information that is meaningful for the browser and server at the application layer.

Routers RT1, RT2, etc.

Each router in the path, except for the last, goes through the following process to forward the packet to its final destination:

- It removes the link layer header.
- It can see that the L3 protocol is IP thanks to a specific field in the link layer header, discussed later in this chapter.
- It determines that the local system is not the destination of the packet because the destination IP address included in the IP header is not one of its own IP addresses.
- It forwards the IP packet to the next router on the path toward Server Y. To do this, it consults its routing tables to select the next hop router and creates a new link layer header (i.e., Figure 13-4(E)). The last step is described in detail in Chapter 35.

Normally, the information on L3 (the IP header) does not change as the packet goes from system to system.[*] Different L2 headers are used on each link.

When the packet finally arrives at Router RT3, the latter realizes that Server Y is directly connected and that there is no need to route the packet another hop.

Once the message reaches the destination server, it traverses the network stack again from the bottom upward:

---

[*] We will see in Part V that only changing fields, such as Time To Live (TTL) and checksum, need to be updated.

Link layer, Server Y

Stripping off the L2 header, this layer checks a field to see which protocol handles the L3 layer. Finding that L3 is handled by IP, the link layer invokes the appropriate function to continue handling the L3 packet (i.e., L2 payload). Most of this chapter discusses the manner in which protocols register themselves and handle the key field indicating which protocol to use.

Network layer, Server Y

This layer recognizes that its own system's IP address, 208.201.239.37, is the destination address in the packet and therefore that the packet should be handled locally. The network layer strips off the L3 header and once again checks a field to see what protocol handles L4. Chapter 24 offers an in-depth description of the interface between L3 and L4 for ingress traffic.

Figure 13-4 shows how a header is added by each network layer as each one takes the data from a higher layer. The last step, from Figure 13-4(d) to Figure 13-4(e), shows the difference between the original frame transmitted to Router RT1 by Host X and the one between Router RT1 and Router RT2.

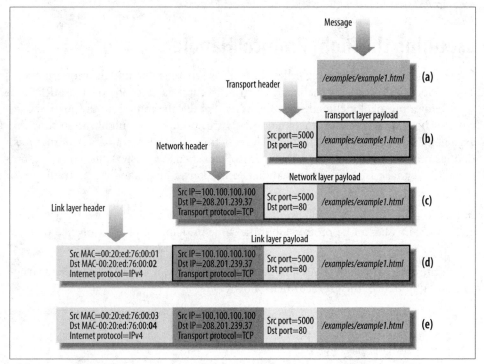

Figure 13-4. Headers compiled by layers: (a…d) on Host X as we travel down the stack; (e) on Router RT1

As we have seen, each layer provides a variety of protocols. Each protocol is handled by a different set of kernel functions. Thus, as the packet travels back up the stack, each protocol must figure out which protocol is being used by the next-higher layer, and invoke the proper kernel function to handle the packet.

On the lowest software layer, L2, the hardware in use defines the protocol. If the frame is received on an Ethernet interface, the receiver knows it contains an Ethernet header, and a Token Ring interface knows it contains a Token Ring header, and so on. There is no ambiguity unless LCC or SNAP is specified. LLC and SNAP are discussed later in this chapter.

But as the packet travels up the network stack, each protocol needs a field in its header to tell it which protocol should handle the next stage of processing. The progress is shown in Figure 13-5. Thus, the transition from L2 in Figure 13-5(a) to L3 in Figure 13-5(b) depends on L2 checking an "Above protocol" field in the L2 header. Similarly, the L3 layer checks a field in its header to facilitate the transition to L4, shown in Figure 13-5(b) and Figure 13-5(c). Finally, L4 uses the Destination Port field of the packet to take the packet out of the kernel and find the process, such as a web server, that handles the packet on the local host.

Executing the Right Protocol Handler

For each network protocol, regardless of its layer, there is one initialization function. This includes L3 protocols such as IPv4 and IPv6, link layer protocols like ARP, and so on. For a protocol included statically in the kernel, the initialization function executes at boot time; for a protocol compiled as a module, the initialization function executes when the module is loaded. The function allocates internal data structures, notifies other subsystems about the protocol's existence, registers files in /proc, and so on. A key task is to register a handler in the kernel that handles the traffic for a protocol.

In this section, for the sake of simplicity, I'll show how a device driver (which operates on L2) invokes an L3 protocol, but the same principle applies to any protocol on any layer.

When the device driver receives a frame, it stores it into an sk_buff buffer data structure and it initializes the protocol field shown here:

```
struct sk_buff
{
        ... ... ...
        unsigned short  protocol;
        ... ... ...
};
```

The value in this field can be an arbitrary value used by the kernel to identify a given protocol, or a field of a MAC header in the incoming frame. The field is consulted by

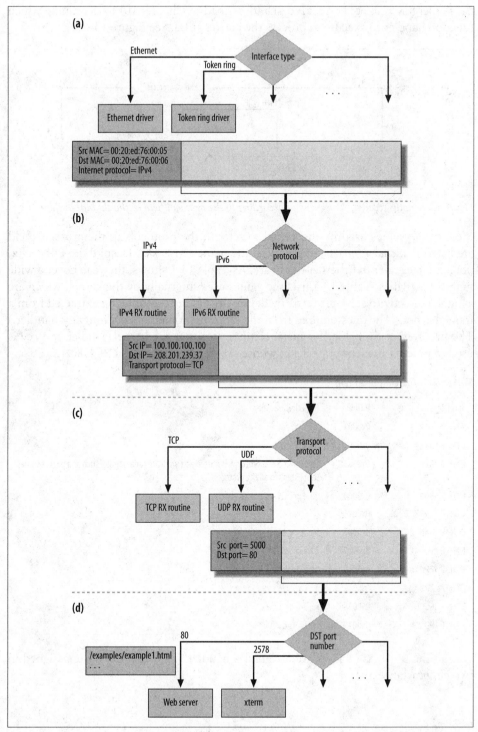

Figure 13-5. Frame decapsulation, layer by layer, at Server Y

the kernel function `netif_receive_skb` (described in Chapter 10) to determine which function handler to execute to process the packet at L3. See Figure 13-6.

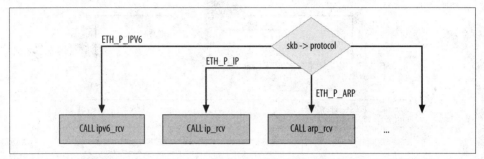

Figure 13-6. netif_receive_skb processes according to the protocol field of the sk_buff buffer

Most of the values used by the kernel to refer to the protocols in the `protocol` field are listed in *include/linux/if_ether.h* with the name `ETH_P_XXX`. Despite the `ETH` prefix, not all names refer to Ethernet hardware. As Table 13-1 shows, they can cover a wide range of activities. Table 13-1 lists the values used internally by the kernel, which are assigned directly to `skb->protocol` by device drivers instead of being extracted from a frame header. (The ones omitted from the table are not assigned a function handler.) The first row of the table, for instance, indicates that the kernel handler `ipx_rcv` is used to process an incoming packet whose `skb->protocol` field is `ETH_P_802_3`.

Table 13-1. Internal protocols

Symbol	Value	Function handler
ETH_P_802_3	0x0001	ipx_rcv
ETH_P_AX25	0x0002	ax25_kiss_rcv
ETH_P_ALL	0x0003	This is not a real protocol. It is used as a wildcard for a handler such as a packet sniffer that listens to all the protocols.
ETH_P_802_2	0x0004	llc_rcv
ETH_P_TR_802_2	0x0011	
ETH_P_WAN_PPP	0x0007	sppp_rcv
ETH_P_LOCALTALK	0x0009	ltalk_rcv
ETH_P_PPPTALK	0x0010	atalk_rcv
ETH_P_IRDA	0x0017	irlap_driver_rcv
ETH_P_ECONET	0x0018	econet_rcv
ETH_P_HDLC	0x0019	hdlc_rcv

Not all the `ETH_P_XXX` values are assigned a handler. They can be left unassigned in two circumstances:

- There is no handler for the protocol (i.e., the kernel does not support it).
- Another protocol handler handles the protocol indirectly, as happens in the case of SNAP. This case is discussed in the sections "Logical Link Control (LLC)" and "Subnetwork Access Protocol (SNAP)."

Unfortunately, it is not always sufficient to extract a field from the L2 header to figure out which handler to invoke; the association between skb->protocol and the protocol handler that will process the frame is not always one-to-one. There are cases where the protocol handler for a given ETH_P_XXX will actually just read other parameters from the frame header (without processing the frame) and hand the frame to another protocol handler that will process it. An example is the ETH_P_802_2 handler.

As described in Chapter 10, netif_receive_skb is the function that dispatches ingress frames to the right protocol handlers. When there is no handler for a specific protocol, the frame is dropped.

In special cases, a single packet can be delivered to multiple handlers. This is the case, for instance, when packet sniffers are running. This mode of operation, sometimes referred to as promiscuous mode, is listed as ETH_P_ALL in Table 13-1. This type of handler is generally not used to process packets for recipients, but just to snoop on a given device or set of devices for the purposes of debugging or collecting statistics.

Special Media Encapsulation

Ethernet is by far the most common mechanism used for implementing both shared and point-to-point network connections. In this book, we always refer to Ethernet device drivers when talking about L2. However, Linux allows you to use any of the most common media available on modern PCs to carry IP traffic (and sometimes any network protocol traffic). Examples of media that can be used to transport IP include the serial and parallel ports (SLIP/PLIP/PPP), FireWire (eth1394), USB, Bluetooth, Infrared Data Association (IrDA), etc.

Such media define network devices as abstractions on top of the generic ports, usually by means of extensions to the generic media device driver. Such virtual devices look like real NICs to the upper layers.

Here is how reception and transmission are implemented on these virtual network devices:

Transmission
  The net_device's hard_start_xmit function pointer of the virtual device is initialized by the device driver to a routine that will encapsulate the IP packet (let's assume it was an IP packet) according to the protocol used by the media.

Reception

When the generic driver receives data from one of its ports, it strips the media headers (as an Ethernet device driver would strip the Ethernet header), initializes skb->protocol, and notifies the upper layer with a call to netif_rx. When these media are used for point-to-point connections only, there is no need for a link layer header, so skb->protocol is statically initialized to ETH_P_IP; in the other cases, the media encapsulation may include a fake Ethernet header too, so skb->protocol is initialized with eth_type_trans routines (as real Ethernet drivers are).

How exactly the generic device driver of a given media type interfaces to the virtual network device is an implementation detail. Depending on the medium, it may offer a synchronous or asynchronous interface, use of buffering both on receive and transmit paths, etc.

Protocol Handler Organization

Figure 13-7 shows how the different protocol handlers are organized in the kernel. Each protocol is described by a packet_type data structure.

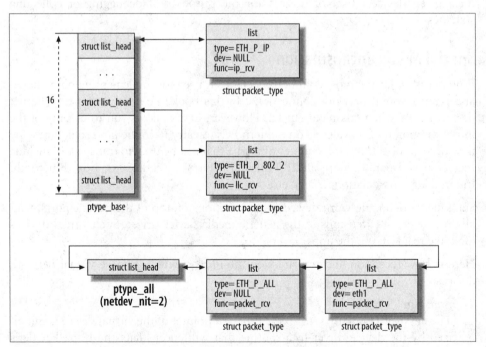

Figure 13-7. Data structure used to store the registered protocol handlers

To make access faster, a very simple hash function is used for most of the protocols. Sixteen lists are organized into an array to which the global variable ptype_base points. When a protocol is registered, using the dev_add_pack function, described in the next section, this function runs a hash function over the protocol type and assigns the packet_type structure to one of the 16 lists. Later on, to find a packet_type structure, the kernel can simply rerun the hash and go through the matching list.

The ETH_P_ALL protocols (see Table 13-1) are organized in their own list to which the global variable ptype_all points.* The number of protocols in this list is stored in netdev_nit. The latter is used by dev_queue_xmit and qdisc_restart to check whether a PF_PACKET socket is open (i.e., a listening sniffer) to which it can deliver a copy of ingress frames (see Chapter 10).

Protocol Handler Registration

At system startup and other times when a protocol is registered, the kernel calls dev_add_pack, passing it a data structure of type packet_type, which is defined in *include/linux/netdevice.h* as follows:

```
struct packet_type
{
    unsigned short       type;
    struct net_device    *dev;
    int                  (*func) (struct sk_buff *, struct net_device *,
                                  struct packet_type *);
    void                 *af_packet_priv;
    struct list_head     *list;
};
```

The fields have the following meanings:

type

> The protocol code. It can take any of the values listed in the first column of Table 13-1 through 13-4 (i.e., ETH_P_IP). The difference between the protocols belonging to different tables will become clear in the following sections.

dev

> Pointer to the device (i.e., *eth0*) for which the protocol is to be enabled. A setting of NULL means "all devices." Thanks to this parameter, it would be possible to have different handlers for different devices, or associate a handler with one specific device. This is not normally done, but could be useful for testing. PF_PACKET sockets commonly use it to listen only on a specific device. For instance, a command such as *tcpdump –i eth0* creates a packet_type instance via a PF_PACKET socket and initializes dev to the net_device instance associated with *eth0*.

---

* The figure shows that the ETH_P_ALL protocol types use the packet_rcv routine. func is initialized by packet_create in *net/packet/af_packet.c* based on the kernel configuration.

func

The function handler called by netif_receive_skb (see Chapter 10) when it needs to process one frame with skb->protocol=type (an example is ip_rcv). Note that one of func's input parameters is a pointer to a packet_type structure: it is used by PF_PACKET sockets to access the af_packet_priv field.

af_packet_priv

Used by PF_PACKET sockets. It is a pointer to the sock data structure associated with the creator of the packet_type structure. It is used to allow the dev_queue_xmit_nit routine (seen in Chapter 10) not to deliver a buffer to the sender as well, and by the PF_PACKET receive routine to deliver ingress data to the right socket.

list

Used to link the data structure to the other instances that collide on the same bucket's list. See Figure 13-7.

When you have multiple instances of packet_type associated with the same type protocol, ingress frames that match type are handed to all protocol handler instances by invoking func for all of them. See Chapter 10 for more details.

To register each protocol, the kernel initializes the packet_type structure and then calls dev_add_pack. Here is an example from *net/ipv4/ip_output.c* that shows how the IPv4 protocol handler is registered by the IPv4 core code.

When the IPv4 protocol is initialized at boot time, the ip_init function is executed. As one result, the function ip_rcv in the IPv4 packet_type structure is registered as the protocol's function handler. All the Ethernet frames received with a "Protocol Above" value of ETH_P_IP will then be processed by the function ip_rcv.

```
static struct packet_type ip_packet_type =
{
    .type = __constant_htons(ETH_P_IP),
    .func = ip_rcv,
}
...
void __init ip_init(void)
{
    dev_add_pack(&ip_packet_type);
    ...
}
```

dev_add_pack is quite simple: it checks whether the handler to add is a protocol sniffer (pt->type==htons(ETH_P_ALL)). If so, the function adds it to the list pointed to by ptype_all and increments the number of protocol sniffers registered (netdev_nit++). If the handler is not a sniffer, it is inserted into one of the 16 lists pointed to by ptype_base depending on the value of the hash code. The data structures pointed to by ptype_base and ptype_all are protected by the ptype_lock spin lock.

```
void dev_add_pack(struct packet_type *pt)
{
    int hash;
```

```
        spin_lock_bh(&ptype_lock);
        if (pt->type == htons(ETH_P_ALL)) {
            netdev_nit++;
            list_add_rcu(&pt->list, &ptype_all);
        } else {
            hash = ntohs(pt->type) & 15;
            list_add_rcu(&pt->list, &ptype_base[hash]);
        }
        spin_unlock(&ptype_lock);
    }
```

The function dev_remove_pack, as the name suggests, is complementary to dev_add_pack.

```
    void dev_remove_pack(struct packet_type *pt)
    {
        __dev_remove_pack(pt);

        synchronize_net();
    }
```

__dev_remove_pack removes the packet_type structure from ptype_all or ptype_base, and synchronize_net is used to make sure that by the time dev_remove_pack returns, no one is holding a reference to the removed packet_type instance (see, for example, the use of RCU locking in netif_receive_skb in Chapter 10).

If dev_add_pack was called within the function init_module, which is in charge of module initialization, dev_remove_pack is most likely within cleanup_module, which is called by the kernel when the module is to be removed. (You can find an example in *net/ax25/af_ax25.c.*) On the other hand, if the protocol was statically included in the kernel, it would be registered automatically at boot time and removed only when the system shuts down. The IPv4 protocol is an example of a protocol that is never removed at runtime.

Ethernet Versus IEEE 802.3 Frames

A number of protocols go under the loose term *Ethernet*. The 802.2 and 802.3 standards are represented by the protocols ETH_P_802_2 and ETH_P_802_3, respectively, but there are many other Ethernet protocols, listed in Table 13-2, as well as the LLC and SNAP extensions. The standards institute a couple of hacks to support all of these variations (h_proto isdiscussed in the following section).

Table 13-2. Valid Ethernet types (when h_proto > 1536)

Protocol	Ethernet type	Function handler
ETH_P_IP	0x0800	ip_rcv
		ic_bootp_recv[a]
ETH_P_X25	0x0805	X25_lap_receive_frame
ETH_P_ARP	0x0806	arp_rcv

Table 13-2. Valid Ethernet types (when h_proto > 1536) (continued)

Protocol	Ethernet type	Function handler
ETH_P_BPQ	0x08FF	bpq_rcv
ETH_P_DNA_RT	0x6003	dn_route_rcv
ETH_P_RARP	0x8035	ic_rarp_recv
ETH_P_8021Q	0x8100	vlan_skb_rcv
ETH_P_IPX	0x8137	ipx_rcv
ETH_P_IPV6	0x86DD	ipv6_rcv
ETH_P_PPP_DISC	0x8863	pppoe_disc_rcv
ETH_P_PPP_SES	0x8864	pppoe_rcv

a The reason why IP has two handlers has to do with the possibility for the kernel to retrieve the IP configuration by means of protocols like RARP/BOOTP. The *ic_bootp_recv* handler is used only at boot time to take care of the dynamic IP configuration, and it is uninstalled once the configuration has been retrieved. See *net/ipv4/ipconfig.c*.

Ethernet was designed before the IEEE created its 802.2 and 802.3 standards. The latter are not pure Ethernet, even though they are commonly called Ethernet standards. Fortunately, the IEEE 802 committee decided to make the protocols compatible. Every Ethernet card is able to receive both the 802 standard frame types and the old Ethernet frames, and the kernel provides a routine (discussed later in this section) that allows device drivers to recognize them thanks to the solution described in this section.

This is the definition of an Ethernet header:

```
struct ethhdr
{
        unsigned char   h_dest[ETH_ALEN];    /* destination eth addr */
        unsigned char   h_source[ETH_ALEN];  /* source ether addr    */
        unsigned short  h_proto;             /* packet type ID field */
} __ATTRIBUTE__ ((packed));
```

As you will see in the next two sections on LLC and SNAP, other fields can follow the ethhdr structure. Here we are focusing on the protocol field, h_proto. Despite its name, it actually can store either the protocol in use or the length of the frame. This is because it is 2 octets (bytes) in size, but the maximum size of an Ethernet frame is 1,500 bytes. (Actually, the size can reach 1,518 if SA, DA, Checksum, and Preamble are included. Frames using 802.1q have four extra bytes of encapsulation and can therefore reach a size of 1,522 bytes.)

To save space, the IEEE decided to use values greater than 1,536 to represent the Ethernet protocol. Some preexisting protocols with identifiers lower than 1,536 (0x600 hexadecimal) were updated to meet the criteria. The 802.2 and 802.3 protocols, however, use the field to store the length of the frame.* Values ranging from 1,501 to 1,535 are not legal in this field.

Figure 13-8 shows the variations possible on an Ethernet header. Simple Ethernet is shown in (a). The 802.2 and 802.3 variant is shown in (b). As you can see, a single field serves as the protocol field in the former and the length field in the latter. In addition, the 802 variant can support LLC, as shown in (c) and SNAP, as shown in (d).

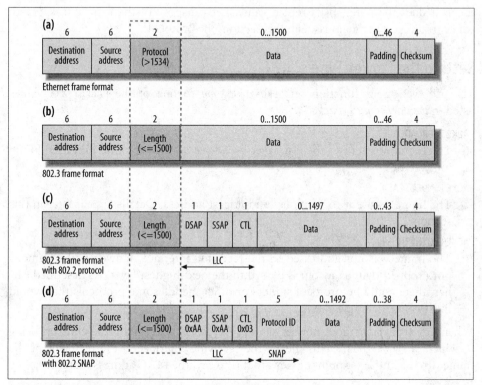

Figure 13-8. Differences between Ethernet and 802.3 frames

Linux deals with the odd distinction between protocol and length in the eth_type_ trans function. A typical context is represented by the following code fragment, issued by the *drivers/net/3c509.c* Ethernet driver when it receives a frame. netif_rx is the function that copies the frame into the input queue and sets the NET_RX_SOFTIRQ flag to let the kernel know about the new frame in the queue (this is described in Chapter 10[†]). Just before invoking netif_rx, the caller performs some important initializations with a call to eth_type_trans.

---

* The reason for this arrangement is a long story. For the curious, I suggest reading *Interconnections, Second Edition: Bridges, Routers, Switches, and Internetworking Protocols* (Addison Wesley), where the author explains it with considerable irony.

```
el3_rx(struct device *dev)
{
        ... ... ...
        skb->protocol = eth_type_trans(skb,dev);
        netif_rx(skb);
        ... ... ...
}
```

eth_type_trans performs two main tasks: setting the packet type[*] and setting the protocol. It does the latter in its return value. Let's dispose of the former task before concentrating on the main issue in this section, the protocol.

Setting the Packet Type

The eth_type_trans function sets skb->pkt_type to one of the PACKET_*XXX* values listed in *include/linux/if_packet.h*:

PACKET_BROADCAST
> The frame was sent to the link layer broadcast address (i.e., FF:FF:FF:FF:FF:FF for Ethernet)

PACKET_MULTICAST
> The frame was sent to a link layer multicast address. Details appear later in this section.

PACKET_OTHERHOST
> The frame was not addressed to the receiving interface. However, the frame is not dropped right away but is passed to the next-highest layer. As described earlier, there could be protocol sniffers or other meddlesome protocols that would like to give the frame a look.

When eth_type_trans does not set skb->pkt_type explicitly, its value ends up being 0, which is PACKET_HOST. This means the receiving interface is the recipient of the frame (from a link layer point of view, that is to say, the MAC address matched).

Most of the information needed to set the correct packet type is specified explicitly in the header. An Ethernet address is 48 bits or 6 bytes long. The two least significant bits of the first byte (in network byte order) have a special meaning (see Figure 13-9):

* Bit 0 distinguishes multicast addresses from unicast addresses. Broadcast addresses are a special case of multicast. When set to 1, this bit denotes multicast; when 0, it denotes unicast. After checking the bit through if(*eth->h_dest&1), the function goes on to see whether the frame is a broadcast frame by comparing the address to the device's broadcast address through memcmp(eth->h_dest,dev->broadcast, ETH_ALEN).

[†] netif_rx is only one of the two interfaces available to device drivers to notify upper layers about the reception of frames. Both of them are described in Chapter 10.

[*] Even though the code calls it the packet type, it actually is the frame type because it is derived from the link layer address.

- Bit 1 distinguishes local addresses from global addresses. Global addresses are worldwide unique, local addresses are not: it is up to the system administrator to assign local addresses properly.[*] When set to 1, this bit denotes a global address; when 0, it denotes a local address.

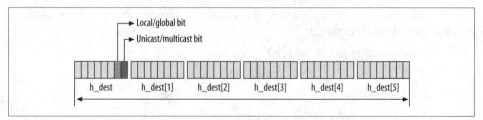

Figure 13-9. Unicast/multicast and local/global bits in the MAC address

Thus, the first part of eth_type_trans is:

```
unsigned short eth_type_trans(struct sk_buff *skb, struct net_device *dev)
{
    struct ethhdr *eth;
    unsigned char *rawp;

    skb->mac.raw=skb->data;
    skb_pull(skb,ETH_HLEN);
    eth= eth_hdr(skb);
    skb->input_dev = dev;

    if(*eth->h_dest&1)
    {
        if(memcmp(eth->h_dest,dev->broadcast, ETH_ALEN)==0)
            skb->pkt_type=PACKET_BROADCAST;
        else
            skb->pkt_type=PACKET_MULTICAST;
    }

    else if(1 /*dev->flags&IFF_PROMISC*/)
    {
        if(memcmp(eth->h_dest,dev->dev_addr, ETH_ALEN))
            skb->pkt_type=PACKET_OTHERHOST;
    }
```

The IFF_PROMISC flag is set in dev->flags when the interface is put into promiscuous mode. As shown in the previous snapshot, eth_type_trans initializes skb->pkt_type to PACKET_OTHERHOST when the destination MAC address does not match the receiving interface's address, regardless of the IFF_PROMISC flag. This will allow PF_SOCKETS handlers to receive a copy of the frame (see netif_receive_skb in Chapter 10), but the upper-layer protocol handlers must discard buffers of PACKET_OTHERHOST type (see, for example, arp_rcv and ip_rcv).

---

[*] There is no relationship between local MAC addresses and nonroutable IP addresses (192.168.*x.x*, etc.): they are similar in concept, but applied to two different layers in the stack.

Setting the Ethernet Protocol and Length

The second part of eth_type_trans retrieves the identifier of the protocol used at the higher layer. Protocol values are also called Ethertypes, and the list of valid types is kept up-to-date at *http://standards.ieee.org/regauth/ethertype*. The distinction between old Ethernet protocols above the value of 1,536 and 802 protocols is made in the following code fragment:

```
if (ntohs(eth->h_proto) >= 1536)
    return eth->h_proto;

rawp = skb->data;

if (*(unsigned short *)rawp == 0xFFFF)
    return htons(ETH_P_802_3);

/*
 *    Real 802.2 LLC
 */
return htons(ETH_P_802_2);
}
```

If values bigger than 1,536 are interpreted as protocol IDs, how does a device driver find the size of the frames it receives? In both cases, whether protocol/length values are less than 1,500 or greater than 1,536, it is the device itself that stores the size of the frame into one if its registers, where the device driver can read it. Devices can figure out the size of each frame thanks to well-known bit patterns used for that purpose. The following piece of code from vortex_rx in *drivers/net/3c59x.c* shows how the driver first reads the size from the device and then allocates a buffer accordingly:

```
/* The packet length: up to 4.5K!. */
int pkt_len = rx_status & 0x1fff;
struct sk_buff *skb;

skb = dev_alloc_skb(pkt_len + 5);
```

Do not get confused by the comment in the previous code. This particular device can receive frames up to 4.5 K in size because it handles FDDI NICs, too.

We saw in Chapter 1 what host and network byte order are. The value returned by eth_type_trans, and therefore the value assigned to skb->protocol, is in network byte order: when it is extracted from the Ethernet header it is already in network byte order, and when eth_type_trans uses a local symbol ETH_P_*XXX* it needs to explicitly convert it from host byte order to network byte order with the htons macro. This also means that when the kernel accesses skb->protocol later and compares it against an ETH_P_*XXX* value, it has to convert either ETH_P_*XXX* to network byte order or skb->protocol to host byte order: it does not matter what order is used, it just matters that both sides of the comparison are expressed in the same order. In other words, these two lines are equivalent:

```
ntohs(skb->protocol) == ETH_P_802_2
skb->protocol == htons(ETH_P_802_2)
```

Since eth_type_trans is called only for Ethernet frames, there are similar functions for other media types, some with names ending in _type_trans and some with other names. The following example, for instance, shows a bit of code taken from the IBM Token Ring driver (*drivers/net/tokenring/ibmtr.c*), before the familiar invocation of netif_rx, skb->protocol is set by tr_type_trans, just as eth_type_trans did for Ethernet devices:

```
static void tr_rx(struct device *dev)
{
    ...
    skb->protocol=tr_type_trans(skb, dev);
    ...
    netif_rx(skb);
    ...
}
```

If you look at tr_type_trans in *net/802/tr.c*, you will see logic similar to that of eth_type_trans, but applied to Token Ring devices.

There are also media types that set skb->protocol directly without any helper function of the _type_trans variety, since they can carry only one protocol (i.e., IrDA, AX25, etc.).

Logical Link Control (LLC)

The LLC layer was designed by the IEEE 802 committee when they standardized LANs. The idea was that instead of having a single higher-layer protocol identifier, it would be more flexible to specify one protocol identifier for the source (SSAP) and another for the destination (DSAP). In most cases, SSAP and DSAP would be the same for any given connection—in fact, SSAP and DSAP are always the same when the global flag is set—but having two separate values gives systems the flexibility to use different protocols.

LLC can provide its upper layer different service types:

Type I
    Connectionless (i.e., datagram protocol), with no support for acknowledgments, flow control, and error recovery

Type II
    Connection oriented, with support for acknowledgments, flow control, and error recovery

Type III
    Connectionless, but with some of the benefits of type II

Figure 13-8(c) shows the header format of a frame using LLC. As you can see, there are three new fields:

SSAP
DSAP

These are 8-bit fields for specifying the protocols used.

Control (CTL)

The size of this field depends on the type of LLC used (type I or type II). I will not go into details on the LLC layer, but will assume this field to be 1 byte long and have the value 0x03 (type I, CTL=UI). This is sufficient for understanding the rest of the chapter.

The LLC header did not prove popular for several reasons. Perhaps the main reason is the 8-bit limit on the SSAP and DSAP identifiers, compounded by reserving two of these bits for the unicast/multicast and local/global flags.* Only 64 protocols could be specified in the remaining 6 bits, which was too limiting.

When using local SAPs (indicated by the local/global flag in the protocol field), the network administrator must make sure all the systems agree on the local SAPs they use, which makes things complicated and less usable. Ambiguity is not possible for global SAP, but global SAP is not being used for new protocols. In the next section, you will see how this limitation was solved by extending the header with the concept of SNAP.

Table 13-3 shows the SAPs registered with the Linux kernel. LLC causes the kernel to use an extra level of indirection when retrieving the handler, compared to the protocols listed in Table 13-2 and registered with dev_add_pack.

Table 13-3. The kernel's 802.2 SAP clients

Protocol	SAP	Function handler
SNAP	0xAA	snap_rcv
IPX	0xE0	ipx_rcv

The IPX case

You may wonder whether a pure 802.3 frame format can be used, given that there is no indication of a protocol ID in Figure 13-8(b). In fact, pure 802.3 frames are not normally used. The one well-known exception involves IPX. IPX packets can be sent using raw 802.3 frames (that is, frames without an LLC header). The receiver recognizes them by means of a hack. The first field of an IPX header is a 16-bit checksum, which normally is turned off by simply setting it to 0xFFFF. Since 0xFF/0xFF† is an invalid SSAP/DSAP combination and there is no Ethertype with that value, IPX

---

* The meaning of those two flags is the same as discussed earlier for MAC addresses, but here it applies to protocols rather than addresses.

† The check against 0xFF/0xFF to recognize IPX packets is used all over the place in the Linux kernel. eth_type_trans is one example.

---

packets using raw 802.3 can be easily recognized. When they are detected, skb->protocol is set to ETH_P_802_3, whose handler is the IPX handler (see Table 13-1).

Linux's LLC implementation

The 802.2 LLC layer was expanded and rewritten during the 2.5 development cycle. The kernel's LLC implementation, which supports types I and II, consists of the following main components:

- Two state machines. These are used to keep track of the states of the local SAPs and the connections created on top of them.
- An LLC receive routine that feeds the right input to the two state machines based on the input frames it receives.
- The AF_LLC socket interface. This can be used to build protocols or services in user space on top of the LLC layer.

Because none of the protocols described in this book uses the LLC layer, I will not go into detail on the definitions of the LLC services (you can refer to the IEEE 802.2 Logical Link Control specification for this[*]), nor will I look at the details of the Linux kernel's LLC implementation. Here we will only see what data structure is used to define a local SAP and briefly how ingress frames are handled.

The data structure used to define a local SAP is llc_sap, which is defined in *include/net/llc.h*. Among its fields are:

struct llc_addr laddr
     SAP identifier.

int (*rcv_func)(struct sk_buff *, struct net_device *, struct packet_type *)
     Function handler. When an SAP is opened via PF_LLC socket, this field is NULL. When the SAP is opened by the kernel, this field points to the routine provided by the kernel (see Table 13-3).

Local SAPs are created with llc_sap_open, and are inserted into the llc_sap_list list. llc_sap_open is called to create two types of SAP:

- Those installed by the kernel itself to install kernel-level handlers[†] (see Table 13-3).
- Those managed with PF_LLC sockets (for example, when a server uses the bind system call on a PF_LLC socket to bind it to a given SAP).

---

[*] Like most IEEE documents, the one about the LLC design is pretty big and not fun to read. However, with this document in your hands, it will be much easier to go through the LLC code, especially through the boring details of the state machines.

[†] This can be accomplished indirectly via the register_8022_client routine, too.

Processing ingress LLC frames

Whenever an incoming frame is classified by eth_type_trans as using the LLC header (because it has a type/length field that is less than 1,536 and no special IPX case is detected), the initialization of skb->protocol to ETH_P_802_2 leads to the selection of the llc_rcv handler (see Table 13-1). This handler will select the right protocol handler based on the DSAP field in the LLC header: to do so, it calls the rcv_func handler registered with llc_sap_open for those SAPs opened by the kernel, and feeds the right input to the right state machine when the SAPs were opened with a PF_LLC socket (see Figure 13-10).

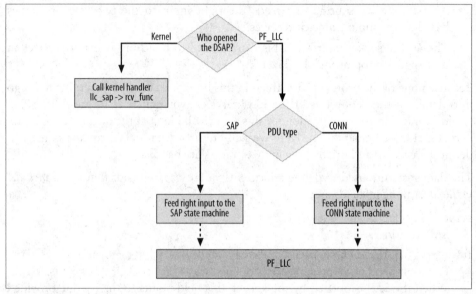

Figure 13-10. The llc_rcv function

Frames are sent out a given SAP when one of the two state machines requires it (for example, to acknowledge the reception of a frame). PF_LLC sockets can use the standard interface (i.e., sendmsg, etc.) to transmit. In both cases, frames are fed directly to dev_queue_xmit once the appropriate link layer headers have been initialized properly.

Subnetwork Access Protocol (SNAP)

Given the limitations of the LLC header, the 802 committee generalized the data link header further. To make the protocol domain bigger, they introduced the concept of SNAP. Basically, when the SSAP/DSAP couple is assigned the value 0xAA/0xAA, it has a special meaning: the five bytes following the CTL field of the LLC header represent a protocol identifier. The unicast/multicast and local/global bits are also not used anymore. Thus, the size of the protocol identifier has jumped from 8 bits to 40.

The reason the committee decided to use five bytes has to do with how protocol numbers are derived from MAC addresses.[*] Unlike SSAP/DSAP, the use of SNAP codes is pretty common.

Since the SNAP identifier 0xAA/0xAA is a special case of SSAP/DSAP, as shown in Table 13-3, it is one of the clients that use llc_sap_open (see snap_init in *net/802/psnap.c*). This means that a protocol using a SNAP code will have another level of indirection, which means three of them!

Before looking at how SNAP clients register with the kernel, let's briefly see how a SNAP protocol ID is defined. As you probably know, MAC addresses are managed by the IEEE, which sells them in chunks of 2^{24}. Since a MAC address is 48 bits long (6 bytes), the IEEE simply has to give each client a 24-bit number (the first three bytes of a MAC address) and let the client use any value for the remaining 24 bits. Suppose I want to buy a chunk of MAC addresses because I want to start selling network cards. We'll call the number assigned to me XX:YY:ZZ. At that point, I would become the owner of all the addresses between XX:YY:ZZ:00:00:00 and XX:YY:ZZ:FF:FF:FF. Together with those 2^{24} MAC addresses, I would be assigned all the 2^{16} SNAP codes between XX:YY:ZZ:00:00 and XX:YY:ZZ:FF:FF.

Effectively, when you get a 24-bit number from the IEEE, it offers you four 24-bit numbers thanks to the four possible combinations of the global/local and unicast/multicast bits (see Figure 13-9).

Similar to the way SAP protocols are registered and unregistered, the SNAP layer provides the register_snap_client and unregister_snap_client functions, which also use a global list (snap_list) to link together all the SNAP protocols registered with the kernel. Table 13-4 shows the clients registered with the Linux kernel.

Table 13-4. SNAP client

Protocol	Snap ID	Function handler
AppleTalk Address Resolution Protocol	00:00:00:80:F3	aarp_rcv
AppleTalk Datagram Delivery Protocol	08:00:07:80:9B	atalk_rcv
IPX	00:00:00:81:37	ipx_rcv

The data structure used to define a SNAP protocol is datalink_proto, defined in *include/net/datalink.h*. Among its fields, you have:

unsigned short header_length
> This is the length of the data link header. It is initialized to 8 in register_snap_client (see Figure 13-8(d)).

---

[*] SNAP codes are defined as a subset of MAC addresses, which are sold by IEEE in chunks. This way, each MAC address owner has a number of SNAP codes assigned to her together with the MAC addresses. For details, I recommend reading *Interconnections*, *Second Edition* (Addison Wesley).

`unsigned_char type[8]`

Protocol identifier. Only five bytes are used (the SNAP protocol ID; see Table 13-4).

`void (*request)(struct datalink_proto *, struct sk_buff *, unsigned char *)`

Initialized to `snap_request` in `register_snap_client`. It initializes the SNAP header (protocol ID only) and passes the frame to the 802.2 code. It is invoked before a transmission to fill in the data link header.

`void (*rcvfunc)(struct sk_buff *, struct net_device *, struct packet_type *)`

Function handler for ingress traffic. See Table 13-4.

I'll focus for just a moment on IPX. It's worth pointing out that this protocol registers the same handler with the kernel at three different points:

- One with an Ethertype (Table 13-2)
- One as an 802.3 SSAP/DSAP protocol (Table 13-3)
- One as a SNAP protocol (Table 13-4)

Figure 13-11 summarizes how the kernel recognizes and handles Ethernet, 802.3, 802.2, and SNAP frames.

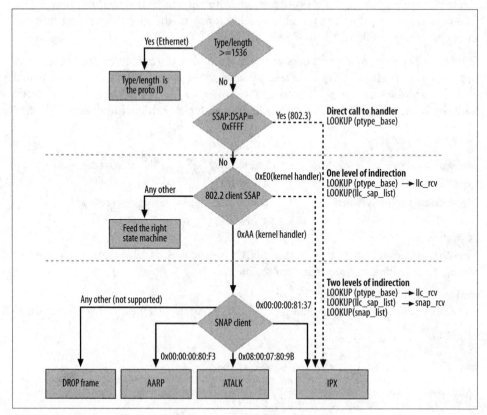

Figure 13-11. Protocol detection for Ethernet/802.3/802.2/SNAP frames

Tuning via /proc Filesystem

For both Ethernet and 802 there is a directory in *proc/sys/net*, */proc/sys/net/ethernet/* (which is empty) and */proc/sys/net/token-ring/* (which includes a single file), registered respectively in the files *net/core/sysctl_net_ethernet.c* and *net/802/sysclt_net_802.c*. These two directories are included only when the kernel is compiled with support for Ethernet and Token Ring, respectively.

Functions and Variables Featured in This Chapter

Table 13-5 lists the main functions introduced in this chapter, together with the most important global variables and data structures.

Table 13-5. Functions and data involved in protocol handler management

Name	Description
Function	
dev_add_pack dev_remove_pack	Add/remove a protocol handler.
register_8022_client unregister_8022_client	Register/unregister an 802.2 protocol. They are defined as wrappers around llc_sap_open and llc_sap_close.
register_snap_client unregister_snap_client	Register/unregister a SNAP client.
llc_sap_open llc_sap_close	Create/remove an SAP.
eth_type_trans	Used by Ethernet devices to extract the higher-layer protocol identifier and classify the frame as unicast/multicast/broadcast.
Variables	
netdev_nit	Number of protocol sniffers registered.
ptype_base	Pointer to the data structure containing the registered protocol handler.
ptype_all	Same as ptype_base but applied to protocol sniffers.
snap_list	List of SNAP clients.
Data structure type	
struct packet_type	Used to store information about an ETH_P_*XXX* protocol handler.
struct datalink_proto	Used to represent a SNAP protocol.

Files and Directories Featured in This Chapter

Figure 13-12 shows the location of the files mentioned in this chapter. In *include/ linux* you can find *if_xxx.h* header files for other media types. The *net/llc* directory includes several more files.

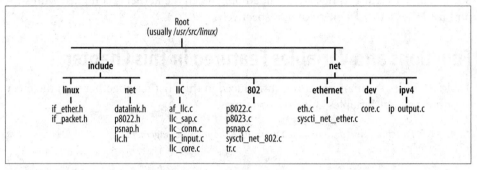

Figure 13-12. Files and directories featured in this chapter

## PART IV

Bridging

At the L3 layer, protocols such as IPv4 connect different networks through the routing subsystem laid out in Part VII. In this part of the book, we will look at the link layer or L2 counterpart of routing: *bridging*. In particular:

Chapter 14, *Bridging: Concepts*
Introduces the concepts of transparent learning and selective forwarding.

Chapter 15, *Bridging: The Spanning Tree Protocol*
Shows how the Spanning Tree Protocol (STP) solves most of bridging's limitations, and concludes with an overview of the latest STP enhancements (not yet available for Linux).

Chapter 16, *Bridging: Linux Implementation*
Show how Linux implements bridging and STP.

Chapter 17, *Bridging: Miscellaneous Topics*
Concludes with an overview of how the bridging code interacts with other networking subsystems and a detailed description of the data structures used by the bridging code.

## CHAPTER 14

Bridging: Concepts

In this first chapter on bridging, we will see what a bridge device is, how it is used, and what limitations it comes with. In particular, I'll describe transparent bridging, address learning, and the use of the so-called forwarding database. I'll conclude the chapter with an explanation of why bridges cannot be used on loop topologies and I will introduce the next chapter, where we will see how the Spanning Tree Protocol (STP) can address this limitation. Other forms of bridging are available, but they are rarely used and not implemented in the Linux kernel.

The network topologies used in this chapter do not necessarily represent real case scenarios; they are selected based only on didactic principles.

Repeaters, Bridges, and Routers

Before introducing bridging, I will clarify the distinction between different network devices that forward packets: repeaters, bridges, and routers. The differences are illustrated in Figure 14-1:

- A *repeater* is a device, typically equipped with two ports, that simply copies what it receives on one port to the other, and vice versa. It copies data bit by bit; it does not have any knowledge of protocols, and therefore cannot distinguish among different frames or packets. Repeaters are rarely used nowadays, because bridges have become pretty affordable and provide better capabilities that justify the cost difference. Multiport repeaters are called *hubs*.

- Unlike a repeater, a *bridge* understands link layer protocols and therefore copies data frame by frame, instead of bit by bit. This means that a bridge must be able to buffer at least one frame per port. Most LANs are implemented with bridges (that more commonly are called *switches*; see the section "Bridges Versus Switches"). This device is the main protagonist of this chapter.

- A *router* is a device that understands L3 network protocols such as IP, and forwards ingress packets based on a routing table. The term *gateway*, which was introduced before *router*, is also commonly used to refer to the same kind of device. Part VII of this book goes into detail on how Linux implements routing.

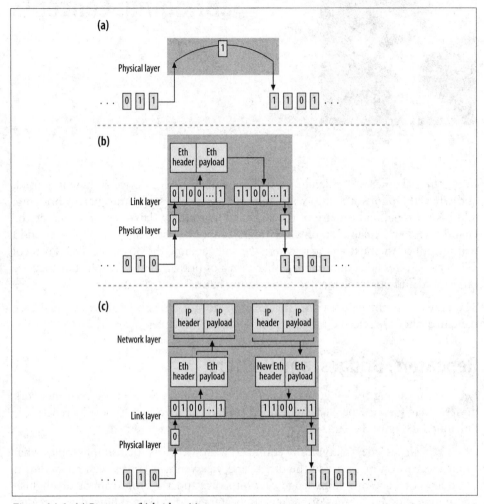

Figure 14-1. (a) Repeater; (b) bridge; (c) router

Figure 14-1(b) shows what is called a store-and-forward bridge, which is the scheme used by Linux: Ethernet frames are copied out of the right ports only after they have been received in their entirety.

Other schemes are possible. For example, a pretty common one called cut-through starts copying frames to the right ports as soon as it has received enough of the ingress frame to identify the destination ports. The meaning of *right ports* will become clearer at the end of this chapter, when we will have seen what address learning is. This scheme is faster because it starts copying earlier, but it cannot discard corrupted ingress frames.[*] The scheme also requires some cooperation from the network interface card (NIC) hardware. In the current model, NICs pass whole frames to the device drivers.

A bridge assigns a link layer address to each of its interfaces, and forwards anything that passes through it but is not addressed to it. (Routers act similarly at the L3 level, as we'll will see in Part VII.) But would any frame be addressed to the bridge's interface? After all, the whole point of a bridge is to help frames get to other destinations. However, a bridge does consume some ingress frames, under two conditions:

To pass it to the upper (i.e., L3) layer
> This is possible only when the bridge implements L3 functionalities, too (i.e., it is a router or host in addition to a bridge) and the ingress frame is addressed to the L2 address configured on the receiving interface.

To pass it to a protocol handler
> We will see this case in Chapter 15 when I will introduce the Spanning Tree Protocol.

Bridges Versus Switches

The terms *bridge* and *switch* can be used to refer to the same device. However, nowadays the term *bridge* is mainly used in the documentation (such as the IEEE specifications referenced at the end of this chapter) that discusses how a bridge behaves and how the STP (which we will see in the next chapter) works. In contrast, references to the actual devices are usually made with the term *switch*.

The only cases where I have seen people referring to a bridge device using the term *bridge* is when the device is equipped with only two ports (and bridges with two ports are not that common nowadays). This is why I often define a switch informally as a multiport bridge. Unless you are familiar with the official IEEE documentation, you will probably use the term *switch*. I personally worked on bridging software for years, and as far as I can remember, I used the term *bridge* only when working on the documentation, never to refer to a device on any network setup.

Generally speaking, I can say that there is really no difference between a bridge and a switch.

Bridges are pretty common nowadays. You can find bridges with a variable number of ports (and matching prices). An Ethernet bridge, nowadays, represents the most common way to implement a LAN.

---

[*] Well, there are variants of cut-through that can handle corrupted frames, too. We do not need to go into that much detail on this point for our generic discussion on bridging.

With a PC running Linux, you can implement a bridge by installing more than one NIC. You can also find multiport Peripheral Component Interconnect (PCI) NICs on the market that allow you to have more network interfaces than PCI slots. You can, for example, have four Ethernet ports in a single PCI NIC.

In the rest of this chapter and in the next ones, I will stick to the term *bridge*, but now you know that the switch that you are using in your office to connect the PCs and the network printer is nothing but a multiport bridge, which probably runs more software than a pure bridge would run—for example, to provide additional features.

Hosts

Any device that operates at a network layer higher than the one used by bridges (i.e., the link layer or L2) is considered a host in the context of this and the following bridging chapters (routers included). A host (i.e., a Linux system) can, if configured appropriately, be both a bridge and a host that a user can use as a standard workstation. But in this chapter and the following ones, we will not consider this case; we'll assume a host does not run any bridging code. Therefore, the PCs in all the figures do not run any bridging code unless stated otherwise in the text.

Merging LANs with Bridges

Let's take the scenario in Figure 14-2 as an example and see how a bridge can be used to merge two LANs and make them look like one. Let's assume the hosts in the two LANs were configured to be part of the same IP subnet. We do not need to include the IP addresses in the figure because we will focus on what happens at the link layer.

You should note that a LAN is nothing but a multiport bridge.

Any frame transmitted on a LAN by any host is received by all other hosts. So when Host A sends out a frame, both the other hosts of LAN1 and the bridge receive it. A bridge copies its ingress frame out on all the other ports (there is just one other port, in this case). At the end, therefore, all hosts of both LAN1 and LAN2 receive a copy of the frame generated by Host A. This means that thanks to the bridge, there is only one big LAN from the perspective of the hosts of LAN1 and LAN2. Bridges are commonly employed to merge physical LANs whose hosts are configured on the same IP subnet, because they give the hosts the illusion of a single LAN.

Note that the bridge forwards the ingress frames as they are received. It does not add, remove, or change anything on them: the hosts in LAN2 receive an exact copy of the original frame generated by Host A.

You may argue that a packet from Host A addressed to Host B is needlessly forwarded to LAN2, which is a waste of bandwidth on LAN2 and a waste of CPU

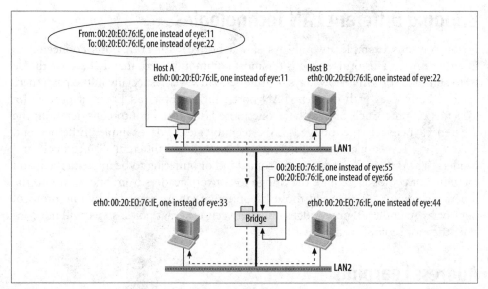

Figure 14-2. Two LANs merged with a bridge

power for the hosts of LAN2 (since all of them will end up dropping any frame that is not addressed to any of them). By assigning the hosts of the two LANs to two different IP subnets and replacing the bridge with a router, as in Figure 14-3, the waste is eliminated, because the router does not forward to LAN2 those packets that are addressed to a host configured on LAN1.

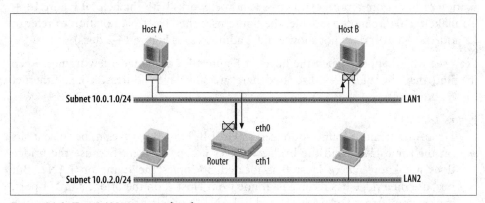

Figure 14-3. Two LANs connected with a router

The topologies of Figures 14-2 and 14-3 are used in different contexts. The first one prefers to have hosts that are located in different LANs share the same L2 and therefore the same IP (L3) subnet. The second one prefers to segregate hosts on different subnets, perhaps for administrative reasons.

Note that the hosts in Figure 14-2 still need a router to reach IP addresses outside their subnet.

Bridging Different LAN Technologies

In the previous examples, we always saw a bridge with both ports connected to Ethernet LANs. This bridge type is the most commonly used, mainly because the de facto standard for LANs nowadays is Ethernet. However, especially in the past, there used to be bridges with different LAN ports; for example, an Ethernet port and a Token Ring port. Such bridges have one more issue to take into consideration: the differences between the bridged LAN technologies. For example, Ethernet and Token Ring LANs operate at different speeds, and use different L2 protocols and headers. The different speeds require some kind of buffering to be implemented, and the different protocols require the bridge to convert headers from one format to the other, including taking care of those L2 options that are provided by one protocol but not by the other. Linux bridges only between Ethernet ports, so we will not consider the more complex case any further.

Address Learning

We saw in the previous section that a bridge that blindly copies ingress frames to all the ports except the one that received the frame may lead to a waste of resources. Fortunately, bridges are not as blind as that. They actually are able to learn the location of hosts (their L2 addresses, to be more exact) and use that knowledge to selectively copy ingress frames only to the right port. This process is called *passive learning*, because it is handled by the bridge alone, without any need for user configuration or help from a protocol. Let's see how it works with the help of Figure 14-4. To make the figure more readable, the figure uses the "Host N" notation to refer to L2 addresses (i.e., it does not show real L2 addresses, as Figure 14-2 does).

Let's see what happens when the hosts of Figure 14-4 exchange a few frames. Keep in mind that the addresses discussed here are link layer addresses (i.e., Ethernet MAC addresses):

Figure 14-4(a)
> Host A transmits a frame addressed to Host B. Host B receives it, because it sits on the same LAN, and the bridge receives a copy as well. Because the bridge does not know where Host B is located, it copies the frame on LAN2. But because the bridge has received a frame from Host A on the bridge's LAN1 port, it now knows that Host A is located in LAN1. Note that this is possible because Ethernet headers include both the source and destination addresses.

Figure 14-4(b)
> Host B transmits a frame addressed to Host A. Both Host A and the bridge receive the frame. Because the bridge knows that Host A is on LAN1, the same LAN it received the frame from, it will not copy the frame on LAN2.

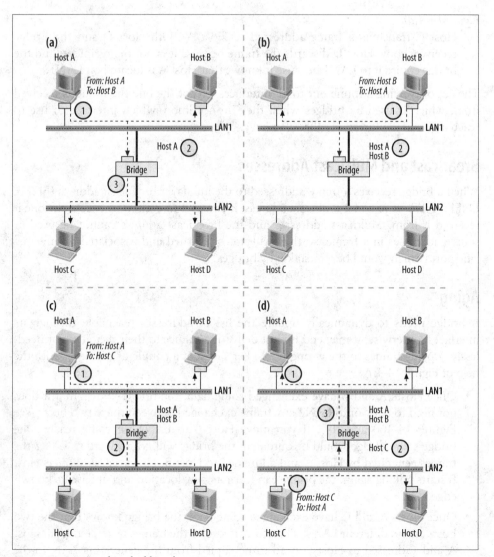

Figure 14-4. Examples of address learning

Figure 14-4(c)

Host A transmits a frame addressed to Host C. Both Host B and the bridge receive the frame. Host B discards it because it is not the recipient, and the bridge copies the frame to LAN2 because it does not know where Host C is located. The bridge already knows that Host A is in LAN1. Therefore, it does not need to add any entry to the list of addresses reachable through its port on LAN1.

Figure 14-4(d)
> Host C transmits a frame addressed to Host A. Both Host D and the bridge receive a copy. Host D discards the frame because it is not the recipient, and the bridge copies it to LAN1 because it knows that Host A is located on LAN1.

The act of copying a frame out to all interfaces except the one the frame is received from, which is used by bridges when they do not know which interface to use to reach a given L2 address, is called *flooding*.

Broadcast and Multicast Addresses

When a bridge receives a frame addressed to the link layer broadcast address (FF:FF: FF:FF:FF:FF) or to an L2 multicast address, it copies it to every port except the one it received it from. Multicast addresses and the broadcast address cannot be used as source addresses in a frame, so they will not be learned and associated to any specific port (which would be a mistake) by bridges.

Aging

A bridge needs to dynamically update the list of addresses reachable through its interfaces; otherwise, it may end up not delivering frames to their recipients or needlessly copying frames to the wrong ports. Let's look at a couple of examples with the help of Figure 14-4:

- Once Hosts A and B have exchanged some data, the bridge knows that it does not need to copy onto LAN2 any frame exchanged between those two hosts (see Figures 14-4(a) and (b)). If you move Host B to LAN2 for some reason, the bridge's knowledge would be outdated: the bridge will not forward to LAN2 the frames generated by Host A and addressed to Host B. However, as soon as Host B starts talking again, the bridge can learn its new location and update its knowledge.

- Once Hosts A and C have exchanged some data, the bridge knows that the two hosts are on different LANs. Therefore, it knows the frames generated from Host A and addressed to Host C need to be copied from the generating LAN to the other one, and vice versa (see Figures 14-4(c) and (d)). Supposing that Host C is moved to LAN1, the bridge would keep copying frames from Host A to LAN2 even if they are not needed. As soon as Host C starts talking again, the bridge can update its lists of addresses and move Host C's address from LAN2's list to LAN1's list.

In both cases, if a host does not generate any frames after it has been moved, the bridge does not have any way of learning its new location.

Therefore, to adapt the bridge's knowledge to topology changes, the addresses learned by the bridge are timed out after a configurable amount of time. This aging mechanism is usually implemented by a simple timer that is started when the address is first learned, and restarted (reset) anytime the host is heard again, confirming or updating its address. The process is shown in Figure 14-5. The lower the timer is, the faster a bridge can learn about changes, but also the more frequently the bridge finds itself not knowing where a given host is located and having to use flooding. The default aging time is 5 minutes. We will see in Chapter 15 how the aging time can be lowered by the STP under specific conditions, and in Chapter 17 how the system administrator can change the default aging time.

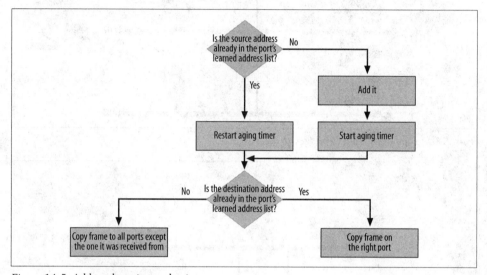

Figure 14-5. Address learning and aging

Multiple Bridges

So far, we have seen only simple scenarios with just one bridge. However, because transparent bridges are transparent to each other, as well as to the hosts and the routers, you can create a larger L2 domain (i.e., a bigger LAN) by employing multiple bridges, as shown in Figure 14-6.

The figure also shows the list of addresses that is learned by each interface of the two bridges, assuming each host has spoken at least once and thus given the bridges a chance to learn their locations. Note, for example, that from Bridge 2's perspective, Hosts A, B, C, and D are all located in LAN2, or in other words, are reachable via Bridge 1's interface on LAN2. After all, a bridge does not really care exactly where a host is located; all it needs to know is what port to use to reach it.

The use of multiple bridges, however, requires care to be taken when designing the topology. Let's see why with the example in Figure 14-7.

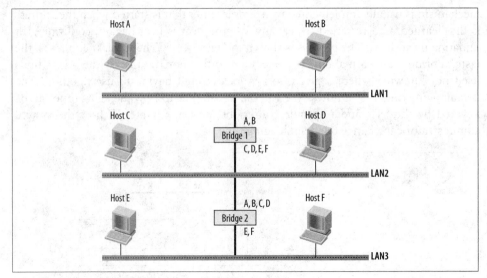

Figure 14-6. Topology with two bridges

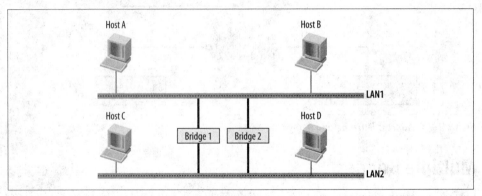

Figure 14-7. Redundant bridges

Multiple bridges on the same LAN can be useful, for instance, to increase the availability of the connectivity between the LANs on which the bridges have interfaces. If one bridge becomes unusable for some reason, the other ones will be able to keep up connectivity. The figure shows a topology with only two bridges, but nothing would forbid you from having more.

Nothing comes for free, though, so as you can imagine, there is a problem with the topology of Figure 14-7. The problem comes from the "transparency" property of bridges that we described earlier as a positive aspect. So next we'll see where our configuration gets us in trouble.

Bridging Loops

Overall, transparency is good because hosts located in different LANs can be transparently merged as if there were only one common LAN. However, transparency is also dangerous because a bridge does not know the origin of an ingress frame. The bridge's job is to learn the location of hosts from ingress packets, build a sort of database of addresses, and copy ingress frames to the right ports based on such a database. When you have more than one bridge sitting on the same LAN, you cannot assume anymore that an ingress frame originated in the same LAN to which the port that received the frame is connected: the frame could have been copied there by another bridge. This lack of information is so dangerous that bridges cannot be used as shown in Figure 14-7 due to the catastrophic consequences of such a setup.

Let's see, for example, what happens in the scenario in Figure 14-8, when Host A transmits a packet and both Bridge 1 and Bridge 2 have empty databases (i.e., no address has been learned yet).

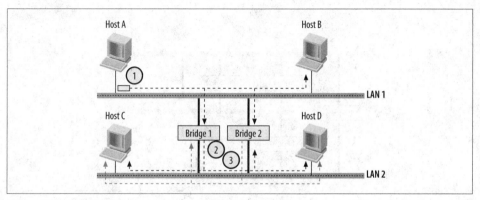

Figure 14-8. Bridging loop

Both bridges will receive the frame, realize that Host A is located in LAN1, and copy the frame on LAN2. Which bridge will do it first is not deterministic; it depends, for instance, on how loaded the two bridges are. Let's suppose they do the copy at almost the same time. The two bridges will therefore receive a copy of the frame on their interfaces on LAN2 and think that Host A has moved to LAN2 (remember that the frame they receive on LAN2 is an exact copy of the original one transmitted by Host A on LAN1). At this point, both bridges will copy the frame to LAN1 (we suppose the destination host has not replied yet and that therefore the bridges do not know where it is located). They will again receive each other's copy, change their minds about the location of Host A, and copy the frames to LAN2.

This is a loop that will flood the two LANs with the same frame circulating endlessly, and making any other transmission on the two LANs impossible. The CPUs of the other hosts in the LANs will also be busy receiving and dropping the huge number of copies of the same frame and, if not protected at the interface layer by some rate limiting means, will collapse.

This simple scenario tells us an important rule: transparent bridges cannot be used on loop topologies.

Loop-Free Topologies

A simple solution to make the topology of Figure 14-8 work would be to disable Bridge 2 and enable it only when Bridge 1 fails. However, this solution would not give us any real redundancy because it would require some kind of manual intervention. Another solution, which is the one commonly used, is to make bridges visible to each other, while still keeping the learning and copying tasks transparent, as described earlier.

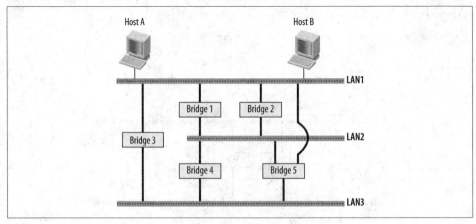

Figure 14-9. Topology with multiple loops

Figure 14-9 shows a more complex scenario.[*] Note that Bridge 5 has an interface on three LANs. It should be clear that all the bridges must cooperate, and you cannot simply turn bridges on or off;[†] you need to be able to define a loop-free topology with a finer granularity. So instead of disabling bridges, you disable bridges' ports. The topology of Figure 14-8 does not represent a common or suggested scenario; however, bridges must be able to work and provide loop-free connectivity even in such a mess.

---

[*] The figure lacks hosts in LAN2 and LAN3 because I want you to focus on the network topology. Any hosts in any LANs in Figure 14-9 would be affected by the consequences of a loop topology.

[†] Well, you can turn bridges off if you like, but you would reduce the degree of redundancy that you can achieve.

Let's return to the simple example in Figure 14-8, and find out the feature of the bridging protocol that makes it safe. If you draw a graph where bridges and LANs are states, and bridge connections to LANs (i.e., bridge ports) are (bidirectional) links, you get Figure 14-10.

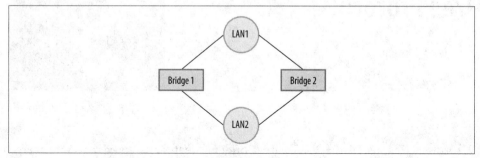

Figure 14-10. Graph associated with the topology of Figure 14-8

All you need to make the graph of Figure 14-10 loop free is to remove a link by disabling a bridge port. The graph for the topology of Figure 14-9 would be more complicated and would include several loops (I can count at least five of them).

Note that there is always more than one way to make any loop topology loop free. For example, to break the loop in Figure 14-10, there are four different choices.

Defining a Loop-Free Topology

If you are familiar with graph theory, you know that given a graph (with costs in the links), finding the best loop-free topology is a classic problem, elegantly solved by a series of different algorithms. However, all those algorithms are centralized: the algorithm runs once with all the necessary information. In our case, the bridges need a distributed algorithm. The bridges must be able to converge to a loop-free topology, disabling the right ports, by exchanging some kind of information.

The algorithm used by bridges to find the best loop-free topology is the Spanning Tree Protocol defined by the 802.1D-1998 IEEE standard, which was extended with the new Rapid Spanning Tree Protocol (RSTP) and became 802.1D-2004. RSTP is sometimes also referred to as 802.1w.

Another interesting extension is the Multiple Spanning Tree Protocol (MSTP), known also as 802.1s. It was integrated into 802.1Q-1998, which then become 802. 1Q-2002 (and should become 802.1Q-2005 sometime this year to reflect the latest changes).

For simplicity, we will refer to those protocols as STP (the original Spanning Tree Protocol), RSTP, and MSTP. Chapter 15 describes STP and gives an overview of the improvements introduced with RSTP and MSTP. Chapter 16 goes into detail on the implementation of STP.

Bridging: The Spanning Tree Protocol

We saw in Chapter 14 that transparent bridging represents an easy way to merge LANs, but it can be used only on loop-free topologies. This limitation eliminates the use of transparent bridges on networks where redundant links are used to increase overall availability.

In this chapter, we will see how the Spanning Tree Protocol (STP) manages to make any topology loop free, and therefore allows the network administrator to use topologies with redundant links. In particular, we will see:

- How the distributed algorithm used by STP leads to a loop-free topology by disabling the right redundant links. The loop-free topology selected by STP is a tree (which by definition is loop free). All the traffic between the hosts of the LANs connected by the bridges travels along the links of this tree.

- How STP dynamically updates the topology to cope with configuration changes and bridge or link failures.

- How STP dynamically updates the forwarding database (i.e., addresses learned on the bridge ports) when changes in the topology are detected.

We cannot go into detail on the STP for lack of space. The goal of this chapter is to give you an overview detailed enough to make you comfortable with the description of the kernel implementation of STP discussed in Chapter 16. For a complete discussion of the 802.1D STP and its enhancements, please refer to the IEEE specifications.

The examples provided in this chapter do not function as a guide on how to configure STP: most of them are used only to show how specific conditions can be met and how STP handles them.

Basic Terminology

Let's define a few key terms that will be used in this and the following chapter:

LAN
> This term should not need any introduction. We will use the term LAN to refer not only to Ethernet-like networks but also to point-to-point connections.

L2 network
> A LAN or a set of LANs merged by bridges. As we saw in Chapter 14, the use of bridges allows multiple LANs to be merged and look like a single bigger LAN (to the eyes of routers and hosts—i.e., to the eyes of devices operating at higher network layers).

Bridged (or switched) network
> An L2 network implemented with bridges.

Bridge port
Interface
> On a bridge device, each network interface is a bridge port. On a more general-purpose system, such as a PC running Linux, a network interface is not necessarily used as a bridge port. In the context of this chapter, the terms *bridge port* and *interface* could be used interchangeably, but in Chapter 16, where we will need to distinguish between bridging and nonbridging interfaces, I will use the term *interface* to refer to nonbridging NICs only. Each port of a bridge can be used to link both hosts and other bridges. We will see several examples in this and the following chapters.

Link
> A connection between two devices. In this chapter, I will use the term to refer to the connection between two bridges.

Stable network
> An L2 network where the STP has converged to the final loop-free topology.

Figure 15-1 shows the terms as they are used in this chapter and their relationship to other everyday networking terms.

Example of Hierarchical Switched L2 Topology

We know that two hosts can be connected to each other with a cross cable; you do not necessarily have to use a device such as a hub or a bridge. You can do the same between bridges and routers. In the examples in this chapter, you will often see such cross-cable links between bridges.

Unlike the scenarios in Chapter 14, where simple two-port bridges link directly to hosts located in the connected LANs, a real bridged network normally has a topology that resembles a tree, where hosts are located only (or mainly) at the leaves' node.

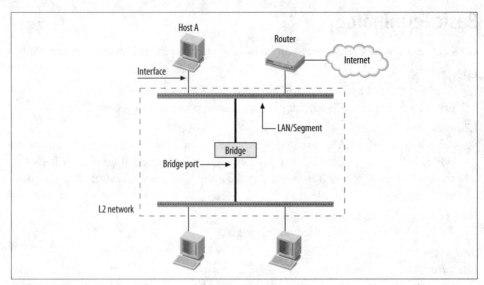

Figure 15-1. Basic terminology

When you have simple scenarios like the ones seen in Chapter 14, you do not usually enable the STP; in fact, most sites could simply use a single flat LAN instead of employing bridges at all. To better understand STP, we need to see what a real-life scenario looks like. Let's take the classic hierarchical bridged and redundant topology in Figure 15-2(a), which is advertised and evangelized by most of the commercial bridge vendors.

The figure leaves out details described later in this chapter, such as the bridge ID and priority, port cost, and priority values, to let you focus on the topology and active links selection. In the subsequent figures in this chapter, we will reuse the symbol definitions in the legend at the bottom of the figure.

At the leaves of the tree (the bottom of the figure) are the hosts. The hosts are linked to so-called access bridges (commonly called access switches): the bridges that give network connectivity to the hosts. Access bridges are mainly used to forward traffic between the hosts linked to the same bridge, but they also have one or more links to the upper-layer bridges. The access bridges in Figure 15-2 are labeled A1, A2, A3, and A4.

Because hosts are always located at the leaves of the topology, you can have as many links to hosts as you like. They will not cause any loops (of course, we assume there are no links between leaves). Because of that, the links to the host are not affected by the STP: none of them needs to be disabled to define a loop-free topology. After all, the ultimate goal of STP it to make the network look like a big single LAN and provide connectivity to all hosts, so why would you disconnect any of the hosts?

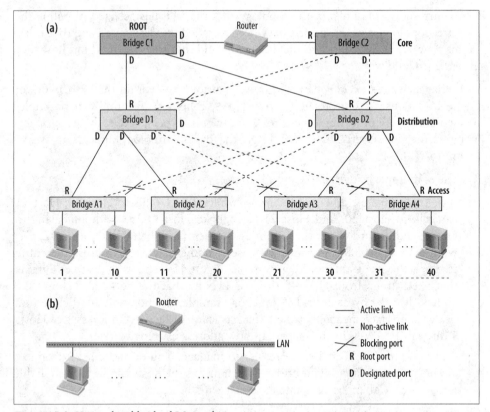

Figure 15-2. Hierarchical bridged L2 topology

A bridge at the distribution layer (D1 and D2 in the figure) is mainly used to bridge traffic between hosts located in some of the access bridges it is directly connected to. For example, D1 will take care of A1 and A2.

Note that D1 is also linked to A3 and A4, although currently D1's links are inactive (dotted lines in the figure). In case the link between D2 and A3 fails, the STP will make sure that the topology is updated so that A3 is again part of the tree. For example, the network could enable the link between D1 and A3; we will see how later in this chapter.

The two distribution bridges D1 and D2 are also linked to the two core bridges C1 and C2. It should be clear what C1 and C2's job is: to connect D1's subtree to D2's subtree. (An alternative solution would be one with a single, and maybe more powerful, core bridge.) Between the distribution and core layers there are also redundant links so that if, for example, the link C1–D1 failed, C2–D1 would take over. The higher the layer where a bridge is located, the bigger the volume of traffic that is processed (because the subtree is bigger).

The figure shows the links of the topology that the STP has selected to define the loop-free topology, and what ports have been assigned the designated and root roles. In this chapter, we will see what the designated and root roles are used for, how they are assigned, and why.

Note that the traffic exchanged between any pair of hosts within the L2 network of Figure 15-2(a) uses L2 protocols to travel (i.e., Ethernet). Routing can be implemented at the core or through the core. From the host's perspective, there is no hierarchy at the link layer, only a flat LAN; the overall topology appears to it like Figure 15-2(b).[*]

The use of multiple bridges has a few advantages:

- It helps segregate traffic. For example, while Host 1 talks to Host 10, Host 11 can talk to Host 20, and Host 21 can talk to Host 40, all without having to receive and discard each other's frames. So the overall bandwidth of the L2 network is increased. But in the worst case, a frame may need to cross the entire tree to get to its destination. For example, Figure 15-3 shows the path of a frame that needs to go from Host 40 to Host 1. Note that the figure also shows the address learned by each bridge port: for example, the notation 1–10 close to a bridge's interface means that the latter has learned the MAC addresses of Hosts 1 through 10. (We saw in Chapter 14 how address learning works.)

- Large numbers of hosts become easier to manage. You do not need to connect all the hosts to a single giant bridge, which means the hosts can be located in different areas. Cabling is also simpler to take care of.

I'll end my overview of L2 bridged topologies here. You would need a whole book to cover bridging protocols and STP in detail, so I'll move ahead with an overview of the algorithm implemented by the STP.

In the rest of this chapter, we will use simpler topologies to describe the protocol. However, what we will see works just the same way in bigger and more complex networks like the one in Figure 15-2.

Basic Elements of the Spanning Tree Protocol

The search for the best nonrooted spanning tree or the best rooted spanning tree is a classic problem in operational research. The literature provides different algorithms that differ in computational complexity. There are a huge number of applications in real life where those algorithms are commonly used.

---

[*] 12-digit MAC addresses (such as 11:22:33:44:55:66) are replaced with simple 2-digit values to make the figure more readable.

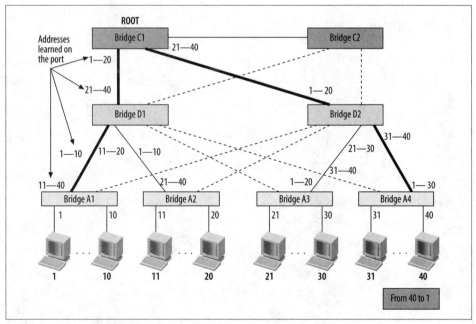

Figure 15-3. Example of bridged network

The STP we describe in this chapter has a somewhat similar goal: given a graph and a root node R, define the best spanning tree rooted in R. However, there is one important difference: the algorithm is not executed on a single host that later distributes the result to all the others; instead, this is a distributed protocol. All bridges in the network must run it. By running this protocol, they enable some of their ports and disable others, and the overall topology that follows is the best rooted spanning tree. The selection of the root node is also part of the protocol: the hosts agree on who is the root node and then decide what links to enable and disable.

Let's try to understand what "best spanning tree" means exactly. Given a graph and a node you want to be the root, the best spanning tree is the loop-free topology (tree) that minimizes the distance of each node from the root node. Depending on the graph, there could be more than one tree with the same goodness score* (Figure 15-4 shows an example with two equally good solutions).

When the links are not assigned a cost, or are all assigned the same cost (which would be equivalent), the distance from a node to the root is measured as the number of links (that is, network hops). However, when you associate a cost with the links, the number of hops is not necessarily an indication of the goodness of the path.

---

* We will see that the STP defines a mechanism to deterministically choose the same tree every time, if more than one optimal instance is available.

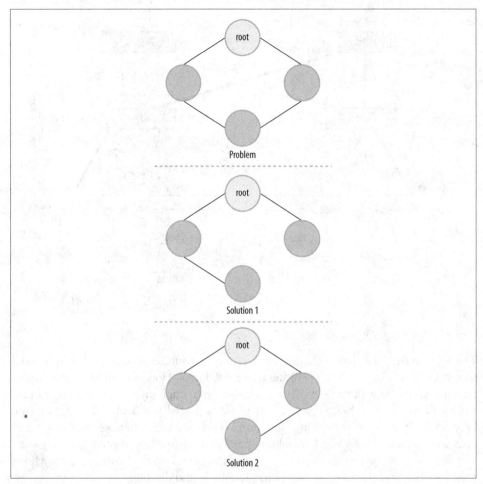

Figure 15-4. Graph with no costs assigned to the links

For example, if we add costs to the topology in Figure 15-4, the associated best rooted spanning tree differs from both of the solutions in Figure 15-4, as shown in Figure 15-5.

We will see in the section "Bridge and Port IDs" how the network administrator can override default costs with other values, basing the choice, for instance, on administrative parameters such as monetary cost and reliability of the connections.

The STP achieves its goal by having each bridge exchange specialized frames called *bridge protocol data units* (BPDUs) with its neighbors. The information exchanged with BPDUs allows bridges to:

- Assign each bridge port a defined state, such as forwarding or blocking, that defines whether data traffic can be accepted on the port

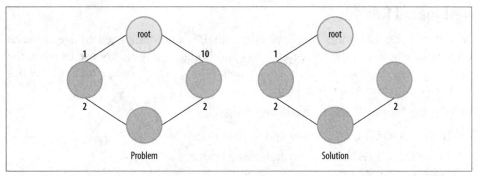

Figure 15-5. Graph with costs assigned to the links

- Select and discard the right links from the loop topology by means of this port state assignment, leading this way to a loop-free topology

Some of the bridge ports are assigned special roles, depending, for example, on whether they lead toward the root of the tree (the so-called *root bridge*) or the leaf nodes of the tree.

Given the precise terminology used in graph theory, it should not be a surprise that the STP also uses a well-defined terminology to refer to nodes (bridges) and links (bridge ports). Before looking at the algorithm, I need to explain:

- What a root bridge and designated bridge are
- What states and roles can be assigned to a bridge's port
- The job of root and designated ports

Root Bridge

The root bridge is not just a placeholder in the topology; it plays a central role in the algorithm. For example, in the next sections, you will see that:

- The root bridge is the only bridge that generates BPDUs. The other bridges transmit BPDUs only when they receive one (i.e., they revise the information they receive by simply updating a couple of fields).
- The root bridge makes sure each bridge in the network comes to know about a topology change when one occurs (see the section "Topology Changes").

Note that the selection of the port states and roles (and therefore of the links that should be enabled or disabled) depends on the location of the root bridge in the topology: this is because first you select the root bridge, and then you build the best tree based on that.

Designated Bridges

While each tree has only one root bridge, there is one designated bridge for each LAN, which becomes the bridge all hosts and bridges on the LAN use to reach the root. The designated bridge is chosen by determining which bridge on the LAN has the lowest path cost to the root bridge.

Thus, using Figure 15-2 as an example:*

- In the A3–D2 LAN, D2 is the designated bridge.
- In the D2–C2 LAN, C2 is the designated bridge.

Spanning Tree Ports

We introduced the root and designated bridge's roles in the previous sections. Let's see here what states and roles can be assigned to a bridge port.

Port states

An STP port is a port in a bridge that runs the STP. This port will process ingress BPDUs and transmit BPDUs according to the rules in the section "When to Transmit Configuration BPDUs."

An STP port can be in any of the following states:

Disabled
> The port is shut down (through administrative action); it does not receive or transmit any traffic.

Blocking
> The port is up, but the STP has blocked it. It cannot be used to forward any data traffic.

Listening
> The port is enabled, but it cannot be used to forward any data traffic.

Learning
> The port is enabled, but it cannot be used to forward any data traffic; however, the bridge's address learning process is active.

Forwarding
> The port is enabled, learning is active, and data traffic can be forwarded.

The use of the intermediate learning state allows a bridge to reduce the amount of flooding that would otherwise be required with an empty forwarding database.

---

* The links in the figure are not assigned costs. You can assume their costs to be 1, and therefore the path cost to be the hop count. This is just an example; 1 is not the default cost assigned to links.

With the exception of ports in the disabled state, ingress BPDUs are processed regardless of the port state. Whether a port in a given state receives ingress BPDUs or transmits BPDUs depends on the port's role, which is introduced in the section "Port roles."

Figure 15-6 shows how the state of a port can change. There is a clear progression from blocking through listening and learning to the most active state, forwarding. The transitions between blocking and forwarding are decided by the protocol based on various factors (see the later section "Defining the Active Topology"). Note that:

- A port on its way to the forwarding state can be moved back to blocking before the forwarding state is entered. This is possible, for instance, when a topology is not stable yet and therefore its state may change repeatedly in a short amount of time.

- The transitions between the intermediate states from blocking to forwarding are driven by a timer (see the section "Timers") and are needed to avoid the risk of temporary loops (see the section "Avoiding Temporary Loops").

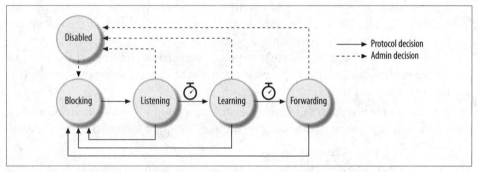

Figure 15-6. Port state transitions

In addition, an administrator can manually remove a port from any of these states and disable it. When a port is administratively disabled, it can be re-enabled only by another administrative intervention; the STP does not have this capability. However, bridges can implement optional features on top of the basic ones defined by the protocol, to enable and disable ports without administrative intervention.

Port roles

STP ports can be assigned one of the following two roles:

Root
> For each bridge, with the exception of the root bridge, the port with the lowest path cost to the root bridge is selected as the root port.

Designated

> On each LAN, the port with the smallest path cost to the root bridge is selected as the designated port. The bridge to which the designated port belongs is called the designated bridge for the LAN. Note that a bridge with ports on different LANs can have more than one designated port, as shown in Figure 15-2. The criteria used to select designated ports are described later in the section "Designated Port Selection."

While root ports lead toward the root of the tree (i.e., the root bridge), designated ports lead toward the leaves. In Figure 15-2, you can see the relationship between root and designated ports.

From a tree's perspective, the two roles can be seen in this way:

- The tree's root has links that go only toward the leaves (i.e., only designated ports*).
- The leaf nodes have links that go only toward the tree's root (i.e., no designated ports and one root port). As a protection against misconfigurations and wrong cabling (such as connecting a bridge to a port where you are supposed to connect a host), a leaf node can run the STP on the ports that connect the hosts, too. In this case, the assumption that a leaf node does not have designated ports would no longer be valid. In other words, if you enable the STP on the ports of the access bridges in Figure 15-2 that connect the hosts, those ports would end up being assigned the designated role.
- Any node between root and leaves has at least one link toward the root (one of which will be selected as the root port), and at least one toward the leaves (a designated port).

There are STP ports that are neither root nor designated ports; this is possible when you have redundant links between bridges. In Figure 15-2, the A1 port that goes to D2 is an example. The newer STP protocols, which I will briefly introduce in the section "Overview of Newer Spanning Tree Protocols," define new roles so that each STP port is assigned one.

We will see how the root and designated port roles are assigned in the sections "Root Port Selection" and "Designated Port Selection," respectively.

---

* If you use shared media such as hubs to connect bridges, as in Figure 15-11(c), the root bridge can have nondesignated ports as well. The newer RSTP protocol would call that port a *backup port* (see the section "Rapid Spanning Tree Protocol (RSTP)."

Bridge and Port IDs

The selection of the root bridge and the port state and roles depends on a set of parameters. Each parameter is assigned a default value that can be changed by user configuration. Here are the main parameters:

Bridge ID

Each bridge is assigned an ID, called the bridge ID, that is defined as an 8-byte value split into two components. The lowest six bytes are assigned the Ethernet MAC address of one of the bridge ports (see Chapter 16), and the highest two bytes are a configurable priority, called the *bridge priority*. The bridge ID is the field used by the root bridge selection algorithm (see the section "Root Bridge Selection").

Port ID

Each port is assigned an ID. A portion of the ID represents a unique identifier called the port number. The way the port number is assigned is implementation dependent, and its value is meaningful only locally on the bridge. For example, the number can reflect the sequence in which ports were created: the first port is assigned 1, the second port 2, etc. Another approach could use the physical location of the port: for example, the first port on the bus is assigned 1, etc. It is desirable to have the port number assignments be deterministic and consistent across reboots so that the system administrator does not need to change the bridge configuration to reflect the changes after a reboot.

Another portion of the ID, called the *port priority*, is used to assign a priority to the port (where a lower value means a higher priority). See Figure 15-7(b).

See the section "Root Port Selection" for an example of when this parameter is used.

Besides the bridge and port priority, the user can configure the following parameters:

Port cost

Each port is assigned a cost. The lower the value, the more preferred the port is. When not explicitly configured, the port is assigned a default cost based on the port's speed. For example, a Fast Ethernet port that runs at 100 Mbits/s is assigned a lower cost than an Ethernet port that runs at 10 Mbits/s. The default cost assignment makes sense in most cases, when the overall cost of going from one point of the tree to another is measured in terms of latency. However, it is possible that in specific contexts, the administrator prefers to explicitly assign costs based on external factors.

Timers

The STP uses a set of per-port and per-bridge timers. All of them have a default configuration that can be customized by the user. See the section "Timers." The timer configuration does not affect the selection of the root bridge and the port state and roles.

We will see later in this chapter how the configuration of these parameters (with the exception of the timers) can be used to influence the selection of the topology.

In 2001, the IEEE released the 802.1t, 802.1D's maintenance document, which changed how bridge and port IDs are defined. The changes in format are shown in Figure 15-7.

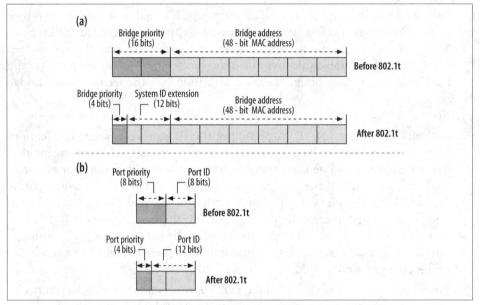

Figure 15-7. Bridge ID and port ID changes introduced by 802.1t

Note that:

- The bridge priority is now only 4 bits in size. For backward compatibility, the bridge priority range is still 0–64 K, but since you have only four bits to play with, you now have priorities in increments of 4,096 (2^{12}).

- There is a new component in the bridge ID, called the system ID extension. This component, which can assume 4,096 different values, allows a network device, for example, to have up to 4,096 different bridge IDs sharing a single MAC address. Before, this would have required 4,096 different MAC addresses. Note that MAC addresses are not random numbers chosen by the administrator; they are worldwide unique numbers (and therefore are a limited resource) that are managed by the IEEE.

- The port number is now a 12-bit value, which allows a bridge to have up to 4,096 ports. Before you could have had only 256 (which was originally considered quite luxurious). The port priority is now a 4-bit value. The priority range is still 1–256 for backward compatibility, so priorities are now assigned in increments of 16.

To understand the reasons for the 802.1t changes, you need to think in terms of high-end commercial devices, not common PCs equipped with just a few NICs. The latter can survive with a limit of 256 bridge ports, or a single bridge ID per MAC address. However, it is not uncommon for big bridges to be equipped with hundreds of ports and to run hundreds of instances of bridges.

Note also that 4,096 is not a random value: it represents the maximum number of Virtual LANs (VLANs) allowed in the 802.1Q protocol.

The 802.1t changes do not have any impact on the STP. From the STP's perspective, a bridge ID is an 8-byte value and a port ID is a 2-byte value. The size or purpose of the user-configuration component does not matter. This means that the 802.1t changes affect only configuration tools, not the protocol's behavior. Tables 15-1 and 15-2 summarize the possible values of the different parameters.

Table 15-1. Bridge IDs and port IDs before 802.1t

	Default value	Min. value	Max. value	Min. increment
Bridge priority	32,768	0	65,535	1
Port cost	Depends on port speed	1	65,535	1
Port priority	128	0	255	1

Table 15-2. Bridge IDs and port IDs after 802.1t

	Default value	Min. value	Max. value	Min. increment
Bridge priority	32,768	0	61,440	4,096
Port cost	Depends on port speed	1	200,000,000	1
Port priority	128	0	240	16

Bridge Protocol Data Units (BPDUs)

Bridges exchange protocol frames, called BPDUs, that include enough information for them to agree on who is the root bridge, and to decide on the roles and states for their local ports. There are two kinds of BPDUs:

Configuration BPDU
> Used to define the loop-free topology. You will see in the section "When to Transmit Configuration BPDUs" what conditions trigger the transmission of these BPDUs.

Topology Change Notification (TCN) BPDU
> Used by a bridge to notify the root bridge about a detected topology change. See the section "Topology Changes."

Figure 15-8 shows the format of both BPDUs. Note that the two types share the same first three fields and can be distinguished by the BPDU type parameter.

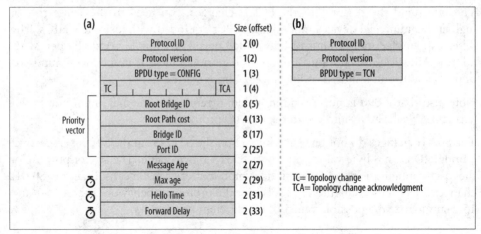

Figure 15-8. a) Configuration BPDU; b) BPDU

Table 15-3 shows the combinations of protocol ID and protocol version used by the three IEEE STPs. In this chapter, we will look only at the basic 802.1D protocol and briefly introduce the other two in the section "Overview of Newer Spanning Tree Protocols."

Table 15-3. BPDU versions

Protocol name	Protocol ID	Protocol version
STP (802.1D-1998)	0	0
RSTP (802.1D-2002 or 802.1w)	0	2
MSTP (802.1Q-2002 or 802.1s)	0	3

Configuration BPDU

Here is the meaning of the fields in the configuration BPDU:

Flags

Only two flags are used: TC (Topology Change) and TCA (Topology Change Acknowledgment). The use of both is described in the section "Topology Changes."

Root Bridge ID

ID of the root bridge. This is what the transmitting bridge thinks the current root bridge is.

Root Path Cost

Cost of the shortest path from the transmitting bridge to the root bridge. The cost is 0 when the transmitting bridge is (or thinks it is to become) the root bridge.

Bridge ID
> ID of the transmitting bridge.

Port ID
> Port identifier. See the section "Bridge and Port IDs" for its syntax.

Message Age
> How much time has passed since the root bridge generated the information in this BPDU. See the section "BPDU Aging."

Max Age
> Maximum lifetime for configuration BPDUs.

Hello Time
> Timeout used by the Hello timer.

Forward Delay
> Timeout used by the Forward Delay timer. See Figure 15-6.

The values of the three timers Max Age, Hello Time, and Forward Delay are not the ones configured locally on the bridge: they are the ones advertised by the root bridge (see the section "Transmitting Configuration BPDUs"). All of them are expressed in ticks (1/256th of second). See the section "Timers."

Priority Vector

Four components of the configuration BPDU—Root Bridge ID, Root Path Cost, Bridge ID, and Port ID—make up the priority vector (see Figure 15-8). Because these four components are in sequence, this vector can be seen as a single 22-byte number. The lower the number is, the more important the bridge is in the topology; in other words, the priority vector determines who wins the bidding for contested roles such as root bridge and designated bridge. In the rest of this chapter, I will refer to priority vectors using a *[BR-Root, Cost, BR-ID, Port-ID]* notation.

In the examples later in this chapter, the figures show only the priority component of the configuration BPDUs transmitted, because that is the portion of the configuration BPDU used by the bridges to select their port's roles and states.

Given two priority vectors PV1=*[BR-Root1, Cost1, BR-ID-1, Port-ID1]* and PV2=*[BR-Root2, Cost2, BR-ID-2, Port-ID2]*, PV1 is said to be superior when it is a lower numeric value than PV2, and inferior when PV1 is a higher numeric value than PV2. In other words, PV1 is superior to PV2 if *BR-Root1 < BR-Root2*, or, in case they are the same, if *Cost1 < Cost2*, or, if they are the same too, if *BR-ID1 < BR-ID2*, or, when the two bridge IDs match too, when *Port-ID1<Port-ID2*.

When to Transmit Configuration BPDUs

A bridge transmits configuration BPDUs out of its designated ports. It does so in the following cases:

- The root bridge runs a timer (the Hello timer) that expires regularly and triggers the transmission of configuration BPDUs. One BPDU is transmitted on each one of its designated ports. Only the root bridge generates new BPDUs, but when a bridge is first enabled, it thinks it is the root bridge (because it has no other priority vector to compare its own to). So it places all of its ports into the designated role, starts its Hello timer, and begins to generate BPDUs (see the section "Root Bridge Selection").

- Nonroot bridges generate BPDUs only in response to ones they receive on their root ports; in other words, they relay BPDUs. BPDUs transmitted by nonroot bridges carry the same information as the BPDUs they received, with the exception of the following fields that they update (see Figure 15-9):

  - The transmitter's bridge ID and port ID are replaced by the bridge with its own information.

  - The bridge updates the cost to be the sum of the cost it received and the cost of the port on the local bridge (its root port) that it received the BPDU on.

  - The message age is updated according to the logic described in the section "BPDU Aging." The latter section explains how the DT quantity is defined.

Regardless of whether a bridge is the root bridge, it transmits a configuration BPDU in the following cases as well:

- When a bridge receives a BPDU with a priority vector that's inferior to the one it would use on the same port, it replies with its own (superior) information. See the section "Examples of STP in Action."

- When a bridge receives a TCN BPDU, it acknowledges its reception right away with the transmission of a configuration BPDU that has a special flag set. This helps propagate changes in topology quickly (see the section "Letting All Bridges Know About a Topology Change").

Regardless of why a configuration BPDU is transmitted out of a given port, the STP enforces rate limiting: a bridge cannot transmit more than one Configuration BPDU per second out of any of its ports (see the section "Transmitting Configuration BPDUs").

BPDU Aging

Because BPDUs are generated only by the root bridge, and are regenerated by the other bridges only upon the reception of a BPDU on their root port, it should be clear that the time taken by the information generated by the root bridge with its

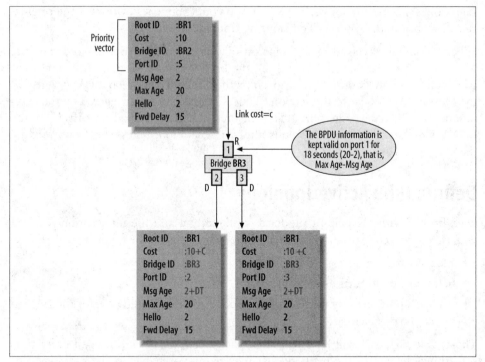

Figure 15-9. BPDU relaying via nonroot bridges

BPDUs to reach the leaf bridges is variable. On a stable network, the time depends mainly on how loaded the bridges are and how fast they can process BPDUs.

BPDUs carrying stale information should not be used to build the loop-free topology. For that reason, configuration BPDUs have a field called Message Age that is compared by the receiving bridge against the other field, Max Age, to discard those BPDUs that have been around for too long and whose priority vector cannot be trusted.

The Message Age field is first initialized to 0 by the root bridge, and is updated by each nonroot bridge prior to forwarding it (see DT in Figure 15-9). The Message Age is supposed to represent the time that has passed since the original root bridge's BPDU was generated. However, to calculate this time is not easy. It should, for example, account for both the transmission delays and the processing time: in other words, the time spent by the frame in the media going from one bridge's port to the next one, and the time spent in the bridge's memory while each bridge processes and regenerates it. But a common approach in commercial bridges is to simply treat the Message Age field as a hop count, just like the Time To Live (TTL) field of the IP header: the Message Age field of the ingress BPDU is incremented by 256 ticks (i.e., 1 second) and copied into the outgoing BPDUs. This means that a BPDU would be dropped after a maximum of 20 hops (20 seconds is the default value for Max Age).

Linux does not use the message age as a hop count, but tries to respect the original rule described in the section "Transmitting Configuration BPDUs."

When the BPDU received by a bridge on one of its port has not expired (i.e., the Message Age is less than the Max Age), the bridge starts a Message Age timer that will expire after an amount of time given by the difference between the Max Age and the Message Age. Refer to the section "Timers" for the actions triggered by the expiration of the Message Age timer. This ensures that the information carried by the BPDU is discarded Max Age seconds after its generation, unless it is confirmed by then.

Defining the Active Topology

Each bridge, with the help of the local configuration and the information received with the ingress configuration BPDUs, is able to accomplish the following:

- Elect the root bridge
- Select one of its ports as the root port
- For each port, identify the designated bridge and designated port for the LAN to which the port belongs

Those tasks, which I will refer to as a *configuration update*, are needed every time something changes in the network that may require a change in the topology. For instance:

- A port is either enabled or disabled.
- A port's Message Age timer expires. In this case, the port is restarted (i.e., assigned the designated role).
- The local configuration of a bridge changes.
- A bridge port receives a configuration BPDU with a superior priority vector compared to the one previously received on the same port.

Note that a configuration update is triggered on the bridge where the configuration is changed or where a port changes administrative state. The other bridges will follow (if necessary) upon seeing these changes reflected in the information carried by the BPDUs they receive.

Let's see how the configuration update's tasks are taken care of, one by one.

Root Bridge Selection

We saw in the section "Bridge and Port IDs" how a bridge ID is defined. An algorithm based only on the use of the MAC address for the selection of the root bridge would be sufficient to ensure a deterministic selection, given that MAC addresses are unique worldwide. However, the addition of the priority component allows administrators to force the topology they like by assigning higher priorities to those bridges they would like to be selected as root. They can even assign strategic priorities to different bridges so that they can also force a given bridge to take over in case the current root bridge fails.

When a bridge is first enabled, it does not know anything about the topology and therefore thinks it's the root bridge. It will therefore assign the designated role to all its ports, start the Forward Delay timer on the ports so that they eventually will be assigned the forwarding state (see Figure 15-6), and start transmitting BPDUs using the bridge's ID as the root Bridge ID field, and a root path cost of 0. This is a convenient way to make it broadcast data about itself and get that data spread around as quickly as possible so that both it and other bridges can discover the truly best root bridge and rebalance the tree.

When the bridge is the one with the best bridge ID, it will keep sending out BPDUs on its designated ports because no other bridge can claim a better priority vector (to be more exact, a better bridge ID) and therefore take over the root role.

If the bridge did not have the best bridge ID, it will eventually receive a configuration BPDU with a better root bridge ID (i.e., a superior BPDU) and:

- Accept and record the better information (including the root bridge ID and timers).
- Update the state and role of its ports accordingly. This is what is called a configuration update.

Root Port Selection

Each bridge must select its own root port, which, as we anticipated in the section "Port roles," is the port with the shortest path (or lowest cost) to the root bridge. The root bridge is the only one that does not have a root port; nonroot bridges have one and only one root port.

For each of its ports, with the exception of the ones that are administratively disabled, a bridge keeps a copy of the best priority vector received with ingress BPDUs. This way, the bridge knows, for each port, what is the best (lowest cost) path to reach the root bridge.

The selection of the root port consists simply of going through all the ports and selecting the one with the best priority vector. If more than one port happens to share the same best priority vector, the local port with the lowest assigned port ID is selected, as shown in Figure 15-10 (note that the receiver port ID is not part of the BPDU).

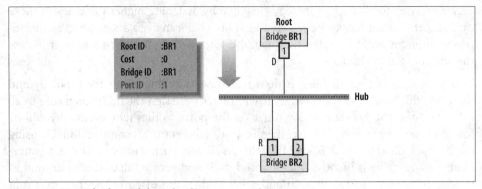

Figure 15-10. Multiple candidates for the root port selection

Designated Port Selection

While there can be one root port per bridge, there is only one designated port per LAN. The STP ensures that each bridge chooses the same port. The designated port should be the one that has the lowest path cost to the root bridge. Thus, it's the port with the best priority vector.

Each bridge is usually on more than one LAN, so it must learn the designated port for each LAN.

On a point-to-point connection between two bridges, there are just two ports. The one that transmits BPDUs with the best priority vector is selected. By contrast, a shared medium such as an Ethernet hub may have more than two bridges. In that case, each bridge will receive each other's BPDUs and, by checking the priority vector, elect the right designated port.

Figure 15-11 shows what would happen when you use a shared medium to connect bridges. Initially only BR2 is connected to the hub and therefore it elects itself as the root bridge. When an administrator later adds BR1, it also thinks it is the root bridge, as you can see from the BPDUs it transmits in Figure 15-11(b). Let's assume that BR2's ID is higher than (i.e., inferior to) BR1's ID, and therefore that the two bridges end up agreeing on BR1 as the root bridge.

Because all of these bridge ports connect to the same hub, when BR1's port 1 transmits a BPDU, BR1 receives its own BPDU on port 2, and vice versa. However, the selection of the designated port based on the best priority vector works in this scenario, too: the fourth field of the priority vector, which is the port ID, makes port 1's BPDU priority vector the best.

However, the shared-medium setup is unpopular for several reasons, so in the rest of this chapter, I will refer only to the point-to-point case.

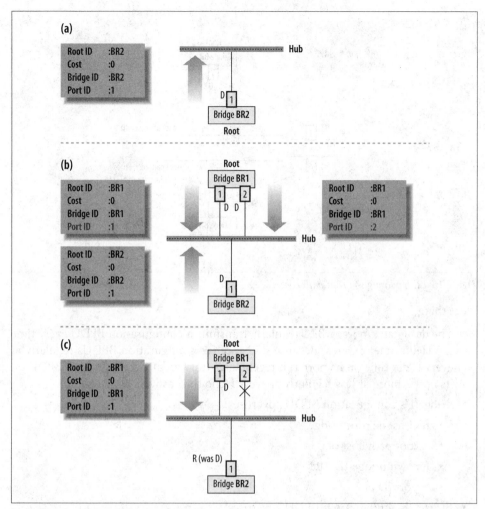

Figure 15-11. Designated port selection

Examples of STP in Action

Let's suppose we had the topology in Figure 15-12. Note that since there are no redundant links, there would be no need for the STP. Let's assume:

- *Bridge ID BR1 < Bridge ID BR2 < Bridge ID BR4* (so BR1 is the root bridge).
- Each bridge can configure the cost of its local interfaces independently from the other bridges. For simplicity and to make the figure easier to read, let's just assume that all the path costs are symmetric (the same on both sides of each link).*

---

* Remember that the path cost of any link is a locally configured parameter and it is not carried in the configuration BPDUs.

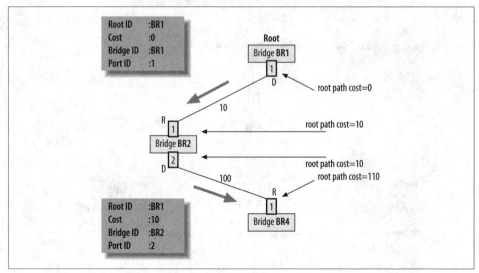

Figure 15-12. Updating the root path cost

Note that:

- The designated port of BR1 regularly transmits a configuration BPDU every time the Hello timer expires. Because BR2 receives configuration BPDUs regularly at every Hello time on its port 1, it regenerates (forwards) a configuration BPDU on its port 2 more or less regularly at every Hello time as well.
- Bridge 1's configuration BPDU advertises:
  - BR1 as the root bridge
  - A root path cost of 0
  - Its own bridge ID BR1
  - A port ID of 1
- Bridge 2's configuration BPDU advertises:
  - BR1 as the root bridge
  - A root path cost of 10 (it adds its own cost to the one sent out by BR1)
  - Its own bridge ID BR2
  - A port ID of 2

Now let's add a new bridge named BR3, and assume that *Bridge ID BR3 < Bridge ID BR4*, as in Figure 15-13.

As we explained in the section "Root Bridge Selection," when BR4 is first enabled it thinks it is the root bridge, and therefore it assigns the designated role to its two ports. It sends out a configuration BPDU on each port, advertising itself as the root bridge, and therefore using a root path cost of 0 in the BPDUs.

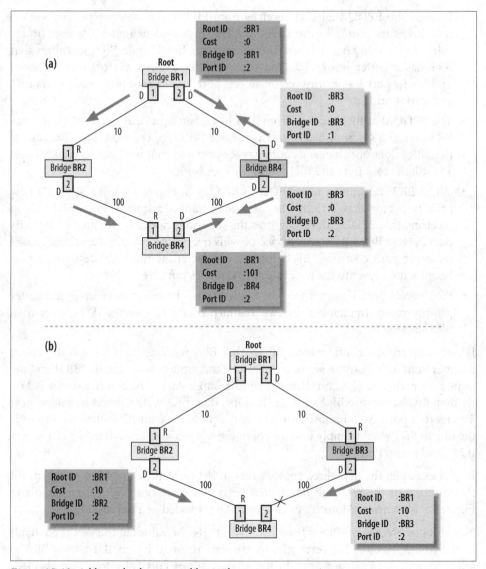

Figure 15-13. Adding a bridge to a stable topology

If we assume BR3 to be connected to BR1 and BR4 with a point-to-point link, as in Figure 15-13, when BR3 is powered up, BR1 and BR4 will enable their ports connected to BR3, assign these ports the designated role, and start transmitting configuration BPDUs.

Let's see how BR1, BR3, and BR4 react upon receiving each other's configuration BPDUs:

- The configuration BPDUs from BR1 and BR4 will have the following priority vectors, respectively: *[BR1, 0, BR1, 2]* and *[BR1, 110, BR4, 2]*.

- Because the BPDU that BR1 receives from BR3 has an inferior priority vector, BR1 keeps its port 2 in the DESIGNATED role and maintains its root bridge role. On the other hand, when BR3 receives the BPDU from BR1, it realizes that BR1 has a better bridge ID (and thus a better priority vector) and therefore updates its port 1's priority vector, selects port 1 as its root port, and selects BR1 as the root bridge.

- The BPDU that BR3 receives from BR4 has a better priority vector than the one BR3 sent to BR4, but not as good as the one BR3 received from BR1. Because of that, BR4 does not change its current root port and root bridge information: port 1 is still the root port and BR1 is still the root bridge.

- When BR3 transmits a new BPDU to BR4, as in Figure 15-13(b), it uses a new priority vector that reflects the new information acquired from BR1. Upon receiving that BPDU, BR4 recognizes the superior priority vector and it blocks its port 2. Note that BR3's priority vector wins over BR4's priority vector because of its lower path cost (i.e., BR3's port 2 is selected as the LAN-designated port because it is closer to the root bridge than BR4's port 2).

- BR4 selects port 1 as its root port because it is the one that receives the better priority vector (remember that we assumed that BR2's bridge ID is lower than BR3's bridge ID).

If you compare the configuration BPDU that BR4 receives from BR2 to the one it receives from BR3, you can see that they share the same root bridge ID (BR1) and the same root path cost (10), but that the third component of the priority vector is better than BR2's, because BR2's bridge ID is less than BR3's. BR4 therefore selects port 1 as its root port. An administrator who had a preference for BR4's link to BR3 over the one to BR2 would simply have to configure a lower cost on that port (see the section "Bridge and Port IDs").

In this example, the first three components of the priority vector were sufficient for the selection of the root and designated ports. Let's see now, with the example in Figure 15-14, when the fourth one, the port ID, is needed as a tiebreaker.

Now BR4 receives two BPDUs from BR2 with the same values in the first three fields of the priority vector. However, the fourth parameter (the port ID) allows BR4 to select its port 1 as its root port. In the section "Root Port Selection," we also saw how a bridge uses the local port ID (as opposed to the remote port ID that is part of the priority vector) as the tiebreaker when all four components of the priority vectors of ingress BPDUs are not sufficient to identify a winning BPDU.

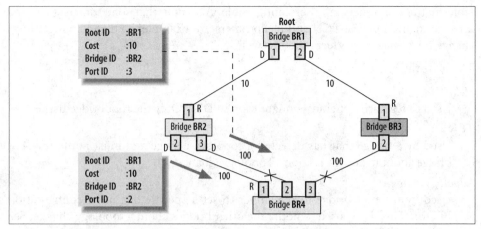

Figure 15-14. Port ID as the tiebreaker

Timers

The STP uses both per-bridge and per-port timers. In Tables 15-4 and 15-5, you can see the default timeouts, and what the allowed values are, for per-bridge and per-port timers, respectively.[*]

Table 15-4. Bridge timers

Timer	Default value (in seconds)	Allowed range
Hello	2	1–10
Topology Change	Forward Delay + Max Age	Not configurable
TCN	Hello time	Not configurable
Addresses Aging	300 or Forward Delay[a]	Not configurable

[a] See the section "Topology Changes."

Table 15-5. Port timers

Timer	Default value (in seconds)	Allowed range
Message Age	20	6–40
Forward Delay	15	4–30
Hold	1	Not configurable

---

[*] If you are interested in how the default timers have been defined, read either the IEEE 802.1d specification or *http://www.cisco.com/warp/public/473/122.html*.

Note that not all timers are user configurable. Also note that some timers share the same configuration (the TCN and Hello timers, for example) so that a configuration change for a timer may affect others as well.

These are the bridge timers:

Hello

Used to regularly generate configuration BPDUs. Only the root bridge uses it.

TCN

Used by a bridge that has detected a topology change and must notify the root bridge about it. See the section "Topology Changes."

Topology change

Used by the root bridge to remember to set a specific flag in its configuration BPDUs. This flag is used to notify the other bridges about a topology change. See the section "Topology Changes."

Aging timer

Used to clean up stale addresses from the forwarding database. This timer is used by the bridge regardless of whether the STP is used. See the section "Short Aging Timer."

Each bridge keeps two copies of its timer configuration: the one configured locally by the administrator, and the one received from the root bridge.

The root bridge is the only one that uses its own configured timers; it makes all the other bridges adopt its configuration. Nonroot bridges use the timer configurations carried by the BPDUs they receive on their root ports. You can see where timer configuration is located in Figure 15-8.

These are the port timers:

Message Age

We saw in the section "BPDU Aging" that the information carried by a BPDU has a limited lifetime. The Message Age timer is used to enforce that lifetime. The timer is restarted each time a BPDU is received on the port. Whenever a BPDU is received, its message age is compared to the network's max age and the frame is dropped if it is too old. The Message Age timer runs on nondesignated ports (i.e., the ones that receive superior BPDUs).

In a stable network without problems, this timer will never expire. However, when the root bridge fails to generate BPDUs, or the latter are received expired or get dropped for some reason, the timer will expire. When the timer expires, the port is restarted, and therefore assigned the designated role.

Forward Delay

Takes care of the state transitions from listening to learning, and from learning to forwarding. Figure 15-15 shows how expiration of the Forward Delay timer is typically handled and how it follows the model of Figure 15-6.

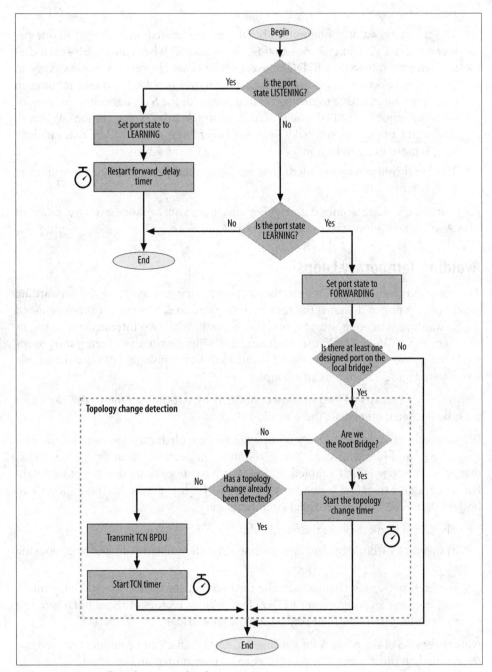

Figure 15-15. Handling the Forward Delay timer

Hold

The transmission of configuration BPDUs is rate limited on each port to one per second. On a stable network—that is, one where STP has converged—each designated port transmits a BPDU at every Hello time. However, when a change in the topology occurs, the convergence to the newer topology can take minutes in complex scenarios due to the distributed nature of the STP algorithm. Because of that, the number of BPDUs sent according to the rules of the section "When to Transmit Configuration BPDUs" can easily get large, and it is here that rate limiting is more likely to kick in.

The Hold timer, when needed, runs on designated ports (the ones transmitting configuration BPDUs).

Per-port timers share configurations. For instance, you cannot have two different Max Age configurations on two different ports.

Avoiding Temporary Loops

The root and designated ports are the only ones that are assigned the forwarding state. When a port is assigned the root or designated role, however, it is not assigned the forwarding state right away: it first has to go through two intermediate states, as shown in Figure 15-6. These intermediate states suppress the risk of temporary loops while the network converges toward a stable loop-free topology. Let's use the simple scenario of Figure 15-16(a) as an example.

The topology consists of two bridges connected by two links. One of the two links must be disabled; otherwise, there would be a loop.

We saw earlier that when a bridge's ports are first enabled, they are assigned the designated role and blocking state. We also saw in the section "Root Bridge Selection" that when a bridge is first enabled, it does not have any knowledge about its neighbor bridges and therefore it thinks it is the root bridge. Figure 15-16(a) shows two bridges that have just been enabled, and therefore:

- They both think they are the root bridge.
- Both ports of both bridges are assigned the designated role and the blocking state.
- For each port, they change the state to listening, start the Forward Delay timer, and transmit a configuration BPDU. The priority vectors of those BPDUs reflect their assumption that their bridges are the root bridge.

Note that none of the ports is forwarding yet. Data traffic can be neither received nor transmitted on those ports. Only BPDUs can be transmitted and received.

When BR2 receives BR1's BPDUs on its ports, it realizes that BR1 has a superior priority vector (a better bridge ID, to be exact). At that point, BR2 starts a configuration update: it selects the root bridge, the root port, and the designated ports, and

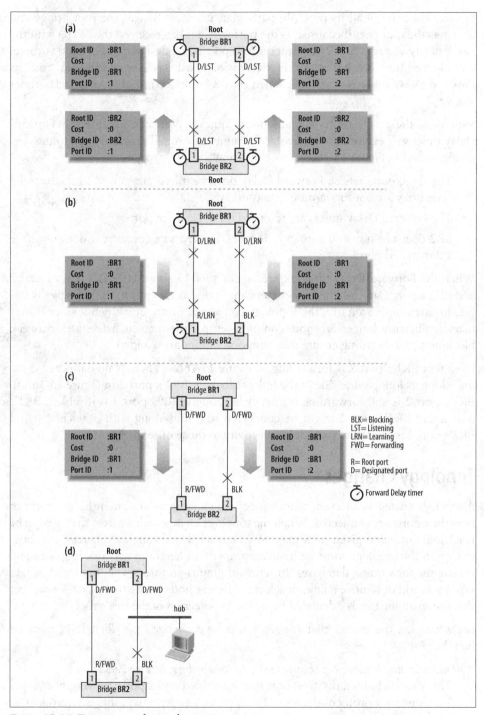

Figure 15-16. Transition to forwarding state

updates the state of all its ports. In particular, it selects BR1 as the root bridge and port 1 as the root port (because it is the port where it has received the BPDU with the best priority vector). Port 2 is neither a root port nor a designated port and is therefore blocked (i.e., it is left out of the tree). When port 1 is assigned the new role, its Forward Delay timer is restarted. When port 2 is blocked, its Forward Delay timer stops.

Supposing these actions took place pretty quickly, you can assume the Forward Delay timer will expire more or less at the same time on all ports, leading to the new configuration in Figure 15-16(b). Note that now:

- The three ports whose Forward Delay timers expired are moved to the learning state (they are not forwarding data traffic yet).
- The Forward Delay timers are restarted on those three ports.
- BR2 does not transmit configuration BPDUs anymore (because it does not have a designated port).

When the Forward Delay timer expires again after 15 seconds, BR1's ports 1 and 2 and BR2's port 1 are assigned the forwarding state. At this point, the topology is stable. In this simple scenario, the topology converged pretty quickly, but since it may take significantly longer on more complex setups, the intermediate states between blocking and forwarding ensure that temporary loops are avoided.

Note that BR1's port 2 is forwarding in Figure 15-16(c). There is no danger of causing a loop as long as one side of the link is blocked (BR2's port 2 in Figure 15-16(c)). BR1's port 2 is still forwarding traffic, even though BR2's port 2 is disabled: BR1's port 2 and BR2's port 2 might be connected to a hub along with other hosts, and BR2's port 2 is needed to provide connectivity to those other hosts.

Topology Changes

A *topology change* is an event that changes which systems are on an L2 network, or how their ports are connected. When the topology changes, an address that used to be reachable through a given path may now be reachable through a different one. So a change in the topology must be handled properly to keep the network loop free and update the forwarding databases. In terms of graphs and trees, the topology changes when you add or remove a link, or select a different node as the tree's root (remember that the spanning tree is calculated based on the selection of the tree's root).

Let's first see the events that trigger a topology change, and then how they are handled:

A nonforwarding bridge port changes state to forwarding, or vice versa
> This case includes a disabled port that is enabled and a port that simply changes state due to a protocol decision. From a tree's perspective, this is equivalent to adding a link to the tree or removing one.

The root bridge ID changes

This can happen, for example, because the current root bridge has been shut down (and therefore another one has taken over the root role), or because a better one has been enabled, or because either the current root bridge or another bridge has changed its priority. A change of the root bridge can, depending on where the new root bridge is located with respect to the old one, trigger quite a few changes of port state and roles all over the network. In theory, a change of root node can produce a very different tree, but in practice, bridges are configured using the parameters we saw in the section "Bridge and Port IDs" so that topology changes do not involve major changes in the tree.

A TCN topology change is received on a bridge port

In this case, the topology change has been detected by another bridge. See the section "Letting All Bridges Know About a Topology Change."

Note that given a loop-free topology, you can create a loop only by adding a link (i.e., a new port enters the forwarding state), not by removing a link (i.e., a forwarding port changes its state to blocking). Removing a link can only partition the tree, whereas adding a link to a tree always creates a loop unless another port has been simultaneously disabled or blocked.

Short Aging Timer

I said earlier that when a topology change is detected, the forwarding database needs to be changed, too. Let's see why with an example. Let's suppose that the link between A2 and D1 in Figure 15-2(a) failed for some reason. All the hosts connected to the access bridge A2 would not be reachable anymore from D1, and D2 should be used instead. The STP will take care of updating the topology by making the bridges go through a configuration update (see the section "Defining the Active Topology"). The new topology could, for instance, look like Figure 15-17. The figure also shows, as an example, the new path between host 40 and host 11.

STP also will make sure to update the stale information in D2 that says that Hosts 11–20 are reachable via its port connected to C1. Stale information is actually not only in that bridge; the forwarding database of other bridges also needs to be cleaned up. Moreover, when there is a change in the topology, the STP needs to converge to a new loop-free topology. During that time, bridge ports may change role and state several times, and thus so will the contents of the forwarding databases.

Stale information in the forwarding database is cleaned up by reducing the time after which an address in the database is removed if it is not used. This is carried out by reducing the Aging timer, which is 5 minutes by default, to the Forward Delay (i.e., 15 seconds by default) when a bridge is notified about a topology change. Topology changes are notified by setting a special flag in the configuration BPDUs (see the next section).

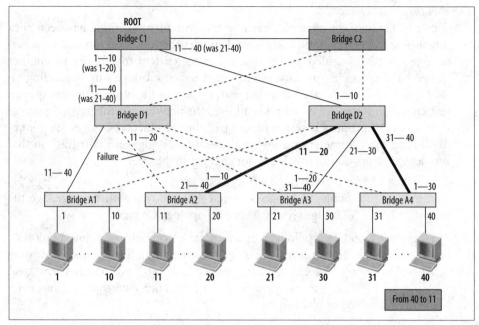

Figure 15-17. Handling a root port failure on A2

Letting All Bridges Know About a Topology Change

When a topology change is detected by a bridge, all bridges must be notified so that they can start using short aging to clean up stale entries in their forwarding databases. Let's see how this is accomplished:

1. The bridge notifies the root bridge about the topology change.
2. The root bridge notifies all the bridges about the topology change.

The first step is done with TCN BPDUs. The bridge that detects the topology change sends a TCN BPDU to its designated bridge through the root port. The bridge sends a TCN BPDU at every Hello time until the designated bridge acknowledges its reception. The designated bridge acknowledges the reception of the TCN BPDU by setting the TCA flag in its next configuration BPDU. At this point, the designated bridge repeats the same process by sending a TCN BPDU to its designated bridge through the root port, etc. This process ends when the TCN finally makes it to the root bridge. The use of the TCN BPDUs is not needed when the topology change is detected by the root bridge itself (because the root bridge does not need to notify itself).

The second step is done by the root bridge by setting a special flag (TC) in its transmitted configuration BPDUs. This flag will be kept toggled on in the BPDUs regenerated by the nonroot bridges so that all bridges in the network will eventually receive the topology change notification. When a bridge sees this flag set, it starts the Short Aging timer.

Example of a Topology Change

If we take the scenario of Figure 15-2(a) and imagine shutting down the link between A2 and D1 (i.e., the root port), A2 would elect the other port as the root port, which would change the state from blocking to forwarding. This would lead to the new scenario in Figure 15-18(a).

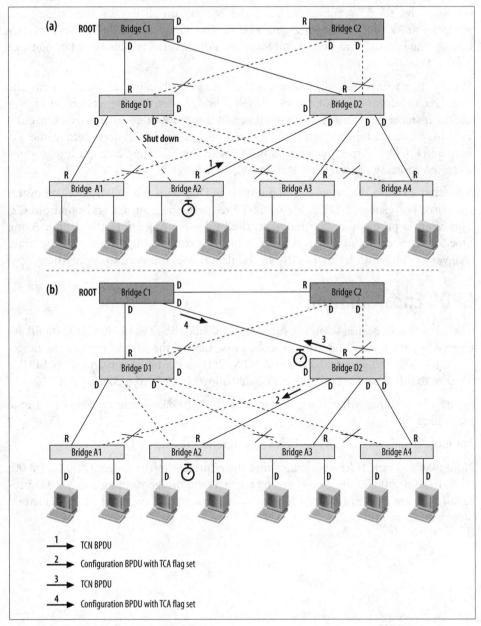

Figure 15-18. Use of the TCN BPDU

A2 starts the TCN timer and transmits a TCN BPDU out of its (new) root port. When D2 receives the TCN BPDU, it acknowledges the reception by sending back a configuration BPDU with the TCA flag set, starts the TCN timer, and transmits a TCN BPDU out of its root port. When A2 receives the acknowledgment from D2, it stops its TCN timer. D2 will do the same when it receives the acknowledgment from C1.

When C1 receives the TCN BPDU, it starts the Topology Change timer, which will remain active for 35 seconds, and sets the TC flag on all BPDUs transmitted out while the timer is pending (see Figure 15-19). The 35 seconds used by the Topology Change timer is not a random value: it is the Forward Delay plus the Max Age (see Table 15-4).

The TC flag will be propagated down the entire tree because all bridges relay the flags received from the root bridge. When a bridge sees this flag set on an ingress BPDU, it starts using the Short Aging timer (if it has not done so already). Once the Topology Change timer expires on the root bridge, the latter stops setting the TC flags in its BPDUs. Upon receiving a BPDU with the TC flag cleared, a bridge stops using the Short Aging timer and starts using default aging.

Note that a bridge can receive configuration BPDUs with the TC flags set on different ports. For example, D2 in Figure 15-19 receives one from C1 and one from C2. This is not a problem: at any moment, the bridge is using either the default Aging timer or the Short Aging timer, so when a bridge already using the Short Aging timer receives a configuration BPDU with the TC flag, it does not need to do anything.

BPDU Encapsulation

The L2 multicast addresses in the range 01:80:C2:00:00:00 to 01:80:C2:00:00:FF are reserved by IEEE for standard protocols. In particular, the first address of the range, 01:80:C2:00:00:00, is used by the 802.1D STP: both configuration and TCN BPDUs are sent to this address. This address is what allows bridges to recognize BPDUs.

Figure 15-20 shows what the encapsulation of a BPDU inside an Ethernet frame looks like.

For more details on the LLC header, you can refer to Chapter 13.

Note that the same IEEE spec states that the addresses in the range 01:80:C2:00:00: 00 to 01:80:C2:00:00:0F should not be relayed by a bridge running the 802.1D protocol: they are either processed locally by the destination protocol (if implemented and enabled) or dropped.

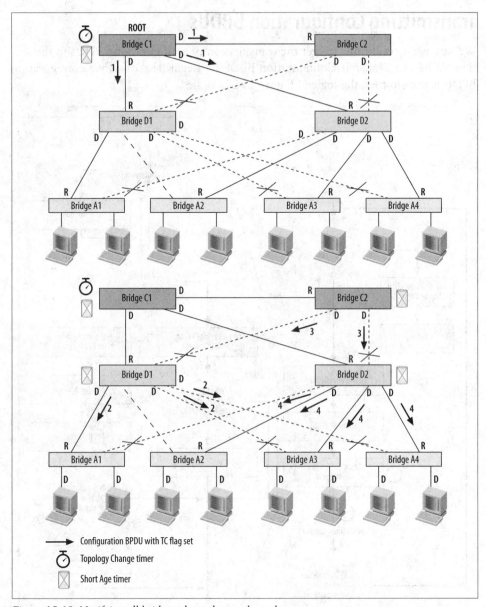

Figure 15-19. *Notifying all bridges about the topology change*

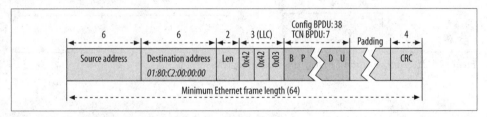

Figure 15-20. *BPDU encapsulation*

Transmitting Configuration BPDUs

We saw what conditions trigger the transmission of configuration BPDUs in the section "When to Transmit Configuration BPDUs." Regardless of why a configuration BPDU is transmitted, the logic of Figure 15-21 applies.

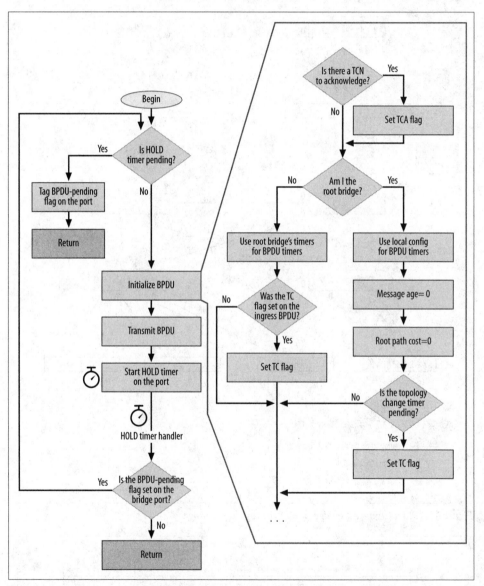

Figure 15-21. Configuration BPDU transmission logic

The per-port Hold timer enforces a rate limit of one BPDU per second. When a BPDU is transmitted, the timer is started. If another transmission is attempted and the timer is already pending, the BPDU is not transmitted and a flag is set in the bridge port configuration block. When the timer expires, it checks the flag and transmits a configuration BPDU if it finds the flag set.

When the root bridge transmits a BPDU, the timers are initialized to the values configured locally; otherwise, the ones received from the root bridge are used instead. Message age and root path cost are both 0 for the root bridge.

Also, the following is not shown in the figure:

- When the bridge needs to acknowledge the reception of a TCN BPDU, it sets the TCA flag.
- The root bridge sets the TC flag if the Topology Change timer is running.
- Nonroot bridges set the TC flag if the last BPDU received on the root port had the TC flag set.

Processing Ingress Frames

We saw in Chapter 14 how a simple bridge handles ingress traffic. Let's now see how a bridge running the STP handles ingress traffic.

Ingress traffic now includes not only data traffic, but BPDUs as well. Bridges handle data traffic the same way, regardless of whether STP is enabled. The only difference is that ports blocked by STP cannot forward any data traffic because they are not considered part of the tree.

Ingress BPDUs

Unlike data traffic, ingress BPDUs are accepted on any port that has not been administratively disabled, including those in the blocking state.

Configuration BPDUs and TCN BPDUs can be distinguished thanks to the BPDU type field, as shown in Figure 15-7. In the section "Letting All Bridges Know About a Topology Change," we already saw how ingress TCN BPDUs are handled. In the next section, we will see how configuration BPDUs are processed.

Ingress Configuration BPDUs

Figure 15-22 shows how ingress configuration BPDUs are processed.

The handling of an ingress BPDU depends on whether its priority vector is:

Better than the one currently known to the receiving bridge's port
    In this case, the BPDU triggers a configuration update that includes the new root port, the designated ports, and the new state for all ports.

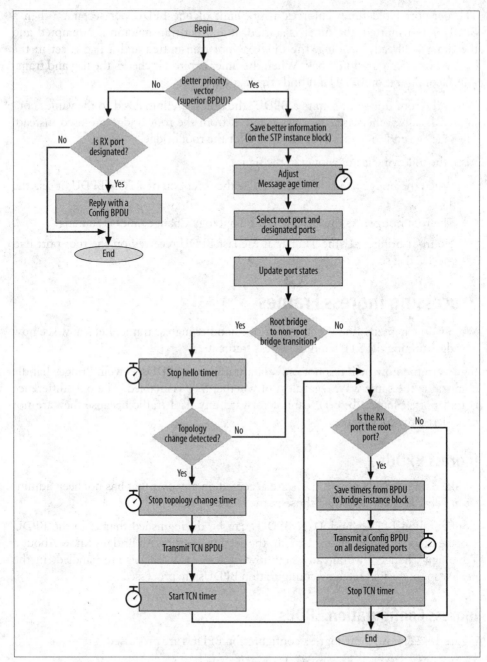

Figure 15-22. Processing ingress configuration BPDUs

The same as the one already known to the receiving bridge's port
> This is what would be received on the root port when the topology has already converged.

Worse than the one known to the receiving bridge's port
> In this case, the bridge replies by sending a configuration BPDU with its own (better) information. This is a common case that happens when a new bridge is added to the topology: initially the bridge does not know anything about the other bridges and therefore advertises its information. It can also happen in numerous other cases, such as when a bridge configuration is changed.

When an ingress BPDU claims a better priority vector than the one known to the receiver port, there is one special case to handle: when the receiving bridge was the root bridge it must lay down its crown. As we mentioned in the section "Topology Changes," this is one of the events that is considered a topology change. In such a case, the bridge that lost the root role must stop the Hello timer (because it is to be run only on the root bridge), send a TCN BPDU out its root port toward the new root bridge, and start the TCN timer to notify the root bridge about the topology change (which will take care of notifying all other bridges).

When the BPDU is received on the root port, the bridge saves the timers from the BPDU (which it will use in its egress BPDUs) and transmits a configuration BPDU out all of its designated ports. When the TCA flag is set, the TCN timer can be stopped.

Convergence Time

We have seen how the STP dynamically updates the topology of the tree based on configuration changes and link or bridge failures. Let's see now how much time STP needs to detect common failures and react accordingly.

When a configuration update takes place on a complex scenario, the network may require minutes before it converges and stabilizes.* During that time the topology is still loop free, but it may not be able to carry traffic properly (because the topology is still changing while the traffic is in transit). In those setups, it is not possible to predict exactly how the topology evolves toward a new stable tree, because the timing of BPDU receptions and transmissions depends on several factors, such as how loaded the bridges are at that moment.

---

* It is possible to configure the bridges to reduce the impact of a failure or configuration change and thus contribute to faster convergence.

However, no matter how well you configure the bridges, there are minimum latencies that cannot be eliminated or reduced. For example:

- When a port changes state, moving, for example, from blocking to forwarding to replace a failing bridge port, the transition to forwarding is not immediate, but takes twice the time of the Forward Delay timer (i.e., 30 seconds by default), as shown in Figure 15-6. The port cannot forward any data traffic during this time.
- Root and nondesignated ports (i.e., the ones that receive BPDUs) realize that they have lost connection to their designated bridge (and therefore to the entire tree except for the portions below the bridge's designated ports*) only when their Message Age timer expires. For example, if the C1 port that goes to D1 in Figure 15-2(a) failed for some reason, D1 may come to know it only after 20 seconds when the Max Age timer expires.

Note that both of these cases are driven by timers. Of course, you can configure both the Forward Delay and Max Age timers to expire faster and therefore reduce the convergence time. However, depending on how complex the network is, you may not always be able to use timers that are too aggressive.

Let's see an example based on Figure 15-2 and see what happens when the D1 bridge fails for some reason. Because both A1 and A2 use D1 to access the rest of the network, all the hosts connected to A1 and A2 are isolated from the rest of the network until STP manages to select a new root port for both A1 and A2. So, how long would it take for STP to make such changes? In the worst-case scenario, this is what would happen:

- D1 stops working properly.
- After 20 seconds, the Message Age timer expires in both A1 and A2 root ports.
- A1 and A2 select the port that goes to D2 as the new root port.
- After another 30 seconds, those new root ports enter the forwarding state.

This means a potential black hole of 50 seconds for the hosts connected to A1 and A2. In a complex network, the topology may require more time than this to converge, even a few minutes.

Overview of Newer Spanning Tree Protocols

The convergence time of the 802.1D-1998 STP was acceptable when it was first defined several years ago by the IEEE committee. However, it has proven too slow over the years, given the higher availability requirements of newer network applications, such as interactive multimedia (IP telephony, video conferencing, etc.), not to mention the user expectations that continuously grow.

---

* Thus, if the bridge is a leaf in the tree (i.e., an access bridge), it is completely isolated.

To address this issue, various commercial bridge producers came out with proprietary enhancements to the STP. Unfortunately, proprietary enhancements often cannot be used in heterogeneous networks that employ devices from different vendors.

Recently the IEEE came out with two newer protocols, Rapid Spanning Tree (RSTP) and Multiple Spanning Tree (MSTP), that address all the significant shortcomings currently known in their older brother, 802.1D. We cannot describe the two protocols here because they would require quite some space (especially MSTP), and anyway, none of them is implemented in Linux (yet). In the following two subsections, we will just explore some of the main improvements offered by the new protocols. For more detail, I suggest the following documents:

- Understanding Rapid Spanning Tree Protocol (802.1w) at *http://www.cisco.com/ warp/public/473/146.html*
- Understanding Multiple Spanning Tree Protocol (802.1s) at *http://www.cisco. com/warp/public/473/147.html*

Rapid Spanning Tree Protocol (RSTP)

The RSTP is backward compatible with 802.1D, so bridges running older and newer protocols can interoperate without problems. However, not all the enhancements introduced by the RSTP would be enabled in such heterogeneous environments. Here are some of the enhancements:

- Each bridge port is now assigned a role. Ports that are neither designated nor root are assigned either the alternate or the backup role. Alternate is used for ports that represent alternate paths toward the root bridge (potential replacements for the current root path), and backup is used for ports that represent alternate paths to the subtree (potential replacements for the designated port). For example:
  - In Figure 15-10, BR2's port 2 would be an alternate port because it provides an alternate path to the root bridge.
  - In Figure 15-11(c), BR1's port 2 would be a backup port because it represents a candidate designated port, but another port on the same bridge has a better priority vector.
- The possible states a port can be assigned have been simplified: the new discarding state includes the old, disabled, blocking and listening states.
- RSTP is able to transition a port to the forwarding state much faster, by means of handshakes between ports and a mechanism called *sync* that makes sure loops are avoided. This new and interesting improvement in RSTP is effective only on point-to-point links.

- When the root port is replaced, it can go to the forwarding state immediately (i.e., no need to wait two times for the Forward Delay timer to expire, as shown in Figure 15-6). This is possible because the protocol has a mechanism to ensure that this immediate transition to forwarding will not cause any loop.

- The previous two enhancements alone imply a significantly faster convergence time, perhaps even a subsecond (depending on the complexity of the topology).

- All bridges now run the Hello timer, and generate configuration BPDUs independently. This allows faster detection of connectivity problems.

- The detection of connectivity problems is no longer dependent on the Max Age timer. Now, when a port that is supposed to receive BPDUs does not receive them for three Hello time periods in a row, it starts the recovery mechanism. The old Max Age timer is still there, but is used only when the new RSTP procedure, previously mentioned, is not applicable.

- Topology changes are handled differently, too. There is no need for TCN BPDUs anymore. Now the bridge that detects a topology change simply transmits a BPDU with the TC flag set from its root and designated ports. Every other bridge that receives such a BPDU simply repeats the process: it transmits a BPDU with the TC flag set out of each of its forwarding ports, except the one from which it received the original. This is a simple mechanism for spreading the topology change notification in all directions. When a bridge receives a BPDU with the TC flag set, it does not start the Short Aging timer, but instead flushes the addresses learned on all its ports, except the one from which the BPDU was received.

- The structure of the BPDUs used by RSTP has changed very little compared to STP. The flags field now uses all 8 bits to accommodate the needs of the newer enhancements.

At the time this chapter was written, there was no open source implementation of RSTP available for Linux. However, you can find a user-space simulator on Source-Forge (*http://rstplib.sourceforge.net*).

Multiple Spanning Tree Protocol (MSTP)

MSTP was designed more or less at the same time RSTP was defined. The main enhancement it introduces is the possibility of defining multiple independent spanning trees. Each spanning tree carries its own subset of data traffic.

The selection of the spanning tree to use for each data packet is based on the VLAN where the packet originated. Figure 15-23 shows hosts configured on two different groups of VLANs, and for each group of VLANs the MSTP builds a separate spanning tree.

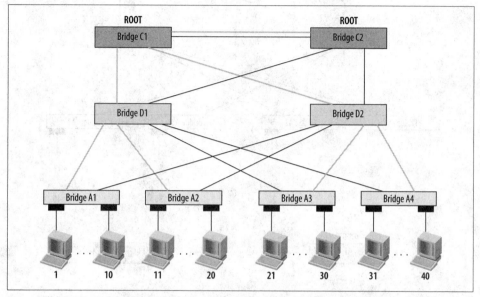

Figure 15-23. Example of bridged network that defines two spanning tree instances

From the hosts' perspective, the result is Figure 15-24.

Nowadays it is pretty common to use VLANs on bridged networks. It's a convenient way to create different L2 broadcast domains on bridged networks. The possibility of defining multiple spanning tree topologies on the same network has several advantages. Among them is better use of the network bandwidth (i.e., better use of redundant links—that is, load balancing). This translates to a lower load on each link.

The MSTP uses the RSTP for each of its spanning tree instances. The protocol is actually more complex than it may seem: the different STP instances are independent, but there is one special instance that plays a central role in the protocol, especially with regard to how BPDUs are exchanged and how backward compatibility with previous protocols is maintained.

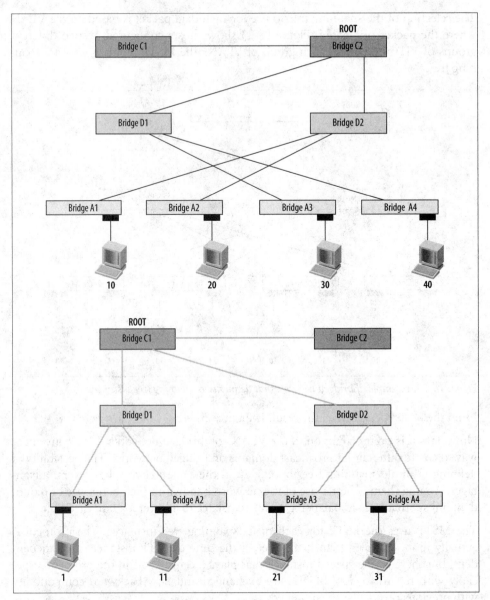

Figure 15-24. The two spanning trees in Figure 15-23

At the time this book was written, there was no open source implementation of the MSTP.

## CHAPTER 16

Bridging: Linux Implementation

This chapter moves on from the general discussion of the bridging specifications and protocols to show how Linux does the job.

We saw in Chapter 10 how the bridging code can capture ingress packets in `netif_receive_skb`. In this chapter, we will see exactly how those ingress packets are processed. We will see how the bridging code manipulates device states and processes ingress traffic, both when the STP is enabled and when it is not.

For a performance evaluation of the bridging code, please refer to the paper "Performance Evaluation of Linux Bridge" by James T. Yu, which you can find with a web search.

Bridge Device Abstraction

In Linux, a bridge is a virtual device. As such, it cannot receive or transmit anything unless you bind one or more real devices to it. We will use the term *enslave* to refer to the process of binding a real device to a (virtual) bridge device.

Let's suppose we want to implement the topology of Figure 16-1. A few points in the figure deserve emphasis:

- The bridge merges two LANs. The hosts of LAN1 and LAN2 are configured on the same subnet, 10.0.1.0/24.
- The bridge is connected to a router so that the hosts of LAN1 and LAN2 can communicate with the hosts of LAN3.
- From the router's perspective, there is a single LAN on *eth0*.

Because Linux implements both routing and bridging, we can merge the two devices into a single Linux system and obtain something like the topology in Figure 16-2(a). The network connection between the bridge and the router is internal to the kernel there.

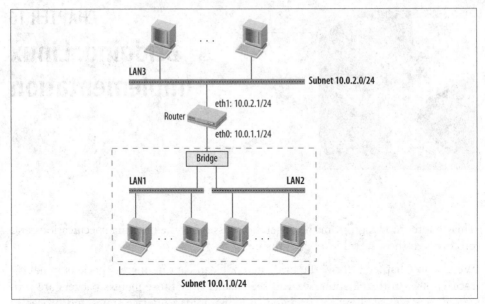

Figure 16-1. Example of use of a bridge

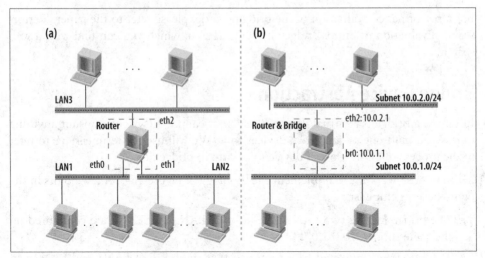

Figure 16-2. Bridge device abstraction

Now the kernel must be able to handle the following two issues:

- At the router level, it sees only two subnets (10.0.1.0/24, 10.0.2.0/24), even though there are three interfaces (*eth0*, *eth1*, *eth2*).

- It should bridge only between *eth0* and *eth1*, and consider the two interfaces as configured on the same IP subnet.

These two issues are handled independently and elegantly, thanks to the way the bridge device is abstracted.

When you create a bridge device, you must tell the kernel which interface to enslave to it. In other words, you must tell the kernel which interfaces to bridge. Sticking to our example, we would create a bridge device, let's call it *br0*, and assign *eth0* and *eth1* to it. Because *eth0* and *eth1* are the bridge interfaces, they do not need any IP configuration—they don't need to be seen at the L3 layer at all, just as none of the bridge interfaces in Figure 16-1 had any IP configuration. Instead, you assign to the bridge device the IP configuration that the router's link to the bridge had in Figure 16-1. The result is the configuration in Figure 16-2(b).

At this point, the routing subsystem can route based on the subnets configured on *eth2* and *br0*. When a transmission on *br0* is attempted, the bridge device driver manages the enslaved devices, applying the logic we saw in Chapter 14: if the forwarding database knows where the destination MAC address is located, the frame is transmitted only on the right bridge port; otherwise, it is flooded to all bridge ports of the bridge device.

We saw in Chapter 11 that transmissions on a device are done with dev_queue_xmit. Figure 16-3(a) shows the devices in our example on which dev_queue_xmit can be asked to transmit frames. dev_queue_xmit invokes the hard_start_xmit routine provided by the device's driver. The function used by the bridging device driver consults the forwarding database and selects the right egress device, or uses flooding if necessary. Details will be provided later in the section "The Big Picture."

We saw in Chapter 10 how a device driver that processes an ingress frame first initializes a few fields of the sk_buff structure and then passes it to the upper layer. One of those fields represents the device on which the frame is received. However, the NIC device driver does not know anything about bridging, so it can't assign an ingress frame to the net_device instance associated with a bridge. In the section "Processing Data Frames," you will see how this issue is taken care of.

The devices enslaved to a bridge device can have their own IP configuration, too. For example, given the topology in Figure 16-2, if we added one more subnet (10.0.3.0/24) and configured *eth0* with an address on it, the topology would appear to the Linux kernel routing layer like the one in Figure 16-4.

eth0 can therefore receive traffic addressed to either the *br0* bridge device or itself. This means that the model in Figure 16-3 changes to that in Figure 16-5.

While the transmitting part does not require any tweaking in the code, the receiving part does. By default, traffic received on an enslaved device is assigned to its assigned bridge device. For example, in Figure 16-5, a frame received on *eth1* would be assigned to *br0*. The decision whether to bridge or route an ingress frame (i.e., the decision whether to hand ingress frames to *eth0* or *br0* in the previous example) can be configured with ebtables (see the section "Data Frames Versus BPDUs").

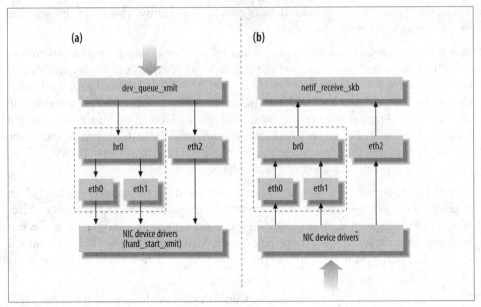

Figure 16-3. (a) Transmitting on a bridge device; (b) receiving on a bridge device

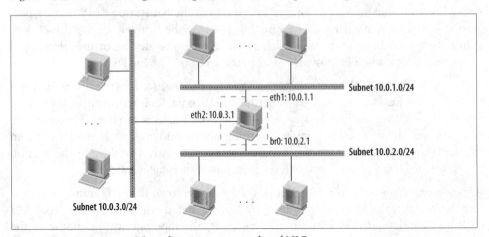

Figure 16-4. Assigning an L3 configuration to an enslaved NIC

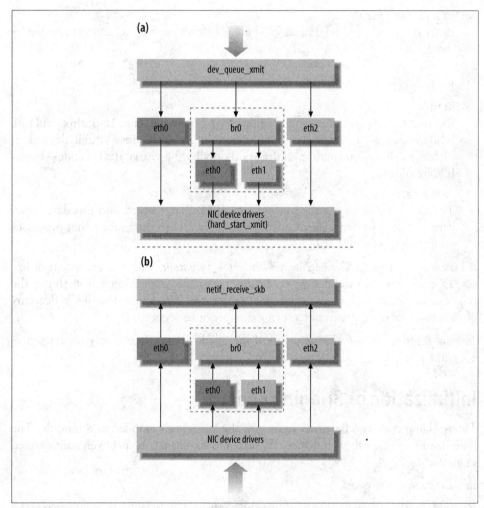

Figure 16-5. Using an NIC both as a standalone interface and as a bridge port

Important Data Structures

The following list explains the main data structures defined and used by the bridging code. All of them have dedicated sections with field-by-field descriptions in Chapter 17.

mac_addr
    MAC address.

bridge_id
    Bridge ID (defined in Chapter 15).

net_bridge_fdb_entry

> Entry of the forwarding database. There is one for each MAC address learned by the bridge.

net_bridge_port

> Bridge port.

net_bridge

> Information applying to a single bridge. As shown in Figure 16-6, this structure is appended to a net_device data structure. As with most virtual devices, it includes private information understood only by the virtual device code—bridging, in this case.

br_config_bpdu

> The key fields of an ingress configuration BPDU are copied into this data structure, and it is passed instead of the original BPDU to the routine that processes configuration BPDUs.

All data structures are defined in *net/bridge/br_private.h*, with the exception of br_config_bpdu, which is defined in *net/bridge/br_private_stp.h*. Figure 16-6 shows the relationships between some of these data structures. The figure does not reflect any of the examples of configurations seen in the previous section.

The age_list list is not used anymore; I included it in the figure only for reference. See the section "net_bridge Structure" in Chapter 17.

Initialization of Bridging Code

The bridging code can be either built into the kernel or compiled as a module. The initialization and cleanup routines, br_init and br_uninit, respectively, are defined in */net/bridge/br.c*.

Initialization consists of:

- Initializing the forwarding database by creating a slab cache (a memory area) to use for allocating net_bridge_fdb_entry structures (br_fdb_init).

- Initializing the function pointer br_ioctl_hook to the routine that will take care of ioctl commands. ioctl commands are described in Chapter 17.

- Initializing the function pointer br_handle_frame_hook to the routine that will process ingress BPDUs. See the section "Handling Ingress Traffic."

- Registering a callback with the netdev_chain notification chain. See the section "netdevice Notification Chain."

When the kernel is compiled with support for Bridging-Firewalling, the option is initialized here with br_netfilter_init. Later, in Figure 16-11 in the section "The Big Picture," you can see where all the Netfilter hooks are located in the core routines used by the bridging code to process ingress and egress traffic.

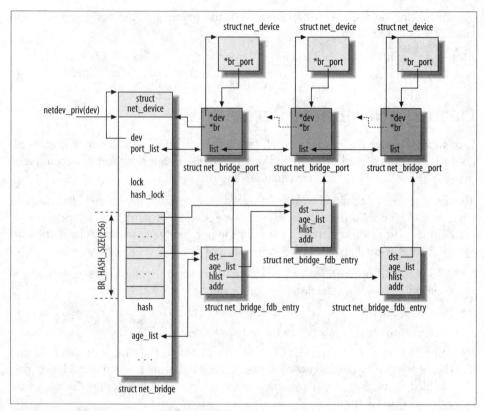

Figure 16-6. Relationships between the main data structure types

Bridging-Firewalling is added to the kernel with the option "Networking support → Networking options → Network packet filtering (replaces ipchains) → Bridged IP/ ARP packet filtering". The Ethernel-Bridging-Tables option (i.e., ebtables) is initialized elsewhere (see the section "Data Frames Versus BPDUs").

The cleanup routine br_deinit simply undoes what was done by br_init.

Creating Bridge Devices and Bridge Ports

There is no hard limit to the number of bridge devices an administrator can create. Each bridge device can have up to BR_MAX_PORTS (1,024) ports.

Bridge devices are created and removed, respectively, with br_add_bridge and br_ del_bridge.

Ports are added to a bridge device with br_add_if and are removed with br_del_if.

All four routines run with the Netlink routing lock held. The lock is acquired with rtnl_lock and is released with rtnl_unlock. br_add_bridge and br_del_bridge take care of locking on their own. For `br_add_if` and `br_del_if`, the `dev_ioctl` function takes care of it (see in Chapter 17).

All four `br_` routines are defined in *net/bridge/br_if.c*. In Chapter 17, you can learn how they are invoked in response to configuration commands in user space.

Creating a New Bridge Device

Even though bridge devices are virtual, the discussion about how a device is enabled, disabled, registered, and unregistered in Chapter 8 still applies. You are encouraged to use that chapter as a reference when reading this section.

The creation and registration of a bridge device follows the model described in Chapter 8. The only difference is that because it is a virtual device, a bridge needs extra initializations in its private area (i.e., the `net_bridge` data structure at the bottom of Figure 16-6). This last task is taken care of by `new_bridge_dev`, which:

- Allocates and initializes a `net_device` data structure using `br_dev_setup` as the setup routine. See the section "Bridge Device Setup Routine."
- Initializes the private structure, as shown in Figure 16-6.
- Initializes the bridge priority to the default value, 32,768 (0x8000).
- Initializes the designated bridge ID with its identifier, the root path cost to 0, and the root port to 0 (i.e., no root port). This is because when a bridge is first enabled, it believes itself to be the root bridge. See the section "Root Bridge Selection" in Chapter 15.
- Initializes the aging time to the default of 5 minutes.
- Initializes the per-bridge timers with `br_stp_timer_init`.

Note that the initialization of spanning tree parameters is done regardless of whether the STP is enabled for the bridge.

Bridge devices can be assigned any name. Common ones are *brN* and *stpN*, when the Spanning Tree Protocol is disabled and enabled, respectively. For example, if you define two bridges that don't use STP, you would conventionally call them *br1* and *br2*. However, your dog's name would be accepted, too.

As with any other network device, bridges are assigned a directory in */sys/class/net/*. See the section "Tuning via /sys Filesystem" in Chapter 17.

Bridge Device Setup Routine

Details about how device drivers use the setup routines when initializing their devices can be found in the section "Device Type Initialization: xxx_setup Functions" in

Chapter 8. Bridge devices use the `br_dev_setup` setup routine. The following snapshot shows the interesting part:

```
void br_dev_setup(struct net_device *dev)
{
    memset(dev->dev_addr, 0 , ETH_ALEN);
    ether_setup(dev);
    ...
    dev->do_ioctl = br_dev_ioctl;
    dev->hard_start_xmit = br_dev_xmit;
    dev->open = br_dev_open;
    dev->change_mtu = br_change_mtu;
    dev->stop = br_dev_stop;
    dev->tx_queue_len = 0 ;
    dev->set_mac_addr = NULL ;
    dev->priv_flags = IFF_EBRIDGE;
}
```

Bridge devices do not implement queuing by default. They let their enslaved devices take care of it, which explains why `tx_queue_len` is initialized to 0. However, the administrator can configure `tx_queue_len` with *ifconfig* or *ip link*.

When the Maximum Transmission Unit (MTU) on a bridge device is changed, the kernel must ensure that the new value is no bigger than the smallest MTU value among the enslaved devices. This is ensured by `br_change_mtu`.

The bridge MAC address `dev_addr` is cleared because it will be derived by the MAC addresses configured on its enslaved devices with `br_stp_recalculate_bridge_id` (see the section "Bridge IDs and Port IDs"). For the same reason, the driver does not provide a `set_mac_addr` function.

The `IFF_EBRIDGE` flag is set so that kernel code can distinguish bridge devices from other types of devices when needed.

The `br_dev_ioctl` routine processes some of the `ioctl` commands you can issue on bridge devices. See Chapter 17.

We saw in Chapter 11 that drivers initialize the `hard_start_xmit` function pointer to the routine they use for transmission. The bridging driver initializes it to `br_dev_xmit`. This function is responsible for implementing the bridge device abstraction we saw in the section "Bridge Device Abstraction." Figure 16-11 later in this chapter shows how that abstraction is implemented.

When a bridge device is administratively enabled or disabled, the kernel calls `dev_open` and `dev_close`, respectively, which invokes `br_dev_open` and `br_dev_close` for bridge devices. See the section "Enabling and Disabling a Bridge Device."

Deleting a Bridge

Before a bridge device can be removed, it must be shut down. If it hasn't been shut down, br_del_bridge returns –EBUSY and refuses to remove the device. To remove it, br_del_bridge invokes del_br, which does most of the work, as follows:

- Removes all its bridge ports. For each bridge port, it also removes the associated links (which appear as directories) in *sys*. See the section "Deleting a Bridge Port."

- For each port, removes all the associated entries in the forwarding database with br_fdb_delete_by_port, stops all the port's timers, and decrements the promiscuity counter. (The promiscuity counter is described in the upcoming section, "Adding Ports to a Bridge.")

- Stops the garbage collection timer br->gc_timer.

- Removes the bridge device directory in the *sys/class/net* directory with br_sysfs_delbr.

- Unregisters the device with unregister_netdevice. This function is described in Chapter 8.

Adding Ports to a Bridge

In the current implementation of bridging, there is a one-to-one relationship between NICs and bridge ports, as shown in Figure 16-6. Some commercial bridges allow an administrator to add an NIC to multiple bridge devices and assign traffic to a particular bridge based on user-chosen criteria, but Linux does not.

Bridge ports are added to a bridge device with br_add_if. The routine internals are shown in Figure 16-7. The routine does not care whether the STP is enabled on the bridge device.

The routine starts with a set of sanity checks. The operation is aborted if any of the following conditions is met:

- The device to be associated with the port is not an Ethernet device (or the loopback device).

- The device to be associated with the port is a bridge. As you can see in Figure 16-6, bridge ports must be assigned to real devices (or to virtual devices that are not bridge devices).

- The bridge port is already assigned to a device (i.e., dev->br_port is not NULL).

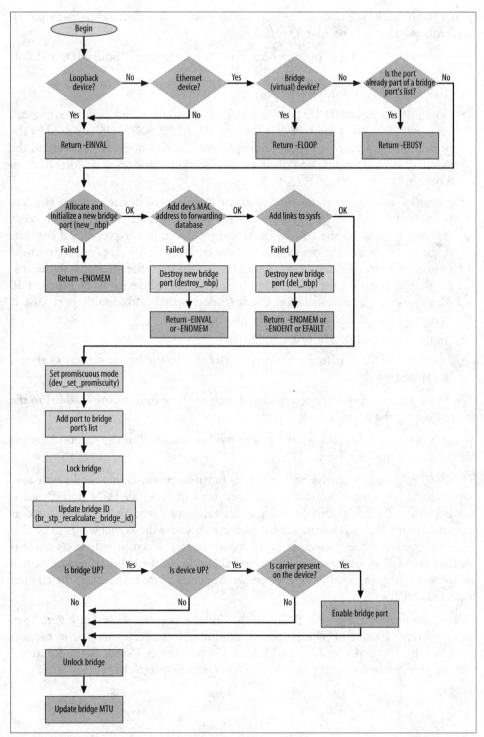

Figure 16-7. br_add_if function

When these checks are passed, the new bridge port is allocated and partially initialized with new_nbp. In particular, that function:

- Assigns a port number to the bridge port. See the section "Bridge IDs and Port IDs."

- Assigns a default priority to the port.

- Computes the port ID by combining the port number and priority using br_make_port_id. Out of the 16 bits in the port ID, 10 (BR_PORT_BITS) are used by the port number and 6 by the port priority. Note that this does not conform to the standard specifications described in the section "Bridge and Port IDs" in Chapter 15.

- Assigns a default cost to the port based on the enslaved device's speed. The cost is selected with br_initial_port_cost (see how new_npb is called), which reads the device speed via the ethtool interface introduced in Chapter 8, and converts it into a cost. When the device driver of the enslaved device does not support the ethtool interface, a default cost cannot be derived from the interface, so the cost is selected based on the assumption that the enslaved device is an Ethernet 10 Mbit/s device. The association between port speed and default port cost is defined in the IEEE 802.1D protocol specification.

- Assigns the initial BR_STATE_DISABLED state.

- Links the bridge port to the enslaved device and to the bridge device, as shown in Figure 16-6.

The MAC address of the device associated with the new bridge port is added to the forwarding database with br_fdb_insert.

br_sysfs_addif adds the necessary links to /sys, as described in the section "Tuning via /sys Filesystem" in Chapter 17.

The NIC associated with the bridge port is put into promiscuous mode with dev_set_promiscuity. Promiscuous mode is used for capturing all LAN traffic, and is needed so that the bridge can do its job of forwarding frames. The mode is stored as a counter rather than a Boolean flag for each port because the kernel wants to be able to handle nested requests to enter promiscuous mode. When promiscuous mode is enabled on a bridge port (as dev_set_promiscuity does), the counter is incremented on the associated enslaved device; when promiscuous mode is disabled, the counter is decremented.

Finally, the new bridge port is added to the bridge's port list shown in Figure 16-6, and the bridge ID and MTU are updated according to the rules we saw in the sections "Bridge IDs and Port IDs" in Chapter 15 and "Bridge Device Setup Routine," with br_stp_recalculate_bridge_id and dev_set_mtu, respectively.

Deleting a Bridge Port

Deleting a bridge mainly requires undoing what was done at port creation time. Figure 16-8 shows the internals of br_del_if.

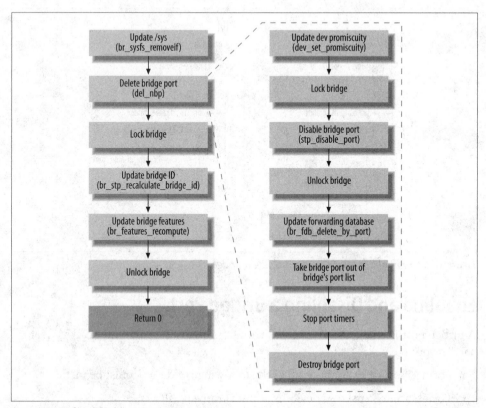

Figure 16-8. br_del_if function

Enabling and Disabling a Bridge Device

We saw in the section "Bridge Device Setup Routine" how dev->open and dev->stop are initialized for bridge devices, and we saw in the section "Enabling and Disabling a Network Device" in Chapter 8 how administrative commands to enable and disable a network device are processed by dev_open and dev_close.

br_dev_open enables a bridge by:

1. Initializing the bridge device features to the minimal, common subset of the features supported by its enslaved devices with br_features_recompute

2. Enabling the device for transmission with netif_start_queue (see the section "Enabling and Disabling Transmissions" in Chapter 11)

3. Enabling the bridge device with br_stp_enable_bridge

When you enable a bridge device, any port that had previously been enslaved to it would also be enabled.

`br_dev_stop` is just the mirror image of `br_dev_open`, as shown in Figure 16-9.

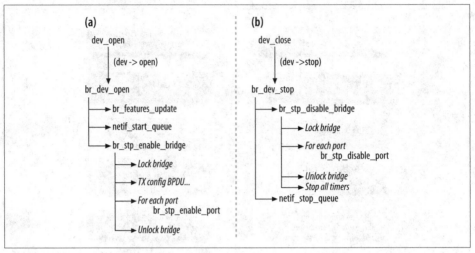

Figure 16-9. (a) Enabling a bridge; (b) disabling a bridge

Enabling and Disabling a Bridge Port

A bridge port is enabled and disabled with `br_stp_enable_port` and `br_stp_disable_port`, respectively.

For a bridge port to be enabled, all of the following conditions must be met:

- The associated enslaved device is administratively UP.
- The associated enslaved device has the carrier status. See the section "Link State Change Detection" in Chapter 8 for how Linux detects changes in the carrier signal status.
- The associated bridge device is administratively UP.

Note that there is no carrier status on the bridge device, because bridges are virtual devices and therefore have no carrier status.

When a bridge port is created with a user-space command and the preceding three conditions are met, the bridge port is enabled right away. See the section "Adding Ports to a Bridge."

Let's suppose that when the port was created, it could not be enabled because at least one of the three required conditions was not met. Here is where the port is enabled when each condition eventually is met:

- When a bridge device that was shut down is activated, all of its disabled ports are enabled.
- When an enslaved device detects the carrier status, the bridging code is notified with a NETDEV_CHANGE notification. See the section "netdevice Notification Chain."
- When an enslaved device that was shut down is activated, the bridging code is notified with a NETDEV_UP notification. See the section "netdevice Notification Chain."

A bridge port is disabled when any of the three conditions listed at the beginning of this section is no longer met.

Figure 16-10 summarizes the steps and associated functions for enabling and disabling a bridge port. Note that when a bridge port is disabled, a nonroot bridge can become the root bridge. That transition is described in the section "Becoming the root bridge."

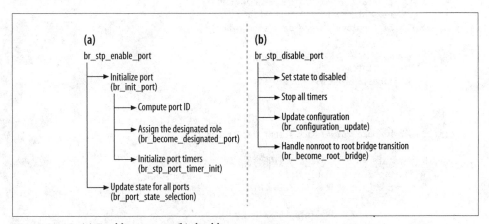

Figure 16-10. (a) Enabling a port; (b) disabling a port

Note that when a port is enabled, it is first initialized and then assigned the right state with br_port_state_selection. This function loops over all bridge ports to apply the right state to each one. But on a bridge that does not run STP, the function actually ends up just putting the new port into the BR_STATE_FORWARDING state. This is because the port is assigned the designated role (although a bridge that does not run the STP should not care about port roles). We need to keep in mind that most routines do not distinguish whether the STP is enabled or disabled. For example, br_state_port_selection loops over all ports because, when the STP is enabled and undergoes a configuration update, it may change the role and therefore the state of many ports (see the section "Configuration Updates").

Changing State on a Bridge Port

A bridge port is either active or inactive: the associated states are BR_STATE_FORWARDING or BR_STATE_BLOCKING. However, while the BR_STATE_BLOCKING state can be assigned right away to a port, the BR_STATE_FORWARDING state is reached only after first going through the intermediate states introduced in the section "Port states" in Chapter 15.

The BR_STATE_FORWARDING and BR_STATE_BLOCKING states are assigned with the br_make_forwarding and br_make_blocking routines, respectively. The same two routines are used regardless of whether the bridge device hosting the port is running the STP.

```
static void br_make_blocking(struct net_bridge_port *p)
{
    if (p->state != BR_STATE_DISABLED &&
        p->state != BR_STATE_BLOCKING) {
        if (p->state == BR_STATE_FORWARDING ||
            p->state == BR_STATE_LEARNING)
            br_topology_change_detection(p->br);

        p->state = BR_STATE_BLOCKING;
        br_log_state(p);
        del_timer(&p->forward_delay_timer);
    }
}

static void br_make_forwarding(struct net_bridge_port *p)
{
    if (p->state == BR_STATE_BLOCKING) {
        if (p->br->stp_enabled) {
            p->state = BR_STATE_LISTENING;
        } else {
            p->state = BR_STATE_LEARNING;
        }
        br_log_state(p);
        mod_timer(&p->forward_delay_timer, jiffies + p->br->forward_delay);
    }
}
```

Note that you cannot assign a port any of the intermediate states between BR_STATE_BLOCKING and BR_STATE_FORWARDING, which is why br_make_forwarding returns if asked to change a port that is not in the BR_STATE_BLOCKING state to BR_STATE_FORWARDING. However, an intermediate state indicates that the port is already on its way to the BR_STATE_FORWARDING state and will get there when the proper timer expires.

In br_make_forwarding, a bridge port skips the BR_STATE_LISTENING state when the STP is not in use. When the STP is not in use, all bridge ports are going to be assigned the forwarding state; therefore, you can skip BR_STATE_LEARNING, too. However, the use of the intermediate state BR_STATE_LEARNING can allow the bridge to learn some MAC addresses and reduce the amount of flooding that would otherwise be needed with an empty forwarding database.

The Big Picture

Figure 16-11 shows the key routines that the bridging code uses to process ingress and egress frames (both data frames and BPDUs).

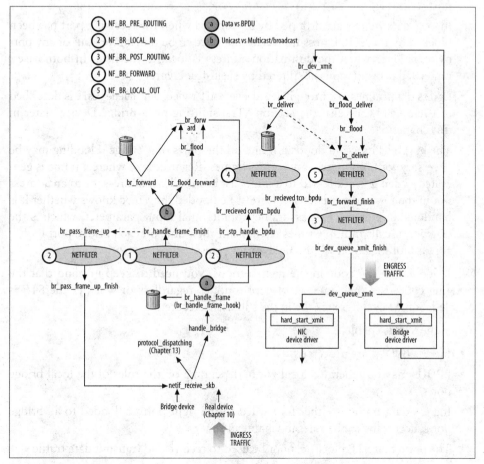

Figure 16-11. The big picture

In particular, note that:

- There are as many hooks as there are at the IP layer (see Figure 18-1 in Chapter 18). One more hook in br_handle_frame (NF_BR_BROUTING), not shown in the figure, is used by ebtables and is described in the section "Data Frames Versus BPDUs."

- Ingress data frames may go through netif_receive_skb twice. netif_receive_skb is described in Chapter 10. See also the section "Processing Data Frames," later in this chapter.

- Ingress frames are passed by netif_receive_skb to the bridging subsystem when a call to handle_bridge indicates it is necessary, or to the upper-layer protocol handlers otherwise (as described in Chapter 13).

- Ingress frames may be dropped by the bridging code, for example, because the port is disabled.

- Ingress data frames are dropped by br_forward when the receiving port has been blocked by the STP. Egress frames do not need to be transmitted out of any port by br_deliver when the destination address is local to the host. In both cases, unneeded transmissions are filtered by should_deliver.

- Egress data frames go through dev_queue_xmit twice. dev_queue_xmit is described in Chapter 11. See also the section "Transmitting on a Bridge Device" later in this chapter.

- The br_flood function floods a frame on the ports of a bridge. Flooding may be necessary for both ingress and egress frames. Regardless of where a frame is generated, when it is addressed to a multicast or broadcast address, or to an address not in the forwarding database, it must be flooded. br_flood knows whether it is handling an ingress or egress frame from its final input parameter, which is the function it calls multiple times to transmit the frame on each bridge port (__br_forward for ingress and __br_deliver for egress).

While looking at the code in the next sections, you need to keep in mind that the bridging code uses the same set of core routines regardless of whether the STP is enabled. Some key differences lie in the subtasks executed.

When the STP is enabled:

- Ingress BPDUs are processed.

- BPDUs may be generated locally too, depending on the roles of the local bridge ports.

- Ingress data traffic is either forwarded to the right port or flooded to all bridge ports, according to the rules in Chapter 14.

- The ports that STP blocks cannot be used to receive and transmit data traffic.

When the STP is disabled:

- Ingress BPDUs are treated as data traffic.

- No BPDUs are generated locally.

- Ingress data traffic is still forwarded to the right port or flooded to all bridge ports, according to the rules in Chapter 14.

- All the bridge ports (unless they're administratively disabled) can be used to receive and transmit data traffic.

Forwarding Database

Each bridge instance has it own forwarding database, which is used regardless of whether STP is enabled or disabled. We will see later in this chapter exactly when the database is consulted and updated. Let's first see its implementation and the core functions for manipulating it. All of the routines used to manage forwarding databases are located in *net/bridge/br_fdb.c*.

The database is embedded in the net_bridge data structure and is defined as a hash table (see Figure 16-6). An instance of a net_bridge_fdb_entry data structure is added to the database for each MAC address that is learned on any of the bridge's ports.

The bridge forwarding database subsystem is initialized with br_fdb_init, which simply creates the br_fdb_cache cache that will be used for the allocation of net_bridge_fdb_entry instances.

Allocations are done with fdb_create, which also initializes a few fields of net_bridge_fdb_entry according to its input parameters.

Lookups

Elements of the forwarding database are identified by their MAC addresses. A lookup in the table consists of selecting the right hash table bucket with br_mac_hash and browsing the bucket's list of net_bridge_fdb_entry instances to find one that matches a given MAC address.

There are two main lookup routines:

fdb_find
> This simply searches net_bridge_fdb_entry for a given MAC address. It is not used to forward data traffic. It is mainly used by bridging management functions.

__br_fdb_get
> Similar to fdb_find, this is called by the bridging code to forward traffic. It does not consider expired entries (see the section "Aging").

For both routines, proper locking is ensured by the caller.

An external subsystem that wishes to make a lookup on the forwarding database can use the br_fdb_get routine, a wrapper that takes care of locking and reference counts and calls __br_fdb_get. br_fdb_get is not called directly, but via br_fdb_get_hook, which is initialized in br_init to be a pointer to br_fdb_get.

Reference Counts

Because external subsystems that query the forwarding database with br_fdb_get are likely to cache the result, a reference count is used to keep track of when entries in the forwarding database are still needed and when they can be freed. Each entry is assigned a reference count. br_fdb_get always increments the reference count when the lookup succeeds. The caller is supposed to decrement it with br_fdb_put when it no longer needs the reference to the lookup result. When the reference count drops to 0, br_fdb_put frees net_bridge_fdb_entry.

Adding, Updating, and Removing Entries

The forwarding database is populated and updated by a different set of routines, depending on whether the MAC addresses are associated with local interfaces or ingress frames.

When you create a bridge port, br_add_if adds the enslaved device's MAC address to the forwarding database with br_fdb_insert. The latter function ignores MAC addresses that are not supposed to be added to the database, such as multicast and broadcast addresses. When the new address happens to be in the database already, it is replaced unless it is associated with another local interface, in which case there is no need for any update. Note that local MAC addresses in the forwarding database allow the bridging code to deliver ingress frames addressed to a local interface locally. So it does not matter what interface the local MAC address is associated with. All that matters is that at least one entry in the database tells the bridging code what traffic to deliver locally.

There is no hard limit on the number of entries that can be added to the forwarding database. This can expose the system to a DOS attack, so we can expect developers to add a hard limit in the near future.

When a local device that is associated with a bridge port—and that therefore has its MAC address in the forwarding database—changes its MAC address,[*] its entry in the database is updated with br_fdb_change_addr (see the section "netdevice Notification Chain"). Because it is possible for multiple local interfaces to be configured with the same MAC address (even though it is not common), bf_fdb_change_addr checks whether another bridge port for the same bridge has the same MAC address before removing the net_bridge_fdb_entry instance: if it finds another bridge port with the same MAC address, it binds the database entry to the interface for the remaining port.

---

[*] Only the system administrator can change the MAC address of an interface, which requires an explicit command like *ip link set eth0 address 00:20:ED:76:1E:12* or *ifconfig eth0 hw ether 00:20:ED:76:1E:12*. Changing the MAC address of an interface is rarely done.

The MAC addresses learned with ingress frames (as described in Chapter 14) are added to the database with br_fdb_update. When the address is already in the database, the reference to the ingress port (dst) is updated if needed and the timestamp of the last update (ageing_timer) is updated.

net_bridge_fdb_entry instances are removed with fdb_delete. That function is never called directly, but always through wrappers like br_fdb_cleanup (described in the next section) and br_fdb_delete_by_port.

Aging

For each bridge instance there is a garbage collection timer (gc_timer) that periodically scans the forwarding database and deletes expired entries. The timer is initialized in br_stp_timer_init when the bridge instance is initialized, and is started when the bridge is enabled with br_stp_enable_bridge.

The timer expires every one-tenth of second and calls br_fdb_cleanup to do the cleanup. That function scans the database and deletes expired entries with fdb_delete.

An entry normally expires if it has not been used for at least 5 minutes. However, when a bridge runs the STP, a shorter aging time of forward_delay seconds is used when a topology change has been detected (see the section "Short Aging Timer" in Chapter 15). The right aging time is used transparently by calling the hold_time routine, which returns the right one to use based on the logic described here.

Handling Ingress Traffic

We saw in Chapter 10 how ingress traffic is processed by netif_receive_skb. In particular, we saw how the function calls handle_bridge (defined in *net/core/dev.c*) before passing each ingress frame to the upper-layer protocol handler.

When the kernel does not have support for bridging, handle_bridge is defined as a NULL pointer and netif_receive_skb hands ingress frames to other protocol handlers. When the kernel does support bridging, and a frame is received on a bridge port, handle_bridge processes the frame with br_handle_frame_hook. The latter pointer is initialized to br_handle_bridge when the bridging module is initialized.

```
#if defined(CONFIG_BRIDGE) || defined (CONFIG_BRIDGE_MODULE)
...
static __inline__ int handle_bridge(struct sk_buff **pskb,
                    struct packet_type **pt_prev, int *ret)
{
    struct net_bridge_port *port;

    if ((*pskb)->pkt_type == PACKET_LOOPBACK ||
        (port = rcu_dereference((*pskb)->dev->br_port)) == NULL)
        return 0;
```

```
        if (*pt_prev) {
            *ret = deliver_skb(*pskb, *pt_prev);
            *pt_prev = NULL;
        }

        return br_handle_frame_hook(port, pskb);
    }
#else
#define handle_bridge(skb, pt_prev, ret)    (0)
#endif
```

In the following subsections, we will see how handle_bridge processes ingress frames, distinguishing between data frames and STP BPDUs (Figure 16-11, circle a). For data frames, the function also distinguishes between unicast frames and multicast or broadcast frames (Figure 16-11, circle b).

Data Frames Versus BPDUs

On a Linux system with support for bridging, not all NICs need to be configured as bridge ports. When one is configured as a bridge port, the br_port pointer of its net_device points to the associated bridge port. Because each bridge port includes a pointer to the bridge instance it is part of, you can easily get from any real device to the bridge instance it belongs to (if any) and check whether STP is enabled for the device by reading a flag in the net_bridge data structure. See Figure 16-6.

BPDUs generated by the STP are distinguished from all other ingress frames and are processed by the STP receiving routine—but only when the STP is enabled on the bridge containing the ingress port.

Figure 16-12 shows how br_handle_frame hands an ingress frame to the right routine, br_handle_frame_finish or br_stp_handle_bpdu, depending on whether STP is enabled.

Any frame received on a disabled port is dropped.

Data frames are accepted on ports in the BR_STATE_FORWARDING state only, and BPDUs are accepted on any enabled port as long as the STP is enabled (otherwise, they are treated just as common data frames).

The logic followed on the left side of Figure 16-12 to recognize BPDUs follows the rules introduced in the section "BPDU Encapsulation" in Chapter 15.

Note that both routines at the bottom of Figure 16-12 are called only if Netfilter does not drop or consume the frame for other reasons.

ebtables is also given a chance to look at frames. ebtables is a framework that provides extra capabilities that Netfilter does not provide.

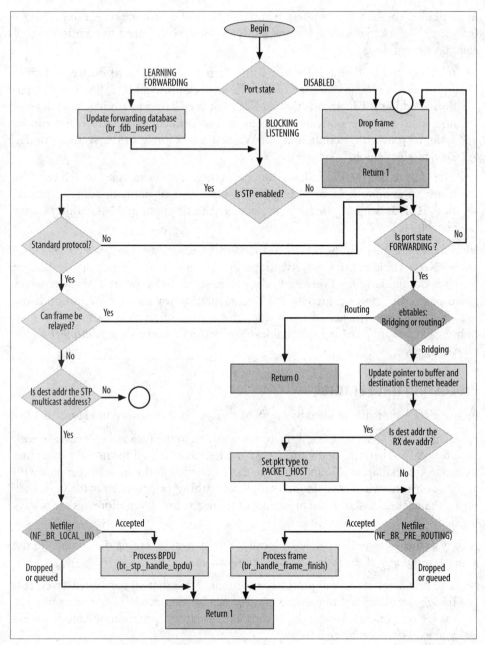

Figure 16-12. *br_handle_frame function*

In particular, ebtables allows filtering and mangling of any frame type, not just those that carry IP packets. For the purposes of our discussion, I need to mention two of ebtables's capabilities:

- It allows you to define rules to tell the kernel what traffic to bridge and what traffic to route, based on such factors as network protocol (i.e., IPv4) or destination IP address. This means that an NIC that is enslaved to a bridge port doesn't just act as a bridge port, but exists as an independent L3 interface and can be assigned its own L3 configuration. We saw an example in the section "Bridge Device Abstraction."

- The destination MAC address can be mangled, for example, to redirect the frame to another host or to implement some sort of network address translation. This is why `br_handle_frame` checks the destination MAC address after ebtables is done.

Support for ebtables can be added to the kernel with the option "Networking support → Networking options → Network packet filtering (replaces ipchains) → Bridge: Netfilter Configuration → Ethernet Bridge tables (ebtables) support". At the ebtables home page, you can find pretty good documentation for this feature, on both the user-space side and the kernel-space side. You can also find clear examples on how to use each feature provided by ebtables. The project's home page is *http://ebtables. sourceforge.net*.

Processing Data Frames

Ingress data frames are handled by `br_handle_frame_finish`, shown in Figure 16-13.

First, the source MAC address of the frame is added to the forwarding database with `br_fdb_update`. Then the destination MAC address is searched for in the forwarding database. If the address is found, the frame is forwarded to the right bridge port with `br_forward`; otherwise, it is flooded to all forwarding bridge ports with `br_flood_frame`. Frames addressed to the broadcast or multicast link layer addresses are always flooded.

A copy of the frame is also delivered locally with `br_pass_frame_up` (i.e., passed to the upper layer) if any of the following conditions are met:

- The bridge interface is in promiscuous mode. Note that all devices enslaved to a bridge port are in promiscuous mode because this mode is necessary for the bridge to work. However, the bridge itself is not in promiscuous mode unless you explicitly configure it to be.

- The frame is flooded for one of the reasons mentioned earlier.

- According to the forwarding database, the destination MAC address belongs to a local interface.

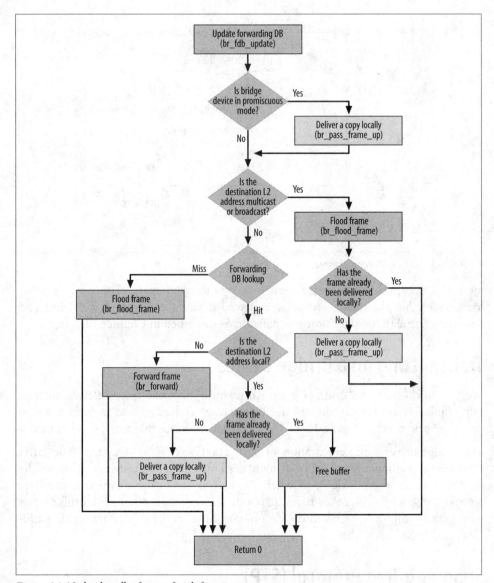

Figure 16-13. br_handle_frame_finish function

It is interesting to see how the local delivery is handled. Figure 16-14, which is a subset of Figure 16-11, shows the exact path of an ingress frame that ends up passed to the upper-layer protocol handler.

When the frame is received by the NIC's device driver, skb->dev is initialized to the real device. The frame is then pushed up the network stack and eventually passed to br_pass_frame_up. That function crosses through another Netfilter hook and then calls br_pass_frame_up_finish. Here skb->dev is replaced with the bridge device the

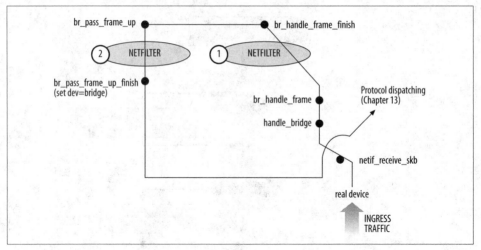

Figure 16-14. Local delivery of ingress data frames

ingress port is part of and `netif_receive_skb` is invoked again. This time, `handle_bridge` sees that the device is not an enslaved device (i.e., `br_port` is NULL) and hands the frame to the right protocol handler, as described in Chapter 13.

Transmitting on a Bridge Device

We saw in the section "Bridge Device Abstraction" that the bridge device abstraction requires transmissions on a bridge device to be converted into transmissions on one or all bridge ports. Figure 16-11 shows the key routines that make this happen.

The bridge driver's implementation of `hard_start_xmit` is `br_dev_xmit`. The latter function simply implements the basic logic used by a bridge to transmit. It copies the frame out of the right bridge port when a lookup in the bridge forwarding database returns success. On the other hand, it floods the frame on all eligible bridge ports when the lookup fails, or when the destination MAC address is either an L2 multicast or L2 broadcast address.

Spanning Tree Protocol (STP)

We saw in Chapter 15 how the STP works. In this chapter, we will mainly see how:

- Ingress BPDUs are processed
- Egress BPDUs are transmitted
- Timers are handled

Key Spanning Tree Routines

Here is a list of the key routines used by the spanning tree code to implement the logic described in Chapter 15:

br_become_root_bridge
br_is_root_bridge

> br_become_root_bridge makes a nonroot bridge the root bridge. This task consists of stopping the TCN timer, because it should not run on the root bridge, and starting the Hello timer, which runs only on the root bridge. The function also updates other timers to locally configured values, and starts a topology change. br_is_root_bridge returns 1 when the input bridge is the root bridge, and 0 otherwise.

br_should_become_designated_port
br_designated_port_selection
br_become_designated_port
br_is_designated_port
br_is_designated_for_some_port

> br_should_become_designated_port returns 1 if the input port should be assigned the designated role, and 0 otherwise. br_designated_port_selection loops over all the bridge ports and it assigns the designated role to those that deserve it (see the section "Designated Port Selection" in Chapter 15).

> br_become_designated_port assigns the designated role to a bridge port. br_is_designated_port returns 1 when the input port is a designated port, and 0 otherwise. Given a bridge, br_is_designated_for_some_port returns 1 if the bridge has at least one port with the designated role, and 0 otherwise.

br_supersedes_port_info

> Given a bridge port and an input configuration BPDU received on the port, this function returns 1 if the BPDU is superior (i.e., has a better priority vector) than the one known to the bridge port, and 0 otherwise.

br_should_become_root_port
br_root_selection

> Given a bridge port and the current root port, br_should_become_root_port compares the priority vector of the first port against the priority vector of the current root port and returns 1 if the first port has a better priority vector (and therefore should be preferred over the current root port). It returns 0 otherwise. Given a bridge, br_root_selection selects the root port as described in the section "Root Port Selection" in Chapter 15.

br_configuration_update

> Given a bridge, determines the root port and designated ports and returns that information.

`br_port_state_selection`

> Given a bridge, selects the right port state for each bridge port.

`br_topology_change_detection`
`br_topology_change_acknowledge`
`br_topology_change_acknowledged`

> `br_topology_change_detection` handles the detection of a topology change, distinguishing between a topology change that is detected by a root bridge and a nonroot bridge. `br_topology_change_acknowledge` acknowledges the reception of a TCN by transmitting a configuration BPDU with the TCA flag set. `br_topology_change_acknowledged` stops the TCN timer.

`br_record_config_information`
`br_record_config_timeout_values`

> Given a bridge port and an ingress configuration BPDU, `br_record_config_information` records the priority vector of the BPDU on the port's `net_bridge_port` data structure and restarts the message age timer, and `br_record_config_timeout_values` records the timer configuration that is in the BPDU (see Figure 15-8 in Chapter 15).

`br_get_port`

> Given a bridge device and a port number, returns the associated `net_bridge_port` structure.

Bridge IDs and Port IDs

We saw in the section "Bridge and Port IDs" in Chapter 15 how bridge IDs and port IDs are defined. While the priority component of both IDs is assigned a default value that can be overridden by the system administrator, the MAC address component of the bridge ID and the port number component of the port ID are initialized by the kernel as follows:

Bridge MAC address

> The lowest MAC address among the ones configured on the enslaved devices is selected. The selection is done with `br_stp_recalculate_bridge_id` anytime a new bridge port is created or deleted, and when an enslaved device changes its MAC address (see the section "netdevice Notification Chain").

Port number

> The first number in the range 1–`BR_MAX_PORTS` that is not already in use is selected. The selection is done with `find_portno` when the bridge port is created (see the section "Adding Ports to a Bridge").

Enabling the Spanning Tree Protocol on a Bridge Device

You will see in Chapter 17 how the STP can be turned on and off for each bridge device. The stp_enabled field of the port's net_bridge structure indicates whether the bridge device is enabled.

When the STP is not in use, most of the data structures listed in the section "Important Data Structures" include fields that are not needed, including timers. In addition, no BPDUs are transmitted and no ingress BPDUs are processed.

You would probably expect that when a bridge is created with STP disabled, only the right fields and timers would be initialized, and that when stp_enabled is set to enable STP later, the necessary additional fields and timers would be initialized and started. However, Linux behaves differently.

When a bridge device or port is initialized, all its fields (including those used by STP) are initialized, regardless of whether STP is enabled. The Hello timer, which is used by STP on root bridges to transmit BPDUs, is also started. This way, if STP is enabled later, all data structures will be ready to go.

Every time the Hello timer expires, according to STP, a bridge is supposed to transmit BPDUs out of its designated ports. Because a bridge's timer runs regardless of whether STP is enabled, the transmit routine always checks the value of stp_enabled and returns immediately when the field says STP is disabled. As soon as STP is enabled, by setting stp_enabled, BPDU transmissions start right away. On a system with few bridge devices, to have a timer that expires regularly to do nothing is not a big waste of resources, but should be avoided anyway. On a system with quite a few bridge instances, having the Hello timer run when it is not needed can be a significant waste of CPU time.

Processing Ingress BPDUs

Ingress BPDUs are passed to br_stp_handle_bpdu (Figure 16-15), which updates the forwarding database and hands them to the right routine based on its type, or discards them when any of the following conditions is met:

- The frame is truncated.
- Either the bridge device or the bridge port that received the frame is disabled.
- The STP is disabled on the bridge device. This case is uncommon because br_handle_frame does not hand BPDUs to br_stp_handle_bpdu when STP is disabled on the bridge device (see the section "Data Frames Versus BPDUs").
- The bridge does not know how to interpret the BPDU message. Because the Linux kernel implements only the IEEE 802.1D STP, it accepts only configuration and TCN BPDUs. Any other BPDU type is discarded.

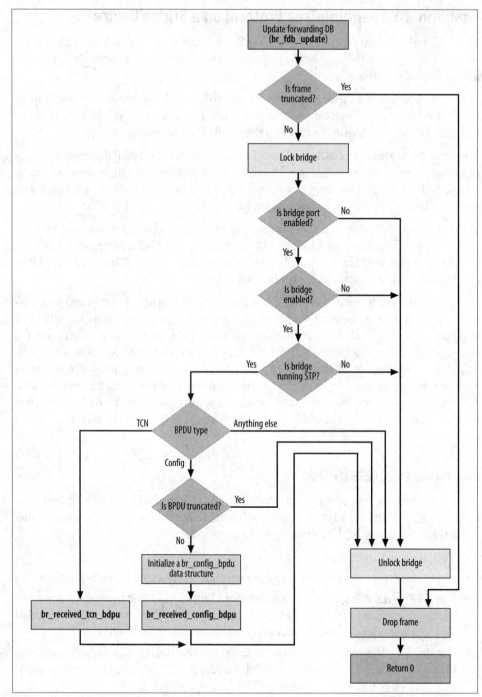

Figure 16-15. br_stp_handle_bpdu function

`br_received_config_bpdu` processes configuration BPDUs according to the logic described in the section "Transmitting Configuration BPDUs" in Chapter 15.

`br_received_tcn_bpdu` processes TCN BPDUs according to the logic described in the section "Letting All Bridges Know About a Topology Change" in Chapter 15.

Note that BPDU processing for any bridge is serialized with the bridge lock: different CPUs cannot process BPDUs concurrently for the same bridge.

Transmitting BPDUs

We saw when configuration and TCN BPDUs are transmitted in the sections "Transmitting Configuration BPDUs" and "Letting All Bridges Know About a Topology Change" in Chapter 15. Here are the transmitting routines:

`br_transmit_config`
> Transmits a configuration BPDU according to the logic in the section "Transmitting Configuration BPDUs" in Chapter 15."

`br_transmit_tcn`
> Transmits a TCN BPDU.

`br_reply`
> Replies to an ingress configuration BPDU with another configuration BPDU. It is a simple wrapper around `br_transmit_config`.

All BPDU transmissions go through the `NF_BR_LOCAL_OUT` Netfilter hook, as shown in Figure 16-16.

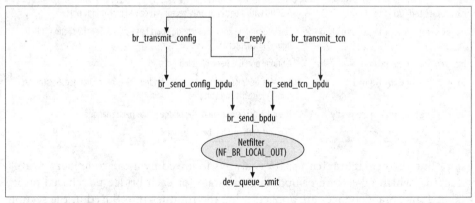

Figure 16-16. Transmit routines

We saw in the section "BPDU Aging" in Chapter 15 that Configuration BPDUs have a limited lifetime enforced through the embedded Message Age field. Here is how nonroot bridges update that field before relaying the BPDU.

When a configuration BPDU is received, br_stp_handle_bpdu saves the Message Age field of the BPDU in a local variable. When br_transmit_config is called to transmit a BPDU out, it updates the Message Age field, adding the amount of time that passed since br_stp_handle_bpdu received the original frame. Because the Message Age timer is expressed in multiples of 1/256th of a second, but the unit of time the kernel manages better is ticks, br_stp_handle_bpdu converts the message age to ticks when saving it. br_transmit_config later computes the elapsed time in ticks, but converts the result back into units of 1/256th of a second so that it can write it to the BPDU. The conversions are made with br_get_tick and br_set_tick.

Configuration Updates

We saw in Chapter 15 how the system administrator can use configuration parameters to affect the topology to which the STP will converge. We also saw how the selection of role and state for a bridge port depends on the current knowledge of the bridge and the information received with ingress configuration BPDUs, in particular the priority vector component (see Figure 15-8 in Chapter 15). Finally, we saw in the section "Defining the Active Topology" in Chapter 15 the events that may trigger a configuration update on a bridge, and what a configuration update consists of.

The routine that takes care of configuration updates is br_configuration_update. Table 16-1 shows where and when that routine is invoked.

Table 16-1. Routines that trigger a configuration update

Where	When
br_received_config_bpdu	A BPDU with a better priority vector is received on a bridge port.
br_message_age_timer_expired	The information known to a bridge port has expired. See the section "BPDU Aging" in Chapter 15.
br_stp_disable_port	A bridge port has been disabled.
br_stp_change_bridge_id	The MAC address component of the bridge ID has been changed. See the section "Bridge IDs and Port IDs."
br_stp_set_bridge_priority	The priority component of the bridge ID has been changed.
br_stp_set_path_cost	The port path cost has been changed.

Each call to br_configuration_update is always followed by a call to br_port_state_selection, which takes care of updating the state for each bridge port based on its assigned role. State changes are applied using the routines introduced in the section "Changing State on a Bridge Port."

In the section "Handling Configuration Changes" in Chapter 17, you can find the user commands that lead to the execution of some of the routines in Table 16-1.

Root Bridge Selection

We saw in the section "Root Bridge Selection" in Chapter 15 how the root bridge is selected. When a bridge is first enabled, it believes it is the root bridge. Thereafter, based on the information received with ingress configuration BPDUs and the configuration applied by the system administrator, the root bridge status can change.

Figure 16-17 shows how events that can change the root status of a bridge do the job.

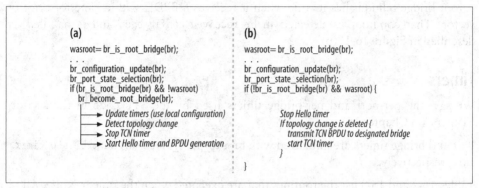

Figure 16-17. (a) Becoming the root bridge; (b)giving up the root bridge role

Becoming the root bridge

The routines that process events that can make a nonroot bridge become the root bridge follow the scheme in Figure 16-17(a): first the root status is saved, and then port roles and states are updated. If this update makes the bridge become the root bridge, the required actions are applied, such as starting and stopping the right timers.

Here are the routines that trigger a configuration update and that may elect a non-root bridge as the new root bridge:

`br_stp_change_bridge_id`
`br_stp_set_bridge_priority`

> These are called when the bridge's MAC address and the bridge's priority are changed, respectively. Because these are the two fields of which bridge IDs are composed, and because the election of the root bridge is based on the bridge ID, any change in them may change the root bridge.

`br_stp_disable_port`

> When you disable the only port that a bridge can use to reach the current root bridge, the spanning tree is partitioned and a new root bridge has to be selected on the partition the current bridge is part of. This is why most of the bridges in the examples in Chapter 15 have redundant links.

`br_message_age_timer_expired`
> When the information a port received by the designated bridge expires (most likely because the designated bridge is not the designated bridge anymore, or because it simply failed), the port is assigned the designated role. Since this is a change in the topology, it is possible that the root bridge changes, too.

Giving up the root bridge role

A root bridge relinquishes its role when it receives a BPDU with a superior priority vector. That condition is detected in `br_received_config_bpdu` and is handled as described in Figure 16-17(b).

Timers

We saw the per-port and per-bridge timers used by the STP code in the section "Timers" in Chapter 15.

Port and bridge timers are initialized with `br_stp_port_timer_init` and `br_stp_timer_init`, respectively.

Tables 16-2 and 16-3 list the routines that are executed when the timers expire. All of these routines, plus the two initialization routines, are defined in *net/bridge/br_stp_timer.c*. All timer handlers run with the bridge lock held.

Table 16-2. Handlers for the STP bridge's timers

Timer	Handler
Hello	`br_hello_timer_expired`
Topology Change Notification	`br_tcn_timer_expired`
Topology Change	`br_topology_change_timer_expired`

Table 16-3. Handlers for the STP port's timers

Timer	Handler
Max Age	`br_message_age_timer_expired`
Forward Delay	`br_forward_delay_timer_expired`
Hold	`br_hold_timer_expired`

Handling Topology Changes

We saw in the section "Topology Changes" in Chapter 15 the events that are considered topology changes. These events are detected by the following routines:

`br_make_blocking`
> Called when the STP has decided to block a forwarding port.

`br_forward_delay_timer_expired`

Called when a port in the BR_STATE_LEARNING state (i.e., not yet forwarding) is moved to the BR_STATE_FORWARDING state.

`br_become_root_bridge`

Called when a nonroot bridge becomes the root bridge. See the section "Becoming the root bridge" for when this routine is invoked.

`br_received_tcn`

Called when a TCN BPDU is received on a bridge port. See the section "Processing Ingress BPDUs" for when this routine is invoked.

netdevice Notification Chain

Because the virtual bridge device is defined as an abstraction on top of real (enslaved) devices, the bridge device is likely to be affected when any of its enslaved devices change status. For this reason, the bridging subsystem's initialization routine, briefly described in the section "Initialization of Bridging Code," registers the br_device_ event callback with the netdevice notification chain. The bridging code is interested only in enslaved devices, so any notification regarding a nonenslaved device is of no interest and does not need attention.

Here is how each received event notification is processed:

NETDEV_CHANGEMTU

The MTU for the bridge device is updated to reflect the minimum MTU among the ones configured on the enslaved devices.

NETDEV_CHANGEADDR

When an enslaved device changes its MAC address, its entry in the forwarding database is updated with br_fdb_changeaddr and the bridge ID is updated with br_stp_recalculate_bridge_id to reflect the rule we saw in the section "Bridge IDs and Port IDs."

NETDEV_CHANGE

This notification can be used for various purposes. The bridging subsystem is interested only in changes to the carrier status.

When an enslaved device loses or detects its carrier status, the associated bridge port is enabled and disabled with br_stp_enable_port and br_stp_disable_port, respectively. When the bridge device this device is associated with is left down by the administrator (i.e., IFF_UP is not set), the notification is ignored.

NETDEV_FEATCHANGE

When features of an enslaved device change, the feature set of the bridge device is updated with br_features_recompute to reflect the set of features common to all of its real devices.

NETDEV_DOWN

When an enslaved device is disabled by the administrator, the associated bridge port must be disabled, too; this is handled by br_stp_disable_port. This is not necessary when the bridge the port is associated with is already down, because that would imply that the bridge port is already down, too.

NETDEV_UP

When an enslaved device is enabled by the administrator (i.e., IFF_UP is set), the associated bridge port is enabled with br_stp_enabled_port if it has the carrier status and the associated bridge device is up, too.

NETDEV_UNREGISTER

When an enslaved device is unregistered, the associated bridge port is removed with br_del_if.

With the exception of NETDEV_UNREGISTER, all events are processed with the bridge lock held.

## CHAPTER 17

Bridging: Miscellaneous Topics

In the previous chapters, we saw how bridging and the STP are implemented, and how they fit into the network stack. In this chapter, we conclude the bridging part of the book with a description of how the subsystem interacts with the user-space commands that configure bridging. I will not describe the commands themselves, because administration is outside the scope of this book.

We will also look at the various files exported in the */sys* directory that can be used to tune bridging. The chapter concludes with a detailed description of the data structures introduced in Chapter 16.

User-Space Configuration Tools

Bridging can be configured with *brctl*, a utility you can download at *http://bridge. sourceforge.net/*. With *brctl*, you can create bridge devices, enslave NICs to bridge devices, and configure bridge parameters and bridge port parameters for the STP.

brctl uses the ioctl interface to talk to the kernel unless the *libsysfs* library is installed, in which case the *sysfs* interface becomes the preferred choice. The *libsysfs* library, which can be downloaded at *http://linux-diag.sourceforge.net/Sysfsutils.html*, provides all the necessary primitives to access and modify the content of the variables exported in */sys*. See the section "Tuning via /sys Filesystem."

In the section "Data Frames Versus BPDUs" in Chapter 16, we introduced ebtables. The user-space configuration tool can be downloaded at *http://ebtables.sourceforge. net*. We will not look at it in this chapter; you can find pretty good documentation on its home page.

Handling Configuration Changes

Table 17-1 lists the *brctl* commands and the callback routines of the kernel bridging code that the configuration layer calls to notify bridging about the changes. For example, when you create the bridge device *br0* with a command like *brctl addbr br0*, the kernel ends up calling br_add_bridge, the routine we described in the section "Creating Bridge Devices and Bridge Ports" in Chapter 16.

Note that some commands do not need to invoke any callback routine. For example, if you change the Hello time with a command such as *brctl sethello br0 3*, the new value will be visible immediately to the bridging code: there is no need for any action to be taken by the STP.

Table 17-1. brctl commands and associated kernel handlers

brctl command	Description	Bridging callback routine
addbr	Create a bridge device.	br_add_bridge
delbr	Delete a bridge device.	br_del_bridge
addif	Create a bridge port.	br_add_if
delif	Delete a bridge port.	br_del_if
setageing	Set the aging time for the addresses in the forwarding database.	N/A
setbridgeprio	Set the bridge priority.	br_stp_set_bridge_priority
setfd	Set the Forward Delay timer.	N/A
sethello	Set the Hello timer.	N/A
setmaxage	Set the Max Age timer.	N/A
setpathcost	Set the port path cost.	br_stp_set_path_cost
setportprio	Set the port priority.	br_stp_set_port_priority
show	Show the bridge device.	N/A
showmacs	Show the forwarding database for a bridge.	N/A
showstp	Show the spanning tree information for a bridge.	N/A
stp	Enable or disable the STP on a bridge.	N/A

The routines in Table 17-1 are used regardless of whether *brctl* talks to the kernel with ioctl commands or via *sysfs*. Regardless of whether a given command requires the invocation of a bridging callback routine, a kernel routine is always called to take care of the *brctl* command.

Old Interface Versus New Interface

Because the kernel code supports both the old and new interfaces, it must be able to handle both versions correctly. Unfortunately, this makes the ioctl code that takes care of bridging configuration commands a little messy. The old interface is completely based on ioctl commands, whereas the new one uses ioctl only for a subset of commands and *sysfs* for the others.

Figures 17(a) and 17(b) show how `ioctl` commands for both interfaces are routed to the right routines for processing (I know, it's not really what you call clear and clean code).

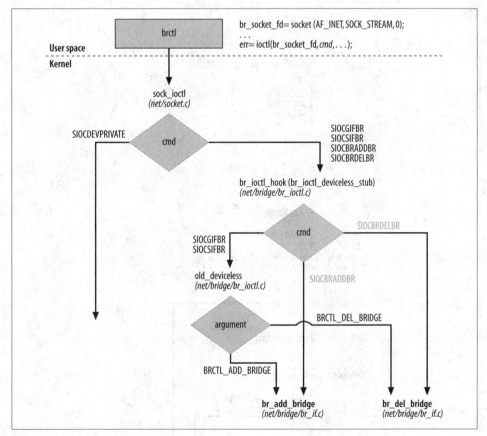

FIgure 17-1(a). Dispatching ioctl commands

The top diamond is the initial dispatching done in `sock_ioctl` in *net/socket.c*. Note that the figure shows only the details needed to route bridging commands, even though some of the routines are shared by other features' commands, too. The commands with a lighter color are the ones used by the new interface.

One detail worth mentioning is that `br_ioctl_deviceless_stub` tries to load the bridge kernel module if it is not already in memory.

The next two sections offer some more details on the two interfaces.

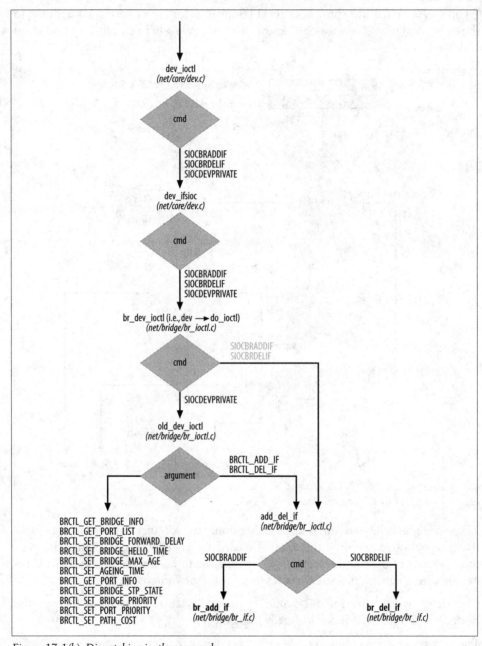

Figure 17-1(b). Dispatching ioctl commands

Creating Bridge Devices and Bridge Ports

I would divide *brctl* commands into two classes: those used to create and delete bridge devices and bridge ports, and those used to configure or dump the configuration of bridge devices and bridge ports (including details on the STP).

Both the old and the new interfaces use `ioctl` commands to implement the first class of commands. The exact `ioctl` command codes used by the old and new interfaces are listed in Table 17-2.

Table 17-2. ioctl commands used for creating bridge devices and ports

brctl command	Old interface (ioctl command, argument)	New interface (ioctl command)
addbr	SIOCSIFBR, BRCTL_ADD_BRIDGE	SIOCBRADDBR
delbr	SIOCSIFBR, BRCTL_DEL_BRIDGE	SIOCBRDELBR
addif	SIOCDEVPRIVATE, BRCTL_ADD_IF	SIOCBRADDIF
delif	SIOCDEVPRIVATE, BRCTL_DEL_IF	SIOCBRDELIF

Note that the old interface needs to pass an argument with the `ioctl` command to identify the precise *brctl* command, whereas for the new interface the `ioctl` command is sufficient.

Configuring Bridge Devices and Ports

The second class of commands is implemented differently in the old and new interfaces: the old interface uses `ioctl` commands, and the new interface uses *sysfs*.

The exact `ioctl` command codes used by the old interface are listed in Table 17-3.

Table 17-3. ioctl commands used by the old interface for configuring bridge devices and ports

brctl command	ioctl command, argument
setageing	SIOCDEVPRIVATE, BRCTL_SET_AGEING_TIME
setbridgeprio	SIOCDEVPRIVATE, BRCTL_SET_BRIDGE_PRIORITY
setfd	SIOCDEVPRIVATE, BRCTL_SET_FORWARD_DELAY
sethello	SIOCDEVPRIVATE, BRCTL_SET_HELLO_TIME
setmaxage	SIOCDEVPRIVATE, BRCTL_SET_MAX_AGE
setpathcost	SIOCDEVPRIVATE, BRCTL_SET_PATH_COST
setportprio	SIOCDEVPRIVATE, BRCTL_SET_PORT_PRIORITY[a]
show	SIOCDEVPRIVATE, BRCTL_GET_BRIDGE_INFO
showmacs	SIOCDEVPRIVATE, BRCTL_GET_FDB_ENTRIES
showstp	SIOCDEVPRIVATE, BRCTL_SET_BRIDGE_INFO
stp	SIOCDEVPRIVATE, BRCTL_SET_BRIDGE_STP_STATE

[a] Version 1.0.6 of *brctl* uses BRCTL_SET_PATH_COST rather than BRCTL_SET_PORT_PRIORITY. This is likely to be a cut-and-paste error.

Note that all *brctl* commands use the SIOCDEVPRIVATE command (even though its use is pretty much deprecated in Linux) and an argument that identifies the exact operation.

The *sysfs*-based configuration simply identifies the right file in */sys* and writes to it using the *libsysfs* library. The operations in Table 17-2 cannot be implemented via *sysfs* because there is no file in its hierarchy for them.

Tuning via /proc Filesystem

The generic bridging code does not create any file in the */proc* filesystem. The firewall bridging extension, however, creates a few files in */proc/sys/net/bridge/* that can be used to make core routines in *net/bridge/br_netfilter.c* return without processing the buffer they receive as input. These files are created by br_netfilter_init, which is called by br_init when the bridging code gets initialized (see *net/bridge/br_netfilter.c*).

Tuning via /sys Filesystem

As I said in the section "User-Space Configuration Tools," *brctl* can configure bridge and STP parameters via the *sysfs* interface. Before seeing how the kernel processes commands from *brctl*, let's see how the information in */sys* is organized.

The kernel creates a directory in */sys/class/net* for each registered network device. This directory is used to export both read-only and read-write parameters that apply to network devices in general. Bridge devices, which are assigned a directory as any other network device, include two special subdirectories in their directory: *bridge* and *brif*. The first exports bridge parameters, and the second includes a soft (symbolic) link to the directory of each enslaved device—that is, each bridge port. Figure 17-2 shows an example of a system with two Ethernet devices, *eth0* and *eth1*, where the admin has created one bridge device, *br0*, and enslaved both *eth0* and *eth1* to *br0*.

The *br0* directory includes another bridge-specific file: *brforward*. This is used to export the bridge forwarding database (in binary format). You can dump it with the *brctl showmacs* command.

The files in the *bridge* directories are fields of the net_bridge data structure, and the files in the *brport* directories are fields of the net_bridge_port data structure.[*]

The bridge device directory (*br0* in the previous example) is populated with bridge parameters and directories by br_sysfs_addbr when the bridge device is created (see

---

[*] change_ack is a shortcut for topology_change_ack.

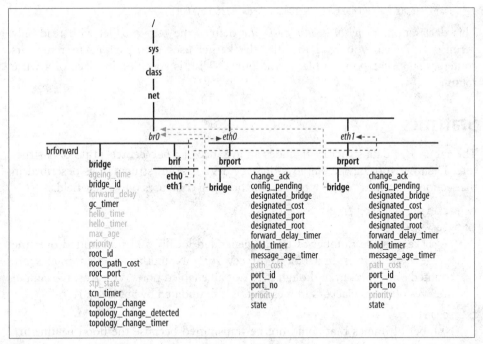

Figure 17-2. Example of bridge information exported with sysfs

the section "Creating a New Bridge Device" in Chapter 16). When a device is enslaved, its directory (*eth0* and *eth1* in the previous example) is populated with br_sys_addif. The latter also populates the bridge's *brif* directory.

All files in Figure 17-2 are read-only, with the exceptions of those with a lighter color, which are writable, too. The writable ones are, for example, those used by *brctl* to configure bridge and bridge port parameters via *libsysfs*.

The kernel code that interacts with the files in the bridge device directories is in *net/bridge/br_sysfs_br.c*, and the code that interact with the files in the bridge port devices (i.e., the enslaved devices) is in *net/bridge/br_sysfs_if.c*.

The code may look complex at first glance, but it is actually pretty simple and well organized. For each file in the *bridge* and *brport* directories (each bridge or port attribute) that is created, the code defines what routines to invoke when a read or write request is issued on the file with an instance of a special macro. Let's skip the details on how those macros are put into a table and used by the br_sysfs_add*xxx* routines introduced earlier, and see a couple of examples of their use.

```
static CLASS_DEV_ATTR(max_age, S_IURGO | S_IWUSR, show_max_age, store_max_age)
```

This declaration in *net/bridge/br_sysfs_br.c* uses the CLASS_DEV_ATTR macro to define the *max_age* file with read-write permissions (write permissions for the superuser only). When you read the file, the kernel uses show_max_age to return its contents, and when you write to the file, the kernel carries out the change with store_max_age.

```
static BRPORT_ATTR(port_no, S_IURGO, show_port_no, NULL)
```

This declaration in *net/bridge/br_sysfs_if.c* defines the *port_no* file, with read-only permission. When you read the file, the kernel uses `show_port_no` to return its contents. Since the *port_no* file is read-only, NULL is specified in place of a write routine.

Statistics

The `net_bridge` data structure includes an instance of a `net_device_stats` data structure. Each network device employs one `net_device_stats` structure, as described in the section "Statistics" in Chapter 12. The bridging code uses only a few fields:

`tx_packets`
`tx_bytes`
> `tx_packets` is the number of frames generated locally and transmitted over the bridge device. It is updated by `br_dev_xmit`. Note that flooded frames are counted only once, even though they exit all enabled ports. `tx_bytes`, the sum of the sizes of the `tx_packets` frames sent, is also updated by `br_dev_xmit`.

`tx_dropped`
> Number of frames that could not be transmitted because the flood routine `br_flood` failed to allocate a buffer.

`rx_packets`
`rx_bytes`
> `rx_packets` is incremented by `br_pass_frame_up` each time an ingress frame received on the bridge device is delivered locally. rx_bytes is the counterpart of `tx_bytes`.

All of the routines referenced here are described in Chapter 16.

No statistics are kept by the STP.

Data Structures Featured in This Part of the Book

The section "Important Data Structures" in Chapter 16 provided a brief overview of the data structures used by the bridging code. This section provides a field-by-field description of them. The trivial ones, such as `mac_addr` and `br_config_bpdu`, do not need dedicated sections.

bridge_id Structure

We saw in the section "Bridge and Port IDs" in Chapter 15 that bridge IDs have two components, the priority and the address:

`unsigned char prio[2]`
> Bridge priority

unsigned char addr[6]
> Bridge MAC address

Note that the data structure definition does not reflect the changes introduced by 802.1t.

net_bridge_fdb_entry Structure

These are the fields that are used to define each entry in the forwarding database:

struct hlist_node list
> Pointer used to link the data structure into the bucket's list of colliding elements.

struct net_bridge_port *dst
> Bridge port.

struct rcu_head rcu
> Used when removing the data structure using the read-copy-update (RCU) scheme (see br_fdb_put in *net/bridge/br_fdb.c*).

atomic_t use_count
> Reference count. See the section "Lookups" in Chapter 30.

unsigned long ageing_timer
> Aging timer. Different parts of the kernel spell this as *aging* or *ageing*. See the section "Aging" in Chapter 16.

mac_addr addr
> MAC address. This is the key field used by the lookup routines.

unsigned char is_local
> When this flag is 1, the MAC address addr is configured on a local device.

unsigned char is_static
> When this flag is 1, the MAC address addr is static and it does not expire. All local addresses (i.e., those where is_local is 1) are static, too.

net_bridge_port Structure

This first block of fields is used regardless of whether the STP is used:

struct net_bridge *br
struct net_device *dev
> br is the bridge device, and dev is the enslaved device. See Figure 16-6 in Chapter 16.

struct list_head list
> Pointer used to link the data structure into the bucket's list of colliding elements.

u8 state
> Port state. Valid values are listed in *include/linux/if_bridge.h* with the BR_STATE_*XXX* enumeration list.

```
struct kobject kobj
```
Used by the generic device infrastructure. This field plays a central role in making all that we saw in the section "Tuning via /sys Filesystem" possible.

```
struct rcu_head rcu
```
Used to safely destroy the structure using the RCU scheme (see del_nbp in *net/bridge/br_if.c*).

This second block is used only when the STP is enabled:

```
u8 priority
```
Port priority.

```
u16 port_no
```
Port number.

```
port_id port_id
```
Port ID. This is computed with br_make_port_id as a combination of priority and port_no.

```
unsigned char topology_change_ack
```
When this flag is set, the TCA flag must be set on configuration BPDUs transmitted on the port.

```
unsigned char config_pending
```
This flag is 1 when a configuration BPDU is waiting to be transmitted because it was previously held back by the Hold timer.

```
port_id designated_port
bridge_id designated_root
bridge_id designated_bridge
u32 designated_cost
```
The four components of the priority vector from the most recent configuration BPDU received on the port (see Figure 16-8 in Chapter 16). They are updated upon reception of each configuration BPDU with br_record_config_configuration.

```
u32 path_cost
```
Port path cost.

```
struct timer_list forward_delay_timer
struct timer_list hold_timer
struct timer_list message_age_timer
```
Port timers. See the section "Timers" in Chapter 15.

net_bridge Structure

This first block of fields is used regardless of whether the STP is in use:

spinlock_t lock
> Lock used to serialize changes to the net_bridge structure or to one of its ports in port_list. Read-only accesses use the rcu_read_lock and rcu_read_unlock primitives.

struct list_head port_list
> List of bridge ports.

struct net_device *dev
> Bridge device (see Figure 16-6 in Chapter 16).

struct net_device_stats statistics
> Statistics. See the section "Statistics."

spinlock_t hash_lock
struct hlist_head hash[BR_HASH_SIZE]
> hash is the forwarding database. hash_lock is the lock used to serialize read-write accesses to its entries. Read-only accesses use the rcu_read_lock and rcu_read_unlock primitives.

struct list_head age_list
> Not used. This list used to be employed to link together all the entries of the forwarding database in ascending order of most recent use (see Figure 16-6 in Chapter 16). This list was used by the aging algorithm to scan the database for expired entries.

unsigned long ageing_time
> Maximum time an entry can stay in the forwarding database without being used. See the section "Aging" in Chapter 16.

struct kobject ifobj
> Used by the generic device infrastructure. This field plays a central role in making all that we saw in the section "Tuning via /sys Filesystem" possible.

unsigned char stp_enabled
> When this flag is set, the STP is enabled for the bridge.

The next block of fields is used only when the STP is in use. The only exception is forward_delay, which is used regardless. Bridge ports are not assigned the forwarding state as soon as STP is enabled; they use the forward_delay timer to go through the intermediate states.

bridge_id designated_root
> Root bridge's ID.

bridge_id bridge_id
> Bridge ID.

`u32 root_path_cost`

   Cost of the best path to the root bridge.

`unsigned long max_age`
`unsigned long hello_time`
`unsigned long forward_delay`

   Bridge timers. These values are configured on the root bridge and are saved locally by br_record_config_timeout_values with the reception of configuration BPDUs on the root port.

`unsigned long bridge_max_age`
`unsigned long bridge_hello_time`
`unsigned long bridge_forward_delay`

   Bridge timers configured locally. These are used only by the root bridge.

`u16 root_port`

   Port number of the root port.

`unsigned char topology_change`

   This flag is set when the latest configuration BPDU received on the root port had the TC flag set. When topology_change is set, the TC flag must be set on any configuration BPDU transmitted by the bridge. See the section "Example of a Topology Change" in Chapter 15.

`unsigned char topology_change_detected`

   This flag is set when a topology change has been detected. See the section "Topology Changes" in Chapter 15 for the conditions that are considered possible topology changes.

`struct timer_list hello_timer`
`struct timer_list tcn_timer`
`struct timer_list topology_change_timer`

   Bridge timers. See the section "Timers" in Chapter 15.

`struct timer_list gc_timer`

   Garbage collection timer for the forwarding database. See the section "Aging" in Chapter 16.

Functions and Variables Featured in This Part of the Book

Table 17-4 summarizes the main functions, variables, and data structures introduced in Part IV. In the sections "Key Spanning Tree Routines" and "Timers" in Chapter 16, you can find some more.

Table 17-4. Functions, variables, and data structures introduced in Part IV

Name	Description
Functions	
br_init br_deinit	Initialize and clean up the kernel bridging module. See the section "Initialization of Bridging Code" in Chapter 16.
br_fdb_init	Initialize the forwarding database.
br_netfilter_init	Initialize the Netfilter hooks used by the bridging code.
br_stp_timer_init br_stp_port_timer_init	Initialize the bridge and bridge port timers.
br_sysfs_addbr br_sysfs_delbr	Handle the extra files in *sysfs* for bridge devices. See the section "Tuning via /sys Filesystem."
br_sysfs_addif br_sysfs_removeif	Handle the extra files in *sysfs* for bridge ports. See the section "Tuning via /sys Filesystem."
br_add_bridge br_del_bridge	Create and delete a bridge device. See the section "Creating Bridge Devices and Bridge Ports" in Chapter 16.
br_add_if br_del_if	Create and delete a bridge port. See the section "Creating Bridge Devices and Bridge Ports" in Chapter 16.
br_stp_recalculate_bridge	Given a bridge, select the numerically lowest MAC address among the ones configured on the bridge ports (i.e., enslaved devices) and use it to compute the bridge ID.
br_min_mtu	Given a bridge, find the lowest MTU among the ones configured on the bridge ports.
br_stp_enable_bridge br_stp_disable_bridge	Enable and disable a bridge device. See the section "Enabling and disabling a bridge instance" in Chapter 16.
br_stp_enable_port br_stp_disable_port	Enable and disable a bridge port. See the section "Enabling and Disabling a Bridge Port" in Chapter 16.

Table 17-4. Functions, variables, and data structures introduced in Part IV (continued)

Name	Description
`__br_fdb_get` `br_fdb_get`	Look up an entry in the forwarding database. See the section "Lookups" in Chapter 30.

`fdb_create`
`br_fdb_insert`
`bf_fdb_change_addr`
`br_fdb_update`
`br_fdb_cleanup`
	Various routines to manipulate the forwarding database. See the section "Forwarding database" in Chapter 16 and its subsections.

`handle_bridge`
`br_handle_frame`
`br_handle_frame_finish`
`br_stp_handle_bpdu`
`br_forward`
`br_flood`
`br_pass_frame_up`
`br_pass_frame_up_finish`
	Various routines used to handle ingress frames. See the section "Handling Ingress Traffic" in Chapter 16.

`br_received_config_bpdu` `br_received_tcn_bpdu`	Process an ingress configuration and TCN BPDU, respectively. See the section "Processing Ingress BPDUs" in Chapter 16.

`br_transmit_config`
`br_transmit_tcn`
`br_reply`
`br_send_bpdu`
	Various transmission routines. See the section "Transmitting BPDUs" in Chapter 16.

`br_make_blocking` `br_make_forwarding`	`br_make_blocking` blocks a port, and `br_make_forwarding` assigns the forwarding state to a port, allowing it to receive and transmit data traffic.
`br_get_tick` `br_set_tick`	Read and write a time interval, taking care of the conversion between 1/256th of a second (used in the configuration BPDUs) and ticks (used by Linux).
Variables	
`BR_MAX_PORTS`	Maximum number of bridge ports that can be added to a bridge device.
`br_handle_frame_hook`	Function pointer initialized to the routine used in the bridging subsystem to process ingress frames. See Figure 16-11 in Chapter 16.
`br_fdb_cache`	Cache used for the allocation of elements of the forwarding databases.
Data structures	

`struct mac_addr`
`struct bridge_id`
`struct bridge_fdb_entry`
`struct net_bridge_port`
`struct net_bridge`
`struct br_config_bpdu`
	Main data structures used by the bridging code. See the section "Important data structures" in Chapter 16.

Files and Directories Featured in This Part of the Book

Figure 17-3 lists the files and directories referred to in the chapters in Part IV.

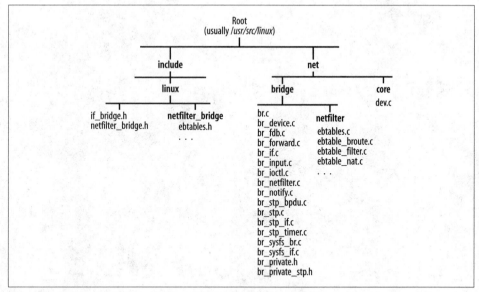

Figure 17-3. Files and directories featured in this part of the book

## PART V

Internet Protocol Version 4 (IPv4)

The Linux kernel supports many Layer three (L3) protocols, such as AppleTalk, DECnet, and IPX, but this book talks just about the one that dominates modern networking: IP. While IPv4 will be described in detail, IPv6 will be only briefly mentioned as needed. I will not spend much time on the theory behind these protocols, with which you should be somewhat familiar, but I will describe the implementation in Linux. I will focus on aspects of the design that are not obvious or that differ substantially from other operating systems. I will also explain the main drawbacks of version 4 of the IP protocol and show how IPv6 tries to address them. Therefore, while there is both some background theory and some code, I expect the reader to be familiar with the basic IP protocol behavior. Here is what is covered in each chapter:

Chapter 18, *Internet Protocol Version 4 (IPv4): Concepts*
    Introduces the major tasks of the IP layer, and the strategies used.

Chapter 19, *Internet Protocol Version 4 (IPv4): Linux Foundations and Features*
    Shows how the IP-layer reception routine processes ingress packets, and how IP options are taken care of.

Chapter 20, *Internet Protocol Version 4 (IPv4): Forwarding and Local Delivery*
    Shows how ingress IP packets are delivered locally to the L4 protocol handler, or are forwarded when the destination IP address does not belong to the local host but the host has enabled forwarding.

Chapter 21, *Internet Protocol Version 4 (IPv4): Transmission*
    Shows how L4 protocols interface to the IP layer to request transmission.

Chapter 22, *Internet Protocol Version 4 (IPv4): Handling Fragmentation*
    Shows how fragmentation and defragmentation are handled.

Chapter 23, *Internet Protocol Version 4 (IPv4): Miscellaneous Topics*
    Shows how configuration tools such as those in the IPROUTE2 package interface to the kernel, shows how the IP header's ID field is initialized on egress packets, and provides a detailed description of the data structures used at the IP layer.

Chapter 24, *Layer Four Protocol and Raw IP Handling*
    Shows how L4 protocols register a handler for ingress traffic.

Chapter 25, *Internet Control Message Protocol (ICMPv4)*
    Describes the implementation of the ICMP protocol.

## CHAPTER 18

Internet Protocol Version 4 (IPv4): Concepts

This chapter explains what the IP protocol is responsible for, and provides a discussion of the IP header fields that support these activities and the impact of these responsibilities on possible implementations. While the chapter discusses some of the choices made in Linux, implementation details are covered in subsequent chapters.

It would be interesting to show how the protocols of the IPsec security suite have been integrated with the IP protocol, but I could not include this topic for lack of space. However, we will sometimes see how the presence of IPsec transformations influences the implementation of core routines.

IP Protocol: The Big Picture

Figure 18-1 shows the important relationships among the components of Linux that handle IPv4. The flow of traffic between major functions is represented by arrows. We will analyze all of these functions in the next few chapters. The figure shows the placement of two subsystems described elsewhere—the Neighboring subsystem and the Traffic Control subsystem—as well as the many hooks where the Netfilter firewalling system can be invoked.[*]

Figure 18-1 is a useful reference when you're examining networking code and wondering whether a particular function is used for input or output, whether it is called during forwarding, and who calls it.

Since the IP layer does not interact directly with the Traffic Control subsystem, that subsystem is left to Part VI. However, in the section "Interface to the Neighboring Subsystem" in Chapter 21, we will see how IP and the Neighboring subsystem interact.

---

[*] The functions used to handle multicast traffic are not included in Figure 18-1 (apart from `ip_mc_output`). The figure includes the main APIs; however, there are others that are used in specific cases. See Chapter 21.

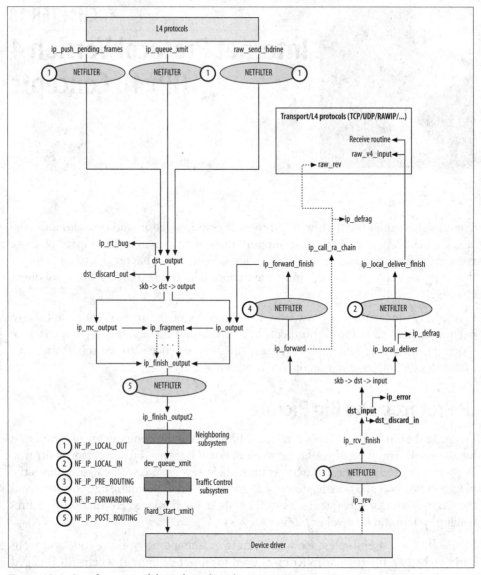

Figure 18-1. Core functions of the IP kernel stack

Among the tasks of the IP protocol are:

Sanity checks

IP datagrams could be discarded immediately upon entering the system, because of an incorrect checksum (that is, transmission has corrupted it), a header field out of range, or other reasons.

Firewalling

As shown in Figure 18-1, the Netfilter firewall subsystem (controlled on the user side by the *iptables* command) can be invoked at many points in the packet's history and can change its destiny. As we will see in Part V, Netfilter can be used at L2 as well.

Handling options

The IP protocol includes a few options that applications can use. Even though the original IP RFC (791) says the implementation of options is mandatory for both hosts and routers, not all of them are actually implemented. Some are universally recognized as obsolete, and others are used only in special cases.

Fragmentation/defragmentation

The len field of the IP header is long enough to allow datagrams up to 64 KB in size, but they almost never reach that limit. In fact, MTU values vary from one part of the network to another depending on the media used for transmission,* so it is quite possible that a packet will be too big for one of the hops along the way. In such cases, the packet has to be split into smaller pieces to be successfully transmitted. Each fragment can be further fragmented before arriving at the destination, which must reassemble the fragments. The use of fragmentation is discouraged nowadays because it introduces problems. We will see them in the section "Packet Fragmentation/Defragmentation."

Receive, transmit, and forward operations

Input packets are handled by reception functions, and output packets by transmission functions. Forwarding is related to transmission, but deals with packets received from other hosts instead of packets generated by higher network layers on the local system.

I briefly introduce the Raw IP protocol in Chapter 24 and IP-over-IP (also called IP tunneling) in Chapter 23.

IP Header

Readers might be familiar with the basic fields of the IP header, but there are a few parameters that are not well known and some others that have changed in meaning over time. Figure 18-2 shows the header, and the text that follows summarizes their purposes:

Version

Version of the protocol. Currently only versions 4 and 6 are implemented. Version 4 is described in this chapter. Version 6 is not covered in this book, although we will sometimes mention how IPv6 differs from IPv4 when this is useful in context.

---

* In Chapter 2, you can find a table with the MTU used by the most common interfaces.

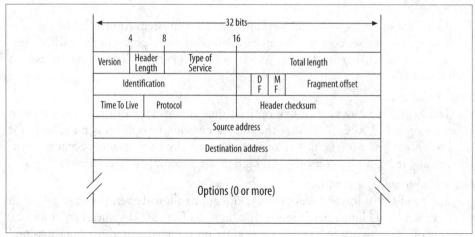

Figure 18-2. IP header

Header Length (IHL)

Length of the header, expressed in units of 32 bits.

Type of Service (TOS)

This 8-bit field is composed of three subfields. I will not go into detail about them because their use is very limited, for many reasons. Originally this field was meant to facilitate Quality of Service (QoS) features by telling routers which criteria were considered most important by the packet's sender: minimum delay, maximum throughput, and so on. The TOS field can still be used in this way, but Internet researchers found it too vague and have decided to implement QoS differently. Therefore, they introduced the Differentiated Services* (diffserv) model, changing the structure and meaning of the field. The new meaning associated with the diffserv model is shown in Figure 18-3(b). DSCP stands for Diff-Serv Code Point. Each possible value has a unique and specific meaning for how the packet should be treated. The two formerly unused bits of the TOS field are now used by the Explicit Congestion Notification (ECN) feature, as shown in Figure 18-3(c). Most of the code used to read and manipulate the ECN flags in the IP and TCP headers is located in *include/net/inet_ecn.h* and *include/net/tcp_ecn.h*. Refer to the RFCs in Figure 18-3 for more detail.

Total Length

Length of the packet, including the header, expressed in bytes.

Identification

Identifier of the packet. As we will see later in this chapter, this field plays a central role in the handling of fragments.

---

* You can find more information about diffserv on the IETF web site, *http://www.ietf.org/html.charters/OLD/diffserv-charter.html*. (For some reasons, the URL with the OLD keyword is more up-to-date than the one without it.)

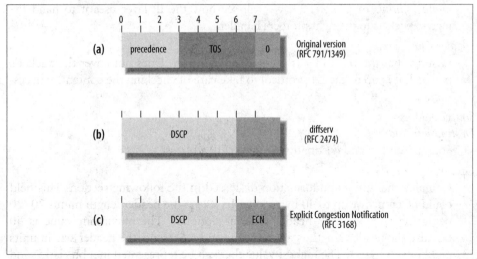

Figure 18-3. Old and new meanings of the TOS field of the IP header

DF (Don't Fragment)
MF (More Fragments)
Fragment Offset

These three fields, together with Identification, are used by the fragmentation/defragmentation feature of the IP protocol. See the section "Packet Fragmentation/Defragmentation."

Time To Live (TTL)

This field is supposed to represent the number of seconds since the IP packet was transmitted, after which it is to be discarded if it has not reached the final destination. However, because routers decrement it by one, regardless of the time they take to forward it, it actually represents a simple hop count. Each router is supposed to decrement this field when it forwards a packet, and the packet is supposed to be dropped when the TTL reaches zero. Its initial value (set by the sender) in theory depends on the type of payload carried. The more sensitive the payload is to end-to-end delay, the smaller the TTL value should be. Most of the time, however, a default value of 64 is used (see *include/linux/ip.h*).[*] Packets are not dropped silently: the source is warned through an Internet Control Message Protocol (ICMP) message.

Protocol

This field represents the protocol identifier of the higher layer (L4). The file */etc/protocols*[†] contains a partial list. You can find more details at *http://www.iana.org/*

---

[*] The default value actually depends on whether the packet is multicast. Multicast IP packets have a default TTL of 1 (which can be changed with the setsockopt system call).

[†] Note that this file is not part of the kernel, but is included in all Linux distributions.

numbers.html. In Chapter 24, we will see how the IP layer uses it to hand the ingress packets to the right protocol handler.

Header Checksum

Ensures that the IP header is accurate after transit. Does not cover the packet's payload; it is up to the L4 protocol to take care of checking the content, if necessary.

Source Address
Destination Address

Source (sender) and destination (receiver) IP addresses.

Options

Contains the optional information discussed in the following section. This field could be empty or up to 40 bytes long. Its size is the header length minus 20 (20 being the size of an IP header without options). The maximum value is 40 because the header length is a 4-bit value and represents the header size in units of 32 bits (4 bytes). The highest value that can be represented in 4 bits is 15, and 15 times 4 bytes is 60 bytes. Since 20 bytes are taken up by the basic IP header, only 40 are left for the options.

IP Options

As described earlier in this chapter, network stacks are required to implement a number of IP options that applications can use if they choose to. To accommodate information related to options, the basic 20-byte IP header is extended up to another 40 bytes.

Most IP options are used very rarely, and in particular contexts. Different options can be combined into the same IP packet. However, with the exception of the "End of Option List" and "No Operation" options, there can be at most one instance of each option in a header. The presence of options also influences the fragmentation/defragmentation process, as we will see in the section "Packet Fragmentation/Defragmentation."

Some options are very simple and can be specified by a single byte; more complex options require a more flexible format and are called *multibyte options*.

Figure 18-4 shows the format of both kinds of options. Note that the option data in a multibyte option does not start at a 32-bit boundary.

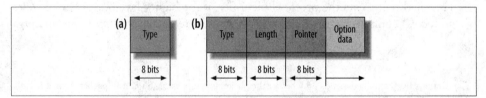

Figure 18-4. (a) Single IP option format; (b) multibyte IP option format

Each option has an 8-bit field named type that can be further decomposed into three subfields, shown in Figure 18-5. The most common values for type are listed in Table 18-1.* It shows the symbols used for options by the Linux kernel and how the value of the symbol breaks down into the three fields in Figure 18-5.

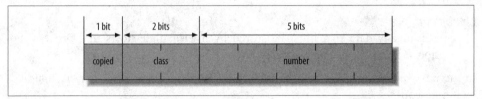

Figure 18-5. Format of the type field of the IP options

When copied is set, the IP layer must copy the option into each fragment when the packet needs fragmentation. class classifies the option according to four criteria; these can be used to filter packets based on IP options, or to apply different QoS parameters to these packets.

Table 18-1. Values of the subcodes of the IP option type field

Option	Symbol used in kernel source code	Number	Copied	Class Control(00) / Reserved(01) / Measurement(10) / Reserved(11)
End of Options List	IPOPT_END	0	0	Control
No Operation	IPOPT_NOOP	1	0	Control
Security	IPOPT_SEC	2	1	Control
Loose Source and Record Route	IPOPT_LSRR	3	1	Control
Timestamp	IPOPT_TIMESTAMP	4	0	Measurement
Record Route	IPOPT_RR	7	0	Control
Stream ID	IPOPT_SID	8	1	Control
Strict Source and Record Route	IPOPT_SSRR	9	1	Control
Router Alert	IPOPT_RA	20	1	Control

In *include/linux/ip.h*, you can find the definitions of the option types, plus some macros that can be used to access their subfields. For instance, the following three macros can be used to extract the number, copied, and class portions, respectively: IPOPT_ NUMBER, IPOTP_COPIED,† and IPOPT_CLASS.

The additional fields shown in Figure 18-4(b), used by multibyte options, are:

Length
    Length of the option in octects, including type and length.

---

* For a more detailed list, you can refer to *http://www.iana.org/assignments/ip-parameters*.

† In the section "IP Options" in Chapter 19, we will see how ip_forward_options uses IPOPT_COPIED.

Pointer

> An offset measured from the beginning of the option and used in various ways as hosts process the option along the way. You will see some examples in upcoming sections. The numbering starts from 1, not 0 (i.e., 1 identifies the location of the type field).

Option data

> Space for any data that must be stored by intermediate hosts that process the option. You will see some examples later.

In the next subsections, we will see how the options in Table 18-1 that are handled by Linux work.

"End of Option List" and "No Operation" Options

The size of the IP header without options is 20 bytes. When the size of the IP options is not a multiple of 4 bytes, the sender pads the IP header with the IPOPT_END option to align it to a 4-byte boundary. This is necessary because the Header Length field of the IP header is expressed in multiples of 4 bytes.

The IPOPT_NOOP option can be used for padding between options, for example, to align the subsequent IP option to a given boundary. In Chapter 19, we will see that Linux uses it also as a convenient way to delete options from an IP header.

Source Route Option

Source routing allows a sender to specify the path that a packet takes to its recipient. A type of source routing is available at both L2 and L3; I'll discuss the L3 implementation here.

Source Routing is a multibyte option in which the source node lists IP addresses to be used on subsequent hops. Of course, if one of the routers in the list goes down, the source-routed packet will not be able to benefit from any dynamic rerouting done on routing protocols. Usually, when a router goes down, the higher-level protocols compute a new source route and resend the packet. Occasionally, they are not allowed to specify a new route, perhaps for security reasons.

Source routing can be of two types: strict and loose. In strict source routing, the sender has to list the IP addresses of every router along the path, and no changes can be made along the way. In loose source routing, one of the intermediate routers can use another router, not specified in the list, as a way to get to the next router in the list. However, all of the routers specified by the sender must still be used in the order specified.

For instance, consider the networks and routers in Figure 18-6. Suppose Host X wants to send a packet to Host Y using the Strict Source Routing option. In this case, Host X must specify all the intermediate router addresses. An example of a strict source route would be R_1 R_2 R_3 Host Y. With loose source routing, something such as R_1 R_3 would be sufficient. The use of nonadjacent routers (i.e., R_1 and R_3 in this example) is allowed and comes with advantages: if R_2 fails, R_2b can be used instead, and vice versa.

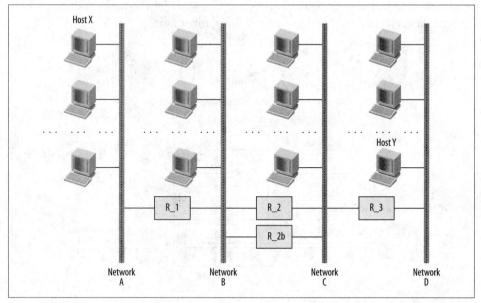

Figure 18-6. Example of IP source routing

Record Route Option

The purpose of this option is to ask the routers along the way between source and destination to store the IP addresses of the outgoing interfaces they use to forward the packet. Because of limited space in the header, only nine addresses at most can be stored (and even fewer, if the header contains other options). Therefore, the packet arrives with the first nine[*] addresses stored in the option; the receiver has no way of knowing what routers were used after that. Since this option makes the header (and therefore the IP packet) grow along the way, and since other options may be present in the header, the sender is supposed to reserve the space that will be used to store the addresses. If the reserved space becomes full before the packet gets to its destination, the additional addresses are not added to the list even if the maximum size of an IP header would permit it. No errors (ICMP messages) are generated when there is no room to store a new address. For obvious reasons, the sender is

[*] (40–3)/4=9, where 40 is the maximum size of the IP options, 3 is the size of the options header, and 4 is the size of an IPv4 address.

supposed to reserve an amount of space that is a multiple of 4 bytes (the size of an IP address).*

Figure 18-7 shows how the IP header portion dedicated to the option changes hop by hop. As each router fills its address, it also updates the pointer field to indicate the end of the data in the option. The offsets at the bottom of the figure start from 1 so that you can compare them to the value of the pointer field.

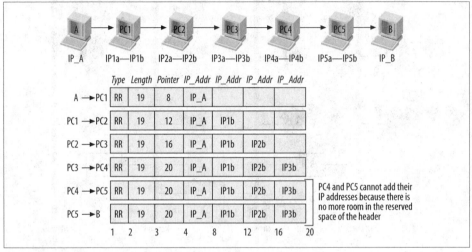

Figure 18-7. Example of Record Route option

Timestamp Option

This option is the most complicated one because it contains suboptions and, unlike the Record Route option, it handles overflows. To manage those two additional concepts, it needs an additional byte in its header, as shown in Figure 18-8.

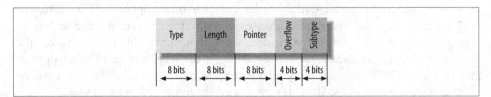

Figure 18-8. IP Timestamp option header

The first three bytes have the same meaning as in the other options: type, length, and pointer. The fourth byte is actually split into two fields of four bits each. The

---

* The value of length is not an exact multiple of 4 because the option header (type, length, and pointer) is 3 bytes long. This means that the 32-bit IP addresses are inconveniently split across 32-bit word boundaries.

rightmost four bits (the least significant ones) represent a subcommand code that can change the effect of the option. Its possible values are:

RECORD TIMESTAMPS
> Each router records the time at which it received the packet.

RECORD ADDRESSES AND TIMESTAMPS
> Similar to the previous subcommand, but the IP address of the receiving interface is saved, too.

RECORD TIMESTAMPS ONLY AT THE PRESPECIFIED SYSTEMS
> Each router records the time at which it received the packet (as with RECORD TIMESTAMPS), but only at specific IP addresses selected by the sender.

In all three cases, the time is expressed in milliseconds (in a 32-bit variable) since midnight UTC of the current day.*

The other four bits represent what is called the overflow field. Because the TIMESTAMP option is used to record information along the route, and because the space available in the IP header for that purpose is limited to 40 bytes, there can be cases where a router is unable to record information for lack of space. While the Record Route option processing simply ignores that case, leaving the receiver ignorant of how many times it happened, the TIMESTAMP option increments the overflow field every time it happens. Unfortunately, overflow is a 4-bit field and therefore can have a maximum value of 15: in modern networks, it itself may easily overflow. When that happens, the router that experiences the overflow has to return an ICMP parameter error message back to the original sender.

While the first two suboptions are similar (they differ only in what to save on each hop), the third suboption is slightly different and deserves a few more words. The packet's original sender lists the IP addresses in which it is interested, following each with four bytes of space. At each hop, the option's pointer field indicates the offset of the next 4-byte space. Each router that appears in the address list fills in the appropriate space with a timestamp and updates the pointer field. See Figure 18-9. The underlined hosts in the sequence at the top of the figure are the hosts that add the timestamps. The offsets at the bottom of the figure start from 1 so that you can compare them to the value of the pointer field.

Router Alert Option

This option was added to the IP protocol definition in 1995 and is described in RFC 2113. It marks packets that require special handling beyond simply looking at the destination address and forwarding the packet. For instance, the Resource Reservation Protocol (RSVP), which attempts to create better QoS for a stream of packets,

---

* UTC stands for Universal Time Clock, also called GMT (Greenwich Mean Time).

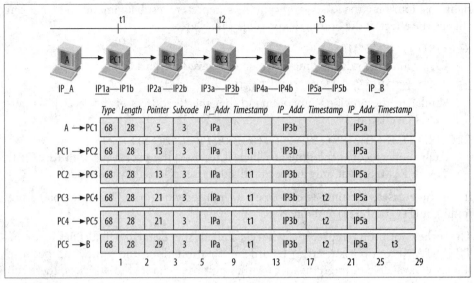

	Type	Length	Pointer	Subcode	IP_Addr	Timestamp	IP_Addr	Timestamp	IP_Addr	Timestamp
A →PC1	68	28	5	3	IPa		IP3b		IP5a	
PC1 →PC2	68	28	13	3	IPa	t1	IP3b		IP5a	
PC2 →PC3	68	28	13	3	IPa	t1	IP3b		IP5a	
PC3 →PC4	68	28	21	3	IPa	t1	IP3b	t2	IP5a	
PC4 →PC5	68	28	21	3	IPa	t1	IP3b	t2	IP5a	
PC5 →B	68	28	29	3	IPa	t1	IP3b	t2	IP5a	t3

Figure 18-9. Example of storing the Timestamp option for pre-specified systems

uses this option to tell routers that it must treat the packets in that stream in a special way. Right now, the last two bytes have only one assigned value, zero. This simply means that the router should examine the packet. Packets carrying other values are illegal and should be discarded, generating an ICMP error message to the source that generated them.

Packet Fragmentation/Defragmentation

Packet fragmentation and defragmentation is one of the main jobs of the IP protocol. The IP protocol defines the maximum size of a packet as 64 KB, which comes from the fact that the len field of the header, which represents the size of the packet in bytes, is a 16-bit value. However, not many interface types can send packets of a size up to 64 KB. This means that when the IP layer needs to transmit a packet whose size is bigger than the MTU of the egress interface, it needs to split the packet into smaller pieces. We will see later in this chapter that the MTU used is not necessarily the one associated to the egress's device; it could be, for instance, the one associated with the routing table entry used to route the packet. The latter would depend on several factors, one of which is the egress device's MTU.

Regardless of how the MTU is computed, the fragmentation process creates a series of equal-size fragments, as shown in Figure 18-10. The MF and OFFSET fields shown in the picture are described later in this section. If the MTU does not divide the original size of the packet exactly, the final fragment is smaller than the others.

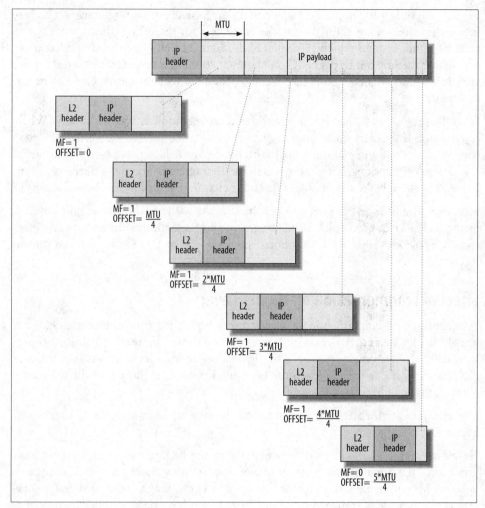

Figure 18-10. IP packet fragmentation

A fragmented IP packet is normally defragmented by the destination host, but intermediate devices that need to look at the entire IP packet may have to defragment it, too. Two examples of such devices are firewalls and Network Address Translation (NAT) routers.

Some time ago, it was an acceptable solution for the receiver to allocate a buffer the size of the original IP packet and put fragments there as they arrived. In fact, the receiver might just allocate a buffer of the maximum possible size, because the size of the original IP packet was known only after receiving the last fragment. That simple approach is now avoided because it wastes memory, and a malicious attack could bring a router to its knees just by sending a burst of very small fragments that lie about their original size.

Because every IP packet can be fragmented, and because each fragment can be further fragmented along the path for the same reason, there must be a way for the receiver to understand which IP packet each fragment belongs to, and at what position inside the original IP packet each fragment should be placed. The receiver must also be told the original size of the IP packet to know when it has received all of the fragments.

Several other aspects have to be considered to accomplish fragmentation. When copying the IP header of the original packet into its fragments, the kernel does not copy all of the options, but only those with the copied field set, as described earlier in the section "IP Options." However, when the IP fragments are merged, the resulting IP packet will look like the original one and therefore include all the options again.

Moreover, the IP checksum covers only the IP header (the payload is usually covered by the higher-layer protocols). When fragments are created, the headers are all different, so a checksum has to be computed for each one of them, and checked on the receiving side.

Effect of Fragmentation on Higher Layers

Fragmenting and defragmenting a packet takes both CPU time and memory. For a heavily loaded server, the extra resources involved may be quite significant. Fragmentation also introduces overhead in the bandwidth used for transmission, because each fragment has to contain both the L2 and L3 headers. If the size of the fragments is small, that overhead can be significant.

Higher layers are theoretically unaware of when the L3 layer chooses to fragment a packet.[*]

However even if TCP and UDP are unaware of the fragmentation/defragmentation processes,[†] the applications built on top of those two protocols are not. Some have to worry about fragmentation for performance reasons. Fragmentation/defragmentation is theoretically a transparent process, but it can have negative effects on performance because it always adds extra delay. A typical application that is very sensitive to delays, and that therefore tries to avoid fragmentation as much as possible, is a videoconferencing system. If you have ever tried one, or even if you have ever had an international phone call, you know what it means to have too big of a delay: conversing becomes very difficult. Some sources of delay cannot be avoided (such as network congestion, in the absence of robust QoS), but if something can be done to reduce that delay, the applications will take extraordinary steps to do it. Many

---

[*] The section "The ip_append_data Function" in Chapter 21 shows how the interface between L3 and L4 has evolved to optimize the fragmentation task for locally generated packets.

[†] As we will see in the section "Putting Together the Transmission Functions" in Chapter 21, L4 protocols actually provide some options that can influence fragmentation.

applications are smart enough to try to avoid fragmentation by taking a few factors into consideration:

- The kernel, first of all, does not have to simply use the MTU of the egress interface, but can also use a feature called *path MTU discovery* to discover the largest packet size it can use while avoiding fragmentation along a particular path (see the section "Path MTU Discovery").

- The MTU can be set to a fairly safe, small value of 576. This reflects the specification in RFC 791 that each host must be prepared to accept packets of up to 576 octets. This restriction on packet size thus drastically reduces the likelihood of fragmentation. Many applications end up using that MTU by default, if not explicitly configured to use a different value.

When a sender decides to use a packet size smaller than its available MTU just to avoid fragmentation, it must also entail the same overhead of including extra headers that fragmentation requires. However, avoiding fragmentation by routers along the way reduces processing considerably along the route and therefore can be critical for improving response time.

IP Header Fields Used by Fragmentation/Defragmentation

Here are the fields of the IP header that are used to handle the fragmentation/defragmentation process. We will see how they are used in Chapter 22.

DF (Don't Fragment)
> There are cases where fragmentation may be bad for the upper layers. For instance, interactive, streaming multimedia can produce terrible performance if it is fragmented. And sometimes, the transmitter knows that the receiver has a simple, lightweight IP protocol implementation and therefore cannot handle defragmentation. For such purposes, a field is provided in the IP packet header to say whether fragmentation is allowed. If the packet exceeds the MTU of some link along the path, it is dropped. The section "Path MTU Discovery" shows a use for this flag associated with path MTU discovery.

MF (More Fragments)
> When a node fragments a packet, it sets this flag to TRUE in each fragment except the last. The recipient knows the size of the original, unfragmented packet when it receives the last fragment created from this packet, even if some fragments have not been received yet.

Fragment Offset
> This represents the offset within the original IP packet to place the fragment. It is a 13-bit field. Since len is a 16-bit field, fragments always have to be created on 8-byte boundaries and the value of this field is read as a multiple of 8 bytes (that is, shifted left 3 bits). An offset of 0 indicates that this fragment is the first within the packet; that information is important because the first fragment contains header information related to the entire original packet.

ID

IP packet ID, which is the same for all fragments of an IP packet. It is thanks to this parameter that the receiver knows what fragments should be rejoined. We will see how the value of this field is chosen in the section "Long-Living IP Peer Information" in Chapter 23. Linux stores the last ID used in a structure named inet_peer where it stores information about the remote hosts with whom it is communicating.

Examples of Problems with Fragmentation/Defragmentation

Fragmentation is a pretty simple process: the node simply has to choose the right value to fit the MTU. It should not come as a surprise that most of the issues have to do with defragmentation. In the next two sections, we cover two of the most common issues: handling retransmissions and reassembling packets properly, along with the special problem of Network Address Translation (NAT).

Another reason not to use fragmentation is that it is incompatible with congestion control algorithms.

Retransmissions

I said earlier that an IP packet cannot be delivered to the next-higher layer until it has been completely defragmented. However, this does not mean that fragments are kept in the host's memory indefinitely. Otherwise, it would be very easy to render a host unusable through a simple Denial of Service (DoS) attack. A fragment might not be received for several reasons: for instance, it might be dropped along the way by a router that has run out of memory to store it due to congestion, it might become corrupted and be discarded due to the CRC (error check), or it could be held up by a firewall because the firewall wants to view the header in the first fragment before forwarding any fragments. Therefore, each router and host has a timer that cleans up the resources used by the fragments of an IP packet if some fragments are not received within a given amount of time.

If a sender could tell that a fragment was lost or dropped along the path, it would be nice if the sender could retransmit just the missing fragment. This is completely unfeasible to implement, though. A sender cannot know even whether its packet was fragmented by a router later on in the path, much less what the fragments are. So each sender must simply wait for a higher layer to tell it to resend an entire packet.

A retransmitted packet does not reuse the same ID as the original. However, it is still possible for a host to receive copies of the same IP fragment with the same packet ID, so a host must be able to handle this situation. Note that the same fragment may be received multiple times even without retransmissions: a common example is when there's a loop at the L2 layer. We saw this case in Part IV. This waste provides another good reason to avoid fragmentation at the source and to try to use packet sizes that minimize the likelihood of fragmentation along the way if delays are bad for the application (e.g., in videoconferencing software).

Since the kernel cannot swap its data out to disk (it swaps only user-space data), the memory waste due to handling fragments has a heavy impact on router performance. Linux puts a limit on the amount of memory usable by fragments, as described in the section "Tuning via /proc Filesystem" in Chapter 23.

Since IP is a connectionless protocol, there is no flow control and it is up to the upper-layer protocols (or the applications) to take care of losses. Some applications, of course, do not care much about the loss of data, and others do.

Let's suppose the upper layer detects the loss of some data by some means (for instance, with a timer that expires due to the lack of acknowledgment) and tries a retransmission. Since it is not possible to selectively resend only the missing fragments, the L4 protocol has to retransmit the entire IP packet. Each retransmission can lead to some special conditions that have to be handled by the receiver side (and sometimes by intermediate routers as well when the latter implement some form of firewalling that requires packets to be defragmented). Here are some of them:

Overlapping
A fragment could contain some of the data that already arrived in a previous packet. Retransmitted packets have a different ID and therefore their fragments are not supposed to be mixed with the fragments of a previous transmission. However, a buggy operating system that does not use a different ID for retransmitted packets, or the wraparound problem I'll introduce in the next section, can make overlapping possible.

Duplicates
This can be considered a special case of overlapping, where the two fragments are identical. A fragment is considered a duplicate if it starts at the same offset and it has the same length. There is no check on the actual payload content. Unless you are in the middle of a security attack, there is no reason why payload content should change between retransmissions of the same packet. The L2 loop mentioned previously can also be a source of duplicates.

Reception once reassembly is already complete
In this case, the IP layer considers the fragment the first of a new IP packet. If all of the new fragments are not received, the IP layer will simply clean up the duplicates during its garbage collection process; otherwise, it re-creates the whole packet and it is the job of the upper-layer protocol to recognize the packet as a duplicate.

Things can get more complicated if you consider that fragments can get fragmented, too.

Associating fragments with their IP packets

Because fragments could arrive out of order, defragmentation is a complex process that requires each packet to be recognized and put in its proper place as it arrives. The insert, delete, and merge operations must be easy and quick.

To identify the IP packet a fragment belongs to, the kernel takes the following parameters into consideration:

- Source and destination IP addresses
- IP packet ID
- L4 protocol

Unfortunately, it is possible for different packets to share all of these parameters. For instance, two different senders could happen to choose the same packet ID for packets that happen to arrive at the same time. One might suppose that the source IP addresses would distinguish the packets, but what if both hosts sat behind a NAT router that put its own IP address on the packets? There is no way the recipient IP layer can distinguish fragments under these conditions. You cannot count on the IP ID field either, because it is a 16-bit field and can therefore wrap around pretty quickly on a fast network.

Since the IP ID field plays a central role in the defragmentation process, let's see how IP fragments are organized in memory and how the IP IDs are generated. The most obvious implementation of an IP ID generator would be one that increments a global counter and uses it as the ID each time the IP layer is asked to send a packet. This would assure sequential IDs and easy implementation. This simple model, however, has some problems:

- For all possible higher-layer protocols to share a global ID, some sort of locking mechanism would be required (especially in multiprocessor machines) to prevent race conditions. However, the use of such a lock would limit symmetric multiprocessing (SMP) scalability.
- IDs would be predictable, which would lead to some well-known methods of attacking a machine.
- The ID value could wrap around quickly and lead to duplicate IDs. Because the ID field is a 16-bit value, allowing a total of 65,535 unique numbers, nodes with high traffic and fast connections might find themselves reusing the same ID for a new packet before the old one has reached its destination. For instance, with an average packet size of 512 bytes, a gigabit interface would send 65,535 packets in half a second A highly loaded server could easily wrap around a global IP ID counter in less than 1 second!

Thus, we have to accept the likelihood that the IP layer occasionally mixes together data from completely different packets. There is something wrong. Only the higher layers can fix the problem—usually with error checking.

The following section shows one way in which Linux reduces the likelihood of (but does not solve) the wraparound problem and ID prediction. The section "Selecting the IP Header's ID Field" in Chapter 23 shows the precise algorithm and code.

Example of IP ID generation

The wraparound problem is partially addressed by means of multiple, concurrent, global counters. Instead of a global IP ID, the Linux kernel keeps a different one for each destination IP address (up to the maximum number of possible IP destinations). Note that by using multiple IP IDs, you make the IDs take a little longer to wrap around, but eventually they will do so anyway.

Figure 18-11 shows an example. Let's suppose we have traffic addressed to two servers with addresses IP1 and IP2. Let's suppose also that for each IP address we have different independent streams of traffic, such as HTTP, Telnet, and FTP. Because the IP IDs are shared by all the streams of traffic going to the same destination, the packets will have sequential IDs if you look at traffic to the destination as a whole, but the traffic of each application will not have sequential IDs. For instance, the IP packets to destination IP1 that are generated by a Telnet session are not sequential. Note that this is merely the solution chosen by Linux, and is not a standard. Other alternatives are available.

Example of unsolvable defragmentation problem: NAT

Despite all manner of cleverness at the IP layer, the rules of fragmentation lead to potential situations that the IP layer cannot solve. Figure 18-12 shows one of them. Let's suppose that R is a router doing NAT for all the hosts on its network. To be more precise, let's suppose R did masquerading:* the source IP addresses in the headers of the IP packets generated by the hosts in the internal network and addressed to the Internet are replaced with router R's IP address, 140.105.1.1.†

Let's also suppose that both PC1 and PC2 need to send some traffic to the same destination server S. What would happen if, by chance, two packets transmitted at more or less the same time had the same IP ID (in this example, 1,000)? Since the router R rewrites the source IP address changing 10.0.0.2 and 10.0.0.3 into 140.105.1.1, server S will think that the two IP packets it received both came from router R. In the absence of fragmentation, this is not a problem because the L4 information (for instance, the port number) distinguishes the two sources. In fact, that is what makes NAT usable in the first place. The problem arises when the two IP packets

---

* What Linux calls masquerading is also commonly called Port Address Translation (PAT).

† Note that since the return traffic from the Internet and addressed to the hosts in the internal network will all have a destination IP address of 140.105.1.1, R uses the destination UDP/TCP port number to find the right internal host to route the ingress traffic to. We do not need to look at how this port business is handled for our example.

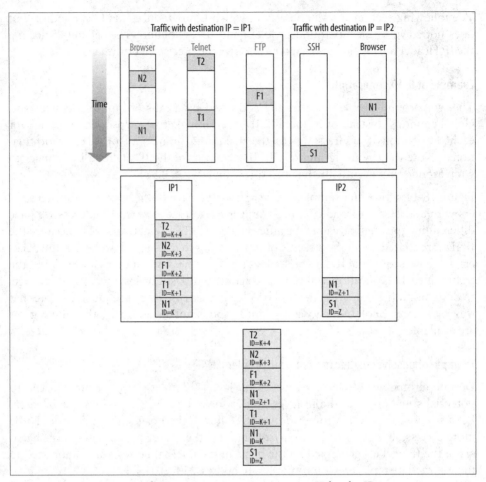

Figure 18-11. Concurrent applications receiving non consecutive IP header IDs

transmitted by R get fragmented before arriving at server S. In this case, server S receives fragments with the same source and destination IP address (140.105.1.1, 151.41.21.194) and the same IP ID (1,000), and therefore tries to put them together and potentially mixes the fragments of two different IP packets. As a consequence of this, both of the packets will be discarded because they are considered corrupted. In the very worst case, the two packets could have the same length and the overlapping could corrupt the payload without corrupting the L4 headers. The IP checksum covers only the IP header and therefore cannot detect this condition. Depending on the application, the consequences could be serious.

After an enumeration of all the problems with fragmentation, we can understand better why the designers of the IPv6 protocol decided to allow IP fragmentation only at the originating hosts, and not at intermediate hosts such as routers.

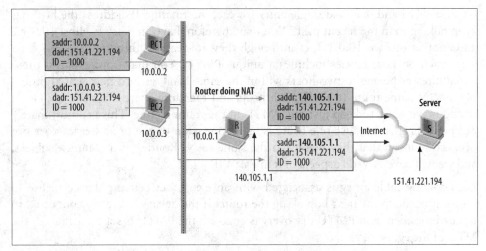

Figure 18-12. Example where NAT and IP fragmentation could give trouble

Path MTU Discovery

After the long discussion of the pitfalls of packet fragmentation, readers can well appreciate the next IP layer feature I'll discuss, path MTU discovery.

When I described the net_device data structure in Chapter 2, I listed the MTUs of the most common interface types. The scope of the MTU is the LAN that the network interface is connected to. If you transmit an IP packet to another host on the same LAN as the interface you use to transmit, and the size of the packet is bigger than the LAN's MTU, the IP packet will have to be fragmented. However, if you chose a size that fits the MTU, you can ensure that no fragmentation will be required. When the destination host is not on a directly attached LAN, you cannot count on the LAN's MTU to derive whether fragmentation will take place. Here is where path MTU discovery comes in.

Path MTU discovery is used to discover the biggest size a packet transmitted to a given destination address can have without being fragmented. That parameter is called the Path MTU (PMTU). Basically, the PMTU is the smallest MTU encountered along all the connections along the route from one host to the other.

Since the path between two endpoints can be asymmetric, it follows that there can be two different PMTUs for any given pair of hosts. Each host computes and uses the one appropriate for sending packets to the other. Furthermore, a change of route can lead to a change of PMTU.

Since each destination IP address can use a different PMTU, it is cached in the associated routing table cache entry. We will see in Part VII that the routes in the routing table can aggregate several IP addresses; for instance, you can have a route that says that network 10.0.1.0/24 is reachable via gateway 10.0.2.1. The routing table cache, on the other hand, has one single entry for each destination IP address the host has been talking to in the recent past.* You may therefore have an entry for host 10.0.1.2 and another one for 10.0.1.3, even though they are reached through the same gateway. Each of those entries includes a unique PMTU. You may object that, if those two addresses belong to two hosts within the same LAN, a third host would probably use the same route to reach both hosts and therefore share the same PMTU. It would make sense to keep just one PMTU in the routing table. This is unfortunately not possible. Just because one route is used to reach a bunch of addresses does not necessarily mean that they belong to the same LAN. Routing is a complex subject, and we will cover several aspects of it in Part VII.

Each routing table entry is associated with an egress device:† the device to use to transmit traffic to the next hop along the route. If the device is directly connected to its correspondent and PMTU discovery is enabled, the PMTU is set by default to the MTU of the egress device.

Directly connected devices include the two endpoints of a telecom cable or devices on an Ethernet LAN. It's particularly important for all devices on the LAN (with no router between them) to share the same MTU for proper operation.

If devices are not directly connected—that is, if at least one router lies between them—or if PMTU discovery is disabled, the PMTU by default is set to 576. This is not a random value, but is defined in the original IP RFC 791.‡ Regardless of the default, an administrator can set the initial PMTU through a user-space configuration program such as *ifconfig*.

Let's see how PMTU discovery works. The algorithm simply takes advantage of the IP header's fields used to handle fragmentation/defragmentation and the associated ICMP messages.

If you transmit an IP packet with the DF flag set in the header and no one complains, it means that no fragmentation has taken place along the path to the destination, and that the PMTU you used is fine. This does not mean you are using the optimal size. You might well be able to increase the PMTU and still not have fragmentation. A simple example is where two Ethernet LANs are connected by a router. On both sides of the network, the MTU is 1,500, but hosts of each LAN use the MTU of 576 to talk to the hosts of the other LAN because they are not directly connected. This is not optimal.

---

* To be more exact, a routing cache entry is associated with a combination of several parameters, including the source IP address, the destination IP address, and the IP TOS.

† We will see in Chapter 31 that if you add support for multipath routing to the kernel, you can define routes with multiple next hops, each one of which can potentially be reachable with a different interface.

‡ If you are interested in more details, I suggest you read RFCs 791, 1191, and 2923.

If you increase the size of the packets in a probe to their optimal size, you will be notified with an ICMP message when you cross the real PMTU. The ICMP message will include the MTU of the device that complained so that the kernel can update the local PMTU accordingly.

Linux can be configured to handle path MTU discovery in one of the following ways:

IP_PMTUDISC_DONT

Never send IP packets with the DF flag set in the header; therefore, do not use path MTU discovery.

IP_PMTUDISC_DO

Always set the DF flag in the header of packets generated on the local node (not forwarded ones), in an attempt to find the best PMTU for every transmission.

IP_PMTUDISC_WANT

Decide whether to use path MTU discovery on a per-route basis. This is the default.

When path MTU discovery is enabled, the PMTU associated with a route can change at any time to include routers with a smaller maximum size, resulting in the source receiving an ICMP FRAGMENTATION NEEDED message (see the discussion of icmp_unreach in Chapter 25). In this case, the PMTU is updated for all the entries in the routing cache with the same destination.[*] Refer to the section "Expiration Criteria" in Chapter 33 for details on how the reception of the ICMP FRAGMENTATION NEEDED message is handled by the routing table. It should be noted that the algorithm always shrinks the PMTU, it never increases it. However, the entries of the routing cache whose PMTU is derived from an ingress ICMP FRAGMENTATION NEEDED message expire after some time, which is equivalent to going back to the (bigger) default PMTU. See the same section just referenced for more details.

The PMTU of a route can also be set manually when adding the route through the *ip route* command.

Even if path MTU discovery was enabled, it is still possible to lock the current PMTU so that it will not be changed. This happens in two main cases:

- When using *ip route* to set the PMTU, it is possible to lock it with the *lock* keyword. The following example adds a route to the 10.10.1.0/24 network via the next hop gateway 100.100.100.1 and locks the PMTU to 750 bytes:

    ip route add 10.10.1.0/24 via 100.100.100.1 mtu lock 750

- If the PMTU you are supposed to use as a consequence of a received ICMP FRAGMENTATION NEEDED message is smaller than the minimum allowed value, the PMTU is set to that minimum value, and locked. The minimum value can be configured with the */proc/sys/net/ipv4/route/min_pmtu* file (see the section

---

[*] There can be more than one route to the same destination, for redundancy or load balancing.

"The /proc/sys/net/ipv4/route Directory" in Chapter 36). In any case, the PMTU cannot be set to a value lower than 68, as requested by RFC 1191, section 3.0 (and indirectly by RFC 791, section "Fragmentation and reassembly"). See also the section "Expiration Criteria" in Chapter 33.

In Linux, the ip_dont_fragment function (shown in Chapter 22) uses the considerations described here to decide whether a packet should be fragmented when it exceeds the PMTU.

The value of the PMTU on a given transmission can also be influenced by the following factors:

- Whether the device's MTU is explicitly configured from user space
- Whether the application has changed the maximum segment size (mss) to use on a given TCP socket

Checksums

A *checksum* is a redundant field used by network protocols to recognize transmission errors. Some checksums cannot only detect errors, but also automatically fix errors of certain types.

The idea behind a checksum is simple. Before transmitting a packet, the sender computes a small, fixed-length field (the checksum) containing a sort of hash of the data. If a few bits of the data were to change during transit, it is likely that the corrupted data would produce a different checksum. Depending on what function you used to produce the checksum, it provides different levels of reliability. The checksum used by the IP protocol is a simple one involving sums and one's complements, which is too weak to be considered reliable. For a more reliable sanity check, you must rely on L2 CRCs or SSL/IPSec Message Authentication Codes (MACs).

Different protocols can use different checksum algorithms. The IP protocol checksum covers only the IP header. Most L4 protocols' checksums cover both their header and the data.

It may seem redundant to have a checksum at L2 (e.g., Ethernet), another one at L3 (e.g., IP), and another one at L4 (e.g., TCP), because they often all apply to overlapping portions of data, but the checks are valuable. Errors can occur not only during transmission, but also while moving data between layers. Moreover, each protocol is responsible for ensuring its own correct transmission, and cannot assume that layers above or below it take on that task.

As an example of the complex scenarios that can arise, imagine that PC A in LAN1 sends data over the Internet to PC B in LAN2. Let's also suppose that the L2 protocol used in LAN1 uses a checksum but that the one on LAN2 doesn't. It's important for at least one higher layer to provide some form of checksum to reduce the likelihood of accepting corrupted data.

The use of a checksum is recommended in every protocol definition, although it is not required. Nevertheless, one has to admit that a better design of related protocols could remove some of the overhead imposed by features that overlap in the protocols at different layers. Because most L2 and L4 protocols provide checksums, having it at L3 as well is not strictly necessary. For exactly this reason, the checksum has been removed from IPv6.

In IPv4, the IP checksum is a 16-bit field that covers the entire IP header, options included. The checksum is first computed by the source of the packet, and is updated hop by hop all the way to its destination to reflect changes to the header applied by each router. Before updating the checksum, each hop first has to check the sanity of the packet by comparing the checksum included in the packet with the one computed locally. A packet is discarded if the sanity check fails, but no ICMP is generated: the L4 protocol will take care of it (for example, with a timer that will force a retransmission if no acknowledgment is received within a given amount of time).

Here are some cases that trigger the need to update the checksum:

Decrementing the TTL
> A router has to decrement a packet's TTL in its IP header before forwarding it. Since the IP checksum also covers that field, the original checksum is no longer valid. You will see in the section "ip_forward Function" in Chapter 20 that the TTL is decreased with ip_decrease_ttl, which takes care of the checksum, too.

Packet mangling (including NAT)
> All of those features that involve the change of one or more of the IP header fields force the checksum to be recomputed. NAT is probably the best-known example.

IP options handling
> Since the options are part of the header, they are covered by the checksum. Therefore, every time they are processed in a way that requires adding or modifying the IP header (i.e., the addition of a timestamp) forces the recomputation of the checksum.

Fragmentation
> When a packet is fragmented, each fragment has a different header. Most of the fields remain unchanged, but the ones that have to do with fragmentation, such as offset, are different. Therefore, the checksum has to be recomputed.

Since the checksum used by the IP protocol is computed using the same simple algorithm that is used by TCP, UDP, and ICMP, a general set of functions has been written to be used by all of them. There is also a specialized function optimized for the IP checksum. According to the definition of the IP checksum algorithm, the header is split into 16-bit words that are summed and ones-complemented. Figure 18-13 shows an example of checksum computation on only two 16-bit words for simplicity. Linux does not sum 16-bit words, but it does sum 32-bit words and even 64-bit longs, which results in faster computation (this requires an extra step between the computation of the sum and its one's complement; see the description of `csum_fold` in the next section). The function that implements the algorithm, called `ip_fast_csum`, is written directly in Assembly language on most architectures.

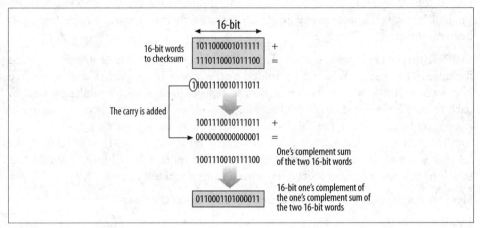

Figure 18-13. IP checksum computation

APIs for Checksum Computation

The L3 (IP) checksum is much faster to compute than the L4 checksum, because it covers only the IP header. Because it's a cheap operation, it is often computed in software.

The set of general functions used to compute checksums are placed in the per-architecture files *include/asm-xxx/checksum.h*. (The one for the i386 platform, for instance, is *include/asm-i386/checksum.h*.) Each protocol calls the general function directly using the right input parameters, or defines a wrapper that calls the general functions. The checksumming algorithm allows a protocol to simply update a checksum, instead of recomputing it from scratch, when changing a previously checksummed piece of data such as the IP header.

The prototype for one IP-specific function in *checksum.h*, `ip_fast_csum`, is shown here. The function takes as parameters the pointer to the IP header (iph), and its length (ihl). The latter can change due to IP options. The return value is the checksum. This function takes advantage of the fact that the IP header is always a multiple of 4 bytes in length to streamline some of the processing.

```
static inline
unsigned short ip_fast_csum(unsigned char * iph, unsigned int ihl)
```

When computing the checksum of an IP header on a packet to be transmitted, the value of iphdr->check should first be zeroed out because the checksum should not reflect the checksum itself. In this algorithm, because it uses simple summing, a zero-value field is effectively excluded from the resulting checksum. This is why in

---

different places in the code you can see that this field is zeroed right before the call to `ip_fast_csum`.

The checksum algorithm has an interesting property that may initially confuse people who read the source code for packet forwarding and reception. If the checksum is correct, and the forwarding or receiving node runs the algorithm over the entire header (leaving the original `iphdr->check` field in place), a result of zero is obtained. If you look at the function `ip_rcv`, you can see that this is exactly how input packets are validated against the checksum. This way of checking for corruption is faster than the more intuitive way of zeroing out the `iphdr->check` field and recomputing.

Here are the main functions used to compute or update an IP checksum:

`ip_compute_csum`

A general-purpose function that computes a checksum. It simply receives as input a buffer of an arbitrary size.

`ip_fast_csum`

Given an IP header and length, computes and returns the IP checksum. It can be used both to validate an input packet and to compute the checksum of an outgoing packet.

You can consider `ip_fast_csum` a variation of `ip_compute_csum` optimized for IP headers.

`ip_send_check`

Computes the IP checksum of an outgoing packet. It is a simple wrapper to `ip_fast_csum` that zeros `iphdr->check` beforehand.

`ip_decrease_ttl`

When changing a single field of an IP header, it is faster to apply an incremental update to the IP checksum than to compute it from scratch. This is possible thanks to the simple algorithm used to compute the checksum. A common example is a packet that is forwarded and therefore gets its `iphdr->ttl` field decremented. `ip_decrease_ttl` is called within `ip_forward`.

There are several other general support routines in the previously mentioned *checksum.h* file, but they are mostly used by L4 protocols. For instance:

`skb_checum`

Defined in *net/core/skbuff.c*, it is a general-purpose checksumming function used by several wrappers (including some of the functions listed earlier), and used mostly by L4 protocols for specific situations.

`csum_fold`

Folds the 16 most-significant bits of a 32-bit value into the 16 least-significant bits and then complements the output value. This operation is normally the last stage of a checksum computation.

csum_partial[_xxx]

> This family of functions computes a checksum that lacks the final folding done by csum_fold. L4 protocols can call one of the csum_partial functions to compute the checksum on the L4 data, then invoke a function such as csum_tcpudp_magic that computes the checksum on a pseudoheader (described in the following section), and finally sums the two partial checksums and folds the result.
>
> csum_partial and some of its variations are written in assembly language on most architectures.

csum_block_add

csum_block_sub

> Sum and subtract two checksums, respectively. The first one is useful when the checksum over a block of data is computed incrementally. The second one might be needed when a piece of data is removed from one whose checksum had already been computed. Many of the other functions use these two internally.

skb_checksum_help

> This function has two different behaviors, depending on whether it is passed an ingress IP packet or an egress IP packet.
>
> On ingress packets, it invalidates the L4 hardware checksum.
>
> On egress packets, it computes the L4 checksum. It is used, for example, when the hardware checksumming capabilities of the egress device cannot be used (see dev_queue_xmit in Chapter 11), or when the L4 hardware checksum has been invalidated and therefore needs to be recomputed. A checksum can be invalidated, for example, by a NAT operation from Netfilter, or when the transformation protocols of the IPsec suite mangle the L4 payload by inserting additional headers between the original IP header and the L4 header. Note also that if a device could compute the L4 checksum in hardware and store it in the L4 header, it would end up modifying the L3 payload, which is not possible when the latter has been digested or encrypted by the IPsec suite, because it would invalidate the data.

csum_tcpudp_magic

> Compute the checksum on the TCP and UDP pseudoheader (see Figure 18-14).

Newer NICs can provide both the IP and L4 checksum computations in hardware. While Linux takes advantage of the L4 hardware checksumming capabilities of most modern NICs, it does not take advantage of the IP hardware checksumming capabilities because it's not worth the extra complexity (i.e., the software computation is already fast enough given the limited size of the IP header). Hardware checksumming is only one example of CPU offloading that allows the kernel to process packets faster; most modern NICs provide some L4 (mainly TCP) offloading, too. Hardware checksumming is briefly described in Chapter 19.

Changes to the L4 Checksum

The TCP and UDP protocols compute a checksum that covers their header, their payloads, and what is known as the *pseudoheader*, which is basically a block whose fields are taken from the IP header for convenience (see Figure 18-14). In other words, some information that appears in the IP header ends up being incorporated in the L4 checksum. Note that the pseudoheader is defined only for computing the checksum; it does not exist in the packet on the wire.

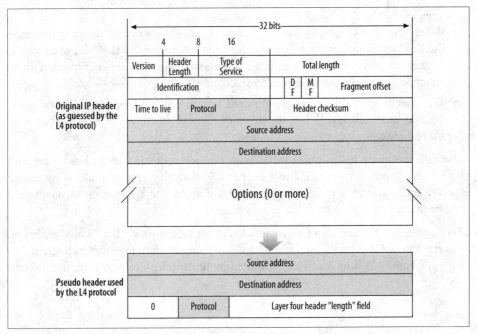

Figure 18-14. Pseudoheader used by TCP and UDP while computing the checksum

Unfortunately, the IP layer sometimes needs to change some of the IP header fields, for NAT or other activities, that were used by TCP and UDP in their pseudoheaders. The change at the IP level invalidates the L4 checksums. If the checksum is left in place, none of the nodes at the IP layer will detect any error because they validate only the IP checksum. However, the TCP layer of the destination host will believe the packet is corrupted. This case therefore has to be handled by the kernel.

Furthermore, there are routine cases where L4 checksums computed in hardware on received frames are invalidated. Here are the most common ones:

- When an input L2 frame includes some padding to reach the minimum frame size, but the NIC was not smart enough to leave the padding out when computing the checksum. In this case, the hardware checksum won't match the one computed by the receiving L4 layer. You will see in the section "Processing Input IP Packets" in Chapter 19 that to be on the safe side, the ip_rcv function always invalidates the checksum in this case. In Part IV, you will see that the bridging code can do something similar.

- When an input IP fragment overlaps with a previously received fragment. See Chapter 22.

- When an input IP packet uses any of the IPsec suite's protocols. In such cases, the L4 checksum cannot have been computed correctly by the NIC because the L4 header and payload are either compressed, digested, or encrypted. For an example, see esp_input in *net/ipv4/esp4.c*.

- The checksum needs to be recomputed because of NAT or some similar intervention at the IP layer. See, for instance, ip_nat_fn in *net/ipv4/netfilter/ip_nat_standalone.c*.

Although the name might prove confusing, the field skb->ip_summed has to do with the L4 checksum (more details in Chapter 19). Its value is manipulated by the IP layer when it knows that something has invalidated the L4 checksum, such as a change in a field that is part of the pseudoheader.

I will not cover the details of how the checksum is computed for locally generated packets. But we will briefly see in the section "Copying data into the fragments: get-frag" in Chapter 21 how it can be computed incrementally while creating fragments.

## CHAPTER 19

Internet Protocol Version 4 (IPv4): Linux Foundations and Features

The previous chapter laid out what an operating system needs to do to support the IP protocol; this chapter introduces the data structures and basic activities through which Linux supports IP, such as how ingress IP packets are delivered to the IP reception routine, how the checksum is verified, and how IP options are processed.

Main IPv4 Data Structures

This section introduces the major data structures used by the IPv4 protocol. You can refer to Chapter 23 for a detailed description of their fields.

I have not included a picture to show the relationships among the data structures because most of them are independent and do not keep cross-references.

iphdr structure
> IP header. The meaning of its fields has already been covered in the section "IP Header" in Chapter 18.

ip_options structure
> This structure, defined in *include/linux/ip.h*, represents the options for a packet that needs to be transmitted or forwarded. The options are stored in this structure because it is easier to read than the corresponding portion of the IP header itself.

ipcm_cookie structure
> This structure combines various pieces of information needed to transmit a packet.

ipq structure
> Collection of fragments of an IP packet. See the section "Organization of the IP Fragments Hash Table" in Chapter 22.

inet_peer structure
> The kernel keeps an instance of this structure for each remote host it has been talking to in the recent past. In the section "Long-Living IP Peer Information" in

Chapter 23 you will see how it is used. All instances of inet_peer structures are kept in an AVL tree, a structure optimized for frequent lookups.

ipstats_mib structure

The Simple Network Management Protocol (SNMP) employs a type of object called a Management Information Base (MIB) to collect statistics about systems. A data structure called ipstats_mib keeps statistics about the IP layer. The section "IP Statistics" in Chapter 23 covers this structure in more detail.

in_device structure

The in_device structure stores all the IPv4-related configuration for a network device, such as changes made by a user with the *ifconfig* or *ip* command. This structure is linked to the net_device structure via net_device->ip_ptr and can be retrieved with in_dev_get and __in_dev_get. The difference between those two functions is that the first one takes care of all the necessary locking, and the second one assumes the caller has taken care of it already.

Since in_dev_get internally increases a reference count on the in_dev structure when it succeeds (i.e., when a device is configured to support IPv4), its caller is supposed to decrement the reference count with in_dev_put when it is done with the structure.

The structure is allocated and linked to the device with inetdev_init, which is called when the first IPv4 address is configured on the device.

in_ifaddr structure

When configuring an IPv4 address on an interface, the kernel creates an in_ifaddr structure that includes the 4-byte address along with several other fields.

ipv4_devconf structure

The ipv4_devconf data structure, whose fields are exported via *proc* in */proc/sys/net/ipv4/conf/*, is used to tune the behavior of a network device. There is an instance for each device, plus one that stores the default values (ipv4_devconf_dflt). The meanings of its fields are covered in Chapters 28 and 36.

ipv4_config structure

While ipv4_devconf structures are used to store per-device configuration, ipv4_config stores configuration that applies to the host.

cork

The cork structure is used to handle the socket CORK option. We will see in Chapter 21 how its fields are used to maintain some context information across consecutive invocations of ip_append_data and ip_append_page to handle data fragmentation.

Checksum-Related Fields from sk_buff and net_device Structures

We saw the routines used to compute the IP and L4 checksums in the section "Checksums" in Chapter 18. In this section, we will see what fields of the sk_buff buffer structure are used to store information about checksums, how devices tell the kernel about their hardware checksumming capabilities, and how the L4 protocols use such information to decide whether to compute the checksum for ingress and egress packets or to let the network interface cards (NICs) do it.

Because the IP checksum is always computed and verified in software by the kernel, the next subsections concentrate on L4 checksum handling and issues.

net_device structure

The net_device->features field specifies the capabilities of the device. Among the various flags that can be set, a few are used to define the device's hardware checksumming capabilities. The list of possible features is in *include/linux/netdevice.h* inside the definition of net_device itself. Here are the flags used to control checksumming:

NETIF_F_NO_CSUM
> The device is so reliable that there is no need to use any L4 checksum. This feature is enabled, for instance, on the loopback device.

NETIF_F_IP_CSUM
> The device can compute the L4 checksum in hardware, but only for TCP and UDP over IPv4.

NETIF_F_HW_CSUM
> The device can compute the L4 checksum in hardware for any protocol. This feature is less common than NETIF_F_IP_CSUM.

sk_buff structure

The two fields skb->csum and skb->ip_summed have different meanings depending on whether skb points to a received packet or to a packet to be transmitted out.

When a packet is received, skb->csum may hold its L4 checksum. The oddly named skb->ip_summed field keeps track of the status of the L4 checksum. The status is indicated by the following values, defined in *include/linux/skbuff.h*. The following definitions represent what the device driver tells the L4 layer. Once the L4 receive routine receives the buffers, it may change the initialization of skb->ip_summed.

CHECKSUM_NONE
> The checksum in csum is not valid. This can be due to various reasons:
> - The device does not provide hardware checksumming.
> - The device computed the hardware checksums and found the frame to be corrupted. At this point, the device driver could discard the frame directly. But some device drivers prefer to set ip_summed to CHECKSUM_NONE and let the software compute and verify the checksum again. This is unfortunate, because after all of the overhead of receiving the packet, all that the kernel does is recheck the checksum and discard the packet (see e1000_rx_checksum

in *drivers/net/e1000/e1000_main.c*). Note that if the input frame is to be forwarded, the router should not discard it due to a wrong L4 checksum (a router is not supposed to look at the L4 checksum). It will be up to the destination host to do it. This is another reason why device drivers do not discard frames that fail the L4 checksum, but let the L4 receive routine verify them.

- The checksum needs to be recomputed and reverified. See the section "Changes to the L4 Checksum" in Chapter 18 for the most common reasons.

CHECKSUM_HW

The NIC has computed the checksum on the L4 header and payload and has copied it into the skb->csum field. The software (i.e., the L4 receive routine) needs only to add the checksum on the pseudoheader to skb->csum and to verify the resulting checksum. This flag can be considered a special case of the following flag.

CHECKSUM_UNNECESSARY

The NIC has computed and verified the checksum on the L4 header and checksum, as well as on the pseudoheader (the checksum on the pseudoheader may optionally be computed by the device driver in software), so the software is relieved from having to do any L4 checksum verification.

CHECKSUM_UNNECESSARY can also be set, for example, when the probability of an error is very low and it would be a waste of time and CPU power to compute and verify the L4 checksum. One example is the loopback device: since the packets sent through this virtual device never leave the local host, the only possible errors would be due to faulty RAM or bugs in the operating system. This option can therefore be used with such special devices, but the standard behavior is to compute the checksum of each received packet and discard corrupted packets at the receiving end.

When a packet is transmitted, csum represents a pointer (or more accurately, an offset) to the place inside the buffer where the hardware card has to put the checksum it will compute, not the checksum itself. This field is therefore used during packet transmission only if the checksum is calculated in hardware. This interaction between L4 and L2, bypassing L3, introduces a couple of additional problems to deal with. For example, a feature such as Network Address Translation (NAT) that manipulates the fields of the IP header used by the L4 layer to compute the so-called checksum on the pseudoheader would invalidate that data structure (see the section "Changes to the L4 Checksum" in Chapter 18).

As in the case of reception, ip_summed represents the status of the L4 checksum. The field is used by the L4 protocols to tell the device whether it needs to take care of checksumming. In particular, this is the meaning of ip_summed during transmissions:

CHECKSUM_NONE

The protocol has already taken care of the checksum; the device does not need to do anything. When you forward an ingress frame, the L4 checksum is already ready because it has been computed by the sender host; therefore, there is no need to compute it. See ip_forward in Chapter 20. When ip_summed is set to CHECKSUM_NONE, csum is meaningless.

CHECKSUM_HW

The protocol has stored into its header the checksum on the pseudoheader only; the device is supposed to complete it by adding the checksum on the L4 header and payload.

ip_summed does not use the CHECKSUM_UNNECESSARY value when transmitting packets (it would be equivalent to CHECKSUM_NONE).

While the feature flags NETIF_F_*XXX*_CSUM are initialized by the device driver when the NIC is enabled, the CHECKSUM_*XXX* flags have to be set for every sk_buff buffer that is received or transmitted. At reception time, it is the device driver that initializes ip_summed correctly based on the NETIF_F_*XXX*_CSUM device capabilities.

At transmission time, the L3 transmission APIs initialize ip_summed based on the checksumming capabilities of the egress device, which can be derived from the routing table: the routing table cache entry that matches the destination includes information about the egress device, and therefore its checksumming capabilities (see ip_append_data for an example).

Given the meaning of the skb->csum and skb->ip_summed fields and the CHECKSUM_HW flag previously described, you can study, for example, how TCPv4 takes care of the checksum on ingress segments in *tcp_v4_checksum_init*, and the checksum of egress segments in *tcp_v4_send_check*.

General Packet Handling

The rest of this chapter covers some general considerations that the kernel has to take into account when handling ingress IP packets, such as checksumming and options. Subsequent chapters go into detail about how they are forwarded, transmitted, and fragmented/defragmented.

Protocol Initialization

The IPv4 protocol is initialized by ip_init, defined in *net/ipv4/ip_output.c*. Because IPv4 support cannot be removed from the kernel (i.e., it cannot be compiled as a module), there is no ip_uninit function.

Here are the main tasks accomplished by ip_init:

- Register the handler for IP packets with the dev_add_pack function (see Chapter 13). This handler is a function named ip_rcv.
- Initialize the routing subsystem, including the protocol-independent cache (see Chapter 32).
- Initialize the infrastructure used to manage IP peers (see the section "Long-Living IP Peer Information" in Chapter 23.

ip_init is invoked at boot time by inet_init, which takes care of the initialization of all the subsystems related to IPv4, including the L4 protocols.

Interaction with Netfilter

We will not examine the Netfilter firewalling subsystem in this book, but we can examine its main working principles now, particularly its relationship to the aspects of the IPv4 implementation we discuss in this part of the book.

Firewalling, essentially, hooks into certain places in the network stack code that packets always pass through when the packets or the kernel meet certain conditions; at those points, the firewall allows network administrators to manipulate the contents or disposition of the traffic. Those points in the kernel, as shown in Figure 18-1 in Chapter 18, include:

- Packet reception
- Packet forwarding (before routing decision)
- Packet forwarding (after routing decision)
- Packet transmission

The reason why it is useful to distinguish between pre-routing and post-routing will become clearer in Part VII.

In each case just listed, the function in charge of the operation is split into two parts, usually called *do_something* and *do_something_*finish. (In a few cases, the names are *do_something* and *do_something2*.) *do_something* contains only some sanity checks and maybe some housekeeping. The code that does the real job is in *do_something_* finish or *do_something2*. *do_something* ends by calling the Netfilter function NF_HOOK, passing in the point where the call comes from (for instance, packet reception) and the function to execute if the filtering rules configured by the user with the *iptables* command do not decide to drop or reject the packet. If there are no rules to apply or they simply indicate "go ahead," the function *do_something_*finish is executed. Given the following general call:

```
NF_HOOK(PROTOCOL, HOOK_POSITION_IN_THE_STACK, SKB_BUFFER, IN_DEVICE, OUT_DEVICE, do_
something_finish)
```

the output value of NF_HOOK can be one of the following:

- The output value of *do_something_*finish when the latter is executed
- -EPERM if SKB_BUFFER is dropped because of a filter
- -ENOMEM if there was insufficient memory to perform the filtering operation

In this chapter, we do not need to worry about those details. We will assume that no filters are configured and therefore that, at the end of *do_something*, the call to the Netfilter function will simply execute *do_something_*finish. We will see the first example at the end of the ip_rcv function.

Interaction with the Routing Subsystem

The IP layer needs to interact with the routing table in several places, such as when receiving and when transmitting a packet. I will cover the details about routing in Part VII when I will describe the routing subsystem; for now I'll just briefly describe three of the functions used by the IP layer to consult the routing table:

ip_route_input
: Determines the destiny of an input packet. As you can see in Figure 18-1 in Chapter 18, the packet could be delivered locally, forwarded, or dropped.

ip_route_output_flow
: Used before transmitting a packet. This function returns both the next hop gateway and the egress device to use.

dst_pmtu
: Given a routing table cache entry, returns the associated Path Maximum Transmission Unit (PMTU).

The ip_route_*xxx* functions, described in detail in Chapters 33 and 35, consult the routing table and base their decisions on a set of fields:

- Destination IP address.
- Source IP address.
- Type of Service (ToS).
- Receiving device in the case of reception.
- List of allowed transmitting devices.

Among the more complex factors that could influence the decision returned by these functions are the presence of policy routing and the presence of a firewall.

The functions store the result of the routing table lookup in skb->dst. This structure includes several fields, including the input and output function pointers that will be called to complete the reception or the transmission of the packet (see Figure 18-1 in Chapter 18 for where those two function pointers are used). The ip_route_*xxx* functions return a negative value if the lookup fails.

Both functions also use a cache to get a stream of packets to the same destination quickly. The destination IP address is the most important criterion for making the decision, and is used as the search key into the cache. But each cache entry also includes several other parameters that distinguish which route is used. For instance, the cache keeps track of each route's PMTU, which was described in the section "Path MTU Discovery" in Chapter 18.

Processing Input IP Packets

Chapter 13 showed that the kernel routes traffic at every level to the proper protocol by invoking the handler function registered by that protocol. In the section "Protocol Handler Registration" in that chapter, we saw how the IP protocol registers its protocol handler ip_rcv, defined in *net/ipv4/ip_input.c*, with the kernel. We can now start to analyze the path of IP packets inside the kernel network stack, starting with the ip_rcv function.

ip_rcv is a classic case of the two-stage process described in the section "Interaction with Netfilter." Its work consists just of applying sanity checks to the packet and then invoking the Netfilter hook. Most processing will take place in ip_rcv_finish, called from the Netfilter hook.

Here is the prototype of ip_rcv. The third input parameter is not used.

```
int ip_rcv(struct sk_buff *skb, struct net_device *dev, struct packet_type *pt)
```

The netif_receive_skb function (described in Chapter 10) sets the pointer to the L3 protocol (skb->nh) at the end of the L2 header. IP layer functions can therefore safely cast it to an iphdr structure.

Most of the fields of sk_buff are set before the call to ip_rcv, as explained in previous chapters, during the sequence of events that take place from the interrupt notification by an NIC to the invocation of the L3 protocol handler. Figure 19-1 shows the values of some of the sk_buff fields when ip_rcv starts. Note that skb->data, which is usually used to point to the payload, here points to the L3 header.

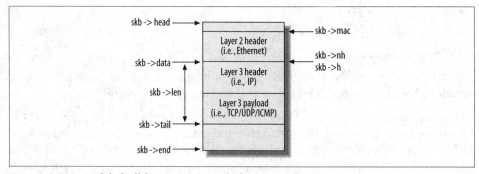

Figure 19-1. Part of sk_buff data structure at the beginning of ip_rcv

In Chapter 10 and Chapter 13 we saw how the NIC's device driver sets the L3 protocol identifier `skb->protocol` and the packet type `skb->pkt_type`. Ethernet drivers, for instance, do that by means of the `eth_type_trans` function.

`skb->pkt_type` is set to `PACKET_OTHERHOST` when the L2 destination address of the frame is different from the address of the receiving interface. Normally those packets are discarded by the NIC itself. However, if the interface has been put into promiscuous mode, it receives all packets regardless of the destination L2 address and passes them up to higher layers. The kernel invokes sniffers that have requested access to all packets, as described in Chapter 10. But `ip_rcv` is not concerned with packets for other addresses and simply drops them:

```
if (skb->pkt_type == PACKET_OTHERHOST)
    goto drop;
```

Note that receiving a packet for a different L2 address is not the same as receiving a packet that should be routed to another system. In the latter case, the packet has the interface's L2 address but an L3 layer address that is different from that of the current recipient. A router is configured to accept such packets and route them, as described in Part VII.

`skb_share_check` checks whether the reference count of the packet is bigger than 1, which means that other parts of the kernel have references to the buffer. As discussed in earlier chapters, sniffers and other users might be interested in packets, so each packet contains a reference count. The `netif_receive_skb` function, which is the one that calls `ip_rcv`, increments the reference count before it calls a protocol handler. If the handler sees a reference count bigger than 1, it creates its own copy of the buffer so that it can modify the packet. Any following handlers will receive the original, unchanged buffer. If a copy is needed but memory allocation fails, the packet is dropped.

```
if ((skb = skb_share_check(skb, GFP_ATOMIC)) == NULL) {
    IP_INC_STATS_BH(IPSTATS_MIB_INDISCARDS);
    goto out;
}
```

The job of `pskb_may_pull` is to make sure that the area pointed to by `skb->data` contains a block of data at least as big as the IP header, since each IP packet (fragments included) must include a complete IP header. If the condition is met, there is nothing to do. Otherwise, the missing part is copied from the data fragments (if any) stored in `skb_shinfo(skb)->frags[]`.* If this fails, the function terminates with an error. If it succeeds, the function must initialize `iph` again because `pskb_may_pull` could change the buffer structure.

```
if (!pskb_may_pull(skb, sizeof(struct iphdr)))
    goto inhdr_error;
iph = skb->nh.iph;
```

---

* Do not confuse data fragments with IP fragments. See Chapter 2 for the use of the `skb_shinfo` macro.

Next come some sanity checks on the IP header. The size of a basic IP header is 20 bytes, and since the size stored in the header is expressed in multiples of 32 bits (4 bytes), if its value is smaller than 5 it means there is an error. The second check in the if statement is rather fussy. Currently there are two versions of the IP protocol: IPv4 and IPv6. The if statement makes sure the packet is an IPv4 packet. But because the two protocols are handled by two different functions, the ip_rcv function should never have been called for IPv6 in the first place.

```
if (iph->ihl < 5 || iph->version != 4)
    goto inhdr_error;
```

Now we repeat the same check as before, but this time we use the full IP header size (including the options). If the IP header claims a size of iph->ihl, the packet should be at least as long as iph->ihl. This check was left until now because the function needs first to make sure the basic header (i.e., the header without options) has not been truncated and that it passes a basic sanity check before reading something from it (ihl in this case).

```
if (!pskb_may_pull(skb, iph->ihl*4))
    goto inhdr_error;
iph = skb->nh.iph;
```

After these two protocol consistency checks have been performed, the function needs to compute the checksum and see whether it matches the one carried in the header. If it doesn't, the packet is dropped. The ip_fast_csum routine was introduced in the section "APIs for Checksum Computation" in Chapter 18.

```
if (ip_fast_csum((u8 *)iph, iph->ihl) != 0)
    goto inhdr_error;
```

After the checksum, there are two other sanity checks:

- Make sure the length of the buffer (i.e., the received packet) is greater than or equal to the length reported in the IP header.

- Make sure the size of the packet is at least as large as the IP header size.

```
{
    __u32 len = ntohs(iph->tot_len);
    if (skb->len < len || len < (iph->ihl<<2))
        goto inhdr_error;
```

Here we need to explain why those two checks are needed. The first one arises from the fact that the L2 protocols (e.g., Ethernet) can pad out the payload,[*] so there may be extra bytes after the IP payload. (This happens, for instance, when the L2 size of the frame is smaller than the minimum required by the protocol. Ethernet frames have a minimum frame length of 64 bytes.) In such a case, the packet would look bigger than the length reported in the IP header. The different sizes and padding are shown in Figure 19-2.

---

[*] From the L2 perspective, the payload is the IP header and everything that follows it.

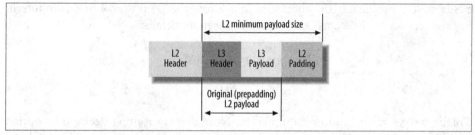

Figure 19-2. L2 padding needed to reach the minimum payload size

The second check derives from the fact that an IP header cannot be fragmented, and that each IP fragment must therefore contain at least an IP header.[*] The reason for the <<2 in the condition is that the size of the header (iph->ihl) is measured in units of 32 bits. This check should fail only in an extremely rare situation. It would mean that the checksum had been computed on a corrupted packet but happened by chance to produce the same checksum as the original packet (i.e., the checksum did not detect the error).

The minimum MTU associated with a route is in fact 68, which comes from RFC 791. Since the IP header can be up to 60 bytes long (20+40) and the minimum fragment length (with the exception of the last one) is 8 bytes, it follows that every IP router must be able to forward an IP packet of 68 bytes without any further fragmentation.

As you can imagine, all of the sanity checks that we have seen so far and that we will see later are very important for the stability of the system. If, by chance, the sk_buff structure was incorrectly initialized, or if the IP header itself was corrupted, the kernel could process packets in a wrong way or could access invalid memory locations, which could indirectly cause a crash.

We said that the L2 protocols could have padded out the packet to reach a specific minimum length. The function pskb_trim_rcsum checks whether that happened and, if it did, trims the packet to the right size with __pskb_trim and invalidates the L4 checksum in case it had been computed by the receiving NIC. __pskb_trim is slightly complex because it may need to deal with fragmented buffers, too.[†]

When the L4 checksum is computed in hardware by the network card, it could include the L2 padding if the card is not smart enough to leave it out. Since here there is no way to know whether that was the case, to be on the safe side, pskb_trim_

---

[*] The IP protocol specification (RFC 791) says that an Internet host must be able to forward a datagram of 68 bytes without having to fragment it: in other words, the L2 protocol must be able to transmit a frame with a payload of at least 68 bytes.

[†] See Chapter 21 for examples of what a fragmented buffer looks like.

rcsum simply invalidates the checksum and forces the L4 protocol to recompute it. See the section "Checksums" in Chapter 18 for more details.

```
        if (pskb_trim_rcsum(skb, len)) {
            IP_INC_STATS_BH(IPSTATS_MIB_INDISCARDS);
            goto drop;
        }
    }
```

Finally we get to the end of the function. Note that no routing decision or option handling has been done so far; that's the job of ip_rcv_finish. As we anticipated earlier in the chapter, the function ends with a call to the Netfilter subsystem, which more or less can be read in this way:

"skb is the packet that was received from device dev; please check whether the packet is allowed to proceed with its travel, or if it needs changes. Take into consideration that we are asking you this from the NF_IP_PRE_ROUTING point within the network stack (which means the packet was received but no routing decision was taken yet). If you decide not to drop the packet, execute ip_rcv_finish."

```
        return NF_HOOK(PF_INET, NF_IP_PRE_ROUTING, skb, dev, NULL,
                    ip_rcv_finish);
```

See the earlier section "Interaction with Netfilter" for background information.

The ip_rcv_finish Function

ip_rcv did not do much more than a basic sanity check of the packet. So when ip_rcv_finish is called, it will take care of the main processing, such as:

- Deciding whether the packet has to be locally delivered or forwarded. In the second case, it needs to find both the egress device and the next hop.

- Parsing and processing some of the IP options. Not all of the options are processed here, however, as we will see when analyzing the forwarding case.

This is the prototype of the ip_rcv_finish function, defined in the same *net/ipv4/ip_input.c* file as ip_rcv.

```
    static inline int ip_rcv_finish(struct sk_buff *skb)
```

The skb->nh field was initialized in netif_receive_skb, which came earlier in the receiving path. At that time, the L3 protocol was not yet known, so it was initialized using nh.raw. Now the function can get a pointer to the IP header.

```
    struct net_device *dev = skb->dev;
        struct iphdr *iph = skb->nh.iph;
```

skb->dst may contain information about the route to be taken by the packet to get to its destination. If that information is not known yet, the function asks the routing subsystem where to send the packet, and if the latter says the destination is unreachable, the packet is dropped. See the section "Local Delivery" in Chapter 35 for an example of when skb->dst is not NULL here.

```
if (skb->dst == NULL) {
    if (ip_route_input(skb, iph->daddr, iph->saddr, iph->tos, dev))
        goto drop;
}
```

Then the function updates some statistics that are used by Traffic Control (the Quality of Service, or QoS, layer).

```
#ifdef CONFIG_NET_CLS_ROUTE
    if (skb->dst->tclassid) {
        struct ip_rt_acct *st = ip_rt_acct + 256*smp_processor_id();
        u32 idx = skb->dst->tclassid;
        st[idx&0xFF].o_packets++;
        st[idx&0xFF].o_bytes+=skb->len;
        st[(idx>>16)&0xFF].i_packets++;
        st[(idx>>16)&0xFF].i_bytes+=skb->len;
    }
#endif
```

When the length of the IP header is bigger than 20 bytes[*] (5×32 bits) it means there are options to process. skb_cow, whose name comes from the well-known phrase "Copy on Write," is called here to make a copy of the buffer if the latter is shared with someone else. Exclusive ownership of the buffer is needed because we are about to process the options and will probably need to change the IP header.

```
if (iph->ihl > 5) {
    struct ip_options *opt;
    if (skb_cow(skb, skb_headroom(skb))) {
            IP_INC_STATS_BH(IPSTATS_MIB_INDISCARDS);
        goto drop;
    }
    iph = skb->nh.iph;
```

ip_option_compile is used to interpret the IP options carried in the header. The next section describes its implementation in detail. Right now we are interested in the output of that function. We saw in Chapter 2 that skb contains a field called cb that can be used to store private data by whomever manages an sk_buff buffer. In this case, the IP layer uses it to store the result of the IP header option parsing plus some other stuff such as fragmentation-related information. The result is stored in a data structure of type struct inet_skb_parm, defined in *include/net/ip.h* and accessed with the macro IPCB (see the section "ipq Structure" in Chapter 23).

If there are any wrong options, the packet is discarded and a special Internet Control Message Protocol (ICMP) message is sent back to the sender to notify the latter about the problem. As we will see in Chapter 25, ICMP messages contain information about where the error was found in the header, something that could help the sender to understand what happened.

---

[*] 20 bytes is the length of an IP header without options.

You will see in the next section that when the first input parameter to ip_options_
compile is NULL, the output of the parsing process is stored in IPCB(skb)->opt; this
explains why the parsed options are retrieved with IPCB.

```
if (ip_options_compile(NULL, skb))
        goto inhdr_error;
```

Note that ip_options_compile simply checks whether the options are correct and
stores them in an ip_option structure inside the private data field pointed to by skb->
cb. The function does not handle any of them. Instead, the upcoming piece of code
partially takes care of that.

In case the packet was source routed, the kernel needs to check whether the configuration of the device allows that option to be used. (If you are not familiar with IP
source routing, check the section "Option: Strict and Loose Source Routing.")

I briefly describe the in_device structure and the associated APIs in the section "in_
device Structure" in Chapter 23. If there was no explicit configuration for IP source
routing, the option would be allowed by default. If, on the other hand, that option
was disabled, the packet is dropped (but no ICMP message is generated). NIPQUAD is a
simple macro defined in *include/linux/kernel.h* that splits a 32-bit variable into four 8-
bit components.

```
        if (opt->srr) {
            struct in_device *in_dev = in_dev_get(dev);
            if (in_dev) {
                if (!IN_DEV_SOURCE_ROUTE(in_dev)) {
                    if (IN_DEV_LOG_MARTIANS(in_dev) && net_ratelimit())
                        printk(KERN_INFO "source route option %u.%u.%u.%u -> %u.
%u.%u.%u\n",
                            NIPQUAD(iph->saddr), NIPQUAD(iph->daddr));
                    in_dev_put(in_dev);
                    goto drop;
                }
                in_dev_put(in_dev);
            }
            if (ip_options_rcv_srr(skb))
                goto drop;
        }
    }
```

When IP source routing is allowed on the device, the code calls ip_options_rcv_srr
to set skb->dst and decide how to handle the packet, which means deciding which
device to use to forward the packet toward the next hop in the source route list. Normally, the requested next hop refers to another host, and the function simply sets
opt->srr_is_hit to indicate the address has been found. The ip_options_rcv_srr
function has to take into account, however, the possibility that the "next hop" may
be an interface on the local host. If that happens, the function writes the IP address
into the destination IP address of the IP header and goes on to check the next address

in the source routing list, if there is one (in the code, this is called a *superfast loop-back forward*). ip_options_rcv_srr keeps browsing the list of next hops in the IP header source routing option block until it finds an IP address that is not local to the host. Normally, there will be no more than one local IP address in that list. However, it is legal to have more than one. In the latter case, going from one next hop to the following one is a no-op—i.e., one more loop inside ip_options_rcv_srr. The srr_is_hit flag is set when the last next-hop found by ip_options_rcv_srr is not a local IP address, which means the packet has not reached its final destination and needs to be forwarded.

If the packet is to be forwarded, as we will see in the section "ip_forward_finish Function" in Chapter 20, the initialization of srr_is_hit tells ip_forward_options to take care of the source routing option by adding the necessary data to the IP header. If the packet is being transmitted (that is, if it originated on this host), opt->faddr will be used instead and the opt->srr_is_hit flag will not be used.

The term MARTIANS is used in the previous code to decide whether a parameter value is wrong. The term is not a fanciful choice by the Linux developers but comes from the RFCs themselves.

ip_rcv_finish ends with a call to dst_input, which actually invokes the function stored in the dst field of the skb buffer. skb->dst was initialized either near the beginning of ip_rcv_finish, or near the end within ip_options_rcv_srr (which is called if the IP source routing option is present in the header). skb->dst->input is set to ip_local_deliver or ip_forward, depending on the destination address of the packet. The call to dst_input therefore completes the processing of the packet (see Figure 18-1 in Chapter 18 and the earlier section "Interaction with the Routing Subsystem").

See also the section "Source Routing" in Chapter 35 for the relationship between the call to ip_route_input in ip_rcv_finish and the one in ip_options_rcv_srr.

IP Options

Because of the overhead associated with the time needed to process IP options, they have never been used much. In the next sections, we will see one by one the IP options handled by the Linux kernel and how they are processed.

Here are the main APIs involved with IP option management, all of them defined in *net/ipv4/ip_options.c*. To understand some of them, remember that not all of the IP options of a packet need to be replicated in all of its fragments.

ip_options_compile
> Parses a block of options from an IP header and initializes an instance of an ip_options structure accordingly. This structure will be used later to process the options; it includes flags and pointers that tell the part of the routing subsystem

that handles forwarding what has to be written into the IP header options space, and where. `ip_options_compile` is described in detail in the section "Option Parsing."

`ip_options_build`

Initializes the portion of an IP header dedicated to the options, based on an input `ip_options` structure. This function is used when transmitting locally generated packets. Thanks to an input parameter, it can distinguish fragments and treat them accordingly: it omits from the header of each fragment those options that do not have to be copied into that fragment (see the section "IP options" in Chapter 18), and overwrites them with null options instead. It also clears the flags of the `ip_options` structure (such as opt->rr_needaddr) that are used to signal the need to add a timestamp or an address to the options.

`ip_options_fragment`

Because the first fragment is the only one that inherits all the options of the original packet, the size of its header is supposed to be greater than or equal to the size of the following ones. Linux simplified this rule, however. By keeping the same header size for all fragments, Linux makes the fragmentation process simpler and more efficient. This is achieved by copying the original header with all its options and overwriting the options that do not need to be replicated (those where `IPOPT_COPY` is not set) with null options (`IPOPT_NOOP`) and clearing all the flags of the `ip_options` structure associated with them (e.g., ts_needaddr), on all fragments but the first one. Null options are described later in the section "Option Parsing."

This last operation is exactly the purpose of `ip_options_fragment`. When we talk about `ip_fragment` in Chapter 22, we will see that after the first IP fragment has been sent, the kernel calls `ip_options_fragment` to change the IP header, and recycles the new adapted header thereafter for all of the following fragments.

`ip_forward_options`

When forwarding a packet, some options may need to be processed. `ip_options_compile` parses the options and initializes a set of flags in the `ip_options` structure used to store the result of the parsing. Later, `ip_forward` will handle them.

`ip_options_get`

This function receives a block of options, parses them with `ip_options_compile`, and stores the result in an `ip_options` structure it allocates. It can receive the input options from either kernel space or user space; there is an input parameter to specify the source. An example of usage is via the `ip_setsockopt` function that is used by L4 protocols such as TCP and UDP to set the IP options on a given socket (see the system call `setsockopt`). `ip_options_get` takes care of the padding described in the section "'End of option list' and 'No operation' options" in Chapter 18.

`ip_options_echo`

> Given an ingress IP packet and its IP options, this function builds the IP options to use to reply back to the sender. For example, the source route options must be reversed on the reply packet. Refer to RFC 1122 (Requirements for Internet Hosts), sections 3.2.1.8, 4.1.3.2, and 4.2.3.8, and to RFC 1812 (Requirements for IP Version 4 Routers).
>
> Some of the places where this routine is invoked include:
>
> - `icmp_reply` to reply to an ingress ICMP request
> - `icmp_send` when an ingress IP packet meets conditions that require the generation of an ICMP message
> - `ip_send_reply`, which is the generic routine provided by IP to reply to an ingress IP packet
> - TCP to save the options of an ingress SYN segment

Now let's see how the functions are used in practice. Because you have not yet seen the internals of all the functions in Figure 18-1 in Chapter 18, you may not understand everything at this stage. You can come back to this second part of the section once you are familiar with the other functions.

As you saw in Figure 18-1 in Chapter 18, different paths can lead to the transmission of a packet, and they handle the IP options in slightly different ways. I will cover two cases and leave you the others as an exercise.

Option Processing

The options of an ingress IP packet are first parsed with the `ip_options_compile` function, described in the next section. As mentioned in the previous section, the options are then processed by different routines at different times, depending on whether a packet is to be forwarded, fragmented, etc. Figure 19-3 summarizes where the key routines introduced in the previous section (with a lighter color) are called for ingress packets and for locally generated packets.

When an ingress packet is to be forwarded, `ip_rcv_finish` calls `ip_forward` (via `dst_input`) to take care of the forwarding process. `ip_forward` handles the Router Alert option, if present, and makes sure that there are no problems with the strict source route option. Then it asks `ip_forward_finish` to complete the job of forwarding. The latter can behave differently depending on whether the header contains options.

Let's suppose the packet had options. In this case, `ip_forward_finish` calls `ip_forward_options` to handle those options that should be processed when forwarding a packet, and then calls `dst_output` to carry out the actual transmission. As shown in Figure 18-1 in Chapter 18, `dst_output` ends up calling `ip_output` when the ingress IP packet needs to be forwarded.

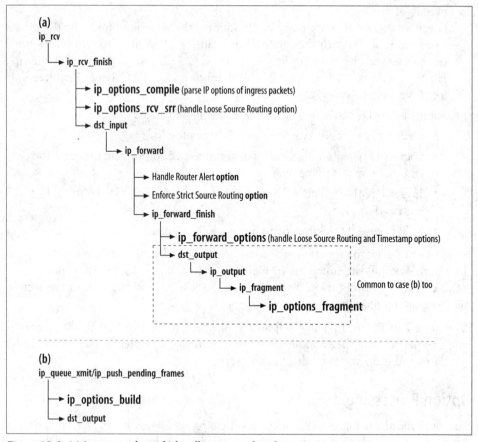

Figure 19-3. (a) Ingress packets; (b) locally generated packets

At this stage, the IP header is ready to be used, because all of the options have been processed. If there was no fragmentation, options processing is finished. However, if the packet needs to be fragmented, ip_output needs to make sure that only the first fragment includes all of the options; the others should have only a subset, according to Table 18-1 in Chapter 18. In this case, ip_output calls ip_fragment. Once the first fragment is done, ip_fragment uses ip_options_fragment to clear the options that are not needed for the subsequent fragments. This way, ip_fragment can keep copying the IP header from the original packet and have all the options correct.

In a locally generated packet, options are handled with ip_options_build. We will see in Chapter 21 how that function is used by ip_queue_xmit and ip_push_pending_frames.

Option Parsing

Parsing, here, means extracting the IP options from the format in which they are stored in an IP packet's header and storing them in a structure called `ip_options` that is more convenient for program code to handle. Storing them in a dedicated data structure is useful because different options are handled in different parts of the IP code. `ip_options_compile` only parses the options, it does not process them. We saw in the previous section where options are processed.

The function `ip_options_compile` is called in two different cases:

- By `ip_rcv_finish` to parse and validate the IP options of the input packets. As shown in Figure 18-1 in Chapter 18, `ip_rcv_finish` is called for all ingress packets, regardless of whether they will be delivered locally or forwarded. When I refer to ingress packets in this section, I am including the case of ingress packets that need to be forwarded because they are not addressed to the local system.

- By `ip_options_get`, for example, to parse the input to the `setsockopt` system call for `AF_INET` sockets.

Let's now analyze how `ip_options_compile` parses the options of an IP packet's header. This is the function's prototype:

```
int ip_options_compile(struct ip_options * opt, struct sk_buff * skb)
```

The values of the two input parameters let the function know the context in which it is being called:

- Ingress packet: `skb` not NULL (in this case, `opt` is NULL)
- Packet being transmitted: `skb` equal to NULL (in this case, `opt` is non-NULL)

This means that depending on the function's context, the IP header is stored in different places. When transmitting a locally generated packet, `opt` is not NULL and `opt->data` contains a pointer to an IP header that was previously partially generated by the caller. If instead the function is processing an ingress packet, the header is contained in the `skb` input buffer and `opt` is NULL. In this second case, the `ip_options` structure is stored in `skb->cb`. `ip_options_compile` initializes local variables such as `optptr` according to where the IP header is located (i.e., `skb->nh` or `opt->__data`). The value of `skb` is also often used by `ip_options_compile` to distinguish between the two previous cases.

In both cases (transmit and forward), you need to fill in `opt`. The only choices to make are where to get the input IP header to parse and where to store the result.

```
if (!opt) {
    opt = &(IPCB(skb)->opt);
    memset(opt, 0, sizeof(struct ip_options));
    iph = skb->nh.raw;
    opt->optlen = ((struct iphdr *)iph)->ihl*4 - sizeof(struct iphdr);
    optptr = iph + sizeof(struct iphdr);
    opt->is_data = 0;
```

```
    } else {
        optptr = opt->is_data ? opt->__data : (unsigned char*)&(skb->nh.iph[1]);
        iph = optptr - sizeof(struct iphdr);
    }
```

If parsing fails, `ip_options_compile` returns immediately. The caller will handle the event in one of the following ways, depending on whether the options were used by a received or transmitted packet:

Bad option in a received packet
> An ICMP message is sent back to the source.

Bad option in a transmitted packet
> The application is notified through an error value returned by the function used to transmit the packet.

Among the possible reasons for a parsing failure are:

- A single option cannot be present more than once in the header. The only exception is the dummy or null option `IPOPT_NOOP`. The latter can be present any number of times and is usually used to enforce some kind of alignment, either on an individual option or on the payload that follows the options (the null option needs no handling).

- The value of a header field has been assigned an invalid value, or a value that the current user is not allowed to use. This case applies to locally generated traffic. Only the superuser is allowed to generate IP packets with option or suboption codes not understood by the kernel. The check for the superuser privilege is done by the `capable` function.

  The original IP RFC says that when receiving an option that is not understood, a router should just ignore it. Linux behaves differently only with locally generated packets (see the earlier reference to `capable`).

Currently, there are only two single-byte options:

- End of options (`IPOPT_END`)
- Null option (`IPOPT_NOOP`)

The main `for` loop simply goes option by option and stores the result of parsing in the output `ip_options` structure opt. The code inside the loop may look complex, but actually it is very easy to read if you take into consideration the following points:

- l represents the size of the block of options that has not been parsed yet.[*]
- `optptr` points to the current position on the block of options being analyzed. `optptr[1]` is the option's length, and `optptr[2]` is the option pointer (where the

---

[*] While reading the code, make sure you do not confuse the variable l, used as the index of the for loop, with the integer 1. They look quite the same and it is easy to lose an hour trying to understand the code if you confuse them. It has already happened to one person.

option starts). Figure 19-4 shows where the array's elements point. The code that handles each option always starts with two sanity checks based on these parameters.

- `optlen` gets initialized to the length of the current option. Do not confuse `optlen` with `opt->optlen`. Note that when `opt` is not NULL, `optlen` is not initialized because that has already been done in `ip_options_get`.

- The flag `is_changed` is used to keep track of when the header has been changed (which requires the checksum to be recomputed).

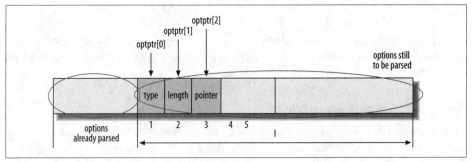

Figure 19-4. ip_options_compile's local variables' values in the middle of an execution

There cannot be other options after the `IPOPT_END` option. Therefore, as soon as one is found, whatever follows it is overwritten with more `IPOPT_END` options.

The basic sanity checks for multibyte options include:

- The option must be at least four bytes long. Since the header of the option is three bytes long, the field `pointer` cannot be smaller than 4. The timestamp option, for instance, requires at least a length of five octets, where four are used just by the header (See Figure 18-8 in Chapter 18).

- Options that reserve space in the header, because they are supposed to be filled in by the next hops or by the destination host, must respect the size required by the option. For instance, the timestamp option is supposed to reserve a space that is a multiple of four bytes (the size of an IPv4 address).

Since the length of each option includes the first two bytes (`type` and `length`) and since it starts counting from 1 (not 0), if `length` is less than 2 or bigger than the block of options left to analyze, there is an error:

```
if (optlen<2 || optlen>l) {
    pp_ptr = optptr;
    goto error;
}
```

Note that some options (such as TIMESTAMP) have a minimum length bigger than 2, and thus the general check just shown is necessary but not always sufficient. The more specific checks are inside the per-option handlers. When an error is found in the options, a special ICMP message has to be sent back to the sender. This ICMP packet includes the original IP header, eight bytes of the IP payload, and an offset that points to where the error was found. The eight bytes of the IP payload consist of the start of the L4 header and usually include the L4 port numbers; this allows the receiver of the ICMP error message to find the socket associated with the faulty IP packet (more details in Chapter 25). Before returning the error message, the code initializes pp_ptr to point to the place where the problem was found.

The switch statement uses, as its discriminator, the option type field. Therefore, each option in handled by a different statement, exactly as was done before for the single-byte options:

```
switch (*optptr)
```

The next sections analyze the multibyte options one by one, and Figures 19-5(a) and 19-5(b) show the big picture. The two obsolete options SEC and SIC are recognized but not processed[*] (see RFC 1812).

Option: strict and loose Source Routing

Only one Source Routing option can appear in a header. The flag opt->srr is used to detect that condition: if the following code does not find any error in the option, it sets that flag. If another option of the same type appears later in the header, the error will be detected.

opt->is_strictroute is used to tell the caller whether the Source Routing option was loose or strict.

The section "ip_forward Function" in Chapter 20 shows how packets are dropped if they cannot reach their destinations while respecting the Source Routing rules.

The option is considered faulty if the length of the option (including type and length) is less than 3. This is because the value has to contain the type, length, and pointer fields. At the same time, pointer cannot have a value smaller than 4 because the first three bytes of the option are already used by the type, length, and pointer fields.

When the input skb parameter is NULL, it means that ip_options_compile has been called to parse the options of an outgoing packet (generated locally, not forwarded). In that case, the first IP address in the array of addresses provided by user space is saved in opt->faddr and then removed from the array by shifting the other elements of the array back one position with a memmove operation. This address will be retrieved later by the functions described in Chapter 21, ip_queue_xmit, and the ip_append_data's users, so they know the destination IP address. An easy-to-follow example of the use of opt->faddr can be found in the function udp_sendmsg.

---

[*] There are some other IP options, such as the IP MTU Discovery Option (RFC 1063), that were defined but never really used or found useful in past years, and that were therefore made obsolete. IP MTU Discovery in particular has been replaced by path MTU discovery (RFC 1191, covered in the section "Path MTU discovery" in Chapter 18).

```
if (!skb) {
    if (optptr[2] != 4 || optlen < 7 || ((optlen-3) & 3)) {
        pp_ptr = optptr + 1;
        goto error;
    }
    memcpy(&opt->faddr, &optptr[3], 4);
    if (optlen > 7)
        memmove(&optptr[3], &optptr[7], optlen-7);
}
opt->is_strictroute = (optptr[0] == IPOPT_SSRR);
opt->srr = optptr - iph;
break;
```

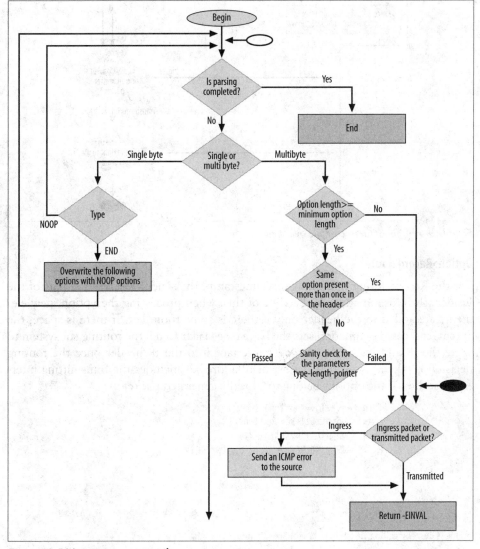

Figure 19-5(a). ip_options_compile overview

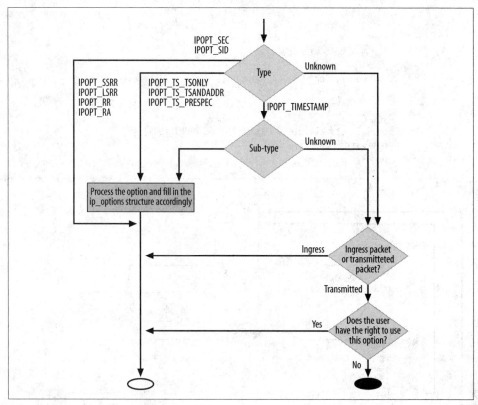

Figure 19-5(b). ip_options_compile overview

Option: Record Route

For the Record Route option, as for Timestamp, the sender reserves the part of the header it will use in advance. Because of this, when processing the option, new elements are added to the header only if there is some room left. If there is space, the ip_options_compile function sets the flag rr_needaddr to tell the routing subsystem to write the IP address of the outgoing interface into the IP header once the routing decision is taken.* Note that the list of IP addresses includes the transmitting interface's address if the options belong to a locally generated packet.

```
if (optptr[2] <= optlen) {
    if (optptr[2]+3 > optlen) {
        pp_ptr = optptr + 2;
        goto error;
    }

    if (skb) {
```

---

* This is done by calling ip_options_build. See Chapter 21.

```
              memcpy(&optptr[optptr[2]-1], &rt->rt_spec_dst, 4);
              opt->is_changed = 1;
          }
          optptr[2] += 4;
          opt->rr_needaddr = 1;
      }
      opt->rr = optptr - iph;
      break;
```

Since skb is non-null only when you are processing the options of an ingress packet, this piece of code simply copies the preferred source IP address into the list of addresses being recorded in the header, and updates the flag is_changed, which will force the IP checksum to be updated. See the section "Preferred Source Address Selection" in Chapter 35 for the reason why the rt_spec_dst IP address is used.

Whether the address is written in the block of code shown here, because the packet is being forwarded, or will be written later thanks to the flag rr_needaddr that is set later, the pointer field of the option is moved ahead four bytes (the size of the IP address). This explains why ip_forward_options (which will be executed if the packet we are processing is being forwarded) will have to go back four bytes to write the IP into the right position.

Option: Timestamp

Because optlen represents the length of the option being analyzed, the if statement simply checks whether any space is left to store the new information. In this case, the length of the option represents the space reserved by the transmitter (not the space used so far).

```
          if (optptr[2] <= optlen) {
              __u32 * timeptr = NULL;
```

The handling of the option depends on the suboption specified by the sub-type field in Figure 18-8 in Chapter 18, but the three suboptions are handled in the same general way. Regardless of the subtype, whoever is going to handle the option needs two pieces of information (which will be stored in the ip_option structure):

- Whether it must record an address, a timestamp, or both
- Where in the IP header the information has to be written (the offset)

If a timestamp needs to be recorded (this would be true for the TS_ONLY and TS_TSANDADDR cases), timeptr would be initialized to point to the right place where it should be written inside the IP header. Note also that timeptr is initialized only when skb is not NULL, which is the case when the option belongs to an ingress packet (as opposed to one that is locally generated).

We already saw in the section "Option Parsing" that ip_options_compile can also be called when handling locally generated packets. In that case, skb would be NULL, so timeptr would not be initialized (i.e., it would be left NULL) and no timestamp would be recorded in the header. There is nothing wrong here, because the timestamp will be put there by ip_options_build. That function will store the timestamp because opt->ts_needtime equals 1.

The only difference between processing an ingress packet to be forwarded and a locally generated packet is that in the former case, a timestamp is added to the IP header and the checksum has to be recomputed (so opt->is_changed needs to be set as well).

When the subcode is IPOPT_TS_PRESPEC, the timestamp has to be added only when the next IP address to match is local to the system. The function used to make that check is inet_addr_type; here are the main return values:

RTN_LOCAL
> The IP address belongs to a local interface.

RTN_UNICAST
> The IP address is reachable according to the routing table and is unicast.

RTN_MULTICAST
> The address is multicast.

RTN_BROADCAST
> The address is broadcast.

Since local broadcasts and registered multicast addresses could be considered local (i.e., addresses the system listens to), the following piece of code that checks RTN_UNICAST does exactly what we want—it determines whether the address is local:

```
{
    u32 addr;
    memcpy(&addr, &optptr[optptr[2]-1], 4);
    if (inet_addr_type(addr) == RTN_UNICAST)
        break;
    if (skb)
        timeptr = (__u32*)&optptr[optptr[2]+3];
}
opt->ts_needtime = 1;
```

Depending on the suboption being processed, the timestamp has to be written at a different offset within the IP header. The first part initializes timeptr accordingly, and the second part copies the timestamp to the right position. Depending on the suboption, the ts_needtime and tr_needaddr flags are also initialized.

```
if (timeptr) {
    struct timeval tv;
    __u32 midtime;
    do_gettimeofday(&tv);
    midtime = htonl((tv.tv_sec % 86400) * 1000 + tv.tv_usec / 1000);
    memcpy(timeptr, &midtime, sizeof(__u32));
    opt->is_changed = 1;
}
```

This last part takes care of the counter overflow we described in the section "Timestamp Option" in Chapter 18.

```
unsigned overflow = optptr[3]>>4;
if (overflow == 15) {
    pp_ptr = optptr + 3;
    goto error;
}
opt->ts = optptr - iph;
if (skb) {
    optptr[3] = (optptr[3]&0xF)|((overflow+1)<<4);
    opt->is_changed = 1;
}
```

Option: Router Alert

As we explained in the section "Router Alert Option" in Chapter 18, the last two bytes of this option must be zero. If this option passes the sanity check, ip_options_ compile initializes the router_alert flag so that later ip_forward will handle it accordingly. (opt->router_alert is simply treated as Boolean, zero, or nonzero.)

```
if (optptr[2] == 0 && optptr[3] == 0)
    opt->router_alert = optptr - iph;
```

Handling parsing errors

If the error was found in a locally generated packet (skb==NULL), the function simply returns an error that will have to be handled by the caller. If instead it was found on a received IP packet, an ICMP error message has to be sent back to the source:

```
error:
    if (skb) {
        icmp_send(skb, ICMP_PARAMETERPROB, 0, htonl((pp_ptr-iph)<<24));
    }
    return -EINVAL;
}
```

CHAPTER 20

Internet Protocol Version 4 (IPv4): Forwarding and Local Delivery

At the end of the ip_rcv_finish function, if the destination address is different from the local interface, the kernel has to forward packets to the appropriate host. On the other hand, if the destination address is local, the kernel has to prepare the packet for use by higher layers. As discussed in the section "The ip_rcv_finish Function" in Chapter 19, the correct choice is taken from the skb buffer through a call to dst_input. Let's see now how the two tasks (forwarding and local delivery) are accomplished.

Forwarding

As with many networking activities described in the previous chapter, forwarding is split into two functions: ip_forward and ip_forward_finish. The second is called at the end of the first, if Netfilter allows it. Both functions are defined in *net/ipv4/ip_forward.c*.

By this time, thanks to the call to ip_route_input in ip_rcv_finish described in Chapter 19, the sk_buff buffer contains all the information needed to forward the packet. Forwarding consists of the following steps:

1. Process the IP options. This may involve recording the local IP address and a timestamp if options in the IP header require them.

2. Make sure that the packet can be forwarded, based on the IP header fields.

3. Decrement the Time To Live (TTL) field of the IP header and discard the packet if the TTL becomes 0.

4. Handle fragmentation if needed, based on the MTU associated with the route.

5. Send the packet out to the outgoing device.

If the packet cannot be forwarded for some reason, the source host has to be notified with an ICMP message that describes the problem encountered. An ICMP message could also be sent as a warning even if the packet will be forwarded, as when a packet is routed with a suboptimal route and triggers a redirect. In the following sections, we'll examine these and other activities in the ip_forward function.

Interaction with IPsec is a major part of forwarding, and is implemented by xfrm4_xxx routines in ip_forward, which are hooks into the IPsec infrastructure. They are not covered in this book for lack of space. The behavior documented here is how forwarding works when IPsec is not configured, in which case those calls simply becomes no-ops.

ICMP Redirect

An ICMP redirect message is sent by a host system (usually a router) when it has been asked to do something that another router is better suited to do (see Chapters 25 and 31 for more details).

When a packet has been source routed, the router assumes the sender had a good reason for requesting the route and does not second-guess it. It honors the requested route and does not send an ICMP redirect message. This special case is covered in the section "ip_forward Function."

ip_forward Function

As we have seen, ip_forward is invoked by ip_rcv_finish (see Figure 18-1 in Chapter 18) to handle all input packets that are not addressed to the local system. The function receives as an input parameter the buffer skb associated with the packet; all the necessary information is inside that structure. skb->dst, the routing information, was initialized by the call to ip_route_input in ip_rcv_finish earlier in the code path (see Chapter 33 for more details).

Figure 20-1 summarizes the internals of the function:

```
int ip_forward(struct sk_buff *skb)
```

The function revolves around manipulations of skb and of a local variable iph, which represents the packet's IP header and is initialized repeatedly from the iph field of skb. (It has to be reinitialized because the header can be changed by some of the functions called from ip_forward.)

If the Router Alert option was found in the IP header, it is handled now.* The function handler for this option is ip_call_ra_chain, which relies on a global list (ip_ra_chain) that contains the list of local sockets that set the IP_ROUTER_ALERT option because they are interested in IP packets that carry the Router Alert IP option. When an ingress IP packet is fragmented, ip_call_ra_chain first defragments the entire IP packet and only then delivers it to the Raw sockets of the ip_ra_chain list, as shown in Figure 18-1 in Chapter 18.

---

* See the section "Router Alert Option" in Chapter 18.

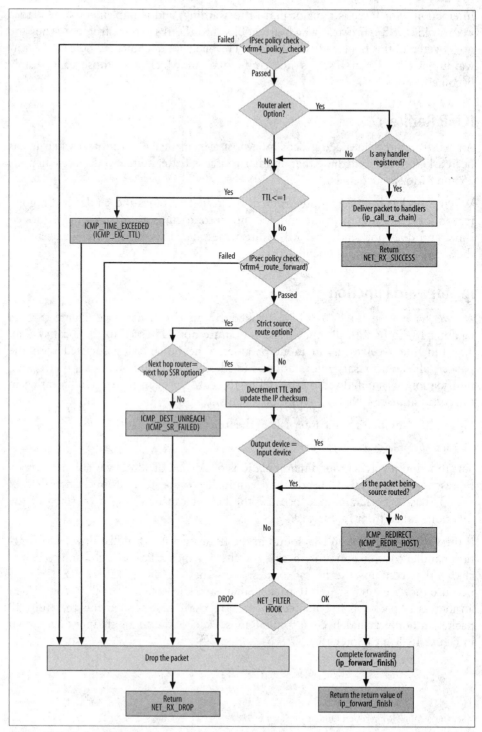

Figure 20-1. ip_forward function

The functions that manage the alert can be found in *net/ipv4/ip_sockglue.c* (see, for example, ip_ra_control and how it is called by ip_setsockopt to apply an option to a socket as requested by the user with a call to the setsockopt system call). ip_forward has no further work to do, and returns success.

If there is no Router_Alert option in the header, or if it is present but no interested processes are running (in which case ip_call_ra_chain returns FALSE), ip_forward continues:

```
if (IPCB(skb)->opt.router_alert && ip_call_ra_chain(skb))
    return NET_RX_SUCCESS;
```

The following check is used just to make sure that the packet we're handling was actually addressed to our host at L2. skb->pkt_type is initialized at the L2 layer (see Chapter 13), and defines the type of frame. It is assigned the value PACKET_HOST when the frame is addressed to the L2 address of the receiving interface. If the lower-level functions do their jobs correctly, there should be no need for this check, but we do it just in case an error left us with a packet we should not have received in the first place.

```
if (skb->pkt_type != PACKET_HOST)
    goto drop;
```

Since we are forwarding the packet, we are operating entirely at the L3 layer and it is not our business to worry about the L4 checksum; we use CHECKSUM_NONE to indicate that the current checksum is OK. If some handling changes the IP header or the TCP header or payload later, before transmission, the kernel will recalculate the checksum there.

```
skb->ip_summed = CHECKSUM_NONE;
```

The real forwarding process starts by decrementing the TTL field. The IP protocol definition says that when TTL reaches the value of 0 (which means you received it with value 1 and it became 0 after you decremented it), the packet has to be dropped and a special ICMP message has to be sent to the source to let it know you dropped the packet.

```
if (iph->ttl <= 1)
        goto too_many_hops;
```

Note that the TTL field has not been decremented yet; it will be done a few lines of code later. The reason for waiting is that the packet may still be shared at this point with other subsystems such as sniffers; the header must be unchanged in that case .

rt points to a data structure of type rtable, which contains all the information needed by the forwarding engine, including the next hop (rt_gateway). If the IP header contains a Strict Source Route option and the next hop (extracted from that option) does not match the one found by the routing subsystem, the Source Routing option fails and the packet is dropped.

```
rt = (struct rtable*)skb->dst;
if (opt->is_strictroute && rt->rt_dst != rt->rt_gateway)
        goto sr_failed;
```

In this case, another ICMP message is transmitted to the sender.

After most of the sanity checks have been fulfilled, the function updates the packet header a bit and then gives it to ip_forward_finish. Since we are about to modify the content of the buffer, we need to make a local copy for ourselves. The copy is actually done by skb_cow only if the packet is shared (if the packet is not shared it can be safely modified) or if the space available at the head of the packet is not sufficient to store the L2 header.

```
if (skb_cow(skb, LL_RESERVED_SPACE(rt->u.dst.dev)+rt->u.dst.header_len))
    goto drop;
```

Now the TTL is decremented by ip_decrease_ttl, which also updates the IP checksum.

```
ip_decrease_ttl(iph);
```

If a better next hop is available than the requested one, the originating host is now notified with an ICMP REDIRECT message—but only if the originating host did not request source routing. The opt->srr field indicates that source routing was requested, in which case the originating host doesn't care whether a supposedly better route is found. In Chapter 35 you will see when exactly the RTCF_DOREDIRECT flag is set on a cached route to indicate that the source of the packet should be sent an ICMP REDIRECT message.

```
if (rt->rt_flags&RTCF_DOREDIRECT && !opt->srr)
    ip_rt_send_redirect(skb);
```

The priority field is set here using the Type of Service field of the IP header. The priority will be used later by Traffic Control (the QoS layer).

```
skb->priority = rt_tos2priority(iph->tos);
```

The function terminates by asking Netfilter to execute ip_forward_finish, if there are no filtering rules that forbid forwarding.

```
return NF_HOOK(PF_INET, NF_IP_FORWARD, skb, skb->dev, rt->u.dst.dev,
        ip_forward_finish);
```

ip_forward_finish Function

If this function is reached, it means the packet has passed all the checks that could stop it and is truly ready to be sent out to another system.

Two possible options from the IP header have been handled so far, as we saw in the section "ip_forward Function": Router Alert and Strict Source Routing. Now we pass the packet to the function ip_forward_options to handle any final work required by the options. It can find out what needs to be done by checking flags (such as opt->rr_needaddr) and offsets (such as opt->rr) initialized earlier by ip_options_compile, which was invoked from ip_rcv_finish. ip_forward_options also recomputes the IP checksum in case it had to update any of the IP header fields. See the section "Option Processing" in Chapter 19.

The packet is finally transmitted with dst_output, described in the next section:

```
static inline int ip_forward_finish(struct sk_buff *skb)
{
    struct ip_options * opt = &(IPCB(skb)->opt);

    IP_INC_STATS_BH(IPSTATS_MIB_OUTFORWDDATAGRAMS);

    if (unlikely(opt->optlen) {
            ip_forward_options(skb);

    return dst_output(skb);
}
```

It may seem we are close to the wire, but there are still a couple of tasks to do before having the device driver do the transmission.

dst_output Function

All transmissions, whether generated locally or forwarded from other hosts, pass through dst_output on their way to a destination host, as shown in Figure 18-1 in Chapter 18. The IP header at this point is finished: it embodies the information needed to transmit as well as any other information the local system was responsible for adding.

```
static inline int dst_output(struct sk_buff *skb)
{
    int err;

    for (;;) {
            err = skb->dst->output(&skb);
            if (likely(err = 0))
                    return err;
            if (unlikely(err != NET_XMIT_BYPASS))
                    return err;
    }
}
```

dst_output invokes the virtual function output, which has been initialized to ip_output if the destination address is unicast and ip_mc_output if it is multicast. Fragmentation is handled in that function. At the end, ip_finish_output is called to interface with the neighboring subsystem (see Figure 18-1 in Chapter 18). ip_finish_output, described in the section "Interface to the Neighboring Subsystem" in Chapter 21, is invoked only if Netfilter gives the green light (otherwise, the packet is dropped).

Note that the output function can potentially be invoked multiple times if it returns the NET_XMIT_BYPASS value. This is, for instance, a simple mechanism to call a sequence of output routines. The IPsec protocol suite uses it to apply transformations before the real transmission.

Local Delivery

Chapter 35 explains how the forwarding (routing) engine knows that the local host is the packet's destination. We saw at the end of the section "The ip_rcv_finish Function" in Chapter 19 that the call to ip_route_input, at the top of ip_rcv_finish, initializes skb->dst->input to ip_local_deliver when the packet has reached its destination host (as opposed to ip_forward, when it needs to be forwarded). Furthermore, Netfilter is given the final right to decide whether the generic do_something function (such as ip_local_deliver) is allowed to call the corresponding do_something_finish function (in this case, ip_local_deliver_finish) to complete the job.

```
int ip_local_deliver(struct sk_buff *skb)
{
    if (skb->nh.iph->frag_off & htons(IP_MF|IP_OFFSET)) {
        skb = ip_defrag(skb, IP_DEFRAG_LOCAL_DELIVER);
        if (!skb)
            return 0;
    }

    return NF_HOOK(PF_INET, NF_IP_LOCAL_IN, skb, skb->dev, NULL,
                   ip_local_deliver_finish);
}
```

In contrast to forwarding, where defragmentation can mostly be ignored, local delivery has to do a lot of work to handle defragmentation. Except for special cases (such as when Netfilter must defragment a packet to examine its contents), forwarding can be performed on each fragment without trying to recombine them. In contrast, the original IP packet must always be defragmented and passed as a whole for local delivery, because that higher L4 layer is supposed to be blissfully ignorant of the need for fragmentation at the IP layer.

Defragmentation is performed within the ip_defrag function, which returns a pointer to the original packet when it has been completely defragmented, and NULL if it is still incomplete. The code shown from ip_local_deliver calls ip_defrag, checks the return value in the local skb variable, and returns if the packet is incomplete. The second input parameter to ip_defrag is described in the section "ipq Structure" in Chapter 23.

Only when the packet is defragmented can the function deliver it. Netfilter is asked to consult its configuration and execute ip_local_deliver_finish if the packet is accepted. We will cover the details of ip_local_deliver_finish in Chapter 24. Defragmentation was introduced in the section "Packet Fragmentation/Defragmentation" in Chapter 18 and will be shown in detail in Chapter 22.

## CHAPTER 21

Internet Protocol Version 4 (IPv4): Transmission

In this chapter, we discuss packet transmission at the L3 layer, which fits into the top-left corner of Figure 18-1 in Chapter 18. *Transmission* refers to packets leaving the local host for another; it can be initiated by the L4 layer or be invoked as the final stage of forwarding. As shown in Figure 18-1 in Chapter 18, the central function that delivers a packet is dst_output; the functions described in this chapter precede it and prepare packets for it. The tasks of the kernel at this stage include:

Looking up the next hop

The IP layer needs to know the outgoing device and the next router to use for the next hop. The route is found through the function ip_route_output_flow, called at the L3 or L4 layer. This chapter does not discuss routing, because that subject is big enough for its own discussion and is therefore covered in Part VII.

Initializing the IP header

Several fields, such as the packet ID, are filled in at this stage. If the packet is a forwarded one, a little work was done on the header earlier (such as updating the TTL, checksum, and options fields). But much more must be done at this point to enable transmission.

Processing options

The software has to honor options that require the addition of an address or timestamp to the header.

Fragmentation

If the IP packet is too big to be transmitted on the outgoing device, it must be fragmented (unless fragmentation is explicitly forbidden).

Checksum

The IP checksum has to be computed after all other work on the header is done. We will see that the IP layer may take care of the L4 checksum as well as the L3 checksum. In both cases, the checksum can be computed either in one shot or incrementally. While the checksum is required, the L3 layer doesn't always have to calculate it, because some devices' hardware does it (as denoted by the CHECKSUM_HW flag).

Checking with Netfilter

As shown in Figure 18-1 in Chapter 18, the Linux firewall system is given a chance to drop or mangle each packet at various stages of processing, including transmission.

Updating statistics

Depending on the result of the transmission (success or failure) and on actions such as fragmentation, the associated SNMP counters have to be updated.

Option processing and fragmentation are by far the most expensive tasks; fragmentation is addressed in Chapter 22, and options were addressed in Chapter 19. In the past there used to be two different functions for transmission, one for packets that could be transmitted quickly because they didn't need fragmentation or IP option processing, and another that provided all the services. The kernel does not explicitly distinguish the two cases anymore.

Key Functions That Perform Transmission

The two functions listed at the top left of Figure 18-1 in Chapter 18 appear in Figure 21-1, classified by the L4 protocols that invoke them. The reason for two sets of functions is that the right-side L4 protocols (TCP and the Stream Control Transmission Protocol, or SCTP) do a lot of work to prepare for fragmentation; that leaves less work for the IP layer. In contrast, raw IP and the other protocols listed on the left side leave all of the work of fragmentation up to the IP layer.

Figure 21-1 shows the main functions that lie between transmission at L4 and the last step of L3, which is invoking the neighbor function discussed in Chapter 27. At the top of the figure, the most common L4 protocols are shown. UDP and ICMP call one set of L3 functions to carry out transmission, whereas TCP and SCTP call another. When the L3 functions described in this chapter finish their work, they pass packets to dst_output. As for raw IP, when it uses the IP_HDRINCL option it is completely responsible for preparing the IP header, so it bypasses the functions described in this chapter and calls dst_output directly. See the section "Raw Sockets" for more details. The Internet Group Management Protocol (IGMP) also makes a direct call to dst_output (after initializing the IP header on its own).

Thus, fragmentation is handled by the two sets of functions as follows:

ip_queue_xmit

The L4 protocol has already divided the data into chunks that are sized properly for fragmentation (if it is needed), taking into account the PMTU as discussed in Chapter 18. The work at the IP layer consists simply of adding IP headers to the data fragments already created.

ip_push_pending_frames *and related functions*

The L4 protocols invoking this function do not consider fragmentation or help perform it. Furthermore, for the sake of efficiency, they introduce complexity by

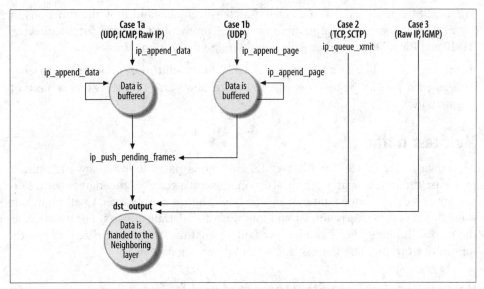

Figure 21-1. Different protocols invoking dst_output differently

their way of passing the data in the packet down to the IP layer. Depending on several factors covered later in this chapter, an L4 protocol can store several transmission requests through multiple calls to ip_append_data without actually transmitting anything.

ip_append_data does not simply buffer transmission requests, but transparently generates data fragments of optimal sizes to make it easier for the IP layer to handle fragmentation later. This saves the IP layer from having to copy data from one buffer to another while making fragments, and leads to a significant performance gain.

When the L4 protocol needs to flush the output queue created with ip_append_data, the protocol invokes ip_push_pending_frames, which in turn does any necessary fragmentation and pushes the resulting packets down to dst_output.

A variant of ip_append_data named ip_append_page is currently used by UDP. We will briefly describe this function later.

Other functions are also used during transmission in specific contexts:

ip_build_and_send_pkt
   Used by TCP to send SYN ACKs.

ip_send_reply
   Used by TCP to send ACKs and Resets. The classification of Figure 21-1 only covers the most common cases: since ip_send_reply uses ip_append_data and ip_push_pending_frame, it follows that TCP does not use only ip_queue_xmit.

These will be pretty easy to understand after you understand how the functions in Figure 21-1 work. It is also possible for an L4 protocol to call dst_output directly; IGMP and RawIP are two protocols that do it (see the section "Raw Sockets").

In this chapter, I briefly cover ip_queue_xmit, but spend more time on ip_append_ data/ip_push_pending_frames because they are key parts of the complex task of fragmentation.

Multicast Traffic

As shown in Figure 18-1 in Chapter 18, the egress paths followed by transmitted multicast and unicast traffic are similar—more similar than for the ingress path. I do not go into detail about multicast in this book, but in this chapter I will point out some differences between unicast and multicast during transmission. For instance, in the section"Building the IP header" we will see that the TTL is initialized differently for multicast traffic. The same is true when forwarding packets.

Relevant Socket Data Structures for Local Traffic

A BSD socket is represented in Linux with an instance of a socket structure. This structure includes a pointer to a sock data structure, which is where the network layer information is stored. The sock data structure is pretty big but is well documented in *include/net/sock.h*. The sock data structure is actually allocated as part of a bigger structure that is specific to the protocol family; for PF_INET sockets the structure is inet_sock, defined in *include/linux/ip.h*. The first field of inet_sock is a sock instance, and the rest stores PF_INET private information, such as the source and destination IP addresses, the IP options, the packet ID, the TTL, and cork (discussed next).

```
struct inet_sock {
    struct sock sk;
    ... ... ...
    struct {
        ... ... ...
    } cork;
}
```

Given a pointer to a sock data structure, the IP layer uses the inet_sk macro to cast the pointer to the outer inet_sock data structure. In other words, the base address of the inet_sock and sock structures is the same, a feature commonly exploited in C programs that deal with complex, nested structures.

The inet_sock's cork field plays an important role in ip_append_data and ip_append_ page: it stores the context information needed by those two functions to do data fragmentation correctly. Among the various information it contains are the options in the IP header (if any) and the fragment length.

Whenever a transmission is generated locally (with only a few exceptions), each sk_buff buffer is associated with its sock instance and is linked to it with skb->sk.

Different functions are used to set and read the value of the fields of the sock and inet_sock structures. Some of them are called by the functions in Figure 21-1. As far as this chapter is concerned, we need to understand the meaning of only a few of them:

sk_dst_set *and* __sk_dst_set
> Once the socket is connected, these functions save the route used to reach the destination in the sock structure. sk_dst_set is a simple wrapper to __sk_dst_set that takes care of locking. If locking is not needed (because it was already taken care of), __sk_dst_set can be called directly.

sk_dst_check *and* __sk_dst_check
> As the names suggest, the validity of the route can be tested with these two APIs. However, if the route is valid, they return it as their return value. This means that these functions can be used to retrieve the route, not just to test the validity. (An invalid route causes them to return NULL.) The two functions are very similar; they differ slightly in terms of how they clear the cached route if they find out that it is not valid anymore.

skb_set_owner_w
> Assigns an sk_buff buffer to a given sock structure. This is useful for accounting.

sock_alloc_send_skb *and* sock_wmalloc
> These functions allocate sk_buff buffers. sock_alloc_send_skb is called to allocate a single buffer or the first fragment of a series (see the discussion of ip_append_data); sock_wmalloc takes care of subsequent fragments. Both end up calling alloc_skb, but the first function is more complex and can fail for more reasons than the second. This is because if allocation of the first buffer succeeds, the following allocations have few reasons to fail.

Another data structure that appears in many of the functions in this chapter is the routing table cache entry associated with the packet, rtable. Many functions refer to it through a variable named rt. It contains information such as the outgoing device, the MTU of the outgoing device, and the next hop gateway. This structure is initialized by ip_route_output_flow and is described in Chapter 36.

The ip_queue_xmit Function

ip_queue_xmit is the function currently used by TCP and SCTP. It receives only two input parameters, and all the information needed to process the packet is accessible (directly or indirectly) through skb.

```
int ip_queue_xmit(struct sk_buff *skb, int ipfragok)
```

Here is what the parameters mean:

skb

> Buffer descriptors for the packet to transmit. This data structure has all the parameters needed to fill in the IP header and to transmit the packet (e.g., the next hop gateway). Remember that ip_queue_xmit is used to handle locally gen-erated packets; forwarded packets do not have an associated socket.

ipfragok

> A flag used mainly by SCTP to say whether fragmentation is allowed.

The socket associated with skb includes a pointer named opt that refers to a struc-ture we saw in the section "Option Parsing" in Chapter 19. The latter structure con-tains the options in the IP header in a format that makes them easier for functions at the IP layer to access. This structure is kept in the socket structure because it is the same for every packet sent through that socket; it would be wasteful to rebuild the information for every packet.

```
struct sock *sk = skb->sk;
struct inet_sock *inet = inet_sk(sk);
struct ip_options *opt = inet->opt;
```

Among the fields of the opt structure are offsets to the locations in the header where functions can store timestamps and IP addresses requested by IP options. Note that the structure does not cache the IP header itself, but only data that tells us what to write into the header, and where.

Setting the route

If the buffer is already assigned the proper routing information (skb->dst), there is no need to consult the routing table. This is possible under some conditions when the buffer is handled by the SCTP protocol:

```
rt = (struct rtable *) skb->dst;
if (rt != NULL)
    goto packet_routed;
```

In other cases, ip_queue_xmit checks whether a route is already cached in the socket structure and, if one is available, makes sure it is still valid (this is done by __sk_dst_check):

```
rt = (struct rtable *)__sk_dst_check(sk, 0);
```

If the socket does not already have a route for the packet cached, or if the one the IP layer has been using so far has been invalidated in the meantime, such as by an update from a routing protocol, ip_queue_xmit needs to look for a new route with ip_route_output_flow and store the result in the sk data structure. The destination is represented by the daddr variable. First, this variable is set to the final destination of the packet (inet->daddr), which is the proper value if the IP header includes no Source Route option. However, ip_queue_xmit then checks for a Source Route option and, if one exists, sets the daddr variable to the next hop in the source route (inet->faddr). In case of a Strict Source Route option, the next hop found by ip_route_output_flow has to match exactly the next hop in the source route list.

```
if (rt == NULL) {
    u32 daddr;

    daddr = inet->daddr;
    if(opt && opt->srr)
        daddr = opt->faddr;

    {
        struct flowi fl = { .oif = sk->sk_bound_dev_if,
                    .nl_u = { .ip4_u =
                                { .daddr = daddr,
                                  .saddr = inet->saddr,
                                  .tos = RT_CONN_FLAGS(sk) } },
                    .proto = sk->sk_protocol,
                    .uli_u = { .ports =
                                { .sport = inet->sport,
                                  .dport = inet->dport } } };

        if (ip_route_output_flow(&rt, &fl, sk, 0))
            goto no_route;
    }
    __sk_dst_set(sk, &rt->u.dst);
    tcp_v4_setup_caps(sk, &rt->u.dst);
}
```

Refer to Chapter 36 for details on the flowi data structure, and to Chapter 33 for details on the ip_route_output_flow routine.

The call to tcp_v4_setup_caps saves the features provided by the egress device in the socket sk; we can ignore this call during our discussion.

The packet is dropped if ip_route_output_flow fails. If the route is found, it is stored with __sk_dst_set in the sk data structure so that it can be used directly next time, and the routing table does not have to be consulted again. If for some reason the route is invalidated again, a future call to ip_queue_xmit will use ip_route_output_flow once more to find a new one.

As the following code shows, the packet is dropped if the IP header carries the Strict Source Routing option, and the next hop provided by that option does not match the next hop returned by the routing table:[*]

```
    skb->dst = dst_clone(&rt->u.dst);

packet_routed:
    if (opt && opt->is_strictroute && rt->rt_dst != rt->rt_gateway)
        goto no_route;
```

---

[*] We saw something similar in the section "ip_forward Function" in Chapter 20.

`dst_clone` is called to increment the reference count on the data structure assigned to `skb->dst`.

When a packet is dropped, an error code is returned to the upper layer and the associated SNMP statistics are updated. Note that in this case the function does not need to send any ICMP to the source (we are the source).

Instead, if everything is OK, we have all the information needed to transmit the packet and it is time to build the IP header.

Building the IP header

So far, `skb` contains only the IP payload—generally the header and payload from the L4 layer, either TCP or SCTP. These protocols always allocate buffers whose size will be able to handle worst case scenarios with regards to the addition of the lower layer headers. In this way they reduce the chances that IP or any other lower layer will have to do memory copies or buffer reallocation to handle the addition of headers that do not fit the free space.

When `ip_queue_xmit` receives `skb`, `skb->data` points to the beginning of the L3 payload, which is where the L4 protocol writes its own data. The L3 header lies before this pointer. So `skb_push` is used here to move `skb->data` back so that it points to the beginning of the L3 or IP header; the result is illustrated in Figure 19-2 in Chapter 19. `iph` is also initialized to the pointer at that location.

```
iph = (struct iphdr *) skb_push(skb, sizeof(struct iphdr) +
                                     (opt ? opt->optlen : 0));
```

The next block initializes a bunch of fields in the IP header. The first assignment sets the value of three fields (`version`, `ihl` and `tos`) in one shot, because they share a common 16 bits. Thus, the statement sets the Version in the header to 4, the Header Length to 5, and the TOS to `inet->tos`.

Some of the values used to initialize the IP header are taken from `sk` and some others from `rt`, both of which were described earlier in the section "Relevant Socket Data Structures for Local Traffic."

```
*((__u16 *)iph) = htons((4 << 12) | (5 << 8) | (inet->tos & 0xff));
iph->tot_len = htons(skb->len);
if (ip_dont_fragment(sk, &rt->u.dst) && !ipfragok)
    iph->frag_off = htons(IP_DF);
else
    iph->frag_off = 0;
iph->ttl      = ip_select_ttl(inet, &rt->u.dst);
iph->protocol = sk->sk_protocol;
iph->saddr    = rt->rt_src;
iph->daddr    = rt->rt_dst;
skb->nh.iph   = iph;
```

If the IP header contains options, the function needs to update the Header Length field `iph->length`, which was previously initialized to its default value, and then call ip_options_build to take care of the options. ip_options_build uses the opt variable, previously initialized to inet->opt, to add the required option fields (such as timestamps) to the IP header. Note that the last parameter to ip_options_build is set to zero, to specify that the header does not belong to a fragment (see the section "IP Options" in Chapter 19).

```
if(opt && opt->optlen) {
    iph->ihl += opt->optlen >> 2;
    ip_options_build(skb, opt, inet->daddr, rt, 0);
}

mtu = dst_pmtu(&rt->u.dst);
```

Then ip_select_ident_more sets the IP ID in the header based on whether the packet is likely to be fragmented (see the section "Selecting the IP Header's ID Field" in Chapter 23), and ip_send_check computes the checksum on the IP header.

skb->priority is used by Traffic Control to decide which one of the outgoing queues to enqueue the packet in; this in turn helps determine how soon it will be transmitted. The value in this function is taken from the sock structure, whereas in ip_forward (which manages nonlocal traffic and therefore does not have a local socket) its value is derived from a conversion table based on the IP TOS value (see the section "ip_forward Function" in Chapter 20).

```
ip_select_ident_more(iph, &rt->u.dst, sk, skb_shinfo(skb)->tso_segs);
ip_send_check(iph);
skb->priority = sk->sk_priority;
```

Finally, Netfilter is called to see whether the packet has the right to jump to the following step (dst_output) and continue transmission:

```
return NF_HOOK(PF_INET, NF_IP_LOCAL_OUT, skb, NULL, rt->u.dst.dev,
        dst_output);
```

The ip_append_data Function

This is the function used by those L4 protocols that want to buffer data for transmission. As stated earlier in this chapter, this function does not transmit data, but places it in conveniently sized buffers for later functions to form into fragments (if necessary) and transmit. Thus, it does not create or manipulate any IP header. To flush and transmit the data buffered by ip_append_data, the L4 layer has to explicitly call ip_push_pending_frames, which also takes care of the IP header.

If the L4 layer wants fast response time, it might call ip_push_pending_frames after each call to ip_append_data. But the two functions are provided so that the L4 layer can buffer as much data as possible (up to the size of the PMTU) and then send it at once to be efficient.

As one consequence of its role in preparing packets, ip_append_data buffers data only up to the maximum size of an IP packet. As explained in the section "Packet Fragmentation/Defragmentation" in Chapter 18, this is 64 KB.

The main tasks of ip_append_data are:

- Organize the input data from the L4 layer into buffers whose size will make it easier to handle IP fragmentation if needed. This includes placing those data fragments into buffers in such a way that the L3 and L2 layers will find it easy to add the lower-layer headers later.

- Optimize memory allocation, taking into account information from upper layers and the capabilities of the egress device. In particular:

  - If upper layers signal that more transmission requests will follow shortly (through the MSG_MORE flag), it could make sense to allocate a bigger buffer.

  - If the egress device supports Scatter/Gather I/O (NETIF_F_SG), fragments can be arranged in memory pages to optimize memory handling.

- Take care of the L4 checksum. We saw in the section "net_device structure" in Chapter 19 how skb->ip_summed is initialized based on the egress device capabilities and other factors.

Given the more complex job of ip_append_data, compared to ip_queue_xmit, its more complex prototype should not come as a surprise:

```
int ip_append_data(struct sock *sk,
                int getfrag(void *from, char *to, int offset, int len,
                        int odd, struct sk_buff *skb),
                void *from, int length, int transhdrlen,
                struct ipcm_cookie *ipc, struct rtable *rt,
                unsigned int flags)
```

Here is the meaning of the input parameters:

sk

Socket behind this packet's transmission. This data structure contains some of the parameters (such as the IP options) that will be needed later to fill in the IP header (by the ip_push_pending_frames function).

from

Pointer to the data (payload) the L4 layer is trying to transmit. This can be either a kernel or a user-space pointer, and it's the getfrag function's job (described next) to handle it correctly.

getfrag

Function used to copy the payload received from the L4 layer into the data fragments that will be created. More details can be found in the section "Copying data into the fragments: getfrag."

length

Amount of data to transmit (including both the L4 header and the L4 payload).

transhdrlen

> Size of the transport (L4) header.

ipc

> Information needed to forward the packet correctly. See the section "ipcm_cookie Structure" in Chapter 23.

rt

> Routing table cache entry associated with the packet (described in Chapter 36). While ip_queue_xmit retrieves this information itself, ip_append_data relies on the caller to collect that information by means of ip_route_output_flow.

flags

> This variable can contain any of the MSG_*XXX* flags defined in *include/linux/socket. h*. Three of them are used by this function:
>
> MSG_MORE
>
> > This flag is used by applications to tell the L4 layer that there will be more transmissions shortly. As we see here, this flag is propagated to the L3 layer. Later we will see how this information can be useful when allocating buffers.
>
> MSG_DONTWAIT
>
> > When this flag is set, the call to ip_append_data must not block. ip_append_data may need to allocate a buffer (with sock_alloc_send_skb) for the socket sk. When the latter has already exhausted its budget, it can either block (with a timer) in the hope that some space will be made available before the timer expires, or fail. This flag can be used to choose between the two previous options.
>
> MSG_PROBE
>
> > When this flag is set, the user does not really want to transmit anything; he is only probing the path. The flag can be used, for instance, to test a PMTU on a path toward a given IP address.* ip_append_data simply returns immediately with a successful return code if this flag is set.

ip_append_data is a long and complex function. The presence of numerous local variables defined, often with similar names, make it hard to follow. We will therefore break it down into the main steps. Given that there are many different combinations of possible outputs, based on the considerations listed near the beginning of this section, we will focus on a few common cases. By the end, you should be able to derive the other cases by yourself.

The next few sections describe what the outcome of ip_append_data should be. After that come several sections describing the initial tasks of the function, finishing with a description of its main loop.

The labels hh_len, exthdrlen, fraghdrlen, trailer_len, copy, and length in Figures 21-2 through 21-7 are either input parameters to ip_append_data or local variables

---

* It may not be clear, by looking at ip_append_data, how MSG_PROBE can be used to test the PMTU. See raw_send_hdrinc in *net/ipv4/raw.c* for an example.

used by ip_append_data (in particular, the value of copy shown in the figures is the one passed to getfrag). All of them are expressed in bytes. The labels X, Y, S, S1, and S2 represent the size of a data block expressed in bytes.

Basic memory allocation and buffer organization for ip_append_data

It is important to understand how the output from ip_append_data—the fragments to be turned into IP packets—is organized in memory. This section and the following two sections cover the data structures that organize the output data and how they are used. The same explanation applies to data formatted by the L4 layer and passed to ip_queue_xmit: this is done, for instance, by TCP instead of using ip_append_data. In every case, the buffers are eventually handed to dst_output, which appears near the center of Figure 18-1 in Chapter 18. Let's see a few examples.

ip_append_data can create one or more sk_buff instances, each representing a distinct IP packet (or IP fragment). This is true regardless of how the data is stored in sk_buff (i.e., regardless of whether it is fragmented).

Suppose we want to transmit an amount of data that lies within the PMTU (that is, it does not need to be fragmented). Let's also assume that because of the configuration of our host, we need to apply at least one of the protocols of the IPsec suite. Finally, let's suppose for the sake of simplicity that we are not trying to achieve memory optimizations in the way we allocate buffers. The results of ip_append_data (shown in Figure 21-2) in this case are as follows:

- Because no fragmentation is needed, we allocate just one buffer.
- The protocols of the IPsec suite may require both a header and a trailer, which wrap around the traditional buffer (including its traditional IP header). We need to take that into account both when allocating the buffer and when copying the data from the L4 layer into the buffer.
- We also preallocate space for the header on the L2 layer. *

By reserving the space needed for all the protocols and layers that will come after the L4 layer, we eliminate the need for time-consuming memory manipulation later. Note also that the pointers to some of the headers (such as h.raw and nh.raw) are initialized; later the associated protocols can fill in their part. The only portion of the packet that is filled in by ip_append_data is the L4 payload. Other parts will be filled in as follows:

- The L4 header will be filled in by the function that calls ip_push_pending_frames. That function can be invoked directly or via a wrapper (for example, UDP uses udp_push_pending_frames).
- The L3 header (including the IP options) will be filled in by ip_push_pending_frames.

---

* The pointers on the left side of the buffer are sk_buff's fields, and the ones on the right side are ip_append_data's local variables.

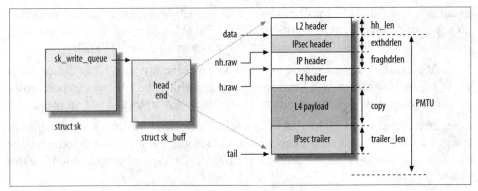

Figure 21-2. IP packet that does not need fragmentation, with IPsec

Part VI covers the L2 part of the header.

Now let's take a slightly more complex example that requires fragmentation. From the previous example, let's remove IPsec and increase the payload size so that it exceeds the PMTU. Figure 21-3 shows the output.[*]

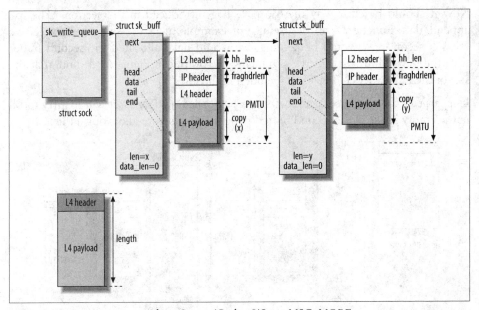

Figure 21-3. Fragmentation without Scatter/Gather I/O, no MSG_MORE

The object on the bottom left is the buffer that `ip_append_data` receives in input, and `length` is another of `ip_append_data`'s input parameters. Two buffers created by the function lie to the right. Note that the first contains a fragment that has the

---

[*] We will see in the section "Buffer allocation" that if the PMTU is not a multiple of eight bytes, the size of all fragments (with the exception of the last one) is shortened to the closest 8-byte boundary.

maximum size (PMTU), and the second contains leftover data. `ip_append_data` creates as many buffers as necessary based on the PMTU; it happens here that a second one holds all the remaining payload, and that it is smaller than the PMTU.

We said previously that `ip_append_data` will not transmit anything; it just creates buffers to be used later for packet fragments. This means that the L4 layer can potentially invoke `ip_append_data` again for either of the previous examples and add more data.

Let's take the second example and show what happens. Since the second buffer is full, we are forced to allocate a new buffer. This might end up with suboptimal fragmentation; it would be better to have every fragment except the last one fill up to the size of the PMTU.

One simple solution to achieve optimal fragmentation, at this point, is to allocate another buffer of maximum size, copy the data there from the second buffer, delete the second buffer, and merge the new data into the new buffer. If there is not enough space, we can allocate a third buffer. But this approach does not offer good performance. It vitiates the essential reason for doing data fragmentation before calling `ip_fragment` (shown in Figure 18-1 in Chapter 18), which is to avoid extra memory copies.

Now it should be clear why the `MSG_MORE` flag introduced in the section "The ip_append_data Function" can be useful. For example, if in the second example, we knew a second call would be coming, we would have allocated the second buffer with the maximum size directly, producing the output in Figure 21-4 (note that the size of the L2 header `hh_len` is not included in the PMTU).

If `ip_append_data` is called again before `ip_push_pending_frames`, it will first try to fill in the empty space in the second buffer in Figure 21-4 before allocating a third.

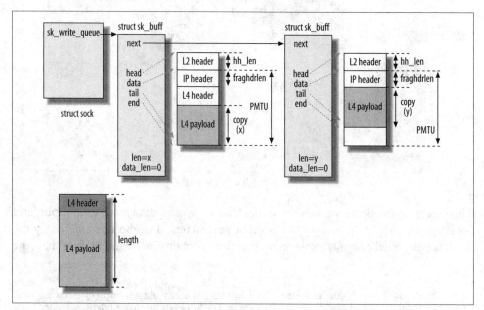

Figure 21-4. Fragmentation without Scatter/Gather I/O, MSG_MORE

Memory allocation and buffer organization for ip_append_data with Scatter Gather I/O

Sometimes it is actually possible to add data to a fragment even if it has not been allocated with the maximum size. That is possible when the device supports Scatter/Gather I/O. This simply means that the L3 layer leaves data in the buffers where the L4 layer placed it, and lets the device combine those buffers to do the transmission. The advantage of Scatter/Gather I/O is that it reduces the overhead of allocating memory and copying data.

Consider this: an upper layer may generate many small items of data in successive operations and the L4 layer may store them in different buffers of kernel memory. The L3 layer is then asked to transmit all of these items in one IP packet. Without Scatter/Gather I/O, the L3 layer has to copy the data into new buffers to make a unified packet. If the device supports Scatter/Gather I/O, the data can stay right where it is until it leaves the host.

When Scatter/Gather I/O is in use, the memory area to which skb->data points is used only the first time. The following chunks of data are copied into pages of memory allocated specifically for this purpose. Figures 21-5 and 21-6 compare how the data received by ip_append_data in its second invocation is saved when Scatter/Gather I/O is enabled, versus when it is disabled:

- Figure 21-5(a) shows memory use after the first call and Figure 21-5(b) shows it after the second call, when Scatter/Gather I/O is *enabled*. A buffer that uses frags is called a paged buffer. Note that the data fragment in Figure 21-5(b) does not need any header: remember that all data fragments of one sk_buff instance are associated with the same IP packet. This also implies that X+S1 is still smaller than the PMTU.

- Figure 21-6(a) shows memory use after the first call and Figure 21-6(b) shows it after the second call, when Scatter/Gather I/O is *disabled*.

Some ancillary data structures support Scatter/Gather I/O. Each buffer except the first (which is allocated in the same way as when there is no support for Scatter/Gather I/O) is stored in skb_shinfo(skb)->frags. These can be found through pointers in the familiar sk_buff structure. As we saw in Chapter 2, each sk_buff structure includes a field of type skb_shared_info, which can be accessed with the macro skb_shinfo. This structure can be used to increase the size of the buffer by adding memory areas that can be located anywhere, not necessarily adjacent to one other. The nr_frags field helps the IP layer remember how many Scatter/Gather I/O buffers hang off of this packet. Note that this field counts Scatter/Gather I/O buffers—not IP fragments, as the name might suggest.

Now we can look at why the kernel needs special support on the device side to use this kind of buffer representation: to be able to refer to memory areas that are not contiguous but whose content is supposed to represent a contiguous data fragment, the device must be able to handle that kind of buffer representation. Note that

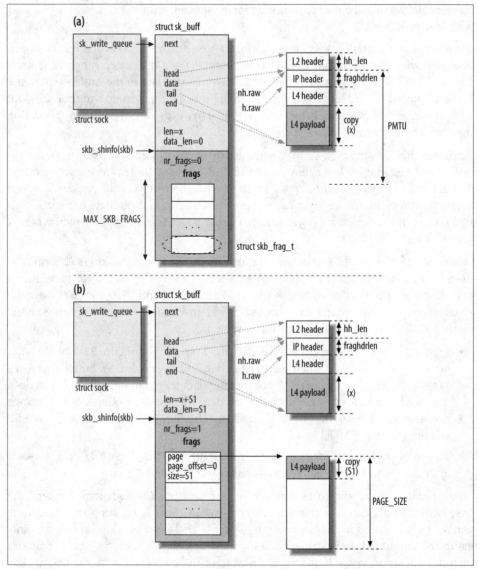

Figure 21-5. ip_append_data with Scatter/Gather I/O

Figure 21-7 shows the simple example where there is one page that contains two adjacent memory areas. But the fragments could easily be nonadjacent, either within a single page or on different pages.

Each element of the frags array is represented by an skb_frag_t structure, which includes a pointer to a memory page, an offset relative to the beginning of the page, and the size of the fragment. Note that since the two fragments in Figure 21-7 are located within the same memory page, their page pointer points to the same memory

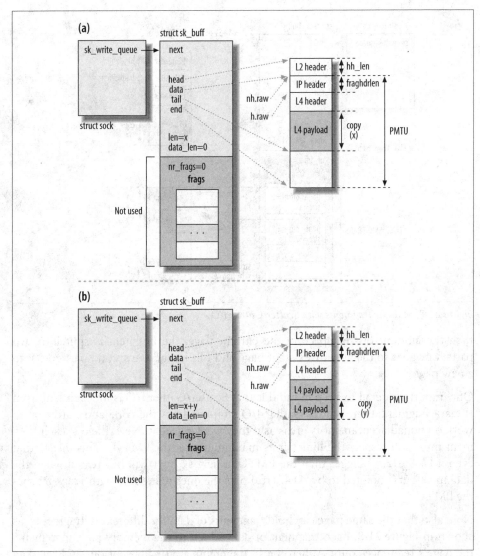

Figure 21-6. ip_append_data without scatter/gather I/O

page. The maximum number of fragments is MAX_SKB_FRAGS, which is defined based on the maximum size of an IP packet (64 KB) and the size of a memory page (which is defined on a per-architecture basis and whose default value on an i386 is 4 KB).

You can find the definitions of all the previously mentioned structures in *include/linux/sk_buff.h*.

Figure 21-7 shows the case where there is only one page, but since there could be several pages, the elements of the frags array include the page pointer to the proper page. A fragment cannot span two pages. When the size of a new fragment is bigger

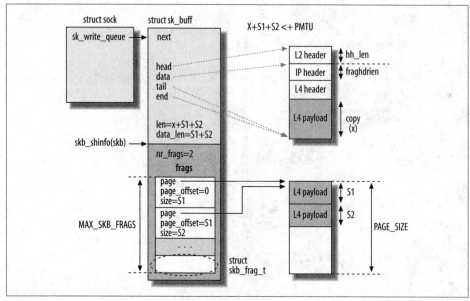

Figure 21-7. Multiple fragments with Scatter/Gather I/O

than the amount of free space in the current page, the fragment is split into two parts: one goes to the already existent page and fills it, and the second part goes into a new page.

One important detail to keep in mind is that Scatter/Gather I/O is independent from IP data fragmentation. Scatter/Gather I/O simply allows the code and hardware to work on nonadjacent memory areas as if they were adjacent. Nevertheless, each fragment must still respect the limit on its maximum size (the PMTU). This means that even if PAGE_SIZE is bigger than the PMTU, a new sk_buff will be created when the data in sk_buff (pointed to by sk_buff->data) plus the ones referenced with frags reaches the PMTU.

Note also that the same page can hold fragments of data for different IP fragments, as shown in Figure 21-8. Each fragment of data added to the memory page increments the page's reference count. When the IP fragments are finally sent out and the data fragments in the page are released, the reference count is decreased accordingly and the memory page is released (see skb_release_data, which is called indirectly by kfree_skb).

The sock structure on the top left of Figure 21-8 includes both a pointer to the last page (sk_sndmsg_page) and an offset (sk_sndmsg_off) inside that page where the next data fragment should be placed.

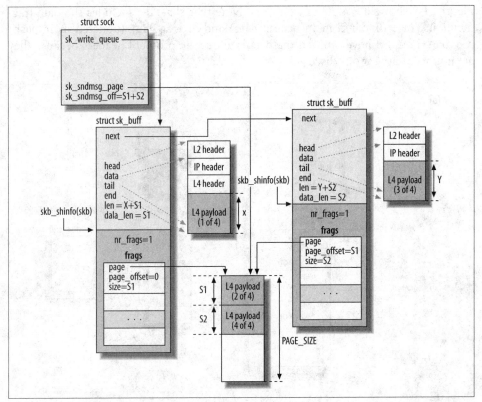

Figure 21-8. Memory page shared between IP fragments

Key routines for handling fragmented buffers

To understand the functions described in this chapter and the ones in Chapter 22, you need to be familiar with the key buffer manipulation routines introduced in Chapter 2, and the following ones:

skb_is_nonlinear
> Returns true when the buffer is fragmented (i.e., skb->data_len is non-null).

skb_headlen
> Given a fragmented buffer, returns the amount of data in the main buffer (i.e., it does not account for the frags fragments nor does it take the frag_list list into account). Do not mistake skb_headlen for skb_headroom: the latter returns the free space between skb->head and skb->data.

skb_pagelen
> Size of a fragmented buffer; it accounts for the data in the main buffer (skb_headlen) and the data in the frags fragments, but it does not consider any buffer linked to the frag_list list.

Figure 21-9 shows a couple of examples. Note that skb->len includes the data fragments in frags (updated in ip_append_data) and in frag_list (updated in ip_push_pending_frames). I have omitted the details about the protocol headers because they are not necessary for our discussion.

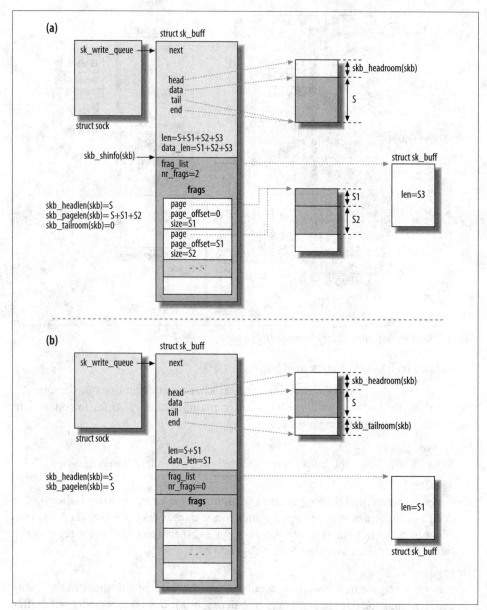

Figure 21-9. Key functions for fragmented buffers: (a) Scatter/Gather; (b) no Scatter/Gather

I also would like to stress this point once more: the data in the frags vector is an extension to the data in the main buffer, and the data in frags_list represents independent buffers (i.e., each one will be transmitted independently as a separate IP fragment).

Further handling of the buffers

Whenever ip_append_data allocates a new sk_buff structure to handle a new data fragment (which will become a new IP fragment), it queues the fragment onto a queue called sw_write_queue that is associated with ip_append_data's input socket sk. This queue is the output of the function. Later functions need only add the IP headers to the data fragments and push them down to the L2 layer (to the dst_output routine, to be exact).

The sk_write_queue list is managed as a First In, First Out (FIFO) queue, as follows:

- New elements (fragments) are added at the tail. It follows that the first element is the one that includes external headers such as IPsec (if any) and the L4 header (or part of it, if the PMTU is relatively small).

- A new element is created and added to the list only when the size of the last fragment in sk_write_queue has reached the maximum size (maxfraglen). (The "size" here refers to the data being transmitted as part of that packet, which is the gray portions of Figure 21-5. It is not the size of the buffer, which might have been allocated to be larger than the available data to accommodate later data.) This is because ip_append_data never creates a fragment bigger than the PMTU associated with the route. When Scatter/Gather I/O is used, new chunks of data are stored in memory pages instead of the area pointed to by skb->data.

Now that we know what kind of output ip_append_data produces, we can look at the code. Once again, keep in mind that the L4 layer can call ip_append_data several times before flushing the buffers with ip_push_pending_frames.

Let's suppose that UDP issued three calls to ip_append_data with the following payload sizes: 300, 250, and 200 bytes. Let's also assume the PMTU is 500 bytes. It should be clear that if UDP had sent a single payload of 750 bytes, the IP layer would have created a first fragment of 500 bytes and a second one of 250 bytes.* However, the application using that UDP socket might actually want to send three distinct IP packets of sizes 300, 250, and 200 bytes. ip_append_data can be told which way to behave. If the application behind the UDP socket prefers to obtain higher throughput, it uses the MSG_MORE flag to tell ip_append_data to create maximum-size fragments (500 bytes) and the result would be a first fragment of 500 bytes and a second one of 250 bytes. If it does not signal the preference for such buffering, UDP transmits each payload individually (see the section "Putting Together the Transmission Functions").

---

* I'm ignoring the header overhead for the sake of simplicity.

Setting the context

The first block of the `ip_append_data` function initializes some local variables and possibly changes some of the input parameters. The exact work done depends on whether the function is creating the first IP fragment (in which case the `sk_write_queue` queue would be empty) or a later one within a packet. With the first element, `ip_append_data` initializes `inet->cork` and `inet` with fields that will be used by the following invocation of `ip_append_data` (and by `ip_push_pending_frames`).

Among the information saved is the IP options and the routing table cache entry. Caching them saves time during subsequent calls to `ip_append_data` for the same packet, but is not strictly necessary because `ip_append_data`'s caller will pass the data again in all of the following calls.

```
if (skb_queue_empty(&sk->sk_write_queue)) {
    opt = ipc->opt;
    if (opt) {
        if (inet->cork.opt == NULL) {
            inet->cork.opt = kmalloc(sizeof(struct ip_options) + 40,
                                sk->sk_allocation);
                    if (unlikely(inet->cork.opt == NULL))
                            return -ENOBUFF;
        }
        memcpy(inet->cork.opt, opt,
                sizeof(struct ip_options)+opt->optlen);
        inet->cork.flags |= IPCORK_OPT;
        inet->cork.addr = ipc->addr;
    }
    dst_hold(&rt->u.dst);
    inet->cork.fragsize = mtu = dst_pmtu(&rt->u.dst);
    inet->cork.rt = rt;
    inet->cork.length = 0;
    sk->sk_sndmsg_page = NULL;
    sk->sk_sndmsg_off = 0;
    if ((exthdrlen = rt->u.dst.header_len) != 0) {
        length += exthdrlen;
        transhdrlen += exthdrlen;
    }
} else {
    rt = inet->cork.rt;
    if (inet->cork.flags & IPCORK_OPT)
        opt = inet->cork.opt;
    transhdrlen = 0;
    exthdrlen = 0;
    mtu = inet->cork.fragsize;
}
```

To understand the rest of the function, you need to understand the meaning of the following key variables. Some of them are received in input by `ip_append_data`; refer to the section "The ip_append_data Function" for their descriptions. It can also be useful to refer back to Figures 21-2 through 21-8.

rt

> Routing table cache entry used to transmit the IP datagram. This structure includes several fields, such as the next hop gateway, the egress device, and the PMTU.

mtu

> The PMTU associated with rt.

opt

> IP options to add to the IP header. When this variable is NULL, there are no options.

exthdrlen *(external header* len*)*
transhdrlen *(transport header* len*)*

> When the L4 layer invokes ip_append_data it passes these two parameters because they need to be taken into account when allocating buffers. transhdrlen is passed directly; exthdrlen is retrieved indirectly via rt. Examples of external headers are the ones used by the protocols in the IPsec suite, such as the Authentication Header (AH) and the Encapsulation Security Payload (ESP). Examples of transport headers are those of the common TCP, UDP, and ICMP protocols.

The way length, exthdrlen, and transhdrlen are initialized may be confusing. I'll explain why their values are changed under some conditions.

As we have already seen, only the first fragment needs to include the transport header and the optional external headers. Because of this, transhdrlen and exthdrlen are zeroed after creating the first fragment. As we will see, this can be done right at the beginning of the function if sk_write_queue is not empty, or inside the big while loop before starting a second iteration.

Because of this initialization, the value of transhdrlen is used by the function to distinguish between the first fragment and the following ones:

- transhdrlen ! = 0 means ip_append_data is working on the first fragment.
- transdhrlen = 0 means ip_append_data is not working on the first fragment.

The same logic cannot be applied to exthdrlen, because the L4 header is needed for every IP packet, but many have no external headers because they don't use special features such as IPsec.

The variables initialized here have several important uses later:

- When deciding how much data to copy into each data fragment, the function needs to take into account that the first fragment includes the L4 header and optional external headers, and therefore that less space is available for the payload (see Figure 21-2).
- When deciding how big to allocate the buffers, the function needs to take into account the extra space needed by the external headers (if any).

- When initializing the `nh.raw` and `h.raw` pointers, the function needs to know whether there are external headers and where they are located to correctly compute the offsets within the packet.

Getting ready for fragment generation

As we will see later, the amount of data copied into each generated fragment may change from fragment to fragment. However, each fragment always includes a fixed portion for the L2 and L3 headers. Figures 21-2 through 21-8 all show this reserved portion.

Before proceeding, the function defines the following three local variables:

```
hh_len = LL_RESERVED_SPACE(rt->u.dst.dev);
fragheaderlen = sizeof(struct iphdr) + (opt ? opt->optlen : 0);
maxfraglen = ((mtu - fragheaderlen) & ~7) + fragheaderlen;
```

`hh_len` is the length of the L2 header. When reserving space for all the headers that precede IP in the buffer, `ip_append_data` needs to know how much space is needed by the L2 header. This way, when the device driver initializes its header, it will not need to reallocate space or move data inside the buffer to make space for the L2 header.

`fraghdrlen` is the size of the IP header, including the IP options, and `maxfraglen` is the maximum size of an IP fragment based on the route PMTU.

As explained in the section "Packet Fragmentation/Defragmentation" in Chapter 18, the maximum size of an IP packet (header plus payload) is 64 KB. This applies not just to individual fragments, but also to the complete packet into which those fragments will be reassembled at the end. Thus, `ip_append_data` keeps track of all the data received for a particular packet and refuses to go over the 64 KB (0xFFFF) limit.

```
if (inet->cork.length + length > 0xFFFF - fragheaderlen) {
    ip_local_error(sk, EMSGSIZE, rt->rt_dst, inet->dport, mtu-exthdrlen);
    return -EMSGSIZE;
}
inet->cork.length += length;
```

The last initialization is the checksum mode, the value of which is saved in `skb->ip_summed`. See the section "L4 checksum."

Copying data into the fragments: getfrag

`ip_append_data` can potentially be used by any L4 protocol. One of its tasks is to copy the input data into the fragments it creates. Different protocols may need to apply different operations to the data copied. One example of such a specialized operation is the computation of the L4 checksum, which is not compulsory for some L4 protocols. Another distinguishing factor could be the origin of the data. This is user space for locally generated packets, and kernel space for forwarded packets or packets generated by the kernel (e.g., ICMP messages).

Instead of having one shared function that takes care of all the possible combinations of protocols and optional operations to apply, it is easier and cleaner to have multiple small functions tailored to each protocol's need. To keep ip_append_data as generic as possible, it allows each protocol to specify the function to use to copy the data by means of the input parameter getfrag. In other words, ip_append_data uses getfrag to copy the input data into the buffers; the result of this copying consists of the memory areas labeled "L4 payload" in Figures 21-2 through 21-9.

Table 21-1 lists the functions used by the most common L4 protocols that invoke ip_append_data. Another function, ip_reply_glue_bits, is used by ip_send_reply (see the section "Key Functions That Perform Transmission").

getfrag receives four input parameters (from, to, offset, and len), and simply copies len bytes from from to to+offset, taking into account that from could be a pointer into user-space memory and thus has to be handled accordingly (it may require translation from user to kernel memory). It also takes care of the L4 checksum: while copying data into the kernel buffer, it updates skb->csum according to the skb->ip_summed configuration.

Table 21-1. getfrag routines

Protocol	API
ICMP	icmp_glue_bits
UDP	ip_generic_getfrag
RAW IP	ip_generic_getfrag
TCP (via ip_send_reply)	ip_reply_glue_bits

In a situation where the origin of the getfrag function's input—user space versus kernel—is always the same, the function does not need to distinguish between the two cases. For example:

- icmp_glue_bits is used by the ICMP protocol when transmitting a message. Because the ICMP message is either built by the kernel or derived from another ICMP message previously received (which therefore is in kernel memory), icmp_glue_bits knows the data is in kernel space.

- When an application issues a sendmsg system call on a UDP or raw IP socket, the kernel ends up calling ip_append_data, passing ip_generic_getfrag as the getfrag function. In this case, the input data is known to always come from user space.

Let's take a closer look at the generic function ip_generic_getfrag:

```
int
ip_generic_getfrag(void *from, char *to, int offset, int len, int odd,
                struct sk_buff *skb)
{
    struct iovec *iov = from;
```

```
        if (skb->ip_summed == CHECKSUM_HW) {
            if (memcpy_fromiovecend(to, iov, offset, len) < 0)
                return -EFAULT;
        } else {
            unsigned int csum = 0;
            if (csum_partial_copy_fromiovecend(to, iov, offset, len, &csum) < 0)
                return -EFAULT;
            skb->csum = csum_block_add(skb->csum, csum, odd);
        }
        return 0;
    }
```

The section "sk_buff structure" in Chapter 19 explained the meaning of CHECKSUM_HW, and how skb->csum and skb->ip_summed are used. In the section "L4 checksum," we will see how ip_append_data decides whether the L4 checksum should be computed in hardware or software (or not computed at all). In the previous snapshot, you can see that ip_generic_getfrag uses two different functions to copy the data (memcpy_fromiovecend and csum_partial_copy_fromiovecend), based on whether the L4 checksum is going to be computed in hardware or must be computed in software.

Buffer allocation

ip_append_data chooses the size of the buffers to allocate based on:

Single transmission versus multiple transmissions
>   If ip_append_data is told there will be other transmission requests soon after (if MSG_MORE is set), it could make sense to allocate a bigger buffer so that data from future transmissions can be merged into the same buffer. See the earlier section "Basic memory allocation and buffer organization for ip_append_data" for further explanation.

Scatter/Gather I/O
>   If the device can handle Scatter/Gather I/O, fragments could be more efficiently stored into memory pages. See the earlier section "Memory allocation and buffer organization for ip_append_data with Scatter Gather I/O" for further explanation.

The following piece of code decides the size of the buffer to allocate (alloclen) based on the two points just stated. The buffer is created with the maximum size (based on the PMTU) if more data is expected and if the device can't handle Scatter/Gather I/O. If either of those conditions is not true, the buffer is made just large enough to hold the current data.

```
        if ((flags & MSG_MORE) &&
            !(rt->u.dst.dev->features&NETIF_F_SG))
            alloclen = mtu;
        else
            alloclen = datalen + fragheaderlen;

        if (datalen == length)
            alloclen += rt->u.dst.trailer_len;
```

Note that when ip_append_data generates the last fragment, it needs to take into account the presence of trailers (such as for IPsec).

datalen is the amount of data to be copied into the buffer we are allocating. Its value was previously initialized based on three factors: the amount of data left (length), the maximum amount of data that fits into a fragment (fraghdrlen), and an optional carry from the previous buffer (fraggap).

The last component, fraggap, requires an explanation. With the exception of the last buffer (which holds the last IP fragment), all fragments must respect the rule that the size of the payload of an IP fragment must be a multiple of eight bytes. For this reason, when the kernel allocates a new buffer that is not for the last fragment, it may need to move a piece of data (whose size ranges from 0 to 7 bytes) from the tail of the previous buffer to the head of the newly allocated one. In other words, fraggap is zero unless all of the following are true:

- The PMTU is not a multiple of eight bytes.
- The size of the current IP fragment has not reached the PMTU yet.
- The size of the current IP fragment has passed the highest multiple of eight bytes that is less than or equal to the PMTU.

Figure 21-10 shows an example where fraggap is nonzero and alloclen has been initialized to mtu. Note that when the kernel moves the data from the current buffer, skb_prev, to the new one, skb, it also needs to adjust the L4 checksum on both skb_prev and skb (see the section "L4 checksum"). The figure shows the buffers as two flat memory areas for simplicity, but they both could be paged (as in Figure 21-5) and nonpages (as in Figure 21-6): the function used to move the fraggap area skb_copy_and_csum_bits can handle both formats. The same function also updates the L4 checksums.

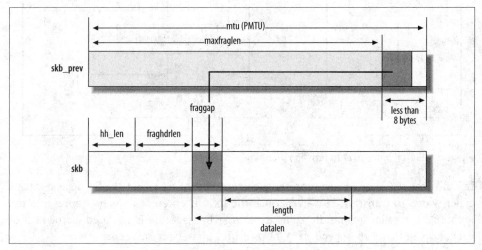

Figure 21-10. Respecting the 8-byte boundary rule on IP fragments

Main loop

The while loop that potentially creates extra buffers may look more complex than it actually is. Figure 21-11 summarizes its job.

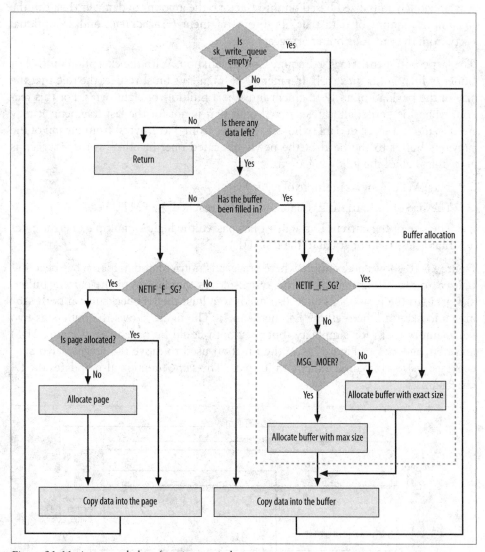

Figure 21-11. ip_append_data function: main loop

Initially, the value of length represents the amount of data that the ip_append_data's caller wants to transmit. However, once the loop is entered, its value represents the amount of data left to handle. This explains why its value is updated at the end of each loop and why ip_append_data loops until length becomes zero.

We already know that MSG_MORE indicates whether the L4 layer expects more data, and that NETIF_F_SG indicates whether the device supports Scatter/Gather I/O. These settings have no effect on the first task within the loop, which is to allocate and initialize sk_buff structures within the first if block inside the loop. Also, the first data fragment is always copied into the sk_buff area (see Figure 21-5(a) and Figure 21-6(a)).

ip_append_data allocates a new sk_buff structure and queues it to sk_write_queue every time one of the following occurs:

- sk_write_queue is empty (that is, for the first fragment).
- The last element of sk_write_queue has been filled in completely.

The piece of code that precedes the loop takes care of the first case by forcing allocation when the queue is empty:

```
if ((skb = skb_peek_tail(&sk->sk_write_queue)) == NULL)
    goto alloc_new_skb;
```

The first part inside the loop handles the second case. First it initializes copy to the amount of space that is left in the current IP fragment: mtu − skb->len. If the data left to add (length) is greater than the amount of free space, copy, there is a need for one more IP fragment. In that case, copy is updated. To enforce the 8-byte boundary rule, copy is lowered to the closest 8-byte boundary. At this point, the kernel can decide whether it needs to allocate a new buffer (i.e., a new IP fragment). This is the logic associated with the if condition that compares copy against 0:

copy > 0
    This means that skb (the last element of sk_write_queue) has some space available. ip_append_data first uses that space. If the space left was not sufficient (i.e., length is greater than the space available), the loop will iterate again, and this time it will fall into the next category (see Figures 21-3 and 21-4).

copy = 0
    This means that it is time to allocate a new sk_buff because the last one has been filled in completely. In this case, the code inside the if block allocates a new buffer, copies the input data into the buffer, and queues the new fragment to sk_write_queue. The following fragments will be either merged to the previous one or copied into memory pages allocated specifically for Scatter/Gather I/O.

copy < 0
    This is a special case of the previous one. When copy is negative, it means that some data must be deleted from the current IP fragment and moved to the new one. See the earlier section "Buffer allocation" for more details.

Every time a new loop ends, the function needs to move ahead the pointer to the data to copy (offset) and to update the amount of data left to copy (length). Once the fragment has been queued with __skb_queue_tail, the function may need to restart the loop if any data is left.

L4 checksum

We saw in the section "net_device structure" in Chapter 19 that the L3 and L4 checksums can be computed by the egress NIC when its device driver advertises that capability by setting the right flags in dev->features. In particular, skb->ip_summed (and eventually skb->csum) must be initialized to show whether the egress device provides support for L4 hardware checksumming. Refer to the aforementioned section for more details.

Whether hardware checksumming can be used is decided when ip_append_data is called for the first fragment (i.e., transhdrlen is nonzero). Hardware checksumming is applicable only when all of the following conditions are met:

- The IP packet built by ip_append_data is not going to be fragmented (i.e., the total data fed to ip_append_data does not exceed the PMTU).
- The egress device supports hardware checksumming.
- There are no transformation headers (i.e., protocols of the IPsec suite). Such transformations can, for example, compress or encrypt the data the NIC is supposed to read when computing the checksum. These transformations also insert additional headers between the IP header and the L4 header. This means that L4 hardware checksumming and IPsec transformations cannot coexist.

Hardware checksumming might also have to be turned off under other conditions.

The first bullet in the previous list requires an explanation. Hardware checksumming does not work when the IP packet is fragmented (as in the example in Figure 21-3). However, because ip_append_data can be called several times before the actual transmission takes place (i.e., before ip_push_pending_frames is called), the IP layer may not know that fragmentation is required when ip_append_data is first called and therefore the initial decision is based only on the input data (length): if fragmentation is required based on length, hardware checksumming is not used.

```
if (transhdrlen &&
    length + fragheaderlen <= mtu &&
    rt->u.dst.dev->features&(NETIF_F_IP_CSUM|NETIF_F_NO_CSUM|NETIF_F_HW_CSUM) &&
    !exthdrlen)
        csummode = CHECKSUM_HW;
```

The local variable csummode initialized here will be assigned to skb->ip_summed on the first buffer. If there is a need for fragmentation and ip_append_data allocates more buffers accordingly (one for each IP fragment), skb->ip_summed on the subsequent buffers will be set to CHECKSUM_NONE. When getfrag is called to copy the data into the buffers, it also takes care of the L4 checksum if it is passed a buffer with skb->ip_summed initialized to CHECKSUM_NONE (see the section "Copying data into the fragments: getfrag").

Note that ip_append_data checksums only the L4 payloads. In the section "Changes to the L4 Checksum" in Chapter 18, we saw that the L4 checksum must include the

L4 header as well as the so-called pseudoheader. If `ip_push_pending_frames` is called by the L4 layer when `sk_write_queue` has only one IP fragment and the egress device supports hardware checksumming, the L4 protocol only needs to initialize `skb->csum` to the right offset and the L4 header's checksum field with the pseudoheader checksum, as we saw in the section "sk_buff structure" in Chapter 19. If instead the egress device does not support hardware checksumming, or the latter is supported but cannot be used because `sk_write_queue` has more than one IP fragment, the L4 checksum must be computed in software. In this case, `getfrag` computes the partial checksums on the L4 payloads while copying data into the buffers, and the L4 protocol will combine them later to get the value to put into the L4 header. See the section "Putting Together the Transmission Functions" to see how UDP takes care of the L4 checksum before invoking `ip_push_pending_frames`.

For an example of how a device driver instructs the NIC to compute the L4 hardware checksum when required, see the `boomerang_start_xmit` routine in *drivers/net/3c59x.c* and `cp_start_xmit` in *drivers/net/8139cp.c*. In both cases, you can also see how a paged `skb` is handled when setting up the DMA transfers.

The ip_append_page Function

We saw in the section "Copying data into the fragments: getfrag" that a transmission request from user space, with a call like `sendmsg`, requires a copy to move the data to transmit from user space to kernel space. This copy is made by the `getfrag` function passed as an input parameter to `ip_append_data`.

The kernel provides user-space applications with another interface, `sendfile`, which allows applications to optimize the transmission and make the data copy. This interface has been widely publicized as "zero-copy" TCP/UDP.

The `sendfile` interface can be used only when the egress device supports Scatter/Gather I/O. In this case, the logic implemented by `ip_append_data` can be simplified so that no copy is necessary (i.e., the data the user asked to transmit is left where it is). The kernel just initializes the `frag` vector with the location of the data buffer received in input, and takes care of the L4 checksum if needed. This simplified logic is what is provided by `ip_append_page`. While `ip_append_data` receives the location of the data with a `void*` pointer, `ip_append_page` receives the location as a pointer to a memory page and offset within it, which makes it straightforward to initialize one entry of `frag`.

The only piece of code that differs from `ip_append_data` with regard to Scatter/Gather I/O is the following:

```
i = skb_shinfo(skb)->nr_frags;
if (len > size)
    len = size;
if (skb_can_coalesce(skb, i, page, offset)) {
    skb_shinfo(skb)->frags[i-1].size += len;
```

```
        } else if (i < MAX_SKB_FRAGS) {
            get_page(page);
            skb_fill_page_desc(skb, i, page, offset, len);
        } else {
            err = -EMSGSIZE;
            goto error;
        }

        if (skb->ip_summed == CHECKSUM_NONE) {
            unsigned int csum;
            csum = csum_page(page, offset, len);
            skb->csum = csum_block_add(skb->csum, csum, skb->len);
        }
```

When adding a new fragment to a page, ip_append_page tries first to merge the new one with the previous fragment already in the page. To do that, it first checks, by means of skb_can_coalesce, whether the point where the new one should be added matches with the point where the last one ends. If merging is possible, all it has to do is update the length of the previous fragment already in the page to include the new data.

When merging is not possible, the function initializes the new fragment with skb_fill_page_desc. In this case, it also increments the reference count on the page with get_page. The reference count must be incremented because ip_append_page uses the page it receives as input, and this page could potentially be used by someone else, too.

ip_append_page is currently used by UDP only. We said that TCP does not use the ip_append_data and ip_push_pending_frames functions because it implements the same logic in tcp_sendmsg. The same applies to this zero-copy interface: TCP does not use ip_append_page, but implements the same logic in do_tcp_sendpage. Unlike UDP, TCP allows the application to use the zero-copy interface only if the egress device supports L4 hardware checksumming.[*]

The ip_push_pending_frames Function

As explained near the beginning of this chapter, ip_push_pending_frames works in tandem with ip_append_data and ip_append_page. When the L4 layer decides it is time to wrap up and transmit the fragments queued to sw_write_queue through ip_append_data or ip_append_page (either because of some protocol-specific criterion or because it is explicitly told by the higher-level application to send the data), it simply calls ip_push_pending_frames:

```
    int ip_push_pending_frames(struct sock *sk)
```

---

[*] Zero-copy can also be used if the device does not require an L4 checksum. See the description of NETIF_F_NO_CSUM in Chapter 19.

The function receives a sock structure in input. It needs access to several fields, notably the pointer to the socket's sk_write_queue structure.

We saw in the section "Memory allocation and buffer organization for ip_append_data with Scatter Gather I/O" that the data in the packet is organized differently in the sk_buff structure, depending on whether Scatter/Gather I/O is used.

The code in this half queues all the buffers that follow the first one into a list named frag_list that is part of the first element, as shown in Figure 21-12, and updates the len and data_len fields of the buffer at the head of the list to account for all of the fragments. This last operation is performed because it is useful to the ip_fragment routine that comes later in the code path (see Figure 18-1 in Chapter 18, and see Chapter 22). As buffers are queued onto frag_list, they are cleared off of sk_write_queue. It requires very little time to create the new list (no data is copied; only pointers are changed) and the result is to free the sk_write_queue list, which therefore allows the L4 layer to consider the data transmitted. The data is now out of the hands of the L4 layer and completely under the care of the IP layer.

Remember, as you look at Figure 21-12, that nr_frags reflects the number of Scatter/Gather I/O buffers, and not the number of IP fragments. Two points are worth mentioning about Figure 21-12:

- The input to ip_push_pending_frames shown in the example in Figure 21-12(a) reflects the no Scatter/Gather case (i.e., no use of the frags vector). With Scatter/Gather, you would have a list of buffers like the one in Figure 21-7.
- The skb_shinfo block is shown only on the buffer in Figure 21-12(b) that uses it, but it is there for all the other sk_buff structures, too.

After that, it is time to fill in the IP header. If there are multiple fragments, only the first is going to have its IP header filled in by ip_push_pending_frames; the others will be taken care of later (we will see how in Chapter 22).

The setting of the TTL field of the IP header (iph->ttl) depends on whether the destination address is multicast. Usually, a smaller value is used for multicast traffic because multicasting is most often used to deliver streaming (and sometimes interactive) data such as audio and video that can become useless if it is received too late. The default values assigned to the TTL field for multicast and unicast packets are 1 and 64, respectively.*

```
        if (rt->rt_type == RTN_MULTICAST)
            ttl = inet->mc_ttl;
        else
            ttl = ip_select_ttl(inet, &rt->u.dst);
        ...
        iph->ttl = ttl;
```

---

* Either value can be changed with ip_setsockopt, but only the unicast value can be set with the /proc interface (see the section "Tuning via /proc Filesystem" in Chapter 23).

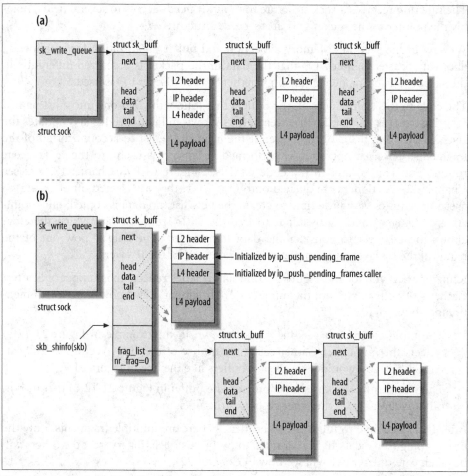

Figure 21-12. (a) Before and (b) after removing buffers from the sk_write_queue queue

If there are IP options in the header, `ip_options_build` is used to take care of them. The last input parameter to `ip_options_build` is set to zero to tell the API that it is filling in the options of the first fragment. This distinction is needed because the first fragment's IP options are treated differently, as we saw in the section "IP Options" in Chapter 18. The length of the header is also updated to reflect the length of the options.

```
if (inet->cork.flags & IPCORK_OPT)
    opt = inet->cork.opt;
...
iph->ihl = 5;
if (opt) {
    iph->ihl += opt->optlen>>2;
    ip_options_build(skb, opt, inet->cork.addr, rt, 0);
}
```

The Don't Fragment flag IP_DF of the IP header is set when the socket's configuration enforces the use of that flag on all packets (i.e., IP_PMTUDISC_DO), and when the route rt has PMTU enabled (i.e., IP_PMTUDISC_WANT) and not locked (see the definition of ip_dont_fragment):[*]

```
if (inet->pmtudisc != IP_PMTUDISC_DO)
      skb->local_df = 1
   ...
   if (inet->pmtudisc == IP_PMTUDISC_DO ||
      skb->len <= dst_mtu(&rt->u.dst) &&
      ip_dont_fragment(sk, &rt->u.dst)))
      df = htons(IP_DF);
   ...
   iph->frag_off = df;
```

The value just assigned to the df variable, reflecting the packet's Don't Fragment status, determines in turn how the IP packet ID is set. The section "Selecting the IP Header's ID Field" in Chapter 23 goes into more detail on how that ID is computed.

```
if (!df) {
      __ip_select_ident(iph, &rt->u.dst, 0);
   } else {
      iph->id = htons(inet->id++);
   }
```

skb->priority is used by Traffic Control to decide which one of the outgoing queues to enqueue the packet in. See the similar initialization by ip_queue_xmit in the section "Building the IP header."

```
iph->version = 4;
iph->tos = inet->tos;
iph->tot_len = htons(skb->len);
iph->protocol = sk->sk_protocol;
iph->saddr = rt->rt_src;
iph->daddr = rt->rt_dst;
ip_send_check(iph);
skb->priority = sk->sk_priority;
skb->dst = dst_clone(&rt->u.dst);
```

Before passing the buffer to dst_output to complete the transmission, the function needs to ask Netfilter permission to do so. Note that Netfilter is queried only once for all the fragments of a packet. In an earlier version of the kernel (2.4), Netfilter was queried for each fragment. This gave Netfilter the chance to filter IP packets with a higher granularity, but it also forced Netfilter to defragment and refragment packets in case there were filters that examined the L4 or higher levels. The overhead was judged too burdensome for the value it offered.

---

[*] The PMTU is one of the metrics that can be assigned to routes. When a metric is locked, it cannot be changed by protocol events. Metrics are introduced in Chapters 30 and 36.

Note that when dst_input is passed a list of sk_buff buffers (as opposed to a single buffer), as shown in Figure 21-12(b), only the first one gets its IP header initialized. We will see in Chapter 22 how such a list is taken care of by ip_fragment.

```
err = NF_HOOK(PF_INET, NF_IP_LOCAL_OUT, skb, NULL,
        skb->dst->dev, dst_output);
```

Before returning, the function clears the IPCORK_OPT field, which invalidates the contents of the cork structure. This is because later packets to the same destination reuse the cork structure, and the IP layer needs to know when old data should be thrown away.

Putting Together the Transmission Functions

To see how the functions we've been examining, ip_append_data and ip_push_pending_frames, work together, let's focus on a function called by the UDP layer, udp_sendmsg, and see how it calls them.

```
int udp_sendmsg(struct kiocb *iocb, struct sock *sk, struct msghdr *msg,
        size_t len)
{
    ... ... ...
    struct udp_opt *up = udp_sk(sk);
    ... ... ...
    int corkreq = up->corkflag || msg->msg_flags&MSG_MORE;
    ... ... ...
    err = ip_append_data(sk, ip_generic_getfrag, msg->msg_iov, ulen,
            sizeof(struct udphdr), &ipc, rt,
            corkreq ? msg->msg_flags|MSG_MORE : msg->msg_flags);
    if (err)
        udp_flush_pending_frames(sk);
    else if (!corkreq)
        err = udp_push_pending_frames(sk, up);
```

The local flag corkreq is initialized based on multiple factors, and will be passed to ip_append_data to signal whether buffering should be used. Among those factors are:

MSG_MORE
> This flag can be set or cleared individually on each transmission request.

corkflag (UDP_CORK)
> This is applied once to a socket and remains active until explicitly disabled.

These two flags have a comparable purpose. After some discussion over which was the best one, in the end both of them were made available in the kernel.

udp_sendmsg first calls ip_append_data, and then forces the immediate transmission of the data with udp_push_pending_frames only if corkreq is false. In case ip_append_data failed for any reason, udp_sendmsg flushes the queue with udp_flush_pending_frames, which is a wrapper for the IP function ip_flush_pending_frames.

Figure 21-13 shows the internals of udp_push_pending_frames. Note how the L4 checksum is handled according to the logic we saw in the section "L4 checksum."

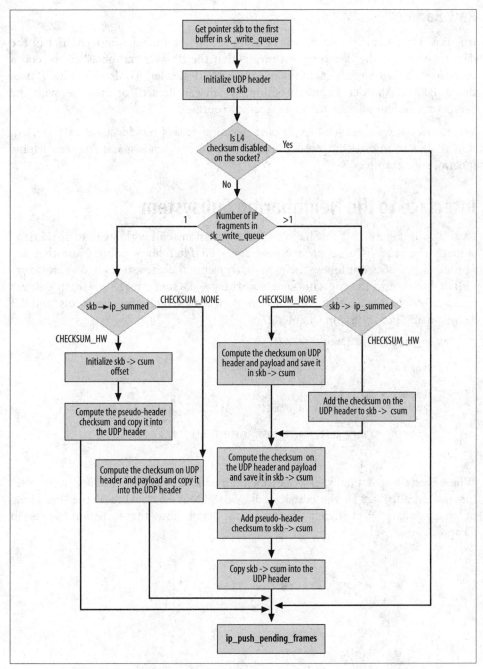

Figure 21-13. udp_push_pending_frames function

For an example of how to use ip_append_page, you can take a look at udp_sendpage.

Raw Sockets

It is possible for raw sockets (sockets using raw IP) to include the IP header in the data they pass to the IP layer. This means that the IP layer can be asked to send a piece of data that already includes an initialized IP header. To do this, raw IP uses the IP_HDRINCL (header included) option, which can be set, for instance, with the setsockopt system call (see the ip_setsockopt routine).

When this option is set, neither ip_push_pending_frames nor ip_queue_xmit is used. Raw IP directly invokes dst_output instead. See the raw_sendmsg and raw_send_hdrinc functions for examples.

Interface to the Neighboring Subsystem

As shown in Figure 18-1 in Chapter 18, transmissions end with a call to ip_finish_output. The latter is a simple wrapper for a Netfilter hook point. Note that ip_finish_output does not follow the naming convention do_something + do_something_finish, but instead the convention do_something + do_something2. ip_finish_output2 is described in the section "Interaction Between Neighboring Protocols and L3 Transmission Functions" in Chapter 27.

```
int ip_finish_output(struct sk_buff *skb)
{
    struct net_device *dev = skb->dst->dev;

    skb->dev = dev;
    skb->protocol = __constant_htons(ETH_P_IP);

    return NF_HOOK(PF_INET, NF_IP_POST_ROUTING, skb, NULL, dev,
            ip_finish_output2);
}
```

When everything is finally in place (including the L2 header), the dev_queue_xmit function is called (via hh->hh_output or dst->neighbour->output) to do the "hard job" of transmission. We already discussed in detail how that function works in Chapter 11.

## CHAPTER 22

Internet Protocol Version 4 (IPv4): Handling Fragmentation

Fragmentation and defragmentation are complex tasks because of the variety of inputs that the IP layer of a host can receive both when fragmenting and when defragmenting a packet. We have seen much of the work that goes into fragmentation as part of the functions shown in previous chapters on IPv4. This chapter describes the ip_fragment function, which is defined in *net/ipv4/ip_output.c*, where all of these efforts reach their final culmination and result in separate packets ready to transmit. This chapter also describes the corresponding ip_defrag function, defined in *net/ipv4/ip_fragment.c*, where incoming fragments are reassembled into a packet prior to being passed to the L4 layer via ip_local_deliver. Helper functions are described in each section as well.

These two functions can be used by other subsystems besides IPv4. For example, Netfilter uses them when it is forced to defragment (and refragment) an IP packet to be able to access header fields above the L3 layer. This is necessary mostly for forwarded packets and was discussed in the section "The ip_push_pending_frames Function" in Chapter 21.

How does the IP layer recognize that a packet is a fragment of a larger packet? Based on what we saw in Chapter 17, we need both the Offset and MF fields of the IP header to tell. If the packet has not been fragmented, Offset=0 and MF=0. If instead we have a fragment on our hands, the following is true:

- The first fragment has Offset=0 and MF=1.
- All the fragments between the first and the last one have both of the fields non-zero.
- The last fragment has MF=0 and Offset nonzero.

We said earlier that ip_local_deliver is one of the places where defragmentation could take place. Here is a snapshot from the function that shows how a fragment is recognized and passed to ip_defrag based on the considerations just listed:

```
if (skb->nh.iph->frag_off & htons(IP_MF|IP_OFFSET)) {
    skb = ip_defrag(skb);
```

```
        if (!skb)
            return 0;
}
```

Similar logic can be found in fragmentation code to correctly tag fragments.

The fragmentation/defragmentation subsystem is initialized by `ipfrag_init`, which is invoked at boot time by `inet_init`. The initialization function does not do much; it mainly starts a timer and initializes one variable to a random value. Both of these tasks are needed to handle an optimization added to protect the kernel from a possible Denial of Service (DoS) attack; see the section "Hash Table Reorganization" for details.

IP Fragmentation

As shown in Figure 18-1 in Chapter 18, the `dst_output` function is called by both locally generated and forwarded packets, so the `ip_fragment` function in the area below `dst_output` can run in both situations. Thus, the input to `ip_fragment` can be:

- Forwarded packets that are whole
- Forwarded packets that the originating host or a router along the way has fragmented
- Buffers created by local functions that, as described in the previous chapter, have started the fragmentation process but have not added the headers that are required for transmission as packets

In particular, `ip_fragment` must be able to handle both of the following cases:

Big chunks of data that need to be split into smaller parts.
    Splitting the big buffer requires the allocation of new buffers and memory copies from the big buffer to the small ones. This, of course, impacts performance.

A list or array of data fragments that do not need to be fragmented further.
    If the buffers were allocated such that they have room to allow the addition of lower-layer L3 and L2 headers, `ip_fragment` can handle them without a memory copy. All the IP layer needs to do is add an IP header to each fragment and handle the checksum.

Previous kernel versions used to handle IP fragmentation entirely at the IP layer. The IP functions used to transmit a packet could receive a payload of any size between 0 and 64 KB, and had to split that payload into multiple IP fragments when the size of the packet exceeded the PMTU. We saw this in the section "Packet Fragmentation/Defragmentation" in Chapter 18.

The approach used by newer kernels is to make the L4 protocols aid in the fragmentation task in advance: instead of passing to the IP layer a single buffer that will have to be fragmented, they can pass a set of buffers appropriate to the PMTU. This way, the IP fragmentation handled at the IP layer consists simply of creating an IP header for each data fragment already formed. This does not mean that the L4 protocols implement IP fragmentation; it simply means that since L4 protocols are aware of IP fragmentation, they try to cooperate and make life easier for the IP layer. The L4 protocols do not touch the IP headers.

Before the introduction of the ip_append_data/ip_append_page functions discussed in Chapter 21, IP fragmentation used to be simpler than IP defragmentation. Now both processes are equally complex.

Fragmentation can currently be done in two ways: the so-called fast (or efficient) way, and the slow (or old-style) way. Both of them are taken care of by ip_fragment. Before seeing how those two approaches differ, let's review the main tasks required to fragment an IP packet:

1. Split the L3 payload into smaller pieces to fit within the MTU associated with the route being used to send the packet (PMTU). As we will see in a moment, this task may or may not involve some memory copies. If the size of the IP payload is not an exact multiple of the fragment size, the last fragment is smaller than the others. Also, since the fragment offset field of the IP header is measured in units of 8 bytes, this value is aligned to an 8-byte boundary. Every fragment, with the possible exception of the last one, has this size. See Figure 18-10 in Chapter 18.

2. Initialize each fragment's IP header, taking into account that not all of the options have to be replicated into all of the fragments. ip_options_fragment, introduced in section "IP Options" in Chapter 18, does this job.

3. Compute the IP checksum. Each fragment has a different IP header, so the checksum has to be recomputed for each one.

4. Ask Netfilter, the Linux filtering system, for permission to complete the transmission.

5. Update all the necessary kernel and SNMP statistics (such as IPSTATS_MIB_FRAGCREATES, IPSTATS_MIB_FRAGOKS, and IPSTATS_MIB_FRAGFAILS).

In kernel versions prior to 2.4, a function named ip_build_xmit_slow created and transmitted IP fragments for locally generated packets in reverse order: last to first. This approach had a couple of advantages:

• The last fragment is the only one that can tell the receiver the size of the original, unfragmented packet. To know this as soon as possible could help the defragmenter handle its memory better.

• It makes it more likely that the defragmenter can build up a packet faster. As described in the section "IP Defragmentation," fragments are added into a list (ipq) in increasing order of offset. If each fragment arrives after the fragment that comes after it, fragments can be added speedily at the head of the list.

While this sort of optimization works when the receiver is a Linux box, it might have no effect or even be a drawback if the receiver uses some other operating system that makes different assumptions.* Therefore, starting with 2.4, the Linux kernel transmits fragments in forward order.

Functions Involved with IP Fragmentation

The previous chapter, which described the functions that transmit data at the IP layer, covered the `ip_append_data`/`ip_append_page` set of functions that do a lot of the groundwork for fragmentation. The rest of this section focuses on `ip_fragment`, which turns the buffers waiting for transmission into actual packets.

Here are a couple of support routines used by the fragmentation code:

ip_dont_fragment
> Decides whether the IP packet can be fragmented, based on Path MTU discovery configuration (see the section "Path MTU Discovery" in Chapter 18).

ip_options_fragment
> Modifies the IP header of the first fragment so that it can be recycled by the following ones. See the section "IP Options" in Chapter 19.

`ip_dont_fragment` and `ip_options_fragment` are defined in *include/net/ip.h* and *net/ipv4/ip_options.c*, respectively.

The ip_fragment Function

We already mentioned in the previous section that `ip_fragment` can take care of fragmentation in two different ways. Let's first see what the common part does. In the next two sections, we will analyze the two cases separately.

```
int ip_fragment(struct sk_buff *skb, int (*output)(struct sk_buff*))
```

Here are the meanings of the function's input parameters:

skb
> Buffer containing the IP packet to fragment. The packet includes an already initialized IP header, which will have to be adapted and replicated into all the fragments. See Figure 21-12(b) in Chapter 21 for an example of what skb may look like.

output
> Function to use to transmit the fragments. In Figure 18-1 in Chapter 18, you can see some of the places where `ip_fragment` is called. You can check them to see what function is used as output (for example, ip_output uses ip_finish_output).

---

* For example, the PIX firewall from Cisco Systems has an option that lets the administrator prevent IP fragments from passing through unless they are received in order from first to last.

`ip_fragment` begins by initializing a few key variables that will be used later. It extracts their values from the device and IP header structures that are obtained via the input `skb` parameter. The egress device `dev` and the PMTU `mtu` are extracted from the routing entry used to transmit the packet (`rt`). You will see in Chapter 36 what other parameters are kept in that data structure.

If the input IP packet cannot be fragmented because the source has set the DF flag, `ip_fragment` sends an ICMP packet back to the source to notify it of the problem, and then drops the packet. The `local_df` flag shown in the `if` condition is set mainly by the Virtual Server code when it does not want the condition just described to generate an ICMP message.

```
dev = rt->u.dst.dev;
iph = skb->nh.iph;

if (unlikely((iph->frag_off & htons(IP_DF)) && !skb->local_df)) {
    icmp_send(skb, ICMP_DEST_UNREACH, ICMP_FRAG_NEEDED,
            htonl(dst_pmtu(&rt->u.dst)));
    kfree_skb(skb);
    return -EMSGSIZE;
}

hlen = iph->ihl * 4;
mtu = dst_mtu(&rt->u.dst) - hlen;
```

Fast fragmentation is used when `ip_fragment` receives an `sk_buff` whose data is already fragmented. This is possible, for example, for packets locally generated by an L4 protocol that uses the `ip_append_data` and `ip_push_pending_frames` functions. It is also possible for packets generated by L4 protocols that use the `ip_queue_xmit` function, because they take care of creating fragments themselves. See Chapter 21.

The slow path is used in all the other cases, among which we have:

- Packets being forwarded
- Locally generated traffic that has not been fragmented before reaching `dst_output`
- All of those cases where fast fragmentation was disabled due to a sanity check on the buffers (see the beginning of `ip_fragment`)

Even if `ip_fragment` was given a buffer whose data was already broken into fragment-size buffers as input, it may not be possible to use the fast path due to an error in the organization of the fragments. An error could be caused by a broken feature that performs a faulty buffer manipulation, or by the transformers used by the IPsec protocols.

In both cases (slow and fast), if any of the fragment transmission fails, `ip_fragment` returns immediately with an error code and the following fragments are not transmitted. When this happens, the destination host will receive only a subset of the IP fragments and therefore will fail to reassemble them.

Slow Fragmentation

Unlike the fast fragmentation done in collaboration with ip_append_page/ip_append_
data, slow fragmentation does not need to keep any state information (such as the
list of fragments, etc.). The process simply consists of splitting the IP packet into
fragments whose size is given by the MTU of the outgoing interface, or by the MTU
associated with the route used if path MTU discovery is enabled.

Before entering the loop, the function needs to initialize a few local variables.

ptr is the offset into the packet about to be fragmented; it will be moved as fragmentation proceeds. left is initialized to the length of the IP packet. In calculating left,
the ip_fragment function subtracts hlen (the L2 header length) because that component is not part of the IP payload and the function must leave room for it because it
will be copied into each fragment.

The IP header places the fragment offset and the DF and MF flags together in a single 16-bit field. The formula in the following code extracts the offset field from it.

The local variable not_last_frag, as the name suggests, is true when more data is
supposed to follow the current fragment in the packet. This is an important bit of
data because the last fragment in the packet indicates the size of the packet, which is
valuable information for allocating memory efficiently; the function acts on this
information later. The not_last_frag variable is not set, however, on the first fragment within the packet (that is, the original packet—if a packet is fragmented into
two pieces, for example, and the second piece is later fragmented, all fragments in
the second piece will have the not_last_frag variable set).

```
left = skb->len - hlen;
ptr = raw + hlen;

offset = (ntohs(iph->frag_off) & IP_OFFSET) << 3;
not_last_frag = iph->frag_off & htons(IP_MF);
```

ip_fragment next starts a loop to create a new buffer for each fragment (skb2). The
input parameter skb contains the original IP packet.

```
while(left > 0) {
    len = left;
```

For each fragment, the length is set to the MTU value defined earlier through the
PMTU field. The size of the fragment is also aligned to an 8-byte boundary, as
imposed by the IP RFC. The only cases where the following condition is not met are
when we are transmitting the last fragment or when fragmentation is not needed. But
the second case should never occur because if fragmentation were not needed, the
function would not execute in the first place.

```
if (len > mtu)
    len = mtu;
```

```
if (len < left) {
    len &= ~7;
}
```

The size of the buffer allocated to hold a fragment is the sum of:

- The size of the IP payload
- The size of the IP header
- The size of the L2 header

The last of those values is initialized just before the while loop and is retrieved from the routing table cache. The IP layer can learn, from the routing table, the L2 device to be used to transmit the fragments. The ip_fragment function can extract the size of the header associated with the device's protocol from the associated net_device data structure. This value is aligned to a 16-byte boundary by the LL_RESERVED_SPACE[_EXTRA] macros and is stored in the local variable ll_rs (Link Layer Reserved Space). This alignment has nothing to do with the 8-byte alignment just performed on the payload. When the kernel is compiled with support for L2 firewalling (i.e., the CONFIG_BRIDGE_NETFILTER kernel option), ll_rs and mtu are updated accordingly to accommodate a possible 802.1Q header.

```
if ((skb2 = alloc_skb(len+hlen+ll_rs,
                      GFP_ATOMIC)) == NULL) {
    NETDEBUG(printk(KERN_INFO "IP: frag: no memory for new fragment!\n"));
    err = -ENOMEM;
    goto fail;
}
```

Now the function needs to copy into the newly allocated buffer skb2 the value of a few fields from the sk_buff structure (the original IP packet) being replicated. Some of them are copied here, and others are taken care of by ip_copy_metadata, which also may copy some fields based on whether specific features (such as Traffic Control and Netfilter) are built into the kernel. The pointers to the L3 (nh.raw) and L4 (n.raw) headers are also initialized.

```
ip_copy_metadata(sk2, skb);
skb_reserve(skb2, ll_rs);
skb_put(skb2, len + hlen);
skb2->nh.raw = skb2->data;
skb2->h.raw = skb2->data + hlen;
```

The newly allocated buffer is associated with the socket attempting the transmission, if any. (This is the case, for instance, when the transmission was requested with the functions on the left side of Figure 18-1 in Chapter 18.)

```
if (skb->sk)
    skb_set_owner_w(skb2, skb->sk);
```

Now it is time to fill in the new buffer skb2 with some real data. (So far the function has taken care of only the management fields of the sk_buff structure.) This is done in two parts:

- The IP header is copied with a simple memcpy.
- Then a piece of payload from the original packet is copied into the fragment.

The latter task cannot use a simple memcpy, because the data may be stored in skb in a variety of ways using a list of fragments or memory page extensions (see Chapter 21). The slow path could be invoked when a packet contains all its data in the memory area pointed to by skb->data (see Figure 21-2 in Chapter 21), or when data has already been fragmented before reaching ip_fragment but one of the sanity checks described earlier rules out the fast path. The logic to handle the various possibilities for data layout is in the helper function skb_copy_bits, which ip_fragment calls.

```
memcpy(skb2->nh.raw, skb->data, hlen);

if (skb_copy_bits(skb, ptr, skb2->h.raw, len))
    BUG();

left -= len;
iph = skb2->nh.iph;
iph->frag_off = htons((offset >> 3));
```

The first fragment (where offset is 0) is special from the IP options point of view because it is the only one that includes a full copy of the options from the original IP packet. Not all the options have to be replicated into all of the fragments; only the first fragment will include all of them.

```
if (offset == 0)
    ip_options_fragment(skb);
```

ip_options_fragment, described in Chapter 19, cleans up the content of the ip_opt structure associated with the original IP packet so that fragments following the first one will not include options they do not need. Therefore, ip_options_fragment is called only during the processing of the first fragment (which is the one with offset=0).

The MF flag (for More Fragments) is set if either of the following conditions is met:

- The packet being fragmenting is not a fragment itself, and the fragment created in this loop is not the last one (left>0).
- The packet being fragmented is a fragment itself, but is not the last one, and therefore all of its fragments must have MF set (not_last_frag=1).

```
if (left > 0 || not_last_frag)
    iph->frag_off |= htons(IP_MF);
```

The following two statements update two offsets. It is easy to confuse the two. offset is maintained because the packet currently being fragmented may be a fragment of a larger packet; if so, offset represents the offset of the current fragment within the original packet (otherwise, it is simply 0). `ptr` is an offset within the packet we are fragmenting and changes as the loop progresses. The two variables have the same value in two cases: where the packet we are fragmenting is not a fragment itself, and where this fragment is the very first fragment.

```
ptr += len;
offset += len;
```

Finally, the slow path needs to update the header length (taking into account the size of the options), compute the checksum with `ip_send_check`, and transmit the fragment using the output function passed as a parameter. The output function used by IPv4 is `ip_finish_output` (see Figure 18-1 in Chapter 18).

```
iph->tot_len = htons(len + hlen);
ip_send_check(iph);

err = output(skb2);
```

Fast Fragmentation

`ip_fragment` tries the fast path when it sees that the `frag_list` pointer of the input skb buffer is not NULL. However, as described earlier in this chapter, it must make sure that the fragments are suitable for the fast path. Here are the sanity checks related to protocol requirements:

- The size of each fragment should not exceed the PMTU.
- Only the last fragment can have an L3 payload whose size is not a multiple of eight bytes.
- Each fragment must have enough space at the head to allow the addition of an L2 header later.

And there are some other buffer management checks as well:

- The fragment cannot be shared, because that would forbid `ip_fragment` from editing it to add the IP header. It is acceptable for `ip_fragment` to receive a shared buffer when using the slow path because the buffer is going to be copied into many other new buffers, but it is not acceptable for the fast path.

```
if (skb_shinfo(skb)->frag_list) {
    struct sk_buff *frag;
    int first_len = skb_pagelen(skb);

    if (first_len - hlen > mtu ||
        ((first_len - hlen) & 7) ||
        (iph->frag_off & htons(IP_MF|IP_OFFSET)) ||
        skb_cloned(skb))
        goto slow_path;

    for (frag = skb_shinfo(skb)->frag_list; frag; frag = frag->next) {
        if (frag->len > mtu ||
            ((frag->len & 7) && frag->next) ||
```

```
        skb_headroom(frag) < hlen)
            goto slow_path;

    if (skb_shared(frag))
        goto slow_path;
    ...
}
```

The initialization of the IP header of the first fragment is completed outside the loop because it can be optimized slightly. For instance, when this function runs, it knows there are at least two fragments, and therefore it does not need to check `frag->next` on the first fragment to initialize `iph->frag_off`: as the first fragment, this fragment must have the IP_MF flag set and the rest of the offset set to 0 (`iph->frag_off = IP_MF`). The other packets must have the IP_MF bit set in `frag_off` without disturbing the rest of the value (`iph->frag_off |= IP_MF`).

Let's suppose the fast path can be used. The rest of the code is pretty simple, and to some extent it is similar to the code seen for the slow path. After the first fragment has been sent (i.e., after the first loop of the `for` block), the IP header is modified with `ip_options_fragment` so that it can be recycled by the following fragments. If we exclude that special case, all we need to do to transmit a fragment is:

- Copy the (modified) header from the first IP fragment into the current fragment.

- Initialize those fields of the IP header that may differ. Among them are the offset and the IP checksum, which is computed with `ip_send_check`. Also, if the fragment is not the last one, set the MF flag.

- Copy from the first fragment to the current fragment the rest of the `sk_buff` fields, using `ip_copy_metadata`. These fields are management parameters; they do not have anything to do with the content of the IP fragment.

- Transmit the fragment with the function `output` passed as a parameter.

In case of errors, memory for all the subsequent fragments in `frag_list` is freed (not shown in the following snapshot). Note that the code inside the `if (frag) {...}` block prepares the fragment that will be transmitted in the following loop iteration, and the call to `output` transmits the current one.

```
skb->data_len = first_len - skb_headlen(skb);
skb->len = first_len;
iph->tot_len = htons(first_len);
iph->frag_off = htons(IP_MF);
ip_send_check(iph);

for (;;) {
    if (frag) {
        frag->ip_summed = CHECKSUM_NONE;
        frag->h.raw = frag->data;
        frag->nh.raw = __skb_push(frag, hlen);
        memcpy(frag->nh.raw, iph, hlen);
        iph = frag->nh.iph;
        iph->tot_len = htons(frag->len);
```

```
              ip_copy_metadata(frag, skb);
              if (offset == 0)
                  ip_options_fragment(frag);
              offset += skb->len - hlen;
              iph->frag_off = htons(offset>>3);
              if (frag->next != NULL)
                  iph->frag_off |= htons(IP_MF);
              ip_send_check(iph);
          }

          err = output(skb);

          if (err || !frag)
              break;

          skb = frag;
          frag = skb->next;
          skb->next = NULL;
      }
```

IP Defragmentation

Defragmentation is needed, obviously, when a packet has reached its final destination and has to be passed to an upper network layer (in Linux, it is handled by the ip_local_deliver function). Routers, by contrast, usually just pass packets through without caring whether they are fragments of a larger packet. But defragmentation can sometimes be required on a router: generally speaking, defragmentation is needed whenever a host has to do some processing on the entire packet. Two such cases on routers are:

- The IP header contains the Router Alert option, which forces the router to process the packet (see ip_call_ra_chain, called from ip_forward, and Figure 18-1 in Chapter 18).

- Netfilter has to look at the packet to decide what to do with it. Given the scheme in Figure 18-1 in Chapter 18, the hook points where Netfilter may force defragmentation are NF_IP_PRE_ROUTING and NF_IP_LOCAL_OUT.

But the way defragmentation works does not depend on the circumstances in which it is triggered, so I will describe the implementation from a high-level standpoint.

Organization of the IP Fragments Hash Table

As IP fragments are received, they are organized into a hash table of struct ipq elements. Figure 22-1 shows an example of how the data structure is organized and used.

```
#define IPQ_HASHSZ    64
static struct ipq *ipq_hash[IPQ_HASHSZ];
```

Each IP packet being defragmented is represented by an `ipq` instance, which consists of a list of fragments. Figure 22-1 shows an example of an IP packet with ID 1234, for which only two fragments have been received so far. At the bottom of the figure you can see where those two fragments fit into the original IP packet, which is 1,250 bytes in length. The figure shows the roles of some of the most important fields in the data structures involved.

Near the bottom of the figure you can see that an offset for each fragment is stored in a field called `cb` within each `sk_buff`. We saw in Chapter 2 that this field is a buffer that can be used by the various network layers to store private information. The data stored in that buffer may change depending on whether the buffer is being received or transmitted.

In the context of IP defragmentation, IP uses the `sk_buff->cb` field to store an `ipfrag_skb_cb` structure, which in turn is a simple wrapper for `inet_skb_parm`, the structure used to store IP options and flags. (The same structure is commonly used by higher layers, too.) The new field added in `ipfrag_skb_cb` is the offset the fragment lies at inside the original IP packet. That data structure can be accessed with the macro `FRAG_CB`, defined in *net/ipv4/ip_fragment.c*. Thus, the IP layer uses `FRAG_CB` for the purpose of defragmentation and `IPCB` (defined in *include/net/ip.h*) for accessing the options for any other purpose; they point to data structures with different names but ultimately to the same locations in memory.

The `ipq_hash` table is protected by `ipfrag_lock`, which can be taken either in shared (read-only) or exclusive (read-write) mode. Do not confuse this lock with the one embedded in each `ipq` element.

Key Issues in Defragmentation

As you read the rest of this section, it will help you to keep in mind the constraints that make defragmentation complex:

- Fragments must be stored in kernel memory until they are totally processed by the network subsystem, and memory is expensive. Therefore, there must be a way to limit memory use.

- The most efficient structure for storing large amounts of information (just think of a router passing through millions of packets per second) is a hash table. A hash table can become unbalanced, however, particularly if malicious attackers figure out the hash algorithm and deliberately try to weigh down particular elements of the hash table to slow down processing. In the section "Hash Table Reorganization" we will see how Linux makes the hash algorithm use an additional random component to make the output produced by a given input less predictable.

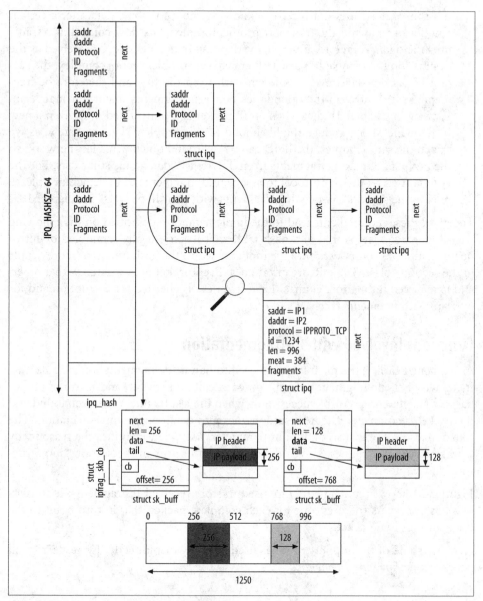

Figure 22-1. Structure used to store IP fragments

- Networking often uses unreliable media, so fragments can be lost. This is particularly true because different fragments within a packet may travel along different paths. Therefore, the IP layer must maintain a timer on each packet and give up at some point, throwing away any fragments received. Checksums must also be employed to maximize the chance that corruption will be detected.

- If a source host does not receive acknowledgment for some data after a certain amount of time and the transport protocol implements flow control, it retransmits the data. Therefore, multiple overlapping fragments may be received at the destination for a single IP packet. To make this problem more complex, the second IP packet may travel a different path from the first and therefore be fragmented differently, so the boundaries between fragments might not match up. We saw in Chapter 18 that when an IP packet is retransmitted, it is given a new IP ID, which helps reduce the likelihood of this problem. Unfortunately, as we saw in the same chapter, the IP ID can wrap around quickly in a fast network, so the problem of mixing fragments from different IP datagrams still exists. For the criteria used by the IP protocol to associate IP fragments to IP detagrams, please refer to the section "Associating fragments with their IP packets" in Chapter 18.

Together, these requirements lead to the implementation described on the following pages. Fragments are stored in a hash table that is periodically scrambled by introducing a random component into the input passed to the hash function (more details in the section "Hash Table Reorganization"). Each packet is associated with a timer, and is removed if the timer expires. Each fragment is checked for corruption and for overlaps with fragments received earlier.

Functions Involved with Defragmentation

As explained earlier, the main function used to handle defragmentation is `ip_defrag`. It receives a single fragment as input on each call and tries to add it to the proper packet. The function returns success only when the last fragment has been found and the packet is complete. The next section goes into detail on its implementation. The function also receives a second input parameter, user, that identifies the reason why defragmentation is requested. See the description of user in the section "ipq Structure" in Chapter 23.

Figure 22-1 shows the data structure used to store received IP fragments; it consists of a hash of data structures, one for each complete packet, that in turn point to the fragments for that packet.

Here are some of the support routines used (directly or indirectly) by `ip_defrag`, all defined in *net/ipv4/ip_fragment.c*:

`ip_evictor`
> Removes ipq structures of incomplete packets one by one, starting from the oldest, until the memory used by the fragments goes below the `sysctl_ipfrag_low_thresh` threshold.

> For `ip_evictor` to work properly, a Last Recently Used (LRU) list has to be kept updated. This is achieved simply by adding new ipq structures at the end of a global list (`ipq_lru_list`), and by moving an ipq structure to the end of that list every time a new fragment is added to it. This means that the element that

remains untouched for the longest time is at the head of ipq_lru_list; thus, packets that have no hope of being completed (because the transmitting host went down, for instance) stand out at the front.

ip_find

Finds the packet (fragment list) associated with the fragment being processed. The lookup is based on four fields of the IP header: the ID, the source and destination IP addresses, and the L4 protocol. This makes it pretty certain (but not absolutely certain) that the right packet is chosen (see the section "Example of an unsolvable defragmentation problem: NAT" in Chapter 18). The lookup key actually includes a local parameter too: the user. This parameter is used to identify the reason behind the defragmentation effort (see the section "ipq Structure" in Chapter 23).

ip_frag_queue

Queues a given fragment to the list of fragments (the ipq structure) associated with the same IP packet. See Figure 22-1 and the section "The ip_frag_queue Function."

ip_frag_reasm

Builds the original IP packet from its fragments, once all of them have been received.

Here are a few other support routines used to handle the deletion of an ipq:

ip_frag_destroy

Removes the ipq structure passed to it, and all of its associated IP fragments, and updates the global counter ip_frag_mem (see the section "The ip_defrag Function"). This function is called from the wrapper ipq_put function, instead of being called directly.

ipq_put

Decrements the reference count on the ipq structure passed to it, and removes the structure and fragments with ip_frag_destroy if no one else is holding a reference to it:

```
static __inline__ void ipq_put(struct ipq *ipq, int *work)
{
        if (atomic_dec_and_test(&ipq->refcnt))
                ip_frag_destroy(ipq, work);
}
```

When the input parameter work is not a NULL pointer, ipq_put returns with work initialized to the amount of memory freed by ip_frag_destroy. This is useful, for instance, to an ip_evictor invocation that was called to free a given amount of memory and therefore needs to know how much each call to ipq_put manages to free.

ipq_kill

Marks an ipq structure as eligible to be removed because some of the fragments did not arrive in time. See the section "Garbage Collection" for details.

In the next two sections, we will see `ip_defrag` and `ip_frag_queue` in more detail. Let's first see how a new fragment list (ipq instance) is created.

New ipq Instance Initialization

The first task of `ip_defrag` is to search for the packet to which it should add the fragment it receives as input. To find the packet, the function invokes `ip_find`. If the fragment happens to be the first of a packet (in terms of the time it arrives, not necessarily its position within the packet), `ip_find` will fail. In this case, `ip_find` creates a new ipq instance using the `ip_frag_create` function. Whether a structure is found or newly created, `ip_find` returns a pointer to it. `ip_defrag` uses this pointer to insert the new fragment into the ipq structure of the proper packet. The only case where `ip_find` fails (returns NULL) is when there is an error trying to create a new ipq element.

While the insertion of a new fragment is handled by `ip_defrag`, the insertion of a new ipq instance is handled by `ip_frag_create` via `ip_frag_intern`. Besides initializing a bunch of parameters in the new structure, this function also starts a garbage collection timer that will clean up the new ipq structure (and all of its fragments) if the associated defragmentation fails to complete within a given amount of time. This timeout, by default, is 30 seconds, but it can be configured via */proc* (see the section "Tuning the /proc Filesystem" in Chapter 23). The function that does the garbage collection, `ip_expire`, also generates an ICMP message to inform the source host about the failed defragmentation attempt.

The ip_defrag Function

The actual `ip_defrag` function is quite simple, because all the complexity is within the four functions it uses internally: `ip_find`, `ip_frag_queue`, `ip_frag_reasm`, and `ip_evictor`.

```
struct sk_buff *ip_defrag(struct sk_buff *skb, u32 user)
```

The fragment skb received in input by `ip_defrag` contains all the information discussed earlier that is needed to identify the ipq instance it belongs to (if one is already created).

The function starts with a check on the memory used up by IP fragments, and may trigger a garbage collection with `ip_evictor` if a configurable threshold has been reached. See the section "Garbage Collection."

If this is the first fragment of a new IP packet, `ip_find` creates a new ipq structure; otherwise, it simply returns the one it finds. In case a new one was created, the latter will be added to ipq_hash later with `ip_frag_queue`.

```
if ((qp = ip_find(iph)) != NULL) {
    struct sk_buff *ret = NULL;
```

Finally, the fragment is enqueued. ip_frag_queue is quite a complex function, and we will analyze it in detail in the next section. The list of fragments, qp, is protected by a lock to make sure there cannot be simultaneous incompatible accesses to the list:

```
spin_lock(&qp->lock);
ip_frag_queue(qp, skb);
```

If both the first and the last fragments have been received and the total size of the fragments equals the size of the original IP packet, it is time to join the fragments together to obtain the original packet and pass it to the higher layer. ip_frag_reasm stops the timer associated with the qp element, glues together the fragments, updates a few global variables, such as the one that represents the memory used by fragments (ip_frag_mem), and takes care of the L4 hardware checksum (see the section "L4 checksum"). We will not describe this function in detail because it is composed mostly of predictable, low-level instructions.

```
    if (qp->last_in == (FIRST_IN|LAST_IN) &&
        qp->meat == qp->len)
        ret = ip_frag_reasm(qp, dev);

    spin_unlock(&qp->lock);
    ipq_put(qp, NULL);
    return ret;
}

    IP_INC_STATS_BH(IPSTATS_MIB_REASMFAILS);
    kfree_skb(skb);
    return NULL;
}
```

The ip_frag_queue Function

The task of adding a new fragment to an ipq structure (the list of fragments associated with the same IP packet) is complex because the data structure used to store fragments is not a trivial array where fragments are copied using the offset field. That solution would have one major problem: because the size of the original IP packet is not known until the last fragment is received, this would force the IP layer to allocate a buffer of a size equal to the maximum IP packet size. As you can imagine, this would waste a lot of memory. Also, while easy to implement, such a solution would not perform well and would make it very easy to bring a router to its knees by means of a DoS attack.

The use of a list to handle fragments optimizes the memory used, but makes it a little bit more complicated to handle the fragments. Let's summarize the main tasks accomplished by ip_frag_queue:

- Figures out where the input fragment falls within the original packet, based on both its offset and its length.

- Based on the considerations detailed at the start of this chapter, determines whether this is the last fragment of a packet and, if so, extracts the length of the IP packet from it.

- Inserts the fragment into the list of fragments associated with the same IP packet, handling possible overlaps. (As I explained in an earlier chapter, fragments can overlap if a packet was believed to be lost and was retransmitted by a host, possibly over a different route with a different PMTU.)

- Updates those fields of the ipq structure that are used by the garbage collection task (i.e., timestamp and memory used).

- Invalidates the L4 checksum computed in hardware if necessary (e.g., when a fragment needs to be truncated by ip_frag_queue).

This is the prototype:

```
static void ip_frag_queue(struct ipq *qp, struct sk_buff *skb)
```

where qp is the IP packet the fragment belongs to (found by the caller by use of the ip_find function) and skb is the new fragment.

The function starts by extracting data from the IP header and doing a number of general checks to make sure the fragment is valid. First comes a general check to make sure the function has not been called by mistake when the IP packet has already been completely received. The COMPLETE flag, usually set after all the fragments have been received, could also be set in other unusual circumstances—for instance, when ipq_kill marks an ipq element as dead.

```
if (qp->last_in & COMPLETE)
    goto err;
```

The offset is stored in the 13 least-significant bits of the 16-bit Offset field in the IP header. Two of the three most-significant bits are used by two flags: DF and MF.* One bit is not used.

Because the offset is expressed in units of eight bytes, the value in the field must be multiplied by 8 before being usable. The header length ihl is expressed in units of four bytes and therefore must be multiplied by 4 before being usable. IP_OFFSET is simply a mask that is used to extract the lower 13 bits from the 16-bit field.

```
offset = ntohs(skb->nh.iph->frag_off);
flags = offset & ~IP_OFFSET;
offset &= IP_OFFSET;
offset <<= 3;
ihl = skb->nh.iph->ihl * 4;
```

Since the IP fragment carries both its offset and its length, we can easily calculate where the fragment ends within the original IP packet. skb->len - ihl is the size of

---

* See the file *include/net/ip.h*, and Figure 18-2 in Chapter 18.

the IP payload, and since that payload is at offset `offset` in the original IP packet, their sum gives the offset where this fragment terminates in the original IP packet.

```
end = offset + skb->len - ihl;
```

If the MF flag is not set, it means that the fragment is the last one; we can therefore extract the total length of the original IP packet, store this length in qp->len, and set the flag `LAST_IN`. If the size of the original packet derived from this last fragment (end) does not match the value we already defined earlier (if any), it means that this fragment or one of the previous ones got corrupted, and therefore this fragment is dropped.

```
if ((flags & IP_MF) == 0) {
    if (end < qp->len ||
        ((qp->last_in & LAST_IN) && end != qp->len))
        goto err;
    qp->last_in |= LAST_IN;
    qp->len = end;
} else {
```

Every fragment except the last must be a multiple of eight bytes. Thus, if the current fragment is not the last one (MF is not set) and its size is not a multiple of eight bytes, the kernel truncates it to make its size a multiple of eight bytes. (The hope here is that another fragment will arrive with the truncated information and will make the reconstructed packet correct.) Since this operation changes the L4 payload (by truncating the data), the function must also invalidate the checksum in case it had already been computed.[*] The receiving L4 layer will have to recompute it.

```
if (end&7) {
    end &= ~7;
    if (skb->ip_summed != CHECKSUM_UNNECESSARY)
        skb->ip_summed = CHECKSUM_NONE;
}
```

If the point where the fragment ends (`offset+len`) is bigger than the current value of qp->len, the latter is updated. Note that qp->len represents the length of the original defragmented packet only if the last fragment has already been received. For this reason, if a fragment ends past qp->len when the last fragment has been received, it means there is an error somewhere and the fragment is dropped.[†]

```
if (end > qp->len) {
    if (qp->last_in & LAST_IN)
        goto err;
    qp->len = end;
}
}
```

---

[*] See comments in ip_rcv and ip_rcv_finish for similar conditions.

[†] In theory, the corrupted packet could have been the one with MF=0 that previously set qp->len, instead of the one we are dropping now.

By definition of the IP protocol, the IP header cannot be fragmented. This means that if a packet has been fragmented, there must be a nonempty payload. It follows that the case of a fragment without a payload (that is, the fragment ends where it starts) would not make sense; therefore, if a fragment meets this condition, it is considered corrupted.

```
if (end == offset)
    goto err;
```

Now the function removes the IP header by moving the skb->data offset forward to the IP payload and updating skb->len; this is done by calling pskb_pull. Then the function calls pskb_trim to set the length of the buffer data portion to the length of the IP payload (end-offset). Note that the second operation is actually needed only in the following two cases:

- The buffer still contains some L2 padding. This should never be the case, because if there was any L2 padding, it would have been removed earlier in the path by ip_rcv.

- The size of the IP fragment is not a multiple of eight bytes. In this case, the function has shortened the length to a multiple of eight bytes, thus leaving some garbage at the end of the buffer.

```
if (pskb_pull(skb, ihl) == NULL)
    goto err;
if (pskb_trim(skb, end-offset))
    goto err;
```

The list of fragments contained in the input qp parameter (see Figure 22-1) is kept sorted, with the lowest fragment offset at the head of the list. Therefore, the function now needs to find where in the list to add the new fragment.

```
prev = NULL;
for(next = qp->fragments; next != NULL; next = next->next) {
    if (FRAG_CB(next)->offset >= offset)
        break;
    prev = next;
}
```

Handling overlaps

Now it is time to handle potential overlaps with previously received frames. This is done in two steps: first the function handles conflicts with fragments that have a smaller starting offset, and then it handles the others, which have higher starting offsets. The next and prev variables, which point inside the qp list described in the previous section, manage the list of old fragments.

If the new fragment does not have to be placed at the head of the list (prev!=NULL), which means we already received at least one fragment with a smaller offset, we need to handle the insertion by removing the common part (if there is any) from one of the overlapping fragments.

To do this, the function just needs to determine the size of the overlapping portion, and remove a block of that size from the head of the new fragment. Note in the following code that the presence of an overlap is marked by i being a positive number:

```
if (prev) {
    int i = (FRAG_CB(prev)->offset + prev->len) - offset;

    if (i > 0) {
        offset += i;
        if (end <= offset)
            goto err;
        if (!pskb_pull(skb, i))
            goto err;
        if (skb->ip_summed != CHECKSUM_UNNECESSARY)
            skb->ip_summed = CHECKSUM_NONE;
    }
}
```

When there is indeed an overlap with the previous fragment in the list, the function updates the offset field it extracted earlier from the header by removing the redundant part from the new fragment using pskb_pull, and invalidates the L4 checksum computed in hardware. If moving the offset ahead means that the start becomes higher than the end of the fragment, it means the new fragment is completely contained in the ones already received, so the function can simply return.

Having dealt with the preceding fragments, the function can now take care of a possible overlap with the following fragments (the ones with higher offsets). There can be two such cases:

- One or more following fragments is completely included in the new one.
- One following fragment overlaps partially with the new one.

Both cases are illustrated in Figure 22-2, where P indicates a new fragment and F an old one. P1 overlaps only with F2 (completely including it), whereas P2 overlaps with both F3 and F4 (which is completely included).

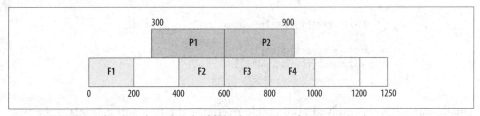

Figure 22-2. Example of single and multiple overlaps among fragments

At this point, next refers to the fragment whose offset value is the first one greater than the offset of the new fragment. The function goes fragment by fragment until it finds an overlap, simply comparing where the new fragment ends and where the ones in the list end. (Remember that the fragments already in the list are sorted in increasing order of offset.)

```
while (next && FRAG_CB(next)->offset < end) {
    int i = end - FRAG_CB(next)->offset;
```

If the size of the overlapping part is smaller than the size of the new fragment, it means that the function reached the last overlapping fragment of the list and that the only action needed is to remove the overlapping part from the fragment already in the list. The new fragment will be added later. Since the function truncates part of a fragment already in the list, both qp->meat and the offset field of the truncated fragment must be updated and the hardware checksum must be invalidated. Note that when the overlap is with a previous fragment, the function removes data from the new one, but that when the overlap is with a following fragment, the function does the opposite.

```
if (i < next->len) {
    if (!pskb_pull(next, i))
        goto err;
    FRAG_CB(next)->offset += i;
    qp->meat -= i;
    if (next->ip_summed != CHECKSUM_UNNECESSARY)
        next->ip_summed = CHECKSUM_NONE;
    break;
} else {
```

If instead the fragment is completely contained in the new one, the function can remove it from the list (once again updating qp->meat as well).[*]

If the fragment being removed is the head of the list, the head pointer has to be updated:

```
struct sk_buff *free_it = next;
next = next->next;

if (prev)
    prev->next = next;
else
    qp->fragments = next;

qp->meat -= free_it->len;
frag_kfree_skb(free_it, NULL);
    }
}
```

Finally, after having resolved all possible overlaps, the function can insert the new fragment into the list and update a few parameters of the qp structure, such as meat, stamp, and last_in. skb->truesize and the memory currently used by fragments (ip_frag_mem) also are updated. qp is also moved to the end of the ipq_lru_list list.

---

[*] frag_kfree_skb updates ip_frag_mem as well.

```
qp->stamp = skb->stamp;
qp->meat += skb->len;
atomic_add(skb->truesize, &ip_frag_mem);

if (offset == 0)
    qp->last_in |= FIRST_IN;
```

L4 checksum

Ingress IP fragments could already have their L4 checksum computed if the ingress device supports L4 hardware checksumming. When the fragments are reassembled by `ip_frag_reasm`, it combines the checksums of the individual fragments with `csum_add` and saves the result in the reassembled buffer. However, when one of the following conditions is met, the hardware checksum on the reassembled buffer is invalidated (i.e., `skb->ip_summed` is set to `CHECKSUM_NONE`):

- A fragment (with the exception of the last one) has been truncated in `ip_defrag` because its size was not a multiple of eight bytes.

- A fragment overlapped with at least one other previously received fragment. Because the overlapping is taken care of by removing the redundant part, the checksum (which covers the redundant part as well) must be invalidated.

Garbage Collection

The kernel implements two kinds of garbage collection for IP fragments:

- System memory usage limit
- Defragmentation timer

As a protection against an abuse of the memory used by the IP defragmentation subsystem, a limit on that memory is imposed and stored in the `sysctl_ipfrag_high_thresh` variable, whose value can be changed at runtime through the */proc* filesystem. The global `ip_frag_mem` variable represents the memory currently used by fragments. It is updated every time a new fragment is added to or removed from the `ipq_hash` table structure. When the system limit is reached, `ip_evictor` is invoked to free some memory.

```
if (atomic_read(&ip_frag_mem) > sysctl_ipfrag_high_thresh)
    ip_evictor();
```

The check on the memory limit is implemented by `ip_defrag` (see the section "The ip_defrag Function").

When the first fragment of a new IP packet is added to the `ipq_hash` table (i.e., when a new `ipq` instance is created), the kernel starts a defragmentation timer. The timer is used to discard all the fragments for the incomplete packet to avoid having incomplete IP packets sit in `ipq_hash` for too long (see the discussion of `sysctl_ipfrag_time` in the section "Tuning via /proc Filesystem" in Chapter 23). If a fragment is lost or delayed long enough, the timer expires and its handler `ip_expire` is called to do the cleanup, which consists of the following operations:

1. Unlinking the `ipq` structure from the `ipq_hash` table and from the `lru_list` list.

2. If `ipq` includes the first fragment of the IP packet, sending an ICMP TIME EXCEEDED message back to the source host. The local host must have received the first fragment to be able to transmit the ICMP message because this message needs to include a portion of the original IP packet in its payload, and only the first fragment includes the original IP header (with all of the options of the unfragmented packet) and all or part of the L4 header (see Figure 21-4 in Chapter 21). The ICMP message is sent only if the device the last fragment was received from is still up and running, because it will most probably be used to transmit the ICMP.

3. Updating the SNMP counters for the failed defragmentation event.

The first operation is accomplished by `ipq_kill` (by calling `ipq_unlink`). Because this function is called in other contexts, too—not just by `ip_expire`—its attempt to stop the `ipq`'s timer is not useless. It will not stop any timer when invoked by `ip_expire`, but it may stop one in the other cases. If a timer is running for the packet, the `ipq`'s reference count was incremented when the timer was started. Therefore, to keep the reference count correct, `ipq_kill` decrements the reference count after deleting the timer.

Besides `ip_expire`, here are two other cases that may lead to a call to `ipq_kill`:

- `ip_frag_reasm` calls it when the last missing fragment is received.
- `ip_evictor` (introduced at the beginning of this section) calls it to kill the `ipq` structures it selects for deletion.

Regardless of the reason why `ipq_kill` was called, the COMPLETE flag is set and the `ipq` structure is unlinked from all lists it was on. This means that the COMPLETE flag does not necessarily refer to completely defragmented IP packets.

Hash Table Reorganization

We saw in Figure 22-1 how incoming fragments are organized in memory while waiting to be defragmented. At the top level, all fragments for all packets are accessed through a hash table named `ipq_hash`. A hash table performs best when the hash function can spread the various elements as uniformly as possible. Allowing a large number of collisions, which would cause IP fragments to be bunched up in a few lists that are hanging off of a few elements of `ipq_hash`, would degrade performance and even allow DoS attacks. To avoid these collisions, the Linux kernel regularly reorganizes all of the IP fragments in the table using a different hash function. This mechanism can be effective only if the reorganization is done frequently and, every time a new function is selected, the new one cannot be guessed from the previous one.

Reorganization of fragments is kicked off by a timer that is started by `ipfrag_init` and that expires every 10 minutes by default. (The expiration time can be configured by means of the */proc* interface, described in "Tuning via /proc Filesystem" in Chapter 23.

The function executed when the timer expires, `ipfrag_secret_rebuild`, is pretty simple. Every time it is executed, it generates a random value with `get_random_bytes` and stores the value in the global variable `ipfrag_hash_rnd`, which is used by the `ipqhashfn` hash function. Then, one by one, each element in the hash table is first unlinked, its hash (i.e., bucket) is recomputed with `ipqhashfn` (that now uses the new value of `ipfrag_hash_rnd`), and finally it is re-inserted into the table.

`ipfrag_hash_rnd` is first initialized in `ipfrag_init`, without using `get_random_bytes`, because the latter function depends on a quality of the system known as "entropy," built up over time by checking system events that traditionally happen at unpredictable times. At boot time, there may not be enough entropy yet to rely on get_random_bytes for a random number.

The reorganizations of the `ipq` structures do not affect the `ipq_lru_list` list.

## CHAPTER 23

Internet Protocol Version 4 (IPv4): Miscellaneous Topics

This chapter wraps up our discussion of the IPv4 layer in the networking code. It covers general topics such as the management of information in the IPv4 layer by the kernel, statistics, and the user interface through */proc*. The chapter also includes a brief discussion of the limitations of the IPv4 protocol, which led to the development of IPv6.

Long-Living IP Peer Information

At the IP layer, there is no concept of a stateful connection. Because IP is a stateless protocol, there are no parameters or connection-related data structures to keep, except for statistics. (These are optional and are not required by the protocol itself.) However, to improve performance, the kernel keeps information about some parameters on a per-destination IP address base. We will see an example in a moment.

Any host that has recently carried on an exchange of data with a Linux box is considered an IP peer. The kernel allocates a data structure for each peer to preserve some long-living information. At the moment, not many parameters are kept in the structure. The most important one is the IP packet ID. We saw in Chapter 18 that each IP packet is identified by a 16-bit field called ID. Instead of having a single shared ID, incremented for each IP packet regardless of the destination, one unique instance is kept for each IP peer. (This solution is an implementation choice; it is not imposed by any standard.) We already had a little discussion on the packet ID in Chapter 18.

Peers are represented by inet_peer structures. These structures, defined in *include/ net/inetpeer.h* and described in the section "inet_peer Structure," are organized in an AVL tree, which is a well-known type of data structure optimized for lookups. I will not go into detail about the AVL data structure; you can find it in any programming book.[*] However, it is worthwhile to underline the trade-offs involved in an AVL tree.

---

[*] The comment at the top of *net/ipv4/inetpeer.c* is quite clear and self-explanatory.

Essentially, the tree is kept balanced thanks to the way in which insert and delete operations are defined. Because the tree is balanced, a search will always take O(lg n) time, where n is the number of elements in the tree. Generally speaking, because keeping the tree balanced comes at a cost, this kind of data structure is usually used when there are many lookups relative to insert/delete/change operations, and when the speed of these lookups is particularly important.

The whole AVL tree and the associated global variables (such as peer_total) are protected by the peer_pool_lock lock. The lock can be acquired in both shared and exclusive modes. Lookups need only read privilege and therefore will acquire the lock in shared mode, whereas insert/delete operations have to acquire the lock in exclusive mode.

Initialization

The peer subsystem is initialized by inet_initpeers, which is defined in *net/ipv4/inetpeer.c* and is invoked by ip_init when the IPv4 protocol is initialized at boot time.

That function accomplishes three main tasks:

- Allocates the cache that will be used to hold inet_peer structures, which will be allocated as peers are recognized.
- Defines a threshold (inet_peer_threshold) that will be used to limit the amount of memory used by inet_peer structures. Its value is computed based on the amount of RAM in the system. When a new entry is created, the global counter peer_total is incremented; it is of course decremented when an element is removed. If peer_total becomes bigger than the threshold, the most recently used element is removed (see inet_getpeer).
- Starts the garbage collection timer. We describe this task in the section "Garbage Collection."

Lookups

The key for a search is the destination's IP address. There are two main functions:

lookup
> This is a macro local to *net/ipv4/inetpeer.c* that implements a simple search in an AVL tree.

inet_getpeer
> This function can be used from other subsystems, such as TCP and routing, to search a given entry. This function is built on top of lookup.

inet_getpeer is passed the search key (the peer's IP address) and a flag (create) that can be used to ask for the creation of a new entry in case the search failed. When a new entry is created, the initial IP packet ID is initialized to a random value by means of secure_ip_id.

Figure 23-1 shows the internals of inet_getpeer. The function is pretty simple and does not need much explanation. However, there is one point worth clarifying: why there are two lookups to see whether there is already an entry with the same destination address as the one being requested. The second check is not superfluous because a similar entry could have been created and added to the tree between the time the read lock was released and the write lock was acquired.

How the IP Layer Uses inet_peer Structures

Among the few fields of the inet_peer structure, only two are currently used by the IP layer: v4addr, which identifies the peer, and ip_id_count.

The value of ip_id_count can be retrieved via inet_getid, which automatically increments its value at the same time. The latter is never called directly. The section "Selecting the IP Header's ID Field" offers a list of the wrappers that are used by the IP layer depending on the context.

Garbage Collection

Because the number of inet_peer instances that can be created is limited, there is a timer (peer_periodic_timer) that is started at subsystem initialization time (inet_initpeers) and that at regular intervals causes the removal of entries that have not been used for a given amount of time. The timer handler is peer_check_expire.

The amount needed to classify an entry as old depends on how loaded the system is. A system is considered loaded when the number of elements (peer_total) is greater than or equal to the threshold (inet_peer_threshold). On a loaded system, entries are removed after an inactivity period of 120 seconds (inet_peer_minttl). On a system that is not loaded, the value lies between 120 seconds and 10 minutes (inet_peer_maxttl) and is inversely proportional to the number of outstanding inet_peer entries (peer_total). To avoid making the timer a CPU hog, the number of elements removable at each timer expiration is set to PEER_MAX_CLEANUP_WORK (30).

When the timer is first started, the timeout is set to expire after inet_peer_minttl, with a little perturbation to avoid synchronization with other timers started at boot time. After that, the timer does not really run at regular intervals. Instead, the expiration time is set to a value between 10 seconds (inet_peer_gc_mintime) and 120 seconds (inet_peer_gc_maxtime), inversely proportional to the number of entries (see peer_check_expire), which means that the more entries there are, the faster they expire.

When an entry expires, it is inserted into the unused list, whose head and tail are pointed to by the two global variables inet_peer_unused_head and inet_peer_unused_tailp. The unused list is protected by the inet_peer_unused_lock lock. If an expired entry is still referenced (that is, the reference count is greater than 1), it cannot be freed and it is kept in the unused list; otherwise it, is freed now.

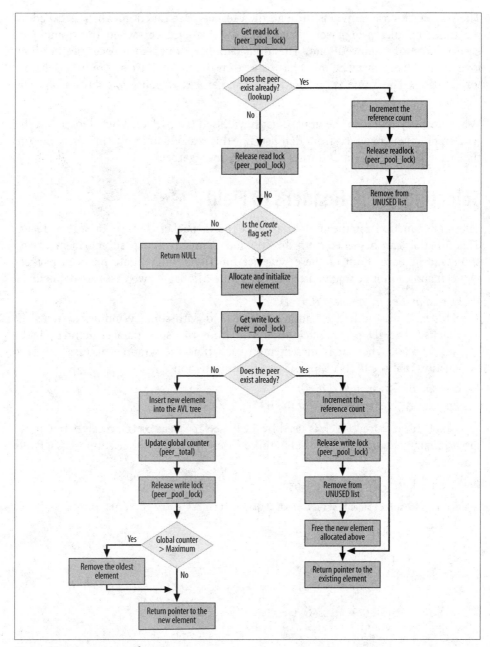

Figure 23-1. inet_getpeer function

When an inet_peer structure is to be removed, because it expired or because it is not used anymore (i.e., its reference count dropped to 0), it is inserted into the unused list but is kept in the AVL tree, too. This means that subsequent lookups on the AVL tree can return inet_peer entries currently in the unused list.

The way entries are purged is through the cleanup_once function, which is called by the timer handler peer_check_expire, and by inet_getpeer when the number of entries passes the allowed limit. The input parameter to cleanup_once specifies how long an inet_peer instance must have spent on the unused list before being eligible for deletion. The value 0, as used by inet_getpeer, means that any instance is eligible.

When an entry that is in the unused list is accessed (i.e., selected by a lookup on the AVL tree), it gets removed from that list. For this reason, an entry can join and leave the unused list several times during its life (see inet_getpeer).

Selecting the IP Header's ID Field

The main function for the initialization of the IP packet ID is __ip_select_ident. This function can be called both directly and indirectly via ip_select_ident or ip_select_ident_more. Both of these wrapper functions differentiate between packets that can and cannot be fragmented (based on the MF flag). Two cases are defined:

Packets cannot be fragmented (DF=1)
This case was added to handle a bug found with some Windows systems' IP stacks.[*] The ID is extracted indirectly from the sock data structures (inet_sk(sk)->sk), where it is incremented each time the wrapper accesses it. This ensures that the IP ID changes at every transmission.

Packets can be fragmented (DF=0)
ip_select_ident takes care of the ID.

ip_select_ident_more, which is used by TCP (see ip_queue_xmit), receives one more input parameter (more) that is used in those cases where the device supports TCP off-loading.

Let's go back to __ip_select_ident:

```
void __ip_select_ident(struct iphdr *iph, struct dst_entry *dst, int more)
{
    struct rtable *rt = (struct rtable *) dst;

    if (rt) {
        if (rt->peer == NULL)
            rt_bind_peer(rt, 1);
        if (rt->peer) {
            iph->id = htons(inet_getid(rt->peer, more));
            return;
        }
    } else
        printk(KERN_DEBUG "rt_bind_peer(0) @%p\n",
```

---

[*] According to the comment in the source code, the issue has to do with the implementation of the TCP/IP header compression algorithm described in RFC 1144.

```
    __builtin_return_address(0));

        ip_select_fb_ident(iph);
    }
```

We saw in the section "Long-Living IP Peer Information" that for each IP peer there is an inet_peer data structure that keeps, among other things, a counter that can be used to set the IP packet ID (iph->id). __ip_select_ident uses this ID when it is available, and falls back to ip_select_fb_ident otherwise.

If the inet_peer structure is not already initialized in the routing cache entry rt, rt_bind_peer first looks for the inet_peer structure associated with the peer, and if it does not exist, the function tries to create it (because the last input parameter to rt_bind_peer is set to 1). Such creation attempts can fail on a loaded system that runs out of memory and thus cannot afford the allocation of a new inet_peer structure. In this case, __ip_select_ident generates an ID with ip_select_fb_ident, which represents the last recourse.

The way ip_select_fb_ident (where fb stands for *fallback*) works is simple: it keeps a static variable, ip_fallback_id, combines it with the destination IP address of the peer, and passes it to the secure_ip_id function we already saw in the section "Lookups." The only drawback of this solution is that because this function can potentially be used for several peers, there is no longer a guarantee that the IDs assigned to consecutive IP packets sent to any given peer within a reasonable amount of time will be different. It is important that different IP packets addressed to the same destination have different IDs because the IP ID is one of the fields used to take care of defragmentation. Thus, if different IP packets with the same ID get fragmented and the fragments get mixed, there is no way for the receiver to distinguish the fragments belonging to the different IP packets (see the section "Associating fragments with their IP packets" in Chapter 18).

IP Statistics

The Linux kernel keeps several sets of statistics about different events and conditions that can be useful for accounting, debugging, or confirming compatibility with standards. In this chapter, we will only briefly see what statistics are kept by the IP protocol layer (without touching on the SNMP infrastructure) and how they are updated. In previous chapters, especially when describing the various functions, we saw a few cases where macros such as IP_INC_STATS were used to update the value of some counters.

Let's start with the data structure that contains all of the counters associated with the IP protocol. It is called ip_statistics and is defined in *net/ipv4/ip_input.c*. It is a vector with two pointers, each one pointing to a vector of ipstats_mib' structures (defined in *include/net/snmp.h*), one per CPU. The allocation of such vectors is done in init_ipv4_mibs in *net/ipv4/af_inet.c*.

```
static int __init init_ipv4_mibs(void)
{
        ...
        ip_statistics[0] = alloc_percpu(struct ipstats_mib);
        ip_statistics[1] = alloc_percpu(struct ipstats_mib);
        ...
}
```

The ipstats_mib structure is simply declared as an array of unsigned long fields of size __IPSTATS_MIB_MAX, which happens to be the size of the IPSTATS_MIB_XXX enumeration list in *include/linux/snmp.h*.

Here is the meaning of the IPSTATS_MIB_XXX values, classified into four groups. For a more detailed description, you can refer to RFC 2011 for IPv4 and RFC 2465 for IPv6. The IPSTATS_MIX_XXX counters that are not used by IPv4 (with the exception of IPSTATS_MIB_INADDRERRORS) are not defined in RFC 2011.

Fields related to received packets

IPSTATS_MIB_INRECEIVES

>Number of packets received. This field does not distinguish between complete IP packets and fragments. It also includes both the ones that will be accepted and the ones that will be discarded for any reason (with the exception of those dropped because an interface in promiscuous mode delivered frames to ip_rcv that were not addressed to the receiving interface). It is updated at the beginning of ip_rcv.

IPSTATS_MIB_INHDRERRORS

>Number of packets (fragments as well as nonfragmented packets) that were discarded because of corrupted IP headers. This field can be updated both in ip_rcv and in ip_rcv_finish for different reasons.

IPSTATS_MIB_INTOOBIGERRORS

>Not used by IPv4. IPv6 uses it to count those ingress IP packets that cannot be forwarded because they would need to be fragmented (which is not an allowed operation for a router in IPv6, unlike IPv4).

IPSTATS_MIB_INNOROUTES

>Not used at the moment. It is supposed to count those ingress packets that could not be forwarded because the local host does not have a valid route.

IPSTATS_MIB_INADDRERRORS

>Not used at the moment by IPv4. IPv6 uses it to count those packets received with a wrong address type.

IPSTATS_MIB_INUNKNOWNPROTOS

>Number of packets received with an unknown L4 protocol (i.e., no handler for the protocol was registered). This field is updated in ip_local_deliver_finish.

---

* MIB, as mentioned earlier, stands for Management Information Base, and is used to refer to a collection of objects (typically counters).

IPSTATS_MIB_INTRUNCATEDPKTS

The packet is truncated (i.e., it does not include a full IP header). It is used by IPv6, but not by IPv4.

IPSTATS_MIB_INDISCARDS

Number of packets discarded. This counter does not include the packets dropped because of header errors; it mainly includes memory allocation problems. This field is updated in ip_rcv and ip_rcv_finish.

IPSTATS_MIB_INDELIVERS

Number of packets successfully delivered to L4 protocol handlers. This field is updated in ip_local_deliver_finish.

IPSTATS_MIB_INMCASTPKTS

Number of received multicast packets. It is used by IPv6, but not by IPv4.

Fields related to transmitted packets

IPSTATS_MIB_OUTFORWDATAGRAMS

Number of ingress packets that needed to be forwarded. This counter is actually incremented before the packets are transmitted and when they theoretically could still be discarded for some reason. Its value is updated in ip_forward_finish (and in ipmr_forward_finish for multicast).

IPSTATS_MIB_OUTREQUESTS

Number of packets that the system tried to transmit (successfully or not), not including forwarded packets. This field is updated in ip_ouput (and in ip_mc_output for multicast).

IPSTATS_MIB_OUTDISCARDS

Number of packets whose transmission failed. This field is updated in several places, including ip_append_data, ip_push_pending_frames, and raw_send_hdrinc.

IPSTATS_MIB_OUTNOROUTES

Number of locally generated packets discarded because there was no route to transmit them. Normally this field is updated after a failure of ip_route_output_flow. ip_queue_xmit is one of the functions that can update it.

IPSTATS_MIB_OUTMCASTPKTS

Number of transmitted multicast packets. Not used by IPv4 at the moment.

Fields related to defragmentation

IPSTATS_MIB_REASMTIMEOUT

Number of packets that failed defragmentation because some of the fragments were not received in time. The value reflects the number of complete packets, not the number of fragments. This field is updated in ip_expire, which is the timer function executed when an IP fragment list is dropped due to a timeout. Note that this counter is not used as defined in the two RFCs mentioned at the beginning of this section.

IPSTATS_MIB_REASMREQDS

>Number of fragments received (and therefore the number of attempted reassemblies). This field is updated in ip_defrag.

IPSTATS_MIB_REASMFAILS

>Number of packets that failed the defragmentation. This field is updated in several places (__ip_evictor, ip_expire, ip_frag_reasm, and ip_defrag) for different reasons.

IPSTATS_MIB_REASMOKS

>Number of packets successfully defragmented. This field is updated in ip_frag_reasm.

Fields related to fragmentation

IPSTATS_MIB_FRAGFAILS

>Number of failed fragmentation efforts. This field is updated in ip_fragment (and in ipmr_queue_xmit for multicast).

IPSTATS_MIB_FRAGOKS

>Number of fragments transmitted. This field is updated in ip_fragment.

IPSTATS_MIB_FRAGCREATES

>Number of fragments created. This field is updated in ip_fragment.

The values of these counters are exported in the */proc/net/snmp* file.

Each CPU keeps its own accounting information about the packets it processes. Furthermore, it keeps two counters: one for events in interrupt context and the other for events outside interrupt context. Therefore, the ip_statistics array includes two elements per CPU, one for interrupt context and one for noninterrupt context. Not all of the events can happen in both contexts, but to make things easier and clearer, the vector has simply been defined of double in size; those elements that do not make sense in one of the two contexts are simply not to be used.

Because some pieces of code can be executed both in interrupt context and outside interrupt context, the kernel provides three different macros to add an event to the IP statistics vector:

```
#define IP_INC_STATS     (field)    SNMP_INC_STATS     (ip_statistics, field)
#define IP_INC_STATS_BH  (field)    SNMP_INC_STATS_BH  (ip_statistics, field)
#define IP_INC_STATS_USER(field)    SNMP_INC_STATS_USER(ip_statistics, field)
```

The first can be used in either context, because it checks internally whether it was called in interrupt context and updates the right element accordingly. The second and the third macros are to be used for events that happened in and outside interrupt context, respectively. The macros IP_INC_STATS, IP_INC_STATS_BH, and IP_INC_STATS_USER are defined in *include/net/ip.h*, and the three associated SNMP_INC_*XXX* macros are defined in *include/net/snmp.h*.

IP Configuration

The Linux IP protocol can be tuned and configured manually by a system administrator in different ways. This tuning includes both changes to the protocol itself and to device configuration. The four main interfaces are:

ioctl *calls made via ifconfig*
> *ifconfig* is the older Unix-legacy tool for configuring IP on network devices.

RTNetlink via ip
> *ip*, which is part of the IPROUTE2 package, is the newer tool that Linux offers for configuring IP on network devices.

/proc filesystem
> Protocol behavior can be tuned via a collection of files in the directory */proc/sys/net/ipv4*.

RARP/BOOTP/DHCP
> These three protocols can be used to dynamically assign an IP configuration to a host and its interfaces.

The last set of protocols in the preceding list have an interesting twist. They are normally implemented in user space, but Linux also has a simple kernel-space implementation that is useful when used together with the nfsroot boot option. The latter allows the kernel to mount the root directory (/) via NFS. To do that, it needs an IP configuration at boot time before the system is able to initialize the IP configuration from user space (which, by the way, could be stored in a remote partition and not even be available to the system when it mounts the root directory). Via kernel boot options, it is possible to give nfsroot a static configuration, or specify what protocols (yes, more than one can be used concurrently) to use to obtain the configuration. The IP configuration code is in *net/ipv4/ipconfig.c*, and the one used by nfsroot is in *fs/nfs/nfsroot.c*. The two files cross-reference variables and functions, but they are actually simple to read. We will not cover them, because network filesystems and user-space clients are outside the scope of this book. Once you know how to read _ _setup macros (described in Chapter 7), reading the code should become a piece of cake. It is clear and well commented.

The third item in the list, */proc*, is covered later in the section "Tuning via /proc Filesystem."

In this section, I will say a bit about the kernel interfaces that support the behavior of the first two items, *ifconfig* and *ip*. The purpose here is not to cover the internals of the user-space commands or the associated kernel counterparts that handle configuration requests. It is to show how user space and kernel space communicate, and the kernel functions that are invoked in response to a user-space command.

Main Functions That Manipulate IP Addresses and Configuration

In *net/ipv4/devinet.c*, you can find several functions that can be used to add an IP address to a network interface, delete an address from an interface, modify an address, retrieve the IP configuration of a device given its device index or net_device data structure, etc. Here I introduce only a few of the functions that will be useful, to help you to understand the functions described later when we talk about the *ip* and *ifconfig* user-space tools.

Before reading these descriptions of functions, it would be worthwhile reviewing the key data structures used by the IP layer, introduced in Chapter 19 and described in detail later in this chapter. For instance, a single IP address is represented by an in_ifaddr structure and the complete IPv4 configuration of a device by an in_device structure.

inetdev_init *and* inetdev_destroy

> inetdev_init is invoked when the first IP configuration is applied to a device. It allocates the in_device structure and links it to the associated net_device instance. It also creates a directory in */proc/sys/net/ipv4/conf/* (see the section "Tuning via /proc Filesystem").
>
> The IP configuration can be removed with inetdev_destroy, which simply undoes whatever was done in inetdev_init, plus removes all of the linked in_ifaddr structures. The latter are removed with inet_free_ifa, which also decrements the reference count on the in_device structure with in_dev_put. When the last reference is released, probably with the last call to inet_free_ifa, the in_device instance is freed with in_dev_finish_destroy.

inet_alloc_ifa *and* inet_free_ifa

> Those two functions allocate and free, respectively, an in_ifaddr data structure. A new one is allocated when a user adds a new address to an interface. A deletion can be triggered by the removal of a single address, or by the removal of all of the devices' IP configurations together. Both routines use the read-copy update (RCU) mechanism as a means to enforce mutual exclusion.

inet_insert_ifa *and* inet_del_ifa

> inet_insert_ifa adds a new in_ifaddr structure to the list within in_device. It detects duplicates and marks the address as secondary if it finds out that it falls within another address's subnet. Suppose, for instance that *eth0* already had the address 10.0.0.1/24. When a new 10.0.0.2/24 address is added, it will be recognized as secondary with respect to the first. Primary addresses are also used to feed the entropy of the kernel random number generator with net_srandom. More information on primary and secondary addresses can be found in Chapter 30.
>
> inet_del_ifa simply removes an in_ifaddr structure from the associated in_device instance, making sure that, if the address is primary, all of the associated secondary addresses are removed too, unless the administrator has explicitly configured the device via its */proc/sys/net/ipv4/conf/dev_name/promote_*

secondaries file not to remove secondary addresses. Instead, a secondary address can be promoted to a primary one when the associated primary address is removed. Given the in_device instance, this configuration can be accessed with the IN_DEV_PROMOTE_SECONDARIES macro. The inet_del_ifa function accepts an extra input parameter that can be used to tell whether the in_device structure should be freed when the last in_ifaddr instance has been removed. While it is normal to remove the empty in_device structure, sometimes a caller might not do it, such as when it knows it is going to add a new in_ifaddr soon.

In both cases, addition and deletion, successful completion leads to a Netlink broadcast notification with rtmsg_ifa (see the section "Change Notification: rtmsg_ifa") and a notification to the other kernel subsystems via the inetaddr_chain notification chain (see Chapter 4).

inet_set_ifa

> This is a wrapper for inet_insert_ifa that creates an in_device structure if none exists for the associated device, and sets the scope of the address to local (RT_SCOPE_HOST) for addresses like 127.*x.x.x*. Refer to the section "Scope" in Chapter 30 for more details on scopes.

Many other, smaller functions can be used to make the code more readable. Here are a few of them:

inet_select_addr

> This function is used to select an IP address among the ones configured on a given device. The function accepts an optional scope as a parameter, which can be used to narrow down the lookup domain. We will see where this function is useful in Chapter 35.

inet_make_mask *and* inet_mask_len

> Given the number of 1s the netmask is composed of, inet_make mask creates the associated netmask. For example, an input of 24 would generate the netmask with the decimal representation 255.255.255.0.

> inet_mask_len is the converse, returning the number of 1s in a decimal netmask. For instance, 255.255.0.0 would return 16.

inet_ifa_match

> Given an IP address and a netmask, inet_ifa_match checks whether a given second IP address falls within the same subnet. This function is often used to classify secondary addresses and to check whether a given IP address belongs to one of the locally configured subnets. See, for instance, inet_del_ifa.

for_primary_ifa *and* for_ifa

> These two functions are macros that can be used to browse all of the in_ifaddr instances associated with a given in_device structure. for_primary_ifa considers only primary addresses, and for_ifa goes through all of them.

Change Notification: rtmsg_ifa

Netlink provides the RTMGRP_IPV4_IFADDR multicast group to user-space applications interested in changes to the locally configured IP addresses. The kernel uses the rtmsg_ifa function to notify those applications that registered to the group when any change takes place on the local IP addresses. The function can be called when two types of events occur:

RTM_NEWADDR
> A new address has been configured on a device.

RTM_DELADDR
> An address has been removed from a device.

The generated message is initialized with inet_fill_ifaddr, the same function used to handle dump requests from user space (with commands such as *ip addr list*). The message includes the address being added or removed, and the device associated with it.

So, who is interested in this kind of notification? Routing protocols are a major example. If you are using Zebra, the routing protocols you have configured would like to remove all of the routes that are directly or indirectly dependent on an address that has gone away. In Chapter 31, you will learn more about the way routing protocols interact with the kernel routing subsystem.

inetaddr_chain Notification Chain

The IP subsystem uses the inetaddr_chain notification chain to notify other kernel subsystems about changes to the IP configuration of the local devices. A kernel subsystem can register and unregister itself with inetaddr_chain by means of the register_inetaddr_notifier and unregister_inetaddr_notifier functions. Here are two examples of users for this notification chain:

Routing
> See the section "External Events" in Chapter 32.

Netfilter masquerading
> When a local IP address is used by the Netfilter's masquerading feature, and that address disappears, all of the connections that are using that address must be dropped (see *net/ipv4/netfilter/ipt_MASQUERADE.c*).

The two NETDEV_DOWN and NETDEV_UP events, respectively, are notified when an IP address is removed and when it is added to a local device. Such notifications are generated by the inet_del_ifa and inet_insert_ifa routines introduced in the section "Main Functions That Manipulate IP Addresses and Configuration."

IP Configuration via ip

Traditionally, Unix system administrators configured interfaces and routes manually using *ifconfig*, *route*, and other commands. Currently Linux provides an umbrella *ip* command to handle IP configuration, with a number of subcommands.

In this section we will see how IPROUTE2 handles the main addressing operations, such as adding and removing an address. Once you are familiar with these operations, you can easily understand and read through the code for the others.

Figure 23-2 shows the files and the main functions of the IPROUTE2 package that are involved with IP address configuration activities. The labels on the lines are *ip* keywords, and the nodes show the function invoked and the file the latter belongs to. For instance, the command *ip address add* would be handled by ipaddr_modify.

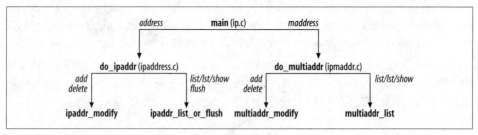

Figure 23-2. IPROUTE2 files and functions for address configuration

Table 23-1 shows the association between the operation specified with a command-line keyword (e.g., *add*) and the kernel handler run by the kernel. For instance, when the kernel receives a request for an RTM_NEWADDR operation, it knows it is associated with an *add* command and therefore invokes inet_rtm_newaddr. Some kernel operations are overloaded, and for these, the kernel needs extra flags to figure out exactly what the user-space command is asking for. See Chapter 36 for an example. This association is defined in *net/ipv4/devinet.c* in the inet_rtnetlink_table structure. For an introduction to RTNetlink, refer to Chapter 3.

Table 23-1. ip route commands and associated kernel operations

CLI keyword	Operation	Kernel handler
add	RTM_NEWADDR	inet_rtm_newaddr
delete	RTM_DELADDR	inet_rtm_deladdr
list, lst, show	RTM_GETADDR	inet_dumpifaddr
flush	RTM_GETADDR	inet_dumpifaddr

The *list* and *flush* commands need some explanation. *list* is simply a request to the kernel to dump information, for instance, about a given device, and *flush* is a request to clear the entire IP configuration on the device.

The two functions `inet_rtm_newaddr` and `inet_rtm_deladdr` are wrappers for the generic functions `inet_insert_ifa` and `inet_del_ifa` that we introduced in the section "Main Functions That Manipulate IP Addresses and Configuration." All the wrappers do is translate the request that comes from user space into an input understandable by the two more-general functions. They also filter bad requests that are associated with nonexistent devices.

IP Configuration via ifconfig

ifconfig is implemented in the *ifconfig.c* user-space file (part of the *net-tools* package). Unlike *ip*, *ifconfig* uses `ioctl` calls to interface to the kernel. However, a set of functions are used by both the *ip* and *ifconfig* handlers. In Chapter 3, we had an overview of how `ioctl` calls are handled by the kernel. Here all we need to know is that the requests related to IPv4 configuration are handled by the `inet_ioctl` function in *net/ipv4/af_inet.c*. Based on the `ioctl` code you can see what helper functions `inet_ioctl` uses to process the user-space commands (e.g., `devinet_ioctl`).

As for IPROUTE2, user-space requests from *ifconfig* are handled on the kernel side by wrappers that end up calling the functions in the section "Main Functions That Manipulate IP Addresses and Configuration."

IP-over-IP

IP-over-IP, also called IP tunneling (or IPIP), consists of transmitting IP packets inside other IP packets. This protocol is useful in some very interesting cases, including in a Virtual Private Network (VPN). Of course, nothing comes for free; you can well imagine the extra weight of the doubling of the protocol: because each IP packet has two IP headers, the overhead becomes huge for small packets. There are subtle complexities in implementation, too. For instance, what is the relationship between the IP options of the two headers?

If you consider just the IPv4 and IPv6 protocols, you already have four possible combinations of tunneling. But not all of these combinations are likely to be used.

To make things more complex (I should actually say "flexible"), keep in mind that there is no limit to the number of recursions in tunneling.*

The different tunnel interfaces that can be created in Linux are not covered in this book. However, given the background on the IP implementation in this part of the book, you can study the code in *net/ipv4/ipip.c* and *include/net/ipip.h* to derive the implementation details.

---

* IPv6 defines the "tunnel encapsulation limit" as the maximum number of nested encapsulations. See section 6.6 of RFC 2473.

IPv4: What's Wrong with It?

We saw in the section "IP Protocol: The Big Picture" in Chapter 18 what the main tasks are of the IP protocol. IPv4 was designed almost 25 years ago (in 1981), and given the speed with which the Internet and network services have evolved since then, the protocol is showing its age. Because IPv4 was not originally designed with today's big network topologies and commercial uses in mind, it has shown several limitations over the years. These have been only partially solved, sometimes with special extensions to the protocol (e.g., classless interdomain routing), DiffServ Code Point (DSCP) replacement to ToS, congestion notification, etc.), and other times by defining specialized external protocols such as IPsec.

Thanks to the experience gained with IPv4, the new IPv6 version of the protocol has been designed to address the known shortcomings of IPv4, taking into consideration such aspects as:

- Functionality
- Ease of configuration
- Performance
- Transition from IPv4 networks to IPv6 networks
- Security

Naturally, the committees designing the new protocol have tried to keep IPv4 and IPv6 as compatible as possible, and the transition from one to another as painless as possible. This compatibility and interaction have to be handled not only at the application layer, but also at the kernel layer.

When analyzing IPv4 packet transmission, we saw that fragmentation and options processing were the two most expensive tasks. It should not come as a surprise, therefore, that IPv6 addressed both points:

- Fragmentation has been limited in IPv6: an IP packet can be fragmented only at the source.
- The presence of IP options may sometimes inhibit the fast processing path: this is true for both software routers like Linux on a PC and commercial hardware IP implementations. For a commercial implementation, it could mean that IP packets without options can be forwarded in hardware at much higher speed, and the ones with options have to be handled in software. The way options are handled by IPv6 is also different: IPv6 uses the concept of *extensions*, whose main advantage is that not all of the routers have to process them.

One other big limitation of IPv4 is the 32-bit size of its addresses and the limited hierarchy they come with. Network Address Translation (NAT) is only a short-term solution that partially solves the problem. NAT comes with some limitations, which are listed on the following page.

- Each protocol has to be treated specially, so some protocols don't always work passing through a NAT router (e.g., H323).

- The NAT router becomes a single point of failure. Because it needs to keep state information for all the connections passing through it, designing a network with redundancy or security in mind is not easy.

- Its tasks are complex and computationally heavy when there is a need to support those complex protocols that have not been designed with NAT support in mind (these are considered to be "not NAT-friendly"*).

The limited number of addresses in IPv4 also contributes (because of its limited hierarchy) to the creation of huge routing tables. A core router can have up to hundreds of thousands of routes. This trend is bad, for a couple of reasons:

- The routes require lots of memory.
- Lookups are slower.

Classless interdomain routing helps in reducing the size of the routing tables, but cannot solve the limited address space problem of IPv4.

In IPv6, the address has been made four times bigger in size, which does not mean four times as many addresses, but rather 2^{96} times as many! This potentially brings systems outside the NAT router and makes them full-fledged citizens of the Internet, with implications for new types of applications.

IPv4 was not designed with security in mind. Because of this, several approaches of different granularity have been developed: application end-to-end solutions such as Secure Sockets Layer (SSL), host end-to-end solutions such as IPsec, etc. Each has its own pros and cons. SSL requires the applications to be written to use that security layer (which sits on top of TCP), whereas IPsec (which is what most people identify VPNs with) does not: IPsec sits at the L3 layer and therefore is transparent to applications. IPsec can be used by both IPv4 and IPv6, but it fits better with IPv6.

With IPv6, the neighboring system has changed as well. It is called *neighbor discovery*, and represents the counterpart to ARP for IPv4. The QoS component is also expanded.

With IPv4 networks, it is already possible to carry out automatic host configuration, thanks to protocols such as DHCP; however, some constraints make that solution less Plug and Play (PnP) than it should be. This issue has been solved by IPv6 too, with the so-called *autoconfiguration* feature.

---

* You can read RFC 3235 if you would like to see what is considered a NAT-friendly protocol or application.

Tuning via /proc Filesystem

The *proc* filesystem was introduced in Chapter 3; it provides a simple interface for users to view and change kernel parameters and is the model for the newer *sysfs* directory. It contains a huge number of files (or rather, virtual data structures that look to the user just like files) that map to variables and functions inside the kernel and that can be used to tune the behavior of the networking component of the kernel as well.

The files used for IPv4 tuning are located mainly in two directories:

/proc/sys/net/ipv4/
> Table 23-2 shows some of the files in this directory that are used by IPv4. The kernel variables associated with those files are declared in *net/ipv4/sysctl_net_ipv4.c* and are statically registered at boot time (see Chapter 3). Note that the directory contains many more files than the ones in Table 23-2. Most of the extra files are associated with L4 protocols, especially TCP.

/proc/sys/net/ipv4/conf/
> This directory contains a subdirectory for each network device recognized by the kernel, plus other special directories (see Figure 36-4 in Chapter 36). Those subdirectories include configuration parameters that are device specific; among them are accept_redirects, send_redirects, accept_source_route, and forwarding. These will be covered in Chapter 36, with the exception of promote_secondaries, which is described in the section "Main Functions That Manipulate IP Addresses and Configuration."

Table 23-2. IPv4-related files in /proc/sys/net/ipv4

/proc filename	Associated kernel variable	Default value
ip_forward	ipv4_devconf.forwarding	0
ip_no_pmtu_disc	ipv4_config.no_pmtu_disc	0
ip_autoconfig	ipv4_config.autoconfig	0
ip_default_ttl	sysctl_ip_default_ttl	IPDEFTTL (64)
ip_nonlocal_bind	sysctl_ip_nonlocal_bind	0
ip_local_port_range	sysctl_ip_local_port_range[0]	1
	sysctl_ip_local_port_range[1]	65535[a]
ipfrag_high_tresh	sysctl_ipfrag_high_thresh	256K
ipfrag_low_tresh	sysctl_ipfrag_low_thresh	192K
ipfrag_time	sysctl_ipfrag_time	IP_FRAG_TIME (30 * HZ)
ipfrag_secret_interval	sysctl_ipfrag_secret_interval	10 * 60 * HZ
ip_dynaddr	sysctl_ip_dynaddr	0
inet_peer_gc_maxtime	inet_peer_gc_maxtime	120 * HZ
inet_peer_gc_mintime	inet_peer_gc_mintime	10 * HZ
inet_peer_maxttl	inet_peer_maxttl	10 * 60 * HZ

Table 23-2. IPv4-related files in /proc/sys/net/ipv4 (continued)

/proc filename	Associated kernel variable	Default value
`inet_peer_minttl`	`inet_peer_minttl`	120 * HZ
`inet_peer_threshold`	`inet_peer_threshold`	65536 + 128[b]

[a] These values are updated by `tcp_init` at boot time based on the amount of memory available in the system. Even if they are updated by TCP, they are used by any L4 protocol that uses ports.

[b] This value is updated by `inet_initpeers` at boot time based on the amount of memory available in the system.

The first three elements in Table 23-2 are members of two data structures of type `ipv4_devconf` and `ipv4_config`, located, respectively, in *include/linux/inetdevice.h* and *include/net/ip.h* and described later in this chapter. The other elements of those structures are either exported elsewhere or not exported at all (we will cover them in the associated chapters). The meaning of the files and kernel variables is as follows:

ip_forward
> Set to a nonzero value to enable the device to forward traffic. See the section "Enabling and Disabling Forwarding" in Chapter 36.

ip_no_pmtu_disc
> When 0, path MTU discovery is enabled.

ip_autoconfig
> This is set to 1 when the IP configuration of the host was done via a protocol such as DHCP. See the section "IP Configuration."

ip_default_ttl
> This is the default value of the IP TTL field used for unicast traffic. Multicast traffic uses the default value of 1 and does not have an equivalent `sysctl` variable to set it.

ip_nonlocal_bind
> When nonzero, it is possible for an application to bind to an address that is not local to the host. This allows, for instance, binding a socket to an address even if the associated interface is down.

ip_local_port_range
> Range of ports that can be used for outgoing connections.

ipfrag_high_thresh
ipfrag_low_thresh
> Thresholds used to limit the amount of memory used by incoming IP fragments. When the memory used by fragments reaches `ipfrag_high_thresh`, old entries are removed until the memory used declines to `ipfrag_low_thresh`. See the section "Garbage Collection."

ipfrag_time

Maximum amount of time incoming IP fragments are kept in memory before expiring.

ipfrag_secret_interval

Interval after which the incoming IP fragments that are in the hash table are extracted and reinserted with a different hash function. See the section "Hash Table Reorganization" in Chapter 22.

ip_dynaddr

This variable is used to handle the case of sockets bound to addresses associated with dial-on-demand interfaces that do not receive any reply until the interface comes up. If `ip_dynaddr` is set, the sockets will retry binding.

inet_peer_threshold

Maximum number of `inet_peer` structures that can be allocated.

inet_peer_gc_maxtime
inet_peer_gc_mintime

Amount of time between regular garbage collection passes. Since the amount of memory usable by the `inet_peer` structures is limited (by `inet_peer_threshold`), there is a regular timer that expires unused entries based on these two variables. `inet_peer_gc_maxtime` is used when the system is not heavily loaded, and `inet_peer_gc_mintime` is used in the opposite case. Thus, the more entries there are, the more frequently the timer expires.

inet_peer_maxttl
inet_peer_minttl

Maximum and minimum TTL of `inet_peer` entries. Its value is supposed to be bigger than `sysctl_ipfrag_time`, for obvious reasons.

Data Structures Featured in This Part of the Book

The section "Main IPv4 Data Structures" in Chapter 19 gave a brief overview of the main data structures. This section has a detailed description of each data structure type. Figure 23-3 shows the file that defines each data structure.

iphdr Structure

The meaning of its fields has already been covered in the section "IP Header" in Chapter 18.

ip_options Structure

This structure represents the options for a packet that needs to be transmitted or forwarded. The options are stored in this structure because it is easier to read than the corresponding portion of the IP header itself.

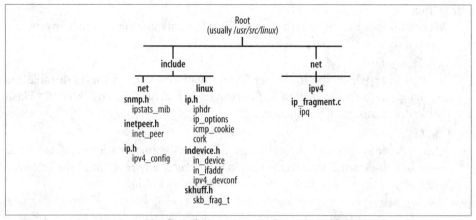

Figure 23-3. Distribution of data structures in kernel files

Let's go field by field. They should be fairly simple to understand if you have read the section "IP Options" in Chapter 18. After this description, you will be able to understand more easily how the parsing is done and how its results are used by the IP layer subsystems, such as the code that processes incoming IP packets. Some of the bit fields are grouped together into an unsigned char; the declarations of these end with :1.

unsigned char optlen

> Length of the set of options. As explained in Chapter 18, this is limited to a maximum of 40 bytes by the definition of the IP header.

unsigned char is_changed:1

> Set if the IP header has been modified (such as an IP address or a timestamp). This is useful to know because if the packet has to be forwarded, this field indicates that the IP checksum has to be recomputed.

__u32 faddr
unsigned char is_strictroute:1
unsigned char srr
unsigned char srr_is_hit:1

> faddr is meaningful only for transmitted packets (that is, those generated locally) and only for those using source routing. The value of faddr is set to the first of the IP addresses provided for source routing. See the section "Option: Strict and Loose Source Routing" in Chapter 19.

> is_strictroute is a flag set to true when Strict Source Route is among the options.

> srr contains the offset of the Source Route option in the header. If the option is not used, the value is zero.

> srr_is_hit is true if the packet was source routed and the IP address of the receiving interface is one of the addresses in the source route list (see ip_options_rcv_srr in *net/ipv4/ip_options.c*).

---

unsigned char rr

When `rr` is nonzero, Record Route is one of the IP options and the value of this field represents the offset inside the IP header where the option starts. This field is used together with `rr_needaddr`.

unsigned char rr_needaddr:1

When `rr_needaddr` is true, Record Route is one of the IP options and there is still room in the header for another route; therefore, the current node should copy the IP address of the outgoing interface into the IP header at the offset specified by `rr`.

unsigned char ts

When `ts` is nonzero, Timestamp is one of the IP options and this field represents the offset inside the IP header where the option starts. This field is used together with `ts_needaddr` and `ts_needtime`.

unsigned char is_setbyuser:1

This field makes sense only for transmitted packets and is set when the options were passed from user space with the system call `setsockopt`. Currently, however, it is never used.

unsigned char is_data:1
unsigned char _data[0]

These fields are used in two situations: when the local node transmits a locally generated packet, and when the local node replies to an ICMP echo request. In these cases, `is_data` is true and `_data` points to an area containing the options to append to the IP header. The `[0]` definition is a common convention used for reserving space for a pointer.

When forwarding a packet, the options are in the associated `skb` buffer (see the `ip_options_get` function in the *net/ipv4/ip_options.c* file).

unsigned char ts_needtime:1

When this option is true, Timestamp is one of the IP options and there is still room in the header for another timestamp; therefore, the current node should add the time of transmission into the IP header at the offset specified by `ts`.

unsigned char ts_needaddr:1

Used with `ts` and `ts_needtime` to indicate that the IP address of the egress device should also be copied into the IP header.

unsigned char router_alert

When this option is true, Router Alert is one of the IP options.

unsigned char __pad1, __pad2

Because memory accesses are faster when the location is aligned to a 32-bit boundary, the Linux kernel data structures are often padded out with unused fields called __pad*n* in order to make their sizes a multiple of 32 bits. This is the only purpose of __pad1 and __pad2; they are not used otherwise.

The flags srr, rr, and ts also are useful when parsing the options in order to detect the ones that are present more than once, which is illegal (see the section "Option Parsing" in Chapter 19).

ipcm_cookie Structure

This structure combines various pieces of information needed to transmit a packet.

```
struct ipcm_cookie
{
    u32             addr;
    int             oif;
    struct ip_options   *opt;
};
```

The destination IP address is addr, the egress device is oif if defined, and the IP options are in an ip_options structure. Note that addr is the only field that is always set. oif is 0 if there are no constraints on which device to use.

ipq Structure

Here is the description of the fields of the ipq structure. For the sake of simplicity, not all fields are shown in Figure 22-1 in Chapter 22.

struct ipq *next
> When the fragments are put into the ipq_hash hash table, conflicting elements (elements with the same hash value) are linked together with this field. Note that this field does not indicate the order of fragments within the packet; it is used simply as a standard way to organize the hash table. The order of fragments within the packet is controlled by the fragments field (see Figure 22-1 in Chapter 22).

struct ipq **pprev
> Pointer back to the head of the list of IP packets that have the same hash value.

struct list_head lru_list
> All of the ipq structures are kept sorted in a global list, ipq_lru_list, based on a least-recently-used criterion. This list is useful when performing garbage collection. This field is used to link the ipq structure to such a list.

u32 user
> The reason why an IP packet is to be defragmented, which indirectly says what kernel subsystem asked for the defragmentation. The list of allowed values for IP_DEFRAG_XXX is in include/net/ip.h. The most common one is IP_DEFRAG_LOCAL_DELIVER, which is used when defragmenting ingress packets that are to be delivered locally.

```
u32 saddr
u32 daddr
u16 id
u8 protocol
```
These parameters represent the source IP address, destination IP address, IP packet ID, and L4 protocol identifier, respectively. As described in Chapter 18, these four parameters identify the original IP packet a fragment belongs to. For that reason, they are also the parameters used by the hash function to optimally spread elements throughout the hash table.

```
u8 last_in
```
Stores three flags, whose possible values are:

COMPLETE

All of the fragments have been received and can therefore be joined together to obtain the original IP packet. This flag can also be used to mark those ipq structures that have been chosen for deletion (see ipq_kill in *net/ipv4/ip_fragment.c*).

FIRST_IN

The first of the fragments (the one with offset=0) has been received. The first fragment is the only one carrying all of the options that were in the original IP packet.

LAST_IN

The last of the fragments (the one with MF=0) has been received. The last fragment is important because it is the one that tells us the size of the original IP packet.

```
struct sk_buff *fragments
```
List of fragments received so far.

```
int len
```
Offset where the fragment with the biggest offset ends. When the last fragment is received (the one with MF=0), len will tell the size of the original IP packet.

```
int meat
```
Represents how many bytes of the original packet we have received so far. When its value is the same as len, the packet has been completely received.

```
spinlock_t lock
```
Protects the structure from race conditions. It could happen, for instance, that different IP fragments are received at the same time by different NICs handled by different CPUs.

```
atomic_t refcnt
```
Counter used to keep track of external references to this packet. As an example of its purpose, the timer timer increments refcnt to make sure that no one is going to free the ipq structure while the timer is still pending; otherwise, the timer might expire and try to access a data structure that does not exist anymore. You can imagine the consequences.

`struct timer_list timer`

Chapter 18 explained why IP fragments cannot stay forever in memory and should be removed after some time if defragmentation is not possible. This field is the timer that takes care of that.

`int iif`

ID of the device from which the last fragment was received. When a list of fragments expires, this field is used to decide which device to use to transmit the FRAGMENTATION REASSEMBLY TIMEOUT ICMP message (see `ip_expire` in the *net/ipv4/ip_fragment.c* file).

`struct timeval stamp`

Time when the last fragment was received (see `ip_frag_queue` in *net/ipv4/ip_fragment.c*).

The `ipq_hash` table is protected by `ipfrag_lock`, which can be taken in either shared (read-only) or exclusive (read-write) mode. Do not confuse this lock with the one embedded in each `ipq` element.

inet_peer Structure

The kernel keeps an instance of this structure for each remote host it has been talking to in the recent past. In the section "Long-Living IP Peer Information," you saw how it is used. All instances of `inet_peer` structures are kept in an AVL tree, a structure optimized for frequent lookups. The functions used to manipulate `inet_peer` instances are in *net/ipv4/inetpeer.c*.

`struct inet_peer *avl_left`
`struct inet_peer *avl_right`

Left and right pointers to the two subtrees.

`__u16 avl_height`

Height of the AVL tree.

`struct inet_peer *unused_next`
`struct inet_peer **unused_prevp`

Used to link the node into a list that contains elements that expired. `unused_prevp` is used to check whether the node is in that list.

A node can be put into that list and then taken back out of it several times without ever being removed completely. See the section "Garbage Collection."

`unsigned long dtime`

Time when this element was added to the unused list `inet_peer_unused_head` via `inet_putpeer`.

`atomic_t refcnt`

Reference count for the element. Among the users of this structure are the routing subsystem and the TCP layer.

`__u32 v4daddr`
> IP address of the remote peer.

`__u16 ip_id_count`
> IP packet ID to use next for this peer (see inet_getid in *include/net/inetpeer.h*).

`__u32 tcp_ts`
`unsigned long tcp_ts_stamp`
> Used by TCP to manage timestamps.

ipstats_mib Structure

The SNMP protocol employs a type of object called an MIB to collect statistics about systems. A data structure called `ipstats_mib` keeps statistics on the IP layer. The section "IP Statistics" covered this structure in more detail.

in_device Structure

The `in_device` structure stores all of the IPv4-related configuration for a network device, such as changes made by a user with the *ifconfig* or *ip* command. This structure is linked to the `net_device` structure via `net_device->ip_ptr` and can be retrieved with `in_dev_get` and `__in_dev_get`. The difference between those two functions is that the first one takes care of all of the necessary locking, and the second one assumes the caller has taken care of it already.

Since `in_dev_get` internally increases a reference count on the `in_dev` structure when it succeeds (i.e., when a device is configured to support IPv4), its caller is supposed to decrement the reference count with `in_dev_put` when it is done with the structure.

The structure is allocated and linked to the device with `inetdev_init`, which is called when the first IPv4 address is configured on the device. Here are the meanings of its fields:

`struct net_device *dev`
> Pointer back to the associated `net_device` structure.

`atomic_t refcnt`
> Reference count. The structure cannot be freed until this field is 0.

`int dead`
> This field is set to mark the device as dead. This is useful to detect those cases where the entry cannot be destroyed because it has a nonzero reference count, but a destroy action has been initiated. The two most common events that trigger the removal of an `in_device` structure are:
> - Unregistration of the device (see Chapter 8)
> - Removal of the last configured IP address from the device (see `inet_del_ifa` in *net/ipv4/devinet.c*)

```
struct in_ifaddr *ifa_list
```
List of IPv4 addresses configured on the device. The `in_ifaddr` instances are kept sorted by scope (bigger scope first), and elements with the same scope are kept sorted by address type (primary first). The `in_ifaddr` data structure is further described in the section "in_ifaddr Structure."

```
struct neigh_parms *arp_parms
```
The meaning of this field is described in detail in Part VI.

```
struct ipv4_devconf cnf
```
See the section "ipv4_devconf Structure"

```
struct rcu_head rcu_head
```
Used by the RCU mechanism to enforce mutual exclusion. It accomplishes the same job as a lock.

The rest of the fields are used by the multicast code. For instance, `mc_list` stores the device's multicast configuration and it is the multicast counterpart of `ifa_list`. `mr_v1_seen` and `mr_v2_seen` are timestamps used by the IGMP protocol to keep track of the reception of versions 1 and 2 IGMP packets.

in_ifaddr Structure

When configuring an IPv4 address on an interface, the kernel creates an `in_ifaddr` structure that includes the 4-byte address along with several other fields. Here are their meanings:

```
struct in_ifaddr *ifa_next
```
Pointer to the next element in the list. The list contains all of the addresses configured on the device.

```
struct in_device *ifa_dev
```
Pointer back to the associated `in_device` structure.

```
u32 ifa_local
u32 ifa_address
```
The values of these two fields depend on whether the address is assigned to a tunnel interface. If so, `ifa_local` and `ifa_address` are the local and remote addresses of the tunnel, respectively. If not, both contain the address of the local interface.

```
u32 ifa_mask
unsigned char ifa_prefixlen
```
`ifa_mask` is the netmask associated with the address. `ifa_prefixlen` is the number of 1s that compose the netmask. Since they are different ways of representing the same information, one of the two is normally computed from the other. This is done, for instance, by the *ip* and *ifconfig* user-space configuration tools described in the section "IP Configuration." *ip* passes the kernel `ifa_prefixlen` and lets the latter compute `ifa_mask`, whereas *ifconfig* does the opposite. The kernel provides some functions to convert a netmask into a prefix length, and vice versa.

u32 ifa_broadcast
:   Broadcast address.

u32 ifa_anycast
:   Anycast address.

unsigned char ifa_scope
:   Scope of the address. The default is RT_SCOPE_UNIVERSE (which corresponds to the value 0) and the field is usually set to that value by *ifconfig/ip*, although a different value can be chosen. The main exception is an address in the range 127.*x.x.x*, which is given the RT_SCOPE_HOST scope. See Chapter 30 for more details.

unsigned char ifa_flags
:   The possible IFA_F_XXX bit flags are listed in *include/linux/rtnetlink.h*. Here is the one used by IPv4:

    IFA_F_SECONDARY
    :   When a new address is added to a device that already has another address with the same subnet, it is tagged as secondary.

    The other flags are used by IPv6.

char ifa_label[IFNAMSIZ]
:   A string used mostly for backward compatibility with 2.0.*x* kernels that allowed aliased interfaces with names such as *eth0:1*.

struct rcu_head rcu_head
:   Used by the RCU mechanism to enforce mutual exclusion. It accomplishes the same job as a lock.

ipv4_devconf Structure

The ipv4_devconf data structure, whose fields are exported via */proc* in */proc/sys/net/ipv4/conf/*, is used to tune the behavior of a network device. There is an instance for each device, plus one that stores the default values (ipv4_devconf_dflt). The meanings of its fields are covered in Chapters 29 and 36, with the exception of promote_secondaries, which is described in the section "Main Functions That Manipulate IP Addresses and Configuration."

ipv4_config Structure

While ipv4_devconf structures are used to store per-device configuration, ipv4_config stores configuration that applies to the host.

Here is a brief description of its fields:

int log_martians
:   This parameter is also present in the ipv4_devconf structure. It is used to decide whether to print warning messages to the console when specific errors occur. Its value is not checked directly, but via the macro IN_DEV_LOG_MARTIANS, which gives higher priority to the per-device instance.

`int autoconfig`
> Not used.

`int no_pmtu_disc`
> Used to initialize the variable `inet_sock->pmtudisc` that stores the PMTU configuration for a socket. See Chapter 18 for more details on path MTU discovery.

cork Structure

The cork structure, defined in *include/linux/ip.h** inside the definition of inet_sock, is used to handle the socket cork option (`UDP_CORK` for UDP, `TCP_CORK` for TCP). We saw in Chapter 21 how its fields are used to maintain some context information across consecutive invocations of `ip_append_data` and `ip_append_page` to handle data fragmentation.

Here is a brief description of its fields:

`unsigned int flags`
> Currently only one flag used by IPv4 can be set: `IPCORK_OPT`. When this flag is set, it means there are options in opt.

`unsigned int fragsize`
> Size of the data fragments generated. This includes both payload and L3 header and is normally the PMTU.

`struct ip_options *opt`
> IP options to use.

`struct rtable *rt`
> Routing table cache entry that will be used to transmit the IP packet.

`int length`
> Size of the IP packet (sum of all the data fragments, not including IP headers).

`u32 addr`
> Destination IP address.

`struct flowi fl`
> Collection of information about the two ends of the connection. More details are in Chapter 36.

skb_frag_t Structure

We saw in Chapter 21 what a paged buffer looks like (see, for example, Figure 21-5 in that chapter). skb_frag_t includes the fields necessary to identify a data block on a memory page:

---

* IPv6 defines its own version of cork in *include/linux/ipv6.h.*

```
struct page *page
```
Pointer to the memory page. On i386, the page size is 4 KB. To find the size of a page on any given architecture *xxx*, look for PAGE_SIZE in *include/asm-xxx/page.h*.

```
__u16 page_offset
```
Offset, relative to the beginning of the page, where the fragment starts.

```
__u16 size
```
Size of the fragment.

Functions and Variables Featured in This Part of the Book

Table 23-3 summarizes the main functions, variables, and data structure introduced or referenced in the chapters of this book covering the IPv4 protocol.

Table 23-3. Functions, variables, and data structures in the IPv4 subsystem

/proc filename	Associated kernel variable
ip_init	Initializes the IPv4 protocol. See the section "IP Options" in Chapter 19.
ip_rcv	Processes ingress IP packets. See the section "Processing Input IP Packets" in Chapter 19.
ip_forward ip_forward_finish	Forward an ingress IP packet or fragment. See the section "Forwarding" in Chapter 20.
ip_local_deliver ip_local_deliver_finish	Deliver an ingress IP packet to the local host. See the section "Local Delivery" in Chapter 20.
ipfrag_init	Initializes the IP Fragmentation/Defragmentation subsystem.
ip_defrag ip_find ip_frag_queue ip_frag_reasm ip_frag_destroy ip_expire ip_evictor	Handle IP defragmentation. See the section "IP Defragmentation" in Chapter 22.
ip_fragment ip_dont_fragment getfrag	Handle IP fragmentation. See the section "IP Fragmentation" in Chapter 22.

Table 23-3. Functions, variables, and data structures in the IPv4 subsystem (continued)

/proc filename	Associated kernel variable
ip_options_compile ip_options_parse ip_options_build ip_forward_options	Handle IP options. See the section "IP options" in Chapter 19.
ip_queue_xmit, ip_append_data, ip_push_pending_frames	Used by L4 protocols to transmit IP packets. See the section "Key Functions That Perform Transmission" in Chapter 21.
dst_output	Invokes the right transmit routine according to the result of a previous routing lookup. See Figure 18-1 in Chapter 18.
ip_finish_output ip_finish_output2	Interface between the IP layer transmission routines and the neighboring subsystem. See the section "Interface to the Neighboring Subsystem" in Chapter 21.
ip_decrease_ttl	Decrements the IP header's TTL field and updates the IP checksum accordingly.
ip_fast_csum ip_send_check, ...	Compute or update an IP checksum. Many more such routines are listed in the section "APIs for Checksum Computation" in Chapter 18.
in_dev_get	Returns the IP configuration block in_device of a network device and increments its reference count.
inet_initpeers	Initializes the IP peer subsystem.
inet_getpeer	Searches an inet_peer structure using an IPv4 address as a key.
ip_select_ident ip_select_ident_more secure_ip_id	Select the IP ID to use for an egress IP packet.
ip_call_ra_chain	Hands ingress IP packets that carry the Router Alert option to the interested local Raw sockets. See the section "ip_forward function" in Chapter 20.
IP_INC_STATS IP_INC_STATS_BH IP_INC_STATS_USER	Increment counters used to keep statistics on IP traffic. See the section "IP Statistics."
inet_rtm_newaddr inet_rtm_deladdr inet_dump_ifaddr	Process *ip addr* commands from the user-space IPROUTE2 package.

Table 23-3. Functions, variables, and data structures in the IPv4 subsystem (continued)

/proc filename	Associated kernel variable
inet_alloc_ifa inet_free_ifa inet_insert_ifa inet_del_ifa inet_set_ifa inet_select_addr inet_make_mask inet_mask_len inet_ifa_match	Add, remove, and manipulate the IP addresses configured on the local devices. See the section "Main functions that manipulate IP addresses and configuration."
for_primary_ifa for_ifa	Browse the IP addresses configured on a network device.
rtmsg_ifa	Generates notifications about changes to the IP address configuration of local devices. See the section "Change notification: rtmsg_ifa."
Variables	
ipv4_devconf ipv4_devconf_dflt	Store a set of parameters that can be tuned on a per-device basis via the */proc* filesystem. See the section "Tuning via /proc filesystem."
ip_frag_mem	Amount of memory held by ingress IP fragments. See the section "Garbage Collection" in Chapter 33.
ipfrag_lock	Lock used for the table of ipq instances. See the section "Organization of the IP Fragments Hash Table" in Chapter 22.
peer_total inet_peer_threshold	peer_total is the number of outstanding inet_peer structures, and inet_peer_threshold is the maximum amount of memory that can be used to allocate inet_peer instances.
peer_pool_lock	Lock used for the AVL tree where inet_peer structures are inserted.
inet_peer_unused_lock	Lock used for the list where unused inet_peer structures are inserted.
ip_statistics	Stores statistics about IP traffic. See the section "IP Statistics."

Table 23-3. Functions, variables, and data structures in the IPv4 subsystem (continued)

/proc filename	Associated kernel variable
Data structures	
`struct iphdr`	Main data structures used by IPv4. They are briefly introduced in Chapter 19 and are described in detail in this chapter.
`struct ip_options`	
`struct ipcm_cookie`	
`struct ipq`	
`struct ip_mib`	
`struct inet_peer`	
`struct in_device`	
`struct ipv4_devconf`	
`struct ipv4_config`	
`struct in_ifaddr`	
`struct cork`	

Files and Directories Featured in This Part of the Book

The *net/ipv4* directory contains more files than the ones listed in Figure 23-4, but they are covered in other chapters, including the chapters comprising Parts VI and VII.

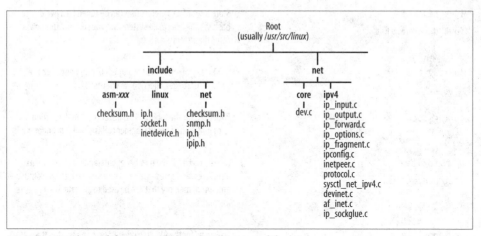

Figure 23-4. Files and directories featured in this part of the book

## CHAPTER 24

Layer Four Protocol and Raw IP Handling

This chapter describes the interface between L3 and L4 protocols. The only L3 protocol considered here is IP. The L4 protocols include the familiar TCP, UDP, and ICMP, along with several other ones. The L4 protocols are not covered in this book for reasons of space and complexity. However, this chapter explains what happens when applications handle their own L4 (and sometimes L3) processing through raw IP.

In particular, this chapter explains:

- How L4 protocols register with the kernel and tell the kernel what kind of traffic they are interested in
- How ingress packets are passed to the correct L4 protocol handler
- How applications tell the kernel to let the application process headers

We saw in Chapter 21 the functions that L4 protocols use to transmit an IP datagram. Since this book focuses on IP, this chapter covers only those L4 protocols that sit on top of IP. The chapter describes the IPv4 interface and then briefly shows where IPv6 differs.

Available L4 Protocols

A few key L4 protocols are statically compiled into the kernel. Several less-common protocols can be compiled as modules. Table 24-1 shows the protocols that are statically compiled in.

Table 24-1. Protocols statically compiled into the kernel

Protocol	RFC# (Year)
UDP	768(1980)
ICMP	792(1981)
TCP	793(1981)

Table 24-2 lists some of the protocols in the second category. They can be added to the kernel from the section "Networking Support → Networking Options" in the kernel configuration.

Table 24-2. Protocols implemented as modules

Protocol	RFC# (Year)
Internet Group Management Protocol (IGMP)	Version 1: 1112(1989)
	Version 2: 2236(1997)
	Version 3: 3376(2002)
Stream Control Transmission Protocol (SCTP)	2960(2000)
Protocol Independent Multicast, version 1 (PIMv1) and version 2 (PIMv2)	2362(1998)
IPsec suite: IP Authentication Header Protocol (AH), IP Encapsulating Security Payload Protocol (ESP), IP Payload Compression Protocol (IPcomp)	AH: 2402(1998)
	ESP: 2406(1998)
	IPcomp: 3173(2001)
Generic Routing Encapsulation (GRE)	2784(2000)
IPv4-over-IPv4 tunnels (IPIP)	1853(1995)
IPv6 over IPv6	2473(1998)
Simple Internet Transition (IPv6-over-IPv4 tunnel, SIT)	1933(1996)

Other protocols are available for the Linux kernel but are either implemented in user space (routing protocols are an example) or are available as kernel patches because they are not yet integrated into the core kernel.

Figure 24-1 shows how the L4 protocols rest on L3 protocols. The three main protocols (ICMP, UDP, and TCP), as well as the IPsec suite, have IPv6 counterparts. There is no IGMPv6 in Figure 24-1 because its functionality is implemented as part of ICMPv6.

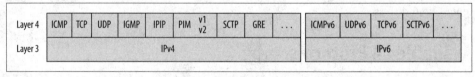

Figure 24-1. L4 protocols on top of IPv4 and IPv6 that are implemented in the Linux kernel

Note that the last four items in Table 24-2 are tunneling protocols. Their IDs identify an L3 protocol. For example, the IPIP protocol is used to transport IPv4 datagrams inside IPv4 datagrams. Note that the value assigned to the protocol field of the IPv4 header when it encapsulates an IP datagram has nothing to do with the value used to initialize the protocol field of an Ethernet header when the Ethernet payload is an IP datagram. Even though the two fields refer to the same protocol (IPv4), they belong to two different domains: one is an L3 protocol identifier, whereas the other is an L4 protocol identifier.

L4 Protocol Registration

The L4 protocols that rest on IPv4 are defined by net_protocol data structures, defined in *include/net/protocol.h*, which consist of the following three fields:

int (*handler)(struct sk_buff *skb)
> Function registered by the protocol as the handler for incoming packets. This is discussed further in the section "L3 to L4 Delivery: ip_local_deliver_finish." It is possible to have protocols that share the same handler for both IPv4 and IPv6 (e.g., SCTP).

void (*err_handler)(struct sk_buff *skb, u32 info)
> Function used by the ICMP protocol handler to inform the L4 protocol about the reception of an ICMP UNREACHABLE message. We will see in Chapter 35 when a Linux system generates ICMP UNREACHABLE messages, and we will see in Chapter 25 how the ICMP protocol uses err_handler.

int no_policy
> This field is consulted at certain key points in the network stack and is used to exempt protocols from IPsec policy checks: 1 means that there is no need to check the IPsec policies for the protocol. Do not confuse the no_policy field of the net_protocol structure with the field bearing the same name in the ipv4_devconf structure: the former applies to a protocol; the latter applies to a device. See the sections "L3 to L4 Delivery: ip_local_deliver_finish" and "IPsec" for how no_policy is used.

The *include/linux/in.h* file contains a list of L4 protocols defined as IPPROTO_*XXX* symbols. (For a more complete list, see the */etc/protocols* file, or RFC 1700 and its successor RFCs.) The maximum value for an L4 protocol identifier is 2^8-1 or 255, because the field in the IP header allocated to specify the L4 protocol is 8 bits. The highest number, 255, is reserved for Raw IP, IPPROTO_RAW.

Not all of the protocols defined in the list of symbols are handled at the kernel layer; some of them (notably Resource Reservation Protocol, or RSVP, and the various routing protocols) are usually handled in user space. This is, for example, why RSVP and routing protocols like OSPF are not included in the list of L4 protocols supported by the kernel that is in the previous section.

Registration: inet_add_protocol and inet_del_protocol

Protocols register themselves with the inet_add_protocol function and, when implemented as modules, unregister themselves with the inet_del_protocol function. Both routines are defined in *net/ipv4/protocol.c*.

All of the inet_protocol structures of the L4 protocols registered with the kernel are inserted into a table named inet_protos, represented in Figure 24-2. In earlier versions of the kernel, this was a hash table, and the word hash still appears in the code that handles the table, but currently it is a simple flat array with one item for each of the possible 256 protocols. The protocol number from *letc/protocols* is the slot in the table where the protocol is inserted. If you'd like to see how the table was handled as a hash table in the 2.4 kernel, look in the 2.4 sources at the ip_run_ipprot function. Figure 24-2 shows the numbers and initials of the most common protocols; for instance, ICMP is protocol 1 and occupies slot 1 in the inet_protos table.

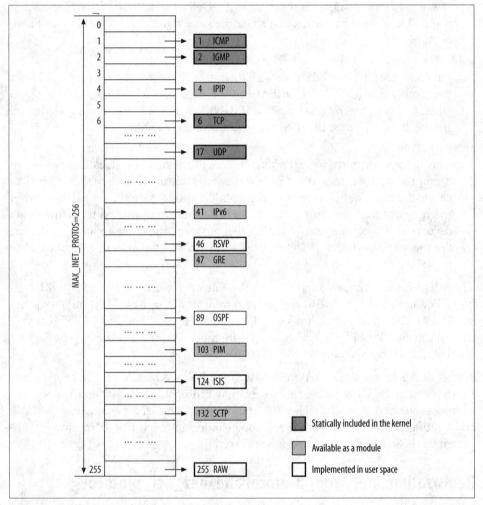

Figure 24-2. IPv4 protocol table

Concurrent accesses to the inet_protos table are managed in this way:

- Read-write accesses (i.e., inet_add_protocol and inet_del_protocol) are serialized with the inet_proto_lock spin lock.

- Read-only accesses (i.e., ip_local_deliver_finish; see the next section) are protected with rcu_read_lock/rcu_read_unlock.

inet_del_protocol, which may remove an entry of the table currently held by an RCU reader, calls synchronize_net to wait for all the currently executing RCU readers to complete their critical section before returning. There is another hash table used by protocols that rest on IPv6. Note that IPv6 appears in the IPv4 inet_protos table as well: the kernel can tunnel IPv6 over IPv4 (also called SIT, for Simple Internet Transition). See the section "IPv6 Versus IPv4."

As mentioned in the previous section, the ICMP, UDP, and TCP protocols are always part of the kernel and therefore are statically added to the hash table at boot time by inet_init in *net/ipv4/af_inet.c*. The following excerpts show the definitions of their structures and the actual inet_add_protocol calls that register them:

```
#ifdef CONFIG_IP_MULTICAST
static struct net_protocol igmp_protocol = {
    .handler =    igmp_rcv,
};
#endif

static struct net_protocol tcp_protocol = {
    .handler =      tcp_v4_rcv,
    .err_handler =  tcp_v4_err,
    .no_policy =    1,
};

static struct net_protocol udp_protocol = {
    .handler =      udp_rcv,
    .err_handler =  udp_err,
    .no_policy =    1,
};

static struct net_protocol icmp_protocol = {
    .handler =    icmp_rcv,
};

static int __init inet_init(void)
{
...

    /*
     *    Add all the base protocols.
     */

    if (inet_add_protocol(&icmp_protocol, IPPROTO_ICMP) < 0)
        printk(KERN_CRIT "inet_init: Cannot add ICMP protocol\n");
    if (inet_add_protocol(&udp_protocol, IPPROTO_UDP) < 0)
        printk(KERN_CRIT "inet_init: Cannot add UDP protocol\n");
    if (inet_add_protocol(&tcp_protocol, IPPROTO_TCP) < 0)
        printk(KERN_CRIT "inet_init: Cannot add TCP protocol\n");
#ifdef CONFIG_IP_MULTICAST
    if (inet_add_protocol(&igmp_protocol, IPPROTO_IGMP) < 0)
        printk(KERN_CRIT "inet_init: Cannot add IGMP protocol\n");
```

```
#endif
...
}
```

The IGMP handler is registered only when the kernel is compiled with support for IP multicast.

As an example of how other protocols are dynamically registered, the following snapshot is taken from the Zebra user-space routing daemon's implementation of the Open Shortest Path First IGP (OSPFIGP) protocol. The code is taken from the *ospfd/ospf_network.c* file in the Zebra package. The socket call effectively registers the user-space daemon with the kernel, giving the kernel a place to send ingress packets that use the protocol specified in the third argument. This protocol is IPPROTO_OSPFIGP, a symbol equal to 89, the number assigned to OSPFIGP in */etc/protocols*. Note also that the socket type is SOCK_RAW, because packets have a private format that the OSPFIGP protocol knows how to handle. The use of raw sockets is described later in the section "Raw Sockets and Raw IP."

```
int
ospf_serv_sock (struct interface *ifp, int family)
{
  int ospf_sock;
  int ret, tos;
  struct ospf_interface *oi;

  ospf_sock = socket (family, SOCK_RAW, IPPROTO_OSPFIGP);
  if (ospf_sock < 0)
  {
    zlog_warn ("ospf_serv_sock: socket: %s", strerror (errno));
    return ospf_sock;
  }
  ... ... ...
}
```

For each L4 protocol there can be only one handler in kernel space (but multiple handlers could be present in user space, as discussed later in the section "Raw Sockets and Raw IP"). inet_add_protocol complains (returns –1) when it is called to install a handler for an L4 protocol that already has one.

L3 to L4 Delivery: ip_local_deliver_finish

The main job of ip_local_deliver_finish, which is defined in *net/ipv4/ip_input.c* and was briefly described in Chapter 20, is to find the correct protocol handler based on the protocol field of the input IP packet's header and to hand the packet to that handler. At the same time, ip_local_deliver_finish needs to handle raw IP and enforce security policies if they are configured. These latter two tasks are described in later sections.

Most packets, of course, are associated with an L4 protocol. `ip_local_deliver_finish` extracts the number of this protocol from the 8-bit field of the IP header shown with shading in Figure 24-3. If the `inet_protos` table doesn't contain a handler for this number—that is, if the kernel received a packet for an L4 protocol that never registered itself in the manner shown in the previous section—and no raw socket is interested in the packet, the packet is dropped and an ICMP unreachable message is sent back to the sender.

In addition to kernel handling, however, applications can also handle packets. This handling can be done instead of the kernel handling or in addition to it. Therefore, regardless of whether a kernel handler is registered, the `ip_local_deliver_finish` function always checks whether an application has set up a raw socket to handle the protocol and, if so, makes a clone of the packet to hand over to the application. This is depicted in Figure 24-4. Finally, whether the packet is processed through a registered L4 protocol or Raw IP, other protocols such as those in the IPsec suite might have to be invoked.

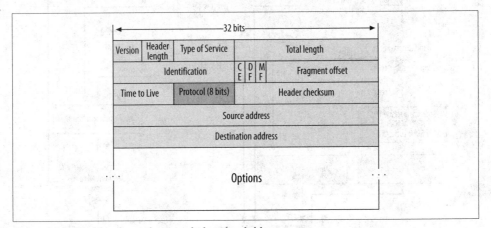

Figure 24-3. IPv4 header and protocol identifier field

Figure 24-4 shows the basic operation of the function.

The function starts as follows:

```
static inline int ip_local_deliver_finish(struct sk_buff *skb)
{
    int ihl = skb->nh.iph->ihl*4;
    __skb_pull(skb, ihl);
    skb->h.raw = skb->data;
```

`skb->h` was initialized in `netif_receive_skb` (described in Chapter 10) to point to the beginning of the IP header. At this point, the kernel no longer needs the IP header because it is finished with the IP layer and is delivering the packet to the next higher layer. Therefore, the `__skb_pull` call shown here shortens the data portion of the packet to ignore the L3 header, and the following statement updates the pointer in

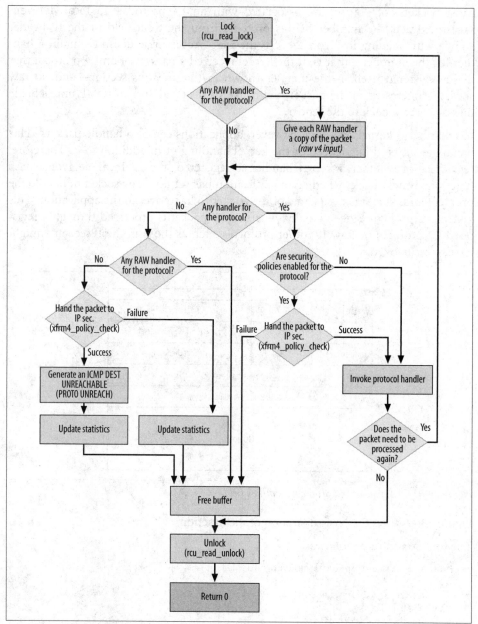

Figure 24-4. ip_local_deliver_finish function

skb to the value of the skb->data pointer, which points to the beginning of the L4 header.

The protocol ID is extracted from the `skb->nh.iph->protocol` variable, which points to the protocol field of the IP header, shaded in Figure 24-3.

Figure 24-4 shows that `ip_local_deliver_finish` may invoke more than one protocol handler (`ipprot->handler`). One might ask how this could happen, because, as shown in Figure 24-3, each packet header has space to list only one L4 protocol. An example where multiple L4 protocols are invoked is the use of IPsec. With IPsec, the kernel needs to process possible AH, ESP, and IPcomp headers before handing the packet to the real L4 protocol. Figure 24-5 shows where the headers and trailers used by the protocols of the IPsec suite sit. The figure also shows that `ip_local_deliver_finish` consults the IPsec security policies with `xfrm4_policy_check` in a couple of places. Because IPsec is not discussed in this book, let's just assume there is no IPsec configuration on the host and therefore that both calls to `xfm4_policy_check` return failure.

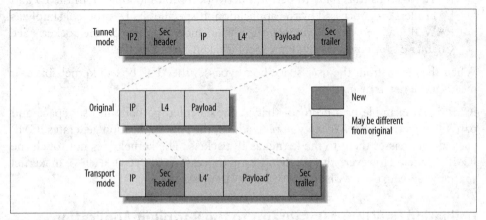

Figure 24-5. IPsec headers/trailers locations

Note in Figure 24-4 that `ip_local_deliver_finish` does not free the buffer after successful processing by the protocol handler: the protocol handler takes care of it.

Raw Sockets and Raw IP

Not all the L4 protocols are implemented in kernel space. For instance, an application can use raw sockets, as shown earlier in the Zebra code, to bypass L4 in kernel space. When using raw sockets, the applications supply the kernel with IP packets that already include all the necessary L4 information. This makes it possible both to implement new L4 protocols in user space and to do extra processing in user space on those L4 protocols normally processed in kernel space. Some L4 protocols, therefore, are implemented entirely in kernel space (e.g., TCP and UDP), some entirely in user space (e.g., OSPF), and some partially in kernel space and partially in user space (e.g., ICMP). Figure 24-6(a)(b)(c) shows the three cases, and Figure 24-6(d) is a special case of Figure 24-6(b). Here is an explanation of what's going on in the figure:

- (a) A web browser communicates with a remote web server. In this case, the communication is done via one or more TCP sockets. TCP is implemented in kernel space: the browser and the web server pass the kernel the TCP payload only, and the kernel takes care of the TCP and IP headers.
- (b) Two routers running OSPF daemons talk to each other. The OSPF protocol is implemented in user space, and passes the kernel the L4 header.* This is an example of the use of raw sockets. See Chapter 13 for information on how raw sockets fit into the stack.
- (c) One host pings another one. The request component is implemented in user space. The reply component is implemented in kernel space.
- (d) A host runs *traceroute* to perform network troubleshooting. Both the L3 and L4 headers are processed by the application. It specifies its L4 protocol simply as RAW IP and sets the IP_HDRINCL (header included) option on the socket.† See Chapter 21 for how the raw IP protocol is taken care of by IP.

When the arrow from the user-space box bypasses the "L4" box in kernel space, it means it is a raw transmission.

ICMP is an example of a protocol that is implemented partially in user space and partially in kernel space. When you ping a host, the *ping* application generates ICMP packets and passes them to the kernel as IP packets. The kernel does not touch the ICMP header. However, the receiving host processes ICMP_ECHO_REQUEST in kernel space by replying back with an ICMP_ECHO_REPLY message.

Delivering Raw Input Datagrams to the Recipient Application

When learning programming, you were probably exposed to the socket call. We'll review it here to show its relation to raw protocols. When an application opens a socket, the call needs to specify the family, socket type, and protocol identifier. Both the socket and the protocol can be of type raw. Let's see the relationship between the two. This is the prototype of the socket system call:

```
socket(int family, int type, int protocol)
```

family is the address family; the allowed values AF_*XXX* are listed in *include/linux/socket.h* (the value used for TCP/IP is AF_INET). type is the socket type; the allowed values SOCK_*XXX* are listed in *include/linux/net.h*. protocol is the L4 protocol identifier; the allowed values IPPROTO_*XXX* of IP protocols are listed in *include/linux/in.h*.

---

* Most implementations of OSPF pass the IP header as well. See the case shown in Figure 24-6(d).

† The IP packet is transmitted with the dst_output routine, described in Chapter 21. dst_output takes care of the Layer three to Layer two address mapping if needed; therefore, case (d) is not really a direct call to L2.

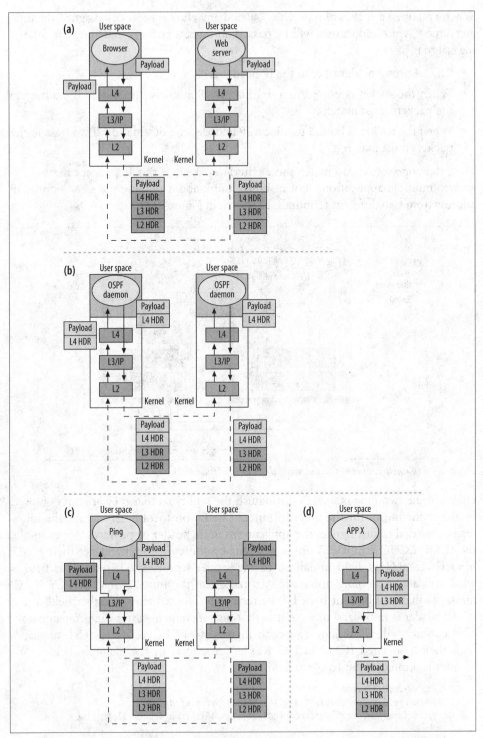

Figure 24-6. Kernel versus user-space implementations of protocols

When you open a socket of type SOCK_RAW and any chosen protocol assigned the integer value *P*, your application will be passed all ingress packets matching the following criteria:

- The L4 protocol identifier in the IP header is *P*.
- When the socket is bound to a destination IP address, the source IP address in the packets must match it.
- When the socket is bound to a local IP address, the destination IP address in the packets must match it.

More than one socket can match these criteria, so a single raw IP packet can be delivered to multiple applications. For instance, think about pinging the same remote IP address from two different terminals, as shown in Figure 24-7.

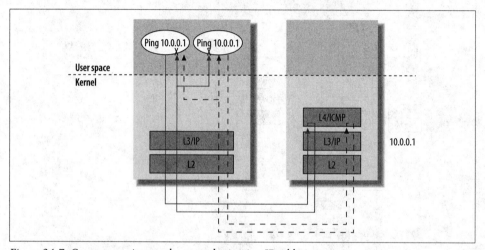

Figure 24-7. Concurrent pings to the same destination IP address

How can the two ping instances distinguish the replies so that they are not confused by the traffic meant for the other instance? The L4 protocol must include the information needed to distinguish the applications in its header or payload. For example, the ICMP ECHO REQUEST messages sent by the *ping* command get their ICMP header's identifier field initialized to the sender's process ID (pid). This field is what will allow the *ping* application to recognize the input ECHO REPLY ICMP messages that will be sent back by the recipient. The sequence number field of the ICMP header is initialized to a counter that *ping* increments after each transmission. This counter will allow *ping* to match ingress ICMP ECHO REQUEST messages with their associated ICMP ECHO REPLY messages. In the example below, this counter is printed as the icmp_seq field.

```
# ping www.oreilly.com
PING www.oreilly.com (208.201.239.36) 56(84) bytes of data
64 bytes from www.oreillynet.com (208.201.239.36): icmp_seq=0 ttl=50 time=245 ms
```

```
64 bytes from www.oreillynet.com (208.201.239.36): icmp_seq=1 ttl=50 time=244 ms
...
```

For more details on ICMP, see Chapter 25. Note the extra overhead involved in delivering the packet to multiple applications and having the applications screen out the unwanted packets, instead of having the kernel do the screening through a port. Because of this overhead, new protocols that need heavy multiplexing/demultiplexing are not normally implemented in user space using raw IP.

In short, every time the kernel receives a packet that carries an L4 protocol not handled by the kernel, all the sockets that registered for that protocol receive a copy of the packet. It is up to them to accept or discard the packet. This means that the applications must have a way to understand if the packet they receive is addressed to them, a task rendered unnecessary in TCP and UDP by the port system.

Raw IP is suitable for *ping* because, while it's possible for a few ping instances to be running at once on the same machine, they normally do not target the same destination IP address and normally send only a few packets each. Similarly, a routing protocol such as OSPF usually runs as a single instance on each host.

When the socket type is SOCK_RAW and the protocol is RAW IP (255) it means that the application takes care of both the L4 header and the IP header. This differs from the Zebra routing application shown earlier in that the protocol is RAW IP instead of a known protocol such as OSPF. Figure 24-6(d) shows the RAW IP case. Such applications set an option on a socket called IP_HDRINCL (header included) to tell the kernel that the application will take care of the IP header and that the kernel therefore does not need to do anything with it. When protocol *P* is RAW IP, the IP_HDRINCL option is turned on by default on the socket. *traceroute*, which needs to plays with the TTL field of the IP header to accomplish its job, is an example of application that uses the IP_HDRINCL option.

When an application uses a raw IP socket, it needs to give the kernel only the protocol ID and the destination IP address (which will be set on the IP header that the kernel will generate): the kernel can ignore all the other parameters and options normally used at the L4 layer.

The table used to store the raw handlers (raw_v4_htable) and the ones used to store the protocol handlers (inet_protos) are of the same size, so ip_local_deliver_finish uses the same value hash to access the two tables. (As I said earlier, this value is no longer an actual hash.) Raw packets are given to raw_v4_input. This function does not operate directly on the input buffer, because the packet belongs to the caller (ip_local_deliver_finish) and may be shared with many applications. Therefore, raw_v4_input makes local copies (clones) and gives them to the main handler, raw_rcv.

IPsec

Before ip_local_deliver_finish delivers a packet to the right protocol handler, it first checks with IPsec whether the packet is allowed to be processed. The same is done when, due to the absence in the kernel of the right protocol handler, the kernel needs to generate an ICMP error message. IPsec keeps a database of security policies divided into ingress and egress policies. Because ip_local_deliver_finish processes incoming traffic, the IPsec function xfrm4_policy_check is invoked with the direction flag XFRM_POLICY_IN. The return value of this function is 1 if the packet is allowed to be processed, and zero if it is not. Security policies are not consulted when the transport protocol's net_protocol instance has no_policy initialized to 1.

The implementation of the protocols of the IPsec suite are not discussed in this book for lack of space.

IPv4 Versus IPv6

IPv6 is very similar to IPv4 as far as the L3 to L4 protocol interface is concerned. L4 protocols can register via inet6_add_protocol and deregister them via inet6_del_protocol, both defined in *net/ipv6/protocol.c*. Handlers are stored in a table called inet6_protos of the same size (MAX_INET_PROTOS) used by IPv4. L4 protocols that run on top of IPv6 are represented by inet6_protocol data structures (defined in *include/net/protocol.h*), whose definition is almost identical to the one used by IPv4. The only differences are in the prototypes of the handler and err_handler function pointers and the use of a flag instead of an integer to store such information as the presence of security policies.

The field used by IPv6 to identify the upper-layer protocol in the IPv6 header is called next_header and is an 8-bit value like the one used by IPv4. See Figure 24-8 for the location of the field in the header.

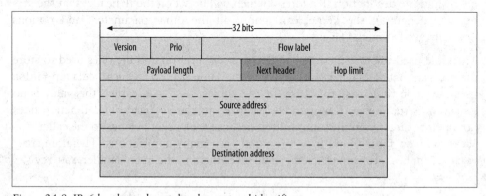

Figure 24-8. IPv6 header and next_header protocol identifier

Tuning via /proc Filesystem

There are no files in */proc* that can be used to tune the interface between L3 and L4.

Functions and Variables Featured in This Chapter

Table 24-3 summarizes the functions, variables, and data structures introduced in this chapter.

Table 24-3. Functions, variables, and data structures featured in this chapter

Name	Description
Functions	
inet_add_protocol inet_del_protocol	Registers and unregisters an L4 protocol handler for the IP stack.
inet_init	Initialization routine for the AF_INET protocol family. It is where the most common L4 protocols are registered.
ip_local_deliver_finish raw_v4_input	ip_local_deliver_finish delivers ingress IP traffic to the right L4 protocol handlers, and it uses raw_v4_input to give a copy to any eligible RAW IP socket.
Variables	
inet_protos	Table of L4 protocol handlers for the IP stack.
raw_v4_htable	Table of raw sockets.
Data structure	
net_protocol	L4 protocol descriptor for the IP stack.

Files and Directories Featured in This Chapter

The code used by the kernel to invoke the L4 protocols handlers is located mainly in two files: *include/net/protocol.h* and *net/ipv{4,6}/protocol.c*. The more lightly shaded files in Figure 24-9 are the ones that implement L4 protocols.

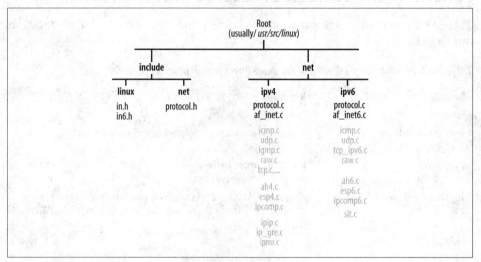

Figure 24-9. Files and directories featured in this chapter

## CHAPTER 25

Internet Control Message Protocol (ICMPv4)

The Internet Control Message Protocol (ICMP) is a transport protocol used by Internet hosts to exchange control messages, notably error notifications and information requests. In this chapter, we will look at ICMPv4, the version used by IPv4. IPv6 uses the ICMPv6 protocol, a protocol that includes other functionalities besides the ones in ICMPv4.

Over the years, the ICMP protocol has increasingly been used as the basis for the development of monitoring and measurement applications. Unfortunately, the ICMP protocol is also often used as the basis for security attacks, such as DoS or remote fingerprint collection. For this reason, network administrators often configure routers and firewalls to filter out most ICMP message types. Sometimes they filter too much, going against the RFC recommendations. Regardless of whether messages are filtered, they are often rate limited. It follows that any application built on top of ICMP is not always reliable for measurement or monitoring purposes. However, because measurements were not in its original design goal, ICMP often does not allow monitoring applications to collect all the information they need. Instead, dedicated applications have been written for that purpose, often based on TCP or UDP.

For readers interested in the security aspects of ICMP, I recommend the paper "ICMP Usage in Scanning" from the Israeli security consultant Ofir Arkin (*http://www.sys-security.com/archive/papers/ICMP_Scanning_v3.0.zip*). It shows how ICMP messages can (and are) used for network scanning purposes and why most of them should be (and are) therefore filtered out by network administrators. The paper includes a detailed summary of the main RFCs on ICMP as well.

In this chapter, we'll see how Linux implements the ICMP protocol. For each ICMP message type, we will briefly see when the kernel generates it and how the kernel processes it when it is received. For more details, refer to the following RFCs:

- RFC 792, Internet Control Message Protocol
- RFC 950, Internet Standard Subnetting Procedure, Appendix I
- RFC 1016, Something a Host Could Do with Source Quench

- RFC 1191, Path MTU Discovery
- RFC 1122, Requirements for Internet Hosts—Communication Layers
- RFC 1812, Requirements for IP Version 4 Routers
- RFC 1256, ICMP Router Discovery Messages
- RFC 1349, Type of Service in the Internet Protocol Suite

In particular, RFC 792 describes the layout of the headers of most ICMP types, and RFCs 1122 and 1812 tell whether hosts and routers should generate and process each ICMP type. Part of that information is included in this chapter, too.

For a detailed list of RFCs related to ICMP messages, you can also consult this URL: *http://www.iana.org/assignments/icmp-parameters*.

ICMP Header

Figure 25-1 shows the structure of the ICMP header.

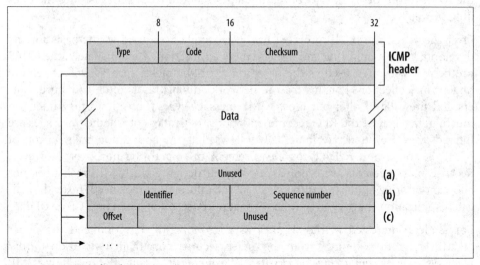

Figure 25-1. ICMP header

The first three fields are common to all ICMP message types:

type
code

> This pair identifies the ICMP message type. Sometimes type alone is sufficient to unequivocally identify the message, and other times code is needed to distinguish between different variants of the same message type. See the section "ICMP Types" for more details.

checksum

> checksum covers the IMCP header and the payload. It uses the same algorithm as other major IP protocols (IP, UDP, TCP, and IGMP): the one's complement sum of the 16-bit words of the IP packet. See the section "Checksums" in Chapter 18 for more details.

The structure of the second half of the ICMP header depends on the message type. Thanks to the value of type and code, the receiver can identify the message type and read the rest of the header accordingly. The following 32 bits can be unused, completely used, or partially used depending on the message type; examples of these three different layouts are shown at the bottom of Figure 25-1.

ICMP messages are classified into two categories: error and query (request/response). In Table 25-1, you can see which ICMP types fall into each category. Query messages use the extra 32 bits of the header to define the two fields identifier and sequence_number (Figure 25-1(b)). These two fields are left unchanged by the receiver (i.e., copied from the request message to the response message) and allow the source to match the response with its original request.

ICMP error messages include a payload, whose content is described in the next section.

In RFC 792, you can find the layout of most ICMP message types' headers.

ICMP Payload

ICMP error messages are sent when the kernel detects an error condition while processing an ingress IP packet. All ICMP error types include the same information in the ICMP payload: the IP header of the IP packet that triggered the transmission of the ICMP message, plus a portion of the IP payload. The resulting IP packet must not exceed 576 bytes in size, including the outer IP header and the ICMP header. (This last rule is stated in RFC 1812, section 4.3.2.3, which updates the header definitions of RFC 792. According to the older RFC 792, the ICMP payload needs to include only the original IP header plus 64 bits of the original transport header.)

Figure 25-2 shows an example of what an ICMP_FRAG_NEEDED error message looks like according to RFC 792. Figure 25-2(a) is the fragment that triggered the transmission of the ICMP message, and Figure 25-2(b) is the ICMP message. Note that the ICMP payload includes the original IP header and a piece of the transport header, too. Linux is compliant with RFC 1812, and therefore includes the extra block shown in Figure 25-2(a), up to a size of 576 bytes.

The protocol field of the original IP header will be used by the target of the ICMP message to identify the right transport protocol (TCP in the example) and a portion of the transport header in the ICMP payload (which includes source and destination port numbers) will allow the same target host to identify a local socket. Thus, the target host will have some help tracking down the reason it caused an error.

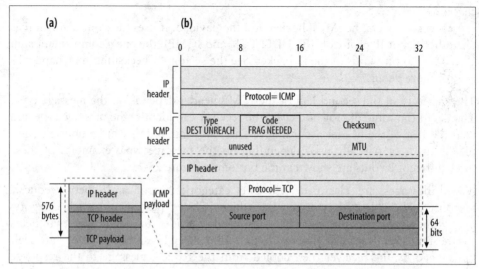

Figure 25-2. Example of ICMP payload for the ICMP_DEST_UNREACH error message

ICMP Types

Table 25-1 lists the ICMP types and the RFCs where they are defined, shows whether they are generally transmitted and processed by the kernel or in user space, and classifies each as an error or query message. The kernel symbols are listed in *include/linux/icmp.h*. The table lists only the ICMP message types the Linux kernel cares about (regardless of whether they are implemented). You can refer to the URL provided in the chapter's introduction for an updated list.

Table 25-1. ICMP types

Type	Name	TX by	RX by	RFC	Error/Query
0	Echo Reply	Kernel	User	792	Query
8	Echo Request	User	Kernel	792	Query
1	Not assigned				
2	Not assigned				
3	Destination Unreachable	Kernel	Kernel	792	Error
4	Source Quench (obsolete; see RFC 1812 section 4.3.3.3)				
5	Redirect	Kernel	Kernel	792	Error
6	Alternate Host Address (obsolete[a])				
7	Not assigned				
9	Router Advertisement	User	User	1256	Query
10	Router Solicitation	User	User		
11	Time Exceeded	Kernel	Kernel	792	Error

Table 25-1. ICMP types (continued)

Type	Name	TX by	RX by	RFC	Error/Query
12	Parameter Problem	Kernel	Kernel	792	Error
13	Timestamp Request	User	Kernel	792	Query
14	Timestamp Reply	Kernel	User	792	Query
15	Information Request				
16	Information Reply (obsolete; see RFC 1122 section 3.2.2.7 and RFC 1812 section 4.3.3.7)				
17	Address Mask Request	Kernel	Kernel	950	Query
18	Address Mask Reply	Kernel	Kernel		

a This option was defined by the same author of RFC 792, but it is not defined in any RFC.

ICMP types 1, 2, and 7 are simply listed as unassigned, and type 6 is not defined in any RFC.

Types 9 and 10 are not handled (and therefore are not defined) in kernel space; the Router discovery messages are processed in user space by applications that implement RFC 1256. For Linux, you can refer to *rdisc*, which is an application that comes as part of the *iputils* package.

RFC 1122 and RFC 1812 tell whether the implementation for each ICMP message type is optional or mandatory, for hosts and routers respectively. Table 25-2 summarizes these requirements. For the exact interpretation of the words *must*, *should* and *may*, you can refer to RFC 2119. The table does not include obsolete options.

Table 25-2. Host and router requirements

Type	Name	Hosts (RFC 1122)	Routers (RFC 1812)	Linux is compliant
0	Echo Reply	Must implement an echo server	Must implement an echo server	Yes
8	Echo Request			
3	Destination Unreachable	Should transmit Must receive	Must transmit	Yes
5	Redirect	Should not transmit Must receive	Must transmit May receive	Yes
9	Router Advertisement	N/A	Must receive	No
10	Router Solicitation			(Support is available in user space)
11	Time Exceeded	Must receive	Must transmit	Yes
12	Parameter Problem	Should transmit Must receive	Must transmit	Yes
13	Timestamp Request	May receive	May receive/transmit	Yes
14	Timestamp Reply	May receive		
17	Address Mask Request	May receive/transmit	Must receive/transmit	No
18	Address Mask Reply			

A router must respect the host requirements when it is the originator of the IP packet that triggered the transmission of an ICMP message. For example, the Destination Unreachable ICMP message is sent to the host whose IP packet could not be delivered. When an offending packet is generated by a router, the router must process the ICMP error message according to the host requirements in Table 25-2. Note that a router cannot be the target of a Destination Unreachable message sent for an IP packet it has not generated (which explains why Table 25-2 does not specify how a router must behave when it receives one).

Similar comments apply to other message types.

ICMP_ECHO and ICMP_ECHOREPLY

These are probably the most common and best-known ICMP types. They are used by different applications, the most famous of which is *ping*.

The ICMP_ECHO message type is used to test the reachability of a remote host. When a host receives an ICMP_ECHO message, it replies with an ICMP_ECHOREPLY message. See the section "ping."

ICMP_DEST_UNREACH

When an IP packet cannot be delivered to its destination, or when the IP payload cannot be delivered to the target application on the remote host, this ICMP type is used to notify the sender about the failed delivery and its cause. This ICMP type has quite a few different subtypes (code values), all listed in Table 25-3. Not all of them are used by Linux.

The header used for this message includes the 32-bit field shown in Figure 25-1(a).

Table 25-3. ICMP codes for ICMP type ICMP_UNREACH

Code	Kernel symbol	Description
0	ICMP_NET_UNREACH	Network unreachable.
1	ICMP_HOST_UNREACH	Host unreachable.
2	ICMP_PROT_UNREACH	Protocol unreachable. The transport protocol used on top of IP is not implemented on the target host.
3	ICMP_PORT_UNREACH	Port unreachable. There is no application listening to the port number specified by the destination port in the transport header.
4	ICMP_FRAG_NEEDED	Fragmentation needed. The IP packet needed to be fragmented but the Don't Fragment (DF) flag was set in the IP header.
5	ICMP_SR_FAILED	Source route failed.
6	ICMP_NET_UNKNOWN	Destination network unknown.
7	ICMP_HOST_UNKNOWN	Destination host unknown.
8	ICMP_HOST_ISOLATED	Source host isolated.

Table 25-3. ICMP codes for ICMP type ICMP_UNREACH (continued)

Code	Kernel symbol	Description
9	ICMP_NET_ANO	Communication with destination network is administratively prohibited.
10	ICMP_HOST_ANO	Communication with destination host is administratively prohibited.
11	ICMP_NET_UNR_TOS	Destination network unreachable for Type of Service.
12	ICMP_HOST_UNR_TOS	Destination host unreachable for Type of Service.
13	ICMP_PKT_FILTERED	Communication administratively prohibited.
14	ICMP_PREC_VIOLATION	Host precedence violation.
15	ICMP_PREC_CUTOFF	Precedence cutoff in effect.

ICMP_SOURCE_QUENCH

This message type was originally defined as a mechanism for routers to inform peers about congestion. However, generating more traffic to help with congestion recovery did not turn out to be that effective, and RFC 1812 made this ICMP message type obsolete.

The original goal of this ICMP type (congestion control) is now taken care of by the Early Congestion Notification (ECN) mechanism described in RFC 3168.

ICMP_REDIRECT

ICMP REDIRECT message types are sent only by routers, and are processed by hosts and optionally by routers.* Linux provides a file in /proc that allows you to enable and disable the processing of ICMP_REDIRECT messages. Routers generate this type of message when they detect that a neighboring host is using suboptimal routing; that is, when a destination can be reached through a better gateway than the one generating the message.

The basic and most common cause for an ICMP_REDIRECT message is an ingress packet that needs to be forwarded out of the same device it was received from. We will see an example later in this section.

There are four subtypes for this ICMP message type, shown in Table 25-4. RFC 1812 states that only ICMP_REDIR_HOST and ICMP_REDIR_HOSTTOS should be generated because there are cases where the use of subnetting makes it harder to handle the other two ICMP codes. Linux follows this recommendation.

---

* See RFC 1812, sections 4.3.3.2 and 5.2.7.2.

Table 25-4. ICMP codes for ICMP type ICMP_REDIRECT

Code	Kernel symbol	Description
0	ICMP_REDIR_NET (obsolete)	Redirect for network address
1	ICMP_REDIR_HOST	Redirect for host address
2	ICMP_REDIR_NETTOS (obsolete)	Redirect for network address and Type of Service
3	ICMP_REDIR_HOSTTOS	Redirect for host address and Type of Service

Figure 25-3 provides a scenario where a router generates an ICMP_REDIRECT message. From the topology it looks clear that Host X should use Router RT2 to reach Host Y. But suppose Host X has been configured only with the default gateway RT1 so that any traffic Host X sends outside its local network goes to Router RT1.

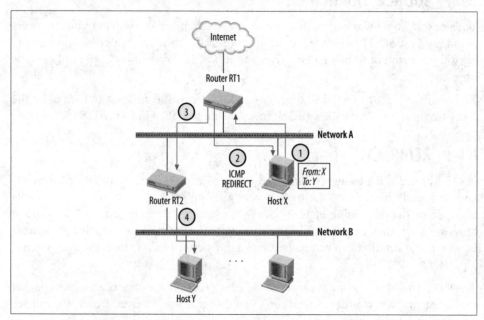

Figure 25-3. Example of ICMP_REDIRECT

This is what happens when Host X transmits an IP packet to Host Y:

1. Host X sends Router RT1 a packet addressed to Host Y.

2. Router RT1 consults its routing table and realizes the next hop is Router RT2. It also realizes that because Router RT2 is on the same subnet as Host X, Host X could have sent the packet directly to Router RT2.

3. Router RT1 sends Host X an ICMP_REDIRECT message to inform it about the better route. Host X will save the route and use it next time.

4. Router RT1 forwards the packet to Router RT2.

Normally, when a router detects that it is being asked to route a packet along a sub-optimal route, it replies back to the sender with an `ICMP_REDIRECT` message that describes the correct route. For security reasons, however, these suggestions are often rejected nowadays: you can imagine how easy it otherwise could be to create trouble by just saying, "Look, to get to that network you should use Router XYZ rather than the one you have been configured with."

In the section "Transmitting ICMP_REDIRECT Messages" in Chapter 31, you can find the exact conditions that trigger the transmission of `ICMP_REDIRECT` messages. Also see the section "ICMP Redirect" in Chapter 20 for the interaction between this ICMP type and the Source Route IP option. In the section "Processing Ingress ICMP_REDIRECT Messages" in Chapter 31, you can find details about whether an ingress `ICMP_REDIRECT` message is processed.

ICMP_TIME_EXCEEDED

This message type has two subtypes, as shown in Table 25-5.

Table 25-5. ICMP codes for ICMP type ICMP_TIME_EXCEEDED

Code	Kernel symbol	Description
0	ICMP_EXC_TTL	TTL exceeded
1	ICMP_EXC_FRAGTIME	Fragment reassembly time exceeded

The IP header includes a field, TTL, that is decremented at each intermediate hop between source and destination. If TTL becomes 0 before the packet reaches the destination host, the IP packet is dropped. The intermediate host that drops the packet sends an `ICMP_EXEC_TTL` message to the sender to inform it that its packet was dropped. We will see in the section "traceroute" how the popular command *traceroute* uses it.

The `ICMP_EXC_FRAGTIME` message is generated when the defragmentation of an IP packet takes too long to complete and is therefore aborted.

ICMP_PARAMETERPROB

When a problem is found while processing the IP header of an ingress IP packet, the host that detects the problem sends an ICMP message of this type back to the source. The ICMP header (see Figure 25-1(c)) includes an offset that indicates where in the IP header the problem was found.

ICMP_TIMESTAMP and ICMP_TIMESTAMPREPLY

The `ICMP_TIMESTAMP` message type can be used to ask a remote host for a timestamp (actually two of them) and use it to synchronize the hosts' clocks. A host that receives an `ICMP_TIMESTAMP` message replies with an `ICMP_TIMESTAMPREPLY` message like that in Figure 25-4.

Type (8 bits) ICMP_TIMESTAMP_REPLY	Code (8 bits) (Not used)	Checksum (16bits)	
Identifier		Sequence number	
Timestamp1: set by the ICMP_TIMESTAMP sender			
Timestamp2: time at which ICMP_TIMESTAMP was received			
Timestamp3: time at which ICMP_TIMESTAMPREPLY was sent			

Figure 25-4. ICMP_TIMESTAMPREPLY structure

While the first timestamp is initialized by the `ICMP_TIMESTAMP` sender, the other two are initialized by the `ICMP_TIMESTAMPREPLY` sender. The second and third timestamps should reflect the time the `ICMP_TIMESTAMP` message was received and the time the associated `ICMP_TIMESTAMPREPLY` was transmitted.

These ICMP types are not of much use because other protocols are better suited for the same purpose (e.g., NTP).

ICMP_INFO_REQUEST and ICMP_INFO_REPLY

According to RFC 1122, these two ICMP message types were made obsolete because other protocols such as DHCP (and the older BOOTP and RARP) can do the same thing, and much more.

ICMP_ADDRESS and ICMP_ADDRESSREPLY

The purpose of these ICMP types is to allow a host to discover the netmasks to use on its interfaces by broadcasting a query on the attached networks. A router that receives an `ICMP_ADDRESS` message replies with an `ICMP_ADDRESSREPLY` message. The reply is usually unicast to the sender, but may be broadcasted when the sender uses a source IP address of 0 (i.e., not configured).

The goal of these two message types is achieved nowadays by other means, such as DHCP.

The Linux kernel does not reply to ingress `ICMP_ADDRESS` messages, but it listens to ingress `ICMP_ADDRESSREPLY` messages to detect misconfigurations (such as wrong netmask configurations).

Among the reasons why Linux does not process `ICMP_ADDRESS` messages is that the same interface can be configured with multiple IP addresses, and therefore there may not be a unique netmask to return to any given request.

According to RFC 1812, the implementation of the `ICMP_ADDRESS` and `ICMP_ADDRESSREPLY` messages is mandatory on routers, so Linux is not compliant. However, since these ICMP message types are not commonly used, this missing compliance does not represent a compatibility problem in any way for Linux.

Applications of the ICMP Protocol

ICMP messages can be transmitted both by the kernel and by user-space applications. The user-space applications use the raw IP socket interface that we briefly introduced in Chapter 13. Two well-known examples of network troubleshooting tools that use the ICMP protocol are *traceroute* and *ping*. Other users of the raw IP socket interface for transmitting or listening to ICMP messages are routing protocols.

ping

ping does not need an introduction. For most people, it represents the first command learned when approaching the networking area. Given an input IP address and a set of optional flags, it transmits an `ICMP_ECHO` message to the input IP address, and prints the round-trip time and other information when it receives the associated `ICMP_ECHOREPLY` message. You can find the history of *ping* at *http://ftp.arl.mil/~mike/ ping.html*, the home page of its creator.

traceroute

traceroute is probably the first command you learned after *ping*. It is used to determine the path between the host where the command is issued and a given destination IP address. The path is represented by the list of IP addresses of the intermediate routers.

traceroute can achieve its goal by using either UDP or ICMP.* By default, it uses UDP, but you can force the use of ICMP with the *–I* switch option. As we will see, the UDP method also depends on an ICMP message for its success. Both methods demonstrate considerable cleverness.

Let's see how the technique based on ICMP works. As we saw in Chapter 20, when the IP header's TTL field of an ingress IP packet is 1 and forwarding is required, the receiver discards the packet and sends back to the source an ICMP message of type `ICMP_TIME_EXCEEDED` and code `ICMP_EXC_TTL`. *traceroute* takes advantage of this rule to discover the intermediate hops one at a time: by sending `ICMP_ECHO` messages to the destination IP address with increasing values of the TTL field (starting with value 1),

---

* There is a third option, based on the use of an IP option (RFC 1393) that is not supported by Linux. The version of *traceroute* that comes with the most common Linux distributions does not support RFC 1393.

it makes sure that all intermediate hosts will generate ICMP_TIME_EXCEEDED messages, and the last one (i.e., the target host) will reply with an ICMP_ECHOREPLY message. Figure 25-5 shows an example.

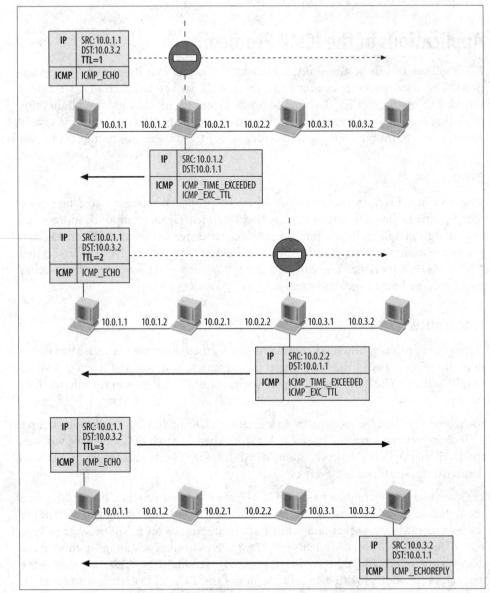

Figure 25-5. Example of traceroute with ICMP

I did not include the value of the TTL field for the ICMP reply messages in the figure because different operating systems use different values (64 and 255 are the most common).

The technique based on the use of the UDP protocol is somewhat similar. It still takes advantage of how the TTL field is handled, but instead of using ICMP_ECHO messages, it uses UDP packets with a high destination port number that is unlikely to be used at the end host. When the IP packet makes it to the end host, the latter will complain with an ICMP message of type ICMP_DEST_UNREACH and code ICMP_PORT_UNREACH. Figure 25-6 shows an example.

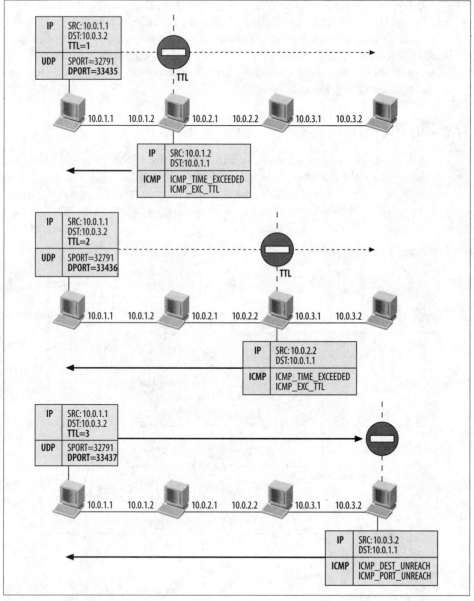

Figure 25-6. Example of traceroute with UDP

In both cases, ICMP and UDP, the intermediate hosts are discovered one by one with independent "probe" packets. Two consequences of this are worth mentioning:

- The round-trip times associated with the intermediate routers reflect the network's congestion state at different times. Therefore, the nth intermediate router will usually have a higher round-trip time than the $(n-1)$th intermediate router, but not always.

- The intermediate routers used to reach the nth hop may not be the same ones used to reach the $(n-1)$th hop. Different factors can contribute to the selection of the route to take toward a given destination, such as dynamic routing changes, load balancers, etc. The source code of the *traceroute* command, which you can download from the most common Linux distribution's download servers, includes a few examples worth reading.

The Big Picture

Figure 25-7 shows the kernel subsystems with which the ICMP protocol interacts. The figure shows only the two common transport protocols, TCP and UDP, but many others also interact with ICMP, such as the various tunnel protocols (IPIP, GRE), the protocols of the IPsec suite (AH, ESP, IPcomp), etc.

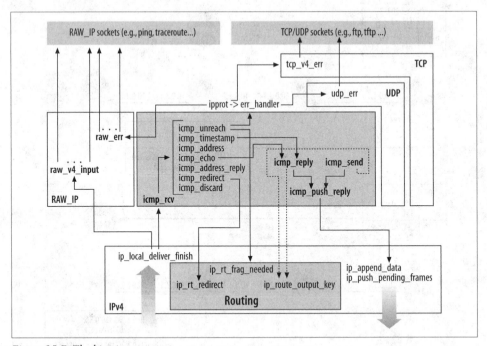

Figure 25-7. The big picture

Here are some examples of interactions between protocols:

IP protocol
The `ip_local_deliver_finish` routine, described in Chapter 24, delivers ingress ICMP messages to the receive routine `icmp_rcv` registered by the ICMP protocol, but it also delivers them to the raw IP sockets that registered against the ICMP protocol (`raw_v4_input`). Transmission requests are submitted to the IP layer via the `ip_append_data` and `ip_push_pending_frames` routines described in detail in Chapter 21. The figure does not show the points where the IP protocol or the routing subsystem call `icmp_send`.

Routing subsystem
ICMP messages are transmitted with `icmp_reply` and `icmp_send`. Both are described in the section "Transmitting ICMP Messages." These routines consult the routing table with the `ip_route_output_key` function described in Chapter 33. Also, the routines that process ingress ICMP messages may need to interact with the routing subsystem, such as by using `ip_rt_redirect` and `ip_rt_frag_needed`, to process the information received with an ICMP message.

Socket layer
When an ingress ICMP message carries an error indication, the socket layer is notified by invoking the `err_handler` function pointer registered by the transport protocol associated with the faulty IP packet.

Ingress ICMP messages are dispatched to the right handler based on the ICMP type.

Protocol Initialization

The ICMPv4 protocol is initialized with `icmp_init` in *net/ipv4/icmp.c*. The ICMP protocol cannot be compiled as a module, so there is no `module_init` or `module_cleanup` function. The meaning of the `__init` macro tagging `icmp_init` can be found in Chapter 7.

Initialization consists of the creation of an array of sockets, one per CPU, which will be used when transmitting ICMP messages generated by the kernel (as opposed to user-generated messages). Those sockets, of type `SOCK_RAW` and protocol `IPPROTO_ICMP`, are not to be inserted into the kernel socket's table because they are not supposed to be used as targets for ingress ICMP messages. For this reason, a call to the unhash function takes the sockets out of the hash tables where they have been added by the generic routine `sock_create_kern`.

```
void __init icmp_init(struct net_proto_family *ops)
{
    struct inet_sock *inet;
    int i;
    for (i = 0; I < NR_CPUS; i++) {
        ...
        err = sock_create_kern(PF_INET, SOCK_RAW, IPPROTO_ICMP,
```

```
                      &per_cpu(__icmp_socket, i));
            if (err < 0)
                panic("Failed to create the ICMP control socket.\n");
            ...
            inet = inet_sk(per_cpu(__icmp_socket, i)->sk);
            inet->uc_ttl = -1;
            inet->pmtudisc = IP_PMTUDISC_DONT;
            per_cpu(__icmp_socket, i)->sk->sk_prot->unhash(per_cpu(__icmp_socket, i)->
    sk);
        }
```

uc_ttl, the TTL value to use for IP packets sent to unicast addresses, is initialized to
−1 to tell the kernel to use the default unicast TTL (sysctl_ip_default_ttl). The setting of IP_PMTUDISC_DONT disables PMTU discovery on the sockets.

The per-CPU sockets can be accessed with the icmp_socket macro defined in *net/
ipv4/icmp.c*, which transparently selects the right socket based on the local CPU ID.

```
    static DEFINE_PER_CPU(struct socket *, __icmp_socket) = NULL;
    #define icmp_socket    __get_cpu_var(__icmp_socket)
```

Data Structures Featured in This Chapter

The three main data structures used by the ICMP code are:

icmphdr
    ICMP header.

icmp_control
    ICMP message type descriptor. Among its fields is the routine used to process
    ingress messages.

icmp_bxm
    Input structure given as a parameter to the two transmit routines described in
    the section "Transmitting ICMP Messages." It includes all the information nec-
    essary to transmit an ICMP message.

icmphdr Structure

We saw in Figure 25-1 the structure of an ICMP message. The following, from
include/linux/icmp.h, is the data structure used to define an ICMP header:

```
    struct icmphdr {
      __u8     type;
      __u8     code;
      __u16    checksum;
      union {
          struct {
              __u16    id;
              __u16    sequence;
          } echo;
          __u32    gateway;
```

```
        struct {
            __u16    __unused;
            __u16    mtu;
        } frag;
    } un;
};
```

First come the three fields common to all ICMP types, and then a union that provides different fields based on the message type. For example, un.frag is used by ICMP_FRAG_NEEDED messages, and un.echo by the query messages (i.e., ICMP_ECHO, ICMP_ECHOREPLY, etc.).

icmp_control Structure

For each ICMP type there is an instance of an icmp_control data structure (defined in *net/ipv4/icmp.c*). Among other fields, it includes a pointer to the routine that is to be called to process ingress ICMP messages. Here are its fields:

int output_entry
int input_entry
> Indexes used by the receive routine icmp_rcv and the transmission routines in the section "Transmitting ICMP Messages" to update the right SNMP counter in an array. See the section "ICMP Statistics."

void (*handler)(struct sk_buff *skb)
> Function invoked by the receiving routine icmp_rcv to process incoming ICMP messages.

short error
> Flag that is set when the ICMP type is classified as an error (as opposed to a query). See Table 25-1.

Here are two examples where the error field is useful, as mentioned in the section "Transmitting ICMP Error Messages":

- The kernel can check to make sure it is not replying to an ingress ICMP error message with another ICMP error message, which is prohibited.

- ICMP types that are classified as errors are given a better TOS (IPTOS_PREC_INTERNETCONTROL) since they are considered more important (see icmp_send*).

Refer to the section "Receiving ICMP Messages" to see how icmp_control data structures are organized.

---

* This is required by RFC 1812 in section 4.3.2.5.

icmp_bxm Structure

icmp_bxm is defined in *net/ipv4/icmp.c*. Here is a description of its fields:

struct sk_buff *skb
> For ICMP messages sent with icmp_send, represents the ingress IP packet that triggered the transmission. For ICMP messages sent with icmp_reply, represents an ingress ICMP message request.

int offset
> Offset between skb->data and skb->nh (i.e., the size of the IP header). This offset is useful when evaluating how much data can be put into the ICMP payload for those ICMP messages that require it (see the section "ICMP Payload").

int data_len
> Size of the ICMP payload.

struct {
    struct icmphdr icmph;
    __u32 times[3];
} data
> icmph is the header of the ICMP message to transmit. times is used by the ICMP_TIMESTAMPREPLY message type (see Figure 25-4).

int head_len
> Size of the ICMP header.

struct ip_options replyopts
unsigned char optbuf
> replyopts stores the IP options to use at the IP layer. It is initialized with ip_options_echo based on the IP options of skb. optbuf is an extension of replyopts that is accessed by ip_options_echo via the __data field of ip_options. See Chapter 19.

Transmitting ICMP Messages

The two classes of ICMP messages introduced in the section "ICMP Header," errors and queries, are transmitted using two different routines:

icmp_send
> Used by the kernel to transmit ICMP error messages when specific conditions are detected.

icmp_reply
> Used by the ICMP protocol to reply to ingress ICMP request messages that require a response.

Both routines receive an skb buffer in input. However, the one used as input to icmp_send represents the ingress IP packet that triggered the transmission of the ICMP message, whereas the one in input to `icmp_reply` represents an ingress ICMP request message that requires a response.

The code in *net/core/icmp.c* processes incoming ICMP messages, and therefore always uses `icmp_reply` to transmit an ICMP message in response to another one received in input. Other kernel network subsystems (i.e., routing, IP, etc.) use `icmp_send` when they need to generate ICMP messages, as shown in Figure 25-8.

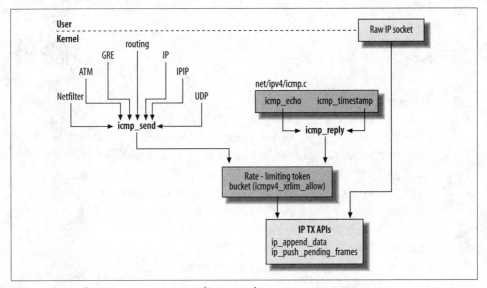

Figure 25-8. Subsystems using icmp_send/icmp_reply

In both cases:

- `ip_route_output_key` is used to find the route to the destination (see Chapter 33).
- The two routines `ip_append_data` and `ip_push_pending_frames` are used to request a transmission to the IP layer. These routines are described in Chapter 21.
- ICMP messages generated in kernel space are rate limited (if the kernel has been configured to do it via */proc*) with `icmpv4_xrlim_allow` (see the section "Rate Limiting").
- Transmissions are serialized with a per-CPU spin lock through `icmp_xmit_lock` and `icmp_xmit_unlock`. The per-CPU spin locks are accessed via the per-CPU ICMP sockets (see the section "Protocol Initialization"). When the spin lock cannot be acquired because it is already held, transmission fails (but neither of the routines returns an error code).

Tables 25-6, 25-7, and 25-8 show where the ICMP types in Table 25-1 are generated by the kernel. For those subsystems covered in this book, it also includes a reference to the routines where the ICMP messages are generated.

Table 25-6. Network subsystems that generate ICMP messages

Type	Name	Generated by
0	ICMP_ECHOREPLY	ICMP (icmp_echo)
3	ICMP_DEST_UNREACH	See Table 25-7
5	ICMP_REDIRECT	Routing (ip_rt_send_redirect)
11	ICMP_TIME_EXCEEDED	See Table 25-8
12	ICMP_PARAMETERPROB	IPv4 (ip_options_compile, ip_options_rcv_srr)
14	ICMP_TIMESTAMPREPLY	ICMP (icmp_timestamp)

Table 25-7. Network subsystems that generate variants of the ICMP_DEST_UNREACH message type

Code	Kernel symbol	Generated by
0	ICMP_NET_UNREACH	Routing (ip_error), Netfilter
1	ICMP_HOST_UNREACH	Routing (ip_error, ipv4_link_failure), Netfilter, GRE, IPIP
2	ICMP_PROT_UNREACH	IPv4 (ip_local_deliver_finish), Netfilter, GRE
3	ICMP_PORT_UNREACH	Netfilter, GRE, IPIP, UDP
4	ICMP_FRAG_NEEDED	IPv4 (ip_fragment), GRE, IPIP, Virtual Server
5	ICMP_SR_FAILED	IPv4 (ip_forward)
9	ICMP_NET_ANO	Netfilter
10	ICMP_HOST_ANO	Netfilter
13	ICMP_PKT_FILTERED	Routing (ip_error), Netfilter

Netfilter generates ICMP_DEST_UNREACH messages when it drops ingress IP packets according to the configuration applied, for instance, with *iptables*. The *–reject-with* option for the REJECT target allows the user to select which ICMP message type to use when rejecting ingress IP packets that match a given rule.

Tunneling protocols such as IPIP and GRE, defined in *net/ipv4/ipip.c* and *net/ipv4/ip_gre.c*, respectively, need to handle ICMP messages according to the rules in RFC 2003, section 4.

Table 25-8. Network subsystems that generate variants of the ICMP_TIME_EXCEEDED message type

Code	Kernel symbol	Generated by
0	ICMP_EXC_TTL	IPv4 (ip_forward)
1	ICMP_EXC_FRAGTIME	IPv4 (ip_expire)

Transmitting ICMP Error Messages

Figures 25-9(a) and 25-9(b) show the internals of `icmp_send`. Here are its input parameters:

`skb_in`
> Input IP packet the error is associated with.

`type`
`code`
> Type and code fields to use in the ICMP header.

`info`
> Additional information: an MTU for `ICMP_FRAG_NEEDED` messages, a gateway address for `ICMP_REDIRECT` messages, and an offset for `ICMP_PARAMETERPROB` messages.

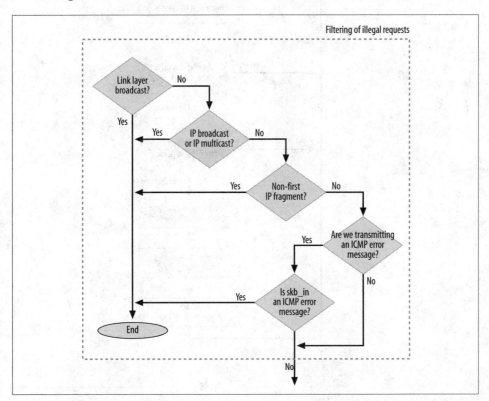

Figure 25-9(a). icmp_send function

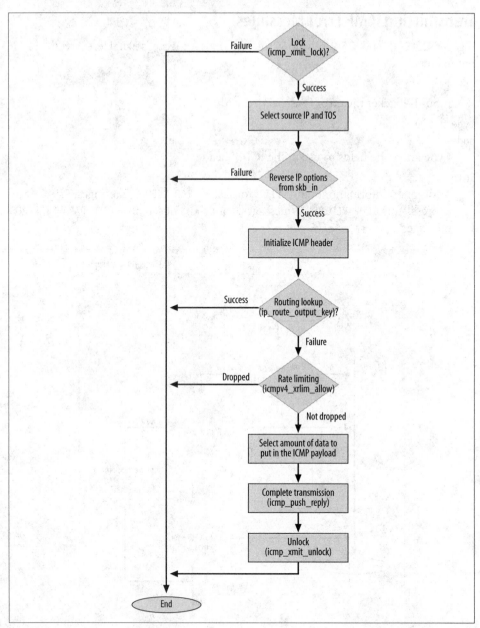

Figure 25-9(b). icmp_send function

`icmp_send` starts with a few sanity checks to filter out illegal requests. The following conditions cause it to abort:

- The IP datagram is received as broadcast or multicast. This case is detected by checking the `RTCF_BROADCAST` and `RTCF_MULTICAST` flags of the routing cache entry associated with `skb_in`.
- The IP datagram is received encapsulated in a broadcast link layer frame. This case is detected by comparing the packet type `skb_in->pkt_type` against `PACKET_HOST`.
- The IP datagram is a fragment, and it is not the first one of the original packet. This case can be detected by reading the offset field of the IP header (see Chapter 22).
- The IP datagram carries an ICMP error message. You must not use an error message to reply to an error message.

It is not the responsibility of the ICMP layer to initialize the IP header. However, a couple of IP header fields will be initialized by the IP layer according to the requirements of ICMP. In particular:

Source IP address
> When the target of the ICMP message is not a locally configured IP address (i.e., `RTCF_LOCAL`), the source IP address to place in the encapsulating header is selected according to the `sysctl_icmp_errors_use_inbound_ifaddr` configuration (see the section "Tuning via /proc Filesystem").

Type of Service (TOS)
> The TOS is copied from the TOS of `skb_in`. In addition, when the ICMP message is classified as an error (see Table 25-1), the precedence's component of the TOS is initialized to `IPTOS_PREC_INTERNETCONTROL` (i.e., this message has higher precedence). See Chapter 18 for more information on TOS.

IP options
> The IP options are copied and reversed from `skb_in` with `ip_options_echo`. See the section "IP Options" in Chapter 19.

Next, the function finds the route to the destination with `ip_route_output_key`, which is a cache lookup routine introduced in Chapter 33.

Note that, as shown in Figure 25-8, transmissions are rate limited with a token bucket algorithm via the `icmpv4_xrlim_allow` routine. When the ICMP message is not suppressed by the token bucket algorithm, the transmission ends with a call to `icmp_push_reply`, which ends up calling the two IP routines shown in Figure 25-8.

Replying to Ingress ICMP Messages

As mentioned in the section "ICMP Header," a subset of the ICMP message types comes in pairs: a request message and a response message. For one example, an

`ICMP_ECHOREPLY` message is sent in answer to an ingress `ICMP_ECHO` message. The transmission of response messages is done as follows:

1. The header of the response message is first copied from the ingress request ICMP message.

2. The type field of the ICMP header is updated (for example, `ICMP_ECHO` is replaced with `ICMP_ECHOREPLY`).

3. `icmp_reply` is called to complete the transmission (i.e., to compute the checksum on the ICMP header, find the route to the destination, fill in the IP header, etc.).

Rate Limiting

ICMP messages are rate limited in two places:

By the routing code
> The routing code rate limits only the outgoing `ICMP_DEST_UNREACH` and `ICMP_REDIRECT` message types. See the section "Routing Failure" in Chapter 35 and the section "Egress ICMP REDIRECT Rate Limiting" in Chapter 33.

By the ICMP code
> The ICMP code can rate limit all outgoing ICMP message types (with only the few exceptions listed later in this section), including the types that are also rate limited by the routing code.

The two types of rate limiting differ in an important way: the routing code rate limits ICMP messages per destination IP address, and the ICMP code rate limits per source IP address. This means that the types that are rate limited by both ICMP and the routing code are rate limited twice.

Let me clarify this point. The kernel keeps the rate-limiting information needed to apply the token bucket algorithm in the `dst_entry` entries of the routing cache. Each `dst_entry` instance is associated with a destination IP address (more details in Chapter 33). This alone tells us that rate limiting is applied on a per-IP-address basis, not on a per-ICMP-message-type basis, but let's see exactly how per-source and per-destination rate limiting differ:

• When a kernel subsystem, such as the IPv4 protocol, processes an input IP packet that meets certain error conditions, it sends an ICMP error message back to the source of the ingress IP packet. The ICMP code consults the routing table, the routing lookup returns a cache entry, and the cache entry is used to store the rate limiting information. This cache entry is associated with the route from the local host to the source of the faulty IP packet—that is, to the source IP address of the faulty IP packet. This is called per-source IP address rate limiting.

• When the routing code cannot route an ingress IP packet, it generates an `ICMP_HOST_UNREACH` message, whereas it generates an `ICMP_REDIRECT` message when the destination IP address of the ingress IP packet is better reached via another gateway. In both cases, the routing code adds an entry to the cache whose associated destination IP address is the destination IP address of the ingress IP packet. This is why this is called per-destination IP address rate limiting. Chapter 35 explains how such cache entries will be used by subsequent matching IP packets.

Implementation of Rate Limiting

Let's see now how the ICMP code applies its rate limiting. As shown in Figure 25-10, any time an ICMP message is transmitted and rate limiting is configured in the kernel, the `icmpv4_xrlim_allow` function is called to enforce rate limiting. Both the ICMP message types to rate limit (`sysctl_icmp_ratemask`) and the rate limit's rate (`sysctl_icmp_ratelimit`) can be configured via */proc* (see the section "Tuning via /proc Filesystem").

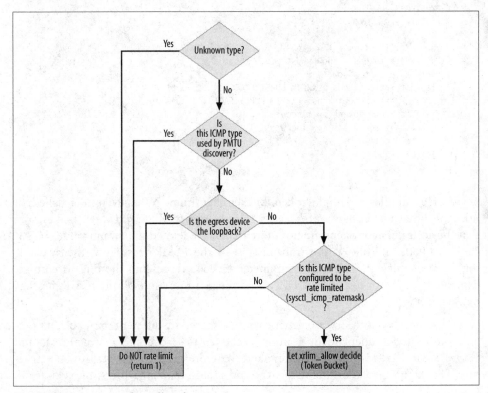

Figure 25-10. icmpv4_xrlim_allow function

`icmpv4_xrlim_allow` does not apply any rate limiting in the following cases:

- ICMP messages whose type is not known to the kernel (they could be important ones).
- ICMP messages used by the PMTU protocol described in RFC 1191 (i.e., type `ICMP_DEST_UNREACH` and code `ICMP_FRAG_NEEDED`).[*] PMTU is briefly described in Chapter 18.
- ICMPs sent out on the loopback device.

`icmpv4_xrlim_allow` is a wrapper for a more general-purpose function, `xlim_allow`, which does the real job. It is called if, according to the `sysctl_icmp_ratemask` bitmap, the ICMP message is to be rate limited.

```
#define XRLIM_BURST_FACTOR 6
int xrlim_allow(struct dst_entry *dst, int timeout)
{
    unsigned long now;
    int rc = 0;

    now = jiffies;
    dst->rate_tokens += now - dst->rate_last;
    dst->rate_last = now;
    if (dst->rate_tokens > XRLIM_BURST_FACTOR * timeout)
            dst->rate_tokens = XRLIM_BURST_FACTOR * timeout;
    if (dst->rate_tokens >= timeout) {
        dst->rate_tokens -= timeout;
        return 1;
    }
    return rc;
}
```

`xrlim_allow` applies a simple token bucket algorithm. Whenever it is called, it updates the available `dst->rate_tokens` tokens (measured in `jiffies`), makes sure that the accumulated tokens are not more than a predefined maximum value (`XRLIM_BURST_FACTOR`), and allows the transmission of the ICMP message if the available tokens are sufficient. The input parameter `timeout` represents the rate to enforce, expressed in Hz (for example, 1*HZ would mean a rate limit of one ICMP message per second).

Note that since `xrlim_allow` is a generic routine shared by different protocols, it operates on protocol-independent routing cache entries (`dst_entry` structures), and `icmpv4_xrlim_allow` is an IPv4 routine and therefore operates on `rtable` data structures. For more details on the `dst_entry` and `rtable` data structures, please refer to Chapter 36.

---

[*] Note that the policy used by the kernel has nothing to do with the one used by the firewall. It is common, for instance, for firewalls to drop all but a few ICMP messages. Sometimes the ones used by PMTU are dropped too, even though it goes against the RFC recommendations.

Receiving ICMP Messages

`icmp_rcv` is the function called by `ip_local_deliver_finish` to process ingress ICMP messages.

The ICMP protocol registers its receiving routine `icmp_rcv` in *net/ipv4/protocol.c*, as described in Chapter 24. See Chapter 20 for more details on local delivery of ingress IP packets.

First, the ICMP message's checksum is verified. Note that even when the receiving NIC is able to compute the L4 checksum in hardware (which would be the ICMP checksum in this case) and that checksum says the ICMP message is corrupted, `icmp_rcv` verifies the checksum once more in software. You can refer to the section "sk_buff structure" in Chapter 19 for more details on L4 checksumming support by NICs.

Not all ICMP message types can be sent to a multicast IP address: only `ICMP_ECHO`, `ICMP_TIMESTAMP`, `ICMP_ADDRESS`, and `IMCP_ADDRESSREPLY`. `icmp_rcv` filters out those messages that do not respect this rule. In particular, ingress broadcast `ICMP_ECHO` messages are dropped if the system has been configured to do so. See the section "Tuning via /proc Filesystem."

When all sanity checks are satisfied, `icmp_rcv` passes the ingress ICMP message to the right helper routine. The latter is accessed via the `icmp_pointers` vector that is initialized at the end of *net/ipv4/icmp.c*. `icmp_pointers` is an array of `icmp_control` data structures. Table 25-9 summarizes part of `icmp_pointers`'s initialization. See the section "icmp_control Structure" for the exact meaning of the `handler` and `error` fields. Any types not in the table are obsolete, unsupported, or not supposed to be processed in kernel space. For all these types, `handler` is initialized to `icmp_discard`.

Table 25-9. Initialization of handler and error

Type	Kernel symbol	Handler	Error
3	ICMP_DEST_UNREACH	icmp_unreach	1
4	ICMP_SOURCE_QUENCH	icmp_unreach	1
5	ICMP_REDIRECT	icmp_redirect	1
8	ICMP_ECHO	icmp_echo	0
11	ICMP_TIME_EXCEEDED	icmp_unreach	1
12	ICMP_PARAMETERPROB	icmp_unreach	1
13	ICMP_TIMESTAMP	icmp_timestamp	0
17	ICMP_ADDRESS	icmp_address	0
18	ICMP_ADDRESSREPLY	icmp_address_reply	0

Figure 25-11 shows the internals of `icmp_rcv`.

Note that neither `ICMP_ADDRESS` nor `ICMP_ADDRESSREPLY` is supported; the two handlers that are registered against them are just placeholders or apply some kind of logging.

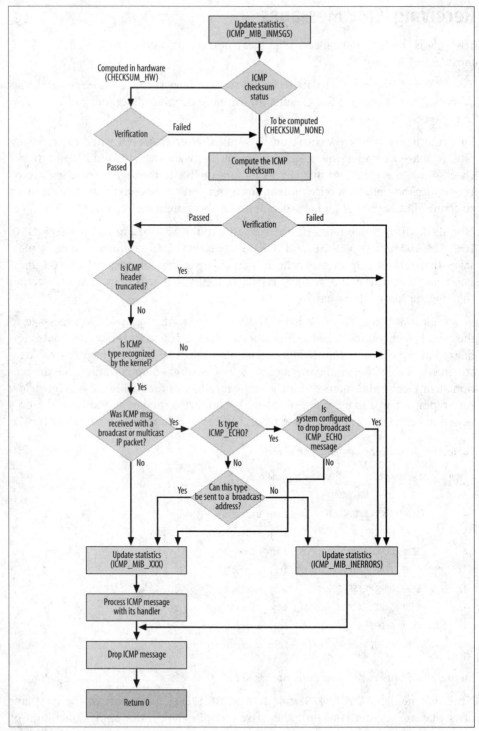

Figure 25-11. icmp_rcv function

Note also that the `icmp_unreach` handler takes care of different ICMP message types, not just `ICMP_DEST_UNREACH`.

Figure 25-12(a) shows how some of `skb`'s pointers are initialized when `icmp_rcv` is invoked, and Figure 25-12(b) shows how they are initialized when the handlers of Table 25-9 are called. This figure can be useful when analyzing the routines in Table 25-9, especially `icmp_unreach`.

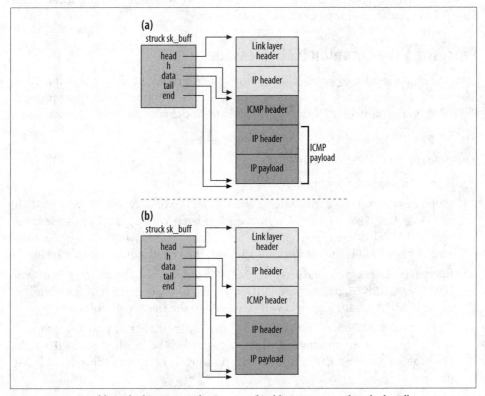

Figure 25-12. (a) skb at the beginning of icmp_rcv; (b) skb as it is passed to the handler

Processing ICMP_ECHO and ICMP_ECHOREPLY Messages

`ICMP_ECHO` messages are processed according to the generic model described in the section "Replying to Ingress ICMP Messages":

```
static void icmp_echo(struct sk_buff *skb)
{
    if (!sysctl_icmp_echo_ignore_all) {
        struct icmp_bxm icmp_param;

        icmp_param.data.icmph       = *skb->h.icmph;
        icmp_param.data.icmph.type  = ICMP_ECHOREPLY;
        icmp_param.skb              = skb;
```

```
            icmp_param.offset        = 0;
            icmp_param.data_len      = skb->len;
            icmp_param.head_len      = sizeof(struct icmphdr);
            icmp_reply(&icmp_param, skb);
        }
    }
```

ICMP_ECHOREPLY messages are not processed by the kernel, but by the applications that generated the associated ICMP_ECHO messages. See the section "Raw Sockets and Raw IP" in Chapter 24 for an example involving *ping*.

Processing the Common ICMP Messages

icmp_unreach is used as a handler for multiple ICMP types, as shown in Table 25-9. The function starts with some common sanity checks, continues with some processing based on the particular message type, and concludes with another common part.

The internals of the routine are shown in Figure 25-13.

The per-type processing is minimal:

- It prints a warning message for ICMP_SR_FAILED ICMPs.

- It updates the routing cache when it receives an ICMP of type ICMP_DEST_UNREACH and code ICMP_FRAG_NEEDED. The cache is updated with ip_rt_frag_needed, but only if PMTU discovery is enabled (i.e., if ipv4_config.no_pmtu_disc is non-zero). When PMTU discovery is not enabled, the kernel simply logs a warning.

- It extracts the pointer field from the ICMP header when the message is of type ICMP_PARAMETERPROB. pointer is an offset relative to the beginning of the IP header in the ICMP payload. The field will be passed to the transport protocol.

- ICMP_SOURCE_QUENCH does not require any specific treatment in icmp_unreach, so it is completely up to the transport protocols to handle it when notified via the err_handler routines. Currently, all transport protocols ignore this type of ICMP message.

For both ICMP_FRAG_NEEDED and ICMP_SR_FAILED, the logging is rate limited via LIMIT_NETDEBUG, which is a generic routine that rate limits networking-related messages to five per second.

The last part of icmp_unreach is again common to all ICMP types that use it as a handler, and consists of the following tasks:

- When the sysctl_icmp_ignore_bogus_error_messages variable is set (by default, it is not), the ICMP message is discarded if it is received with a broadcast IP packet.

- The function makes sure the ICMP payload includes the whole IP header of the IP packet that triggered the generation of the ICMP message, plus 64 bits from the transport payload of the same IP packet. This information is necessary to

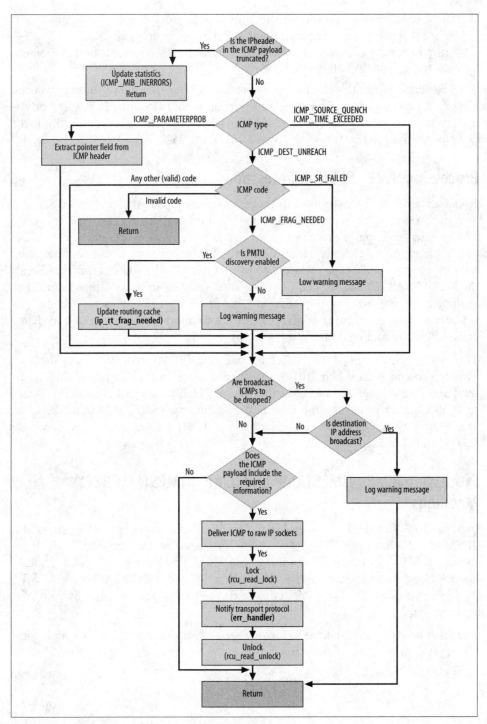

Figure 25-13. icmp_unreach function

allow the transport protocol to identify a local socket (i.e., the application). When this condition is not met, the ICMP message is dropped. Note that the 64-bit requirement comes from RFC 792, but RFC 1812 changed the requirement (see the section "ICMP Payload").

- The function notifies the transport protocol about this ICMP message via the err_handler function. The right transport protocol is identified using the protocol field of the IP header in the ICMP payload. See the section "Passing Error Notifications to the Transport Layer" and Figure 25-2.

Processing ICMP_REDIRECT Messages

icmp_redirect, the function used to process incoming ICMP_REDIRECT messages, is a wrapper around ip_rt_redirect with some additional sanity checks. The logic used by the latter function is described in the section "Processing Ingress ICMP_REDIRECT Messages" in Chapter 31. ip_rt_redirect adds an entry to the routing cache with rt_intern_hash, which is described in Chapter 33. The route is initialized with the RTCF_REDIRECTED flag toggled on, to be distinguished from the other routes. For example, we will see in the section "Examples of eligible cache victims" in Chapter 30 how the routing code uses this information when it is forced to delete entries from the routing cache.

The system administrator can also influence when ICMP redirects are generated. Through the /proc filesystem, it is possible to specify for each interface whether to send and accept ICMP redirects (see the section "The /proc/sys/net/ipv4/conf Directory" in Chapter 36). Using the firewall capabilities, as well, the administrator can specify from whom to accept particular types of ICMP packets and therefore whose ICMP_REDIRECT messages to trust.

Processing ICMP_TIMESTAMP and ICMP_TIMESTAMPREPLY Messages

Ingress ICMP_TIMESTAMP messages are handled by replying with an ICMP_TIMESTAMPREPLY message, using the scheme discussed in the section "Replying to Ingress ICMP Messages." The second and third timestamps are not initialized according to the rules we saw in the section "ICMP_TIMESTAMP and ICMP_TIMESTAMPREPLY": they are initialized to the same timestamp with do_gettimeofday.

Note that head_len is initialized to include not only the default ICMP header length, but also the three 32-bit timestamps.

Processing ICMP_ADDRESS and ICMP_ADDRESSREPLY Messages

Because the Linux kernel does not generate ICMP_ADDRESS messages, ingress ICMP_ADDRESSREPLY messages cannot be answers to queries generated locally (not in kernel space, at least). However, when forwarding and logging of Martian addresses* are enabled on the ingress device, Linux listens to ICMP_ADDRESSREPLY messages with icmp_address_reply. The latter function checks whether the mask advertised with the message is correct with regard to the IP addresses configured on the receiving interface: if the receiving interface does not have any IP address configured on the same subnet of the source IP address used by the ICMP message sender (which also implies the exact same netmask), the kernel logs a warning.

The sanity check on the received reply is not done when the routing cache has the RTCF_DIRECTSRC flag set. This flag is set only when the destination address is reachable by the local host via a next hop that has local scope (i.e., that exists only internally to the Linux box).

ICMP Statistics

The ICMP protocol keeps the statistics defined in RFC 2011, storing them in icmp_mib data structures. The kernel maintains statistics on a per-CPU basis, and for each CPU it distinguishes between statistics updated in software interrupt context and those updated outside that context. In other words, for each counter there are two instances per CPU: one of those two instances is used by code running in software interrupt context and the other is used by code not running in software interrupt context. All of those icmp_mib instances are allocated by init_ipv4_mibs in *net/ipv4/af_inet.c*. icmp_statistics is a two-element array, whose first element represents the per-CPU array of icmp_mib instances used by code that runs in software interrupt context, and whose second element represents the other per-CPU array.

```
static int __init init_ipv4_mibs(void)
{
    ...
    icmp_statistics[0] = alloc_percpu(struct icmp_mib);
    icmp_statistics[1] = alloc_percpu(struct icmp_mib);
    ...
}
```

The icmp_mib structure consists of an array of unsigned long members, one for each counter defined in RFC 2011 for the ICMP protocol:

```
#define SNMP_MIB_DUMMY  __ICMP_MIB_MAX
#define ICMP_MIB_MAX    (ICMP_MIB_MAX + 1)
struct icmp_mib {
    unsigned long mibs[ICMP_MIB_MAX];
} __SNMP_MIB_ALIGN__;
```

---

* See the definition of *log_martians* in the section "File descriptions" in Chapter 36.

The counters are identified via the enumeration list `ICMP_MIB_XXX`, defined in *include/linux/snmp.h*:

```
enum
{
    ICMP_MIB_NUM = 0,
    ICMP_MIB_INMSG,
    ...
    ICMP_MIB_OUTADDRMASKREPS,
    __ICMP_MIB_MAX
}
```

Note that the size of the `icmp_mib` array is one unit bigger than the size of the `ICMP_MIB_XXX` enumeration list. The extra element is used to account for ICMP message types not recognized by the kernel.

At any time, when the kernel needs to update a given counter, it selects the right element of `icmp_statistics` based on the interrupt context, and then the right `icmp_mib` instance based on the current CPU. The kernel provides a set of macros in *include/net/icmp.h* that need only the counter identifier in input (i.e., `ICMP_MIB_XXX`) and transparently take care of the two selections just described:

`ICMP_INC_STATS`

    This macro can be used both in and outside of software interrupt context.

`ICMP_INC_STATS_BH`

    This macro can be used when the code that needs to update a counter always runs in software interrupt context.

`ICMP_INC_STATS_USER`

    This macro can be used when the code that needs to update a counter never runs in software interrupt context.

The three macros are defined as wrappers around generic macros provided by the SNMP subsystem:

```
#define ICMP_INC_STATS(field)       SNMP_INC_STATS(icmp_statistics, field)
#define ICMP_INC_STATS_BH(field)    SNMP_INC_STATS_BH(icmp_statistics, field)
#define ICMP_INC_STATS_USER(field)  SNMP_INC_STATS_USER(icmp_statistics, field)
```

Here is the meaning of the `ICMP_MIB_XXX` values. For a more detailed description, you can refer to RFC 2011.

Fields related to received ICMP messages

    `ICMP_MIB_INMSG`

        Number of received ICMP messages. It includes those messages that are accounted by `ICMP_MIB_INERRORS`.

    `ICMP_MIB_INERRORS`

        Number of ICMP messages dropped because of some problem. `icmp_rcv` and the handlers in Table 25-9 drop ingress messages when they have a truncated ICMP header. The L4 layer `err_handler` function described in the section "Passing Error Notifications to the Transport Layer" drops ingress messages when they have a truncated ICMP payload.

ICMP_MIB_IN*XXX*

> Besides the two general-purpose counters just listed, there is one per-ICMP message type. ICMP_MIB_IN*XXX* counts the number of ICMP messages of type *XXX* received.

ICMP_MIB_IN*XXX counterpart for each* ICMP_MIB_OUT*XXX counter:*

ICMP_MIB_OUTMSG

> Number of transmitted ICMP messages.

ICMP_MIB_OUTERRORS

> Number of faulty ICMP transmissions. Not used.

ICMP_MIB_OUT*XXX*

> Besides the two general-purpose counters just listed, there is one per-ICMP message type. ICMP_MIB_OUT*XXX* counts the number of ICMP messages of type *XXX* transmitted.

ICMP_MIB_IN*XXX* counters are updated in icmp_rcv.

ICMP_MIB_OUT*XXX* counters are updated within icmp_reply and icmp_send by invoking icmp_out_count:

```
static void icmp_out_count(int type)
{
    if (type <= NR_ICMP_TYPES) {
        ICMP_INC_STATS(icmp_pointers[type].output_entry);
        ICMP_INC_STATS(ICMP_MIB_OUTMSGS);
    }
}
```

In both cases, for any ICMP type t, the right counter to increment is identified by means of the input_entry and output_entry fields of the icmp_control data structure associated with t. The values of these counters are exported in the */proc/net/snmp* file. You can also read them with *netstat –s* (and with SNMP agents, of course).

Passing Error Notifications to the Transport Layer

We saw in the section "L4 Protocol Registration" in Chapter 24 that when transport protocols register with the kernel, they provide an instance of an inet_protocol data structure. It includes one function pointer, err_handler, which is called by the ICMP protocol to propagate to the transport layer error notifications received with ingress ICMP messages. RFCs 1122 and 1256 specify, for hosts and routers, respectively, whether each ICMP message type should be propagated to the transport layer. All the error message types that require a notification to be sent to the transport layer are processed by icmp_unreach. At the end of that function, the transport layer is notified with err_handler.

When the transport layer processes the notification, it uses the `icmp_err_convert` array defined in *net/ipv4/icmp.c* to convert the ICMP_DEST_UNREACH code into an error code that is better understood by the socket layer (see udp_err in *net/ipv4/udp.c* for an example). The transport layer passes that error code to the socket associated with the error (which is identified thanks to the ICMP payload, as described in the section "ICMP Payload"). Raw IP sockets are notified as well, by means of raw_err. Table 25-10 shows the conversion that is applied by `icmp_err_convert`. Note that the err_handler routines registered by tunneling protocols such as IPIP and GRE may generate new ICMP messages (see ipip_err in *net/ipv4/ipip.c* for an example).

Table 25-10. Initialization of icmp_err_convert

Code	Kernel symbol	errno	Fatal (0=No, 1=Yes)
0	ICMP_NET_UNREACH	ENETUNREACH	0
1	ICMP_HOST_UNREACH	EHOSTUNREACH	0
2	ICMP_PROT_UNREACH	ENOPROTOOPT	1
3	ICMP_PORT_UNREACH	ECONNREFUSED	1
4	ICMP_FRAG_NEEDED	EMSGSIZE	0
5	ICMP_SR_FAILED	EOPNOTSUPP	0
6	ICMP_NET_UNKNOWN	ENETUNREACH	1
7	ICMP_HOST_UNKNOWN	EHOSTDOWN	1
8	ICMP_HOST_ISOLATED	ENONET	1
9	ICMP_NET_ANO	ENETUNREACH	1
10	ICMP_HOST_ANO	EHOSTUNREACH	1
11	ICMP_NET_UNR_TOS	ENETUNREACH	0
12	ICMP_HOST_UNR_TOS	EHOSTUNREACH	0
13	ICMP_PKT_FILTERED	EHOSTUNREACH	1
14	ICMP_PREC_VIOLATION	EHOSTUNREACH	1
15	ICMP_PREC_CUTOFF	EHOSTUNREACH	1

Tuning via /proc Filesystem

There are no compile-time kernel options for the ICMP protocol; all the tuning parameters are defined in *net/ipv4/sysctl_net_ipv4.c* and are exported via the */proc* filesystem in the directory */proc/sys/net/ipv4*:

icmp_echo_ignore_all

This flag is used by `icmp_echo`, the handler for incoming ICMP_ECHO ICMP messages, to decide whether to reply. This kind of filtering is usually done for security reasons by firewalls; however, the ICMP subsystem provides the capability, too.

icmp_echo_ignore_broadcasts

When this flag is set, ICMP_ECHO messages sent to broadcast addresses are ignored. See the section "Directed Broadcasts" in Chapter 30 for an example. The value of this field is checked in icmp_rcv.

icmp_ignore_bogus_error_responses

When this flag is clear, ICMP error message types with a broadcast destination IP address are ignored. icmp_unreach handles the flag.

icmp_errors_use_inbound_ifaddr

This flag is used to change how the source IP address is chosen when the local host transmits an ICMP error message. When the flag is not set, Linux selects the source IP address from the interface that is going to be used to transmit the ICMP message (see Part VII). When the flag is set, Linux selects the source IP address from the interface that received the IP packet that triggered the transmission of the ICMP message.

In most cases, the two interfaces match, but they could differ, for example, when two hosts are reachable with asymmetric routes (see the section "Essential Elements of Routing" in Chapter 30).

icmp_ratelimit
icmp_ratemask

These two variables are used by ICMP to rate limit outgoing ICMP messages (see the section "Rate Limiting"). sysctl_icmp_ratemask is simply a bitmap where each bit (starting from the least-significant bit) represents an ICMP type: if the bit corresponding to type *XXX* is set, outgoing ICMP messages of type *XXX* are rate limited.

Table 25-11 summarizes the variables and associated files.

Table 25-11. /proc/sys/net/ipv4 files usable for tuning the ICMP subsystem

Kernel variable	Filename	Default value
sysctl_icmp_echo_ignore_all	icmp_echo_ignore_all	0
sysctl_icmp_echo_ignore_broadcasts	icmp_echo_ignore_broadcasts	0
sysctl_icmp_ignore_bogus_error_responses	icmp_ignore_bogus_error_responses	0
sysctl_icmp_errors_use_inbound_ifaddr	icmp_errors_use_inbound_ifaddr	0
sysctl_icmp_ratelimit	icmp_ratelimit	1 * HZ
sysctl_icmp_ratemask	icmp_ratemask	0x1818[a]

[a] Given that each bit represents an ICMP type, and given the types in Table 25-1, this bitmap includes the following types: ICMP_DEST_UNREACH, ICMP_SOURCE_QUENCH, ICMP_TIME_EXCEEDED, and ICMP_PARAMETERPROB.

Functions and Variables Featured in This Chapter

Table 25-12 summarizes the main functions, variables, and data structures introduced in this chapter.

Table 25-12. Functions, variables, and data structures introduced in this chapter

Name	Description
Functions	
icmp_init	Initializes the ICMPv4 protocol. See the section "Protocol Initialization."
icmp_rcv	Processes ingress ICMP messages. See the section "Receiving ICMP Messages."
icmp_send icmp_reply	Transmit an ICMP message. See the section "Transmitting ICMP Messages."
icmp_xmit_lock icmp_xmit_unlock	Get and release the per-CPU ICMP-socket's transmit lock.
icmpv4_xrlim_allow xrlim_allow	Rate limit ICMP message transmissions. See the section "Rate Limiting."
icmp_out_count	Updates SNMP counters for transmitted ICMP messages.
icmp_err_convert	Converts ICMP error codes to socket error codes. See the section "Passing Error Notifications to the Transport Layer."
ICMP_INC_STATS ICMP_INC_STATS_BH ICMP_INC_STATS_USER	Increment counters used to keep statistics on ICMP messages. See the section "ICMP Statistics."
Variables	
icmp_statistics	SNMP counters. See the section "ICMP Statistics."
Data structures	
struct icmphdr struct icmp_control struct icmp_bxm	Main data structures used by ICMPv4. See the section "Data Structures Featured in This Chapter."
icmp_mib	Array of counters. See the section "ICMP Statistics."

Files and Directories Featured in This Chapter

The ICMP subsystem uses only five files—two for IPv4, two for IPv6, and one shared by the two IP versions—as shown in Figure 25-14.

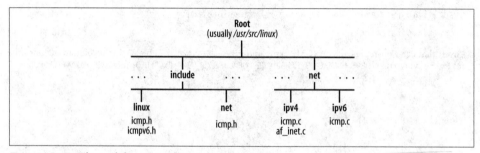

Figure 25-14. Files and directories featured in this chapter

Neighboring Subsystem

Packets use a Layer three protocol such as IP to reach a LAN, and then a Layer two protocol such as Ethernet to go from the router on the local network to the system where the endpoint application is running. But a step is missing in this scenario. How do the router and the application host know who each other are? In more technical terms, how can a host find the L2 address (such as a MAC address) that corresponds to a given IP address? The action of finding the L2 address associated with a given L3 address is referred to as "resolving the L3 address." The missing piece is filled in by a *neighboring protocol*.

The most familiar neighboring protocol is Address Resolution Protocol (ARP), and Chapter 28 describes it in general terms. The corresponding protocol used in IPv6 is Neighbor Discovery (ND). But the key principles and tasks of a neighboring protocol, and a neighboring subsystem within an operating system, can be generalized.

Here is what each chapter discusses:

Chapter 26, *Neighboring Subsystem: Concepts*
Describes why and when a neighboring protocol is used and lays out its major tasks.

Chapter 27, *Neighboring Subsystem: Infrastructure*
Discusses the infrastructure that is common to all neighboring protocols.

Chapter 28, *Neighboring Subsystem: Address Resolution Protocol (ARP)*
Describes how ARP, the most common neighboring protocol and the one readers are most likely to have interacted with, uses the infrastructure.

Chapter 29, *Neighboring Subsystem: Miscellaneous Topics*
Covers the command-line and user-space interface (including the neighboring subsystem's directories in the */proc* filesystem).

## CHAPTER 26

Neighboring Subsystem: Concepts

This chapter describes why and when a neighboring protocol is used and lays out its major tasks. It is deliberately a general overview that makes only passing references to particular neighboring protocols such as ARP. It covers such general issues as:

- The tasks taken on by a general neighboring infrastructure
- Why caching is valuable
- The states a neighbor entry in the cache can take
- Reachability detection and Network Unreachability Detection (NUD)
- What proxying is for

The terminology used in the Linux kernel source code follows the IPv6 neighbor discovery model described in RFC 2461 in the section "Neighboring Protocols," but we will try to keep the discussion as protocol-independent as possible.

The terms *L2 address*, *Layer two address*, *hardware address*, *MAC address*, and *link layer address* are commonly used to refer to the same concept. In this chapter, we will mostly use the first term.

What Is a Neighbor?

A host is your *neighbor* if it is connected to the same LAN (i.e., you are directly connected to it through either a shared medium or a point-to-point link) and it is configured on the same L3 network. For example, on an IP network, you can say that two hosts are neighbors if they are connected to the same LAN and each has at least one interface on the same IP subnet. Two such hosts can speak directly using the protocol associated with the medium that connects them (e.g., Ethernet). Another way to define a neighbor is to say that a host must be only one L3 hop away from its neighbor; its L3 routing table must provide a way for it to talk directly to the neighbor. Hosts that are not neighbors must communicate through a gateway or router.

Two hosts can still be neighbors if they are separated by a system on the L2 layer (a bridge). Part IV goes into more detail on this point, but we'll look at some simple examples here based on the IP networks of Figure 26-1.

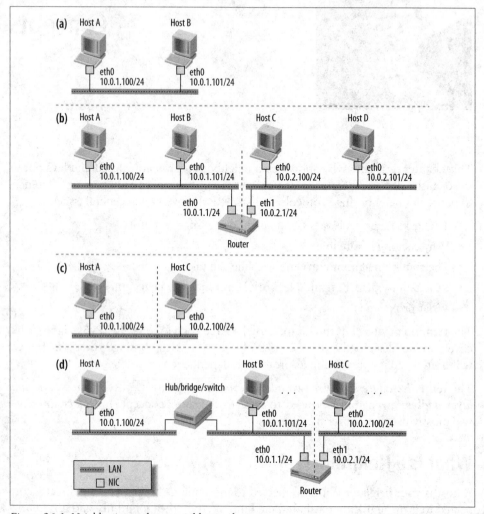

Figure 26-1. Neighboring and non-neighboring hosts

Each topology in Figure 26-1 shows a different relationship between L3 and L2 addresses, which has implications for reaching neighbors:

Figure 26-1(a)

Host A and Host B belong to the same 10.0.1.0/24 IP subnet and therefore can talk directly, being just one L3 hop away from each other. They are neighbors.

Figure 26-1(b)

This shows a slightly more complex case. Host A and Host B still belong to the same subnet and can therefore talk directly to each other. Host A and Host C, on the other hand, belong to two different IP subnets; because of this they need to rely on a router (assuming they have been configured properly) to talk to each other. In this case, Host A and Host C can be considered two L3 hops away from each other.

Figure 26-1(c)

This shows a case of two hosts, connected to the same hub, that cannot talk to each other. Even if each host can receive whatever the other host transmits, they cannot talk to each other at the L3 layer because they have been configured with different IP subnets. Thus, Host A thinks it can reach only hosts within the subnet 10.0.1.0/24. It will not even try to send anything if the destination address is outside that subnet. This problem can be solved easily in numerous ways; we will see one in the following section, and more in other chapters.

Figure 26-1(d)

This shows a case where the subnet 10.0.1.0/24 actually consists of two LANs merged into one subnet through a hub or a bridge. We saw how they differ in Chapter 14, but from this chapter's perspective they can be considered equivalent. Note that the two interfaces used to merge the two LANs do not have IP addresses: this is because all three device types operate below the IP layer.

When two hosts are one L3 hop away from each other, they are usually one L2 hop away as well, as in Figure 26-1(a), (b), and (c). But this is not necessarily always the case, as shown in Figure 26-1(d), where Host A and router are one L3 hop apart (and therefore are neighbors) but two L2 hops apart.

Furthermore, the relationship between physical subnets (LANs) and logical subnets (i.e., IP subnets) is not always one-to-one, as shown in Figure 26-2(a). You can have multiple IP subnets on one LAN, or multiple LANs on one IP subnet. For example, Figure 26-1(c) shows two IP subnets on the same LAN, and Figure 26-1(d) shows two LANs connected by a hub on the same IP subnet (on the left side).While the former is not common, the latter is commonly used when configuring Proxy ARP or bridging. You can see an example of Proxy ARP configuration in the section "Final Common Processing" in Chapter 28, and examples of bridging in Part IV.

Figure 26-2(b) shows two groups of hosts configured to lie on different IP subnets. Even if the hosts of the two groups share the same LAN and are therefore able to talk to each other directly, they have to go through the router, which listens on both sides. The router could have two different Network Interface Cards, or NICs (as shown in Figure 26-2(b)), or a single NIC with multiple IP configurations. This scenario is pretty uncommon: it could be used, for example, to address a temporary shortage of equipment or a failure. For example, if you had the scenario in Figure 26-2(a) and LAN1 failed, you could move LAN1's hosts to LAN2 (including the Router's *eth0* interface*), and everything would work again without any need to change the IP subnet configuration of the hosts that were on LAN1. The hosts that were already on LAN2 will still access the other hosts through the router. Even if this scenario is uncommon, the kernel must be able to handle it properly. The implications of this scenario, especially when the router uses a single interface to access both subnets (i.e., *eth0* is removed and its address is added to *eth1*), will be addressed in the section "Tunable ARP Options" in Chapter 28.

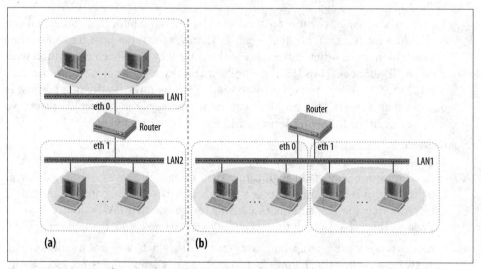

Figure 26-2. (a) IP_subnet-LAN 1:1; (b) IP_subnet-LAN n:1

In the rest of this chapter we will not explicitly mention the case of Figure 26-2(b), but you should keep in mind that setups like that one are possible and are not illegal.

Reasons That Neighboring Protocols Are Needed

In this section, we'll look at the basic reasons for the neighboring subsystem. They stem from the fundamental division of networks into layers, and the existence of shared media such as Ethernet.

When L3 Addresses Need to Be Translated to L2 Addresses

The reason for the distinction between the network Layer two (Ethernet, 802.11 wireless, Token Ring, point-to-point, etc.) and Layer three (IP or proprietary) protocols is that many different L2 protocols exist to take data between neighbors, whereas the routing L3 layer should not have to worry what medium is being used

---

* An alternative would be not to move the upper router's interface and simply add one IP address to the lower interface.

for transmission. The higher layer should be able to employ the same software to send packets between two systems whether they're on an Ethernet or a point-to-point connection.

Figure 26-3 shows the different situations that require different responses by the neighboring subsystem.

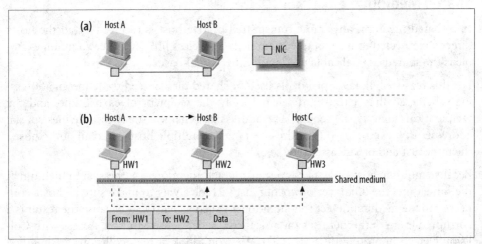

Figure 26-3. Point-to-point connection versus shared medium

Figure 26-3(a) shows a point-to-point connection, such as a dial-up line. The L2 protocol is fairly simple, handling such issues as error checking and taking turns if it's running on a half-duplex medium. The neighboring protocol is minimal, because it simply has to invoke the L2 protocol. There is no choice of which neighbor to send a packet to.

Figure 26-3(b) shows a more complicated situation: a host on an Ethernet or other shared medium that operates through broadcasts. If Host A has data for Host B, it must just place the data on the cable (or the radio waves, in the case of wireless) and let all systems on the shared medium receive it. It must indicate an L2 address so that one host knows the data is meant for it. Other hosts check the address and ignore the data. The neighboring protocol chooses the L2 address corresponding to the L3 address in the packet.

If Host A and Host B are separated by a bridge, the latter accepts the L2 address and directs it to the right host;* the neighboring subsystem doesn't have to worry about it. In fact, the bridge is invisible to the neighboring subsystem.

There is usually a one-to-one relationship between an L3 address and its corresponding L2 frame. A system with multiple L3 addresses (usually a router) provides

---

* We saw in Part IV how bridges and switches manage to direct frames only to the right host when possible, reducing in this way the useless delivery of frames to every host in the LAN.

multiple interfaces so that the one-to-one relationship between L3 addresses and L2 addresses is preserved. But as the later section "Special Cases" explains, multiple multicast addresses at the L3 layer can map to the same L2 address. It is also possible for an interface to be configured with multiple IP addresses.

Shared Medium

In a shared medium, any frame transmitted by one host is received by all the hosts directly connected to it. A simple example is a wireless link. Another common example is the shared coaxial cable used with Ethernet 10-base2.

For this reason, link layer protocols used in shared media need to define an addressing scheme so that a transmitter can specify the recipient of each frame, and the recipient can identify the sender. The addressing scheme usually also defines special addresses that can be used to address a frame to multiple hosts or to all of the hosts: the multicast and broadcast addresses.

Because multiple hosts may need to transmit and therefore use the shared medium at the same time, the link layer protocol must include a way to make sure all hosts connected to the medium detect this situation—called a *collision*—because the result is a corrupted frame. Ethernet uses the so-called Carrier Sense Multiple Access with Collision Detection protocol (CSMA/CD). We won't look at how collisions are handled because that is off-topic for this chapter. Information on all things Ethernet-related can be found in *Ethernet: The Definitive Guide* (O'Reilly).

On the other hand, point-to-point media, such as serial lines, are designed for communication between two endpoints only. In this case, there is no need to use a link layer address to identify the source and destination endpoints. The two endpoints can communicate in either half duplex or full duplex, depending on whether they share the same wire or have one each. In either case, there is no need for a collision detection mechanism: the two endpoints are either assigned one wire each (full duplex) or have a mechanism that each end can use to take ownership of the shared wire. As a consequence, there is no need for a neighboring protocol when two hosts are connected through a point-to-point medium.

Ethernet was first designed to work with a shared medium, allowing hosts to share the same medium and rely on CSMA/CD to handle collisions. This was the shared coaxial cable era (i.e., 10Base-2). However, over time the use of shared coaxial cables has been replaced with the use of unshielded twisted pair (UTP) wire, or RJ-45 wire, for a variety of reasons. The latter allows Ethernet interfaces to be configured in both half-duplex and full-duplex mode, because the UTP cable includes enough wires to allow both ends to speak at the same time. Ethernet in full-duplex mode can be used only on point-to-point connections between two Ethernet interfaces. In such a case, each end of the connection is assigned one wire for transmission and one for reception, so there is no need for CSMA/CD.

Nowadays, Ethernet LANs are mainly implemented with switches:* you connect each host to a switch with a UTP cable. In these scenarios, you can either configure the interfaces in half-duplex mode, in which case CMSA/CD is used to handle collisions between the switch port and the host's Ethernet adapter, or you can configure the two interfaces in full-duplex mode and allow both the host and the switch to transmit simultaneously. Both endpoints must use the same duplex configurations. In most cases, there is no need to explicitly configure the duplex mode on the two ends of the connection, because a duplex detection mechanism takes care of it.

Note that the frames generated by the hosts are never addressed to the switch (although there are exceptions to this general rule); the switch is used by a host to reach the other hosts connected to the same switch. Therefore, even though you do not need CSMA/CD when the interfaces are in full-duplex mode, you still need the source and destination addresses, and therefore a neighboring protocol. This also means that the multicast and broadcast capabilities that were provided by a really shared medium, such as the coaxial cable, are now provided by the switch by other means: when the switch receives a frame addressed to a multicast or broadcast link layer address, it copies it to all ports except for the one from which the frame is received. We saw in Part IV that switches are actually smarter than this.

Given that modern LANs are mainly implemented with Ethernet switches, and hosts are connected to switches with point-to-point links (UTP), the use of CSMA/CD has become of secondary importance in the design of newer Ethernet standards. Also for this reason (among others), newer Ethernet standards designed for higher speeds made the use of CSMA/CD optional or removed it altogether.

Table 26-1 indicates which flavors of Ethernet support CSMA/CD. Note that Gigabit Ethernet still supports CSMA/CD (shared), even though it is mainly used for full-duplex point-to-point connections. 10 Gigabit Ethernet, standardized mainly for use with WANs (as opposed to LANs), does not support CSMA/CD at all, and can be used for point-to-point links over fiber-optic media only. For each element of Table 26-1 there are actually many variants, but I did not include them because they are not needed for our discussion.

Table 26-1. Ethernet flavors and point-to-point/shared medium capabilities

Ethernet flavor	Point-to-point only	Shared (i.e., supports CSMA/CD)
Ethernet (10 Mbit/s)		X
Fast Ethernet (100 Mbits/s)		X
Gigabit Ethernet		X
10 Gigabit Ethernet	X	

---

* In this book, bridges and switches are used to refer to the same type of device. See Part IV for more details.

Why Static Assignment of Addresses Is Not Sufficient

We already saw in Chapter 13 the roles of L2 and L3 addresses and protocols. L3 addresses, such as IP addresses, are logical; this means that any valid address can be assigned to any interface. L2 addresses, on the other hand, are bound to NICs and are not supposed to be configurable: they are assigned to the interfaces by the vendors and are unique worldwide. However, most NICs can be configured to use arbitrary L2 addresses via common tools like *ifconfig*. This may be useful when dealing with local IEEE addresses, as described in Chapter 13. But when you change the L2 address of an NIC to a value that you do not own, you do it at your own risk: you are not assured anymore that the address is unique and can therefore operate correctly on a shared medium where NICs are identified by their L2 addresses. Normally this is done in special configurations by highly educated administrators, such as virtual servers or high-availability setups.

Because L3 addresses are logical, they can change for many reasons. Here are some common cases where an L3 address can change. These require the mapping between the L3 address and the associated L2 address to change as well.

Dynamic configuration
> In IP networks, a host can be assigned a dynamic IP address by means of a protocol such as DHCP. The same host can be given a different IP address every time it asks for one, but the hardware address is hardcoded into the Ethernet or wireless card, so the L3-to-L2 mapping must be updated accordingly.

Replacement of a faulty interface
> The L2 address changes once the NIC is replaced, but the administrator would probably prefer to keep the same logical configuration on the network, and therefore the same L3 address.

Moving an L3 address
> A server may go down and require the same traffic to be handled by a different server; this means the old L3 address should be associated with a new server and a new interface. The change is required also if an administrator keeps the L3 address on the same host but uses a different interface.

To keep all of these changes isolated from both the L2 and L3 layers—because they have plenty of work to do without handling all the eventualities and caching involved—a protocol is needed to manage the association of L3 to L2 addresses. That is the neighboring protocol discussed in this part of the book.

Special Cases

Sometimes there is no need for any protocol to resolve the L3 address to an L2 address. These cases include the following:

- There is only one host that data can be sent to on a point-to-point medium, such as a dial-up connection or a cable connecting a system temporarily to one that an administrator wants to monitor. Here, there is no addressing scheme at all at the L2 level. (However, even point-to-point media use L2 addresses in some contexts.)

- There may be special L3 addresses whose associated L2 addresses can be obtained with a simple formula; because there is no ambiguity and no dynamic allocation, no protocol is needed.

- Multicast addresses can be statically translated without any protocol. On IPv4/ ARP networks, multicast addresses are resolved using the function arp_mc_map, which in turn invokes the very simple function ip_eth_mc_map when the device is an Ethernet NIC. The mapping in ip_eth_mc_map is done by a formula, without any protocol, as explained here and illustrated in Figure 26-4:

  - The most-significant 24 bits are assigned the static value 01:00:5E allocated by IANA.

  - Bit 23 (the most-significant bit of the lower 24) is set to 0.

  - The least-significant 23 bits are copied from the least-significant 23 bits of the IP address.

  Note that the same Ethernet multicast address can be assigned to multiple IP addresses (because the most-significant 9 bits of the IP address are not used).

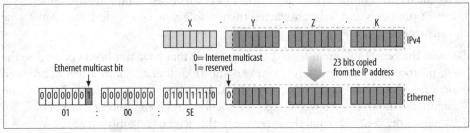

Figure 26-4. Generation of an Ethernet multicast address from an IPv4 multicast address

- Broadcast addresses (IP subnet broadcasts) are statically resolved to the link layer broadcast address (FF:FF:FF:FF:FF:FF for Ethernet). The L2 broadcast address of each device can also be explicitly configured, if needed.

Solicitation Requests and Replies

When an L3-to-L2 mapping cannot be resolved through a static translation as described in the previous section, a neighboring protocol is needed to do the mapping. Different protocols may use different mechanisms. But for all of these protocols, it's useful to be familiar with the following terminology, which we'll use extensively in this part of the book:

Solicitation request (also called a neighbor solicitation*)*
  This refers to the transmission of a packet on the network to ask all of the hosts whether any knows the L2 address associated with a given L3 address. This request can be sent as unicast, multicast, or broadcast, depending on both the protocol and the context.

Solicitation reply (also called a neighbor advertisement*)*
  This is the packet that is normally sent in reply to a solicitation request. But it could also be generated independently (see the section "Gratuitous ARP" in Chapter 28 for an example). Under normal conditions, the host associated with the target L3 address generates the reply, but it is possible to have another host reply in its place (see the section "Proxying the Neighboring Protocol"). It is normally sent as unicast, but under specific conditions broadcasts are possible, too.

Linux Implementation

Early Linux kernels had L3 protocols call functions provided by neighboring protocols directly. The IPv4 subsystem, therefore, interacted directly with the ARP code. In recent versions of the kernel, developers have identified common requirements for different protocols and have abstracted them into a new layer called the *neighboring infrastructure*.

Because the kernel still includes old pieces of code that have not been updated to the new, protocol-independent layer, you can still find direct calls to a few deprecated functions of the ARP code (e.g., arp_find), but they are exceptions. The section "Common Interface Between L3 Protocols and Neighboring Protocols" in Chapter 27 discusses in detail the interface to the neighboring infrastructure.

Figure 26-5 shows the key parts of Linux's neighboring subsystems and the other parts of the kernel with which they interact. The L3 protocols interact with the neighboring layer via a common interface, which uses the right neighboring protocol (ARP, ND, etc.) depending on the L3 protocol that is asking for the service.[*]

When transmitting a packet, the following steps take place:

 1. The routing subsystem of the local host selects the L3 destination address (the next hop).

---

[*] The figure does not include DECnet and ATM, because they are not covered in this book.

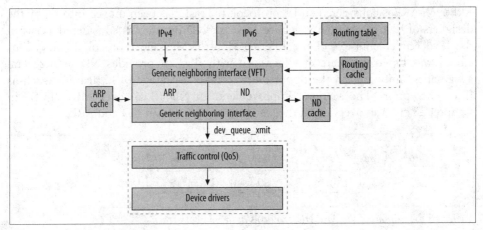

Figure 26-5. The big picture

2. If according to the routing table, this hop is on the same network (if, that is, the next hop is a neighbor), the neighboring layer resolves the destination's L3 address to its L2 address. This association is cached for future use. Thus, if one application sends several packets of data in a short amount of time to another application, the neighboring protocol is used only once, to send the first packet.

3. Eventually, a function such as dev_queue_xmit (described in Chapter 11) takes care of the transmission, handing the packet to the Traffic Control or Quality of Service (QoS) layer. Although Figure 26-5 shows only dev_queue_xmit, the neighboring layer can actually invoke other functions as well (mostly wrappers around dev_queue_xmit), as we will see later in this chapter.

Note that dev_queue_xmit is called when the packet to transmit is ready to go, so if an L2 header is needed, the neighboring layer must add it before calling the function. Certain types of transmissions—point-to-point connections, broadcasts, and multicasts—do not require any L2 layer header and therefore do not need an L3-to-L2 mapping; these transmissions are covered in the section "Special Cases." Other transmissions use a shared medium and therefore need an L2 header, either from the neighboring subsystem's cache or through a request issued by the neighboring subsystem to the network.

Neighboring Protocols

Two protocols are in use in IP networks today. The vast majority of systems use ARP with IPv4. A more general-purpose protocol called Neighbor Discovery (ND) was developed for IPv6. Other neighboring protocols are also implemented in the Linux kernel for use with proprietary networks, such as the one used by DECnet, but we will not cover them in this book due to their limited use.

Although ARP is considered an L3 protocol, the task has been moved into L4 by the designers of IPv6. As shown in Figure 26-6, the ND protocol is considered a part of the IPv6 implementation of the Internet Control Message Protocol (ICMP). This choice was based on years of experience with IPv4. It provides ND with several advantages, among them the opportunity to take advantage of L3 features such as IPsec encryption. The section "Improvements in ND (IPv6) over ARP (IPv4)" in Chapter 28 gives an overview of the key differences between ND and ARP.

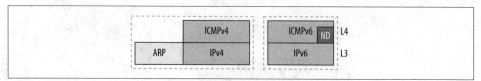

Figure 26-6. Positions of the ARP/ND protocols in the network stack

As mentioned, Linux also provides a common infrastructure to reduce overhead and code replication for services that are very similar across all neighboring protocols. The generic neighboring infrastructure provides services that can be tailored by different protocols to suit their needs. Here are some of the services provided by the infrastructure to the protocols:

- A per-protocol cache to store the results of L3-to-L2 translations.
- Functions to add, remove, change, and look up a specific translation entry in the cache. Because the lookup function influences the performance of the system most of all, it must be fast.
- An aging mechanism for the entries in the per-protocol cache.
- A choice of policies to follow when there is a request for a new translation entry to be created in the cache, and the cache is full.
- A per-neighbor request queue. When a packet is ready to be sent and the L2 address is not already in the cache, the packet must be buffered until a solicitation request is sent and the reply is received. See the section "Queuing" in Chapter 27.

To let each protocol tailor the behavior of the neighboring subsystem, it defines a set of placeholder or virtual functions for which each protocol plugs in the functions it wants to use. This is similar to the way much of the Linux kernel allows customization. The neighboring layer also provides a bunch of tuning parameters that can be configured via user-space commands, /proc, or the protocol itself. Finally, the functions to access the cache are common to all of the protocols, but different protocols may use keys (addresses) of different sizes. Therefore, the infrastructure provides a generic way to define which type of key to use. Later chapters will cover all of these points in detail.

Each protocol can run and be configured independently from the others. The section "Protocol Initialization and Cleanup" in Chapter 27 shows how a neighboring protocol registers and unregisters itself with the kernel.

Proxying the Neighboring Protocol

When a host intercepts traffic addressed to another host and processes it in place of the latter, it is said to act as a *proxy*. The term does not, of course, cover a malicious host that launches a man-in-the-middle attack. Rather, a common example of a proxy is a caching HTTP server that cuts down on network traffic by intercepting requests directed to popular web servers and serving up pages from those web servers that are stored in its own cache.

If hosts and applications do not need to be explicitly configured to benefit from the services provided by a proxy, this proxy is said to be *transparent*. The caching HTTP server just mentioned is an example of a transparent proxy. But as Figure 26-7 shows, a service could be provided by either a transparent proxy or a nontransparent proxy. The figure shows two examples of an HTTP proxy in use:

- (a) The proxy is installed on the router used by a local network to access the Internet. All browser requests from hosts on the network go through the router, so the administrator can configure the router to intercept and proxy all HTTP requests. This is considered transparent proxying because no configuration or specially programmed browser is needed on Host B.

- (b) The browser of Host B is configured to use the proxy on the host named Proxy to browse the Internet. The host Proxy uses the router when it is needed (that is, when there is a cache miss).

Of course, several other options are possible. For instance, the proxy may be a separate machine, while the router is configured to relay HTTP requests to the proxy. I will not go into detail on this topic, because it is a large topic outside the context of this book. Proxies for neighboring protocols are normally transparent.

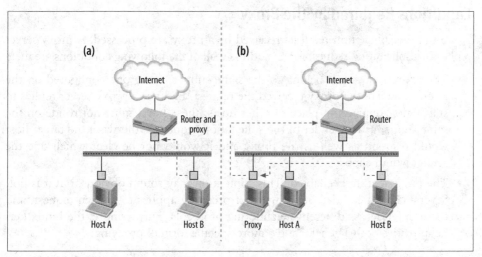

Figure 26-7. (a) Transparent proxy; (b) nontransparent proxy

The previous example showed one popular type of proxying: HTTP or web proxying. Now let's consider proxying in relation to this part of the book. A proxying server for a neighboring protocol is a host that is configured to reply to solicitation requests for addresses it does not own, in place of other hosts that actually have those addresses. Thanks to the proxy, hosts located on different LANs can talk to each other as if they were on the same LAN.

For instance, proxy ARP is commonly used in IPv4 networks to help in transitions from flat to subnetted networks. The hosts do not need special protocols or configuration because the proxy is transparent to them. But if the proxy server goes down, the connectivity to the hosts being proxied is lost, too. This can be mitigated by providing multiple proxy servers. In that case, a host may receive multiple solicitation replies to its (broadcast) requests. By selecting the first one, a host probably gets the fastest or least-loaded proxy server.

The use of proxies can also simplify the configuration of hosts taken care of by a proxy; one example is provided in the section "Proxy VS Router" in Chapter 28.

Among the neighboring protocols implemented in the Linux kernel, only IPv4 and IPv6 can use the proxy feature. The common infrastructure is shared by both protocols, each of which tailors proxying behavior to its needs. The differences are explained in the section "Improvements in ND (IPv6) over ARP (IPv4)" in Chapter 28.

In the section "Acting As a Proxy" in Chapter 27, we will see the implementation of the protocol-independent component of this feature in detail (timers, queues, etc.). In the section "Proxy ARP" in Chapter 28, we will see details on the specific case of IPv4 and ARP.

Conditions Required by the Proxy

Not all of the solicitation requests received by a proxy are processed. A proxy server replies to a solicitation request for an address if all of the following conditions are met:

- The address does not belong to the same subnet as the one configured on the interface where the proxy received the request. Because a proxy server replies to solicitation requests in place of other hosts, these hosts must not reside on the same subnet as the sender of the solicitation request. Otherwise, the target host would respond as well as the proxy and it would not be clear which one the sender would choose.

- The proxy feature is enabled. This stipulation may sound obvious, but it is not. Several criteria can determine whether proxying applies to a given request, and these differ across different neighboring protocols. Furthermore, the Linux kernel provides both a general and a more-specific form of proxying:

Device based

> All valid requests received on the device are processed. This is the most common case in IPv4 networks. IPv6 does not use it.

Destination based

> Both the destination address and the device are taken into account during the decision whether to proxy. This means that a proxy can reply to requests for selected IP addresses. Destination-based proxying is standard in IPv6 networks, but is available for IPv4, too.

Figure 26-8 shows the precedence between the two kinds of proxying. When a host receives a solicitation request for an address outside the local subnet, the host may process it if proxying is enabled. First the subsystem checks whether proxying is enabled globally on the device, and if not, whether the device is configured to proxy that particular address.

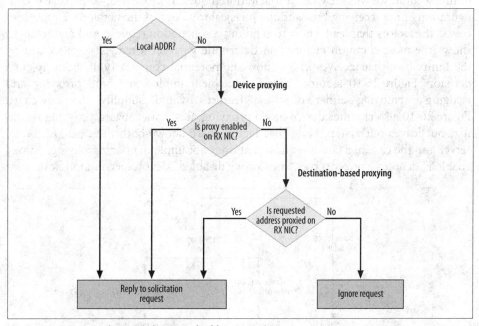

Figure 26-8. Priority between device and address proxying

- Forwarding is enabled on the proxy server on which the request was received.

Because the proxy server interpolates itself between hosts, it has to accept forwarded traffic between the two endpoints.[*]

---

[*] This does not mean that by enabling proxying on the proxy host, you also automatically enable forwarding. The two features are configured separately, but proxying requires forwarding to function properly.

ARP solicitation requests are always sent to the L2 broadcast address. This ensures that all of the hosts sharing the same medium receive it. Thus, a proxy can intercept requests addressed to those hosts it proxies for without having to put any of its interfaces into promiscuous mode. When doing reachability confirmation (see the section "Reachability Confirmation"), ARP uses unicasts rather than broadcasts.

ND uses L3 multicast addresses to handle solicitation requests and replies. When a router wants to proxy a given IP address, it needs to subscribe to the associated L3 multicast address.

When Solicitation Requests Are Transmitted and Processed

In this section, we will see when a solicitation request is processed, based on the configuration of the receiving host and the physical topology of the network. Figure 26-9 covers the factors that lead a host to send out a solicitation request, and Figure 26-10 shows the most-common factors that determine whether a request is processed by the Linux host that receives it. To show the potential complexity of the recipient's decision, Figure 26-10 assumes that the recipient implements both proxying and bridging[*]; removing either of these features would simplify the flowchart. Figure 26-10 also assumes device-based proxying; destination-based proxying is similar, but leaves out a step. Note that Figure 26-10 shows both the case of a proxy server and the case of a common host that does not implement any proxying: "proxy enabled" denotes a proxy server, and "proxy disabled" denotes a common host.

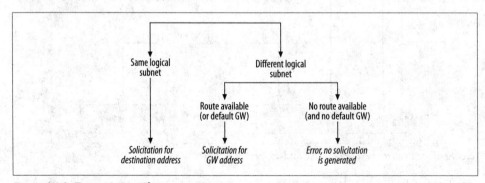

Figure 26-9. Transmitting solicitation requests

This is a protocol-independent analysis; particulars about ARP are shown in Chapter 28.

---

[*] I added bridging to Figure 26-10 to show that bridging is handled before the neighboring protocols, and therefore the latter may not always see ingress solicitation requests. Bridging is described in detail in Part IV.

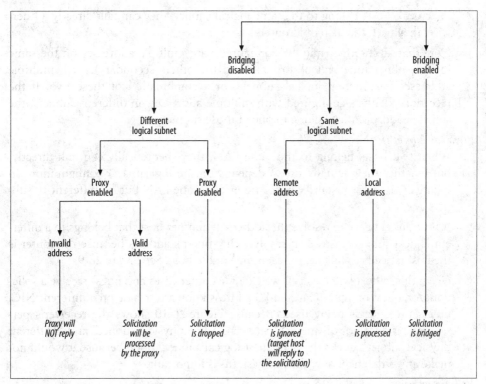

Figure 26-10. Processing ingress solicitation requests

When bridging is enabled, solicitation requests are not processed by the receiving host, but are instead forwarded (bridged) to the right interfaces according to the bridging configuration. Bridging takes place before the neighboring protocol has a chance to look at the ingress packets. In other words, as the figure shows, bridging is handled before proxying in the Linux implementation of handling solicitation requests. See Part IV for details.

Let's suppose bridging is disabled. Keeping in mind that a host that sits on a shared medium can receive solicitation requests for addresses that belong to other hosts, here are the variables that can influence whether a Linux host replies to an ingress solicitation request:

Logical subnet (e.g., IP subnet)
   "Same logical subnet" in Figure 26-10 is true when the solicited address and the L3 address configured on the NIC that receives the solicitation request belong to the same logical subnet (according to the configuration of the receiving host). If we take IPv4 as an example, 10.0.0.1 (as the solicited address) and 10.0.0.2/24 (as the address configured on the receiving NIC) would belong to the same 10.0.0.0/24 IP subnet.

When two hosts belong to the same logical subnet, they can talk directly. Otherwise, they need the help of a router.

Note that an interface may be configured with multiple addresses on the same logical subnet (one will be primary and the others secondary), with multiple addresses on different logical subnets, or a combination of these two. If the receiving NIC was configured with multiple addresses on different subnets, the solicited address must belong to one of those subnets.

Physical subnet (LAN)

When two hosts belong to the same LAN, they theoretically can talk directly, but whether they actually do so depends on the logical (L3) configuration. In Figure 26-1(c), for instance, hosts are on the same LAN but on different IP subnets.

A host does not try to resolve the address of another host that belongs to a different logical subnet; instead, it resolves the router's address because the router is the host it needs to talk to, to reach the remote host. See Figure 26-9.

Given this, a host will never (if we exclude corner cases and bugs) receive a solicitation request on an NIC for an L3 address known to reside on a different NIC, unless proxying is being used. Because Figure 26-10 shows the receiver's perspective, it does not distinguish between "Same physical subnet" and "Different physical subnet" under the "Different logical subnet" node because it would not make any difference: only the proxy status is important.

Proxy requirement

Not all of the solicitation requests received by a proxy are processed. See the section "Conditions Required by the Proxy" for details.

The section "Processing Ingress ARP Packets" in Chapter 28 shows how the various situations in Figure 26-10 are handled by the ARP protocol.

Neighbor States and Network Unreachability Detection (NUD)

Figure 26-11 is a simplified summary of the steps the kernel has to go through when transmitting a packet to a given L3 address.

Figure 26-12 is a simplified model that shows the states a neighbor can go through.

The two simple models in Figures 26-11 and 26-12 would work in most cases, but the Linux kernel uses a more sophisticated model to handle all possible states. The next section will expand the model in Figure 26-12, and later sections will focus on the details in Figure 26-11.

As you can see, an important part of managing neighbors is to know whether they are *reachable*.

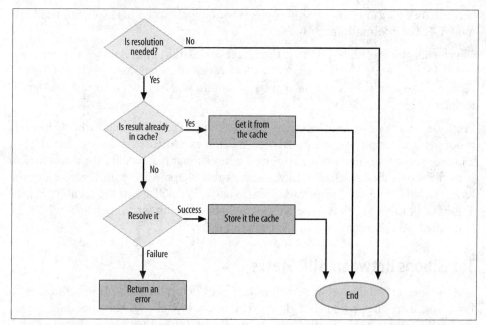

Figure 26-11. L3-to-L2 address resolution steps

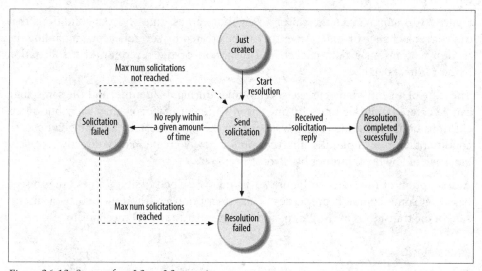

Figure 26-12. States of an L3-to-L2 mapping

Reachability

Reachability, from the neighboring subsystem's perspective, can be described through a real-life analogy. Suppose you are in a dark room with other people, including me. If you say "Everybody out of the room!" everybody will leave the room because they all can hear you. But if you want only me to go out, you will need one more piece of information: my name.

Thus, a solicitation reply sent to a broadcast destination address does not carry the same amount of information as one with a unicast destination address: anyone can receive a broadcast, but you need the exact address if you want to talk to a given recipient.

From the neighboring perspective, a host is considered reachable if the kernel has proof that the recipient can correctly receive frames addressed at its unicast address, and vice versa. In other words, you need bidirectional reachability for the kernel to consider a neighbor reachable. In the rest of this chapter, we will therefore use the term *reachable* to mean bidirectional reachability. We will see in the section "Reachability Confirmation" that there are two possible ways in which reachability can be confirmed: L4 confirmation and a solicitation reply.

Transitions Between NUD States

IPv6 defines an NUD mechanism that can help determine quickly whether neighbors have disconnected or gone down. The Linux kernel uses the same mechanism for both IPv4 and IPv6. Similar models are used by the other protocols we will not cover in the book, such as DECnet.

Figure 26-13 summarizes the states a neighbor can assume and the conditions that can trigger a change of state. An entry can be created by several events, including the request to transmit a data packet to a neighbor, or the reception of a solicitation request from a neighbor.

The state of an entry may change several times during its lifetime, and the same state can be entered multiple times by one entry. Different protocols may carry out different transitions, including some not shown in the figure, to take advantage of special conditions. For example, the link that puts a newly created entry directly into NUD_ STALE is used by IPv4, but not by IPv6.

A description of the states in Figure 26-13 follows. The possible values are grouped based on some common properties. This description will be followed by a discussion of the transitions in the graph, and in particular the NUD mechanism.

Basic states

The states in Figure 26-13 are defined as follows. We start with the default state of a newly created entry:

NUD_NONE
   The neighbor entry has just been created and no state is available yet.

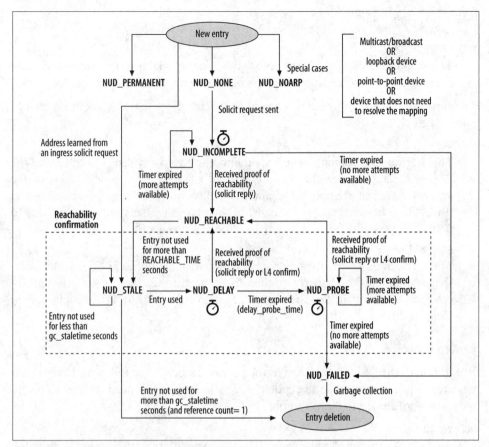

Figure 26-13. Transitions among NUD states

This next set comes from the IPv6 neighboring definition and has been adopted by the latest Linux ARP/IPv4 implementation as well:

NUD_INCOMPLETE

A solicitation has been sent, but no reply has been received yet. In this state, there is no hardware address to use (not even an old one, as there is with NUD_STALE).

NUD_REACHABLE

The address of the neighbor is cached and the latter is known to be reachable (there has been a proof of reachability).

NUD_FAILED

Marks a neighbor as unreachable because of a failed solicitation request, either the one generated when the entry was created or the one triggered by the NUD_PROBE state.

```
NUD_STALE
NUD_DELAY
NUD_PROBE
```
Transitional states; they will be resolved when the local host determines whether the neighbor is reachable. See the section "Reachability Confirmation."

The next set of values represents a group of special states that usually never change once assigned:

```
NUD_NOARP
```
This state is used to mark neighbors that do not need any protocol to resolve the L3-to-L2 mapping (see the section "Special Cases"). The section "Start of the arp_constructor Function" in Chapter 28 shows how and why this state is set in IPv4/ARP. But even though the name of this state suggests that it applies only to ARP, it can actually be used by any neighboring protocol.

```
NUD_PERMANENT
```
The L2 address of the neighbor has been statically configured (i.e., with user-space commands) and therefore there is no need to use any neighboring protocol to take care of it. See the section "System Administration of Neighbors" in Chapter 29.

Derived states

In addition to the basic states listed in the previous section, the following derived values are defined just to make the code clearer when there is a need to refer to multiple states with something in common:

```
NUD_VALID
```
An entry is considered to be in the NUD_VALID state if its state is any one of the following, which represent neighbors believed to have an available address:

```
    NUD_PERMANENT
    NUD_NOARP
    NUD_REACHABLE
    NUD_PROBE
    NUD_STALE
    NUD_DELAY
```

```
NUD_CONNECTED
```
This is used for the subset of NUD_VALID states that do not have a confirmation process pending:

```
    NUD_PERMANENT
    NUD_NOARP
    NUD_REACHABLE
```

```
NUD_IN_TIMER
```
The neighboring subsystem is running a timer for this entry, which happens when the status is unclear. The basic states that correspond to this are:

```
NUD_INCOMPLETE
NUD_DELAY
NUD_PROBE
```

Let's look at an example of why a derived state is useful in kernel code. When a neighbor instance is removed, the host needs to stop all the pending timers associated with that data structure. Instead of comparing the neighbor's state to the three states known to have a pending timer associated with them, it is just cleaner to define NUD_IN_TIMER and compare the neighbor's state against it using the bitwise operator &.

Initial state

When a neighbor instance is created, the NUD_NONE state is assigned to it by default, but the state can also be explicitly set to something different when the creation is caused by an explicit user command (see Chapter 29).

As explained in the section "Neighbor Initialization" in Chapter 27, the protocol's constructor method may also change the state depending on the characteristics of the associated device (e.g., point-to-point) and L3 address (e.g., broadcast).

Reachability Confirmation

We saw in the section "Why Static Assignment of Addresses Is Not Sufficient" that it is possible for an L3-to-L2 mapping to change. Because of this, it makes sense to confirm the information stored in the cache regularly, if the information has not been used for some time. This is called *reachability confirmation*.

Note that a change in reachability status is not necessarily due to the reasons listed in the section "Reasons That Neighboring Protocols Are Needed"; a router, bridge, or other network device may just be experiencing some problems. While the reachability confirmation is in progress, the cached information is temporarily used under the assumption that it is most likely still valid.

The three NUD states NUD_STALE, NUD_DELAY, and NUD_PROBE support the task of reachability confirmation. The key reason for the use of these states is that there is no need to start a reachability confirmation process until a packet needs to be sent to the associated neighbor.

Let's define once again the exact meaning of these three NUD states, and then look at the two ways a mapping can be confirmed:

NUD_STALE

The cache contains the address of the neighbor, but the latter has not been confirmed for a certain amount of time (see the discussion of reachable_time in the section "neigh_parms Structure" in Chapter 29). The next time a packet is sent to the neighbor, the reachability verification process will be started.

NUD_DELAY

This state, closely tied to NUD_STALE, represents an optimization that can reduce the number of transmissions of solicitation requests.

This state is entered when a packet is sent to a neighbor whose associated entry is in the NUD_STALE state. The NUD_DELAY state represents a window of time where external sources could confirm the reachability of the neighbor. The simplest sort of external confirmation is when the neighbor in question sends a packet, thus indicating that it is running and accessible.

This state gives some time to the upper network layers to provide a reachability confirmation, which may relieve the kernel from sending a solicitation request and thus save both bandwidth and CPU usage. This state may look like a small optimization, but if you think in terms of big networks, you can imagine the gain it can provide.

If no confirmation is received, the entry is put into the next state, NUD_PROBE, which resolves the status of the neighbor through explicit solicitation requests or whatever other mechanism a protocol might use.

NUD_PROBE

When the neighbor has been in the NUD_DELAY state for the allotted amount of time and no proof of reachability has been received, its state is changed to NUD_PROBE and the solicitation process starts.

The reachability status of a neighbor can be confirmed in two main ways. As we will see, these two methods do not have the same level of authority. They are:

Confirmation from a unicast solicitation's reply

When your host receives a solicitation reply in answer to a solicitation request it previously sent out, it means that the neighbor received the request and was able to send back a reply; this in turn means that either it already had your L2 address or it learned your address from your request (see the section "Creating a neighbour Entry" in Chapter 27. It also means that there is a working path in both directions. Note, however, that this is true only when the solicitation's reply is sent as a unicast packet. The reception of a broadcast reply would move the state to NUD_STALE rather than NUD_REACHABLE. (You can find more discussion of this from the standpoint of ARP in the section "Processing Ingress ARP Packets" in Chapter 28.)

External confirmation

If your host is sure it received a packet from the neighbor in response to something previously sent, it can assume the neighbor is still reachable. Figure 26-14 shows an example, where the TCP layer of Host A confirms the reachability of Host B when it receives a SYN/ACK in reply to its SYN. Note that if Host B was not a neighbor of Host A, the reception of the SYN/ACK from Host B would confirm the reachability of the next hop gateway used by Host A to reach Host B.

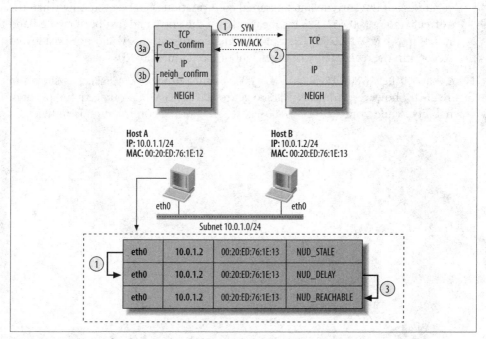

Figure 26-14. Example of external neighbor reachability confirmation

Confirmation is done via `dst_confirm`, which confirms the validity of the routing table cache entry used to route the SYN packet toward Host B. `dst_confirm` is a simple wrapper around `neigh_confirm`, which accomplishes the task we described earlier: it confirms the reachability of the neighbor and therefore the L3-to-L2 mapping. Note that `neigh_confirm` only updates the `neigh->confirmed` timestamp; it will be the `neigh_periodic_timer` function (which is executed by the expiration of the timer started when the neighbor entered the `NUD_DELAY` state) that actually upgrades the neighbor entry's state to `NUD_REACHABLE`.[*]

Note that the correlation between the two packets in Figure 26-14 could not be performed at the IP layer because the latter doesn't have any knowledge of data

---

[*] The delay between the reception of the confirmation from the L4 layer and the setting of the state to `NUD_REACHABLE` does not affect traffic in any way.

streams. This is why the L4 layer takes care of the confirmation. TCP SYN/ACK exchanges are only one example of an L4 protocol providing external confirmation. Given a socket, and therefore the associated routing cache entry and its next-hop gateway, a user-space application can confirm the reachability of the gateway by using the MSG_CONFIRM option with transmission calls such as send and sendmsg.

While the reception of a solicitation's reply can move the state to NUD_REACHABLE regardless of the current state, external confirmations can be used only when the current state is NUD_STALE. This means that if the entry had just been created and it was in the NUD_INCOMPLETE state, external confirmations would not be allowed to confirm the reachability of the neighbor (see Figure 26-13).

Note that NUD_DELAY/NUD_PROBE and NUD_NONE can lead to NUD_REACHABLE, as shown in Figure 26-13; however, from NUN_NONE to get to NUD_REACHABLE, you need full proof of reachability, while from NUD_DELAY/NUD_PROBE, any kind of confirmation is sufficient.

## CHAPTER 27

Neighboring Subsystem: Infrastructure

In Chapter 26, we saw the main problems that the neighboring protocols are asked to solve. You also learned that the Linux kernel abstracted out parts of the solution into a common *infrastructure* shared by various neighboring protocols. In this chapter, we will see how the infrastructure is designed. In particular, we will see how protocols interface to the common infrastructure, how caching and proxying are implemented, and how external subsystems such as higher-layer protocols notify the neighboring protocols about interesting events. We will conclude the chapter with a description of how L3 protocols such as IPv4 actually interface with their neighboring protocols, and how queuing is implemented for buffers awaiting address resolution.

Main Data Structures

To understand the code for the neighboring infrastructure, we first need to describe a few data structures used heavily in the neighboring subsystem, and see how they interact with each other.

Most of the definitions for these structures can be found in the file *include/net/ neighbour.h*. Note that the Linux kernel code uses the British spelling *neighbour* for data structures and functions related to this subsystem. When speaking generically of neighbors, this book sticks to the American spelling, which is the spelling found in RFCs and other official documents.

struct neighbour

> Stores information about a neighbor, such as the L2 and L3 addresses, the NUD state, the device through which the neighbor can be reached, etc. Note that a neighbour entry is associated not with a host, but with an L3 address. There can be more than one L3 address for a host. For example, routers, among other systems, have multiple interfaces and therefore multiple L3 addresses.

struct neigh_table

Describes a neighboring protocol's parameters and functions. There is one instance of this structure for each neighboring protocol. All of the structures are inserted into a global list pointed to by the static variable neigh_tables and protected by the lock neigh_tbl_lock. This lock protects the integrity of the list, but not the content of each entry.

struct neigh_parms

A set of parameters that can be used to tune the behavior of a neighboring protocol on a per-device basis. Since more than one protocol can be enabled on most interfaces (for instance, IPv4 and IPv6), more than one neigh_parms structure can be associated with a net_device structure.

struct neigh_ops

A set of functions that represents the interface between the L3 protocols such as IP and dev_queue_xmit, the API introduced in Chapter 11 and described briefly in the upcoming section "Common Interface Between L3 Protocols and Neighboring Protocols." The virtual functions can change based on the context in which they are used (that is, on the status of the neighbor, as described in Chapter 26).

struct hh_cache

Caches link layer headers to speed up transmission. It is faster to copy a cached header into a buffer in one shot than to fill in its fields one by one. Not all device drivers implement header caching. See the section "L2 Header Caching."

struct rtable
struct dst_entry

When a host needs to route a packet, it first consults its cache and then, in the case of a cache miss, it queries the routing table. Every time the host queries the routing table, the result is saved into the cache. The IPv4 routing cache is composed of rtable structures. Each instance is associated with a different destination IP address. Among the fields of the rtable structure are the destination address, the next hop (router), and a structure of type dst_entry that is used to store the protocol-independent information. dst_entry includes a pointer to the neighbour structure associated with the next hop. I cover the dst_entry data structure in detail in Chapter 36. In the rest of this chapter, I will often refer to dst_entry structures as elements of the routing table cache, even though dst_entry is actually only a field of the rtable structure.

Figure 27-1 shows how dst_entry structures are linked to hh_cache and neighbour structures.

The neighboring code also uses some other small data structures. For instance, struct pneigh_entry is used by destination-based proxying, and struct neigh_statistics is used to collect statistics about neighboring protocols. The first structure is described in the section "Acting As a Proxy," and the second one is described

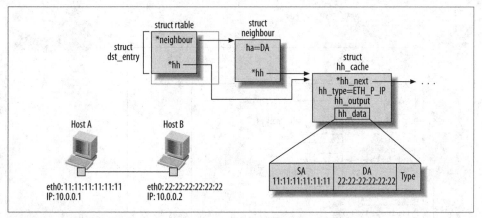

Figure 27-1. Relationship among dst_entry, neighbour, and hh_cache structures

in the section "Statistics" in Chapter 29. Figure 27-2 also includes the following data structure types, described in greater detail in Chapters 22 and 23:

in_device, inet6_dev
> Used to store the IPv4 and IPv6 configurations of a device, respectively.

net_device
> There is one net_device structure for each network device recognized by the kernel. See Chapter 8.

Figure 27-2 shows the relationships between the most important data structures. Right now it might seem a big mess, but it will make much more sense by the end of this chapter.

Here are the main points shown in Figure 27-2:

- In the central part of the figure, you can see that each network device has a pointer to a data structure that holds the configuration for each L3 protocol configured on the device. In the example shown in the figure, IPv6 is configured on one device and IPv4 is configured on both. Both the in_device structure (IPv4 configuration) and inet6_dev structure (IPv6 configuration) include a pointer to the configuration used by their neighboring protocols, respectively ARP and ND.

  All of the neigh_parms structures used by any given protocol are linked together in a unidirectional list whose root is stored in the protocol's neigh_table structure.

- The top and bottom of the figure show that each protocol keeps two hash tables. The first one, hash_buckets, caches the L3-to-L2 mappings resolved by the protocol or statically configured. The second one, phash_bucket, stores those IP addresses that are proxied, as described in the section "Per-Device Proxying and Per-Destination Proxying." Note that phash_bucket is not a cache, so its elements do not expire and don't need confirmation. Each pneigh_entry structure

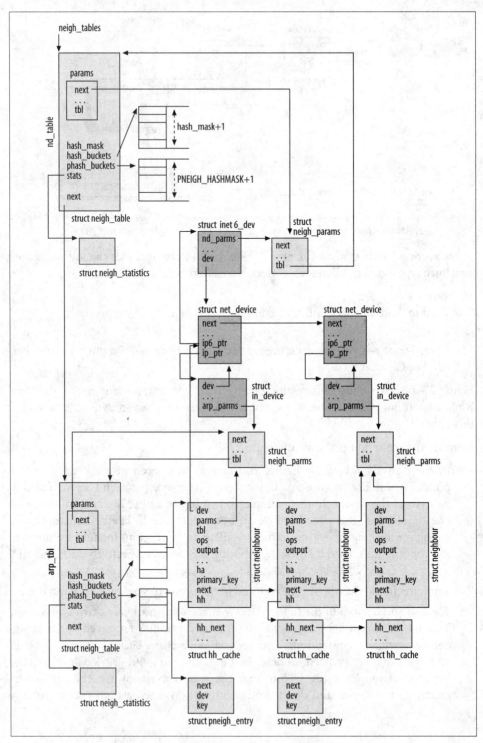

Figure 27-2. Data structures' relationships

includes a pointer (not depicted in Figure 27-2) to its associated net_device structure. Figure 27-6 gives more detail on the structure of the cache hash_buckets.

- Each neighbour instance is associated with one or more hh_cache structures, if the device supports header caching. The section "L2 Header Caching," and Figures 27-1 and 27-10, give more details about the relationship between neighbour and hh_cache structures.

Common Interface Between L3 Protocols and Neighboring Protocols

The Linux kernel has a generic neighboring layer that connects L3 protocols to the main L2 transmit function (dev_queue_xmit) via a virtual function table (VFT). A VFT is the mechanism frequently used in the Linux kernel for allowing subsystems to use different functions at different times. The VFT for the neighboring subsystem is implemented as a data structure named neigh_ops. A pointer to one of these structures is embedded as a field named ops in each neighbour structure.

The flexibility of the VFT interface allows different L3 protocols to use different neighboring protocols. This in turn allows different neighboring protocols to behave quite differently while allowing the neighboring subsystem to provide a common generic interface between the neighboring protocols and the L3 protocols.

In this section, we examine the VFT-based interface between the L3 protocols and the neighboring protocols, the advantages of using the VFT, when it is first initialized, and how it is updated during the lifetime of a neighbor. The section concludes with a brief overview of the functions used to control the initialization of the VFT. To better understand this section, you are invited to first read the section "neigh_ops Structure" in Chapter 29.

Let's start with an overview of how the routines in the VFT are invoked. Given a neighbour instance and its embedded VFT neighbour->ops, the function to which the output field points could in theory be invoked directly like this:

```
neigh->ops->output
```

But this construct is not found in the Linux code because even this is not general enough. The function in the output field of the neigh_ops structure is only one of four functions that perform similar tasks, each function having its own field in neigh_ops. The individual protocol has to decide which of the four functions to use. The proper function depends on events, the context, and the configuration of the interface and device. So, to leave the neighboring infrastructure protocol-independent, the neighbour structure contains its own output field. The individual protocol assigns the proper function from one of the fields in neigh->ops to neigh->output. This allows the code to be simpler and clearer. For instance, instead of doing:

```
if (neighbour is not reachable)
    neigh->ops->output(skb)
else
if (the device used to reach the neighbor can use cached headers)
  neigh->ops->hh_output(skb)
else
  neigh->ops->connected_output(skb)
```

the neighboring infrastructure can just call:

```
neigh->output
```

as long as neigh->output has been initialized by the protocol to the right neigh_ops method. Of course, each neighboring protocol uses its own logic to initialize neigh->output; it does not necessarily have to follow the rules in this snapshot.

When a neighbor is created, its neighbour->ops field is initialized to the proper neigh_ops structure, as shown in Figure 27-3(a). This assignment does not change during the neighbor's lifetime. However, as depicted in Figure 27-3(b), neigh->output can be changed to different functions many times during the lifetime of the neighbor structure, driven both by events that take place during protocol operation, and (much less often) by user commands. The following sections will go into detail on both initializations shown in Figure 27-3.

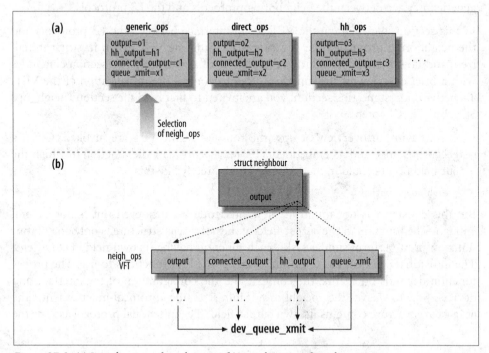

Figure 27-3. (a) Initialization of neigh->ops; (b) initialization of neigh->output

Initialization of neigh->ops

On certain types of devices, the initialization of the functions listed in Figure 27-3(b) could be further optimized to speed up transmissions. These include, for instance, the situations described in the section "Special Cases" in Chapter 26, where there is no need to map an L3 address to an L2 address. In those cases, the neighboring subsystem can almost be bypassed altogether and only the queue_xmit function described in Chapter 11 is needed. The protocol code needs to know this kind of detail, but the general neighboring infrastructure does not, so the protocol can just initialize neigh->output to neigh->ops->queue_xmit and everything remains transparent to the upper layers. Simple!

For this reason, each protocol provides for three different instances of the neigh_ops VFT:

- A generic table that can be used in any context (*xxx*_generic_ops). This is the one that is normally used to handle neighbors whose L2 addresses need to be resolved.

- An optimized set of functions that can be used when the device driver provides its own set of functions to manipulate L2 headers and thus take advantage of the speedup coming from the use of cached headers (*xxx*_hh_ops).

- A table that can be used when the device does not need to map L3 addresses to L2 addresses (*xxx*_direct_ops). An example is the use of ISDN with raw IP encapsulation.

When the neighbor instance is created, the protocol initializes the neigh_ops VFT to the right instance depending on several factors. See the section "neigh_ops Structure" in Chapter 29.

In the specific case of IPv4/ARP, a fourth instance of neigh_ops called arp_broken_ops is used to initialize those neighbour instances associated with old devices that have not been adapted to the new neighboring infrastructure and therefore would not work otherwise. This once again shows how generic the neighboring infrastructure is: by initializing the neigh_ops VFT in the right way, the kernel is even able to use the old ARP code.

Initialization of neigh->output and neigh->nud_state

The state of a neighbor (neigh->nud_state) and the neigh->output function depend on each other. When nud_state changes, output often has to be updated accordingly. As a simple example, if the state becomes stale, confirmation of reachability is required. But the neighboring infrastructure doesn't waste time confirming reachability right away; there might be no further traffic and the effort might be wasted. Instead, the neighboring infrastructure stops using the optimized output function that blindly plugs in the current address, and switches to the slower output function that checks the address. In the example in Figure 27-3(a), we would change connected_output from *c1* to *o1*.

For help in understanding this section, check Figure 26-13 in Chapter 26 for the possible states that neigh->nud_state can assume, based on device type and protocol events.

The neighboring subsystem provides a generic routine, neigh_update, that moves a neighbor to the state provided as an input argument. A later section in this chapter describes neigh_update in detail, but let's first look at the most common changes of state and the helper routines that can be called, either directly or via neigh_update, to take care of them.

Let's start with the most common case: a device that needs a neighboring protocol, an address that does not belong to any of the special cases described in Chapter 26, and a change of state caused by a transition (that is, we exclude creation and deletion).[*] Figure 26-12 in Chapter 26 can then be simplified to produce Figure 27-4. The figure also shows the kernel functions where the transitions are handled. However, not all of the transitions made by calls to neigh_update are shown, because most are too generic to add any value to the figure; only the transition triggered by the reception of a solicitation reply is shown.

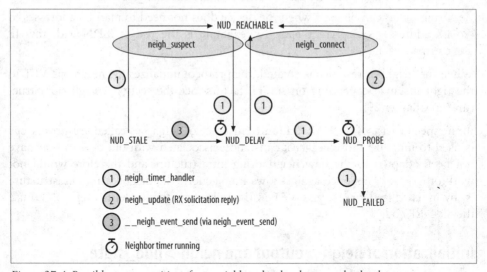

Figure 27-4. Possible state transitions for a neighbor that has been resolved at least once

---

[*] For the first initialization of neigh->output, check the source code of the constructor routines (e.g., arp_constructor/ndisc_constructor for ARP/ND). For ARP, see the section "Initialization of a neighbour Structure" in Chapter 28.

Note that some of the transitions in Figure 27-4 are asynchronous: they are taken care of by a timer and are therefore triggered by timestamp comparisons.[*] Other transitions are taken care of synchronously by the protocols (e.g., neigh_event_send[†]).

Common state changes: neigh_connect and neigh_suspect

The main ways a neighbor can enter the NUD_REACHABLE state (all described in Chapter 26) are:

Reception of a solicitation reply
> When a solicitation reply is received, either to resolve a mapping for the first time or to confirm a neighbor in the NUD_PROBE state, the protocol updates neigh->nud_state via neigh_update. This update is synchronous and happens right away.

L4 confirmation
> The first time neigh_timer_handler is executed after the reception of an L4 reachability confirmation, the state is changed to NUD_REACHABLE (see the section "Reachability Confirmation" in Chapter 26). An L4 confirmation is asynchronous and may be slightly delayed.

Manual configuration
> When a new neighbour structure is created by the user through a system administration command, this command can specify the state, and NUD_REACHABLE is a valid state. In this case, neigh_connect is invoked via neigh_update.

Whenever the NUD_REACHABLE state is entered, the neighboring infrastructure calls the neigh_connect function to make the neigh->output function point to neigh_ops->connected_output.

When a neighbor in the NUD_REACHABLE state moves to NUD_STALE or NUD_DELAY, or is simply initialized to a state different from one of the states in NUD_CONNECTED (for example, by a call to neigh_update), the kernel invokes neigh_suspect to enforce confirmation of reachability (see the section "Reachability Confirmation" in Chapter 26). neigh_suspect does this by setting neighbour->output to neigh_ops->output.

Both neigh_connect and neigh_suspect also update the neighbour->output and neighbour->hh_output functions of all of the hh_cache structures linked to the input neighbour instance (see Figure 27-1). Neither function, however, updates the NUD state of a neighbour instance, because that is already taken care of by their callers. Later in this chapter I'll use the forms "connect the neighbor" and "suspect the

---

[*] The routines used to compare timestamps, such as time_after_eq and time_before_eq, are defined in *include/linux/jiffies.h*.

[†] Part of neigh_event_send is also depicted in Figure 27-13 as part of the expanded neigh_resolve_output flowchart.

neighbor" to refer to the invocation of neigh_connect and neigh_suspect, respectively, for that neighbor.

Some transitions (changes of NUD state) can happen at any time and more than once during the lifetime of a neighbour instance. Others can take place only once. With some knowledge of networking, it is not hard to look at Figure 26-13 in Chapter 26 and identify the transitions that belong to each of the two categories. For those neighbour instances initialized to permanent states (for instance, NUD_NOARP), neigh->output can be initialized to neigh_ops->connected right away and it will never change.

Routines used for neigh->output

As explained in the previous section, neigh->output is initialized by the neighbor's constructor function, and later is manipulated as a consequence of protocol events via the two routines neigh_connect and neigh_suspect. neigh->output is always set to one of the virtual functions of neigh_ops. This section lists the functions that can be assigned to the neigh_ops virtual functions. The dev_queue_xmit function, which is not really part of the neighboring subsystem, is defined in *net/core/dev.c*. The other routines are defined in *net/core/neighbour.c*.

dev_queue_xmit
> The L3 layer always calls this function when transmitting a packet, regardless of the kind of device or L2 and L3 protocols used. A neighboring protocol initializes the function pointers of neigh_ops to dev_queue_xmit when all the information needed to transmit on the egress device is present and there is no extra work for the neighboring subsystem to do. If you look at arp_direct_ops in Chapter 28, you can see that all four transmission virtual functions are set to dev_queue_xmit. That function is described in Chapter 11.

neigh_connected_output
> This function just fills in the L2 header and then calls neigh_ops->queue_xmit. Therefore, it expects the L2 address to be resolved. It is used by neighbour structures in the NUD_CONNECTED state.

neigh_resolve_output
> This function resolves the L3 address to the L2 address before transmitting, so it is used when that association is not ready yet or needs to be confirmed. Except for the situations in the section "Special Cases" in Chapter 26, neigh_resolve_output is usually the default routine used when a new neighbour structure is created and its L3 address needs to be resolved.

neigh_compat_output
> This function is present for backward compatibility. Before the neighboring infrastructure was introduced, it was possible to call dev_queue_xmit even if the L2 address was not ready yet.

neigh_blackhole

> This function is used to handle the temporary case where a neighbour structure cannot be removed because someone is still holding a reference to it. neigh_blackhole discards any packet received in input. This is necessary to ensure that no attempt to transmit a packet to the neighbor will take place, because the neighbor's data structures are about to be removed. See the section "Neighbor Deletion."

The section "Initialization of a neighbour Structure" in Chapter 28 shows how ARP uses these functions to initialize the different instances of the neigh_ops VFT. The choices made by the functions are also shown in the flowchart in Figure 27-13.

Updating a Neighbor's Information: neigh_update

neigh_update, defined in *net/core/neighbour.c*, is a generic function that can be used to update the link layer address of a neighbour structure. This is its prototype, with a brief description of the input parameters:

```
int neigh_update(struct neighbour *neigh, const u8 *lladdr, u8 new,
                 u32 flags)
```

neigh

> Pointer to the neighbour structure to update.

lladdr

> New link layer (L2) address. lladdr may not always be initialized to a new value. For instance, when neigh_update is called to delete a neighbour structure (by setting its state to NUD_FAILED, as described in the section "Neighbor Deletion," it is passed a NULL value for lladdr.

new

> New NUD state.

flags

> Used to convey information such as whether an existing link layer address can be overridden, etc. Here are the available flags, from *include/net/neighbour.h*:

NEIGH_UPDATE_F_ADMIN

> Administrative change. This means the change derives from a user-space command (see the section "System Administration of Neighbors" in Chapter 29).

NEIGH_UPDATE_F_OVERRIDE

> The current L2 address can be overridden by lladdr. Administrative changes use this flag to distinguish between *replace* and *add* commands, among other things (see Table 29-1 in Chapter 29). Protocol code can use this flag to enforce a minimum lifetime for an L2 address (see, for example, the section "Final Common Processing in Chapter 28).

The next three flags are used only by IPv6 code:

NEIGH_UPDATE_ISROUTER

> The neighbor is a router. This flag is used to initialize the IPv6 flag NTF_ROUTER in neighbour->flags.

NEIGH_UPDATE_F_OVERRIDE_ISROUTER

> The IPv6 NTF_ROUTER flag can be overridden.

NEIGH_UPDATE_F_WEAK_OVERRIDE

> If the link layer address lladdr supplied in input differs from the current known link layer address of the neighbor neigh->ha, the address is suspected (i.e., its state is moved to NUD_STALE so that reachability confirmation is triggered).

The IPv6's ND protocol uses flags in the protocol header that can influence the setting of the NEIGH_UPDATE_F_XXX flags just listed. The discussion that follows skips over the parts of neigh_update that deal with the IPv6-only flags.

neigh_update is used by all of the administrative interfaces to change the link layer address of a neighbour structure, as shown in Figure 29-1 in Chapter 29. The function can also be used by the neighboring protocols themselves, but it is not the only function that changes state.

Figures 27-5(a) and 27-5(b) show a high-level description of neigh_update's internals. The flowchart is divided into different areas, each area taking care of a different task:

- Sanity checks
- Changes applied to a neighbor whose current state is not NUD_VALID
- Selection of the L2 address to use for a change applied to a neighbor whose current state is NUD_VALID
- Setting a new link layer address
- Change of NUD state
- Handling an arp_queue queue

The following subsections explain the code in detail.

neigh_update optimization

Before changing the state of a neighbor, neigh_update first checks to see whether it is possible to avoid the change. An optimization discards the change of state if both of the following conditions are met (see (c)):

- The link layer address has not been modified (that is, the input lladdr is the same as the current neigh->ha).
- The new state is NUD_STALE and the current one is NUD_CONNECTED, which means that the current state is actually better than the new one.

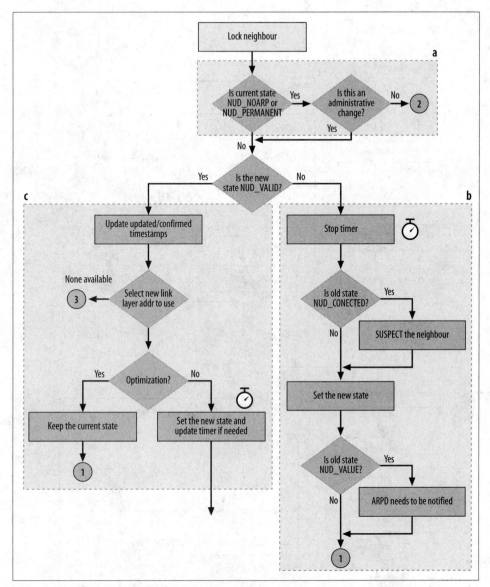

Figure 27-5(a). neigh_update function

Initial neigh_update operations

In this section, we trace the decisions made by neigh_update as it handles various values for the current state (neighbour->nud_state) and the requested state (the new parameter).

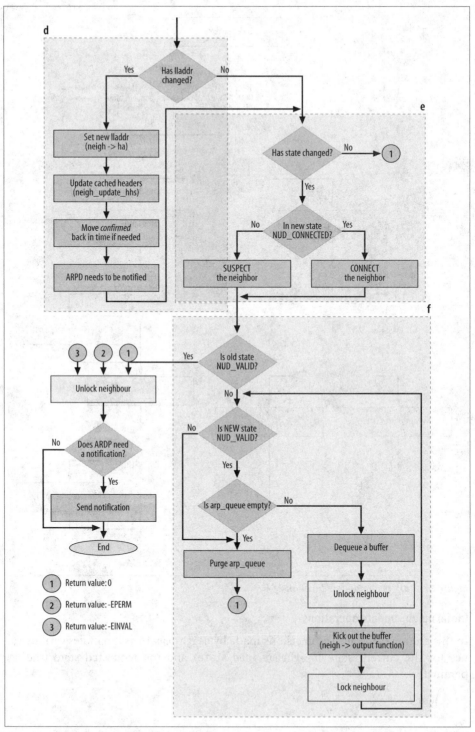

Figure 27-5(b). neigh_update function

Only administrative commands (NEIGH_UPDATE_F_ADMIN) can change the state of a neighbor that is currently in the NUD_NOARP or NUD_PERMANENT state. A sanity check at the beginning of neigh_update causes it to exit right away if these constraints are violated.

When the new state new is not a valid one—if it is NUD_NONE or NUD_INCOMPLETE—the neighbor timer is stopped if it is running, and the entry is marked suspect (that is, requiring reachability confirmation) through neigh_suspect if the old state was NUD_CONNECTED. See the section "Initialization of neigh->output and neigh->nud_state." When the new state is a valid one, the neighbor timer is restarted if the new state requires it (NUD_IN_TIMER).

When neigh_update is asked to change the NUD state to a value different from the current one, which is normally the case, it needs to check whether the state is changing from a value included in NUD_VALID to another value not in NUD_VALID (remember that NUD_VALID is a derived state that includes multiple NUD_XXX values). In particular, when the old state was not NUD_VALID and the new one is NUD_VALID, the host has to transmit all of the packets that are waiting in the neighbor's arp_queue queue. Since the state of the neighbor could change while doing this (because the host may be a symmetric multiprocesing, or SMP, system), the state of the neighbor is rechecked before sending each packet.

Changes of link layer address

The reason for calling neigh_update is to change the NUD state, but it can also change the destination link layer address by which a neighbor is reached. The function will do this if a new link layer address is provided (that is, if the lladdr parameter is not NULL) and if the input parameter flags allows it. When the link layer address is changed, all of the cached headers need to be updated accordingly. This is taken care of by neigh_update_hhs.

When no link layer address is supplied to neigh_update (i.e., lladdr is NULL), and the current NUD state is not a valid one, neigh_update discards the input frame skb and returns with an error (no change of state is applied if there is no valid link layer address for the neighbor).

Notifications to arpd

Some sites with large networks choose to manage ARP requests through a user-space daemon called *arpd* instead of making the kernel do it. When the kernel is compiled with support for *arpd*, and its use is configured (that is, app_probes > 0), neigh_update notifies the daemon about the following events:[*]

- When a state is modified from NUD_VALID to a state that is not valid
- When the link layer address is changed

---

[*] See the section "ARPD" in Chapter 28, and the section "neigh_parms Structure" in Chapter 29.

General Tasks of the Neighboring Infrastructure

This section describes a few general concepts that you should be familiar with before delving into specific functions within the neighboring infrastructure: caching, reference counting, and timers.

Caching

The neighboring layer implements two kinds of caching:

Neighbor mappings
>As with any other kind of data that can be used multiple times, it makes sense to cache the results of the L3-to-L2 mappings. Negative results (where an attempt to resolve the address failed) are not cached. But the neighbour structures associated with failed mappings are set to the NUD_FAILED state so that the garbage collection timer can clean them up (see the section "Garbage Collection").

L2 headers
>The neighboring infrastructure caches L2 headers to speed up the time required to encapsulate an L3 packet into an L2 frame. Otherwise, the infrastructure would have to initialize each field of the L2 header one by one.

Because the caching of neighbor mappings is central to the operation of the neighboring subsystem, this section describes it in detail. (The later section "L2 Header Caching" describes L2 header caching.) The contents of a neighbour structure are described in the section "neighbour Structure" in Chapter 29, and the structure's creation and deletion are described in later sections in this chapter. Here we will stay at a higher level, describing how those structures are organized and accessed by the neighboring infrastructure.

The neighboring infrastructure places neighbour structures into caches, one per protocol, which are implemented as typical hash tables where elements that collide into the same bucket are linked into a singly linked list. New elements are added at the head of the lists (see the function neigh_create in the section "The neigh_create Function's Parameters"). The inputs to the hash function that distributes elements into buckets are the L3 address, the associated device, and a random value that is recomputed regularly to reduce the effectiveness of a hypothetical Denial of Service (DoS) attack. Figure 27-6 shows the structure of the cache. In Figure 27-2, you can see its relationship to other key data structures, such as the per-protocol neigh_table structure.

Hash tables are allocated and freed with neigh_hash_alloc and neigh_hash_free, respectively. Each hash table is created with a size of two elements at protocol initialization time (see neigh_table_init). When the number of elements in the table grows bigger than the number of buckets, the table is reorganized as follows. First, the size of the table is doubled (thus, the size of the hash table is always a power of 2). The

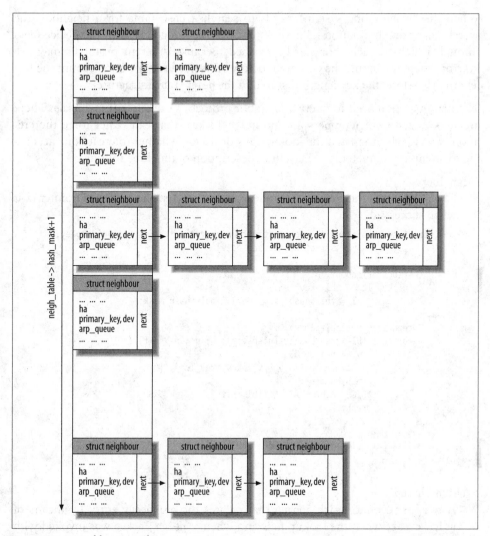

Figure 27-6. neighbour's cache

random value used for hashing is recalculated. Finally, the elements are redistributed throughout the table using the same previously mentioned variables: L3 address, device, and random number. This extension of the hash table is performed by neigh_hash_grow, which is called by neigh_create when necessary.

Note that extension of the hash table is easily triggered. Therefore, it rarely has more than one or two structures per bucket.

The maximum number of elements in a table is controlled by the gc_thresh*X* variables described in the section "Garbage Collection." These limits are needed to prevent possible DoS attacks.

When the "neighboring system" needs to search a hash table for a neighbor, the search key is the destination L3 address (primary_key) together with the device (dev) through which the neighbor can be reached. Because different protocols may use keys of different lengths, the common lookup APIs need to take into account the key length. Therefore, the key length is stored in the neigh_table structure.

The main function used to query a neighbor protocol's cache is neigh_lookup. There are two others, both wrappers around neigh_lookup, that can either force the creation of a neighbour entry if the lookup fails or decide whether to create one according to an input parameter. Here is a brief description of the three routines:

neigh_lookup
    Checks whether the element being searched for exists, and returns a pointer to it
    when successful.

```
struct neighbour *neigh_lookup(struct neigh_table *tbl, const void *pkey,
                struct net_device *dev)
{
    struct neighbour *n;
    int key_len = tbl->key_len;
    u32 hash_val = tbl->hash(pkey, dev) & tbl->hash_mask;

    read_lock_bh(&tbl->lock);
    for (n = tbl->hash_buckets[hash_val]; n; n = n->next) {
        if (dev == n->dev &&
            !memcmp(n->primary_key, pkey, key_len)) {
            neigh_hold(n);
            NEIGH_CACHE_STAT_INC(tbl, hits);
            break;
        }
    }
    read_unlock_bh(&tbl->lock);
    return n;
}
```

__neigh_lookup
    A wrapper around neigh_lookup that creates the neighbour entry by means of
    neigh_create when the lookup fails and when __neigh_lookup was invoked with
    the creat input flag set.

__neigh_lookup_errno
    Uses neigh_lookup to see whether the entry exists, and always creates a new
    neighbour instance when the lookup fails. This function is basically the same as
    __neigh_lookup without the input creat flag.

Chapter 28 describes another function, arp_find, which is a wrapper around __neigh_lookup and is kept for backward compatibility, for use by legacy code. Another function, neigh_lookup_nodev, is currently used only by DECnet.

Each protocol also maintains a separate cache and an associated set of lookup APIs used for destination proxying. You can find more details about them in the section "Acting As a Proxy."

Timers

The neighboring subsystem uses several timers. Some are global, whereas others are created on a one-per-neighbor basis. Some run periodically, and others are started only when needed. The following is a brief overview of the timers we will see in more detail in later sections:

Transitions between states (neighbour->timer)

Some transitions between NUD states are driven by the passage of time rather than by events in the system. These transitions include:

From NUD_REACHABLE *to* NUD_DELAY *or* NUD_STALE

This transition takes place when a certain amount of time goes by without sending or receiving traffic from a neighbor; the neighboring subsystem automatically suspects that the neighbor may not be reachable.

From NUD_DELAY *to* NUD_PROBE *or* NUD_REACHABLE

This is the next state after the neighbor's reachability is suspected; either it must be confirmed by an external event or the neighboring subsystem must launch an explicit probe. The timer simply detects the condition required to change state and takes care of it. For example, we saw in Figure 26-14 in Chapter 26 how neigh_confirm may be called when TCP provides confirmation of reachability. neigh_confirm updates a timestamp in the neighbour structure but does not change the state. Instead, when this timer detects the new timestamp, it changes the neighbor's state.

A timer in each neighbour structure controls both of these transitions. Its callback is initialized to neigh_timer_handler when the neighbour entry is created with neigh_alloc. You can find more information on this in Figure 27-4, and in the section "Reachability Confirmation" in Chapter 26.

Failed solicitation requests

If no answer to a solicitation request is received within a given amount of time, a new solicitation is sent. The maximum number of solicitation requests that can be sent is given by the *XXX*_probes fields of the neigh_parms structure, described in the section "neigh_parms Structure" in Chapter 29.

After the final failed attempt, the neighbor entry is moved to the NUD_FAILED state (see Figure 27-13). After the state becomes NUD_FAILED, it is up to the garbage collection timer to remove the entry.

Garbage collection (neigh_table->gc_timer)

A periodic timer is used to make sure that no memory is wasted by unused data structures. The callback handler is neigh_periodic_timer. The section "Garbage Collection" describes the garbage collection mechanism in detail.

neigh_periodic_timer also updates the value of reachable_time in the neighbour structure to a random value* every 300 seconds. The value is random rather than fixed because you want to avoid having too many entries expiring at the same time: in a pretty big network, that could create a burst of traffic and CPU usage.

Proxy (`neigh_table->proxy_timer`)

> For a proxy that might receive a large number of solicitation requests, it may be useful to delay the processing of requests. This timer is used to enforce the delay. See the section "Delayed Processing of Solicitation Requests."

Reference Counts on neighbour Structures

Many kernel subsystems involved in the creation of neighbors keep a reference to the `neighbour` structure in some data structure; the routing subsystem does so, for instance. Therefore, the `neighbour` structure includes a reference count named `refcnt`, which is incremented and decremented with `neigh_hold` and `neigh_release`, respectively.

The most common event that increments a neighbor reference count is a packet transmission. Whenever a packet is sent out, the associated `sk_buff` buffer holds a reference to a `neighbour` structure, so `neighbour->refcnt` is incremented to make sure that the transmission can complete without problems. Once the packet has been transmitted, the count is decremented again.

This was an example of a short-term reference; others can last significantly longer. One example is the reference kept by the routing table cache (under both IPv4 and IPv6[*]), as depicted in Figure 27-10.

The reference count is also incremented every time a per-neighbor timer is fired up, as shown in the following snapshot taken from `neigh_update`:

```
if (new & NUD_IN_TIMER) {
        neigh_hold(neigh);
        neigh->timer.expires = jiffies +
                        ((new & NUD_REACHABLE) ?
                        neigh->parms->reachable_time : 0);
        add_timer(&neigh->timer);
}
```

When an entry is to be removed for some reason (see `neigh_ifdown` in the section "Interactions with Other Subsystems") but it cannot be freed because someone still holds a reference to it, it is marked as dead with `neighbour->dead` set to 1. The garbage collection timer will soon take care of it, as explained in the section "Garbage Collection."

---

[*] To be more exact, it is a random value in the range `base_reachable_time/2` to `(3×base_reachable_time)/2`, as computed by the `neigh_rand_reach_time` routine.

[*] Both IPv4's `rt_intern_hash` (described in Chapter 33) and IPv6's `ip6_route_add` end up calling `__neigh_lookup_errno`.

Creating a neighbour Entry

Like most cached items, the creation of neighbour entries is event driven: an instance is created when the system needs a neighbor and there is a cache miss. Specifically, a new instance is created when one of the following takes place:

Transmission request

> When there is a transmission request toward a host whose L2 address is not known, the address needs to be resolved. This is the most common case and is depicted in Figure 27-13(a). When the target host is not directly connected to the sender, the L2 address to resolve will be that of the next hop gateway, not that of the target host.

Reception of a solicitation request

> Because the host sending the request identifies itself in that request, the recipient automatically creates a cache entry on the assumption that communication between the two systems is imminent. (For details involving ARP, see Figure 28-2 in Chapter 28). However, information learned in this way (passively) is not considered as authoritative as information learned with an explicit solicitation request and reply (see the section "Transitions Between NUD States" in Chapter 26 for more details).

Manual coding

> An administrator can create a cache entry through an *ip neigh add* command, as described in the section "System Administration of Neighbors" in Chapter 29.

When one of these events happens, and a query to the neighboring subsystem cache returns a miss, the neighboring protocol tries to resolve the association (normally by sending a solicitation request) and stores the resulting neighbour entry in the per-protocol cache.

The neigh_create Function's Parameters

Now that we know what triggers the creation of a neighbour structure, we can look at the main functions involved with its creation.

The data structure itself is created with neigh_create, whose return value is a pointer to the neighbour data structure. Here is the prototype and a description of the three input parameters:

```
struct neighbour * neigh_create(struct neigh_table *tbl, const void *pkey,
                struct net_device *dev)
```

tbl

> Identifies the neighboring protocol used. The way this parameter is set is simple: if it is being called from IPv4 code (i.e., from arp_rcv) it is set to arp_tbl, etc.

pkey

> L3 address. It is called pkey because it is the field that will be used as the search key for the cache lookup.

dev

> Device the entry is associated with. Because each neighbour entry is associated with an L3 address and the latter is always associated with a device, it follows that a neighbour instance is always associated with a device.

New neighbour data structures are allocated with neigh_alloc, which is also used to initialize a few parameters such as the embedded timer, the reference count, a pointer to the associated neigh_table (neighboring protocol) structure, and global statistics about the number of neighbour structure allocations.

neigh_alloc uses a memory pool created at subsystem initialization time (see the section "Protocol Initialization and Cleanup"). The function fails only if the number of structures currently allocated is greater than some configurable threshold and, on top of that, an attempt by the garbage collector (via neigh_forced_gc) to free some memory failed (see the section "Synchronous cleanup: the neigh_forced_gc function").

pkey is copied into the data structure with the help of key_len, which provides the size of the data to be copied. This is necessary because the neighbour structures are used by protocol-independent cache lookup routines and the various neighboring protocols use addresses of different sizes.

```
memcpy(n->primary_key, pkey, key_len);
```

Also, because the neighbour entry holds a reference to the net_device structure dev, the kernel increases the reference count on the latter with dev_hold to make sure the device will not be removed until the neighbour structure ceases to exist.

Neighbor Initialization

There are two kinds of initialization for a neighbour structure: one done by the neighboring protocol and one done by the device.

```
if (tbl->constructor && (error = tbl->constructor(n)) < 0) {
    rc = ERR_PTR(error);
    goto out_neigh_release;
}
```

The protocol's initialization is carried out by the neigh_table->constructor function invoked, as shown here, from the function's tbl parameter. Chapter 28 explains how the ARP constructor does the job.

Device initialization is done through the neigh_setup virtual function:

```
if (n->parms->neigh_setup &&
    (error = n->parms->neigh_setup(n)) < 0) {
    rc = ERR_PTR(error);
    goto out_neigh_release;
}
```

This function is actually defined by only a few devices. For instance, the shaper virtual device (an old piece of code in *drivers/net/shaper.c* that has been rendered obsolete by the Traffic Control subsystem but is needed for backward compatibility) uses the setup function to make sure the device is associated with a specific instance of the neigh_ops structures provided by ARP (see the section "Initialization of neigh->ops"). Some WAN devices use a setup function for similar reasons.

The neigh_create function ends by setting the entry's confirmed field to indicate that the neighbor is reachable. Normally, this field is updated by a proof of reachability and is set to the current time expressed in jiffies. But here, at the point of creation, the function subtracts a small amount of time (one-half the value reachable_time) to make the state move to NUD_STALE a little faster than usual and to require proof of reachability.

```
n->confirmed = jiffies - (n->parms->base_reachable_time<<1);
```

Once the entry has been initialized, it is added to the main cache using the hash function provided by the neighboring protocol.

Neighbor Deletion

A neighbour data structure can be removed for three main reasons:

- The kernel tries to send a packet to a host that is not reachable. There are many reasons this could happen: the host went down, its cable came unplugged, it was a wireless device that moved out of range, its network configuration got corrupted, or somebody manually created an entry for a nonexistent host. Whatever the cause, the neighboring subsystem notices the failure and puts the associated neighbour structure into the NUD_FAILED state so that it is cleaned up by asynchronous garbage collection, described in the section "Asynchronous cleanup: the neigh_periodic_timer function."
- The host associated with the neighbor structure has changed its L2 address (perhaps because its NIC was replaced) but still has the same L3 configuration. Thus, the neighbour structure has an outdated L2 address. A host with an outdated neighbor entry has to put it into the NUD_FAILED state and create a new one.[*]
- The structure gets old and the kernel needs its memory. It is therefore removed by garbage collection, described in the section "Synchronous cleanup: the neigh_forced_gc function."

The transition to NUD_FAILED is taken care of by the NUD algorithm introduced in the section "Transitions Between NUD States" in Chapter 26. Asynchronous garbage collection is performed by the neigh_periodic_timer function, which is associated

---

[*] Some device drivers let the administrator change the MAC address either temporarily (i.e., it returns to its original value after a power cycle) or permanently. This operation is limited to special scenarios and is not needed by the average user.

with the neigh_table->gc_timer timer (see the sections "Timers" and "Garbage Collection" for more details).

A structure is removed only when its reference count goes to zero. Thus, the function that carries out the deletion, neigh_destroy, is called only from neigh_release, which is called every time a reference to a structure is released. neigh_release decrements the structure's reference count and calls neigh_destroy to actually remove the structure when the count goes down to zero:

```
static inline void neigh_release(struct neighbour *neigh)
{
        if (atomic_dec_and_test(&neigh->refcnt))
                neigh_destroy(neigh);
}
```

neigh_destroy carries out the following tasks:

- Stops any pending timer. This is a belt-and-suspenders precaution. In theory, no timer should be pending when executing neigh_destroy because the condition required by neigh_release to invoke neigh_destroy is a reference count value of 0, and timers always hold a reference when running.

- Releases any references to external data structures, such as the associated device and cached L2 headers. See Figures 27-1 and 27-10.

  The section "L2 Header Caching," later in this chapter, explains the purpose of the cache and shows the relationship between the neighbour structure and the hh_cache structures that contain the headers. Each hh_cache structure is strictly coupled with a neighbour entry and therefore should not be used once the neighbour entry has been removed or marked NUD_FAILED. Thus, when a neighbour entry is deleted, any hh_cache structures to which it refers are unlinked from the cache and freed if their reference counts allow it, and neigh_destroy sets the hh_cache->hh_output field in the cached header to neigh_blackhole (for that function, see the section "Routines used for neigh->output"). After this, any transmission attempt using the neighbour entry will silently fail and the packet will be dropped. At the L3 layer, the results of dropping the packet can be seen in the section "Interaction Between Neighboring Protocols and L3 Transmission Functions."

- If a destructor method has been provided by the neighboring protocol, executes it to give the protocol a chance to do its own cleanup.

- If the arp_queue queue is not empty, purges it (i.e., removes all of its elements). arp_queue is described in the section "Egress Queuing."

- Decrements the global counter indicating the number of neighbour entries used by the host.

- Frees the neighbour data structure (i.e., gives it back to its memory pool).

Garbage Collection

Garbage collection refers to the process of eliminating resources that are not in use anymore. Like many Linux kernel subsystems (networking and others), the neighboring subsystem maintains a timer that runs periodically and executes a function whenever the timer expires, to clean up the unused data structures.

The garbage collection algorithm used by the neighboring infrastructure has two main components:

Synchronous cleanup
> This takes place immediately when the neighboring infrastructure needs to allocate a new neighbour structure and the memory pool for such structures is used up.

Asynchronous cleanup
> This takes place periodically to remove neighbour structures that have not been used for a certain amount of time. This time is configurable and is stored in the gc_staletime variable. The neigh_periodic_timer function, described in the section "Timers," enforces this rule.

This relatively complex system was chosen because, in the case of the neighboring subsystem, the designers thought it would be more efficient than simpler designs such as deleting a structure the moment its reference count went down to zero. While the asynchronous cleanup tries to free structures that have no further value, the synchronous cleanup tries to sacrifice some of the less-needed entries to free some memory. Therefore, the criteria used to select the eligible structures are different in the two types of cleanup.

It is interesting to note that an asynchronous cleanup can be triggered by an external subsystem, too. For instance, when the routing subsystem cannot insert a new routing entry into its cache, it tries to remove unused cache entries (see the description of the rt_intern_hash function in Chapter 33), which indirectly causes neighbour structures to be freed, too.

The parameters that tune garbage collection behavior are:

- From neigh_table:
    - —gc_interval
    - —gc_thresh1, gc_thresh2, gc_thresh3
    - —last_flush
    - —gc_timer
- From neigh_parms:
    - —gc_staletime

The following two sections explain their meaning and use. Also consult the section "neigh_table structure," the section "neigh_parms structure," and Table 29-3 in Chapter 29 for information on these variables.

Figures 27-7 and 27-8 show the behavior of neigh_periodic_timer and neigh_forced_ gc, the two routines described in the next two sections.

Synchronous cleanup: the neigh_forced_gc function

Figure 27-7 shows the internals of neigh_forced_gc.

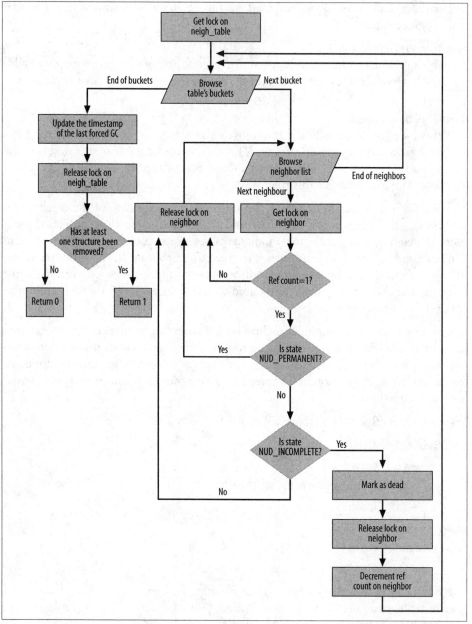

Figure 27-7. neigh_forced_gc function

If there is no memory to allocate a new neighbour instance, the host cannot transmit any packet to neighbors for which there is not already a neighbour structure in the cache. Without a policy to handle this case, the consequences would be pretty bad: no communication could take place with a new host until another neighbour structure happened to be removed for some reason.

The neigh_alloc function, which we have seen is responsible for allocating memory in the neighboring subsystem, is the natural place to kick off synchronous garbage collection. To determine whether there is a danger situation and do garbage collection before memory is actually exhausted, neigh_alloc checks two variables named gc_thresh2 and gc_thresh3. (Another variable, gc_thresh1, is currently declared in the kernel but is not used.)

When the number of neighbour instances is greater than gc_thresh3, the neigh_alloc function forces garbage collection. When the number of instances is between gc_thresh2 and gc_thresh3, garbage collection is forced if the previous garbage collection took place at least 5 seconds earlier. The reason for the second check is to rate limit the time spent doing garbage collection.

The default values for gc_thresh2 and gc_thresh3 are 512 and 1,024, respectively. These look like big numbers, but are designed to support proxy ARP. Without a proxy ARP server, each host usually creates ARP entries for only a few local machines and the router, so it would never get near those thresholds. But when proxy ARP is in use, hosts request more L3 addresses because they rely less on the default gateway. The reception of a solicitation request by the proxy ARP server leads to the indirect creation of a neighbour entry for the sender's address. See the earlier section "Creating a neighbour Entry," and the description of arp_process in Chapter 28. In a medium-size network, the thresholds are pretty safe and the cache is not likely to overflow.

The routine invoked to do synchronous cleanup is neigh_forced_gc, which is depicted in Figure 27-7. neigh_forced_gc removes all of the eligible elements from the hash table. Eligible elements are the ones that meet both of the following requirements:

- The reference count is 1, meaning that nobody is using the element, and the subsystem holding the remaining reference is free to delete the element.

- The element is not in the NUD_PERMANENT state. Elements in that state have been statically configured and therefore do not expire.

Elements are added by neigh_create at the head of the bucket's lists in the hash table.

Asynchronous cleanup: the neigh_periodic_timer function

Figure 27-8 shows the internals of neigh_periodic_timer.

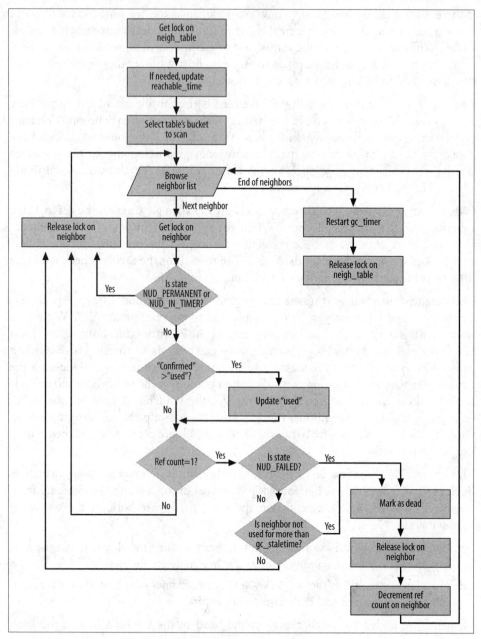

Figure 27-8. neigh_periodic_timer function

gc_timer is a per-protocol timer that expires periodically. When the timer expires, it invokes the garbage collection routine neigh_periodic_timer. The kernel actually invokes a function specified in a field of the neigh_table structure (one of which exists for each neighboring protocol), so each protocol could theoretically have its own implementation of the garbage collection handler, but in practice the field is initialized to the same routine across all the protocols in the neigh_table_init function.

How often gc_timer expires depends on the size of the hash_buckets table: because neigh_periodic_timer scans only one bucket of the table every time it is called, and because the whole table is scanned (by design choice) once every base_reachable_time/2 seconds, it follows that the timer must be set to expire every (base_reachable_time/2)/*number_of_buckets*.

Every time neigh_periodic_timer is called, it remembers the last bucket scanned, thanks to neigh_table's field, hash_chain_gc, and scans the following one.

The neigh->confirmed timestamp is updated every time the reachability of the neighbor is confirmed, for example, by calling neigh_confirm, as we saw in the section "Reachability Confirmation" in Chapter 26. Even though its name suggests it, the neigh->used timestamp is not updated every time the neighbour structure is used (i.e., with the transmission of each packet to the neighbor). Because of this, it is possible that at some point, neigh->confirmed represents a more updated timestamp marking the last use of the neighbour structure. For this reason, neigh_periodic_timer updates neigh->used if that is needed (i.e., if neigh->confirmed is greater than neigh->used). It is important to keep neigh->used updated because that's the timestamp used by neigh_periodic_timer to eliminate old entries.

As Figure 27-8 shows, eligible elements marked for deletion by neigh_periodic_timer meet both of the following criteria:

- The reference count is 1, meaning it is no longer used.
- The entry either is in the NUD_FAILED state, which means that resolution failed, or has simply not been used for more than the configurable gc_staletime time.

Acting As a Proxy

The section "Proxying the Neighboring Protocol" in Chapter 26 described why proxies are useful and gave a few examples of their use. It also showed the criteria by which neighboring protocols decide whether a given solicitation request is taken care of by the proxy. This section goes into detail on the implementation of proxying.

We saw in the section "Conditions Required by the Proxy" in Chapter 26 that two kinds of proxying can be configured: a host either can proxy all requests received on a particular NIC (per-device proxying) or, more selectively, can proxy requests for a particular address received on a particular NIC (per-destination proxying).

The precedence shown in Figure 26-8 in Chapter 26 is enforced in protocol-specific code. ARP's implementation is shown in Chapter 28, and you can look at the routine neigh_recv_ns for IPv6's implementation. The section "Per-Device Proxying and Per-Destination Proxying" also goes into more detail about these two types of proxying.

Before digging into the code, let me introduce a naming convention used extensively there. The neighboring subsystem contains pairs of functions and data structures whose names differ only in the presence or absence of an initial *p* (e.g., neigh_lookup versus pneigh_lookup). The *p* stands for *proxy*. Because addresses intercepted by proxies are handled differently, there is a dedicated set of functions to manipulate them.

Delayed Processing of Solicitation Requests

Solicitation requests handled by the proxy can be processed right away or after a configurable delay. The main reason for introducing a delay is to give proxy entries lower priority than more authoritative hosts, such as the real owners of the solicited L3 addresses. A host that sends a request locks the first reply for a small amount of time and waits in case another arrives, to enforce the priority; details are described in the section "Final Common Processing" in Chapter 28.

The delay applied is a random value between 0 and the configured value proxy_delay (see the function pneigh_enqueue). The use of a random value reduces the likelihood of synchronized requests by multiple hosts, and the congestion that could result. For example, if a power failure occurs at a site, and upon recovery it powers up hundreds of hosts at the same time, all of the hosts probably solicit the same set of servers or default gateways. A random delay smoothes out the spike in traffic that would result.

To apply a delay, the neighboring subsystem creates a queue storing ingress solicitation requests, and a timer. The timer expires after the configured delay has passed and triggers the execution of a special handler that dequeues the elements from the queue. They are then processed as if they had just been received from the network.

Figure 27-9 depicts the model just described.

The major variables and virtual functions involved in handling the proxy delay are:

- From neigh_table (per-protocol parameters)

    proxy_queue

    > Queue where the ingress solicitation requests are temporarily buffered. Elements are added to the end of the list. When the proxy_queue list has reached the maximum length specified in proxy_qlen (discussed later), new elements are dropped; they do not replace the oldest ones.

    proxy_timer

    > Timer used to enforce the delay. The timer is initialized by neigh_table_init and the default handler is neigh_proxy_process.

    proxy_redo

    > Function that processes the dequeued requests. As shown in Figure 27-9, it consists of just a call to the same function that processes freshly received packets.

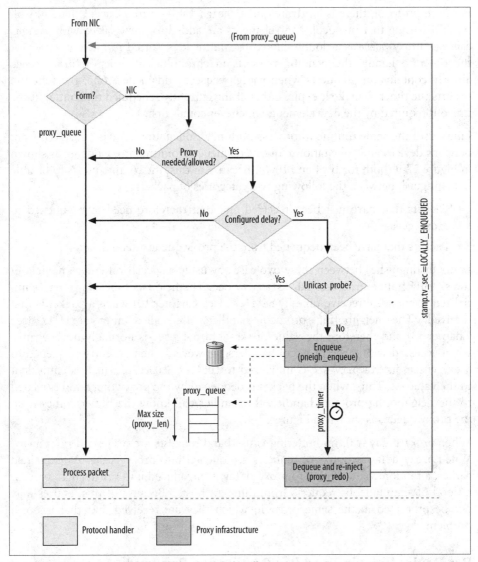

Figure 27-9. Generic model of a protocol proxy handler

- From `neigh_parms` (per-device parameters)

`proxy_delay`
Configurable delay used to load the timer.

`proxy_qlen`
Maximum length of the temporary storage queue.

For a more detailed, field-by-field description of the most important data structures, refer to Chapter 29.

For each protocol, there is a private queue (neigh_table->proxy_queue) shared by all the NICs using that protocol. New elements are added to proxy_queue with pneigh_ enqueue. proxy_queue is a doubly linked list that is kept sorted to make it easier for the timer to handle the pending requests in chronological order. If proxy_queue already contains any requests when pneigh_enqueue adds a new one, the function restarts the timer to make it expire either at the currently scheduled timeout or at the timeout required by the new element, whichever comes first.

Linux uses the same routine to process both new solicitation requests received from network devices and solicitation requests dequeued from the proxy queue, as shown in Figure 27-9 (both for IPv4 and IPv6). Because of this, the routine needs to be able to distinguish between the following two categories of packets:

- Packets that have just been received and that therefore need to be queued to proxy_queue
- Packets that have been dequeued from the proxy queue after a delay

Linux distinguishes between these two cases by using a special value for one field of the sk_buff buffer structure: skb->stamp.tv_sec. The field is a timestamp that is initialized to the local receive time by netif_rx (see Chapter 10) when a packet is first received. The neighboring protocol handlers are called after netif_rx (see Chapter 13) and therefore the value of skb->stamp.tv_sec is normally non-negative when accessed within the protocol handlers. However, when an entry is queued to proxy_queue, its stamp.tv_sec is initialized to LOCALLY_ENQUEUED, which is equivalent to the value −2. Thus, when the packet is dequeued by the proxy timer and is passed to the neighboring protocol handler, the handler will know the buffer comes from the proxy queue, as shown in Figure 27-9.

When proxy_delay is 0, no buffering is used and requests are processed right away. When proxy_delay is nonzero, requests are queued into proxy_queue. As explained earlier, a random value from 0 to proxy_delay is introduced into the delay to prevent a flood of simultaneous requests from different hosts.[*] Because of this, entries may not be processed in the same order in which they are received, but that is not a problem.

Per-Device Proxying and Per-Destination Proxying

When proxying is globally enabled on a device, state information is simple: the device just needs to be associated with a flag that says whether proxying is enabled. Per-destination proxying, on the other hand, needs to store the proxied addresses. These L3 addresses for which the host should intercept solicitation requests are

---

[*] The random delay is one of the topics covered in RFC 2461. That document deals with IPv6/ND, but Linux does the same for IPv4/ARP.

stored in the `neigh_table->phash_buckets` hash table (see Figure 27-2), which can be searched with `pneigh_lookup`, the proxying counterpart of `neigh_lookup`.

Like `neigh_lookup`, which is described in the section "Caching," `pneigh_lookup` accepts an input parameter that can be used to force the creation of a `neighbour` structure if the search fails. Unlike `hash_buckets`, `phash_buckets` does not have a maximum size. Furthermore, there is no garbage collection because it would not make sense given the different nature of its elements: these addresses are explicitly configured to be proxied, so they remain valid until they are explicitly configured not to be proxied anymore. In IPv4, these addresses can be configured only manually. In IPv6, these addresses can also be configured by the protocol under certain conditions.

New entries can be added to the table dynamically by the neighboring protocols or statically by an administrative command (see the section "System Administration of Neighbors" in Chapter 29). Entries can be removed with `pneigh_delete`.

L2 Header Caching

L2 headers tend to be the same on all packets sent from one host to another. This is in contrast to L3 headers, which usually have different IDs, different fragment offsets when fragmentation occurs, and other ways of changing from one packet to the next. Therefore, the kernel doesn't bother caching L3 headers, but it does cache L2 headers. Complex L2 protocols may not have consistent headers, but the most common ones, such as Ethernet, do. (See Chapter 13 for more details on Ethernet.) When caching is used, the device driver of the egress device has to support it.

After sending the first packet to a given destination, a driver saves the L2 header in a dedicated structure named `hh_cache`. The next time a packet is sent to the same neighbor, the sender does not need to fill in the L2 header field by field, but simply copy it in one shot from the cache. The relationship of `hh_cache` to other neighboring protocol structures was introduced earlier in the section "Main Data Structures," and in Figure 27-2 in that section. The structure is described in more detail in the section "hh_cache Structure" in Chapter 29.

Header caching at the L2 layer is tied to caching by the routing subsystem at the L3 layer, described in Chapter 33. As shown in Figure 27-1, each `dst_entry` element of the IPv4 routing cache includes a pointer to the `neighbour` structure associated with the next hop, and that entry includes a list of `hh_cache` cached headers. While multiple headers could be cached for each neighbor, usually only one is cached. Figure 27-1 shows the case of an Ethernet header.[*]

---

[*] The Ethernet header does not include the preamble and the checksum, because they are taken care of by the NIC itself.

The relationship between the data structures in different caches is shown in action in Figure 27-10. The figure shows a simple scenario: two LANs connected by a router. From Host C's perspective, Host A, Host B and Router are reachable via the next hop Router. If Host C had exchanged some data with each of those three hosts, its routing cache would have a dst_entry (routing cache element) for each one. As explained previously, each dst_entry has a link to the neighbour structure of the associated next hop, which in this case is Router. Note that both the neighbour and the dst_entry structures have a link to the hh_cache entry. Note also that one cached header is sufficient because all three hosts (Host A, Host B, and Router) are reachable via the same next hop.

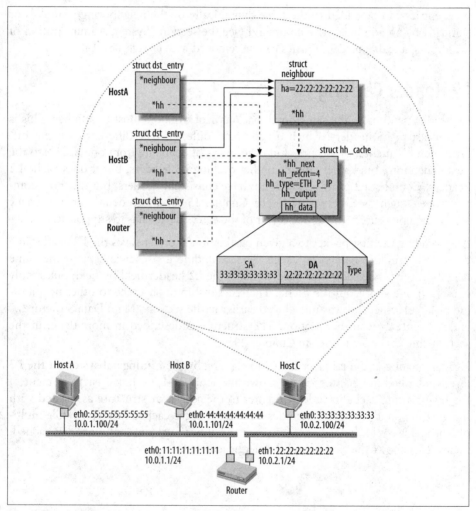

Figure 27-10. Example of caches used with routing

The reference count on the hh_cache structure (hh_refcnt) in Figure 27-10 is 4, which is the number of dotted links. Both the references held by the dst_entry structures and the reference held by the neighbour structure are set via neigh_hh_init, as described in the section "Link Between Routing and L2 Header Caching." Reference counts on hh_cache structures are incremented via direct calls to atomic_inc. As shown in the section "Reference Counts on Neighbour Structures," the kernel provides a special wrapper for neighbour structures.

The use of L2 header caching is transparent to L3 protocols, as shown in the later section, "Interaction Between Neighboring Protocols and L3 Transmission Functions."

Methods Provided by the Device Driver

For L2 caching to be used, the device driver has to cooperate by providing a routine that stores the L2 header in an hh_cache structure. In Chapter 2, I described the methods or virtual functions in the net_device data structure. It is worthwhile reviewing some of those methods now in light of the knowledge you have developed from reading this chapter. We will take the ones defined for Ethernet devices as examples for this section; these methods are initialized in ether_setup (see Chapter 8).

hard_header

> Fills in the L2 header field by field. When the device does not use any L2 header (see the section "Special Cases" in Chapter 26), this method is initialized to NULL. The neighbor's constructor method checks hard_header to select the right neigh_ops method from the virtual table; a NULL entry is treated specially. See the ARP example in the section "Start of the arp_constructor Function" in Chapter 28. ndisc_constructor acts similarly for the ND protocol.

> hard_header is used when header caching is not supported by the device driver (as in neigh_connected_output), or when the header is not ready yet and therefore is not present in the cache (as in neigh_resolve_output). When invoked, hard_header usually receives an skb buffer in input. The skb->data field points to the beginning of the L3 header. hard_header uses skb_push to make the space needed to prepend the L2 header.

hard_header_cache

> Caches an L2 header in an hh_cache structure. This is done, of course, only the first time a packet is sent to a neighbor, and only when all of the header's fields are ready (for instance, not before address resolution has completed).

header_cache_update

> Updates an existing hh_cache entry by replacing its cached header with a new one. This function is usually called from within neigh_update_hhs, which is used

by neigh_update to update a neighbor entry (see the section "Updating a Neighbor's Information: neigh_update").

hard_header_parse

Retrieves the source L2 address from a buffer and returns its length.

rebuild_header

Deprecated and kept only for backward compatibility with pre-2.2 kernel device drivers. Devices using this function cannot use the cached resolved address in dst_entry->neigh.

Link Between Routing and L2 Header Caching

When a neighbor entry has just been created, neigh->output points to neigh_resolve_output, which is in charge of associating the neighbor with the L2 header. Thus, transmitting functions at the L3 layer (described in Chapter 21 and in the section "Interaction Between Neighboring Protocols and L3 Transmission Functions" in this chapter) transparently trigger address resolution.

Here is a snapshot from neigh_resolve_output, where dst is the routing table cache entry briefly introduced in the section "Main Data Structures":

```
if (dev->hard_header_cache && !dst->hh) {
        write_lock_bh(&neigh->lock);
        if (!dst->hh)
                neigh_hh_init(neigh, dst, dst->ops->protocol);
        err = dev->hard_header(skb, dev, ntohs(skb->protocol),
                                neigh->ha, NULL, skb->len);
        write_unlock_bh(&neigh->lock);
} else {
        read_lock_bh(&neigh->lock);
        err = dev->hard_header(skb, dev, ntohs(skb->protocol),
                                neigh->ha, NULL, skb->len);
        read_unlock_bh(&neigh->lock);
}
```

If the device can use header caching (that is, hard_header_cache is set) but the header has not been cached yet (!dst->hh), neigh_resolve_output has to initialize and cache the L2 header. It does so by calling the neigh_hh_init function, which creates the hh_cache entry and links it to the dst->hh routing table cache entry (the operation shown by dotted lines in Figure 27-10).

If, instead, caching is not supported by the device, the L2 header is filled in with hard_header.

In both cases, the neighbour structure is accessed under the protection of a lock. But the first case accesses the structure in exclusive mode to write the header; the second accesses it in shared mode. Note that in the first case, neigh_resolve_output checks the status of dst->hh once more after having acquired the lock. This is a standard way to avoid a race condition with locks; it is done in this case because dst->hh may have been initialized by another CPU between the previous check and the acquisition of the lock.

For the internals of neigh_resolve_output, see Figure 27-13.

Cache Invalidation and Updating

A cached header may include many different fields, but the two that are most likely to change and therefore invalidate the cached header are the source and destination addresses.

When a local device changes its L2 address, all of the cached headers associated with the address become out of date. When the neighboring subsystem is notified about this event (NETDEV_CHANGEADDR, described in the section "Updates via neigh_changeaddr (netdevice notification chain)"), it flushes all of the neighbour entries associated with the device, thereby also invalidating all of the associated cached L2 headers.

When the system detects that the L2 address of a neighbor has changed, it invokes neigh_update_hhs. This function updates all of the cached headers used by that neighbour structure by invoking, in turn, the header_cache_update function provided by the device driver and introduced in the section "Methods Provided by the Device Driver." See the section "Updating a Neighbor's Information: neigh_update."

Protocol Initialization and Cleanup

Each neighboring protocol has an initialization function that is executed at boot time if the protocol is included in the kernel, or at module load time if the protocol has been compiled as a module. As for other kernel subsystems, the initialization function allocates all of the resources that are needed by the subsystem to function properly. The four initialization functions of the four neighboring protocols implemented in the Linux kernel are listed in Table 27-1.

Table 27-1. Neighboring protocol init/cleanup functions

Protocol	Init function	Cleanup function	File
ARP	arp_init[a]	None	*net/ipv4/arp.c*
Neighbor Discovery (ND)	ndisc_init	ndisc_cleanup	*net/ipv6/ndisc.c*
DECnet	dn_neigh_init	dn_neigh_cleanup	*net/decnet/dn_neigh.c*
ARP over IP (clip)[b]	atm_clip_init	atm_clip_exit	*net/atm/clip.c*

[a] arp_init is described in the section "ARP Protocol Initialization" in Chapter 28.

[b] clip represents a special case under ARP, not an independent protocol. Therefore, unlike the other three protocols, clip does not register with neigh_table_init, but accomplishes its initialization (such as memory pool allocation) by itself. Basically, it initializes its neigh_table structure and lets the ARP protocol (arp_bind_neighbour) take care of it.

Here are some of the common tasks accomplished by these functions:

- Initialize the neigh_table structure with neigh_table_init.
- Register a group of variables in the */proc* filesystem if needed (usually to allow tuning by an administrator).
- Register a protocol handler. IPv4 registers arp_rcv to use ARP (see Chapter 13). Neighbor handling in IPv6 is part of the more general-purpose protocol, ICMPv6, so IPv6 registers an ICMPv6 protocol handler, which invokes IPv6's counterpart of arp_rcv (ndisc_rcv) for those ICMPv6 messages that have to do with its neighboring protocol, ND.

neigh_table_init accomplishes the following:

- Allocates a memory pool to reserve memory for neighbour structures.
- Allocates a neigh_statistics structure that collects statistics about the protocol. See the section "neigh_statistics Structure" in Chapter 29.
- Allocates the two hash tables hash_buckets and phash_buckets, used respectively as the cache for resolved associations and as a database of proxied addresses. See Figure 27-2.
- Creates a file under */proc/net* that can be used to dump the contents of the cache. The name of the file is taken from neigh_table->id.
- Starts the gc_timer garbage collector timer. See the section "Garbage Collection."
- Initializes (but does not start yet) the proxy_timer proxy timer and the associated queue, proxy_queue. See the section "Delayed processing of solicitation requests."
- Adds neigh_table structures to the neigh_tables global list. The latter is protected by a lock, as shown in Figure 27-2.
- Initializes a few other parameters, such as reachable_time.

When a protocol is run through a module and the module is unloaded, neigh_table_clear is called to undo what neigh_table_init did at initialization time and to clear any other resources allocated by the protocol during its lifetime, such as timers and queues.

Table 27-1 shows the protocol cleanup functions that use neigh_table_clear to clean up protocol resources. IPv4 is the only one that cannot be compiled as a module, so ARP does not have a cleanup function.

Interaction with Other Subsystems

The neighboring subsystem interacts with other subsystems, both by generating and by receiving notifications when specific events take place. Here are some of the other subsystems involved in these interactions:

Routing

The relationship between caching at this layer and header caching at the neighbor layer is described in the section "L2 Header Caching."

Traffic equalizer (TEQL)

TEQL is one of Traffic Control's queuing disciplines that can be configured through the IPROUTE2 package's *tc* command. This feature groups a set of links at the L3 layer and uses them in round-robin fashion when transmitting packets to a given destination. The impact on the neighboring protocol is that the resolution of a single IP address (the master address) may actually trigger the resolution of multiple slave IP addresses.

Because each link in the group has to resolve the L3-L2 address binding, the first round over the devices in the group will need that binding to be resolved when moving from one slave to another.

IPsec

IPsec defines a series of transformations that need to be applied to a packet before it can be transmitted—notably encryption. Because of this, if the effects of IPsec were added to Figure 27-1, it would show multiple dst_entry structures in a linked list, and only the last one would have a pointer to a neighbour structure (see Figure 33-5 in Chapter 33).

Netfilter (iptables)

Netfilter hooks are placed at various points affecting the ingress, egress, and forwarding of packets; as these potentially affect all traffic, they affect solicitation requests and responses on the neighboring layer, too. The interaction between Netfilter and the neighboring protocols is taken care of independently from the neighboring infrastructure, partly because different neighboring protocols sit at different layers of the network stack.

Figure 28-13 in Chapter 28 shows how Netfilter and ARP interact by means of the three dedicated hook points NF_ARP_IN, NF_ARP_OUT, and NF_ARP_FORWARD. Unlike ARP, ND sits on top of its L3 protocol, IPv6, so it can be firewalled with the default NF_IP6_PRE_ROUTING, NF_IP6_POST_ROUTING, NF_IP6_LOCAL_IN, and NF_IP6_LOCAL_OUT hooks used for IPv6 traffic. To get an idea where those IPv6 hook points are positioned inside the IPv6 stack, take as a reference the IPv4 counterpart depicted in Figure 18-1 in Chapter 18.

In the following subsections, we'll see some of these interactions from the point of view of the neighboring subsystem.

Events Generated by the Neighboring Layer

When a neighbor is classified as unreachable, and therefore enters the NUD_FAILED state, the neighboring layer executes the neigh_ops->error_report function, which notifies the upper layer about the failure. For example, in the case of an ARP failure, the IPv4 layer would be notified. All of this is taken care of by `neigh_timer_handler`, the timer handler described in the section "Timers."

Events Received by the Neighboring Layer

As we have seen, entries maintained by the neighboring system become invalid whenever one of their main constituents—L3 address, L2 address, or device—changes. Therefore, the kernel must make sure the neighboring protocols are notified whenever one of these pieces of information changes. This is accomplished through two main functions provided by the neighboring subsystem:

`neigh_ifdown`
> A generic function that external kernel subsystems can invoke to notify the neighboring subsystem about changes to devices and L3 addresses. Notifications about changes to L3 addresses are sent by L3 protocols.

`neigh_changeaddr`
> A function that neighboring protocols can invoke to update a protocol's cache when the L2 address of a local device has changed. Each protocol can register with the kernel to be notified of these events. See the section "Received Events" in Chapter 28 for an example involving ARP. Notifications about changes to L2 addresses are sent by the kernel when a user command changes the hardware address of a device.

Updates via neigh_ifdown

Figure 27-11 summarizes the activities and functions that generate the external events in which the neighboring protocols are interested. Among the main events are:

Device shutdown
> Each neighbor entry is associated with a single device. Therefore, if a device is shut down, all of the associated entries have to be removed. To be more exact, the event represents not the shutdown of the device itself, but the clearing of the L3 configuration on the device that results, and that renders the association between the L3 address and L2 address invalid.
>
> The opposite case, of a device being added to the system, is not of interest to the neighboring subsystem.

L3 layer address change
> If an administrator changes the configuration of an interface, hosts that were reachable through that interface before might no longer be reachable through it. For that reason, changing an interface's address triggers a call to `neigh_ifdown`.

Protocol shutdown
> If an L3 protocol installed as a module is removed from the kernel, all of the associated neighboring entries become unusable and have to be removed.

Figure 27-11 shows two functions that do this kind of cleanup: dn_neigh_cleanup for the removal of DECnet and ndisc_cleanup for the removal of IPv6. IPv4 is not represented because it is not implemented as a module and is never removed.

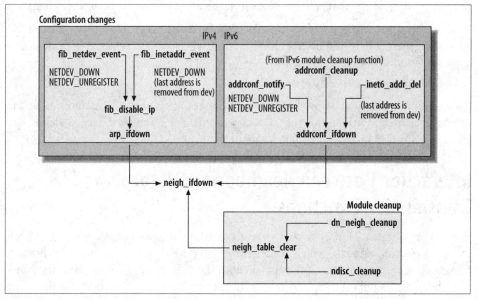

Figure 27-11. Contexts where neigh_ifdown is called

The function neigh_ifdown is pretty simple. It browses all the neighbour structures and makes the ones associated with the device that has triggered the event unusable. (They are not removed right away because references to them may be left in the neighboring subsystem.) Here are the main activities neigh_ifdown performs on each affected neighbour structure:

- Stops all pending timers.
- Changes the entry's state to NUD_NOARP so that any traffic that tries to use that entry does not trigger a solicitation request.
- Sets neigh->output to neigh_blackhole so that packets sent to the neighbor are dropped rather than delivered. See the description of this function in the section "Routines used for neigh->output."
- Invokes skb_queue_purge to drop all pending packets in the arp_queue queue. After neigh_ifdown clears the entries associated with the guilty device from the cache, the function calls pneigh_ifdown to do the same for the proxy cache, and the proxy's proxy_queue queue is purged.

Updates via neigh_changeaddr (netdevice notification chain)

The netdevice chain keeps track of numerous networking-related events, listed in Chapter 4. Neighboring protocols register with the kernel in their initialization routines (arp_init, ndisc_init, etc.) to ask for notifications from the netdevice chain.

The most important event for the neighboring subsystem is NETDEV_CHANGEADDR, which is generated by the do_setlink function when the L2 address of a device is changed with a command such as:

```
ip link set eth0 lladdr 01:02:03:04:05:06
```

When neigh_changeaddr is invoked by the change, it browses all the entries in the protocol cache and marks the ones associated with the changed device as dead. The garbage collection process then takes care of them.

Interaction Between Neighboring Protocols and L3 Transmission Functions

We saw in Chapter 21 that packet transmission in the IPv4 subsystem ends with a call to ip_finish_output2, which passes the packet down to the L2 layer. In this section, we'll see how this function interacts with the neighboring subsystem. The function that has a similar name and task within the IPv6 subsystem behaves the same way, except that it calls the ND protocol instead of IPv4's ARP protocol.

The input skb buffer, ip_finish_output2, includes the packet data (but without an L2 header), along with information such as the device to use for transmission and the routing table cache entry (dst) that was used by the kernel to make the forwarding decision. As we saw in Figure 27-1, that dst entry includes a pointer to the neighbour entry associated with the next hop (which can be either a router or the final destination itself). The decisions made by ip_finish_output2 that are of interest to us in this chapter are summarized in Figure 27-12.

If a cached L2 header is available (hh is not NULL), it is copied into the skb buffer. (skb->data points to the start of the user data, which is where the L2 header should be placed.) Finally, hh_output is invoked.

If no cached L2 header is available, ip_finish_output2 invokes the neigh->output method. As explained earlier in this chapter, the precise function associated with neigh->output depends on the state of the neighbour entry. If the L2 address is ready, the function will probably be neigh_connected, so the header can be filled in right away and the packet transmitted. Otherwise, neigh->output will probably be initialized to neigh_resolve_output, which will put the packet in the arp_queue queue, try to resolve the address by sending a solicitation request, and wait until the solicitation reply arrives, whereupon the packet is transmitted. Whether the packet is sent immediately or queued, ip_finish_output2 returns the same value, indicating success. The packet is not the IP subsystem's responsibility after this point; when the

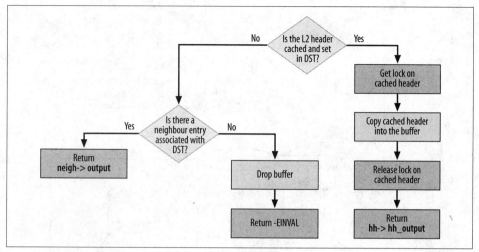

Figure 27-12. ip_finish_output2 function: compact version

solicitation reply arrives, the neighboring subsystem dequeues the packet from arp_
queue and sends it to the device.

As described earlier in the sections "Neighbor Deletion" and "Updates via neigh_
ifdown," if the necessary neighbour entry (the one associated with the routing table
cache element used to transmit the dst->neighbour packet) ceases to exist when ip_
finish_output2 is invoked, the packet is dropped. This condition is supposed to be
impossible, but the code is ready to handle this exception if it takes place.

Figures 27-13(a) and 27-13(b) offer a more detailed version of Figure 27-12 that
shows what happens depending on which function is assigned to neigh->output and
on the state of the neighbour entry. If you look at the source code, you can see that
the part of the flowchart that represents neigh_resolve_output consists mostly of the
expansion of neigh_event_send, with the exception of the part that is marked with
the dotted box.

When a new neighbour entry is in the NUD_NONE state, its state is changed to NUD_
INCOMPLETE and its timer is fired. The timer is initialized to expire right away. neigh_
timer_handler, the timer handler, then generates a solicitation request to resolve the
address.

dev_queue_xmit was introduced in Chapter 21. As shown in Figure 18-1 in
Chapter 18, dev_queue_xmit is the interface between the neighboring subsystem and
the Traffic Control subsystem, which stands between the neighboring protocol and
the device driver.

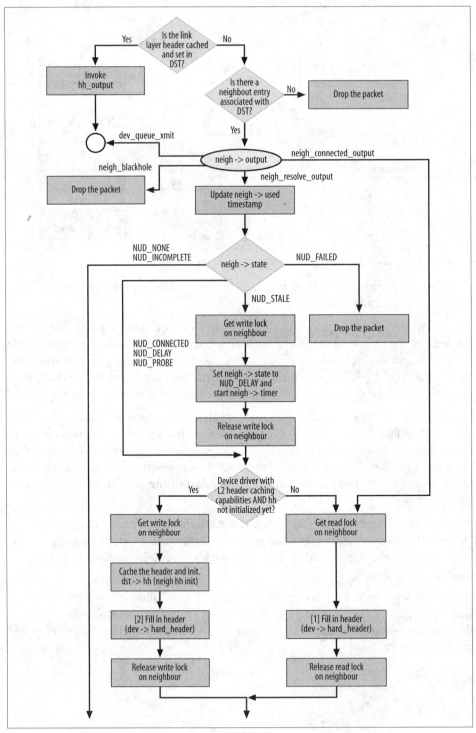

Figure 27-13(a). ip_finish_output2 function: expanded version

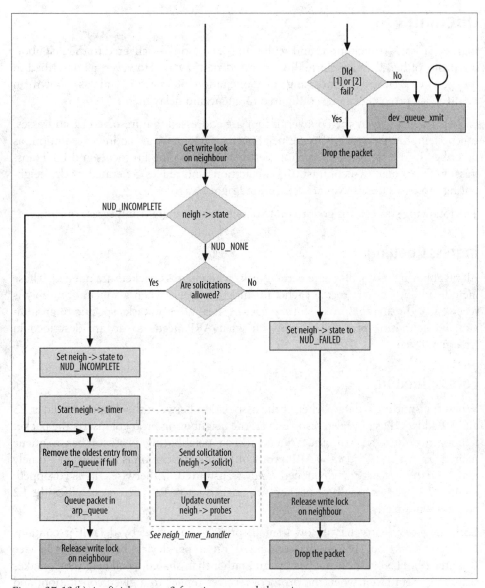

Figure 27-13(b). ip_finish_output2 function: expanded version

Queuing

Ingress packets—solicitations and replies to solicitations—delivered to the neighboring protocol handlers are normally processed right away. However, as described in the section "Delayed Processing of Solicitation Requests" and as shown in Figure 27-9, proxying can be configured to queue and delay them.

Packets transmitted by the L3 layer, if they are addressed to unresolved L2 addresses, can be temporarily queued by the neighboring layer to await address resolution, as described in the section "Interaction Between Neighboring Protocols and L3 Transmission Functions." (In contrast, the solicitations and replies generated by the neighboring protocols themselves are transmitted right away.)

The following subsections go into more detail on both ingress and egress queuing.

Ingress Queuing

All neighboring protocols share certain tasks when ingress packets are queued. These include adding packets to the cache, flushing arp_queue when a solicitation reply is received, and using the proxy's proxy_queue. There are also tasks specific to an individual neighboring protocol. Details on what ARP needs to do are described in Chapter 28.

Egress Queuing

When transmitting a data packet, if the association between the destination layer L3 and L2 address has not been resolved yet, the neighboring protocol inserts the packet temporarily into the arp_queue queue. (Each neighboring protocol has a queue named arp_queue, not just the ARP protocol.) If the association is resolved in a timely manner, the packet is dequeued and transmitted; otherwise, it is dropped. Figure 27-13 shows how IPv4 packets are queued into ARP's arp_queue when the L2 address is not ready.

Each neighbour entry has its own small, private arp_queue; by default it contains three elements, but it can be configured on a per-device basis via /proc (see Chapter 29). Having these queues private, rather than shared by all neighbors, makes searching them faster when the protocol receives replies to a given solicitation, and also assures a better level of fairness. If there is no space left when new elements are added to a private queue, new elements simply replace older ones (see __neigh_event_send).

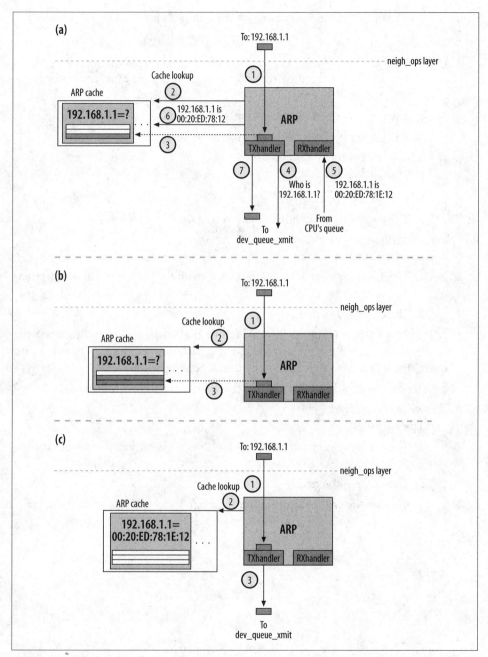

Figure 27-13. Packets handled in three common situations

Figure 27-13 shows three common cases, ignoring proxies for the sake of simplicity:

(a) Empty cache
    The steps are as follows.

1. The L3 layer submits a request to transmit a packet to the L3 destination address 192.168.1.1.

2. The cache is queried, generating a cache miss.

3. The packet is temporarily inserted into the queue.

4. A solicitation request is sent.

5. The solicitation reply arrives.

6. The cache is populated.

7. The packet waiting in the queue is sent out.

(b) Address resolution pending
    The steps are as follows.

1. The L3 layer submits a request to transmit a packet to the L3 destination address 192.168.1.1.

2. The cache is queried.

3. The address is not in the cache, but the kernel has already started the task of resolving the address, so the packet is temporarily inserted into the queue to wait for the reply to the pending request.

This case can occur when another packet is waiting at step (5) of case (a).

(c) Address already resolved
    The steps are as follows.

1. The L3 layer submits a request to transmit a packet to the L3 destination address 192.168.1.1.

2. The cache is queried.

3. Because the cache returns a hit, the packet can be sent out right away.

## CHAPTER 28

Neighboring Subsystem: Address Resolution Protocol (ARP)

Chapter 27 described the services provided by the infrastructure common to all neighboring protocols. This chapter will show how ARP, the protocol used by IPv4, fits into the modular design of the infrastructure. Readers familiar with ARP may have seen the outlines of its behavior in the description of the general neighboring subsystem in the previous chapters, although the nomenclature used to describe the subsystem is drawn more from IPv6's ND protocol than from ARP.

The presence of a common infrastructure makes the design and implementation of ARP simpler. To cover ARP in this chapter, we look at the following points:

- How the `neigh_table` structure `arp_tbl` is initialized to tune the behavior of the common neighboring infrastructure for ARP

- How the `neigh_parms` structure is initialized to tune the behavior of the common neighboring infrastructure for ARP (e.g., to set timer expiration periods)

- How the reception of ARP packets (i.e., `ARPOP_REQUEST`/`ARPOP_REPLY`) interacts with the neighboring subsystem, and how the `solicit` method works

- How the `neigh_ops` structure is initialized depending on the device type and the type of L3 address (unicast, multicast, or broadcast)

- How proxy ARP uses the common infrastructure

- How the behavior of ARP can be further tailored by means of compile options and the explicit configuration of special features

- How the kernel can hand some work over to a user-space daemon, *arpd*, to handle a particularly heavy workload

- The relationship between ARP and Reverse ARP (RARP)

- What events ARP can notify to other kernel subsystems, and vice versa

The chapter concludes with a brief overview of the improvements made by IPv6's ND over ARP.

ARP Packet Format

Figure 28-1 shows an ARP packet encapsulated in an Ethernet frame.

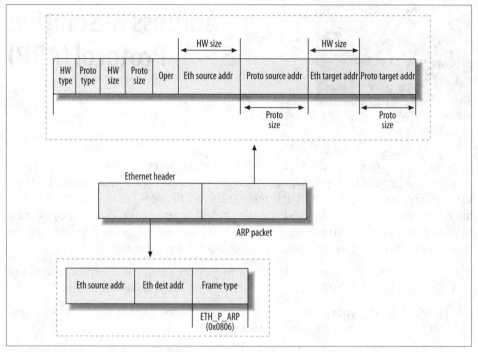

Figure 28-1. ARP packet encapsulated in an Ethernet frame

Here is a field-by-field description of the ARP packet's fields, represented in Linux with an arphdr structure:*

Hardware type
> Hardware type identifier (e.g., Ethernet). See the ARPHDR_XXX values in *include/ linux/if_arp.h*.

Protocol type
> L3 protocol identifier (e.g., IPv4). See the ETH_P_XXX values in *include/linux/if_ ether.h*.

Hardware size
> Size in octets of an L2 address (e.g., 6 for Ethernet).

---

* The arphdr structure does not contain placeholders for the last four fields of the ARP frame (the addresses); those are extracted by simply reading past the end of the Oper field, which is made possible thanks to the HS and PS fields.

Protocol size

    Size in octets of an L3 address (e.g., 4 for IPv4).

Oper

    Operation code, described following this list.

SHA, SPA (Sender Hardware Address, Sender Protocol Address)

    Hardware and protocol addresses of the sender.

THA, TPA (Target Hardware Address, Target Protocol Address)

    Hardware and the protocol addresses of the "target" (or receiver). The sender of a solicitation request normally sets THA to 0, because this address is just what the sender is trying to discover with the solicitation. But sometimes the sender tries to confirm an existing neighbour entry by sending a request containing the current, known THA.

Because ARP is normally used only for IPv4, kernel code uses the abbreviations SIP and TIP (Source IP address and Target IP address) to refer to SPA and STA.

A large number of ARP message types are offered in the ARPOP_*XXX* list of opcodes described in *include/linux/if_arp.h*. Two are used by RARP and are described later, in the section "Reverse Address Resolution Protocol (RARP)". Several are used by a relatively recent protocol named InARP, which is an extension to ARP (defined in RFC 2390) that is used by Frame Relay and ATM and is beyond the scope of this book. Here we will cover the two that are basic to ARP:

ARPOP_REQUEST

    This is used to send a solicitation in an attempt to resolve an L3 address to an L2 address. For a new neighbor entry, a host sends the message to the broadcast address associated with the device's hardware. To confirm an existing neighbour entry, the host sends the message directly to the neighbor's L2 address. A request is equivalent to what IPv6 calls *neighbor solicitation*.

    Solicitations also can be used for other reasons, such as those discussed in the section "Gratuitous ARP."

ARPOP_REPLY

    This is the message sent in answer to an ARPOP_REQUEST. Normally it is sent directly to the host that sent the request. But sometimes it can be sent to the broadcast address; a host can do this to update the caches of its neighbors after it changes its configuration. A broadcast reply is equivalent to what IPv6 calls *neighbor advertisement*.

Destination Address Types for ARP Packets

The *address type* of an L3 address can be unicast, broadcast, or multicast. The type is saved in the neighbour structure (as the neigh->type field), as explained in the section "Initialization of a neighbour Structure," and can be determined by invoking the routine inet_addr_type. Each type is handled by ARP as follows:

Unicast

This is the most common case, and is resolved by ARP's normal solicitation method.

Broadcast

ARP simply maps the L3 broadcast address directly to the L2 broadcast address associated with the device.

Multicast

ARP uses the routine `arp_mc_map` to derive the L2 multicast address from the L3 multicast address. ARP does not need to generate a solicitation request, because the L2 address can be derived by a formula that depends on the hardware type (Ethernet, Token Ring, etc.). See the section "Special Cases" in Chapter 26.

Example of an ARP Transaction

Figure 28-2 shows a simple case where one host asks for the L2 address associated with the IP address 10.0.0.4, and the owner of that address replies. The MAC target (the address to resolve) in the request is 0, to indicate that it should be filled in by whoever (probably the owner of the target IP address) replies.

If you look carefully at Figure 28-2, you can see that the sender hardware address is present twice: once in the Ethernet header and once in the ARP payload. They usually match, but not always (see the section "Acting As a Proxy" in Chapter 27).

More-detailed examples appear later in the section "Examples."

Gratuitous ARP

Normally an ARPOP_REQUEST is sent because the sender wants to talk to a given IP address and needs to find out the associated L2 address. But sometimes the sender generates an ARPOP_REQUEST to inform the receivers about some information, instead of asking for information. This is called *gratuitous ARP* and is commonly used in the following situations:

- Change of L2 address
- Duplicate address detection
- Virtual IP

Each is described in the subsections that follow.

Change of L2 Address

We already saw in the section "Reasons That Neighboring Protocols Are Needed" in Chapter 26, that a change of L2 address (which invalidates neighbour entries for other nodes on the network) cannot be detected without the help of a protocol.

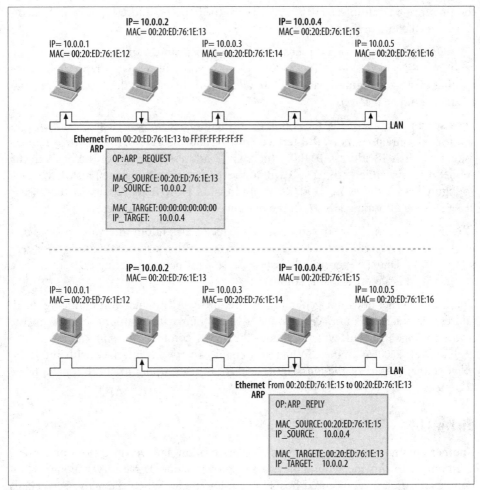

Figure 28-2. Example of ARP usage

Instead of waiting for the old association to expire and forcing each node to start a new protocol transaction (and therefore suffer a temporary black hole), it makes sense to trigger the update of the association in advance. The node that changed the address accomplishes the update through gratuitous ARP. See *net/irda/irlan/irlan_eth.c* for an example.

Duplicate Address Detection

No two hosts on a local network should have the same L3 address, but this problem can happen, especially in big networks with a mix of static and dynamic (that is, DHCP-based) configurations. The most common reasons for duplicate addresses are the presence of multiple DHCP servers with overlapping address pools, and incorrect manual configurations.

To detect the presence of a duplicate address, a host can use gratuitous ARPs. If you send an ARP solicitation for your own address, you will receive a reply only when another host is configured with your IP address. If there is no duplicate address, no replies should be received.

Let's see an example using the topology in Figure 28-3. When Host A boots up, as soon as it configures its *eth0* interface with IP address 10.0.0.4, it sends a request asking who has IP address 10.0.0.4 (its own IP address). If none of the hosts in the subnet was misconfigured, Host A will not receive a reply. But since Host Bad_guy is configured with the same 10.0.0.4 IP address as Host A, it replies to the ARPOP_REQUEST, thus informing Host A of the presence of a duplicate address.

Of course, allowing hosts to send out ARP packets at random intervals on large networks is bad for performance. Instead, as shown in the section "Requests with zero addresses," a DHCP sever usually issues the request before granting an address to a client, which is a more scalable solution.

The Linux kernel does not generate any gratuitous ARP when you configure an IP address on the local interfaces. However, most Linux distributions come with the *iputils* package installed, which includes the *arping* command. *arping* can be used to generate ARP_REQUEST frames. When you enable a network interface with the */sbin/ifup* command (part of the *initscripts* package), it uses *arping* to check for duplicate addresses.

Virtual IP

Another common use for gratuitous ARP is to allow failover in a pool of servers. Commonly, to provide redundancy, a site provides one active server along with a number of similarly configured hosts in standby mode. When the active server fails for some reason, a mechanism often referred to as a *heartbeat timer* (implemented through some protocol on the pool of servers) detects the failure and triggers the election of a new active server. This new server generates a gratuitous ARP to update the ARP cache of all the other hosts in the network. Because the new server has taken the IP address of the old server, the ARPOP_REQUEST is not answered, but all the recipients update their caches accordingly.

Note that in this way, the IP layer and higher layers can keep communicating without even noticing the change. Of course, because heartbeats are sent out at regular intervals, a small window of time exists after the old server fails and the new one takes over, during which traffic is not delivered. So some nodes may discover the failure and mark their neighbor entries as failed until the new ARPOP_REQUEST arrives.

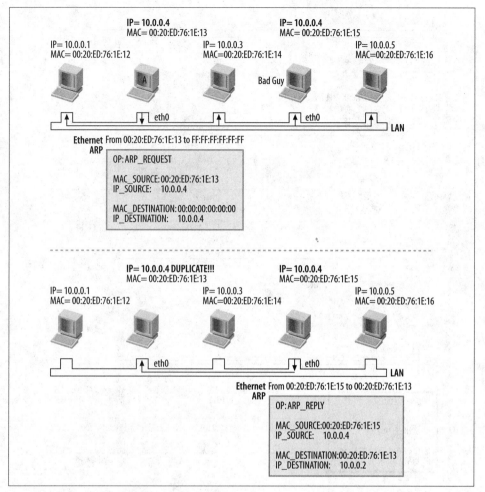

Figure 28-3. Example of duplicate address detection

The example in Figure 28-4* shows two routers, one taking the active role and the other taking the standby role (a). The server labeled Active has the IP address 10.0.0.1. The hosts of LAN2 use this router to communicate with the hosts of LAN1, and vice versa.

A failover system is in place so that when the Active router fails, the Standby router takes over the IP address 10.0.0.1 and becomes the Active router (b). When the Standby router becomes the new Active router, sends out a gratuitous ARP request that changes the entries of all local hosts (c) so that 10.0.0.1 is associated with the L2

---

* The MAC addresses in the figure are truncated for convenience. For example, 00:...:03 stands for 00:00:00: 00:00:03. I used simple MAC addresses like that one to simplify the figure.

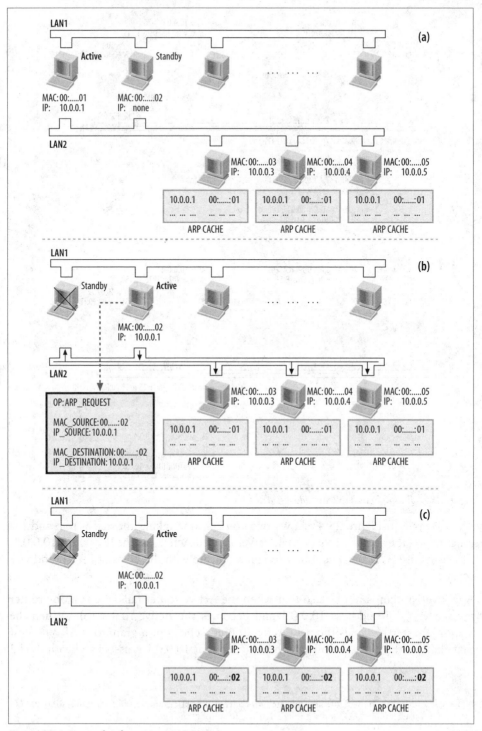

Figure 28-4. Example of gratuitous ARP

address of the new active router. Subsequent IP traffic from LAN2 comes to this router. The new Active router also sends a gratuitous ARP request to LAN1, but this is not shown in the figure. The figure also does not show another detail that a real-life administrator would configure: each router would have a second IP address on each of its interfaces, used mainly to provide connectivity when the current role is not active.

Responding from Multiple Interfaces

Linux has a rather unusual design: it considers an IP address as belonging to a host rather than an interface, even though administrators always assign IP addresses to particular interfaces.* This has impacts that some administrators complain about:

- A Linux host replies to any ARP solicitation requests that specify a target IP address configured on any of its interfaces, even if the request was received on this host by a different interface. To make Linux behave as if addresses belong to interfaces, administrators can use the ARP_IGNORE feature described later in the section "/proc Options."

- Hosts can experience the *ARP flux* problem, in which the wrong interface becomes associated with an L3 address. This problem is described in the text that follows.

Imagine you have a host with two NICs on the same LAN, and that another host sends an ARP request for one of the addresses. The request is received by both interfaces, as shown in Figure 28-5, and both interfaces reply.

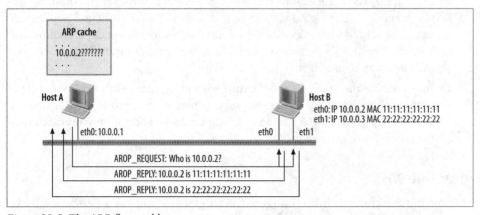

Figure 28-5. The ARP flux problem

---

* Using the options described in the section "Tunable ARP Options," you can make Linux behave as if IP addresses belonged to the interfaces. For an interesting discussion of this design, including its advantages and disadvantages, you can refer to the (pretty long) thread "ARP responds on all devices" on the *netdev* mailing list, which is archived at *http://oss.sgi.com/archives/netdev*.

The host sending the solicitation therefore receives two replies to its request. One comes from the NIC with the correct L2 address (*eth0*) but the other bears the other NIC's address (*eth1*). Which address is entered by the correspondent in its ARP cache depends on the order in which the requests happen to be received and the host's way of handing duplicate replies—in short, it's nondeterministic.

The ARP flux problem can be solved with the features described in the section "Tunable ARP Options."

Tunable ARP Options

The kernel allows the user to tune the ARP behavior via both the */proc* filesystem and compile-time options. We will see details on how to configure those features, their allowed settings, and their defaults in the section "Tuning via /proc Filesystem" in Chapter 29, but let's introduce the main ones here.

Compile-Time Options

Two ARP options can be enabled at compile time:

ARPD (CONFIG_ARPD)

> This allows a user-space daemon to handle ARP, which can improve performance on a very large and busy network. See the section "ARPD."

UNSOLICITED ARP (CONFIG_IP_ACCEPT_UNSOLICITED_ARP)

> By default, when a host receives an ARPOP_REPLY for which it had no pending ARPOP_REQUEST, the kernel drops the reply. Sometimes, however, it could be useful to accept it. This feature, which establishes that unsolicited replies are accepted, is actually not supported by Linux anymore: the code is commented out (in the function arp_process) and the kernel configuration menu does not provide any way to enable it.
>
> Do not confuse the effect of this feature with gratuitous ARP. ARP_UNSOLICITED accepts unsolicited ARPOP_REPLY packets, whereas gratuitous ARP causes a "push" update via an ARPOP_REQUEST. As Figure 28-18 shows, only unicast unsolicited requests are accepted.

/proc Options

Most of those features can be configured both globally and on a per-device basis. Code can check whether they are enabled by using the IN_DEV_XXX macros defined in *include/linux/inetdevice.h* (e.g., IN_DEV_ARP_ANNOUNCE, IN_DEV_ARP_IGNORE, and IN_DEV_ARPFILTER). Please refer to the definition of those macros to see which features are global and which are local. All of the macros take, as their input parameter, the device's IP configuration block (net_device->ip_ptr), which is normally retrieved with the routine in_dev_get.

Some of those options have been introduced to address issues specific to Linux Virtual Servers (LVS). In the LVS HOWTO, in the section "LVS: the ARP problem," you can find detailed information on what these features are for and how they can be configured. You will also find information about previous approaches.

ARP_ANNOUNCE

This option controls which source IP addresses can be put in the ARP headers of solicitation requests, when the host generating the request offers multiple addresses. Table 28-1 lists the allowed levels and tells how the IP address is selected from the ones configured on the local system. The section "Solicitations" shows how ARP uses it. ARP_ANNOUNCE is handled in the arp_solicit function.

Table 28-1. ARP_ANNOUNCE levels

Value	Meaning
0 (Default)	Any local IP address is fine.
1	If possible, pick an address that falls within the same subnet of the target address. If not possible, use level 2.
2	Prefer primary addresses.

ARP_IGNORE

This option controls the criteria that determine whether to process ARPOP_REQUEST packets.

Normally, all requests that can be handled by a host are processed. As explained in the section "Responding from Multiple Interfaces," IP addresses in Linux belong to the host, not to its interfaces. Because of that, an ARPOP_REQUEST will be processed by a host as long as the target IP address is configured on any of the interfaces, including the loopback interface.* In some cases, such as with LVS, that would be a problem. By configuring ARP_IGNORE properly, an administrator can solve the problem. See the LVS HOWTO for a detailed description of the problem and the possible solutions.

Figure 28-6 shows an example of virtual server configuration. The address by which the server is known to the world is shown as VIP, which is configured on an NIC on the virtual server and as the loopback address on the two real servers. All replies to requests for the address VIP should come from only the virtual server. But when the virtual server receives a request for the services it provides, it forwards it to one of the real servers using a well-defined selection algorithm. The receiving hosts accept the packets because they have VIP locally configured. Both real servers configure ARP_ IGNORE on their *eth0* interface so that they will not respond to ARPOP_REQUEST for the VIP address.

---

* 127.*x.x.x* addresses are an exception; ARP requests for them are never handled.

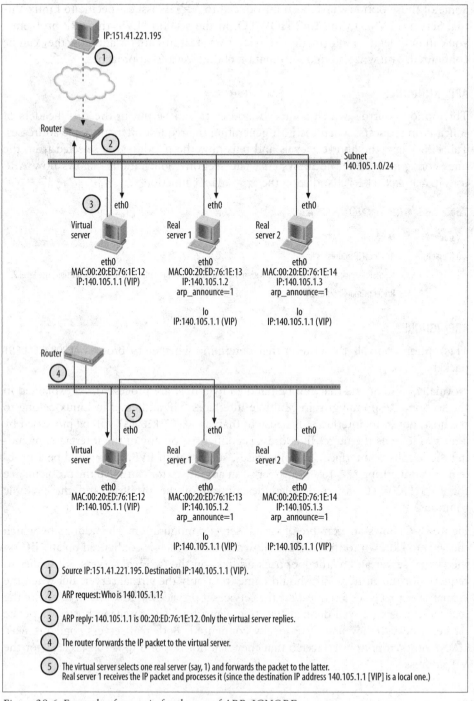

IP:151.41.221.195

Router

Subnet
140.105.1.0/24

eth0

eth0

eth0

Virtual
server

Real
server 1

Real
server 2

eth0
MAC:00:20:ED:76:1E:12
IP:140.105.1.1 (VIP)

eth0
MAC:00:20:ED:76:1E:13
IP:140.105.1.2
arp_announce=1

eth0
MAC:00:20:ED:76:1E:14
IP:140.105.1.3
arp_announce=1

lo
IP:140.105.1.1 (VIP)

lo
IP:140.105.1.1 (VIP)

Router

eth0

eth0

eth0

Virtual
server

Real
server 1

Real
server 2

eth0
MAC:00:20:ED:76:1E:12
IP:140.105.1.1 (VIP)

eth0
MAC:00:20:ED:76:1E:13
IP:140.105.1.2
arp_announce=1

eth0
MAC:00:20:ED:76:1E:14
IP:140.105.1.3
arp_announce=1

lo
IP:140.105.1.1 (VIP)

lo
IP:140.105.1.1 (VIP)

1 Source IP:151.41.221.195. Destination IP:140.105.1.1 (VIP).

2 ARP request: Who is 140.105.1.1?

3 ARP reply: 140.105.1.1 is 00:20:ED:76:1E:12. Only the virtual server replies.

4 The router forwards the IP packet to the virtual server.

5 The virtual server selects one real server (say, 1) and forwards the packet to the latter.
   Real server 1 receives the IP packet and processes it (since the destination IP address 140.105.1.1 [VIP] is a local one.)

Figure 28-6. Example of scenario for the use of ARP_IGNORE

ARP_IGNORE is handled in the arp_process function. Possible values are listed in Table 28-2.

Table 28-2. ARP_IGNORE values

Value	Meaning
0 (Default)	Reply for any local address.
1	Reply only if the target IP is configured on the receiving interface.
2	Like 1, but the source IP (sender's address) must belong to the same subnet as the target IP.
3	Reply only if the scope of the target IP is not the local host (e.g., that address is not used to communicate with other hosts).
4–7	Reserved.
8	Do not reply.
>8	Unknown value; accept request.

ARP_FILTER

This option controls whether an interface should reply to an ingress ARPOP_REQUEST in scenarios where multiple NICs are connected to the same LAN and are configured on the same IP subnet. In this scenario, where each NIC receives a copy of the ARPOP_REQUEST, you want only one interface (chosen deterministically, not at random) to reply. This feature is useful mainly in networks where the IP source routing options are used.

Let's take the example in Figure 28-7. When Host A tries to resolve the 10.0.0.1 IP address, both of Host B's interfaces receive the ARPOP_REQUEST. For both requests, Host B consults the routing table and replies only to the request that was received on the interface that would be used by Host B to reach the sender's IP address (10.0.0.3). Host B's routing table shows that the 10.0.0.3 address is reachable via both *eth0* and *eth1*. However, we will see in Part VII that when multiple routes are available toward any given IP address, a routing lookup always returns the same one[*] (i.e., the first one that matches).

When configured, ingress ARPOP_REQUEST packets are processed only if the kernel knows how to reach the sender's IP address, and if the device used to reach the sender's IP address is the same as the device where the request was received.

Note that ARP filtering has nothing to do with the filtering that can be done with Netfilter. The two are configured and enforced independently.

Unlike the previous two options, ARP_FILTER can only be enabled or disabled; there are no intermediate states. It is handled in the arp_process function.

---

[*] Unless the kernel comes with support for multipath caching. That feature is described in Chapter 33.

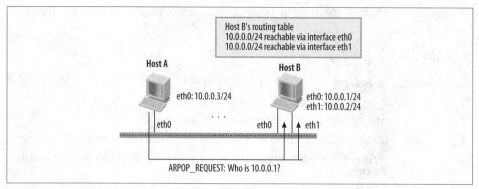

Figure 28-7. Example of scenario for the use of ARP_FILTER

Medium ID

This is a feature that can be used to handle certain rare cases where a subnet spans different LANs, and where a host offering proxy ARP has multiple NICs on that subnet serving the different LANs. The term *medium* refers to a network served by a single broadcast address. If a hub or switch ties two such media together, a situation could arise where a proxy ARP host acts as a proxy inappropriately, responding to a request on behalf of a host on a different LAN that could handle the request itself.

We already saw in Chapter 26 that a proxy ARP server does not reply to an ARPOP_ REQUEST that is received on the same device through which the solicited IP address can be reached. However, when multiple NICs are connected to the same LAN, this condition may not be sufficient to ensure proper behavior. Let's look at the example in Figure 28-8.*

Host B is configured with two NICs on the same LAN (medium). *eth0* is used to reach all of the IP addresses in the 10.0.0.0/24 subnet, and *eth1* is used to communicate to Host C only, thanks to the /30 netmask. Host B acts as a proxy for both LAN1 and LAN3.

Let's assume now that Host A needs to transmit something to HostC but does not have its L2 address. Host A will send a broadcast ARPOP_REQUEST, which will be received by both *eth0* and *eth1* on Host B as well as by Host C. Host B should not reply to the ARPOP_REQUEST because Host C will do so by itself.

---

* This is an extended version of the example provided by Julian Anastasov and Alexey Kuznetsov at *http:// www.ssi.bg/~ja/medium_id.txt*. The document also describes a common scenario where this feature can be useful.

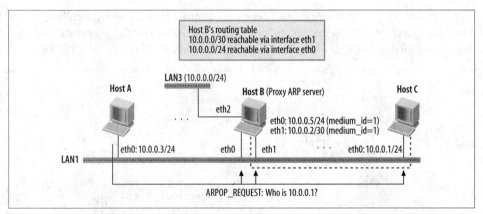

Figure 28-8. Example of use of medium ID

Let's suppose Host B is a proxy ARP server with proxying enabled on all of its interfaces, and see how it behaves when it receives the ARPOP_REQUEST on both of its interfaces:

Request received on eth0
> According to the routing table, the solicited address 10.0.0.1 is reachable via a different interface (*eth1*). Therefore, Host B processes the request. Note that Host B has two routes that match the destination address 10.0.0.1, but the one with netmask /30 is more specific and therefore wins.

Request received on eth1
> In this case, the receiving interface and the one used to reach 10.0.0.1 match, so Host B does not process the request.

As you can see, there is a need for a way to tell the proxy ARP server that its two interfaces reside on the same broadcast domain, and that therefore neither of the two ARPOP_REQUESTs should be processed. This is done by assigning an ID called the *medium ID* to interfaces connected to the same LAN. In this case, the same medium ID should be assigned to both *eth0* and *eth1* on Host B. A host replies to an ingress solicitation request only when the solicited address is reachable through a device with a medium ID different from the one associated with the ingress device. Medium IDs are positive numbers; other values have special meanings as shown in Table 28-3.

Table 28-3. Value of medium ID

Value	Meaning
−1	Proxy ARP is disabled.
0 (default)	Medium ID feature is disabled.
>0	Valid medium ID.

The medium ID configuration is not necessary in the topology in Figure 28-9, where Host B's interfaces are connected to two different LANs. For details on the purpose and use of medium IDs, see *http://www.ssi.bg/~ja/medium_id.txt*.

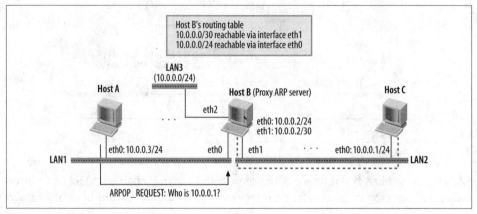

Figure 28-9. Redesign of the topology in Figure 28-8 that does not need the medium ID configuration

Figure 28-10 shows the logic implemented by arp_fwd_proxy, the routine invoked by arp_process to see whether a given ARP request can be proxied based on the proxy ARP and Medium ID configuration.

ARP Protocol Initialization

The ARP protocol is initialized by arp_init in *net/ipv4/arp.c*.

The skeleton of a general protocol initialization routine was shown in the section "Protocol Initialization and Cleanup" in Chapter 27. In this chapter we'll examine what is ARP-specific.

The first step in the function is to register a table of virtual functions and other general parameters used by ARP; this is done by neigh_table_init. The contents of the table, arp_tbl, are described in the next section.

We saw in Chapter 13 how dev_add_pack is used to install a protocol handler. If you remember how that routine is used, from the following definition of arp_packet_type it should be clear that ARP packets will be processed by the arp_rcv function (defined in the same *net/ipv4/arp.c* file).

```
static struct packet_type arp_packet_type = {
     .type:    __constant_htons(ETH_P_ARP),
     .func:    arp_rcv,
};
```

arp_proc_init creates the */proc/net/arp* file, which can be read to see the contents of the ARP cache (including proxy destinations).

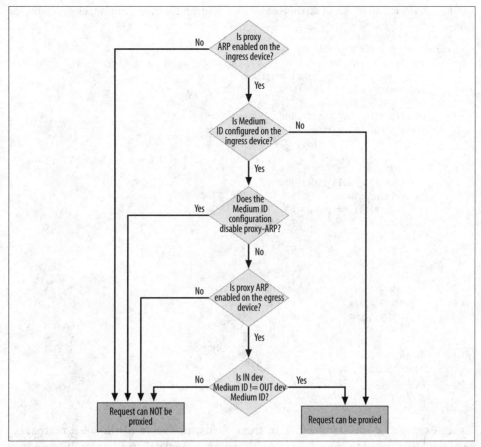

Figure 28-10. arp_fwd_proxy function

When the kernel is compiled with support for sysctl, the directory */proc/sys/net/ ipv4/neigh* is created to export the default tuning parameters of the neigh_parms structure by means of neigh_sysctl_register. Note that the first input parameter to the latter is set to NULL, which, as we will see in the section "Directory creation," in Chapter 29, means that the caller (arp_init) wants to register the default directory.

register_netdevice_notifier registers a callback function with the kernel to receive notifications about changes to the configurations and status of devices. See the section "External Events" for more details.

The arp_tbl Table

This is the basic data structure that contains essential variables to which the ARP protocol refers. The role of the structure, which is of type neigh_table, was described in the section "Main Data Structures" in Chapter 27. ARP initializes its table as follows:

```
struct neigh_table arp_tbl = {
    .family:        AF_INET,
    .entry_size:    sizeof(struct neighbour) + 4,
    .key_len:       4,
    .hash:          arp_hash,
    .constructor:   arp_constructor,
    .proxy_redo:    parp_redo,
    .id:            "arp_cache",
    .parms: {
        .tbl:                   &arp_tbl,
        .base_reachable_time:   30 * HZ,
        .retrans_time:          1 * HZ,
        .gc_staletime:          60 * HZ,
        .reachable_time:        30 * HZ,
        .delay_probe_time:      5 * HZ,
        .queue_len:             3,
        .ucast_probes:          3,
        .mcast_probes:          3,
        .anycast_delay:         1 * HZ,
        .proxy_delay:           (8 * HZ) / 10,
        .proxy_qlen:            64,
        .locktime:              1 * HZ,
    },
    .gc_interval:   30 * HZ,
    .gc_thresh1:    128,
    .gc_thresh2:    512,
    .gc_thresh3:    1024,
};
```

As an example of the significance of these fields, the value of the base_reachable_time field (described in the section "neigh_parms Structure" in Chapter 29) indicates that ARP considers an entry NUD_REACHABLE only if the last proof of reachability arrived within the last 30 seconds. Similarly, the retrans_time field (described in the same section) indicates that if no reply is received to a solicitation, a new one will be sent after 1 second.

In the following sections, we'll examine the hash, constructor, and proxy_redo methods. We will also see how arp_rcv processes ingress ARP packets.

Initialization of a neighbour Structure

As we saw in earlier chapters, a neighbour structure stores all of the information needed to perform the neighboring protocol's job—translating an L3 address to an L2 address—for a single L3-to-L2 address mapping. Each protocol specifies the function used to create a neighbour structure in its neigh_table->constructor virtual function. ARP's initialization function, as you can see from the definition of the arp_tbl structure in the previous section, is arp_constructor.

Basic Initialization Sequence

Figure 28-11 shows the basic steps in creating a neighbor entry.

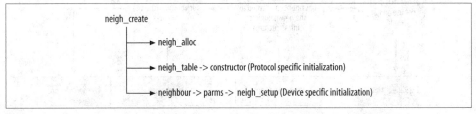

Figure 28-11. Initialization sequence for a new neighbour structure

We saw in the section "Creating a neighbour Entry" in Chapter 27 that a neighbor can be created for different reasons and in different initial states. Because of that, the default values assigned to the fields of the neighbour structure can be overridden by the caller. For instance, neigh->nud_state is set to NUD_NONE when the neighbour structure is created as a consequence of a transmission request toward the associated neighbor. But it could also be NUD_PERMANENT or NUD_STALE if the entry was created from the command line. Broadcast and multicast IP addresses do not need any help from ARP to be translated to an L2 broadcast or multicast corresponding address, so in these cases, nud_state is set to NUD_NOARP.

Particularly important are the initializations of the following fields:

nud_state
> The initial state of the neighbour structure depends on the type of L3 address and the reason the entry was created.

output
> output is initialized based on the value assigned to nud_state.

ha
> This field is the L2 address, which is what the ARP protocol is there to discover. Once again, ARP is not needed for the addresses described in the section "Special Cases" in Chapter 26, and the L2 address can be derived from the L3 address right away.

ops
> As described in Chapter 27, this collection of virtual functions determines the operations invoked by the IP subsystem. Figure 28-12 summarizes the criteria used by ARP (more exactly, arp_constructor) to select which instance of neigh_ops to use, among the four defined in *net/ipv4/arp.c*.

When not explicitly set by neigh_create, the fields just described inherit the values assigned by neigh_alloc, which is called by neigh_create before it invokes the constructor virtual function.

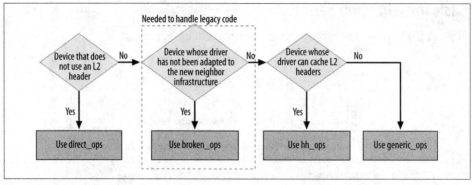

Figure 28-12. Initialization of neigh->ops in arp_constructor

Virtual Functions in the ops Field

In the section "Common Interface Between L3 Protocols and Neighboring Protocols" in Chapter 27, we saw an overview of the functions provided by the neighboring infrastructure in *net/core/neighbour.c* for the output, connected_output, hh_output, and queue_xmit methods used by a neighboring protocol. In this chapter, we focus on the ones provided by the ARP protocol. The four sets of methods that can be assigned to neigh->ops (depending on the state of the neighbour) are:

```
static struct neigh_ops arp_generic_ops = {
    .family:             AF_INET,
    .solicit:            arp_solicit,
    .error_report:       arp_error_report,
    .output:             neigh_resolve_output,
    .connected_output:   neigh_connected_output,
    .hh_output:          dev_queue_xmit,
    .queue_xmit:         dev_queue_xmit,
};

static struct neigh_ops arp_hh_ops = {
    .family:             AF_INET,
    .solicit:            arp_solicit,
    .error_report:        arp_error_report,
    .output:             neigh_resolve_output,
    .connected_output:    neigh_resolve_output,
    .hh_output:          dev_queue_xmit,
    .queue_xmit:         dev_queue_xmit,
};

static struct neigh_ops arp_direct_ops = {
    .family:             AF_INET,
    .output:             dev_queue_xmit,
    .connected_output:    dev_queue_xmit,
    .hh_output:          dev_queue_xmit,
    .queue_xmit:         dev_queue_xmit,
};
```

```
struct neigh_ops arp_broken_ops = {
    .family:              AF_INET,
    .solicit:             arp_solicit,
    .error_report:         arp_error_report,
    .output:              neigh_compat_output,
    .connected_output:     neigh_compat_output,
    .hh_output:           dev_queue_xmit,
    .queue_xmit:          dev_queue_xmit,
};
```

The three fields with an ARP-specific initialization are set to the same value in all four neigh_ops instances (except that arp_direct_ops does not need some of the fields, and therefore omits their definitions).

family
> AF_INET simply indicates that ARP works with IPv4.

solicit
> arp_solicit is called to generate a solicitation request, either to resolve an address for the first time or to confirm one that is already in the cache. In the latter case, it is triggered by the expiration of a timer, as discussed in the section "Timers" in Chapter 27.
>
> The transmission is done with arp_send, which is described in the section "Transmitting ARP Packets: Introduction to arp_send."

error_report
> arp_error_report notifies the upper networking layers when there is an error in an ARP transaction. See the section "Generated Events."

Start of the arp_constructor Function

The first task of arp_constructor is to retrieve an in_dev structure from the device associated with the neighbor. This structure stores the IP layer configuration of the network device, which includes the ARP configuration information, too. If it does not exist, the device the neighbor is associated with does not have an IP configuration and therefore the use of ARP does not make sense; the function therefore terminates with an error.

If the device has an IP configuration, the ARP configuration information is stored in the neighbour entry via the neigh->parms pointer.

```
static int arp_constructor(struct neighbour *neigh)
{
    u32 addr = *(u32*)neigh->primary_key;
    struct net_device *dev = neigh->dev;
    struct in_device *in_dev;
    struct neigh_parms *parms

    neigh->type = inet_addr_type(addr);
```

```
    rcu_read_lock();
    in_dev = rcu_dereference(__in_dev_get(dev));
    if (in_dev == NULL) {
        rcu_read_unlock();
        return -EINVAL;
    }

    parms = in_dev->arp_parms;
    __neigh_parms_put(neigh->parms);
    neigh->parms = neigh_parms_clone(parms);

    rcu_read_unlock();

    if (dev->hard_header == NULL) {
        /* Case1: Device that does not use L2 */
    } else {
        /* Case2: Device that does use L2 */
    }
```

The following steps depend on whether the device driver provides an L2 protocol header, dev->hard_header.

Devices That Do Not Need ARP

When dev->hard_header is not set, it means that the device driver does not provide a function to fill in the L2 header. This in turn means that the device does not have an L2 header, so the state of the neighbour entry should be set to NUD_NOARP. Moreover, neigh_ops is initialized to arp_direct_ops, which consists of a neigh_ops structure with all the functions initialized to dev_queue_xmit: because there is no need for a neighboring protocol, arp_direct_ops simply goes straight to the lower layer.

```
    neigh->nud_state = NUD_NOARP;
    neigh->ops = &arp_direct_ops;
    neigh->output = neigh->ops->queue_xmit;
```

Note that neigh->ops is not necessarily set to arp_direct_ops every time state is set to NUD_NOARP. There are cases, such as IP broadcast addresses, where the L2 layer uses a header (dev->hard_header is not NULL) but ARP is not needed.

Also note that neigh->ha is not initialized, because it is not needed.

Devices That Need ARP

As shown in Figure 28-12, once arp_constructor establishes that a device needs ARP, it has to further differentiate between devices whose drivers have been updated to the new neighboring infrastructure and those that still use the old one (see the functions noted as obsolete in *net/ipv4/arp.c*).

Device types are identified by the ARP header type, a list of ARPHDR_*XXX* values included in *include/linux/if_arp.h*. arp_constructor uses these types to distinguish between old- and new-style drivers.

At the moment, only the amateur radio devices and some WAN cards are still using the old code. For these, neigh->ops is initialized to arp_broken_ops, which consists of virtual functions based on the old code.

```
        switch (dev->type) {
        default:
            break;
        case ARPHRD_ROSE:
#if defined(CONFIG_AX25) || defined(CONFIG_AX25_MODULE)
        case ARPHRD_AX25:
#if defined(CONFIG_NETROM) || defined(CONFIG_NETROM_MODULE)
        case ARPHRD_NETROM:
#endif
            neigh->ops = &arp_broken_ops;
            neigh->output = neigh->ops->output;
            return 0;
#endif
        ;}
#endif
```

For other devices, the kernel initializes neigh->ops based on the capabilities of the device driver. If the device driver provides a function to manage L2 header caching (dev->hard_header_cache), arp_hh_ops is used. Otherwise, the generic arp_generic_ops is selected. To know whether a given device provides this service, look at the device's associated *xxx*_setup function (e.g., ether_setup for Ethernet cards, as described in Chapter 8).

```
    if (dev->hard_header_cache)
        neigh->ops = &arp_hh_ops;
    else
        neigh->ops = &arp_generic_ops;
```

The initialization of neigh->output, as described earlier in the section "Basic Initialization Sequence," depends on nud_state. For example, when the neighbour structure is ready to be used (NUD_VALID), the output function can be initialized directly to connected_output. See the section "Routines used for neigh->output" in Chapter 27 for more details about neigh->output.

```
        if (neigh->nud_state&NUD_VALID)
            neigh->output = neigh->ops->connected_output;
        else
            neigh->output = neigh->ops->output;
```

The loopback device (lo) and devices configured with the IFF_NOARP flag do not need to use ARP to resolve the address. However, because the neighboring subsystem still needs an address to put into the L2 header, this function assigns the one associated with the device.

```
neigh->type = inet_addr_type(addr);
... ... ...
if (neigh->type == RTN_MULTICAST) {
    neigh->nud_state = NUD_NOARP;
    arp_mc_map(addr, neigh->ha, dev, 1);
} else if (dev->flags&(IFF_NOARP|IFF_LOOPBACK)) {
    neigh->nud_state = NUD_NOARP;
    memcpy(neigh->ha, dev->dev_addr, dev->addr_len);
} else if (neigh->type == RTN_BROADCAST || dev->flags&IFF_POINTOPOINT) {
    neigh->nud_state = NUD_NOARP;
    memcpy(neigh->ha, dev->broadcast, dev->addr_len);
}
```

Transmitting and Receiving ARP Packets

The functions used to send and receive ARP packets are:

arp_send

> The neighboring subsystem calls neigh_ops->solicit to transmit a solicitation request. In the case of ARP, the solicit function (arp_solicit) is a simple wrapper around arp_send. arp_send fills in the ARP header and payload and uses the dev_queue_xmit function to transmit the request.

arp_rcv

> Because ARP is a protocol in its own right (unlike ND for IPv6), it registers a handler in arp_init. The next section describes arp_rcv in detail, along with how the two main ARP packet types are processed.

As shown in Figure 28-13, both transmission and reception of ARP packets can be controlled by Netfilter.

The dotted lines between arp_rcv and arp_send indicate that in some cases, the reception of an ARP packet triggers the transmission of at least one other ARP packet. This occurs when:

- Bridging is configured. A bridge receiving an ARP packet may just forward it to other bridge interfaces without processing it.
- The ingress packet is an ARPOP_REQUEST and the neighboring subsystem decides it can reply according to its configuration. The subsystem generates an ARPOP_REPLY.

As Figure 28-13 shows, arp_send is also triggered by external events and a few kernel features such as bonding; details are provided in later sections.

Transmitting ARP Packets: Introduction to arp_send

arp_send is the routine provided by ARP to transmit both solicitation requests and replies, as shown in Figure 28-14. Chapter 27 explained on a protocol-independent

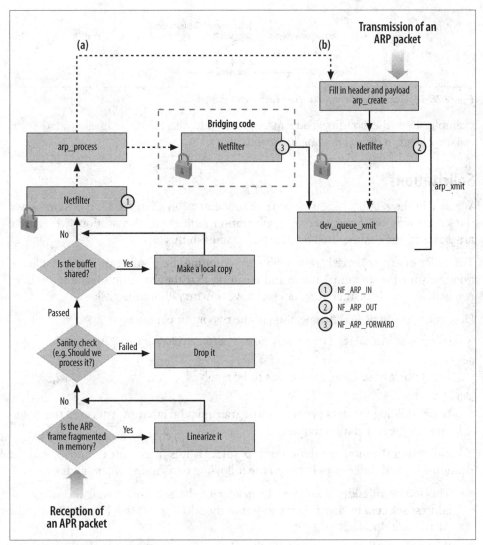

Figure 28-13. (a) arp_rcv; (b) arp_send

level how the neighbor infrastructure takes care of solicitation transmissions and retransmissions. Here we'll see how arp_send accomplishes its job.

As shown in Figure 28-13(b), arp_send is split into two parts: arp_create initializes the ARP packet, and arp_xmit hooks into Netfilter and then invokes dev_queue_xmit.

arp_send is split into these two parts so that drivers that need to manipulate a packet—for instance, by inserting extra headers—can call arp_create and arp_xmit separately. The driver can thus perform some customization in between. See, for

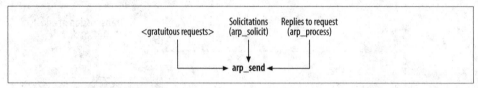

Figure 28-14. Examples of contexts where arp_send is used

example, how the bonding code manages to add the 802.1Q tag if needed (rlb_update_client in *drivers/net/bonding/bond_alb.c*).

Solicitations

We saw in the section "Creating a neighbour Entry" in Chapter 27, the times when the kernel may need to generate a solicitation request. In this section, we analyze arp_solicit, the routine used by ARP to accomplish this task.

The caller of arp_solicit is responsible for counting the number of probes (solicitation transmission attempts) made and ensuring that the maximum has not yet been reached. arp_solicit, therefore, doesn't have to worry about this task.

Here is its prototype and the meaning of the two input parameters:

```
static void arp_solicit(struct neighbour * neigh, struct sk_buff *skb)
```
neigh
> Neighbor whose L3 address needs to be resolved.

skb
> Buffer holding the data packets whose transmission attempts triggered the generation of the solicitation request.

To understand the implementation of arp_solicit, it is important to understand the relationships and differences between the following two groups of parameters:

- The source IP addresses in the IP header of the skb buffer, and the source IP address selected by arp_solicit to put in the ARP header (see Figure 28-1 for the ARP header format).

  When the traffic is generated locally, the source IP address in the IP header is local to the system. When the packet is being forwarded, the source IP address is that of the original sender.

- The destination IP address in the IP header of the skb buffer, and the destination IP address that arp_solicit is asked to resolve (neigh->primary_key).

  The address that ARP is asked to resolve is the address of the next hop used to route skb. This matches the destination IP address in the IP header only when the next hop is also the final destination.

The main tasks of arp_solicit are:

- Select the source IP address to put in the ARP header. This can be influenced by the ARP_ANNOUNCE configuration mentioned in the section "/proc Options." Figure 28-15 shows the internals of arp_solicit and in particular how the source IP address is selected.
- Update the number of solicitation requests generated.
- Transmit the solicitation using arp_send.

The next section will go into detail on the selection of the source IP address. Let's briefly see how the other two tasks are accomplished.

arp_solicit differentiates between requests that should be generated by the kernel and requests that should be generated from user space. The latter can happen when an *arpd* ARP daemon is running; this requires that the kernel be compiled with the ARPD option, and is discussed in the section "ARPD." The two cases are handled as follows:

- For kernel-generated requests, the solicitation is transmitted with arp_send.
- For user-space requests, arp_solicit makes a call to neigh_app_ns to notify the interested user-space application about the need to generate a solicitation request. If the kernel has not been compiled with support for ARPD, arp_solicit simply returns without making the solicitation request.

ARP_ANNOUNCE and selection of source IP address

Most hosts have just one IP address, so this can be copied into the ARP header. When a host offers multiple IP addresses, the choice can be influenced by ARP_ANNOUNCE. arp_solicit simply applies the logic described in Table 28-1 and depicted in Figure 28-15. In order to accomplish its job, it makes use of three routines made available by the routing and configuration subsystems:

inet_addr_type
> Given an IP address in input, this function returns the address type. In the context of this chapter, we are interested in the value RTN_LOCAL, which indicates an address that belongs to the local host.

inet_addr_onlink
> Given a device and two IP addresses, this function checks whether the two addresses belong to the same subnet.

inet_select_addr
> Given a device, an IP address (usually not local to the system), and a scope, this function searches the device configuration for an IP address that falls within the same subnet as the ingress address and with a scope that is the same or smaller. The scope typically covers a site, a link, or a host. An input address of 0 makes any primary address configured on the input device eligible for selection. You can find a more detailed description in Chapter 30.

Note that when ARP_ANNOUNCE is configured at level 0 or 1 and the source IP address in the IP header cannot be used, arp_solicit falls back to level 2. inet_select_addr is invoked with a scope of RT_SCOPE_LINK. Given a device *dev* and a target IP address *IP*, inet_select_addr browses the IP addresses configured on *dev* and selects the first one that matches the subnet of the target IP address *IP* and has a scope greater than or equal to RT_SCOPE_LINK. Scopes are described in the section "Scope" in Chapter 30.

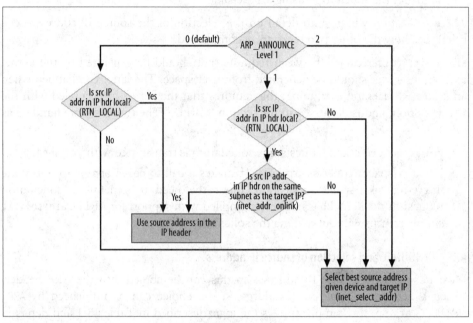

Figure 28-15. Selection of source IP in arp_solicit

Processing Ingress ARP Packets

As explained in the section "ARP Protocol Initialization," ARP registers the arp_rcv routine as its protocol handler. Let's see how this handler processes incoming ARP packets.

The ARP packet can be accessed from the skb buffer that is the function's input argument; in particular, the ARP header is at skb->nh.arph. The function's first task is to make sure the ARP packet is not fragmented; that is, that it can be accessed linearly in memory. This task is necessary because sometimes the skb buffer is fragmented in memory.* If it is, arp_rcv calls the generic routine pskb_may_pull to make sure there is enough room in the main buffer for the ARP header and payload.

---

* This has nothing to do with IP packet fragmentation. Details are in Chapter 2.

```
int arp_rcv(struct sk_buff *skb, struct net_device *dev, struct packet_type *pt)
{
    struct arphdr *arp;

    /* ARP header, plus 2 device addresses, plus 2 IP addresses.  */
    if (!pskb_may_pull(skb, (sizeof(struct arphdr) +
                (2 * dev->addr_len) +
                (2 * sizeof(u32)))))
        goto freeskb;
```

An input ARP packet is dropped by arp_rcv if one of the following conditions is met:

- It was received on a device that does not use ARP (i.e., one tagged with the IFF_ NOARP flag).

    The loopback interface is a special case within this category. Packets sent to and from the loopback interface are classified with the PACKET_LOOPBACK type. Since such an interface is virtual and does not have a hardware address, there is no need to use ARP.

- It was not addressed to the receiving interface (i.e., the destination address was not the receiving interface's address or the broadcast address).

In case the buffer was shared (that is, someone else holds a reference to it), arp_rcv clones the buffer with skb_share_check. Cloning is necessary to make sure that no one will change the content of skb (in particular, its header pointers) while processing the ARP packet. See the section "Cloning and copying buffers" in Chapter 2 for more details.

Refer to the section "ARP Packet Format" for the meaning of SIP and TIP. Once an ingress ARP packet is ready to be processed, supposing Netfilter does not kidnap it, arp_process takes care of it, as shown in Figure 28-13.

Figure 28-16 shows the structure of the arp_process function. It starts with some sanity checks common to all the ARP packet types it understands, and then continues with operations specific to particular packet types. The final part of the function is another common piece of code that updates the cache with the new information, unless the entry to update is locked (see the section "Final Common Processing"). Requests for multicast IP addresses are dropped because they are illegal: we saw in the section "Special Cases" in Chapter 26 that multicast IP addresses do not need the use of ARP to be translated to link layer addresses.

Initial Common Processing

arp_process processes both ARPOP_REQUEST and ARPOP_REPLY packet types. Any other ARP packet type is dropped. Packets with a multicast or broadcast destination address, which can be detected with the LOOPBACK and MULTICAST macros,[*] are also

---

[*] LOOPBACK recognizes the addresses 127.*x.x.x* and MULTICAST recognizes the addresses 224.*x.x.x* (class D).

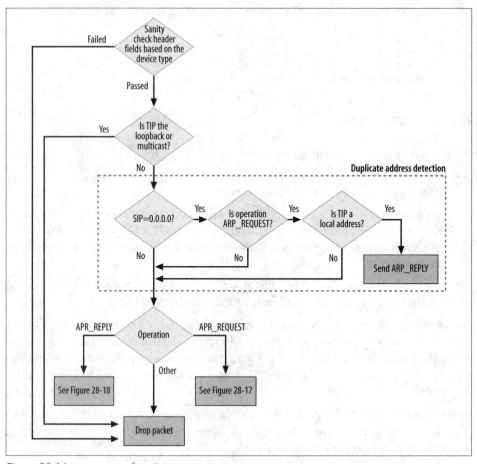

Figure 28-16. arp_process function

dropped because ARP is not needed for them, as described in the earlier section "Destination Address Types for ARP Packets," and the section "Special Cases" in Chapter 26.

Some device types are supported by the kernel only when it has been explicitly compiled with support for them. They are not included by default because they are not used very often, so the kernel developers decided to reduce the kernel size by making their support optional. The `switch` statement shown here simply goes one by one through these device types (using a `#ifdef` to make sure each one has been compiled into the kernel) and checks whether the protocol specified on the ARP packet is correct for that device type. This part of the code is long and repetitive.

```
switch (dev_type) {
default:
    if (arp->ar_pro != htons(ETH_P_IP)) ||
        htons(dev_type) != arp->ar_hrd)
```

```
            goto out;
        break;
#ifdef CONFIG_NET_ETHERNET
    case ARPHRD_ETHER:
    ... ... ...
        if (arp->ar_hrd != htons(ARPHRD_ETHER) &&
            arp->ar_hrd != htons(ARPHRD_IEEE802)) ||
            arp->ar_pro != htons(ETH_P_IP))
            goto out;
        break;
#endif
#ifdef CONFIG_TR
    case ARPHRD_IEEE802_TR:
            ... ... ...
#endif
            ... ... ...
#endif
    }
```

The last task in this section of arp_process is to initialize a few local variables from fields of the ARP header to make later code cleaner. This part of the function is not shown here, but is fairly easy to understand by consulting Figure 28-1. arp_ptr points to the end of the hardware header.

Processing ARPOP_REQUEST Packets

Figure 28-17 is a high-level description of how ARPOP_REQUEST packets are processed by arp_process. arp_process processes both requests for local IP addresses and requests for nonlocal IP addresses. The latter case—that is, the left side of the figure—is described in the section "Proxy ARP." Table 28-4 explains the meanings of SIP and TIP.

Table 28-4. Parameters extracted from the ARP packet

ARP packet field	Local variable name
Sender Ethernet address	sha
Sender IP address	sip
Target Ethernet address	tha
Target IP address	tip

An ARPOP_REQUEST is processed only if all of the following are true:

- The kernel knows how to reach the address requested by the sender (that is, there is a valid route to the address in the routing table).

```
    if (arp->ar_op == htons(ARPOP_REQUEST) &&
        ip_route_input(skb, tip, sip, 0, dev) == 0) {
        /* Process packet */
    }
```

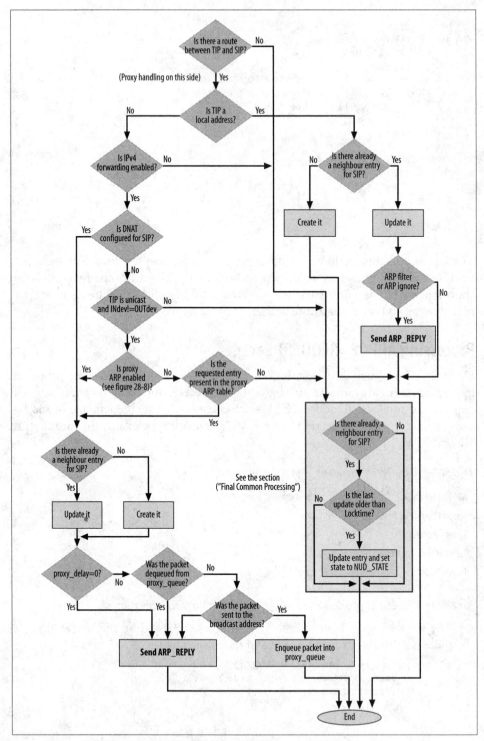

Figure 28-17. ARPOP_REQUEST handling by arp_process

This is a simple way to filter out requests for IP addresses about which the local system has no knowledge. When the local system is a host, it replies only to requests for IP addresses configured on the local interfaces. When the local system is a proxy ARP server, it also replies to requests for IP addresses that fall within any of the subnets configured on the local interfaces (i.e., IP addresses belonging to neighbor hosts).

We will see in Part VII that the routing subsystem adds an entry to the routing table for each IP address configured locally, and one for the subnet associated to each of those IP addresses. In both cases, therefore, a routing lookup is sufficient to filter out the requests for those IP addresses the local host should not reply to.

- Either the requested address is on the system, or it is a remote address handled by this host as a proxy ARP host. In this section, we address the local case, identified by the RTN_LOCAL flag. The section "Proxy ARP" describes the remote case.

- There is no configuration explicitly forbidding the transmission of an ARPOP_REPLY (see the earlier sections "ARP_IGNORE" and "ARP_FILTER").

If everything is OK, arp_process calls arp_send with the right input parameters. arp_send was described in the section "Transmitting ARP Packets: Introduction to arp_send."

```
rt = (struct rtable*)skb->dst;
addr_type = rt->rt_type;

if (addr_type == RTN_LOCAL) {
    n = neigh_event_ns(&arp_tbl, sha, &sip, dev);
    if (n) {
        int dont_send = 0;

        if (!dont_send)
            dont_send |= arp_ignore(in_dev,dev,sip,tip);
        if (!dont_send && IN_DEV_ARPFILTER(in_dev))
            dont_send |= arp_filter(sip,tip,dev);
        if (!dont_send)
            arp_send(ARPOP_REPLY,ETH_P_ARP,sip,dev,
                             tip,sha,dev->dev_addr,sha);
        neigh_release(n);
    }
    goto out;
} else {

        /* Handle Proxy ARP if all the required conditions */
        /* are met. See the section "Proxy ARP"           */
```

Passive learning and ARP optimization

The section "Creating a neighbour Entry" in Chapter 27 mentioned that at the end of an ARP transaction, both the requester and the replier learn something. The sender achieves its essential goal of learning the target's address from the ARPOP_REPLY; this is called *active learning*. But the target host that receives the ARPOP_REQUEST learns the sender's address from the request itself; this is called *passive learning*. It is a valuable optimization of the neighboring protocol.

Passive learning is taken care of by neigh_event_ns. The latter checks if it already has an entry associated to the requester; it then updates an existing entry or creates a new entry if one doesn't already exist.

Whether updating an existing entry or creating a new one, the function sets the state of the neighbor to NUD_STALE. ARP does not take the optimistic step of calling it NUD_REACHABLE because that state is reserved for hosts that have provided proof of reachability, a stricter requirement described in Chapter 27.

neigh_event_ns returns NULL when it fails to create an entry (usually because of a lack of memory—that is, no space is available in the cache). In this case, a reply is not sent to the requester. This policy is a little conservative; a more aggressive approach would be to reply anyway on the basis that even though we are temporarily unable to create an entry on our system for the neighbor, we should not deprive it of the ability to transmit data to us.

neigh_event_ns calls one of the lookup functions described in the section "Caching" in Chapter 27. Because these always increment the entry's reference counter when the search succeeds, neigh_event_ns needs to decrement the reference count correspondingly.

Requests with zero addresses

When the source IP address in an ARP request is set to 0 (0.0.0.0 in standard quad notation), it could be a corrupted packet, because 0.0.0.0 is not a valid IP address. However, it could also be a special packet used by DHCP to detect duplicated addresses. See the earlier section "Duplicate Address Detection" for the conditions under which these packets are sent, and RFC 2131, section 2.2, for the use of a 0 address.

A DHCP server or client can optionally send an ARPOP_REQUEST for a DHCP-assigned IP address to double-check whether, by mistake, the same address is already in use by another host. That special ARPOP_REQUEST is sent with a source IP address of 0.0.0.0 so that it will not create any trouble for the other hosts on the subnet.

The following code in arp_process runs when the source IP address (sip) is 0, and lets the local host claim an address when the packet's sender is making this type of request:

```
if (sip == 0) {
    if (arp->ar_op == htons(ARPOP_REQUEST) &&
        inet_addr_type(tip) == RTN_LOCAL &&
        !arp_ignore(in_dev, dev, sip, tip))
```

```
                    arp_send(ARPOP_REPLY,ETH_P_ARP,tip,dev,tip,sha,
                              dev->dev_addr,dev->dev_addr);
          goto out;
     }
```

Processing ARPOP_REPLY Packets

Incoming `ARPOP_REPLY` packets are processed if one of the following conditions is met:

- There is a pending `ARPOP_REQUEST` that matches the received `ARPOP_REPLY`. In other words, the `ARPOP_REPLY` is a reply to an `ARPOP_REQUEST` the kernel generated earlier. This is the most common case.

- There is no pending `ARPOP_REQUEST`, but the kernel has been compiled with support for `UNSOLICITED_ARP` (see the section "Compile-Time Options"). In this case, a new neighbor entry is created by calling `__neigh_lookup` with a non-NULL last parameter.

```
     #ifdef CONFIG_IP_ACCEPT_UNSOLICITED_ARP
         if (n == NULL &&
             arp->ar_op == htons(ARPOP_REPLY) &&
             inet_addr_type(sip) == RTN_UNICAST)
             n = __neigh_lookup(&arp_tbl, &sip, dev, -1);
     #endif
```

The right and left sides of Figure 28-18, respectively, show how these two cases are handled.

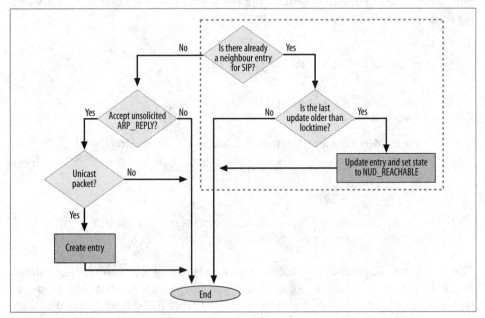

Figure 28-18. ARPOP_REPLY handling by arp_process

Regardless of why the packet is accepted, the existing neighbour entry is updated by the common code described in the next section (and is shown in the dotted box in the figure) to reflect the information in the ARPOP_REPLY packet.

Final Common Processing

The last part of arp_process is executed for all ARPOP_REPLY packets, and for ARPOP_REQUEST packets that have not been processed because they did not meet the conditions listed in the section "Processing ARPOP_REQUEST Packets."

Remember that when a host replies to an ARPOP_REQUEST, it inverts the source and destination fields of the ARP header, as well as fills in the empty spaces.

Another concept to understand, in reading this code, is the *locktime*. This is unrelated to the semaphore type of locking used frequently by the kernel. Rather, it's a simple kind of timeout that takes care of the chance that a host could receive more than one ARPOP_REPLY for the same ARPOP_REQUEST. This could happen if there is some kind of misconfiguration or if there are multiple proxy ARP servers on the same LAN; the arp_process function reacts by using only the first reply and rejecting subsequent replies.

The mechanism is as follows: the neighboring subsystem introduces the locktime parameter in the neigh_table structure; the parameter can also be tuned by /proc. The following code sets override to a time in the future that reflects locktime. (locktime is expressed in jiffies, so a value of HZ means 1 second.) The neigh_update function is called to update an entry only if it wasn't called for that same entry during the preceding locktime.

Thus, the final code is:

```
n = __neigh_lookup(&arp_tbl, &sip, dev, 0);
...
if (n) {
    int state = NUD_REACHABLE;
    int override;

    override = time_after(jiffies, n->updated + n->parms->locktime);

    if (arp->ar_op != htons(ARPOP_REPLY) ||
        skb->pkt_type != PACKET_HOST)
        state = NUD_STALE;

    neigh_update(n, sha, state, override ? NEIGH_UPDATE_F_OVERRIDE : 0);
    neigh_release(n);
}
```

The code has to select the right state to assign to the neighbour entry being updated. As explained in the section "Reachability" in Chapter 26, unicast and broadcast replies have different levels of authority. A unicast reply (PACKET_HOST) sets the neighbor state to NUD_REACHABLE, and a broadcast reply sets it to NUD_STALE. Updates caused by ARPOP_REQUEST packets always set the state to NUD_STALE.

Proxy ARP

In the section "Processing Ingress ARP Packets," we saw how requests for local addresses were handled by arp_process. Now we will see how and when requests for remote addresses are handled by the same function.

We saw in the sections "Conditions Required by the Proxy" in Chapter 26 and "Per-Device Proxying and Per-Destination Proxying" in Chapter 27, that the kernel supports two types of proxying: device-based and destination-based (or global). Per-device proxy ARP is disabled on a host by default. It can be enabled either globally or on a per-device basis via the /proc interface. The kernel can check whether proxying ARP is enabled on a given device through the IN_DEV_PROXY_ARP macro defined in include/linux/inetdevice.h. Per-destination proxying can be configured with either the arp or the ip neigh command (see the section "System Administration of Neighbors" in Chapter 29).

ARP adds one more condition under which it does proxying: Destination Network Address Translation. We will see in the section "Destination NAT (DNAT)" why the kernel needs to proxy requests when DNAT is configured.

For an ARPOP_REQUEST to be eligible for handling by a proxy server, the following conditions must be true:

- Forwarding is enabled on the receiving device, or globally on the proxying host.
- The target IP address is unicast (because other address types don't need ARP to be resolved, as we saw in the section "Special Cases" in Chapter 26). In code terms, addr_type==RTN_UNICAST.
- The device receiving this request is not the one through which the target IP address can be reached (because if it was, no proxying would be needed: the target host can reply by itself). In code terms, rt->u.dst.dev!=dev.

The following code from the arp_process function shows how it checks for the conditions just listed:

```
if (addr_type == RTN_LOCAL) {
    ... ... ...
} else if (IN_DEV_FORWARD(in_dev)) {
    if ((rt->rt_flags&RTCF_DNAT) ||
        (addr_type == RTN_UNICAST  && rt->u.dst.dev != dev &&
        (arp_fwd_proxy(in_dev, rt) ||
            pneigh_lookup(&arp_tbl, &tip, dev, 0)))) {
```

If the basic conditions are met, the proxy host checks its configuration of device-based and destination-based proxying. The logic is shown in Figure 26-8 in Chapter 26. The following conditions determine whether the proxy host responds to the address.

- Proxy ARP is enabled either on the device or globally.

- The ingress and egress interfaces are not on the same medium, as explained in the section "Medium ID."
- The target address is in the database of addresses being proxied. This database is organized by destination address and is queried through the pneigh_lookup function.

Let's suppose that arp_process has the green light to process the ARPOP_REQUEST.

First, neigh_event_ns is used to create (or just update) a neighbour entry for the sender's IP address, just as it does when ARP is processing requests for local addresses as described in the section "Passive learning and ARP optimization."

Processing of proxy ARP can be delayed to prevent bursts of traffic on the network, as described in the section "Delayed Processing of Solicitation Requests" in Chapter 27. Thus, if a packet comes directly from another host and delayed processing is configured, it is enqueued on the proxy queue. If the packet comes from the queue (that is, it was previously enqueued and the time has come to handle it) or if delayed processing is not configured, the packet is processed now.

```
        n = neigh_event_ns(&arp_tbl, sha, &sip, dev);
        if (n)
            neigh_release(n);

        if (skb->stamp.tv_sec == LOCALLY_ENQUEUED ||
            skb->pkt_type == PACKET_HOST ||
            in_dev->arp_parms->proxy_delay == 0) {
            arp_send(ARPOP_REPLY,ETH_P_ARP,
                                sip,dev,tip,sha,dev->dev_addr,sha);
        } else {
            pneigh_enqueue(&arp_tbl, in_dev->arp_parms, skb);
            in_dev_put(in_dev);
            return 0;
        }
        goto out;
    }
}
```

Destination NAT (DNAT)

Destination NAT, also called Route NAT in IPROUTE2 terminology, allows a host to define dummy (NAT) addresses: ingress packets addressed to them are detected by the host and forwarded to another address. DNAT is used mainly by routers, and bears no relation to the Destination NAT implemented by Netfilter.[*]

---

[*] All flavors of NAT supported by Linux—SNAT, DNAT, Masquerading, etc.—are implemented by Netfilter. Because this book does not cover the Netfilter internals, I have not included a discussion on NAT in the book either. For a discussion of the differences between the NAT flavors, you can refer to the Netfilter project's home page, *http://www.netfilter.org*.

It should be noted that although the ARP code in Linux handles DNAT, the routing code seems to have dropped support for it. Therefore, this feature is currently broken in kernel 2.6.

Figure 28-19 illustrates DNAT. The router RT has been configured with the dummy NAT address 10.0.0.5. Whenever RT receives traffic addressed to 10.0.0.5, it changes the destination address to 10.0.1.10 and forwards the traffic to the host with that address. Of course, the configuration ensures that reverse traffic is also taken care of.

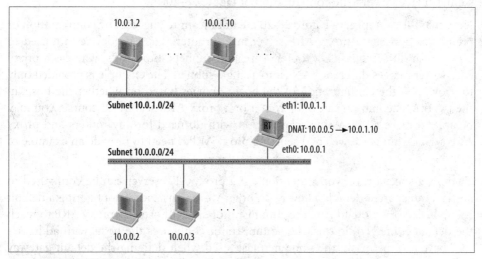

Figure 28-19. DNAT example

All of this is done using proxy ARP. In the 10.0.0.0/24 subnet, no host is configured with the 10.0.0.5 address. However, that address is publicized as the address of a given host (for instance, a web server). Whenever a host on the subnet 10.0.0.0/24 wants to talk to 10.0.0.5, it sends an ARP request for that address like any other. Because the ARP request is sent to the Ethernet broadcast address, RT receives it and proxies it by replying to the ARP request, providing the L2 address of its *eth0* interface. From that moment on, RT proxies traffic between the requester and 10.0.1.10.

When a host configures a dummy NAT address, a special routing table entry is created and tagged with the RTCF_DNAT flag so that ARP can check and proxy the address.

Proxy ARP Server as Router

At this point, a proxy and a router may seem similar, and to some extent they are. In fact, routers are usually the hosts that handle proxy ARP under IPv4, and (as described in RFC 2461) only routers are allowed to do it under IPv6. But proxying and routing differ in the following aspect: while a proxy ARP server is usually transparent to the hosts being served by it, a router is not. Each host needs to be explicitly configured to use the router. In the most common scenario, a proxy server acts as a transparent router between hosts located in different LANs but configured with the same IP subnet, as shown in Figure 28-20.

Figure 28-20(a) shows a simple topology where two subnets with a /25 netmask communicate via a router. Figure 28-20(b) shows how the same topology allows hosts on the two subnets to communicate via a proxy rather than a router by simply changing their netmasks from /25 to /24; this change joins the 10.0.1.0/25 and 10.0.1.128/25 subnets. Figure 28-20(c) is the topology that the hosts of the two subnets perceive with the configuration of Figure 28-20(b).

Note that the examples in Figure 28-20 are not meant to suggest any configuration or preference between a proxy ARP server and a router. The two devices are used to accomplish different tasks: a router segregates subnets into LANs, whereas a proxy ARP server merges different LANs into a single subnet. The example is provided only to show how the configuration of the hosts changes based on whether the hosts in the two LANs communicate via a router or a proxy ARP server. Of course, you may be able to place all hosts in a single LAN with no need for any routers and proxy ARP servers, but since we are discussing proxy ARP, I need to provide an example of its use.

There is a special case worth mentioning: a proxy ARP server can be configured to act as a transparent default gateway. In other words, instead of configuring a default route on each host on a LAN, the administrator can let hosts use proxy ARP to reach the default route. To do this, the administrator configures the hosts with addresses that have a /0 netmask, the same netmask used when defining the default gateway route. In this way, the proxy ARP server handles all traffic to unknown addresses, effectively becoming the default gateway. The proxy ARP server can even change its address without any impact on the hosts, as long as it updates all the old neighbour entries in the host's caches (see the section "Gratuitous ARP" for how this can be done). However, this clever-looking scenario is not very efficient, for reasons I'll explain next.

A network topology that includes a proxy ARP server, like the one in Figure 28-20(b), registers a high volume of solicitation requests and replies. When the number of hosts being proxied is high, the percentage of bandwidth used by solicitations may become considerable.

Given a network like the one in Figure 28-20(a), the worst-case scenario is where the /25 subnet contains a full 126 hosts (the number that fits in 7 bits, minus the default and broadcast addresses), and each host needs to resolve the address of every other host. This would lead to (126–1) * (126–1) different solicitation requests. However, a worst-case scenario like that one is far from average, because a host usually has to access only a few local machines, such as servers. Most of a host's traffic goes to hosts beyond the router, so the L3 and L2 address of this gateway router is all the host needs.

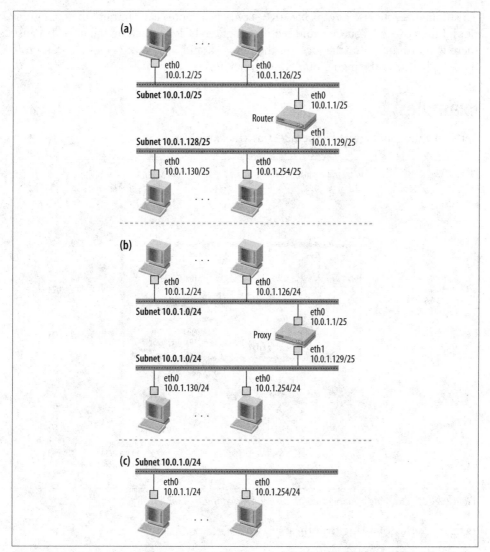

Figure 28-20. Proxy versus router

If we keep the same network topology but change the /24 netmask to a /0 netmask, the worst-case scenario explodes—and the average scenario starts to approach the worst-case scenario. Any time a host wants to communicate with another host, regardless of whether the latter is remote or local, there will always be a separate solicitation. Instead of making a single solicitation for the default gateway, which can be used to reach any host beyond the router, a host must make a separate solicitation for each host, because it has no knowledge about the router.

To summarize, the use of a proxy ARP server as a router can simplify the configuration of the hosts on a subnet, and require a lighter TCP/IP stack on the hosts because there is no routing. But the load on the network and on the proxy's CPU can grow quite high, due to the higher number of solicitations.

Examples

Let's take the topology of Figure 28-21 as an example.

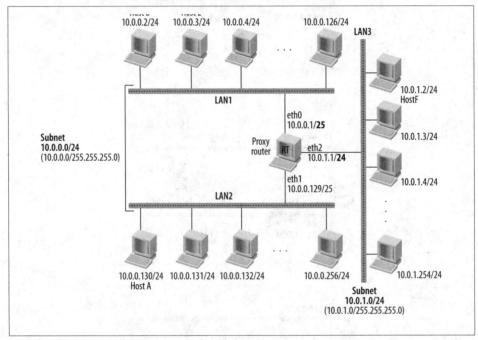

Figure 28-21. Example of network with proxy ARP configured on host RT

Let's make the following hypotheses:

- All the hosts use Ethernet cards.
- All the hosts of LAN1 and LAN2 are configured with a netmask of 255.255.255.0 (/24). They do not have any routes in their routing tables, nor do they have a default gateway configured. In other words, hosts in LAN1 and LAN2 can communicate only with other hosts within their same logical subnet.
- All neighbor caches are empty, which means that no one host knows any link layer address of any other host.
- Bridging is disabled everywhere. This excludes the top-right case of Figure 26-10 in Chapter 26. If the implications of this hypothesis are not clear, you should read Part IV.

Note that even if both hosts on LAN1 and LAN2 have been configured as belonging to the same logical subnet (network 10.0.0.0/24, netmask 255.255.255.0), they actually belong to different LANs. This means that as far as the configuration is concerned, they share the same subnet and can communicate with each other without the help of any router. However, by looking at the network topology, it is clear that they cannot do that without the help of RT.

For RT to give the hosts of LAN1 and LAN2 the illusion that they are on the same subnet, RT needs to have some extra knowledge: the real netmask of the LANs it wants to merge, which is 255.255.255.128 or /25. If RT was not a proxy ARP server, RT or the hosts in LAN1 and LAN2 would be considered misconfigured.[*]

For RT to make hosts in LAN1 and LAN2 communicate transparently, RT needs to have some more knowledge about the network topology, and more exactly it needs to know who is where. Note that the simple solution where RT forwards on one side whatever it receives on the other has nothing to do with proxying; Part IV covered that scenario. If RT wants to represent (e.g., reply in place of) the hosts of LAN1 to the requests of/from LAN2, it needs to know who is on what side. For instance, RT should not reply to requests generated on LAN1 and addressed to other hosts within LAN1 (because the hosts of LAN1 already belong to the same subnet, 10.0.0.0/24). Thanks to the right netmasks on its *eth1* and *eth2* NICs, RT knows that:

- On *eth0,* there are hosts with addresses ranging from 10.0.0.1 to 10.0.0.126 (10.0. 0.127 is the broadcast and 10.0.0.0 is the network).

- On *eth1,* there are hosts with addresses ranging from 10.0.0.129 to 10.0.0.254 (10.0.0.255 is the broadcast and 10.0.0.128 is the network).

Let me remind you that a router is needed to forward packets from one subnet to another one (i.e., sender and receiver are not in the same subnet). Note that the two NICs of router RT that go to LAN1 and LAN2 would be misconfigured if proxy ARP was not enabled on RT.

Let's now analyze a few common cases. You can refer to Figure 26-9 and Figure 26-10 in Chapter 26 for the expected behaviors:

- (a) From LAN1 to LAN1 (e.g., from Host D to Host E)

  Since Host D (10.0.0.2) is in the same subnet (10.0.0.0/24) as Host E, it can send a solicitation request (ARPOP_REQUEST) for the IP address 10.0.0.3. All of the hosts in LAN1 will receive that request, but only Host E will reply to Host D specifying its L2 address. Note that RT would not reply even if proxying was enabled on *eth0*. The reason is that RT received the solicitation on *eth0* (LAN1), and since it knows that 10.0.0.3 is located within the same subnet of the sender, it

---

[*] The statement is correct if we exclude the use of special features, like bridging.

does not need to intercept the request: Host E resides in the network the solicitation comes from and therefore it can answer by itself.

- (b) From LAN1 to an illegal IP address in LAN1 (e.g., from Host D to 10.0.0. 128)

From A2's perspective, 10.0.0.128 is a valid host address; from RT's perspective it is not (it is a network address). No one is going to reply. This is true regardless of whether RT is a proxy.

The tricky part here is that even if the hosts of LAN1 and LAN2 are configured with a 10.0.0.0/24 netmask, they have been physically divided on the two sides accordingly to RT's configuration. RT does not reply because it recognizes 10.0. 0.128 as a network address.

- (c) From LAN1 to LAN2 (e.g., from Host D to Host A)

Since the host with address 10.0.0.130 is on another LAN, the host would not be able to receive the request and reply. However, since RT is configured with proxy enabled on *eth0*, it will reply with the address of its *eth0* interface. This means that when Host D sends data to Host A, it will actually send it to RT, which will simply forward it to Host A. The opposite would have happened if Host A had asked for Host D's address.

- (d) From LAN1 to LAN3 (e.g., From Host D to Host F)

Since Host F is not on the same subnet as Host D (10.0.1.2 is not in 10.0.0.0/24) and no routes are defined in Host D to reach LAN3 (10.0.1.0/24), the IP layer of the kernel in Host D would reply with a message saying that no route is available to reach Host F, and Host D would not even generate a solicitation request.[*]

External Events

ARP can both receive and generate notifications when special conditions come into being. The section "Interaction Between Neighboring Protocols and L3 Transmission Functions" in Chapter 27 gives an overview of how neighboring protocols interact with the rest of the kernel. Here we will see in particular how ARP takes care of these notifications.

Received Events

We saw in the section "ARP Protocol Initialization" that ARP registers with the kernel for the notification of device events and that arp_netdev_event is the handler that takes care of those events. Among the various event types that the function receives, ARP is interested only in NETDEV_CHANGEADDR, which is generated when the L2 address

---

[*] Note that it would be true even if Host F were physically in LAN1 while still keeping its address of LAN3 (which would, in most cases, be a misconfiguration, as shown in Figure 26-1(c) in Chapter 26).

of a device is changed (e.g., via manual configuration). The kernel routine that processes the user-space request to change a device link layer address, and that therefore generates the NETDEV_CHANGEADDR notification, is do_setlink, defined in *net/core/rtnetlink.c*.

```
static int
arp_netdev_event(struct notifier_block *this, unsigned long event, void *ptr)
{
    struct net_device *dev = ptr;

    switch (event) {
    case NETDEV_CHANGEADDR:
        neigh_changeaddr(&arp_tbl, dev);
        rt_cache_flush(0);
        break;
    default:
        break;
    }

    return NOTIFY_DONE;
}
```

neigh_changeaddr is described in the section "Events Received by the Neighboring Layer" in Chapter 27.

rt_cache_flush flushes the IPv4 routing cache so that the IP layer is forced to start using the new L2 address. This function does not selectively delete the entries associated with the device that generated the notification, but simply removes everything in the cache. Chapter 33 contains details about the meaning of the input parameter and the routing cache in general.

Generated Events

The error_report virtual function, which is part of the neigh_ops structure, was mentioned in the section "Events Generated by the Neighboring Layer" of Chapter 27. In ARP, this function is carried out by arp_error_report. The ARP subsystem invokes the routine when an ARP transaction fails. Its two main tasks are:

- Remove the entry associated with the unreachable neighbor from the routing table cache.[*]
- Notify the sender about the unreachable neighbor by means of an ICMP UNREACHABLE message.

Wake-on-LAN Events

Some sophisticated NICs support a feature called Wake-on-LAN (WOL).

---

[*] To be exact, the entry is removed from the protocol-independent cache, which is covered in detail in Chapter 33.

WOL, briefly introduced in Chapter 6 is a feature that allows an NIC to wake up a system in standby mode when it receives a specific type of frame. Among the various types of frames that cause wake-ups are ARP packets. The feature is implemented at the hardware level because a system in standby mode does not have a device driver running in the CPU that can process incoming packets. WOL-enabled NICs need to have their own source of power to be able to scan for those special frames. I will not go into detail on this feature because it is handled entirely by the NIC's drivers, not by the ARP module. For details, browse the code for the WAKE_ARP keyword.

ARPD

The number of neighbors on a network segment can range from a few to many thousands. On large networks, the memory required by neighbour data structures can therefore grow quite big and affect system performances. Increasing the values of the gc_thresh*n* configuration parameters in the neigh_table structure simply changes the maximum number of entries that can be created, but it does not solve the performance problem of over-consumption of limited kernel memory.

arpd is a user-space daemon that can offload work from the kernel by keeping its own (bigger) cache. A user-space implementation of ARP cannot be as fast as a kernel implementation, but the difference is acceptable in most cases.

To use *arpd*, a kernel has to be compiled with support for the ARPD feature. The kernel documentation calls ARPD an experimental feature, but it has actually been around for a long time.

Two *arpd* daemons are currently available for download. One is old and does not work properly, and the other is part of the IPROUTE2 package and does work. I will refer to the second one in this section.

The *arpd* daemon is responsible for intercepting ARP requests from other systems and maintaining its own database in lieu of a kernel cache. We won't say much about the internals of the daemon in this chapter, but we will focus on the interaction between the daemon and the kernel. While *arpd* maintains its own relationship with the network, the kernel can also continue to handle ARP requests, and is responsible for notifying *arpd* about events the kernel knows about. They communicate via a Netlink socket, which is supported by default in the 2.6 kernel.

Figure 28-22 gives the big picture of the interaction between the neighboring subsystem, ARP, and *arpd*. Essentially, the neighboring subsystem sends notifications to the daemon and the daemon listens for them. The next two sections go into more detail on this interaction.

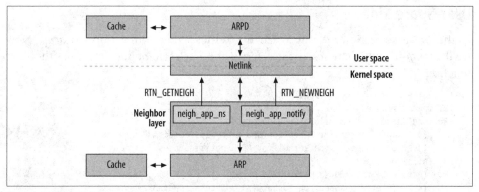

Figure 28-22. Interaction between ARP and arpd daemon

Kernel Side

When ARPD is enabled, the neighboring subsystem sends messages to the user-space daemon. Here we review the routines used to send those messages and the conditions under which the routines are invoked:

neigh_apps_ns

> This is called from the protocol's solicit function (arp_solicit) when the number of solicitations (probes) the kernel is allowed to send is exhausted and the number of user-space-generated solicitations is not. The rule for using *arpd* is that the kernel must use up all the probes for a neighbor before invoking the daemon. However, nothing prevents an administrator from configuring ARPD so that the kernel generates no probes at all, and invokes *arpd* right away.
>
> neigh_app_ns generates messages of type RTM_GETNEIGH.

neigh_app_notify

> This is used to send ARPD two kinds of notifications:
>
> - A neighbour entry has been moved to the NUD_FAILED state and will soon be deleted by the garbage collector. This change of state and the call to neigh_app_notify are handled in this case by neigh_periodic_timer (described in Chapter 27).
>
> - The state of a neighbor has changed from a valid one (the derived state NUD_VALID) to an invalid one, or the neighbor's L2 address has changed. These changes of state and the calls to neigh_app_notify are handled in this case by neigh_update.
>
> neigh_app_notify generates messages of type RTM_NEWNEIGH.

User-Space Side

In the previous section we saw when the kernel sends notifications to *arpd*. Now we'll see how *arpd* handles them. Here's the skeleton of the daemon (the main function):

```
1. Parse command-line options
2. Open database
3. Load database from file if option present
     (3.1) Open socket for reception and transmission of ARP packets
     (3.2) Open socket with kernel for ARPD notifications
4. Infinite loop
     (4.1) Poll the two sockets
     (4.2) If events appear on socket (1), process input ARP packet
     (4.3) If events appear on socket (2), process input kernel message
```

A simplified model of this behavior is shown in Figure 28-23. (Figure 28-23(a) represents 4.2, and Figure 28-23(b) represents 4.3.) It should clearly show a correspondence to the kernel behavior described in the previous section.

The daemon accepts a few command-line options to tune its behavior. For instance, the administrator can specify:

- How many probes to send before giving up
- Whether the kernel should generate probes too, or just the daemon
- Uploading entries into the cache from a file

The current *arpd* daemon implements its ARP cache using a generic Berkeley DB Database, which is the reason why, when an administrator installs the IPROUTE2 package, it includes a dependency on the Berkeley DB package.

One difference between *arpd* and the kernel's ARP subsystem is worth mentioning: unlike the kernel ARP cache, the *arpd* cache stores negative results. When an attempt to resolve an address fails, the daemon stores that information in its cache and does not retry the resolution for a certain amount of time.

Reverse Address Resolution Protocol (RARP)

RARP is an old protocol that can be used to autoconfigure a dynamic host. Its function was replaced by *bootp* and then DHCP. Although RARP has a different purpose from ARP, RARP also uses ARP packets (with different operation codes from ARPOP_ REQUEST and ARPOP_REPLY) and shares the same transmit routine arp_send. RARP is not included by default on the Linux kernel; it has to be added explicitly at compilation time.

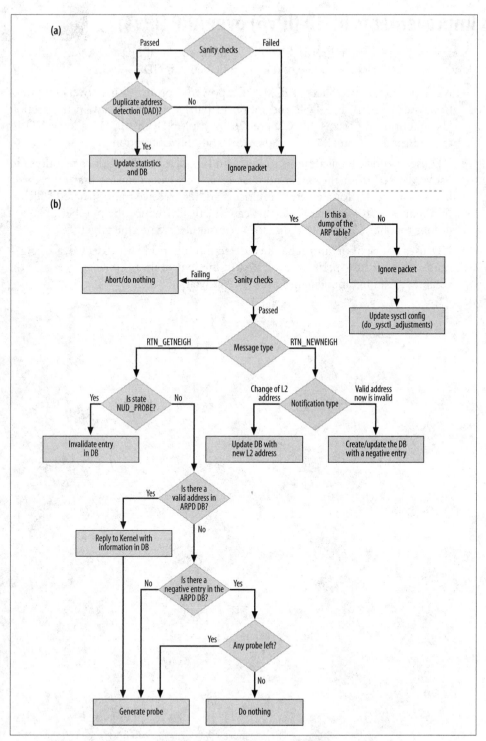

Figure 28-23. (a) Processing ARP packets; (2) processing kernel messages

Improvements in ND (IPv6) over ARP (IPv4)

As explained in Chapter 26, the IPv6 neighboring protocol ND has a very different design from ARP. Here are some of the improvements in ND:

- ND is a function provided by ICMPv6, a powerful protocol that covers the functionalities of ARP, ICMPv4, and more. In particular, as we saw in the section "Neighboring Protocols" in Chapter 26, putting ND into ICMP allows ND to take advantage of any L3 feature provided, notably encryption.

- ND uses multicast solicitations rather than broadcasts. The multicast address to use is derived from the target address to solicit, which means that only those hosts that register for a given IP multicast address receive the associated solicitation requests. In a big network, this can drastically reduce the number of solicitations that hosts receive and discard because they are not the target.

- ND uses a neighbor unreachability detection algorithm to detect dead neighbors. This is not part of every ARP implementation, but as we saw in Chapter 27, Linux implements it for ARP as well.

Neighboring Subsystem: Miscellaneous Topics

With this chapter, we conclude the part of this book on the neighboring protocol. The chapter shows how the user-space commands used to configure neighboring protocols interact with the kernel, summarizes the variables and functions introduced in the previous three chapters in easy-to-read tables, and concludes with a detailed description of the main data structures used by the neighboring subsystem.

System Administration of Neighbors

Neighbor entries can be added, removed, and modified with two user-space tools:

arp
> This is the older tool. It is part of the *net-tools* package, which includes other common commands such as *ifconfig*, *route*, *netstat*, etc. *arp* handles entries only for the IPv4 neighboring protocol ARP, as the name indicates. Like its companions, *arp* uses ioctl calls to communicate with the kernel.

ip
> This is considered the current tool. The *ip* command is part of the IPROUTE2 package and is used to configure a wide range of networking subsystems (routing, traffic control, etc.). It can be used to configure any neighboring protocol, and it talks to the kernel using the Netlink socket.

Both tools can also be used to configure destination-based proxying.

This chapter does not go into detail on the commands' syntax, features, or implementation, but it is worth knowing what is executed on the kernel side when the commands manipulate a neighbour entry.

The next three sections give you an overview of how configuration commands are propagated to the kernel. In the case of IPROUTE2, I'll also show briefly how the user-space code is organized.

Common Routines

Even though *ip* and *arp* use different mechanisms to talk to the kernel and therefore, as we will see in the next two sections, use different kernel handlers to process the configuration commands, in the end they actually talk to the neighboring layer via the same set of routines:

Lookup routines

Before applying a change to an existing entry or adding a new one, the kernel needs to do a lookup in the cache. These lookups are done using the functions described in the section "Caching" in Chapter 27.

`neigh_update`

`neigh_update` is a generic routine that can accomplish a variety of different operations depending on its input parameters. The function is described in the section "Updating a Neighbor's Information: neigh_update" in Chapter 27.

`pneigh_update`

`pneigh_update` is used instead of `neigh_update` by destination proxying. See the section "Acting As a Proxy" in Chapter 27.

The lookup routines, when necessary, create or delete `neighbour` entries with the `neigh_add` and `neigh_destroy` routines described in Chapter 27.

Figure 29-1 summarizes the relationships described in this section and the previous one.

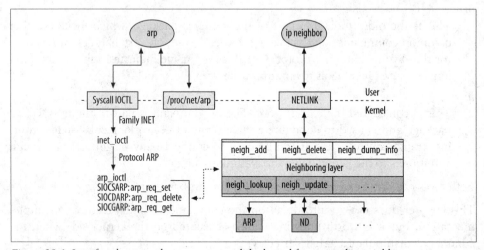

Figure 29-1. Interface between the user space and the kernel for arp and ip neighbour

New-Generation Tool: IPROUTE2's ip Command

ip is a generic command that replaces a number of traditional Unix commands such as *ifconfig*, *route*, and *arp*. The first argument of the *ip* command—*address*, *route*, *neighbour*, etc.—indicates the object that *ip* acts on, and thus whether it does the job of *ifconfig*, *route*, *arp*, and so on. In terms of the kernel, the *ip* object determines what subsystem the command interacts with.

The commands used to configure neighboring protocols are the ones that start with *ip neighbour*. Figure 29-2 shows the key files and functions of the IPROUTE2 package that implement the configuration of neighboring protocols.

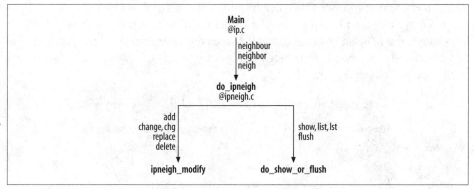

Figure 29-2. Structure of IPROUTE2 package's neighbor files and functions

The second argument to *ip* is the command that indicates what the administrator wants to do to the subsystem. Table 29-1 summarizes the commands and indicates the corresponding operation, flags, and handler in the kernel code. Thus, the command *ip neighbour add ...*, which adds a new entry to the neighboring subsystem, sends the kernel a RTM_NEWNEIGH command with both the NLM_F_CREATE (create an entry if one doesn't exist) and NLM_F_EXCL (leave an entry alone if it does exist) flags set. The command is taken care of by the kernel handler neigh_add.

Table 29-1. Parameters set by do_ipneigh in IPROUTE2 and associated kernel handlers

Command-line keyword	Operation	Flags	Kernel handler
add	RTM_NEWNEIGH	NLM_F_CREATE NLM_F_EXCL	neigh_add
change, chg	RTM_NEWNEIGH	NLM_F_REPLACE	neigh_add
replace	RTM_NEWNEIGH	NLM_F_CREATE NLM_F_REPLACE	neigh_add
delete	RTM_DELNEIGH	None	neigh_delete
show, list, lst	RTM_GETNEIGH	NLM_F	neigh_dump_info
flush	RTM_GETNEIGH	NLM_F	neigh_dump_info

If you look at one of the kernel functions listed, such as neigh_add, thanks to Table 29-1 you should be able to identify what each part of the function does. Of course, a minimal knowledge of the Netlink layer is also required, for example, to understand how input data is parsed. Netlink is introduced in Chapter 3; however, its internals could not be covered for lack of space.

Old-Generation Tool: net-tools's arp Command

People who prefer the old Unix commands to the IPROUTE2 package use *arp* on the rare occasion that they need to manipulate a host's ARP tables by hand (the command has nothing to offer other neighboring protocols, of course). Table 29-2 lists the main *arp* commands along with the kernel handlers that process them. The table also shows the *ip neigh* command that achieves the same functionality. Note that no *arp* command corresponds to *ip neigh change* or *ip neigh_replace* (instead, one would issue a delete followed by an add).

Table 29-2. arp commands, corresponding ip commands, and kernel functions invoked

	User-space command	Kernel function invoked by net-tools
net-tools	IPROUTE2	
arp -s ...	ip neigh add ...	arp_req_set
arp -d ...	ip neigh del ...	arp_req_delete
arp	ip neigh show ...	*/proc/net/arp* file

The arp_req_*xxx* routines are defined in *net/ipv4/arp.c*. In the same file, you can find the routines that manipulate the virtual */proc/net/arp* file. *arp* reads this file instead of issuing ioctl calls to the kernel to obtain information, even though the kernel provides a routine named arp_req_get that can perform the request. See the definition of the arp_seq_ops structure in *net/ipv4/arp.c* to find out more about the use of the */proc* file.

Tuning via /proc Filesystem

As we saw in an earlier chapter, the neighboring protocols follow the common kernel practice of offering a convenient interface in the */proc* directory to let administrators tune the subsystem's parameters. The neighboring subsystem's parameters reside in four directories, two for IPv4 and two for IPv6:

/proc/sys/net/ipv4/neigh
/proc/sys/net/ipv6/neigh

> Generic parameters of the neighboring subsystem, such as the timers used to control when cache operations take place

/proc/sys/net/ipv4/conf
/proc/sys/net/ipv6/conf

> Particular behaviors within the protocol, such as the ones described in the section "Tunable ARP Options" in Chapter 28

Each directory contains a subdirectory for each NIC device on the system, a *default* subdirectory, and (in the case of the *conf* directory) an *all* subdirectory that can be used to apply a change to all the devices at once. Under *conf*, the *default* subdirectory shows the global status of each feature, while under *neigh*, the *default* subdirectory shows the default setting (i.e., configuration parameters) of each feature. The values of the default subdirectories are used to initialize the per-device subdirectories when the latter are created.

The directories for individual devices take precedence over the more general directories. But not all devices pay attention to all the parameters; if a parameter is not relevant to a device, the associated directory contains a file for the parameter but the kernel ignores it. For instance, the gc_thresh1 value is not used by any protocol, and only IPv4 uses locktime.

Figure 29-3 shows the layout of the files and the routines that register them.

The three files *arp*, *arp_cache*, and *ndisc_cache* at the top-right corner of Figure 29-3 are not used to configure anything, but just to export read-only data. Note that they are in the */proc/net* directory, not in */proc/sys*. */proc/net/arp* is used by the *arp* command to dump the contents of the ARP cache (there is no counterpart for ND), as discussed in the section "Old-Generation Tool: net-tools's arp Command." The */proc/net/stat/xxx_cache* files export statistics about the protocol caches. Most of their files represent fields of neigh_statistics structures, described in the section "neigh_statistics Structure."

The /proc/sys/net/ipv4/neigh Directory

This directory contains parameters from neigh_parms structures, which were introduced in Chapter 27. As that chapter explained, each device has one neigh_parms structure for each neighboring protocol that it interacts with (see Figure 27-2 in Chapter 27). We have also seen that another neigh_parms instance is included in the neigh_table structure to store default values.

However, not all fields of the neigh_parms structure are exported to */proc*. For instance, reachable_time is a derived field whose value is indirectly calculated from base_reachable_time and therefore cannot be changed by the user. In addition, tbl and neigh_setup are used by the kernel to organize its data structures and do not have anything to do with the protocol itself, so they are not exported.

In addition to exporting most of the parameters in the neigh_parms structure to */proc*, the neighboring subsystem exports a few from the neigh_table structure, too.

Initialization of global and per-device directories

Because the default values are provided by the protocol itself, the *default* subdirectory is installed when the protocol is initialized (see the arp_init and ndisc_init functions) and populated with files whose names are based on those of the

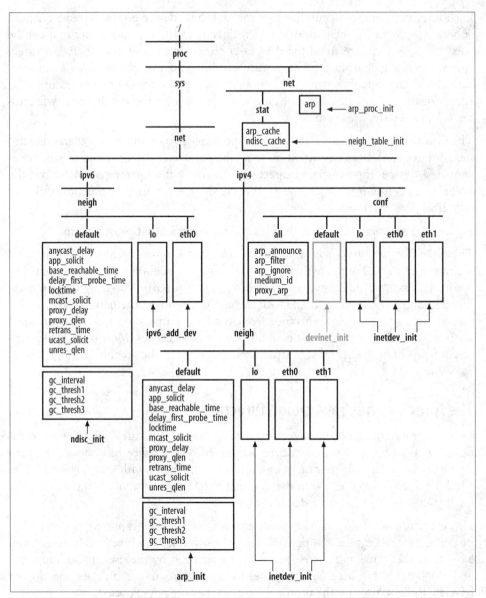

Figure 29-3. Example of /proc/sys file registration for the neighboring subsystem

associated fields in the `neigh_parms` structure. You can find the default values of the fields in Table 29-3 directly in the initializations of the *xxx_tbl* tables; Chapter 28 shows an example for ARP.

The relationships between the kernel variables and the names of the files in */proc/sys/ net/ipv4/neigh/xxx/* are shown in Table 29-3. See the initialization of `neigh_sysctl_ template` in *net/core/neighbour.c*; a guide to reading the template is in Chapter 3.

Table 29-3. Kernel variables and associated files in /proc/sys/net/ipv4/neigh subdirectories

Kernel variable name	Filename	Default value for IPv4/IPv6
mcast_probes	mcast_solicit	3
ucast_probes	ucast_solicit	3
app_probes	app_solicit	0
retrans_time	retrans_time	100 * HZ
base_reachable_time	base_reachable_time	30 * HZ
delay_probe_time	delay_first_probe_time	5 * HZ
gc_staletime	gc_stale_time	60 * HZ
queue_len	unres_qlen	3
proxy_qlen	proxy_qlen	64
anycast_delay	anycast_delay	1 * HZ
proxy_delay	proxy_delay	(8*HZ)/10
locktime	locktime	1 * HZ
gc_interval	gc_interval	30 * HZ
gc_thresh1	gc_thresh1	128
gc_thresh2	gc_thresh2	512
gc_thresh3	gc_thresh3	1,024

Each device's directories are created when the device is first configured. The first time an address is configured on device *D*, a directory with the name *D* is created under */proc/sys/net/ipv4/neigh*. All of the parameters apply to the device rather than to a specific address, so there is only a single directory for each device, even if it is configured with multiple addresses.

Figure 29-3 shows the directory tree you would see if a host had three devices named *eth0*, *eth1*, and *eth2*; if *eth0* and *eth1* had been given IPv4 addresses; if *eth0* had also been given an IPv6 address; and if *eth2* has not been configured yet.

The two functions in charge of configuring IPv4 and IPv6 devices are inetdev_init and ip6_add_dev, respectively. Each calls neigh_sysctl_register to create the device's subdirectory under */proc*, as described in the following section.

Directory creation

Both the *default* and the per-device directories in */proc/sys/net/ipv4/neigh* are created with the neigh_sysctl_register function. The latter differentiates between the two cases by using the value of the input parameter dev. If we take IPv4 as an example, you can compare the way arp_init (a protocol initialization function) and inetdev_init (a device's configuration block initializer) call neigh_sysctl_register. neigh_sysctl_register needs to differentiate between the two cases to:

- Pick the name of the directory to create. It will be *default* when dev is NULL, and extracted from the device itself (dev->name) otherwise.

- Decide what parameters to add as files to that directory; the default directory will include a few more parameters than the others (four to be exact). While the parameters extracted from neigh_parms are meaningful when configured on a per-device basis, the ones in neigh_table are not. Thus, the four parameters taken from neigh_table go only in the *default* directory (see the end of Table 29-3). Those four parameters are related to the garbage collection process:

    —gc_interval

    —gc_thresh1, gc_thresh2, gc_thresh3

Here is the meaning of the input parameters to neigh_sysctl_register:

struct net_device *dev
> Device associated with the directory being created. When dev is NULL, it means the function has been invoked to create the *default* directory.

struct neigh_parms *p
> Structure whose parameters will be exported. A device using ARP, for instance, passes in_dev->arp_parms. When dev is NULL, this is the neigh_parms instance embedded in the protocol's neigh_table structure (neigh_table->neigh_parms), which stores the protocol's defaults.

int p_id
> Protocol identifier. See the NET_*XXX* values in *include/linux/sysctl.h*. ARP, for instance, uses NET_IPV4.

int pdev_id
> Class identifier of parameters being exported. See the NET_IPV4_*XXX* values in *include/linux/sysctl.h*. ARP, for example, uses NET_IPV4_NEIGH.

char *p_name
> String indicating the L3 protocol that refers to the neighboring protocol fields. ARP, for example, uses "ipv4".

proc_handler *handler
> Function that the kernel invokes when the value of one of the exported fields is modified by the user. Only IPv6 passes a non-NULL value, and the function it provides is simply a wrapper to the default handler that the kernel would install otherwise. See ndisc_ifinfo_sysctl_change in *net/ipv6/ndisc.c* for an example.

The only tricky part in the function is how the four gc_*xxx* parameters are extracted from the neigh_table structure. It relies on a trick of memory layout: the four parameters related to garbage collection are stored in the neigh_table structure right after the neigh_parms structure, as shown here:

```
struct neigh_table
    ...
        struct neigh_parms parms;
        int gc_interval;
        int gc_thresh1;
        int gc_thresh2;
```

```
        int gc_thresh3;
        ...
```

Thus, all the function needs to do to retrieve the `neigh_table` values is to go past `neigh_parms`, cast the pointer to an integer, and extract four integers in a row:

```
if (dev) {
    dev_name_source = dev->name;
    t->neigh_dev[0].ctl_name = dev->ifindex;
    memset(&t->neigh_vars[12], 0, sizeof(ctl_table));
} else {
    t->neigh_vars[12].data = (int *)(p + 1);
    t->neigh_vars[13].data = (int *)(p + 1) + 1;
    t->neigh_vars[14].data = (int *)(p + 1) + 2;
    t->neigh_vars[15].data = (int *)(p + 1) + 3;
}
```

The /proc/sys/net/ipv4/conf Directory

The files in the */proc/sys/net/ipv4/conf* subdirectories are associated with the fields of the `ipv4_devconf` structure, which is defined in *include/linux/inetdevice.h*. Not all of its fields are used by the neighboring protocols (see Chapters 23 and 36 for the other fields). Table 29-4 lists the parameters relevant to the neighboring protocols; their meanings were described in the section "Tunable ARP Options" in Chapter 28.

Table 29-4. Kernel variables and associated files in /proc/sys/net/ipv4/conf subdirectories

Kernel variable name	Filename	Default value for IPv4/IPv6
ipv4_devconf.arp_announce	*arp_announce*	0
ipv4_devconf.arp_filter	*arp_filter*	0
ipv4_devconf.arp_ignore	*arp_ignore*	0
ipv4_devconf.medium_id	*medium_id*	0
ipv4_devconf.proxy_arp	*proxy_arp*	0

As shown in Figure 29-3, in addition to the per-device subdirectories, there are also two special ones named *default* and *all*. See Chapter 36 for more details.

Data Structures Featured in This Part of the Book

In the section "Main Data Structures" in Chapter 27, we had a brief overview of the main data structures used by the neighboring subsystem. This section presents a detailed description of each data structure's field.

Figure 29-4 shows the files that define each data structure. The ones with a lighter color are not part of the neighboring subsystem, but I referred to them in this part of the book.

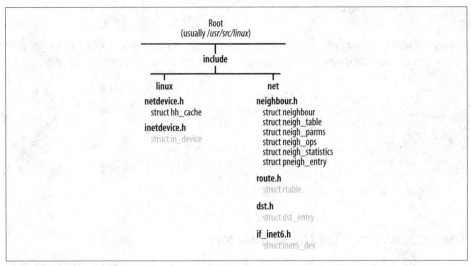

Figure 29-4. Distribution of data structures in kernel files

neighbour Structure

Neighbors are represented by struct neighbour structures. The structure is complex and includes status fields, virtual functions to interface with L3 protocols, timers, and cached L2 headers.

Here is a field-by-field description:

struct neighbour *next

Each neighbour entry is inserted in a hash table. next links the structure to the other ones that collide and share the same bucket. Elements are always inserted at the head of the list (see the section "Creating a neighbour Entry," and Figure 27-2 in Chapter 27).

struct neigh_table *tbl

Pointer to the neigh_table structure that defines the protocol associated with this entry. If the neighbor is an IPv4 address, for instance, tbl points to arp_tbl.

struct neigh_parms *parms

Parameters used to tune the neighboring protocol behavior. When a neighbour structure is created, parms is initialized with the values of the default neigh_parms structure embedded in the protocol's associated neigh_table structure. When the protocol's constructor method is called by neigh_create (e.g., arp_constructor for ARP), that block is replaced with the configuration block of the associated device, if any. While most devices use the system defaults, a device can start up with different parameters or be configured by the administrator later to use different parameters, as discussed earlier in this chapter.

`struct net_device *dev`

The device through which the neighbor is reachable. Only one device can be used to reach each neighbor. Thus, the value NULL never appears here as it does in other kernel subsystems that use it as a wildcard to refer to all devices.

`unsigned long confirmed`

Timestamp (in `jiffies`) when the reachability of the entry was most recently confirmed. L4 protocols can update it with `neigh_confirm` (see Figure 26-14 in Chapter 26). The neighboring infrastructure updates it in `neigh_update`, described in .

`unsigned long updated`

Timestamp of the most recent time the entry was updated by `neigh_update` (the only exception is the first initialization by `neigh_alloc`). Do not confuse `updated` and `confirmed`, which keep track of very different things. The `updated` field is set when the state of a neighbor changes, whereas the `confirmed` field merely records one particular change of state: the one that occurs when the entry was most recently confirmed to be valid.

`unsigned long used`

Most recent time the entry was used. Its value is not always updated synchronously with the data transmissions. When the entry is not in the `NUD_CONNECTED` state, this field is updated by `neigh_event_send`, which is called by `neigh_resolve_output`. In contrast, when the entry is in the `NUD_CONNECTED` state, its value is sometimes updated by `neigh_periodic_timer` to the time the entry's reachability was most recently confirmed.

`__u8 flags`

Possible values for this field are listed in *include/linux/rtnetlink.h* and *include/net/neighbour.h*:

`#define NTF_PROXY 0x08`

When the *ip neigh* user-space command is used to add entries to the proxy tables (for instance, *ip neigh add proxy 10.0.0.2 dev eth0*), this flag is set in the data structure sent to the kernel, to let the kernel handler `neigh_add` know that the new entry has to be added to the proxy table (see the section "System Administration of Neighbors").

`#define NTF_ROUTER 0x80`

This flag is used only by IPv6. When set, it means the neighbor is a router. Unlike `NTF_PROXY`, this flag is not set by user-space tools. The IPv6 neighbor discovery code updates its value when receiving information from the neighbor.

`__u8 nud_state`

Indicates the entry's state. The possible values are defined in *include/net/neighbour.h* and *include/linux/rtnetlink.h* with names of form `NUD_XXX`. The role of states is described in the section "Transitions Between NUD States" in

Chapter 26. Figure 26-13 in Chapter 26 shows how the state changes depending on various events.

__u8 type

This parameter is set when the entry is created with neigh_create by calling the protocol constructor method (e.g., arp_constructor for ARP). Its value is used in various circumstances, such as to decide what value to give nud_state. type can assume the values in Table 36-12 in Chapter 36, listed in *include/linux/rtnetlink.h*.

In the context of this chapter, not all of the values of that table are actually used: we are mostly interested in RTN_UNICAST, RTN_LOCAL, RTN_BROADCAST, RTN_ANYCAST, and RTN_MULTICAST.

Given an IPv4 address (such as the L3 address associated with a neighbour entry), the inet_addr_type function finds the associated RTN_*XXX* value (see Chapter 28). For IPv6, there is a similar function called ipv6_addr_type.

__u8 dead

When dead is set to 1 it means the structure is being removed and cannot be used anymore. See neigh_ifdown in the section "External Events" in Chapter 32, and neigh_forced_gc and neigh_periodic_timer for examples of usage.

atomic_t probes

Number of failed solicitation attempts. Its value is checked by the neigh_timer_handler timer, which puts the neighbour entry into the NUD_FAILED state when the number of attempts reaches the maximum allowed value.

rwlock_t lock

Used to protect the neighbour structure from race conditions.

unsigned char ha[]

The L2 address (e.g., Ethernet MAC address for Ethernet NICs) associated with the L3 address represented by primary_key (discussed shortly). The address is in binary format. The size of the vector ha is MAX_ADDR_LEN (defined as 32 in *include/linux/netdevice.h*), rounded up to the first multiple of a C long. An Ethernet address requires only six octets (i.e., 48 bits), but other link layer protocols may require more. For each hardware address type, the kernel defines a symbol that is assigned the size of the address. Most symbols use names like *XXX*_ALEN or *XXX*_ADDR_LEN. Ethernet, for example, defines the ETH_ALEN symbol in *include/linux/if_ether.h*.

struct hh_cache *hh

List of cached L2 headers. See the section "L2 Header Caching" in Chapter 27.

atomic_t refcnt

Reference count. See the sections "Caching" and "Reference Counts on neighbour Structures" in Chapter 27.

int (*output)(struct sk_buff *skb)

Function used to transmit frames to the neighbor. The actual routine this function pointer points to can change several times during the structure's lifetime, depending on several factors. It is first initialized by the `neigh_table`'s constructor method (see the section "Initialization of a neighbour Structure" in Chapter 28). It can be updated by calling `neigh_connect` or `neigh_suspect` when the neighbor state goes to `NUD_REACHABLE` or `NUD_STALE` state, respectively.

`struct sk_buff_head arp_queue`

Packets whose destination L3 address has not been resolved yet are temporarily placed into this queue. Despite the name of this field, it can be used by all neighboring protocols, not just ARP. See the section "Egress Queuing" in Chapter 27.

`struct timer_list timer`

Timer used to handle several tasks. See the section "Timers" in Chapter 15.

`struct neigh_ops *ops`

VFT containing the methods used to manipulate the `neighbour` entry. Among the methods, for instance, are several used to transmit packets, each optimized for a different state or associated device type. Each protocol provides three or four different VFTs; which is used for a specific `neighbour` entry depends on the type of L3 address, the type of associated device, and the type of link (e.g., point-to-point). See the upcoming section "neigh_ops Structure," and the section "Initialization of neigh->ops" in Chapter 27.

`u8 primary_key[0];`

L3 address of the neighbor. It is used as the key by the cache lookup functions. It is an IPv4 address for ARP entries and an IPv6 address for neighbor discovery entries.

neigh_table Structure

This structure is used to tune the behavior of a neighboring protocol. There are a few instances of `neigh_table` in the kernel, each for a different protocol:

`arp_tbl`

ARP protocol used by IPv4 (see *net/ipv4/arp.c*)

`nd_tbl`

Neighbor discovery protocol used by IPv6 (see *net/ipv6/ndisc.c*)

`dn_neigh_table`

Neighbor discovery protocol used by DECnet (see *net/decnet/dn_neigh.c*)

`clip_tbl`

ATM over IP protocol (see *net/atm/clip.c*)

These `neigh_table` structures are initialized when the associated subsystems are initialized in the kernel, and are inserted into a global list pointed to by `neigh_tables`, as shown in Figure 27-2 in Chapter 27.

The data structures contain most (if not all) of the information required by the neighboring protocol. Therefore, each `neighbour` entry has a `neigh->tbl` pointer to its associated neigh_table; for instance, a neighbour entry associated with an IPv4 address will have a pointer to the arp_tbl structure, whereas an IPv6 entry will have a pointer to nd_tbl.

To understand the field-by-field descriptions more easily, refer to the initializations of the four tables as examples—in particular, arp_tbl, which is also discussed in the section "The arp_tbl Table" in Chapter 28.

struct neigh_table *next
> Links all the protocol tables in a list.

rwlock_t lock
> Lock used to protect the table from possible race conditions. It is used in read-only mode by functions such as neigh_lookup that only need read permission, and in read/write mode by other functions such as neigh_periodic_timer.
>
> Note that the whole table is protected by a single lock, as opposed to something more granular such as a different lock for each bucket of the table's cache.

char *id
> This is just a string that identifies the protocol. It is used mainly as an ID when allocating the memory pool used to allocate neighbour structures (see neigh_table_init).

struct proc_dir_entry *pde
> File registered in */proc/net/stat/* to export statistics about the protocol. For instance, ARP creates */proc/net/stat/arp_cache*. The file is created by neigh_table_init when the protocol is initialized.

int family
> Address family of the entries represented by the neighboring protocol. Its possible values are listed in the file *include/linux/socket.h*, with names in the form AF_*XXX*. For IPv4 and IPv6, the associated values are AF_INET and AF_INET6, respectively.

int entry_size
> Size of the structures inserted into the cache. Since a neighbour structure includes a field whose size depends on the protocol (primary_key), entry_size is set to the sum of the size of a neighbour structure and the size of the primary_key provided by the protocol. In the case of IPv4/ARP, for instance, this field is initialized to sizeof(struct neighbour) + 4, where 4 is, of course, the size in bytes of an IPv4 address. The field is used, for instance, by neigh_alloc when clearing the content of the entries retrieved from the cache.[*]

---

[*] When a neighbour structure is put back into the memory pool by neigh_destroy, its content is not cleared.

int key_len

Length of the key used by the lookup functions (see the section "Caching" in Chapter 27). Because the key is the L3 address, this is 4 for IPv4, 8 for IPv6, and 2 for DECnet.

__u32 (*hash)(const void *pkey, const struct net_device *)

Hash function applied to the search key (e.g., L3 address) to select the right bucket of the hash table when doing a lookup.

int (*constructor)(struct neighbour *)

The constructor method is invoked by neigh_create when creating a new entry, and initializes the protocol-specific fields of a new neighbour entry. For example, the one used by ARP (arp_constructor) is described in detail in the section "Initialization of a neighbour Structure" in Chapter 28.

struct neigh_parms parms

This data structure contains some parameters used to tune the behavior of the protocol, such as how much time to wait before resending a solicitation request after not receiving a reply, and how many packets to keep in a queue waiting for the reply before transmitting them. See the section "neigh_parms Structure."

struct neigh_parms *parms_list

Not used.

kmem_cache_t *kmem_cachep

Memory pool used when allocating neighbour structures. It is allocated and initialized at protocol initialization time by neigh_table_init. You can check its status by dumping the contents of the /proc/slabinfo file.

atomic_t entries

Number of neighbour instances currently in the protocol's cache. Its value is incremented when allocating a new entry with neigh_alloc and decremented when deallocating an entry with neigh_destroy. See the description of gc_thresh1, gc_thresh2, and gc_thresh3 later in this section.

unsigned long last_rand

Time (expressed in jiffies) when the variable reachable_time of the neigh_parms structures associated with the table (there is one for each device) was most recently updated.

struct neigh_statistics *stats

Various statistics about the neighbour instances in the cache. See the section "neigh_statistics Structure."

struct neighbour **hash_buckets

Hash table that stores the neighbour entries.

unsigned int hash_mask

Size of the hash table. See Figure 27-6 in Chapter 27.

__u32 hash_rnd

> Random value used to distribute neighbour entries in the cache when its size is increased. See the section "Caching" in Chapter 27.

The following variables and functions are used by the garbage collection algorithm described in the section "Garbage Collection" in Chapter 27:

int gc_interval

> This controls how often the gc_timer timer expires, kicking off garbage collection. It used to be 30 seconds but now it is shorter. The timer causes garbage collection on only one bucket of the hash table each time. See the section "Garbage Collection" in Chapter 27 for more information.

int gc_thresh1
int gc_thresh2
int gc_thresh3

> These three thresholds define different levels of memory usage granted to the neighbour entries currently cached by the neighboring protocol.

unsigned long last_flush

> This variable, measured in jiffies, represents the most recent time neigh_forced_gc was executed. In other words, it represents the most recent time a garbage collection process was forced because of low memory conditions.

struct timer_list gc_timer

> Garbage collector timer. See the section "Garbage Collection" in Chapter 27.

unsigned int hash_chain_gc

> Keeps track of the next bucket of the hash table the periodic garbage collector timer should scan. The buckets are scanned sequentially.

The following fields are used when the system acts as a proxy. See the section "Acting As a Proxy" in Chapter 27.

struct pneigh_entry **phash_buckets

> Table that stores the L3 addresses that must be proxied.

int (*pconstructor)(struct pneigh_entry *)
void (*pdestructor)(struct pneigh_entry *)

> pconstructor is the counterpart of constructor. Right now, only IPv6 uses pconstructor; it registers a specific multicast address when the associated device is first configured.

> pdestructor is called when releasing a proxy entry. It is used only by IPv6 and undoes the work of the pconstructor method.

struct sk_buff_head proxy_queue

> Received solicit requests (e.g., received ARPOP_REQUEST packets in the case of ARP) are queued into this queue when proxying is enabled and configured with a non-null proxy_delay delay. New elements are queued at the tail.

void (*proxy_redo)(struct sk_buff *skb)
> Function that processes the solicit requests (e.g., ARPOP_REQUEST packets for ARP) after they are extracted from the proxy queue neigh_table->proxy_queue. See the section "Delayed Processing of Solicitation Requests" in Chapter 27.

struct timer_list proxy_timer
> This timer is started when there is at least one element in proxy_queue. The handler that is executed when the timer expires is neigh_proxy_process. The timer is initialized at protocol initialization by neigh_table_init. Unlike the timer neigh_table->gc_timer, this one is not periodic and is started only if needed (for instance, a protocol might start it when the first element is added to proxy_queue). The section "Acting As a Proxy" in Chapter 27 describes why and when elements are queued to proxy_queue and how proxy_timer processes them.

neigh_parms Structure

The neigh_parms data structure stores the configurable parameters of the neighboring protocol. For each configured L3 protocol that uses a neighbor protocol, there is one instance of neigh_parms for each device[*] plus one that stores the default values.

Here is the field-by-field description:

struct neigh_parms *next
> Pointer that links neigh_parms instances associated with the same protocol family. This means that each neigh_table has its own list of neigh_parms structures, one instance for each configured device (see Figure 27-2 in Chapter 27).

int (*neigh_setup)(struct neighbour *)
> Initialization function used mainly by those devices that are still using the old neighboring infrastructure. This function is normally used just to initialize neighbour->ops to the arp_broken_ops instance (see the section "neigh_ops Structure" later in this chapter, and the section "Initialization of neigh->ops" in Chapter 27). Look at shaper_neigh_setup in *drivers/net/shaper.c* for an example. To see when this initialization function is called during the initialization phase of a new neighbour instance, see Figure 28-11 in Chapter 28.
>
> Do not confuse this virtual function with net_device->neigh_setup. The latter is called when the first L3 address is configured on a device, and normally initializes neigh_parms->neigh_setup, too. net_device->neigh_setup is called only once for each device, and neigh_parms->neigh_setup is called once for each neighbour structure that will be associated with the device.

---

[*] This statement is not 100% correct. Because a neigh_parms structure is used to tune the behavior of a neighboring protocol, its presence is needed only if there is at least one device whose L3 configuration uses the neighboring subsystem.

`struct neigh_table *tbl`

> Back pointer to the `neigh_table` structure that holds this structure.

`int entries`

`void *priv`

> Not used.

`void *sysctl_table`

> This table, initialized at the end of the file *net/ipv4/neighbour.c*, is involved in allowing users to modify the values of those parameters of the `neigh_parms` data structure that are exported via */proc*, as described in the section "Tuning via /proc Filesystem."

`int base_reachable_time`

`int reachable_time`

> `base_reachable_time` is the interval of time (expressed in `jiffies`) since the most recent proof of reachability was received. Note that this interval is used as a base value to compute the real one, which is stored in `reachable_time`* and is given a random (and uniformly distributed) value ranging between `base_reachable_time` and 3/2 `base_reachable_time`. This random value is updated every 300 seconds by `neigh_periodic_timer`, but it can also be updated by other events (especially for IPv6).

`int retrans_time`

> When a host does not receive a reply to a solicitation request within `retrans_time`, a new one is sent, up to a given number of maximum attempts. `retrans_time` is expressed in `jiffies`.

`int gc_staletime`

> A neighbour structure is removed if it has not been used for `gc_staletime` time and no one holds a reference to it. `gc_staletime` is expressed in `jiffies`.

`int delay_probe_time`

> This indicates how long a neighbor in the `NUD_DELAY` state waits before entering the `NUD_PROBE` state. See Figure 26-13 in Chapter 26.

`int queue_len`

> Maximum number of elements that can be queued in the `arp_queue` queue.

`int proxy_qlen`

> Maximum number of elements that can be queued in the `proxy_queue` queue.

---

* With ND/IPv6, `reachable_time` can also be explicitly exchanged between routers and hosts using a field in the protocol header.

```
int ucast_probes
int app_probes
int mcast_probes
```
ucast_probes is the number of unicast solicitations that can be sent to confirm the reachability of an address.

app_probes is the number of solicitations that can be sent by a user-space application when resolving an address (see the section "ARPD" in Chapter 28 for the IPv4/ARP case).

mcast_probes is the number of multicast solicitations that can be sent to resolve a neighbor's address. For ARP/IPv4, this is actually the number of broadcast solicitations, because ARP does not use multicast solicitations. IPv6 does.

Note that mcast_probes and app_probes are mutually exclusive (only one can be non-null).

```
int anycast_delay
```
Not used.

```
int proxy_delay
```
Amount of time (expressed in jiffies) that neighboring protocol packets handled by a proxy should be kept in a queue before being processed. See the section "Delayed Processing of Solicitation Requests" in Chapter 27.

```
int locktime
```
Minimum time, expressed in jiffies, that has to pass between two updates of the fields of a neighbour entry (typically nud_state and ha). This window helps avoid some nasty ping-pong effects that can take place, for instance, when more than one proxy ARP server is present on the same network segment and all of them reply to the same query solicitations with conflicting addresses. Details of this behavior are discussed in the section "Final Common Processing" in Chapter 28.

```
int dead
```
Boolean flag that is set to mark the neighbor instance as "Being removed." See neigh_parms_release.

```
atomic_t refcnt
```
Reference count.

```
struct rcu_head rcu_head
```
Used to take care of mutual exclusion.

The use of the reference count refcnt deserves a few more words. Please refer to Figure 27-2 in Chapter 27 during this discussion. Because there is an instance of neigh_parms per device per protocol, and one instance embedded in the neigh_table structure to hold the default values, plus a pointer in each neighbour structure, it may be confusing to understand who points to whom and who is who. Let's try to clarify these points.

Each neigh_table, and therefore each protocol, has its own instance of neigh_parms. That instance holds the default values that the protocol provides. Each device's net_ device can be configured with more than one L3 protocol. For each L3 protocol configured, net_device has a pointer to a protocol-specific structure that stores the configuration (e.g., in_device for IPv4). That structure includes a pointer to an instance of neigh_parms that is used to store the device-specific configuration of the neighboring protocol used by the L3 protocol (e.g., ARP for IPv4).

Table 29-5 lists the main protocol initialization routines, which allocate neigh_parms structures. For the two IP protocols, you can see the result in Figure 29-3.

Table 29-5. L3 protocol init functions

Protocol	Function	File
IPv4	inetdev_init	*net/ipv4/devinet.c*
IPv6	ipv6_add_dev	*net/ipv6/addrconf.c*
DECnet	dn_dev_create	*net/decnet/dn_dev.v*

Let's stick to IPv4 for the rest of the description. The neigh_parms instance used by ARP is allocated by inetdev_init, the IPv4 routine called when an IPv4 configuration is first applied to a device. The initial content of the new neigh_parms instance is copied from neigh_table->parms, where neigh_table is arp_tbl for ARP. Whenever a neighbour instance in created, neigh->parms is initialized to point to the neigh_parms instance of the associated device. As we saw in the section "Tuning via /proc Filesystem," both the global defaults (neigh_table->parms) and the per-device configuration can be changed by the administrator.

Because each per-device neigh_parms structure is referenced by all the neighbour instances associated with the device, neigh_parms->refcnt is used to keep track of them. The routines that directly or indirectly update the reference count are:

neigh_parms alloc
neigh_parms_destroy

> Allocate and destroy an instance of neigh_parms. neigh_parms_destroy is called only when the structure can be freed because the reference count is 0.

__neigh_parms_put
neigh_parms_put

> __neigh_parms_put only decrements the reference count, and neigh_parms_put also invokes neigh_parms_destroy if the reference count becomes 0.

neigh_parms_release

> Marks the instance as dead and indirectly invokes neigh_parms_put.

neigh_parms_clone

> Increases the reference count on a structure and returns a pointer to it.

neigh_rcu_free_parms
    Called by neigh_parms_release to actually delete the structure (here is where
    neigh_parms->rcu_head is used).

neigh_ops Structure

The neigh_ops structure consists of pointers to functions invoked at various times
during the lifetime of a neighbour entry. Most of them are virtual functions that act as
the interface between the L3 protocol and the dev_queue_xmit API introduced in
Chapter 11. Some of them are provided by the overarching neighboring infrastructure (neigh_xxx functions), and others are provided by individual neighboring protocols (e.g., arp_xxx for ARP). See the section "Initialization of a neighbour Structure"
in Chapter 28.

The main difference between the functions lies in the context where they are used.
The section "Special Cases" in Chapter 26 covered the two most common cases.

Here is the field-by-field description:

int family
    We already saw this field when describing the analogous family field of the
    neigh_table structure.

void (*destructor)(struct neighbour *)
    Function executed when a neighbour entry is removed by neigh_destroy. It basi-
    cally is the complementary method of neigh_table->constructor. But for some
    reason, constructor is in the neigh_table structure and destructor is in the
    neigh_ops structure.

void (*solicit)(struct neighbour *, struct sk_buff*)
    Function used to send solicitation requests.

void (*error_report)(struct neighbour *, struct sk_buff*)
    Function invoked when a neighbor is classified as unreachable. See the section
    "Events Generated by the Neighboring Layer" in Chapter 27.

The following four methods are used to transmit data packets, not neighboring protocol packets. The difference between them lies in the context where they are used.
See the section "Common Interface Between L3 Protocols and Neighboring Protocols" in Chapter 27.

int (*output)(struct sk_buff*)
    This is the most generic function and can be used in all the contexts. It checks if
    the address has already been resolved and starts the resolution in case it has not.
    If the address is not ready yet, it stores the packet in a temporary queue and
    starts the resolution. Because it does everything necessary to ensure the recipient
    is reachable, it is a relatively expensive operation. Do not confuse neigh_ops->
    output with neighbour->output.

```
int (*connected_output)(struct sk_buff*)
```
Used when the neighbor is known to be reachable (i.e., the state is NUD_
CONNECTED). It simply fills in the L2 header, because all the required information
is available, and therefore is faster than output.

```
int (*hh_output)(struct sk_buff*)
```
Used when the address is resolved and a copy of the whole header has already
been cached from a previous transmission. See the section "Interaction Between
Neighboring Protocols and L3 Transmission Functions" in Chapter 27.

```
int (*queue_xmit)(struct sk_buff*)
```
The previous functions, with the exception of hh_output, do not actually transmit the packets. All they do is make sure the header is compiled and call the
queue_xmit method when the buffer is ready for transmission. See Figure 27-3(b)
in Chapter 27.

hh_cache Structure

The data structure used to store a cached L2 header is struct hh_cache, defined in
include/linux/netdevice.h. (The name comes from "hardware header.") The following
is a description of its fields; the section "L2 Header Caching" in Chapter 27 describes
how it is used.

```
unsigned short hh_type
```
Protocol associated with the L3 address (see the ETH_P_*XXX* values in the file
include/linux/if_ether.h).

```
struct hh_cache *hh_next
```
More than one cached L2 header can be associated with the same neighbour
entry. However, there can be only one entry for any given value of hh_type (see
neigh_hh_init).

```
atomic_t hh_refcnt
```
Reference count.

```
int hh_len
```
Length of the cached header expressed in bytes.

```
int (*hh_output)(struct sk_buff *skb)
```
Function used to transmit the packet. As with neigh->output, this method is initialized to one of the methods of the neigh->ops VFT.

```
rwlock_t hh_lock
```
Lock used to protect the hh_cache structure from possible race conditions. For
instance, an IP function that wants to transmit a packet (see the section "Interaction Between Neighboring Protocols and L3 Transmission Functions" in
Chapter 27) acquires the read lock before copying the header from the hh_cache
structure to the skb buffer. The lock is held in exclusive mode when a field of the
structure needs to be updated: for instance, the lock is acquired when hh_output

needs to be initialized to a different function* or when the hh_cache->hh_data header needs to be updated because the destination link layer address has changed.

unsigned long hh_data[HH_DATA_ALIGN(LL_MAX_HEADER) / sizeof(long)]
Cached header.

neigh_statistics Structure

This structure stores statistics about the neighboring protocols, available for users to peruse. Each protocol keeps its own instance of the structure. This is the definition of the structure from *include/net/neighbour.h*. The following is a description of its fields:

unsigned long allocs
Total number of neighbour structures allocated by the protocol. Includes ones that have already been removed.

unsigned long destroys
Number of removed neighbour entries. Updated in neigh_destroy.

unsigned long hash_grows
Number of times that the hash table has been increased in size. Updated in neigh_hash_grow (see the section "Caching" in Chapter 27).

unsigned long res_failed
Number of times an attempt to resolve a neighbor address failed. This value is not incremented every time a new solicitation is sent; it is incremented by neigh_timer_handler only when all the attempts have failed.

unsigned long lookups
Number of times the neigh_lookup routine has been invoked.

unsigned long hits
Number of times neigh_lookup returned success.

unsigned long rcv_probes_mcast
unsigned long rcv_probes_ucast
These two fields are used only by IPv6 and represent the number of solicitation requests (probes) received that were sent to multicast and unicast addresses, respectively.

unsigned long periodic_gc_runs
unsigned long forced_gc_runs
The number of times neigh_periodic_timer and neigh_forced_gc have been invoked, respectively. See the section "Garbage Collection" in Chapter 27.

---

* A good illustration of the use of the hh_lock field can be found in neigh_destroy in *net/core/neighbour.c*. Here the lock is used to handle the case of a neighbour entry that cannot be removed because its reference count number is nonzero.

The kernel keeps an instance of these counters for each CPU. The counters are updated with the NEIGH_CACHE_STAT_INC macro, defined in *include/net/neighbour.h*. Note that the macro updates the counter on the current CPU.

The fields of the neigh_statistic structure are exported in the per-protocol */proc/net/stat/{protocol_name}_cache* files.

Data Structures Featured in This Part of the Book

Table 29-6 summarizes the main functions, variables, and data structures introduced or referenced in the chapters of this book covering the neighboring subsystem.

Table 29-6. Functions, variables, and data structures in the neighboring subsystem

Functions	Description
dev_queue_xmit neigh_compat_output neigh_resolve_output neigh_connected_output neigh_blackhole	Main routines used for packet transmission. See the section "Routines used for neigh->output" in Chapter 27.
neigh_update neigh_update_hhs neigh_sync	Update the information stored in a neighbour structure. See the section "Updating a Neighbor's Information: neigh_update" in Chapter 27.
neigh_confirm	Confirms the reachability of a neighbor.
neigh_create neigh_destroy	Create and delete a neighbour structure as a consequence of protocol events. See the sections "Creating a neighbour Entry" and "Neighbor Deletion" in Chapter 27.
neigh_add neigh_delete	Create and delete a neighbour structure as a consequence of a user-space command. See the section "System Administration of Neighbors."
neigh_alloc	Allocates a neighbour structure.
neigh_connect neigh_suspect	Used to implement reachability. See the section "Initialization of neigh->output and neigh->nud_state" in Chapter 27.
neigh_table_init	Registers a neighboring protocol.
neigh_ifdown	Handles changes of state in the L3 address when notified by external subsystems. See the section "Updates via neigh_ifdown" in Chapter 27.
neigh_proxy_process	Function handler executed when the proxy timer expires. See the section "Delayed Processing of Solicitation Requests" in Chapter 27.
neigh_timer_handler	See the section "Timers" in Chapter 15.
neigh_periodic_timer neigh_forced_gc	Used by the garbage collection algorithm. See the section "Garbage Collection" in Chapter 27.

Functions	Description
neigh_lookup *__neigh_lookup* *__neigh_lookup_ errno* *arp_find*	Check for an entry in the cache. See the section "Caching" in Chapter 27.
neigh_hold *neigh_release*	Increment/decrement the reference count on a neighbour structure.
pneigh_enqueue *pneigh_lookup*	Used for destination-based proxying. See the sections "Delayed Processing of Solicitation Requests" and "Per-Device Proxying and Per-Destination Proxying" in Chapter 27, and the section "Proxy ARP" in Chapter 28.
arp_rcv *ndisc_rcv*	Protocol handlers for ARP and ND packets, respectively.
ip_finish_output2 *ip6_output_finish*	Transmission functions for IPv4 and IPv6, respectively. See the section "Interaction Between Neighboring Protocols and L3 Transmission Functions" in Chapter 27.
neigh_hh_init	Initializes an hh_cache structure with an L2 header and binds it to the associated routing table cache entry. See the section "Link Between Routing and L2 Header Caching" in Chapter 27.
Variables	
neigh_tables	List of registered protocols.
arp_tbl nd_tbl dn_neigh_table clip_tbl	The four neigh_table structures that define the four neighboring protocols implemented in the kernel.
Data structures	
struct neighbour struct neigh_table struct neigh_parms struct neigh_ops struct hh_cache struct neigh_ statistics	Main data structures, described in Chapter 27 and detailed in reference style in the section "Functions and Variables Featured in This Part of the Book."

Files and Directories Featured in This Part of the Book

Figure 29-5 shows the main files and directories referred to in the chapters on the neighboring subsystem.

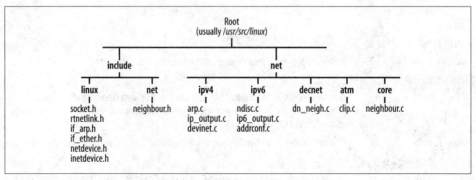

Figure 29-5. Files and directories featured in this part of the book

## PART VII

Routing

Layer three protocols, such as IP, must find out how to reach the system that is supposed to receive each packet. The recipient could be in the cubicle next door or halfway around the world. When more than one network is involved, the L3 layer is responsible for figuring out the most efficient route (so far as that is feasible) and for directing the message toward the next system along that route, also called the *next hop*. This process is called *routing*, and it plays a central role in the Linux networking code. Here is what is covered in each chapter:

Chapter 30, *Routing: Concepts*
Introduces the functionality that a basic router, and therefore the Linux kernel, must provide.

Chapter 31, *Routing: Advanced*
Introduces optional features the user can enable to configure routing in more complex scenarios. Among them we will see policy routing and multipath routing. We will also look at the other subsystems routing interacts with.

Chapter 32, *Routing: Linux Implementation*
Gives you an overview of the main data structures used by the routing code, describes the initialization of the routing subsystem, and shows the interactions between the routing subsystem and other kernel subsystems.

Chapter 33, *Routing: The Routing Cache*
Describes the routing cache, including the protocol-independent cache (destination cache, or DST). The description covers how elements are inserted and deleted from the cache, along with the garbage collection and lookup algorithms.

Chapter 34, *Routing: Routing Tables*
Describes the structure of the routing table, and how routes are added to and deleted from it.

Chapter 35, *Routing: Lookups*

Describes the routing table lookups, for both ingress and egress traffic, with and without policy routing.

Chapter 36, *Routing: Miscellaneous Topics*

Concludes this part of the book with a detailed description of the data structures introduced in Chapter 32, and a description of the interfaces between user space and kernel. This includes a description of the old and new generations of administrative tools, namely the *net-tools* and IPROUTE2 packages.

## CHAPTER 30

Routing: Concepts

Figure 30-1 shows where the routing subsystem (the gray box) fits into the network stack. The figure does not include all the details (Netfilter, bridging, etc.) but shows the other major kernel subsystems that are traversed before and after routing.

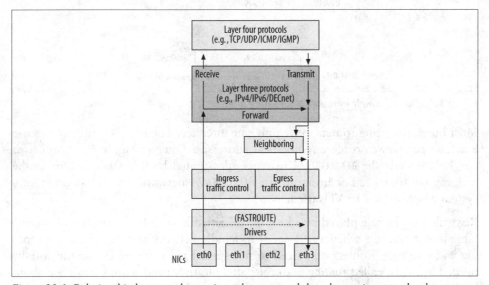

Figure 30-1. Relationship between the routing subsystem and the other main network subsystems

To explain some of the features or the details of their implementation, I'll often show snapshots of user-space configurations. You are encouraged to use Chapter 36 as a reference if you need to learn more about the user-space tools I employ in the examples.

The discussion on routing will focus on IPv4 networks. However, I will point out the aspects of IPv6 that differ significantly.

Routers, Routes, and Routing Tables

In its simplest form, a router can be defined as a network device that is equipped with more than one network interface card (NIC), and that uses its knowledge of the network to forward ingress traffic appropriately.*

The information required to decide whether an ingress packet is addressed to the local host or should be forwarded, together with the information needed to correctly forward the packets in the latter case, is stored in a database called the Forwarding Information Base (FIB). It is often referred to simply as the *routing table*.

Figure 30-2 shows a simple scenario with a LAN whose hosts are configured on the 10.0.0.0/24 subnet, and a router, RT, that is used by the hosts of the LAN to reach the Internet.

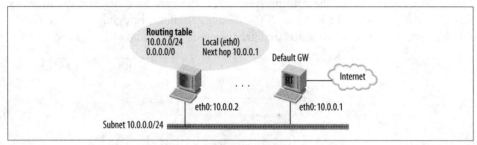

Figure 30-2. Basic example of router and routing table

Most hosts, not being routers, have only one interface. The host is configured to use a default gateway to reach any nonlocal addresses. Thus, in Figure 30-2, traffic for any host outside the 10.0.0.0/24 network (designated by 0.0.0.0/0) is sent to the gateway on 10.0.0.1. For hosts on the 10.0.0.0/24 network, the neighboring subsystem described in Part VI is used.

Regardless of the role played by a host in the network, each host maintains a routing table that it consults whenever it needs to handle network traffic, both when sending and receiving. Routers may need to run specialized software that is not usually needed by hosts, called *routing protocols*; after all, they need more knowledge about how to reach remote networks, and the nonrouter hosts depend on them for that. The routing protocols are beyond the scope of this book.

The routing capabilities required by hosts may be reduced even further under specific scenarios, such as the one described in the section "Proxy ARP Server as Router" in Chapter 28. In this chapter, however, we will stick to the common case just laid out.

---

* Unlike IPv4, IPv6 explicitly defines the router role by using a special flag in the IP header.

The routing table is nothing but a collection of routes. A *route* is a collection of parameters used to store the information necessary to forward traffic toward a given destination. In Chapter 32, we will see in detail how Linux defines a route, but we can anticipate here the minimum set of parameters needed to define a route. Let's use Figure 30-2 again as a reference.

Destination network
> The routing table is used to forward traffic toward its destination. It should not come as a surprise that this is the most important field used by the routing lookup routines. Figure 30-2 shows a routing table with two routes: one that leads to the local subnet 10.0.0.0/24 and another one that leads everywhere else. The latter is called the *default route* and is recorded as a network of all zeros in the table (see the section "Default Gateway Selection").

Egress device
> This is the device out of which packets matching this route should be transmitted. For example, packets sent to the address 10.0.0.100 would be sent out *eth0*.

Next hop gateway
> When the destination network is not directly connected to the local host, you need to rely on other routers to reach it. For example, the host in Figure 30-2 needs to rely on the router RT to reach any host located outside the 10.0.0.0/24 subnet. The next-hop gateway is the address of that router.

Nonrouting Multihomed Hosts

Earlier, I said that a router usually has more than one NIC, given that its main job is to forward data received on one interface out to another. However, nonrouting hosts—especially servers—can also have multiple NICs without actually doing any packet forwarding. It is not uncommon for a big server to have multiple NICs for one or more of the following reasons:

High availability
> If one interface goes down or fails, traffic can be taken over by a second one (which may be connected to a different LAN as well).

Greater routing capabilities
> The server may be configured with more routes than just one default. For instance, it may use static routes or multiple NICs to reach specific hosts or subnets for particular reasons (for instance, to facilitate system logging). Figure 30-3 shows an example where a multihomed host has a second NIC connected to another LAN to let it reach Host A. Note that the multihomed host does not forward traffic between the two LANs; otherwise it would be a router by definition.

Channeling
> It is possible to bind together multiple interfaces and make them look like a single one to the routing subsystem. This extra layer (which is transparent to the

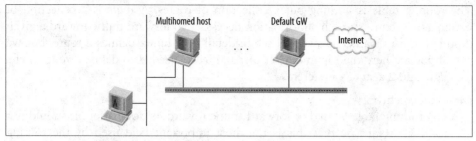

Figure 30-3. Example of a multihomed host

routing subsystem) can increase the overall bandwidth over a given connection, which can be a valuable feature for highly loaded servers.

In none of the preceding cases is the host considered a router, because it does not forward traffic from one interface to another. Another way to say this is that such a host never receives traffic addressed to any host but itself (where "itself" includes broadcast and multicast traffic), except in error or under very specific conditions (proxying, promiscuous interfaces, etc.). Multicast and broadcast traffic can be considered traffic addressed to the host.

Varieties of Routing Configurations

Routing is a complex topic; we will not be able to analyze all the possible scenarios, problems, and solutions. However, it is important to be aware of some of them to go through the source code and understand why some seemingly superfluous conditions are taken into consideration and handled specially.

Figure 30-4 shows three configurations you should understand to make sense of the design of the routing subsystem. The routers in these configurations are named R*n*. Let's see what is so special about these cases:

- (a) This is the most common case, where different interfaces are configured on different subnets, and each subnet is associated with a different LAN.

- (b) Router RT has two interfaces on the same LAN (shown below the router), but they are configured on two different subnets.

- (c) Router RT still has one address on each subnet 10.0.2.0/24 and 10.0.3.0/24, but both of those addresses have been configured on the same NIC. This can be accomplished in two different ways: by using the multiple IP address capability introduced with IPROUTE2, or by creating old-style aliasing interfaces. We will briefly compare the two approaches later in this chapter.

Cases (b) and (c) are not common, but they are perfectly legitimate and show how flexible Linux and IP are. Their implications may not be clear to you yet. We will point them out and justify them later in this chapter, but let's start with a couple of simple implications.

- A LAN is a broadcast domain. All the hosts that belong to the same L2 broadcast domain receive each other's broadcast. This means that in cases (b) and (c), if RT (or any other host in network 10.0.2.0/24) sends a packet to the broadcast address 10.0.2.255, all the hosts of subnet 10.0.3.0/24 will receive it (even though they will discard it), including, of course, RT.

- The ingress interface is not necessarily different from the egress interface, although it usually is. Forwarding usually consists of receiving a packet on one interface and retransmitting it out to another one. In case (c), however, RT can receive a packet on one subnet and forward it to the other one on the same LAN using the same NIC.

In Chapter 26, we saw the implications of the setups in Figure 30-4(b) and 30-4(c) on lower-layer neighboring protocols. In this chapter, we will look at the implications with regard to routing.

Questions Answered in This Part of the Book

At this point, you may be asking yourself general questions such as:

- If a router is supposed to forward packets, how does the kernel know that forwarding is enabled?
- Is routing something you enable globally or between interface pairs?
- Are there tuning parameters that can significantly influence the performance of a Linux router?
- What is the syntax of the routing table?

Or more specific ones such as:

- What is the algorithm used to find the information needed to forward a packet?
- Is the routing table used only to forward traffic, or is there any other use for it?
- How does the kernel interact with dynamic routing protocol daemons running in user space?

With this and the following routing chapters, you'll be able to answer both kinds of questions.

Essential Elements of Routing

In this section, I'll introduce some terms and basic elements of the routing landscape. It's important to have a clear understanding of the meanings of a few key terms that are used extensively in this part of the book, and that appear as part of the variable and function names in the associated kernel code. Fortunately, the routing code uses naming conventions pretty consistently.

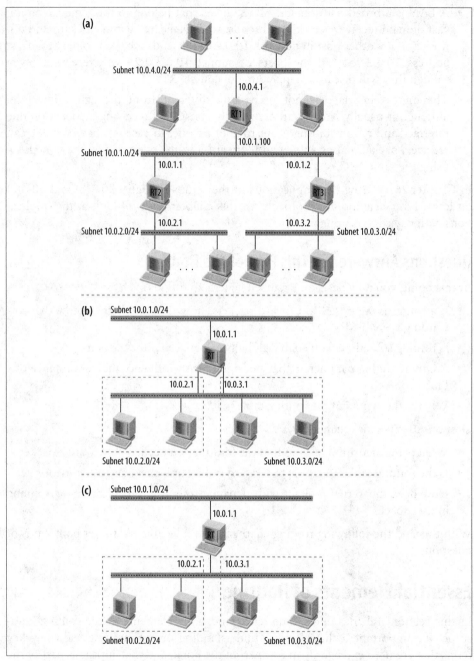

Figure 30-4. Examples of network topologies.

A few definitions are simple and are shown in the following list. Other concepts are presented in their own subsections.

Internet Service Provider (ISP)
Company or organization that provides access to the Internet.

Forwarding Information Base (FIB)
This is simply the routing table. See the earlier section "Routers, Routes, and Routing Tables."

Symmetric routes and asymmetric routes
Usually, the route taken from Host A to Host B is the same as the route used to get back from Host B to Host A; the route is then called *symmetric*. In complex setups, the route back may be different; in this case, it is *asymmetric*.

Metrics
A metric is an optional parameter that can be configured on a route. Do not confuse these metrics with the ones used by routing protocols: the latter use metrics to quantify how good a route is. Examples of routing protocol metrics are the end-to-end delay, the number of hops, a configuration weight or cost, etc.

When you configure a route with IPROUTE2, you can provide additional parameters called metrics, as defined in the section "Essential Elements of Routing." One of them—Path Maximum Transmission Unit, or Path MTU—is described in Chapter 18. Others are used by the Transmission Control Protocol (TCP) as starting values for internal variables that may later be adjusted by the protocol. You can refer to any book on TCP for their meaning and use:

- Window
- Round trip
- Round-trip time variation
- Slow-start threshold
- Congestion window
- Maximum segment size to advertise
- Reordering

Realm
A numerical domain identifier. See the section "Routing Table Based Classifier" in Chapter 31.

Address class
IP addresses are classified into various classes, shown in Table 30-1. Table 30-2 shows, for each class of IP addresses, the size of the network and host components (note that classes D and E are special cases of class C).

Table 30-1. Classification of IPv4 addresses based on class

Class	First address	Last address	Leftmost bits of addresses
A	0.0.0.0	127.255.255.255	0----
B	128.0.0.0	192.255.255.255	10---
C	192.0.0.0	223.255.255.255	110--
D (Multicast)	224.0.0.0	239.255.255.255	1110-
E (Reserved)	240.0.0.0	255.255.255.255	11111

Table 30-2. Network and host components

Class	Size of network address component	Size of host address component	Number of hosts (including network and broadcast addresses)
A	8	24	16,777,216 (2^{24})
B	16	16	65,535 (2^{16})
C	24	8	256 (2^8)

Routable and nonroutable addresses

The IP specifications have set aside certain ranges of addresses (shown in Table 30-3) as nonroutable, which means they are reserved for use on a LAN. Routable addresses must be handed out by centralized bodies and are unique worldwide. Anyone, in contrast, can configure nonroutable addresses, and these are the ones most users have on their systems behind their routers. Nonroutable addresses cannot be used to provide any Internet service because they are not unique and Internet routers are not supposed to pass traffic to them.

The 127.0.0.0/8 subnet is a special range of addresses whose scope[*] is just the host where they are configured. No packet can leave a host with one of these addresses as either the source or the destination.

Table 30-3. Nonroutable and loopback IPv4 addresses

Addresses	Class
10.0.0.0/8	1 x Class A
172.16.0.0/16 to 172.31.0.0/16	16 x Class B
192.168.0.0/16	256 x Class C
127.0.0.0/8 (Loopback)	1 x Class A

Figure 30-5 shows a topology with two subnets using the same range of nonroutable IP addresses 10.0.1.0/24, and one subnet using the routable subnet 100.0.1.0/24. For hosts from either 10.0.1.0/24 subnet to communicate with hosts outside their subnet, their routers must use some form of Network Address Translation (NAT) to

---

[*] The section "Scope" describes the exact meaning of the term when applied to IP addresses.

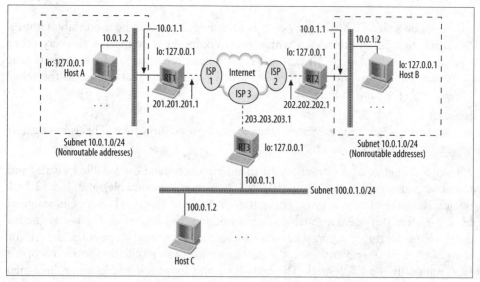

Figure 30-5. Routable versus nonroutable addresses

hide the local, nonroutable subnets. Note also that each host is configured by default with the 127.0.0.1 address. The interfaces that connect the three routers to their ISPs are configured with routable IP addresses assigned by the ISPs.

Scope

Both routes and IP addresses are assigned *scopes*, which tell the kernel the contexts in which they are meaningful and usable. If you understand the concept of scope, you will have an easier time understanding the various sanity checks done by the routing code, and the distinctions it makes between differently scoped routes and IP addresses.

The scope of a route in Linux is an indicator of the distance to the destination network. The scope of an IP address is an indication of how far from the local host the address is known, which, to some extent, also tells you how far the owner of that address is from the local host.

Chapter 32 offers a more detailed list of scopes, but let's see a few examples here, using a terminology very similar to the one used in the code so that it will be easier to associate the code with these concepts.

Let's start with common scopes for IP addresses:

Host

> An address has host scope when it is used only to communicate within the host itself. Outside the host this address is not known and cannot be used. An example is the loopback address, 127.0.0.1.

Link

> An address has link scope when it is meaningful and can be used only within a LAN (that is, a network on which every computer is connected to every other one on the link layer). An example is a subnet's broadcast address. Packets sent to the subnet broadcast address are sent by a host on that subnet to the other hosts on the same subnet.*

Universe

> An address has universe scope when it can be used anywhere. This is the default scope for most addresses.

Note that the scope does not reflect the distinction between nonroutable (private) and routable (public) addresses. Both 10.0.0.1 (which is nonroutable) and 165.12.12.1 (which is routable) can be given either link or universe scope. The scope is assigned by the system administrator when she configures the addresses (or is assigned a default value by the configuration commands). Since universe scope is the default for both of the addresses mentioned, the administrator must explicitly specify a scope if something different is desired. The broadcast and loopback addresses are assigned the proper scope automatically by the kernel.

Let's see now the meaning of the same three scopes when applied to routes:

Host

> A route has host scope when it leads to a destination address on the local host.

Link

> A route has link scope when it leads to a destination address on the local network.

Universe

> A route has universe scope when it leads to addresses more than one hop away.

We will see in the section "Adding an IP address" in Chapter 32 that Linux creates a route for each local address configured, plus one for the broadcast address of each configured subnet. That section should help you understand the relationship between the scopes of addresses and of routes.

Use of the scope

The scope of both addresses and routes is used extensively by the routing code and other parts of the kernel.

First of all, remember that in Linux, even though an administrator configures IP addresses on interfaces, addresses belong to the host, not to the interfaces. See the section "Responding from Multiple Interfaces" in Chapter 28 for more details.

---

* There are exceptions, of course. See the section "Directed Broadcasts" for an example.

It is not uncommon for a host to be configured with multiple addresses, either on a single interface or on multiple interfaces. When the local system transmits a packet, the kernel needs to select what source IP address to use. This is trivial when the host has only one NIC with a single IP address configured, but it is less obvious when you run a complex setup with multiple addresses of different scopes. Depending on the location of the destination address, you may prefer to select a source IP address with a specific scope, which the destination can then use to return traffic or for other purposes at the remote site.

The routing code also uses scopes to enforce simple yet powerful sanity checks on the configuration. Suppose you need to transmit a packet to remote Host B, which is not directly reachable in any of the subnets configured on the local host. A routing lookup will return you the address of the gateway to use—say, RT. Now you know that to reach Host B, you need to send your packet to RT, which will take care of forwarding it. To avoid a loop, RT must be closer to the destination than you are. In other words, the scope of the route to Host B must be wider than the scope of the route toward RT. (There are exceptions, which are often required by special configurations.)

Let's look at an example using the topology of Figure 30-6. For Host A to reach Host B, a routing lookup on the former returns the default route via 10.0.1.1, whose scope is RT_SCOPE_UNIVERSE. The gateway's address 10.0.1.1 is reachable directly via A's *eth0* interface, according to the other route shown in the figure. This second route has scope RT_SCOPE_LINK, which is narrower than the previous scope and therefore enables the interface to be used to send the packet to the address with the broader scope.

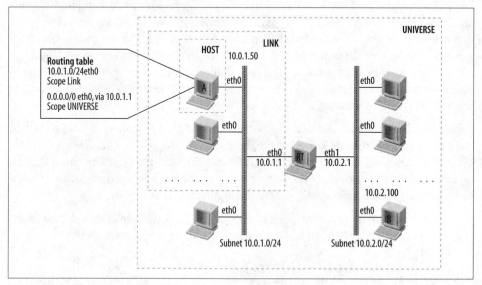

Figure 30-6. Simple network topology

In the section "Egress lookup" in Chapter 33, you can find an example of using scope involving ARP.

Default Gateway

The default gateway, often referred to as the 0.0.0.0/0 route, is the one used when there is no explicit route to a destination.* A single host connected to the Internet is usually configured with a route to the local network (which is indirectly derived from the NIC's configuration) and one default route (usually given by the ISP) that is used to reach the Internet. A router, on the other hand, may or may not be configured with default routes; it depends on where the router is placed in the network topology and what role the router plays.

The Linux kernel does not have any restriction on the number of default gateways you can configure. See Chapter 35 for details.

Directed Broadcasts

A broadcast packet is simply a packet sent to a subnet's broadcast address. Subnet broadcasts are usually generated by hosts located within the same subnet. This means that the broadcast packet is addressed to all the hosts in its own subnet.

A directed broadcast, on the other hand, is addressed to the broadcast address of a remote subnet. An example of the use of a directed broadcast is the remote announce feature used by SAMBA servers to advertise resources (printers or folders) on remote subnets.

Let's illustrate directed broadcasts by referring to Figure 30-7(a). When Host A sends an IP packet to the address 10.0.0.255, it generates a local broadcast (this case is not in the figure). When it sends a packet to the address 10.0.1.255 instead, it generates a directed broadcast. In our example, Host A and the destination network (10.0.1.0/24) are separated by only one hop, but they could have been more distant; the definition of a directed broadcast includes any case where the sender does not belong to the local network to which it addresses the broadcast.

A host can identify a directed broadcast only if the host is on the subnet to which the broadcast is directed. For example, in Figure 30-7(c), RT1 cannot tell whether 100.0.1.127 is a subnet broadcast, but RT2 can. Directed broadcasts can therefore be recognized as such only by the last gateway on the path to the destination subnet, because that gateway has one IP address configured on that subnet.

You may wonder why this is important. Essentially, a misuse of directed broadcasts can generate Denial of Service (DoS) attacks, and it is unfortunately difficult to

---

* There are topologies where a default gateway is not needed. See the section "Proxy ARP Server as Router" in Chapter 28 for an example.

distinguish benign directed broadcasts from malign ones. One case, however, is known to probably be malign: ICMP ECHO REQUEST packets (i.e., pings) sent as directed broadcasts.

Let's take the example in Figure 30-7(a) and (b) and imagine 10.0.0.200 sending an ICMP ECHO REQUEST to the broadcast address 10.0.1.255 (which is not its own subnet), using the source IP address 10.0.0.100 (which is not its own address). This would make each host in the remote subnet 10.0.1.0/24 reply to the ICMP ECHO REQUEST by sending an ICMP ECHO REPLY to the victim host with IP address 10.0.0.100. The latter would simply discard those packets, since it never sent any ICMP ECHO REQUEST, but even discarding a huge number of packets is CPU-consuming. As you can imagine, if there were a lot of hosts in the 10.0.1.0/24 subnet, the victim could be flooded with garbage traffic.

The routing subsystem of the Linux kernel does not allow you to discard any directed broadcasts. (You can, however, use the filtering subsystem to weed them out.) Linux does handle ICMP ECHO REQUESTS addressed to a broadcast address specially: the administrator can indicate whether a host should reply to an ICMP ECHO REQUEST when the destination address is a local subnet broadcast.

Primary and Secondary Addresses

Sometimes it's necessary to configure multiple IP addresses on the same NIC. This may be required, for instance, because:

- You run multiple services on the same host and you prefer to advertise each service with a different IP address. This can also simplify the firewall rules.
- You may be short of hardware and forced to temporarily merge two subnets onto the same hub or switch. In that case, a single NIC would be sufficient to provide connectivity to both subnets.

You may be surprised to hear that, when you configure multiple IP addresses on the same NIC, the kernel's routing code may not consider them equivalent even when they are assigned the same scope. Distinctions can be made by calling some addresses *primary* and others *secondary*.

When you configure an IP address on an interface, you are always required to provide a netmask as well. When you do not provide it and the system does not complain, it means the system has selected a default netmask for you. (It may, for example, be based on the class the IP address belongs to. See the section "Essential Elements of Routing.") Without a netmask, the routing subsystem wouldn't know which addresses are directly reachable through that interface. So every address is accompanied by a netmask, and if you configure multiple IP addresses on the same interface, you need to specify a netmask for each one. Those netmasks may or may not be the same, depending on the configuration you want to enforce.

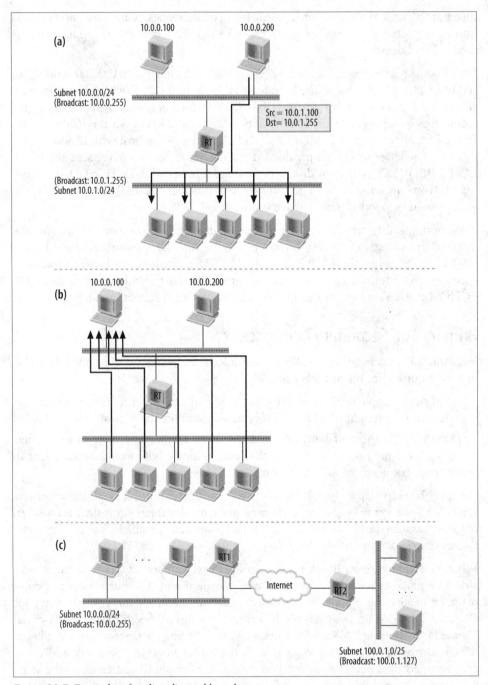

Figure 30-7. Examples of malign directed broadcasts

An address is considered secondary if it falls within the subnet of another already configured address on the same NIC. This includes the case where the subnets are the same. Thus, the order in which addresses are configured is important: you do not explicitly say that a given address is primary or secondary when you configure it, but the decision is made automatically based on the presence of an existing address encompassing the subnet.

Let's see a couple of examples.

The following is the configuration of a single NIC named *eth0* after it is configured with two addresses having the same netmask, first 10.0.0.1/24 and then 10.0.0.2/24. Since the two addresses fall within the same 10.0.0.0/24 subnet, the first one configured will be primary and the other one will be secondary.

```
[root@router kernel]# ip address add 10.0.0.1/24 broadcast 10.0.0.255 dev eth0
[root@router kernel]# ip address list dev eth0
4: eth0: <BROADCAST,MULTICAST,UP> mtu 1500 qdisc pfifo_fast qlen 100
    link/ether 00:60:97:77:d1:8c brd ff:ff:ff:ff:ff:ff
    inet 10.0.0.1/24 brd 10.0.0.255 scope global eth0

[root@router kernel]# ip address add 10.0.0.2/24 broadcast 10.0.0.255 dev eth0
[root@router kernel]# ip address list dev eth0
4: eth0: <BROADCAST,MULTICAST,UP> mtu 1500 qdisc pfifo_fast qlen 100
    link/ether 00:60:97:77:d1:8c brd ff:ff:ff:ff:ff:ff
    inet 10.0.0.1/24 brd 10.0.0.255 scope global eth0
    inet 10.0.0.2/24 brd 10.0.0.255 scope global secondary eth0
```

Each interface can have as many primary and secondary addresses as you like. For a particular netmask (the /24 netmask in this case), only one address can be primary. If we added a third address—say, 10.0.0.3/24—it would be classified as a secondary address associated with the primary address 10.0.0.1/24.

On the other hand, 10.0.0.1/24 and 10.0.0.3/25 are on different subnets (because of the different netmasks) even though they cover an overlapping range of addresses. Therefore, if we added the 10.0.0.3/25 address to the previous two, it would be classified as another primary address on *eth0*. This would be the output of *ip address list*:

```
[root@router kernel]# ip address add 10.0.0.3/25 broadcast 10.0.0.127 dev eth0
[root@router kernel]# ip address list dev eth0
4: eth0: <BROADCAST,MULTICAST,UP> mtu 1500 qdisc pfifo_fast qlen 100
    link/ether 00:60:97:77:d1:8c brd ff:ff:ff:ff:ff:ff
    inet 10.0.0.1/24 brd 10.0.0.255 scope global eth0
    inet 10.0.0.2/24 brd 10.0.0.255 scope global secondary eth0
    inet 10.0.0.3/25 brd 10.0.0.127 scope global eth0
```

In the section "Helper Routines" in Chapter 35 we will see how the kernel manages to select one IP address when there are multiple primary addresses with overlapping subnets.

In short, it is not only the IP address that decides the primary-secondary status: you also need to take into account the netmask because it identifies the subnet. When configuring multiple IP addresses on an interface, it is important to understand the difference between primary and secondary addresses. It is also important when looking at the routing code. We will see in Chapter 32 that the response to many events and conditions depends on whether the IP address is primary or secondary. Here are some examples:

- Primary addresses contribute to the entropy of the CPU that happens to run the code that applies the configuration.
- When you delete a primary address, all the associated secondary addresses are also removed. There is an option, configurable via /proc, that allows secondary addresses to be promoted to primary when the current primary address is removed (see Chapter 18).
- When a host selects the source IP address for locally generated traffic, it considers only primary addresses.

Old-generation configuration: aliasing interfaces

You may have noticed that in the previous sections, I always used the *ip address* command to configure addresses. That's for a good reason: *ifconfig*, the old-generation interface configuration command and the most common tool used by Unix administrators for this purpose, cannot distinguish between primary and secondary addresses. *ifconfig* does not even show the secondary addresses, so the output of *ifconfig* and *ip address list* would not match in the examples in the previous sections. Chapter 36 offers a deeper comparison between *ifconfig*, offered by Linux's net-tools package, and the new-generation *ip address* tool, offered by the IPROUTE2 package.

Before the introduction of IPROUTE2 and its advanced routing capabilities, Linux used the concept of *aliasing* interfaces, which is still available with newer kernels for backward compatibility. The only way to configure multiple addresses on a single NIC with *ifconfig* was to define virtual devices like *eth0:0, eth0:1*, etc. Each virtual device could be used as a real NIC: you could configure an address on it, use it as a device when configuring routing, and so on.

Relationship between aliasing devices and primary/secondary status

Because the kernel supports both the advanced capabilities of IPROUTE2 and old-style aliasing, those two models need to coexist somehow. We will see the details of the kernel internals in Chapter 32, but we can examine here how the two coexist from a user-space perspective.

When you configure an aliasing device, the primary/secondary status is still assigned based on the same rule we introduced in the section "Primary and Secondary Addresses." However, the output of *ip address list* now adds a reference to the aliasing device. The following snapshot shows an example where we start with an interface with one configured address (*eth1*), add an address within the same subnet on an aliasing device (*eth1:1*), and then add another address in a different subnet on another aliasing device (*eth1:2*). Because of the differing subnets, *eth1:1* becomes secondary and *eth1:2* becomes primary.

```
[root@router kernel]# ip address list
...
11: eth1: <BROADCAST,MULTICAST,UP> mtu 1500 qdisc pfifo_fast qlen 1000
    link/ether 00:0a:41:04:bd:16 brd ff:ff:ff:ff:ff:ff
    inet 192.168.1.101/24 brd 192.168.1.255 scope global eth1
...
[root@router kernel]# ifconfig eth1:1 192.168.1.102 netmask 255.255.255.0
[root@router kernel]# ifconfig eth1:2 192.168.1.103 netmask 255.255.255.128
[root@router kernel]# ip address list
...
11: eth1: <BROADCAST,MULTICAST,UP> mtu 1500 qdisc pfifo_fast qlen 1000
    link/ether 00:0a:41:04:bd:16 brd ff:ff:ff:ff:ff:ff
    inet 192.168.1.101/24 brd 192.168.1.255 scope global eth1
    inet 192.168.1.103/25 brd 192.168.1.255 scope global eth1:2
    inet 192.168.1.102/24 brd 192.168.1.255 scope global secondary eth1:1
...
```

An obvious question is whether you can configure multiple addresses on an aliasing device using IPROUTE2. This is not possible, because IPROUTE2 does not treat aliasing devices as real, independent devices as *ifconfig* does: an aliasing device to IPROUTE2 is just a label on an address.

```
[root@router kernel]# ip address add 192.168.1.104/24 dev eth1:1
Cannot find device "eth1:1"
```

Routing Table

The routing table is the core of the routing sysbsystem. In its simplest definition, it consists of a database of routes that is available to other subsystems—IPv4, for example—through various functions, the most important being the one used to do lookups.

As you may already imagine, routes do not consist only of the basic information shown in the section "Routers, Routes, and Routing Tables." Over time, due both to code optimizations and to the introduction of new features, the amount of information that makes up an entry in the routing table has grown quite a bit. We will look at those details in Chapter 34.

In the following subsections, we will briefly see:

- How Linux routes packets addressed to local addresses
- What algorithm is used to look up addresses in the routing table
- What administrative actions can be applied to traffic matching a route besides the default forwarding action
- What extra information is stored in a route by upper protocols for their convenience

Special Routes

When a packet is received, a router needs to determine whether to deliver it locally to the next-higher layer (because the local host is the final destination) or to forward it. A simple way to accomplish this is to store all the local addresses in a list and scan the list for each packet as part of the routing lookup. Of course, a list would not be the best choice; there are better data structures that can provide faster lookup time. Linux uses a separate hash-based routing table where it stores only local addresses. To be more exact, it stores all of those addresses that it listens to, which includes both the locally configured addresses and the subnet broadcasts.

This means that by default, Linux uses two routing tables:

- A table for local addresses. A successful lookup in this table means that the packet is to be delivered on the host itself. We will see in Chapter 32 how the kernel populates this table.

- A table for all other routes, manually configured by the user or dynamically inserted by routing protocols.

Route Types and Actions

We saw in the section "Routers, Routes, and Routing Tables" what a basic route consists of. By default, the action taken to process a packet that matches a given route is to forward it according to the forwarding information returned from the routing table for that route: the next-hop router and the egress device.

However, Linux allows you to optionally define other kinds of actions as well.* Here are the main ones:

Black hole
 Packets matching this type of route are silently discarded.

Unreachable
 Packets matching this type of route are discarded and generate an Internet Control Message Protocol (ICMP) host unreachable message.

Prohibit
 Packets matching this type of route are discarded and generate an ICMP packet filtered message.

Throw
 This type is used in conjunction with policy routing, a feature covered in Chapter 31. When policy routing is configured, a matching route of this type will make the lookup abandon the current table and continue with the following one (if any).

---

* We will see in Chapter 36 that you can configure these alternative route types only using the new-generation configuration tool IPROUTE2.

Routing Cache

Depending on the role played by the router, the number of routes in its routing table can range from a few units to a few hundred thousand. Because of that, it should be obvious that it would be beneficial to maintain a smaller table that caches the results of lookups, both positive and negative. Linux splits the routing cache into two components (where a protocol, in this context, means an L3 protocol such as IPv4 and IPv6):

- A protocol-dependent cache
- A protocol-independent destination cache, often called just DST

The first component represents the skeleton of the cache, where each element is defined as a collection of protocol-specific fields. The second component, which is embedded in the first, stores only protocol-independent information. Both the protocol-dependent cache and the protocol independent component of it are described in Chapter 33.

We will see in Chapter 31 that it is possible to create multiple independent routing tables on a Linux system that supports the policy routing feature. Regardless of the number of routing tables, Linux uses only one routing cache. If policy routing is supported, the cache does not provide any fairness, so it is possible that the routes of one routing table use many more entries of the cache than other routing tables (i.e., the space in the cache is not equally distributed among the routing tables). This approach, however, ensures greater routing throughput overall.

Routing Table Versus Routing Cache

The routing table and the routing cache, besides differing in size and structure, also differ in the granularity of their objects. The routing table uses subnets, aggregates of consecutive addresses. Entries of the cache, on the other hand, are associated with single IP addresses. Because of this, the lookup algorithm used by the routing table and the routing cache also differs, as we will see in the section "Lookups."

Let's view an example. Suppose our routing table includes, among other routes, the one in Table 30-4, which is the only one that leads to the subnet 10.0.1.0/24.

Table 30-4. Example of routing table entry

Destination	Next hop	Device to use
10.0.1.0/24	10.0.0.1	*eth0*

Let's also suppose the kernel was asked to transmit two packets to the addresses 10.0.1.100 and 10.0.1.101, respectively. Since the route in Table 30-4 would match in both cases, the kernel would use it to route the two packets and would install two entries into the routing cache that would look like those in Table 30-5.

Table 30-5. Example of routing cache entry

Destination	Next hop	Device to use
10.0.1.100	10.0.0.1	*eth0*
10.0.1.101	10.0.0.1	*eth0*

The elements in Table 30-5 are a simplified version, of course. In Chapter 33, we will see that entries of the routing cache include the source address, too.

Routing Cache Garbage Collection

Garbage collection is responsible for eliminating data structures, owned by the routing subsystem, that are no longer in use. However, data structures may be removed even if they are in use, for example, to free the memory needed to store something more important. The effects of the deletions done by the garbage collection will not lead to any loss of data, because all the information eliminated can be re-created. The deletion of an element from the cache can lead only to a cache miss in the worst case.

There are two kinds of garbage collection:

Synchronous

When the routing subsystem sees the need to free some memory, a cleanup is done right away. There are two cases where the routing code may force garbage collection without waiting for the regular timer to do it:

- When a new entry is to be added to the routing cache and the number of entries currently in the cache has reached a particular threshold, which is configurable by the user.

- When memory is needed by the neighboring subsystem cache. We saw in Chapter 27 that the routing cache and the neighboring subsystem cache keep references to each other. The creation of a new routing cache entry could trigger the creation of a new neighbor cache entry. If the neighboring protocol—say, ARP—failed to allocate the memory it needed, the routing subsystem would force a garbage collection to indirectly free data structures owned by the neighboring protocol and therefore help the latter find the memory it needed.

Asynchronous

To keep the cache size reasonable, a periodic timer is used to trigger regular cleanups. By default, routing cache entries do not expire. However, it is possible for external subsystems to tell the routing cache to expire certain entries after a given amount of time. The routing subsystem runs a timer that periodically scans the cache, looking for entries that:

- Are expired and should be removed

- Are not expired, but could be sacrificed if the kernel needs to free some memory

Examples of events that can expire cache entries

An entry is set to expire only in specific cases, including:

- When the local system receives an ICMP UNREACHABLE or ICMP FRAG-MENTATION NEEDED message, it hands it to the ICMP layer. Such a message notifies the local host about a packet that it previously sent out whose size exceeded the MTU of a router along the path to the destination address. The ICMP handler will scan the routing cache, update the PMTU field of all the affected entries, and set the latter to expire after a certain configurable amount of time, which is 10 minutes by default.

  ICMP also notifies the L4 protocol associated with the packet that triggered the ICMP message. For instance, TCP may use these notifications for the Path MTU discovery algorithm. See Chapters 18 and 25 for more details on path MTU discovery.

- A destination IP address can be classified as unreachable when the neighboring protocol has failed to resolve the L3-to-L2 mapping (see Chapter 27) or when the local host is at one end of an IP tunnel, and the other end becomes unreachable for some reason (for example, a routing problem or misconfiguration).

  When a destination IP address is classified as unreachable, all the entries of the cache associated with the address need to be flushed and therefore will be set to expire right away.

Examples of eligible cache victims

There may be cases where the kernel needs to free some cache entries to make room for new ones, and the periodic timer is not able to guarantee by itself that the cache will always have some free room (i.e., to keep its size below some threshold). In those cases, the host must delete entries that the periodic timer would not pick because they are still valid. Even if the garbage collection system needs to select victims from valid entries, it can reduce the damage by selecting those that can be re-created quickly with only a small overhead.

Good candidates for removal include routes to broadcast and multicast addresses. Normally, when the routing subsystem deletes a routing cache entry, it may indirectly remove the L3-to-L2 association as well. When this happens, the next time the host needs to send data to the L3 address, the neighboring subsystem will need to resolve the L3-to-L2 association again. However, broadcast and multicast addresses can be resolved with low overhead because they do not need any solicitation request (see the section "Special Cases" in Chapter 26).

Particularly bad (high-overhead) candidates for removal include:

REDIRECT *routes*
> This kind of route has been learned through an ICMP REDIRECT message; if it is removed, the host will use suboptimal routing for further traffic along that route. Removing the entry may also be a waste of time because the host will most likely receive another ICMP REDIRECT that just leads to reinserting the route.

Routes manually configured by the administrator
> These are routes that a user, via a command such as *ip route get 10.0.0.1 monitor*, has asked the kernel to send a notification (via the Netlink socket) when it changes state. The user probably considers this route important for some reason. See Table 36-11 in Chapter 36 for more information.

In any case, entries with non-null reference counts are never considered eligible for deletion.

Lookups

As mentioned in the section "Routing Cache," Linux uses both a routing cache and a routing table. Figure 30-8 summarizes the steps in a routing table lookup. To keep the "Route/deliver packet" simple, it does not reflect the variety of routes described earlier in the section "Special Routes."

Lookups in the routing cache are based on an exact match in a simple hash table. Lookups in the potentially much bigger and more complex routing table are based on a Longest Prefix Match (LPM) algorithm, described in the following section. As we will see in Chapter 34, a routing table is organized as a complex mesh of data structures. This makes LPM faster and easier to implement, scales well with a large number of routes, and reduces the duplication of instances of data structures that can be shared.

Longest Prefix Match

If there were only one route toward each destination, routing lookups would be trivial. As soon as you found a route whose destination subnet included your destination address—the key of the lookup—you would be done. However, routing is a complex topic. Without going into detail on the network topologies or specific cases where this complexity occurs, suffice it to say that it is not uncommon to have multiple routes to the same destinations. The overlapping between the routes can be anywhere from one address to an entire subnet.

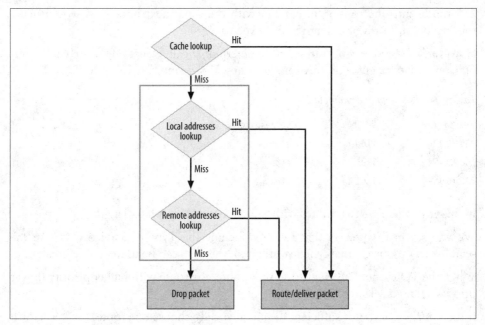

Figure 30-8. Routing lookup

In case of multiple matches, the routing algorithm needs a rule to deterministically decide which of the eligible routes should be selected as the best candidate. Here is where LPM comes into play and partially solves the problem: the best route is the most specific one. This means the one with the smallest subnet size, or equivalently, the longest netmask.

Let's look at an example. Suppose our routing table had two routes that matched the lookup for the destination address 10.0.0.100, as shown in Table 30-6.

Table 30-6. Routing table example 1

Destination	Next hop	Device to use
10.0.0.0/16	10.0.1.1	*eth0*
10.0.0.0/24	10.0.0.1	*eth1*

Since the second route has 24 bits (out of 32) in common with the destination address and the first one has only 16, the second one is said to have the longest prefix match and wins. It is not uncommon to define routes like the ones in Table 30-6, where one route leads to a subset of addresses of another one. This can be necessary, for instance, to route traffic addressed to a specific subnet differently from the rest of the network, due to administrative or security reasons. But it is also the easiest way to configure routing: the alternative would be to split the 10.0.0.0/16 range into multiple /24 ranges (i.e., from 10.0.0.0/24 to 10.0.255.0/24) and therefore put

255 routes into the routing table, 254 with the same next hop. This would make routing lookups slower and more CPU expensive.

However, LPM alone is not sufficient to deterministically select one route when multiple ones match a given destination. Let's take the example in Table 30-7.

Table 30-7. Routing table example 2

Destination	Next hop	Device to use
10.0.0.0/16	10.0.1.1	*eth0*
10.0.0.0/24	10.0.0.1	*eth1*
10.0.0.0/24	10.0.0.2	*eth1*

In this case, there are two routes with the same matching prefix length.

We will see in Chapter 35 that lookups include the Type of Service (TOS) in the search key: this means that when configured, the TOS can be used as a tie breaker.

When the TOS is not sufficient to select a route, the route with higher priority (lower priority value) is selected.

If the priority is also not sufficient to unequivocally choose one route, the kernel will simply choose the first one. This means that it matters in which order routes to the same destination and with the same prefix length are added to the routing table.

Packet Reception Versus Packet Transmission

The routing table is used to route both packets that are transmitted and those that are received, because either type may be delivered locally or forwarded. But besides those obvious uses of the routing table, there are others that are less obvious.

Figure 30-9 shows a couple of examples of routing table use. It distinguishes between lookups triggered by the reception of data (left side) and the transmission of data (right side). Note that the routing information required to forward an input packet is collected when the packet is first received, which explains why the Forwarding block does not have an arrow toward the Routing block in Figure 30-9. The figure also includes pointers to those chapters where you can find more details about a given kernel component. Here are some details concerning the activities shown:

- Address Resolution Protocol (ARP) packets are not routed, but ARP may need to do a route lookup to enforce some sanity checks. See Chapter 28.
- IP-over-IP is a simple tunneling protocol that encapsulates IP packets within larger IP packets. When the IP handler is handed an ingress IP-over-IP packet, it redelivers the payload to the IP layer. The inner IP packet is routed like any other ingress packet, so the routing subsystem needs to make another routing lookup.

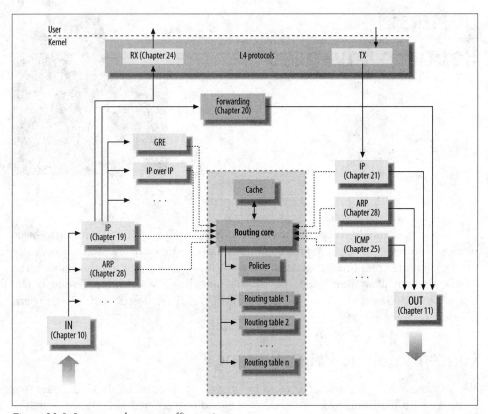

Figure 30-9. Ingress and egress traffic routing

- Routing a packet normally requires only one lookup, regardless of where the packet originated (locally or remotely). That lookup returns all the information needed to route the packet, including the kernel functions that will take care of it. There are a few exceptions: you may have a feature that for some reason needs to make additional lookups, as with the case of IP-over-IP just described.

- The routing core first checks whether the cache already contains the required information, and falls back to the routing table otherwise.

## CHAPTER 31

Routing: Advanced

The previous chapter gave an introduction to basic routing. This chapter introduces routing features such as policy routing and multipath that can be used to configure routing in more complicated scenarios. It also shows how routing interacts with the Traffic Control subsystem in charge of QoS, and the firewall code (Netfilter). The chapter concludes with two smaller features: ICMP redirects and reverse path filtering.

Concepts Behind Policy Routing

We saw in the section "Special Routes" in Chapter 30 that the Linux kernel uses two routing tables by default, one for local routes and one configurable by the administrator. When the kernel is compiled with support for policy routing, you can have up to 255 distinct and independent routing tables. In this chapter, we will see what policy routing can be used for, and in Chapter 35 we will see its implications on the design of the routing subsystem.

The main idea behind policy routing is to allow the user to configure routing based on more parameters than just the destination IP addresses.

The Internet thrived for years with most routers configured just to route packets based on the destination IP address. (For the sake of simplicity, I'll leave out particular factors such as crossing ISP or country boundaries.) And basing the route on only the destination address can (with the help of some external configuration parameters) lead to pretty optimal routing tables for a surprisingly wide range of situations.

But the commercial world needs to take many other things into account, such as separating streams of traffic for security or accounting purposes, or sending real-time streaming traffic over a separate route. Here is where policy routing comes into play. Because there are such varied criteria for routing, for the purposes of this chapter I'll just say that any routing based on more than just the destination address is policy routing.

An example of the use of policy routing is for an ISP to route traffic based on the originating customer, or on Quality of Service (QoS) requirements. The customer can often be easily identified by the port on which the traffic arrives at the ISP's router, the source IP address, or a combination of the two. A router can also use a combination of source and destination addresses to identify a profile of traffic or an aggregate of traffic from a given source. The QoS requirements can be derived from the DiffServ Code Point (DSCP) field of the IP header and from a combination of the fields of the higher-layer headers (these identify the applications).

Since this book is about kernel internals, we want to know how those policies are passed to the kernel, see how they are embedded in the routing table, and find out how they affect the routing lookups. We will learn all of this, but let's start with an example, using the topology of Figure 31-1 as a reference.

Let's focus on the configuration of the router RT, which is used to connect Campus 1 and Campus 2 to both Campus 3 and the Internet (let's not bother about how the routers manage to translate the nonroutable addresses 10.0.*x.x*; this is just an example). Let's also suppose we want to enforce the following two policies:

- Traffic directed to Campus 3 will go through router RT1 when originated from Campus 1, and through RT2 when originated from Campus 2. One reason could be that the administrator of Campus 2 is willing to pay more and therefore is allowed the use of the faster network that connects RT to Campus 3.

- Traffic directed to the Internet (e.g., any destination except the three campuses) will go through DG1 (default gateway 1) for Campus 1, and through DG2 for Campus 2. This could be needed, perhaps, to enforce security or bandwidth policies.

This example is a simple one with just a few routes and only two policies. Of course, the advantage of providing independent routing tables appears only in much bigger and more complex scenarios. And even this example is incomplete—we are ignoring, for instance, incoming routes from the Internet to the campuses.

There are two conceivable ways to configure routing on router RT, one of which (multiple tables) is the approach used by Linux.

Single table approach

Table 31-1 is a simplified version of the routing table configured on RT to enforce the two policies listed earlier. Note that because Campus 1 is the only network connected to RT's *eth0*, and Campus 2 is the only one connected to RT's *eth1*, the routes do not need to specify the source IP addresses. Instead of routing just on the destination address—because the same destination address can match multiple routes—multiple criteria are checked to choose a unique route. In this case, the incoming device is checked along with the destination address.

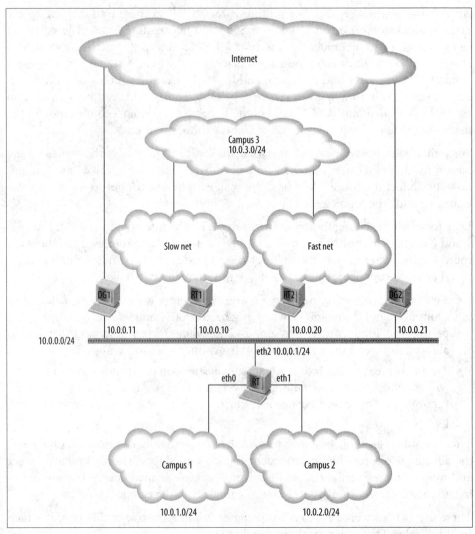

Figure 31-1. Example of topology that may require policy routing

Table 31-1. Single routing table example

Ingress device	Source IP	Destination IP	Next hop	Egress device
Routes to Campuses 2 and 3 for traffic originated in Campus 1				
eth0	Not specified	10.0.3.0/24	10.0.0.10 (RT1)	*eth2*
eth0	Not specified	10.0.2.0/24	Not specified	*eth1*
Routes to Campuses 1 and 3 for traffic originated in Campus 2				
eth1	Not specified	10.0.3.0/24	10.0.0.20 (RT2)	*eth2*

Table 31-1. Single routing table example (continued)

Ingress device	Source IP	Destination IP	Next hop	Egress device
eth1	Not specified	10.0.1.0/24	Not specified	eth0
Default routes for Campus 1 and Campus 2				
eth0	Not specified	0.0.0.0/0	10.0.0.11 (DG1)	eth2
eth1	Not specified	0.0.0.0/0	10.0.0.21 (DG2)	eth2

Multiple table approach

Because so many criteria could potentially be involved in every route lookup, it's faster and easier for a host to maintain independent routing tables and choose the right one from particular criteria. For instance, the source IP address or the ingress device could be used to choose a routing table, and that table could contain more criteria to help make the final route selection.

Thus, when multiple routing tables are used, the kernel has to select the right routing table before it can do a lookup—the choice of a routing table is where *policies* come into effect. Thus, the rules for router RT in our example could be determined by the following rules, in conjunction with Tables 31-2 and 31-3:

- Traffic coming in on *eth0* is checked against Routing Table 1 (Table 31-2).
- Traffic coming in on *eth1* is checked againstRouting Table 2 (Table 31-3).

Table 31-2. RT1 used to route traffic from Campus 1

Destination IP	Next hop	Egress device
10.0.2.0/24	None	eth1
10.0.3.0/24	10.0.0.10 (RT1)	eth2
0.0.0.0/0	10.0.0.11 (DG1)	eth2

Table 31-3. RT2 used to route traffic from Campus 2

Destination IP	Next hop	Egress device
10.0.1.0/24	None	eth0
10.0.3.0/24	10.0.0.20 (RT2)	eth2
0.0.0.0/0	10.0.0.21 (DG2)	eth2

The first entry in Tables 31-2 and 31-3 does not need to be explicitly configured because the kernel derives it from the configuration of interfaces *eth0* and *eth1*, respectively. We will see how this is achieved in Chapter 32.

As we will see in Chapter 33, Linux maintains only one routing cache that is updated by all the routing tables. These tables also share the memory pools used to allocate the building blocks of the tables. Linux does not enforce any fairness mechanism to share these common resources equitably among the various routing tables. In addition to simplifying the implementation, this actually maximizes overall routing throughput, because more system resources are allocated to the routing tables with higher needs. However, it may have an externally detectable effect: that is, when one Linux host using different routing tables manages traffic from different sources, the overall experience from a customer perspective may be different from the experience provided by independent routers or even by a single host that stringently separates the resources used by routes.

Lookup with Policy Routing

When policy routing is in use, a lookup for a destination consists of two steps:

1. Identify the routing table to use, based on the policies configured. This extra task inevitably increases routing lookup times.
2. Do a lookup on the selected routing table.

Of course, before taking these two steps, the kernel always tries the routing cache.

Policies can be assigned an administrative type, like routes (see the section "Route Types and Actions" in Chapter 30). This allows the kernel to make a quick decision based on a type assigned to an entire policy, without waiting to look up the route. For example, the kernel generates an ICMP HOST UNREACHABLE message when the matching policy is configured with an UNREACHABLE type, instead of waiting and finding a matching route configured with an UNREACHABLE type.

Figure 31-2 is a revised version of Figure 30-9 in Chapter 30, with added support for policy routing and details about the optional policy types.

Routing Table Selection

The policies that let the kernel select the routing table to use can be based on the following parameters:

Source and/or destination IP address
It is possible to specify both the source IP address and the destination IP address, each with a netmask.

Ingress device
Depending on the context, the receiving device can be a more appropriate criterion for routing policy than the source IP address. There are cases where a packet with one source IP address could arrive on more than one interface, but we would like the configuration to be based on the receiving device—for instance, if traffic on one device was considered real time and higher priority. In that case, the source IP address would not be of much help. The use of the

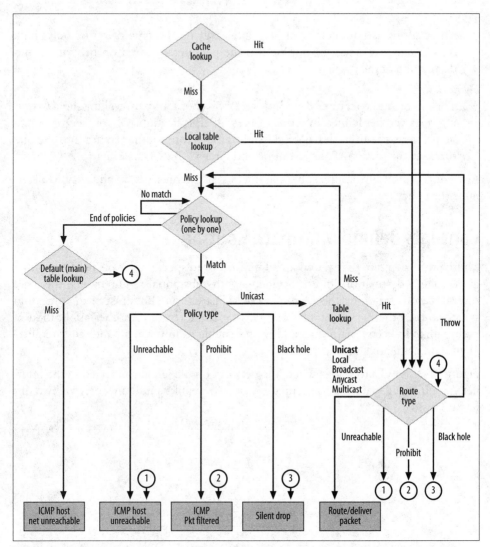

Figure 31-2. Policy routing lookup

device rather than of the source IP address could be preferable in these cases as well:

- When multiple, discontinuous ranges of source IP addresses are on the same device that we want to associate with the same routing table. In this case, instead of adding a rule for each distinct range of IP addresses, you can simplify the configuration by using a single rule based on the device.

- When the selection of the routing table has more to do with the physical network topology than with the source of the traffic.

TOS

The use of this parameter can help in classifying the type of traffic (e.g., bulk data, interactive, etc.), as opposed to the parameters based on the source and destination of the traffic.

Fwmark

This is one of the features that shows the power of Linux firewalling. Policy routing rules can be defined in terms of firewall classification. Of course, for this to be possible, the firewall has to classify traffic before routing comes into the picture. See the section "Policy Routing and Firewall-Based Classifier."

Any combination of the preceding parameters also represents a valid way to determine the policy.

Concepts Behind Multipath Routing

Multipath is a feature that allows an administrator to specify multiple next hops for a given route's destination. In environments with substantial requirements, there are several reasons for doing this. A router could just use one ISP most of the time, and switch to the other when the first one fails for some reason. Another application of multipath is to keep a path on standby and enable it only when bandwidth requirements surpass a predefined threshold.

Figure 31-3 shows a topology where the network on the left is connected to the Internet via router RT, which is configured to use two uplinks simultaneously via two different ISPs.

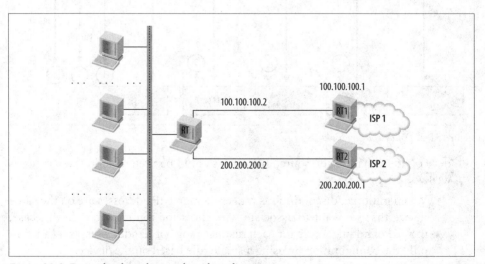

Figure 31-3. Example of topology with multipath

Let's suppose we want to have RT use both RT1 and RT2 as default gateways, keeping them always available. On RT, we could define a multipath route, simply by providing the route with more than one next hop. The following user-space command, using the newer IPROUTE2 package, would enable multipath:

```
ip route add default scope global nexthop via 100.100.100.1 weight 1 nexthop via 200.
200.200.1 weight 2
```

Note that even if the route includes multiple next hops, the route is still considered a single route. Therefore, given a route (in our example, the default route 0.0.0.0/0) with more than one next hop, the kernel needs a mechanism to select the next hop to use each time the route matches a route lookup. There are different ways to do that, each one with its pros and cons. For an interesting analysis of the most common algorithms for multipath routing, I suggest you read RFCs 2991 and 2992.

Linux provides flexibility among algorithms by allowing the administrator to assign each next hop a weight with the weight keyword. The number of times a next hop is selected is proportional to its weight in relation to all the other next hops. If all the next hops are assigned the same weight, the algorithm falls back to the so-called *equal cost multipath* algorithm.

Note, however, that the granularity used to distribute traffic among the next hops is measured not in packets, but in the number of routing cache entries. This is because once a next hop is selected, an entry is added to the cache. Because the routing subsystem always consults the cache before invoking any check on routing tables, subsequent packets belonging to the same traffic flow (aggregate of traffic) will be handled straight from the cache. As explained in Chapter 36, a flow is a collection of packets that match a set of criteria. These consist mainly of the source or destination addresses, the ingress or egress devices, and the IP TOS field. You will see in the section "Per-Flow, Per-Connection, and Per-Packet distribution" that when Multipath support for the cache is enabled, traffic can also be distributed on a per-connection basis instead of on a per-flow basis.

From purely a throughput point of view, this granularity may be suboptimal, because different flows may have very different bandwidth requirements, and therefore the kernel may be unfair even when all of the next hops are configured with the same weight—and what is worse, the unfairness would not be deterministic. So Linux provides an option that allows you to use per-packet rather than per-flow granularity (see the section "Equalizer algorithm"). However, in most cases, given the high number of flows that usually traverse a router, the next hops are likely to get, on average, a load that is proportional to their weights.

Next Hop Selection

The selection of the next hop is based on a weighted round-robin algorithm.

We saw in the previous section a sample user-space command that specified a weight for each next hop. Usually, an administrator assigns a weight to each path to indicate whether it is preferred. That is the weight used by the round-robin algorithm. The method used to define the weight is an administrative issue based on criteria such as bandwidth and cost, so I will not go into detail about it.

The easiest way to select the next hops, proportionally to their weights, would be to simply have each one consume its tokens one by one and then restart. For instance, if we had two next hops with weights of 3 and 5, respectively, we could select the first one three times, the second one five times, and then again the first one three times, etc. But the distribution of traffic with this approach could be too bursty.

Therefore, Linux adds a randomness component to the selection of the next hop. Given the weight W_i for the ith next hop, and given the sum W of all the next hops, Linux selects a next hop randomly W times, and each next hop is selected a number of times equal to its weight W_i. The randomness introduced is not too accurate, but it is an acceptable approximation, and it falls back to a simple sequential selection (from first to last next hop) when all the next hops are assigned the same weight 1.

Here is how it is implemented. The kernel defines the round-robin budget as the sum of all the next hop weights. The budget (number of tokens) of each next hop is initialized to the value of its weight. At each round, the kernel generates a random value ranging from 0 to the total round-robin budget. Then it browses the next-hop list until it finds one with a budget greater than or equal to the generated random value. After each next-hop selection, it decrements both the round-robin budget and the selected next hop's budget.

Note that it is possible for none of the next hops to match on the first round. Imagine a case with three next hops whose weights are 1, 2, and 3. The total budget would be 6. Valid random values are the ones in the range 0 to 5. However, values 4 and 5 would not select any next hop because none has a budget that big. When this happens, the kernel subtracts the weight of each nonmatching next hop from the total budget and checks again.

Let's continue our example to show how this works. Suppose our random number was 5. We start browsing the list of next hops. The first one has a budget of 1, which is not sufficient. We therefore do not select it, and reduce our requirement from the following next hop by lowering the random value to 5–1, or 4. The following next hop has a budget of 2, which again is not sufficient. So we lower the random value again to 4-2, or 2. The last next hop has a budget of 3, which is greater than or equal to 2 and therefore is selected. This, by the way, is the worst case in terms of performance: the last of the next hops is the one selected.

Next hops of a multipath route can be temporarily unavailable (see the section "Effects of Multipath on Next Hop Selection" in Chapter 35). These, of course, will not be taken into consideration by the next-hop selection algorithm.

Cache Support for Multipath

By default, the routing cache does not support multipath. Therefore, as we saw in the section "Concepts Behind Multipath Routing," once the algorithm in the section "Next Hop Selection" has chosen one of the next hops, it will be used for all subsequent traffic matching the same lookup key because a route is added to the cache with a reference to that next hop.

Starting with version 2.6.12, the Linux kernel comes with an option that allows the user to enable multipath support for the cache, and also allows the system administrator to select what algorithm to use to distribute traffic between the different next hops specified by a given multipath route.

Here are the available algorithms:

Random
> The next hop to use is selected randomly. This is fast because it does not require any state information to be kept. On average, it distributes traffic equally on all next hops.

Weighted random
> Next hops are assigned a weight, and traffic is distributed randomly to all next hops proportionally to their weights.

Round robin
> Standard round-robin algorithm, distributing each transmission to the next route in order.

Device round robin
> Instead of distributing traffic based on the routes, traffic is distributed in round-robin fashion on the interfaces. Multiple next hops sharing a common device are considered one unit.

When you configure a route with IPROUTE2's *ip route* command, you can use the new mpath keyword to select the algorithm to use. This is an example of a route configured to use the round-robin algorithm:

```
ip route add 10.0.1.0/24 mpath rr nexthop via 192.168.1.1 weight 1
                         nexthop via 192.168.1.2 weight 2
```

When the mpath keyword is not provided, multipath caching is kept disabled on the route.

The weighted random and device round-robin algorithms are described in more detail in the next subsections.

Weighted random algorithm

Assume we have a multipath route with four next hops, assigned the weights 1, 1, 2, and 4. Let's align the four weights along a line as shown in Figure 31-4. The sum of the weights is 8, so if you generate a random number in the range 0–8 you can unequivocally identify a next hop in the line. For example, the value 2.8 would select the third-next hop. It should be clear that the next hops are selected proportionally to their weights.

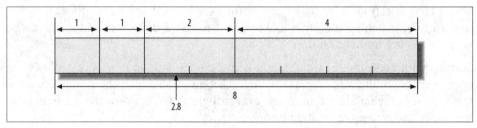

Figure 31-4. Example of weighted random selection

Device round-robin algorithm

The next hops of a multipath route can be reachable through a single device, each can be reachable through a different device, or you can have a hybrid situation. These three cases are shown in Figure 31-5.

A pure round-robin algorithm would distribute traffic equally to the various next hops, but not necessarily equally to the various devices associated with those next hops. For example, a multipath route with three next hops, two of which share the same egress device, as in Figure 31-5(c), would load one of the two egress devices twice as much as the other.

Thus, the goal of the device round-robin algorithm is to distribute traffic equally among a pool of devices, instead of on a per-multipath-route basis. All traffic that matches any route configured to use this algorithm is considered a single aggregate of traffic to distribute equally among devices. Therefore, the decision concerning which device to use for a given multipath route depends not only on the devices previously used to route traffic with the same multipath route, but also on the devices used by other multipath routes.

Note that while a pure round-robin algorithm assumes that the bottleneck in the forwarding path is the target routers' CPUs, device round robin aims at optimizing the use of the devices' bandwidths, giving less importance to the target CPUs.

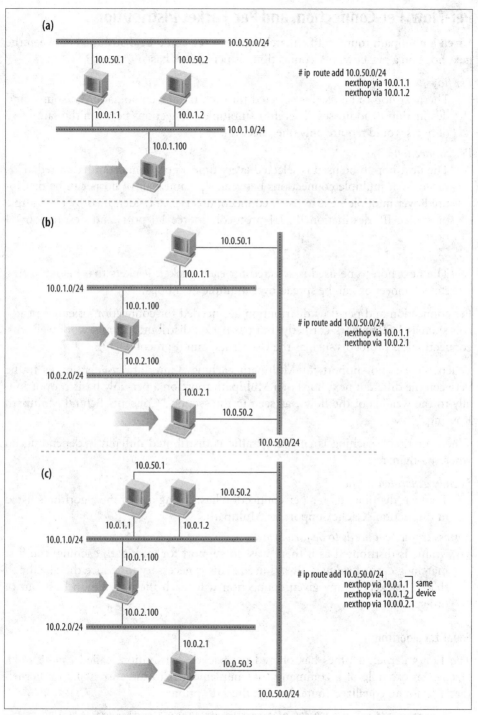

Figure 31-5. Different ways to assign next hops to interfaces

Per-Flow, Per-Connection, and Per-Packet Distribution

Given a multipath route, traffic matching the route could be distributed between the next hops on a per-flow, per-connection, or per-packet basis:

Per flow
> The next hop to be used is selected for each unique combination of source and destination IP addresses. Therefore, multiple connections between the same pair of hosts would require only one selection.

Per connection
> The next hop to be used is selected every time a new connection is started. This means that multiple connections between the same pair of hosts can be distributed over multiple next hops. A connection is typically identified by the 5-tuple of source IP, destination IP, L4 protocol, source L4 port, and destination L4 port.

Per packet
> The next hop to be used is selected for each packet. Packets that belong to the same connection can be spread over multiple next hops.

Per-connection and per-flow distribution are needed for connection-oriented protocols such as TCP to work correctly, but per-packet distribution could work well with connectionless protocols such as the User Datagram Protocol (UDP).

When there is no support for Multipath caching, Linux always distributes traffic between the different next hops of a Multipath route on a per-flow basis proportionally to the weights of the flows, as seen in the section "Concepts Behind Multipath Routing."

When multipath caching is enabled, traffic is distributed differently depending on where it originates:

Locally generated traffic
> Traffic is distributed on a per-connection basis using one of the algorithms listed in the section "Cache Support for Multipath."

Ingress traffic that needs to be forwarded
> Traffic is distributed as if there was no support for multipath caching: the first matching cached route is always used. This is necessary to reduce the likelihood that IP packets of any given connection will reach the destination host out of order.

Equalizer algorithm

The Linux kernel at times has offered per-packet distribution, called *equalization*. Here is an example of a command (not implemented in the current Linux kernel) that asks for an equalized route through the eql option:

```
# ip route add eql 100.100.100.0/24 nexthop via 10.0.0.2 nexthop via 10.0.0.3
# ip route list
```

```
100.100.100.0/24 equalize
    nexthop via 10.0.0.2  dev eth0 weight 1
    nexthop via 10.0.0.3  dev eth0 weight 1
...
```

Given how much time has passed since support for this option was announced as being in the works, it is not likely to be added anytime soon, probably because there is no need for it.

Interactions with Other Kernel Subsystems

Between the time a packet makes its appearance in the system, because it was either received on one interface or generated locally, and the time it is delivered to the next hop (if forwarded) or locally (if addressed to the local host), several network subsystems may place their hands on it. Among them are the Firewall and Traffic Control subsystems. Both of them can classify traffic based on various databases of information and store the result of their classification into a field of the buffer descriptor. The routing subsystem code can also classify traffic and store the result in the buffer descriptor.

Figure 31-6 is a simplified overview of how routing, Firewall, and Traffic Control interact, and when a given subsystem comes into the picture. The figure shows how an input packet goes through the various subsystems and gets its firewall and routing tags initialized.

In the next subsections, we will take a closer look at how policy routing and Firewall compute their tags and make them available to other kernel subsystems for use.

Routing Table Based Classifier

Among the many classifiers available to the Traffic Control subsystem is one called the routing table based classifier that can classify routes based on *realms*. Realms are numerical tags that can be assigned to both policies and routes. Each route and policy can be assigned up to two realms: an ingress realm and an egress realm.

In the following subsections, we will first see how realms are configured to get more familiar with the feature. Then I'll describe the logic used by the routing code to derive the classification tag (which will be used by Traffic Control) from the realms' configuration.

The file *ip-cref.ps* included with the IPROUTE2 package offers some examples of the purpose and use of realms. In this book, we will consider only how realms are configured via IPROUTE2 commands.

Both routes and policies are configured with the *ip* command. The first keyword that follows *ip* determines the object type you want to configure. The *route* keyword denotes a route, and the *rule* keyword denotes a policy.

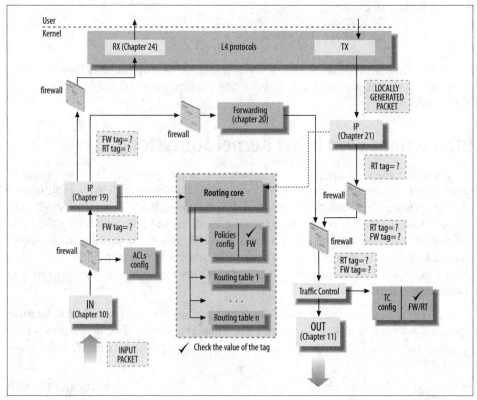

Figure 31-6. Interactions among routing, Traffic Control, and Firewall (Netfilter)

Configuring policy realms

Routing policies are configured with the IPROUTE2's *ip rule* command. Its syntax is:

```
ip rule add ... realms [source_realm/]destination_realm
```

As you can see, the source realm is optional while the destination realm is not, which means that if you provide only one value, you configure the destination realm.

Here are a couple of examples of commands that configure policy realms. The following associates the policy destination realm 128 with all traffic that originates in the subnet 10.0.1.0/24:

```
ip rule add from 10.0.1.0/24 realms 128
```

The following command associates the policy source realm 64 and the policy destination realm 128 with traffic that originates in the 10.0.1.0/24 subnet and that is addressed to the 10.0.2.0/24 subnet:

```
ip rule add from 10.0.1.0/24 to 10.0.2.0/24 realms 64/128
```

Configuring route realms

A route's realms are configured very similarly to policy realms. The syntax of the IPROUTE2 command for this purpose is:

```
ip route add ... realms [source_realm/]destination_realm
```

Note that even though the command's help message does not show both the source and destination realms, the syntax is just the same as for policies.

Here is an example command for traffic directed to the 10.0.1.0/24 subnet that forwards the traffic to the gateway with address 10.0.0.3 and assigns to the destination realm 100:

```
ip route add 10.0.1.0/24 via 10.0.0.3 realms 100
```

In the following command, traffic directed to the 10.0.1.0/24 subnet is forwarded to the gateway with address 10.0.0.3 and assigned to the source realm 100 and the destination realm 200:

```
ip route add 10.0.1.0/24 via 10.0.0.3 realms 100/200
```

Computing the routing tag

Because realms can be assigned to both individual routes and whole policies, a routing decision can come up with two realms for a single direction: for instance, an ingress destination realm derived from the policy and another ingress destination realm derived from the route. In such a case, the realm derived from the route is given higher priority. Usually, such a decision is necessary only for a destination realm; administrators rarely define source realms on the basis of the route.

If a realm is missing—not provided by either route or policy—the kernel computes the reverse route (from the local host back to the source of the packet being classified) and checks whether it can use the associated realms. For instance, if the kernel cannot derive a source realm for ingress traffic, it figures out and uses the destination realm for egress traffic on the reverse path. This heuristic assumes that the realm configurations on the two directions should be symmetric.

Let's look at a simple example using the topology in Figure 31-7, which shows a router between two networks. The policy routing configuration says that traffic coming from subnet 10.0.1.0/24 belongs to Realm A, and that traffic coming from subnet 10.0.2.0/24 belongs to Realm B. Assume that no route realm is configured; only the two policy realm configurations shown in Figure 31-7. Both of those policies provide only the source realm—so when forwarding, a realm is specified for ingress but not for egress. Let's suppose now that the router receives a packet from host 10.0.1.100 (Realm A) directed to the destination address 10.0.2.200 (Realm B). When the routing subsystem makes a lookup to route the packet, it also computes the routing tag. The following list explains what happens.

1. The routing lookup returns route R2 and policy P1. Because no realm is configured on route R2, the source realm A from policy P1 is used.

2. Because the destination realm is not initialized, the kernel computes the reverse route from 10.0.2.200 to 10.0.1.100. The routing lookup this time returns route RT1 and policy P2. Once again, no realm is configured on the matching route RT1, so the kernel relies on the policy realm, which is B. However, because this was found during a reverse lookup, the source realm B on the reverse path is used as a destination realm on the forward path.

In the end, the routing tag is initialized to source realm A and destination realm B. When the QoS layer is traversed later, it can use those two realms to correctly classify the packet.

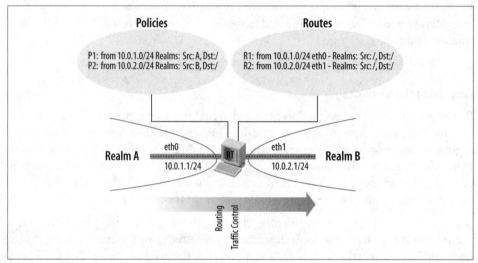

Figure 31-7. Example of realm configuration

Figure 31-8 summarizes the logic used to compute the tag.

Policy Routing and Firewall-Based Classifier

The Netfilter firewall software can classify traffic to see whether, based on its filtering criteria, it needs to drop or mangle packets. The firewall can also be configured to simply classify a packet using its powerful classification engine just to provide a service to other kernel subsystems. The firewall has multiple hooks in the network stack. If Routing or Traffic Control runs after one of the hooks that places a tag, those subsystems can see and act on the tag. Figure 31-6, earlier in the chapter, showed the sequence in which various subsystems and firewall hooks access packets.

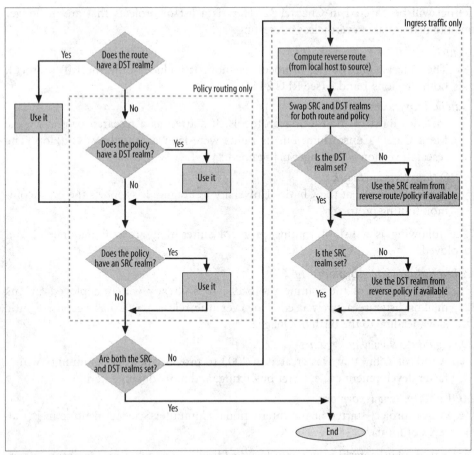

Figure 31-8. Logic used to compute the routing tag

Routing Protocol Daemons

Routes can be inserted into the kernel routing tables from three main sources:

- Static configuration via user commands (e.g., *ip route*, *route*)
- Dynamic configuration via routing protocols such as Border Gateway Protocol (BGP), Exterior Gateway Protocol (EGP), and Open Shortest Path First (OSPF), implemented as user-space routing daemons
- ICMP redirect messages received and processed by the kernel due to suboptimal configurations

We will cover the first source in Chapter 36, and we will see the third one later in this chapter. Let's take a look at the second source now, and in particular the routing daemons available for Linux systems. The details of their interaction with the kernel will be covered in Chapter 32. Here is a list of projects that are no longer maintained but are nevertheless interesting:

Routed
> The oldest Unix routing protocol daemon. It includes only the RIP protocol, both Versions 1 and 2 (see RFC 2453).

GateD (http://www.gated.org)
> Includes most of the routing protocols. It started as a research project by the Merit GateD Consortium, but its rights were later acquired by NextHop. The research version is no longer maintained.

BIRD (http://bird.network.cz)
> A project started at the Charles University in Prague. It supports the most common routing protocols.

The following is a list of routing protocol suites that are still maintained and deployed:

Zebra (http://www.zebra.org)
> Includes most of the routing protocols. It is already widely deployed and its mailing lists are actively used. However, the release cycle has become a little slow, leading to the birth of Quagga.

Quagga (http://www.quagga.net)
> A fork of Zebra that was created in 2003 to provide the user community with a faster development cycle, faster bug fixing, and more documentation.

XORP (http://www.xorp.org)
> A new project started at the International Computer Science Institute in Berkeley, California.

Refer to the URLs within the parentheses to find exactly what protocols and extensions each package provides.

The routing daemon implementations are not covered in this book because they do not belong to the kernel, but we briefly look here at how they talk to the kernel. It is important to know, for instance, how the daemons inject into the routing tables the routes that they learn from their peers or from user configuration, and how they remove defunct routes.

Each daemon maintains its own routing tables in user space. These are not used to select any routes directly—only the kernel's routing tables in kernel memory are used for that. However, the daemons are one of the sources used to populate the kernel tables, as mentioned earlier in this section. Most of the daemons introduced earlier implement multiple routing protocols. Each routing protocol, when running, keeps its own routing table. Depending on the design of the daemon, each protocol might install routes into the kernel's routing table on its own (as shown on the left side of Figure 31-9), or the protocols may share a common layer within the daemon that does the talking to the kernel (as shown on the right side of Figure 31-9). The approach used is a user-space design choice outside the scope of this book.

Communication between routing protocols and the kernel is bidirectional:

- The routing protocols install routes into the kernel's routing table and remove routes they have determined to be expired or no longer valid.
- The kernel notifies routing protocols about the installation or removal of new routes, and about a change of state in a local device link (which of course indirectly affects all the associated routes). This is possible only when the routing daemons talk to the kernel via a Netlink socket; that is, a bidirectional channel.

The IPROUTE2 package allows the user not only to configure routes, but also to listen to the aforementioned notifications generated by the kernel and by routing daemons. Thus, an administrator can log them or dump them on the screen for debugging purposes.

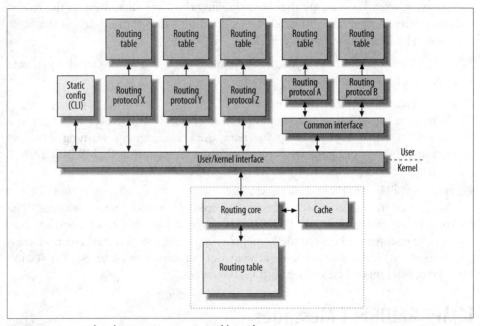

Figure 31-9. Interface between user space and kernel

Verbose Monitoring

When support for this option is added to the kernel and the option is enabled (it is disabled by default), the kernel prints warning messages on the console when input packets have suspicious or invalid source or destination IP addresses. These messages are rate limited to one every five seconds, to avoid potential DoS attacks.

Ingress packets that are dropped by sanity checks in the routing subsystem, due to faulty source or destination addresses, trigger a warning message. The kernel can make some of these checks easily using the classifications listed in Table 30-1 and Table 30-3 in Chapter 30. In summary, these classifications are:

- Source address: Multicast, Loopback, Reserved, Invalid (zeronet)
- Destination address: Loopback, Reserved, Invalid (zeronet)

The kernel makes additional sanity checks on ingress packets based on the routing table. In particular:

- When reverse path filtering is enabled (an anti-IP-spoofing check), the source IP address must be reachable through the same interface from which the packet was received. See the section "Reverse Path Filtering."
- The source IP address cannot be a subnet broadcast address or one of the addresses configured on the receiving interface. This check can help prevent IP spoofing attempts (i.e., another host claiming the same IP address as the receiving interface), and can also detect cases of address duplication such as might be caused by DHCP misconfiguration.

When the Verbose Monitoring feature is enabled, the ICMP layer can also generate warning messages under specific conditions:

Transmission of ICMP REDIRECT messages
When the kernel has sent a certain number of ICMP REDIRECT messages to a remote host that appears to ignore them, the kernel prints a warning. The precise number is configurable. See the section "Transmitting ICMP_REDIRECT Messages."

Reception of ICMP REDIRECT message
Whenever an ingress ICMP redirect is rejected, the kernel prints a warning. The processing of ingress ICMP REDIRECT messages is a little more complex than their transmission, because the kernel may reject ingress ICMP REDIRECT messages for several reasons, some of them configurable by the user. See the section "Processing Ingress ICMP_REDIRECT Messages."

ICMP_REDIRECT Messages

The ICMP protocol defines a number of different messages to control traffic flow and notify hosts of network problems. One such message, REDIRECT,[*] is used to notify a source of traffic about its suboptimal use of routing. Refer to Chapter 25 for a detailed description of the ICMP messages. In this chapter, we focus on the tuning

---

[*] There are four ICMP REDIRECT message subtypes. In this chapter, we look only at REDIRECT HOST, used to redirect traffic addressed to a specific IP address. See Chapter 25 for the other subtypes.

parameters provided by the routing subsystem to decide whether to process ingress ICMP REDIRECT messages and whether to transmit one when the default required conditions are met.

The decision about whether an ICMP REDIRECT should be sent, and whether an ingress ICMP REDIRECT should be processed, can be influenced by user configuration. In particular, the user can say whether:

- Ingress or egress ICMP REDIRECT messages can be accepted or generated. As we will see in Chapter 36, this is configurable on a per-device basis.

- For ingress ICMP packets, it is also possible to specify whether to accept only secure redirects. An ICMP REDIRECT is considered secure when the new gateway advertised by the message is already known by the local host as a gateway. This can be determined, for instance, by checking in the routing table whether the suggested gateway is already used as the next hop for any of the configured routes.

- Each device can be configured with a flag that says whether the device is attached to a shared medium.

The last bullet deserves a little explanation, which is provided in the next section.

Shared Media

In the early 1990s, IP protocol designers started looking at the tendency (then somewhat new, but now almost universal) of creating LANs on media such as Ethernet and attaching these LANs to other networks. Sometimes administrators would connect groups of hosts configured on different IP subnets to a single LAN while separating them with routers. There are many reasons related to history or convenience for doing this; nowadays there is rarely any reason to do it and it is rarely found. Nonetheless, the routing subsystem must be designed to handle it.

When hosts configured on different subnets are plugged into the same LAN, IP routing documents call it a *shared medium*. Note that this term refers to network configuration rather than the device's capabilities. In other words, in the normal case where all the hosts sharing an L2 connection also share an IP subnet, this term does not apply; nor do the issues here. In this section, the issue concerning us is that ICMP REDIRECT messages are more likely to be generated.

Figure 31-10 shows an example of a shared medium. Three different subnets are configured on the hosts connected to the same LAN. The two routers RT1 and RT2 are used to connect the IP subnets: each router is part of two subnets, having one NIC configured with an address on each side.

A typical way to configure routing in Figure 31-10 (although not the only way) is described next.

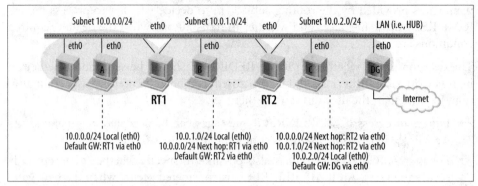

Figure 31-10. Sample configuration for a shared media topology

- The hosts of subnet 10.0.0.0/24 define RT1 as their default gateway and are configured to send all traffic to other subnets through that gateway. The other two subnets and the gateway used to reach the Internet are reachable via RT1.

- The hosts of subnet 10.0.1.0/24 have a similar configuration, using RT2 as their default gateway. However, they need one extra route through RT1 to reach subnet 10.0.0.0/24.

- Hosts of subnet 10.0.2.0/24 use DG as their default gateway, and are configured with two explicit routes to reach the other two subnets via RT2.

The key aspect of this routing scenario is that it specifies inefficient routes. The hosts of subnet 10.0.0.0/24 and 10.0.0.2/24, for instance, could exchange packets on the L2 layer without any routing, but the configuration tells them to use two routers. A cleverer configuration would consist in configuring only the default gateway on the hosts, and have the default gateways take care of the routes to the other subnets in the LAN.

Luckily, the routing subsystem has ways to overcome this inefficiency on its own and gradually find the directly connected hosts. The mechanism is ICMP REDIRECT messages. We'll ignore the presence of DG and the Internet connection.

Suppose Host A wants to talk to Host B. According to its routing table, Host A sees that Host B is reachable via router RT1. However, when RT1 receives a packet sent by Host A and addressed to Host B, it realizes that Host A could have sent the packet directly to Host B because both of them (Host A and Host B) are reachable via the same device *eth0*. This looks like the classic condition that triggers the generation of an ICMP REDIRECT: suboptimal routing. However, there's a catch: even if Host A and Host B are connected to the same shared medium and can therefore talk to each other from a link layer point of view (i.e., Ethernet), from the IP layer perspective that's not possible. Host A does not know that the hosts of the 10.0.1.0/24 subnet are reachable via *eth0*. All Host A knows is that the 10.0.1.0/24 subnet is reachable via RT1.

To understand why, look back, if necessary, to the section "When Solicitation Requests Are Transmitted and Processed" in Chapter 26. For a host to talk to another one based on L3 addresses, it must first make an L3-to-L2 address resolution. A sending host can do that only for hosts that belong to one of the subnets it is connected to; for all others, finding the host is a router's business. In our case, Host B does not belong to Host A's subnet. This means that for an ICMP REDIRECT that tells Host A to talk to Host B directly to work, hosts must be able to accept what is called a *foreign redirect*: a redirect whose suggested new next hop does not belong to any of the local subnets known to the receiver of the redirect.

Foreign redirects are meaningful only in shared media scenarios like the one depicted in Figure 31-10. This is because after Host A receives the redirect and accepts it, it sends an ARP request for Host B's address.* In the topology of Figure 31-10, thanks to the shared medium, Host B will receive the ARP request. But if Host B was located in another LAN, it would not be able to receive any ARP requests from Host A.†

It is interesting to see what happens if Host A wants to talk to Host C and uses RT1. According to RT1, Host C is reachable via RT2. So RT1 sends an ICMP REDIRECT to Host A, providing RT2 as the suggested new gateway. RT2 will detect the same suboptimal routing condition later when it is asked by Host A to send another packet to Host C, so RT2 will send an ICMP REDIRECT and Host A will finally realize that it can reach Host C directly. In short, the process of resolving shared media connections through foreign redirects is iterative.

In this section, you have seen the implications of configuring the hosts connected to the same shared medium on different IP subnets. RFC 1620 goes into more detail on the subject and is well worth reading. In the next two sections, you will see how the user can explicitly configure an interface to be connected to a shared medium, to influence the transmission and the processing of ingress ICMP REDIRECT messages so that scenarios like the one in this section are taken care of properly.

Transmitting ICMP_REDIRECT Messages

It may seem superfluous to check the shared media configuration when the routing subsystem has already seen that the ingress and egress devices match. In fact, that check is not superfluous. The use of forwarding shortcuts, as a result of using the ICMP REDIRECT messages described in the previous section, may not always be desirable. The shortcuts allow hosts to bypass certain routers, but the system admin-

---

* We said earlier that an IP host would never ARP for an IP address that does not belong to one of its locally configured subnets. Note that the behavior described here (i.e., a host that ARPs for an IP address located on a foreign subnet) is possible because the redirected route is installed directly in the routing cache, therefore bypassing the routing table (that is the one that would make it impossible to ARP a foreign IP).

† It is interesting to note that IPv6 has optimized ICMP redirects. Under IPv6, a redirect includes the L2 address of the suggested new gateway. So a host that receives an ICMP REDIRECT does not need to resolve the L3-to-L2 association to know the new gateway's address.

istrator might be using those routers to apply policies to all traffic. An example would be where RT1 and RT2 were firewalls[*] or proxy hosts.

Figure 31-11 shows the logic that the routing code follows when it routes an ingress packet that needs to be forwarded. There is only one part of the flowchart that I have not described yet: the check made when the device is not configured as a shared medium. In that case, the sender is sent an ICMP REDIRECT message only if the next hop found by consulting the routing table belongs to the same subnet as the sender (which is identified by the sender's source IP address). When this is not true, the sender would not (according to the router's knowledge) be able to reach the new next hop. And this is exactly why the check for shared media precedes the check for a gateway on the same subnet.

Note that since support for Fast NAT has been dropped in kernel 2.6 (see the section "Recently Dropped Options" in Chapter 32), the check on NAT/MASQ is never successful.

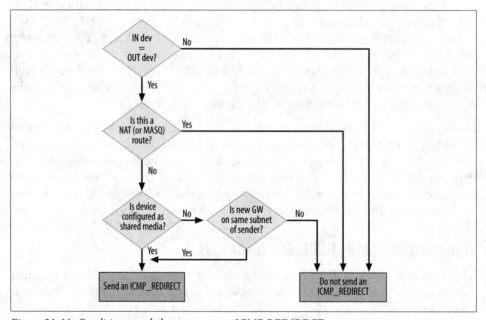

Figure 31-11. Conditions needed to generate an ICMP REDIRECT

See Chapter 20 and the section "Forwarding" in Chapter 35 for details on how the ip_forward routine decides whether to transmit ICMP REDIRECT messages. Also, see Chapter 25 for more details on the ICMP code that takes care of transmission.

---

[*] The use of firewalls in scenarios like Figure 31-10, where all hosts share an L2 broadcast domain, would be a bad choice anyway. But it can give you an idea of why routing shortcuts are not always desirable.

Processing Ingress ICMP_REDIRECT Messages

For an ingress ICMP REDIRECT to be accepted, it needs to pass a few sanity checks and comply with the user configuration. Figure 31-12 shows all the logic with a flowchart. We'll go over it piece by piece.

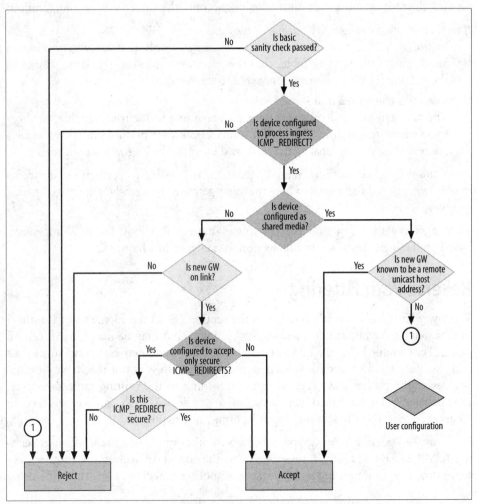

Figure 31-12. Conditions needed to process an ingress ICMP REDIRECT

First come a few basic sanity checks to pass, and one user configuration to comply with:

- The new gateway advertised by the ICMP REDIRECT should be different from the current one (otherwise, there is no need for an ICMP REDIRECT).
- The new gateway IP address cannot be Multicast, Invalid (zeronet), or Reserved.
- The receiving interface must be configured to accept ingress ICMP REDIRECTs.

Second, the routing subsystem must take into account the shared media configuration:

If the device is not configured as a shared medium
> In this case, the host can accept a new gateway only if it knows, once again according to the routing table, that the gateway resides on the same subnet as the old one (i.e., it is directly connected to the host).

If the device is configured as a shared medium
> The new gateway is accepted as long as, according to the routing table, the host knows how to reach it. Two other sanity checks are performed: the gateway's address must not be local to the host, and must not be a broadcast address.

As mentioned in the section "Shared Media," it is possible to configure a device so that it accepts redirects only when the new gateway is already known to it as a gateway.

The ip_rt_redirect function that processes ingress ICMP REDIRECT messages, based on the logic described in this section, is analyzed in Chapter 25.

Reverse Path Filtering

We saw what an asymmetric route is in the section "Essential Elements of Routing" in Chapter 30. Asymmetric routes are not common, but may be necessary in certain cases. The default behavior of Linux is to consider asymmetric routing suspicious and therefore to drop any packet whose source IP address is not reachable through the device the packet was received from, according to the routing table. However, this behavior can be tuned via */proc* on a per-device basis, as we will see in Chapter 36. See also the section "Input Routing" in Chapter 35.

In Figure 30-7(a) and (b) in Chapter 30, we saw an example of a malicious user sending ICMP ECHO REQUEST messages with the source IP address of another host within the same subnet. Figure 31-13 shows another malicious user, this time using as its source IP address (e.g., its victim) an address in the target subnet. As Figure 31-13(a) shows, this attempt is detected and dropped by Linux by default. Figure 31-13(b) shows what would have happened if the ICMP ECHO REQUEST message was not dropped by the router RT.

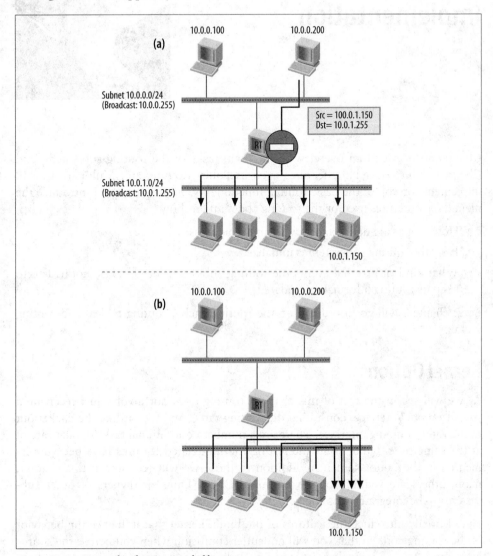

Figure 31-13. Example of reverse path filtering

The example uses a directed broadcast ICMP packet, but reverse path filtering applies to any kind of traffic.

## CHAPTER 32

Routing: Linux Implementation

Chapter 30 provided an overview of the main tasks of the routing subsystem, and Chapter 31 introduced the features such as Policy Routing and Multipath that IP implements on top of the basic routing functionality. In this chapter, I introduce the main data structures used by the routing code. I then show:

- How scopes are defined for routes and IP addresses
- How the routing subsystem is initialized
- What kind of external events the routing subsystem needs to be notified of to keep its routing information updated

Later chapters will go into detail on the routing cache, routing tables, and routing lookups.

Kernel Options

As we will see in the rest of this chapter, routing does not involve just receiving a packet on one interface, consulting the routing table, and forwarding the packet out of the right outgoing interface. There are a number of additional tasks to take care of at the same time. Quite a few interesting routing-related features have been implemented in the Linux kernel. In addition to those we will see later in this chapter, many others are waiting for the green light from Linus or owners of other subsystems to be integrated into the kernel.

Here I briefly introduce the features of the Linux kernel that influence the behavior of the routing code so that you will not suffer confusion when you peruse the source code. Each feature is further described in dedicated sections in this and later chapters.

Routing options can be classified into two categories:

- The ones that are always supported, and that only need to be enabled or configured by the user, such as via *proc*.

- The ones whose support may be added or removed by recompiling the kernel with the right options. The `CONFIG_WAN_ROUTER` option and the options under the `CONFIG_IP_ROUTE_MULTIPATH_CACHED` menu can be compiled as modules; the others must be compiled into the main kernel.

We will look at both categories of options in the rest of this and the following chapters, but in this section we will start with an overview of the compile-time options. These options can be configured from the Networking Options menu, as shown in the *make xconfig* snapshot in Figure 32-1.

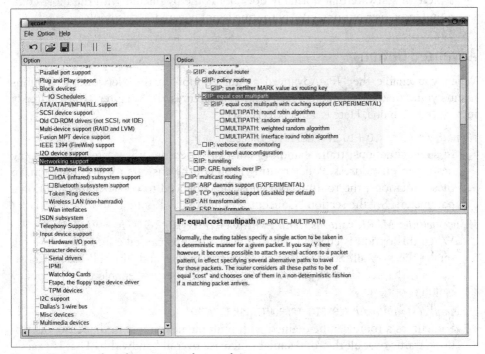

Figure 32-1. Kernel configuration (make xconfig)

The following two sections include the `CONFIG_XXX` kernel symbol associated with each option within parentheses. You can use the symbol to identify the kernel code that is conditionally executed only when support for the feature is included in the kernel. When an entire file is used by a specific feature, though, you will not find `CONFIG_XXX` in the file.

Basic Options

Here are a few basic routing options. None of them is covered in this chapter.

IP: multicast routing (CONFIG_IP_MROUTE)
> IP: PIM-SM version 1 support (`CONFIG_IP_PIMSM_V1`)
>
> IP: PIM-SM version 2 support (`CONFIG_IP_PIMSM_V2`)

If you enable IP multicast routing, you can then selectively enable either of the two versions of the Protocol Independent Multicast (PIM) protocol supported by the kernel. Multicast routing is not covered in this book.

WAN router (CONFIG_WAN_ROUTER)
This option allows configuration of X.25, Frame Relay, HDLC, and other non-IP protocols to perform routing on WAN devices. In the kernel configuration menu, you can see the list of available drivers under "Network device support → Wan interfaces." To be able to configure WAN devices you need to download a piece of software that normally does not come by default with the most common Linux distributions.* WAN routing is not covered in this book.

Advanced Options

When you enable the "IP: Advanced router" option in the Networking Options menu, you can then enable a few additional features. In Chapter 31, we already introduced each one. Here is a brief overview:

IP: policy routing (CONFIG_IP_MULTIPLE_TABLES)
In some situations, traffic handling must be based on other criteria besides the destination IP address. Policy routing is one of the answers to this limitation. In these situations, the routing code must be enhanced to consider the additional parameters. See the section "Concepts Behind Policy Routing" in Chapter 31.

IP: use netfilter MARK value as routing key (CONFIG_IP_ROUTE_FWMARK)
When this option is enabled, routing table lookups can take into account a tag set by the firewall. See the section "Policy Routing and Firewall-Based Classifier" in Chapter 31. You can see this option if you first enable the "IP: policy routing" option.

IP: equal cost multipath (CONFIG_IP_ROUTE_MULTIPATH)
Sometimes a route can be defined with multiple next hops. In that case, distributing traffic over all the routes might increase overall bandwidth. That is exactly what this feature is about. In the section "Concepts Behind Multipath Routing" in Chapter 31, we saw that the implementation of this feature is not as trivial as it may look.

IP: equal cost multipath with caching support (CONFIG_IP_ROUTE_MULTIPATH_CACHED)
Add support for Multipath to the routing cache. This option can be selected only if the previous one is first enabled. When you select it, you get a submenu with a list of the available algorithms that can be used for the selection of the next hop from the cached routes. See the section "Cache Support for Multipath" in Chapter 31.

---

* See the file *documentation/networking/wan-router.txt*.

IP: verbose route monitoring (CONFIG_IP_ROUTE_VERBOSE)

There are a few places where weird conditions are detected, as when doing a sanity check on the traffic processed. In those cases, it can be useful to have some extra warning messages printed; that is the purpose of this feature. The output of those messages is rate limited to one every five seconds to avoid DoS attacks.

Recently Dropped Options

Following are a couple of features currently supported in the 2.4 kernel series, but not included in the 2.6 series:

IP: fast network translation (CONFIG_IP_ROUTE_NAT)

NAT is a feature typically configured on routers to modify the source or destination IP addresses of the forwarded IP packets according to a specific configuration. The NAT implemented by the routing code has nothing to do with the one implemented by the firewall code and has been determined to be superfluous. Its support was removed completely in kernel version 2.6.9.

Fast switching (CONFIG_NET_FASTROUTE)

This feature allows data traffic to be forwarded between NICs directly at the device driver layer. The packets are forwarded to the outgoing interface without having to pass through the higher layer (IP) and without any need to consult the routing table. In Figure 30-1 in Chapter 30, this feature is represented by the dotted line inside the driver box. The feature is currently supported by only one family of NICs, the Tulip cards.[*]

This feature, which was removed in kernel version 2.6.8, is not compatible with other important features for the simple reason that this low-level switching would bypass them. Examples of such features are the Netfilter firewall, advanced routing, and virtual devices (i.e., bonding).

Forwarding between high-speed interfaces (CONFIG_NET_HW_FLOWCONTROL)

This feature allows network cards to start and stop the kernel from sending them packets to transmit, based on the availability of buffer space in their memory. Not all network cards support it. An example of cards that support it is the Tulip family (*drivers/net/tulip/*). Given the introduction of NAPI, described in Chapter 10, this interesting but almost unused feature has been dropped in kernel version 2.6.10.

---

[*] There is a patch you can download and apply to the kernel that allows the Tulip 8390 card to use the "fast switching" feature on 2.4 kernels. A link to this patch is provided by the help window you can open when you enable this feature (e.g., with *make xconfig*).

Main Data Structures

The routing code uses a huge number of different data structures that reference each other. To understand the current routing code and any future improvements, it is important to see the relationships between them clearly.

Any code's performance can be significantly affected by the data structures used and the overall code design. This is especially true for kernel code. A kernel subsystem such as routing, which is the core of the network stack, therefore needs to make sure that it not only provides robust functionality, but also considers performance. We will see in the following chapters how the data structures listed in this section come together to make it easier to implement algorithms that are optimized from the point of view of CPU and RAM consumption, as well as caching.

The following list explains the main data structures defined and used by the routing code. The most important ones have dedicated sections with field-by-field descriptions in Chapter 36. The rt, fib, and fn prefixes in the data structures' names stand for *route*, *Forwarding Information Base*, and *function*, respectively.

struct ip_rt_acct
> Used by the routing table based classifier (see the section "Routing Table Based Classifier" in Chapter 31) to keep statistics, expressed in both bytes and number of packets, about the traffic for routes that have been associated with a tag. The structure contains an array of counters, with 256 elements for each processor.* The size is 256 because route tags lie in the range from 0 to 255. The vector is allocated by ip_rt_init for IPv4; nothing is allocated for IPv6. The four fields of ip_rt_acct are updated in ip_rcv_finish. See the section "Policy Routing and Routing Table Based Classifier" in Chapter 35.

struct rt_cache_stat
> Stores statistics about routing lookups. There is one instance of this data structure for each processor. Even though the name suggests that only counters related to the routing table cache are counted, a few instances are used for more general statistics about routing lookups. See the section "Statistics" in Chapter 36.

struct inet_peer
> Maintains long-living information about remote IP peers. This data structure is described in the section "Long-Living IP Peer Information" in Chapter 23.

struct fib_result
> Structure returned by a lookup in the routing table. The contents do not simply represent the next hop but also include some more parameters that are needed, for instance, by policy routing.

---

* Do not get confused by the fact that the data structure and the array have the same name.

struct `fib_rule`

Represents the rules used by policy routing to select the routing table to use in routing traffic. See the section "Concepts Behind Policy Routing" in Chapter 31.

struct `flowi`

`flowi` is to some extent similar to an Access Control List (ACL): it defines an aggregate of traffic based on the value of selected L3 and L4 header fields, such as IP addresses, L4 port numbers, etc. It is used, for example, as a search key for routing lookups.

The following data structures are the building blocks of routing tables. Their relationships are described in greater detail in Chapter 34.

struct `fib_node`

A routing table entry; the data structure used to store the information generated, for example, when adding a route with the command *route add* or *ip route add*.

struct `fn_zone`

A zone represents a set of routes with the same netmask length. Because the netmask is a 32-bit value (for IPv4), there are 33 zones for each routing table. Thus, routes to the subnets 10.0.1.0/24 and 10.0.2.0/24 would go into the 24-bit zone list (the 25th zone), and routes to the subnet 10.0.3.128/25 would go into the 25-bit zone list.

struct `fib_table`

A routing table. Do not confuse it with the routing table cache.

struct `fib_info`

Some parameters can be shared between different routing table entries. These parameters are stored in `fib_info` data structures. When the set of parameters used by a new routing entry match those of an already existing entry, the existing `fib_info` structure is recycled. A reference count keeps track of the number of users. Figure 34-1 in Chapter 34 shows an example.

struct `fib_alias`

Routes that lead to the same destination network but differ with regard to other parameters, such as the TOS, are distinguished by means of `fib_alias` instances.

struct `fib_nh`

The next hop. If you define a route with a command such as *ip route add 10.0.0.0/24 scope global nexthop via 192.168.1.1*, the next hop will be 192.168.1.1. Normally there is only one next hop for a route, but when the multipath feature is compiled into the kernel, you can configure routes with more than one next hop. See the section "Concepts Behind Multipath Routing" in Chapter 31.

struct `fn_hash`

Contains the pointers to the heads of the 33 `fn_zone` lists, and a list that links together the active zones (the ones with at least one element). The elements of the latter are sorted by decreasing netmask length. See Figure 34-1 in Chapter 34.

The next block of structures is used by the protocol routing cache code and the protocol-independent routing cache code (DST), described in more detail in Chapter 33:

struct dst_entry

The protocol-independent part of the routing table cache entries (DST). Fields of the routing table cache entries that apply to any L3 protocols (e.g., IPv4, IPv6, DECnet) are put into this structure, which is then normally embedded in the data structures used by the L3 protocols to represent a routing table cache entry.

struct dst_ops

Virtual function table (VFT) used by the DST core code to notify the protocol of specific events (for instance, link failures). Each L3 protocol provides its own set of functions to handle those events in the way it prefers. Not all of the fields of the VFT are used by all of the protocols. See the section "Interface Between the DST and Calling Protocols" in Chapter 33.

struct rtable

Used by IPv4 to represent a routing table cache entry.[*]

The following structures are commonly used in configuration:

struct kern_rta

When the kernel receives a request to add or delete a route from an IPROUTE2 command in user space, it parses the request and stores it into a kern_rta structure. See the section "inet_rtm_newroute and inet_rtm_delroute functions" in Chapter 36.

struct rtentry

Used by the *route* command when sending the kernel a request to add or delete a route. IPROUTE2's *ip route* command uses a different data structure.

struct fib_iter_state

Stores context information used while browsing the data structure instances that compose a routing table. It is used by the code that handles the */proc* interface.

The next block of data structures is used by the multipath caching feature, described in Chapter 33:

struct ip_mp_alg_ops

Multipath caching algorithm. It consists of function pointers.

struct multipath_device

Used by the device round-robin caching algorithm to keep information about a device.

---

[*] IPv6 uses struct rt6_info.

```
struct multipath_candidate
struct multipath_dest
struct multipath_bucket
struct multipath_route
```
> Used by the weighted random caching algorithm to keep the state information
> needed by the algorithm.

Lists and Hash Tables

Two other general-purpose data structures are used by the routing code. We will see
them often in this part of the book, so they deserve a little introduction.

```
hlist_head
hlist_node
```
> Hash tables are implemented with these two data structure types. The buckets of
> the table are defined as type `hlist_head`, and the actual elements that are added
> to the table embed an element of type `hlist_node` that is used to link them to the
> table. The only difference between the types is that `hlist_head` includes only a
> forward pointer, whereas `hlist_node` has both forward and back pointers.

Thus, the lists in hash table buckets are bidirectional. Because the head does not
have a backward pointer, the list is not circular, so it is expensive to reach the tail of
the list, but for a hash table this is not a problem. By leaving the backward pointer
out of the bucket's head, this implementation reduces the size of the bucket by 50%,
and therefore doubles the number of buckets it can store with the same amount of
memory.

Figure 32-2 shows an example of a hash table built with `hlist_head` and `hlist_node`
structures. Note that the `hlist_node` structure does not necessarily need to be the
first field of the structure it links.

Not all hash tables defined by the routing code use the model in Figure 32-2: in
Chapter 34, you will see a few examples of use involving the routing tables and the
organization of its data structures; in Chapter 33, you will see that the routing cache
uses its own definition instead.

Lists with two pointers in the head element can also be implemented, using `list_head` structures. You can find more details about both kinds of lists in *include/linux/
list.h*. It includes definitions of the most common manipulation routines (add,
remove, browse, etc.).

Route and Address Scopes

The concept of scope was introduced in the section "Scope" in Chapter 30. Let's see
here how the scopes described in that section are defined by the kernel, and see some
examples of their use.

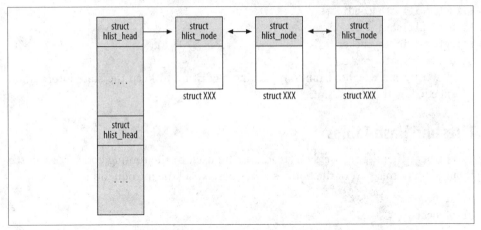

Figure 32-2. Generic hash table and use of lists

The kernel defines an `rt_scope_t` enum that lists possible scopes in *include/linux/ rtnetlink.h*. Its values range from 0 to 255, where 0 (`RT_SCOPE_UNIVERSE`) represents the broadest scope. The kernel actually uses only a few values. The others are left to the discretion of the user; at the moment, there are no practical uses for them.

Route Scopes

The scope of a route is saved in the `fa_scope` field of the `fib_alias` data structure (see Figure 34-1 in Chapter 34). Here are the main scopes used by the IPv4 routing code, in order of increasing scope:

RT_SCOPE_NOWHERE
> This value, which was not listed in Chapter 30, is treated by the code as illegal. The literal meaning is that the route does not lead anywhere, which basically means there is no route to the destination.

RT_SCOPE_HOST
> Examples of these routes are the ones created automatically when configuring IP addresses on the local interfaces (see the section "Adding an IP address").

RT_SCOPE_LINK
> This includes routes to the local network (as defined by the netmask) and to the subnet broadcast addresses derived from locally configured addresses (see the section "Adding an IP address").

RT_SCOPE_UNIVERSE
> This is used for all routes that lead to remote destinations not directly connected (i.e., the ones that require a next-hop gateway).

Address Scopes

The scope of an address is saved in the `ifa_scope` field of the `in_ifaddr` structure. There is an `in_ifaddr` instance for each IP address configured on a device (see Chapter 19). We saw examples of addresses for each main scope in Chapter 30.

The next-hop gateway in a route is another object type that is assigned a scope. Each route can be assigned zero, one, or multiple next hops. Each next hop is defined with an instance of a `fib_nh` structure (see Figure 34-1 in Chapter 34). Two of the `fib_nh`'s fields are `nh_gw` and `nh_scope`: `nh_gw` is the IP address of the next-hop gateway, and `fib_scope` is the scope of that address (which consists of the scope of the route needed to reach the next-hop gateway from the local host).

Relationship Between Route and Next-Hop Scopes

While the scope of a route and the scope of locally configured addresses are either explicitly set by the user or assigned a default value by the kernel, the scope of a route's next hop (`fib_nh` structure) is always assigned by the kernel.

In the section "Adding a Route" in Chapter 34, you will see how `fn_hash_insert` manages to insert a new route into a routing table. Here it suffices to say that `fn_hash_insert` uses `fib_create_info` to allocate the necessary data structures for the new route and to initialize the next hop's scope. This last task is taken care of by `fib_create_info`, with the help of `fib_check_nh`. The next hop's `nh_scope` scope is derived from the scope of the route being configured: normally, given a route and its next hop, the value assigned to `nh_scope` is the scope of the route that would be used to reach the next hop. There are special cases that require different rules, such as routes to locally configured addresses and other direct routes, which do not include a next hop.

Now that we know how `nh_scope` is initialized, let's see how its value can be used to enforce sanity checks on the routes.

The routing code enforces sanity checks on the scopes of routes and next hops in different places. Most of those sanity checks are based on an interesting property of the relationship between the scope of a route and the scope of its next hops. When a host forwards an IP packet, it is supposed to get closer to the final destination.[*] Based on this simple property, it follows that the scope of a route should always be greater than or equal to the scope of the next hop used by the route.

---

[*] This does not necessarily mean physically closer. Sometimes, complex routing scenarios may need to force packets to go through specialized devices, which may require suboptimal routes. However, given the path that a packet is supposed to follow to go from source to destination, every system that forwards it must make it go one more hop toward its final destination.

Let's see a couple of examples using the topology in Figure 32-3. Remember that for every route, nh_scope is the next hop's scope and nh_gw is the next hop's IP address.

- When Host A sends a packet to Host C, the matching route has scope RT_SCOPE_ UNIVERSE and the next hop to use is RT. The scope of the route to RT must be narrower than RT_SCOPE_UNIVERSE for the routing to converge. Thus, a lookup in the routing table for a route from Host A to Host RT will return a route with scope RT_SCOPE_LINK, which is a narrower scope than RT_SCOPE_UNIVERSE and therefore correct. Because an RT_SCOPE_LINK route does not need a gateway (and in fact you do not need a gateway for Host A to reach Host RT), the kernel initializes nh_gw to 0 and the nh_scope scope to a scope smaller than RT_SCOPE_LINK (e.g., RT_SCOPE_HOST).

- When Host A sends a packet to itself, the matching route has scope RT_SCOPE_ HOST. In this case, you do not need a gateway, so nh_gw is set to 0. nh_scope is set to a scope smaller than RT_SCOPE_HOST: RT_SCOPE_NOWHERE.

The recursion just described ends when the result of a routing lookup is a direct route (i.e., no next-hop gateway is necessary). Here are the two possible cases:

The route returned by the routing lookup has scope RT_SCOPE_HOST
In this case, the destination is a locally configured address, so the host can deliver the packet locally.

The route returned by the routing lookup has scope RT_SCOPE_LINK
Because the destination is directly connected and there is no need for a gateway, the host can send the packet to the destination directly using an L2 protocol.[*]

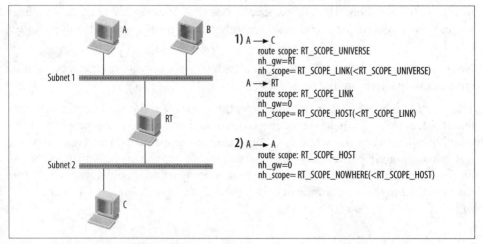

Figure 32-3. Example of initialization of next hop's scopes

---

[*] This includes the case of onlink routes, described in Chapter 33.

Primary and Secondary IP Addresses

We saw in the section "Primary and Secondary Addresses" in Chapter 30 that an IP address can be configured as primary or secondary on a device. The kernel often needs to browse all the addresses configured on a device to find one that matches a given condition. Let's see how the two types of addresses are distinguished and how addresses are browsed.

Secondary IPv4 addresses are tagged with the IFA_F_SECONDARY flag in their in_ifaddr data structures (see Chapter 19). Because there are only two configurations—primary and secondary—there is no need for an IFA_F_PRIMARY flag: if an address is not secondary, it is considered primary.

The kernel provides macros in *include/linux/inetdevice.h* that make it easier to browse interfaces meeting specific criteria. For each criterion selected, there are usually two macros that are used to bracket a loop: the programmer places the code to process a single address in a block that is started by one macro and terminated by another. The effect is to run a loop applying the code to each address meeting selected criteria.

Here is an example of the macros in use:

```
for_ifa {

        do something with ifa

} endfor_ifa
```

The for_ifa macro starts a loop with the variable ifa to represent each address selected. The code between the macros does not need to be placed in brackets, but it usually is, to make variables such as ifa local and usable only within the loop.

A few such macros include:

for_ifa
endfor_ifa
> Given a device, these two macros can be used to browse all of its in_device data structures.[*]

for_primary_ifa
endfor_ifa
> Given a device, these two macros can be used to selectively browse only the in_device instances associated with primary IP addresses.

---

[*] We saw in Chapter 19 that in_device is the data structure used to store the IP configuration of a network device.

Generic Helper Routines and Macros

The routing code uses quite a few small routines and macros that make the code more readable. This section lists some of the generic ones; more-specialized ones will be introduced later in the section "Helper Routines." It is important to keep in mind that the same function or macro can have different definitions, depending on such factors as:

- Support for policy routing in the kernel
- Support for multipath routing in the kernel
- L3 protocol (e.g., IPv4 versus DECnet)

The generic routines follow:

FIB_RES_XXX

> Given a fib_result structure, these macros extract specific fields. For example, FIB_RES_DEV extracts the nh_dev field. These macros are defined in *include/net/ip_fib.h*.

change_nexthops
for_nexthops
endfor_nexthops

> Used to browse all the fib_nh structures of a given fib_info instance. change_nexthops starts a loop over the structures, designating the local variable nh to represent each structure; as the name of the macro suggests, it can be used to alter the structures. for_nexthops is very similar and ends with the same endfor_nexthops macro. The only difference is that for_nexthop defines the local variable nh as a pointer to a constant and therefore the code inside the loop cannot change the content of any of the fib_nh instances browsed.

> For IPv4, these macros are defined in *net/ipv4/fib_semantics.c*. Note that for each macro there are two versions: one used when there is Policy Routing support in the kernel and one when there is no Policy Routing. The second one is optimized by taking into account that without Policy Routing you always have at most one fib_nh instance per fib_info instance (that is, at most one next hop per route).

inet_ifa_byprefix

> Given a device, a prefix, and a mask, this function browses all the primary IP addresses configured on the input device looking for an address that matches the input prefix and mask. In case of success, it returns the address that matches.

fib_get_table

> Given a routing table identifier (a number from 0 to 255), this function returns the associated fib_info structure from the fib_tables array shown in Figure 34-1 in Chapter 34. It is defined in *include/net/ip_fib.h*.

`fib_new_table`

> This function creates and initializes a new routing table and links it to the `fib_tables` vector (see Figure 34-1 in Chapter 34).

`LOOPBACK`
`ZERONET`
`MULTICAST`
`LOCAL_MCAST/BADCLASS`

> These macros, defined in *include/linux/in.h*, are used to quickly classify some well-known categories of IP addresses. See Tables 30-1 and 30-2 in Chapter 30.
>
> `LOOPBACK` identifies 127.*x.x.x* addresses.
>
> `ZERONET` identifies 0.*x.x.x*/8 addresses, which in most cases are not legal.
>
> `MULTICAST` identifies addresses in the class D range.
>
> `LOCAL_MCAST` identifies a subset of the class D range used for local multicast: 224.0.0.0/24.
>
> `BADCLASS` identifies addresses in the class E range.

Global Locks

The routing code uses a few locks for protection against race conditions. The following list includes only global locks; those that are embedded in the data structure (i.e., applied to single entries) will be addressed in the associated data structure descriptions.

`fib_hash_lock`

> This read-write spin lock (rwlock) protects all the routing tables. For instance, the insertion of a new `fib_node` instance requires the lock to be taken in exclusive mode, and a routing table lookup requires the lock to be acquired just in shared mode. Since there is only one lock for all the routing tables, it means that it is not possible to add two routing entries to two distinct routing tables at the same time. However, this does not really represent a bottleneck, because configuration changes are rare events and the user can live with a shared lock without any major impact on router performance.

`fib_info_lock`

> This rwlock protects all the `fib_info` data structures. It is used, for instance, when accessing `fib_info` structures through the hash tables described in the section "Organization of fib_info Structures" in Chapter 34.

`fib_rules_lock`

> This rwlock protects the `fib_rules` global list of `fib_rule` data structures.

`rt_flush_lock`

> This spin lock is used by `rt_cache_flush` to protect the manipulation of the `rt_deadline` global variable and the `rt_flush_timer` timer. The cache is protected by

the per-bucket locks. See Figure 33-1 and the section "Flushing the Routing Cache," both in Chapter 33.

`fib_multipath_lock`
> This spin lock is used when modifying fields of the `fib_info` structure that are used by the multipath feature.

`alg_table_lock`
> This spin lock serializes access to the `ip_mp_alg_table` vector. It is used by the `multipath_alg_register` and `multipath_alg_unregister` functions. See the section "Registering a Caching Algorithm" in Chapter 33.

Routing Subsystem Initialization

The initialization of the IPv4 routing code starts in *net/ipv4/route.c* with `ip_rt_init`, which is called by the IP subsystem when it is initialized with `ip_init` in *net/ipv4/ip_output.c* at boot time. `ip_init` is described in Chapter 19; here we will see `ip_rt_init`.* Figure 32-4 shows how the main routing initialization routines are invoked.

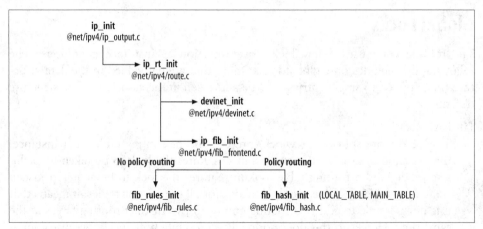

Figure 32-4. Sequence of calls for the main routing initialization functions

In `ip_rt_init`, the IPv4 routing code initializes its data structures and global variables. Among other things, the function:

- Defines the size of the routing cache based on the available RAM.
- Creates the memory pool that will be used to allocate elements of the routing cache.
- Initializes the routing cache

---

* IPv6 does something similar in *inet6_init* by calling `ip6_route_init`.

- Defines the gc_thresh threshold used by the garbage collection algorithm (see the section "rt_garbage_collect Function" in Chapter 33).
- Starts the timer rt_periodic_timer (see the section "Garbage Collection" in Chapter 33).
- Starts the rt_secret_timer timer (see the section "Flushing the Routing Cache" in Chapter 33).
- Adds a few files to the */proc* filesystem (see the section "Tuning via /proc Filesystem" in Chapter 36).

Two routines are of particular interest:

ip_fib_init
> Initializes the default routing tables and registers two handlers with the two notification chains* netdev_chain and inetaddr_chain (see the section "External Events").

devinet_init
> Registers another handler with the notification chain netdev_chain, registers the handlers for the address and route commands (i.e., *ip addr ...* and *ip route ...*) with the Netlink socket, and creates the */proc/sys/net/conf* and */proc/sys/net/conf/ default* directories. See Chapter 36 for the last two tasks.

When the kernel is compiled with support for IPsec, ip_rt_init also invokes a couple of IPsec initialization routines (xfrm_init and xfrm4_init).

See the section "Routing Cache Initialization" in Chapter 33 for the details on how the rt_hash_*xxx* global variables are initialized by ip_rt_init.

Policy routing is initialized with fib_rules_init, defined in *net/ipv4/fib_rules.c*. The initialization consists simply of registering a handler with the netdev_chain notification chain. The registered handler is fib_rules_event, and is described in the section "Impacts on the policy database."

External Events

The routing subsystem plays a central role in the network stack. Because of this, it needs to know when changes take place that may affect the routing table and routing cache. Changes to the network topology are taken care of by optional routing protocols running in user space. On the other hand, changes to the local host configuration require kernel attention.

In particular, the routing subsystem is interested in two kinds of events:

- Changes in the status of a network device

---

* Notification chains are described in Chapter 4.

- Changes in IP configuration on a network device

To receive notifications when these take place, the routing subsystem registers with the `netdev_chain` and `inetaddr_chain` notification chains, respectively. The sections "Changes in Device Status" and "Changes in IP Configuration" go into more detail on the handlers registered for the two classes of events.

Figure 32-5 shows a high-level description of the two handlers registered in `ip_rt_init` and described in the sections "Impacts on the routing tables" and "Impacts on the IP configuration." Some of the events are handled by calling certain helper routines with varying input parameters. Some of those routines are described in the upcoming section "Helper Routines." See the description of `fib_sync_down` in that section for the meaning of the `force` parameter shown in Figure 32-5.

We will see that a variety of events can flush the routing cache. Refer to the section "Flushing the Routing Cache" in Chapter 33 for a complete list of such events.

Helper Routines

In the following sections, we will see in detail how `fib_netdev_event` and `fib_inetaddr_event` are implemented. This section gives an overview of some of the routines called by those two handlers; you can use this section as a reference when reading about the handlers themselves.

void rt_cache_flush(int delay)
> Schedules a flush of the routing cache after a given amount of time, which is specified with an input parameter. See the section "Flushing the Routing Cache" in Chapter 33.

int fib_sync_down(u32 local, struct net_device *dev, into force)
> Updates the routing tables when a device is shut down or a local address is removed. Here is the meaning of the input parameters:

local
> IP address that has been removed.

dev
> Device that has been shut down.

force
> Determines when certain activities are performed. Refer to Figure 32-5 to see when each of the following values is used. The meanings are as follows.
>
> 0: An IP address has been deleted.
>
> 1: A device has been shut down.
>
> 2: A device has been unregistered.

The `force` parameter is overloaded; it is used to decide two things:

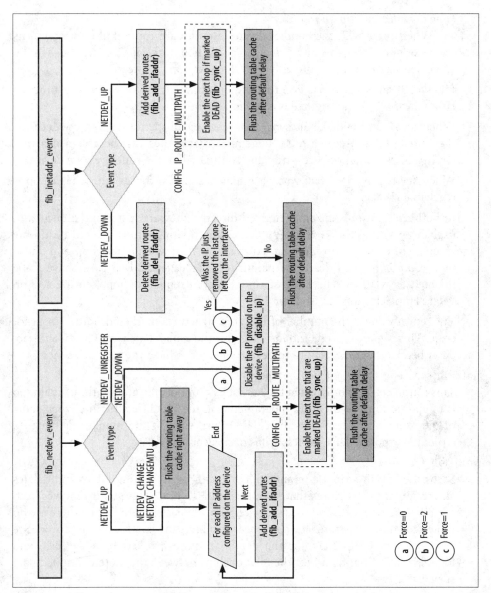

Figure 32-5. fib_netdev_event and fib_inetaddr_event functions

The scope of the routes to delete

When force is 0, the handler deletes all eligible routes except for the ones that lead to locally configured addresses (i.e., scope RT_SCOPE_HOST). When force is 1 or 2, the handler deletes all eligible routes regardless of the scope.

How to handle multipath routes

When force is 2, the handler deletes a multipath route if at least one of its next hops uses the input device dev. When force is 0 or 1, the handler deletes a multipath route only if all the next hops are dead.

fib_sync_down is usually called to handle only one type of event at a time, so either the dev or local argument is set and the other is null.

When local is provided, fib_sync_down removes all the routes that use local as their preferred source address. Remember that routes can be assigned a preferred address, and not necessarily one configured on the route's egress device.

When dev is provided, fib_sync_down removes all the routes whose next hop is reachable via dev.

In both cases, routes are not removed directly; they are just marked dead (not usable) by setting the RTNH_F_DEAD flag. A multipath route is marked dead only when all of its next hops are marked as such. Also, when a next hop of a multipath route is marked dead, the parameters fib_power and nh_power have to be updated as well, to reflect the status of the current next hop (see the section "Next Hop Selection" in Chapter 35).

The return value is the number of fib_info structures marked dead by fib_sync_down. This value is used, for instance, by the caller (such as fib_disable_ip, described later in this section) to decide whether to flush the routing cache.

int fib_sync_up(struct net_device *dev)

This routine is used only when the kernel has support for multipath. Its main job is to update some of the route's parameters in the fib_info structure when some of the route's next hops are alive. The return value is the number of fib_info structures whose RTNH_F_DEAD flag has been cleared.

void fib_flush(void)

Scans the ip_fib_main_table and ip_fib_local_table routing tables and deletes all the fib_info structures that have their RTNH_F_DEAD flags set. It removes both the fib_info structure and the associated fib_alias structure. When there are no more fib_alias structures for a fib_node instance, the latter is also removed. See Table 34-1 in Chapter 34 for the default routine invoked by fib_flush, and Figure 34-1 in Chapter 34 for the relationships between the aforementioned data structures.

When there is support for multipath in the kernel, fib_flush scans all the routing tables.

When at least one fib_info instance is removed, the routing cache is then flushed with rt_cache_flush.

The return value is the number of fib_info instances removed.

```
static void fib_disable_ip(struct net_device *dev, int force)
```
Disables the IP protocol on the device received in input by calling fib_sync_down. When the number of deleted routes is positive (as determined from the return value of fib_sync_down), the function also flushes the routing table immediately: fib_sync_down marks routes as dead, and fib_flush actually removes these routes. fib_disable_ip also flushes the routing cache immediately and asks ARP to clear from its cache all the entries that refer to the device where the IP protocol is being shut down.

Note that the input parameter force is passed as it is to fib_sync_down. Figure 32-6 shows the internals of fib_disable_ip.

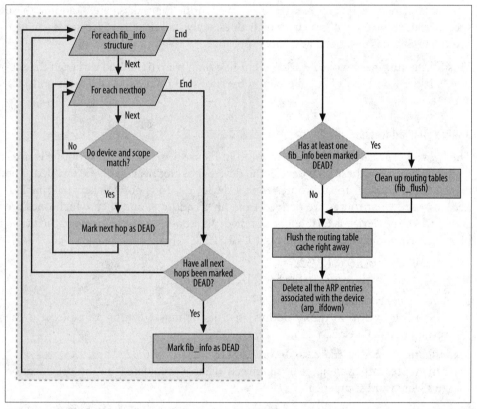

Figure 32-6. fib_disable_ip function

Changes in IP Configuration

Whenever a device's IP configuration changes, the routing subsystem receives a notification and handles it by running fib_inetaddr_event. Figure 32-5 summarizes the actions triggered by all the possible events that can be conveyed by this notification chain. Here is how the main events are handled:

NETDEV_UP

A new IP address has been configured on a local device. The handler must add the necessary routes to the local_table routing table. The routine responsible for this is fib_add_ifaddr.

NETDEV_DOWN

An IP address has been removed from a local device. The handler must remove these routes that were added by the previous NETDEV_UP event. The routine responsible for this is fib_del_ifaddr.

As mentioned in the section "Special Routes" in Chapter 30, every time an IP address is configured on an interface, the kernel adds a set of special routes to a separate routing table named ip_fib_local_table. The routine that takes care of adding these special routes is fib_add_ifaddr, which does it by calling fib_magic for each new route. fib_magic is described in Chapter 36.

Most of the routines invoked during event handling were described earlier in the section "Helper Routines." The following subsections describe fib_add_ifaddr and fib_del_ifaddr.

Adding an IP address

The logic of fib_add_ifaddr is summarized in Figure 32-7. When this routine is notified about a new address on a device, the device may not necessarily be enabled. The choice about whether to add routes to that device depends on whether it is enabled. Let's first see what routes are derived from an IP address, and then which ones are added when the device is enabled or disabled. As a basic example, here are the possible routes pertaining to the IP address 10.0.1.1/24:

Route to the address 10.0.1.1/32
This is simply the route to the specified host address.

Route to the network address 10.0.1.0/24
This is derived from the IP address and its netmask. In our example, it is the result of 10.0.1.1 & 255.255.255.0.

Routes to the broadcast addresses 10.0.1.255/32 and 10.0.1.0/32
This represents a compromise between what is mandated by the specification and what is most practical.

Linux is generous in handling the different requirements: it adds routes to both versions of the broadcast address in the ip_fib_local_table routing table. Note that routing can distinguish between the network address and limited broadcast address because they have different netmasks (10.0.1.0/24 versus 10.0.1.0/32). In addition, a user can configure a broadcast address explicitly. In this case, the fib_add_ifaddr routine adds a route to that address in addition to the other two.

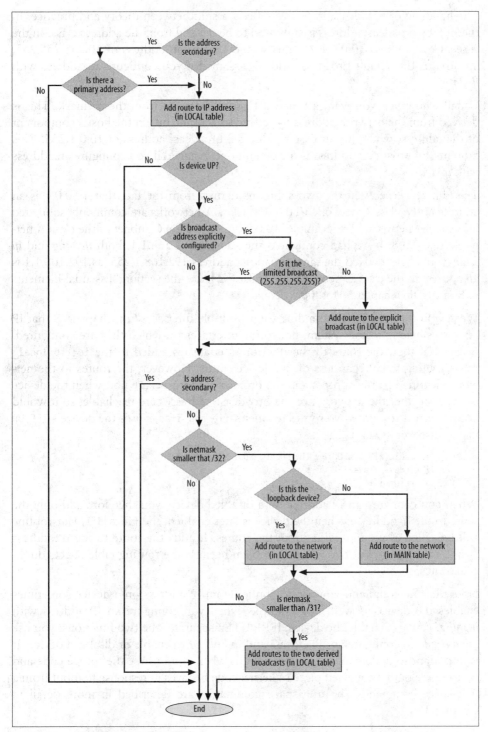

Figure 32-7. fib_add_ifaddr function

The handling of broadcast addresses reflects a split between theory and practice. In theory, the broadcast address is supposed to be derived from the address class. In the case of our address 10.0.0.1/24, this would lead to an address of 10.255.255.255, and that is the default broadcast address assigned if you configure an address with *ifconfig*.

Usually, however, you want a broadcast address derived from the netmask. This is derived from the network address by setting to 1 all the bits in the host's component of the address, which in our case produces a broadcast address of 10.0.1.255. This more useful broadcast address is the default one assigned if you configure an address with *ip addr*.

This difference between the two solutions derives from the fact that 10.0.0.1 is an address in the class A network 10.0.0.0/8. Class A networks are commonly subnetted into smaller networks. For example, 10.0.0.0/24 is a class C subnet of the class A network 10.0.0.0/8. If we had configured the address 192.168.1.1, both *ifconfig* and *ip addr* would have derived the same broadcast address 192.168.1.255, as 192.168.1.1 is an address in the class C network 192.168.1.0/24. See the section "Essential Elements of Routing" in Chapter 30 for more details.

We saw in the section "Responding from Multiple Interfaces" in Chapter 28 that IP addresses belong to the system, not to the interfaces on which they are configured. Because of that, the route to the IP address is always added to the ip_fib_local_ table routing table regardless of the device status. However, the routes to the network identified by the address and the broadcast addresses are not: when the device is down, neither the network nor the broadcast addresses are reachable, so it would not be correct to create two routes for them. fib_add_ifaddr uses the device's IFF_UP flag to discover its status.

```
fib_magic(RTM_NEWROUTE, RTN_LOCAL, addr, 32, prim);
if (!(dev->flags&IFF_UP))
    return;
```

When you configure an IP address on a disabled device, you therefore add only the route to the IP address. When the device is later enabled, the fib_add_ifaddr routine will be called again and will add all the routes. It adds the route to the IP address again at this point, but this is not a problem because the routing table rejects duplicate routes.

Note that the command you use to configure an IP address on a device sometimes enables the device as well. For example, when you configure an IP address with *ifconfig*, you also enable the device. IPROUTE2 separates the two functions: you use *ip addr add* to configure an IP address and *ip link set* to enable or disable a device. It is important to understand these distinctions when you browse the source code and try to figure out how a given piece of kernel code behaves in response to input from a user-space command. The user-space commands are described in more detail in Chapter 36.

Table 32-1 shows some sample commands and the routes created.

Table 32-1. Examples of IP configurations and the associated derived routes

Command	Main	Local
`ip addr add 10.0.1.1/24 dev eth0`	10.0.1.0/24	10.0.1.1/32 (address)
		10.0.1.0/32 (broadcast)
		10.0.1.255/32 (broadcast)
`ip addr add 10.0.1.1/24 broadcast 10.0.1.100 dev eth0`	10.0.1.0/24	10.0.1.1/32 (address)
		10.0.1.100/32 (broadcast)
		10.0.1.0/32 (broadcast)
		10.0.1.255/32 (broadcast)
`ip addr add 10.0.1.1/32 dev eth0`		10.0.1.1/32 (address)
`ip addr add 10.0.1.1/32 broadcast 10.0.1.255 dev eth0`		10.0.1.1/32 (address)
		10.0.1.255/32 (broadcast)

When the explicit broadcast happens to match the limited broadcast address 255.255.255.255, no route is added toward the explicit broadcast address because the latter is checked by the lookup routines, as we will see in the sections "Input Routing" and "Output Routing" in Chapter 35).

```
if (ifa->ifa_broadcast && ifa->ifa_broadcast != 0xFFFFFFFF)
    fib_magic(RTM_NEWROUTE, RTN_BROADCAST, ifa->ifa_broadcast, 32, prim);
```

The explicit configuration of a broadcast address allows you to define a broadcast address even on a /32 subnet where you theoretically have only one IP address, as in the fourth example in Table 32-1 (note that the broadcast address 10.0.1.255 does not fall within the subnet 10.0.1.1/32).

Under some conditions, the function may not need to add the routes to the broadcast addresses. These depend on the length of the netmask, which is stored in the local variable prefixlen:

- When prefixlen is 32, there is only one valid address in the subnet, so there is no need for either the derived broadcast or the network routes.

- When prefixlen is 31, there is only one bit to play with, so there are just two addresses within the subnet. The one with the clear bit identifies the network, and the one with the set bit is the host address (the one the function is configuring). In this case, routes are needed for these two addresses, but not for any derived broadcast addresses.

- When prefixlen is smaller than 31, there is room for other addresses, because the local address together with the network and broadcast addresses use only three out of four or more addresses. Thus, the kernel adds a route to both the derived broadcast addresses and the network.

The following code shows how these cases are handled for primary addresses:

```
if (!ZERONET(prefix) && !(ifa->ifa_flags&IFA_F_SECONDARY) &&
    (prefix != addr || ifa->ifa_prefixlen < 32)) {
    fib_magic(RTM_NEWROUTE, dev->flags&IFF_LOOPBACK ? RTN_LOCAL :
        RTN_UNICAST, prefix, ifa->ifa_prefixlen, prim);
    if (ifa->ifa_prefixlen < 31) {
        fib_magic(RTM_NEWROUTE, RTN_BROADCAST, prefix, 32, prim);
        fib_magic(RTM_NEWROUTE, RTN_BROADCAST, prefix|~mask, 32, prim);
    }
  }
}
```

Secondary addresses have none of these issues. When you add a secondary address there must already be a primary address on the same subnet (prefix) configured on the same device. If there is no such primary address, you have made an error and the configuration cannot be accepted. Thus, routes to the network and to the derived broadcasts are not needed for secondary addresses: these routes were already added when the associated primary address was configured.

Removing an IP address

When you remove an IP address from an interface, the routing subsystem is notified so that it can clean up its routing tables and cache. The routine that takes care of this is fib_del_ifaddr, whose logic is described in Figure 32-8.

The routine starts with a sanity check. If you try to remove a secondary address, there must be a primary address on the same subnet. If there isn't, something must have gone wrong earlier somewhere and the routine returns an error.

When fib_del_ifaddr is invoked, the IP address whose associated route is being removed has already been removed from the list of configured addresses on the affected device (see, for example, when inet_del_ifa triggers the NETDEV_DOWN notification).

Because routes to broadcast addresses and the network address may not always have been added along with the primary address, as we saw in the previous section, fib_del_ifaddr scans all the configured addresses on the device and checks what needs to be removed. You can see, for example, in Table 32-1 what routes are added when configuring a local IP address.

In most cases, when a secondary address is removed, the routing subsystem needs to remove only the route to the IP address. The routes to the network and broadcast addresses are not removed because they are still needed by the primary address (and other secondary addresses, if any). However, it is possible that when removing a secondary IP address, it is not even necessary to remove the route to its IP address: this is the case, for example, when an administrator configures the same address with two different netmasks, as in the following example:

```
# ip addr add dev eth0 192.168.0.1/24
# ip addr add dev eth0 192.168.0.1/16
```

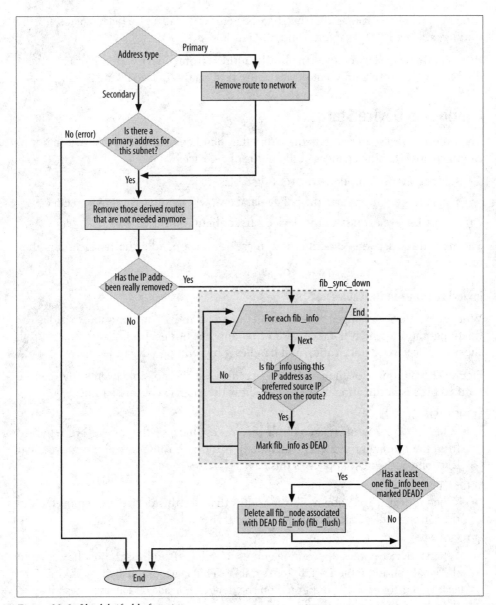

Figure 32-8. fib_del_ifaddr function

The example does not represent a common scenario, but the code must be able to handle it.

The routes to the network and broadcast addresses derived by the two commands (as described in the section "Adding an IP address") are different, but they share a route to the IP address.

After removing the routes that need to be removed, `fib_del_ifaddr` cleans up the routing table with `fib_sync_down` and `fib_flush`.

When `fib_del_ifaddr` removes the last IP address from a device, `fib_inetaddr_event` disables the IP protocol on that device with `fib_disable_ip` (see Figure 32-5).

Changes in Device Status

The routing subsystem registers three different handlers with the `netdev_chain` notification chain to handle changes in the status of a device:

- `fib_netdev_event` updates the routing tables.
- `fib_rules_event` updates the policy database, when policy routing is in effect.
- `ip_netdev_event` updates the device's IP configuration.[*]

The next three sections describe how these routines handle the notifications they receive.

Impacts on the routing tables

Whenever a device changes state or something else in its configuration (besides the IP configuration, which is taken care of by another notification chain), the routing subsystem receives a notification and handles it by running `fib_netdev_event`.

Figure 32-5 summarizes the actions triggered by all the possible events that can be notified by this notification chain. Here is how the main events are handled:

NETDEV_UNREGISTER
> When a device is unregistered, all the routes that use this device are removed from the routing tables (cache included). Multipath routes are also removed if at least one of the next hops uses this device.

NETDEV_DOWN
> When a device goes down, all the routes that use this device are removed from the routing tables (cache included) with `fib_disable_ip`.

NETDEV_UP
> When a device comes up, routing entries for all its IP addresses must be added to the local routing table `ip_fib_local_table`. This is accomplished by calling `fib_add_ifaddr` for each IP configured on the device. `fib_add_ifaddr` was described in the section "Adding an IP address."

NETDEV_CHANGEMTU
NETDEV_CHANGE
> When a configuration change is applied to a device, the routing table cache is flushed. Among the most common notified changes are modifications of the MTU or the PROMISCUITY status.

---

[*] This handler is registered by `ip_rt_init`, but it actually belongs to the IP subsystem.

Note that the routing subsystem is not interested in the NETDEV_REGISTER event. NETDEV_UP is already sufficient to trigger the necessary actions for a newly activated device.

Unregistering a device and shutting down a device can have different effects on the routing table. Some of the reasons a device can be unregistered include a user removing the driver from the kernel or unplugging a hotplug device such as a PCMCIA Ethernet card. Some of the reasons a device can be shut down include a user unplugging the cable or issuing an administrative command. In each case, different routes are removed from the routing tables.

Let's look at an example. The first column in Table 32-2 shows the routes that would be added to the routing table with the following two commands, and the last two columns show what routes would be removed when the device *eth0* is shut down or unregistered, respectively.

```
# ip addr add dev eth0 192.168.1.100
# ip route add  10.0.1.0/24 via 192.168.1.111
```

Table 32-2. Routes dropped when a device is shut down or unregistered

Route	Routing table	Shut down	Unregistered
192.168.1.0/24	Main	Yes	Yes
192.168.1.0/32	Local	Yes	Yes
192.168.1.255/32	Local	Yes	Yes
192.168.1.100/32	Local	No	Yes
10.0.1.0/24	Main	Yes	Yes

The route to the IP address is not removed when the device is shut down because its IP address belongs to the host, not to the interface. This address exists as long as its associated device exists. See the section "Responding from Multiple Interfaces" in Chapter 28.

Impacts on the policy database

A policy (i.e., a rule) can be associated with a device. You can specify, for instance, that traffic received on *eth0* and addressed to the subnet 10.0.1.0/24 should be assigned a specific priority. Therefore, when a device is unregistered, all the associated policies (i.e., fib_rule data structures) are marked as unusable by setting their device ID, the r_ifindex field of the data structure, to the invalid value −1 with fib_rules_detach.

On the other hand, when a device is registered, if there is any disabled policy associated with this device it is re-enabled with fib_rules_attach. Because the device ID of disabled policies is −1, the kernel uses the device's name saved in fib_rule's r_ifname field to recognize the device with which a policy is associated.

Impacts on the IP configuration

Here is how the handler's `inetdev_event` routine handles the notifications received from the `netdev_chain` chain:

`NETDEV_UNREGISTER`

Disables the IP protocol on the device.

`NETDEV_UP`

Enables the multicast configuration (if present) with `ip_mc_up`. When the device going up is the loopback device, configure the 127.0.0.1/8 address on it.

This notification is ignored if the device going up has a configured MTU smaller than the minimum value of 68 that is necessary to enable the IP protocol. This is only a sanity check.

`NETDEV_DOWN`

Disables the multicast configuration (if present) with `ip_mc_down`.

`NETDEV_CHANGEMTU`

Checks whether the device's MTU has been set to a value smaller than the minimum necessary to run the IP protocol (68), and if so, disables the IP protocol on the device.

`NETDEV_CHANGENAME`

Updates the name of the directories */proc/sys/net/ipv4/conf/devname* and */proc/sys/net/ipv4/neigh/devname* to reflect the new device name. These directories are described in Chapters 23 and 29, respectively.

For both `NETDEV_UNREGISTER` and `NETDEV_CHANGEMTU`, the IP protocol is disabled with `inetdev_destroy`. That function removes all IP configurations from the device and clears the ARP cache accordingly with `arp_ifdown`.

Interactions with Other Subsystems

The section "Interactions with Other Subsystems" in Chapter 31 anticipated the main interactions that the routing subsystem has with other ones, such as Traffic Control and Firewall. In the following subsections, we will see some more details. The interaction with the routing table based classifier is deferred until Chapter 35 because it requires some background on the routing table structure and on how lookups are implemented.

Netlink Notifications

When a route is added or removed, a notification is sent to the Netlink group `RTMGRP_IPV4_ROUTE` using the routine `rtmsg_fib`. Notifications for creation and deletions are respectively generated in `fn_hash_insert` and `fn_hash_delete`, two important routines that we will see in Chapter 34. See also the section "Change Notifications" in Chapter 36.

Policy Routing and Firewall-Based Classifier

As anticipated in the section "Interactions with Other Kernel Subsystems" in Chapter 31, policy routing can use a tag initialized by the firewall code as a discriminator to decide which routing table to use for both ingress and egress traffic. Routing based on firewall tagging requires special support to be compiled into the kernel. When available, the firewall tag is part of the cache and routing table lookup keys (represented by flowi structures). The firewall subsystem copies the tag into the skb->nfmark buffer field, where it can be used as a discriminator by Policy Routing to decide which routing table to use to route ingress and egress traffic.

In Chapter 33, you will see how the two cache lookup routines ip_route_input and __ip_route_output_key check the value of the firewall tag. Chapter 34 shows how the two routing table lookup routines ip_route_input_slow and ip_route_output_slow initialize the nfmark field of the lookup key flowi with the firewall tag skb->nfmark. A 0 value for skb->nfmark means that no tag exists.

Figure 31-4 in Chapter 31 shows when, inside the network stack, the firewall can tag a buffer based on its configuration, and when the policy routing engine uses it for its policy rules lookup.

Routing Protocol Daemons

Routes can be added both by users with commands such as *ip route* or *route* and by routing protocols running in user space, such as BGP, IGRP, and OSPF. We saw the big picture in the section "Routing Protocol Daemons" in Chapter 31. In this section, we will go into a little more detail on the user/kernel interface, and Chapter 36 will go into more detail on the utilities themselves. However, we will not cover the internals of any routing protocol in detail because it is outside the scope of the book.

Routing protocols run in user space, but they need to inject their knowledge into the kernel to have their routes be incorporated into the kernel's routing tables. While the routing protocol code is independent from the underlying operating system, the way those protocols inject routes into the kernel has to adapt to the user/kernel interfaces provided by the underlying operating system.

If you like browsing source code, I urge you to look at how the platform-independent code (basically, the routing protocols) interact with the platform-dependent code to inject routes into the kernel's routing table. You will see, for instance, how different operating systems may require different interfaces. Even different versions of the same operating system may require or make available different interfaces.

With regard to Linux, the old-generation ioctl interface is still available, but the new Netlink is preferred by the kernel because it is more powerful. While ioctl is pretty common to all the Unix flavors, Netlink is Linux-specific and plays the same role in the Linux world that the routing socket plays in the BSD world. It is important to note that when Netlink is compiled into the kernel, it is preferred over ioctl because of its better control and bidirectional capabilities. (For instance, with Netlink—as with the routing socket on BSD—when the kernel detects changes on an NIC, it can communicate it to a user-space application over a Netlink socket so that the application can take some action.)

Table 32-3 lists the most common routing daemons and shows which ones can handle the ioctl interface and Netlink. Chapter 36 goes into more detail on these interfaces.

Table 32-3. Interfaces to the Linux kernel used by the most common routing daemons

Daemon	ioctl	Netlink
ROUTED (v 0.17)	Yes	No
GATED (v3.6)	Yes	Yes
BIRD (v1.0.9)	Yes	Yes
ZEBRA (v0.94)	Yes	Yes
QUAGGA (v 0.98.0)	Yes	Yes
MRT (v2.2.0)	Yes	Yes
XORP (v1.0)	No[a]	Yes

[a] XORP uses ioctl, but not to insert or delete routes. The purpose and operation of XORP are described in an interesting document, *http://www.xorp.org/releases/current/docs/fea/fea.pdf*.

## CHAPTER 33

Routing: The Routing Cache

The routing cache is used to reduce the lookup time on the routing tables. The center of the routing cache is the Protocol Independent Destination Cache, which is simply called DST. Even if policy routing is in effect—creating multiple routing tables—a single routing cache is always shared by all the routing tables.

The main job of the cache is to store information that allows the routing subsystem to find destinations for packets, and to offer this information through a set of functions to higher layers. The cache also offers some functions to manage cleanup. The cache stores the information about the routing table cache entries that applies to all L3 protocols and can therefore be included in any data structure used to represent a routing table cache entry.

In this chapter, we will see:

- How the cache is implemented
- How new elements are inserted and existing ones are deleted
- How ingress and egress lookups are implemented, and where they differ
- How external subsystems can interact with the cache via an interface provided by the DST
- How different kinds of garbage collection keep the size of the cache under control
- How the DST provides a rate-limiting mechanism for egress ICMP REDIRECT messages

Routing Cache Initialization

The routing cache is implemented as a hash table. It is initialized in `ip_rt_init`, which is the initialization function of the routing subsystem and is described in the section "Routing Subsystem Initialization" in Chapter 32.

The size of the cache depends on the amount of physical memory available in the host. On your system, you can find the size of the hash table in the messages printed at boot time, or later in the output of the *dmesg* command. Look for the string "IP: routing cache hash table of ...", which is printed by ip_rt_init itself. The size is stored in rt_hash_mask, and the base two logarithm of it is saved in rt_hash_log (that is, $2^{rt\_hash\_log}$=rt_hash_mask). The default size assigned by the kernel can be overridden by the user boot option *rhash_entries*, which stores the hash table size to use in the variable rhash_entries.

In particular, ip_rt_init initializes the following:

rt_hash_table
> The routing cache, defined as a hash table.

rt_hash_mask
rt_hash_log
> The size (number of buckets) of the hash table rt_hash_table, and the base two logarithm of that number, which often is useful when a value has to be shifted by that number of bits.

rt_hash_rnd
> A parameter that is assigned a new random value every time the routing cache is flushed with rt_run_flush. This parameter is used to prevent DoS attacks, as part of an algorithm that distributes elements in the routing cache to make their distribution less deterministic. This variable is first initialized by ip_rt_init based on parameters related to available memory and the current jiffies. Later, after the system has been up for a while and there is a chance for it to build up good entropy, the variable is reset using the get_random_bytes routine.

Hash Table Organization

The data structures described in this section vary slightly among L3 protocols. In IPv4, hash table buckets are of type rt_hash_bucket, a structure that includes only a pointer to the list of colliding elements and a lock. The use of the lock is described in the section "Cache Locking."

Elements of the cache are of type rtable. This structure includes some protocol-dependent fields, described in the section "rtable Structure" in Chapter 36, and a protocol-independent data structure of type dst_entry, shown in Figure 33-1. The dst_entry structure includes the interface to the neighboring layer and its cache, transformers (such as IPsec), and routing cache management. The section "dst_entry Structure" in Chapter 36 describes the data structure in detail, and Chapter 27 goes over the interface to the neighboring layer.

The first field of the rtable structure is a union; this makes it easy for the rtable and dst_entry structures to share values such as the pointer to the next colliding hash

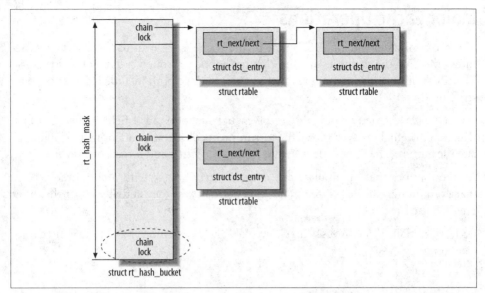

Figure 33-1. Routing cache structure

table entry. The names of the pointers differ (dst_entry uses next, whereas rtable uses rt_next), but they refer to the same memory location.

```
struct rtable
{
        union
        {
                struct dst_entry dst;
                struct rtable *rt_next;
        } u;
        ... ... ...
}
```

A pointer to an rtable structure can be safely typecast to a pointer to a dst_entry, and vice versa.

When accessing the table for an insertion, deletion, or lookup, the routing subsystem selects the bucket of the table through a combination of the source and destination IP addresses, the TOS field, and the ingress or egress device. The ingress device ID is used when routing ingress traffic, and the egress device ID is used when routing egress traffic that is locally generated. However, while there is always a known ingress device for ingress traffic, the egress device may not yet be known for egress traffic. The egress device is known only after the routing lookup, unless the routing lookup key includes the egress device (which is possible for locally generated traffic, but not necessary).

Major Cache Operations

The protocol-independent (DST) part of the cache is a set of `dst_entry` data structures. Most of the activities in this chapter happen through a `dst_entry` structure. The IPv4 and IPv6 data structures `rtable` and `rt6_info` both include a `dst_entry` data structure.

The `dst_entry` structure offers a set of virtual functions in a field named `dst_ops`, which allows higher-layer protocols to run protocol-specific functions that manipulate the entries. The DST code is located in *net/core/dst.c* and *include/net/dst.h*.

All the routines that manipulate `dst_entry` structures start with a `dst_` prefix. Note that even though they operate on `dst_entry` structures, they actually affect the outer `rtable` structures, too.

DST is initialized with `dst_init`, invoked at boot time by `net_dev_init` (see Chapter 5).

Cache Locking

Read-only operations, such as lookups, use a different locking mechanism from read-write operations such as insertion and deletion, but they naturally have to cooperate. Here is how they are handled:

Read-only operations
> These use the routines presented in the section "Cache Lookup" and are protected by a read-copy-update (RCU) read lock, as in the following snapshot:
>
> ```
> rcu_read_lock( );
> ...
> perform lookup
> ...
> rcu_read_unlock( );
> ```
> This code actually does no locking, because read operations can proceed simultaneously without interfering with each other.

Read-write operations
> The insertion of an entry (see the section "Adding Elements to the Cache") and the deletion of an entry (see the section "Deleting DST Entries") use the spin lock embedded in each bucket's element and shown in Figure 33-1. Note that the provision of a per-bucket lock lets different processors write simultaneously to different buckets.

Chapter 1 explains the RCU algorithm used to implement locking in the routing table cache, and how read-write spin locks coexist with RCU.

Cache Entry Allocation and Reference Counts

A memory pool used to allocate new cache entries is created by `ip_rt_init` at boot time. Cache entries are allocated with `dst_alloc`, which returns a void pointer that is cast by the creator to the right data type. Despite the function's name, it does not allocate `dst_entry` structures, but instead allocates the larger entries that contain those structures: `rtable` structures for IPv4 (as shown in Figure 33-1), `rt6_info` for IPv6, and so on. Because the function can be called to allocate structures of different sizes for different protocols, the size of the structure to allocate is indicated through an `entry_size` virtual function, described in the section "Interface Between the DST and Calling Protocols."

Adding Elements to the Cache

Every time a cache lookup required to route an ingress or egress packet fails, the kernel consults the routing table and stores the result into the routing cache. The kernel allocates a new cache entry with `dst_alloc`, initializes some of its fields based on the results from the routing table, and finally calls `rt_intern_hash` to insert the new entry into the cache at the head of the bucket's list. A new route is also added to the cache upon receipt of an ICMP REDIRECT message (see Chapter 25). Figures 33-2(a) and 33-2(b) shows the logic of `rt_intern_hash`. When the kernel is compiled with support for multipath caching, a cache miss may lead to the insertion of multiple routes into the cache, as discussed in the section "Multipath Caching."

The function first checks whether the new route already exists by issuing a simple cache lookup. Even though the function was called because a cache lookup failed, the route could have been added in the meantime by another CPU. If the lookup succeeds, the existing cached route is simply moved to the head of the bucket's list. (This assumes the route is not associated with a multipath route; i.e., that its DST_BALANCED flag is not set.) If the lookup fails, the new route is added to the cache.

As a simple way to keep the size of the cache under control, `rt_intern_hash` tries to remove an entry every time it adds a new one. Thus, while browsing the bucket's list, `rt_intern_hash` keeps track of the most eligible route for deletion and measures the length of the bucket's list. A route is removed only from those that are eligible for deletion (that is, routes whose reference counts are 0) and when the bucket list is longer than the configurable parameter `ip_rt_gc_elasticity`. If these conditions are met, `rt_intern_hash` invokes the `rt_score` routine to choose the best route to remove. `rt_score` ranks routes, according to many criteria, into three classes, ranging from most-valuable routes (least eligible to be removed) to least-valuable routes (most eligible to be removed):[*]

---

[*] See the section "Examples of eligible cache victims" in Chapter 30.

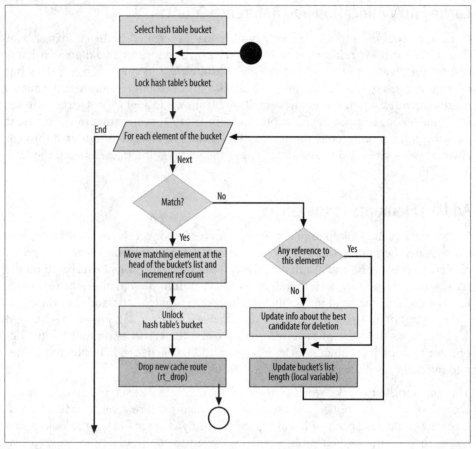

Figure 33-2(a). rt_intern_hash function

- Routes that were inserted via ICMP redirects, are being monitored by user-space commands, or are scheduled for expiration.

- Output routes (the ones used to route locally generated packets), broadcast routes, multicast routes, and routes to local addresses (for packets generated by this host for itself).

- All other routes in decreasing order of timestamp of last use: that is, least recently used routes are removed first.

rt_score simply stores the time the entry has not been used in the lower 30 bits of a local 32-bit variable, then sets the 31st bit for the first class of routes and the 32nd bit for the second class of routes. The final value is a score that represents how important that route is considered to be: the lower the score, the more likely the route is to be selected as a victim by rt_intern_hash.

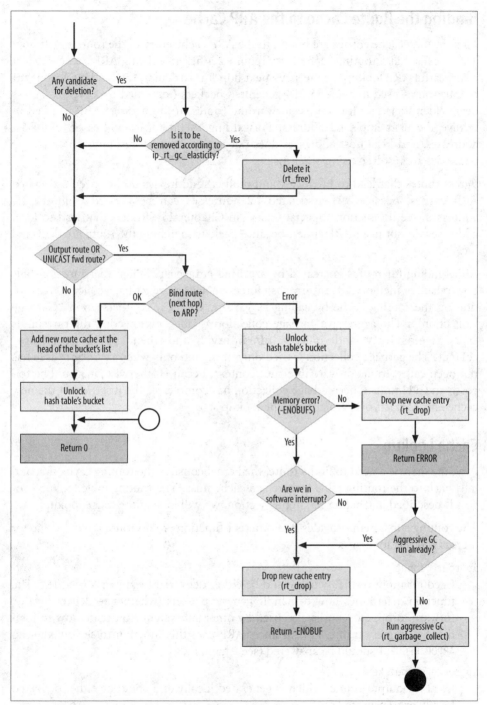

Figure 33-2(b). rt_intern_hash function

Binding the Route Cache to the ARP Cache

Most routing cache entries are bound to the ARP cache entry of the route's next hop. This means that a routing cache entry requires either an existing ARP cache entry or a successful ARP lookup for the same next hop. In particular, the binding is done for output routes used to route locally generated packets (identified by a NULL ingress device identifier) and for unicast forwarding routes. In both cases, ARP is asked to resolve the next hop's L2 address. Forwarding to broadcast addresses, multicast addresses, and local host addresses does not require an ARP resolution because the addresses are resolved using other means.

Egress routes that lead to broadcast and multicast addresses do not need associated ARP entries, because the associated L2 addresses can be derived from the L3 addresses (see the section "Special Cases" in Chapter 26). Routes that lead to local addresses do not need ARP either, because packets matching the route are delivered locally.

ARP binding for routes is created by arp_bind_neighbour. When that function fails due to lack of memory, rt_intern_hash forces an aggressive garbage collection operation on the routing cache by calling rt_garbage_collect (see the section "Garbage Collection"). The aggressive garbage collection is done by lowering the thresholds ip_rt_gc_elasticity and ip_rt_gc_min_interval and then calling rt_garbage_collect. The garbage collection is tried only once, and only when rt_intern_hash has not been called from software interrupt context, because otherwise, it would be too costly in CPU time. Once garbage collection has completed, the insertion of the new cache entries starts over from the cache lookup step.

Cache Lookup

Anytime there is a need to find a route, the kernel consults the routing cache first and falls back to the routing table if there is a cache miss. The routing table lookup process is described in Chapter 35; in this section, we will look at the cache lookup.

The routing subsystem provides two different functions to do route lookups, one for ingress and one for egress:

ip_route_input
> Used for input traffic, which could be either delivered locally or forwarded. The function determines how to handle generic packets (whether to deliver locally, forward, drop, etc.) but is also used by other subsystems to decide how to handle their ingress traffic. For instance, ARP uses this function to see whether an ARPOP_REQUEST should be answered (see Chapter 28).

ip_route_output_key
> Used for output traffic, which is generated locally and could be either delivered locally or transmitted out.

Possible return values from the two routines include:

0

The routing lookup was successful. This case includes a cache miss that triggers a successful routing table lookup.

-ENOBUF

The lookup failed due to a memory problem.

-ENODEV

The lookup key included a device identifier and it was invalid.

-EINVAL

Generic lookup failure.

The kernel also provides a set of wrappers around the two basic functions, used under specific conditions. See, for example, how TCP uses `ip_route_connect` and `ip_route_newports`.

Figure 33-3 shows the internals of two main routing cache lookup routines. The egress function shown in the figure is `__ip_route_output_key`, which is indirectly called by `ip_route_output_key`.

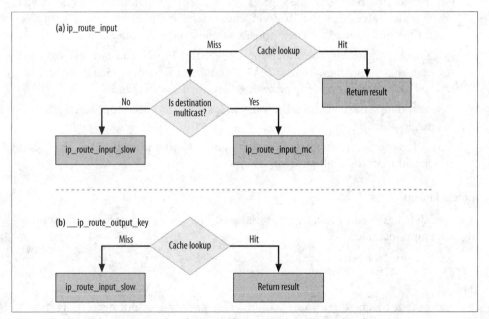

Figure 33-3. (a) ip_route_input_key function; (b) __ip_route_output_key function

The routing cache is used to store both ingress and egress routes, so a cache lookup is tried in both cases. In case of a cache miss, the functions call `ip_route_input_slow` or `ip_route_output_slow`, which consult the routing tables via the `fib_lookup` routine that we will cover in Chapter 35. The names of the functions end in `_slow` to underline the difference in speed between a lookup that is satisfied from the cache and one that requires a query of the routing tables. The two paths are also referred to as the fast and slow paths.

Once the routing decision has been taken, through either a cache hit or a routing table, and resulting either in success or failure, the lookup routines return the input buffer skb with the skb->dst->input and skb->dst->output virtual functions initialized. skb->dst is the cache entry that satisfied the routing request; in case of a cache miss, a new cache entry is created and linked to skb->dst.

The packet will then be further processed by calling either one or both of the virtual functions skb->dst->input (called via a simple wrapper named dst_input) and skb->dst->output (called via a wrapper named dst_output). Figure 18-1 in Chapter 18 shows where those two virtual functions are invoked in the IP stack, and what routines they can be initialized to depending on the direction of the traffic.

Chapter 35 goes into detail on the slow routines for the routing table lookups. The next two sections describe the internals of the two cache lookup routines in Figure 33-3. Their code is very similar; the only differences are:

- On ingress, the device of the ingress route needs to match the ingress device, whereas the egress device is not yet known and is therefore simply compared against the null device (0). The opposite applies to egress routes.

- In case of a cache hit, the functions update the in_hit and out_hit counters, respectively, using the RT_CACHE_STAT_INC macro. Statistics related to both the routing cache and the routing tables are described in Chapter 36.

- Egress lookups need to take the RTO_ONLINK flag into account (see the section "Egress lookup").

- Egress lookups support multipath caching, the feature introduced in the section "Cache Support for Multipath" in Chapter 31.

Ingress lookup

ip_route_input is used to route ingress packets. Here is its prototype and the meaning of its input parameters:

```
int ip_route_input(struct sk_buff *skb, u32 daddr, u32 saddr,
        u8 tos, struct net_device *dev)
```

skb
> Packet that triggered the route lookup. This packet does not necessarily have to be routed itself. For example, ARP uses ip_route_input to consult the local routing table for other reasons. In this case, skb would be an ingress ARP request.

saddr
daddr
> Source and destination addresses to use for the lookup.

tos

TOS field, a field of the IP header.

dev

Device the packet was received from.

ip_route_input selects the bucket of the hash table that should contain the route, based on the input criteria. It then browses the list of routes in that bucket one by one, comparing all the necessary fields until it either finds a match or gets to the end without a match.

The lookup fields passed as input to ip_route_input are compared to the fields stored in the fl field* of the routing cache entry's rtable, as shown in the following code extract. The bucket (hash variable) is chosen through a combination of input parameters. The route itself is represented by the rth variable.

```
        hash = rt_hash_code(daddr, saddr ^ (iif << 5), tos);
        rcu_read_lock();
        for (rth = rcu_dereference(rt_hash_table[hash].chain; rth;
            rth = rcu_dereference(rth->u.rt_next)) {
            if (rth->fl.fl4_dst == daddr &&
                rth->fl.fl4_src == saddr &&
                rth->fl.iif == iif &&
                rth->fl.oif == 0 &&
#ifdef CONFIG_IP_ROUTE_FWMARK
                rth->fl.fl4_fwmark == skb->nfmark &&
#endif
                rth->fl.fl4_tos == tos) {
                rth->u.dst.lastuse = jiffies;
                dst_hold(&rth->u.dst);
                rth->u.dst.__use++;
                RT_CACHE_STAT_INC(in_hit);
                rcu_read_unlock();
                skb->dst = (struct dst_entry*)rth;
                return 0;
            }
            RT_CACHE_STAT_INC(in_hlist_search);
        }
        rcu_read_unlock();
```

In the case of a cache miss for a destination address that is multicast, the packet is passed to the multicast handler ip_route_input_mc if one of the following two conditions is met, and is dropped otherwise:

- The destination address is a locally configured multicast address. This is checked with ip_check_mc.
- The destination address is not locally configured, but the kernel is compiled with support for multicast routing (CONFIG_IP_MROUTE).

---

* See the description of the flowi structure in the section "Main Data Structures" in Chapter 32.

This decision is shown in the following code:

```
if (MULTICAST(daddr)) {
    struct in_device *in_dev;

    rcu_read_lock();
    if ((in_dev = __in_dev_get(dev)) != NULL) {
        int our = ip_check_mc(in_dev, daddr, saddr,
                        skb->nh.iph->protocol);
        if (our
#ifdef CONFIG_IP_MROUTE
            || (!LOCAL_MCAST(daddr) && IN_DEV_MFORWARD(in_dev))
#endif
            ) {
            rcu_read_unlock();
            return ip_route_input_mc(skb, daddr, saddr,
                        tos, dev, our);
        }
    }
    rcu_read_unlock();
    return -EINVAL;
}
```

Finally, in the case of a cache miss for a destination address that is not multicast, ip_route_input calls ip_route_input_slow, which consults the routing table:

```
    return ip_route_input_slow(skb, daddr, saddr, tos, dev);
}
```

Egress lookup

__ip_route_output_key is used to route locally generated packets and is very similar to ip_route_input: it checks the cache first and relies on ip_route_output_slow in the case of a cache miss. When the cache supports Multipath, a cache hit requires some more work: more than one entry in the cache may be eligible for selection and the right one has to be selected based on the caching algorithm in use. The selection is done with multipath_select_route. More details can be found in the section "Multipath Caching."

Here is its prototype and the meaning of its input parameters:

```
    int __ip_route_output_key(struct rtable **rp, const struct flowi *flp)
```

rp

When the routine returns success, *rp is initialized to point to the cache entry that matched the search key flp.

flp

Search key.

A successful egress cache lookup needs to match the RTO_ONLINK flag, if it is set:

```
        !((rth->fl.fl4.tos ^ flp->fl4_tos) &
            (IPTOS_RT_MASK | RTO_ONLINK)))
```

The preceding condition is true when both of the following conditions are met:

- The TOS of the routing cache entry matches the one in the search key. Note that the TOS field is saved in the bits 2, 3, 4 and 5 of the 8-bit tos variable (as shown in Figure 18-3 in Chapter 18).*

- The RTO_ONLINK flag is set on both the routing cache entry and the search key or on neither of them.

You will see the RTO_ONLINK flag in the section "Search Key Initialization" in Chapter 35. The flag is passed via the TOS variable, but it has nothing to do with the IP header's TOS field; it simply uses an unused bit of the TOS field (see Figure 18-1 in Chapter 18). When the flag is set, it means the destination is located in a local subnet and there is no need to do a routing lookup (or, in other words, a routing lookup could fail but that would not be a problem). This is not a flag the administrator sets when configuring routes, but it is used when doing routing lookups to specify that the route type searched must have scope RT_SCOPE_LINK, which means the destination is directly connected. The flag is then saved in the associated routing cache entries when they are created. Lookups with the RTO_ONLINK flag set are made, for example, by the following protocols:

ARP
> When an administrator manually configures an ARP mapping, the kernel makes sure that the IP address belongs to one of the locally configured subnets. For example, the command *arp –s 10.0.0.1 11:22:33:44:55:66* adds the mapping of 10.0.0.1 to 11:22:33:44:55:66 to the ARP cache. This command would be rejected by the kernel if, according to its routing table, the IP address 10.0.0.1 did not belong to one of the locally configured subnets (see arp_req_set and Chapter 26).

Raw IP and UDP
> When sending data over a socket, the user can set the MSG_DONTROUTE flag. This flag is used when an application is transmitting a packet out from a known interface to a destination that is directly connected (there is no need for a gateway), so the kernel does not have to determine the egress device. This kind of transmission is used, for instance, by routing protocols and diagnostic applications.

Multipath Caching

The concepts behind this feature are introduced in the section "Cache Support for Multipath" in Chapter 31. When the kernel is compiled with support for multipath

---

* The TOS field, as shown in Figure 18-3 in Chapter 18, is an 8-bit field, of which bit 0 is ignored and bit 1 through 7 are used. However, the routing code uses only the bits 1, 2, 3 and 4. It does not take the precedence component (bits 5, 6, 7) into consideration for egress routes. Those bits are masked out with the macro RT_TOS.

caching, the lookup code adds multiple routes to the cache, as shown in the section "Multipath Caching" in Chapter 35. In this section, we will examine the key routines used to implement this feature, and the interface provided by caching algorithms.

Registering a Caching Algorithm

Caching algorithms are defined with an instance of the `ip_mp_alg_ops` data structure, which consists of function pointers. Depending on the needs of the caching algorithm, not all function pointers may be initialized, but one is mandatory: `mp_alg_select_route`.

Algorithms register and unregister with the kernel, respectively, using `multipath_alg_register` and `multipath_alg_unregister`. All the algorithms are implemented as modules in the *net/ipv4/* directory.

Interface Between the Routing Cache and Multipath

For each function pointer of the `ip_mp_alg_ops` data structure, the kernel defines a wrapper in *include/net/ip_mp_alg.h*. Here is when each one is called:

`multipath_select_route`
> This is the most important routine. It selects the right route from the ones in the cache that satisfy a given lookup (because they are associated with the same multipath route). This routine is called by `__ip_route_output_key`, the lookup function we saw earlier.

`multipath_flush`
> Clears any state kept by the algorithm when the cache is flushed. It is called by `rt_cache_flush` (see the section "Flushing the Routing Cache").

`multipath_set_nhinfo`
> Updates the state information kept by the algorithm when a new multipath route is cached.

`multipath_remove`
> Removes the right routes in the cache when a multipath route is removed (for example, by `rt_free`).

None of the algorithms supports `multipath_remove`, and only the weighted random algorithm uses `multipath_flush` and `multipath_set_nhinfo`.

In later sections, we will see what state information the various algorithms need to keep, and how they implement the `mp_alg_select_route` routine.

Helper Routines

Here are a couple of routines used by the multipath code:

`multipath_comparekeys`

Compares two route selectors. It is used mainly by the `mp_alg_select_route` algorithm's functions to find cached routes that are associated with the same multipath route as another cached route.

`rt_remove_balanced_routes`

Given an input cached route, removes it and all the other cached routes on the same hash table's bucket that are associated with the same multipath route. The last input parameter to `rt_remove_balanced_routes` returns the number of cached routes removed. The function's return value is the next `rtable` instance in the hash bucket's list that follows the input parameter's route. This return value is used by the caller to resume its scan on the table from the right position. When `rt_remove_balanced_routes` removes the last `rtable` instance of the bucket's list, it returns NULL.

Common Elements Between Algorithms

Keeping the following three points in mind will help you understand the code that deals with multipath caching, and in particular, the implementation of the `mp_alg_select_route` routine provided by the caching algorithms:

- Entries of the routing cache associated with multipath routes can be recognized thanks to the `DST_BALANCED` flag, which is set prior to their insertion into the cache (see the section "dst_entry Structure" in Chapter 36). We will see exactly how and when this is done in Chapter 35. This flag is often used in the routing cache code to apply different actions, depending on whether a given entry of the cache is associated with a multipath route.

- The `dst_entry` structure used to define cached routes includes a timestamp of last use (`dst->lastuse`). Each time a cached route is returned by a cache lookup, this timestamp is updated for the route. Cache entries associated with multipath routes need to be handled specially. When the cache entry returned by a lookup is associated with a multipath route, all the other entries of the cache associated with the same multipath route must have their timestamps updated, too. This is necessary to avoid having routes purged by the garbage collection algorithm.

- The input to the `mp_alg_select_route` routine is the first cache entry that matches the lookup key. Given how elements are added to the routing table cache, all the other entries of the cache associated with the same multipath route are located within the same bucket. For this reason, `mp_alg_select_route` will browse the bucket list starting from the input cache element and identify the other routes thanks to the `DST_BALANCED` flag and the `multipath_comparekeys` routine.

Random Algorithm

This algorithm does not need to keep any state information, and therefore it does not need any memory to be allocated, nor does it take up significant CPU time to make its decisions. All the algorithm does is browse the routes of the input table's bucket, count the number of routes eligible for selection, generate a random number with the local routine random, and select the right cache entry based on that random number.

The algorithm is defined in *net/ipv4/multipath_random.c*.

Weighted Random Algorithm

This is the algorithm with the most complicated implementation. Each next hop of a multipath route can be assigned a weight. The algorithm selects the right next hop (i.e., the right route in the cache) randomly and proportionally to the weights.

For each multipath route's next hop there is an instance of the fib_nh data structure that stores the weight, among other parameters. We will see in Chapter 34 where those data structures are located in the routing table. In particular, you can refer to Figure 34-1 in that chapter.

The section "Weighted Random Algorithm" in Chapter 31 explains the basic concepts behind this algorithm. To help make a quick decision, the algorithm builds a local database of information that it uses to access fib_nh instances and to read the weights of the next hops. Figure 33-4 shows what that database would look like after configuration of the following two multipath routes:

```
# ip route add 10.0.1.0/24 mpath wrandom nexthop via 192.168.1.1 weight 1
                                         nexthop via 192.168.2.1 weight 2
# ip route add 10.0.2.0/24 mpath wrandom nexthop via 192.168.1.1 weight 5
                                         nexthop via 192.168.2.1 weight 1
```

The database is actually not built right away when the multipath routes are defined: it is populated at lookup time.

Remember that the input to the mp_alg_select_route routine (wrandom_select_route in this case) is the first cached route of the routing cache that matches the search key. All other eligible cached routes will be in the same routing cache bucket.

Selection of the route by mp_alg_select_route is accomplished in two steps:

1. mp_alg_select_route first browses the routing cache's bucket, and for each route, checks whether it is eligible for selection with the multipath_comparekeys routine. In the meantime, it creates a local list of eligible cached routes, with the main goal of defining a line like the one in Figure 31-4 in Chapter 31. Figure 33-5 shows what the list would look like for the example in that chapter. Each route added to the list gets its weight using the database in Figure 33-4 and initializes the power field accordingly.

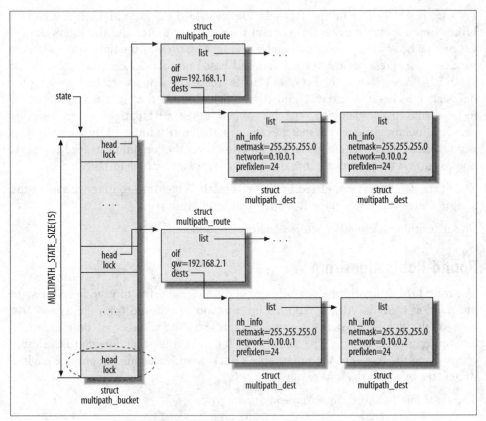

Figure 33-4. Next-hop database created by the weighted random algorithm

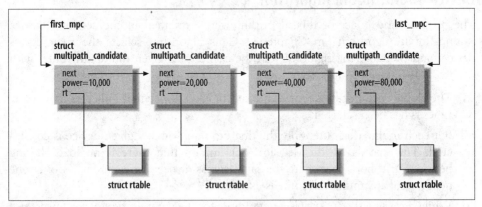

Figure 33-5. Example of temporary list created for the next-hop selection

2. `mp_alg_select_route` generates a random number and, given the list of eligible routes, selects one route using the mechanism described in the section "Weighted Random Algorithm" in Chapter 31.

Let's see how a lookup on the state database works. Let's keep in mind that cached routes (that is, rtable instances) contain the next hop router and the egress device. Given a cached route, __multipath_lookup_weight first selects the right state's bucket based on the egress device: state is indexed based on that device. Once a bucket of state has been selected, the list of multipath_route elements is scanned, looking for one that matches the gateway and device fields. Once the right multipath_route instance has been identified, the list of associated multipath_dest structures is scanned, looking for one that matches the destination IP address of the input lookup key fl. From the matching multipath_dest instance, the function can read the next-hop weight via the pointer nh_info that points to the right fib_nh instance.

The state database is populated by the multipath_set_nhinfo routine we saw in the section "Interface Between the Routing Cache and Multipath."

This algorithm is defined in *net/ipv4/multipath_random.c*.

Round-Robin Algorithm

The round-robin algorithm does not need additional data structures to keep the state information it needs. All the required information is retrieved from the dst->__use field of the dst_entry structure, which represents the number of times a cache lookup returned the route. The selection of the right route therefore consists simply of browsing the routes of the input table's bucket, and selecting, among the eligible routes, the one with the lowest value of __use.

The algorithm is defined in *net/ipv4/multipath_rr.c*.

Device Round-Robin Algorithm

The purpose and effect of this algorithm were explained in the section "Device Round-Robin Algorithm" in Chapter 31. This algorithm selects the right egress device, and therefore the right entry in the cache for a given multipath route, with the drr_select_route routine as follows:

1. The global vector state keeps a counter for each device that indicates how many times is has been selected.

2. For each multipath route, only the first next hop on any given device is considered. This speeds up the decision but implies that there is no load sharing between next hops that share the same egress device: for each device, only one next hop of any multipath route is used.

3. While browsing the routes (i.e., next hops) for the computation of the lowest use count, routes associated with devices that have not been used yet are given higher preference. When a new device is selected, a new entry is added to state.

4. The first route analyzed for the device with the lowest use count is selected.

The algorithm is defined in *net/ipv4/multipath_drr.c*.

Interface Between the DST and Calling Protocols

The DST cache is an independent subsystem; it has, for instance, its own garbage collection mechanism. As a subsystem, it provides a set of functions that various protocols can use to change or tune its behavior. When external subsystems need to interact with the routing cache, such as to notify it of an event or read the value of one of its parameters, they do it via a set of DST routines defined in the files *net/core/dst.c* and *include/net/dst.h*. These routines are wrappers around a set of functions made available by the L3 protocol that owns the cache, by initializing an instance of a dst_ops VFT, as shown in Figure 33-6.

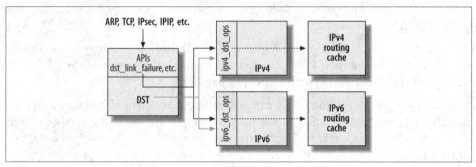

Figure 33-6. dst_ops interface

The key structure presented by DST to higher layers is dst_entry; protocol-specific structures such as rtable are merely wrappers for this structure. IP owns the routing cache, but other protocols often keep references to routing cache elements. All of those references refer to dst_entry, not to its rtable wrapper. The sk_buff buffers also keep a reference to the dst_entry structure, not to the rtable structure. This reference is used to store the result of the routing lookup.

The dst_entry and dst_ops structures are described in detail in the associated sections in Chapter 36. There is an instance of dst_ops for each protocol; for example, IPv4 uses ipv4_dst_ops, initialized in *net/ipv4/route.c*:

```
struct dst_ops ipv4_dst_ops = {
    .family =           AF_INET,
    .protocol =         __constant_htons(ETH_P_IP),
    .gc =               rt_garbage_collect,
    .check =            ipv4_dst_check,
    .destroy =          ipv4_dst_destroy,
    .ifdown =           ipv4_dst_ifdown,
    .negative_advice =  ipv4_negative_advice,
    .link_failure =     ipv4_link_failure,
    .update_pmtu =      ip_rt_update_pmtu,
    .entry_size =       sizeof(struct rtable),
};
```

Whenever the DST subsystem is notified of an event or a request is made via one of the DST interface routines, the protocol associated with the affected dst_entry instance is notified by an invocation of the proper function among the ones provided by the dst_entry through its instance of the dst_ops VFT. For example, if ARP would like to notify the upper protocol about the unreachability of a given IPv4 address, it calls dst_link_failure for the associated dst_entry structure (remember that cached routes are associated with IP addresses, not with networks), which will invoke the ipv4_link_failure routine registered by IPv4 via ipv4_dst_ops.

It is also possible for the calling protocol to intervene directly in DST's behavior. For example, when IPv4 asks DST to allocate a new cache entry, DST may then realize there is a need to start garbage collection and invoke rt_garbage_collect, the routine provided by IPv4 itself.

When a given type of notification requires some kind of processing common to all the protocols, the common logic may be implemented directly inside the DST APIs instead of being replicated in each protocol's handler.

Some virtual functions in the DST's dst_ops structure are invoked through wrappers in higher layers; functions that do not have a wrapper are invoked directly through the syntax dst->ops->*function*. Here is the meaning of the dst_ops virtual functions and a brief description of the IPv4 subsystem's routines (listed in the preceding snapshot of code) that would be assigned to them:

gc

Takes care of garbage collection. It is run when the subsystem allocates a new cache entry with dst_alloc and that function realizes there is a shortage of memory. The IPv4 routine rt_garbage_collect is described in the section "Synchronous Cleanup."

check

A cached route whose dst_entry is marked as dead is normally not usable. However, there is one case, where IPsec is in use, where that's not necessarily true. This routine is used to check whether an obsolete dst_entry is usable. For instance, look at the ipv4_dst_check routine, which performs no check on the submitted dst_entry structure before removing it, and compare it to the corresponding xfrm_dst_check routine used to do "xfrm" transforms for IPsec. Also see how routines such as sk_dst_check (introduced in Chapter 21) check the status of a cached route. There is no wrapper for this function.

destroy

Called by dst_destroy, the routine that the DST runs to delete a dst_entry structure, and informs the calling protocol of the deletion to give it a chance to do any necessary cleanup first. For example, the IPv4 routine ipv4_dst_destroy uses the notification to release references to other data structures. dst_destroy is described in the section "Deleting DST Entries."

ifdown

> Called by `dst_ifdown`, which is invoked by the DST subsystem itself when a device is shut down or unregistered. It is called once for each affected cached route (see the section "External Events"). The IPv4 routine `ipv4_dst_ifdown` replaces the `rtable`'s pointer to the device's IP configuration `idev` with a pointer to the loopback device, because that is always sure to exist.

negative_advice

> Called by the DST function `dst_negative_advice`, which is used to notify the DST about a problem with a `dst_entry` instance. For example, TCP uses `dst_negative_advice` when it detects a write timeout.

> The IPv4's routine `ipv4_negative_advice` uses this notification to delete the cached route. When the `dst_entry` is already marked as dead (through its `dst->obsolete` flag, as we will see in the section "Deleting DST Entries"), `ipv4_negative_advice` simply releases the `rtable`'s reference to the `dst_entry`.

link_failure

> Called by the DST function `dst_link_failure`, which is invoked when a transmission problem is detected due to an unreachable destination.

> As an example of this function's use, the neighbor protocols ARP and Neighbor Discovery—used by IPv4 and IPv6, respectively—invoke it to indicate that they never received a reply to solicitation requests they generated to resolve an L3-to-L2 address association. (They can usually tell this because of a timeout; see, for example, `arp_error_report` in *net/ipv4/arp.c* for the behavior of the ARP protocol.) Other higher-layer protocols, such as the various tunnels (IP over IP, etc.), do the same when they have problems reaching the other end of a tunnel, which could be several hops away; see, for example, `ipip_tunnel_xmit` in *net/ipv4/ipip.c* for the IP-over-IP tunneling protocol.

update_pmtu

> Updates the PMTU of a cached route. It is usually invoked to handle the reception of an ICMP Fragmentation Needed message. See the section "Processing Ingress ICMP_REDIRECT Messages" in Chapter 31. There is no wrapper for this function.

get_mss

> Returns the TCP maximum segment size that can be used on this route. IPv4 does not initialize this routine, and there is no wrapper for this function. See the section "IPsec Transformations and the Use of dst_entry."

Besides the wrappers around the functions just shown, the DST also manipulates `dst_entry` instances through functions that do not need to interact with other subsystems. For example, the section "Asynchronous Cleanup" shows `dst_set_expires`, and Chapter 26 shows how `dst_confirm` is used to confirm the reachability of a neighbor. See the files *net/core/dst.c* and *include/net/dst.h* for more details.

IPsec Transformations and the Use of dst_entry

In the previous sections, we saw the most common use for dst_entry structures: to store the protocol-independent information regarding a cached route, including the input and output methods that process the packets to be received or transmitted after a routing lookup.

Another use for dst_entry structures is made by IPsec, a suite of protocols used to provide secure services such as authentication and confidentiality on top of IP. IPsec uses dst_entry structures to build what it calls *transformation bundles*. A *transformation* is an operation to apply to a packet, such as encryption. A *bundle* is just a set of transformations defined as a sequence of operations. Once the IPsec protocols decide on all the transformations to apply to the traffic that matches a given route, that information is stored in the routing cache as a list of dst_entry structures.

Normally, a route is associated with a single dst_entry structure whose input and output fields describe how to process the matching packets (forward, deliver locally, etc., as shown in Figure 18-1 in Chapter 18). But IPsec creates a list of dst_entry instances where only the last instance uses input and output to actually apply the routing decisions; the previous instances use input and output to apply the required transformations, as shown in Figure 33-7 (the model in the figure is a simplified one).

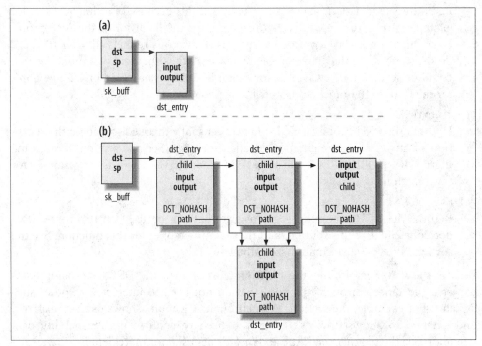

Figure 33-7. Use of dst_entry (a) without IPsec; (b) with IPsec

dst_entry lists are created using the child pointer in the structure. Another pointer named path, also used by IPsec, points to the last element of the list (the one that would be created even when IPsec is not in use).

Each of the other dst_entry elements in the list—that is, each element except the last—is there to implement an IPsec transformation. Each sets its path field to point to the last element. In addition, each sets its DST_NOHASH flag so that the DST subsystem knows it is not part of the routing cache hash table and that another subsystem is taking care of it.

The implications of IPsec on routing lookups are as follows: both input and output routing lookups are affected by the data structure layout shown for IPsec configuration in Figure 33-7(b). The result returned by a lookup is a pointer to the first dst_entry that implements a transformation, not the last one representing the real routing information. This is because the first dst_entry instance represents the first transformation to be applied, and the transformations must be applied in order.

You can find interactions between the IP or routing layer and IPsec in several other places:

- For egress traffic, ip_route_output_flow (which is called by ip_route_output_key, introduced in the section "Cache Lookup") includes extra code (i.e., a call to xfrm_lookup) to interact with IPsec.

- For ingress traffic that is to be delivered locally, ip_local_deliver_finish calls xfrm4_policy_check to consult the IPsec policy database.

- ip_forward makes the same check for ingress traffic that needs to be forwarded.

Sometimes the IP code makes a direct call to the generic xfrm_xxx IPsec routines, and sometimes it uses IPv4 wrappers with the names xfrm4_xxx.

External Events

When dst_init initializes the DST subsystem, it registers with the device event notification chain netdev_chain, introduced in Chapter 4. The only two events the DST is interested in are the ones generated when a network device goes down (NETDEV_DOWN) and when a device is unregistered (NETDEV_UNREGISTER). You can find the complete list of NETDEV_XXX events in *include/linux/notifier.h*.

When a device becomes unusable, either because it is not available anymore (for instance, it has been unregistered from the kernel), or because it has simply been shut down for administrative reasons, all the routes using that device become unusable as well. This means that both the routing tables and the routing cache need to be notified about this kind of event and react accordingly. We will see how the routing tables are handled in Chapter 34. Here we will see how the routing cache is cleaned up. The dst_entry structures for cached routes can be inserted in one of two places:

- The routing cache.
- The dst_garbage_list list. Here deleted routes wait for all their references to be released, to become eligible for deletion by the garbage collection process.

The entries in the cache are taken care of by the notification handler fib_netdev_event (described in the section "Impacts on the routing tables" in Chapter 32), which, among other actions, flushes the cache. The ones in the dst_garbage_list list are taken care of by the routine that DST registers with the netdev_chain notification chain. As shown in the following snippet from *net/core/dst.c*, the handler DST uses to process the received notifications is dst_dev_event:

```
static struct notifier_block dst_dev_notifier = {
    .notifier_call = dst_dev_event,
};

void __init dst_init(void)
{
    register_netdevice_notifier(&dst_dev_notifier);
}
```

dst_dev_event browses the dst_garbage_list list of dead dst_entry structures and invokes dst_ifdown for each one. The last input parameter to dst_ifdown tells it what event it is being called to handle. Here is how it handles the two event types:

NETDEV_UNREGISTER
> When the device is unregistered, all references to it have to be removed. dst_ifdown replaces them with references to the loopback device, for both the dst_entry structure and its associated neighbour instance, if any.[*]

NETDEV_DOWN
> Because the device is down, traffic cannot be sent to it anymore. Therefore, the input and output routines of dst_entry are set to dst_discard_in and dst_discard_out, respectively. These two routines simply discard any input buffer passed to them (i.e., any frame they are asked to process).

We saw in the section "IPsec Transformations and the Use of dst_entry" that a dst_entry structure could be linked to other ones through the child pointer. dst_ifdown goes child by child and updates all of them. The input and output routines are updated only for the last entry, because that entry is the one that uses the routines for reception or transmission.

We saw in Chapter 8 that unregistering a device triggers not only a NETDEV_UNREGISTER notification but also a NETDEV_DOWN notification, because a device has to be shut down to be unregistered. This means that both events handled by dst_dev_event occur when a device is unregistered. This explains why dst_ifdown checks its

[*] See the section "L2 Header Caching" in Chapter 27.

unregister parameter and deliberately skips part of its code when the parameter is set, while running other parts only when it is set.

Flushing the Routing Cache

Whenever a change in the system takes place that could cause some of the information in the cache to become out of date, the kernel flushes the routing cache. In many cases, only selected entries are out of date, but to keep things simple the kernel removes all entries. The main events that trigger flushing are:

A device comes up or goes down
> Some addresses that used to be reachable through a given device may not be reachable anymore, or may be reachable through a different device with a better route.

An IP address is added to or removed from a device
> We saw in the sections "Adding an IP address" and "Removing an IP address" in Chapter 32 that Linux creates a special route for each locally configured IP address. When an address is removed, any associated route in the cache also has to be removed. The removed address was most likely configured with a netmask different from /32, so all the cache entries associated with addresses within the same subnet should go away* as well. Finally, if one of the addresses in the same subnet was used as a gateway for other indirect routes, all of them should go away. Flushing the entire cache is simpler than keeping track of all of these possible cases.

The global forwarding status, or the forwarding status of a device, has changed
> If you disable forwarding, you need to remove all the cached routes that were used to forward traffic. See the section ""Enabling and Disabling Forwarding" in Chapter 36.

A route is removed
> All the cached entries associated with the deleted route need to be removed.

An administrative flush is requested via the /proc interface
> This is described in the section "The /proc/sys/net/ipv4/route Directory" in Chapter 36.

The routine used to flush the cache is rt_run_flush, but it is never called directly. Requests to flush the cache are done via rt_cache_flush, which will either flush the cache right away or start a timer, depending on the value of the input timeout provided by the caller:

---

* This is not true when you remove a secondary address. See the section "Removing an IP address" in Chapter 32.

Less than 0

> The cache is flushed after the number of seconds specified by the kernel parameter `ip_rt_min_delay`, which can be tuned via */proc* as described in the section "The /proc/sys/net/ipv4/route Directory" in Chapter 36.

0

> The cache is flushed right away.

Greater than 0

> The cache is flushed after the specified amount of time.

Once a flush request is submitted, a flush is guaranteed to take place within `ip_rt_max_delay` seconds, which is set to 8 by default. When a flush request is submitted and there is already one pending, the timer is restarted to reflect the new request; however, the new request cannot ask the timer to expire later than `ip_rt_max_delay` seconds since the previous timer was fired. This is accomplished by using the global variable `rt_deadline`.

In addition, the cache is periodically flushed by means of a periodic timer, `rt_secret_timer`, that expires every `ip_rt_secret_interval` seconds (see the section "The /proc/sys/net/ipv4/route Directory" in Chapter 36 for its default value). When the timer expires, the handler `rt_secret_rebuild` flushes the cache and restarts the timer. `ip_rt_secret_interval` is configurable via */proc*.

Garbage Collection

As explained in the section "Routing Cache Garbage Collection" in Chapter 30, there are two kinds of garbage collection:

- To free memory when a shortage is detected. This is actually split into two tasks, one synchronous and one asynchronous. The synchronous task is triggered at irregular times by particular conditions, and the asynchronous task runs more or less regularly at the expiration of a timer.

- To clean up `dst_entry` structures that the kernel asked to be removed, but that could not be deleted right away because someone still held a reference to them.

This section covers both the synchronous and asynchronous cases of the first type of garbage collection. The section "Deleting DST Entries" goes into detail on the other type.

Both synchronous and asynchronous garbage collection use a common routine to decide whether a given `dst_entry` instance is eligible for deletion: `rt_may_expire`. The routine accepts two parameters (`tmo1`, `tmo2`) that represent the minimum time that candidates must have spent in the cache before being eligible for deletion. Specifically, `tmo2` applies to those candidates that are considered particularly good for deletion, and `tmo1` applies to all the other candidates, as described in the section

"Examples of eligible cache victims" in Chapter 30. The ip_rt_gc_timeout parameter specifies the time for other entries in the cache.

The lower those two values are, the more likely it is that entries will be deleted. That's why, as shown in the section "Asynchronous Cleanup," rt_check_expire halves the local variable tmo every time an entry is not removed. As we will see in the section "rt_garbage_collect Function," rt_garbage_collect does the same with both thresholds.

Synchronous Cleanup

A synchronous cleanup is triggered when the DST subsystem detects a shortage of memory. While it is up to the DST to decide when to trigger garbage collection, the routine that takes care of it is provided by the protocol that owns the cache. Everything is controlled through the dst_ops virtual functions introduced in the section "Interface Between the DST and Calling Protocols." We saw there that dst_ops has a function called gc, which IPv4 initializes to rt_garbage_collect. gc is invoked in the following two cases:

- When a new entry is added to the routing cache and a memory shortage comes up. When adding an entry, rt_intern_hash has to bind the route to the neighbour data structure associated with the next hop (see the section "Binding the Route Cache to the ARP Cache"). If there is not enough memory to allocate a new neighbour data structure, the routing cache is scanned in an attempt to free some memory. This is done because there could be some cache entries that have not been used for a while, and removing them could allow the associated neighbour entries to be removed, too. (I said "could" allow it, because as we know, a data structure cannot be removed until all the references to it have been removed.)

- When a new entry is added to the routing cache and the total number of entries exceeds the threshold gc_thresh. The dst_alloc function that allocates the entry triggers a cleanup to keep down memory use by restricting the cache to a fixed size. gc_thresh is configurable via /proc (see the section "Tuning via /proc Filesystem" in Chapter 36).

The next section gives the internals of rt_garbage_collect.

rt_garbage_collect Function

The logic of rt_garbage_collect is described in Figures 33-8(a) and 33-8(b).

The garbage collection done by the rt_garbage_collect routine is expensive in terms of CPU time. Therefore, the routine returns without doing anything if less than ip_rt_gc_min_interval seconds have passed since the last invocation, unless the number

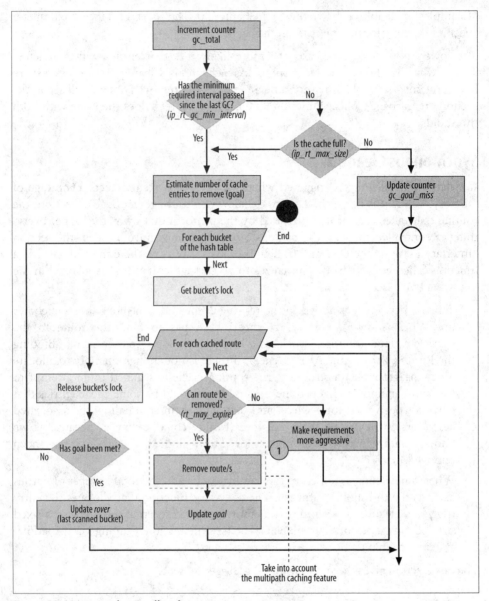

Figure 33-8(a). rt_garbage_collect function

of entries in the cache reached the maximum value `ip_rt_max_size`, which requires immediate attention.

`ip_rt_max_size` is a hard limit. Once that threshold is reached, `dst_alloc` fails until `rt_garbage_collect` manages to free some memory.

Here is the logical structure of `rt_garbage_collect`:

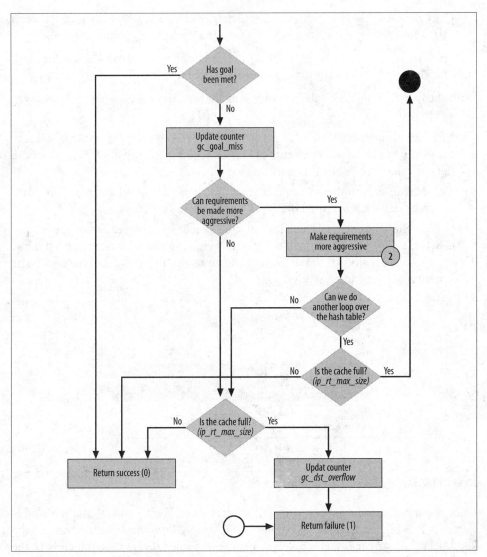

Figure 33-8(b). rt_garbage_collect function

- First it computes the number of cache entries it would like to remove (goal). From this value and the number of entries currently in the cache (ipv4_dst_ops.entries), it derives the number of entries that would be left once goal entries are removed, and stores this number in equilibrium.

- It browses the hash table and tries to expire the most-eligible entries, checking their eligibility with rt_may_expire. Entries eligible for deletion are deleted with rt_free directly or with rt_remove_balanced_route, depending on whether they are associated with multipath routes (see the section "Helper Routines").

- Once the table has been scanned completely, it checks whether the goal has been met, and if not, it repeats the loop with more-aggressive eligibility criteria.

The number of entries to remove (goal) depends on how heavily loaded the hash table is. The goal is to expire entries faster when the table is more heavily loaded.

With the help of Figure 33-9, let's clarify some of the thresholds used by rt_garbage_ collect to define goal:

- The size of the hash table is rt_hash_mask+1, or $2^{rt\_hash\_log}$. rt_garbage_collect is called when the number of entries in the cache is bigger than gc_thresh, whose default value is the size of the hash table.

- The maximum number of entries that the cache can hold is ip_rt_max_size, which by default is set to 16 times the size of the hash table.

- When the number of entries in the cache is bigger than ip_rt_gc_ elasticity*$(2^{rt\_hash\_log})$, which by default is eight times the size of the hash table, the cache is considered to be dangerously large and the garbage collection starts setting goal more aggressively.

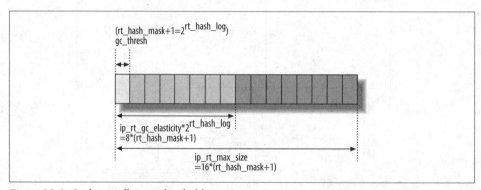

Figure 33-9. Garbage collection thresholds

Once the thresholds have been defined, rt_garbage_collect browses the hash table elements looking for victims. The table is not simply browsed from the first to the last bucket. rt_garbage_collect keeps a static variable, rover, that remembers the last bucket that was scanned at the previous invocation. This is because the table does not necessarily need to be scanned completely. By remembering the last scanned bucket, the routine handles all the buckets fairly, instead of always selecting victims from the first buckets. Victims are identified by rt_may_expire. This routine, already described in the section "Garbage Collection," is passed two time thresholds that define how two categories of entries should be considered eligible for deletion. While scanning elements of a bucket, one of the thresholds is lowered (halved) every time an element is not selected. At the end of each bucket's list, the function checks again whether the number of deleted entries meets the goal set at the beginning of the function (goal). If not, the function goes ahead with the next bucket. This continues until the whole table has been scanned. At that point, the function lowers the value of the second time threshold passed to rt_max_expire, to make it even more likely to find eligible victims. Then a new scan over the table starts, if it would not be too time consuming. The new scan is considered too time consuming and is skipped if the routine was called in software interrupt context, or if the previous scan took more than one jiffies of time (e.g., 1/1000 of a second on an x86 platform).

Asynchronous Cleanup

Synchronous garbage collection is used to handle specific cases of memory shortage; but it would be better to avoid waiting for extreme conditions to emerge before taking action: in other words, it is better to make extreme conditions less likely. This is what the asynchronous cleanup does by means of a periodic timer.

The timer, rt_periodic_timer, is started by ip_rt_init when the routing subsystem is initialized, and invokes the handler rt_check_expire every time it expires. Each time it is invoked, rt_check_expire scans just a part of the cache. It keeps a static variable (rover) to remember the last bucket it scanned at the previous invocation and starts scanning each time from the next one. rt_check_expire restarts the timer and returns when it has finished scanning the entire table or has run for at least one jiffies.

Entries are removed with rt_free if their time in the cache has expired, or if they are considered eligible by rt_may_expire. When the entry is associated with a multipath route, the deletion is taken care of by rt_remove_balanced_route.

```
            while ((rth = *rthp) != NULL) {
                if (rth->u.dst.expires) {
                    if (time_before_eq(now, rth->u.dst.expires)) {
                        tmo >>= 1;
                        rthp = &rth->u.rt_next;
                        continue;
                    }
                } else if (!rt_may_expire(rth, tmo, ip_rt_gc_timeout)) {
                    tmo >>= 1;
                    rthp = &rth->u.rt_next;
                    continue;
                }
                /* Cleanup aged off entries. */
#ifdef CONFIG_IP_ROUTE_MULTIPATH_CACHED
                /* remove all related balanced entries if necessary */
                if (rth->u.dst.flags & DST_BALANCED) {
                    rthp = rt_remove_balanced_route(
                        &rt_hash_table[i].chain,
                        rth, NULL);
                    if (!rthp)
                        break;
                } else {
                    *rthp = rth->u.rt_next;
                    rt_free(rth);
```

```
            }
#else /* CONFIG_IP_ROUTE_MULTIPATH_CACHED */
            *rthp = rth->u.rt_next;
            rt_free(rth);
#endif /* CONFIG_IP_ROUTE_MULTIPATH_CACHED */
        }
        ...
        if (time_after(jiffies, now)))
            break;
```

The timer expires by default every `ip_rt_gc_interval` seconds, whose value is 60 by default but can be changed via the */proc/sys/net/ipv4/route/gc_interval* file (see the section "Tuning via /proc Filesystem" in Chapter 4). The first time the timer fires, it is set to expire after a random number of seconds between `ip_rt_gc_interval` and `2*ip_rt_gc_interval` (see `ip_rt_init`). The reason for using the random value is to avoid the possibility that timers from different kernel subsystems might expire at the same time and use up the CPU. This is conceivable if many subsystems start up at the same time during the boot process and schedule times at regular intervals.

Expiration Criteria

By default, routing cache entries never expire because `dst_entry->expires` is 0.* When an event that can expire cache entries occurs (see the section "Examples of events that can expire cache entries" in Chapter 30), entries are expired by setting their `dst_entry->expires` timestamp field to a nonzero value with `dst_set_expires`†:

- When an ICMP UNREACHABLE or FRAGMENTATION NEEDED message is received, the PMTU of all the related routes (those that have the same destination IP as the one specified by the IP header carried in the payload of the ICMP message) must be updated to the MTU specified in the ICMP header. Thus, the ICMP core code calls `ip_rt_frag_needed` to update the routing cache. The affected entries are set to expire after the configurable time `ip_rt_mtu_expires`, which by default is 10 minutes and can be changed with */proc/sys/net/route/mtu_expires*. See Chapter 25 for more details.

- When the TCP code updates the MTU of a route with the path MTU discovery algorithm, it calls the `ip_rt_update_mtu` function, which in turns calls `dst_set_expires`. Refer to Chapter 18 for more details on path MTU discovery.

- When a destination IP address is classified as unreachable, the associated `dst_entry` structure in the cache is marked as unreachable by directly or indirectly calling the `link_failure` method of the `dst_ops` data structure (see the section "Interface Between the DST and Calling Protocols").

---

* The `dst_entry->expires` field is set in `dst_alloc` with a global `memset` call.

† Note that when `dst_set_expires` is called to expire an entry immediately, it replaces the input value of 0 with 1, to distinguish this situation from the 0 that means never to expire.

Deleting DST Entries

In the previous sections, we saw how rtable cache entries are deleted by synchronous or asynchronous cleanups and background garbage collection. In this section, we will see how the embedded dst_entry structures are taken care of. The function that deletes a dst_entry is dst_free.

The reference count on a dst_entry is incremented and decremented with dst_hold and dst_release, respectively. But when dst_release is called to release the last reference, the entry is not deleted automatically. Instead, it is removed indirectly when the associated rtable structures are removed with rt_free and rt_drop. These functions schedule the execution of dst_free via dst_rcu_free, which takes care of the RCU mechanisms (see the section "Cache Locking").

We saw in the section "IPsec Transformations and the Use of dst_entry" that dst_entry structures are not always embedded into rtable structures. Standalone instances are removed by calling dst_free directly.

The removal of a dst_entry is not complex, but there are a couple of points that need to be covered to understand how dst_free and its helper routines work:

- When an entry cannot be removed because it is still referenced, it is marked as dead by setting its obsolete flag to 2 (the default value for dst->obsolete is 0). An attempt to delete an entry that is already dead fails.

- As we saw in the section "IPsec Transformations and the Use of dst_entry," a dst_entry instance could have children. When deleting the first dst_entry of a list, the routing subsystem has to delete all the others as well. But at the same time, you need to keep in mind that any entry cannot be removed so long as some references are left to it.

Given these two points, let's see now how dst_free works.

When dst_free is called to remove an entry whose reference count is 0, it removes the entry right away with dst_destroy. The latter function also tries to remove any children linked to the structure. When one of the children cannot be removed because it is still referenced, dst_destroy returns a pointer to the child so that dst_free can take care of it.

When dst_free is called to remove an entry whose reference count is not 0—which includes the case just described, when dst_destroy could not delete a child—it does the following:

- Marks the entry as dead by setting its obsolete flag.

- Replaces the entry's input and output routines with two fake ones, dst_discard_in and dst_discard_out. These ensure that no reception or transmission is attempted on the associated routes (see the description of input and output in the section "dst_entry Structure" in Chapter 36). This initialization is typical of a device that is not yet operative, or in a down state (the flag IFF_UP is not set).

We saw in the section "External Events" that when the two events handled by dst_dev_event occur, dst_ifdown is called to take care of the dst_entry structures in the dst_garbage_list. In particular, it replaces their current input and output methods with dst_discard_in and dst_discard_out. This is not superfluous, because dst_free does this only when the dst_entry it is called to free is associated with a device being shut down, which is not necessarily always the case when one of the dst_dev_event events occurs.

- Adds the structure to the global list dst_garbage_list. This list links all entries that should be removed, but cannot be removed yet due to nonzero reference counts.

- Adjusts the dst_gc_timer timer to expire after the minimum configurable delay (DST_GC_MIN) and fires it if it is not already running.

The dst_gc_timer timer periodically browses the dst_garbage_list list and removes, with dst_destroy, entries with a reference count of 0. When the timer handler dst_run_gc cannot remove all the entries in the list, it starts the timer again but makes it expire a little later. To be precise, it adds DST_GC_INC seconds to its expiration delay, up to a maximum delay of DST_GC_MAX. But each time dst_free adds a new element to dst_garbage_list, it resets the expiry delay to the default minimum value DST_GC_MIN.

Figures 33-10(a) and 33-10(b) summarize the logic of dst_free.

Variables That Tune and Control Garbage Collection

In summary, here are the meanings of the main global variables and parameters that control the DST garbage collection task:

dst_garbage_list

> The list of dst_entry structures waiting to be removed. When dst_gc_timer expires, the handler takes care of them. Entries are put into this list (instead of being removed directly) only when the reference count __refcnt is greater than 0, preventing their deletion. New entries are inserted at the head of the list.

dst_gc_timer_expires
dst_gc_timer_inc

> dst_gc_timer_expires is the number of seconds the timer waits before expiring. Its value ranges between DST_GC_MIN and DST_GC_MAX and is increased with units of dst_gc_timer_inc by dst_run_gc every time that function runs and cannot manage to empty the dst_garbage_list list. dst_gc_timer_inc must be in the range DST_GC_MIN to DST_GC_MAX as well.

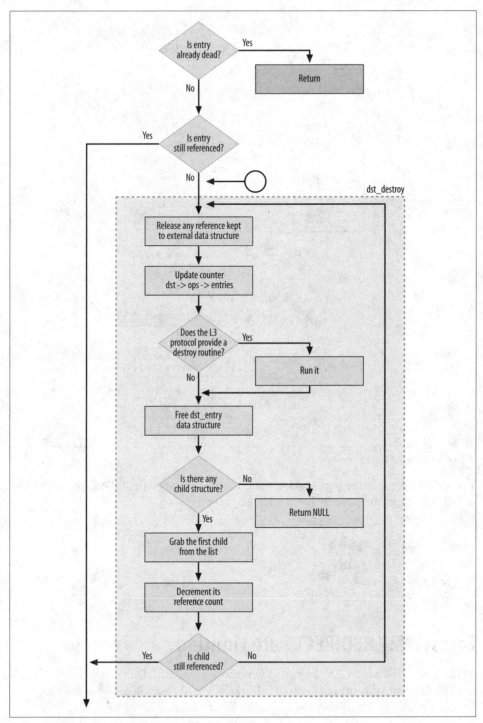

Figure 33-10(a). dst_free function

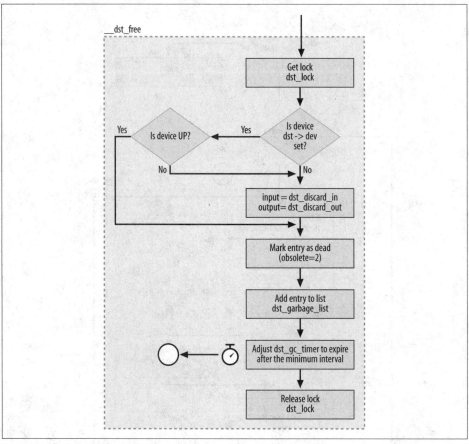

Figure 33-10(b). dst_free function

The values of the three constants mentioned in the previous bullets, as defined in *include/net/dst.h*, are listed in Table 33-1.

Table 33-1. DST_GC_XXX constants

Name	Value
DST_GC_MIN	HZ/10
DST_GC_MAX	120*HZ
DST_GC_INC	HZ/2

Egress ICMP REDIRECT Rate Limiting

As discussed in Chapter 25, the kernel generates ICMP REDIRECT messages when it detects suboptimal routing. These ICMP messages are handled by the routing sub-system, which rate limits them as suggested by section 4.3.2.8 of RFC 1812.

The algorithm used is a simple exponential backoff algorithm. If the destination keeps ignoring ICMP REDIRECT messages, the kernel keeps sending them up to ip_rt_redirect_number, doubling each time the interval between consecutive messages. After ip_rt_redirect_number such messages have been sent, the kernel stops sending them until ip_rt_redirect_silence seconds pass while no input packet arrives that would trigger the generation of an ICMP REDIRECT. Once ip_rt_redirect_silence seconds are passed, the kernel starts sending ICMP REDIRECT messages again, if they are needed.

The initial delay for the exponential backoff algorithm is given by ip_rt_redirect_load. All three ip_rt_redirect_*xxx* parameters are configurable via */proc*. See Chapter 36 for the default values of those variables.

All the logic for egress REDIRECT messages is implemented in ip_rt_send_redirect, which is the routine called by the kernel when it detects the need for an ICMP REDIRECT (see Chapter 20).

Two dst_entry fields implement this feature:

rate_last
> Timestamp when the last IMCP REDIRECT was sent.

rate_tokens
> Number of ICMP REDIRECT messages already sent to the destination associated to this dst_entry instance. rate_tokens-1, therefore, represents the number of consecutive ICMP REDIRECT messages that the destination has ignored.

## CHAPTER 34

Routing: Routing Tables

Given the central role of routing in the network stack and how big routing tables can be, it is important to have efficiently designed routing tables to speed up operations, particularly lookups. This chapter describes how Linux organizes routing tables, and how the data structures that compose a routing table are accessed with different hash tables, each one specialized for a different kind of lookup.

Organization of Routing Hash Tables

To support the key goal of returning information quickly for a wide variety of operations, Linux defines a number of different hash tables that point to the same data structures describing routes:

- A set of hash tables that access routes based on their netmask length (described in the section "Organization of Per-Netmask Tables")
- A set of hash tables that search `fib_info` structures directly (described in the section "Organization of fib_info Structures")
- One hash table, indexed on the network device, used to quickly search the next hops of the configured routes (described in the section "Organization of Next-Hop Router Structures").
- One hash table that, indegiven a route and a device, quickly identifies the gateway used by the route's next hop

Organization of Per-Netmask Tables

At the highest level, routes are organized into different hash tables based on the lengths of their netmasks. Because IPv4 uses 32-bit addresses, 33 different netmask lengths (ranging from /0 to /32, where /0 represents default routes) can be associated with an IP address. The routing subsystem maintains a different hash table for each netmask length. These hash tables are then combined into other tables, described in subsequent sections in this chapter.

Figure 34-1 shows the relationships between the main data structures in a routing table. All of these data structures were briefly introduced in Chapter 32, and are described in detail in Chapter 36. In this chapter, we will concentrate on the relationships between the data structures.

Basic structures for hash table organization

Routing tables are described with `fib_table` data structures. The `fib_table` structure includes a vector of 33 pointers, one for each netmask, and each pointing to a data structure of type `fn_zone`. (The term *zone* refers to the networks that share a single netmask.) The `fn_zone` structures organize routes into hash tables, so routes that lead to destination networks with the same netmask length share the same hash table. Therefore, given any route, its associated hash table can be quickly identified by the route's netmask length. Nonempty `fn_zone` buckets are linked together, and the head of the list is saved in `fn_zone_list`. We will see in Chapter 35 how this list is used.

There is one exception to the general organization of these per-netmask hash tables. The table for the /0 zone, used for default routes, consists of a single bucket and therefore collapses into a simple list. This design choice was made because a host rarely maintains many default routes.

Routes are described by a combination of different data structures, each one representing a different piece of information. The information that defines a route is split into several data structures because it is possible for multiple routes to differ by only a few fields. Thus, by splitting routes in pieces instead of maintaining one large, flat structure, the routing subsystem makes it easier to share common pieces of information among similar routes, and therefore to isolate different functions and define cleaner interfaces among the functions.

For each unique subnet there is one instance of `fib_node`, identified by a variable named `fn_key` whose value is the subnet. For example, given the subnet 10.1.1.0/24, `fn_key` is 10.1.1. Note that the `fib_node` structure (and therefore its `fn_key` variable) is associated to a subnet, not to a single route; it's important to keep this in mind to avoid confusion later. The importance of this detail derives from the possibility of having different routes to the same subnet.

Different routes leading to the same subnet (i.e., the same `fn_key`) share the same `fib_node`. Each route is assigned its own `fib_alias` structure. You can have, for instance, different routes leading to the same subnet and differing only with regard to the TOS values: each `fib_alias` instance would therefore be assigned a different TOS value. Each `fib_alias` instance is associated with a `fib_info` structure, which stores the real routing information (i.e., how to get to the destination).

Given a `fib_node` instance, the associated list of `fib_alias` instances is sorted in increasing order of IP TOS (i.e., the `fa_tos` field). `fib_alias` instances with the same

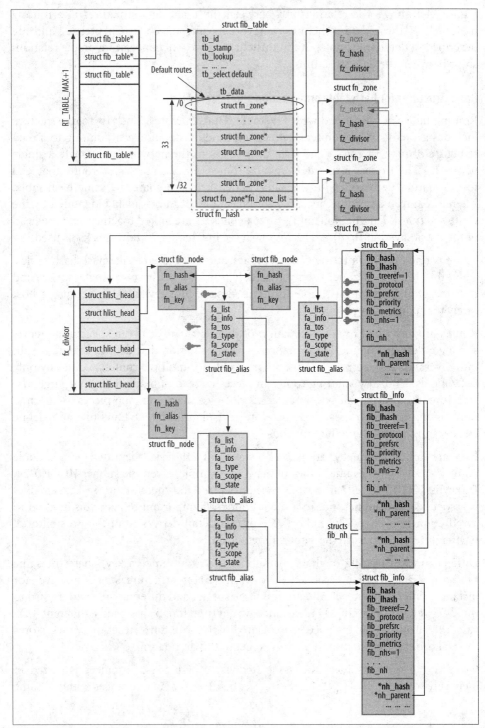

Figure 34-1. Routing table organization

value of `fa_tos` are sorted in increasing order of the associated `fib_info`'s `fib_protocol` field.

I explained earlier in this chapter that the routing subsystem is broken into multiple data structures to optimize their use and make the logic cleaner. Thus, the association between `fib_alias` and `fib_info` is not one-to-one; several `fib_alias` structures can share a `fib_info` structure. When different routes happen to share the same parameter values of an existing `fib_info` structure, they simply point to the same `fib_info` instance. Sharing is remembered through a reference count on the `fib_info` structure.

If, for instance, five routes to five different networks happen to use the same next-hop gateway, the information about the next hop would be the same for all of them and therefore it will make sense to share it. In this case, therefore, there are five `fib_node` structures and five `fib_alias` structures, but only one `fib_info` structure.

The sample configuration in Figure 34-1 shows a number of relationships among different structures making up the hash tables described in this section. In this figure:

- There are four routes (i.e., four `fib_alias` instances).
- These four routes lead to three different subnets (i.e., three `fib_node` instances) because two `fib_alias` instances share a common `fib_node` instance.
- Two of the four routes share the same next-hop routers. Thus, the `fa_info` fields of these two `fib_alias` structures point to the same `fib_info` structure on the bottom-right side of the figure.

The data structure fields in the figure where a key appears on the right side are the fields used by the lookup routines you will see in Chapter 35.

Dynamic resizing of per-netmask hash tables

The size of the hash table `fz_hash` is increased when the number of elements passes a given threshold. A hash table can be resized repeatedly up to a given upper limit. The section "Adding a Route" will explain exactly how the insertion of a new element into the hash table triggers resizing.

Each of the 33 hash tables pointed to by `fn_hash`[*] is resized independently. A table is resized when the number of entries reaches twice the size of the number of buckets, which is a value stored in `fz_divisor`, as shown in Figure 34-1. This heuristic is chosen mainly to limit the lookup time on the hash table. Keeping the number of elements below this threshold keeps lookups fast (assuming elements are well distributed).

---

[*] Do not confuse `fn_hash` with `fz_hash`.

The maximum size of a table is derived from architecture-specific parameters related to memory management. On an i386, the maximum size is 8 MB. Because each element of the table consists of a pointer, which has a size of 4 bytes on a 32-bit processor, an i386 system can support a hash table with more than 2 million buckets.

When a hash table is first created by fn_new_zone, the table is given a default size of 16 buckets. (The only exception, as mentioned in the previous section, is the /0 zone used for default routes.) The first two times the table is expanded, the size is increased to 256 and 1,024, respectively. Subsequent increases will always double the current size.

There is currently no shrink mechanism. So, if a zone's hash table goes from 280 elements down to 10, the size of the table will not decrease from 256 to 16.

Organization of fib_info Structures

As shown in Figure 34-1, each fib_info structure includes two fields, fib_hash and fib_lhash, that are used to insert the structures into two more-comprehensive hash tables, shown in Figure 34-2. These hash tables are:

fib_info_hash
> All fib_info structures are inserted into this hash table. Lookups on this table are done with fib_find_info.

fib_info_laddrhash
> fib_info structures are inserted into this table only when the associated routes have a preferred source address. The use of the preferred source address is described in the section "Preferred Source Address Selection" in Chapter 35. That address is normally derived automatically from the device configuration, but it can also be explicitly configured.
>
> This hash table is mainly used to facilitate the removal of routes affected by the deletion of a locally configured IP address (see fib_sync_down).

In both tables, new elements are added at the head of a bucket's list by fib_create_info.

Dynamic resizing of global hash tables

The total number of fib_info structures, in all routing tables, is stored in the counter fib_info_cnt. Its value is incremented by fib_create_info when an instance is created and decremented by free_fib_info when an instance is deleted.

When creating a new instance, fib_create_info checks whether fib_info_cnt has reached fib_hash_size, which is the size of the hash table, as shown in Figure 34-2. When this size is reached, both fib_info_hash and fib_info_laddrhash are doubled in size. The old hash tables are removed with fib_hash_free, the new ones are

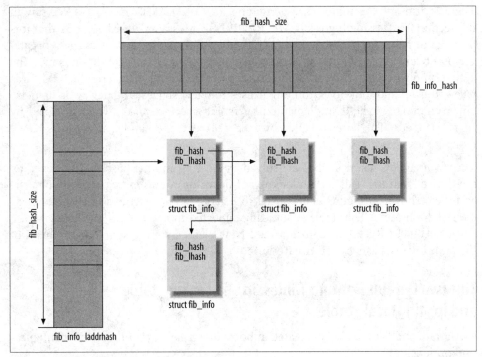

Figure 34-2. fib_info structures' organization

allocated with `fib_hash_alloc`, and all the `fib_info` instances are moved from the old tables to the new ones with `fib_hash_move`.

Note that the resizing discussed in this section has nothing to do with the one discussed in the section "Dynamic resizing of per-netmask hash tables."

Organization of Next-Hop Router Structures

As shown in Figure 34-1, each `fib_info` structure can include one or more `fib_nh` structures, each one representing a next-hop router. The information for a next-hop router includes the device through which it can be reached. Thus, it is easy to find a device when the router is known, but the structure does not provide a quick way to find a router when the device is known. The latter ability is important in two cases:

When a device is shut down
> The networking subsystem has to disable all the routes associated with the device. This is done by `fib_sync_down`, described in Chapter 32.

When a device is enabled or re-enabled
> The networking subsystem has to enable or re-enable all the routes associated with next-hop routers reachable via this device. This is done by `fib_sync_up`, also described in Chapter 32.

There is also another minor case pertaining to ICMP_REDIRECT messages. We saw in the section "Processing Ingress ICMP_REDIRECT Messages" in Chapter 31 that it is possible to have the kernel accept only ICMP redirects whose new suggested gateway is already known locally as a router. To check whether this condition is met, the kernel simply needs to browse all the routes associated with the device the ICMP was received from and look for a route that uses the new suggested gateway as its next-hop router. This logic is implemented by ip_fib_check_default, which is called by ip_rt_redirect. The latter is called by icmp_redirect, the handler for ingress ICMP redirect messages.

The requirements just described are solved by creating another hash table indexed by the device identifier; this makes lookups of next-hop routes extremely fast. The nh_hash field shown in Figure 34-1 is used to insert fib_nh structures in the fib_info_devhash hash table. That table is statically allocated in *net/ipv4/fib_semantics* with a size of DEVINDEX_HASHSIZE (256) buckets. New elements are inserted at the head of the table bucket's lists by fib_create_info.

The Two Default Routing Tables: ip_fib_main_table and ip_fib_local_table

Two routing tables are always created at boot time regardless of the kernel configuration options:

ip_fib_local_table
> The kernel installs routes to local addresses here, including the associated subnet's address and the subnet's broadcast addresses (see the section "Routes Inserted by the Kernel: The fib_magic Function" in Chapter 36). This routing table cannot be explicitly configured by the user.

ip_fib_main_table
> All other routes go here (user-configured routes and routes generated by routing protocols).

The section "Special Routes" in Chapter 30 explains the relationship between these two routing tables. In Chapter 35, we will see how routing lookups use them.

Routing Table Initialization

Routing tables are initialized with fib_hash_init, defined in *net/ipv4/fib_hash.c*. It is called by ip_fib_init, which initializes the IP routing subsystem, to create the ip_fib_main_table and ip_fib_local_table tables (see the section "Routing Subsystem Initialization" in Chapter 32).

The first time fib_hash_init is called, it creates the memory pool fn_hash_kmem that will be used to allocate fib_node data structures.

`fib_hash_init` first allocates a `fib_table` data structure and then initializes its virtual functions to the routines shown in Table 34-1. The function also clears the content of the bottom part of the structure (`fn_hash`), which, as shown in Figure 34-1, is used to distribute the routing entries on different hash tables based on their netmask lengths.

Table 34-1. Initialization of the fib_table's virtual functions

Method	Routine used
tb_lookup	fn_hash_lookup
tb_insert	fn_hash_insert
tb_delete	fn_hash_delete
tb_flush	fn_hash_flush
tb_select_default	fn_hash_select_default
tb_dump	fn_hash_dump

Adding and Removing Routes

In Chapter 36, we will see how routes are added, deleted, and modified by user commands and routing daemons. Both are satisfied through a single set of routines in the kernel's routing subsystem. In this section, we will see what the kernel has to do when asked to add or remove a route from one of its routing tables. As shown in Table 34-1, `fn_hash_insert` and `fn_hash_delete` are the routines used to insert and delete routes, and we will analyze them in the sections "Adding a Route" and "Deleting a Route." `fn_hash_insert` has several related uses, all involving changes of routes.

Here are a few operations common to the two routines:

- Given a route to add or remove, derive the search key and use it to make a `fib_node` lookup and a `fib_alias` lookup. These lookups are similar to the ones done to route data packets, but are done for a different purpose: to check whether a route being added is a duplicate of an existing route, or whether a route being removed really exists.

- Populate (in case of insert) and clean up (in case of delete) the right hash tables.

- Flush the routing cache if necessary.

- Generate a Netlink broadcast notification to tell the interested listeners that a route has been added to or removed from a routing table (see the section "Netlink Notifications" in Chapter 32).

Adding a Route

The insertion of a new route is taken care of by `fn_hash_insert`, whose logic is described in Figures 34-3(a) and 34-3(b). This routine is actually called for many operations: in addition to the insertion of new routes, it handles appending, prepending, changing, and replacing. The different cases are distinguished by the NLM_F_XXX flags passed. The combination of flags associated to each operation is listed in Table 36-1 in Chapter 36.

The different requirements of different operations complicate the function's logic. For instance, as mentioned in the section "Organization of Routing Hash Tables," different routes with different TOS values can lead to the same destination. When the kernel adds a new route, it returns an error if there is already a route with the same destination and TOS. However, the same condition is actually a requirement when replacing a route. Therefore, based on the command type, the route lookup done by fn_hash_insert is expected to return a different result.

As explained in the section "Dynamic resizing of per-netmask hash tables," the insertion of a new route may trigger the resizing of a zone's hash table, which is taken care of by fn_rehash_zone. As explained in the section "Organization of Next-Hop Router Structures," new fib_info structures are added to the fib_info_devhash hash table when the associated routes specify a preferred source address. Each fib_nh structure representing one of the route's next hops is also added to the fib_info_devhash hash table.

When a replace operation replaces an existing route with a new one, the kernel flushes the routing cache so that the old route is no longer used.

Regardless of the type of operation, a Netlink notification is generated to notify all of the interested subsystems.

Deleting a Route

The deletion of a route is taken care of by fn_hash_delete, whose logic is described in Figure 34-4. Deleting a route is simpler than adding one; for example, there is only one type of operation.

First fn_hash_delete computes the search key and uses it for a lookup to see whether the entry to remove actually exists. When the victim fib_alias structure is found, the function deletes it, notifies interested listeners with a Netlink broadcast, and flushes the routing cache in case the route has been used (i.e., it has the FA_S_ACCESSED flag set).

The deletion of a fib_alias instance can lead to the deletion of a fib_info instance and a fib_node instance as well (use Figure 34-1 as a reference):

- When the associated fib_node instance is left empty because the deleted fib_alias was its last instance, the fib_node gets deleted, too.

---

* The flowchart does not follow the source code flow precisely, but preserves the logic.

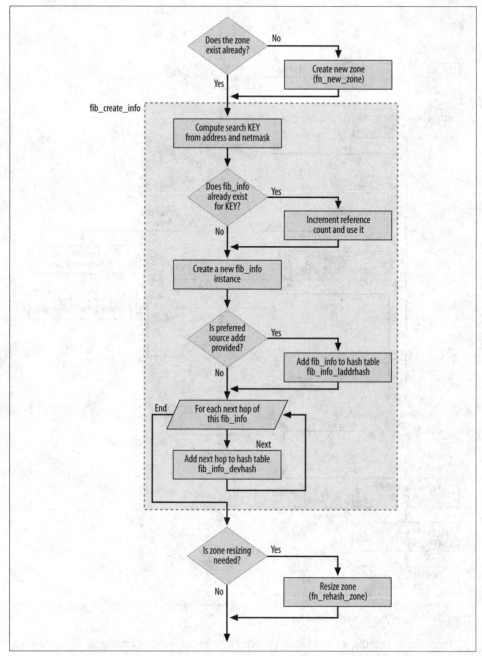

Figure 34-3(a). fn_hash_insert function

- When the associated `fib_info` instance is left with a null `fib_treeref` reference count, it is freed because it is not needed anymore. In particular, `fn_free_alias`

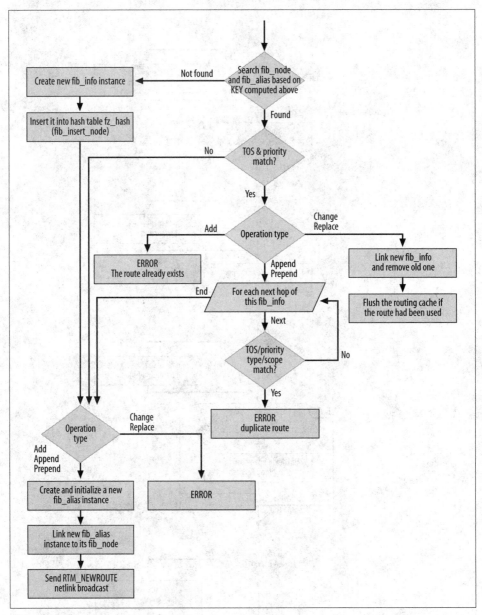

Figure 34-3(b). fn_hash_insert function

frees the matching fib_alias instance right away, and decrements the reference count fib_treeref on the associated fib_info instance with fib_release_info. When that reference count drops to zero, the fib_info instance is taken out of all of the hash tables it was inserted into, is marked dead by setting its fib_dead flag, and is freed with free_fib_info at the first invocation of fib_info_put. The next hops associated with the `fib_info` instance are also taken out of the hash table, as described in the section "Organization of Next-Hop Router Structures."

Manipulations of the `fa_list` and `fn_alias` lists are protected by the `fib_hash_lock` lock (see Figure 34-1).

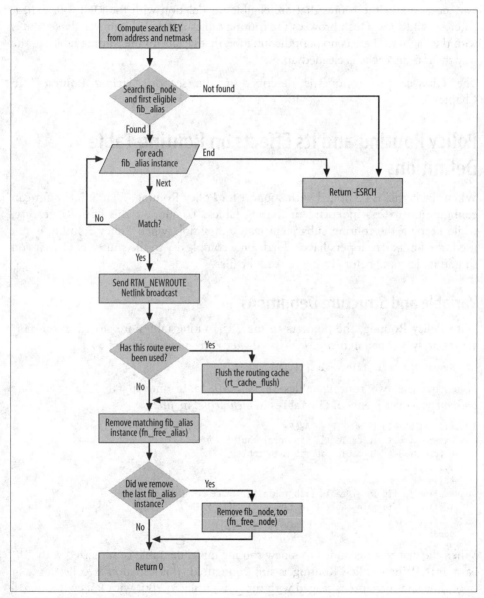

Figure 34-4. fn_hash_delete function

Garbage Collection

Routes should be deleted when they are invalidated by configuration changes or changes of status for local devices. Several functions in the routing subsystem browse the routing tables (or a portion of them). Under certain conditions, one of them, fib_sync_down, marks the routes that are eligible for deletion with the RTNH_F_DEAD flag. Later, a call to fib_flush browses the routing tables again and removes those routes with the flag set. There is no periodic function that cleans up the routing tables in the way the routing cache is cleaned up.

The fib_sync_down routine is described in the section "Helper Routines" in Chapter 32.

Policy Routing and Its Effects on Routing Table Definitions

When the kernel is compiled with support for Policy Routing, an administrator can configure up to 255 independent routing tables. To support this optional feature, while keeping the routing subsystem lean and simple when Policy Routing is not used, the Linux developers have added some complexity to the source code that you should understand before trying to read the files.

Variable and Structure Definitions

With Policy Routing, the pointers to the 255 routing tables are stored in the fib_tables array, defined in *net/ipv4/fib_frontend.c* and shown in Figure 34-1.

```
struct fib_table *fib_tables[RT_TABLE_MAX+1];
```

Note that the two routing tables ip_fib_main_table and ip_fib_local_table are defined as two elements of fib_tables in *include/net/ip_fib.h*:

```
#ifndef CONFIG_IP_MULTIPLE_TABLES
extern struct fib_table *ip_fib_local_table;
extern struct fib_table *ip_fib_main_table;
... ... ...
#else
#define ip_fib_local_table (fib_tables[RT_TABLE_LOCAL])
#define ip_fib_main_table (fib_tables[RT_TABLE_MAIN])
... ... ...
#endif
```

When the first route is added to a new routing table, the table is initialized with fib_hash_init. When Policy Routing is not configured, this function is called only at boot time and therefore is tagged with the __init macro.[*] But with Policy Routing, a

---

[*] Chapter 7 describes the use and meaning of the __init macro.

new routing table can be created at any time, so `fib_hash_init` cannot be so tagged. This explains its conditional prototype definition:

```
#ifdef CONFIG_IP_MULTIPLE_TABLES
struct fib_table * fib_hash_init(int id)
#else
struct fib_table * __init fib_hash_init(int id)
#endif
{
    ... ... ...
}
```

Even with Policy Routing support, all configured routes are added to `ip_fib_main_table` unless an ID for a different routing table is explicitly specified. The table ID can be provided only with the new *ip* command, not with the traditional *route* command.

Double Definitions for Functions

The Policy Routing feature is not transparently integrated into the routing code. For example, the variables, routines, or pieces of code that are needed only when there is Policy Routing support in the kernel are protected by the preprocessor conditional variable `CONFIG_IP_MULTIPLE_TABLES`.[*]

There are also a few global variables and functions that have a double definition, one to use when there is no policy routing support in the kernel and another one to use when there is support. Two important ones, defined in *net/ipv4/fib_rules.c* and in *include/net/ip_fib.h*, are:

`fib_lookup`
    Used to make routing table lookups, and described in Chapter 35

`fib_select_default`
    Used to select a default route when forwarding a packet when there is no explicit route to its destination

Besides these two functions, there are double definitions for a few others, such as `fib_get_table` (which returns the routing table given the table ID) and `fib_new_table` (which creates a new routing table).

It is important to be aware of the double definitions of these routines when browsing the source code, particularly with tools such as TAGS and *cscope*. Otherwise, you may be looking at the wrong instance while analyzing a given code path.

---

[*] Do not mistake multiple tables with multipath; they are two totally different and independent features.

CHAPTER 35

Routing: Lookups

In Chapter 33, we saw how lookups are triggered by both ingress and egress traffic. The cache is always searched first, and when there is a miss, the routing tables are consulted through the `ip_route_input_slow` and `ip_route_output_slow` functions. In this chapter, we will analyze these functions; in particular, we will cover:

- How ingress and egress routing differ
- How a routing table is searched with `fib_lookup`
- How policy routing lookups differ from normal lookups
- When and how multipath routing is handled
- How the selection of a default gateway works

High-Level View of Lookup Functions

Regardless of the direction of the traffic, a routing table lookup is made with `fib_lookup`. However, as mentioned in the section "Double Definitions for Functions" in Chapter 34, there are two versions of `fib_lookup`, one used when the kernel has support for Policy Routing (*net/ipv4/fib_rules.c*) and one when that support is not included (*include/net/ip_fib.h*). The selection of the right routine is made at compile time, so when `ip_route_input_slow` and `ip_route_output_slow` call `fib_lookup`, they transparently invoke the right one.

Let's briefly see the key functions used to make a route lookup. You will find it helpful to refer to Figure 34-1 in Chapter 34 during this discussion.

The `fib_lookup` routine is a wrapper around the lookup function provided by each routing table. The version provided when there is no policy routing simply runs the lookup function for the local and main tables, and the other has more complicated logic that allows it to consult the tables provided by policy routing.

As shown in Figure 35-1, the lookup function invoked from `fib_lookup` is `fn_hash_lookup`, which is the routine to which the `fib_table`'s function pointer `tb_lookup` is initialized (see the section "Routing Table Initialization" in Chapter 34). This function identifies the fib_node instance whose key matches the destination address. Then fn_hash_lookup asks fib_semantic_match to do a lookup on the fib_alias instances associated with the matching fib_node. If one is identified, fib_semantic_match may also need to select the right next hop when Multipath is configured.

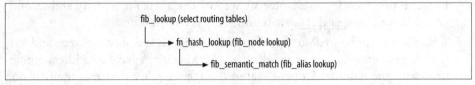

Figure 35-1. Relationships among the main lookup routines

All the functions introduced here are described in detail in later sections. In particular, they cover:

- How ingress and egress lookups use fib_lookup (the sections "Input Routing" and "Output Routing")
- How fn_hash_lookup is implemented (the section "The Table Lookup: fn_hash_lookup")
- The fib_semantic_match function (the section "Semantic Matching on Subsidiary Criteria")
- How the version of fib_lookup that supports Policy Routing differs from the basic function (the section "fib_lookup Function")

Helper Routines

Here are a few routines used by some of the functions we will cover in this chapter:

fib_validate_source
> Validates the source IP address of a packet received on a given device, to detect spoofing attempts. Among other things, this function makes sure that unless asymmetric routing is enabled, the source IP address of the packet is reachable through the same interface the packet was received from (see the section "Reverse Path Filtering" in Chapter 31). It also returns the preferred source address spec_dst to use for the reverse direction, as described in the upcoming section "Preferred Source Address Selection," and initializes the routing tag, as described in the section "Routing Table Based Classifier" in Chapter 31.

inet_select_addr
> Given a device dev, an IP address dst, and a scope scope, returns the first primary address with scope scope, to use in sending a packet to the address dst out of device dev.

This routine is needed because a device can be configured with multiple addresses, and each can have its own scope.

The reason for the dst argument is that if dev is configured with different IP addresses on different subnets, dst allows this function to return an IP address configured on the same subnet as dst.

In the section "Scope" in Chapter 30, we saw that there are primary and secondary addresses; inet_select_addr returns only primary addresses.

If no address configured on dev meets the conditions specified by scope and dst, the function tries the rest of the devices, checking if any have an address configured with the required scope. Because the loopback_dev device is the first one inserted into the dev_base list, it will be the first one to be tried.

rt_set_nexthop

Given a routing cache entry rtable and a routing table lookup result res, completes the initialization of rtable's fields, such as rt_gateway and the metrics vector of the embedded dst_entry structure. This function also initializes the routing tag described in the section "Routing Table Based Classifier" in Chapter 31.

The Table Lookup: fn_hash_lookup

All routing table lookups, regardless of the tables provided by Policy Routing and the direction of the traffic, are done with fn_hash_lookup. This function is registered as the handler for the tb_lookup function pointer of the fib_table structure in fib_hash_init (see the section "Routing Table Initialization" in Chapter 34).

The function's lookup algorithm uses the LPM algorithm introduced in Chapter 30. The execution of this algorithm is facilitated by the organization of routes into per-netmask hash tables, as shown in Figure 34-1 in Chapter 34. fn_hash_lookup searches for the fib_node instance that has the information to route packets to a particular destination.

The prototype for fn_hash_lookup is:

```
static int
fn_hash_lookup(struct fib_table *tb, const struct flowi *flp, struct fib_result *res)
```

Here is the meaning of its input parameters:

tb

The routing table to search. Because fn_hash_lookup is a generic lookup routine that runs on one table at a time, the tables to search are decided by the caller, depending on Policy Routing support and related factors.

flp

Search key.

res

Upon success, res is initialized with the routing information.

And these are the possible return values:

0: success

res has been initialized (by `fib_semantic_match`) with the forwarding information.

1: failure

No route matched the search key.

Less than 0: Administrative failure

This means the lookup cannot succeed because the route found is of no value: for instance, the associated host may be flagged as unreachable.

The LPM algorithm loops over the routes, starting with the zone that represents the longest netmask. This is because longer netmasks mean more specific routes, which in turn means that the packet is likely to get closer to the final destination. (For instance, a /27 netmask that can cover only 30 hosts is preferred over a /24 netmask that potentially covers 254.) Thus, the search browses all the active zones, starting from the ones with the longest netmasks. As we saw in the section "Organization of Routing Hash Tables" in Chapter 34, all the active zones are sorted by netmask length and `fn_zone_list` stores the head of the list.

```
struct fn_hash *t = (struct fn_hash*)tb->tb_data;
read_lock(&fib_hash_lock);
for (fz = t->fn_zone_list; fz; fz = fz->fz_next) {
    struct hlist_head *head;
    struct hlist_node *node;
    struct fib_node *f;
```

The function ANDs the destination IP address with the netmask of the active zone being checked, and uses the result as a search key. For example, if the function is currently checking the /24 zone, and the destination address `flp->fl4_dst` is 10.0.1. 2, the search key k is initialized to 10.0.1.2 & 255.255.255.0, which comes out to 10. 0.1.0. This means that the following piece of code searches for a route to the subnet 10.0.1.0/24:

```
u32 k = fz_key(flp->fl4_dst, fz);
```

Because routes are stored in a hash table (`fz_hash`), head selects the right bucket of the table by applying a hash function to the key k. The next step is to browse the list of routes (`fib_node` structures) associated with the selected table's bucket and look for one that matches k.

```
head = &fz->fz_hash[fn_hash(k, fz)];
hlist_for_each_entry(f, node, head, fn_hash) {
    if (f->fn_key != k)) {
        continue;

    err = fib_semantic_match(&f->fn_alias,
                             flp, res,
```

```
                                        f->fn_key, fz->fz_mask,
                                        fz->fz_order);

                if (err < 0)
                        goto out;
        }
    }
    err = 1;
out:
    read_unlock(&fib_hash_lock);
    return err;
}
```

We saw in the section "Organization of Routing Hash Tables" in Chapter 34 that a fib_node covers all the routes that lead to the same subnet but that could differ on other fields such as TOS. Now, if fn_hash_lookup manages to find a fib_node that matches the search key k, the function still needs to check each potential route to find one that also matches the other search key fields received in input through the flp parameter. This detailed check is taken care of by fib_semantic_match, described in the next section.

If fib_semantic_match returns success, it also initializes the input parameter res that stores the result of the lookup, and fn_hash_lookup returns this result to its caller. fn_hash_lookup loops through all the zones until fib_semantic_match either returns a successful result or discovers that the table's routes are unusable (i.e., they do not match).

Semantic Matching on Subsidiary Criteria

fib_semantic_match is called to find whether any routes (fib_alias structures) among the ones associated with a given fib_node match all the required search key fields. We saw in the previous section that the main field, the final destination IP address to which the packet must be routed, was matched by fn_hash_lookup before invoking this function. So it falls to fib_semantic_match to check the other criteria.

Once fib_semantic_match has identified the right instance of fib_alias, it simply needs to extract the routing information from the associated fib_node. The only additional task required is the selection of the next hop. This last task is needed only when the matching route uses Multipath, and it can be handled in two ways:

- By fib_semantic_match, when the search key provides an egress device.
- By fib_select_multipath, when the search key does not provide an egress device. fib_select_multipath is called by the ip_route_input_slow or ip_route_output_slow routine.

The logic of fib_semantic_match is shown in Figure 35-2.

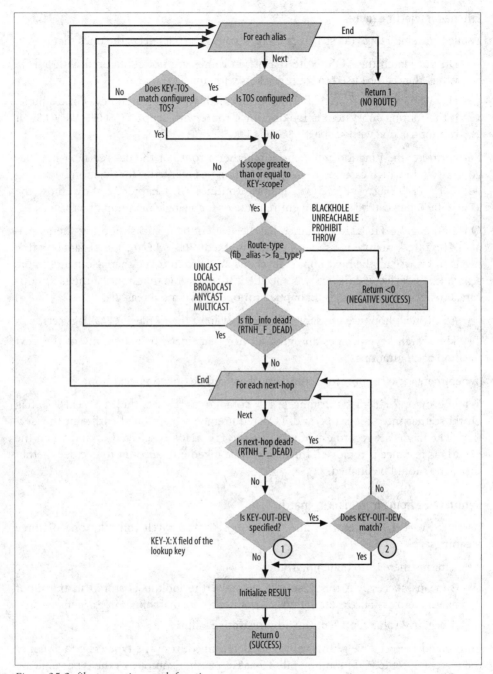

Figure 35-2. fib_semantic_match function

Criteria for rejecting routes

While browsing `fib_alias` structures, `fib_semantic_match` rejects the ones that:

- Do not match the TOS. Note that when routes are not configured with a TOS value, they can be used to route packets with any TOS.

- Have a narrower scope than the one specified with the search key. For example, if the routing subsystem is looking for a route with scope `RT_SCOPE_UNIVERSE`, it cannot use one with scope `RT_SCOPE_LINK`.

Furthermore, the function must check whether a route or the desired next hop has gone away, in which case the routing subsystem has marked it for deletion by setting its `RTNH_F_DEAD` flag. The section "Helper Routines" in Chapter 32 shows how the `RTNH_F_DEAD` flag can be set for an entire route or for a single next hop of a route.

Once an eligible `fib_alias` instance has been identified, and supposing the associated `fib_info` structure is usable (i.e., not marked `RTNH_F_DEAD`), `fib_semantic_match` needs to browse all the next hops' `fib_nh` instances to find one that also matches the search key's device, if a device was specified. It is possible that none of the next hops can actually be used. This could happen for one of two main reasons:

- All the next hops are unusable (that is, they have their `RTNH_F_DEAD` flags set).

- The search key specifies an egress device that does not match any of the next hop configurations.

When there is no support for Multipath, there can be only one next hop.

While browsing `fib_alias` instances, `fib_semantic_match` sets the `FA_S_ACCESSED` flag on those that meet the scope and TOS requirements mentioned earlier in this section. The flag is set regardless of whether the `fib_alias` is selected. If and when the `fib_alias` instance is removed, this flag will be taken into account to decide whether the cache should be flushed.

Return value from fib_semantic_match

As stated earlier, the return value from `fib_semantic_match` can take one of three meanings:

- 1 means there is no matching route.

- 0 means success. In this case, the result of the lookup is stored in the input parameter res. The result includes a pointer to the matching `fib_info` instance.

- A negative value represents an administrative failure.

Both 0 and the negative return values are determined from the type (fa->fa_type) of the matching route (fa) found by `fib_semantic_match`. Examples of the type value are `RTN_UNICAST` and `RTN_LOCAL`. From this type, `fib_semantic_match` can decide whether the lookup should succeed or fail, and can pass back an error code that allows the kernel to take the proper action in case of failure.

For example, a route of type `RTN_UNREACHABLE` causes `fib_semantic_match` to return the error –EHOSTUNREACH, which then leads the kernel to generate an ICMP unreachable message. A route of type `RTN_THROW` causes `fib_semantic_match` to return the error -EAGAIN, which instructs the Policy Routing version of `fib_lookup` in *net/ipv4/ fib_rules.c* to retry the lookup with the next routing table.

Because the `fa->fa_type` type field drives the value returned, the error codes are embodied in a `fib_props` array, defined and initialized in the file *net/ipv4/fib_ semantics.c* (see the section "rtable Structure" in Chapter 36). The array contains an element for each possible route type that specifies the associated error code and an `RT_SCOPE_XXX` scope. Deriving the error code and scope is as simple as referencing the element of `fib_props` corresponding to the index `fa->fa_type`.

Table 35-1 shows how `fib_props` is initialized.

Table 35-1. Initialization of fib_props

Route type	Error	Scope
RTN_UNSPEC	0	RT_SCOPE_NOWHERE
RTN_UNICAST	0	RT_SCOPE_UNIVERSE
RTN_LOCAL	0	RT_SCOPE_HOST
RTN_BROADCAST	0	RT_SCOPE_LINK
RTN_ANYCAST	0	RT_SCOPE_LINK
RTN_MULTICAST	0	RT_SCOPE_UNIVERSE
RTN_BLACKHOLE	-EINVAL	RT_SCOPE_UNIVERSE
RTN_UNREACHABLE	-EHOSTUNREACH	RT_SCOPE_UNIVERSE
RTN_PROHIBIT	-EACCES	RT_SCOPE_UNIVERSE
RTN_THROW	-EAGAIN	RT_SCOPE_UNIVERSE
RTN_NAT	-EAGAIN	RT_SCOPE_NOWHERE
RTN_XRESOLVE	-EINVAL	RT_SCOPE_NOWHERE

Note that the first few elements have a value of 0 for `error`: in these cases, `fib_ semantic_match` returns success. The others have an error code used by the routing code to handle the routing failure correctly.

fib_lookup Function

As mentioned in the section "Special Routes" in Chapter 30, the kernel uses two routing tables by default when there is no support for Policy Routing. A routing table lookup simply consists of two table lookups (two calls to `fn_hash_lookup`), so the `fib_ lookup` function defined in *include/net/ip_fib.h* is quite brief:

```
static inline int fib_lookup(const struct flowi *flp, struct fib_result *res)
{
```

```
        if (ip_fib_local_table->tb_lookup(ip_fib_local_table, flp, res) &&
            ip_fib_main_table->tb_lookup(ip_fib_main_table, flp, res))
                return -ENETUNREACH;
        return 0;
}
```

The search key is flp. The function first checks the ip_fib_local_table routing table, and if that fails, it checks the ip_fib_main_table routing table. If neither table manages to find a match, fib_loopkup returns –ENETUNREACH (unreachable destination network).

Setting Functions for Reception and Transmission

Both received packets and locally generated packets need to be routed: in the case of received packets, to find out whether they should be locally delivered or forwarded, and in the case of locally generated packets, to find out whether they should be delivered locally or transmitted out.

In both cases, given a packet to route skb, the result of the routing lookup is saved in skb->dst. This is a data structure of type dst_entry, described in detail in the section "dst_entry Structure" in Chapter 36. This data structure includes several fields; two of them are function pointers named input and output that process the packet in accordance with the result of the routing lookup. The next section goes into detail on the initializations of these function pointers.

Then the sections "Input Routing" and "Output Routing" describe in detail the routines ip_route_input_slow and ip_route_output_slow, used respectively to find routes for ingress and egress packets when the cache lookup fails. These two functions can be a bit scary because of their size and the extent to which they apply macros, conditional code (such as #ifdef), and special feature handling (e.g., Multipath), but they actually are simpler than they look. In addition, programmers who do not like the use of goto statements in the source code may be disappointed by their heavy use. I have included a flowchart for each function, which you might want to look at for high-level descriptions before reading about the functions.

In the rest of this section, we will see how the virtual function each calls (dst->input and dst->output) are initialized, and learn more about when they are invoked. The functions to which they are set depend on a few factors, including:

• Whether the packet is being transmitted, received, or forwarded

• Whether the address is unicast or multicast

• Whether an error is detected during the routing lookup

Tables 35-2 and 35-3 list the routines to which dst->input and dst->output can be initialized.

Table 35-2. Routines used for dst->input

Function	Description
ip_local_deliver	Deliver the packet locally. See Chapter 20.
ip_forward	Forward a unicast packet. See Chapter 20.
ip_mr_input	Forward a multicast packet.
ip_error	Handle an unreachable destination. See the section "Routing Failure."
dst_discard_in	Simply drop any input packet.

Table 35-3. Routines used for dst->output

Function	Description
ip_output	Wrapper around ip_finish_ouput. See Chapter 21.
ip_mc_output	Handle egress packet with multicast destination address.
ip_rt_bug	Print a warning message, because it is not supposed to be called.
dst_discard_out	Simply drop any input packet.

Not all combinations of the functions in Tables 35-2 and 35-3 are possible; Figure 35-3 summarizes the meaningful ones. These combinations do not include the dst_discard_*xxx* routines because they are found only in special cases independent from routing lookups (see the section "Special Cases").

Figure 35-3 shows how dst->input and dst->output are initialized for ingress and egress traffic. Let's see one case at a time.

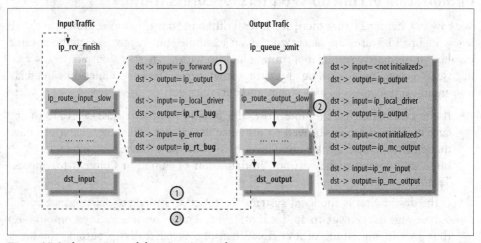

Figure 35-3. dst->input and dst->output initialization

Initialization of Function Pointers for Ingress Traffic

We saw in Chapter 19 that ingress IP traffic is processed by `ip_rcv_finish`. This function consults the routing table to decide whether the packet is to be delivered locally or dropped. This decision is taken by `ip_route_input`, which first checks the cache and then the routing tables (`ip_route_input_slow`) in case of a cache miss. `ip_route_input_slow` can create three main combinations of `dst->input` and `dst->ouput`:

- If the packet is to be forwarded, the function initializes `dst->input` to `ip_forward` and `dst->output` to `ip_output`. `dst_input` will therefore call `ip_forward`, which indirectly ends up calling `dst_output` and therefore `ip_output`. This is case (1) in Figure 35-3.

- If the packet is to be delivered locally, the function initializes `dst->input` to `ip_local_deliver`. There is no need to initialize `dst->output`, but it's initialized anyway to `ip_rt_error`, which is a routine that prints an error message when called. This can help detect bugs where `dst->output` is wrongly called when dealing with packets being delivered locally.

- If the destination address is not reachable according to the routing table, `dst->input` is initialized to `ip_error`, which generates an ICMP message whose type depends on the exact result returned by the routing lookup. Since `ip_error` frees the `skb` buffer, there is no need to initialize `dst->output` because it would not be called even by mistake.

Initialization of Function Pointers for Egress Traffic

We saw in Chapter 21 that there are several different transmission routines on the IP layer. Figure 35-3 uses `ip_queue_xmit` as an example, but regardless of the routine invoked, it ultimately results in a routing lookup with `__ip_route_output_key`, which in case of a cache miss relies on `ip_route_output_slow`. The latter function can create four main combinations of `dst->input` and `dst->output`:

- If the destination is a remote host, the function initializes `dst->output` to `ip_output`. Here there is no need to initialize `dst->input`. However, it would have made sense to use a fake initialization to something like `ip_rt_error` to catch bugs, as we saw in the section "Initialization of Function Pointers for Ingress Traffic."

- If the destination is the local system, the function initializes `dst->output` to `ip_output` and `dst->input` to `ip_local_deliver`. This is an interesting combination that goes in something of a circle. When `dst_output` calls `ip_output`, the latter transmits the packet out the loopback device, leading to the execution of `ip_rcv` and `ip_rcv_finish`. `ip_rcv_finish` sees that the ingress buffer already has routing information in `skb->dst`, and therefore calls `dst_input`, which in turn invokes `ip_local_deliver`. This is case (2) in Figure 35-3.

- If the destination address is a locally configured multicast IP address, the function initializes `dst->output` to `ip_mc_output`. Multicast code then takes care of the packet. `dst->input` is not initialized.

- The same multicast case is handled slightly differently when the kernel is compiled with support for multicast routing. In this case, `dst->output` is still initialized to `ip_mc_output`, but `dst->input` is initialized as well, to the routine `ip_mr_input`.

Special Cases

When a cached route `dst` is not supposed to be used, `dst->output` is initialized to `dst_discard_out` and `dst->input` is initialized to `dst_discard_in`. Both routines simply drop any packet they are passed. One example of their use is when a cached route is to be removed but cannot be destroyed because there are still references left to it (see the section "Deleting DST Entries" in Chapter 33).

These two routines are also used when a new entry is allocated and is not ready to be used because it is not fully initialized yet (see `dst_alloc`).

General Structure of the Input and Output Routing Routines

We saw in the section "Cache Lookup" in Chapter 33 that ingress and egress routing lookups that cannot be satisfied by the cache are taken care of by `ip_route_input_slow` and `ip_route_output_slow`, respectively.

Both routines are pretty long. To make them more readable, part of their code has been moved to two inline[*] functions, called `ip_mkroute_input` and `ip_mkroute_output`, respectively. Both routines differentiate between the case where the kernel supports multipath caching and the case where it does not. In the latter case, they become an alias to the two routines `ip_mkroute_input_def` and `ip_mkroute_output_def`, respectively. Regardless of whether multipath caching is supported, the routing cache entry is allocated and initialized with `__mkroute_input` and `__mkroute_output`. Regardless of whether it is `ip_route_input_slow` or `ip_route_output_slow` that triggers the insertion of a new entry into the cache, that operation is performed by `rt_intern_hash`.

Figure 35-4 summarizes the material in this section and shows how symmetrical the skeletons of the two slow routines are.

---

[*] Note that since they are inline routines, they can use goto statements that refer to labels defined in the slow routines they are part of.

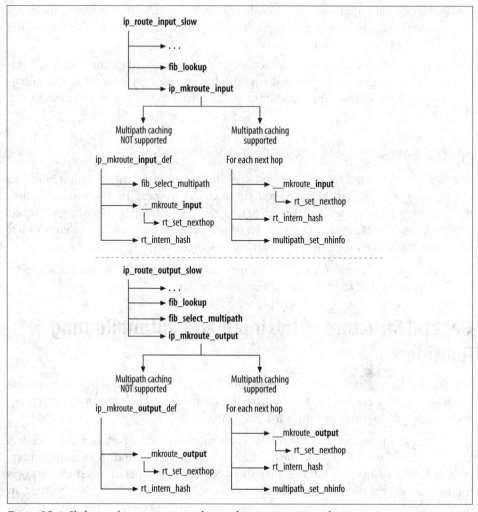

Figure 35-4. Skeleton of ip_route_input_slow and ip_route_output_slow

The differences with regard to Multipath, like the call to `fib_select_multipath` in `ip_mkroute_input_def` that is missing in `ip_mkroute_output_def`, will be explained in the section "Multipath Caching."

Input Routing

Ingress IP packets for which no route can be found in the cache by `ip_route_input` are checked against the routing tables by `ip_route_input_slow`, which is defined in *net/ipv4/route.c* and whose logic is shown in Figures 35-5(a) and 35-5(b). In this section, we describe the internals of this routine in detail.

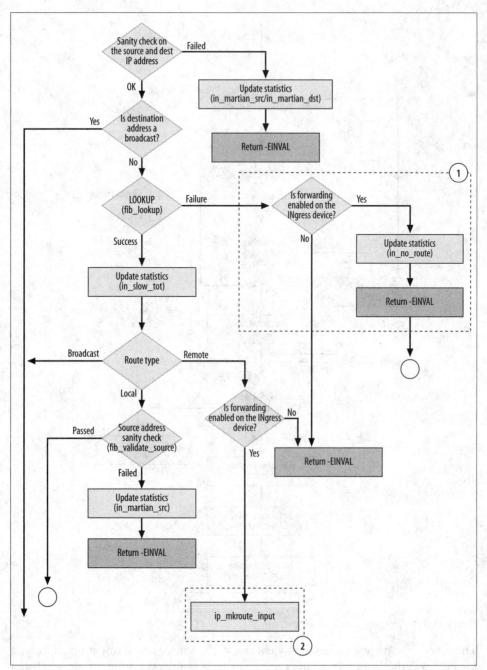

Figure 35-5(a). ip_route_input_slow function

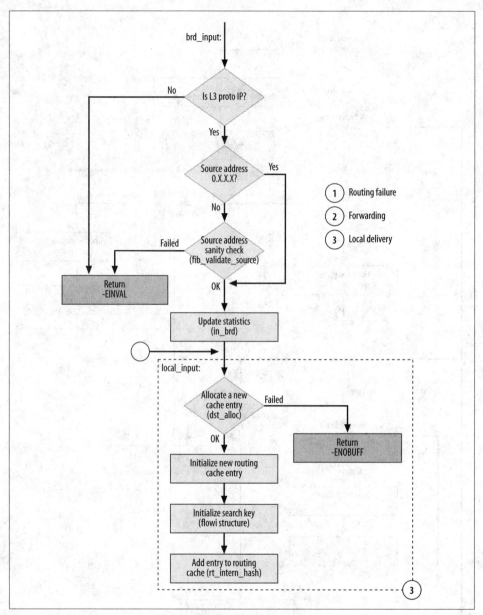

Figure 35-5(b). ip_route_input_slow function

The function starts with a few sanity checks on the source and destination addresses; for instance, the source IP address must not be a multicast address. I already listed most of those checks in the section "Verbose Monitoring" in Chapter 31. More sanity checks are done later in the function.

The routing table lookup is done with `fib_lookup`, the routine introduced in the section "fib_lookup Function." If `fib_lookup` cannot find a matching route, the packet is dropped; additionally, if the receiving interface is configured with forwarding enabled, an `ICMP_UNREACHABLE` message is sent back to the source. Note that the ICMP message is sent not by `ip_route_input_slow` but by its caller, who takes care of it upon seeing a return value of `RTN_UNREACHABLE`.

In case of success, `ip_route_input_slow` distinguishes the following three cases:

- Packet addressed to a broadcast address
- Packet addressed to a local address
- Packet addressed to a remote address

In the first two cases, the packet is to be delivered locally, and in the third, it needs to be forwarded. The details of how local delivery and forwarding are handled can be found in the sections "Local Delivery" and "Forwarding." Here are some of the tasks they both need to take care of:

Sanity checks, especially on the source address
Source addresses are checked against illegal values and are run through `fib_validate_source` to detect spoofing attempts.

Creation and initialization of a new cache entry (the local variable `rth`)
See the following section, "Creation of a Cache Entry."

Creation of a Cache Entry

I said already in the section "Cache Lookup" in Chapter 33 that `ip_route_input` (and therefore `ip_route_input_slow`, in case of a cache miss) can be called just to consult the routing table, not necessarily to route an ingress packet. Because of that, `ip_route_input_slow` does not always create a new cache entry. When invoked from IP or an L4 protocol (such as IP over IP), the function always creates a cache entry. Currently, the only other possibility is invocation by ARP. Routes generated by ARP are cached only when they would be valid for proxy ARP. See the section "Processing ARPOP_REQUEST Packets" in Chapter 28.

The new entry is allocated with `dst_alloc`. Of particular importance are the following initializations for the new cache entry:

`rth->u.dst.input`
`rth->u.dst.output`
These two virtual functions are invoked respectively by `dst_input` and `dst_output` to complete the processing of ingress and egress packets, as shown in Figure 18-1 in Chapter 18. We already saw in the section "Setting Functions for Reception and Transmission" how these two routines can be initialized depending on whether a packet is to be forwarded, delivered locally, or dropped.

`rth->fl`

> This `flowi` structure is used as a search key by cache lookups. It is important to note that `rth->fl`'s fields are initialized to the input parameters received by `ip_route_input_slow`: this ensures that the next time a lookup is done with the same parameters, `ip_route_input` will be able to satisfy it with a cache lookup.

`rth->rt_spec_dst`

> This is the preferred source address. See the following section, "Preferred Source Address Selection."

Preferred Source Address Selection

The route added to the routing cache is unidirectional, meaning that it will not be used to route traffic in the reverse direction toward the source IP address of the packet being routed. However, in some cases, the reception of a packet can trigger an action that requires the local host to choose a source IP address that it can use when transmitting a packet back to the sender.[*] This address, the *preferred source IP address*,[†] must be saved with the routing cache entry that routed the ingress packet. Here are two cases where that address, which is saved in a field called `rt_spec_dst`, comes in handy:

ICMP

> When a host receives an ICMP ECHO REQUEST message (popularly known as "pings" from the name of the command that usually generates them), the host returns an ICMP ECHO REPLY unless it is explicitly configured not to. The `rt_spec_dst` of the route used for the ingress ICMP ECHO REQUEST is used as the source address for the routing lookup made to route the ICMP ECHO REPLY. See `icmp_reply` in *net/ipv4/icmp.c*, and see Chapter 25. The `ip_send_reply` routine in *net/ipv4/ip_output.c* does something similar.

IP options

> A couple of IP options require the intermediate hosts between the source and the destination to write the IP addresses of their receiving interfaces into the IP header. The address that Linux writes is `rt_spec_dst`. See the description of `ip_options_compile` in Chapter 19.

The preferred source is selected through the `fib_validate_source` function mentioned in the section "Helper Routines" and called by `ip_route_input_slow`.

`ip_route_input_slow` initializes the preferred source IP address `rt_spec_dst` based on the destination address of the packet being routed:

---

[*] The preferred source IP address to use for traffic generated locally (i.e., packets whose transmission is not triggered or influenced by the reception of another packet) may be different. See the section "Selecting the Source IP Address."

[†] RFC 1122 calls it the "specific destination."

Packet addressed to a local address

In this case, the local address to which the packet was addressed becomes the preferred source address. (The ICMP example previously cited falls into this case.)

Broadcast packet

A broadcast address cannot be used as a source address for egress packets, so in this case, `ip_route_input_slow` does more investigation with the help of two other routines: `inet_select_addr` and `fib_validate_source` (see the section "Helper Routines").

When the source IP address is not set in the received packet (that is, when it is all zeroes), `inet_select_addr` selects the first address with scope `RT_SCOPE_LINK` on the device the packet was received from. This is because packets are sent with a null source address when addressed to the limited broadcast address, which is an address with scope `RT_SCOPE_LINK`. An example is a DHCP discovery message.

When the source address is not all zeroes, `fib_validate_source` take cares of it.

Forwarded packet

In this case, the choice is left to `fib_validate_source`. (The IP options example previously cited falls into this case.)

The preferred source IP to use for packets matching a given route can be explicitly configured by the user with a command like this:

```
ip route add 10.0.1.0/24 via 10.0.0.1 src 10.0.3.100
```

In this example, when transmitting packets to the hosts of the 10.0.1.0/24 subnet, the kernel will use 10.0.3.100 as the source IP address. Of course, only locally configured addresses are accepted: this means that for the previous command to be accepted, 10.0.3.100 must have been configured on one of the local interfaces, but not necessarily on the same device used to reach the 10.0.1.0/24 subnet. (Remember that in Linux, addresses belong to the host, not to the devices; see the section "Responding from Multiple Interfaces" in Chapter 28.) An administrator normally provides a source address when she does not want to use the one that would be picked by default from the egress device.

Figure 35-6 summarizes how `rt_spec_dst` is selected.

Local Delivery

The following types of packets are delivered locally by initializing `dst->input` appropriately, as we saw in the section "Initialization of Function Pointers for Ingress Traffic":

- Packets addressed to locally configured addresses, including multicast addresses
- Packets addressed to broadcast addresses

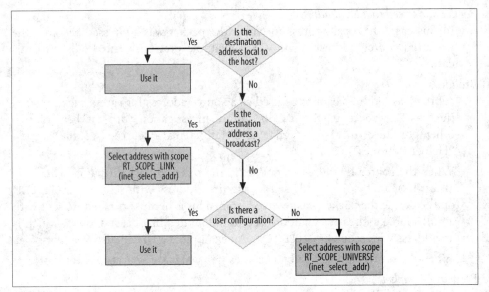

Figure 35-6. Selection of rt_spec_dst

ip_route_input_slow recognizes two kinds of broadcasts:

Limited broadcasts

> This is an address consisting of all ones: 255.255.255.255.[*] It can be recognized easily without a call to fib_lookup. Limited broadcasts are delivered to any host on the link, regardless of the subnet the host is configured on. No table lookup is required.

Subnet broadcasts

> These broadcasts are directed at hosts configured on a specific subnet. If hosts are configured on different subnets reachable via the same device (see Figure 30-4(c) in Chapter 30), only the right ones will receive a subnet broadcast. Unlike a limited broadcast, subnet broadcasts cannot be recognized without involving the routing table with fib_lookup. For example, the address 10.0.1.127 might be a subnet broadcast in 10.0.1.0/25, but not in 10.0.1.0/24.

ip_route_input_slow accepts broadcasts only if they are generated by the IP protocol. You might think that this a superfluous check, given that ip_route_input_slow is called to route IP packets. However, as I said in the section "Cache Lookup" in Chapter 33, the input buffer to ip_route_input (and therefore to ip_route_input_slow in case of a cache miss) does not necessarily represent a packet to be routed.

If everything goes fine, a new cache entry, rtable, is created, initialized, and inserted into the routing cache.

Note that there is no need to handle Multipath for packets that are delivered locally.

---

[*] There is an obsolete form of limited broadcast that consists of all zeros: 0.0.0.0.

Forwarding

If the packet is to be forwarded but the configuration of the ingress device has disabled forwarding, the packet cannot be transmitted and must be dropped. The forwarding status of the device is checked with `IN_DEV_FORWARD`. Figure 35-7 shows the internals of `ip_mkroute_input`; in particular, it shows what that function looks like when there is no support for multipath caching (i.e., when `ip_mkroute_input` ends up being an alias to `ip_mkroute_input_def`). In the section "Multipath Caching," you will see how the other case differs.

If the matching route returned by `fib_lookup` includes more than one next hop, `fib_select_multipath` is used to choose among them. When multipath caching is supported, the selection is taken care of differently. The section "Effects of Multipath on Next Hop Selection" describes the algorithm used for the selection.

The source address is validated with `fib_validate_source`. Then, based on the factors we saw in the section "Transmitting ICMP_REDIRECT Messages" in Chapter 31, the kernel may decide to send an `ICMP_REDIRECT` to the source. In that case, the ICMP message is sent not by `ip_route_input_slow` directly, but by `ip_forward`, which takes care of it upon seeing the `RTCF_DOREDIRECT` flag.

As we saw in the section "Creation of a Cache Entry," the result of a routing lookup is not always cached.

Routing Failure

When a packet cannot be routed, either because of host configuration or because no route matches, the new route is added to the cache with `dst->input` initialized to `ip_error`. This means that all the ingress packets matching this route will be processed by `ip_error`. That function, when invoked by `dst_input`, will generate the proper `ICMP_UNREACHABLE` message depending on why the packet cannot be routed, and will drop the packet. Adding the erroneous route to the cache is useful because it can speed up the error processing of further packets sent to the same incorrect address.

ICMP messages are rate limited by `ip_error`. We already saw in the section "Egress ICMP REDIRECT Rate Limiting" in Chapter 33 that `ICMP_REDIRECT` messages are also rate limited by the DST. The rate limiting discussed here is independent of the other, but is enforced using the same fields of the `dst_entry`. This is possible because given any route, these two forms of rate limiting are mutually exclusive: one applies to `ICMP_REDIRECT` messages and the other one applies to `ICMP_UNREACHABLE` messages.

Here is how rate limiting is implemented by `ip_error` with a simple token bucket algorithm.

The timestamp `dst.rate_last` is updated every time `ip_error` is invoked to generate an ICMP message. `dst.rate_tokens` specifies how many ICMP messages—also known as the number of tokens, or the budget—can be sent before the rate limiting

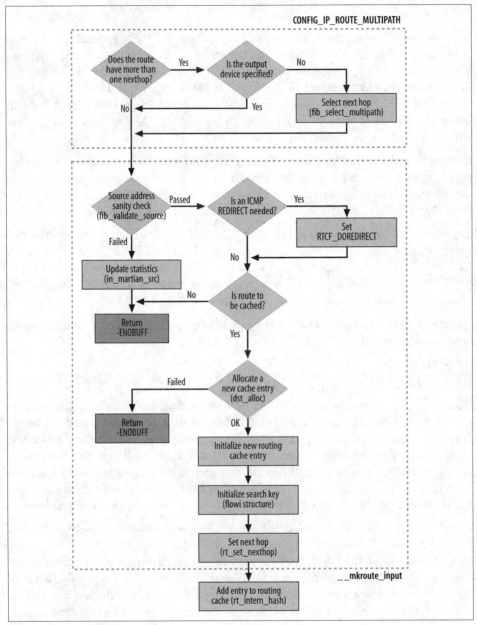

Figure 35-7. ip_mkroute_input function

kicks in and new ICMP_UNREACHABLE transmission requests will be ignored. The budget is decremented each time an ICMP_UNREACHABLE message is sent, and is incremented by ip_error itself. The budget cannot exceed the maximum number ip_rt_error_burst, which represents, as its name suggests, the maximum number of ICMP messages a host can send in 1 second (i.e., the burst). Its value is expressed in Hz so that it is easy to add tokens based on the difference between the local time `jiffies` and `dst.rate_last`.

When `ip_error` is invoked and at least one token is available, the function is allowed to transmit an `ICMP_UNREACHABLE` message. The ICMP subtype is derived from `dst.error`, which was initialized by `ip_route_input_slow` when `fib_lookup` failed to find a route.

Output Routing

Packets generated locally are routed with `ip_route_output_slow` if `__ip_route_output_key`, the routine we introduced in the section "Initialization of Function Pointers for Egress Traffic," encounters a cache miss. The structure of `ip_route_output_slow` somewhat resembles `ip_route_input_slow`. A high-level overview of the function is shown in Figures 35-8(a) and 35-8(b).

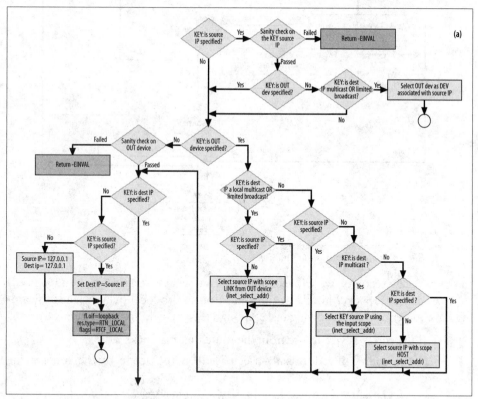

Figure 35-8.(a). ip_route_output_slow function

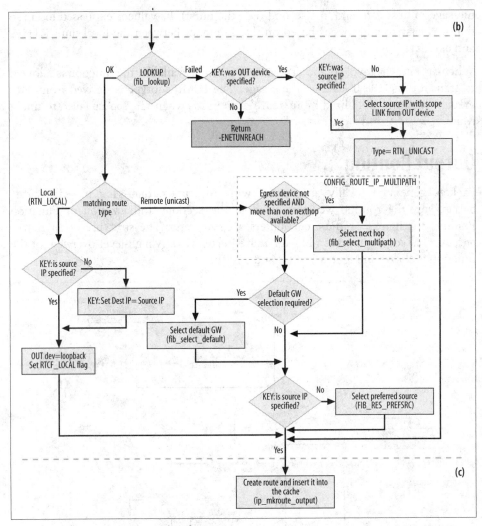

Figure 35-8(b). p_route_output_slow function

In the next few sections, we will examine in detail what `ip_route_output_slow` needs to do to deliver a packet locally or transmit it out. Both local delivery and forwarding have to perform the following tasks, though they may do so in different ways:

- Select the egress device to use from the route that matches.
- Select the source IP address to use, based on the scope of the route being searched.
- Create and initialize a new cache table entry and insert it into the cache.

Figure 35-8 is split into three parts by dotted lines. The top part, *a*, fills in the fields of the search key that are not already initialized when it is passed to the function.

The central part, *b*, makes a routing table lookup and, if needed, selects the next hop in a multipath route or the default gateway. The bottom part, *c*, creates the new cache table entry. The bottom part also initializes dst->input and dst->output based on the result of the forwarding decisions taken earlier in the function and tracked by the function mostly through a local flags variable.

In a few cases, a packet can be routed without the need for any routing lookup (i.e., no need to call fib_lookup, the central part of the figure). These are three such cases, all depicted in Figure 35-8:

Packets addressed to a multicast or limited broadcast address, when the egress device is not provided with the search key
> This case is a hack that gets around a problem with assumptions made by multimedia tools such as *vic* and *vat*. A comment in the function's code explains the problem. See the section "Special Cases" in Chapter 26.

Packets addressed to a local multicast address (i.e., 224.0.0.X) or the limited broadcast address (i.e., 255.255.255.255) going out on a given device
> Because the egress device is provided by the caller along with the search key, and because local multicasts and limited broadcasts are addresses with scope RT_SCOPE_LINK, the next hop is represented by the destination address itself. Therefore, the routing subsystem already has all the information needed to route the packet and does not need to do a lookup.* See the section "Essential Elements of Routing" in Chapter 30 for a discussion of multicast addresses.

Packets addressed to the unknown address (0.0.0.0†).
> Those packets are delivered locally. They are not sent out.

Search Key Initialization

This is how ip_route_input_slow initializes the search key that it passes to fib_lookup for the routing table lookup. The same key will be saved along with the new cached route for subsequent lookups using the cache.

```
        u32 tos    = RT_FL_TOS(oldflp);
        struct flowi fl = { .nl_u = { .ip4_u =
                     { .daddr = oldflp->fl4_dst,
                     .saddr = oldflp->fl4_src,
                     .tos = tos & IPTOS_RT_MASK,
                     .scope = ((tos & RTO_ONLINK) ?
                             RT_SCOPE_LINK :
                             RT_SCOPE_UNIVERSE),
#ifdef CONFIG_IP_ROUTE_FWMARK
                     .fwmark = oldflp->fl4_fwmark
```

---

* Note that the L3-to-L2 address mapping is also automatic, as explained in the section "Special Cases" in Chapter 26.

† 0.0.0.0 is also an obsolete form of a limited broadcast address, but Linux does not honor that form.

```
#endif
                    } },
            .iif = loopback_dev.ifindex,
            .oif = oldflp->oif };
```

The source and destination IP addresses and the firewall mark are just copied from the function's input. The setting of the TOS and scope, however, needs a little explanation:

TOS

> The two least significant bits of the fl4_tos field can be used by the caller to store flags that ip_route_output_slow can take into account to determine the scope of the route to search. This is possible because the TOS field itself does not need the whole octet. See the section "Egress lookup" in Chapter 33, and see Figure 18-3 in Chapter 18.
>
> The RF_FL_TOS macro is defined in *net/ipv4/route.c* as follows:
>
> ```
> #define RF_FL_TOS(oldflp) \
>     ((u32)(oldflp->fl4_tos & (IPTOS_RT_MASK | RTO_ONLINK))
> ```

Scope

> When the RTO_ONLINK flag is set, the scope of the route to search is set to RT_SCOPE_LINK; otherwise, it is initialized to RT_SCOPE_UNIVERSE. See the section "Egress lookup" in Chapter 33 for an example involving ARP.

Because ip_route_output_slow is called only to route locally generated traffic, the source device in the search key fl is initialized to the loopback device. As we will see, when the destination address is also local, the egress device is also initialized to the loopback device.

Figure 35-8(a) shows how basic fields of the search key are initialized when they are not provided with the input key.

Selecting the Source IP Address

The source IP address used for the search key is also the source IP address put into the IP header of the transmitted packets. In the initial part of ip_route_output_slow, therefore, the function selects the source IP address, if present, from the search key fl.fl4_src; later it initializes rth->rt_src to the same value.

When the search key does not provide a source IP address,[*] the function chooses it by calling inet_select_addr[†] with input that depends on the destination address type. In particular, ip_route_output_slow invokes inet_select_addr with the following scopes to handle special cases:

---

[*] See the section "Preferred Source Address Selection" for examples of when the source IP address may be provided with the search key.

[†] I introduced this routine in the section "Helper Routines."

- `RT_SCOPE_HOST` when the packet is to be delivered locally (see the section "Local Delivery").
- `RT_SCOPE_LINK` when the packet is sent to an address that is meaningful only on the local link, such as broadcasts, limited broadcasts, and local multicasts. This scope is also used when `fib_lookup` fails but a packet is transmitted anyway, because the search key provides the egress device and the destination is therefore supposed to be on the link (see the section "Transmission to Other Hosts").

When the packet to route does not fall into the two special cases just listed, `ip_route_output_slow` selects the source IP address by calling `FIB_RES_PREFSRC`, passing to it the result res of the search made by `fib_lookup` for a route. `FIB_RES_PREFSRC` uses various measures to pick the preferred source IP address: it returns a preferred source address if one is explicitly configured for that route by the user; otherwise, it gets one by calling `inet_select_addr` with the scope of the matching route (res->scope).

`ip_route_output_slow` gives higher priority to addresses configured on the egress device (if this device is known), by passing it as the first input parameter to `inet_select_addr`. However, other devices' addresses can be selected as well.

Figure 35-9 summarizes the logic used to select the source IP address.

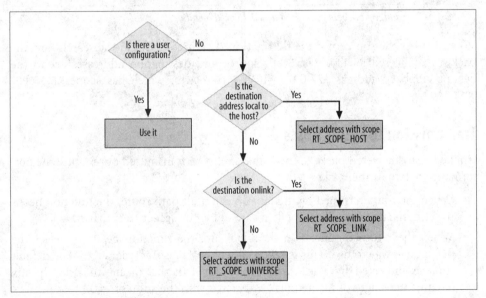

Figure 35-9. Source IP selection

Local Delivery

A packet is delivered locally when `fib_lookup` says the destination address is locally configured, or when no destination address is provided (i.e., the search contains the unknown address 0.0.0.0). In this case:

- The egress device is set to the loopback address. This means that this packet will not leave the local host; the transmission of the packet will reinject it into the IP stack.

- dst->input is initialized to ip_local_deliver, as described in the section "Local Delivery" in Chapter 20. Thanks to this, when the packet is reinjected and ip_rcv_finish invokes dst_input, the ip_local_deliver function will handle the packet.

Figure 35-10 shows the effect of these two actions as the packet moves from the output functions to the input functions in the kernel network code.

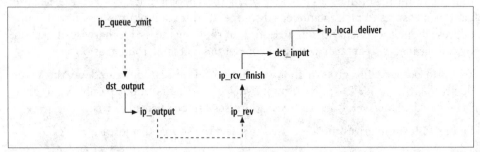

Figure 35-10. Handling packets generated and delivered locally

When neither the source nor the destination IP address is set in the search key, the packet is delivered locally, with both source and destination addresses set to the default loopback address 127.0.0.1 (INADDR_LOOPBACK), which has scope RT_SCOPE_HOST.

Transmission to Other Hosts

Unlike locally delivered packets, those that are to be transmitted out require the performance of two further tasks:

- When the route returned by the lookup is a multipath route, the function needs to select the next hop. This is taken care of by fib_select_multipath.

- When the returned route is a default route, the function needs to select the default gateway to use. This is taken care of by fib_select_default. (The default route is indicated by a res.prefixlen field of 0; this means that the "prefix length," the length of the netmask associated with the address, is 0.)

Both of these tasks are discussed in the following sections.

Even when a route lookup with fib_lookup fails, it may be possible to successfully transmit a packet. When the egress device is provided with the search key, ip_route_output_slow assumes the destination is directly reachable on the egress device. In this case, a source IP address with scope RT_SCOPE_LINK is also set, if one is not already there; an address from the egress device is used, if possible.

Interaction Between Multipath and Default Gateway Selection

This snapshot from ip_route_output_slow shows when the two key functions fib_select_multipath and fib_select_default are called to take care of respectively, multipath and default gateway selection. res is the result returned by fib_lookup.

```
#ifdef CONFIG_IP_ROUTE_MULTIPATH
    if (res.fi->fib_nhs > 1 && fl.oif == 0)
        fib_select_multipath(&fl, &res);
    else
#endif
    if (!res.prefixlen && res.type == RTN_UNICAST && !fl.oif)
        fib_select_default(&fl, &res);
```

Note that there is no need for these two routines when the search key specifies an egress device to use (fl.oif). In this case, res already contains the final forwarding decision. Therefore, the main tasks performed by fib_lookup, and the fib_semantic_match function it calls (see Figure 35-1), are to select:

- The next hop, when the matching route is a multipath route. fib_semantic_match accomplishes this by selecting the first next hop router that matches the egress device (see the section "Semantic Matching on Subsidiary Criteria"). This is done in conditional code that is present only when the kernel is compiled with multipath support.

- The default route, when the matching route is a default route. fib_semantic_match accomplishes this by selecting the first default route that matches the egress device. fib_semantic_match does not differentiate between routes with different netmask lengths, which means it does not treat default routes specially, so this case is handled transparently by fib_semantic_match.

Multipath is described in the section "Effects of Multipath on Next Hop Selection"; default gateway selection is described in the section "Default Gateway Selection."

The code snippet shown at the beginning of this section could be misinterpreted when taken out of context, and could lead to two misunderstandings:

- It suggests that Multipath cannot be used for default routes, because the logic in the snapshot shows that the execution of fib_select_multipath precludes a call to the following fib_select_default function.

  However, Multipath can actually be used on a default route. The *ip* command provided by the IPROUTE2 package (which is required for configuring Multipath) allows you to configure the default route with multiple next hops. Therefore, calling fib_select_multipath on this route is sufficient to complete the routing decision.

  net-tools's route tool allows an administrator to configure several default routes, each one with a single next hop. In this case, Multipath is not in the picture (fib_nhs is always 1). So fib_select_default is sufficient to complete the routing decision.

- It suggests that an administrator cannot configure multiple next hops on an egress device, because `fib_select_multipath` is called only when the egress device is null.

  However, it is possible to configure a multipath route with more than one next hop using the same egress device. A routing lookup whose search key contains a non-null egress device (`fl.oif`) is handled by `fib_semantic_match`, which simply returns the first available next hop that matches the device. `fib_select_multipath` is not involved in the selection.

Default Gateway Selection

The selection of the right default gateway is done with `fib_select_default`, which is invoked by `ip_route_output_slow` when both of the following conditions are met:

The route returned by `fib_lookup` *has a /0 netmask (*`res.prefixlen` *is 0)*
A default route matches any destination address, but it is checked last thanks to having a netmask of /0, the shortest possible netmask. If none of the configured routes matches the destination address, only default routes will match. However, because all default routes would match, `fib_lookup` always returns the first one it checks. This is why `fib_select_default` is called to make the best choice among the available ones.

The route returned by `fib_lookup` *is of type* `RTN_UNICAST`
Local routes, broadcast routes, and multicast routes do not need a gateway; its use with them could even be considered nonsensical.

As we mentioned in the section "Double Definitions for Functions" in Chapter 34, there are two versions of `fib_select_default`. This is the one used when there is no support for Policy Routing (defined in *include/net/ip_fib.h*[*]):

```
static inline
void fib_select_default(const struct flowi *flp, struct fib_result *res)
{
    if (FIB_RES_GW(*res) && FIB_RES_NH(*res).nh_scope == RT_SCOPE_LINK)
        ip_fib_main_table->tb_select_default(ip_fib_main_table, flp, res);
}
```

`flp` is the search key, and `res` is the lookup result returned by a previous call to `fib_lookup` in `ip_route_output_slow`.

Note that when the conditions required to execute `tb_select_default` are not met, the caller does not receive any error or warning; `fib_select_default` simply returns the same `fib_result` instance that was provided as input.

---

[*] See the section "Default Gateway Selection with Policy Routing" for the other definition.

`tb_select_default` is initialized to `fn_hash_select_default`, which is defined in *net/ipv4/fib_hash.c* and described in the following section. Note that `fib_select_default` does a lookup on the `ip_fib_main_table` only when res a route whose next hop gateway has scope `RT_SCOPE_LINK`; the reason for this is described in the section "Use of the scope" in Chapter 30.

fn_hash_select_default Function

The `fn_hash_select_default` function receives in input a `fib_result` structure, res, where the result of a previous `fib_lookup` invocation was stored. This structure is used as the starting point for the search of the default route by `fn_hash_select_default`.

To be selected, the default route must have the same scope as res->scope, a priority that is less than or equal to res->fi->fib_priority, and a next hop with scope `RT_SCOPE_LINK` (i.e., it must be directly connected).

The selection of the route also takes into consideration the reachability status of the next hops. `fib_detect_death` is used to give higher preference to routes whose next hops have an L3 address that is already resolved to an L2 address (i.e., NUD_REACHABLE state). This check ensures that when the currently used default route becomes unusable—for example, because the next hop gateway failed—a new one is selected, if available.

The previously selected default route is saved in the global variable `fn_hash_last_dflt`.

The entire routine runs with the `fib_hash_lock` held.

Effects of Multipath on Next Hop Selection

In both `ip_route_input_slow` and `ip_route_output_slow`, `fib_select_multipath` is called only when:

- Multipath support is included in the kernel (`CONFIG_IP_ROUTE_MULTIPATH`).
- The routing lookup with `fib_lookup` returns a route with more than one next hop (`fib_nhs> 1`).
- The egress interface was not provided with the search key.
- The destination address is not a local, broadcast, or multicast address.

The following code shows how `fib_select_multipath` is called to select the next hop:

```
#ifdef CONFIG_IP_ROUTE_MULTIPATH
    if (res.fi->fib_nhs > 1 && fl.oif == 0)
        fib_select_multipath(&key, &res);
#endif
```

We already saw in the section "Next Hop Selection" in Chapter 31 how Linux selects the next hop to use when more than one is available. Let's see now how that algorithm is implemented.

We saw in the section "Organization of Routing Hash Tables" in Chapter 34 that a route is represented by the closely coupled data structures `fib_node` and `fib_info`, and that each `fib_info` includes an array of `fib_nh` data structures (one for each next hop specified in the route).

First, let's clarify which fields of the `fib_info` and `fib_nh` structures are used to decide whether a next hop must be chosen among a pool of available next hops, and if so, which one is chosen.

These are the fields used to store the multipath configuration:

`fib_info->fib_nhs`
> Number of next hops defined by the route.

`fib_info->fib_nh`
> Array of `fib_nh` structures. The size of the array is given by `fib_info->fib_nhs`.

The following fields are used to implement the weighted random roundrobin algorithm:

`fib_info->fib_power`
> This is initialized to the sum of the weights (`fib_nh->nh_weight`) of all the next hops of this `fib_info` instance, excluding ones that are disabled for some reasons (tagged with the `RTNH_DEAD` flag). Every time `fib_select_multipath` is called to select a next hop, `fib_power` is decremented. Its value is reinitialized when it reaches zero.

`fib_nh->nh_weight`
> Weight of this next hop. When not explicitly configured, it is set to a default value of 1. As we will see, this value is used to make `fib_select_multipath` select the next hops proportional to their weights (relative to `fib_info->fib_power`).

`fib_nh->nh_power`
> Tokens allowing this next hop to be selected. This value is first initialized to `fib_nh->nh_weight` when `fib_info->fib_power` is initialized. Its value is decremented every time this next hop is selected by `fib_select_multipath`. When the value reaches zero, this next hop is no longer selected until `nh_power` is reinitialized to `fib_nh->nh_weight` (which happens when `fib_info->fib_power` is reinitialized).

Now we'll look at how the implementation works.

Everything starts with all the next hops having a number of tokens (`nh_power`) that is the same as their weights. This number, as we've seen, is 1 by default. The `change_nexthops` loop sets the next hops' `nh_power` field while accumulating the total weights in the function's local variable, `power`.

```
spin_lock_bh(&fib_multipath_lock);
if (fi->fib_power <= 0) {
    int power = 0;
    change_nexthops(fi) {
        if (!(nh->nh_flags&RTNH_F_DEAD)) {
            power += nh->nh_weight;
            nh->nh_power = nh->nh_weight;
        }
    } endfor_nexthops(fi);
```

`fib_info->fib_power` is initialized to the sum of the next hop's weight. Because it is decremented each time `fib_select_multipath` makes a decision (in code shown later in this section), each next hop will be selected a number of times equal to its weight by the time `fib_power` reaches 0. This also ensures that by the time `fib_info->fib_power` reaches 0, each next hop has been selected a number of times proportional to its weight.

```
        fi->fib_power = power;
        if (power <= 0) {
            spin_unlock_bh(&fib_multipath_lock);
            res->nh_sel = 0;
            return;
        }
    }
```

The selection of a next hop by `fib_select_multipath` is pseudorandom: every time `fib_select_multipath` is called, it generates a random number w ranging from zero to `fib_info->fib_power-1`, and then browses all the next hops until it finds one that has a number of tokens (`fib_nh->nh_power`) greater than or equal to w. Note that w is reduced at each loop, making each loop more likely to find a next hop that matches this condition.

```
w = jiffies % fi->fib_power;
change_nexthops(fi) {
    if (!(nh->nh_flags&RTNH_F_DEAD) && nh->nh_power) {
        if ((w -= nh->nh_power) <= 0) {
            nh->nh_power--;
            fi->fib_power--;
            res->nh_sel = nhsel;
            spin_unlock_bh(&fib_multipath_lock);
            return;
        }
    }
} endfor_nexthops(fi);
res->nh_sel = 0;
spin_unlock_bh(&fib_multipath_lock);
```

Multipath Caching

Figure 35-4 shows when the `fib_select_multipath` routine described in the previous section is called for both ingress and egress traffic, as well as how support for multipath caching influences the way the routing cache is populated by `ip_mkroute_input` and `ip_mkroute_output`. Let's analyze the ingress and egress cases separately.

Ingress traffic

When the kernel does not have support for multipath caching, `ip_mkroute_input` calls `fib_select_multipath` when the conditions listed in the previous sections are met, and selects one next hop according to the logic described earlier.

When the kernel has support for multipath caching, it does not select one next hop with `fib_select_multipath`. Instead, it loops over all the next hops of the Multipath route and adds an entry to the cache for each one. For each route, it also calls `multipath_set_nhinfo`, described in the section "Interface Between the Routing Cache and Multipath" in Chapter 33. That function can be used by the caching algorithm to update the local information it uses to select the next hop. For example, the weighted random algorithm uses the function to populate its database of next hops (see the section "Weighted Random Algorithm" in Chapter 33).

Egress traffic

As shown in Figure 35-4, the egress case is pretty similar to the ingress case. The only difference is that even when the kernel supports Multipath caching, `fib_select_multipath` is called and the latter invocation of `ip_mkroute_output` overrides the selection made by `fib_select_multipath`.

In both cases—res->nh_sel, that is, the result of the next hop selection—is initialized to the last next hop of the multipath route. For subsequent packets, the selection will be done at cache lookup time. See the section "Multipath Caching" in Chapter 33.

Policy Routing

A routing lookup in a kernel that has support for Policy Routing has to take into account the possible presence of multiple tables. The next two sections show how the Policy Routing versions of `fib_lookup` and `fib_select_default` differ from the basic versions we saw earlier in this chapter.

fib_lookup with Policy Routing

When Policy Routing is configured, this function contains an extra step: it needs to find out what routing table to use based on the configured policies.

We saw in the section "Main Data Structures" in Chapter 32 that routing policies are defined with `fib_rule` data structures. All the `fib_rule` instances are linked together with the global list `fib_rules`. The list is kept sorted in increasing order as indicated by the `priority` field. This allows the configuration to define the order in which the rules should be checked, therefore reducing lookup time. The more commonly matched rules or most important rules (as defined by the administrator, depending on the context) are closer to the head of the list. The `priority` is a 32-bit field, which means a host can theoretically have up to 2^{32} policies. Of course, because policies are stored in a sorted, flat list, a high number of policies can decrease routing performance significantly.

Without any user configuration, `fib_rules` includes the three default instances defined in *net/ipv4/fib_rules.c*, as shown in Figure 35-11:

local_rule
> This is the highest-priority rule and is therefore at the head of the list. It always matches, and its purpose is to force the first lookup to be on the `ip_fib_local_table` routing table. This makes sense because the packets addressed to the local system don't need any further routing decision.

main_rule
> This is the second table to be checked (unless the administrator inserts some user-defined tables in between) and always matches as well. It causes a search on the main routing table `ip_fib_main_table`.

default_rule
> This is the default table and is put at the end of the list.

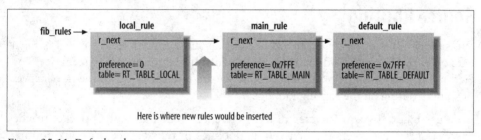

Figure 35-11. Default rules

Figure 35-12 shows the logic implemented by `fib_lookup`. It browses policies one by one until it either finds a match with the packet it is routing or gets to the end of the list of policies without any match. When a matching policy is found, the action that follows depends on the policy type (see the section "Lookup with Policy Routing" in Chapter 31). In particular, the policy actions `RTN_UNREACHABLE`, `RTN_BLACKHOLE`, and `RTN_PROHIBIT` lead to the return of an error, whose value may be used by the caller of `fib_lookup` to generate the appropriate ICMP message. The policy action `RTN_UNICAST` leads to a lookup with `tb_lookup`, which consists of a call to the `fn_hash_lookup` function described in the section "The Table Lookup: fn_hash_lookup." This function can return various results. Besides the errors already described in its dedicated section, it is interesting to note that:

- When the lookup succeeds, `res->r` is initialized to the matching policy.

- When the lookup fails, `fib_lookup` continues its loop over the policies if the error type is –EAGAIN. This is because that error is returned when the action type associated with the matching route found by `fn_hash_lookup` is RTN_THROW (see the section "Route Types and Actions" in Chapter 30).

Default Gateway Selection with Policy Routing

The selection of a default route with Policy Routing works just the same as when there is no Policy Routing. The only difference is that `fib_select_default`, defined in *net/ipv4/fib_rules.c*, uses the matching policy (res->r) to identify the routing table to use.

```
void fib_select_default(const struct flowi *flp, struct fib_result *res)
{
    if (res->r && res->r->r_action == RTN_UNICAST &&
        FIB_RES_GW(*res) && FIB_RES_NH(*res).nh_scope == RT_SCOPE_LINK) {
        struct fib_table *tb;
        if ((tb = fib_get_table(res->r->r_table)) != NULL)
            tb->tb_select_default(tb, flp, res);
    }
}
```

Source Routing

We saw in Chapter 18 that IP packets can be source routed. Because this is taken care of by the IP protocol directly without involving the routing subsystem, it is covered in the part of the book about IP. Here we are interested just in the implications of source routing on the routing lookups.

Let's use Figure 18-1 in Chapter 18 as a reference. When an ingress packet reaches `ip_rcv_finish`, it triggers the first routing lookup. In the absence of source routing, this is the only routing lookup needed. However, before `ip_rcv_finish` calls `dst_input`, it checks whether the IP header specifies source routing and, if so, takes care of it.

Source routing here is handled by `ip_options_rcv_srr`. It extracts the next hop to use from the IP header and makes a second routing lookup with `ip_route_input`. This second lookup replaces the existing skb->dst with a newer one. See the sequence of calls in Figure 35-13.

When locally generated traffic carries the Source Routing IP option, it triggers only one routing lookup because the correct next hop is selected before the lookup (see `ip_queue_xmit` for an example).

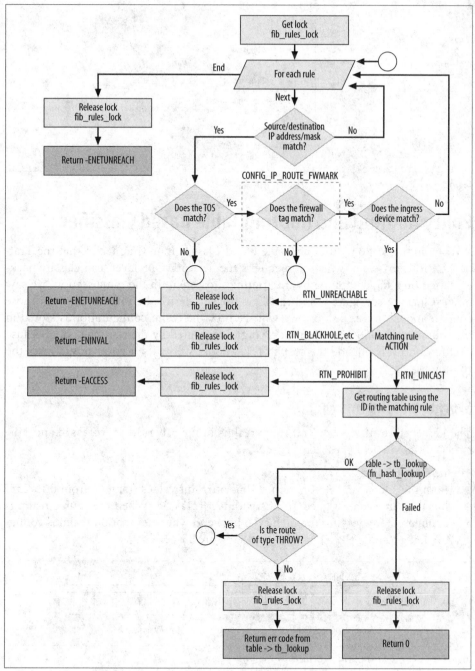

Figure 35-12. Policy Routing version of fib_lookup function

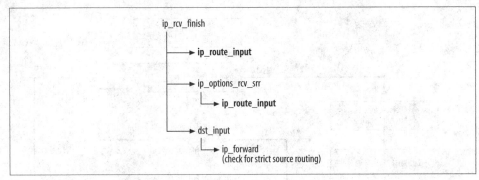

Figure 35-13. Source routing for ingress traffic

Policy Routing and Routing Table Based Classifier

We saw in the section "Routing Table Based Classifier" in Chapter 31 that the Traffic Control subsystem, which implements the network QoS layer, can classify packets based on a tag computed by the routing subsystem. In the same section, we saw how realms are configured, and the logic used to derive the routing tag from those configurations. In this section, we will see how the realm configuration is stored in the routing table and how the routing tag is computed by the routing code. Because Traffic Control is outside the scope of this book, we will not cover how it uses the routing tag.

Storing the Realms

The kernel stores the policy and route realms in the fib_rule->r_tclassid and fib_nh->nh_tclassid fields, respectively.

fib_rule->r_tclassid
:   Both the source and destination realms are 8-bit values (ranging from 0 to 255) but they are each assigned 16 bits within r_tclassid. When the source realm is configured, it goes into the higher 16 bits, and when destination realm is configured, it goes into the lower 16 bits. See Figure 35-14.

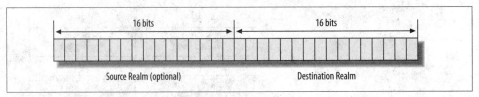

Figure 35-14. r_tclassid field structure

`fib_nh->nh_tclassid`

> Normally, only the destination realm is used to compute the routing tag; the matching route is selected based on the destination address. However, as we saw in the section "Computing the routing tag" in Chapter 31, sometimes the kernel needs to make a reverse path lookup. When that happens, the destination realm of a route is derived from the source realm of the reverse route. `nh_tclassid` is a 32-bit variable.

Helper Routines

Before seeing how `dst.tclassid` is initialized, let's look at a few helper routines that are used in accomplishing that task:

`fib_rules_tclass`

> This is used to retrieve the `r_tclassid` field from a `fib_rule` data structure. Because the result returned by `fib_lookup` includes a pointer to the `fib_rule` instance that matched, `fib_rules_tclass` is useful to extract the matching rule after a lookup. Note that this function is called only when there is support for Policy Routing in the kernel, which makes `fib_rule` structures meaningful.

`fib_combine_itag`

> Figure 35-15 shows the logic of this function, which is used to help find realms when a reverse path lookup is necessary.
>
> When Policy Routing is not enabled, it simply swaps the source and destination route realms.
>
> When Policy Routing is enabled, the function takes policy source realm (S2 in Figure 35-15) as the destination realm. It also takes the destination route realm (D1) as the source realm if it is provided, and takes the destination policy realm (D2) otherwise.
>
> The result is returned in the input parameter `itag`, which will be used by the caller when invoking `rt_set_nexthop` (see the section "Computing the Routing Tag").
>
> This function is called by `fib_validate_source` after a reverse path lookup. `fib_validate_source` receives the source and destination IP addresses as input, swaps them, and calls `fib_lookup` to do a reverse path lookup. The result returned by `fib_lookup`, therefore, also has the source and destination realms swapped. Because the realm fields are 16 bits wide and the realms returned by `fib_lookup` are swapped, `fib_combine_itag` uses 16-bit shifts to adjust everything.

`set_class_tag`

> Given a route (and therefore the associated `dst_entry.tclassid`) and a tag previously initialized by the caller, `set_class_tag` uses the second parameter to fill in the realms not already initialized in `dst_entry.tclassid`.

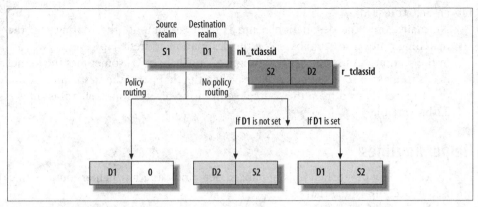

Figure 35-15. fib_combine_itag function

Computing the Routing Tag

The routing tag has to be calculated by the ip_route_input_slow and ip_route_
output_slow functions we saw earlier in this chapter. The logic used was described in
the section "Computing the Routing Tag" in Chapter 30.

The information required to compute a routing tag is the skb packet to route and the
skb->dst result of the routing lookup. The routing tag is saved in skb->dst.tclassid.
Once ip_route_input_slow and ip_route_output_slow have successfully found the
forwarding information, they initialize a new routing cache entry, including the routing tag, and add it to the cache. Part of the cache entry initialization is done with rt_
set_nexthop, which among other things takes care of the routing tag dst_entry.
tclassid. Figure 35-4 shows exactly when rt_next_hop is called.

```
static void rt_set_nexthop(struct rtable *rt, struct fib_result *res, u32 itag)
{
    struct fib_info *fi = res->fi;

    if (fi) {
        ... ... ...
#ifdef CONFIG_NET_CLS_ROUTE
        rt->u.dst.tclassid = FIB_RES_NH(*res).nh_tclassid;
#endif
    }
    ... ... ...

#ifdef CONFIG_NET_CLS_ROUTE
#ifdef CONFIG_IP_MULTIPLE_TABLES
    set_class_tag(rt, fib_rules_tclass(res));
#endif
    set_class_tag(rt, itag);
#endif
    ... ... ...
}
```

The preceding snapshot shows that tclassid is first initialized with the destination route's realm, when the kernel has support for the routing table based classifier (otherwise, there would be no need for that). Note that set_class_tag is called with different inputs based on whether the kernel has Policy Routing support:

With Policy Routing support
> The components of dst.tclassid that are not yet initialized are filled in from the policy realms.

Without Policy Routing support
> The components of dst.tclassid that are not yet initialized are filled in using the input parameter itag previously computed by the caller:

> - ip_route_input_slow (called via __mkroute_input) passes a value of itag computed with fib_combine_itag.

> - ip_route_output_slow (called via __mkroute_output) passes 0, because the packets it routes are generated locally and therefore the kernel does not use any reverse lookup to try to fill in the missing realms.

CHAPTER 36

Routing: Miscellaneous Topics

In the previous chapters, we saw how the various routing features work and how they interact with each other and with other kernel subsystems. In this chapter, we conclude the routing part of the book with a description of how the subsystem interacts with the user-space commands that configure routing. I will not describe the commands themselves, because administration is outside the scope of this book. We will also look at the various files exported in the */proc* directory that can be used to tune routing. The chapter concludes with a detailed description of the data structures already introduced in Chapter 32.

User-Space Configuration Tools

Routing can be configured with both the *net-tools* and IPROUTE2 packages, which use ioctl and Netlink interfaces, respectively. The following subsections give more details on these two packages, but focus on the IPROUTE2's *ip* command, which is the newer and more powerful way to configure routing on Linux.

The two sets of tools can coexist without problems, if you know their limitations and use them accordingly. *net-tools* does not allow you to configure any of the advanced routing features, such as Multipath and Policy Routing; nor can you see these features in the results displayed by *net-tools*' utilities. However, the routing configuration applied by IPROUTE2 is backward compatible with *net-tools*.

Figure 36-1 summarizes what we will see in the subsections. The figure shows the main functions used by the two kernel interfaces to manipulate routing tables, and the ioctl commands used by *net-tools*. (IPROUTE2 allows you to configure other objects too, such as policy rules, but these are not shown in the figure to keep it simple.)

A few points are worth mentioning:

- Both tools end up adding or removing routes using the same routines: fn_hash_ insert and fn_hash_delete, which we saw in Chapter 34.

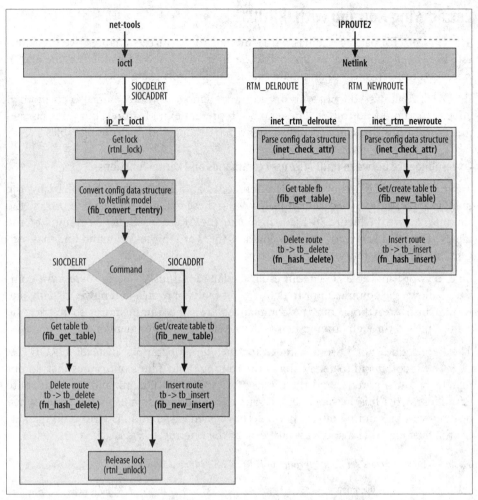

Figure 36-1. ioctl- based versus Netlink-based routing table manipulation

- Because of the previous point, the input received from the two user-space tools must be saved in the same data structures before invoking the common fn_hash_ *xxx* routines. Because the two tools use different message types to talk to the kernel, and because Netlink is the newer and preferred interface, the input from ioctl commands is converted to Netlink format with fib_convert_rtentry. The conversion also takes care of parsing the request—converting the string entered by the user into the kernel data structure shown later in this chapter—so there is no need for an explicit call to the parsing routine inet_check_attr (which is instead called by the inet_rtm_*xxx* routines).

- A lock is used to serialize routing configuration changes. Figure 36-1 does not show any locking associated with the two inet_rtm_*xxx* routines, because the lock is acquired by the routing Netlink socket code before invoking them (see rtnetlink_rcv for details).

Configuring Routing with IPROUTE2

The IPROUTE2 package comes with different tools. In this chapter, we are interested in the *ip* command, and in particular in its two subcommands *ip route* and *ip rule*, used respectively to manipulate routes and policy routing rules.

IPROUTE2 allows you not only to add and remove a route, but also to modify, append, and prepend routes. These do not represent extra features, but just management operations that can make life easier when dealing with big routing tables.

Correspondence between IPROUTE2 user commands and kernel functions

Tables 36-1 and 36-2 show the operation codes and flags set by IPROUTE2 for the main *ip route* and *ip rule* commands. Knowing these will make it easier to browse the routines shown in Figure 36-1 and listed in the "Kernel handler" columns of the tables. The "CLI keyword" column contains the word in the command line that triggers the proper operation.

One keyword in Table 36-1 requires an explanation: *flush*. The *ip route flush* command allows the administrator to define what kinds of routes to remove. Usually one would flush everything, but the command allows the administrator to restrict the routes flushed through criteria such as device and destination network.

The kernel does not have a handler for the *flush* operation. Instead, IPROUTE2 issues a *list* command to get a copy of the routing table, filters out routes that do not match the flush criteria, and then issues an RTM_DELROUTE command for each route left. This works fine in small setups, but can introduce significant overhead when dealing with big routing tables. It would have been easier and faster to send the kernel the flushing criteria and let it take care of the filtering.

Table 36-1. Parameters set by do_iproute in IPROUTE2's iproute.c file

CLI keyword	Operation	Flags	Kernel handler
add	RTM_NEWROUTE	NLM_F_EXCL NLM_F_CREATE	inet_rtm_newroute
change	RTM_NEWROUTE	NLM_F_REPLACE	inet_rtm_newroute
replace	RTM_NEWROUTE	NLM_F_CREATE NLM_F_REPLACE	inet_rtm_newroute
prepend	RTM_NEWROUTE	NLM_F_CREATE	inet_rtm_newroute
append	RTM_NEWROUTE	NLM_F_CREATE NLM_F_APPEND	inet_rtm_newroute
test	RTM_NEWROUTE	NLM_F_EXCL	inet_rtm_newroute
delete	RTM_DELROUTE	None	inet_rtm_delroute
list/lst/show	RTM_GETROUTE	None	inet_dump_fib
get	RTM_GETROUTE	NLM_F_REQUEST	inet_rtm_getroute
flush	RTM_GETROUTE	None	None

Table 36-2. Parameters set by do_iprule in IPROUTE2's iprule.c file

CLI keyword	Operation	Flag	Kernel handler
add	RTM_NEWRULE	None	inet_rtm_newrule
delete	RTM_DELRULE	None	inet_rtm_delrule
list/lst/show	RTM_GETRULE	None	inet_dump_rules

Note that some kernel handlers take care of more than one user command type from the "CLI keyword" column. The kernel can distinguish the different commands thanks to the combination of the operation and flags parameters.

As shown in Figure 36-1, the kernel handlers that manipulate routes are inet_rtm_newroute and inet_rtm_delroute, described in the next subsection. I'll leave it as an exercise to see how the handlers in Table 36-2 are implemented (use the section "Policy Routing" in Chapter 35 as a reference).

For readers who are curious about investigating the IPROUTE2 utility code itself, Figure 36-2 shows the files and routines in this package that take care of parsing and sending the requests of the various *ip route* and *ip rule* commands to the kernel. For example, if you type the command *ip route add ...*, the routine main in *ip.c* would process the command with do_iproute defined in *iproute.c*. Because the operation is *add*, do_iproute would process the command with iproute_modify.

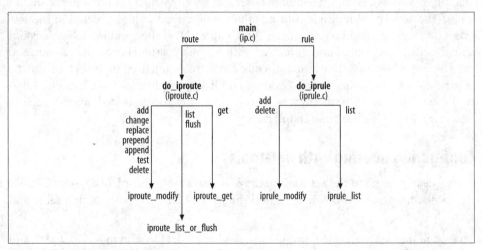

Figure 36-2. IPROUTE2 files and functions for routing

inet_rtm_newroute and inet_rtm_delroute functions

These two routines take care of adding and removing a route, respectively, when the kernel receives a user request from the IPROUTE2 tools, as shown in Figure 36-1 and Table 36-1.

Both routines use `inet_check_attr` to fill in a `kern_rta` structure, which stores the results from parsing the input from the user command. All the fields of `kern_rta` are pointers: they point directly to fields inside the data structure received from user space. A NULL pointer means that the associated field has not been configured.

In this section, we'll examine `inet_rtm_newroute`. The operation of `inet_rtm_delroute` is symmetrical.

```
int inet_rtm_newroute(struct sk_buff *skb, struct nlmsghdr* nlh, void *arg)
{
    struct fib_table * tb;
    struct rtattr **rta = arg;
    struct rtmsg *r = NLMSG_DATA(nlh);

    if (inet_check_attr(r, rta))
        return -EINVAL;

    tb = fib_new_table(r->rtm_table);

    if (tb)
        return tb->tb_insert(tb, r, (struct kern_rta*)rta, nlh, &NETLINK_CB(skb));
    return -ENOBUFS;
}
```

First the function parses the input message `nlh` with `inet_check_attr` and stores the result in `rta`. When adding a route, the user can specify which routing table it should go in. The concept of multiple routing tables is described in higher detail in the section "Concepts Behind Policy Routing" in Chapter 31. If the specified table does not already exist, it is created and initialized with `fib_new_table`. Having the reference to the routing table now, the function calls the virtual function `tb_insert` to do the insertion. We saw in the section "Adding and Removing Routes" in Chapter 34 that `tb_insert` invokes `fh_hash_insert`, whose internals are described in the section "Adding a Route" in the same chapter.

Configuring Routing with net-tools

The *route* command in the *net-tools* package is available in most Unix systems, and is the most common way to configure and dump the content of the routing table and its cache.

The *route add* and *route del* commands send the ioctl commands `SIOCADDRT` and `SIOCDELRT`, respectively, to the kernel to add and remove a route. The dump of the routing table and routing cache, however, is done in a different way: *route* simply dumps the contents of the */proc/net/route* and */proc/net/rt_cache* files.*

---

* See the file *lib/inet_gr.c* in the *net-tools* package.

The kernel handler that takes care of the two ioctl commands is ip_rt_ioctl, defined in *net/ipv4/fib_frontend.c*. Figure 36-1 showed part of its internals.

Only users with network administration privileges (CAP_NET_ADMIN) can use the *route* command. The call to capable is used to enforce this rule.[*] Then, because the data structure that carries the information about the route to delete or add is in user space, it has to be copied into an address in kernel space with copy_from_user.

```
... ... ...
if (!capable(CAP_NET_ADMIN))
    return -EPERM;
if (copy_from_user(&r, arg, sizeof(struct rtentry)))
    return -EFAULT;
... ... ...
```

Change Notifications

We saw in Chapter 3 that Netlink defines multicast groups for the purpose of sending out notifications about particular kinds of events, and user programs can register to be part of those groups. Among those groups is the RTMGRP_IPV4_ROUTE group, which is used for notifications regarding changes to the IPv4 routing tables. These changes are sent to the multicast group RTGRM_IPV4_ROUTE with the rtmsg_fib routine.

Examples of interested listeners for these events are routing daemons, which need to know such things as when routes are added or deleted by other daemons or by manual user configuration. Users can also use IPROUTE2's *ip monitor route* command to test the feature. Figure 36-3 shows an example: every time a change is applied to a routing table on one terminal, a notification is printed on the other terminal where the *ip monitor route* command is executing.[†] The terminal and the kernel communicate via a Netlink socket.

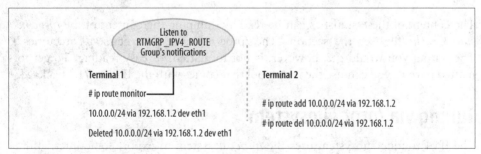

Figure 36-3. Example of use of the ip monitor route command

---

[*] For more details on user privileges and process capabilities, refer to *Understanding the Linux Kernel* (O'Reilly).

[†] Not all changes currently generate notifications. For example, when a device goes down, removal of the associated IPv4 routes is not communicated to the IPv4 protocol. This behavior could change, however. For example, IPv6 is already notified.

Routes Inserted by the Kernel: The fib_magic Function

We saw in Figure 36-1 that the Netlink socket can be used to exchange messages between the kernel and user space. There are cases, however, where different parts of the kernel use Netlink messages to communicate with each other. This makes it easy, for instance, to react to kernel-generated events with the same code that is normally used to react to user-generated events.

For instance, we saw in the section "Adding an IP address" in Chapter 32 that when a new address is configured on an interface, a set of routing entries may be generated. An easy way to install those routes is to simulate the reception of a user-space command that requests the insertion of new routes. This is accomplished with the fib_magic routine, which creates the same message that would have been generated if the route was entered explicitly with the *route add* or *ip route add* command.

fib_add_ifaddr and fib_del_ifaddr are two good examples of the use of fib_magic. See the section "Changes in IP Configuration" in Chapter 32 for more details on those two functions.

Statistics

The routing code keeps statistics about different aspects of the routing code, such as lookups and garbage collection. Statistics are maintained on a per-processor basis. ip_rt_init, described in the section "Routing Subsystem Initialization" in Chapter 32, allocates for each CPU a copy of the rt_cache_stat data structure, where the CPU keeps its own statistics. The rt_cache_stat fields are incremented with the RT_CACHE_STAT_INC macro, which transparently updates the counter for the right CPU. The section "rt_cache_stat Structure" describes the fields of rt_cache_stat in detail.

The content of these statistics can be read by dumping the content of the */proc/net/stat/rt_cache* file (see the section "The /proc/net and /proc/net/stat Directories"). The output you would get, however, is not formatted for easy reading. To get formatted output, you can use the *lnstat* tool that comes with the IPROUTE2 package.

Tuning via /proc Filesystem

The IPv4 routing subsystem uses the */proc* filesystem to export some internal data structures in read-only mode (e.g., the cache), and other structures in read-write mode so that they can be used for tuning.

Figure 36-4 shows where these files are located and the routines that register them. The files shown without a reference to a creating routine are statically defined by sysctl_init at boot time.

/proc/sys/net/ipv4/
/proc/sys/net/ipv4/conf
/proc/sys/net/ipv4/route

These directories are used to export internal data structures used for tuning. The files in these directories are therefore writable. Later sections list their files, the associated kernel variables, and the variables' default values when applicable.[*]

/proc/net/
/proc/net/stat

Files in these directories are not used for tuning, but rather, to execute kernel routines to get some kind of information. See the section "The /proc/net and /proc/net/stat Directories."

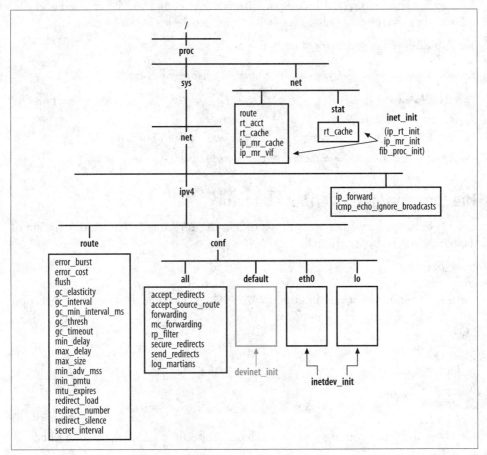

Figure 36-4. /proc files used by the IPv4 routing subsystem

---

[*] Take into account that the default value set by the kernel may be different from the default value you get when you boot a Linux system. The reason is that each Linux distribution is free to change the default value of each sysctl variable at boot time by means of the initialization files and scripts. See, for instance, */etc/sysctl.conf*. Also, different kernel versions could use different default values.

The /proc/sys/net/ipv4 Directory

This directory contains a lot of files, but the only ones used by routing subsystems are:

ip_forward
> Contains a Boolean flag that can be used to globally enable and disable IP forwarding. Its value can be overwritten on a per-device basis (see the section "Enabling and Disabling Forwarding").

icmp_echo_ignore_broadcasts
> An ICMP tuning parameter. It was introduced in the section "Directed Broadcasts" in Chapter 30, which explained that the routing code uses it to decide how to handle directed broadcasts. Broadcast filtering can be enabled and disabled only here, and only globally (not on a per-device basis).

See Table 36-3 for a summary of these files.

Table 36-3. /proc/sys/net/ipv4/ files usable for tuning the routing subsystem

Kernel variable name	Filename	Default value
ipv4_devconf.forwarding[a]	ip_forward	0
sysctl_icmp_echo_ignore_broadcasts	icmp_echo_ignore_broadcasts	0

[a] See Chapter 19 for a description of the ipv4_devconf data structure.

The /proc/sys/net/ipv4/route Directory

The IPv4 routing subsystem uses all the files in this directory. Here is a description of the files, grouped by functionality:

error_burst
error_cost
> Used to implement rate limiting for ICMP_UNREACHABLE messages. See the section "Routing Failure" in Chapter 35.

max_size
gc_thresh
gc_min_interval
gc_timeout
gc_elasticity
gc_interval
> Used by the routing cache garbage collection algorithm, described in Chapter 33.

flush
min_delay
max_delay

Used to control the flushing of the routing cache.

Unlike the other files in this directory, flush is only writable* and triggers an action; it is not a simple tuning parameter. When the user writes *n* into this file, the function ipv4_sysctl_rtcache_flush is invoked to schedule a flush of the routing table cache after *n* seconds. When a negative value is written to *flush*, the kernel schedules a flush after the default delay min_delay. max_delay is the maximum time that can pass between when the user schedules a flush and when the kernel actually flushes the cache. See the section "Flushing the Routing Cache" in Chapter 33.

min_adv_mss

This value is associated with the TCP Maximum Segment Size (MSS) parameter. Each route has an associated MSS value. When the next hop of a dst_entry is initialized (with rt_set_nexthop), before it is added to the routing table cache with rt_intern_hash, the MSS is initialized to either the outgoing device's MTU or min_adv_mss, whichever is greater. See the comment in tcp_advertise_mss and its initialization in rt_set_nexthop.

min_pmtu
mtu_expires

When the PMTU associated with a routing cache entry is changed, the routing cache is scheduled to expire after mtu_expires seconds. See the section "Examples of events that can expire cache entries" in Chapter 30.

min_pmtu is the minimum PMTU value that the path MTU discovery protocol can set for a route.

redirect_load
redirect_number
redirect_silence

Used to implement rate limiting for ICMP_REDIRECT messages. See the section "Egress ICMP REDIRECT Rate Limiting" in Chapter 33.

secret_interval

The routing cache is flushed regularly every secret_interval/HZ seconds. See the section "Flushing the Routing Cache" in Chapter 33.

Table 36-4 lists the kernel variables and default values.†

---

* The file actually has read permissions, but if you try reading its contents, the kernel complains.

† Most of the parameters that represent periods of time are configured in seconds, but stored in jiffies (the number of seconds * HZ). When you read these values by dumping the contents of the associated files, you may get the value in seconds or jiffies depending on what routine the kernel uses to dump them (e.g., proc_handler routine). For example, proc_dointvec prints the kernel value as is (with the assumption that it is an integer value), where as proc_dointvec_jiffies converts a value assumed to be expressed in jiffies (i.e., ticks) to seconds for display.

Table 36-4. /proc/sys/net/ipv4/route files usable for tuning the routing subsystem

Kernel variable name	Filename	Default value
ip_rt_error_burst	error_burst	5 * HZ
ip_rt_error_cost	error_cost	HZ
flush_delay	flush	N/A[a]
ip_rt_gc_elasticity	gc_elasticity	8
ip_rt_gc_interval	gc_interval	60 * HZ
ip_rt_gc_min_interval	gc_min_interval_ms[b]	HZ / 2
ipv4_dst_ops.gc_thresh	gc_thresh	Depends on RAM[c]
ip_rt_gc_timeout	gc_timeout	RT_GC_TIMEOUT (300 * HZ)
ip_rt_min_delay	min_delay	2 * HZ
ip_rt_max_delay	max_delay	10 * HZ
ip_rt_max_size	max_size	Depends on RAM
ip_rt_min_advmss	min_adv_mss	256
ip_rt_min_pmtu	min_pmtu	512+20+20[d]
ip_rt_mtu_expires	mtu_expires	10 * 60 * HZ
ip_rt_redirect_load	redirect_load	HZ / 50
ip_rt_redirect_number	redirect_number	9
ip_rt_redirect_silence	redirect_silence	((HZ/50)<<(9+1))
ip_rt_secret_interval	secret_interval	10 * 60 * HZ

[a] See the description of flush earlier in this section.

[b] There is another file, gc_min_interval, associated with the same kernel variable. That file is deprecated and will be removed.

[c] Initialized at boot time based on the hash table size, whose value depends on the amount of RAM installed.

[d] 512 is the default MSS used by TCP according to RFCs 793 and 1112; the additional 20+20 is the size of the IP and TCP headers, when they are both without options.

The /proc/sys/net/ipv4/conf Directory

This directory includes files that can be used to tune the IPv4, IPsec, and ARP protocols, as well as to control routing on a per-device basis. The protocol-related parameters are covered in the associated chapters, so in this chapter, we will cover only the ones used to tune routing.

The *proc/sys/net/ipv4/conf* directory includes subdirectories for each registered network device, including the loopback device, which in turn contain files for each tuning parameter. This allows you to configure the routing parameters on a per-device basis for the previously mentioned protocols. Each directory contains the same set of files. All the parameters are grouped by the kernel in a data structure of type ipv4_ devconf, defined in *include/linux/inetdevice.c* and shown in Table 36-5. The default value is the value exported to the corresponding file in the */proc/sys/net/ipv4/conf/default* directory.

Table 36-5. /proc/sys/net/ipv4/conf subdirectory files usable for tuning the routing subsystem

Kernel variable name (field of ipv4_devconf)	Filename	Default value
accept_redirects	*accept_redirects*	1
accept_source_route	*accept_source_route*	1
forwarding	*forwarding*	0
mc_forwarding	*mc_forwarding*	0
rp_filter	*rp_filter*	0
secure_redirects	*secure_redirects*	1
shared_media	*shared_media*	1
send_redirects	*send_redirects*	1
log_martians	*log_martians*	0
tag (not used)	*tag*	0

Special subdirectories

In addition to a directory for every device, the */proc/sys/net/ipv4/conf* directory includes two special directories:

default

> All the parameters not explicitly configured by the user are initialized to the default values exported in this directory. These values are maintained by the kernel in a separate ipv4_devconf instance, ipv4_devconf_dflt (see Table 36-5).

all

> This directory is used for global configurations (i.e., what the user writes here applies to all devices). These values are also maintained by the kernel in a separate data structure whose name is the same as the structure type itself, ipv4_devconf.

Both the *default* and per-device directories are created by calling devinet_sysctl_register. The *all* directory is statically defined (see the definition of devinet_sysctl_table in *net/ipv4/devinet.c*).

devinet_sysctl_register is called by devinet_init when the routing code gets initialized at boot time (see the section "Routing Subsystem Initialization" in Chapter 32) to register the *default* directory. Because the function is called by inetdev_init, it is called once for each device (when the first IPv4 address is configured on the device).

Use of the special subdirectories

Different features behave differently when combining the per-device and global configuration values, as well as when propagating the changes to the variables exported in the *all* directory. For example:

- For some of the fields, the per-device and global values are ANDed. In this case, the feature is enabled only if both the global and per-device configurations are enabled.
- For some of the fields, the values are ORed. In this case, enabling the value in either file is sufficient.
- For some of the fields, the global values are not taken into consideration.

How the files are consulted for a given feature depends on what makes sense for that feature.

For each parameter, there is a macro, IN_DEV_XXX, defined in *include/linux/inetdevice.h*, that can be used to derive the current operative state for a given device. The macros take as their input parameter the IPv4 configuration block of the device, which is an instance of in_device. You can look at those macros to figure out what criteria (AND, OR, or NONE) each parameter uses to combine the per-device and global configuration. Here is an example for each of the three cases:

```
#define IN_DEV_RPFILTER(in_dev) \
(ipv4_devconf.rp_filter && (in_dev)->cnf.rp_filter)

#define IN_DEV_PROXY_ARP(in_dev) \
(ipv4_devconf.proxy_arp || (in_dev)->cnf.proxy_arp)

#define IN_DEV_MEDIUM_ID(in_dev) ((in_dev)->cnf.medium_id)
```

The logic used by the preceding examples is not the only one implemented by the IN_DEV_XXX macros. For example, IN_DEV_RX_REDIRECTS is more complex and is defined as a wrapper around several parameters, not just as an AND or OR condition between two values.

There is one more case to consider. For some parameters, changes to the files in the *all* directory are propagated to the per-device directories right away (instead of being consulted by the IN_DEV_XXX macros). In that case, the associated IN_DEV_XXX macro does not need to check the global value. See the section "Enabling and Disabling Forwarding" for an example.

File descriptions

Here is a brief description of the files listed in Table 36-5:

accept_redirects
send_redirects

ICMP redirects, described in Chapter 31, are sent by routers to hosts to inform them about suboptimal routing. accept_redirects is a Boolean flag that can be used to enable or disable ICMP redirect processing for an interface.* send_ redirects is used for the other side of the coin: when it is true, the system is allowed to generate ICMP redirects when the required conditions of suboptimal routing are detected.

accept_source_route

The IP Source Routing option can be enabled and disabled with this flag. When it is disabled, ip_rcv_finish drops all the IP packets carrying such an option. IP options are discussed in Chapter 18.

forwarding
mc_forwarding

These are Boolean flags used to enable and disable unicast and multicast forwarding, respectively. For mc_forwarding to be used, the kernel must be compiled with the necessary multicast options.

rp_filter

When this flag is true, an ingress packet is dropped if the source of the packet is reachable through an asymmetric route (according to the routing table of the local host). See the section "Reverse Path Filtering" in Chapter 31.

secure_redirects
shared media

When secure_redirects is set, ICMP_REDIRECT messages are accepted only when the suggested gateway is already known locally as a gateway.

Normally, ICMP_REDIRECT messages that suggest the use of a new next hop whose IP address is not in the same subnet as the current next hop are rejected, as specified in RFC 1122. However, there are cases where accepting them would make sense. When shared_media is true, those ICMP_REDIRECT messages will be accepted. RFC 1620 explains quite nicely why this option makes sense in some cases.

See the section "ICMP_REDIRECT Messages" in Chapter 31 for more information on this feature.

log_martians

When this flag is set, the kernel generates log messages when it receives packets with illegal IP addresses. See the section "Verbose Monitoring" in Chapter 31.

---

* See also the section "Enabling and Disabling Forwarding."

The /proc/net and /proc/net/stat Directories

The */proc/net* directory offers a few files that execute kernel handlers when you try to dump their contents. The following is the file-by-file description:

route
rt_cache

> You can read those two files to get a dump of the routing table (if_fib_main_table) and the routing cache, respectively. They do not display the contents of user-defined routing tables, which can be created when the kernel has support for Policy Routing. IP addresses are printed in hexadecimal format.

stat/rt_cache

> Collection of statistics. See the sections "Statistics" and "rt_cache_stat Structure."

rt_acct

> Accounting information collected by the routing table based classifier introduced in Chapter 31. For better-formatted output, use IPROUTE2's *rtacct* command.

ip_mr_cache
ip_mr_vif

> Used by multicast routing (not covered in this book).

Table 36-6 summarizes the association between files and kernel handlers.

Table 36-6. Kernel handlers for the files in /proc/net used by the routing subsystem

Filename	Kernel file where it is defined
route	net/ipv4/fib_hash.c (fib_proc_init)
rt_cache	net/ipv4/route.c (ip_rt_init)
rt_acct	net/ipv4/route.c (ip_rt_init)
ip_mr_cache	net/ipv4/ipmr.c (ip_mr_init)
ip_mr_vif	net/ipv4/ipmr.c (ip_mr_init)
stat/rt_cache	net/ipv4/route.c (ip_rt_init)

As shown in Figure 36-4, the files in the two directories */proc/net* and */proc/net/stat* are created indirectly by inet_init, with the help of routines such as ipv4_proc_init and ip_init. inet_init is marked with the module_init macro and therefore is executed at boot time (see Chapter 7).

Enabling and Disabling Forwarding

As mentioned earlier in this chapter, the kernel exports parameters via */proc* that can be used to enable and disable IP forwarding, both globally and on a per-device basis. In this chapter, we will address only IPv4 forwarding.

Even though an administrator can change the forwarding state globally, there really is no global forwarding state. The routing code uses only the per-device forwarding states: global configuration changes are just a convenient way to apply the same change to all devices in one shot. In particular, when the kernel receives an IP packet whose destination address does not belong to the local system, it either forwards the packet or drops it based on the forwarding state of the receiving interface. This is not a decision made on a global basis or on the forwarding state of the device that would be used to transmit the packet out toward its destination.

It is important to understand the relationship between per-device and global configurations, to know how the system is going to behave when you change their values. Here are the relevant */proc* files:

/proc/sys/net/ipv4/conf/device_name/forwarding
> Enable and disable forwarding on the device *device_name*. A value of zero means disabled; any other value means enabled.

/proc/sys/net/ipv4/conf/all/forwarding
> Changes to this file are applied to all network devices (including the ones not in the UP state) but do not affect the forwarding state of devices registered in the future.

/proc/sys/net/ipv4/conf/default/forwarding
> This is the default forwarding state of those devices that do not have an explicit configuration. Unlike the previous file, its value affects only the forwarding state of those devices registered in the future (not the ones already present).

/proc/sys/net/ipv4/ip_forward
> Changes to this file have the same effect as changes to */proc/sys/net/ipv4/conf/all/ forwarding*. You can look at the former as an alias to the latter.

Changes to the *forwarding* files are processed by `devinet_sysctl_forward`, which distinguishes between the three cases internally. Changes to the *ip_forward* file are processed by `ipv4_sysctl_forward`. Every time there is a change of forwarding state for at least one device, the routing cache is flushed with `rt_cache_flush`.

Changes to either */proc/sys/net/ipv4/conf/all/forwarding* or */proc/sys/net/ipv4/ip_ forward* will trigger the execution of `inet_forward_change`, which:

1. Updates the `ipv4_devconf.accept_redirect` configuration parameter.

    This is done to enforce the rule by which only hosts are supposed to accept ICMP redirects, not routers. If global forwarding gets enabled, it means the system is now to be considered a router and therefore the default configuration for honoring ICMP redirects must be disabled. (The administrator can, of course, re-enable it if needed).

2. Updates the default forwarding state.

   Note that changing the global forwarding configuration forces the default to change, but not vice versa.

3. Updates the forwarding state of all devices.

Data Structures Featured in This Part of the Book

The section "Main Data Structures" in Chapter 32 gave a brief overview of the main data structures, and Figure 34-1 in Chapter 34 can help you understand the relationships between them. This section provides a detailed description of each data structure type. Figure 36-5 shows the file that defines each data structure.

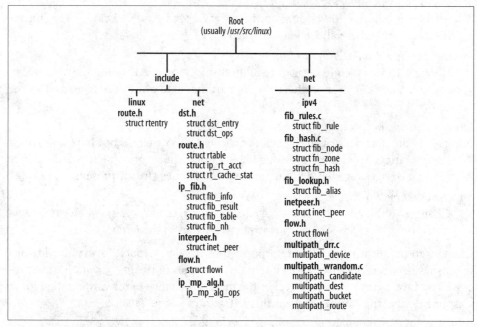

Figure 36-5. Distribution of data structures in kernel files

fib_table Structure

A fib_table structure is created for each routing table instance. The structure consists mainly of a routing table identifier and a set of function pointers used to manage the table:

unsigned char tb_id

   Routing table identifier. In *include/linux/rtnetlink.h,* you can find the rt_class_t list of predefined values, such as RT_TABLE_LOCAL.

unsigned tb_stamp

> Not used.

int (*tb_lookup)(struct fib_table *tb, const struct flowi *flp, struct fib_result *res)

> The function called by the fib_lookup routine described in Chapter 35.

int (*tb_insert)(struct fib_table *table, struct rtmsg *r,struct kern_rta *rta, struct nlmsghdr *n, struct netlink_skb_parms *req)
int (*tb_delete)(struct fib_table *table, struct rtmsg *r, struct kern_rta *rta, struct nlmsghdr *n, struct netlink_skb_parms *req);

> tb_insert is called by inet_rtm_newroute and ip_rt_ioctl to process the *ip route add/change/replace/prepend/append/test* and *route add* user-space commands. Similarly, tb_delete is called by inet_rtm_delroute (in answer to *ip route del ...* commands) and by ip_rt_ioctl (in answer to *route del ...* commands) to delete a route from a table. Both are also called by fib_magic (see the section "Routes Inserted by the Kernel: The fib_magic Function").

int (*tb_dump)(struct fib_table *table, struct sk_buff *skb,
  struct netlink_callback *cb)

> Dumps the content of a routing table. It is invoked to handle user commands such as "*ip route get ...*".

int (*tb_flush)(struct fib_table *table)

> Removes the fib_info structures that have the RTNH_F_DEAD flag set. See the section "Garbage Collection" in Chapter 33.

void (*tb_select_default)(struct fib_table *table, const struct flowi *flp, struct fib_result *res)

> Selects a default route. See the section "Default Gateway Selection" in Chapter 35.

unsigned char tb_data[0]

> Pointer to the end of the structure. It is useful when the structure is allocated as part of a bigger one, because it allows code to point to the part of the outer data structure that immediately follows this one. See Figure 34-1 in Chapter 34.

fn_zone Structure

A *zone* is the collection of routes that have the same netmask length. The routes of a routing table are organized into zones, as described in Chapter 32. Zones are defined with fn_zone structures, which contain the following fields:

struct fn_zone *fz_next

> Pointer used to link together the active zones (i.e., the ones with at least one route). The head of the list is kept in fn_zone_list, which is a field of the fn_hash data structure.

`struct hlist_head *fz_hash`
> Pointer to the hash table that stores the routes that fall into this zone.

`int fz_nent`
> Number of routes in the zone (i.e., number of `fib_node` instances that are in the zone's hash table). Its value is used, for instance, to detect the need to resize the hash table (see the section "Dynamic resizing of per-netmask hash tables" in Chapter 34).

`int fz_divisor`
> Size (number of buckets) of the hash table `fz_hash`. See the section "Dynamic resizing of per-netmask hash tables" in Chapter 34.

`u32 fz_hashmask`
> This is simply `fz_divisor-1`, and is provided so that cheap binary AND operations can be used instead of expensive modulo operations to compute a value modulo `fz_divisor`. `n%fz_divisor` is the same as `n&fz_hashmask` (for instance, `100%16 = 100&15`), and the latter takes less CPU time.

`int fz_order`
> The number of bits (all consecutive) that are set in the netmask `fz_hashmask`, also seen in the code as `prefixlen`. For instance, given the netmask 255.255.255.0, `fz_order` would be 24.

`u32 fz_mask`
> The netmask built using `fz_order`. For example, an `fz_order` of 3 produces a binary `fz_mask` of 11100000.00000000.00000000.00000000, or decimal 224.0.0.0.

Along with the structure are two macros used to access the `fz_hashmask` and `fz_mask` fields:

```
#define FZ_HASHMASK(fz) ((fz)->fz_hashmask)
#define FZ_MASK(fz) ((fz)->fz_mask)
```

fib_node Structure

There is a `fib_node` instance for each unique destination network for which the kernel has a route. Different routes that lead to the same destination network but that differ with regard to other configuration parameters share the same `fib_node` instance. Here is the field-by-field description:

`struct hlist_node fn_hash`
> `fib_node` elements are organized into hash tables. This pointer is used to link the elements that collide in a single bucket of a hash table.

`struct list_head fn_alias`
> Each `fib_node` structure is associated with a list of one or more `fib_alias` structures. This is the pointer to the head of that list.

---

su32 fn_key
 This is the prefix of the route (the network address, indicated by the route's net-
 mask). It is used as a search key. See the section "Basic Structures for Hash Table
 Organization" in Chapter 34.

fib_alias Structure

fib_alias instances are used to distinguish between different routes to the same destination network that differ with regard to other configuration parameters (besides
the destination address). Here is the field-by-field description:

struct list_head fa_list
 Used to link the fib_alias instances associated with the same fib_node structure.

struct fib_info *fa_info
 Pointer to the fib_info instance that stores the information about how to process packets matching this route.

u8 fa_tos
 Route's Type of Service (TOS) bitfield. When the value is zero, it means the TOS
 has not been configured and therefore any value can match on a routing lookup.
 Do not confuse fa_tos with the r_tos field of fib_rule. The fa_tos field allows
 the user to specify conditions on the TOS for individual routing entries. In contrast, the r_tos field of fib_rule specifies conditions on the TOS for policy rules.

u8 fa_type
 See the description of the rt_type field in the section "rtable Structure."

u8 fa_scope
 Scope of the route. See the section "Scope" in Chapter 30.

u8 fa_state
 Bitmap of flags. The only flag defined so far is the following:

 FA_S_ACCESSED
  Whenever the fib_alias instance is accessed with a lookup, it is marked
  with this flag. The flag is useful when a change is applied to a fib_node data
  structure: it is used to decide whether the routing cache should be flushed. If
  fib_node has been accessed, it probably means entries in the routing cache
  need to be cleared if the route changes; thus, a flush is triggered.

fib_info Structure

The parameters that define a route are contained in the combination of fib_node and
fib_alias structures, described in the previous sections. Important routing

information such as the next hop gateway is stored in a `fib_info` structure. Here is the field-by-field description:

`struct hlist_node fib_hash`
`struct hlist_node fib_lhash`

Used to insert the data structure into the two hash tables described in the section "Organization of fib_info Structures" in Chapter 34.

`int fib_treeref`
`atomic_t fib_clntref`

Reference counts. `fib_treeref` is the number of `fib_node` data structures holding a reference on this `fib_info` instance, and `fib_clntref` is the number of references being held as a result of successful routing lookups.

`int fib_dead`

A flag that tags routes being removed. When set to 1, it warns that the structure is not to be used because it is about to be removed. See the section "Deleting a Route" in Chapter 34.

`unsigned fib_flags`

Set of `RTNH_F_XXX` flags, listed in Table 36-7. The only flag currently used is `RTNH_F_DEAD`, which is set for a multipath route when all the associated `fib_nh` structures have their `RTNH_F_DEAD` flags set (see the section "Generic Helper Routines and Macros" in Chapter 32).

Table 36-7. Values for the nh_flags field of fib_nh

Flag	Description
RTNH_F_DEAD	This flag is used mainly by the multipath code to keep track of dead next hops. See the description of `fib_sync_down` in the section "Generic Helper Routines and Macros" in Chapter 32.
RTNH_F_PERVASIVE	This flag is supposed to mark entries that require recursive lookups but is currently not used. The latest IPROUTE2 releases do not accept the `pervasive` keyword anymore.
RTNH_F_ONLINK	When this flag is set, the kernel is asked not to check for consistency on the next hop address (i.e., not to check whether the next hop address is reachable on the outgoing device). It is set with the `onlink` keyword and is used, for instance, when defining routes on tunnel virtual devices.

`int fib_protocol`

Protocol that installed the route. The possible values for this field, `RTPROT_XXX`, are defined in *include/linux/rtnetlink.h* and are listed in Tables 36-8 and 36-9 (ROUTED is missing from these tables because it does not use Netlink to interface with the kernel). See the section "Routing Protocol Daemons" in Chapter 31 for a brief overview of these protocols.

Values of `fib_protocol` greater than `RTPROT_STATIC` are used only by routes not generated by the kernel (i.e., those generated by user-space routing daemons).

One example of a use for this field is to allow routing daemons to restrict operations to their own routes when dealing with the kernel. See the section "Interaction between daemons and kernel" in Chapter 31 for more details.

Table 36-8. Values of fib_protocol used by the kernel

Value	Description
RTPROT_UNSPEC	Field is invalid.
RTPROT_REDIRECT	Route installed by ICMP redirects; not used by current IPv4.
RTPROT_KERNEL	Route installed by kernel. See the section "Routes Inserted by the Kernel: The fib_magic Function."
RTPROT_BOOT	Route installed by user-space commands such as *ip route* and *route*.
RTPROT_STATIC	Route installed by administrator. Not used.

Table 36-9. Values of fib_protocol used by user space

Value	Description
RTPROT_GATED	The route was added by GateD.
RTPROT_RA	The route was added by RDISC (IPv4) and ND (IPv6) router advertisements. There is a mechanism, the ICMP Router Discovery Protocol defined in RFC 1256, that lets hosts find neighboring routers. *rdisc*, which is part of the *iputils* package, is the user-space tool that implements ICMP Router Discovery Messages.
RTPROT_MRT	The route was added by the Multi-Threaded Routing Toolkit (MRT).
RTPROT_ZEBRA	The route was added by Zebra.
RTPROT_BIRD	The route was added by BIRD.
RTPROT_DNROUTED	The route was added by the DECnet routing daemon.
RTPROT_XORP	The route was added by the XORP routing daemon.

u32 fib_prefsrc

Preferred source IP address. See the section "Selecting the Source IP Address" in Chapter 35.

u32 fib_priority

Priority of the route. The smaller the value, the higher the priority. Its value can be configured with IPROUTE2 using the metric/priority/preference keywords. When not explicitly set, it has the default value 0 to which it is initialized by the kernel.

u32 fib_metrics[RTAX_MAX]

When you configure a route, the *ip route* command allows you to also specify a set of metrics. fib_metrics is a vector used to store them. Metrics not explicitly configured are initialized to zero. See the section "Essential Elements of Routing" in Chapter 30 for a list of the available metrics. Table 36-10 shows the relationships between the metrics listed in that section and the associated kernel symbols RTAX_*XXX* defined in *include/linux/rtnetlink.h*.

Table 36-10. Routing metrics

Metric	Kernel symbol
Not a metric	RTAX_LOCK
Path MTU	RTAX_MTU
Maximum Advertised Window	RTAX_WINDOW
Round Trip Time	RTAX_RTT
RTT Variance	RTAX_RTTVAR
Slow Start threshold	RTAX_SSTHRESH
Congestion Window	RTAX_CWND
Maximum Segment Size	RTAX_ADVMSS
Maximal Reordering	RTAX_REORDERING
Default Time To Live (TTL)	RTAX_HOPLIMIT
Initial Congestion Window	RTAX_INITCWND
Not a metric	RTAX_FEATURES

`int fib_power`

This field is part of the data structure only when the kernel is compiled with support for multipath. See the section "Concepts Behind Multipath Routing" in Chapter 31.

`struct fib_nh fib_nh[0]`
`int fib_nhs`

`fib_nh` is a variable-length vector of `fib_nh` structures, and `fib_nhs` is its size. `fib_nhs` can be greater than 1 only when the kernel supports the Multipath feature. See the section "Concepts Behind Multipath Routing" in Chapter 31, and see Figure 34-1 in Chapter 34.

`u32 fib_mp_alg`

Multipath caching algorithm. The `IP_MP_ALG_XXX` IDs of the algorithms introduced in the section "Cache Support for Multipath" in Chapter 31 are listed in *include/linux/ip_mp_alg.h*. This field is part of the data structure only when the kernel is compiled with support for multipath caching.

`#define fib_dev fib_nh[0].nh_dev`

Macro used to access the nh_dev field of the first `fib_nh` instance of the `fib_nh` vector. See Figure 34-1 in Chapter 34.

`#define fib_mtu fib_metrics[RTAX_MTU-1]`
`#define fib_window fib_metrics[RTAX_WINDOW-1]`
`#define fib_rtt fib_metrics[RTAX_RTT-1]`
`#define fib_advmss fib_metrics[RTAX_ADVMSS-1]`

Macros used to access specific elements of the `fib_metrics` vector.

fib_nh Structure

For each next hop, the kernel needs to keep more than just the IP address. The fib_nh structure stores that extra information in the following fields.

struct net_device *nh_dev
> This is the net_device data structure associated with the device ID nh_oif (described later). Since both the ID and the pointer to the net_device structure are needed (in different contexts), both of them are kept in the fib_nh structure, even though either one could be used to retrieve the other.

struct hlist_node nh_hash
> Used to insert the structure into the hash table described in the section "Organization of Next-Hop Router Structures" in Chapter 34.

struct fib_info *nh_parent
> Pointer to the fib_info structure that contains this fib_nh instance. See Figure 34-1 in Chapter 34.

unsigned nh_flags
> A set of RTNH_F_XXX flags defined in *include/linux/rtnetlink.h* and listed in Table 36-7 earlier in this chapter.

unsigned char nh_scope
> Scope of the route used to get to the next hop. It is RT_SCOPE_LINK in most cases. This field is initialized by fib_check_nh.

int nh_weight
int nh_power
> These two fields are part of the fib_nh data structure only when the kernel is compiled with support for multipath, and are described in detail in the section "Concepts Behind Multipath Routing" in Chapter 31. nh_power is initialized by the kernel; nh_weight is set by the user with the keyword weight.

__u32 nh_tclassid
> This field is part of the fib_nh data structure only when the kernel is compiled with support for the routing table based classifier. Its value is set with the realms keyword. See the section "Policy Routing and Routing Table Based Classifier" in Chapter 35.

int nh_oif
> ID of the egress device. It is set with the keywords oif and dev.

u32 nh_gw
> IP address of the next hop gateway provided with the keyword via. Note that in the case of NAT, this represents the address that the NAT router advertises to the world, and to which replies are sent before the router sends them on to the host on the internal network. For example, the command *ip route add nat 10.1.1.253/32 via 151.41.196.1* would set nh_gw to 151.41.196.1. Note that NAT support in the routing code, known as FastNAT, has been dropped in 2.6 kernels.

---

fib_rule Structure

Policy routing rules (also called policies) are configured with the *ip rule* command. If the IPROUTE2 package is installed on your Linux system, you can type *ip rule help* to see the syntax of the command. Policies are stored in fib_rule structures, whose fields are described here:

struct fib_rule *r_next
> Links these structures within a global list that contains all fib_rule structures (see Figure 35-8 in Chapter 35).

atomic_t r_clntref
> Reference count. It is incremented by fib_lookup (in the Policy Routing version only), which explains why fib_res_put (which decrements it) is always called after a successful lookup.

u32 r_preference
> Priority of the rule. This can be configured using the keywords priority, preference and order when the administrator adds a policy with IPROUTE2. When not explicitly configured, the kernel assigns a priority that is one unit smaller than the priority of the last user-added rule (see inet_rtm_newrule). Priorities 0, 0x7FFE, and 0x7FFF are reserved for special rules installed by the kernel (see the section "fib_lookup with Policy Routing" in Chapter 35, and the definitions of the three default rules local_rule, main_rule, and default_rule in *net/ipv4/fib_rules.c*).

unsigned char r_table
> Routing table identifier. Ranges from 0 to 255. When it is not specified by the user, IPROUTE2 uses the following defaults: RT_TABLE_MAIN when the user command adds a rule, and RT_TABLE_UNSPEC in other cases (e.g., when deleting a rule).

unsigned char r_action
> The values allowed for this field are the rtm_type enum listed in *include/linux/rtnetlink.h* (RTN_UNICAST, etc.). The meanings of these values are described in the section "rtable Structure."
>
> This field can be explicitly set by the user using the type keyword when configuring a rule. When it is not explicitly configured by the user, IPROUTE2 sets it to RTN_UNICAST when adding rules, and RTN_UNSPEC otherwise (e.g., when deleting rules).

unsigned char r_dst_len
unsigned char r_src_len
> Length of the destination and source IP addresses, expressed in bits. They are used to compute r_srcmask and r_dstmask. When not initialized, they are set to zero.

u32 r_src

u32 r_srcmask

IP address and netmask, respectively, of the source network from which packets must come.

u32 r_dst

u32 r_dstmask

IP address and netmask, respectively, of the destination network to which packets must be directed.

u32 r_srcmap

Field that used to be set with the user-space keywords nat and map-to and was used by the Routing NAT implementation. Routing NAT support has been removed, so this field is not used anymore. See the section "Recently Dropped Options" in Chapter 32.

u8 r_flags

Set of flags. Currently not used.

u8 r_tos

IP header's TOS field. Included because the definition of a rule can include a condition placed on the IP header TOS field.

u32 r_fwmark

When the kernel is compiled with support for the "Use Netfilter MARK value as routing key" feature, it is possible to define rules in terms of firewall tags. This is the tag specified by the fwmark keyword when the administrator defines a policy rule.

int r_ifindex

char r_ifname[IFNAMSIZ]

r_ifname is the name of the device the policy applies to. Given r_ifname, the kernel finds the associated net_device instance and copies the value of its ifindex field into r_ifindex. The value -1 for r_ifindex is used to disable the rule (see the section "Impacts on the policy database" in Chapter 32.

__u32 r_tclassid;

This field is included in the data structure only when the kernel is compiled with support for the routing table based classifier. Its meaning is described in the section "Policy Routing and Routing Table Based Classifier" in Chapter 35.

int r_dead

When a rule is available for use, this field is 0. When the rule is removed with inet_rtm_delrule, this field is set to 1. Every time a reference to the fib_rule data structure is removed with fib_rule_put, the reference count is decremented, and when it gets to zero the structure is supposed to be freed. At that point, however, if r_dead is not set, it means that something wrong happened (for instance, code has set the reference count incorrectly).

fib_result Structure

The fib_result structure is initialized by fib_semantic_match to the result of a routing lookup. See Chapters 33 and 35 (in particular, the section "Semantic Matching on Subsidiary Criteria") for more details. The fields in the structure are:

unsigned char prefixlen
> Prefix length of the matching route. See the description of fz_order in the section "fn_zone Structure."

unsigned char nh_sel
> Multipath routes are defined with multiple next hops. This field identifies the next hop that has been selected.

unsigned char type
unsigned char scope
> These two fields are initialized to the values of the fa_type and fa_scope fields of the matching fib_alias instance.

__u32 network
__u32 netmask
> These two fields are included in the data structure definition only when the kernel is compiled with support for multipath caching. See the section "Weighted Random Algorithm" in Chapter 33 for how they are used by the weighted random multipath caching algorithm.

struct fib_info *fi
> The fib_info instance associated with the matching fib_alias instance.

struct fib_rule *r
> Unlike the previous fields, this one is initialized by fib_lookup. This field is included in the data structure definition only when the kernel is compiled with support for Policy Routing.

rtable Structure

IPv4 uses rtable data structures to store routing table entries in the cache.* To dump the contents of the routing cache, you can view /proc/net/rt_cache (see the section "Tuning via /proc Filesystem"), or issue the *ip route list cache* or *route –C* commands. Here is a field-by-field description of the data structure:

union {...} u
> This union is used to embed a dst_entry structure into the rtable structure (see the section "Hash Table Organization" in Chapter 33). One of its fields, rt_next, is used to link the rtable instances that collide into the same hash table's bucket.

---

* IPv6 uses rt6_info, and DECnet (not covered in this book) uses dn_route.

`struct in_device *idev`

Pointer to the IP configuration block of the egress device. Note that when the route is used for ingress packets that are to be delivered locally, the egress device is the loopback device.

`unsigned rt_flags`

The flags you can set in this bitmap are the RTCF_*XXX* values defined in *include/linux/in_route.h* and listed in Table 36-11.

Table 36-11. Possible values for rt_flags

Flag	Description
RTCF_NOTIFY	Interested user-space applications are notified of any change to the routing entry via Netlink. This option is not yet completely implemented. The flag is set with commands such as *ip route get 10.0.1.0/24 notify*.
RTCF_REDIRECTED	The entry has been added in response to a received ICMP_REDIRECT message (see ip_rt_redirect and its caller).
RTCF_DOREDIRECT	This flag is set by ip_route_input_slow when an ICMP_REDIRECT message must be sent back to the source. ip_forward, described in detail in Chapter 20, decides whether to actually send the ICMP redirect based on this flag and other information. For instance, if the packet was source routed, no ICMP redirect would be generated.
RTCF_DIRECTSRC	This flag is used mostly to tell the ICMP code that it should not reply to Address Mask Request Messages. The flag is set every time a call to fib_validate_source says that the source of the received packet is reachable with a next hop that has a local scope (RT_SCOPE_HOST). See Chapters 25 and 35 for more detail.
RTCF_SNAT RTCF_DNAT RTCF_NAT	These flags are not used anymore by IPv4. They were used by the FastNAT feature that has been removed from the 2.6 kernels (see the section "Recently Dropped Options" in Chapter 32).
RTCF_BROADCAST	The destination address of the route is a broadcast address.
RTCF_MULTICAST	The destination address of the route is a multicast address.
RTCF_LOCAL	The destination address of the route is local (i.e., configured on one of the local interfaces). This flag is also set for local broadcast and multicast addresses (see ip_route_input_mc).
RTCF_REJECT	Not used. According to the syntax of IPROUTE2's *ip rule* command, there is a *reject* keyword, but it is not accepted.
RTCF_TPROXY	Not used.
RTCF_DIRECTDST	Not used.
RTCF_FAST	Not used. This flag is obsolete; it used to be set to mark a route as eligible for Fast Switching, a feature that has been dropped in the 2.6 kernels.
RTCF_MASQ	Not used anymore by IPv4. The flag was supposed to mark packets coming from masqueraded source addresses.

`unsigned rt_type`

Type of route. It indirectly defines the action to take when the route matches on a routing lookup. The possible values for this field are the RTN_*XXX* macros defined in *include/linux/rtnetlink.h* and listed in Table 36-12.

Table 36-12. *Possible values for rt_type*

Route type	Description
RTN_UNSPEC	Defines a noninitialized value. This value is used, for instance, when removing an entry from the routing table, because that operation does not require the type of entry to be specified.
RTN_LOCAL	The destination address is configured on a local interface.
RTN_UNICAST	The route is a direct or indirect (via a gateway) route to a unicast address. This is the default value set by the *ip route* command when no other type is specified by the user.
RTN_MULTICAST	The destination address is a multicast address.
RTN_BROADCAST	The destination address is a broadcast address. Matching ingress packets are delivered locally as broadcasts, and matching egress packets are sent as broadcasts.
RTN_ANYCAST	Matching ingress packets are delivered locally as broadcasts, and matching egress packets are sent as unicast. Not used by IPv4.
RTN_BLACKHOLE RTN_UNREACHABLE RTN_PROHIBIT RTN_THROW	These values are associated with specific administrative configurations rather than destination address types. See the section "Route Types and Actions" in Chapter 30.
RTN_NAT	The source and/or destination IP address must be translated. Not used because the associated feature, FastNAT, has been dropped in the 2.6 kernels.
RTN_XRESOLVE	An external resolver will take care of this route. This functionality is currently not implemented.

__u16 rt_multipath_alg

> Multipath caching algorithm. It is initialized based on the algorithm configured on the associated route (see fib_mp_alg in the section "fib_info Structure").

__u32 rt_dst
__u32 rt_src

> Destination and source IP addresses.

int rt_iif

> ID of the ingress device. Its value is extracted from the net_device data structure of the ingress device. For traffic generated locally (and hence not received on any interface), the field is set to the ifindex field of the outgoing device. Do not confuse this field with the iif field of the flowi data structure fl described later in this chapter. The latter field is set to zero (loopback_dev) for locally generated traffic.

__u32 rt_gateway

> When the destination host is directly connected (it is on-link), rt_gateway matches the destination address. When a gateway is needed to reach the destination, rt_gateway is set to the next hop gateway identified by the route.

struct flowi fl

> Search key used for the cache lookups, described in the section "flowi Structure."

`__u32 rt_spec_dst`

RFC 1122-specific destination, explained in the section "Preferred Source Address Selection" in Chapter 35.

`struct inet_peer *peer`

The `inet_peer` structure, introduced in Chapter 19, stores long-living information about the IP peer, which is the host with the destination IP address of this cached route. There is an `inet_peer` structure for each remote IP address to which the local host has been talking in the recent past.

dst_entry Structure

The data structure `dst_entry` is used to store the protocol-independent information concerning cached routes. L3 protocols keep their own, additional private information in separate structures. (For example, IPv4 uses `rtable` structures.)

Here is the field-by-field description:

`struct dst_entry *next`

Used to link the `dst_entry` instances that collide into the same hash table's bucket. See Figure 33-1 in Chapter 33.

`struct dst_entry *child`
`unsigned short header_len`
`unsigned short trailer_len`
`struct dst_entry *path`
`struct xfrm_state *xfrm`

These fields are used by IPsec code.

`atomic_t __refcnt`

Reference count. See the section "Deleting DST Entries" in Chapter 33.

`int __use`

Number of times this entry has been used (i.e., number of times that a cache lookup has returned it). Do not confuse this value with `rt_cache_stat[smp_processor_id()].in_hit`: the latter (described in the section "Statistics") represents the global number of cache hits for the device.

`struct net_device *dev`

Egress device (i.e., where to transmit to reach the destination).

`short obsolete`

Used to define the usability status of this `dst_entry` instance: 0 (the default value) means the structure is valid and can be used, 2 means the structure is being removed and therefore cannot be used, and -1 is used by IPsec and IPv6 but not by IPv4.

int flags

> Set of flags. DST_HOST is used by TCP and means the route leads to a host (i.e., it is not a route to a network or a broadcast/multicast address). DST_NOXFRM, DST_NOPOLICY, and DST_NOHASH are used only by IPsec.

unsigned long lastuse

> Timestamp used to remember the last time this entry was used. It is updated when there is a successful cache lookup and it is used by the garbage collection routines to select the best structures to free.

unsigned long expires

> Timestamp that indicates when the entry will expire. See the section "Expiration Criteria" in Chapter 33.

u32 metrics[RTAX_MAX]

> Vector of metrics, used mostly by TCP. This vector is initialized with a copy of the fib_info->fib_metrics vector (if it is defined), and default values are used where needed. See the function rt_set_nexthop and Chapter 35. See Table 36-10 for a description of the vector's possible values.

> The RTAX_LOCK value needs a little explanation. RTAX_LOCK is not a metric but a bitmap: when the bit in position *n* is set, it means that the metric with enum value *n* has been configured with the *lock* options/keyword. In other words, a command like *ip route add ... advmss lock ...* sets the 1<<RTAX_ADVMSS bit. When a metric is locked, it cannot be changed by protocol events.

unsigned long rate_last
unsigned long rate_tokens

> These two fields are used to rate limit two types of ICMP messages. See the section "Egress ICMP REDIRECT Rate Limiting" in Chapter 33 and the section "Routing Failure" in Chapter 35.

short error

> When the fib_lookup API (used only by IPv4) fails, the error is saved into error (with a positive sign) and used later by ip_error to decide how to handle the failure (i.e., to decide which ICMP to generate).

struct neighbour *neighbour
struct hh_cache *hh

> neighbour is the data structure that contains the L3-to-L2 address mapping for the next hop. hh is the cached L2 header. See the chapters in Part VI for details.

int (*input)(struct sk_buff*)
int (*output)(struct sk_buff**)

> Functions used to process ingress and egress packets, respectively. See the section "Cache Lookup" in Chapter 33.

__u32 tclassid

> Routing table based classifier's tag. See the section "Policy Routing and Routing Table Based Classifier" in Chapter 35.

`struct dst_ops *ops`

VFT whose functions are used to manipulate `dst_entry` structures.

`struct rcu_head rcu_head`

Takes care of mutual exclusion.

`char info[0]`

This field can be useful as a pointer to the end of the data structure. It is only a placeholder.

dst_ops Structure

The `dst_ops` structure is the interface between the protocol-independent cache and L3 protocols that use a routing cache. See the section "Interface Between the DST and Calling Protocols" in Chapter 33. Here is the field-by-field description:

`unsigned short family`

Address family. See AF_*XXX* values in *include/linux/socket.h*.

`unsigned short protocol`

Protocol ID. See ETH_P_*XXX* values in *include/linux/if_ether.h*.

`unsigned gc_thresh`

This field, used by the garbage collection algorithm, specifies the size (number of buckets) of the routing cache. The initialization is done in `ip_rt_init` (the IPv4 routing subsystem initialization function).

`int (*gc)(void)`
`atomic_t entries`

gc is the garbage collection function invoked by `dst_alloc` when the number of `dst_entry` instances (entries) already allocated by the protocol is greater than or equal to the threshold `gc_thresh`.

`struct dst_entry * (*check)(struct dst_entry *, __u32 cookie)`
`void (*destroy)(struct dst_entry *)`
`void (*ifdown)(struct dst_entry *, struct net_device *dev, int how)`
`struct dst_entry * (*negative_advice)(struct dst_entry *)`
`void (*link_failure)(struct sk_buff *)`
`void (*update_pmtu)(struct dst_entry *dst, u32 mtu)`
`int (*get_mss)(struct dst_entry *dst, u32 mtu)`

See the section "Interface Between the DST and Calling Protocols" in Chapter 33.

`int entry_size`

Size of the outer L3 routing cache structure (e.g., rtable for IPv4).

`kmem_cache_t *kmem_cachep`

Memory pool used to allocate routing cache elements.

flowi Structure

With the `flowi` data structure, it is possible to define classes of traffic based on the combination of fields such as ingress and egress devices, parameters from the L3 and L4 protocol headers, etc. It is commonly used as a search key for lookups, as a traffic selector for IPsec policies, and other advanced uses. Here is a brief description of its fields:

`int oif`
`int iif`
> Egress and ingress device IDs.

`union {...} nl_u`
> Union whose fields are structures that can be used to specify the values of L3 parameters. The protocols currently supported are IPv4, IPv6, and DECnet.

`__u8 proto`
> L4 protocol.

`__u8 flags`
> The only flag defined in this variable, `FLOWI_FLAG_MULTIPATHOLDROUTE`, originally was used by the multipath code, but it is not used anymore.

`union {...} uli_u`
> Union whose fields are mainly structures that can be used to specify the values of L4 parameters. The protocols currently supported are TCP, UDP, ICMP, DECnet, and the IPsec suite.

Because the data structure is not flat, but contains unions and structs, the kernel provides a set of macros that can be used to access some of its fields.

rt_cache_stat Structure

`rt_cache_stat` stores the counters used for the statistics introduced in the section "Statistics." Here are its counters:

`in_hit`
`out_hit`
> Number of received and locally generated packets, respectively, that have been routed with a successful lookup on the routing cache (see `ip_route_input` and `ip_route_output_key`).

`in_slow_tot`
`in_slow_mc`
> `in_slow_tot` is the number of packets that required a lookup on the routing table because the cache lookup failed (see `ip_route_input_slow`). Only successful routing table lookups are counted. The counter is called slow because a lookup on the routing tables can be much slower than a lookup on the routing cache. This

counter includes broadcasts, but it does not include multicast traffic, which is counted in in_slow_mc.

out_slow_tot
out_slow_mc

out_slow_tot and out_slow_mc play the same role as in_slow_tot and in_slow_mc for the egress traffic

in_no_route

Number of ingress packets that could not be forwarded because the routing table did not know how to reach the destination IP address (which is possible only if no default gateway is configured or usable). See ip_route_input_slow. There is no counter to keep track of the locally generated packets that could not be sent for lack of a route.

in_brd

Number of broadcast packets received correctly (no sanity check failed). There is no counter for the number of transmitted broadcasts.

in_martian_dst
in_martian_src

These two counters represent the number of packets that were dropped because the sanity check failed on the destination or source IP addresses, respectively. Examples of sanity checks are that the source IP address cannot be multicast or broadcast and that the destination address cannot belong to the so-called zero-network—that is, it cannot look like 0.*n.n.n*.

gc_total
gc_ignored
gc_goal_miss
gc_dst_overflow

These four fields are updated by rt_garbage_collect, described in the section "rt_garbage_collect Function" in Chapter 33.

gc_total keeps track of the number of times rt_garbage_collect is invoked.

gc_ignored is the number of times rt_garbage_collect returns immediately because it was called too recently.

gc_goal_miss is the number of times the cache has been scanned by rt_garbage_collect without meeting the goal set at the beginning of the function.

gc_dst_overflow is the number of times gc_garbage_collect fails by not reducing the number of cache entries below the ip_rt_max_size threshold.

in_hlist_search
out_hlist_search

These are updated by the routines used for the cache lookups, ip_route_input and __ip_route_output_key, respectively. They represent the number of cache elements that have been tested and did not match (not just the number of cache misses).

ip_mp_alg_ops Structure

ip_mp_alg_ops represents the interface between the routing cache and the Multipath caching feature. It consists of the following function pointers:

```
void (*mp_alg_select_route) (const struct flowi *flp, struct rtable *rth,
struct rtable **rp)
void (*mp_alg_flush) (void)
void (*mp_alg_set_nhinfo) (__u32 network, __u32 netmask, unsigned char
prefixlen, const struct fib_nh *nh)
void (*mp_alg_remove) (struct rtable *rth)
```

These functions are invoked by the algorithm-independent wrappers described in the section "Interface Between the Routing Cache and Multipath" in Chapter 33.

Functions and Variables Featured in This Part of the Book

Table 36-13 summarizes the main functions, variables, and data structures introduced or referenced in the chapters of this book covering the routing subsystem. You can find more in the section "Generic Helper Routines and Macros" and "Helper Routines" in Chapter 32, and the two "Helper Routines", in Chapter 35.

Table 36-13. Functions, variables, and data structures in the routing subsystem

Functions	
for_ifa, endfor_ifa for_primary_ifa, endfor_ifa	Macros used to browse the IPv4 addresses configured on a network device. See the section "Primary and Secondary IP Addresses" in Chapter 32.
FIB_RES_*XXX*	Set of macros used to access the fields of the fib_result structure. See the section "Generic Helper Routines and Macros" in Chapter 32.
LOOPBACK ZERONET MULTICAST LOCAL_MCAST/BADCLASS	Macros used to recognize special IP addresses. See the section "Generic Helper Routines and Macros" in Chapter 32.
fib_hash_lock fib_info_lock fib_rules_lock rt_flush_lock fib_multipath_lock alg_table_lock	Locks used to protect various pieces of data. See the section "Global Locks" in Chapter 32.

Table 36-13. Functions, variables, and data structures in the routing subsystem (continued)

Functions	
ip_rt_init ip_fib_init devinet_init fib_rules_init fib_hash_init dst_init	Initialization routines. See the section "Routing Subsystem Initialization" in Chapter 32.
dst_alloc	Allocate an entry for the routing cache. See the section "Cache Entry Allocation and Reference Counts" in Chapter 33.
rt_periodic_timer rt_secret_timer	Timers. See the sections "Garbage Collection" and "Flushing the Routing Cache" in Chapter 33.
fib_netdev_event fib_inetaddr_event	Handlers for the netdev_chain and inetaddr_chain notification chains. See the section "External Events" in Chapter 32.
fib_add_ifaddr fib_del_ifaddr	Used to update the routing table upon the addition or removal of an IP address from the configuration of a local network device. See the sections "Adding an IP address" and "Removing an IP address" in Chapter 32.
fib_magic	Used by the kernel to insert routes under specific conditions. See the section "Routes Inserted by the Kernel: The fib_magic Function."
fib_rules_detach fib_rules_attach	Enables and disables routing policies when network devices are registered and unregistered, respectively. See the section "Impacts on the policy database" in Chapter 32.
rtmsg_fib	Used to send notification on a specific Netlink multicast group when routes are added or removed. See the section "Netlink Notifications" in Chapter 32.
ip_route_input __ip_route_output_key ip_route_output_flow ip_route_output_key ip_route_connect ip_route_newports	The first two functions are routing cache lookup routines, and the others are wrappers around them. See the section "Cache Lookup" in Chapter 33.
ip_route_input_slow ip_route_output_slow	Routing table lookup routines. See Chapter 35.
ip_route_input_mc	Lookup routines used for multicast destinations.
ip_mkroute_input ip_mkroute_input_def ip_mkroute_output ip_mkroute_output_def fib_select_default fib_select_multipath	Various support routines used by ip_route_input_slow and ip_route_output_slow. See Chapter 35.
fib_lookup fn_hash_lookup fib_semantic_match	Routines called at different stages during a routing table lookup. See the section "High-Level View of Lookup Functions" in Chapter 35.

Table 36-13. Functions, variables, and data structures in the routing subsystem (continued)

Functions	
`fn_hash_insert`	Add a new route to a routing table. See the section "Adding a Route" in Chapter 34.
`fn_hash_delete`	Remove a route from a routing table. See the section "Deleting a Route" in Chapter 34.
`rt_intern_hash`	Add an entry to the routing cache. See the section "Adding Elements to the Cache" in Chapter 33.
`multipath_alg_register` `multipath_alg_unregister`	Register and unregister a multipath caching algorithm. See the section "Registering a Caching Algorithm" in Chapter 33.
`multipath_select_route` `multipath_flush` `multipath_set_nhinfo` `multipath_remove`	Various routines used to manage cache entries associated with multipath routes. See the section "Interface Between the Routing Cache and Multipath" in Chapter 33. More routines are listed in the section "Helper Routines" in the same chapter.
`rt_free` `dst_free`	Free an `rtable` and a `dst_entry` structure, respectively.
`rt_garbage_collect` `rt_may_expire`	Garbage collection routines used for the routing cache. See the section "rt_garbage_collect Function" in Chapter 33.
`dst_input` `dst_output`	Complete the reception and transmission of a packet, respectively. See the section "Cache Lookup" in Chapter 33. See also the section "Setting Functions for Reception and Transmission" in Chapter 35.
`rt_garbage_collect` `dst_destroy` `dst_ifdown` `dst_negative_advice` `dst_link_failure` `dst_set_expires`	Routines used for the initialization of the `dst_ops` instance associated with the IPv4 protocol. See the section "Interface Between the DST and Calling Protocols" in Chapter 33.
`dst_dev_event`	Handler used by the DST subsystem to process notifications from the `netdev_chain` notification chain. See the section "External Events" in Chapter 32.
`RT_CACHE_STAT_INC`	Update per-CPU statistics. See the section "Statistics."
Variables	
`ip_fib_local_table` `ip_fib_main_table`	Routing tables. See the section "The Two Default Routing Tables: ip_fib_main_table and ip_fib_local_table" in Chapter 34.
`rt_hash_table`	Routing cache. See Chapter 33.
`rt_hash_mask`	Size of the routing cache (i.e., number of buckets of the hash table).
`dst_garbage_list`	List of `dst_entry` instances that cannot be removed because they are still referenced. See Chapter 33.
`fib_tables`	List of `fib_table` instances. See Figure 34-1 in Chapter 34.
`fib_rules`	List of routing policies. See the section "fib_lookup with Policy Routing" in Chapter 35.
`fib_info_cnt`	Number of outstanding `fib_info` instances. See the section "Dynamic resizing of global hash tables" in Chapter 34.
`fib_info_hash` `fib_info_laddrhash`	Hash tables used to search `fib_info` instances. See the section "Organization of fib_info Structures" in Chapter 34.

Table 36-13. Functions, variables, and data structures in the routing subsystem (continued)

Functions	
`fib_info_devhash`	Hash table used to search `fib_nh` instances. See the section "Organization of Next-Hop Router Structures" in Chapter 34.
`fib_props`	Vector whose elements are used by the lookup routine `fib_semantic_match` to map route types to return values. See the section "Return value from fib_semantic_match" in Chapter 35.

Data structures	
`fib_table structure`	Key data structures used by the routing code. They are described in detail in the section "Data Structures Featured in This Part of the Book."
`fn_zone structure`	
`fib_node structure`	
`fib_alias structure`	
`fib_info structure`	
`fib_nh structure`	
`fib_rule structure`	
`rtable structure`	
`dst_entry structure`	
`dst_ops structure`	
`flowi structure`	
`rt_cache_stat structure`	
`ip_mp_alg_ops structure`	

Files and Directories Featured in This Part of the Book

Figure 36-6 lists the files and directories referred to in the chapters in Part VII.

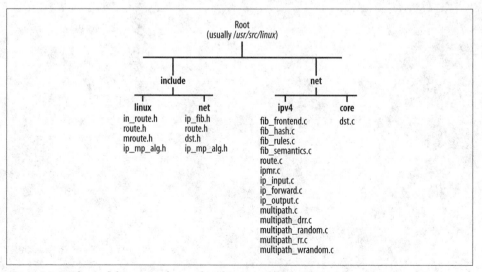

Figure 36-6. Files and directories featured in this part of the book

Index

Numbers

802.1d device (see bridge)
802.1D-1998 standard, 309
802.1D-2004 standard, 309
802.1Q device, 101, 102
802.1Q-2002 standard, 309
802.1s standard, 309
802.1w standard, 309
802.3 standard, compared to Ethernet
        protocols, 281–287
802.4 device (see Token Bus device)
802.5 device (see Token Ring 4 MB/s device)

A

aarp_rcv function, 291
accept_fastpath function pointer, net_device
        structure, 56
accept_redirects file, 963, 965
accept_redirects variable, 963
accept_source_route file, 963, 965
accept_source_route variable, 963
access bridges, 312
addbr command, brctl utility, 392, 395
addif command, brctl utility, 395
addifr command, brctl utility, 392
addr field
    bridge_id structure, 399
    cork structure, 565
    net_bridge_fdb_entry structure, 399
addrconf.c file, 44
address class, 783
address learning by bridge, 302–305
Address Resolution Protocol (see ARP)

addr_len field, net_device structure, 47, 142
AF_PACKET sockets, 268
af_packet_priv field, packet_type
        structure, 280
ageing_time field, net_bridge structure, 401
ageing_timer field, net_bridge_fdb_entry
        structure, 399
age_list field, net_bridge structure, 401
age_list structure, 360
aging
    of addresses, by bridge, 304, 336, 341
    of BPDUs, 326
Aging timer, STP, 336, 341
AH (IP Authentication Header
        Protocol), 570
alg_table_lock lock, 844, 986
aliasing interfaces, 101, 792
allmulti field, net_device structure, 51
alloc_etherdev function, 139
alloc_fcdev function, 139
alloc_fddidev function, 139
alloc_hippi_dev function, 139
alloc_irdadev function, 139
alloc_netdev function, 138, 140, 145, 172
allocs field, neigh_statistics structure, 771
alloc_skb function, 33–35
alloc_trdev function, 139
alloc_xxxdev functions, 172
anycast_delay field, neigh_parms
        structure, 767
anycast_delay file, 755
anycast_delay variable, 755
AppleTalk Address Resolution Protocol, 291
AppleTalk Datagram Delivery Protocol, 291

We'd like to hear your suggestions for improving our indexes. Send email to *index@oreilly.com.*

B

backlog queue, 223, 231–235
backlog_dev field, softnet_data
        structure, 207
BADCLASS macro, 843, 986
base_addr field, net_device structure, 44,
        142
base_reachable_time field, neigh_parms
        structure, 766
base_reachable_time file, 755
base_reachable_time variable, 755
bf_fdb_change_addr function, 404
BH (see bottom half)
Big Endian format, 15
big_endian.h file, 16
BIRD routing protocol daemon, 820, 860
black hole route, 794
bonding device, 43, 101
    notifications on, 170
    processing of ingress frames, 237
    tx_queue_len value for, 53
books (see publications)
BOOTP protocol, IP configuration
        using, 545
boot-time initialization routines, 128–130
boot-time kernel options, 85, 93, 116–122
boot-time PCI device activities, 112
bottom half (BH), 4
bottom half handlers, 184–186
    implementations of, 186
    old style, concurrency and, 187
    requirements for, 190
    software interrupts for (version 2.4 and
        higher), 193–196
    tasklets for, 196–198
    version 2.2 and earlier, 190–193
BPDUs (Bridge Protocol Data Units), 316,
        323–328
    aging of, 326
    compared to data frames, 376
    configuration BPDUs, 323, 324–326
    encapsulation of, 344
    ingress BPDUs, handling, 347, 383
    processing of, 371–372
    TCN BPDU, 323
    transmitting, 385
bpq_rcv function, 282
br field, net_bridge_port structure, 399
br_add_bridge function, 361, 392, 403
br_add_if function, 361, 364, 374, 392, 403
br_become_designated_port function, 381
br_become_root_bridge function, 381, 389

br.c file, 360
br_change_mtu function, 363
br_config_bpdu structure, 360, 404
br_configuration_update function, 381, 386
brctl utility, 391
    commands, list of, 391
    configuring bridge devices and ports, 395
    creating bridge devices and ports, 395
br_deinit function, 361, 403
br_del_bridge function, 361, 364, 392, 403
br_del_if function, 361, 392, 403
br_deliver function, 372
br_designated_port_selection function, 381
br_dev_close function, 363
br_dev_ioctl function, 363
br_dev_open function, 363, 367
br_dev_setup function, 363
br_dev_stop function, 368
br_dev_xmit function, 363, 380
br_fdb_cache variable, 404
br_fdb_change_addr function, 374
br_fdb_cleanup function, 375, 404
br_fdb_delete_by_port function, 375
_ _br_fdb_get function, 373, 404
br_fdb_get function, 373, 374, 404
br_fdb_init function, 373, 403
br_fdb_insert function, 366, 374, 404
br_fdb_put function, 374
br_fdb_update function, 375, 404
br_features_recompute function, 367
br_flood function, 372, 404
br_forward function, 372, 404
br_forward_delay_timer_expired
        function, 388, 389
br_get_port function, 382
br_get_tick function, 386, 404
br_handle_bridge function, 375
br_handle_frame function, 376, 404
br_handle_frame_finish function, 376, 378,
        404
br_handle_frame_hook function
        pointer, 360
br_handle_frame_hook variable, 404
br_hello_timer_expired function, 388
br_hold_timer_expired function, 388
bridge, 101, 297–299
    access bridges, 312
    adding ports to, 364
    address learning by, 302–305
    aging mechanism for addresses, 304, 336,
        341

br_pass_frame_up function, 378, 379, 404
br_pass_frame_up_finish function, 379, 404
br_port field, net_device structure, 53, 376
br_port_state_selection function, 369, 382
br_private.h file, 360
br_private_stp.h file, 360
br_received_config_bpdu function, 385,
    386, 404
br_received_tcn function, 389
br_received_tcn_bpdu function, 385, 404
br_record_config_information function, 382
br_record_config_timeout_values
    function, 382
br_reply function, 385, 404
br_root_selection function, 381
br_send_bpdu function, 404
br_set_tick function, 386, 404
br_should_become_designated_port
    function, 381
br_should_become_root_port function, 381
BR_STATE_BLOCKING state, 370
BR_STATE_DISABLED state, 366
BR_STATE_FORWARDING state, 369,
    370, 376, 389
BR_STATE_LEARNING state, 370, 389
BR_STATE_LISTENING state, 370
BR_STATE_XXX enumeration list, 399
br_stp_change_bridge_id function, 386, 387
br_stp_disable_bridge function, 403
br_stp_disable_port function, 368, 386, 387,
    403
br_stp_enable_bridge function, 367, 403
br_stp_enable_port function, 368, 403
br_stp_handle_bpdu function, 376, 383,
    386, 404
br_stp_port_timer_init function, 388, 403
br_stp_recalculate_bridge function, 403
br_stp_recalculate_bridge_id function, 363,
    366, 382
br_stp_set_bridge_priority function, 386,
    387, 392
br_stp_set_path_cost function, 386, 392
br_stp_set_port_priority function, 392
br_stp_timer_init function, 375, 388, 403
br_supersedes_port_info function, 381
br_sysfs_addbr function, 403
br_sysfs_addif function, 366, 403
br_sysfs_delbr function, 403
br_sysfs_removeif function, 403
br_tcn_timer_expired function, 388
br_topology_change_acknowledge
    function, 382

br_topology_change_acknowledged
    function, 382
br_topology_change_detection function, 382
br_topology_change_timer_expired
    function, 388
br_transmit_config function, 385, 386, 404
br_transmit_tcn function, 385, 404
br_uninit function, 360
buffers (see sk_buff structure)
bug catching, 17
BUG_ON macro, 17
BUG_TRAP macro, 17
byteorder.h file, 16
byte-ordering conversions, 15
bytes, 3

C

caching
    hash tables implementing, 6
    in neighboring subsystem, 666–668
    L2 headers, 683–687
    memory caches, 5
    multipath caching, 836, 873–878, 943
    multipath routing, 811–812
    (see also ARP cache; DST; routing cache)
call_usermodehelper function, 96, 104
Carrier Sense Multiple Access with Collision
        Detection protocol
        (CSMA/CD), 630–631
cb field, sk_buff structure, 29
change_mtu function pointer, net_device
        structure, 56, 142
change_nexthops macro, 842, 942
channeling, 779
check virtual function, dst_ops
        structure, 880, 983
checksum field, ICMP header, 587
CHECKSUM_HW flag, 442, 443
CHECKSUM_NONE flag, 441, 443
checksums, 432–438
    algorithms for, 432
    for frame transmission, 250
    functions for, 434–436
    L3 checksum, 473
    L4 checksum, 437–438, 473, 502, 533
    net_device structure fields for, 441
    reliability of, 432
    sk_buff structure fields for, 441–443
    status values for, 441
    updating, when required, 433
CHECKSUM_UNNECESSARY flag, 442,
    443

dev_add_pack function, 279, 280, 293, 444
dev_addr field, net_device structure, 47, 363
dev_alloc_name function, 139, 172
dev_alloc_skb function, 33–35
dev_base variable, 43, 145, 146, 172
dev_base_lock variable, 172
dev_boot_phase variable, 96, 104
dev_boot_setup variable, 135
dev_close function, 160
dev_cpu_callback function, 95
dev_deactivate function, 161
dev_ethtool function, 168, 172
__devexit macro, 127, 132, 134
__devexitdata macro, 127, 134
__devexit_p macro, 127, 134
dev_get_by_index function, 147
dev_get_by_name function, 147
dev_hold function, 158, 172
device driver
    disabling transmissions, 89
    initializations by, 143
    loading, causing registration of
        device, 137
    notifying kernel of frame
        reception, 178–183
    unloading, causing unregistration of
        device, 138
device round-robin algorithm, multipath
        routing, 811, 812, 878
device status changes, handling, 856–858
device-based proxying, 639
device_initcall macro, 126
devices (see network devices; virtual devices)
dev_id field
    irqaction structure, 92
    net_device structure, 44
dev_index_head hash table, 146, 172
devinet_init function, 845, 987
devinet_sysctl_forward function, 967
__devinit macro, 127, 132, 134
__devinitdata macro, 124, 127, 132, 134
dev_ioctl function, 362
dev_kfree_skb function, 35, 264
dev_kfree_skb_any function, 264
dev_kfree_skb_irq function, 255, 257, 264
dev_mcast file, 103
dev_mcast_init function, 95, 103
dev_name_head hash table, 146, 172
dev_new_index function, 155
dev_open function, 159
dev_proc_init function, 95, 103
dev_put function, 158, 172

dev_queue_xmit function, 239, 243,
        249–255, 264
    bridging code using, 372
    connected to L3 protocols via neighboring
        layer, 655
    neighboring subsystem and, 635, 660,
        693, 772
dev_remove_pack function, 281, 293
dev_set_mtu function, 366
dev_set_promiscuity function, 366
dev_shutdown function, 157
dev_watchdog function, 259
dev_weight file, 263
DF (Don't Fragment) field, IP header, 413,
        423, 507
DHCP protocol
    duplicate addresses and, 703
    IP configuration using, 545, 632
DiffServ Code Point (see DSCP)
directed broadcasts, 788
directives, conditional, 11–13
directories
    bridging, list of, 405
    component initialization, list of, 135
    device registration and initialization, list
        of, 173
    ICMP, list of, 622
    IPv4, list of, 568
    L4 protocols, list of, 583
    neighboring subsystem, list of, 774
    network device initialization, list of, 105
    networking, list of, 66
    notification chains, list of, 83
    PCI layer, list of, 115
    protocol handlers, list of, 294
    routing, list of, 989
    transmission and reception, list of, 265
disabling network devices, 137
divert field, net_device structure, 53
Diverter
    allocating configuration block for, 155
    net_device fields for, 53
    processing ingress frames, 238
dma field, net_device structure, 44
DMA, Scatter/Gather, 155
DMA transmission, 89
dma.c file, 44
DNAT (Destination NAT), 736
dn_dev_create function, 768
dn_neigh_cleanup function, 687
dn_neigh_init function, 687

J

jiffies global variable, 17

K

kconfig files, 24
kernel component, 5
    (see also subsystems)
kernel (see Linux kernel)
kernel_param structure, 119, 135
kern_rta structure, 836
key_len field, neigh_table structure, 763
keywords, registering, 117
kfree function, 5
kfree_skb function, 35
kmalloc function, 5
kmem_cache_alloc function, 5, 6
kmem_cache_create function, 5
kmem_cache_destroy function, 5
kmem_cache_free function, 5
kmem_cachep field
    dst_ops structure, 983
    neigh_table structure, 763
kmod kernel module loader, 98
kobj field, net_bridge_port structure, 400
kobject_hotplug function, 99
ksoftirqd function, 202
ksoftirqd kernel threads, 202–204

L

L2 address
    change of, gratuitous ARP used for, 702
    configuring, 632
    static translation of L3 address to, 633
    translating L3 address to, 628–634
L2 bridged topology, 311–314
L2 headers, caching, 683–687
L2 (link layer), 3, 4
    communication choices made by, 272,
        273
    data units for (frames), 267
    protocol choices for, 268, 274
L2 network, 311
L3 address
    changing, situations for, 632
    duplicate, gratuitous ARP used
        for, 703–704
    static translation to L2 address, 633
    translating to L2 address, 628–634
    (see also IP addresses)
L3 (network layer), 3, 4

communication choices made by, 271,
        273
    data units for (packets), 267
    L3 to L4 packet delivery, 574–582
    VFT interface with neighboring
        subsystem, 655–665
L4 checksum, 437–438
L4 (transport layer), 3, 4
    communication choices made by, 271
    data structures for, list of, 583
    data units for (segments), 267
    files and directories for, list of, 583
    functions for, list of, 583
    L3 to L4 packet delivery, 574–582
    passing error notifications to, 619
    protocol registration, 571–574
    protocols, xx
    protocols for, list of, 569–570
    raw IP and, 577–581
    raw sockets and, 577–581
    variables for, list of, 583
LANs, 311
    loop topology, 307
    loop-free topology, 308
    merging with bridges, 300
    of different technologies, bridging, 302
last_flush field, neigh_table structure, 764
last_in field, ipq structure, 559
last_rand field, neigh_table structure, 763
last_rx field, net_device structure, 50
lastuse field, dst_entry structure, 875, 982
late_initcall macro, 126
Layer two address (see L2 address)
layers of TCP/IP network stack, terminology
        for, 3
len field
    ipq structure, 560
    sk_buff structure, 25
length field, cork structure, 565
likely macro, 13
limited broadcasts, 930
link between bridges, 311
link layer address (see L2 address)
link layer multicast, net_device fields for, 51
link layer (see L2)
link scope for IP addresses, 786
link scope for routes, 786, 838
link state change detection, 163–165
link_failure virtual function, dst_ops
        structure, 881, 983
__LINK_STATE_LINKWATCH_EVENT
        flag, 148

tx_dropped field, net_device_stats structure, 398

tx_packets field, net_device_stats structure, 398

tx_queue_len field, net_device structure, 52, 142, 363

tx_timeout field, net_device structure, 259

tx_timeout function pointer, net_device structure, 56, 142

type field
    datalink_proto structure, 292
    fib_result structure, 978
    ICMP header, 586
    neighbour structure, 701, 760
    net_device structure, 46, 142
    packet_type structure, 279

Type of Service field (see TOS field)

typographical conventions used in this book, xxii

U

u field, rtable structure, 978

ucast_probes field, neigh_parms structure, 767

ucast_probes variable, 755

UDP protocol, 569
    MSG_DONTROUTE flag and, 873
    (see also L4)

udp_flush_pending_frames function, 508

udp_push_pending_frames function, 508

uli_u field, flowi structure, 984

Understanding Multiple Spanning Tree Protocol (802.1s), 351

Understanding Rapid Spanning Tree Protocol (802.1w), 351

Understanding the Linux Kernel (O'Reilly), xvi

uninit function pointer, net_device structure, 55, 142, 149, 156, 169

universe scope for IP addresses, 786

universe scope for routes, 786, 838

university projects, Linux used by, xv

unlikely macro, 13

unreachable route, 794

unregister_8022_client function, 293

unregister_inet6addr_notifier function, 79

unregister_inetaddr_notifier function, 79, 548

unregister_netdev function, 149, 172

unregister_netdevice function, 141, 149, 157, 169, 172

unregister_netdevice_notifier function, 79, 152

unregister_snap_client function, 291, 293

unregister_sysctl_table function, 62, 64

unregistration of network devices, 149–154, 156–159
    compared to disabling devices, 136
    conditions for, 138
    NICs, 141
    virtual devices, 169

unres_qlen file, 755

unshielded twisted pair (UTP) wire, 630

unused_next field, inet_peer structure, 561

unused_prevp field, inet_peer structure, 561

updated field, neighbour structure, 759

update_pmtu virtual function, dst_ops structure, 881, 983

__use field, dst_entry structure, 981

use_count field, net_bridge_fdb_entry structure, 399

used field, neighbour structure, 759

user field, ipq structure, 559

users field, sk_buff structure, 26, 40

user-space tools
    brctl utility, 391, 395
    bridge configuration using, 391–396
    device-related information, configuring, 166–169
    ethtool tool, 166–168
    hotplug helper, 96, 98–100, 103
    ifconfig command, 67, 166, 550
    initialization events handled by, 96–100
    ioctl commands, 59, 67, 71, 392–393, 545
    kmod kernel module loader, 98
    list of, 18, 58
    mii-tool tool, 168
    modprobe helper, 96, 98, 103
    neighbor system administration, 749–752
    Netlink, 60, 70, 71, 858
    net-tools package, 749, 752, 952, 956
    procfs (/proc filesystem), 58, 60
    routing, 952–958
    sysctl command, 59, 60, 61–67
    sysfs (/sys filesystem), 7, 59
    (see also IPROUTE2 package; routing protocol daemons)

UTP (unshielded twisted pair) wire, 630

About the Author

Christian Benvenuti received his masters degree in computer science at the University of Bologna in Italy. He collaborated for a few years with the International Center for Theoretical Physics (ICTP) in Trieste, where he developed ad-hoc software based on the Linux kernel, was a scientific consultant for a project on remote collaboration, and served as an instructor for several training sessions on networking. The trainings, held mainly in Europe, Africa, and South America were all based on Linux systems and addressed to scientists from developing countries, where the ICTP has been promoting Linux for many years. He occasionally collaborates with a nonprofit organization founded by ICTP members, Collaborium.org, to continue promoting Linux on developing countries.

In the past few years he worked as a software engineer for Cisco Systems in the Silicon Valley, where he focused on Layer 2 switching, high availability, and network security.

Colophon

Our look is the result of reader comments, our own experimentation, and feedback from distribution channels. Distinctive covers complement our distinctive approach to technical topics, breathing personality and life into potentially dry subjects.

Philip Dangler was the production editor, and Audrey Doyle was the copyeditor for *Understanding Linux Network Internals*. Sada Preisch proofread the book. Mary Brady and Colleen Gorman provided quality control. Rachel Monaghan, Lydia Onofrei, and Laurel Ruma provided production assistance. Angela Howard wrote the index.

Karen Montgomery designed the cover of this book, based on a series design by Hanna Dyer and Edie Freedman. The cover image is a 19th-century engraving from *Men: A Pictorial Archive from 19th Century Sources*). Karen Montgomery produced the cover layout with Adobe InDesign CS using Adobe's ITC Garamond font.

David Futato designed the interior layout. The chapter opening images are from *Men: A Pictorial Archive from 19th Century Sources*. This book was converted by Keith Fahlgren to FrameMaker 5.5.6 with a format conversion tool created by Erik Ray, Jason McIntosh, Neil Walls, and Mike Sierra that uses Perl and XML technologies. The text font is Linotype Birka; the heading font is Adobe Myriad Condensed; and the code font is LucasFont's TheSans Mono Condensed. The illustrations that appear in the book were produced by Robert Romano, Jessamyn Read, and Lesley Borash using Macromedia FreeHand MX and Adobe Photoshop CS. The tip and warning icons were drawn by Christopher Bing.

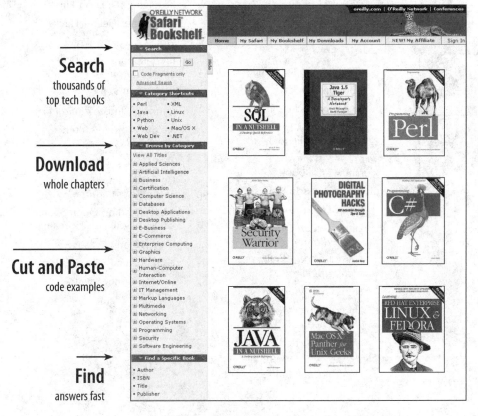

Related Titles from O'Reilly

Linux

Building Embedded Linux Systems

Building Secure Servers
with Linux

The Complete FreeBSD,
4th Edition

Even Grues Get Full

Exploring the JDS Linux
Desktop

Extreme Programming Pocket
Guide

GDB Pocket Reference

Knoppix Hacks

Knoppix Pocket Guide

Learning Red Hat Enterprise
Linux and Fedora,
4th Edition

Linux Cookbook

Linux Desktop Hacks

Linux Desktop Pocket Guide

Linux Device Drivers,
3rd Edition

Linux in a Nutshell,
5th Edition

Linux in a Windows World

Linux iptables Pocket
Reference

Linux Network Administrator's
Guide, *3rd Edition*

Linux Pocket Guide

Linux Security Cookbook

Linux Server Hacks, *Volume 2*

Linux Unwired

Linux Web Server CD
Bookshelf, *Version 2.0*

LPI Linux Certification
in a Nutshell

Managing RAID on Linux

More Linux Server Hacks

OpenOffice.org Writer

Programming with Qt,
2nd Edition

Root of all Evil

Running Linux, *5th Edition*

Samba Pocket Reference,
2nd Edition

Test Driving Linux

Understanding the Linux
Kernel, *3rd Edition*

Understanding Open Source
& Free Software Licensing

User Friendly

Using Samba, *2nd Edition*

Version Control with
Subversion

Our books are available at most retail and online bookstores.

To order direct: 1-800-998-9938 • *order@oreilly.com* • *www.oreilly.com*

Online editions of most O'Reilly titles are available by subscription at *safari.oreilly.com*